The SA

Social Media

The SAGE Handbook of
Social Media

Paperback Edition

Edited by
Jean Burgess,
Alice Marwick and
Thomas Poell

Los Angeles | London | New Delhi | Singapore | Washington DC | Melbourne

Los Angeles | London | New Delhi
Singapore | Washington DC | Melbourne

SAGE Publications Ltd
1 Oliver's Yard
55 City Road
London EC1Y 1SP

SAGE Publications Inc.
2455 Teller Road
Thousand Oaks, California 91320

SAGE Publications India Pvt Ltd
B 1/I 1 Mohan Cooperative Industrial Area
Mathura Road
New Delhi 110 044

SAGE Publications Asia-Pacific Pte Ltd
3 Church Street
#10-04 Samsung Hub
Singapore 049483

Editor: Michael Ainsley
Editorial Assistant: Colette Wilson
Production Editor: Sushant Nailwal
Copyeditor: Sarah Bury
Proofreader: Dick Davis
Indexer: Caroline Eley
Marketing Manager: Lucia Sweet
Cover Design: Wendy Scott
Typeset by: Cenveo Publisher Services
Printed in the UK

At SAGE we take sustainability seriously.
Most of our products are printed in the UK
using FSC papers and boards. When we
print overseas we ensure sustainable
papers are used as measured by the
PREPS grading system. We undertake an
annual audit to monitor our sustainability.

Library of Congress Control Number: 2017937664

British Library Cataloguing in Publication data

A catalogue record for this book is available from the British Library

ISBN 978-1-4129-6229-2
ISBN 978-1-5264-8687-5 (pbk)

Contents

List of Figures

List of Tables

Notes on the Editors and Contributors

THE EDITORS

Jean Burgess is Professor of Digital Media and Director of the QUT Digital Media Research Centre (DMRC), Queensland University of Technology, Australia. She is author or editor of more than 100 publications on digital and social media, including *YouTube: Online Video and Participatory Culture* (Polity Press), *Twitter and Society* (Peter Lang), *Studying Mobile Media* (Routledge) and *The Handbook of New Media Dynamics* (Wiley-Blackwell).

Alice Marwick (PhD, New York University) is a Fellow at the Data & Society Research Institute, where she leads the Media Manipulation project, and an Assistant Professor of Communication at the University of North Carolina at Chapel Hill. Her current book project examines how the networked nature of online privacy disproportionately impacts marginalized individuals in terms of gender, race, and socio-economic status. She is the author of *Status Update: Celebrity, Publicity and Branding in the Social Media Age* (Yale, 2013), an ethnographic study of the San Francisco tech scene which examines how people seek social status through attention and visibility online. Marwick was previously Assistant Professor of Communication and Media Studies and the Director of the McGannon Center for Communication Research at Fordham University. She has written for popular publications such as *The New York Times*, *The New York Review of Books* and *The Guardian*, in addition to academic publications such as *Public Culture* and *New Media and Society*.

Thomas Poell is Assistant Professor of New Media & Digital Culture and Program Director of the Research Master Media Studies at the University of Amsterdam. He has published widely on social media and popular protest, as well as on the role of these media in the development of new forms of journalism. His next book, co-authored with José van Dijck and Martijn de Waal, will be titled *The Platform Society: Public Values in a Connective World*.

THE CONTRIBUTORS

Kath Albury is Professor of Media and Communication in the Faculty of Health, Arts and Design at Swinburne University of Technology, Australia. Her research focuses on practices of mediated self-representation, particularly in relation to sexuality and gender.

Jessica Baldwin-Philippi is an Assistant Professor in Fordham University's Communication and Media Studies department. Her work is fundamentally concerned with how engagement with new technologies can restructure forms of political participation and ideas about citizenship. Her book, *Using Technology, Building Democracy: Digital Campaigning and the*

Construction of Citizenship (Oxford, 2015) investigates the digital strategies and tactics electoral campaigns have adopted at both the local and national level.

Niels Brügger is Professor and head of the Centre for Internet Studies as well as of the internet research infrastructure NetLab, Aarhus University, Denmark. His research interests are web historiography, web archiving, and media theory. Within these fields he has published monographs and a number of edited books as well as articles and book chapters. Recent publications include *The Web as History: Using Web Archives to Understand the Past and the Present* (edited with Ralph Schroeder, UCL Press, 2017) and *Web 25: Histories from the First 25 Years of the World Wide Web* (ed., Peter Lang, New York 2017). He is co-founder and Managing Editor of the newly founded international journal *Internet Histories: Digital Technology, Culture and Society* (Taylor & Francis/Routledge).

Taina Bucher is Associate Professor in Communication and IT at the University of Copenhagen. Her research focuses on the power and politics of algorithms in social media and journalism. In her forthcoming book (Oxford University Press, 2018) she explores how algorithms variously govern participation, how people make sense of algorithms in everyday life, and the ways in which algorithms are impacting the news media industry. Her work on programmed friendship, the attention economy, the politics of API, Twitter bots and computational journalism has been published in journals such as *New Media & Society, Information, Communication & Society, Television & New Media, Culture Machine* and *Computational Culture*.

Rhiannon Bury is Associate Professor of Women's and Gender Studies at Athabasca University, Canada's Open University. She has published work on television and fandom in a number of journals, including *New Media & Society, Critical Studies in Television*, and *Convergence: The International Journal of Research into New Media Technologies*. Her first book, *Cyberspaces of Their Own: Female Fandoms Online*, was published by Peter Lang in 2005. Her most recent book, *Television 2.0: Viewer and Fan Engagement with Digital TV*, will be published by Peter Lang in 2017.

Nick Couldry is a sociologist of media and culture. He is Professor of Media Communications and Social Theory at the London School of Economics and Political Science. He is the author or editor of twelve books, including, most recently, *The Mediated Construction of Reality* (with Andreas Hepp, Polity Press, 2016), *Ethics of Media* (co-edited with Mirca Madianou and Amit Pinchevski, Palgrave, 2013), *Media, Society, World: Social Theory and Digital Media Practice* (Polity Press, 2012) and *Why Voice Matters: Culture and Politics After Neoliberalism* (Sage, 2010).

Francesco D'Orazio is a researcher and product designer who specializes in futures research and exploring the opportunities emerging at the intersection of social software, data science and audience behaviour. He has a PhD in Social Sciences and Digital Media from Università degli Studi di Roma 'La Sapienza'. He was a Fellow at the McLuhan Program in Culture and Technology at the University of Toronto, where he focused on Immersive Media, the evolution of Audiences and the rise of Social Software. He is co-founder and Vice President of Product at audience intelligence firm Pulsar and co-founder of the Visual Social Media Lab. His work focuses on designing systems and research frameworks that help analyse social data and extract insights from the web in real-time using computational social science and data visualization.

Most of his research work on social data has been focusing on virality, social influence, content diffusion and audience insights.

Gabriele de Seta holds a PhD degree in Sociology from the Hong Kong Polytechnic University and is currently a postdoctoral fellow at the Institute of Ethnology, Academia Sinica in Taipei, Taiwan. His scholarly work, grounded on ethnographic engagement across multiple sites, focuses on digital media practices and vernacular creativity in contemporary China. Gabriele's ongoing research projects cover topics ranging from experimental music scenes and urban life in East Asian cities to new media aesthetics and digital folklore on Chinese online platforms. He also experiments with ways of bridging anthropology and art practice. More information is available on his website: http://paranom.asia.

Aaron Delwiche (PhD, University of Washington) is a professor in the Department of Communication at Trinity University in San Antonio, Texas. He teaches courses on topics such as virtual world development, transmedia storytelling and mobile gaming. In 2016, with support from the Lennox Foundation, he organized a seminar series on 'Propaganda and Political Persuasion'. Aaron is the co-editor of the *Participatory Cultures Handbook* (Routledge, 2012). His recent publications include a chapter on transmedia storytelling in the anthology *The Rise of Transtexts: Challenges and Opportunities* (Routledge, 2016) and an article charting the comic book scanner subculture in the journal *First Monday*. Aaron's current research investigates the emergence of bots and sockpuppets, arguing that these technologies constitute a "fake audience" which poses a fundamental threat to global civil society.

Brooke Erin Duffy (PhD, University of Pennsylvania) is an assistant professor in the Department of Communication at Cornell University (USA). Her research interests include digital/social media industries, gender and feminist media studies, cultural work and creative labour, and critical consumer culture. She is the author of *(Not) Getting Paid to Do What You Love: Gender, Social Media, and Aspirational Work* (Yale University Press, 2017) and *Remake, Remodel: Women's Magazines in the Digital Age* (University of Illinois Press, 2013). Her work has been published in such journals as *Critical Studies in Media Communication, Communication, Culture & Critique*, the *International Journal of Cultural Studies, Feminist Media Studies, Social Media + Society*, and *Information, Communication, and Society*, among others.

Simon Faulkner is a Senior Lecturer in Art History and Visual Culture at Manchester School of Art (Manchester Metropolitan University). His recent individual research has been focused on relationships between visual practices and the Israeli–Palestinian conflict. This research has addressed a range of artistic and photographic work, and has been particularly concerned with the ways that visual images have been used for political purposes within the divided geography of Palestine/Israel. This work has resulted in a number of publications, including *Between States* (Black Dog Publishing, 2015), written with Israeli artist David Reeb. Since 2014, he has also been a co-director of the Visual Social Media, the work of which is focused on researching social media images.

Terry Flew is Professor of Media and Communications and Assistant Dean (Research) in the Creative Industries Faculty at the Queensland University of Technology, Brisbane, Australia. Professor Flew is an internationally recognized leader in media and communications, with research interests in digital media, global media, media policy, creative industries, and media economics. He is the author of nine books, including *Understanding Global Media* (Palgrave,

2018), *Politics, Media and Democracy in Australia* (Routledge, 2017), *Media Economics* (Palgrave, 2015), and *Global Creative Industries* (Polity Press, 2013). During 2011–2012 was appointed Commissioner with the Australian Law Reform Commission by the Attorney-General of Australia, chairing the National Classification Scheme Review. He has been a member of the International Communications Association Executive Board since 2012.

Jeremy Foote studies the social construction of knowledge and beliefs. His current work focuses on how online knowledge communities get started. He is a PhD student at Northwestern University, in the Media, Technology, and Society Program.

Robert W. Gehl received a PhD in Cultural Studies from George Mason University in 2010. He is currently an associate professor in the Department of Communication at the University of Utah. His research draws on science and technology studies, software studies, and critical/cultural studies. He has published critical research exploring corporate and alternative social media, knowledge management, crowdsourcing, media theory, and the Dark Web. This work appears in journals such as *New Media & Society, Communication Theory, Social Text, Fibreculture, Television and New Media, European Journal of Cultural Studies*, and the *Canadian Journal of Communication*. His book, *Reverse Engineering Social Media* (Temple University Press, 2014), explores the architecture and political economy of social media and is the winner of the Association of Internet Researchers Nancy Baym Book award. At Utah, he teaches courses in communication technology, software studies, new media theory, and political economy of communication.

Tarleton Gillespie is a principal researcher at Microsoft Research, an affiliated associate professor in Cornell's Department of Communication and Department of Information Science, co-founder of the blog Culture Digitally, the author of *Wired Shut: Copyright and the Shape of Digital Culture* (MIT Press, 2007) and co-editor of *Media Technologies: Essays on Communication, Materiality, and Society* (MIT Press, 2014). His next book (Yale University Press, forthcoming 2018) examines how the governance of what users say and do by social media platforms has broader implications for freedom of expression and the character of public discourse.

Gerard Goggin is Professor of Media and Communications, University of Sydney, and an Australian Research Council Future Fellow. He is widely published on mobile media and communication, Internet, and disability and technology. Key books include *Digital Disability* (2003), *Cell Phone Culture* (Routledge, 2006), *Routledge Companion to Mobile Media* (Routledge, 2009), *Internationalizing Internet Studies* (Routledge, 2009), *Global Mobile Media* (Routledge, 2011), and *Routledge Companion to Global Internet Histories* (Routledge, 2017). Gerard is one of the founder co-editors of the journal *Internet Histories*.

John Hartley is John Curtin Distinguished Professor at Curtin University, Australia, and Distinguished Visiting Research Fellow at Cardiff University, Wales. He is the author or editor of 30 books and many articles on popular culture and media, the creative industries and journalism. He has a continuing interest in the creative economy in China. His current research interests are in Cultural Science, an attempt to analyse culture, communication, media and knowledge using evolutionary and complexity theories. Recent books include *Cultural Science* (with Jason Potts, Bloomsbury, 2014) and *Creative Economy and Culture* (with Wen Wen and Henry Li, Sage, 2015). Hartley was foundation dean of the Creative Industries Faculty at QUT, and founding head of the School of Journalism at Cardiff University. He was awarded the Order of

Australia for service to education (2009). He is an elected Fellow of the Australian Academy of Humanities, The Learned Society of Wales, and the International Communication Association.

Anne Helmond is Assistant Professor of New Media and Digital Culture at the University of Amsterdam. She is a member of the Digital Methods Initiative, where she focuses her research on the infrastructure of social media platforms and apps. Her research interests include digital methods, software studies, platform studies, app studies, infrastructure studies and web history. In her research on platforms she has developed the notion of 'platformization' to understand the dual logic of social media platforms' extension into the rest of the web and, simultaneously, their drive to make external web data 'platform ready'. Her work has been published in the peer-reviewed journals *New Media & Society*, *Theory, Culture and Society*, *Social Media + Society*, *First Monday*, and *Computational Culture*.

Alfred Hermida (PhD, City, University of London) is an associate professor and Director of the School of Journalism at the University of British Columbia, and co-founder of The Conversation Canada. With two decades of experience in digital journalism, his research explores the digital transformation of media, with a focus on emerging news practices, media innovation, social media and data journalism. He is author of *Tell Everyone: Why We Share and Why It Matters* (DoubleDay, 2014), winner of the 2015 National Business Book Award, co-author of *Participatory Journalism: Guarding Open Gates at Online Newspapers* (Wiley Blackwell, 2011), and co-editor of *The SAGE Handbook of Digital Journalism* (SAGE, 2016). A former BBC journalist for 16 years, he was a founding news editor of the BBC News website in 1997.

Benjamin Mako Hill works to understand why some attempts at peer production – like Wikipedia and Linux – build large volunteer communities while the vast majority never attract even a second contributor. He is an Assistant Professor in the Department of Communication at the University of Washington. He is also a faculty associate at the Berkman Klein Center for Internet and Society at Harvard University. He has been a leader, developer and contributor to the free and open source software community for more than a decade. Hill has a Masters degree from the MIT Media Lab and a PhD from MIT in an interdepartmental programme between the Sloan School of Management and the Media Lab.

Jannis Kallinikos is Professor in the Department of Management at the London School of Economics and Political Science. His research focuses on the impact of information and communication technologies on organizations and economic institutions. He has published widely in Management, Information Systems and Sociology journals and written several monographs, including *The Consequences of Information: Institutional Implications of Technological Change* (Edward Elgar, 2007), *Governing Through Technology: Information Artefacts and Social Practice* (Palgrave, 2011). He has, together with Paul Leonardi and Bonnie Nardi, co-edited *Materiality and Organizing: Social Interaction in a Technological World* (Oxford University Press, 2012).

Deborah Lupton is Centenary Research Professor in the News & Media Research Centre, Faculty of Arts & Design, University of Canberra. She is a co-leader of the Digital Data & Society Consortium. Her latest books are *Medicine as Culture* (3rd edition, Sage, 2012), *Fat* (Routledge, 2013), *Risk* (2nd edition, Routledge, 2013), *The Social Worlds of the Unborn* (Palgrave Macmillan, 2013), *Digital Sociology* (Routledge, 2015), *The Quantified Self: A Sociology of Self-Tracking* (Polity Press, 2016) and *Digital Health: Critical and Cross-Disciplinary Perspectives* (Routledge, 2017). Her current research interests all involve aspects of digital sociology: Big Data cultures, self-tracking practices, digital food cultures, the digital surveillance of children, digitized academia, and digital health technologies.

Tom McDonald is an Assistant Professor at The University of Hong Kong. He obtained his PhD from University College London, in 2013, where he also worked on the Why We Post project, a European Research Council funded global comparative ethnographic study exploring the impact of social media use across a range of different societies. He has conducted extensive ethnographic research in rural China. His first solely-authored monograph, *Social Media in Rural China: Social Networks and Moral Frameworks* (UCL Press), was published in 2016. He also co-authored the volume *How the World Changed Social Media* (UCL Press, 2016). McDonald is currently working on a new project investigating the use of digital money by migrant workers in China.

Mark McLelland is Professor of Gender and Sexuality Studies at the University of Wollongong and a former Toyota Visiting Professor of Japanese at the University of Michigan. He is author or editor of over 10 books concerning the history of sexuality in Japan, Japanese popular culture, new media and the Internet, most recently: *The End of Cool Japan: Ethical, Legal and Cultural Challenges to Japanese Popular Culture* (Routledge, 2017) and *The Routledge Companion to Global Internet Histories* (with Gerard Goggin, Routledge, 2017).

Kate M. Miltner is a PhD Candidate at the USC Annenberg School of Communication and Journalism. Her research focuses on the intersection of technology, identity, culture, and inequality. She has a BA in English from Barnard College, Columbia University, and received her MSc in Media and Communications from the London School of Economics and Political Science. She has also had research appointments at Microsoft Research New England and Twitter. Kate has published scholarly work on a variety of topics relating to digital culture, including internet memes, online antagonism, animated GIFs, selfies, and Big Data; her work has appeared in the peer-reviewed journals *Social Media & Society*, *International Journal of Communication*, *First Monday*, *Feminist Media Studies*, and *Mobile Media and Communication*. Kate's research has also been featured in *Wired*, *Slate*, *The Atlantic*, *The Guardian*, *Time*, and the BBC. You can find more about her at katemiltner.com.

Zizi Papacharissi is Professor and Head of Communication, and Professor of Political Science at the University of Illinois at Chicago. She edits the *Journal of Broadcasting and Electronic Media*, and is the founding and current editor of the open access and free journal *Social Media and Society*. She has authored or edited nine books, over 60 journal articles and book chapters, and presently serves on the editorial board of 15 journals. Her research focuses on the social and political consequences of technologies.

Isabella Peters is Professor of Web Science at ZBW Leibniz Information Centre for Economics and Chair of the Web Science research group at Kiel University. She received her PhD in Information Science from Heinrich Heine University in Düsseldorf. Her research focuses on user-generated content and its potential in knowledge representation and information retrieval as well as in scholarly communication on the social web, e.g. altmetrics. In 2016 she was one of the members of the Expert Group on Altmetrics initiated by the European Commission.

Jack Linchuan Qiu is Professor at the School of Journalism and Communication, the Chinese University of Hong Kong, where he serves as Director of the C-Centre (Centre for Chinese Media and Comparative Communication Research). His publications include *Goodbye iSlave*

(University of Illinois Press, 2016), *World's Factory in the Information Age* (Guangxi Normal University Press, 2013), *Working-Class Network Society* (MIT Press, 2009), *Mobile Communication and Society* (co-authored, MIT Press, 2006), some of which have been translated into German, French, Spanish, Portuguese, and Korean. He is on the editorial boards of 10 international academic journals, including six indexed in the SSCI, and is Associate Editor for *Journal of Communication*. He also works with grassroots NGOs and provides consultancy services for international organizations.

Kelly Quinn is a Clinical Assistant Professor in the Department of Communication at the University of Illinois at Chicago. Her work focuses on new media, such as social network sites and microblogging, and how these intersect with such diverse areas as the life course, social capital, friendship, and privacy. Quinn's recent work has centred on midlife and older adults and the cognitive and social impacts of their social media use. She serves on the editorial board for *Emerald Studies in Media and Communications*, and her publications have been included in *Information, Communication & Society*, the *Journal of Broadcast and Electronic Media*, and the *International Journal of Emerging Technologies and Society*, as well as several edited volumes.

Richard Rogers is University Professor and holds the Chair in New Media & Digital Culture at the University of Amsterdam. He is Director of Govcom.org, the group responsible for the Issue Crawler and other info-political tools, and the Digital Methods Initiative, dedicated to the study of the natively digital. Among other works, Rogers is author of *Information Politics on the Web* (MIT Press, 2004), awarded the 2005 best book of the year by the American Society of Information Science & Technology (ASIS&T) and *Digital Methods* (MIT Press, 2013), awarded the 2014 Outstanding Book of the Year by the International Communication Association (ICA). His latest book is *Issue Mapping for an Ageing Europe* (with Natalia Sanchez and Aleksandra Kil, Amsterdam University Press, 2015).

Michael Serazio is an Assistant Professor in the Department of Communication at Boston College (USA). His research interests include media production, advertising, popular culture, political communication, and new media. He is the author of *Your Ad Here: The Cool Sell of Guerrilla Marketing* (New York University Press, 2013), which investigates the integration of brands into entertainment content, social patterns, and digital platforms. He has scholarly work appearing or forthcoming in the *Journal of Communication*, the *International Journal of Communication*, *Critical Studies in Media Communication*, the *Journal of Consumer Culture*, the *Journal of Broadcasting and Electronic Media*, *Communication Culture & Critique*, and *Television & New Media*, and has also written essays on media and culture for *The Atlantic*, among other publications.

Aaron Shaw studies collective action, organization, and participation online, usually in collaborative peer production communities like Wikipedia. He is an Assistant Professor of Communication Studies and Director of the Media, Technology and Society program at Northwestern University. At Northwestern he is also an affiliate of the Sociology Department, the Buffett Institute, the Institute for Policy Research, and the SONIC lab. Elsewhere, he is a faculty affiliate of the Berkman Klein Center for Internet & Society at Harvard University. Aaron received his PhD in Sociology from the University of California Berkeley.

Jolynna Sinanan is a Vice Chancellor's Postdoctoral Research Fellow in the Digital Ethnography Research Centre and the School of Media and Communications at RMIT University, Melbourne. Prior to this position she was a Research Fellow in Anthropology at

University College London with the European Research Council funded project *Why We Post*, which compared uses of social media across eight countries. She is the co-author of *Visualising Facebook* (UCL Press, 2017) and *Webcam* (with Daniel Miller, Polity Press, 2014), and *How the World Changed Social Media* (UCL Press, 2016).

Michael Stevenson is an Associate Professor in the Media Studies department at the University of Amsterdam, and a founding member of the Digital Methods Initiative. He researches the history of web culture, and the discourse and practice of web exceptionalism. He is currently working on a four-year research project called 'The web that was', about the technology and culture of the early web with a focus on the web's shared history with the Perl programming language. The project is funded by the Dutch National Science Foundation (NWO).

Crispin Thurlow is Professor of Language and Communication in the Department of English at the University of Bern, Switzerland. His books include the edited collection *Digital Discourse: Language and the New Media* (Oxford University Press, 2011). He is on the editorial board of a number of international journals, including *Language in Society*, *Critical Discourse Studies*, *Discourse, Context & Media*, and the *Journal of Computer Mediated Communication*. More information about his research and teaching can be found at: www. crispinthurlow.net.

Daniel Trottier (PhD, Queen's Canada) is an Associate Professor of Global Digital Media in the Department of Media and Communication at Erasmus University Rotterdam. In addition to leading a five-year project on digital vigilantism, he has participated in European Commission projects on security, privacy and digital media. He has authored in peer-reviewed journals on this and other topics, as well as *Social Media as Surveillance* (Ashgate, 2012), *Identity Problems in the Facebook Era* (Routledge, 2013) and *Social Media, Politics and the State* (co-edited with Christian Fuchs, Routledge, 2014). He previously held appointments as a Postdoctoral Fellow at the Communication and Media Research Institute (CAMRI) at the University of Westminster, the Department of Informatics and Media at Uppsala University Sweden, and the Department of Sociology at the University of Alberta, Canada.

Siva Vaidhyanathan is the Robertson Professor of Media Studies and the Director of the Center for Media and Citizenship at the University of Virginia. He is the author of four books and the co-editor of another. His Twitter feed is @sivavaid.

José van Dijck is distinguished university professor of Media Studies at the University of Utrecht. She previously taught at the University of Amsterdam where she served as Chair of the Department of Media Studies and Dean of the Faculty of Humanities. Her visiting appointments include MIT, the Annenberg School for Communication (Philadelphia), Georgia Tech, and the University of Technology in Sydney. In 2015, she was elected as President of the Royal Netherlands Academy of Arts and Sciences. Her work covers a wide range of topics in media theory, media technologies, social media, and digital culture. Van Dijck's book *The Culture of Connectivity: A Critical History of Social Media* (Oxford University Press, 2013) was distributed worldwide and was recently translated into Spanish. Her next book, co-authored with Thomas Poell and Martijn de Waal, will be titled *The Platform Society: Public Values in a Connective World*.

Farida Vis is Director of the Visual Social Media Lab and Faculty Research Fellow in the Information School at The University of Sheffield (UK). The VSML brings together a group of interdisciplinary researchers from academia and industry interested in analysing social media images. In the VSML she is principal investigator on a number of funded projects. Her research is focused on developing methods for researching social media, the datafication of society and emerging algorithmic regimes. Taking seriously the need to engage beyond academia, she sits on the World Economic Forum's Global Futures Council on The Future of Information and Entertainment (2016–2018), having previously served on the Global Agenda Council on Social Media (2013–2016). She sits on the Board of Directors of the Big Boulder Initiative, an US-based organization focused on the sustainable future of the social data industry. The VSML is a member of the First Draft News Partner Network.

Jill Walker Rettberg is professor of Digital Culture at the University of Bergen. She is the author of *Seeing Ourselves Through Technology: How We Use Selfies, Blogs and Wearable Devices to See and Shape Ourselves* (Palgrave 2014) and *Blogging* (Polity Press, 2008, 2nd ed 2014), and co-edited *Digital Culture, Play, and Identity: A World of Warcraft Reader* (MIT Press, 2008). Her research has centered on storytelling and self-representation in social media, as well as on digital art, electronic literature and the implications of digital visual technologies. Rettberg has been an active research blogger at jilltxt.net since 2000.

Katrin Weller is senior researcher at GESIS Leibniz Institute for the Social Sciences and head of the team Social Analytics and Services within the Computational Social Science department. In 2015, she was one of the inaugural researchers to be awarded with the John W. Kluge Center's Fellowship in Digital Studies for a research stay at the Library of Congress, Washington DC. She received her PhD in Information Science from Heinrich Heine University Düsseldorf in 2010. Her research focuses on social media users and usage in different contexts, including social media in scholarly communication and altmetrics. She has also done field work on the conditions of conducting research with social media data, including the ethics of social media research and data archiving. Katrin is co-editor of *Twitter and Society* (Peter Lang, 2014).

Rowan Wilken (PhD) is Principal Research Fellow and Associate Professor in the School of Media and Communication, at RMIT University, Melbourne, Australia. His present research interests include mobile and locative media, domestic technology consumption, theories and practices of everyday life, and old and new media. He has published widely on mobile and location-based media. He is the co-editor (with Justin Clemens) of *The Afterlives of Georges Perec* (Edinburgh University Press, 2017), and co-editor (with Gerard Goggin) of *Locative Media* (Routledge, 2015) and *Mobile Technology and Place* (Routledge, 2012), and is the author of *Teletechnologies, Place, and Community* (Routledge, 2011). At present he is working on two books: a research monograph, *Cultural Economies of Locative Media* (to be published by Oxford University Press), and an edited book (with Gerard Goggin and Heather Horst), *Location Technologies in International Context* (to be published by Routledge).

Haiqing Yu is Associate Professor of contemporary Chinese media and culture in the School of Humanities and Languages, University of New South Wales, Australia. Her research focuses on the 'effect' and 'affect' of digitally mediated social economy, social movements, and cultural transformation. It explores Chinese digital and informal economy, associations, and social activism; rural e-commerce and its impact on gender and ethnicity; social enterprise, digital economy, and disability; social media and Chinese diaspora. Her published works have also explored the implications of the Internet and mobile communication on Chinese journalism, youth culture/sexuality, HIV-related health communication, and everyday life politics. Her publications include: *Media and Cultural Transformation in China* (Routledge, 2009) and *Sex in China* (co-author with Elaine Jeffreys, Polity Press, 2015).

Editors' Introduction

Jean Burgess, Alice Marwick and Thomas Poell

THE SOCIAL MEDIA PARADIGM

The world is in the midst of a social media paradigm – a distinctive moment in the history of media and communications shaped by the dominance of social media technologies. By social media technologies, we mean those digital platforms, services and apps built around the convergence of content sharing, public communication, and interpersonal connection. These technologies have been widely but unequally taken up by the world's diverse populations, and have an influence on all of our lives through pervasive 'social media logics' like connectivity (van Dijck & Poell, 2013).

Through its logic of convergence (Burgess, 2017), the social media paradigm brings with it entanglements between commercial, public and personal contexts. Well-known platforms like Twitter, Facebook and WeChat, once seen as mere sources of teenage distraction, have become embedded into the ICT infrastructures of corporations, societal organizations,

and public institutions. Especially with the rapid uptake of mobile media, these platforms, their uses and their politics are also increasingly embedded in our everyday life, work and relationships at a very personal and embodied level.

The social media paradigm is also shaping the interests and knowledge practices of media and communication studies. From the mid to the late 1990s, proto-social media like social networking sites and content sharing platforms (from Friendster to MySpace) were objects of burgeoning interest in internet studies, media studies and communication studies. Since then, social media has become a recognizable field of study within these disciplines. As of 2015, this sub-field even has its own journal, *Social Media + Society* (also published by Sage),[1] as well as a number of edited collections, and now this *Handbook*.

At the same time, research on social media has transitioned from being a niche topic within internet studies to a site of transformation and methodological innovation for more mainstream social scientists. Through its embedding across areas of society like government and politics, health and medicine, and education, social media is becoming an area of interest for researchers focused on those topics, even if they have not previously been particularly interested in studying the internet. In the field of political science, for example, social media is unavoidable because of the way it is now playing such an obvious and contentious role in electoral politics, protest, and political journalism. In public and sexual health research, it is increasingly impossible to understand sexual cultures and practices without understanding the role of mobile dating apps. And because social media is understood as important for networking and the dissemination of knowledge for practitioners in almost every profession (including science), most college graduates and doctoral students are encouraged to develop social media literacy in the course of their education.

Most recently, as part of a broader 'datafication' of society and a turn to digital methods, the social media paradigm has driven significant change in *how* humanities and social science research is done. This shift has been the focus of a number of stand-alone articles and edited volumes (see, for example, Snee, Hine, & Morey, 2015). Cross-disciplinary journals, such as *Big Data and Society*, have been launched to deal with the dual challenges posed by the datafication of *society* on the one hand, and the datafication of social science *research* on the other. These shifts are felt particularly acutely in the domain of social media research because the discourses, interactions and relationships of social media users are themselves monitored, collected and ordered as data that can be aggregated, analysed and monetized by social media platforms, while the mechanisms for doing so in turn provide access to research data for social scientists. This datafication of social media use has attracted computational and information scientists to the data-driven analysis of social networks

and behaviour; and it has attracted media and communications researchers to questions around the political economy and ethics of social media's data cultures (see, for example, Langlois, Redden, & Elmer, 2015).

So, then, social media as a field of research is a potentially dynamic and diverse 'trading zone' (Rieder & Röhle, 2012) among many different social science and humanities disciplines, and even in Science, Technology, Engineering and Mathematics (STEM). As a common object of study that affords a wide variety of research questions and approaches, it presents us with exciting opportunities for discovery, dialogue and transdisciplinary collaboration, as well as the need for critical reflection on issues like privacy, ethics and the political aspects of data-mining. We hope this book will bring new and established voices from a range of disciplinary perspectives into this conversation.

SCOPE AND APPROACH

Given the rapid pace of popular technological developments, terminology is a constantly-shifting target. When interpersonal communication scholars and information scientists turned their attention to e-mail, forums and bulletin boards in the early 1980s (Rice, 1980; Kerr & Hiltz, 1982), they used the term 'computer-mediated communication' (CMC) to describe, as Joseph Walther (1992: 52) puts it, 'synchronous or asynchronous electronic mail and computer conferencing, by which senders encode in text messages that are relayed from senders' computer to receivers''. While internet communication is no longer entirely textual and no longer requires a user to sit at a computer terminal or use a modem to 'log on', many of today's social media practices were first identified and explored by CMC scholars, such as the use of emoticons (or emoji), trolling and flaming. We might best describe CMC today as a method rooted in interpersonal communication studies. Nancy Baym's popular book *Personal Connections in the Digital Age* (now in its second edition, 2015) takes this approach among several to analyse contemporary social technologies.

But why *social* media? 'New media', once a useful way to distinguish internet communication from broadcast media, now seems as dated as 'cyberspace' or 'the information superhighway', and firmly rooted in the 1990s. 'Digital media' is more precise, but covers an enormous scope, from video games to internet radio to e-books. 'Web 2.0', was used in the mid-2000s as a catch-all for a group of nascent social technologies, including Wikipedia, MySpace and Flickr. However, the '2.0' never referred to any particular technological development. It was a rhetorical move by entrepreneurs and venture capitalists to attract investment to the internet after the dot-com crash, and disappeared quickly, leaving unread business books and failed startups in its wake (Marwick, 2013).

'Social media', the current term of art, describes digital internet technologies that facilitate communication and collaboration by users. One might say that the term social media is so broad as to be useless, but because such technologies develop so quickly, this definition is expansive and vague by design. Similarly, scholars often operationalize 'social media' as 'Facebook and Twitter'. While Facebook is still the largest social media site in the world, and Twitter is popular to study since vast volumes of tweets are accessible to researchers, 'social media' must also encompass social networking sites like VK and LinkedIn; photo and video sharing apps like Instagram and Snapchat; music-sharing sites like Soundcloud; video sites like YouTube; blogs; texting apps like Signal, LINE and What'sApp; forums like Reddit and 4chan; location-based technologies like Foursquare and NextDoor; groupware like Slack and Discord; and annotation and aggregation sites like Pinterest and Genius (and dozens more by the time you read this), all of which may be mobile apps, websites or desktop software. A single one of these

apps and platforms can encompass thousands of different functions, communities and practices. In this book, rather than focusing on any one (or two, or three) technologies, our contributors examine a range of common practices, beliefs and concerns that they observe across social media technologies.

Since social media is an object of study, rather than a single discipline with a methodological history and agreed-upon canon, this volume is by necessity interdisciplinary. Contributors come from communication, media studies, journalism, information science, linguistics, science and technology studies, sociology, and gender studies, to name but a few. While interdisciplinarity is often championed by universities and in graduate classes, in practice it is much harder to achieve. Ethnographers trained in media anthropology, fan studies or audience studies may disagree with anthropologists on what 'counts' as ethnography. Computational social scientists may clash with digital humanists over what constitutes data. A cultural theorist might dislike the writing style of a communication scholar's paper (and vice versa!), while a sociologist might throw up their hands at how an information scientist thinks about class. However, what the contributors to this volume have in common is that they draw widely from different traditions and disciplines. Because social media combines the *social* with the *technical*, developing a full understanding of the use and effects of social media requires a promiscuous attitude towards scholarship. We ask our readers to suspend, to the best of their abilities, disciplinary prejudices when reading chapters in this *Handbook* from scholars outside their home field.

Much research and scholarship on social media focuses on the US context. This is unsurprising given the Anglo-centric bias across adjacent academic fields, including media studies (Thussu, 2009), cultural studies (Shome, 2009) and social computing (Philip, Irani, & Dourish, 2012, and compounded by the fact that many of the most-researched social media technologies originate in Silicon Valley and were popularized in the USA, including Facebook, Twitter, YouTube and Snapchat. Unfortunately, this focus has limited our understanding of social media technologies. Not only are practices local to English-speaking contexts often generalized far beyond what is rational, studies are often limited to WEIRD populations – those residing in Western, educated, industrialized, rich and developed countries (Henrich, Heine, & Norenzayan, 2010) – which are by no means representative. Such myopia also misses many significant social media sites. Russia's most popular social network, for instance, is VK (a mix of Facebook and filesharing), while China's internet giants Baidu, Alibaba, Tencent and Sina have more than 2 billion users. We have attempted to include, whenever possible, studies and perspectives from other contexts. De Seta's chapter on trolling, for instance, looks at how trolling in China complicates definitions and models of the practice drawn from English-speaking sites and cultures.

Finally, we must note the centrality of *mobile* communication to the social media experience for most people. Worldwide, 50% of overall internet traffic is mobile, and 88% of social media users access social media sites and apps using mobile phones (Kemp, 2017). Many of today's most popular social media apps, including WhatsApp, WeChat and Instagram, were designed for mobiles and have limited functionality on the desktop. Overwhelmingly, smartphone owners use their phones to access social media; to decouple social media from mobile use is impossible. Thus, our assumptions about *how* and *where* people access social media, in what contexts, and with who, must move beyond desktop and laptop usage.

media platforms and technologies that exist, the broad range of social media practices that can be observed across the globe, and the different ways in which these practices and technologies have been studied. While the *Handbook* overall still skews towards an Anglo-centric focus – reflecting both our own institutional contexts and the state of the field – it is structured so that the global and cultural diversity of platforms, practices and approaches is more evident. Our diverse international contributors have made sustained efforts to include examples from comparatively less-studied parts of the world, and they sketch avenues for future research into new platforms and practices. In this regard, the *Handbook* can be read as an invitation to further broaden the scope of social media as a multi-disciplinary field of study.

The first section of the book is devoted to histories and pre-histories, prompting the reader to shift their attention from the 'present', 'latest' and 'most current' to the complex lineages of contemporary social media. The subsequent section highlights the diverse repertoire of available approaches and methods, from ethnography and digital methods to political economic and historical analysis. The following two sections zoom in on the key technologies, business models, cultures and practices that define social media. Although this inventory is by no means comprehensive, the chapters offer inspiring examples of how social media can be empirically and conceptually explored in new ways. The final section on social and economic domains features chapters that examine how social media become involved in various professional domains, including marketing, education and journalism, providing starting points for further research on the role of these media in public life.

STRUCTURE AND CONTENTS

In developing this *Handbook*, we have tried to do justice to the wide variety of social

Histories and Pre-Histories

One of the potential weaknesses of research on social media is a lack of attention to its histories. The traps lie both in potential igno-rance of previous work done on a specific area of interest in other disciplines (as when researchers study online deliberation from a political science perspective without making themselves aware of the relevant work already done by communications scholars) and in being interested only in contemporary phenomena, without recognizing now those phenomena represent both continuity and change in the relationships between societies and communications technologies. The chap-ters in this section will help to build a more in-depth understanding of both these issues.

The opening chapter, 'Pushing Back: Social Media as an Evolutionary Phenomenon' by John Hartley, constitutes a genuine *tour de force*. Replacing the 'transmission' model of communication with a 'translation' or semiotic model, Hartley provocatively sug-gests that 'mass communication' and 'social media' predate the Neolithic Revolution. From his long-term perspective, he under-stands social media as group-forming institu-tions of inclusion and exclusion. As such they can be considered as the prime directive for humans, since, in Hartley's words, 'culture-made groups are the survival vehicles for knowledge and technology'.

With the second chapter, the *Handbook* moves into the more familiar terrain of bul-letin board systems (BBS). Aaron Delwiche traces the rise and fall of these systems, from their beginnings as technologies for computer enthusiasts to their mainstream acceptance. The chapter closes with a discussion of the collapse of the BBS scene, when the privati-zation and commercialization of the internet took off.

Shifting the focus to East Asia, Mark McLelland, Haiqing Yu and Gerard Goggin examine the historical development of social media in China and Japan in Chapter 3. These histories illustrate that there is not one uni-versal trajectory along which social media develop, but that language, place and culture continue to shape local and regional patterns of internet development. This conclusion is also reached by Michael Stevenson in the closing chapter of the histories section, in which he stresses that web history shows us that social media were not 'inevitable'. The chapter traces the lineage of social media to older ideas, values, media forms and technol-ogies, especially from the early web of the 1990s. Considering this history, Stevenson argues that utopian 'visions' of the web's purpose and nature should not simply be dis-missed, but understood as productive forces that set expectations, prompt community for-mation, create inequalities of attention and steer financial speculation.

Approaches and Methods

The study of social media is methodologically diverse, dynamic and challenging. This sec-tion brings together chapters that elaborate on the underpinning knowledge structures, approaches and techniques of particular social media research methods – from the concep-tual to the qualitative and the computational.

In the first chapter of this section, Richard Rogers elaborates on Digital Methods – that is, critical humanities methods that use the internet's affordances to study the very socio-cultural phenomena that they mediate – and updates them for a social media-dominated Web. His chapter brings to light the specific challenges of cross-platform analysis in a context where the characteristics of (often proprietary) platforms play such a central role in mediating social and cultural life, and it suggests a number of practical approaches and techniques that can be used in such work.

The existence and availability of large-scale sets of social media data have attracted immense interest in computational social sci-ence, or the use of computational methods to test social theories. In their chapter, Jeremy Foote, Aaron Shaw and Benjamin Mako Hill demonstrate such methods using a dataset of social media scholarship. Their analysis finds that while early social media research used social network analysis and quantitative methods, the most cited and influential work has come from marketing and medical research. In his chapter 'Digital Discourse: Locating Language in New/Social Media', Crispin Thurlow traces the foundations of digital discourse analysis in sociolinguistics and critical discourse studies.

Nick Couldry and Jannis Kallinikos approach the study of social media through one of sociology's most fundamental concepts – ontology. They rehearse the question of what social media even *are*, and what can be understood to be their constitutive elements or objects of study. They conclude that, rather than taking such matters at face value, social media research needs to trace the political logics of social media's infrastructures, processes and interactions, in order to pin down the 'evasive sociality' of social media, and to empirically observe and critiques its operations and incentives.

In addressing social media's recent 'visual turn', Simon Faulkner, Farida Vis and Francesco D'Orazio survey the available approaches to the analysis of social media images, dividing them into three categories: large-scale (computational) image analysis; analysis at multiple scales using mixed methods; and close qualitative analysis. They illustrate how these approaches can be combined through their own case study of image-sharing practices: the visual representation on Twitter of Alan Kurdi's death.

Jolynna Sinanan and Tom McDonald tackle the role of ethnography in social media research. Ethnography is treated here as the defining practice and output of anthropology. Through a survey of the literature on its application in media anthropology as well as reflections on their own work within the international Why We Post project, the authors consider how ethnography is being used to shed light on everyday social media practice, and how social media are shifting the practice of ethnography within Anthropology.

It is one thing to argue that social media researchers must attend to the history of the platforms and practices they study, but it is quite another to figure out where to find the archives, tools and approaches to do so in practice. In his chapter, pioneering web historian Niels Brügger reflects on the general challenge of archiving and understanding the ephemeral web, and the acute challenges of doing so in an appified and proprietary social media-dominated environment, leaving the reader with useful pointers for moving forward with this kind of work.

Siva Vaidhyanathan uses the example of Facebook Basics in India to discuss political economy approaches to social media. Considering research in critical theory, Marxist-influenced Critical Political Economy and cultural studies, he suggests a model of scholarship rooted in the work of Thorstein Veblen that engages with the complexity of labour, use, technology, states and corporations that mark today's social media landscape.

Platforms, Technologies and Business Models

One of the distinctive challenges of approaching social media as an object of study is finding ways to account for the role of platforms – complex assemblages of technologies, business models and user practices – in mediating and being shaped by the specific and diverse forms of interaction and communication that they support. This section is devoted to chapters that critically explore these issues, each bringing together political economy and software or technology studies in particular combinations in order to do so.

Taina Bucher and Anne Helmond lead off the section by bringing software studies and internet studies together in an advanced concept of affordances that can account for the materiality and the medium specificity of social media platforms. In doing so, they revisit older debates about the concept, and refresh it through close forensic analyses of specific features and their uses. Tarleton

Gillespie extends his popular work on the politics of platforms to examine how platforms both govern and are governed. Platforms are governed by information policy, such as the United States' 'safe harbor provision' for information intermediaries. But Gillespie also shows how platforms themselves govern, in terms of content regulation and behaviour policing. By examining the complexities of moderation and enforcement, Gillespie delves into questions of accountability and responsibility in social media.

Each of the next three chapters deals with some aspect of the political economy of social media in the context of a globalizing world. Rowan Wilken provides a detailed account of the interconnected global business interests operating at every layer of the mobile app economy through which so many people experience social media. The chapter covers major US players like Apple, Google, Facebook and Twitter, but then considers the different dynamics of other major markets, such as China and Russia.

Jack Qiu elaborates a multi-dimensional model that describes the various forms of labour operating in and through social media's material and symbolic economies, focusing particularly on the Chinese context – where much of the hardware that powers the social media paradigm is produced, and where distinctive formations of class consciousness, creativity and political protest are expressed through social media platforms like QQ and WeChat.

In her chapter 'Silicon Valley and the Social Media Industry', Alice Marwick considers the influence of the United States' dominant cultures of production (especially the 'Californian Ideology' associated with Silicon Valley) on social media and on global markets and their local economies. She describes how Silicon Valley functions as a kind of global imaginary, articulating to various local contexts through their own start-up and entrepreneurial scenes.

Robert Gehl's chapter, 'Alternative Social Media: From Critique to Code', examines alternative social media platforms, those developed outside systems of hegemonic corporate social media. Gehl argues that sites like Ello and Diaspora represent the primary critiques of social media, from political economy (surveillance, user data collection) to technical infrastructures (algorithms, centralization) and cultural practices (real-name policies and context collapse).

Cultures and Practices

In this section our authors trace a range of themes that cross platforms, cultures and, indeed, internet eras. Each chapter represents both a substantive body of scholarship and is focused on a topic of great popular interest or public concern.

In 'Personal Connection and Relational Maintenance in Social Media Use', Kelly Quinn and Zizi Papacharissi use an interpersonal communication approach to examine how social media affects how social relationships are formed and developed, focusing on friendship. Rihannon Bury's chapter draws from her new Television 2.0 project to look at fandom, and how sites that enable people to share content, including YouTube, peer-to-peer file sharing networks and social media platforms, are changing viewing and participatory fan practices. Her rich ethnographic evidence shows the complex relationship between broadcast and social media for both self-professed fans and more casual viewers.

The next two chapters draw from participatory cultural practices that can be both playful and problematic. Gabriele de Seta provides a comprehensive look at 'troll studies' so far, and draws from his research on Chinese digital culture to examine the cultural situatedness of the term. Arguing for analysis of digital practice that draws from individual and reflexive experience, de Seta shows that while trolling *per se* does not exist in the Chinese context, similar practices are articulated locally, affected by national media ecologies and platform-specific norms and interactions. Similarly, Kate Miltner's examination of memes serves both as a 'primer on internet memes and internet meme research' and a deft overview of how memes function and differ in democratic and authoritarian regimes, as play, activism, and as part of capitalist political economy.

Jill Walker Rettberg's beautifully-written chapter, 'Self-Representation in Social Media', untangles two concepts that are often muddled together: self-representation and self-presentation. Using a Kendall Jenner Instagram photo as an object to think with, Rettberg unpacks how scholars from each tradition might approach such an artefact. She traces visual, written and quantitative self-representation, from diaries and self-portraits to the Big Data era of the self made of metrics and numbers. Kath Albury's essay on 'Sexual Expression in Social Media' takes a similar historical approach to argue that sexual expression has been part of internet communication since early textual chat rooms and discussion groups. The popularity of social media has made such expression much more visible, promoting freedom of expression for sexual minorities, but raising ethical concerns around young people, LGBT individuals and BDSM practitioners – and often social anxiety as well.

In the last essay in the section, surveillance studies scholar Daniel Trottier skilfully traces the difference between examining privacy and surveillance with regard to social media. He presents an overview of contemporary surveillance practices that occur on social media, focusing on how these practices force a reconsideration of privacy as a legal and cultural value.

Social and Economic Domains

Over the past decade, social media have become increasingly involved in a wide range of public domains, from journalism to politics and from education to health care. In the process, social media practices have transformed as well as clashed with established institutional routines. The chapters in this section examine how the rise of social media provides new opportunities, but also introduces new sets of problems in key public domains.

The section's first chapter by Michael Serazio and Brooke Duffy focuses on social media marketing. After a useful inventory of the threats to the traditional advertising model, the chapter explores how social media, such as Facebook and Instagram, are employed in the marketing triad of earned, owned and paid media. Such social media marketing strategies entail activating online influencers, soliciting user-generated content and circulating promotional content.

Alfred Hermida, in turn, examines the integration of social media in journalistic practices. He describes these media as 'the land of opportunity' for news organizations and journalists, as they allow for an expansion of audiences and enable new forms of engagement. At the same time, he notices that they force these organizations and journalists to operate outside the framework of institutional journalism, creating new tensions as journalistic norms and established representations of the news are challenged. In the following chapter, Terry Flew makes very similar observations in his investigation of the evolving relationship between social media and the cultural and creative industries. He maintains that the use of social media expands reach and engagement, undermines traditional creative business models and leads to new types of model. Services such as Netflix that revolve around algorithm-based decision-making are a prominent example of this trend.

Shifting the focus from the creative industries to politics, Jessica Baldwin-Philippi contends that the adoption of digital tools in political campaigns has led to strategic and technical innovation. Investigating social media campaign strategies in the years following the revolutionary 2008 US elections, she discusses the (often unintended) consequences of opening up campaigns to public feedback and of giving analytics an increasingly central role in campaigning. Remaining within the political realm, the subsequent chapter by Thomas Poell and José van Dijck analyses how the intensive use of social media transforms the organization and communication of protest. In critical dialogue with the idea that traditional modes of organization in social movements are being replaced by platform-enabled mass user activity, the authors argue that leadership and collective identities continue to play a vital role in online contention. Moreover, they show that social media do not simply enable mass protest activity, but fundamentally shape it.

Deborah Lupton, a leading authority on digital technologies and health tracking, contributes a chapter on 'Lively Data, Social Fitness and Biovalue'. The chapter investigates the connections between practices and discourses of self-tracking and those of social media. Developing the concept of 'social fitness', Lupton explores the new forms of value that personal health and medical data have generated and she critical reflects on the political implications of the ideal of the socially fit citizen.

The two final chapters of the *Handbook* focus on the world of education and academia. Through case studies on AltSchool and Massive Open Online Courses (MOOCs), such as those offered by Coursera, José van Dijck and Thomas Poell investigate how learning metrics and predictive analytics are employed in primary and higher education. They also examine the new business models developed by such corporations. The chapter closes with a discussion of the impact of platformization on education as a public good. In the last chapter of the *Handbook*, Katrin Weller and Isabella Peters study the use of social media in scholarly communication. Rather than focusing on differences and transformations, the authors show the similarities between traditional and social media forms of scholarly communication.

They point out that in both cases researchers leave traces through which impact can be measured and the researcher's identity shaped. The chapter discusses how altmetrics enable such understanding of scholarly social media communication.

Note

1   See http://journals.sagepub.com/home/sms

REFERENCES

Baym, N. K. (2015). *Personal Connections in the Digital Age* (2nd ed.). Malden, MA: Polity Press.

Burgess, J. (2017). Convergence. In L. Ouellette & J. Gray (Eds.), *Keywords for Media Studies*. New York: New York University Press, pp. 47–48.

Henrich, J., Heine, S. J., & Norenzayan, A. (2010). The weirdest people in the world? *Behavioral and Brain Sciences*, *33*, 61–135.

Kemp, S. (2017). *Digital in 2017: Global Overview* (p. January 24, 2017). New York: We Are Social. Retrieved from: http://wearesocial.com/blog/2017/01/digital-in-2017-global-overview

Kerr, E. B., & Hiltz, S. R. (1982). *Computer-Mediated Communication Systems: Status and Evaluation*. London: Academic Press.

Langlois, G., Redden, J., & Elmer, G. (Eds.) (2015). *Compromised Data: From Social Media to Big Data*. London: Bloomsbury.

Marwick, A. (2013). *Status Update: Celebrity, Publicity and Branding in the Social Media Age*. New Haven, CT: Yale University Press.

Philip, K., Irani, L., & Dourish, P. (2012). Postcolonial computing: A tactical survey. *Science, Technology, & Human Values*, *37*(1), 3–29.

Rice, R. E. (1980). The impacts of computer-mediated organizational and interpersonal communication. In M. Williams (Ed.), *Annual Review of Information Science and Technology* (Vol. 15, pp. 221–249). White Plains, NY: Knowledge Industry Publications.

Rieder, B., & Röhle, T. (2012). Digital methods: Five challenges. In D. Berry (Ed.),

Understanding Digital Humanities. London: Palgrave Macmillan.

Shome, R. (2009). Post-colonial reflections on the 'Internationalization' of Cultural Studies. *Cultural Studies*, *23*(5–6), 694–719.

Snee, H., Hine, C., & Morey, Y. (Eds.) (2015). *Digital Methods for Social Science: An Interdisciplinary Guide to Research Innovation*. London: Palgrave Macmillan

Thussu, D. K. (2009). *Internationalizing Media Studies*. New York: Routledge.

van Dijck, J., & Poell, T. (2013). Understanding social media logic. *Media and Communication*, *1*(1), 2–14.

Walther, J. B. (1992). Interpersonal effects in computer-mediated interaction: A relational perspective. *Communication Research*, *19*(1), 52–90.

PART I

Histories and Pre-histories

Pushing Back: Social Media as an Evolutionary Phenomenon

John Hartley

A universe comes into being when a space is severed into two. A unity is defined. The description, invention and manipulation of unities is at the base of all scientific inquiry. (Humberto Maturana and Fransisco Varela, 1980: 73)

SOCIAL MEDIA: LONG STORY!

Taking the long-term view, 'social media' is a tautology. All media are social. All sociality is mediated. Pragmatically, the current arrangements known as 'social media', which distinguish online media from other types of media entertainment and social networks from physical ones, are not geared to the long-term view. It may be that most readers who encounter this chapter are also focused on the here and now. However, the chapter heads in the opposite direction, out of the endless present tense of social science, to push back as far as possible in order to understand what it might mean to claim, as Zizi Papacharissi does in the opening statement of

the new journal *Social Media and Society* (2015: 1), that 'we have always been social'. If so, one methodological imperative is that *we must all be interdisciplinary now*. We must find ways to translate and enjoy each other's knowledge and expertise, especially across polarised disciplinary or ideological boundaries. In that interdisciplinary universe, we need to pay more attention to *how we know what we know* – to 'noetics' (Ong, 2012) or the science of science, even as we deploy methods specific to a particular approach. Taking the long view imposes a new kind of 'discipline', which is both comparative (to *combine* different perspectives) and integrative (to *synthesise* difference).

Let's take Papacharissi's 'always' literally, and see where it leads, pushing back beyond history, even Fernand Braudel's (2012) 'extreme long term' (*la très longue durée*), beyond anthropology and even the confines of *H. sapiens*, to a much more fundamental level, as explored in biosemiotics: that of life itself:

Semiotics, in the process of delimiting and defining itself, has shown a noticeable trend towards a view which states that semiosis begins where life itself begins. (Kull, 1999: 115)

In other words, 'life' and 'sign' may prove to be one and the same phenomenon. It's not just that 'we' are social and thus communicative, via media from language to the internet, but also that all life is founded upon signals communicated in, by and among biogeochemical material processes, where the 'self-creation' and self-organisation of complex systems, or *autopoiesis* (Maturana and Varela, 1980: 73–123), produces discrete entities, bounded by difference-from-environment, from molecular level upwards.

If you like, you may proceed even further back in time and in causal sequence, from biogeochemistry to elementary physics, which may also be founded on communication. Elementary particles communicate with each other through 'messenger particles' (gravitons, photons, Higgs bosons, etc.) that carry force over a force field (gravitational field, electromagnetic field, Higgs field). Physics is known as the 'fundamental' or 'enabling' science because it describes mathematically a framework of perfect communication – of all particles with all particles – which then constructs the concepts of information and message, based on difference from randomness (Hartley and Potts, 2016). Rethinking physical reality itself in terms of communication bases the natural world – physical and biological – not only on fields but also on relations.

Traces of life from 4.1 billion years ago have been found in Western Australia (Bell et al., 2015). Communication as '*matter-energy*' + *life* + *sign* can be illustrated with something that emerged about halfway along terrestrial life's timeline. About 2 billion years ago Eukaryotic organisms appeared. Eukaryotic cells have a nucleus; those of the other two bio-domains, archaea and bacteria, do not. Eukaryotes are the cellular 'complex systems' from which we are all descended, including algae, plants, fungi and animals. Eukaryotes are quite complex structures, with nuclei and other 'organelles' within each cell.[1] In order to constitute and maintain themselves as entities, eukaryotic cells require communicative relationships. Internally, cell-signalling coordinates the cell's actions. In the case of multicellular eukaryotes like us, they must communicate with other parts of the same organism as well as the trillions of microorganisms living within it, such as gut bacteria. Externally, cells must communicate with the environment and its biotic load.

Communication connects organisms to systemic relations at much higher levels of organisation too: relations of descent and reproduction (in time), prey and predator (in space), cooperation and competition (dynamics of change), and environmental adaptation or niching (selection). The very constitution of eukaryotes (including *H. sapiens*), then, is based on these *communicative relations*, internal and external, which, at maximum, interrelate every living organism with every other, present and past, differentiating life into an evolved new 'envelope' of planetary extent: the 'biosphere' (Vernadsky, 1998; and see Figure 1.1).

'SOCIAL INSTINCTS'

Thus 'social media' must include cellular secretions – think pheromones. The very glimpse of such possibilities permits an approach to communication – the thing that makes the media into media and sociality social – that is naturalistic and scientific, but can include relations, meanings, and identities, deriving its approach from bioscience not directly from physics, especially the model taken from the war-effort information science of the 1940s that still underlies the dominant 'transmission' model of communication (Carey, 1989). That model (Shannon, 1948) reduces communication to transmission of information from sender to receiver

Phylogenetic Tree of Life

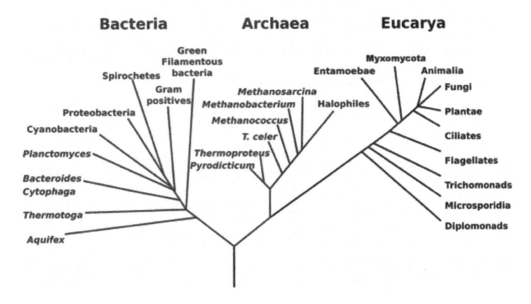

Figure 1.1   The biosphere: 'To the best of our current knowledge, all organisms that are alive today or that have lived on this planet in the past are part of one large, genetically connected group: *Life on Earth*' (*Tree of Life Web Project*). **Image: Phylogenetic Tree of Life (after Woese et al., 1990), courtesy of Wikimedia Commons (Public domain)**[2]

through a channel (or wire). This reduces *relations* to 'interference' and 'noise' and communication itself to individualistic behaviour.

As James Carey (2000) went on to warn, such a model of science is better suited to control than to democracy, because it replaces communication with behaviour and uses science to manipulate that. In critiquing 'a science designed to rule over citizens', Carey offers an alternative: a 'science of enlightenment or citizenship, a science in society'. He writes:

Science, under the dominant construction of what science is, deeply undercuts the democratic impulse of journalism. For a science of journalism is a science about journalism: a science of bureaucracy, of systems, of procedures, of management and of control. It is not a science of creation and construction, a science of understanding and common action. A science from without cannot connect with the creative impulse from within. (Carey, 2000: 22)

We can now do better, using relational models to develop a communication-based science of 'creation and construction', of 'understanding and common action' that connects with 'the creative impulse', developed from interdisciplinary contact (and some feats of mutual translation) with evolutionary and complexity sciences.

The evolutionist Charles Darwin (1871) called the framework of *human* communication the 'social instinct'.

As humanity advances in civilisation, and small tribes are united into larger communities, the simplest reason would tell each individual that they ought to extend their social instincts and sympathies to all the members of the same nation, though personally unknown to them. This point being once reached, there is only an artificial barrier to prevent their sympathies extending to the humanity of all nations and races. ...

The highest stage in moral culture at which we can arrive, is when we recognise that we ought to control our thoughts, and 'Not even in inmost thought to think again the sins that made the past so pleasant to us'.[3] (Darwin, 1871, 1(3): 100–101)[4]

Extending the 'social instinct' to non-kin and even to unmet strangers ('all the members of the same nation') is an important move, both for humans and for bioscience. It draws attention away from the *individual* and the so-called 'selfish gene' celebrated by Richard Dawkins (1976), to focus instead on the *group*, up to population level ('all nations and races'). Instead of Dawkins' individualistic gene-centred view of evolution, Darwin is pointing to a culture-centred view, where communicative sociality – language, relationship, identity – binds groups, via social media, in such a way that their knowledge and technologies can be shared, stored and transmitted through time and across space, typically in competition with other groups.

Culture makes groups, which are the 'survival vehicles' (Pagel, 2012) for all who live within their boundaries. This approach to culture – emphasising what it is *for* rather than restricting it to the products of professional practitioners – is elaborated in Hartley and Potts (2014: Chapter 3), where we introduce the concept of 'demes'. This term for culture-made groups is based on both bioscience (demes = interbreeding subpopulations) and political science (demos = citizens), to identify 'inter-knowing' subpopulations or 'we'-groups. Demes are at once rule-bound and dynamic, cooperative and competitive – up to the point of destructive conflict between adversarial demes. Within a deme too, 'cooperation' is not all lovey-dovey, since *H. sapiens*, like previously evolved hominins going back 2 million years, had use of lethal hand-weapons as well as tools and, with language, to deceit as well as truth. In that situation, whatever knowledge could save a group could also destroy it: *Hamlet* style, anyone can secretly murder the monarch in their sleep and marry their consort. Since strength alone cannot determine group leadership,

the 'social media' of any 'we'-group are crucial to the maintenance of both trust and scepticism, testing individuals' communicative intentions (Tomasello, 2014) even while telling group-binding stories, building and breaking alliances for social coordination at different scales, as well as extending knowledge and technology across increasingly large communities of non-kin and personal strangers. The most 'efficient' evolved mechanism for holding groups together (while distinguishing them from others) is language and its semiotic load, such that 'being human' and 'language' are one and the same. As Raymond Williams put it (1977: 21): 'A definition of language is always, implicitly or explicitly, a definition of human beings in the world'. Thinking about 'language' (group) rather than 'behaviour' (individual) is essentially a systems approach to culture, and its germ is present in Darwin.

PLANETARY SCALE

Bioscience shares components with other evolutionary sciences, from computer- and web-science (cybernetics) to economics and linguistics. It connects foundational 'systems' approaches to aspects of culture, for example: Niklas Luhmann (2012), who analysed 'society' as *autopoietic* or self-creating, by means of communication (following Maturana and Varela); Yuri Lotman (1990), who construed the *semiosphere* as a dynamic meaning-system (or system-of-systems) of planetary extent; Brian Arthur (2009), who analysed technology in terms of '*combinatorial* evolution'. Stuart Kauffman (2016), theorist of biological and machine systems, has recently extended his scope to 'humanity in a creative universe', moving beyond the Enlightenment tradition of reductive science to a 'new mythic structure' for understanding the biosphere and noösphere. Such work (there are many more examples) indicates that the study of social media is not an abrupt discovery of something new, but that they result from evolving complex systems, and interlock with others. The principle of biogenesis suggests the continuity of life, by which life cannot be understood except by the existence of prior life (Vernadsky, 1998: 54–55) (Figure 1.1). Similarly, social media are both self-creating and of evolutionary provenance, and must be explained accordingly.

Further, systems interact with other, incommensurate, systems. Lotman's approach to culture suggests that meaning is generated across the boundaries between *two or more pre-existing semiotic systems* (Lotman, 1990) in a web of interacting cultural systems of planetary extent. Similarly, social media interact with other systems, cultural and technological. Relations between systems are as important as relations within them.

These processes are indifferent to individuals – specimens or species – so you can't really do evolutionary analysis without a 'macro' model of both planetary space and geological time in which to situate your 'micro' processes and specimens, as well as the 'meso' institutions or populations in which they cluster (cf. Dopfer et al., 2004). But for most of human history, the full macro-system was simply not known. Once they migrated 'out of Africa' (say, 70,000 years ago), humans finally girdled the Earth when Polynesians settled the Earth's last large uninhabited landmass, Aotearoa New Zealand (a mere 1000–1500 years ago), but they took with them no shared understanding of the planet as such. They developed a planetary patchwork of mutually suspicious cultures whose competitive interactions were marked by adversarial conflict and occasional catastrophe. Despite *humans* being planetary, *culture* and *knowledge* long remained parochial.

Planetary extent was 'realised' in knowledge only in modernity, following early-modern European exploration and consequent imperial exploitation from the 1500s to the 1900s. *Knowledge* of the planet as a single system was thus only attained as part of Western expansionism once observations 'here' (e.g., meteorology, geology, fauna, flora, fossils, natural processes) could be correlated with similarly conceptualised observations of phenomena found 'there'. At an accelerating rate, the Earth became a coherent unit of exploration, discovery and thence knowledge. Finally, Darwin was able to conceptualise the 'social instinct' as a planetary phenomenon, with 'sympathies extending' to 'all nations and races', such that 'our thoughts' would come under the control of that knowledge, to value the macro (group) over the micro (individual) for the sake of survival though different but shared culture.

'WORLD-HISTORICAL FACTS'

Geology emerged as a global science in the eighteenth century, in the pursuit of rocks that might yield wealth (coal, oil, metals, etc.). During the nineteenth century, such global 'findings' began to be consolidated into disciplinary knowledge systems (Wallerstein, 2004) by globetrotting scholars. Alexander von Humboldt's explorations in South America led to his 'invention' of 'nature' (Wulf, 2015) and, in *Cosmos* (1858), to a very early conceptualisation of the 'causal interconnectivity of the universe' (Walls, 2009). Darwin and Alfred Russel Wallace elaborated evolutionary science using insights they'd gathered from voyages to the Galapagos Islands, South America and the Malay Archipelago; and, in Darwin's case, return visits to his home in Kent by barnacles, live and fossilised, from all over the world (Stott, 2004).

Karl Marx was an early 'collector' and synthesiser of global knowledge, reading ravenously through the burgeoning 'imperial archive' (Richards, 1993) under the dome of the British Museum Reading Room, navel of world knowledge, to develop his notion of 'world-historical' capitalism:

The more the original isolation of the separate nationalities is destroyed by the developed mode of production and intercourse and the division of labour between various nations naturally brought forth by these, the more history becomes world history. Thus, for instance, if in England a machine is invented, which deprives countless workers of bread in India and China, and overturns the whole form of existence of these empires, this invention becomes a world-historical fact. (Marx, 1845: Chapter 1.B)

Despite this discovery of world-historical 'facts' in the socioeconomic and historical domain by 1845, the implications of global scale have taken much longer to work through into widespread consciousness, especially in the arena of public thought and discourse. Darwin's (1871: 101) vision of the diffusion of species-sociality has not yet been realised. Marx was surely among the 'few people' who 'honoured and practised' global consciousness back in the 1840s, but strenuous efforts were made from that day to this to *stop* what Darwin saw as a natural process of knowledge diffusion, 'through instruction and example to the young, and eventually through public opinion'. Aggressive parochialism, which is Mark Pagel's (2012) evolutionary definition of culture, expressed as ideological conflict (internal) and warfare (external), still rules the roost. Meanwhile, the very idea of comprehensive, integrated knowledge ('scientific progress') is widely resisted, not least because it was established on the wings of nation-state imperialism, colonialism, militarism and class/gender/race antagonism, but also because it challenges the knowledge systems that maintained 'parochial' cultures, including religion and 'we'-group self-aggrandisement, thus resisting global consciousness in relation to society. In short, 'world-historical' facts have been resisted by both 'sides' of the political spectrum.

Global consciousness was adopted first in the natural sciences connected with the geosphere; and thence in those that served large-scale organised economic activities such as mining, manufacturing and trade. The next wave of knowledge-globalisation

took in the biosciences, which were synthesised into an evolutionary framework in the 1940s (Huxley, 1942). Here too the integration of knowledge is followed by large-scale economic exploitation. In the most recent wave, the post-1940s globalisation of telecommunications, broadcasting and user-centred social media took human meanings, relationships and identity around the world. Again, economic exploitation followed, such that the largest global corporations are currently the ones that 'mine' the resources of personal identity, relationships and meanings most efficiently. Individual subjectivity and global scale have at last integrated, if only in the culturally impoverished form of corporately owned 'big data' and in what we now call 'social media'.

However, even though that process may be accelerating, it too is resisted. The struggle between (closed) system-control and (open) user-democracy has continued. Conceptually, it is proving as hard to separate culture from capitalism as it was to distinguish science from imperialism, because the international trade in cultural products and media platforms is market-based, putting pressure on national jurisdictions to 'open' their citizens as well as their economies to the global market. But market forces don't have everything their own way. Emergent countries such as China and India and non-Western cultural systems such as Islam resist open media markets for strategic as well as ideological reasons, seeing such 'soft power' systems as a means to improve their own competitiveness. The galloping corporatisation of the internet, against which Jonathan Zittrain warned us way back (2008), and its more recent appropriation by surveillance-state agencies, is still resisted by myriad activists, associations and local cultures, both traditional (first peoples; civic organisations) and alternative (green activism; subcultures, WikiLeaks). Ordinary users, consumers and citizens are also resistant to such developments when they are experienced as over-intrusive because of surveillance, invasions of privacy and corporate appropriation of the 'social instinct' (and its expression) through intellectual property regimes, proprietorial platforms and marketing; or where they are corroded from within, as it were, by personal hate-speech, abuse, trolling, flaming, cyberbullying, online harassment, racism, sexism and intolerance of others, all of which Emma Jane (2015) sums up in the interdisciplinary term 'e-bile'.

Where the semiosphere (including social media) differs from the biosphere and geosphere is that here is the domain of consciousness, subjectivity and sociality itself, where all 'agents' (users) are active and productive makers of the very sphere that produces them. *They* ('consumers') cannot be 'mined' and 'exploited' in the same way that other 'resources' from the geo-biosphere have been; and *we* ('citizens') cannot – yet – be trusted to form a single, global, e-bile-free 'we'-group who agree with Darwin (1871) that 'the highest stage in moral culture at which we can arrive, is when we recognise that we ought to control our thoughts'.

Despite the global extent of computers, telecommunications, media and the internet, the cultural 'sphere' remains riven by what Alice Marwick (2013: 362) calls 'the structural oppression of difference', even as knowledge of the planetary extent of culture is increasingly widespread. It is still hard even to represent the semiosphere as a single unit, since its variable components use different languages, technologies and software, and different politics to produce what look at first sight like different realities, where 'difference' is construed as adversarial and antagonistic. To the extent that knowledge of culture at planetary scale and evolutionary time may produce understanding that supersedes this parochial aggressiveness, it can nevertheless be observed that the expanding knowledge systems of modernity, which *should* periodically be self-corrected by bouts of reflexivity, activism, decolonisation and revision, *can* extend planetary-scale knowledge from the geosphere (resources) and biosphere (life) into the semiosphere (cultural and mediated

meaning), to the sphere of knowledge itself – the noösphere – as globalisation accelerates further, across the economy, technology and media-culture.

ECONOMY VS CULTURE: 'MOST IMPORTANT' OR 'WORST MISTAKE'?

Pushing back to observe continuities as well as breaks in human history and material evolution can provide important insights for contemporary understanding. Social media are no exception. One way to try to understand them is to look for continuities with earlier periods, which may provide clues about where to look for causation. For a long time, since Marx in fact, social life has been supposed to be 'powered' (in every sense of the word) by the economy. We're not used to thinking about communication, culture and meaning as the drivers of change in human society. But recent discoveries, going back 12,000 years, suggest that they are primary, causing other kinds of social change, including economics and politics.

Most Important...

These discoveries are changing our perception of what has been claimed by many as the 'most important' of all 'world-historical facts': the so-called Neolithic Revolution, which saw the invention of farming (the economy) and adoption of settlement (politics). The idea of the Neolithic Revolution has become axiomatic, but it carries with it assumptions that may be mistaken; and correcting them may change our understanding of what we're looking at when we look at social media (i.e., a paradigm shift). It may be that we've been confusing causes and effects.

Here is how the story of the Neolithic Revolution is told, in this case sampled from the Khan Academy, where Senta German celebrates 'the cultural advances brought about by the Neolithic revolution', which she calls *the most important development in human history*. She explains:

> The way we live today, settled in homes, close to other people in towns and cities, protected by laws, eating food grown on farms, and with leisure time to learn, explore and invent is all a result of the Neolithic revolution. ... Before the Neolithic revolution, it's likely you would have lived with your extended family as a nomad, never staying anywhere for more than a few months, always living in temporary shelters, always searching for food and never owning anything you couldn't easily pack in a pocket or a sack. The change to the Neolithic way of life was huge and led to many of the pleasures (lots of food, friends and a comfortable home) that we still enjoy today. (German, n.d.)

Great story! (unless you're an Indigenous person living a traditional or nomadic life; or a migrant or refugee), speaking powerfully for the continuity of history from that day to this. But where did the idea of the Neolithic Revolution itself come from? Why is it thought so important? Did it actually occur? The term was coined by Australian archaeologist and socialist Vere Gordon Childe (1925/1958; 1936/1965).[5] Childe was a progressive cultural evolutionist, especially in relation to the mutually determining forces of technology and food production. He proposed the continuity of technological evolution, through the evidence of:

> ... insignificant bits of flint and stone, bronze and baked clay [in which] are revealed the preconditions of our gigantic engines and of the whole mechanical apparatus that constitutes the material basis of modern life. (1925/1958: xv)

According to Marxist theory, the 'material basis of modern life' was the economy or 'mode of production'. Childe's 'Neolithic Revolution' named the shift from a hunter-gatherer economy to agriculture, when 'mankind' (humanity) became:

> ... master of his own food supply through the possession of domestic animals and cultivated plants, and shaking off the shackles of environment by his

> skill in fashioning tools for tree-felling and carpentry, by organization for co-operative labour, and by the beginnings of commerce. (Childe, 1925/1958: 1)

Childe pushed the lines of continuity back in time to show that the Stone Age was part of the story of how we came to be modern ('our gigantic engines'). The mode of production (domesticating animals and cultivating plants), technology (tools), along with the social organisation of cooperation and trade (political economy), were all well established before copper and bronze were first smelted – about 5000 years ago.

Childe's great work performed a Huxleyan 'modern synthesis' for archaeology. He created a coherent story of developmental causation (a.k.a. modernist progress) out of a previous patchwork of mutually disconnected digs and findings, many of which sought biblical or racist explanations of the past. Childe was careful and erudite, integrating and synthesising previous knowledge. He developed an inferential method for associating archaeological finds with the material conditions of 'prehistoric cultures' (his term) that convinced many professionals, and he was a good science communicator at a time when poplar learning was being stimulated and extended to 'the masses' via cheap paperbacks. The 'Neolithic Revolution' became 'common knowledge', faithfully taught in academies ever since.

In line with his commitment to modernist progress, Childe didn't much like the Stone Age, at least prior to the Neolithic Revolution, seeing Mesolithic hunter-gatherer societies, dependent on the environment and with low levels of technological and social organisation, as closer to animality (i.e., 'primitive') than to 'civilisation'. For him, the Neolithic Revolution introduced *growth*, enabling the gigantic engine of history to sputter into accelerating motion. But Childe's dream of 'shaking off the shackles of environment' proved to be a modernist delusion. His desire to find a complete break between the Stone Age and civilisation was also mistaken. We are just as dependent on the environment as ever – including the geology, climate and biota that we are busy manipulating. In fact, Childe's characterisation of the invention of agriculture as a 'Revolution' owed more to the Marxist theory of his own times than to Mesolithic realities. He wanted the term to carry its full Marxist weight, where 'revolution' describes the rapid transition from one economic epoch to another. It had to be rapid, transformative and general, precipitating new class antagonisms (in this case between surplus-producing farmers and surplus-consuming specialists such as elite warriors and priests). But was it?

Agriculture's diffusion from the 'Fertile Crescent' across Eurasia and Africa was uneven. It was invented more than once, across different continents and islands, using different crops: wheat (Eurasia), rice (East Asia), maize and potato (America), millet (Africa), etc., or the much less nutritious taro (Papua New Guinea).[6] Some cultures developed herding but not crop cultivation (Saami), while in other places, like Aboriginal Australia, Inuit Canada or Kalahari Africa, agriculture was invented not at all. But Aboriginal people who live traditionally, not to mention young people everywhere, do not reject as primitive or superseded the idea of living 'with your extended family as a nomad, never staying anywhere for more than a few months, always living in temporary shelters, always searching for food and never owning anything you couldn't easily pack in a pocket or a sack', as the Khan Academy textbook has it. This is not a primitive dystopia but a description of aspects of the oldest continuing cultures in the world, which value community, 'country', 'dreamtime' and ceremony above a suburban semi-detached. It also describes one of the world's *newest* 'cultures' – that of millions of displaced migrant-refugees in the Middle East, Europe, Africa and elsewhere, for whom 'nomadic' life is the new normal, and of course it also describes the mode of life of many modern young adults and students who may find transition to settled life

more uncertain than did previous generations, even as their intellectual and social horizons expand via social media. Thus the presumption that farming and modern life are different in kind from 'hunter-gathering' (now known as 'work-shopping'), and that nomadic life is somehow indicative of primitive cultures, can only be understood as ideological: it's a preferred narrative about the primacy of economics (mode of production), not a description of how human societies work.

Worst Mistake...

The progressivism inherent in the idea that today's 'pleasures (lots of food, friends and a comfortable home)' are confined to post-farming cultures has been thoroughly critiqued. Jared Diamond (borrowing ideas from anthropologists like Marshall Sahlins and Eric Wolf) is a well-known critic:

> Now archaeology is demolishing another sacred belief: that human history over the past million years has been a long tale of progress. In particular, recent discoveries suggest that the adoption of agriculture, supposedly our most decisive step toward a better life, was in many ways a catastrophe from which we have never recovered. With agriculture came the gross social and sexual inequality, the disease and despotism, that curse our existence. (Diamond, 1987)[7]

Note that Diamond isn't disagreeing with Childe's thesis about the *importance* of the Neolithic Revolution. It's just that he values its outcomes negatively instead of positively. Like Childe before him, he accepts the Marxist narrative of increased class antagonism. Thus, his intervention (including subsequent criticisms of his work) does not alter the idea of a 'Revolution' but strengthens it. Alternative narratives are not sought. Even counter-evidence doesn't upset the model, which has reified into myth. So, for example, Samuel Bowles (2011) found that the first farming was *not* more productive than foraging, but he still calls the period in which farming was adopted the 'Holocene technological revolution' and repeats the idea that this was 'arguably the greatest ever revolution in human livelihoods'. His own results, however, suggest *piecemeal* not *revolutionary* adoption and ascribe 'causes' that come from culture (childrearing) and politics (military procurement), not economics (productivity). He concludes:

> Social and demographic aspects of farming, rather than its productivity, may have been essential to its emergence and spread. Prominent among these aspects may have been the contribution of farming to population growth and to military prowess, both promoting the spread of farming as a livelihood. (Bowles, 2011)

Gordon Childe himself did not stop at farming. He was interested in 'civilisation', which included settlement. He coined the term 'Urban Revolution' to mark the change from dispersed settlement patterns to trading towns. Among these, he was most impressed by the Achaean (Homeric) 'city state', where 'an international commercial system linked up a turbulent multitude of tiny political units' (1958: 172). The 'Urban Revolution' (his term) introduced the development of *international markets*, which managed to combine political competitiveness with economic cooperation through trade. Here, then, is the full progressivist picture, a 'grand narrative' (Lyotard, 1979), which completes its modernist look with a sustaining clamour of contested critique: the economy led to growth, class division and changes in the organisation of 'political units', accompanied by the development of mutually antagonistic classes (internally) and competitive states (externally), which nevertheless continued to trade in ideas as well as goods.

WHICH CAME FIRST – BASE OR SUPERSTRUCTURE?

The question that any student of social media needs to ask is whether it is safe to rely on

that story. My answer is no, but not because it's a story. The reason for scepticism goes beyond postmodern suspicion of the totalitarian tendencies in 'grand narrative' (Lucy, 2016). The problem is not only with the politics of progress, but also with the arrow of causation. If you are a student of social media, you're going to need a theory of *cultural* causation. But Childe's model places culture – 'civilisation' – at the end of a causal chain that separates it from most of human history (the tens of thousands of years before the Neolithic Revolution and among those cultures that didn't have one) and it places causal priority on labour (mode of production) over both knowledge and sociality, including mediation. But what if the arrow of causation points the other way? What if the 'Neolithic Revolution' was in fact *caused by social media*; and *mode of production* was a side effect, or means to an end?

In both of his revolutions – economic (mode of production) and political (ordered settlement) – Childe explains causal sequence in human history (and Diamond follows him) by using Marx's 'base and superstructure' model. In a justly famous passage Marx wrote:

> In the social production of their existence, humans enter into definite, necessary relations, which are independent of their will, namely, relations of production corresponding to a determinate stage of development of their material forces of production. ... The mode of production of material life conditions the social, political and intellectual life-process in general. It is not the consciousness of humanity that determines their being, but on the contrary it is their social being that determines their consciousness. (1857/1976: 4–5)

Marx was not interested in 'structure' or 'consciousness' as such; he was more interested in the causes and dynamics of historical *change*. He wanted a scientific explanation for social change and he thought the 'base and superstructure' model supplied it:

> At a certain stage of their development, the material productive forces of society come into conflict with the existing relations of production [property

relations]. ... From forms of development of the productive forces these relations turn into their fetters. At that point an era of social revolution begins. With the change in the economic foundation the whole immense superstructure is more slowly or more rapidly transformed. (1857/1976: 4–5)

That's a terrific piece of synthesising analysis: its ambition, reach and rhetoric still command admiration after all these years. Like his previous comments on 'world-historical' facts, it is also an amazingly early attempt to put history on the footing of a 'natural science', complete with laws arising from observations, and to consider it at planetary scale. But is it true? Does the conflict between forces and relations of production drive historical change, transforming in turn the 'whole immense superstructure' of culture, communication and consciousness? As it transpires, perhaps not.

THE *CULTURAL REVOLUTION?*

Göbekli Tepe changes everything. (Ian Hodder, director of archaeology, Stanford University)[8]

Social groups (demes) certainly were transformed in the Neolithic period, but the crucial question for present purposes is about the chain of causation. Did farming produce surpluses, classes, growth, settlement, states, and thus set humanity on the uneven road to modernity? And even if it did (albeit not as a 'revolution'), what 'caused' the invention of farming and then of cities? Did *culture* (communication) precipitate the need for large-scale resource-gathering and ordered settlement? And was it ceremonial activity, perhaps marking the demic boundaries of large, highly organised groups and 'broadcasting' their strengths, that necessitated more intensive modes of food gathering, herding and residential settlement? Such possibilities were out of the question for Childe.

The reason why such questions can be asked at all is that we now know that monumental building *preceded* the agricultural 'revolution'. The first great stone buildings in the world were put up not by surplus-generating farmers, but thousands of years earlier – further back in time before Stonehenge (Parker Pearson, 2012) and Saqqara's pyramids (Romer, 2012) than these sites are remote from today. The first stone monuments were erected by *Mesolithic hunter-gatherers* before pottery was invented, before metals and before farming. The arrow of causation may have to be reversed: the causal force for this epoch-making change was not 'surplus labour' but the *concentration of groups and intensification of communication*. It was this in turn that precipitated large-scale food requirements and the need to house large bodies of people in one place.

How do we know? Recent discoveries, especially at Göbekli Tepe ('Potbelly Hill') in Turkey, excavated by the late Klaus Schmidt,[9] suggest that the Childean chain of causation is the wrong way round (Hartley and Potts, 2014: 59–67). The limestone monuments here are about 12,000 years old (Stonehenge and the Great Pyramid are not even 5000). Its monumental scale – both the size of individual 20-foot-high carved stones and the number of circles created – is astonishing, as is the precision and beauty of construction. Göbekli Tepe seems to be have been designed as an expression of 'symbolic culture' (as Schmidt called it) and communal activities that were organised around *gathering* people, resources, knowledge and performance into one place, for one purpose: *communication*, both internal, to confirm the 'we'-group with feasting and shared ritual, not to mention the collaborative work and organisation of making the monument, and external 'costly signalling', especially broadcasting this deme's prowess to foes or competing neighbours who may have been building something of their own.

Altogether, this was a boundary-making exercise, possibly one designed to include the dead (burial levels are not yet excavated). Indeed, it may have been a prehistoric technology for *linking* the living with the dead, making demic 'honorary relatives' (Pagel, 2012) out of ancestors, by drawing a new, capacious boundary around the 'we'-group to include within the community both time (beyond death) and place, 'sanctifying' (as we might now say)[10] the country where they inhabited. Once boundaries were drawn around such a community, it proved practical to do the same to the land required to support it. The crowd was so big that they had to invent farming and settlement to cope with the pressures created by congregating, building stone monuments, feasting and ritual activities. The economy and settlement were merely a means to an end. Mesolithic nomads, without metals or even pottery, began the process of 'abstracting' symbolic culture into *new media* – in this case, limestone – so that everyone could find their thrill on Potbelly Hill.

Nevertheless, there were unintended consequences. Once farming had been invented and put on an efficient footing, the resources were so much the greater for continuing with cultural and political activities. Nick Card, director of the Ness of Brodgar dig in Scotland, another recently unearthed wonder that is older than Stonehenge (and may explain its prehistory), told PBS in 2015 that the artefacts unearthed over the years of the dig had led him to change his view of its function, from 'something to do with life and death' to the suggestion that 'people traveled long distances to the imposing complex to perform rituals, but also to feast, trade goods, gossip and celebrate'.[11] Perhaps there's no need to choose between these options. After all, even the most revered ancient Greek temples like the Parthenon were also treasuries – Bronze Age Reserve Banks – storing 'cash reserves for the construction of buildings and the erection of statues, as well as for a series of wars'.[12] We need to understand that trade, gossip, celebration (including celebrities), treasures, life and death are all of a piece: they are culture, not 'mode of production'. Oddly, we presume that such functions

among the ancients were religious; but we assume the same functions now – in social media for instance – are profane.

Best Story

Belittling the present in the name of the past is one thing; it is accompanied by an equally bad habit of belittling the past in the name of the present. Modern science habitually makes a distinction between story (culture) as unreliable and imagined ('old wives' tales'), as if those attributes were not also present in science (as per the theory of the Neolithic Revolution); and science (knowledge) as reliable and evidential, as if these attributes are not present in stories. These are print-era prejudices (Ong, 2012), based on the difference between oral-aural mediation of knowledge (language, drama, song, spectacle, ceremony, audio-visual media) and the more easily abstracted written/printed mediation of knowledge, out of which modern science emerged in the seventeenth and eighteenth centuries.

One way of countering such prejudice is (as above) to draw attention to storytelling in science. Another is to apply the scientific method to storytelling itself, linking bioscience to linguistics, for example, as have Sara da Silva and Jamie Tehrani (2016). Their 'phylogenetic' method of analysis, showing how stories found across different languages may indicate a 'common ancestor' language, and thus a date for the origin of particular stories (not just storytelling in general), has produced remarkable results. The oldest story they identify is 'The Smith and the Devil', about a man who learns the secret of smelting metal with fire by doing a deal with the devil (and then outwits him to keep both the secret and his soul). Variations on this 'fairy tale' are still forceful in the modern Western imagination. The modern Faustian version[13] moralises about the dangers of untrammelled knowledge, but equally it tells of the power of knowledge (fire, metallurgy, transformation of materials), the impact of such knowledge on individuals and society, and the social ambivalence of the specialist crafts where such knowledge is mastered.

Silva and Tehrani (2016) report that 'the Smith and the Devil' is at least 6000 years old. It appears in the language repertoire at about the same time as smelting (first lead and tin, then copper and the hard/sharp alloy bronze), in the right place – Anatolia ('Asia Minor') – at the right time, when the 'proto-Indo-European' (PIE) language split from Hittite. The story imputes the origin of knowledge to a supernatural agent, but that only reflects the state of scientific understanding at the time (humans were and remain unsure about where 'life' stops). The attempt to ascribe causal sequence was present, as was the threat of disruptive knowledge to existing society: after all, metallurgy was responsible for the 'creative destruction' of an entire epoch (the 'Stone' Age). Where the story still outpaces science is its imaginative and emotional charge in making clear the disruptive danger of innovation, the human risks of knowing more than your deme, even though specialisation of knowledge is necessary within a group. The story of the smith and the devil, or of other disruptive agents, like Dr Faustus or Don Juan, shows how a deme seeks simultaneously to hold itself together by sharing the tale and its worldview, even as the energies of innovation tear it apart, leaving the figure of the Trickster-artist-entrepreneur (Hartley, 2012: 199–214) to exploit and benefit from the gap between present rules and future possibilities, at mortal risk to themselves.

CHILDREN MUST BE SCENE BUT NOT EARN?

The sanctioned time for stories is childhood. But empirical social science barely notices children when modelling social structures and agency. They only enter the picture as behavioural problems – vulnerable victims or disruptive youth. Cultural science, on the other hand, accords a central conceptual place to children. The activities associated with growing up, playing, socialising, copying, making mischief, daydreaming, going around in gangs or cliques while creating new slang, crazes, celebrities, and associations, give to them as a group the cultural function of forming new future-facing demes, thereby maintaining dynamism in cultural systems (Hartley and Potts, 2014: Chapter 8). Thus, an evolutionary perspective on *social media* would ask how young people form groups.

When children start to make groups among non-kin they are experimenting with deme-formation, and also developing real links for future social networks. Thus, children create the next set of demes or culture-made groups, bound together by lived sociality and mutual knowledge that can only be acquired by living in the process and learning the language. Their groups are divided from others (foreign and parental versions) by asymmetries of trust, comprehension and cooperation, codes for which are learned in childish play, including playing with online social media. Here, 'play' is mistaken in social science as 'inconsequential' and 'unproductive' behaviour, using *economic measures* to determine culture, and thus posing a 'biological puzzle' for those who seek a 'rational choice' account of it (Konner, 2010: 500). Play (including its modern, mediated forms, from gaming and sport to entertainment, music and dance) needs to be reconceptualised, using *cultural functions* to explain a dynamic process of group-formation and thence transmission of knowledge, know-how and technologies through time (Hartley and Potts, 2014: 175–183), where, again, economic productivity is a consequence, not a cause.

Despite their centrality to the reproduction of a culture, children and young people are generally *represented* in media and scholarship in rather different guise, that of 'innocence'. Instead of being seen as future-forming agents, they are looked at with anxiety and rarely permitted, even in semiosis, a creative, productive role. Childish innocence is the preferred image of euphoria for capitalist marketing. But when children *are* productive, economically and creatively, from underclass child-labour in farm and factory to 'under-age' models and actors, they attract discourses of anxiety, protection and correction. Economic productivity in children is represented as going beyond the limit of the social (and thereby setting that demic limit). 'Letting children be children!' means confining them to uselessness: politically unenfranchised, economically unproductive, behaviourally inconsequential, sexually impotent and creatively of no account, most themselves when most idle and irresponsible. They are very much a latter-day Veblenesque 'leisure class', their conspicuous wastefulness an index of their society's affluence (or, where they are exploited as a labour force, its poverty).

Actual living humans have to reverse these values as they traverse from child to adult, exchanging unknowing unproductivity for economic and social responsibility. It's a hard trick to pull off, and they must perform it in public, always being looked at and looking (Hickey-Moody, 2015: 145), as they make themselves up under surveillance by both peers and by agencies interested in enforcing certain choices upon them. As they experiment with the possibilities of social media, they are building selves and society: longing for love, fearing death, combining identity ('me') and belonging ('we') in new demic groups. Their creative and communicative dynamism demonstrates that the uncertainty, anxiety and differentiation associated with coming of age is one of the engines of economic productivity in the creative epoch.

Science has inherited a view of children as underperforming or incomplete economic assets, to which the only response is control, combined with a knowledge-regime that discounts whatever they produce. But such a tradition not only mistakes the role children are playing in social reproduction, it also misconstrues social media and associated institutions such as celebrity, entertainment and games, dismissing them as inconsequential leisure, distraction, even dangerous delusion. But if we think of young people as cultural agents for the growth of knowledge and creative of groups, meanings, sociality, relationships and identity, then we may need to re-set the predominant governance mechanisms. If there's a point where systems are flexible enough to sustain themselves, the 'control' setting needs to be counterbalanced with an 'open' setting, and children themselves – as a deme – test where that point can be set. It may even be that social media are a 'natural experiment' in this very enterprise. We need to rethink how our inherited knowledge systems understand (and discount) 'primitive' culture, fictional stories and 'childish' behaviour. All of these might have something to teach us.

'GOOD ANCESTORS'

In his postscript to *The Gift*, Lewis Hyde makes a compelling case for valuing those who build futures:

> Those who have the wit and power and vision to build beyond their own day: for artists, those will be the good ancestors of the generations of practitioners that will follow when we are gone. (Hyde, 2007: 385)

Who are the 'good ancestors' of social media? It's a long way from Göbekli Tepe to Taylor Swift, you may say. But both of them may be performing the same cultural function: using the highest-technology social media of the day to call together and to represent in symbolic form the creation and unity of the deme, which, for all 'we' know, extends to the whole of humanity. We don't know who was top of the bill at Potbelly Hill, but it's a good bet that it was an all-singing, all-dancing venue.[14] So why not a Mesolithic – and megalithic – Taylor Swift? I'm not the only one to have noticed this: a former Presidential advisor has too, when writing in the *Washington Post* about Yuval Harari's *Sapiens* (2014):

> Then, to cut a long story short, came coinage, empires, monotheism, cathedrals, global capitalism, Newton's *Principia Mathematica*, the moon landing and Taylor Swift. (*Washington Post*, 2015)[15]

As 'arguably the most famous and influential entertainer on earth' (*Vanity Fair*, August 2015), Taylor Swift is the current queen of social media. She has followers in the multiple millions on Twitter, Facebook, Tumblr and Instagram. Media commentary uses her as a representation of worldwide unity for young and old, quoting insiders who:

> liken her deeply personal storytelling to new chapters of a book the whole world wants to read. ... 'We're all talking about it. In my lifetime, I haven't experienced that since Michael Jackson – that one artist who stands above and unites us all.' (*Vogue*, 2015)[16]

Commentary about Swift often mentions her 'squad' of celebrity BFFs, through which she 'models' how social media bring women together in friendship – another kind of deme-formation. She is quoted as saying:

> 'When you've got this group of girls who need each other as much as we need each other, in this climate, when it's so hard for women to be understood and portrayed the right way in the media ... now more than ever we need to be good and kind to each other and not judge each other...'. (*Vanity Fair*, 2015)[17]

Of course, scepticism is never far from the surface. The Murdoch media are always on hand to put the record straight. No sooner had Swift's 'squad' been recognised as a thing than the *New York Post* announced that it 'has become a cult', reinforcing her 'Stalin-like control of the entertainment industry'. The squad's unpaid appearance on one of Swift's videos was not Hyde's gift economy but 'indentured servitude'. News Corp's message to fans: 'Taylor Swift and her squad were

once the goal of millennials everywhere, but now they're just plain creepy.'[18] Or, we may say, the 'good ancestors' of a new deme.

O, O, THOSE AWFUL DAWKS

Talking of sceptics, there's only one way to close a chapter like this. It has to be about evolutionary phenomena *in* social media: in this case none other than Richard Dawkins, well-known evolutionary scientist, together with his own 'squad', who I'm going to call the 'Dawks'. This is not very polite, because Dawk is {Dawkins + dork + Orcs},[19] but I coin it in homage to the American critic Edmund Wilson's wonderfully acerbic review of J.R.R. Tolkein's *The Fellowship of the Ring* (Wilson, 1956). Wilson blames Tolkein's readers, especially among the English, for *pretentiousness* and *infantilism*. These barbs seem ready-sharpened for battle with 'those awful Dawks' – the e-bile trolls of social media who're 'gonna hate', as Taylor Swift puts it in 'Shake it Off'. The Dawks 'follow' the burning eye, not of Sauron,[20] but of a character I'm going to call 'Sciron', denoting an ancient scientist who once excelled in his craft but later thinks he's replaced God, and who in the end is only ever seen in the form of an angry eye trying to impose his will on naive mortals.

While I was writing this chapter, Dawkins and the Dawks were having fun. Richard found a piece of research that set him off. Sciron's Angry Eye flared into life on Twitter. Anna Hickey-Moody, an Australian academic at the University of London, had 'developed a philosophically informed, cultural studies approach to youth, disability and gender' (according to her Goldsmiths' profile). In the course of that work, her paper on 'Carbon fibre masculinity' (Hickey-Moody, 2015) was uploaded to ResearchGate.net (a 'social networking site for scientists and researchers'). In the course of a consideration of the links among carbon-fibre technologies, homosociality, disability and the case of Olympic athlete and domestic murderer Oscar Pistorius, Hickey-Moody invoked Continental theory (specifically, Deleuze). That is what seems to have caught Sciron's eye. He repeatedly tweeted contemptuous dismissal of the research as 'pretentious bullshit-peddling' (Figure 1.2), invoking the 'Sokal hoax' (Lucy, 2016), to the delight of various dutiful Dawks.

There followed a predictable outburst of copycat trolling, mixed with messages of support for both Dawkins and Hickey-Moody, which soon spilt over from Twitter to Facebook and various online forums.[21] Hickey-Moody suggested that her critics should read more and respect (demic) boundaries of expertise and discipline. She wrote directly to Dawkins: 'Your very enthusiastic followers have located images of me and posted them to my twitter page along with personal insults and abuse.' She asked him to apologise. Dawkins replied that 'I greatly deplore any personal abuse' but held off from 'issuing an apology for my tweets' on the grounds of Hickey-Moody's suspected 'affinities' with philosophers disapproved of by Dawkins.[22] Dawkins continued to tweet about how much he loathes 'pretension' (pretentiousness), with a meant-to-be-funny phallic flourish featuring a space rocket and a link to Hickey-Moody's paper, unrepentantly captioned: 'AND it's stiff with carbon fibre. OMG' (Figure 1.2).

Over on chat forums like *Utopia Talk*, some Dawks took this as a prompt to express misogynistic abuse (although some attempt was made to understand the issue), including:

– srsly just kill yourself cow
– Facilitating the decline of academia by supporting this cunt
– Rofl@fat angry ugly lesbian with hyphenated last name.
– This is the kind of education the queen is against.
– I sure as hell don't want to be the one to tell this … can I use woman? … this woman that her research is not scientific. She'd probably come at me with hedge clippers. (*Utopia Talk*)

One of these same commentators remarked, however: 'you can tell by dawkins' angry

homosocial trolls attacking her on social media that she hits the bullseye', which elicited in response only: 'Bulls are the male cows'.

Over on *The Skeptics' Guide to the Universe*, one contributor offered a reflexive comment that echoed Charles Darwin's test for high 'moral culture' – 'when we recognise that we ought to control our thoughts' (1871) – and indeed it seemed to temper subsequent discussion on this thread:

Oh no, a scholar published a theoretical article where she attempts to apply a point of view to her research subject that you guys don't like! The logical conclusion is that she must have mental issues and is definitely horrible at what she does. What has this world come to, when people whose job is to think are not constrained by others' views on what people should think about and how they should do that. (*Skeptics' Guide to the Universe*)

The furore led to re-posts of mainstream journalism and blogs, especially items from *The Guardian* and a critique from blogger Rebecca Watson (Skepchick).[23] In a lengthy profile by Sophie Elmhirst in *The Guardian*, Dawkins is reported as playing down his controversialism on Twitter:

In conversation, Dawkins seemed concerned that an article about him would draw disproportionately on his Twitter feed – in his eyes, an insignificant late chapter in the context of his whole career. 'I'm a scientist,' he said, as if this fact might be forgotten. (*The Guardian*)

That is a definite risk. Doubtless Dawkins would use the science-teacher's defence that he mentions in his *Guardian* profile: 'Very often I'm not making a point, but asking a question' (see Figure 1.2 for the tenor of those). But his *communicative intentions* are not 'read' in quite the same way in the Twittersphere, where users trump producers in the matter of deciding what something means. Here, he is Sciron of the Angry Eye! And of course Dawkins is not just a misunderstood scientist. He's a professional controversialist, riding the wave of celebrity to create an adversarial social-media 'deme' with very definite boundaries: inside are

Figure 1.2 'Goodness, how I loathe pretension.' A selection of tweets, from/to Richard Dawkins, December 17–19, 2015. Source: Courtesy of Anna Hickey-Moody

scientific rationalists, atheists … and truth; outside are bilge, rubbish, pretension, bullshit … a.k.a postmodernism, cultural studies and identity politics. Dawkins sees only one of these groups as a 'tribe'. His own deme is labelled 'individuals':

> Identity Politics is surely one of the great evils of our age. Stand for yourself as an individual, not a representative of a tribe. (Twitter: Figure 1.2)

Dawkins does not admit as 'research' (much less science) methods derived from 'theory' in the humanities, but instead acts as what in cultural science is called the Bad Neighbour or *Malvoisine* (Hartley and Potts, 2014: Chapter 4). He seeks to 'cooperate' with such disciplines Sciron-style, by destroying, at least rhetorically, those who are 'still defending the pretentious bilge exposed by the great Sokal hoax'. But as McKenzie Wark has helpfully argued, a useful outcome of the Sokal affair would be rapprochement between postmodernism (language arts) and sciences: 'to get those who study the language arts to pay more attention to how other modes of knowledge actually work'; and at the same time not to accept attempts to 'preserve scientific authority in the public realm from legitimate and even in a broad sense "scientific" scrutiny' (in Lucy, 2016: 185). The Sokal affair is ultimately about who has the authority to speak about truth; and that is what Dawkins wants. There's no room here for consilience between evolutionary science and cultural studies. Instead of that, he enjoins Hickey-Moody to 'Give up & do some honest work'.

SCIRON – OR CULTURAL SCIENCE?

Readers of this chapter will by now have gathered that I think this is not the right way forward. Citizens of social media are unlikely to be recruited to new ideas by such foe-creating strategies, and meanwhile evolutionary theory

suffers reputational risk if it is associated with misogyny, parochial aggressiveness and *ad hominem* attacks. If we're trying to create, with James Carey, 'a science of creation and construction, a science of understanding and common action … a science of enlightenment or citizenship, a science in society' (2000: 22), then attempts to impose control and to close down communication between natural and cultural sciences don't advance the cause of knowledge; it just stirs up the Dawks. The BBC announced that 2015 was 'The year that angry won the internet'.[24] The hosepipe of hate is not a sustainable scenario for social media.

But in the epoch of a global, creative economy and with knowledge technologies such as social media linking more people to more knowledge than ever before, it is important for professional researchers, scientists, theorists, commentators, polemicists and citizens *not* to pursue aggressive parochialism, but to recognise that *difference* – the more mutually incomprehensible the better, perhaps – is the catalyst of new ideas. 'We' all now live in the same semiosphere, the same noösphere, and have begun to recognise the importance of social media, rhetoric and 'fictions' in organising human thought and collective action. So, yeah, 'we have always been social', but the question now is – what are we (so many more of us than ever) going to do about it? Science, evolution and complexity are not the enemies of culture, communication and media. Science and stories are one and the same thing (Haraway, 1990). Can we use both to tell a new, inclusive, *Swiftian* truth about *knowledge* (learning from difference, not belittling or oppressing it) – as best we can, knowing it'll all be wrong again soon enough – without coming across to each other as Dawks?

This chapter has operated on a theory of culture and a new approach to 'cultural science' that is based on the causal primacy of communicative sociality and group-formation, held together by, among other things, language, story and other such social-media institutions, both technologically equipped and otherwise. In this account, the earliest charismatic monuments erected by our species, from Göbekli Tepe to Stonehenge and the Pyramids, are nothing less than *mass media*, within a network of social media, broadcasting messages about community to whole populations. Culture and communication systems perceive the world for us and shape our demes as high-trust 'we'-groups with a common but dynamic identity, which are distinguished from adversarial or low-trust 'they'-groups by recognised differences. Social media are group-forming institutions of inclusion and exclusion, and demic groups are powerful both internally (they 'crowdsource' some new ideas while controlling others) and externally (they protect 'our' knowledge and culture from incursions while plundering 'theirs'). Equally, they are vulnerable to lethal force and duplicity, both internal and external. They don't even exist 'in nature' (Harari, 2014) – they're made not found – so they need elaborate rituals, stories, ceremonies and 'sacred sites' to sustain their centrality for the group. Since culture-made groups are the survival vehicles for knowledge and technology, they are, as it were, the prime directive for humans. Among their side effects or unintended consequences are the economy, politics, and the specialisation (and thus industrialisation) of knowledge. How these domains will evolve when the dynamics of change are generalised throughout the population, including children and postmodernists, rather than remaining in the hands of Faustian experts and their Dawkish retainers, remains to be seen. Perhaps later chapters of this very book will show us.

Notes

1   Every nucleic cell – and organism – that ever lived (and that's a big number) owes its life to mitochondria. Originally independent bacteria, then accidental 'visitors' that overstayed in cells, mitochondria are: 'essential to the *life* … and *death* … of a cell'. They supply cellular energy and they also exercise the power of life and death over every potential new human: 'Mitochondria are also thought to influence, by exercising a veto, which eggs in a woman should be released during ovulation and which should be destroyed by programmed cell death (apoptosis)': http://bscb.org/learning-resources/softcell-e-learning/mitochondrion-much-more-than-an-energy-converter/

2   Quotation source: http://tolweb.org/tree/home.pages/structure.html. Image source: https://en.wikipedia.org/wiki/File:Phylogenetic_tree.svg. See also: https://en.wikipedia.org/wiki/Tree_of_life_(biology); and https://en.wikipedia.org/wiki/Carl_Woese

3   The internal quotation is from Tennyson, *Idylls of the King* (1859), pp. 244–245. It is in the voice of Guinevere, repenting (but still yearning for) her 'golden days' with Lancelot. See Valerie Purton's (2013: xii) discussion of this passage and on Darwin as a reader of Tennyson. Darwin's 'highest stage in moral culture' reveals not (only) his own 'advanced human being' but (also) Tennyson's 'desperate soul striving, almost certainly in vain'.

4   I have modernised gendered pronouns (to plurals) and rendered generic 'man' as 'humanity'.

5   For a 1968 summary of Childe's publications by Judith Treistman, to which this section is indebted, see: *Encyclopedia.com*: www.encyclopedia.com/doc/1G2-3045000185.html; see also Childe's entry in Wikipedia.

6   Jared Diamond at: www.pbs.org/gunsgermssteel/show/transcript1.html.

7   See Jason Antrosio (2013) for a useful review of the salient literature.

8   See: www.academia.edu/4681349/Göbekli_Tepe_Changes_Everything.

9   See, for instance: http://beforeitsnews.com/blogging-citizen-journalism/2013/08/gobekli-tepe-fantastic-new-photos-of-12000-year-old-temple-complex-the-oldest-known-2448608.html. For a tribute to Schmidt, who died in 2014, see: http://antiquity.ac.uk/tributes/schmidt.html

10 If you search for Göbekli Tepe online, you will encounter claims – first made by *National Geographic Magazine* – that it was 'the world's first temple'. With John Romer (2012) I'm wary of imposing such terminology on prehistoric peoples, so Occam's razor applies here to talk of religion, temples, or gods.

11 Lorna Baldwin (2015) 'Keeping up with the Joneses, Neolithic Scotland edition.' *PBS Newshour*: www.pbs.org/newshour/updates/uncovering-neolithic-mysteries-one-dig-season-time/#

12 *Greek Reporter*, July 9, 2015: http://greece.greekreporter.com/2015/07/09/parthenon-might-have-served-as-athens-treasury/

13 For a Faustian timeline, see: http://aix1.uottawa.ca/~jesleben/faust/fausttimeline.html

14 A photograph by Vincent J. Musi, published in *National Geographic* (2006), bore the caption: 'Pillars at the temple of Gobekli Tepe may represent priestly dancers' (www.alamy.com/stock-photo-pillars-at-the-temple-of-gobekli-tepe-may-represent-priestly-dancers-43993327.html).

15 Michael Gerson (2015) 'Myths, meaning and Homo sapiens.' *The Washington Post*, June 11: www.washingtonpost.com/opinions/myths-meaning-and-homo-sapiens/2015/06/11/28660902-106f-11e5-a0dc-2b6f404ff5cf_story.html. Gerson was Assistant to President George W. Bush for policy and strategic planning.

16 Jada Yuan (2015) 'On the Road with Best Friends Taylor Swift and Karlie Kloss.' *Vogue*, February 13: www.vogue.com/9287379/taylor-swift-karlie-kloss-best-friends-march-2015-cover/

17 Josh Duboff (2015) 'Taylor Swift: Apple Crusader, #GirlSquad Captain, and the Most Influential 25-Year-Old in America.' *Vanity Fair*, August 31: www.vanityfair.com/style/2015/08/taylor-swift-cover-mario-testino-apple-music

18 Lindsay Putnam (2015) 'Taylor Swift's "squad" has become a cult.' *New York Post*, September 1: http://nypost.com/2015/09/01/taylor-swifts-squad-has-become-a-cult/. For an alternative take on 'creepy', see: www.thestar.com/entertainment/2016/01/13/a-romance-for-the-ages-regardless-of-ages-menon.html

19 For 'dork', see: https://en.wiktionary.org/wiki/dork. For Orcs, Google reports: '(in fantasy literature and games) a member of an imaginary race of human-like creatures, characterized as ugly, warlike, and malevolent'.

20 We learn from Sauron's Wikipedia entry that Tolkein's Evil Eye originally possesses 'great knowledge of the physical substances of the world'. Despite his fall into evil, Sauron 'would always retain the "scientific" knowledge he derived from the great Vala of Craft'. As for Sauron's motives for turning evil, 'Tolkien noted that "it had been his virtue (and therefore also the cause of his fall…) that he loved order and coordination, and disliked all confusion and wasteful friction".' Thus, he retained 'fair motives': he 'was not indeed wholly evil, not unless all "reformers" who want to hurry up with "reconstruction" and "reorganization" are wholly evil, even before pride and the lust to exert their will eat them up' (https://en.wikipedia.org/wiki/Sauron).

21 Forums include *Utopia Talk* (http://atarchive.gotdns.org/UtopiaForums/boardthread?id=politics&thread=75778); and *The Skeptics' Guide to the Universe* (http://sguforums.com/index.php/topic,45821.msg9372536.html#msg9372536).

YouTube featured a hostile compilation by Thunderf00t, whose channel boasts nearly half a million subscribers and over 100 million views, called *Feminism: So CRAZY that EVERYTHING is sexist!* (January 3, 2016: www.youtube.com/watch?v=tRoKnmhGRyQ), which soon attracted over 40,000 views and 1500 comments.

22 See: https://twitter.com/annahm (December 18, 2015).

23 Rebecca Watson (2011) 'The Privilege Delusion.' *Skepchick* Blog, July 5: http://skepchick.org/2011/07/the-privilege-delusion/ (Watson was the object of Dawkins' scorn in the infamous 'Dear Muslima' episode, for which Dawkins apologised); Adam Lee (2014) 'Richard Dawkins has lost it: Ignorant sexism gives atheists a bad name.' *Guardian*, September 18: www.theguardian.com/commentisfree/2014/sep/18/richard-dawkins-sexist-atheists-bad-name?; and Sophie Elmhirst (2015) 'Is Richard Dawkins destroying his reputation?' *Guardian*, June 9: www.theguardian.com/science/2015/jun/09/is-richard-dawkins-destroying-his-reputation

24 Mike Wendling (2015) '2015: The year that angry won the internet.' *BBC Trending*, December 30: www.bbc.com/news/blogs-trending-35111707

REFERENCES

Antrosio, J. (2013) 'Agriculture as "Worst Mistake in the History of the Human Race"?' *Living Anthropologically*: www.livinganthropologically.com/anthropology/worst-mistake-in-the-history-of-the-human-race/

Arthur, W.B. (2009) *The Nature of Technology: What It Is and How It Evolves*. New York and London: Allen Lane.

Bell, E., P. Boehnke, T.M. Harrison and W. Mao (2015) 'Potentially biogenic carbon preserved in a 4.1 billion-year-old zircon.' *PNAS*, 112(47), 14518–14521. Accessible at: www.pnas.org/content/112/47/14518.full

Bowles, S. (2011) 'Cultivation of cereals by the first farmers was not more productive than foraging.' *PNAS*, 108(12), 4760–4765. Accessible at: www.pnas.org/content/108/12/4760.full

Braudel, F. (2012) 'History and the Social Sciences: The *Longue Durée*,' trans. I. Wallerstein. Appendix to R.E. Lee (ed.) (2012), *The Longue Durée and World-Systems Analysis* (pp. 241–276). Albany, NY: SUNY Press. First published (1958) as 'Histoire et Sciences sociales: *La longue durée.' Annales E.S.C.*, XIII(4), 725–753.

Carey, J. (1989) *Communication as Culture.* Boston, MA: Unwin Hyman.

Carey, J. (2000) 'Some personal notes on US journalism education'. *Journalism*, 1(1), 12–23.

Childe, V.G. (1925/1958) *The Dawn of European Civilization* (6th edn, 1958). New York: Knopf.

Childe, V.G. (1936/1965) *Man Makes Himself* (4th edn, 1965). London: Watts.

Childe, V.G. (1958) *The Prehistory of European Society.* London: Cassell.

Darwin, C. (1871) *The Descent of Man.* London: John Murray. Accessible at: http://darwin-online.org.uk/content/frameset?pageseq=1&itemID=F937.1&viewtype=text

Dawkins, R. (1976) *The Selfish Gene.* Oxford: Oxford University Press.

Diamond, J. (1987) 'The worst mistake in the history of the human race.' *Discover Magazine*, May, 64–66. Accessible at: http://discovermagazine.com/1987/may/02-the-worst-mistake-in-the-history-of-the-human-race

Dopfer, K., J. Foster and J. Potts (2004) 'Micro–Meso–Macro'. *Journal of Evolutionary Economics*, 14, 263–279.

German, S. (n.d.) 'The Neolithic Revolution'. Khan Academy. Accessible at: www.khanacademy.org/humanities/prehistoric-art/neolithic-art/a/the-neolithic-revolution

Harari, Y.N. (2014) *Sapiens: A Brief History of Humankind.* London: Vintage.

Haraway, D. (1990) *Primate Visions: Gender, Race and Nature in the World of Modern Science.* New York: Routledge.

Hartley, J. (2012) *Digital Futures for Cultural and Media Studies.* Malden, MA, and Oxford: Wiley-Blackwell.

Hartley, J. and J. Potts (2014) *Cultural Science: A Natural History of Stories, Demes, Knowledge and Innovation.* London: Bloomsbury Academic.

Hartley, J. and J. Potts (2016) '"Paris with snakes"? The future of communication is/as "Cultural Science".' *The Unbearable Lightness of Communication Research*: Special issue of *The International Communication Gazette*, 78(7), 627–35.

Hickey-Moody, A. (2015) 'Carbon fibre masculinity: Disability and surfaces of homosociality'. *Angelaki: Journal of the Theoretical Humanities*, 20(1), 139–153.

Humboldt, A. von (1858) *Cosmos: A Sketch or a Physical Description of the Universe* (Vol. 1) (5 vols). Online at: Project Gutenberg: www.gutenberg.org/cache/epub/14565/pg14565-images.html

Huxley, J. (1942) *Evolution: The Modern Synthesis.* London: Allen & Unwin.

Hyde, L. (2007) 'On being good ancestors: Afterword to the 25th anniversary edition.' *The Gift: Creativity and the Artist in the Modern World* (2nd edn, pp. 369–385). New York: Vintage Books.

Jane, E.A. (2015) 'Flaming? What flaming? The pitfalls and potentials of researching online hostility.' *Ethics and Information Technology*, 17(1), 65–87.

Kauffman, S. (2016) *Humanity in a Creative Universe.* Oxford: Oxford University Press.

Konner, M. (2010) *The Evolution of Childhood: Relationships, Emotion, Mind.* Cambridge, MA: Harvard University Press.

Kull, K. (1999) 'Towards biosemiotics with Yuri Lotman.' *Semiotica*, 127(1/4), 115–131.

Lee, R.E. (ed.) (2012) *The Longue Durée and World-Systems Analysis.* Albany, NY: SUNY Press. Editor's Introduction (pp. 1–7), accessible at: www.sunypress.edu/pdf/62451.pdf

Lotman, Y. (1990) *Universe of the Mind: A Semiotic Theory of Culture.* Bloomington, IN: Indiana University Press.

Lucy, N. (2016) *A Dictionary of Postmodernism.* Ed. J. Hartley. Oxford: Wiley-Blackwell.

Luhmann, N. (2012) *Theory of Society, Vol. 1.* Stanford, CA: Stanford University Press.

Lyotard, J. (1979) *The Postmodern Condition: A Report on Knowledge.* Manchester: Manchester University Press (UK); Minneapolis, MN: University of Minnesota Press (USA), 1984.

Marwick, A. (2013) 'Online identity'. In J. Hartley, J. Burgess and A. Bruns (eds), *A Companion to New Media Dynamics* (pp. 355–364). Malden, MA, and Oxford: Wiley-Blackwell.

Marx, K. (1845) *The German Ideology.* Accessible at: www.marxists.org/archive/marx/works/1845/german-ideology/ch01b.htm

Marx, K. (1857/1976) *Preface and Introduction to A Contribution to the Critique of Political*

Economy. Peking: Foreign Languages Press. Accessible at: www.marx2mao.com/M&E/PI.html

Maturana, H. and F. Varela (1980) *Autopoiesis and Cognition: The Realization of the Living*. Dordrecht, Holland: Reidel; Boston, MA: Kluwer.

Ong, W.J. (2012) *Orality and Literacy: Technologizing the Word* (30th Anniversary Edition with Additional Chapters by John Hartley). London: Routledge.

Pagel, M. (2012) *Wired for Culture: The Natural History of Human Cooperation*. London: Allen Lane.

Papacharissi, Z. (2015) 'We have always been social.' *Social Media + Society*, 1(1), 1–2. Accessible at: http://sms.sagepub.com/content/1/1/2056305115581185.full.pdf+html

Parker Pearson, M. (2012) *Stonehenge: Exploring the Greatest Stone Age Mystery*. London: Simon & Schuster.

Purton, V. (ed.) (2013) *Darwin, Tennyson and Their Readers: Explorations in Victorian Literature and Science*. London and New York: Anthem Press.

Richards, T. (1993) *The Imperial Archive: Knowledge and the Fantasy of Empire*. London: Verso.

Romer, J. (2012) *A History of Ancient Egypt: From the First Farmers to the Great Pyramid*. London: Penguin Books.

Shannon, C. (1948) 'A mathematical theory of communication.' *Bell System Technical Journal*, 27(3), 379–423. Accessible at: https://archive.org/details/bstj27-3-379

Silva, S. and J. Tehrani (2016) 'Comparative phylogenetic analyses uncover the ancient roots of Indo-European folktales.' *Royal Society Open Science*, 2016(3), 150645. Accessible at: http://rsos.royalsocietypublishing.org/content/3/1/150645

Stott, R. (2004) *Darwin and the Barnacle: The Story of One Tiny Creature and History's Most Spectacular Scientific Breakthrough*. London: Faber & Faber; New York: W.W. Norton.

Tennyson, A. (1859) *Idylls of the King*. London: Edward Moxon.

Tomasello, M. (2014) *A Natural History of Human Thinking*. Cambridge, MA: Harvard University Press.

Vernadsky, V.I. (1998) *The Biosphere*. New York: Copernicus (Springer-Verlag).

Wallerstein, I. (2004) *World-Systems Analysis: An Introduction*. Durham, NC: Duke University Press.

Walls, L.D. (2009) *The Passage to Cosmos: Alexander von Humboldt and the Shaping of America*. Chicago, IL: University of Chicago Press.

Williams, R. (1977) *Marxism and Literature*. Oxford: Oxford University Press.

Wilson, E. (1956) 'O, O, Those Awful Orcs: A review of *The Fellowship of the Ring*.' *The Nation*, April 14. Accessible at: www.jrrvf.com/sda/critiques/The_Nation.html

Woese, C., O. Kandler and M. Wheelis (1990) 'Towards a natural system of organisms: Proposal for the domains Archaea, Bacteria, and Eucarya.' *PNAS*, 87(12), 4576–459. Accessible at: www.pnas.org/content/87/12/4576

Wulf, A. (2015) *The Invention of Nature: The Adventures of Alexander von Humboldt, the Lost Hero of Science*. London: John Murray.

Zittrain, J. (2008) *The Future of the Internet – and How to Stop It*. New Haven, CT: Yale University Press.

Early Social Computing: The Rise and Fall of the BBS Scene (1977–1995)

Aaron Delwiche

In 1976, the long sixties were over. American troops had left Vietnam after almost two decades of grueling warfare, and 18-year-olds had finally been awarded the right to vote in state and federal elections. Alex Haley's (1976) novel *Roots: The Saga of an American Family* spent more than five months at the top of the bestseller list, and 16,000 activists marched in Springfield, Illinois to show their support for the Equal Rights Amendment. Much had changed during the previous decades on almost every front, but our global communication landscape remained largely unchanged in fundamental ways. Although the long sixties had incubated a vibrant underground press, inexpensive public access television, and community radio projects, these experiments were the exception rather than the rule. For the most part, television, radio, magazines, and newspapers were viewed as vehicles for one-to-many mass communication rather than as platforms for conversation and distributed creativity.

As A. J. Liebling famously observed, 'freedom of the press is guaranteed only to those who own one.' In the wake of the 1973 oil crisis, few citizens had enough money to purchase a press, let alone a radio station, a television station, or a satellite. Lee Felsenstein (1993) describes the epiphany he had one evening when watching the blue cathode light emitting through his neighbor's windows. 'They were all getting their information from Walter Cronkite in New York,' says Felsenstein, but 'we had no ready way of getting information to each other.' This was about to change.

During the next two decades, the cultural and political revolutions of the 1960s would be followed by a technological revolution that radically decentralized communication power. The personal computer, the smart modem, and bulletin board systems were vanguard technologies of the digital revolution. For computer enthusiasts around the world, bulletin board systems were a thrilling on-ramp to a global network of engaged, interactive human beings. Between 1978 and 2001, there were more than 93,000 bulletin board systems in existence (Scott, 2001). At the peak of the BBS scene, in 1994, there were approximately 45,000 bulletin board systems in the United States alone (Scott, 2001). Far from a purely American phenomenon, these systems were linked to millions of computer users around the world (Bush, 1993), and they displayed many similarities to European computer networks such as the Minitel in France (Schofield, 2012).

This chapter discusses the rise and fall of the BBS scene in the closing decades of the twentieth century. This period is significant because almost all of the conversations associated with contemporary social media were originally articulated in connection with computer bulletin board systems. Concerns about the ways teenagers use the technology? Check. Prurient discussions about sexual gratification on the local news? Check. Entrepreneurial enthusiasm for the way this 'game changing' technology threatens traditional business models? Check. Anxieties about falling in love with someone without meeting them face to face? Check. Utopian excitement about ways the new technology can help dissidents and traditionally disenfranchised citizens? Check. In fact, BBSs were some of the very first social media (Driscoll, 2014), and they arrived on the scene decades before Twitter, Snapchat, and Facebook.

At the heart of this claim is the term 'social media.' The phrase is widely used but rarely defined. When pressed for a definition, many recite a list of contemporary platforms, but defining a medium by its current technological instantiation makes little sense in a world characterized by the exponential growth of information technology. As those who study media often explain, some of yesterday's most popular platforms have been ignored, and tomorrow's champions have not yet arrived (Obar & Wildman, 2015). For this reason, the best definitions are not tethered to a specific implementation. Carr and Hayes (2015: 50)

define social media as 'Internet-based channels that allow users to opportunistically interact and selectively self-present, either in real-time or asynchronously, with both broad and narrow audiences who derive value from user-generated content and the perception of interaction with others'. If not for the requirement that social media channels be Internet-based, Carr and Haye's definition is an apt description of the bulletin board systems that flourished from 1977 through 1997.

The following pages trace the fascinating story of computer bulletin boards, from their emergence as a fringe technology for computer enthusiasts to mainstream acceptance at both a national and global level. As the BBS scene matured, the user base grew more diverse, and these systems affected the world of politics and culture. Courts struggled to understand the legal implications of these new technologies, and law enforcement raced to keep up with an emerging computer underground. And then, just as the BBS scene was poised on the brink of global success, it was vaporized – blindsided by the privatization of the global Internet.

COMMUNITY MEMORY AND THE FIRST BULLETIN BOARD SYSTEMS

It all started in 1973 with Community Memory, a bold attempt to revitalize communities by establishing 'strong, free non-hierarchical channels of communication' (Schuler, 1994). Community Memory was created when a small collective of technologically literate radicals erected coin-operated computer terminals in record stores, libraries, and laundromats throughout the San Francisco Bay Area (Slaton, 2001). Citizens were encouraged to use these terminals as vehicles for anonymous communication about topics of interest – there were no limits placed on potential topics. Users could read messages for free, post new messages for one quarter, and create new forums for one dollar (Schuler, 1994). As Judith Milhon later observed, 'the idea was to make a new medium so useful, yet so yummy, that people would want to use it again and again' (Slaton, 2001). From the very beginning, it was the users themselves who shaped the network's evolution. Whether discussing People's Park, sharing vegetarian recipes, or reviewing concerts from local performers, Community Memory was composed entirely of what we would today refer to as 'user-generated content' (Felsenstein, 1993). The project was centered in the Bay Area, but Community Memory's creators believed that it had the potential to shake up the nation. 'Without making Ma Bell any richer,' they wrote, 'we could have a national news network, a means of coordination for national political action, a fast mail service, and a way to hold long term dialogue on problems of greater than local interest' (Szpakowski, 2006).

Community Memory disbanded before it could fulfill this vision, but it served as a 'proof of concept' and paved the way for similar experiments. In 1978, hoping to facilitate communication between Chicago residents interested in the world of computers, Ward Christensen and Randy Seuss developed something they called 'The Computerized Hobbyists Bulletin Board System (CBBS).' After connecting to the system with his or her computer, an individual user could read messages posted by other people and post messages for others to read. The project was a success. News of the system traveled far beyond Chicago, and the board soon began receiving telephone calls from computer users across the country (Seger, 1983). Realizing that they had stumbled into something exciting, Christensen and Seuss (1978) documented their project in the pages of *Byte Magazine*, predicting a world in which multiple bulletin boards could be linked to function as 'nodes in a communication network of automated message and process switching' (1978: 151).

At the core of this system was a piece of technology called a modem. By converting digital information into sound waves, modems made it possible for a computer in one location to exchange information with a computer on the opposite side of town – or the opposite side of the world. At first, people did not realize the revolutionary implications of this breakthrough, and the BBS scene grew slowly. Modems were expensive and they lacked a common standard that could transcend the balkanization of different computer platforms. However, in 1981, the Hayes Smart Modem added a layer of data abstraction that facilitated communication across platforms (Gilbertson, 2010). It also included something called a 'command set' – a set of special instructions that hobbyists could use to modify and extend their modem's functionality. Soon, almost all modems were Hayes-compatible, fueling the growth of the bulletin board scene and the computer industry that served it (Ceruzzi, 1998; Preimesberger, 2012).

BULLETIN BOARD SYSTEMS ARRIVE ON THE SCENE

By 1983, CBBS was receiving 50 calls a day, and more than 800 microcomputer bulletin boards had sprouted up across the country (Seger, 1983). Behind each of these boards was a system operator (sysop) responsible for purchasing and configuring the BBS computer, and for paying telephone expenses. Why would someone do this if there was no profit to be found in these primitive systems? One early chronicler of the BBS scene noted, 'the majority of bulletin boards ... are run by rather altruistic individuals who derive great satisfaction from computerized communication' (Seger, 1983).

BBS software continued to evolve over the years, expanding the reach and participatory potential of these systems. These early bulletin boards fostered discussion on a wide range of topics, but there were fundamental similarities across all bulletin boards. First, the process of connecting to a BBS was almost always the same. The user would instruct the modem to dial the telephone number of the BBS. To avoid toll charges, this was typically a local number. If the BBS line was not busy, the modem would emit a series of beeps (the handshake), followed by a squealing static sound that signaled connection. At this point, the host BBS would take over the computer screen, displaying a configuration of text-based menus. Second, regardless of the system's topical focus, users could expect to engage in the same sorts of activities. Almost all bulletin board systems encouraged users to send and receive electronic messages (an early form of electronic mail), to participate in threaded discussion forums, to exchange public domain software, to exchange text files (e.g., recipes, computer tutorials, political manifestos, and movie reviews), and to enjoy single-player games.[1]

Because the first wave of bulletin board systems could only sustain one telephone connection at a time, this was *asynchronous* communication – users were not communicating with one another in real time. Over time, modems became faster, operating systems became more sophisticated, and graphics capabilities improved dramatically. This paved the way for new BBS functionality. Users engaged in *synchronous* chat, they played games with one another in real time, and they exchanged low-resolution images (Scott, 2008).

As news of bulletin board systems spread, reporters struggled to explain the technology to those who were wrapping their head around the concept for the first time. They invariably stressed the range of topics, the engagement of users, and the civic potential of these networks. Phoebe Hoban (1984) suggested that bulletin board systems could be viewed as a version of the Sunday *New York Times* 'constantly being rewritten by a cross-section of New York's population' while featuring 'discussions on literally every possible topic' (1984: 19). Another reporter described

bulletin boards as a 'humbling and electrifying' antidote to the passivity encouraged by traditional media. 'This kind of news isn't passive,' he wrote. 'It consumes back. ... Imagine a newspaper reading you, asking you what you know, how you feel about the stories in it' (Katz, 1993). Other commentators were quick to recognize the potential of these systems, predicting that bulletin board systems would someday be used to manage college courses, to organize field offices, to deliver product lists to consumers, and to organize community groups and clubs (Glossbrenner, 1984). One excited hobbyist proclaimed '10 years from now, people will probably check their bulletin boards as often as they check their mailboxes' (Seger, 1983).

Some of the first civic applications of computer bulletin boards were implemented by public agencies. In 1981, the Chicago Public Library became the first library to offer a bulletin board system, logging close to 1,000 calls a month on a small personal computer said to be 'the only Apple in town' (Dewey, 1984). The board announced upcoming events, included movie reviews and book reviews commissioned by free-lance writers, and encouraged users to download public domain software for their own machines (Shea, 1984). Four years later, 20 libraries had rolled out some type of bulletin board for their patrons (Dewey, 1986). In 1989, the city of Santa Monica created the Public Electronic Network (PEN) and made the system available for free to anyone living and working in the city. In addition to dial-up BBS access, the system also erected public terminals in libraries, parks, government buildings, and senior recreation centers. Homeless residents used the network to educate other citizens about the challenges they faced, explaining that the lack of showers, clean clothing, and a place to store belongings makes it very difficult to find a job (McKeown, 1991). Inspired by these conversations, a coalition of homeless and non-homeless users formed a network called SWASHLOCK (SHowers,

WASHers, and LOCKers) and successfully lobbied the Santa Monica City Council to create a homeless services drop-in center that included job counselors and a PEN terminal (Kantor, 1992; Wittig, 1991).

Individuals and small activist groups were also excited by the way bulletin boards could be used to engage the community. In Colorado Springs, a retired West Point instructor named Dave Hughes realized that we were on the brink of 'a coming global revolution in human communications.' He launched a BBS called *Old Colorado City Electronic College* in the hopes of promoting electronic democracy. A few months later, when the city council proposed regulations that would stop residents from working out of their homes, Hughes encouraged his board's users to spread word of the controversial regulations (Rheingold, 1991). More than 175 citizens showed up at the next public meeting, and the ordinance went down in flames. 'In the end,' said Hughes, 'the city council never knew what hit them' (Kelly, 1984: 36). Meanwhile, on the West Coast, a group of antiwar activists affiliated with the Disarmament Resource Center created a bulletin board called *PeaceNet* (Rae, 1984). One of the very first computer networks for progressive activists, PeaceNet eventually evolved into the Institute for Global Communications and served 'tens of thousands of individuals, nonprofits, and progressive causes in more than 130 countries' (Drew, 2013: 91).

For those who were paying attention to these experiments, it was clear that something exciting was underway. Declaring bulletin boards 'a new and important subculture,' the computer scientist Jacques Vallee (1984) argued that user-generated content on bulletin boards represented a revolutionary paradigm shift because 'the entertainment value was provided by the people who contributed to its message base around the clock' (1984: 156). More than one writer made the logical connection to Gutenberg's printing press, suggesting that the rise of networked

personal computers was creating an entirely new medium for exchanging information (Rheingold, 1991; Wood & Blankenhorn, 1990).

Bulletin boards and online systems also established a reputation for citizen journalism. When the 1989 Loma Prieta earthquake hit the San Francisco Bay Area, television networks encountered technical difficulties and were slow to cover the crisis. As one *Washington Post* reporter marveled, 'the network that first began to spread the news of the earthquake was the enormously energetic world of personal computer bulletin boards.' In the thousands of bulletin board messages generated after the quake, people assured their loved ones that they were safe, shared information about aftershocks, and provided first-hand accounts of the damage wrought by the quake (Reid, 1989). Optimists viewed such developments as evidence of an emerging 'network nation' in which citizens were 'linked electronically to one another through the medium of their computers' (Kelly, 1984).

Of course, not all residents of the network nation were filled with love for their neighbors. Racist bulletin boards attracted the ire of Canadian authorities by disseminating anti-Semitic tracts and files claiming that the Holocaust was a hoax. Canadian customs authorities blocked physical versions of these documents, but digital versions could travel across the border with impunity (InfoWorld, 1984).Glenn Miller, leader of the North Carolina Klan, created *Aryan Nation Liberty Net* to 'press the Klan's cause and out-maneuver the "Jewish-controlled mass media"' (*Newsweek*, 1984). Within a year, the network included the *White Aryan Resistance BBS* in California, the *Aryan Nations BBS* in Idaho, two KKK-linked bulletin boards in Texas, and a KKK-node in North Carolina. According to the investigative journalist Chip Berlet (2001), this network was stitched together on Apple and Radio Shack computers running standard BBS software.

BULLETIN BOARD SYSTEMS IN THE MAINSTREAM

At the start of the Reagan Administration's second term, experts estimated that there were well over 2,000 boards in the United States (Spurrier, 1985). This would not have happened without the passionate commitment of system operators who devoted considerable amounts of their time and money: approximately two hours a day for system maintenance, $3,000 for startup equipment costs, and $50 a month to keep the system humming (Glossbrenner, 1984; *Information Today*, 1984). From the user perspective, BBS software was increasingly sophisticated, greeting visitors with color menus, blocky computer graphics, and even sound (Stone, 1985).

From the very beginning, bulletin board systems were used to distribute software. On most bulletin boards, one could find libraries of public domain software that users could legally download and install on their own computer. The term *shareware* was often used to describe the games and utilities distributed in this way. Developers shared software with the community for free, encouraging users to send a small amount of money if they found the program to be useful. By 1992, there were hundreds of thousands of shareware programs available for download (Green, 1992). Many shareware authors were able to make a decent living from this system, and analysts estimated that the shareware market was worth approximately $15 million (Earnshaw, 1989). It would be misleading to suggest that all of the software distributed online fell into this category. On the fringes of the BBS scene, boards affiliated with the computer underground made it possible for users to illegally download copyrighted software such as mainstream productivity applications and high-end computer games.

Although computing technologies are sometimes viewed as the exclusive property of male computer hobbyists in their early 20s, the bulletin-board scene was populated by a wide variety of users. After studying usage figures from almost two-dozen library bulletin board systems, Dewey (1986: 16) noted, 'callers more and more are reflecting a cross-section of people who normally visit libraries.' System operators also began to notice that a significant number of users were handicapped or elderly (Wood & Blankenhorn, 1990). Because adaptive computing technologies helped disabled people become more independent, disabled users were among the very first to recognize the benefits of online communication (Markoff, 1983). For similar reasons, bulletin boards also appealed to older users as a vehicle for intellectual stimulation and a lifeline to the outside world (Evasuk, 1992). In the words of one journalist, 'People can explore their town, city, or even the world without ever leaving their terminal' (Hoban, 1984).

For many teenagers – both boys and girls – bulletin boards were a vital form of social support. 'Back then, if you had a modem and were "connected,"' recalls one member of the teen BSS scene, 'the BBS was a vital part of your life. ... Back before people were literally living on the Internet, the BBS world was a regular part of my life' (Chickenhead, 2004). As young people spent more and more time in front of a computer screen, outreach workers used bulletin boards such as *CyberCrisis* to connect with isolated teens in need of support (Duvall, 1995). A 13-year old girl in Del Mar, California, launched a system called *Teen Line* that allowed teenagers to chat with one another about family, school, and personal lives (Smith, 1985). The response to such efforts was overwhelmingly positive, particularly among shy teenagers who found face-to-face interaction to be excruciatingly difficult (Bula, 1993).

As is often the case with teen uses of emerging technologies, the response from adults was mixed. Writing for *The Futurist*, one reporter argued that teen-oriented computer bulletin boards provided a vital form of social support while also 'preparing teenagers for their future business lives' in a workplace that would soon be dominated by personal computers (Smith, 1985). Other journalists emphasized that 'bulletin boards are addictive' (Seger, 1983: 216), pointing to the example of users who spent several hours online each day (Hoban, 1984). In Texas, one teenager argued 'electronic messaging can be just as addicting as drugs or alcohol for teenagers,' blaming his compulsive behavior on peer pressure (Smith, 1985: 28).

The diversity of the BBS scene was also reflected in the sexual orientation of its members. Gay and lesbian users constituted 'the second wave of online pioneers,' and in 1984 approximately 10% of the nation's bulletin board systems were exclusively focused on the gay community (Kohn, 1984). A survey conducted by *The Advocate*, found that gay citizens were four times more likely than other Americans to own a 'microcomputer' (O'Laughlin, 1983). 'Computers and gay people have both been around for a long time,' argued Dave Kinnick (1989: 43) in the pages of *The Advocate*, 'but only recently have they formed this intimate union. The pairing has a lot going for it.'

Before the advent of the BBS, much of the gay scene revolved around bars in larger cities. For many, bulletin boards were a welcome alternative. They were accessible to gay youth who could not legally enter the bars, they were accessible to older gay citizens who felt alienated by the emphasis on physical beauty, and they provided much needed community for gays who lived in rural areas (Kinnick, 1989). For many lesbians, bulletin boards were a welcome source of interaction in a society that 'takes to women's bars and meeting grounds even less kindly than it takes to gay male meeting places' (Kinnick, 1989: 43).

Similar social configurations were emerging in the French computer network Minitel. A group of 'self-avowed lesbian activists' called Les Goudous Telematiques (the GTs) used French bulletin boards to build a virtual community that 'stretched beyond Paris into provincial towns and villages'

(Chaplin, 2014). Considering the effect of Minitel on the gay community, Mattias Duyves (1993) marveled at the 'amazing opportunities the little machine offered for the making of personal and anonymous contacts' such as 'a change in sexual partner, the financing of services such as a gay radio station and help for AIDS sufferers' (1993: 194).

THE RISE OF COMMERCIAL ONLINE SERVICES

Although bulletin boards were reaching an increasingly diverse audience, certain constraints were still holding the technology back. For many years, the experience was stymied by the fact that BBS software could only support one caller at a time, resulting in constant busy signals. In an attempt to share the wealth, sysops limited registered users to a certain amount of session time, although this was relatively easy to circumvent simply by creating a second account (Spurrier, 1985). Frustrated by the need to repeatedly dial the same number, hobbyists developed auto-dialers that repeatedly called the phone number until a connection was established (Hoban, 1984). In addition to these hassles, many users were intimidated by jargon and unfamiliar terms like *baud rate*, *protocol*, *buffer*, and *Kermit* (Randall, 1989).

Partly in response to the need for a less complicated on-ramp, commercial online services began building steam in the late 1980s. The three major players were Prodigy (a joint venture between CBS, IBM and Sears, Roebuck and Company), CompuServe (originally marketed via Radio Shack as MicroNET), and GEnie (a service created by General Electric). All three services offered moderately accessible interfaces, greater breadth and depth of content, more toll-free phone numbers, and fewer busy signals (Freed, 1995). They also capitalized on the growing fear of computer viruses, promising users that all of the software downloaded from their service would be completely trustworthy (Schopp, 1993). The major deterrent to using these services was the hourly connect charges (Rothman, 1987). All three services charged peak hourly rates ranging from $12 to $35 per hour.

Although they offered similar functionality, the mainstream services had different brand identities. Prodigy was viewed as too permeated with advertising, and driven by an overriding profit ethic (Katz, 1993). The network also developed a reputation for censorship and enraged users by canceling the accounts of subscribers who complained about the company's billing structure (Takahashi, 1990). CompuServe was arguably the most successful of the three services. Referred to as 'the computer nerd's online service,' it was the first service to expand into Europe (Carlson, 2009; Vaughan-Nichols, 2012). CompuServe claimed approximately 992,000 subscribers, Genie claimed to have 600,000 subscribers, and Prodigy had more than 1.3 million subscribers (James, Wotring, & Forrest, 1995).

During the 1992 campaign season, candidates on both sides of the aisle realized that online services might be an effective way of communicating with voters. Governor Clinton and President Bush fielded questions from Prodigy subscribers, the Clinton campaign posted position papers to Compuserve and GEnie, and Jerry Brown engaged in online discussions with CompuServe and Genie users (Campbell, 1993). In one of the first online polls of its type, Prodigy subscribers voiced a narrow preference for Governor Clinton over President Bush (Bloomberg News, 1992). This was the first political campaign to be so clearly shaped by online interaction, and pundits characterized candidates' involvement as 'an electronic town hall spanning the nation' (Schwartz, 1992). Such moves were hailed for the way they made it possible for candidates to 'bypass the editing function of the traditional media and to reach voters directly' (Campbell, 1993).

BULLETIN BOARD SYSTEMS AND SEX

"Why do you think the net was born?" asked the cast of the musical *Avenue Q*. "Porn. Porn. Porn." Indeed, historians have long noticed the close relationship between sexuality and emerging technologies, with one scholar referring to pornographers as "shock troops of advancing technology" (Gross, 2010). Consider the case of the printing press. Originally used to publish Gutenberg's bible, it was soon applied to concerns of the flesh with erotic works by Pietro Aretino and Giulio Romano paving the way for generations of pornographers. Or, consider the birth of cinema. While it might sound hyperbolic to argue that "production of erotic films commenced *almost immediately* after the invention of the motion picture," (Pornographic film, 2017), the claim is not that much of a stretch. Within two years of the very first public motion picture screening, Eugène Pirou and Albert Kirchner's *Le Coucher de la Mariée* (1896) depicted the actress Louise Willy performing a scandalous strip tease in the bathroom – one of the very first examples of erotic film. We can even see the same trend in the case of the humble Polaroid instant camera. Amateur photographers understood that "whatever happened in front of the lens never needed to be seen by a lab technician," and this epiphany paved the way for "camera club" sessions and thousands of "naughty first-generation Polaroid photos" (Bonanos, 2012).

Considered in the light of these historical examples, it should not be surprising that bulletin board systems were remarkably effective tools for disseminating erotica and pornography. By the 1990s, mainstream computer magazines regularly included pages of advertisements touting sex-oriented bulletin boards. Modems were still slow, so low-resolution pictures and videos were accompanied by racy text files. A *Time Magazine* article titled 'Orgies Online,' estimated that more than half of the 46,000 small bulletin boards offered 'some form of digital titillation' and described an Oregon-based site which generated $3.5 million in annual revenue by charging for access to the system operator's 'bulging database of R-rated and X-rated digital images and film loops' (Elmer-Dewitt, 1993). One of the most well-known systems was *Rusty-N-Edie's BBS*. Launched by 'a couple burn-outs from the 60s,' the site boasted 'more than three gigabytes of adult graphics.' The system operators proclaimed 'We live by the three no's: "No censorship, no rules, no hassle"' (*BBS Callers Digest*, 1992). This was not without risk. A system operator in Broken Arrow, Oklahoma, was fined $500 and given two years' probation on obscenity charges for posting files that were deemed 'too graphic' (Wood & Blankenhorn, 1990).

In addition to distributing erotic images and stories, bulletin board systems also hosted steamy electronic mail and chat sessions. Although newspapers could not resist the temptation to draw attention to cybersex, it was difficult to deny that cybersex was the 'safest sex' in town (Chamberlin, 1991; Lacey, 1992). As with bulletin board systems in the United States, entrepreneurs recognized that networked computers could be used to service the adult imagination. Minitel Rose offered up chat lines for every possible niche, and some users spent thousands of francs each month on the service. Mattias Duyves (1993) estimated that – in 1987 – approximately 200,000 erotic messages were sent over Minitel each day. The *Sunday Times* in London claimed 'more than half the traffic [on Minitel] consists of calls from people who are interested in sex' (Schofield, 2012).

INCREASINGLY GLOBAL REACH

The first computerized bulletin boards emerged in Berkeley and Chicago, but the BBS scene was a global phenomenon. Sysops began to form large 'echo networks' which shared files and discussion groups with other systems in the network. With this type of network, one could transmit a message from San Antonio to Beijing in just a few days. There were many echo networks, including Relaynet, Interlink, SmartNet, and Canada Remote Systems (Wood & Blankenhorn, 1990), but FidoNet was by far the largest and most influential. Described as 'the world's first (and probably last) amateur computer network based on anarchism' (Sprouse, 1990), FidoNet was created by a 'queer punk' media activist named Tom Jennings. The original computer bulletin boards were digital islands that could only support one user at a time, but Jennings' FidoNet protocol transformed the BBS landscape into a global network of interconnected machines. In this store and forward network, a system operator in one location would send an enormous bundle of data over the telephone line to a nearby system operator. The recipient would add his or her messages to the bundle of data, and then pass it on to the next system operator. As Bush (1993) explained, 'as calls within a city of the United States are generally free, but calls between cities are not, it seemed obvious to concentrate the intercity traffic into one call per night.' It is important to note that much of this traffic cost money, and – for the most part – it was system operators who footed the bill for long distance and toll charges (Sheppard, 2004).

One of the most remarkable things about this network was the content-neutral strategy that system operators (sysops) used to minimize long-distance telephone fees. The network only worked if sysops agreed to forward data packets to the nearest node, even if the nearest BBS represented a radically different point of view. Empowering an unlikely alliance of groups on all sides of the political spectrum, FidoNet's philosophy decoupled ideology from data exchange. Driven by a vision of cooperative anarchy, Jenning's system required that (a) each FidoNet node would be fully self-sufficient, and (b) each node could 'communicate with any other node without the aid or consent of technical or political groups at any level' (Bush, 1993). In many ways, this was the human equivalent of the breakthrough that revolutionized the modem: a protocol for exchanging information consciously decoupled from the constraints of a single ideology or proprietary operating system.

By any measure, FidoNet was extraordinarily successful. In early 1985, there were just 200 nodes. In April 1993, this number had climbed to 20,000. By 1996, more than 30,000 FidoNet systems connected millions of users around the world – a decentralized, asynchronous framework that anticipated the Internet. For the first time, hobbyists around the world were brought into contact with others who shared their unique interests. An amateur chef in Santa Fe, New Mexico, might post a question and receive answers from a kindred spirit in Rome, Italy (Scott, 1993). These global connections fueled innovation and cross-cultural knowledge exchange. Programmers outside the United States were thrilled to be connected with one another in this way, arguing that before FidoNET they would have waited three to six months for news of technical developments to filter into their awareness. 'The result,' commented one coder, 'is that any programmer in Australia can be as up-to-date as any other programmer in the world' (Powell, 1987).

As FidoNet grew, it was adopted by government agencies such as the National Park Service, the National Oceanic and Atmospheric Association (NOAA), and private corporations (Calvo, 1986). The system was also popular among the nonprofit community in developing countries (Borsook, 1996), with nodes in North America, Europe, Australia and New Zealand, Asia, Latin America, and Africa (Bush, 1993). Commenting on the network's impressive rate of growth, one technology journalist predicted that 'every man, woman and child on earth will be connected by 2002' (Ginn, 1991).

Similar experiments were underway across the Atlantic. In response to the oil shock of 1973, the French government invested significant resources in revitalizing the nation's telecommunication infrastructure (Fletcher, 2002). France Telecom began developing Minitel in 1977, and it was released to the public in 1982 (Chaplin, 2014). Originally imagined as a replacement for French phone directories, Minitel positioned itself as an information utility (Dvorak, 2012). Citizens could use the free terminals to buy groceries, send messages, read news updates, and pay bills (McClearn, 2012). Unlike the decentralized ground-up structure of the North American BBS scene, Minitel was completely top-down. Service providers were required to ask for permission from France Telecom, and only registered newspapers were allowed to provide services on the network (Schofield, 2012).

In 1986, more than 3 million Minitel terminals were in use throughout France (Chaplin, 2014). Eight years later, more than a third of French citizens over the age of 15 had used Minitel (Kling & Hill, 1997). However, by the late 1990s, the system seemed increasingly quaint and too bureaucratic, with *Le Monde* writing that 'Minitel is more expensive than the Internet, more crude and too French' (McClearn, 2012: 12). In June 2012, France Telecom killed off the service, migrating what was left of its information pages to the Internet (Mailland, 2016).

BULLETIN BOARD SYSTEMS AND LEGAL HASSLES

One challenge posted by an open communication system was that no one ever knew what type of information would be published online. When one patron posted death threats against Ronald Reagan on a library BBS, secret service agents confiscated the diskettes as evidence in the case (Dewey, 1986). Thomas Tcimpidis, a 33-year-old system operator in Los Angeles, had his home raided and his PC seized because one of his users posted a list of telephone credit card numbers

(Pollack, 1984). The Tcimpidis case was widely viewed as a turning point. System operators realized that they faced legal consequences – fines and even jail time – for illegal activity that occurred on their systems (Pemberton, 1985).

In the early 1990s, several bulletin board systems encountered legal problems. In 1992, arguing that the BBS was illegally distributing copyrighted software to subscribers, FBI agents confiscated personal computers and modems that were used to power *Davy Jones Locker* (Hyatt, 1992). The system operator who ran the board was eventually sentenced to six months of home detention and two years' probation (Kleiner, 1995). In 1993, the Ohio-based *Rusty-N-Edie's* was raided for allegedly distributing copyrighted software. Despite protestations of innocence from the sysops and subscribers alike, FBI agents confiscated all of the board's computers, monitors, and hard drives (Nash & Lindquist, 1993). The following month, *Playboy* sued the board's operators for copyright infringement, arguing that more than 412 downloadable adult images had been illegally scanned from the pages of *Playboy*. The case was eventually settled in 1998, with the sysops agreeing to pay $500,000 to resolve the lawsuit (Associated Press, 1998).

In 1990, the Secret Service raided the office of an Austin-based game company, seizing computers, hard drives, floppy disks, modems, monitors, and a laser printer. No employees of the game company were arrested, no charges were filed, and there were no formal criminal accusations (Sterling, 1992). Eventually, the Secret Service explained that one of the company's employees maintained a separate bulletin board system that focused on issues related to the computer underground. Although most of the confiscated equipment was eventually returned, the company was forced to lay off half of its employees (Jackson, 2010). In response to the troubling regulatory landscape that faced sysops and ordinary computer users alike, John Perry Barlow and Mitch Kapor formed the Electronic Frontier Foundation with the task of 'assuring the application of the US Constitution to digital media' (Barlow, 1990). The Supreme Court agreed. In 1997, in Reno v. ACLU, they agreed that the Internet was protected by the First Amendment and should be treated like a newspaper rather than a broadcast station.

THE COMPUTER UNDERGROUND

Released in 1984, the movie *War Games* told the story of a 15-year old hacker accidentally bringing the world to the brink of nuclear war when he stumbled across a BBS linked to the North American Aerospace Defense Command (NORAD). In addition to cementing the foundations for the enduring hacker stereotype, *War Games* introduced viewers to the world of modems, bulletin boards, and auto-dialers. It also spawned a wave of anxious coverage of the hacker threat. Less than a year later, Emmanuel Goldstein (a pen name for Eric Corley) launched the magazine *2600* to document the emerging computer underground.

The term *hacker* typically connotes destructive and illegal digital behavior, but this is not the only meaning of the term. Others argue that the *hacker ethic* is a positive stance, characterized by a commitment to sharing, openness, decentralization, expanded access to technology, and the creation of beautiful things (Levy, 1984). An honest observer of the computer underground that flourished on bulletin boards would have to concede that both types of hacker were actively involved in the scene. Many users were simply motivated by curiosity and a desire to understand new things. Others were engaged in piracy and driven by the thrill of cracking a supposedly locked computer system. Some were excited about all of these things.

Douglas Thomas (2002) argues that bulletin board systems were the ideal medium for the emergence of an underground hacker subculture. 'Because of the difficulty in regulating them (or even knowing about their existence) and their ability to offer complete anonymity to their users,' he explains, 'the boards provided the ideal "safe space" for hackers to congregate, to share information, learn from one another, and build their reputations' (Thomas, 2002: 119). By 1984, there were more than 200 hacking-themed boards in the United States and experts estimated that computer tampering cost up to $3 billion per year (Myers, 1984). Underground hacking boards distributed pages of phone numbers for 'major computers around the country,' including 'all of the Fortune 500 companies and a large amount of military systems' (Zap, 1988).

In addition to electronic mail, software downloads, and discussion forums, most bulletin board systems included an area where users could download text files. For the most part, text file archives contained innocuous documents ranging from recipes and instruction manuals to adventure game walkthroughs, lists of bulletin board access numbers, or articles about technology and popular culture retyped by hand and uploaded to the board. However, among the computer underground, one could find archives of T-files, G-files or Philes that plowed more controversial ground: instructions on how to build a 'blue box' that could be used to make free international phone calls, a recipe for manufacturing Methamphetamine from easily obtained ingredients, a guide on how to override software copy protection, and tips for making nitroglycerin from nitric acid, wheat germ, and sodium bicarbonate (Scott, 2016). As Jason Scott (2016) explains, 'they were textfiles of any sort, written to explain in detail an important new computer discovery, a great new concept, or an old piece of knowledge that needed to be passed on. It included stories, poems, songs, ramblings, and long treatises on theories that the writer couldn't possibly have known. They were full of bravado, of half-truths, of promises, and occasionally, of brilliance that shines to this day.'

When hackers first appeared on the scene, researchers realized that 'nearly all are teenage boys,' and noted that many of their posts were sophomoric, 'strewn with profanities questioning the masculinity of other system users' (Schiffres, 1985). Three decades before the word *doxing* entered the popular vocabulary, bitter users decided to punish *Newsweek* reporter Richard Sandza for an article that criticized the underground BBS scene. They published the journalist's credit card number and social security number on the boards, allegedly having acquired the information by cracking the computers of the credit reporting agency TRW (Schiffres, 1985). Almost from the very beginning of the BBS scene, system operators began to complain about immature, thoughtless, and malevolent users (Hoffman, 1985; Spurrier, 1985). The system operator responsible for creating the first public library BBS told of one high school that was forced to shut down the BBS at the end of the day because students flooded them with vulgar messages, graffiti, and bank access numbers (Dewey, 1986). In order to deny access to other users, auto-dialers were used to tie up a BBS all night, a retaliatory strategy 'dreaded by sysops everywhere' (Dewey, 1986: 16). During this period, system operators complained about flame wars in which participants exchanged 'unnecessarily argumentative or antagonistic messages.' One system operator speculated that angry, hateful invective was made easier by the fact that users could not actually see one another face to face (Wright, 1992).

It was sophomoric, vindictive hackers – not the knowledge-seekers – who captured the popular imagination in much that was written about the computer underground in the 1980s. For example, the *ABA Banking Journal*'s 'Beware the Hacker Attack' argued that personal computers and modems were a gateway drug on the road to computer crime. 'Inevitably, as [BBS users] phone bills begin to rise,' warned the article, 'they begin to look for ways to avoid paying long distance calls.' Before they knew it, hackers would be stealing telephone credit card access numbers to fuel their addiction (Miller, 1984). In 1983, seven young computer enthusiasts – mostly teenagers – were said to have penetrated computer systems at the Los Alamos Nuclear Facility, the Memorial Sloan-Kettering Cancer Care Center, and Pacific Security bank. Referred to as 414s, based on their shared Milwaukee area code, the young 'bandits' insisted that their worst transgression was creating a few accounts named Joshua – a reference to the movie *War Games*. Commenting on the incident, one computer security expert compared the emergence of inexpensive computers to a 'flood' of cheap, semi-automatic weapons (Covert, 1983). Jacque Vallee (1984) argued that the public *loved* this type of media coverage because 'it is mysterious, full of technical intrigue and ingenious plots, and its victims are usually big companies, giving the man in the street his vicarious revenge over faceless institutions with their massive computers' (1984: 136).

THE SHORT-LIVED BOOM: INTERNET KILLED THE VIDEO STAR

With the introduction of *Microsoft Windows* and multi-tasking, it became possible to handle multiple callers simultaneously on a single personal computer. Although this reduced computing costs, sysops began paying more for multiple telephone lines – a trend which stimulated the rise of paid bulletin board systems (Fire Escape, 1998; Sheppard, 2004). For example, the 85-line Channel 1 in Cambridge, MA, received more than 2,500 calls a day and generated $20,000 each month (Berck, 1992). However, system operators realized that their businesses did not necessarily scale well. 'The larger we get, the more the problems of size are exposed,' noted one successful sysop (Hardenburgh, n.d.). In addition to consuming electricity,

computers generated so much heat that it was necessary to 'open the windows in the dead of the Ohio winter to keep the heat under control.' Controlling heat during the summer months required a four-ton air conditioner unit and three huge humidifiers running around the clock (Hardenburgh, n.d.). In an attempt to offset the costs of their business, more and more system operators adopted complex fee structures and added hundreds of telephone lines. By the mid-1990s, industry analysts estimated that three out of four bulletin boards charged subscription fees (Scott, 1993).

In the mid-1990s, the emerging BBS industry was described as a $2 billion industry – a figure that include revenues from paid BBS subscriptions and the sale of affiliated technologies (Metcalfe, 1994b). Making the leap from 'an obscure hobby' to a 'cultural revolution' (Plotnikoff, 1995), this digital landscape was home to more than 60,000 bulletin boards and approximately 17 million users (Metcalfe, 1994b). Meanwhile, the software used to run the bulletin boards was in high demand, and generated approximately $20 million in sales each year (Berck, 1992). 'Today, the word *hobby* hardly applies,' argued Lamont Wood and Dana Blankenhorn (1990) about the rise of for-profit bulletin boards. 'BBSes are a way of life for thousands of people. For some, it's a business, perhaps even a career' (1990: 298).

This way of life was about to be extinguished. As Randy Seuss noted, 'once BBSers were able to leave the local community via the Internet, it was unstoppable' (Zelchenko, 1998: para. 5). In 1994, the *New York Times* noted that the global Internet population had nearly doubled in a single year, from 15 million to 25 million users (Pacheco, 1994). The sysop of a popular BSS *The Ledge* remembers that, in 1996, 'one by one, my subscribers began to vanish and open up dial-up accounts with Internet service providers that were popping up everywhere.' Commenting on the 'great migration' of users to the Internet, one hobbyist (Fire Escape, 1998) observed 'many sysops are currently just holding their breath and veering their eyes, hoping that the Internet will just "go away".' It did not. One industry pundit grudgingly conceded that the world-wide web was "the BBS of the future" (Rickard, 1994).

Arguing that bulletin board systems were on the brink of a comeback, one sysop optimistically predicted that 'we can all sit back and watch the bloated internet crumble under its own weight while our dialup customers continue to call BBS's like they have done for over a decade!' (Robbins, 1996). The computer journalist Bill Machrone (1995) predicted that the biggest Internet groups would 'collapse under their own weight' because people would 'prefer their local BBS, a place like *Cheers* (where everybody know your name) – even if the BBS becomes a web site' (1995: 83). Offering one of the most unique reasons to resist the Internet, William Zachmann (1991) argued that 'electronic mail is inherently exclusionary' because it is only delivered to the recipient(s), reinforcing corporate 'chain of command' and hierarchical communication channels. In contrast, the BBS approach was said to make information available to everyone (1991: 95). The controlled environment of e-mail, said the journalist, appeals to 'those who are incompetent or simply lazy' (1991: 95).

Motivated by a combination of desperation and profit, the largest bulletin board systems transformed themselves into Internet Service Providers (Metcalfe, 1994a; Rubin, 1995). As with the growth of the telephone and radio industries in the previous century, these small-scale operations had little hope of competing with corporate giants. The lucky ones were acquired during the Internet boom; others simply shuttered their doors. Perhaps most telling, *Boardwatch* (the flagship journal of the BBS community) replaced its regular list of BBS phone numbers with a column that profiled interesting web sites (Romonesko, 1996).

Outmatched by 'the glitz and resources of the World Wide Web,' the small bulletin boards struggled to stay afloat (Romonesko, 1996: 1E). System operators for the remaining boards reported that their users primarily connected to the system for sentimental reasons. Commenting on the death of the scene, an 84-year-old computer hobbyist explained, 'BBSs became web pages. The web became one big BBS, or a million tiny ones, depending on how you look at it' (Zelchenko, 1998: para. 2).

CONCLUSION

This chapter focused primarily on the social and cultural topography of the bulletin board scene, with only passing attention to particular technical details. However, the connection between the BBS and contemporary social media is directly tied to the significant ways that computing tools have changed in recent decades. It's not just that computers are more powerful each year – it's the fact that the rate of change itself is speeding up. Kurzweil (2001: para 1) calls this 'exponential growth in the rate of exponential growth.'

Modem speeds are measured in 'baud' or 'bits per second.' When Christensen and Seuss developed the first bulletin board in 1977, they used a modem that was capable of transferring 300 bits per second. This works out to approximately 42 characters per second – less than one third the length of a typical tweet. As with processing power and storage space, the pace of improvements in connection speeds was astonishing. Each new version was at least twice as fast as its predecessor, the amount of time between releases shortened, and overall costs steadily declined.

For much of the BBS scene, computer networks were primarily used to exchange chunks of text. Suddenly, modems were fast enough to exchange low-resolution images and blocky computer graphics. Computer networks became vehicles for visual communication. By the early 1990s, it was possible to transfer audio files and even short video clips over a dial-up connection. The content was pixelated, but the image quality was irrelevant. The network was absorbing the characteristics of global broadcasters. This might seem quaint in a contemporary world in which teenagers carry high-definition supercomputers known as cellphones and Internet Service Providers are rolling out one-gigabit-per-second connection speeds (Glaser, 2016). Not so long ago, though, these technological developments were unthinkable. Contemporary connection speeds are more than *three million times faster* than the modem that Ward Christensen and Randy Seuss used to power their first computer bulletin board.

Why does this matter? It matters because this is the key that helps us recognize the enduring characteristics of our social media landscape. Our contemporary media landscape has changed considerably during the past two decades. At first glance, the world of BBS users seems so radically different than the world of users camped out on popular social media platforms. But the current communication landscape is *exactly* what one might expect would happen to the BBS scene when you fold in connection speeds that are *three million times faster* than original modems, computer processors that are *345,000 times more powerful* than the Apple II that powered the BBS in the Chicago Public library (Morgan, 2014), and an ecosystem that has *grown 100-fold* from approximately 30 million digitally networked users in 1990 to 3.3 billion digitally networked users in 2016.

Whether sending messages, talking about politics, playing games, consuming stories, or downloading content, contemporary computer users are doing the exact same things online that they did in the 1980s. The machines are faster, the graphics are better, and computers have insinuated themselves ever further into the nooks and crannies of our daily lives, but the human desire to interact with other human beings stays the same. The drive to communicate endures.

Notes

1 Although bulletin board systems facilitated information exchange, most users only *downloaded* software, images and text files. Only a handful actually uploaded files, and – of those – only a small percentage uploaded *original* content (Hoffman, 1985).
2 Luckily for communication historians and computer hobbyists of all stripes, Scott has dedicated an enormous amount of energy to archiving thousands of text files from 1980 through 1995.

REFERENCES

Associated Press (1998) Owners of Internet site settle with 'Playboy' over use of photos. *Cincinnati Enquirer*, March 6.

Barlow, J. (1990) A not terribly brief history of the Electronic Frontier Foundation. *Electronic Frontier Foundation*, November 8.

BBS Callers Digest (1992) Advertisement for Rusty n Edie's BBS. *BBS Callers Digest*, May: 2.

Berck, J. (1992) All about electronic bulletin boards. It's no longer just techno-hobbyists who meet by modem. *New York Times*, July 19.

Berlet, C. (2001) When hate went online. Paper presented to Northeast Sociological Association, Spring Conference, Fairfield, CT: Sacred Heart University, April 28.

Bloomberg News (1992) Among Prodigy users, it's Clinton by a hair. *Bloomberg News*, October 4.

Bonanos, C. (2012) Before sexting, there was Polaroid. *The Atlantic*, October 1. Web.

Borsook, P. (1996) The anarchist. *Wired Magazine*. April.

Bula, F. (1993) The invisible city of computer networking: Bulletin boards are key stroke to involving teens. *Vancouver Sun*, January 2.

Bush, R. (1993) FidoNet: Technology, use, tools, and history. Technical document. *Fidonet.org*.

Calvo, M. (1986) Business acceptance of FidoNet growing. *Information World*, 8(16), April 21.

Campbell, A. (1993) Political campaigning in the Internet age: A proposal for protecting political candidates' use of on-line computer services. *Villanova Law Review*, 38: 517.

Carlson, D. (2009) Compuserve. David Carlson's Virtual World: The Online Timeline. Web.

Carr, C. T. & Hayes, R. A. (2015) Social media: Defining, developing, and divining. *Atlantic Journal of Communication*, *23*(1): 46–65.

Ceruzzi, P. (1998) *A History of Modern Computing*. Cambridge, MA: MIT Press.

Chamberlin, P. (1991) Safe sex becomes an on-line buzz. *Sydney Morning Herald*, May 2.

Chaplin, T. (2014) Lesbians online: Queer identity and community formation on the French Minitel. *Journal of the History of Sexuality*, *23*(3): 451–472.

Chickenhead (2004) The BBS universe from the perspective of a simple pleb. *Textfiles.com*. Web.

Christensen, W. & Seuss, R. (1978) Hobbyist computerized bulletin board. *Byte*, November: 150–157.

Covert, C. (1983) High-tech hijinks: Seven curious teenagers wreak havoc via computer. *Detroit Free Press*, August 28.

Dewey, P. (1984) Public-access micros: A little equipment can serve scores of walk-in patrons and a whole community of dial-in participants. *American Libraries*, November: 704.

Dewey, P. (1986) Electronic bulletin boards: Applications in libraries. *Library Computing*, November.

Drew, J. (2013) *A Social History of Contemporary Democratic Media*. London: Routledge.

Driscoll, K. (2014) *Hobbyist inter-networking and the popular Internet imaginary: Forgotten histories of networked personal computing, 1978–1998*. Doctoral dissertation, University of Southern California, Los Angeles, California.

Duvall, M. (1995) Teens find help with crises on bulletin board. *Calgary Herald*, October 5.

Duyves, M. (1993) The Minitel: The glittering future of a new invention. In R. Mendès-Leite & P. de Busscher (Eds), *Gay Studies from the French Cultures: Voices from France, Belgium, Brazil, Canada, and the Netherlands*. New York: Harrington Park Press.

Dvorak, J. (2012) Minitel R.I.P. (1982–2012). *PC Mag.Com*. June 27. Web.

Earnshaw, G. (1989) Share your program and make a fortune. *Sydney Morning Herald*, January 9.

Elmer-Dewitt, P. (1993) Orgies on-line. *Time Magazine*, *141*(22).

Evasuk, S. (1992) Computer bulletin board aims to keep seniors in touch. *The Toronto Star*, Aubust 3.

Felsenstein, L. (1993) The commons of information. *Dr. Dobb's Journal*, May: 18–24.

Fire Escape (1998) From the BBS backroads to the information super highway (or Where Did All the BBSes Go?!?). *Textfiles.com*. Web.

Fletcher, A. (2002) France enters the information age: A political history of Minitel. *History and Technology*, *18*(2): 103–117.

Freed, L. (1995) An online service of your own. *PC Magazine*. August: NE6.

Gilbertson, S. (2010) February 16, 1978: Bulletin board goes electronic. *Wired Magazine*, February.

Ginn, A. (1991) Computer. Fido goes walkies a million times. *The Guardian*, August 15.

Glaser, A. (2016) Going for Google, Comcast preps gigabit Internet that works with regular cable. *Wired Magazine*, April 30. Web.

Glossbrenner, A. (1984) Going by the board. *PC Magazine*, March 20: 471–474.

Green, C. (1992) Use of inexpensive 'shareware' surges with growth in modems. *The Financial Post (Toronto)*, March 24.

Gross, D. (2010) In the tech world, porn quietly leads the way. *CNN*, April 23. Web.

Harrer, J. (2000) The History of Mustang. USBBS Historical BBS Blog & Memorial BBS List.

Hoban, P. (1984) The latest bulletins. *New York*, September 24: 19.

Hoffman, D. (1985) Across the boards. *PC Magazine*, *4*(12): 311.

Hyatt, J. (1992) PC bulletin board hit by FBI raid. *Boston Globe*, June 14.

Info World (1984) Bulletin board controversy: Group transmits racist literature into Canada. *Info World*, *6*(39), September 24.

Information Today (1984) Survey calls BBSs 'costly.' *Information Today*, October: 9.

Jackson, S. (2010). Steve Jackson Games vs. the Secret Service. *Steve Jackson Games*. Web.

James, M. L., Wotring, C. E., & Forrest, E. J. (1995) An exploratory study of the perceived benefits of electronic bulletin board use and their impact on other communication activities. *Journal of Broadcasting & Electronic Media*, *39*(1): 30–50.

Kantor, A. (1992) Electronic democracy. *PC Magazine*, December 22: 31.

Katz, J. (1993) Bulletin boards: News from Cyberspace. *Rolling Stone*, 654: 35.

Kelly, K. (1984) The birth of a network nation. *New Age Journal*, October: 32–42.

Kinnick, D. (1989) Sex byting: A guide for the menu-driven. *The Advocate*, January: 42–44.

Kleiner, K. (1995) Software pirate sunk by new law. *New Scientist*, March 25.

Kling, R. & Hill, R. (1997) Electronic commerce, the world-wide web, Minitel and EDI. *Information Society*, *13*(1): 33–41.

Kohn, A. (1984) Bulletin boards for gay computer hackers. *The Advocate*, September 18: 24.

Kurzweil, R. (2001) The law of accelerating returns. *Kurzweil: Accelerating Intelligence*, March 7.

Lacey, L. (1992) Call me Modem, or sex and the single nerd. *Globe and Mail (Canada)*, April 11.

Levy, S. (1984) *Hackers: Heroes of the Computer Revolution*. New York, NY: Anchor Press/Doubleday.

Machrone, B. (1995) Where everyone knows your name. *PC Magazine*, *14*(6): 83.

Mailland, J. (2016) 101 Online. American Minitel networks and lessons from its failure. *IEEE Annals of the History of Computing*, January–March.

Markoff, J. (1983) Well-net personal computer network serves the disabled. *Info World*, *5*(33), August 15.

McClearn, M. (2012) The Minitel (1978–2012). *Canadian Business*, August 8. Web.

McKeown, N. (1991) Social norms and implications of Santa Monica's PEN (Public Electronic Network). *99th Annual Convention of the American Psychological Association*. San Francisco, CA.

Metcalfe, B. (1994a) There were four kinds of people in cyberspace. *InfoWorld*, *16*(15): 49.

Metcalfe, B. (1994b) Sysops are reaping the benefits in the wake of a BBS explosion, *InfoWorld*, *16*(36): 52.

Miller, D. (1984) Beware of the 'hacker attack'. *ABA Banking Journal*, *76*(11): 50.

Morgan, T. (2014) Oracle cranks up the cores to 32 with Sparc M7 chip. *Enterprise Tech: Inside Advanced Scale Challenges*, August 13.

Myers, E. (1984) Pirates on the boards. *Datamation*, *30*: 61–64.

Nash, K. & Lindquist, C. (1993) First raid tests felony law. *Computerworld*, March 15.

Newsweek (1984) Neo-Nazi Aryan Nations' electronic bulletin board. *Newsweek*, December 24: 20.

Obar, J. A. & Wildman, S. (2015) Social media definition and the governance challenge: An introduction to the special issue. *Telecommunications Policy*, *39*(9): 745–750.

O'Laughlin, R. (1983) Gay press works to develop an electronic community. *Info World*, *5*(2), October 17.

Pacheco, D. (1994) Fast growth spells trouble for Internet traditionalists. *Denver Post*, July 26.

Pemberton, J. K. (1985) Information mischief? Information villainy? The Tcimpidis case. *Database*: 86–7.

Plotnikoff, D. (1995) Untangling the web: From fresh newbie cruisers to veteran BBS-era users, if you've ever used a modem there's a magazine for you. *San Jose Mercury News*, July 10.

Pollack, A. (1984) Free-speech issues surround computer bulletin board use. *New York Times*, November 12. Web.

Pornographic film. (2017) In *Wikipedia, The Free Encyclopedia*, June 30. Web.

Powell, G. (1987) Bulletin boards will live. *Sydney Morning Herald*, August 31.

Preimesberger, C. (2012) 30 years ago: How Hayes modems, bulletin boards presaged the web. *eWeek*, September 12.

Rae, J. (1984) Grapevine: Swaps, nets, users' groups. *InfoWorld*, April 9: 26.

Randall, N. (1989) The world through a wire. *Compute*, April: 21.

Reid, T. (1989) Bulletin board systems: Gateway to citizenship in the network nation. *Washington Post*, November 6.

Rheingold, H. (1991) The great equalizer. *Whole Earth Review*, *71*(5): 11.

Rickard, J. (1994) Webulism and the cable fable. *Boardwatch*, December.

Robbins, M. (1996) Internet's effect on BBS use. (Coming full circle again). *Textfiles.com*. Web.

Romonesko, J. (1996) Endangered species? Once popular online hangouts, Twin Cities computer bulletin board systems face an uncertain future as the glitz of the world wide web takes. *St. Paul Pioneer Press* (Minnesota), June 24.

Rothman, J. (1987) The modem: One peripheral every Amiga owner should have. *Amazing Computing*, February: 9.

Rubin, C. (1995) Distilled online wisdom: *Boardwatch* magazine. *Guerilla Marketing*. Web.

Schiffres, M. (1985) The shadowy world of computer hackers. *U.S. News & World Report*, 58–60.

Schofield, H. (2012) Minitel: The rise and fall of the France-wide web. *BBC News*, June 28. Web.

Schopp, S. (1993) Electronic bulletin boards and the music educator. *Music Educators Journal*, 79(9): 64–67.

Schuler, D. (1994) Community networks: Building a new participatory medium. *Communications of the ACM*, 37: 38–51.

Schwartz, E. (1992) Putting the PC into politics. *Bloomberg News*, March 15.

Scott, J. (2001) Textfiles.com BBS list. *Textfiles. com*. Web.

Scott, J. (2008) Your news in full-color GIF. *Textfiles.com*. Web.

Scott, J. (2016) Statement. *Textfiles.com*. Web.

Scott, M. (1993) Cyberspace trekkers will find FidoNet as inviting as a favorite armchair. *Vancouver Sun (British Columbia)*, July 24.

Seger, K. (1983) The electronic bulletin board. *PC Magazine*, 1(9): 214–220.

Shea, T. (1984) Educating a community. *Info World*, 6(14), April 2.

Sheppard, J. (2004) Ten years on the ledge. *Textfiles.com*. Web.

Slaton, J. (2001) Remembering community memory: The Berkeley beginnings of online community. *SF Gate*, December 13.

Smith, R. (1985) Computer bulletin boards: New wave in teen communications. *Futurist*, 19(4): 28–29.

Sprouse, M. (1990) *Threat by Example*. San Francisco, CA: Pressure Drop Press.

Spurrier, J. (1985) BBS Land. *Microtimes*, March: 30.

Sterling, B. (1992) The Hacker Crackdown: Law and Disorder on the Electronic Frontier. London: Penguin.

Stone, M. (1985) Taking notice of bulletin boards. *PC Magazine*, April 30: 261–262.

Szpakowski, M. (2006) Excerpts about Community Memory in the Resource One Newsletter. *Community Memory: 1972–1974, Berkeley and San Francisco, California*, November 4.

Takahashi, D. (1990) Prodigy service cut is censorship, subscribers say. *Los Angeles Times*, November 7.

Thomas, D. (2002) *Hacker Culture*. Minneapolis, MI: University of Minneapolis Press.

Vallee, J. (1984) The Network Revolution: Confessions of a Computer Scientist. Harmondsworth: Penguin.

Vaughan-Nichols, S. (2015) Before the web: Online services of yesteryear. *ZDNet*, December 4.

Wittig, M. (1991) Electronic city hall. *Whole Earth Review*, 71(Summer): 24–27.

Wood, L. & Blankenhorn, D. (1990) State of the BBS nation: Behold the lowly bulletin board, now encompassing the globe. *Byte Magazine*, January: 298–304.

Wright, K. (1992) A little respect please. *BBS Magazine*, 3(5): 10.

Zachmann, W. (1991) Corporate e-mail and bulletin boards. *PC Magazine*, 10(4): 95–96.

Zap, C. (1988) An interpretation of computer hacking. Reprinted in E. Goldstein (2008) *The Best of 2600: A Hacker Odyssey*. Hoboken, NJ: John Wiley & Sons.

Zelchenko, P. (1998) Jack Rickard, editor of *Boardwatch* magazine saw it coming… *Chicago Tribune*, October 30.

Alternative Histories of Social Media in Japan and China

Mark McLelland, Haiqing Yu,
and Gerard Goggin

INTRODUCTION

In her essay for the inaugural edition of the journal *Social Media and Society*, Nancy Baym critiques the idea that there is something inherently new or special about recent social media platforms such as Facebook. She notes that older forms of media like televisions and telephones have always had social applications and that a range of earlier Internet functions have long enabled 'connecting with friends and family, discovering what is going on in the world [and] sharing and expressing what maters' (Baym, 2015: 1). For Baym, the rise of the term 'social media' is more about the corporatization of the Internet and the manner in which companies such as Facebook have developed platforms that 'harness what people were already doing' and turned these practices into 'revenue streams' (Baym, 2015: 1). She notes many of the drawbacks of the corporate model of social networking, not least its domination by a few venture-capitalist companies whose 'take-it-or-leave-it' terms of service divest users from their content and promote cultures of mass surveillance where individuals lose control over their data. We need a better model for rethinking communication media, she concludes, not one that treats 'humans as data profiles to be matched with advertisers' (2015: 2).

Baym's well-founded critique of the development of the term 'social media' as well as the commercialism that underpins today's immensely popular and revenue-producing platforms is based on the American experience. Indeed, Baym notes that some of the world's most successful social media platforms have been developed by 'small groups of (usually) (young) (White) (American) men' (2015: 1). But we are moving away from a time when discussions about the Internet and the effects of its myriad applications can be discussed or judged from an exclusively North American (or even wider Anglophone) perspective.

As emergent research is illustrating, there is a wide range of social media platforms that have been established and developed across many different countries. Many of these social media ventures have their own specific antecedents in earlier Internet technologies and cultures, including bulletin board systems (BBS), chat rooms, messaging platforms, mobile social software ('mososo'), web cultures, and so on. Quite a number of social media platforms and forms – especially national social media – have had relatively limited careers, especially with the advent of the present global and regional titans of Weibo, Twitter, Facebook, Instagram, WeChat, and others. Other social media platforms still have substantial national, cross-national, and regional user bases, significance, and cultural influence. Leading examples include the Russian social media network Vkontakte (В Контакте) known as VK, the African MixIt messaging software, and the Korean 'over-the-top' chat, messaging, and digital culture apps Kakao Talk and Line (which took over from the pioneering Cyworld). ('Over-the-top' is the term for text, audio, and video applications that deliver content and connectivity via the Internet, across different devices – without the involvement of infrastructure or access operators).

There are also some very interesting and important historiographic questions to ask when social media are inaugurated in different places (cf. Lee, 2016 and Brügger, 2013), where we discern the 'breaks' or how we understand 'continuity', or, indeed, how we make sense of the persistence of, say, BBS in some countries (China, Taiwan, Turkey) and the greater prominence of blogs in some countries and contexts (Iran, Taiwan) (Goggin & McLelland, 2017a). How do we understand the interplay among different media forms, formats, and preferences, in the kind of 'remediations' that particular facets of social media represent? Mobile phones have a greater role in the social media histories of some countries (Japan, Korea, Indonesia, India, Burma) than others, where PCs might be decisive at particular points; or the prominence of the press might parlay into

some social media forms taking on notable social, cultural, and political functions.

Such apparently historiographic issues in the development of social media take on heightened importance when we consider the uses and abuses of taken-for-granted, or even unnoticed, histories. Consider, for instance, the ways that particular kinds of histories help us imagine, invent, domesticate, use or resist, and deploy ideas, values, and frameworks for how we see, relate to, and live with social media. These kinds of social imaginaries have been drawn to our attention by the important work of Internet historians and scholars such as Janet Abbate (1999), Patrice Flichy (2007), Sandra Braman (2011, 2012), Fred Turner (2006), Thomas Streeter (2011), Robin Mansell (2012), and others. However, we are only at the early stage of documenting, theorizing, and debating non-Western and alternative Internet imaginaries, let alone social media imaginaries.

Thus a basic sense of the range, importance, and influence of these alternative histories of social media is vital, if we are to understand – not misconstrue – the contemporary dynamics of social media. Accordingly, in this chapter, which draws on our earlier work aimed at internationalizing Internet studies and reframing the Internet in terms of its global histories (Goggin & McLelland, 2009 & 2017b), we discuss a range of alternative histories of social media outside the usual North American and European paradigms. In particular, we examine two distinct though also related Asian cases: Japan and China. Japan and China are significant case studies for several reasons. First, both were perceived as coming late to the Internet age, having to overcome complex coding problems for the input, transfer and display of Han (Chinese) characters, which the scripts of both languages share. Both societies also largely missed out on the stage of office automation, particularly the use of typewriters, which were typical of mid-twentieth century business environments in North America and Europe. There was consequently less familiarity with the keyboard as a text input medium requiring the development of 'new literacy and communication practices different from the US' (Sugimoto & Levin, 2000: 137). However, once these coding issues had been resolved, both societies took to computer-mediated communication. By 2000, approximately 30% of the Japanese population were using the Internet, with 93% by 2015 (ITU, 2016). China's usage climbed from 1.78% of the population using the Internet in 2000, to approximately 28% in 2009, and 50% by 2015 (ITU, 2016). In relative terms, Japanese share of Internet usage has slipped down the global scale as global language users of Spanish, Arabic and Portuguese increasingly come online, while Chinese users represent the second most prevalent population with the largest number of Internet users in any country (Internet World Stats, 2016a, 2016b; ITU, 2016).

Each case has its own complex dynamics, but there are interesting comparisons and contrasts to be made. Taken together, we hope that this two-country comparative discussion illustrates the importance and productiveness of generating alternative social histories to the dominant accounts – which tend to assume, to their peril, that Western social media platforms and corporations have trumped their non-Western counterparts.

JAPAN

Japan is significant for any history of social media because, despite the relatively slow development of PC-based Internet culture during the 1990s, the mobile Internet took off exponentially at the turn of the century – driven largely by young people's desire for enhanced connection via cell phones. Indeed, there is a marked difference between the kinds of reports about Japan's adoption of the Internet that appear in computing magazines pre- and post-1999. It was in that year that NTT's (Japan's largest telephone company and network provider) rolled out its *i-mode* (that is, information or Internet-mode) cell phones that anticipated many of the functions of today's smartphones by several years. The innovation of the *i-mode* system that saw Internet connectivity skyrocket in Japan tends to be what is now remembered, at least in the Anglophone literature, about Japan's Internet history. It was the roll out of mobile Internet and the pioneering handsets and applications developed for them that got Japan 'back in the race' (Coates, 2000). However, prior to 1999 the discourse about Japan and the Internet in magazines such as *Wired* was very much framed in terms of bureaucratic incompetence, missed opportunities and 'catch-up' based on American models (see, for example, Abate, 1996; Johnstone, 1994).

The problem with these accounts is that they were so fixated on pointing out what Japan was *not* doing (in terms of models already developed in the USA) that they missed what was actually going on – in particular the important cultural and technological steps that had to be taken in Japan in order for computer-mediated communication (CMC), particularly online socializing, to become widely intelligible and acceptable among the general population. Although it is arguable that on a bureaucratic level there were indeed many missed opportunities (Contreras, 2014), the grassroots appropriation of CMC in Japan was pioneering in a Japanese context – and, importantly, was always already 'social'.

One reason why a highly developed technological society such as Japan came relatively late to the Internet (the first publicly accessible service provider did not commence till 1993) was the necessity of developing software and transmission protocols for the input and display of a complex character-based script. Closely aligned with these encoding difficulties was the fact that Japan had not gone through the same kind of office automation characteristic of Western societies. Although in the Western context the movement from manual typewriter to electric typewriter to personal computer was fairly seamless – given that the QWERTY keyboard remained the main human–machine interface on all these devices – the lack of a standardized input and display system presented a challenge to users of non-alphabet-based Asian languages (Contreras, 2014).

Although a system that allowed users to input Japanese text phonetically using the QWERTY keyboard and then press a conversion key to show various options in Japanese script on screen had been developed in 1979, computer literacy remained low in Japan for the next decade. This was partly because there were no standard conversion protocols, meaning computer companies developed their own mutually incompatible systems, making it difficult to network devices (Contreras, 2014; Seo, 2013: 186). There was also some cultural resistance to reproducing *personal* communication via mechanical means, some older people complaining that printed characters were '"cold" and lacked individuality' (Gottlieb, 2000: 136–137).

Japan's earliest computer networks were established around 1985 and included Keio University academic, Jun Murai's JUNET (Japan UNIX Network), which established links between one private and two public universities, an American-Japanese collaboration known as TWICS, which catered mainly to English-language users, and Japan's first major local network, Computer Communication of Oita Amateur Research Association (COARA). The last was a public-private enterprise initially aimed at networking local businesses to encourage regional revitalization established in Oita province of Japan's south-western island of Kyushu. However, by the late 1980s, two computer companies, NEC and Fujitsu, had been established and were successfully marketing *pasokon tsūshin* or 'personal computer communication' networks utilizing the telephone line and modems. These were basically bulletin board systems (BBS) that enabled users to seek out information from various news feeds as well as participate in online discussions and

send email to other users – but, in the early years at least, only with those on the same system. Yet, once computerized communication became more available, it proved popular, with commentators noting that the new '*wāpuro ningen*' (word-processer human) was likely to write more, and to write more often (Gottlieb, 2000: 141, 147–148).

At this time reports in the Anglophone press, which focused on bureaucratic infighting and the tardiness with which telephone infrastructures and payment systems were responding to consumer demand, missed what was actually happening on the ground in Japan in the late 1980s and early 1990s. This was still a time when Japan's computer networks largely functioned as 'intranets' since the necessary protocols to connect with the global Internet were not yet in place, in part to do with the lack of standard protocols for the input and conversion of Japanese script (Fouser, 2001; Nishigaki, 1998). Many commentators were simply oblivious as to how fundamental Roman script was, in the form of the American Standard Code for Information Interchange (ASCII), which was literally built into the architecture of the Internet, including programming languages as well as domain names and web addresses (Pargman & Palme, 2009).

Japanese scholarship was, however, clear in recognizing the arrival of new and potentially revolutionary forms of communication – often captured by the transliterated term 'network' (*nettowāku*) – including Kumon's *The Network Society* (1988), Kawakami's *The Social Psychology of Electronic Networking* (1993), and Yamane's *Declaration of a Network Republic* (1996). These and other important analyses were clear that the 'networking' taking place via these computer systems was very much about person-to-person communication and not at all like the one-to-many mode of information dissemination characteristic of traditional mass media (Izumi, 1996). The realization that CMC offered the potential for a wide range of people with divergent experiences to come together online in 'people-to-people, two-way communication' encouraged even sites originally founded with business applications in mind to broaden their user-base, as happened with COARA which became a 'network community' for local residents as early as 1987 (Izumi, 1996: 5; Rheingold, 1993: 205–206). As Toru Ono, one of the network's founders, pointed out in his book, *The COARA Electric Nation: How Computer Communication Makes the Regional Global*, 'knowledge' is not simply about information exchange but emerges from human interaction (Ono, 1994: 62). Similarly TWICS, the main English-language network at this time, was, according to its systems operator, always 'oriented more toward people and communication rather than data and information' (cited in Rheingold, 1993: 215).

These early networks were extremely important in building a community consciousness among various constituencies, notably feminist women and those facing adversity, such as parents of still-born infants and those suffering chronic illness (Tamura, 2017). They were also key in developing communication among otherwise dispersed sexual minorities, such as transgender people (the Eon BBS founded in 1990) and gay men (Gay Net Japan, founded in 1988, grew out of contacts made via the TWICS network).

Although these early networks were important in normalizing the idea of CMC in Japan and crucial in bringing about a new kind of online sociality, they were not taken up by the population as a whole. By 1995, for instance, the two largest commercial networks – NEC's PC-Van (founded 1986) and Fujitsu's Nifty-Serve (founded 1987) – had only around a million users each. This was due to a number of factors, not least an inflexible pricing system set by the fixed-line providers and the non-intuitive means of inputting Japanese text using the Roman alphabet. A 1997 survey found that in Japan 50.8% of respondents indicated they had never used a computer in comparison to 21.8% of Americans (Fouser, 2001: 274). It is no surprise, then, that in Japan, the PC did not emerge as the main interface through which the mass of consumers first accessed the Internet. Rather, a range of hand-held and mobile devices has proven more popular. The different orthographies in the East Asian region necessarily impacted upon the take-up of computerization in general and the Internet in particular, and led to different developmental trajectories and patterns of use that diverge in many important ways from those characteristic of the USA and Europe.

The importance of understanding the particular developmental trajectories of the mobile Internet in Japan is highlighted by the popularity in the mid-1990s of paging devices among high-school girls. Okada (2005) notes how in the mid-1990s schoolgirls in Japan appropriated paging devices originally developed for the (male) business market, using the keypad on telephones to send simple text messages to the LCD displays of friends' pagers. This led to a distinct *poke-kotoba* (pager-lingo) among the subculture and assisted young people in organizing their private lives outside parental supervision and control. This innovative use of pagers 'created new literacy practices among young Japanese people' (Sugimoto & Levin, 2000: 138) and impacted upon the functions of early models of cell phones known as *keitai* (literally 'carried in the hand') in Japanese, which included SMS services and, from 1999, via *i-mode*, Internet-enabled email which allowed subscribers to write longer messages and also include graphics, audio, video and web links (Matsuda, 2005: 35). The success of *i-mode* can partly be put down to its use of a modified form of HTML, allowing for increased data speed that enhanced the functionality of the handsets and the kinds of services that were on offer. Young people's use of the service was also innovative in the development of a wide range of text-based emoticons that could be added to email to overcome the perception that computer-based communication was somehow impersonal (Sugimoto & Levin, 2000: 144–146).

In Japan, the rapid uptake in mobile Internet was driven by the desire for 'social media' among the youth market. Mobile Internet providers were further able to appeal to a youth market by circumventing the high cost of accessing the Internet due to fixed-line charges via an innovative payment system where browsing was free but the user paid per packet downloaded to the phone, receiving an itemized bill each month (Okazaki, 2006). A range of other services, such as subscriptions to news sites, ticket purchases and music downloads, took advantage of this billing method, obviating the need for credit cards. Given the long commute times in Tokyo, this encouraged commuters to surf the Internet via their *keitai* screens, updating their websites, engaging in chat, looking up news and sports, TV and show schedules, downloading music and ring tones, and sending recommendations to friends via email. The *keitai* also saw an innovation in input method for the Japanese language, using a limited numerical keypad where each number on the pad is associated with a sequence of phonetic *kana* syllables, such as – ka, ki, ku, ke, ko – with the desired syllable being selected according to the number of button presses. Once the phonetic spelling of the desired term is visible on screen, conversion to the required *kanji* (Chinese character) can be achieved by the use of an arrow button, allowing the entire process to be navigated just by using one thumb – giving rise to the moniker *yubi-zoku* or 'thumb tribe' to describe young people who soon became proficient in this input style.

Indeed, since 2000, the uptake among young people of mobile connection to the Internet has been evident across East Asia and has resulted in a 'juvenation' of the technology, that is, a movement away from a business model of mobile telecommunications towards a model that focuses on young people's recreational patterns of use – SMS, gaming, ring tones, downloads, and so on. This movement has very much been dominated by young people's desire for connection with each other, to stay abreast of the latest trends, and to communicate about topics important to them. While not unique to Japan (since Japanese patterns of usage are similar in some respects to South Korea), it is clear that pre-existing Japanese cultural norms and practices exerted a strong influence on the development of *keitai* technology and its deployments. In Japan (and to an extent in other East Asian societies), mobile telephony, unlike the Internet, was not 'conceived by an elite and noncommercial technological priesthood and disseminated to the masses' but emerged out of young Japanese consumers' love of 'gadget fetishism and technofashion' (Matsuda, 2005: 9).

The astonishing uptake of the mobile Internet in Japan, from only one million *i-mode* subscribers in 1999 to over 40 million in 2003 (Okazaki, 2006: 127), is also related to a host of other specific factors, not least the problematic blurring of public and private space occasioned by the advent of the mobile phone. In Japan, spoken communication via mobiles that takes place 'in public' on buses and trains is frowned upon and needs to be handled with particular decorum. As Matsuda (2005: 24) points out, 'The physical noise is not the problem. Rather, *keitai* conversations disrupt the order of urban space' by confusing the boundaries of private and public. Okabe and Ito (2005) point out how from 1996, when young people became the main demographic to take up the mobile phone, there developed a voluble media discourse about their use in public settings. One way around this impasse is of course the use of SMS and email, which can be used with limited disturbance to those around, once again emphasizing the very social nature of the technology – enabling private conversations to take place in public.

Although, as we have seen above, Internet uptake in Japan was always already social from the initial roll-out of 'personal computer communications' in the late 1980s, it was the widespread adoption of the mobile Internet at the turn of the century that saw the population of Japanese Internet users surge. Japan's forward-looking *i-mode* system and specially designed handsets anticipated the smart phone by several years, and normalized the use of keyboard and screen for the navigation and communication of both commodities and personal information. Japan's *keitai* did not evolve out of an established culture of PC use, but instead owed their success to the innovative ways in which young people were already using technologies such as pagers to send messages and keep in contact – pointing to a very different evolution of social media from that which is familiar to us from the USA or Europe.

CHINA

The case of China is pertinent to our discussion of alternative histories of social media, not only because it has the largest number of social media users in the world, but also because of its self-sustained social media ecosystem enabled by an enormous 'intranet'. This gigantic intranet, which is protected by the notorious 'Great Firewall', screens out most of the world's popular social media applications (such as Facebook, Twitter, Instagram, and YouTube), as well as many other Western websites that are deemed harmful to China and the Chinese people. Scholarship on Internet censorship in China is abundant, with some researchers focusing on the technologies and features of the censorship and governance regime, some on the dichotomy between control and resistance, and some on its international impact and implication. There has been an increased public-private alliance in constructing a 'healthy' and 'civilized' Internet, that is, a sanitized and pacified online environment in China (e.g., Lagerkvist, 2011). It is beyond the scope of this chapter for an informed discussion of the dynamics and nuances of Chinese Internet control and the censorship regime. Suffice to say that such Internet

censorship turns out to be a blessing for domestic Internet Service Providers, whose copycat versions of global Social Networking Systems (SNS) are both improved and localized products that are now able to compete with their Western counterparts. The Chinese social media market is currently dominated by five applications: QQ (granddaddy of Chinese social media), Qzone (father of Chinese social media), WeChat (Chinese replacement of WhatsApp), Weibo (Chinese replacement of Twitter), and Renren (Chinese replacement of Facebook). (The brief descriptions of the major social media platforms in brackets indicate only their major functions. They are all cross-platform social media and social commerce applications akin to a hybrid of Twitter, Facebook, WhatsApp, eBay, and YouTube.) There are many other SNSs competing for niche markets.

Of these, QQ is the earliest, as it started in 1999. All the other social media applications are the products of China's social media boom beginning in 2005. However, the history of social media in China did not start in 1999, if we consider 'social' as being connected virtually through textual and, later, audio-visual interfaces. Any discussion of early social media history in China has to examine pre-1999 'social' media, such as email and BBS, and look into the role of technology and human agency in social innovation.

The early history of social media in China can be roughly divided into three eras: predawn (1986–1993), early dawn (1994–1996), and sunrise (1997–1999). The early Chinese social media developed out of a nebulous environment in which the Party-state, the fledgling IT industry, and computer and information technology enthusiasts (both professional and amateurs) were exploring the power and mystery of computer and Internet-mediated communication. It arose out of a 'lawless' state, as the first campaign to 'civilize' Chinese cyberspace did not start until 2000. This was the 'Network Civilization Project', jointly launched in

Beijing by eight key ministries and government agencies, including the Ministry of Culture, State Administration of Radio, Film, and Television, Chinese Telecom, Chinese Mobile, and All Chinese Universities Association, with the aim to educate Chinese people on 'civil surfing, civil web building, and civil networks' (CNNIC, 2009c). Since then the Chinese Internet control and censorship regime has become more stringent and sophisticated.

The predawn (1986–1993) and early dawn (1994–1996) eras of the Chinese Internet age had a very high barrier to entry for the ordinary Chinese. Bandwidth, cost, lack of knowledge of the Web, and lack of skills in Chinese script input systems were four major bottlenecks that limited the use of the Internet to a small group of people. For most people, cost and the lack of an efficient Chinese script input system were the biggest roadblocks.

In the early days, computer-mediated communication was realized through telephone dial-ups, at an exuberant cost. Until the late 1990s, telephone line leasing from China Telecom was between 5,000 and 10,000 yuan for initial installation fees only, with a long and complicated application process. Once the line was connected, one had to bear the expensive ongoing cost, as the telephone dial-up connection to other modems and later the Internet was charged on a time-metered system. Long distance charges when dialling up out of the local calling area was charged at 1 yuan or more per minute. An average Chinese person, whose annual income was only around 5,500 yuan in mid-1990s, could not afford this. Home phone ownership was low. Mobile phone ownership was even lower. Indeed, until 1999, the mobile phone was a luxury item used only by high-income earners, successful businessmen and high-ranking government officials.

It was not only slow and expensive to use dial-up connections to access other modems and the Internet, but also technically difficult to type Chinese characters and create Chinese content in computer-mediated communication applications. As in the case of Japan, the necessity of developing software and transmission protocols for the input and display of a complex character-based script prompted researchers and private entrepreneurs to develop Chinese character input systems using the standard QWERTY keyboard, with some using pinyin (the romanization of Chinese characters), some using strokes, or a combination of pinyin and strokes. Even though the Five Strokes Input System was developed in 1983, it was difficult to learn and master without proper training. Computer literacy remained low in China for the next decade. The invention of the Intelligent ABC system in 1993 made it possible for everyone with a knowledge of standard Chinese to type Chinese text phonetically, press the space key to display various options in Chinese characters of the same sound, and choose the right character by pressing the number preceding it. Although this system was still slow, it was now possible for amateurs to read and write Chinese scripts on screen. (There are now about a dozen simplified Chinese character input systems in pinyin, strokes, and their combination respectively. The most popular ones, such as the Sogou pinyin, known as 'Intelligent Pinyin' systems, allow people without any training to type quickly by using pinyin initials of all characters in a sentence. The earliest 'Intelligent Pinyin' system was invented in 2000.) The lack of facilities, high cost of accessing the web, and lack of skills in Chinese script input systems meant that computer-mediated communication was limited to a very small number of leading scientists in research institutions in Beijing and Shanghai via dedicated satellite connections. The Chinese government bore the expense. The early use of computer-mediated communication was for research and academic exchange, via emails and file transfers.

Email was the earliest 'social media' in the pre-Internet era in China. It remained 'the most-used and most important Internet service' in China until the early 2000s (Shi, 2015: 127).

The first email from China was sent by Wu Weimin from the High Energy Physics Institute of Chinese Academy of Sciences to a computer in Geneva in 1986 as an experiment (CNNIC, 2009a). But the first officially recognized email from China was sent by two scientists from the Beijing-based Institute of Computer Application to Karlsruhe University in Germany in 1987, with only one line 'Across the Great Wall we can reach every corner in the world' (CNNIC, 2009a). This event is often heralded as China's first step towards its Internet age. With the establishment of computer exchange networks in major Chinese cities and of intra-campus and inter-campus research networks in China's leading universities and academic research institutes, email connections were established in 1992 in Beijing to enable academic exchange with overseas universities and institutions. This access was later extended to universities in eight major cities, such as Shanghai, Guangzhou and Xi'an (CNNIC, 2009a).

Even though email is by no means 'social media' by today's standard, due to its lack of interactivity and dialogic transmission system, it offered the first taste of 'being social' among Chinese scientists, academics, university students, and telecom-geeks (enthusiasts obsessed with trying out new telecommunication technologies as a hobby). Emailing gave early users of radio, computer and later Internet networks the buzz of connecting with people from afar through texts. It offered the early users a taste of the Internet as 'an attractive medium for social exchanges' (Shi, 2015: 131), particularly after China was fully connected to the World Wide Web in 1994.

This took place on 20 April 1994 when the National Computing and Networking Facility of China (NCFC) project, led by HU Qiheng, set up the first direct TCP/IP (Transmission Control Protocol/Internet Protocol) connection via a 64K international dedicated line to the Internet through Sprint Co. Ltd of the United States, after years of negotiation with the US government and lobbying the international scientific community (CNNIC, 2009b). After that, major networks, including China Education and Research Network (CERnet), China Science and Technology Network (CSTnet), China Golden Bridge Network (CGBnet), and China Public Computer Internet (ChinaNet), were built and began providing services to nationwide research institutions and university campuses, government agencies (including banks and customs), and the general public in 1996. Within a year, Chinese Internet users grew from several thousand to 0.2 million (Shanghai Technology, n.d.).

The full connection to the Internet remained an ivory tower celebration until 1996 when the Internet was open to the public and began to be marked by commercial operations via the newly built ChinaNet. Anybody could connect to the Internet and have an email account upon subscribing to China Telecom's dial-up services via the telephone line. Email took off as the most talked-about topic and service in China, reported as the most-used application by more than 90% of Chinese Internet users (CNNIC, 1999). Few people cared about the (high) cost and (slow) speed in dialing up and sending/receiving emails. Chinese people did not have any significant cultural reservation about online socializing with strangers through computer-mediated communication. They embraced social media technologies imported from the West with great enthusiasm, and created a Chinese 'online carnival' in the 2000s (Herold & Marolt, 2011).

The emailing craze and the commercial operation of the Internet in China offered Internet Service Providers (ISPs, both private and public) the opportunity to kick off a booming Internet business. The pioneer of private ISPs is Ying Haiwei, established in 1997 in Beijing. It was modelled after AOL to offer a range of paid services and connections for commercial and individual users, including email and BBS. Its paid email service was very soon challenged by a free email service called 163.com, developed by another private ISP Netease at the end of 1997. Free email service eventually became the mainstream business model and pushed paid email service out of the market in the early 2000s (Shi, 2015: 129–130).

Another early form of 'social media' and precursor to the World Wide Web and others aspects of the Internet are bulletin board systems (BBSs), first computer-based using the Unix system and Mosaic web browser and then, since 1994, TCP/IP based. The computer-based BBSs were amateur in nature, as they were mostly set up as a hobby by young techno-enthusiasts such as the HAM (amateur radio) community and CFido (Chinese Fido Net) participants, who experimented with radio and computer software (such as Shareware or Freeware) for fun and networking, without any commercial interest or political agenda (Lin, 2009: 4). The TCP/IP-based BBSs are Internet enabled, which allows same single connection to multiple services by multiple telephone lines and modems for messaging and file transfer. For many early users, BBSs were the Internet.

Amateur 'social media' started in 1991, with the first CFido BBS 'Great Wall' established by a Taiwanese living in Beijing. CFido BBSs were the social media for young techno-enthusiasts between 1993 and 1998. As the earliest form of BBS, CFido was not Internet-based. CFido BBSs were established to connect with other computers via telephone lines and analog dial-up modems. They were mostly run as a hobby by radio and computer enthusiasts to offer free point-to-point communication to other enthusiasts. The CFido BBS operators had to bear the cost of telephone line leasing, the ongoing cost, as well as that of the computer (around 15,000 yuan in the mid-1990s). The setup expense alone was beyond an average Chinese's annual income. The long-distance dial-up fee was difficult to bear by most young techno-enthusiasts. Hence the early BBSs were often a local phenomenon, such as Beijing's 'Great Wall', Shantou's 'Hand in Hand', Guangzhou's 'New Moon',

and Shenzhen's 'PonySoft' (Lin, 2009: 4–5). They offered similar-minded techno-enthusiasts a forum to communicate and exchange information about computing technologies and software. These people often met offline for social gatherings, since they usually lived in the same area. BBS operators were often treated as 'celebrities' by their peers.

As the earliest form of 'social media', CFido could only allow a small number of people (sometimes just two or three) online at the same time. The offline meetings were more 'social' than online co-presence. But it nurtured many of the leading figures in the Chinese ICT industry and Internet business, such as DING Lei (founder of Netease), MA Huateng (aka Pony Ma, founder of Tencent Inc.), QIU Bojun (founder of Kingsoft), LEI Jun (CEO of Kingsoft and founder of Xiaomi Inc.), and CHEN Danian (co-founder of Shanda Networking). Their early experience with computer networks, their entrepreneurism enabled by China's open and reform policies from 1979 onwards, and particularly after 1993, and their indigenous localization of Western ICT technologies and services all set the foundation and direction of Chinese social media development.

China's first TCP/IP-based BBS – the Dawn BBS – was opened upon China's full functional connection with the World Wide Web in April 1994, hosted by the National Research Centre for Intelligent Computing Systems (CNNIC, 2009b). It was the first public and Internet-based BBS in China, and offered services such as news updates, online forums and chat rooms. Soon afterwards, various university campus-based BBSs and public BBSs were set up. The most 'luxurious' BBS was Shuimu Tsinghua, set up by students at the prestigious Tsinghua University in 1995, serving mainly users of the CERnet, with more than 100 discussion groups, email services, online chatting services, and games (Zhao, 1996: 65). It remained the most popular campus-based but open-to-the-public BBS until 2005, when Tsinghua University authorities decided to stop public access and subscription to the BBS by enforcing a real-name and student-ID registration system and by taking control of the BBS servers under the instruction of the Ministry of Education. Under the increasingly stringent Internet censorship regime, other CERnet-based BBSs followed a similar path towards their demise in the eyes of the public. These BBSs, however, remain an important entertainment, information, and socialization hub for Chinese universities' students.

Other renowned public BBS in the 1990s include: 'SRS BBS', established in 1996 by the Stone company, its popularity peaking in 1997 when a user famously posted to its 'Sports Salon' section lamenting the failure and fate of the Chinese men's soccer team (Lin, 2009: 71–74); 'MOP', starting in 1997 as a BBS for console gamers and later becoming the top entertainment-oriented BBS in China; 'Xici', kicking off in 1998 as the first open-platform online forum in China; 'Tianya Forum', established in 1999 as a BBS for stock investors but quickly evolving into a popular BBS with a sociocultural focus; and 'Strong Nation Forum', a leftist political and social affairs BBS set up by the Party's flagship newspaper *People's Daily* in 1999 in response to the NATO bombing of the Chinese embassy in Belgrade (Damm, 2015: 187; Peng, 2005: 70, 201). During this period, all major web portals and search engines set up BBSs as part their services. These BBS pioneers have continued to grow and re-invent themselves in the 2000s in competition with QQ and many other social media services. Even QQ gradually transformed itself from simply an instant messaging tool to one of the largest instant message-based BBSs and SNS by the mid-2000s.

These interactive and user-generated online forums were marked by 'impurity' from the very beginning, compared to CFido. As discussed earlier, the earliest BBSs were expensive and technologically tricky to set up, marked with an amateur 'sharing' spirit, and underpinned by a belief in freedom of information for fun and networking. The BBSs in operation after 1996, however, were set up by either government agencies or private entrepreneurs, all with clear political agendas and commercial interests. Emailing services followed the same pattern, as they moved from ivory towers to the market after 1996. The eventual triumph of the free email business model over paid email services in the late 1990s signalled another aspect of the 'impurity' of Chinese social media: 'free' does not equate with 'freedom', but user profiles and statistics, which can be traded for both commercial and political purposes. Of course, this is not unique to China but rather a prevailing concern worldwide about big data, surveillance, and privacy (see, for example, van Dijck, 2014).

QQ occupies a special place in China's techno-cultural sphere. It marks the start of 'social media for the people', due to its low threshold in technological know-how, simple Chinese character encoding system, and low cost. It is also the first truly 'social' networking service in China. QQ also marked a departure from other early forms of 'social media' in China with a 'youth and entertainment focus' (Koch et al., 2009: 280), and remained for a few years, at least until 2005, the first major 'entertainment highway' for young people.

Originally called OICQ (until 2001), QQ was developed by Shenzhen-based Tencent, one of China's biggest Internet companies, in 1999. It was modelled on the then popular ICQ, but also allowed users to interconnect with pagers and mobile phones, personalize their QQ chat rooms, identify friends who were offline, and, most of all, to chat in Chinese using a Chinese encoding software that allowed easy and quick input of Chinese characters (Lin, 2009: 95–96). Although QQ was launched in 1999, QQ games and QQ mobile were not launched until 2003. Tencent launched the most popular SNS in China, Qzone, in 2005, and mobile Qzone in 2007. Upon its public launch in 1999, QQ quickly became popular among young Chinese

Internet users who enjoyed using instant messaging to conveniently and cheaply communicate with friends, despite a mixed response to the new social media application from the society (Koch et al., 2009). It soon became, and has continued to be, a must-have application in all Internet cafés in China, on home and office computers, and on young people's mobile phones. For many people, QQ was the first and only portal of the Internet, an extension of their social networks, a practical and emotional tool and space to live out both sociality and intimacy, both harsh and dream worlds, and the only stable identifier in a flux and floating life (Wallis, 2013: 100–116). QQ was particularly favoured by the so-called 'information have-less' – a term coined by Jack Qiu to refer to 'low-end ICT users, service providers and laborers who are manufacturing these electronics' (2009: 3–4), including internal migrants, laid-off workers, retirees, students, unemployed and under-employed youth.

1999 is a landmark in the history of Chinese social media. It is marked not only by the birth of QQ, but also ChinaRen. Like QQ, ChinaRen was also a copycat version of a Western SNS. It was modelled on Friendster, but incorporated elements of AOL into its services. It was more than a social networking site, as it provided a comprehensive range of localized content and services that targeted college students, such as social networking, online forums, music, games, social life, and news. It was a sensation among young Internet users around 2000, even though its popularity quickly declined after it was bought by Sohu.com in September 2000 and later replaced by more specialized SNS, such as Douban (2005–), Xiaonei (2005–2009; renamed 'Renren' since 2009), Qzone (2005–), Sina Weibo (2009–), and WeChat (2011–). QQ has continued to improve its service and enjoyed its popularity among Chinese-speaking communities, while ChinaRen is rarely talked about nowadays.

QQ was the product of Pony Ma and his team, who were early Chinese ICT enthusiasts and amateur hosts of pre-Internet BBSs, while ChinaRen was established by America-trained techno-entrepreneurs Chen Yizhou (Joseph Chen) and his team. Both were launched at a time when revamping the pricing and Chinese language encoding systems were urgently needed to popularize the Internet in China. Both SNSs played an important role in educating the Chinese about 'e-life', which was a buzzword used by entrepreneurs in the IT industry to describe Internet-mediated communication, entertainment, and commercial activities.

Social media like QQ, ChinaRen, and their precursors (email and BBS), were all products of Chinese copycat entrepreneurship with important elements of indigenous innovation when Western products and services were introduced and localized for the Chinese market. The PC was the main interface to access social media and the Internet. The providers of these services in the early eras of Chinese Internet and social media aimed to offer social exchange and entertainment with no strings attached. This industry was soon marked by 'impurity' when political and commercial interests became the driving force behind the boom of social media applications, particularly on mobile devices since 2005. As China's Internet censorship regime developed and grew more sophisticated, social networking for fun and entertainment has become a political decision as well as commercial pursuit, for service providers and users alike.

The early history of social media in China (pre-2000) demonstrates the role of grassroots entrepreneurship in technological and social innovation. It debunks the normative interpretation of Chinese media and communication, which credits the Chinese state as promoter, controller, and censor of the Internet, and argues for attention to local dynamics, individual agency, and indigenous innovation in domesticating Western technologies and concepts. Key to the development of the Internet and social media are

ICT intermediaries, particularly those who are keen observers of and innovators in global technological and business fields. The entrepreneurship of these intermediaries is grounded in their local and national cultural, political, and socioeconomic contexts and market conditions. It is this localized pragmatism and entrepreneurship that have driven social media development along distinctive paths in China and Japan.

CONCLUSION

In this chapter, we have provided brief but richly-textured and critical histories of social media in two countries which have loomed largely in earlier phases (Japan) and later phases (China) of development. These concrete case studies of the development of social media reveal how cultural, social, media, economic, political, and market histories are crucial to understanding particular social media histories.

What clearly emerges is the way that particular infrastructural politics and policies are bound up with information technology, computers, networking, and media varies considerably – yet they all exert an enduring influence on contemporary developments. Such dynamics thread through the particular Internet technologies, cultures, and meanings that predominate in different countries that prefigure social media. The influence of messaging (the iconic QQ technology) in China provided an early impetus for Internet entertainment that has become central to contemporary social media. Yet QQ is also an obvious predecessor to the rise of messaging-inflected platforms such as Weibo and WeChat.

Mobile phones and mobile phone culture are another important area for understanding social media histories, especially across many non-Western countries where social media has emerged at roughly the same time as mobile media. Japan is often celebrated

both internationally and in East Asia as a model for early mobile use. Yet we see that in China the PC remained the only interface for the Internet until 2000, when China Mobile started its Wireless Application Protocol (WAP) business, providing access via the mobile phone. QQ mobile, launched in 2003, played an important role in popularizing WAP phones such as the Nokia 7110. However, the PC was still the main interface for people to access the Internet until 2009. By contrast, mobile telephony was a symbol of wealth and power, a luxury item for high-income earners, until 1999 when such gadgets became more affordable. The emergence of *shanzhai* (copycatting) mobile phones, beginning in 2003, made it easier to own a look-a-like model of the latest foreign brand phone (an economic factor now behind the young Chinese craze for gadget fetishism). Today, China leads the world as the largest smart phone and mobile Internet market, with its own highly competitive applications and brands.

Another important area often overlooked in Internet and digital histories is the role of language and script – and this very much applies to social media histories. Given the complex input and display issues associated with non-Roman scripts such as Chinese and Japanese, the introduction of computer-mediated communication in East Asia was less straightforward than in North America and Europe (Goggin & McLelland, 2017b). Computer users in East Asian societies had first to become familiar with Roman script, the QWERTY keyboard, and the non-intuitive 'conversion' input style required for local language display before CMC could be embraced by a broad majority.

In closing, Japan has long featured in the annals of digital technology research and discourse, its place only comparatively recently taken over by China, a country now attracting intense attention as the market with the greatest number of social media users internationally. There are many other countries, especially Asian countries, that have not been so prominent, yet whose social media histories offer instructive and rich insights. As we have seen in both cases, there remains a kind of weird fascination, even 'techno-orientalism' (Morley & Robins, 1992; Roh, Huang, & Niu, 2015), via a fantasy image of social media that tells us more about how we imagine global social media in general, especially in Western contexts, than it actually helps us to understand social media in particular, or non-Western Asian countries, let alone the realities and materialities of contemporary social media internationally.

REFERENCES

Abate, T. (1996). The Midnight hour: Japan ventures onto the Net in the dark of night. *Scientific American*, January 1, p. 37. Retrieved from: www.scientificamerican.com/article/the-midnight-hour/

Abbate, J. (1999). *Inventing the Internet*. Cambridge, MA: MIT Press.

Baym, N. K. (2015). Social media and the struggle for society. *Social Media + Society*, *1*(1), doi:10.1177/2056305115580477.

Braman, S. (2011). The framing years: Policy fundamentals in the Internet design process, 1969–1979. *The Information Society*, *27*(5), 295–310.

Braman, S. (2012). Internationalization of the Internet by design: The first decade. *Global Media and Communication*, *8*(1), 27–45.

Brügger, N. (2013). Web historiography and Internet studies: Challenges and perspectives. *New Media & Society*, *15*, 752–764.

CNNIC. (1999). Chinese Internet development statistic report, January. [Zhongguo hulian wangluo fazhan zhuangkuang tongji baogao, 1999/1]. Retrieved from: www.cnnic.net.cn/hlwfzyj/hlwxzbg/200905/P020120709345373005822.pdf

CNNIC. (2009a). Internet events 1986–1993 [1986 nia–1993nian hulianwang dashi ji]. Retrieved from: www.cnnic.org.cn/hlwfzyj/hlwdsj/201206/t20120612_27414.htm

CNNIC. (2009b). Internet events 1994–1996 [1994 nia–1996 nian hulianwang dashi ji].

Retrieved from: www.cnnic.org.cn/hlwfzyj/hlwdsj/201206/t20120612_27415.htm

CNNIC. (2009c). Internet events 2000–2001 [2000nian–2001nian hulianwang dashi ji]. Retrieved from: www.cnnic.net.cn/hlwfzyj/hlwdsj/201206/t20120612_27417.htm.

Coates, K. (2000). Back in the race: Japan and the Internet. In P. Bowles & L. T. Woods (Eds.), *Japan after the economic miracle: In search of new directions* (pp. 71–84). Dordrecht: Kluwer.

Contreras, J. (2014). Divergent patterns of engagement in Internet standardization: Japan, Korea and China. *Telecommunications Policy*, *38*, 914–932.

Damm, J. (2015). Communities online. In A. Esarey & R. Kluver (Eds.), *The Internet in China: Cultural, political, and social dimensions (1980s–2000s)* (pp. 184–196). Great Barrington: MA, Berkshire Publishing.

Flichy, P. (2007). *The Internet imaginaire*. Cambridge, MA: MIT Press.

Fouser, R. (2001). 'Culture', computer literacy and the media in creating public attitudes to CMC in Japan and Korea. In C. Ess (Ed.), *Culture, technology, communication: Towards an intercultural global village* (pp. 261–278). Albany, NY: SUNY Press.

Goggin, G., & McLelland, M. (Eds.). (2009). *Internationalizing Internet studies: Beyond anglophone paradigms*. New York: Routledge.

Goggin, G., & McLelland, M. (2017a). Introduction: Global coordinates of Internet histories. In G. Goggin & M. McLelland (Eds.), *Routledge companion to global Internet histories*. New York: Routledge.

Goggin, G., & McLelland, M. (Eds.). (2017b). *Routledge companion to global Internet histories*. New York: Routledge.

Gottlieb, N. (2000). *Word processing technology in Japan: Kanji and the keyboard*. Richmond: Curzon.

Herold, D. K., & Marolt, P. (Eds.). (2011). *Online society in China: Creating, celebrating, and instrumentalising the online carnival*. London and New York: Routledge.

Internet World Stats. (2016a). Internet world users by language (top 10 languages). Retrieved from: www.internetworldstats.com/stats7.htm

Internet World Stats. (2016b). Top 20 countries with the highest number of Internet users.

Retrieved from: www.internetworldstats.com/top20.htm

ITU (International Telecommunications Union). (2016). Percentage of individuals using the Internet. Retrieved from: www.itu.int/en/ITU-D/Statistics/Pages/stat/default.aspx

Izumi, Aizu. (1996). Emergence of Netizens in Japan and its cultural implications for the Net society. Retrieved from: www.ais.org/~jrh/acn/text/acn12-2.articles/acn12-2.a04.txt

Johnstone, B. (1994). Wiring Japan: A bitter cultural clash has reduced Japan to a third-rate power in networking. *Wired*, January 2. Retrieved from: http://archive.wired.com/wired/archive/2.02/wiring.japan_pr.html

Kawakami, Yoshiro. (1993). *Denshi Nettowākingu no Shakai Shinri: Konpyūta Komyunikēshon e no Pasupōto [The social psychology of electronic networking: A passport for computer communication]*. Tokyo: Seishin Shobō.

Koch, P. T., Koch, B. J., Huang, K., & Chen, W. (2009). Beauty is in the eye of the QQ user: Instant messaging in China. In G. Goggin & M. McLelland (Eds.), *Internationalizing Internet studies: Beyond anglophone paradigms* (pp. 265–284). London and New York: Routledge.

Kumon, Shumpei. (1988). *Nettowāku Shakai [The network society]*. Tokyo: Chūōkōronsha.

Lagerkvist, J. (2011). New media entrepreneurs in China: Allies of the party-state or civil society. *Columbia Journal of International Affairs*, 65(1), 169–182.

Lee, K.-S. (2016). On the historiography of the Korean Internet: Issues raised by the historical dialectic of structure and agency. *The Information Society*, 32(3), 217–222.

Lin, J. (2009) *Bubbling 15 years: Chinese Internet 1995–2009* [Feiteng 15 nian: Zhongguo hulianwang 1995–2009]. Beijing: China CITIC Press.

Mansell, R. (2012). *Imagining the Internet: Communication, innovation and governance*. Oxford: Oxford University Press.

Matsuda, M. (2005). Discourses of Keitai in Japan in Mizuko Ito, Daisuke Okabe and Misa Matsuda (eds) *Personal, Portable, Pedestrian: Mobile Phones in Japanese Life* (pp. 19–39) Cambridge: MIT Press.

Morley, D., & Robins, K. (1992). Techno-orientalism: Foreigners, phobias, and futures. *New Formations*, 16, 136–157.

Nishigaki T. (1998). Multilingualism on the Net. Paper presented at UNESCO INFOethics 1998. Downloaded from: www.unesco.org/webworld/infoethics_2/eng/papers/paper_5.htm

Okabe, D., & Ito, M. (2005). Keitai in public transportation. In M. Ito, D. Okabe, & M. Matsuda (Eds.), *Personal, portable, pedestrian: Mobile phones in Japanese life* (pp. 205–218). Cambridge, MA: MIT Press.

Okada, T. (2005). Youth culture and the shaping of Japanese mobile media: Personalization and the *keitai* as multimedia. In M. Ito, D. Okabe, & M. Matsuda (Eds.), *Personal, portable, pedestrian: Mobile phones in Japanese life* (pp. 19–40). Cambridge, MA: MIT Press.

Okazaki, Shintaro. (2006). What do we know about mobile Internet adopters? A cluster analysis. *Information & Management*, 43(2), 127–141.

Ono, T. (1994). *Denshi no Kuni 'COARA' Pasokon Tsūshin ga Tsukuru Gurōbaru na Chihō [The 'COARA' Electric Nation: How computer communication makes the regional global]*. Tokyo: AI Shuppan.

Pargman, D., & Palme, J. (2009). ASCII Imperialism. In M. Lampland & S. L. Star (Eds.), *Standards and their stories: How quantifying, classifying and formalizing practices shape everyday life* (pp. 177–199). Ithaca, NY: Cornell University Press.

Peng, L. (2005). *The first ten years of Chinese online media [Zhongguo wangluo meiti de diyige shinian]*. Beijing: Tsinghua University Press.

Qiu, J. (2009). *Working-class network society: Communication technology and the information have-less in urban China*. Cambridge, MA: MIT Press.

Rheingold, H. (1993). *The virtual community: Homesteading on the electronic frontier*. New York: Harper Collins.

Roh, D. S., Huang, B., & Niu, G. A. (Eds.). (2015). *Techno-orientalism: Imagining Asia in speculative fiction, history, and media*. New Brunswick, NJ: Rutgers University Press.

Seo, D. B. (2013). *Evolution and standardization of mobile communications technology*. Hershey, PA: Information Science Reference.

Shanghai Technology. (n.d.). Internet development and its current state in China [Internet zai woguo de fazhan jingcheng ji xianzhuang]. Retrieved from: www.stcsm.gov.cn/jsp/course/

browser/03/content.jsp?past_cid=257& past_id=62&past_num=2

Shi, S. (2015). Email. In A. Esarey & R. Kluver (Eds.), *The Internet in China: Cultural, political, and social dimensions (1980s–2000s)* (pp. 126–133). Great Barrington, MA: Berkshire Publishing.

Streeter, T. (2011). *The net effect: Romanticism, capitalism, and the Internet*. New York and London: New York University Press.

Sugimoto, T., & Levin, J. (2000). Multiple literacies and multimedia: A comparison of Japanese and American Uses of the Internet. In G. Hawisher & C. Selfe (Eds.), *Global literacies and the world-wide web* (pp. 133–153). London and New York: Routledge.

Tamura, T. (2017). Talking about ourselves on the Japanese digital network. In G. Goggin & M. McLelland (Eds.), *Routledge companion to global Internet histories* (pp. 313–330). New York: Routledge.

Turner, F. (2006). *From counterculture to cyberculture: Stewart Brand, the Whole Earth Network, and the rise of digital utopianism*. Chicago, IL: University of Chicago Press.

Van Dijck, J. (2014). Datafication, dataism and dataveillance: Big Data between scientific paradigm and ideology. *Surveillance & Society, 12*(2), 197–208.

Wallis, C. (2013). *Technobility in China: Young migrant women and mobile phones*. New York and London: New York University Press.

Yamane, K. (1996). *Nettowāku Kyōwakoku Sengen: Pasokon Tsūshin no Ima, Korekara [Declaration of a Network Republic: Personal computer communication now and in the future]*. Tokyo: Chikuma Shobō.

Zhao, H. (1996). Online 'bulletin board' [wangshang 'bugao lan']. *Chinese Computer Users [Zhongguo jisuanji yonnghu], 17*, 64–66.

4

From Hypertext to Hype and Back Again: Exploring the Roots of Social Media in Early Web Culture[1]

Michael Stevenson

INTRODUCTION

Social media emerged in the early 2000s with the launch of sites like Facebook, YouTube and Wikipedia. According to computer industry commentator Tim O'Reilly (2005), such platforms were part of a larger paradigm shift called 'Web 2.0.' They signaled a move away from a web of static pages and towards a more dynamic, open and participatory media environment (ibid.; Kelly, 2005). As many scholars have pointed out, and as O'Reilly himself notes, the rise of Web 2.0 was more evolution than radical change. Many of the features and forms we associate with Web 2.0 and social media – personalization, networking features, user-generated content, many-to-many communication, and so on – were pioneered on the web in the 1990s or with earlier forms of networked computing such as Bulletin Board Systems (BBSs; see Chapter 2 in this volume). This raises the question of what was actually new or different about Web 2.0 and social media platforms. How should

we think of the relationship between social media and the early web, and what can we learn from this history?

In this chapter I argue that Web 2.0 and social media must be seen as a particular constellation of previously existing ideas, values, media forms, and technologies. First, as I will show, values like participation and openness are often associated with Web 2.0 but were very much a part of web culture early on. Second, as sophisticated as the technological infrastructures of social media are, they also strongly echo the technical vision that accompanied the web's invention in 1989, and are rooted in other earlier technological developments such as the rise of open-source software. Third, much like their social media counterparts later on, early web companies gained both cultural legitimacy and speculative financial investment from their portrayal as 'exceptional' media that would reshape the media landscape while enhancing individual freedom and bottom-up organization.

In addition to showing us where social media come from, web history reminds us that these media were not inevitable. A widespread belief is that technology develops in a linear fashion, and nowhere is that assumption more pronounced than in popular web discourses. O'Reilly and others argue, for example, that Web 2.0 represents a natural progression driven by the medium's innate qualities. What these narratives about the 'nature' of the web hide is that a range of actors – web users, producers and investors, to name a few – are constantly making decisions about which technologies or media to promote and use, how to use them, which ones to invest in, and so on. Such choices are not simply the product of individuals making rational decisions; rather, they are shaped by culturally specific values, beliefs and practices, political and commercial interests, as well as the material constraints of available technology. So instead of our interaction with the medium being driven by some technological force such as the web's true nature, it is the opposite: these decisions and the cultural, political and economic values they stem from have real impacts on how the web develops through time.

While we must be skeptical of concepts like Web 2.0 and the various past and present 'visions' of the web's purpose or nature, we should also not dismiss them. It is exactly because the web is shaped socially that such popular narratives must be understood critically. They set expectations, galvanize communities of producers and users, create inequalities of attention, steer financial speculation, etc. As I will argue, visions of the web's purpose are very much a part of the cultural, technological and economic history of the web, and a crucial element in the rise of social media and Web 2.0 in the mid-2000s.

This chapter is organized in an overlapping chronology, from the web's inception in 1989 to the hype surrounding Web 2.0 in the mid-2000s, with each section revealing some of the ideological and technological roots of social media. Section 1 details two utopian visions of digital culture – as an 'information universe' and a 'virtual community' – that arose in the late 1980s and early 1990s, and that continue to resonate today. In the second section, I turn to the dot.com bubble and the discursive construction of the web as an 'exceptional' medium seemingly destined to replace existing mass media. At the center of this discourse was *Wired*, the tech culture magazine that laid out the basic framework by which the web and subsequent technologies (not least social media) have been legitimated as disruptive departures from the traditional media landscape. Section 3 spans the mid- to late-1990s, when various groups of publishers, designers and amateur bloggers sought to define particular new media forms and practices as 'native' to the web. Such efforts served to establish norms and conventions, distinguishing and legitimizing certain practices and forms in the eyes of peers, audiences, customers and investors. While much of what was called 'web-native' culture in the late 1990s, such as blogging, is echoed in social media platforms, there are important differences that highlight how perceptions of the web's essential character continue to change. Section 4 discusses the rise of open source software, an important technological precursor to social media, and Slashdot, the innovative tech news and community website that prefigured many of the features we associate with 'participatory' social media platforms. The concluding section focuses on Web 2.0, discussing how this supposed paradigm shift brought together many of the preceding ideas and developments. In short, the chapter argues against a commonly held perception that Web 2.0 and social media represent radical (yet inevitable) departures from old media and the early web. Rather, web history shows us that both the web and how we perceive it continually evolves, and that to understand the medium in its past or present form requires attention to the cultural, economic and technological factors that shape it.

1. EARLY VISIONS OF DIGITAL CULTURE

Before the World Wide Web was a household name or had even been released publicly, ambitious ideas of what could be done with networked media were already in place. In particular, excitement around the web's potential derived from two key ideas, that of an 'information universe' and of a 'virtual community.' On the one hand, Berners-Lee's notion of a highly organized and automated 'information universe' gave direction to the creation of web standards and protocols, and similarities can be seen in a range of later technical projects, including Berners-Lee's own work in connection with the 'semantic web' (Berners-Lee, Hendler, and Lassila, 2001) and, in a commercial context, Facebook's 'open graph.' On the other hand, the once-popular sense that the web was a 'virtual' space separate from the offline world has largely been forgotten, but many of the ideas, practices and values associated with Rheingold's notion of 'virtual community' were revitalized in the 2000s in connection with Web 2.0 platforms and social media.

Berners-Lee's Information Universe

The World Wide Web was 'born' in late 1990, with the first website up and running in December of that year (Berners-Lee, 2000; see Figure 4.1). Invented by Tim Berners-Lee, the web consisted of a few core technologies that made it easy to navigate documents stored on networked computers. First was a standard for locating specific documents within existing domains, or the Uniform Resource Locator (URL). Second was the HyperText Transfer Protocol (HTTP), which is a set of conventions that standardizes how one computer (the client) requests and downloads a document from another computer (the server). This protocol is also what makes it possible for documents to be

World Wide Web

The WorldWideWeb (W3) is a wide-area hypermedia information retrieval initiative aiming to give universal access to a large universe of documents.

Everything there is online about W3 is linked directly or indirectly to this document, including an executive summary of the project, Mailing lists , Policy , November's W3 news , Frequently Asked Questions .

What's out there?
        Pointers to the world's online information, subjects , W3 servers, etc.
Help
        on the browser you are using
Software Products
        A list of W3 project components and their current state. (e.g. Line Mode ,X11 Viola , NeXTStep , Servers , Tools ,Mail
        robot ,Library)
Technical
        Details of protocols, formats, program internals etc
Bibliography
        Paper documentation on W3 and references.
People
        A list of some people involved in the project.
History
        A summary of the history of the project.
How can I help ?
        If you would like to support the web..
Getting code
        Getting the code by anonymous FTP , etc.

Figure 4.1   info.cern.ch, the first WWW page

connected to one another via hyperlinks, and why a website's address always begins with HTTP. Third, Berners-Lee created HTML (HyperText Markup Language) as a way to write web-specific documents that contained hyperlinks. HTML is a markup language, meaning it describes how a document should look by giving specific instructions to the computer retrieving a document. To this day, these relatively simple protocols and standards are still at the root of much of our online activity, not least social media.

In some ways, the web is simply an application that sits on top of the internet, alongside other applications like email or Internet Relay Chat (and largely forgotten ones like Gopher and Usenet). However, it is one that from the beginning was tied to an ambitious vision of transforming how knowledge is produced and managed. Berners-Lee proposed and built the web at the European Organization for Nuclear Research (called CERN), and the technology's stated purpose was to share information resources among scientists at the lab (Berners-Lee, 1989). But in thinking about its potential, Berners-Lee went much further than the physics laboratory. In an introductory technical paper he wrote with Robert Calliau and other colleagues, Berners-Lee described the larger 'dream' driving the project, dubbed 'the information universe':

> Pick up your pen, mouse, or favorite pointing device and press it on a reference in this document – perhaps to the author's name, or organization, or some related work. Suppose you are then directly presented with the background material – other papers, the author's coordinates, the organization's address, and its entire telephone directory. Suppose each of these documents has the same property of being linked to other original documents all over the world. You would have at your fingertips all you need to know about electronic publishing, high-energy physics, or for that matter, Asian culture. (Berners-Lee et al., 1991: 461)

The dream was a universal document system and information resource. It was imagined as a kind of ultimate reference medium, linking together every other informational medium from telephone books and library catalogs to encyclopedias and scientific databases. It was a scientist's dream, and in fact consciously echoed the dreams of previous scientists. The web, the authors suggested, was set to fulfill the vision set out in 1945 by Vannevar Bush, who had suggested a hypertext-like system could enable more collaboration in the scientific community (Bush, 1945). It also resembled Xanadu, a hypertext system devised by Ted Nelson as part of his general advocacy of using computers for individual empowerment (Nelson, 1974). But where previous hypertext projects remained speculative fictions or stalled during development, the web would succeed. Berners-Lee began to publicize the project in 1991, and in 1993 CERN released the source code for the World Wide Web server and browser to the public domain, meaning these could be used and adapted on a royalty-free basis. Beginning with the release of the Mosaic browser (which allowed for in-line multimedia, and thus a richer user experience) in mid-1993, the growth of the web was meteoric.

What Berners-Lee created was not just a clever solution to the problem of sharing documents remotely, but a system that was utopian in its scope and ambition. Even today, a similar dream of an accessible and universal information system guides Berners-Lee's work at the World Wide Web Consortium (the W3C), the body that develops standards and protocols for the web. But this 'dream' of a perfectly organized information universe is not limited to the work of non-profits; it is clearly echoed in the products created by prominent Web 2.0 and social media companies. For example, Google's (n.d.) stated 'mission' is 'to organize the world's information and make it universally accessible and useful,' while Facebook's efforts to create a 'social graph' involves not only a universal mapping of social relationships but also of the connections between people and a range of places, events, interests, and so on.

The technology of the web and the utopian vision surrounding it was clearly grounded in the needs and ideas of scientists, and perhaps this is why Berners-Lee did not immediately see the web's potential in the realm of entertainment media or as the basis for social media. Nonetheless, social media should be understood in part as an extension of this initial work, both in the sense of Berners-Lee's technical inventions and his larger ambitions for the web.

The Virtual Community and the WELL

While Berners-Lee was working at CERN and imagining the web as an 'information universe,' another vision of the future of networked computing was emerging on the other side of the Atlantic Ocean. Distinct from the scientist's dream of a comprehensive knowledge resource and working environment, this was a vision of community, collaboration and creative expression. Similar values would eventually be tied to Web 2.0 and social media. However, in the early- and mid-1990s this technological vision was associated with an influential BBS called the Whole Earth 'Lectronic Link (the WELL).

The WELL largely served users living in the San Francisco Bay Area, including many of the people working in the computer industry and research centers of Silicon Valley. Much like the *Whole Earth Catalog* that inspired it, the WELL brought together a somewhat strange mix of hippies and technology enthusiasts, as well as a dedicated community of fans of psychedelic rock. Like other BBSs at the time, the WELL consisted of various discussion forums (called 'conferences') on topics ranging from technology to parenting. Unlike most of its contemporaries, it gained notoriety and cultural credibility largely through publicity and the presence of a few high-profile users. This group included technology entrepreneurs, journalists and emerging 'gurus' of digital culture such as John Perry Barlow and Mitch Kapor, the founders of the digital rights organization The Electronic Frontier Foundation. Most of all, the WELL's status as a key object in the history of online culture derives from the work of Howard Rheingold, another influential WELL user who wrote about the BBS in his book *The Virtual Community* (2000; originally published in 1993).

Rheingold is a noted journalist and thinker in the Bay Area's technology scene, and someone who epitomizes the Californian 'free thinker' persona with brightly-colored shirts and painted shoes to go along with his mostly optimistic views on technology. Introducing the book, subtitled 'Homesteading on the Electronic Frontier,' Rheingold wrote:

> People in virtual communities use words on screens to exchange pleasantries and argue, engage in intellectual discourse, conduct commerce, exchange knowledge, share emotional support, make plans, brainstorm, gossip, feud, fall in love, find friends and lose them, play games, flirt, create a little high art and a lot of idle talk. People in virtual communities do just about everything people do in real life, but we leave our bodies behind. (2000: xvii)

Rheingold's argument was not only that one could find real community online, but that virtual communities could provide a solution to increasing individualization and atomization of society, a trend famously described by the sociologist Robert Putnam (2001) as 'bowling alone' (i.e., the decline of activities that maintain community such as bowling leagues). On the WELL, he argued, one lived in a gift economy, where one would 'do things for one another out of a spirit of building something between them, rather than a spreadsheet-calculated quid pro quo' (Rheingold, 2000: 49). And while he also saw potential dangers such as increased surveillance, Rheingold hoped the virtual community could 'revitalize democracy' (ibid.: 295) by providing a participatory alternative to the mass media, which he argued was ruined by consumerism and partisanship.

Many years later, social media companies promote similar notions of giving voice to individuals and improving (inter-)cultural discussion and understanding, although with an important additional emphasis on users' immediate social network. For example, Facebook has variously articulated its mission as giving 'people the power to make the world more open and connected' and working to 'bring the world closer together' (Johnson, 2017).

It's important to note that although the WELL often serves as the default example of online culture in the 1980s and early 1990s, there were many other instances of networked computing being used to build and maintain communities. These include the BBSs discussed elsewhere in this volume and by Driscoll (2014), but also non-US examples like the publicly funded Minitel network in France as well as the Amsterdam, Netherlands initiative De Digitale Stad (DDS). Funded partially by the city government, DDS consciously borrowed Rheingold's concept, adapting the idea somewhat to envision using 'digital cities' as a way to enhance local community and to encourage intercultural awareness via virtual 'travel' to other cities and cultures (see Hinssen, 1995). Such initiatives are notable not only for how they foreshadowed social media, but also how they differ from what came later. Not least, Minitel and DDS remind us that, unlike broadcast media, there are no popular publicly-funded social media, even if this once seemed possible.

Rheingold's vision of virtual community was powerful and prescient, but also flawed. In addition to what critics have called a naiveté or 'starry-eyed' utopianism on the part of Rheingold and other early internet commentators (Morozov, 2011: xiii), the idea of the 'virtual' should be approached critically, as should Rheingold's sense that collaboration on the WELL was a gift economy. While it seemed that the flourishing community on the WELL was made possible by the borderless nature of cyberspace, the truth was quite the opposite. As Turner (2006) argues, the WELL was so coveted by its users precisely because of its geography: the computer industry in Silicon Valley was and still is marked by rapid employment turnover, meaning workers must maintain a large number of social ties as they move from one job to another. The WELL, in addition to 'community' in the sense of friendship and discussion, was an invaluable resource for staying in the loop (Turner, 2006; for a related discussion of 'venture labor' during the dot.com bubble, see Neff, 2012). These connections to geography and work life make sense when we look ahead to social media: the distinction between offline and online networks is often hard to draw, and social network sites are an important source of 'weak ties' that act as a 'bridging' form of social capital, for example, helping (former) college students to find 'jobs, internships and other opportunities' (Ellison, Steinfield, and Lampe, 2007: 1164).

Despite its flaws, the concept of virtual community provided an important 'frame' for understanding networked computing right at the moment that the web was coming into view (Turner, 2006: 159), and its utopian undertones continue to resonate today. It was a powerful notion both for former hippies like Rheingold, who hoped to recover a lost sense of community and public discourse online, as well as for corporations, which thought the sponsorship of online 'communities' was a promising form of commercializing the new medium (ibid.: 161). And although the concept's popularity soon declined, the underlying sense of the web as a medium of collaboration and community resurfaced in the early 2000s and played a major role in how social media were perceived and understood. In fact, it was another book by Rheingold that set the tone. In 2002 he wrote *Smart Mobs*, in which he surveyed the changing media landscape – in particular the rise of mobile computing and the use of reputation systems to engender trust in online communities – and argued that the emerging technologies had 'one thing in common: *They enable people to act together in new ways and in situations where collective action was not possible before*' (Rheingold, 2002: xviii, italics in original). With smart mobs, as with virtual communities, unprecedented voluntary cooperation was seen as the revolutionary product of technological change. Although the sense of the web as a virtual space was quickly fading, the spirit of Rheingold's notion of virtual community was once again very much alive.

2. THE POLITICS OF DOT.COM EUPHORIA: WEB EXCEPTIONALISM AND CYBERLIBERTARIANISM

Although Berners-Lee and Rheingold had ambitious visions for the future of networked computing, neither likely could have predicted the massive amounts of hype and financial speculation that soon followed. Soaring stock prices were fueled by a belief that the web was fated to replace existing media. In line with this belief that the web was an 'exceptional' medium (Stevenson, 2014b) set to displace existing media, an important component of 1990s digital culture was the discursive construction of the web as a medium of individual and economic 'freedom' (Chun, 2006). This emphasis on freedom was part of a political outlook that critics called 'cyberlibertarianism,' which combines libertarianism – a political philosophy that prioritizes individual freedoms over collective duties and is generally opposed to centralized state power – with technological utopianism and countercultural values (Barbrook and Cameron, 1996; Borsook, 2000; Winner, 1995; for an overview and a wider perspective on the 'non-politics' of digital culture, see Liu, 2004: 239–282). Understanding the interrelated history of web exceptionalism, dot.com hype and cyberlibertarianism is important for, among other things, understanding how today's social media companies portray themselves and how they operate in the political realm.

For example, Facebook's recent Internet.org initiative raises important questions about the belief in the emancipatory power of technology, ongoing attempts to 'lock in' large populations to a single platform, as well as how the libertarian politics of Silicon Valley companies become implicated in social and political domains such as international development (see, for example, Morozov, 2013).

The dot.com bubble was ushered in on August 9, 1995, when the web software company Netscape Communications held its Initial Public Offering (IPO) and doubled its share price in a single day. The excitement and financial speculation was unprecedented, as there was little evidence that the company's business model – based on the popularity of its Netscape Navigator web browser (previously called 'Mosaic') and potential sales of its 'Enterprise' web server software – would ever work. What it did have was a near monopoly in terms of browser market share that allowed Netscape to present itself as the web's primary 'platform,' but this was at a time when just 3% of Americans had ever logged onto the World Wide Web (Pew Research Center, 1995), and thus does not fully explain the company's rapid financial success. Rather, as Streeter (2010) argues, the excitement around Netscape relied not only on its demonstrated dominance on the web, but the 'romantic' sense that the web was a 'rebellious' force set to reshape the media landscape.

This perception of the web's inevitable triumph was widespread due to its promotion in national newspapers, magazines and broadcast news, especially after Netscape's IPO. However, it was clearly a perception that was born within and around the computing and multimedia industry. As the web came into view, the most prominent voice expressing this idea was *Wired*, the tech culture magazine created by Louis Rossetto and Jane Metcalfe, which claimed to report on and represent 'the most powerful people on the planet today – the DIGITAL GENERATION' (Rosetto, 1993). *Wired* was an upstart independent publication, and the founders wanted it to be a forum for the tech world's most disruptive thinkers and entrepreneurs, much like *Rolling Stone* had been for the music world before (Wolf, 2003). *Wired* was not the first magazine to focus on the cultural and political aspects of computing technology (there were predecessors such as *Mondo 2000*; see Boulware, 1995). However, its mix of high production values, a distinctive visual and editorial style as well as its connections to a network of influential tech journalists and entrepreneurs – in large part those who populated the WELL – helped the magazine become a key player in the emerging industry (Turner, 2006; Wolf, 2003). The magazine sought to be an arbiter of taste for the new media and offer what it saw as rare insight into the radical changes wrought by new technology. In one of its more famous moves, *Wired* portrayed Marc Andreessen (the young co-founder of Netscape) as a young David taking on Microsoft's Goliath, and helped fan the flames of hype on the way to Netscape's historic IPO a year later (Streeter, 2010). While the magazine arguably no longer has the same cult status it did in the 1990s, it remains an important 'cultural intermediary' in digital culture that can help make or break new startups. More generally, *Wired*'s legacy can be seen in how subsequent actors in new media culture have similarly appealed to the web's 'nature' and a rhetoric of freedom in an effort to legitimize particular new technologies and media forms (Stevenson, 2016). Again, Facebook serves as an important example: in various interviews and other publicity, Mark Zuckerberg has often stated that the company's mission is to promote connectivity, openness and transparency, values that he understands as part of a larger and inevitable cultural shift inherent to the rise of the internet (see, for example, Zuckerberg's interview in *Wired*: Vogelstein, 2009). Such instances demonstrate the continued prevalence of web exceptionalism, and highlight its importance to how new media companies and technologies are promoted and legitimized.

Because of its high visibility, *Wired* was the focal point of some of the first critiques of the technological and political worldview it represented. Most famously, *Wired* and the rest of the 'virtual class' came under attack from the Marxist cultural critics Richard Barbrook and Andy Cameron in a piece called 'The Californian Ideology' (1996). In this classic touchstone of new media criticism, Barbrook and Cameron argue that the 'faith' represented by *Wired* is both contradictory and flawed:

> [T]he Californian Ideology promiscuously combines the free-wheeling spirit of the hippies and the entrepreneurial zeal of the yuppies. This amalgamation of opposites has been achieved through a profound faith in the emancipatory potential of the new information technologies. In the digital utopia, everybody will be both hip and rich. (Barbrook and Cameron, 1996: 1)

Wired, in line with other proponents of cyberlibertarianism (e.g., Dyson et al., 1994), essentially argued that technology and the free market would bring about positive social change. Cyberlibertarian thinkers suggested that utopia was possible in cyberspace, but were remarkably silent on traditional social issues like worker's rights and social justice (Liu, 2004: 264–265). What Barbrook and Cameron were most critical of was the fact that *Wired* and its allies had successfully crafted the perception that the only way forward was to let technology and the market do their work, and that any intervention on the part of government would amount to 'holding back' the digital revolution. The Californian Ideology automatically excluded public initiatives, and the authors put the French Minitel model forward as evidence that such alternatives were possible. In this way, Barbrook and Cameron argued that *Wired*'s digital utopianism simply served as a 'false consciousness' that aided the economic interests of Silicon Valley companies like Netscape.

Today, the most vocal criticism of cyberlibertarianism comes in the form of Evgeny Morozov's polemics against technological 'solutionism,' or the false belief among Silicon Valley types – not least social media companies – that technical fixes can and should be developed for social and political problems. In 1990s web culture, such techno-libertarian problem-solving was on display, for example, in the use of 'ignore' functions to combat verbal abuse in chat rooms and forums, much like block lists and similar features on various social media today. A critique is that such solutionism puts the onus on victims of abuse, and that they do nothing to resolve conflict, that is, they do not form a social solution to a social problem. For Morozov, the problem of solutionism goes well beyond web communities, as more domains of social life become dependent on social media and related technology.

By the mid-1990s, then, important roots of social media were in place. On the one hand, there were two separate, influential visions of the web's significance – the 'information universe' and 'virtual community' – that helped guide the medium's development. On the other hand, there were the twin beliefs in the web's exceptional nature and in its capacity to bring about positive social change, both of which became entangled with the financial speculation of the dot.com bubble. Today, social media companies and initiatives are similarly portrayed in terms of how they form an exception to mass media and an integral part of the unfolding media landscape, and they depend on these perceptions for both cultural legitimacy and financial investment.

3. DEFINING 'WEB-NATIVE' CULTURE

Although an increasing number of tech journalists, entrepreneurs and investors were convinced the web would revolutionize the media industry and that new media companies would challenge their established print and broadcast counterparts, no one was quite sure what the web would look like. While today it seems obvious to say that the web is a 'social'

medium and that media companies should adapt, in the mid-1990s this was not necessarily a given. Then, many existing print and broadcast companies and institutions wondered how to reproduce their products online, while influential tech 'gurus' argued that the only successful strategy would be to take advantage of the medium's affordances for interactivity. But even among those who thought the web required a new approach, there were important disagreements of what exactly that was. As early as 1994, one could begin to see what amounted to competitions or struggles to define 'quality' online, and these activities clearly expressed different ideas about the web's character, especially in relation to mass and mainstream media. What is important is that while each of these approaches to 'web-native' culture reveal similarities with today's social media, they also offer visions of how *else* the web might be approached, designed and used. They thus give insight not only into where social media come from, but also how social media and the web might otherwise look.

The HotWired Debate

One important debate about the web's identity occurred when *Wired*, the magazine that had hyped the web and argued it would revolutionize the media landscape, decided that it would invest heavily in its web presence. Beginning in early 1994, publisher and editor-in-chief Louis Rossetto made the decision to build the web's first commercial site, and the first web-only professional publication (Stevenson, 2014a; Wolf, 2003). To develop a business plan, he called on Jonathan Steuer, a young Stanford graduate student with the necessary technical expertise, and a former investment banker named Andrew Anker. In addition to several editors from *Wired*'s fast-growing network and engineers brought in by Steuer, the new site was to be headed by Howard Rheingold, who brought with him the credibility gained from his publications and his presence on the WELL. In an interview with the *New York Times*, Rossetto proclaimed that the site would point the way to the future: it would 'not be a magazine with buttons' and instead would break new ground in terms of 'context, community and interactivity' (Markoff, 1994).

Although begun with great enthusiasm, the site's development quickly stalled around a series of major disagreements that divided the team into two camps. On the one hand, Rheingold and Steuer wanted to build a site that put readers' voices and digital artwork alongside the online magazine's output, and in some sense orchestrate a 'worldwide jam session' of virtual community and participation (Wolf, 2003: 108). On the other hand, community was important to Rossetto only to the extent that it made the audience feel a bond with the *Wired* brand: for instance, a community feature Rossetto later supported was a *Wired* 'café' where audiences could chat with digital culture celebrities who were covered by the magazine. Such community features, in Rossetto's mind, should never overshadow the professional content being produced. The debates hardly ended there, and questions surrounding the site's interface, business model and editorial direction all became battlefields for the two camps (Wolf, 2003: 93–114). Similar debates about the relative value of editorial versus amateur content would continue to animate web culture, not least when Web 2.0 platforms and social media began to give user-generated content a privileged place in the mid-2000s (e.g., Keen, 2007).

In line with the larger sense that the web was an inherently different medium than existing mass media, Rheingold's and Rossetto's ideas were grounded in their individual perceptions of the web's character and significance (Stevenson, 2014b). For Rheingold, the web was an extension of the communities he had observed on BBSs, and any successful website would reflect the web's open nature. For Rossetto, the web was

an equalizer, giving independent publications like *Wired* the chance to compete with large media corporations, and a space where *Wired*'s superior knowledge of a new breed of active consumers (in other words, the magazine's tech-savvy audience) would allow the magazine to become a dominant player in the emerging media landscape. Where Rheingold saw the web as 'social' in the sense of egalitarian community and individual expression, Rossetto believed the social and participatory affordances of the medium were important only as a means for professional publications to better connect with their audiences and (once the technology had advanced sufficiently) sell targeted advertising. Their competing ideas can be compared to different understandings of social media today: on the one hand, social media are portrayed as productive of bottom-up community and organic social networks (Shirky, 2008), while on the other hand, they can be (and increasingly are) understood as tools that increase the media power of celebrities and other 'traditional' media actors and institutions (Marwick and boyd, 2011).

The HotWired debate was never an even competition, as Rossetto was firmly in charge; Rheingold and Steuer were (respectively) forced out and demoted before the site finally launched in October 1994 (Keegan, 1995). Rossetto's vision was implemented, although some of his decisions (such as forcing readers to register in order to view the site) would backfire and be reversed. The site recorded a few important firsts, such as the first banner advertisement, but was ultimately crushed under the weight of high production costs. Even after the initial debate, HotWired was the site of a number of important discussions and developments in web culture and web design. For example, it was the birthplace of Suck.com, an influential website that published daily essays satirizing and parodying the emerging web culture (Sharkey, 2005). And in 1997, HotWired implemented a social network-like feature in which HotWired 'participants' could create a profile page and list their favorite websites. Although largely remembered for its failed ambitions, HotWired's history reminds us that the 'participatory' logic we ascribe to Web 2.0 and social media has long been a part of how the web has been imagined, and that not all perceptions of the web as 'social' are necessarily the same (Stevenson, 2014a).

Designing a 'Professional' Web in the dot.com Bubble

Alongside the relatively high-profile debate between Rossetto and Rheingold, the issue of the web's social and participatory character was also entangled in the dynamics of a growing industry. Web production companies began to appear as early as 1994 (when, for example, a web production and marketing company called Organic Online was contracted to create advertisements and websites for HotWired's sponsors), and these would serve a range of companies and institutions for years to come. As Megan Ankerson (2010) has argued, the web's dominant aesthetics through the years can be mapped against changing industry dynamics: in addition to the rapid increase (and subsequent decrease) of economic capital during the bubble, the rise of web production companies, their alignments and competition with traditional advertising agencies, as well as changes in bandwidth technology and internet penetration could all be seen to impact web design practices. Perhaps most notably, as competition increased during the 'euphoric' stage of the bubble, producers sought to differentiate themselves by becoming experts in animated Flash websites (ibid.). Flash sites were generally intended to be large-scale, immersive and visual experiences, and demanded heavy budgets and rare skill sets. By promoting Flash sites as more cutting-edge and 'professional' than simple HTML, producers and designers were able to take advantage of their clients' desire to stand out. At the same time, these sites

served to create a clear boundary between producers/creators and users/viewers. It was only after the dot.com crash that usability became a central focus for the industry, setting the stage for the forms of 'permanently beta' web production that characterized Web 2.0 (Neff and Stark, 2003).

Ankerson's case study on Flash reminds us that there is nothing natural about dominant perceptions of web culture or about what counts as quality design practices at any given time. Rather, such perceptions and standards of quality are defined through cultural processes and often shaped according to the economic, ideological and professional interests of those involved. Another important case discussed by Ankerson (2015) is the controversy surrounding two projects designed to capture and publish a single day in the emerging history of the web. The first of these was *A Day in the Life of Cyberspace*, instigated by MIT professors to celebrate their Media Lab's tenth anniversary. The project would showcase life online, with 'bits' added from online citizens from around the globe. Not everyone on the project wanted to publish users' unedited contributions, and professional photographer Rick Smolan left *A Day in the Life* to work on his own project, called *24 Hours in Cyberspace*. In contrast to MIT's participatory platform, Smolan's project imagined a highly professional, global media production, translating the high standards and production values of existing media industries into a polished, interactive product online. Similar to the debate at HotWired, there was a sharp contrast in how participants valued editorial expertise and control (Ankerson, 2015). In an ironic development that demonstrates the complexity of the history of the web and social media, the software developed for Smolan's 'read-only' project was later commercialized and marketed to non-professionals, thus becoming a support for the 'read/write' web as celebrated in the context of Web 2.0 and social media (ibid.). As Ankerson argues, while it is tempting to oppose the early, static and professional Web

1.0 to today's social and participatory Web 2.0, these oppositions do not hold up so well upon closer historical inspection.

The Rise of Blogging: Personal Publishing, Content Management and Web Filtering

In many ways today's social media can be seen to extend blogging, the web genre that rose to prominence in the late 1990s. Distinct from online diaries, which were relatively common on the web as well (see, for example, the online diary history project: http://diaryhistoryproject.org/), weblogs mixed individual expression with linking and other practices related to establishing and maintaining ties within a blogging 'community.' This self-awareness and feeling of belonging formed what bloggers argued was the genre's authenticity, and what they believed was a contrast to the extravagance of dot.com websites and the impersonal voice of mass media (see, for example, Rodzvilla, 2002). Although opinions differ as to who the first blogger was, the label is usually granted to one of three people: Justin Hall, Dave Winer and Jorn Barger. What's more important than 'firsts,' though, is how their individual stories illustrate the genre's key elements and the different ways in which blogging can be thought of in relation to social media.

For Justin Hall, the web was first and foremost a vehicle for self-expression. Having grown up frequenting BBSs and inspired by *Wired*'s talk of digital revolution, Hall started his website links.net from his college dorm room in 1994 (Rosenberg, 2009). On the site, Hall shared links to content on the web (the most popular of which were links to adult content) while also sharing intimate details of his own life. Hall went on to document events from his personal life, from internal conflicts during his employment at HotWired to the ups and downs of his personal relationships. In addition to Hall's youthful enthusiasm and status as one of the web's first

'micro-celebrities' (Senft, 2008), his story is notable as a very early example of oversharing, a story that he himself has recently documented in an excellent video autobiography (see http://overshare.links.net/; for another classic story of blogging and oversharing, see Gould, 2008).

For Dave Winer, a software developer and tech columnist, a crucial question was what news should look like online. The prevailing organizational metaphor at the time was spatial, as evidenced by the term 'cyberspace.' This spatial logic was apparent in how, for example, the personal homepage hosting service Geocities (created in 1995) was divided into 'neighborhoods,' and in the general prevalence of spatial and domestic metaphors (such as 'front door,' 'lobby,' and so on). Against this background, Winer made an important contribution by adding a feature to his Frontier publishing suite that organized new content in reverse-chronological order, so that the newest content was always at the top of the page (Winer credited the idea to HotWired, another sign of that site's influence). This newspage addition was an important technical development in the establishment of the early blogging community (Ammann, 2009), and in general Winer's Frontier content management system foreshadowed the various easy-to-use weblog publishing applications that would become available from 1999 (starting with Pyra, the company that would later become Blogger and was sold to Google).

For Jorn Barger, who built his site *Robot Wisdom* with Winer's Frontier suite and coined the term 'weblog' in late 1997, the web's virtues were openness and transparency, as enabled by its hypertextual form. Linking, if done right, would ideally lead to the best content and bring light to the most accurate and useful information. Barger set out to create a movement (not unlike an artistic or literary movement) dedicated to filtering the web, one that would ensure the web provided an open alternative to the editorial hierarchies and deliberate misinformation that characterized older media environments (Ammann, 2009). Although Barger's influence within the blogging community would wane amid various conflicts (not least with Winer), his efforts and his 'rules of art' for weblogs are significant for how they evoked Berners-Lee's original vision of the web as a highly sophisticated information resource, and prefigured forms of collaborative information management such as social bookmarking.

Although the genre would diversify at the same time that it 'stabilized' (Siles, 2012), these three early bloggers helped shape the genre's core conventions and expectations of it. They each believed the form would take advantage of the web's specific affordances and thereby offer a distinct alternative to mass media, although how much of an alternative this was would later be called into question and critiqued (Lovink, 2008). Blogging would be a source of personal expression, with collections of posts and links providing an unfiltered view of the self. Blogs would be written with professional-grade publishing infrastructure and presented in a reverse-chronological format that better suited the medium. And blogs would ultimately be a collaborative effort, where the sum was greater than the parts. This vision of a collaborative effort echoed Rheingold's earlier vision of virtual community, but it also echoed Berners-Lee's 'information universe,' as a key feature was that blogs would work together to curate and annotate the best links. With such advantages in mind, early blogger Rebecca Blood called blogs 'native to the Web' (Blood, 2002). The term 'web-native' suggests a kind of 'pure' web form, one that connects a set of cultural values such as individual expression and collaboration with perceived characteristics of the medium. In this way, the efforts of the early bloggers were similar to that of HotWired's creators and the producers of *24 Hours in Cyberspace* and *A Day in the Life of Cyberspace*: their accomplishment was not just about the media product they created, but an ability to tie it to a larger story about the web's nature and future direction.

4. OPEN-SOURCE SOFTWARE AND THE DATA TURN

While new genres like blogging developed and understandings of the web's nature continued to evolve, the technologies underlying web production also changed, greatly impacting the medium's capacity and scope and paving the way for the kinds of dynamic, data-intensive social media platforms we use today. Alongside many advances in infrastructure – the further growth of personal computing, increases in internet penetration and bandwidth, the rise of mobile internet, etc. – the 1990s saw the proliferation of professional grade software that was affordable and in many cases free-to-use. In this respect the most important development was the rise of 'free' or 'open source' software (F/OSS), meaning 'nonproprietary but licensed software' (Coleman, 2012: 1).

F/OSS is generally licensed in a way that source code is made freely available and software can be adapted to a user's particular needs. 'Open source' also connotes a distributed, partially self-organizing form of production (Benkler, 2007; Raymond, 2005): beginning with the operating system Linux, one began to see large-scale software projects being carried out by large numbers of developers across the world, using the internet to coordinate and collaborate. Such open source production distinguished itself from traditional software not only by the fact that collaborators generally volunteered their time and that they had a large say in the direction of a project, but also through continuous updates ('rapid prototyping') to the software that ran counter to the idea that software is ever 'finished.' In addition to connoting a particular mode of production, the label 'open source' was created in 1998 to promote the idea that freely available software could be highly profitable, as developers could earn money from services attached to their non-proprietary software (this was a controversial move within the free software community – see Kelty, 2008: 99–117). As the dot.com bubble began to peak in 1999, 'open source' companies like Red Hat held successful IPOs and F/OSS was declared the next big thing.

The rise of F/OSS impacted web culture in the 1990s and early 2000s in two significant ways. First, in a material sense, the fact that open source software was such high quality and did not have to cost much more than the time necessary to master it, meant that a greater user base had the opportunity to produce highly sophisticated websites and web applications. Second, it provided an analogy that, coupled with existing visions of the web's participatory potential, made it seem as if the web would make traditional media companies obsolete. If a group of volunteers spread across the world could outperform traditional software companies like Microsoft and Oracle, why couldn't a group of bloggers outperform CNN?

Slashdot as Early Example of a Participatory Media Platform

The tech news site Slashdot.org is an important touchstone for understanding how open source affected web production and provided a new impulse for envisioning the web's impact on the media landscape. The site was built in 1997 by a 21-year-old programmer named Rob Malda to publish, as he put it on the site's masthead, 'News for Nerds. Stuff that Matters.' The site's audience quickly grew, not least because of growing excitement around Linux and other free software. Built largely using the scripting language Perl, the site was continually updated with new features, most notably a streamlined system for submitting stories to Malda and the site's other editors and a custom-built, automated moderation system that

distributed the work of moderation to the site's 'trusted' users (Stevenson, 2015). The site's infrastructure helped the site's editors deal with the twin problems of information overload and entropy: measures were taken, for example, to ensure submissions could be efficiently organized and searched by editors, while the moderation system allowed users to choose whether to see all comments or just recommended ones, thus minimizing the impact of spam, trolls and other undesirable content. On top of these key features, Malda regularly added features for personalizing and customizing Slashdot, so that readers would see news based on their preferences, as well as expanding the ability of users to add content through journals and a social networking feature (ibid.). Such complex systems of collaborative media production and consumption had not previously been built, and although similar forms of collaborative filtering were increasingly being used by e-commerce sites like Amazon in their efforts to 'profile' consumers and recommend products (Elmer, 2003), Slashdot represented the first application of such technology in the context of web publishing. As early as 1999, the site's success prompted commentators to call Slashdot 'open source' news (Glave, 1999), and Slashdot eventually formed a central example in Bruns's theories of 'gatewatching' (Bruns, 2005) and 'produsage' (Bruns, 2008).

Slashdot not only foreshadowed many of the elements we recognize as part of social media platforms today, but also hinted at criticisms that these later platforms are regularly faced with. One recurring debate surrounded the fact that Slashdot's many features required surveillance in the form of authentication (i.e., registering and logging into the site) and browser cookies (used so that the server could 'remember' a user's activities and preferences) (Stevenson, 2015). This breach of privacy was mitigated by the fact that users were still allowed to read content and comment anonymously, but nonetheless it highlighted the potential clash between creating desirable interactivity, on the one hand, and the potential for personal data to be used for commercial or other purposes. Another critique was that Slashdot did not offer enough user freedom, as editorial control was ultimately in Malda's hands even if certain elements, such as moderation, were distributed and automated. This critique was voiced by Kevin Rose, founder of Slashdot's competitor Digg (Andrews, 2005), and the subsequent exchanges between Malda and Rose (held primarily in the media, e.g., Kushner, 2007) were an early example of debate surrounding 'algorithmic gatekeeping,' or automated forms of information management for selecting, ranking and recommending content (Bozdag, 2013).

Slashdot was an early example of 'informated media,' notable not just for enabling user participation but for doing so in a way that automatically incorporated data generated from user activity (Stevenson, 2015). This interest in experimenting with web technology to create new media forms was also apparent in Everything2 (http://everything2.com/), a site created by Malda's friend Nate Oostendorp. Everything2 was an ambitious project, a 'flexible web database' of individual nodes (or 'things') and their links to other nodes, each of which would be written by the site's users in an attempt to 'find the best way to store and link ideas' (Oosterdorp, 1999). Although it never gained the audience or attention its creators hoped for, Everything2 (like Slashdot) was notable for how it integrated a vision of participation and community with one of a highly-ordered information medium – that is, how it articulated a hybrid version of Rheingold's vision of community and Berners-Lee's vision of the web as an information universe.

5. WEB 2.0 AND SOCIAL MEDIA

So far, this chapter has recounted several interrelated strands of 1990s web history:

early visions of the medium's potential as 'information universe' and 'virtual community,' the widespread belief that the web would transform the media landscape and an accompanying financial speculation, the various attempts to define the dominant forms of (social) media on the web, and the rise of open-source infrastructures and recommendation systems that would form the technological basis for social media platforms. These cultural, economic and technological developments all played a role in shaping how the web would eventually be understood as 'social.' The wave of social media platforms that began to appear in the early 2000s and promised a more participatory media environment were imagined, financed and built in ways that display continuity with the early web.

Despite the many connections between 1990s web culture and our present social media era, the transition was hardly routine. In 2000 and 2001, the internet bubble burst. Dot.com stock prices began to drop, and initial successes like Pets.com (an online pets supply store) and Webvan (a grocery delivery company) declared bankruptcy and became symbols of how badly investors had been swindled. But as Dale Dougherty (an executive at O'Reilly Media) noted in 2003, certain companies like Google seemed to have come out of the stock market crash stronger, and what appeared to make these companies successful was similar to what enabled a new wave of web platforms and services like Wikipedia, del.icio.us and (a year later) flickr to grow so quickly: namely, an ability to 'harness' mass user activity in a way that improved the overall product, as well as the principle that the product itself was never 'finished.' With that insight, Dougherty coined the term 'Web 2.0' and O'Reilly Media held its first annual Web 2.0 conference in 2004. In the widely cited article called 'What is Web 2.0?,' O'Reilly (2005) argued that the term was more than a marketing buzzword, and outlined the new 'rules' for building a successful web business. At the top of the list was the idea of profiting from user contributions: the basis of Google's search engine was the implicit participation of webmasters whose links could be repurposed to index and rank websites, much like Amazon repurposed user activity (such as browsing, ranking and buying products) in order to make better recommendations. As with Slashdot's rise to prominence a few years earlier, a key analogy for this kind of automated media production was once again open source software development. O'Reilly argued that the key to harnessing collective intelligence was building an 'architecture of participation' by lowering the threshold for users to contribute. In addition to leveraging user activity, an important characteristic of Web 2.0 companies was an emphasis on building valuable databases. Web 2.0 thus brought together the two distinct visions of the web's nature outlined at the beginning of this chapter. On the one hand, Web 2.0 platforms like Wikipedia, Digg and flickr, along with later social media like Facebook, suggested an egalitarian or communitarian structure where anyone could participate and no central authority controlled the activities of users: although the term 'virtual' had waned, these companies and platforms certainly encourage characterizations of their users as a 'community' in the sense that Rheingold meant it (for example, see the many 'community guidelines' or variations thereof found on social media platforms). On the other hand, social media and Web 2.0 platforms are essentially intricately organized information systems, and because of this resonate strongly with the 'information universe' imagined by Berners-Lee: the indexes and archives being created by Google, Facebook and others represent impressive attempts to create useful reference media out of the vast databases each of these companies own. Similar to Berners-Lee's ambition of creating a 'semantic web,' their efforts represent a desire to create universal data formats to allow search engines and other applications to distinguish between entities and to map their relationships – such

work clearly has commercial implications, but must also be understood critically in terms of the epistemological and ontological assumptions they carry (for an introduction to the semantic web and discussion of its relationship to Web 2.0, see, for example, McCool (2005, 2006); for a critique of epistemology and ontology of the semantic web and similar schemes, see Cramer (2007)).

Similarities with the 'virtual community' and 'information universe' should not obscure the fact that Web 2.0 is as much a business concept as it is a grand vision of the web's distinctive nature. Where 'participation' often has a positive connotation and implies collective action (such as with democratic or civic participation), here the meaning was much more neutral. Effectively building an architecture of participation, O'Reilly argued, was not so much a matter of inspiring volunteers but of ensuring that 'participation' happened even when users acted out of self-interest – for example, although one might actively rate or review products on Amazon (and even receive the prestige and perks of being a 'Vine Voice' or trusted reviewer), one already contributes to Amazon's efforts to improve its recommendations simply by browsing the site or buying a product. Terranova (2004) argues that such models benefit from users' 'free labor,' while Gehl (2014: 23) similarly points out that social media and Web 2.0 platforms profit from users' 'affective processing' of the valuable archives they control. Likewise, the utopian connotations of knowledge graphs and social graphs are countered by the obvious commercial aims guiding Facebook's and Google's actions. As Gehl argues in relation to Facebook, it is important to see how the particular variables and values it incorporates into its database – from demographics such as age, education and occupation to various 'likes' or interests such as one's favorite music or movies – match closely with the needs of advertisers (Gehl, 2014: 92–116).

Finally, it's worth noting that O'Reilly's Web 2.0 article closely followed the format of *Wired*'s celebrations of the emerging dot. com bubble, in that it portrayed a radically altered media landscape as a foregone conclusion. Web 2.0 was not just a dry description of business concepts, but a reconfiguration of the web's promise of a more open and participatory media environment. As new as Web 2.0 seemed, and as disruptive as the latest social media startups appear to be today, it is important to understand that these concepts and companies emerge from historical processes, not least from evolving understandings of what the web is and what 'works' on it, which themselves are products of cultural, social and economic processes. Meanwhile, our understanding of web history is itself still taking shape, and it is hard to overstate how much work is being carried out, or will be, to preserve and study the medium's history. The importance of such work should not be underestimated, as any attempt to understand and determine the future of the web and social media will benefit greatly from further efforts to uncover their past.

Note

1   Research for this chapter was supported by the Dutch national science foundation (NWO) in connection with the Veni research project 'The web that was'.

REFERENCES

Ammann, Rudolf. (2009). Jorn Barger, the newspage network and the emergence of the weblog community. *Proceedings of the 20th ACM Conference on Hypertext and Hypermedia* (pp. 279–288). Presented at the HT 09, ACM, Torino, Italy.

Andrews, Robert. (2005). Digg just might bury Slashdot. *Wired*. November 17. http://archive. wired.com/science/discoveries/news/2005/ 11/69568

Ankerson, Megan Sapnar. (2010). Web industries, economies, aesthetics: Mapping the look of the web in the dot-com era. In Niels Brügger (Ed.), *Web History* (pp. 173–194). New York: Peter Lang.

Ankerson, Megan Sapnar. (2015). Social media and the 'read-only' web: Reconfiguring social logics and historical boundaries. *Social Media + Society*, 1. http://sms.sagepub.com/ content/1/2/2056305115621935

Barbrook, Richard, and Andy Cameron. (1996). The Californian Ideology. *Science as Culture*, 26(6): 1.

Benkler, Yochai. (2007). *The Wealth of Networks: How Social Production Transforms Markets and Freedom*. New Haven, CT: Yale University Press.

Berners-Lee, Tim. (1989). Information management: A proposal. CERN. www.w3.org/ History/1989/proposal.html

Berners-Lee, Tim. (2000). *Weaving the Web: The Original Design and Ultimate Destiny of the World Wide Web*. San Francisco, CA: HarperBusiness.

Berners-Lee, Tim, Robert Cailliau, Jean-Francois Groff, and Bernd Pollermann. (1991). Worldwide web: The information universe. *Internet Research*, 20(4): 461–471.

Berners-Lee, Tim, James Hendler, and Ora Lassila. (2001). The semantic web. *Scientific American*, 284(5): 34–43.

Blood, Rebecca. (2002). Introduction. In John Rodzvilla (Ed.), *We've Got Blog: How Weblogs are Changing Our Culture* (pp. ix–xiii). Cambridge, MA: Perseus Publishing.

Borsook, Paulina. (2000). *Cyberselfish: A Critical Romp through the Terribly Libertarian Culture of High Tech*. London: Little, Brown & Company.

Boulware, Jack. 1995. "Mondo 1995: Up and Down With the Next Millennium's First Magazine." *San Francisco Weekly*, October 11. https://archives.sfweekly.com/sanfrancisco/ mondo-1995/Content?oid=2132494.

Bozdag, Engin. (2013). Bias in algorithmic filtering and personalization. *Ethics and Information Technology*, 15(3): 209–227.

Bruns, Axel. (2005). *Gatewatching: Collaborative Online News Production*. New York: Peter Lang.

Bruns, Axel. (2008). *Blogs, Wikipedia, Second Life, and Beyond: From Production to Produsage*. New York: Peter Lang.

Bush, Vannevar. (1945). As we may think. *The Atlantic*, July. www.theatlantic.com/magazine/ archive/1945/07/as-we-may-think/303881/

Chun, Wendy Hui Kyong. 2006. *Control And Freedom: Power And Paranoia In The Age Of Fiber Optics*. Cambridge, MA: MIT Press.

Coleman, E. Gabriella. (2012). *Coding Freedom: The Ethics and Aesthetics of Hacking*. Princeton, NJ: Princeton University Press.

Cramer, Florian. (2007). Critique of the 'semantic web.' December 18. www.nettime.org/Lists-Archives/nettime-l-0712/msg00043.html

Driscoll, K. (2014) Hobbyist inter-networking and the popular Internet imaginary: Forgotten histories of networked personal computing, 1978–1998. Doctoral dissertation, University of Southern California, Los Angeles, California.

Dyson, Esther, George Gilder, George Keyworth, and Alvin Toffler. (1994). Cyberspace and the American Dream: A Magna Carta for the Knowledge Age. The Progress & Freedom Foundation, August. www.pff.org/issues-pubs/futureinsights/fi1.2magnacarta.html

Ellison, Nicole B., Charles Steinfield, and Cliff Lampe. (2007). The benefits of Facebook 'Friends:' Social capital and college students' use of online social network sites. *Journal of Computer-Mediated Communication*, 12(4): 1143–1168. doi:10.1111/j.1083-6101.2007.00367.x.

Elmer, Greg. (2003). A diagram of panoptic surveillance. *New Media Society*, 5(2): 231–247.

Gehl, Robert W. (2014). *Reverse Engineering Social Media: Software, Culture, and Political Economy in New Media Capitalism*. Philadelphia, PA: Temple University Press.

Glave, James. (1999). Slashdot: All the news that fits. *Wired*, August 26. www.wired.com/culture/lifestyle/news/1999/08/21448

Google inc. (n.d.). Company overview. www.google.com/about/company/

Gould, Emily. (2008). Exposed. *The New York Times*, May 25, sec. Magazine. www.nytimes.com/2008/05/25/magazine/25internet-t.html

Hinssen, Peter. (1995). Life in the digital city. *Wired*, June. www.wired.com/1995/06/digcity/

Johnson, Khari. (2017). "Facebook Gives up on Making the World More Open and Connected, Now Wants to Bring the World Closer Together." *VentureBeat*. June 22. https://venturebeat.com/2017/06/22/facebook-gives-up-on-making-the-world-more-open-and-connected-now-wants-to-bring-the-world-closer-together/.

Keegan, Paul. (1995). The Digerati! *The New York Times Magazine*, May 21. www.hist.umn.edu/shank/hist3842/Digerati!.html.

Keen, Andrew. (2007). *The Cult of the Amateur: How Today's Internet is Killing Our Culture*. New York: Doubleday.

Kelly, Kevin. (2005). We are the web. *Wired* August 1. http://www.wired.com/wired/archive/13.08/tech.html

Kelty, Christopher. (2008). *Two Bits: The Cultural Significance of Free Software*. Durham, NC: Duke University Press Books.

Kushner, David. (2007). The Slashdot supremacy. October 31. http://spectrum.ieee.org/consumer-electronics/gadgets/the-slashdot-supremacy

Liu, Alan. (2004). *The Laws of Cool: Knowledge Work and the Culture of Information*. Chicago, IL: University of Chicago Press.

Lovink, Geert. (2008). *Zero Comments: Blogging and Critical Internet Culture*. New York: Routledge.

Markoff, John. (1994). The view from cyberspace: The revolution will be digitized. *The New York Times*. May 29. www.nytimes.com/1994/05/29/weekinreview/conversations-louis-rossetto-view-cyberspace-revolution-will-be-digitized.html?scp=1&sq=rossetto&st=nyt&pagewanted=all

Marwick, Alice and danah boyd, (2011). To see and be seen: Celebrity practice on Twitter. *Convergence*, 17: 139–158.

McCool, Rob. (2005). Rethinking the semantic web: Part I. *IEEE Internet Computing*, 9(6): 86–88.

McCool, Rob. (2006). Rethinking the semantic web: Part 2. *IEEE Internet Computing*, 10(1): 93–96. doi:10.1109/MIC.2006.18

Morozov, Evgeny. (2011). *The Net Delusion: The Dark Side of Internet Freedom*. New York: PublicAffairs.

Morozov, Evgeny. (2013). *To Save Everything, Click Here: The Folly of Technological Solutionism*. New York: PublicAffairs.

Neff, Gina. (2012). *Venture Labor: Work and the Burden of Risk in Innovative Industries*. Cambridge, MA: MIT Press.

Neff, Gina, and David Stark. (2003). Permanently beta: Responsive organization in the internet era. In Philip N. Howard and Steve

Jones (Eds.), *Society Online: The Internet in Context* (pp. 173–188). London: Sage.

Nelson, Ted. (1974). *Computer Lib/Dream Machines*. Self-published.

Oosterdorp, Nate. (1999). Everything. *Everything*, November 13. http://everything2.com/user/nate/writeups/Everything

O'Reilly, Tim. (2005). What is Web 2.0? *O'Reilly*. September 30. www.oreillynet.com/pub/a/oreilly/tim/news/2005/09/30/what-is-web-20.html

Pew Research Center. (1995). *Americans Going Online… Explosive Growth, Uncertain Destinations*. Pew Research Center for the People and the Press. October 16. www.people-press.org/1995/10/16/americans-going-online-explosive-growth-uncertain-destinations/

Putnam, Robert D. (2001). *Bowling Alone*. New York: Simon & Schuster.

Raymond, Eric S. (2005). The Cathedral and the Bazaar. *First Monday*, Special issue 2: Open Source (October). http://firstmonday.org/htbin/cgiwrap/bin/ojs/index.php/fm/article/view/1472/1387

Rheingold, Howard. (2000). *The Virtual Community: Homesteading on the Electronic Frontier* (second edition). Cambridge, MA: MIT Press.

Rheingold, Howard. (2002). *Smart Mobs: The Next Social Revolution*. Cambridge, MA: Perseus.

Rodzvilla, Jon (Ed.). (2002). *We've Got Blog: How Weblogs are Changing Our Culture*. Cambridge, MA: Perseus Publishing.

Rosenberg, Scott. (2009). *Say Everything: How Blogging Began, What It's Becoming, and Why It Matters*. New York: Crown Publishing Group.

Rossetto, Louis. 1993. "Why Wired?" *Wired* 1(1), March.

Senft, Theresa. (2008). *Camgirls: Celebrity and Community in the Age of Social Networks*. New York: Peter Lang.

Sharkey, Matt. (2005). The Big Fish. *Keepgoing.org*. www.keepgoing.org/issue20_giant/

Shirky, Clay. (2008). *Here Comes Everybody: The Power of Organizing Without Organizations*. London: Penguin Press.

Siles, Ignacio. (2012). The rise of blogging: Articulation as a dynamic of technological stabilization. *New Media & Society*, 14(5): 781–797. doi:10.1177/1461444811425222

Stevenson, Michael. (2014a). Rethinking the participatory web: A history of HotWired's 'New Publishing Paradigm,' 1994–1997. *New Media & Society*, October.

Stevenson, Michael. (2014b). Web-native culture and new media rupture-talk. *Contemporanea*, 14: 500–508.

Stevenson, Michael. (2015). Slashdot, open news and informed media: Exploring the intersection of imagined futures and web publishing technology. In Wendy Hui Kyong Chun, Anna Watkins Fisher, and Thomas Keenan (Eds.), *New Media, Old Media: A History and Theory Reader* (second edition). London: Routledge.

Stevenson, Michael. (2016). "The Cybercultural Moment and the New Media Field." *New Media & Society* 18 (7): 1088–1102. doi:10.1177/1461444816643789.

Streeter, Thomas. (2010). *The Net Effect: Romanticism, Capitalism, and the Internet*. New York: New York University Press.

Terranova, Tiziana. (2004). *Network Culture: Politics for the Information Age*. London: Pluto Press.

Turner, Fred. (2006). *From Counterculture to Cyberculture: Stewart Brand, the Whole Earth Network, and the Rise of Digital Utopianism*. Chicago: University of Chicago Press.

Vogelstein, Fred. 2009. "The Wired Interview: Facebook's Mark Zuckerberg." *Wired*. June 29. http://www.wired.com/business/2009/06/mark-zuckerberg-speaks/.

Winner, Langdon. (1995). Peter Pan in cyberspace: Wired magazine's political vision. *Educom Review*, 30(3). http://net.educause.edu/apps/er/review/reviewArticles/30318.html

Wolf, Gary. (2003). *Wired: A Romance*. New York: Random House.

PART II

Approaches and Methods

5

Digital Methods for Cross-platform Analysis

Richard Rogers

DIGITAL METHODS AFTER SOCIAL MEDIA

Increasingly employed as an umbrella term for tool-based methods employed in the digital humanities and e-social sciences, digital methods have as their point of departure a series of heuristics with respect to how to study online media (Rogers, 2013b). The first historicises the web as an object of study, one that has undergone a transformation from a (virtual) site for the study of online culture specifically to a source of data about broader societal and cultural trends. Second, to extract the data one not only employs crawlers, scrapers, API logins and manual means, but also pays special attention to 'query design' and 'search as research' for creating tweet collections or sets of Facebook pages for social media analysis. To study those 'natively digital' source sets, digital methods learn from the methods of the medium, e.g., recommendation systems

such as trending topics or newsfeeds. How may platform treatments of retweets and likes (for example) be repurposed for studying the unfolding of historical events (on Twitter), or the most engaged with memes in a political campaign (on Facebook)? Digital methods, finally, consider the conditions of proof. When does it makes sense to ground the findings (about the versions of historical events represented by Google search results, for example) in the particular characteristics and influences of online data, and when is 'online groundedness' less robust than mixed methods approaches?

One of the earliest digital methods maps the hyperlinking patterns between websites involved in the same social issue area so as to study the politics of association of actors from the purposively made as well as the missing links. The IssueCrawler, the software tool developed in the early 2000s or the so-called web 1.0 era, provides a 'programmed method' for studying associations in issue networks online, or clutches

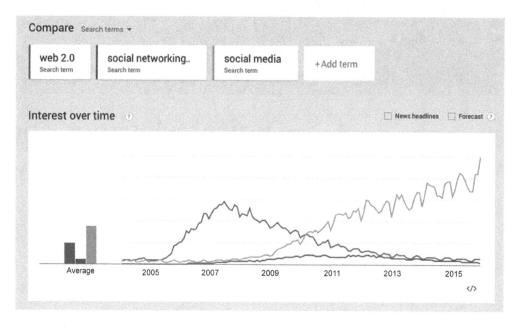

Figure 5.1   Comparison of search volume for [web 2.0], [social networking sites] and [social media], according to Google Trends, 19 November 2015

of NGOs, funders, think tanks, academics as well as databases, widgets and other online objects, working on or serving a particular issue (Bruns, 2007; Rogers, 2009a; Borra and Rieder, 2014). Once the links between actors have been found, one may begin to study association as well as the organisation of networked publics (Latour, 2005; Ito, 2008).

More recently, by calling for a move from 'so-called web 1.0 http or html approaches to 2.0 cross platform based methods,' Greg Elmer and Ganaele Langlois (2013: 45) argue that to study the web these days requires new methods that step past the hyperlink as the pre-eminent digital object tying it all together. They issue a much larger invitation to rethink the web more generally as an object of study, recognising its increasing platformisation, or the mass movement by web users to social media (Helmond, 2015). In the shift from an info-web (1.0) to a social web (2.0), recommendations are made through the participation of platform users rather than only by site webmasters (to use a throwback term).[1] That is, recommendations,

especially in the news feeds of platforms, follow from 'friends'' activity, such as 'liking' and 'sharing'. The content recommendations thereby distinguish themselves epistemologically from those derived from site owners or webmasters' linking to another webpage for referencing or other purposes.[2] Following Tim O'Reilly, here the terms 'web 1.0' and 'web 2.0' have been used (or overused) to periodise not only the transition from the info-web to the social web, but also from the open web to the closed web or the walled gardens of platforms (O'Reilly, 2005; Dekker and Wolfsberger, 2009).

On the Web's 25th anniversary in 2014, Tim Berners-Lee, who 'slowly, but steadily' has come to be known as its inventor, called for its 're-decentralisation', breaking down new media concentration and near monopolies online working as walled gardens without the heretofore open spirit (Berners-Lee, 2014) (Agar, 2001: 371). The web's 'app-ification' is analogous. Next to increased government Internet censorship, mass surveillance and punitive copyright laws, Berners-Lee (2014) lists 'corporate walled gardens' or social media platforms as grave concerns related to the very future of the web and its mobile counterpart.

Langlois and Elmer's point, however, implies that one should not only periodise and critique the dominant phases of the web, but also do the same for its methods of study. There are those digital methods that rely on hyperlinks, and thereby are in a sense still committed to an info-web, and those that have taken on board 'likes', 'shares' and other forms of valuation and currency (such as 'comments' and 'liked comments') on online platforms. Indeed, this analytical periodisation is reflected in the much broader study of value online, reflected in the rise of the 'like economy' over the 'link economy' (Gerlitz and Helmond, 2013). As a case in point, Google's Web Search once valued links higher than other signals (Hindman, 2008; Rieder, 2012). Through the rise of user clicks as a source adjudication measure, one could argue that Google Web Search, too, is valuing the social web over the document or semantic matching of the info-web (van Couvering, 2007). Metrification online, which starts with like counts and follower numbers and progresses towards Klout scores, similarly considers and makes rankings social. Thus the new analytics, both Google's updated ones as well as Klout's, are oriented to a web gone social.

The notion of web 2.0 (and the related idea of the social web) brought with it as its apparent forerunner web 1.0 (with a more informational set of metaphors), but beyond the versioning rhetoric web 2.0 itself has been supplanted first by 'social network(ing) sites' and 'platforms' and later just by 'social media' (boyd and Ellison, 2007; Beer, 2008; Scholz, 2008; Allen, 2013) (see Figure 5.1). The early distinction between social networking sites and social network sites, ushered in by boyd and Ellison, was normative as well as analytical. Social media users ought to have an interest to connect with others online other than for the purposes of 'networking', which would suggest a kind

of neoliberal activity of making sure that even one's social life (online) is productive. In a sense, the authors also anticipated the nuancing of social media into platform types, such as the ones for business (LinkedIn), family (Facebook) and professional doings (Twitter), though social media user practices in each remain diverse. Whether for networking or to connect with one's existing network, the analytical call made by boyd and Ellison seemed to be directed to the study of profiles and friends (together with friending).

The purposive use of the term 'platform', as Tarleton Gillespie (2010) has pointed out, could be viewed as particularly enticing for users to populate an otherwise empty database, thereby generating value for the companies. Platforms connote voice-giving infrastructure, where one can express one's viewpoints (political or otherwise), rise up, and make an online project of oneself. Polishing the profile, friending, uploading videos and photos, and liking, sharing and commenting become not only newly dominant forms of sociality, but a kind of labour for a platform owned by others (Scholz, 2016). Cooperative, user-owned platforms would provide alternatives. Other critical calls for the analysis of Facebook have been made, certain of which have resulted in invitations to leave the platform, to liberate oneself or even to commit so-called Facebook suicide, which would allow you 'to meet your real neighbours', as suicidemachine.org's software project's slogan has it (Portwood-Stacer, 2013; Facebook Liberation Army, 2015).

As web 2.0 has given way to social network(ing) sites, platforms and, finally, social media, social media methods also have evolved. In particular, digital methods for social media analysis initially relied on social network analysis (the study of interlinked friends) as well as profiles and the presentation of self. For example, Netvizz, the Facebook data extraction software, originally was considered a tool to map one's own Facebook friend network (Rieder, 2013). The early digital methods work on social networking sites similarly studied friends and profiles. Dubbed 'post-demographics', this approach to studying profiles considered preferences and tastes as a starting point of analysis as opposed to gender, age, education and such (Rogers, 2009b). One study examined the interests of presidential candidates' MySpace 'friends'. Did Barack Obama's friends and John McCain's friends share the same favourite television shows, movies, heroes, and books, or was there a distinctive politics to media taste and consumption? (For the most part, they did not share tastes and thus TV shows and the other preferences could be considered to have politics of consumption (Rogers, 2013b).) In the case of Netvizz friend-network mapping, as well as post-demographics, these methods could be called digital methods for social media 1.0, for they concerned themselves with profiles, friends and networking.

More recently, attention to social media in digital methods work has been directed towards events, disasters, elections and revolutions, first through the so-called 'Twitter revolution' surrounding the Iran election crisis (2009) and later the Arab Spring (2011–2012). Instead of starting with user profiles, friend networks or networking, such studies collect tweets containing one or more hashtags such as #iranelection (perhaps together with queried keywords), or focus on one particular Facebook page, such as We are all Khaled Said (Gaffney, 2010; Lotan et al., 2011; Rieder et al., 2015).

Many of the more recent methods to analyse platforms rest upon and also derive from the individual APIs that Twitter, Facebook, Instagram, YouTube and others have to offer. As data are increasingly offered and delivered by polling one API, and no longer screen-scraped or crawled from multiple websites (as in the days of the info-web), most work is a study of a page or multiple pages (and groups) on Facebook, or one concerning tweets containing one or more hashtags and keywords on Twitter. In social media analysis with digital methods, in other words, 'single-platform studies' have become the norm.

If there were a significant turning point towards single-platform studies steered by the API (rather than by scraping), it may have been the critique of a 2008 social network analysis of tastes and ties that used college students' Facebook data (Lewis et al., 2008; Zimmer, 2010; Marres and Weltevrede, 2013). It concerned a set of presumably anonymised users from a so-called renowned university in the northeast of the United States. Not so unlike the effects of the release of AOL user search histories in 2006, its publishing prompted detective work to uncover the identities of the users, who turned out to be Harvard College students from the graduating class of 2009 (Zimmer, 2008). Michael Zimmer, both in the detective work as well as in the reflection upon the way forward for social media method, entitled his critique, 'But the data is already public', echoing one of the remarks by an author of the study. In giving rise to a sharper focus on ethics in web studies more generally, coinciding with a decline in scraping, Zimmer argued that in the Harvard study users' so-called contextual privacy was violated, for not only did they not give informed content, but they did not expect their publicly available data to be stored in a researcher's database and matched with their student housing data for even greater analytical scrutiny of their ties and tastes (Nissenbaum, 2009). The actual data collection is described by the researchers as 'downloading' the profile and friend network data directly from Facebook, prior to the release of Facebook API 1.0 in 2010. In other words, the data were obtained or scraped in some non-API manner, albeit with permission from Facebook as well as Harvard for the project funded by the National Science Foundation and approved by the university's ethics review board. Ultimately, in the evolution of its API to version 2.0 (in 2014), Facebook would remove permissions to access friends' data such as ties and tastes (i.e., friends and likes, together with profiles), thereby making (sociometric) social network analysis like the one performed in the Harvard study improbable, including even those of one's own network with all friends' privacy settings adhered to, as one would do with Netvizz (Facebook, 2016). 'Internal' studies still may be performed, which Facebook data scientists also took advantage of with their 'emotional contagion' experiment (Kramer et al., 2014). The data science study (of some 700,000 users with a corpus of 3 million posts) analysed the risks associated with the Facebook news feed. Is user exposure to positive or negative posts psychologically risky (Meyer, 2015)? The study found that negative posts run the risk of 'emotional contagion'. In order to make the findings, Facebook selectively removed negative posts from users' news feeds. The ethics of the study were similarly questioned, for the users were unaware (and not informed) that their news feeds were being altered and their moods measured, however seemingly impractical and obtrusive it would be to gain such permission (Puschmann and Bozdag, 2014). Among the ethical issues raised, one concerned whether researchers can rely on the terms of service as cover for the otherwise lack of informed consent. Are users agreeing to being analysed for more than improvement of the site and services, as is usually stated? To the letter, they are not.

It is worthwhile to recall from the AOL case that the 62-year-old search engine user told the *New York Times* that she never imagined that her queries would be made public, or that she would have to explain to anyone that her information-seeking about medical conditions was undertaken for her friends (Barbaro and Zeller, 2006). In joining a lawsuit brought against AOL at the Federal Trade Commission, the Electronic Frontier Foundation published highly personal and salacious query histories from unnamed individuals; another user's search engine query history was made into the mini-documentary, 'I Love Alaska: The heartbreaking search history of AOL user #711391', by the Dutch

artists and filmmakers Lernert Engelberts and Sander Plug (2009), who were asked subsequently by the broadcasting company to seek out the identity of the woman, now intimately known. (Ultimately, they did not.) Neither the study of Harvard College's 2009 graduating class nor the emotional contagion study appears to have led to the subjects being identified and in some way harmed through outing. It is also not straightforward to claim that informed consent would have been enough to preclude harm, given that the users may be unable to foresee the potential hazards of participation (van de Poel, 2009).

HASHTAG AND (LIKED) PAGE STUDIES

With the decline of scraping and the rise of issues surrounding human subject research in social media, the API-led studies (on events, disasters, elections, revolutions and social causes) rely increasingly on such content-organising elements as the hashtag (for Twitter) and the (liked) page (for Facebook). Each is taken in turn, so as eventually to discuss with which limitations one may study them concurrently across platforms.

The Twitter hashtag, put forward by Chris Messina in 2007, was originally conceived as a means to set up 'channel tags', borrowing from similar practices in Internet Relay Chat (IRC). The proposal was to organise 'group-like activity' on Twitter that would be 'folksonomic', meaning user-generated rather than an editorial or taxonomic practice by the company or its syndicated partners, as in Snapchat's 'Stories' (Messina, 2007). Messina also proposed to provide a ranked list of the channel tags by activity, i.e., most active ones in the past twenty-four hours, showing on the interface where the activity is. This feature is similar to trending topics which Jack Dorsey, co-founder of Twitter, described a year later as 'what the world considers important in this moment'

(Dorsey, 2008). With hashtags and trending topics, Twitter not only gained new functionality but became a rather novel object of study for what could be termed both on-the-ground and 'remote event analysis'. As such, it thus distinguishes itself from Dorsey's original Twitter, created to provide what he called 'personal immediacy – seeing what's happening in my world right now' (Dorsey, 2008). Dorsey himself, in the interviews he gave for the *Los Angeles Times* after his temporary ouster as CEO, acknowledged the shift away from this more intimate Twitter, saying Twitter thrives on 'natural disasters, man-made disasters, events, conferences, presidential elections' (Sarno, 2009). In the event, the study of Twitter as a space for ambient friend-following yielded, at least for a share of Twitter studies, to that of event-following, which is another way of distinguishing between digital methods for social media analysis 1.0 and 2.0 (Rogers, 2013a).

Not so unlike Google Trends that list the year's most sought key words (with a geographical distribution), Twitter's initial cumulative list of the year's trending topics, published in 2009, provides a rationale for the attention granted to the study of the single hashtag for events. In the announcement made by the Twitter data scientist, Abdur Chowdhury (who incidentally was head of AOL Research when the search history data were released), one notes how serious content began to take a prominent place in a service once known primarily for its banality. In 2009 'Twitter users found the Iranian elections the most engaging topic of the year. The terms #iranelection, Iran and Tehran were all in the top-21 of Trending Topics, and #iranelection finished in a close second behind the regular weekly favorite #musicmonday' (Chowdhury, 2009). Some years later the universal list of trending topics became personalised according to whom one follows and one's geographical coordinates, however much one may change one's location and personalise trending topics exclusively by new location. In some sense the change from

universal to personalised results (like Google Web Search's similar move in December 2009, which Eli Pariser (2011) relies upon for his notion the 'filter bubble') made trends more unassailable, for no longer could one call into question why a particular hashtag (like #occupywallstreet) was not trending when it perhaps should have been (Gillespie, 2012). Trending topics are in a sense now co-authored by the Twitter user, making them less compelling to study at least as a cultural barometer. (The exception is trending topics that are location-based only.)

While the single hashtag, or more likely a combination of hashtags and keywords, remain a prominent starting point for making tweet collections to study events, disasters, elections, revolutions and social causes, as well as subcultures, movements, stock prices, celebrity awards and cities, researchers have widely expanded their repertoire for assembling them, first through techniques of capturing follower, reply and mention networks, and subsequently using the 1% random sample made available by Twitter, geotagged tweets and the Twitter ID numberspace in combination with time zones to identify national Twitter spheres (Crampton et al., 2013; Gerlitz and Rieder, 2013; Bruns et al., 2014).

Network analysis remains a preferred analytical technique in digital methods work, and as such it endures in the transition to method 2.0, but one somewhat novel strand of work worthy of mention here concerns Twitter content studies, discussed by way of a brief analytical tool description (Venturini et al., 2014b; Kennedy and Hill, 2016). The Twitter Capture and Analysis Tool (TCAT) can be installed on one's own server to capture tweets for analysis (Borra and Rieder, 2014). Researchers thereby make individual tweet collections, instead of having one or more larger databases that are collaborative-like repositories. Such archival fragmentation could not be avoided, because Twitter, once rather open, changed its terms of service upon becoming a publicly traded

Figure 5.2   Netvizz output showing the share, like and comments count (as well as its sum of 'engagement') of two URLs on Facebook

url	normalized_url	share_ count	like_ count	comment_ count	total_ count
http://www.nytimes.com/ 2015/12/08/opinion/how-isis- makes-radicals.html	http://www.nytimes.com/ 2015/12/08/opinion/how-isis- makes-radicals.html	1775	2667	1087	5229
https://theintercept.com/ drone-papers/	https://www.theintercept.com/ drone-papers/	5995	5623	2396	14014

company, no longer allowing the sharing of tweet collections (Puschmann and Burgess, 2013). Thus researchers must curate their own. The TCAT tool, installed on a server (with GitHub instructions), enables tweet collection-making (gathered from both the streaming and the REST API) and provides a battery of network analyses: social graph by mentions, social graph by in_reply to status_ id, co-hashtag, bipartite hashtag-user, bipartite hashtag-mention, bipartite hashtag-URL and bipartite hashtag-host. There are also modules, however, that direct attention towards forms of content analysis that are 'quanti-quali' and referred to as 'networked content analysis' (Niederer, 2016). By quanti-quali is meant that a quantitative, winnowing analysis (not so unlike sampling) is performed so as to enable not only a 'computational herme-neutics' but also a thicker description (Mohr et al., 2015). Quanti-quali is preferred over the more usual quali-quanti moniker, owing to the order of the methodological steps (Venturini et al., 2014a). Departing from a collection of 600,000 tweets gathered through a single hashtag, an example of such an approach is the #iranelection RT project, which sought to turn Twitter into a story-telling machine of events on the ground and in social media by ordering the top three retweeted tweets per day, and placing them in chronological order, as opposed to the reverse chronological order of Twitter (Rogers et al., 2009). #iranelection RT relied on manual retweeting (where the user types RT in the tweet), whereas the TCAT module outputs, chronologically, 'identical tweet frequency', or narrowly defined 'native'

retweets. Other forms of quanti-quali content analysis with a tweet collection are hashtag as well as URL frequency list-making to study hierarchies of concern and most-referred-to content. It is the starting point for a form of content analysis that treats a hashtag as (for example) an embedded social cause or move-ment (#blacklivesmatter) and URLs a web-page such as a news story or YouTube video. The (often fleeting) 'hashtag publics' mobi-lise around a social cause not only phatically (and affectively) but also with content (Bruns and Burgess, 2011; Bruns and Burgess, 2015; Papacharissi, 2015). Networked content analysis considers how and to what substan-tive ends the network filters stories, mobi-lises particular media formats over others and circulates urgency (geographically), attract-ing bursty or sustained attention that may be measured. Techniques of studying social causes using hashtags in Twitter as well as Instagram are discussed below, including how to consider whether to downplay or embrace medium effects.

While, since June 2013, Facebook has included hashtags as proposed means of organising 'public conversations', the straightforward 'cross-platform analysis' of Twitter and Facebook using the same hashtags is likely fraught. The study of Facebook 'content' relies far more on other activities, such as liking, sharing and com-menting, which is known as studying 'most engaged with content' (and is available in the Netvizz data outputs) (see Figure 5.2). For cross-platform work, the co-appearances of URLs (aka co-links) amplified perhaps by 'likes' (Facebook's as well as Twitter's hitherto favorites) may yield far more material for comparative resonance analysis.

From the beginning Facebook (unlike Friendster and MySpace before it) positioned itself as a social network site that would reflect one's own proper circle of friends and acquaintances, thereby challenging the idea that online friends should be considered 'friends' with quotation marks and thereby a problematic category worthy of special 'virtual' study. In a sense, such a friend designation could be interpreted as another mid-2000 marker of the end of cyberspace. Together with the demise of serendipitous (and aimless) surfing, the rise of national jurisdictions legislating (and censoring) the Internet and the reassertion of local language (and local advertising) as organising principles of browsing, Facebook also re-ordered the web, doing away with cyberspace in at least two senses. As AOL once did with its portal, Facebook sought to attract and keep users by making the web 'safe,' first as a US college website offering registration only to on-campus users with an .edu email address, and then later as it expanded beyond the colleges by ID-ing users or otherwise thwarting practices of anonymisation (Stutzman et al., 2013). This was an effort to prevent so-called 'fakesters', and thus distinguish itself from online platforms like MySpace, which were purportedly rife with lurkers and stalkers as well as publicised cases of sex offenders masquerading as youngsters (boyd, 2013). Facebook's web was also clean, swept of visual clutter. In contrast to MySpace, it did not offer customisation, skinning or 'pimping', so one's profile picture and the friend thumbnails would be set in a streamlined, blue interface without starry nights, unicorns and double rainbows surrounding the posts.

Facebook's safe and de-cluttered web brought a series of 'cyberspace' research practices down to earth as well, cleaning up or at least making seem uncouth such practices as scraping websites for data. For one, scraping social network sites for data became a (privacy and proprietary) concern and also a practice actively blocked by Facebook. Data would be served on Facebook's terms through its API (as mentioned above), and the politics and practices of APIs (more generally) would become objects of study (Bucher, 2013). In this case, terms-of-service-abiding, non-scraping data extraction tools (such as Netvizz) would reside on Facebook itself as apps, and require vetting and approval by the company. Be it through the developers' gateway or a tool on Facebook, one would log in, and the data available would respect one's own as well as the other users' privacy settings, eventually putting paid to the open-ended opportunities social network sites were thought to provide to social network research. With the API as point of access, Facebook as an object of study has undergone a transition from the primacy of the profile and friends' networks (tastes and ties) to that of the page or group, and with it from the presentation of self to social causes (which I'm using as a shorthand for events, disasters, elections, revolutions, and so forth). In a sense the company's acquisition, Instagram, could be said to have supplanted Facebook as the preferred object of study of the self through its ambassadorship of selfie culture, however much its initiator would like the company to take the route of Twitter, at once debanalising and becoming a news and event-following medium, too (Goel, 2015; Senft and Baym, 2015).

If, with the API, Facebook analysis is steered towards the pages of social causes, 'liking' is no longer considered as frivolous, and like-based engagement analyses gain more weight. As a case in point liking a page with photos of brutal acts of violence requires the like button to be re-appropriated, as Amnesty International (and other advocacy organisations) are wont to do by asking one not to take liking lightly (or communicate only phatically) but to see liking as an act of solidarity with a cause or support for a campaign. While it has been dismissed as a form of slacktivism (which requires little or no effort and has little or no effect), liking as a form of engagement has been studied more extensively, with scholars attributing to button clicking on Facebook distinctive forms of liking causes: '(1) socially responsible liking, (2) emotional liking, (3) informational liking, (3) social performative liking, (5) low-cost liking and 6) routine liking' (Brandtzaeg and Haugstveit, 2014: 258). In the event, low-cost liking would be especially slacktivist, though all forms of liking in the list also could be construed as a form of attention-granting with scant impact, as was once said of the 'CNN effect' when all the world's proverbial eyes are watching – but not acting (Robinson, 2002). The question of whether liking as a form of engagement substitutes for other forms, however, has been challenged, for social media activism, it is argued, aids in accumulating action and action potential (Christensen, 2011). It is also where the people are (online).

FROM SINGLE PLATFORM TO CROSS-PLATFORM STUDIES

Social movement, collective action and more recently 'connective action' researchers in particular have long called for multiple platform, and multi-media, analysis (to use an older term). In an extensive study based on interviews, Sasha Costanza-Chock (2014), for one, has deemed the immigrant rights movement in the United States a form of 'transmedia organising'. The cross-platform approach is a deliberate strategy, and each platform is approached and utilised separately for its own qualities and opportunities. Here one may recall the distinction made by Henry Jenkins (2006) between cross-media (the same story for all platforms) and transmedia (the story unfolds differently across platforms). Thus social media, when used as a 'collapsed category', masks significant differences in 'affordances' (Costanza-Chock, 2014: 61–66). (I return to a similar problem

concerning collapsed digital objects such as hashtags or likes across platforms with different user cultures.) If we are to follow Jenkins, as well as Costanza-Chock, a discussion of cross-platform analysis would be more aptly described as trans-platform analysis.

Researchers studying social causes on platforms have also called for 'uncollapsing' social media. Lance Bennett and Alexandra Segerberg, who coined the notion of 'connective action' as a counter-point to collective action, argue that to understand the forces behind social change one should study *those multiple platforms* that allow for 'personalized public engagement', instead of choosing one platform and its API in advance of the analysis (Bennett and Segerberg, 2012). It is, in other words, an implicit critique of the single-platform studies (as collapsed social media studies) that rely solely on Twitter for one issue (e.g., Fukushima in Japan) or Facebook for another (e.g., rise of right-wing populism), when one could have ample cause to study them across media. It is not only the silo-ing of APIs that prompts single-platform studies; as pointed out, the question of the comparability of the 'same' objects across platforms (likes, hashtags) is at issue.

One of Bennett and Segerberg's preferred tools is the IssueCrawler, developed at the Digital Methods Initiative, which could be described as web 1.0 analytical software, relying on the info-web's link and performing hyperlink analysis. For multiple-platform (and transmedia) analysis à la Bennett and Segerberg it could be employed as an exploratory instrument at the outset of a study of a cause (on the web), in order to ascertain which websites (including blogs) and platforms are the focus of attention. In other words, hyperlink analysis could be construed as a web 1.0 methodological starting point for multi-platform analysis. As described below, other 'inter-linkings' (broadly conceived) may be studied, such as co-linked and inter-liked content.

PLATFORM CULTURES OF USE

The purpose of the exercise here is to develop cross-platform methods, or digital methods for cross-platform studies, where one learns from medium methods and repurposes them for social and cultural research. It begins with a sensitivity to distinctive user cultures and subcultures, whereby hashtags and likes, digital objects used to organise and boost content (among other reasons), should not necessarily be treated as if they are employed equivalently across all platforms, even when present. For example, Instagram has inflated hashtag use compared to Twitter's, allowing up to 30 tags (and far more characters per photo caption post than Twitter grants for a tweet). That is, users may copy and paste copious quantities of hashtags in Instagram posts (see Table 5.1). Twitter recommends that one '[does not] #spam #with #hashtags. Don't over-tag a single Tweet. (Best practices recommend using no more than 2 hashtags per Tweet.)' (Twitter, 2016). While present, hashtags are under-utilised on Facebook.

A series of questions arises concerning the meaning of the term 'cross' in 'cross-platform analysis'. First, across which platforms are 'hashtags' worthy of study (Twitter, Instagram, Tumblr), which ones 'likes' (Facebook, Instagram, YouTube, Twitter, Pinterest), which ones 'retweets' or 'repins' (Twitter, Pinterest), which one '@mentions' (Twitter), which ones 'links', including shortened URLs (not Instagram), and so forth (see Table 5.1)? The point is that platforms have similar affordances, such as like buttons and hashtags, but one should not necessarily collapse them by treating them equally across platforms. More specifically, if one were to perform cross-platform analysis of the same hashtags across multiple platforms, how would one build into the method the difference in hashtag use in Twitter and Instagram? Because of hashtag proliferation on Instagram, does one devalue or otherwise correct for hashtag abundance on the one platform while valuing it steadily on another? One could strive to identify cases of copy-and-pasting hashtag strings, and downplay their value, certainly if posts are being 'stuffed' with hashtags.

Second, certain platforms (and perhaps more so certain topics such as large media events on most any platform) may indeed have user cultures and automation activity that routinely befoul posts as well as activity measures. Hashtag hijacking is a case in point, especially when one is studying an event or a social issue and encounters unrelated hashtags purposively inserted to attract attention and traffic, such as when spammers monitor trending hashtags and use them tactically to promote their wares. Hashtag junk may distract at least the researcher.

Third, while a more complex topic, bots and the activity traces they leave behind are often similarly considered worth special consideration during the analysis (Marres, 2015). From a digital forensics point of view, bots that like and follow may have specific (network) signatures, e.g., they do not tend to be followed, or to be liked, meaning the bot often only has outlinks. For the purposes of this discussion, they may inflate activity in causes and such inflation may be considered artificial (though of course there are bots created for events and issues, too, and their activities are thereby purposive). Thus manipulation as well as artificiality are additional (intriguing) complications in both single-platform and cross-platform analysis.

Fourth, platforms have 'device cultures' that affect how one interprets the data from the API.[3] That is, all platforms filter posts, showing particular content and letting other content slide downwards or off screen, so to speak (Eslami et al., 2015). Users thereby cannot 'like' all content equally. That which is liked may tend to be liked more often, and thus there may be power law and long tail effects that differ per platform. But we may not know how preferred posting affects activity measures. APIs will return like and share counts (for example) per post, but they do not let us know the extent to which all the content has been equally visible to those who would be able to like, share, comment, and so forth. And filtering styles and thus visibility effects differ per platform.

Above a series of questions has been posed concerning the limitations of comparing evaluations of content, recommended with the same type of button on different platforms, given that the platforms may have different user, spamming, bot and device cultures. How to nevertheless undertake cross-platform analysis? When studying recommendations and the content that rises, metrically, to the top of the platforms, it may be instructive to begin by examining briefly which digital objects are available in each of the platforms (as above and in Table 5.1) and subsequently enquire into how dominant devices (or in this case metrics such as Klout) handle these objects. Subsequently, it is asked, how to repurpose the metrics?

CROSS-PLATFORM ANALYSIS: CO-LINKED, INTER-LIKED AND CROSS-HASHTAGGED CONTENT

Klout, as the term indicates, measures a user's 'clout', slang for influence, largely from data culled online, where the user is not only an individual but can be a magazine, institution, professional sports team, etc. Klout scores are measured on the basis of activity on Twitter, Facebook, YouTube, Google+, LinkedIn, Instagram, and Foursquare (Rao et al., 2015). It is an influence measure that takes into account particular appearance signals across the seven platforms (e.g., mentions on Twitter), and those mentions by highly influential user accounts grant more influence or clout to the user in question. It also grounds (and augments) the online appearance measures with 'offline factors' that take into account a user's 'real world influence' from Wikipedia as well as resonance in news articles (Rao et al., 2015: 3). Job titles, years of experience

and similar from LinkedIn are also factored in. It is also a computationally intensive, big data undertaking and an aggregated form of cross-platform analysis.

If one were to learn from Klout for social research, one manner would be to shift the focus from power (measures of increases or decreases in one's influence) to matters of concern (increases or decreases in attention, including that from significant others) – be these to events, disasters, elections, revolutions, social causes, and so forth. The shift in focus would be in keeping with how social media is often currently studied, as discussed above. That is, one could apply Klout's general procedure for counting user appearances, and ask, which causes are collectively significant across social media platforms, and which (key) actors, organisations and other users are linked to them, thereby granting them attention. Just as importantly, the attention granted to a cause by key actors, organisations and users may be neither undivided nor sustained. Such an observation would invite inquiries into partial attention as well as attention span, which together could begin to form a means to study engagement across social media.

When can so-called info-web methods based on the hyperlink still be applied to the study of the web and its platforms? By 'http or html approaches' to web 1.0, I mean software like the Issuecrawler and other hyperlink analysis tools, which, generally speaking, crawl a seed list of websites, locate hyperlinks either between them or between them and beyond them, and map the interlinkings, showing uni-directional, bi-directional as well as the absence of linking between websites (see Figure 5.3). Problems arise. Through automated hyperlink analysis, the researcher may miss relationships between websites which are not captured by hyperlinks, such as sites mentioning each other in text without linking. One may also miss links between websites because servers are down, or javascript or other code impenetrable to crawlers are employed on one or

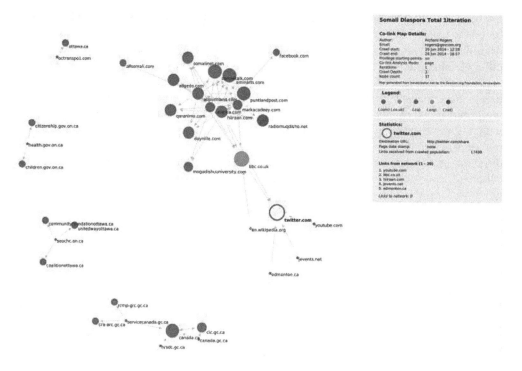

Figure 5.3   IssueCrawler map showing Twitter.com as significant node, albeit without showing individual, significant Twitter users

(*Source:* Issuecrawler.net, June 2014)

more websites in the network. Elmer and Langlois (2013) thereby proposed to follow keywords across websites as well as platforms.

As the info-web has evolved into a social web, hyperlink analysis generally captures links between pages or hosts on the web, but not on social media platforms, where only the host is returned (Facebook.com) rather than individual user profiles, such as a Facebook account, page or group or an individual Twitter user. (Similarly, Google continually

Table 5.1   Elements of cross-platform analysis (adapted from Rieder, 2015)

	Twitter	*Facebook*	*Instagram*
Query design	Hashtag(s), keyword(s), location(s), user(s)	Group(s), page(s)	Hashtag(s), location(s)
Data capture	In advance (for overtime data); on demand (for very recent data)	On demand (for overtime and recent data)	On demand (for overtime location data and recent hashtag data)
Platform user accounts (with primary actions)	user (follow)	user (friend, follow), group (join), page (like)	user (follow)
Content (media contents and digital objects)	tweet (text, photo, video, hashtag, @mention, URL, geotag)	post (text, video, photo, URL)	photo, video (text, hashtag, geotag, @mention)
Activities (resonance measures)	like (fav), retweet	like, comment, share	like, comment

experiments with how its web search returns Twitter and Facebook content, although it still privileges web content.) These drawbacks have occasioned researchers to move in two directions at once: develop crawlers and hyperlink analytical machines that pinpoint deep links between social media platforms and websites as well as within platforms (such as the Hyphe project[4]), and to consider new means to study relationships between platforms as well as between platforms and the web that do not rely on hyperlinks only. Joining in part with the call by Elmer and Langlois (2013), here the proposal would be to study content across the platforms (and the web): which content is co-linked, inter-liked and/or cross-hashtagged?

Co-linked content are URLs (often shortened on social media) that are linked by two or more users, platform pages or webpages. Inter-liked content is content liked by users and pages across platforms. Cross-hashtagged content is content referred to by hashtags across platforms. As they are often embedded social issues (and events), the hashtags themselves could be considered the content.

RESEARCH STRATEGIES FOR CROSS-PLATFORM ANALYSIS

We might ask, then, how to perform cross-platform analysis, and which platforms may be productively compared. When discussing the kind of research done with social media, even with the shift to the study of social causes over the self, it is worthwhile to point out that one may emphasise medium research, social research, or a combination of the two. For medium research, the question concerns how the platform affects the content, be it its presence or absence as well as its orderings. Additionally, specific cultures of use per platform, and (strategic) transmedia deployment, may inform the medium research, as discussed above. For social research, the

question concerns the story the content tells, despite the platform effects. For a combination of medium and social research, the questions are combined; how does the platform affect the availability of content, and what stories do the content tell, given platform effects? Thus for cross-platform analysis, the following steps may be taken.

1   Choose a contemporary issue (revolution, disaster, election, social cause, and so forth) for cross-platform analysis. One may choose to follow an active or unfolding issue (an issue in motion, so to speak), or one from recent history (an issue from the past, where overtime analysis is desirable). Here one should consider which platforms provide overtime data (Facebook), and which do not without great effort (Twitter).

2   Design a query strategy. For social issues and causes, consider querying for a program and an anti-program (Rogers, 2017). For example, in the 2015 US Supreme Court ruling for same-sex marriage the competing Twitter and Instagram hashtags reflected hashtag publics forming around a program and an anti-program, #lovewins and #jesuswins, respectively. If hashtags are preferred, for an election, consider querying a set of candidates or parties, e.g., #Trump and #Hillary (perhaps together with additional hashtags as well as keywords). For a disaster (or tragedy), consider querying its name(s), e.g., #MH17. URLs and/or domain names can be used as queries for a number of platforms.

3   Develop an analytical strategy. For social issues and causes, consider which program or anti-program is finding favour (including among whom and where). Does it have a set of networked publics and a particular geography? For an election, consider creating portrayals of the candidates via the associated issues, or comparing their relative resonance with current election polls. For a revolution, consider its momentum and durability (including the subjects that continue to matter and those that do not endure). For a disaster, consider how it is (continually) remembered or forgotten, and to which extent it has been and still is addressed and by whom.

4   Consider the configuration of use. It may be instructive for the analysis to look into how the platform is configured and set up by the

initiator(s). Is it a group or a page, with or without moderation? Is it centrally organised or a collective effort? Are comments allowed? Does the user have a distinctive follower strategy?

5   Cross-platform analysis. Undertake the platform analysis, according to the query design strategy as well as the analytical strategy discussed above, across two or more platforms. For each platform consider engagement measures, such as the sum of likes, shares, comments (Facebook), likes and retweets (Twitter) and co-hashtags (Instagram). Which (media) content resonates on which platforms? Consider which content is shared across the platforms (co-linked, inter-liked and cross-hashtagged), and which is distinctive, thereby enabling both networked platform content analysis as well as medium-specific (or platform-specific) effects.

6   Discuss your findings with respect to medium research, social research or a combination of the two. Does a particular platform tend to host as well as order content in ways distinctive from other platforms? Are the accounts of the events distinctively different per platform or utterly familiar no matter the platform?

In practice certain platforms lend themselves to comparison more artfully than others, given both the availability of objects such as the hashtag or geotag as well as roughly similar cultures of use. Through the vehicle of the hashtag, Twitter and Instagram (as well as Tumblr) are often the subject of cross-platform analysis. One queries the APIs with such tools as TCAT (for Twitter) as well as relatively simple Instagram and Tumblr hashtag explorers made available by the Digital Methods Initiative, creating collections of tweets and posts for further quantitative and qualitative analysis. Take, for example, certain significant events in the so-called migration crisis in Europe, one concerning the death of refugee children (Aylan Kurdi and his brother) and another the sexual assaults and rapes on New Year's Eve in Cologne (Geboers et al., 2016). For each case Twitter and Instagram are queried for hashtags (e.g., #aylan), whereupon tweet and post collections are made. For Twitter, one 'recipe' to sort

through the contents of the collections would include the following:

(a) Hashtag Frequency counts ascertain the other hashtags that co-occur, and is useful to explore the issue space. For the Cologne rape cases, the hashtag #einearmlänge co-occurs greatly, which was a trending topic referring to the remarks by the Cologne mayor that (as a solution) women should remain an arm's length away from so-called strangers.

(b) Mention Frequency lists the usernames of those who tweet and who are mentioned so one notes which users may dominate a space.

(c) Retweet Frequency provides a ranked list of retweeted tweets, showing popular or significant content.

(d) URL Frequency is a ranked URL list showing popular or significant media (such as images and video). The most referenced media, especially images, become a focal point for a cross-platform analysis with Twitter.

For Instagram, hashtag frequency is undertaken together with image and video frequency. (One is also able to query Instagram for geo-coordinates, which is not undertaken here.) Ultimately, the means of comparison are hashtag as well as image and video use, where the former suffers somewhat from hashtag stuffing in Instagram.

The question of platform effects is treated in the qualitative analysis, where in both the Aylan as well as the Cologne New Year's Eve cases the incidence of news photos was much greater in Twitter than in Instagram, where there were more derivatives, meaning annotated, photoshopped, cartoon-like or other DIY materials with (implied or explicit) user commentary. Twitter thereby becomes a professional medium (with effects) and Instagram more a user-generated content medium, becoming a particular, user-led form of news-following platform to which its founder has been aspiring. The Aylan case, however, appears to reduce this medium-specificity, because there is a relatively greater amount of images which have been edited so as to come to grips with the tragedy of the drowned toddler.

CONCLUSIONS: DIGITAL METHODS FOR CROSS-PLATFORM ANALYSIS

In the call for methodological attention to the platformisation of the web, Elmer and Langlois (2013) discuss how analyses based on the hyperlink do not embrace the analytical opportunities afforded by social media. Hyperlink analysis, and its tools such as the IssueCrawler, rely on an info-web (aka web 1.0), where webmasters make recommendations by linking to another website (or non-recommendations through not making links, thereby showing lack of interest or affiliation). Focusing on links only misses the novel objects of web 2.0, social networking sites, platforms and social media (as the social web has been called), such as the like, share and tweet. While Elmer and Langlois (2013) called for the analysis of the keyword over the hyperlink, but also perhaps over other social media objects, around the same time as their publication the API had arrived (Facebook's version 1.0 in 2010, Twitter's in 2006), and gradually became the preferred point of access to data over scraping, which the platforms actively sought to thwart. The API is of course controlled by the service in question, be it Twitter, Facebook or others, and steers research in ways more readily palpable perhaps than scraping, for the data available on the interface (that could be scraped) and through the developer's entry point may differ considerably. The ethics turn in web research, bound up with the rise of the social web and its publicly available, personal data, in turn has shaped the accessibility of certain data on the APIs such that Facebook no longer allows one to collect friends' 'tastes and ties', or likes, profile interests as well as friends. Such unavailability comes on the heels of a critique of a study of the same name that collected (or scraped, albeit with permission) Facebook profiles and friends' data from Harvard students and enriched it with their student housing information, without their knowledge. Concomitant with the decline in the study of

the self in social media analysis with digital methods (given the increasing dearth of available data through API restrictions) has been the rise in attention to events, disasters, elections, revolutions and social causes. Not only is it in evidence in Facebook research on (Arab Spring) pages (and to an extent groups), but also in Twitter (revolutions), where Jack Dorsey, its co-founder, signalled the shift in the interviews in the *Los Angeles Times* in 2009, mentioning that Twitter did well events such as disasters, elections as well as conferences. Instagram, according to its founder Kevin Systrom, would like to follow the same trajectory, becoming a platform of substance and thereby for the study of events (Goel, 2015). The API, however, appears to have shaped social media studies beyond its selective availability of data. Rather, the APIs serve as silos for what I call 'single-platform studies', which are reflected in the available tools discussed. Netvizz is for Facebook studies, TCAT for Twitter studies, the Instagram hashtag explorer for Instagram, and so forth. Unlike the web 1.0 tools such as IssueCrawler, which find links between websites and between websites and platforms, the social web has not seen tools developed for cross-platform analysis. Where to begin?

The purpose here is to develop techniques for multiple platform analysis that bear medium-sensitivity. Stock is taken of the objects that platforms share, whereupon cultures of use are taken into consideration. In other words, Twitter, Facebook and Instagram share the hashtag, however much, on the one, no more than two are recommended, on another it is rarely used and on the third it is used in overabundance. The cross-platform approaches that are ultimately described rely on hashtags for making collections of tweets (in Twitter) and posts (in Instagram), whereupon the media format (images, but also videos) common to the two are compared in the study of events. During the European refugee crisis of 2015–2016, the death of the toddler, Aylan Kurdi, and the sexual assaults of women in Cologne stand out as major (social media) events for analysis with a quanti-quali approach and a networked content analysis, which are forms of analysis with affinities with computational hermeneutics.

SUGGESTED RESOURCES

For tool tutorials, see the DMI 'tools walk-through' playlist on YouTube, www.youtube.com/playlist?list=PLKzQwIKtJvv9lwyYxh4708Nqo6YC6-YH4

1 **Instagram**
Instagram hashtag explorer, aka Visual Tagnet Explorer
http://tools.digitalmethods.net
Video tutorial for Instagram hashtag explorer, 'Analyze Instagram Activity Around a Hashtag or Location.' Note: since Instagram has blocked researcher use of its API in June 2016, one workaround is to locate and insert a token.
www.youtube.com/watch?v=o07aUKd Rv0g

2 **Twitter**
DMI-TCAT (Twitter Capture and Analysis Tool)
https://github.com/digitalmethods initiative/dmi-tcat/wiki
Video tutorial for TCAT, 'Overview of Analytical Modules'
www.youtube.com/watch?v=ex97 eoorUeo

3 **Facebook**
Netvizz (Facebook Data Extraction Tool)
https://apps.facebook.com/netvizz/
Netvizz video tutorials:
'Introduction to Netvizz 1.2+'
www.youtube.com/watch?v=3vkKP cN7V7Q
'Downloading data and producing a macro view'
www.youtube.com/watch?v=dfoYAP istYg

4 **Gephi-related**
Gephi (The Open Graph Viz Software)
https://gephi.org
'Gephi Tutorial for working with Twitter mention networks'
www.youtube.com/watch?v=snPR 8CwPld0
'Combine and Analyze Co-Hashtag Networks (Instagram, Twitter, etc.) with Gephi'
www.youtube.com/watch?v=ngqW jgZudeE

Notes

1 There certainly were social aspects to the early web, however much its dominant devices (Google web search, and Altavista before it) were oriented less to sociality than information compared to online platforms of a later period.

2 More specifically, these days recommendations could be said to be co-authored by the user and the system, whereas previously they were made by the site owner.

3 'Device culture' studies would inquire into the chain of interactions between user and platform that results in data collected and system-analysed so that ultimately content is recommended recursively back to the user (Rogers et al., 2013; Weltevrede, 2016).

4 See the Hyphe project at the MediaLab, Sciences Po, Paris, http://hyphe.medialab.sciences-po.fr/.

REFERENCES

Agar, John (2001). 'Review of James Gillies and Robert Cailliau, *How the Web was Born*. Oxford: Oxford University Press, 2000,' *The British Journal for the History of Science* 34(3): 370–373.

Allen, Matthew (2013). 'What Was Web 2.0? Versions as the Dominant Mode of Internet History,' *New Media & Society*, 15(2): 260–275.

Barbaro, Michael and Tom Zeller Jr (2006). 'A Face is Exposed for AOL Searcher no. 4417749,' *The New York Times*, p. A1.

Beer, David (2008). 'Social Network(ing) Sites… Revisiting the Story so far: A Response to danah boyd & Nicole Ellison,' *Journal of Computer-Mediated Communication*, 13(2): 516–529.

Bennett, W. Lance and Alexandra Segerberg (2012). 'The Logic of Connective Action: Digital Media and the Personalization of Contentious Politics,' *Information, Communication & Society*, 15(5): 739–768.

Berners-Lee, Tim (2014). 'Tim Berners-Lee on the Web at 25: the past, present and future,' *Wired*, 23 August.

Borra, Erik and Bernhard Rieder (2014). 'Programmed Method: Developing a Toolset for Capturing and Analyzing Tweets,' *Aslib Journal of Information Management*, 66(3): 262–278.

boyd, danah (2013). 'White Flight in Networked Publics? How Race and Class Shaped American Teen Engagement with Myspace and Facebook,' in Lisa Nakamura and Peter A. Chow-White (eds.), *Race after the Internet*. New York: Routledge, pp. 203–222.

boyd, danah and Nicole Ellison (2007). 'Social Network Sites: Definition, History and Scholarship,' *Journal of Computer-Mediated Communication*, 13(1), article 1.

Brandtzaeg, Petter Bae and Ida Maria Haugstveit (2014). 'Facebook Likes: A Study of Liking Practices for Humanitarian Causes,' *International Journal of Web Based Communities*, 10(3): 258–279.

Bruns, Axel (2007). 'Methodological for Mapping the Political Blogosphere: An Exploration Using the IssueCrawler Research Tool,' *First Monday*, 12(5).

Bruns, Axel and Jean Burgess (2015). 'Twitter Hashtags from Ad Hoc to Calculated Publics,' in Nathan Rambukkana (ed.), *Hashtag Publics: The Power and Politics of Discursive Networks*. New York: Peter Lang, pp. 13–28.

Bruns, Axel and Jean Burgess (2011). 'The use of Twitter hashtags in the formation of ad hoc publics,' Proceedings of the 6th European Consortium for Political Research (ECPR) General Conference 2011, University of Iceland, Reykjavik.

Bruns, Axel, Jean Burgess and Tim Highfield (2014). 'A "Big Data" Approach to Mapping the Australian Twittersphere,' in Paul Longley Arthur and Katherine Bode (eds.), *Advancing Digital Humanities: Research, Methods,*

Theories. Basingstoke: Palgrave Macmillan, pp. 113–129.

Bucher, Taina (2013). 'Objects of Intense Feeling: The Case of the Twitter API,' *Computational Culture: A Journal of Software Studies*, 4.

Chowdhury, Abdur (2009). 'Top Twitter Trends of 2009,' Twitter blog, 15 December, https://blog.twitter.com/official/en_us/a/2009/top-twitter-trends-of-2009.html.

Christensen, Henrik Serup (2011). 'Political Activities on the Internet: Slacktivism or Political Participation by Other Means?' *First Monday*, 16(2).

Constanza-Chock, Sasha (2014). *Out of the Shadows, Into the Streets! Transmedia Organising and the Immigrant Rights Movement*. Cambridge, MA: MIT Press.

Crampton, Jeremy W., Mark Graham, Ate Poorthuis, Taylor Shelton, Monica Stephens, Matthew W. Wilson and Matthew Zook (2013). 'Beyond the geotag: situating 'big data' and leveraging the potential of the geoweb,' *Cartography and Geographic Information Science*, 40(2): 130–139.

Dekker, Annet and Annette Wolfsberger (2009). *Walled Garden*. Amsterdam: Virtual Platform.

Dorsey, Jack (2008). 'Twitter Trends & a Tip,' Twitter blog, 5 September, https://blog.twitter.com/official/en_us/a/2008/twitter-trends-a-tip.html.

Elmer, Greg and Ganaele Langlois (2013). 'Networked Campaigns: Traffic Tags and Cross Platform Analysis on the Web,' *Information Polity*, 18(1): 43–56.

Engelberts, Lernert and Sander Plug (2009). 'I Love Alaska: The Heartbreaking Search History of AOL User #711391,' Minimovies Documentary. Amsterdam: Submarine Channel.

Facebook (2016). 'Facebook Platform Changelog,' Facebook for Developers, webpage, https://developers.facebook.com/docs/apps/changelog.

Facebook Liberation Army (2015). *Directives*. Amsterdam: Waag Society, http://fla.waag.org/downloads/FLA-Infographic.pdf.

Gaffney, Devin (2010). '#iranElection: Quantifying online activism,' *Proceedings of WebSci10*. New York: ACM.

Geboers, Marloes, Jan-Jaap Heine, Nienke Hidding, Julia Wissel, Marlie van Zoggel and Danny Simons (2016). 'Engagement with

Tragedy in Social Media,' Digital Methods Winter School '16, Amsterdam, https://wiki. digitalmethods.net/Dmi/WinterSchool2016 EngagementWithTragedySocialMedia.

Gerlitz, Carolin and Anne Helmond (2013). 'The Like Economy: Social Buttons and the Data-intensive Web,' *New Media & Society*, 15(8): 1348–1365.

Gerlitz, Carolin and Bernhard Rieder (2013). 'Mining One Percent of Twitter: Collections, Baselines, Sampling,' *M/C Journal*, 16(2).

Gillespie, Tarleton (2010). 'The Politics of "Platforms",' *New Media & Society*, 12(3): 347–364.

Gillespie, Tarleton (2012). 'Can an Algorithm be Wrong?' *Limn*, 2.

Goel, Vindu (2015). 'Instagram to Offer Millions of Current Events Photos,' *New York Times*, 23 June.

Helmond, Anne (2015). 'The Web as Platform: Data Flows in Social Media,' PhD dissertation, University of Amsterdam.

Hindman, Matthew (2008). *The Myth of Digital Democracy*. Princeton, NJ: Princeton University Press.

Ito, Mizuko (2008). 'Introduction,' in Kazys Varnelis (ed.), *Networked Publics*. Cambridge, MA: MIT Press, pp. 1–14.

Jenkins, Henry (2006). *Convergence Culture*. New York: New York University Press.

Eslami, Motahhare, Aimee Rickman, Kristen Vaccaro, Amirhossein Aleyasen, Andy Vuong, Karrie Karahalios, Kevin Hamilton and Christian Sandvig (2015). '"I always assumed that I wasn't really that close to [her]": Reasoning about Invisible Algorithms in News Feeds,' *CHI 2015, Crossings*, Seoul, South Korea. New York: ACM.

Kennedy, Helen and Rosemary Lucy Hill (2016). 'The Pleasure and Pain of Visualizing Data in Times of Data Power,' *Television & New Media*, first published 7 September, pp. 1–14, 10.1177/1527476416667823.

Kramer, Adam D.I., Jamie E. Guilloryb and Jeffrey T. Hancock (2014). 'Experimental Evidence of Massive-scale Emotional Contagion through Social Networks,' *PNAS*, 111(24): 8788–8790.

Latour, Bruno (2005). *Reassembling the Social*. New York: Oxford University Press.

Lewis, Kevin, Jason Kaufman, Marco Gonzalez, Andreas Wimmer and Nicholas Christakis (2008). 'Tastes, Ties, and Time: A New Social Network Dataset Using Facebook.com,' *Social Networks*, 30(4): 330–342.

Lotan, Gilad, Erhardt Graeff, Mike Ananny, Devin Gaffney, Ian Pearce and danah boyd (2011). 'The Revolutions were Tweeted: Information Flows during the 2011 Tunisian and Egyptian Revolutions,' *International Journal of Communication*, 5: 1375–1405.

Marres, Noortje (2015). 'Why Map Issues? On Controversy Analysis as a Digital Method,' *Science, Technology, & Human Values*, 40(5): 655–686.

Marres, Noortje and Esther Weltevrede (2013). 'Scraping the Social? Issues in Live Social Research,' *Journal of Cultural Economy*, 6(3): 313–335.

Messina, Chris (2007). 'Groups for Twitter; or A Proposal for Twitter Tag Channels,' *Factory Joe blog*, 25 August, http://factoryjoe.com/blog/2007/08/25/groups-for-twitter-or-a-proposal-for-twitter-tag-channels/.

Meyer, Michelle N. (2015). 'Two Cheers for Corporate Experimentation: The A/B Illusion and the Virtues of Data-Driven Innovation,' *Colorado Technology Law Journal*, 13(2): 273–332.

Mohr, John W., Robin Wagner-Pacifici and Ronald L. Breiger (2015). 'Toward a Computational Hermeneutics,' *Big Data & Society*, 2(2).

Niederer, Sabine (2016). 'Networked Content Analysis: The Case of Climate Change,' PhD dissertation, University of Amsterdam.

Nissenbaum, Helen (2009). *Privacy in Context: Technology, Policy, and the Integrity of Social Life*. Stanford, CA: Stanford University Press.

O'Reilly, Tim (2005). 'What is Web 2.0: Design Patterns and Business Models for the Next-Generation of Software,' O'Reilly, Sebastopol, CA: O'Reilly Media, www.oreilly.com/pub/a/web2/archive/what-is-web-20.html.

Papacharissi, Zizi (2015). *Affective Publics*. New York: Oxford University Press.

Pariser, Eli (2011). *The Filter Bubble*. New York: Penguin.

Portwood-Stacer, Laura (2013). 'Media Refusal and Conspicuous Non-consumption: The Performative and Political Dimensions of Facebook Abstention,' *New Media & Society*, 15(7): 1041–1057.

Puschmann, Cornelius and Jean Burgess (2013). 'The Politics of Twitter Data,' in Katrin Weller, Axel Bruns, Jean Burgess, Merja Mahrt and Cornelius Puschmann (eds.), *Twitter and Society*. New York: Peter Lang, pp. 43–54.

Puschmann, Cornelius and Engin Bozdag (2014). 'Staking Out the Unclear Ethical Terrain of Online Social Experiments,' *Internet Policy Review*, 3(4).

Rao, Adithya, Nemanja Spasojevic, Zhisheng Li and Trevor DSouza (2015). 'Klout Score: Measuring Influence across Multiple Social Networks,' *2015 IEEE International Big Data Conference – Workshop on Mining Big Data in Social Networks*. New York: ACM.

Rieder, Bernhard (2012). 'What is PageRank? A Historical and Conceptual Investigation of a Recursive Status Index,' *Computational Culture*, 2.

Rieder, Bernhard (2013). 'Studying Facebook via Data Extraction: The Netvizz Application,' in *Proceedings of the 5th Annual ACM Web Science Conference*. New York: ACM Press, pp. 346–355.

Rieder, Bernhard (2015). 'Social Media Data Analysis,' lecture delivered at the University of Amsterdam, December.

Rieder, Bernhard, Rasha Abdulla, Thomas Poell, Robbert Woltering and Liesbeth Zack (2015). 'Data Critique and Analytical Opportunities for Very Large Facebook Pages: Lessons Learned from Exploring 'We are all Khaled Said,' *Big Data & Society*, 2(2): 1–22.

Robinson, Piers (2002). *The CNN Effect: The Myth of News, Foreign Policy and Intervention*. London: Routledge.

Rogers, Richard (2009a) 'Mapping Public Web Space with the Issuecrawler,' in C. Brossard and B. Reber (eds.), *Digital Cognitive Technologies: Epistemology and Knowledge Society*. London: Wiley, pp. 115–126.

Rogers, Richard (2009b). 'Post-demographic Machines,' in Annet Dekker and Annette Wolfsberger (eds.), *Walled Garden*. Amsterdam: Virtual Platform, pp. 29–39.

Rogers, Richard (2013a). 'Debanalizing Twitter: The Transformation of an Object of Study,' *Proceedings of WebSci13*. New York: ACM.

Rogers, Richard (2013b). *Digital Methods*. Cambridge, MA: MIT Press.

Rogers, Richard (2017). 'Foundations of Digital Methods: Query Design,' in Mirko Schaefer and Karin van Es (eds.), *The Datafied Society: Studying Culture through Data*. Amsterdam: Amsterdam University Press.

Rogers, Richard, Esther Weltevrede, Erik Borra, Marieke van Dijk and the Digital Methods Initiative (2009). 'For the ppl of Iran: #iranelection RT,' in Gennaro Ascione, Cinta Massip and Josep Perello (eds.), *Cultures of Change: Social Atoms and Electronic Lives*. Barcelona: Actar and Arts Santa Monica, pp. 112–115.

Rogers, Richard, Esther Weltevrede, Sabine Niederer and Erik Borra (2013). 'National Web Studies: The Case of Iran Online,' in John Hartley, Axel Bruns and Jean Burgess (eds.), *A Companion to New Media Dynamics*. Oxford: Blackwell, pp. 142–166.

Sarno, David (2009). 'Jack Dorsey on the Twitter Ecosystem, Journalism and How to Reduce Reply Spam: Part II,' *Los Angeles Times*, 19 February.

Scholz, Trebor (2008). 'Market Ideology and the Myths of Web 2.0,' *First Monday*, 13(3).

Scholz, Trebor (2016). 'Platform Cooperativism. Challenging the Corporate Sharing Economy,' New York: Rosa Luxemburg Stiftung.

Senft, Theresa and Nancy Baym (2015). 'What Does the Selfie Say? Investigating a Global Phenomenon,' *International Journal of Communication*, 9: 1588–1606.

Stutzman, Fred, Ralph Gross and Alessandro Acquisti (2013). 'Silent Listeners: The Evolution of Privacy and Disclosure on Facebook,' *Journal of Privacy and Confidentiality*, 4(2), article 2.

Twitter (2016). 'Using Hashtags on Twitter,' Help Center, San Francisco, CA: Twitter, Inc., https://support.twitter.com/articles/49309

Van Couvering, Elizabeth (2007). 'Is Relevance Relevant? Market, Science, and War: Discourses of Search Engine Quality,' *Journal of Computer-Mediated Communication*, 12(3), article 6.

Van de Poel, Ibo (2009). 'The Introduction of Nanotechnology as a Societal Experiment,' in Simone Arnaldi, Andrea Lorenzet and Federica Russo (eds.), *Technoscience in Progress: Managing the Uncertainty of Nanotechnology*. Amsterdam: IOS Press, pp. 129–142.

Venturini, Tommaso, Dominique Cardon and Jean-Philippe Cointet (2014a). 'Présentation – Méthodes digitales: Approches quali/quanti des données numériques,' *Réseaux*, 188(6): 9–21.

Venturini, Tommaso, Nicolas Baya Laffite, Jean-Philippe Cointet, Ian Gray, Vinciane Zabban and Kari De Pryck (2014b). 'Three Maps and Three Misunderstandings: A Digital Mapping of Climate Diplomacy,' *Big Data & Society*, 1(2).

Weltevrede, Esther (2016). 'Repurposing Digital Methods: The Research Affordances of Engines and Platforms,' PhD dissertation, University of Amsterdam.

Zimmer, Michael (2008). 'More on the "Anonymity" of the Facebook Dataset – It's Harvard College,' Michaelzimmer.org blog, http://michaelzimmer.org/2008/10/03/moreon-the-anonymity-of-the-facebook-dataset-its-harvard-college/

Zimmer, Michael (2010). 'But the Data is Already Public: On the Ethics of Research in Facebook,' *Ethics and Information Technology*, 12(4): 313–325.

6

A Computational Analysis of Social Media Scholarship

Jeremy Foote, Aaron Shaw
and Benjamin Mako Hill

INTRODUCTION

The combination of large-scale trace data generated through social media with a series of advances in computing and statistics have enabled the growth of 'computational social science' (Lazer et al., 2009). This turn presents an unprecedented opportunity for researchers who can now test social theories using massive datasets of fine-grained, unobtrusively collected behavioral data. In this chapter, we aim to introduce non-technical readers to the promise of these computational social science techniques by applying three of the most common approaches to a bibliographic dataset of social media scholarship. We use our analyses as a context for discussing the benefits of each approach as well as some of the common pitfalls and dangers of computational approaches.

The chapter walks through the entire process of computational analysis, beginning with data collection. We explain how we gather a large-scale dataset about social media research from the *Scopus* website's application programming interface. The dataset we collect contains metadata about every article in the Scopus database that includes the term 'social media' in its title, abstract, or keywords. Using this dataset, we perform multiple computational analyses. First, we use network analysis (Wasserman & Faust, 1994) on article citation metadata to understand the structure of references between the articles. Second, we use topic models (Blei, 2012), an unsupervised natural language processing technique, to describe the distribution of topics within the sample of articles included in our analysis. Third, we perform statistical prediction (James et al., 2013) in order to understand what characteristics of articles best predict subsequent citations. For each analysis, we describe the method we use in detail and discuss some of its benefits and limitations.

Our results reveal several patterns in social media scholarship. Bibliometric network data reveals disparities in the degree that disciplines cite each other and illustrates that marketing and medical research each enjoy surprisingly large influence. Through descriptive analysis and topic modeling, we find evidence of the early influence of social network research. When we use papers' characteristics to predict which work gets cited, we find that publication venues and linguistic features provide the most explanatory power.

In carrying out our work in this chapter, we seek to exemplify several current best practices in computational research. We use data collected in a manner consistent with the expectations of privacy and access held by the subjects of our analysis as well as the publishers of the data source. We also make our analysis fully reproducible from start to finish. In an online supplement, we provide the full source code for all aspects of this project – from the beginning of data collection to the creation of the figures and the chapter text itself – as a resource for future researchers.

COLLECTING AND DESCRIBING DATA FROM THE WEB

A major part of computational research consists of obtaining data, preparing it for analysis, and generating initial descriptions that can help guide subsequent inquiry. Social media datasets vary in how they make it into researchers' hands. There are several sources of social media data which are provided in a form that is pre-processed and ready for analysis. For example, The Stanford Large Network Dataset Collection (Leskovec & Krevl, 2014) contains pre-formatted and processed data from a variety of social media platforms. Typically, prepared datasets come formatted as 'flat files' such as comma-separated value (CSV) tables, which many types of statistical software and programming tools can import directly.

More typically, researchers retrieve data directly from social media platforms or other web-based sources. These 'primary' sources provide more extensive, dynamic, and up-to-date datasets, but also require much more work to prepare the data for analysis. Typically, researchers retrieve these data from social media sites through application programming interfaces (APIs). Web sites and platforms use APIs to provide programmers with limited access to their servers and databases. Unfortunately, APIs are rarely designed with research in mind and are often inconvenient and limited for social scientists as a result. For example, Twitter's search API returns a small, non-random sample of tweets by default (what a user might want to read), rather than all of the tweets that match a given query (what a researcher building a sample would want). In addition, APIs typically limit how much data they will provide for each query and how many queries can be submitted within a given time period.

APIs provide raw data in formats like XML or JSON, which are poorly suited to most data analysis tasks. As a result, researchers must take the intermediate step of converting data into more appropriate formats and structures. Typically, researchers must also construct measures from the raw data, such as user-level statistics (e.g., number of retweets) or metadata (e.g., post length). A number of tools, such as NodeXL (Hansen, Shneiderman, & Smith, 2010), exist to make the process of obtaining and preparing digital trace data easier. However, off-the-shelf tools tend to come with their own limitations and, in our experience, gathering data amenable to computational analysis usually involves some programming work.

Compared to some traditional forms of data collection, obtaining and preparing social media data has high initial costs. It frequently involves writing and debugging custom software, reading documentation about APIs, learning new software libraries, and testing datasets for completeness and accuracy. However, computational methods scale very well and gathering additional data often simply means expanding the date range in a program. Contrast this with interviews, surveys, or experiments, where recruitment is often labor-intensive, expensive, and slow. Such scalability, paired with the massive participation on many social media platforms, can support the collection of very large samples.

Our Application: The Scopus Bibliographic Database

We used a series of Scopus Bibliographic Database APIs to retrieve data about all of the publications in their database that contained the phrase 'social media' in their abstract, title, or keywords. We used the Python programming language to write custom software to download this data. First, we wrote a program to query the Scopus Search API to retrieve a list of the articles that matched our criteria. We stored the resulting list of 23,131 articles in a file. We used this list of articles as input to a second program, which used the Scopus Citations Overview API to retrieve metadata about all of the articles that cited these 23,131 articles. Finally, we wrote a third program that used the Scopus Abstract Retrieval API to download abstracts and additional metadata about the original 23,131 articles. Due to rate limits and the process of trial and error involved in writing, testing, and debugging these custom programs, it took a few weeks to obtain the complete dataset.

Like many social media APIs, the Scopus APIs return data in JSON format. Although

not suitable for analysis without processing, we stored this JSON data in the form it was given to us. Retaining the 'raw' data as it was provided by APIs allows researchers to construct new measures they might not have believed were relevant in the early stages of their research and to fix any bugs that they find in their data processing and reduction code without having to re-download raw data. Once we obtained the raw data, we wrote additional Python scripts to turn the downloaded JSON files into CSV tables which could be imported into Python and R, the programming languages we used to complete our analyses.

Results

The Scopus dataset contains a wide variety of data, and many different descriptive statistics could speak to various research questions. Here we present a sample of the sorts of summary data that computational researchers might explore. We begin by looking at where social media research is produced. Table 6.1 shows the number of papers produced by authors located in each of the six most frequently seen countries in our dataset.[1] We can immediately see that the English-language world produces much of the research on social media (which is perhaps unsurprising given that our search term was in English), but that a large amount of research comes from authors in China and Germany.

Next we look at the disciplines that publish social media research. Figure 6.1 shows the

Table 6.1 Top author countries by number of social media papers

Country	Number of Papers
United States	7812
United Kingdom	1711
Australia	1096
China	926
Germany	787
Canada	771

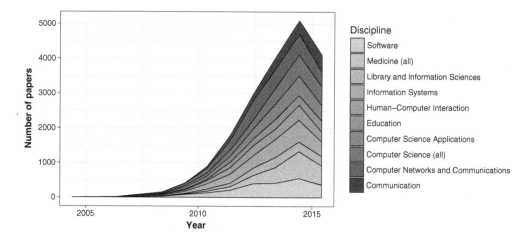

Figure 6.1   Social media papers published in the top ten disciplines (as categorized by Scopus), over time

number of papers containing the term 'social media' over time.

The plot illustrates that the quantity of published research on social media has increased rapidly over time. The growth appears to slow down more recently, but this may be due to the speed at which the Scopus database imports data about new articles. Figure 6.1 shows the top ten disciplines, as categorized by Scopus. We see that the field started off dominated by computer science publications, with additional disciplines increasing their activity in recent years. This story is also reflected in the top venues, listed in Table 6.2, where we see that computer science venues have published social media research most frequently.

We then consider the impact of this set of papers as measured by the citations they have received. Like many phenomena in social systems, citation counts follow a highly skewed distribution with a few papers receiving many citations and most papers receiving very few.

Table 6.3 provides a list of the most cited papers. These sorts of distributions suggest the presence of 'preferential attachment' (Barabási & Albert, 1999) or 'the "Matthew effects"' (Merton, 1968), where success leads to greater success.

Discussion

The summary statistics and exploratory visualizations presented above provide an overview of the scope and trajectory of social media research. We find that social media

Table 6.2   Venues with the most social media papers

Publication Venue	Papers
Lecture Notes in Computer Science	935
ACM International Conference Proceeding Series	288
Computers in Human Behavior	257
CEUR Workshop Proceedings	227
Proceedings of the Hawaii International Conference on System Sciences	179
Journal of Medical Internet Research	170

Table 6.3 Most cited social media papers

Title	Publication Venue	Cited by
Users of the world, unite! The challenges and opportunities of Social Media	Business Horizons	1876
Why we twitter: Understanding microblogging usage and communities	Proceedings of WebKDD/ SNA-KDD 2007	645
Social media? Get serious! Understanding the functional building blocks of social media	Business Horizons	468
Social media: The new hybrid element of the promotion mix	Business Horizons	450
Role of social media in online travel information search	Tourism Management	389
Networked narratives: Understanding word-of-mouth marketing in online communities	Journal of Marketing	335

research is growing – both overall and within many disciplines. We find evidence that computer scientists laid the groundwork for the study of social media, but that social scientists, learning scientists, and medical researchers have increasingly been referring to social media in their published work. We also find several business and marketing papers among the most cited pieces of social media research even though neither these disciplines nor their journals appear among the most prevalent in the dataset.

These results are interesting and believable because they come from a comprehensive database of academic work. In most social science contexts, researchers have to sample from a population and that sampling is often biased. For example, the people willing to come to a lab to participate in a study or take a phone survey may have different attributes from those unwilling to participate. This makes generalizing to the entire population problematic. When using trace data, on the other hand, we often have data from all members of a community, including those who would not have chosen to participate. One of the primary benefits of collecting data from a comprehensive resource like Scopus is that it can reduce some types of bias in the data collection process. For example, we do not have backgrounds in education or medical research; had we tried to summarize the state of social media research

by identifying articles and journals manually, we might have overlooked these disciplines.

That said, this apparent benefit can also become a liability when we seek to generalize our results beyond the community that we have data for. The large N of big data studies using social media traces may make results appear more valid, precise, or certain, but a biased sample does not become less biased just because it is larger (Hargittai, 2015). For example, a sample of 100 million Twitter users might be a worse predictor of election results than a truly random sample of only 1,000 likely voters because Twitter users likely have different attributes and opinions than the voting public. Another risk comes from the danger that data providers collect or filter data in ways that aren't apparent. Researchers should think carefully about the relationship of their data to the population they wish to study and find ways to estimate bias empirically.

Overall, we view the ease of obtaining and analyzing digital traces as one of the most exciting developments in social science. Although the hurdles involved represent a real challenge to many scholars of social media today, learning the technical skills required to obtain online trace data is no more challenging than the statistics training that is part of many PhD programs. Below, we present examples of a few computational analyses that can be done with this sort of data.

NETWORK ANALYSIS

Social network analysis encompasses the most established set of computational methods in the social sciences (Wasserman & Faust, 1994). At its core, network analysis revolves around a 'graph' representation of data that tries to capture relationships (called edges) between discrete objects (called nodes). Graphs can represent any type of object and relationship, such as roads connecting a group of cities or shared ingredients across a set of recipes. Graph representations of data, and the network analytic methods built to reason using these data, are widely used across the social sciences as well as other fields, including physics, genomics, computer science, and philosophy. 'Social network analysis' constitutes a specialized branch of network analysis in which nodes represent people (or other social entities) and edges represent social relationships like friendship, interaction, or communication.

The power of network analysis stems from its capacity to reduce a very large and complex dataset to a relatively simple set of relations that possess enormous explanatory power. For example, Hausmann et al. (2014) use network data on the presence or absence of trading relationships between countries to build a series of extremely accurate predictions about countries' relative wealth and economic performance over time. By reasoning over a set of relationships in a network, Hausmann and his colleagues show that details of the nature or amount of goods exchanged are not necessary to arrive at accurate economic conclusions.

Network analysis has flourished in studies of citation patterns within scholarly literature, called 'bibliometrics' or 'scientometrics.' Bibliometric scholars have developed and applied network analytic tools for more than a half-century (Kessler, 1963; Hood & Wilson, 2001). As a result, bibliometric analysis provides an obvious jumping-off point for our tour of computational methods. Because network methods reflect a whole family of statistics, algorithms, and applications, we focus on approaches that are both well suited to bibliometric analysis and representative of network analyses used in computational social science more broadly.

Our Application: Citation Networks

Our network analysis begins by representing citation information we collected from the Scopus APIs as a graph. In our representation, each node represents a paper and each edge represents a citation. Scopus provides data on incoming citations for each article. Our full dataset includes 35,620 incoming citations to the 23,131 articles in Scopus with 'social media' in their titles, abstracts, or keywords. 19,267 of these articles (83%) have not been cited even once by another article in Scopus and 18,324 (79%) do not cite any other article in our sample. The recent development of social media and the rapid growth of the field depicted in Figure 6.1 might help explain the sparseness (i.e., lack of connections) of the graph. As a result, and as is often the case in network analysis, a majority of our dataset plays no role in our analysis described in the rest of this section.

Once we create our citation graph, there are many potential ways to analyze it. One important application, common to bibliometrics, is the computational identification of communities or clusters within networks. In network studies, the term 'community' is used to refer to groups of nodes that are densely connected to each other but relatively less connected to other groups. In bibliometric analyses, communities can describe fields or sub-fields of articles which cite each other, but are much less likely to cite or be cited by papers in other groups. Although there are many statistical approaches to community detection in network science, we use a technique from Rosvall and Bergstrom (2008) that has been identified as appropriate for the study of bibliometric networks (Šubelj, van Eck, & Waltman, 2016). By looking at the most frequently occurring journals and publication venues in each community, we are able to identify and name sub-fields of social media research as distinct communities.

A citation graph is only one possible network representation of the relationships between articles. For example, the use of common topics or terminology might constitute another type of edge. Alternatively, journals or individual authors (rather than articles) might constitute an alternative source of nodes. In bibliometric analyses, for example, it is common for edges to represent 'co-citation' between articles or authors. Using this approach, papers are said to be tied together by a co-citation if they have both been cited in a third document (Small, 1973). Due to limited space, we only present the simplest case of direct citations.

Results

As is common in social networks, the large majority of articles with any citations connect to each other in one large '"component" or sub-network.' Figure 6.2 shows a visualization of this large component. The optimal way to represent network data in two-dimensional space is a topic of research and debate. Figure 6.2 uses a force-directed drawing technique (Fruchterman & Reingold, 1991), the most widely used algorithm in network visualization, using the free/open source software package Gephi (Bastian, Heymann, & Jacomy, 2009). The basic idea behind the algorithm is that nodes naturally push away from each other, but are pulled together by the edges between them. Shades in each graph in this section reflect the communities of documents identified by Rosvall and colleagues' 'map' algorithm (Rosvall & Bergstrom, 2008; Rosvall, Axelsson, & Bergstrom, 2010).

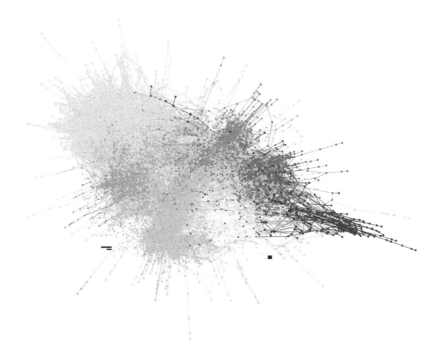

Figure 6.2   Network visualization of the citation network in our dataset. The layout is 'force directed' meaning that nodes (papers) with more edges (citations) appear closer to the center of the figure

Table 6.4   Description of each of the citation network clusters identified by the community detection algorithm, together with a list of the three most common journals in each community

Community	Description	Journals
Community 1	biomedicine; bioinformatics	Journal of Medical Internet Research; PLoS ONE; Studies in Health Technology and Informatics
Community 2	information technology; management	Computers in Human Behavior; Business Horizons; Journal of Interactive Marketing
Community 3	communication	Information Communication and Society; New Media and Society; Journal of Communication
Community 4	computer science; network science	Lecture Notes in Computer Science; PLoS ONE; WWW; KDD
Community 5	psychology; psychometrics	Computers in Human Behavior; Cyberpsychology, Behavior, and Social Networking; Computers and Education
Community 6	Multimedia	IEEE Transactions on Multimedia; Lecture Notes in Computer Science; ACM Multimedia

Although the algorithm identified several dozen communities, most are extremely small, so we have shown only the largest six communities in Figure 6.2. Each of these communities are summarized in Table 6.4 where the right-most column lists the three most common journals for the articles included in each community.

At this point, we could look in more depth at the attributes of the different communities. For example, in a bibliometric analysis published in the journal *Scientometrics*, Kovács, Looy, and Cassiman (2015) reported summary statistics for articles in each of the major communities identified (e.g., the average number of citations) as well as qualitative descriptions of the nodes in each community. We can see from looking at Table 6.4 that the communities point to the existence of coherent thematic groups. For example, Community 1 includes biomedical research, while Community 3 contains papers published in communication journals. Earlier, we relied on an existing category scheme applied to journals to create Figure 6.1; all articles published in particular journals were treated as being within one field. Network analysis, however, can identify groups and categories of articles in terms of who is citing whom and, as a result, can reveal groups that cross journal boundaries. *PLoS ONE*,

for example, is a 'megajournal' that publishes articles from all scientific fields (Binfield, 2012). As a result, *PLoS ONE* is one of the most frequently included journals in both Community 1 and Community 4. In a journal-based categorization system, articles may be misclassified or not classified at all.

Network analysis can also reveal details about the connections between fields. Figure 6.3 shows a second network we have created in which our communities are represented as nodes and citations from articles in one community to articles in the other communities are represented as edges. The thickness of each edge represents the number of citations and the graph shows the directional strength of the relative connections between communities. For example, the graph suggests that the communication studies community (Community 3) cites many papers in information technology and management (Community 2) but that this relationship is not reciprocated.

Discussion

Like many computational methods, the power of network techniques comes from representing complex relationships in simplified forms.

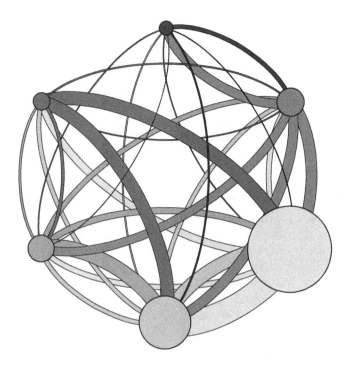

Figure 6.3 Graphical representation of citations between communities using the same grayscale mapping described in Table 6.4. The size of the nodes reflects the total number of papers in each community. The thickness of each edge reflects the number of outgoing citations. Edges are directional, and share the color of their source (i.e., citing) community

Although elegant and powerful, the network analysis approach is inherently reductive in nature and limited in many ways. What we gain in our ability to analyze millions or billions of individuals comes at the cost of speaking about particular individuals and sub-groups. A second limitation stems from the huge number of relationships that can be represented in graphs. A citation network and a co-citation network, for example, represent different types of connections and these differences might lead an algorithm to identify different communities. As a result, choices about the way that edges and nodes are defined can lead to very different conclusions about the structure of a network or the influence of particular nodes. Network analyses often treat all connections and all nodes as similar in ways that mask important variation.

Network analysis is built on the assumption that knowing about the relationships between individuals in a system is often as important, and sometimes more important, than knowing about the individuals themselves. It inherently recognizes interdependence and the importance of social structure. This perspective comes with a cost, however. The relational structure and interdependence of social networks make it impossible to use traditional statistical methods. SNA practitioners have had to move to more complex modeling strategies and simulations to test hypotheses.

TEXT ANALYSIS

Social media produces an incredible amount of text, and social media researchers often analyze the content of this text. For example, researchers use ethnographic approaches

(Kozinets, 2002) or content analysis (Chew & Eysenbach, 2010) to study the texts of interactions online. Because the amount of text available for analysis is far beyond the ability of any set of researchers to analyze by hand, scholars increasingly turn to computational approaches. Some of these analyses are fairly simple, such as tracking the occurrence of terms related to a topic or psychological construct (Tausczik & Pennebaker, 2010). Others are more complicated, using tools from natural language processing (NLP). NLP includes a range of approaches in which algorithms are applied to texts, such as machine translation, optical character recognition, and part-of-speech tagging. Perhaps the most common use in the social sciences is sentiment analysis, in which the affect of a piece of text is intuited based on the words that are used (Asur & Huberman, 2010). Many of these techniques have applications for social media research.

One natural language processing technique – topic modeling – is used increasingly often in computational social science research. Topic modeling seeks to identify topics automatically within a set of documents. In this sense, topic modeling is analogous to content analysis or other manual forms of document coding and labeling. However, topic models are a completely automated, 'unsupervised' computational method – i.e., topic modeling algorithms do not require any sort of human intervention, such as hand-coded training data or dictionaries of terms. Topic modeling scales well to even very large datasets, and is most usefully applied to large corpora of text where labor-intensive methods like manual coding are simply not an option.

When using the technique, a researcher begins by feeding topic modeling software the texts that she would like to find topics for and by specifying the number of topics to be returned. There are multiple algorithms for identifying topics, but we focus on the most common: *latent Dirichlet allocation* or LDA (Blei, Ng, & Jordan, 2003). The nuts and bolts of how LDA works are complex and beyond the scope of this chapter, but the basic goal is fairly simple: LDA identifies sets of words that are likely to be used together and calls these sets 'topics.' For example, a computer science paper is likely to use words like 'algorithm', 'memory', and 'network.' While a communication article might also use 'network,' it would be much less likely to use 'algorithm' and more likely to use words like 'media' and 'influence.' The other key feature of LDA is that it does not treat documents as belonging to only one topic but as consisting of a mixture of multiple topics with different degrees of emphasis. For example, an LDA analysis might characterize this chapter as a mixture of computer science and communication (among other topics).

LDA identifies topics inductively from the observed distributions of words in documents. The LDA algorithm looks at all of the words that co-occur within a corpus of documents and assumes that words used in the same document are more likely to be from the same topic. The algorithm then looks across all of the documents and finds the set of topics and topic distributions that would be, in a statistical sense, most likely to produce the observed documents. LDA's output is the set of topics: ranked lists of words likely to be used in documents about each topic, as well as the distribution of topics in each document. DiMaggio, Nag, and Blei (2013) argue that while many aspects of topic modeling are simplistic, many of the assumptions have parallels in sociological and communication theory. Perhaps more importantly, the topics created by LDA frequently correspond to human intuition about how documents should be grouped or classified.

The results of topic models can be used in many ways. Our dataset includes 73 publications with the term 'LDA' in their abstracts. Some of these papers use topic models to conduct large-scale content analysis, such as looking at the topics used around health on Twitter (Prier et al., 2011; Ghosh & Guha, 2013). Researchers commonly use topic modeling for prediction and machine learning tasks, such as predicting a user's gender or personality type (Schwartz et al., 2013). Papers in the dataset also use LDA to predict transitions between topics (Wang, Agichtein, & Benzi, 2012), to recommend friends based on similar topic use (Pennacchiotti & Gurumurthy, 2011), and to identify interesting tweets on Twitter (Yang & Rim, 2014).

Our Application: Identifying Topics in Social Media Research

We apply LDA to the texts of abstracts in our dataset in order to identify topics in social media research. We show how topics are extracted and labeled and then use data on topic distributions to show how the focus of social media research has changed over time. We begin by collecting each of the abstracts for the papers in our sample. Scopus does not include abstract text for 2,801 of the 23,131 articles in our sample. We examined a random sample of the entries with missing abstracts by hand, and found that abstracts for many simply never existed (e.g., articles published in trade journals or books). Other articles had published abstracts, but the text of these abstracts, for reasons that are not clear, were not available through Scopus.[2] We proceed with the 20,330 articles in our sample for which abstract data was available. The average abstract in this dataset is 177 words long, with a max of 1,353 words and a minimum of 5 ('The proceedings contain 15 papers.').

We then remove 'stop words' (common words like 'the,' 'of,' etc.) and tokenize the documents by breaking them into unigrams and bigrams (one-word and two-word terms). We analyze the data using the Python *LatentDirichletAllocation* module from the *scikit-learn* library (Pedregosa, 2011). Choosing the appropriate number of topics to be returned (typically referred to as k) is a matter of some debate and research

(e.g., Arun et al., 2010). After experimenting with different values of k, plotting the distribution of topics each time in a way similar to the graphs shown in Figure 6.4, we ultimately set k as twelve. At higher values of k, additional topics only rarely appeared in the abstracts.

Results

Table 6.5 shows the top words for each of the topics discovered by the LDA model, sorted by how common each topic is in our dataset. At this point, researchers typically evaluate the lists of words for coherence and give names to each of the topics. For example, after looking at the words associated with Topic 1 we gave it the name 'Media Use.' Of course, many other names for this topic could be chosen. We might call it 'Facebook research' because it is the only topic which includes the term 'facebook.' Researchers often validate these names by looking at some of the texts which score highest for each topic and subjectively evaluating the appropriateness of the chosen name as a label for those texts. For example, we examined the abstracts of the five papers with the highest value for the 'Media Use' topic and confirmed that we were comfortable claiming that they were examples of research about media use. In this way, topic modeling requires a mixture of both quantitative and qualitative interpretation. The computer provides results, but making sense of those results requires familiarity with the data.

The top panel of Figure 6.4 shows how the distribution of topics identified by LDA in our analysis has changed over time. The LDA algorithm gives each abstract a probability distribution over each of the topics, such that it sums to 1 (e.g., a given abstract may be 80% 'Social Network Analysis,' 20% 'Education,' and 0% everything else). To construct Figure 6.4, we sum these percentages for all of the documents published in each year and plot the resulting prevalence of each topic over time.[3]

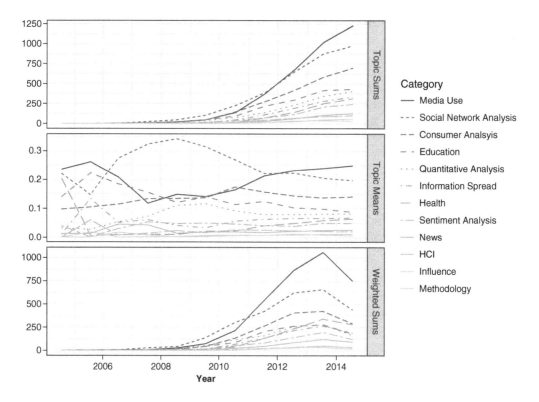

Figure 6.4 Statistics from our LDA analysis, over time. The top panel shows topic sums which capture the amount that each topic is used in abstracts, by year. The middle panel shows topic means which are the average amount that each topic is used in a given abstract. The bottom panel shows the amount that each topic is used in abstracts, by year, weighted by citation count

The figures provide insight into the history and trajectory of social media research. Looking at the top figure, it appears that the 'Social Network Analysis' topic was the early leader in publishing on social media, but was overtaken by the 'Media Use' topic around 2012. This pattern is even more apparent when we look at the mean amount that each topic was used each year (the middle panel of Figure 6.4). In the bottom panel, we take a third look at this data by weighting the topics used in each paper by the log of the number of citations that the paper received. This final statistic characterizes how influential each topic has been. The overall story is similar, although we see that the 'Health' topic and the 'Media Use' topic are more influential than the non-weighted figures suggest.

Discussion

Some of the strengths of topic modeling become apparent when we compare these LDA-based analyses with the distribution of papers by discipline that we created earlier (Figure 6.1). In our earlier attempt, we relied on the categories that Scopus provided and found that early interest in social media was driven by computer science and information systems researchers. Through topic modeling, we learn that these researchers engaged

Table 6.5 Top 20 terms for each topic. Topics are presented in the order of their frequency in the corpus of abstracts

Media Use	Social Network Analysis	Consumer Analsyis	Education	Quantitative Analysis	Information Spread
social	social	media	students	based	twitter
media	data	social	learning	approach	tweets
'social media'	media	'social media'	knowledge	method	time
use	'social media'	new	research	proposed	information
study	information	marketing	education	data	messages
online	users	2015	technology	model	events
facebook	network	business	social	text	public
research	networks	brand	use	images	videos
communication	user	communication	media	results	crisis
public	paper	information	'social media'	media	users
political	web	consumers	design	user	mobile
article	analysis	companies	tools	search	data
findings	based	organizations	technologies	using	event
'use social'	online	management	development	image	location
2014	'social networks'	consumer	digital	topic	used
people	different	customer	2015	propose	2014
new	research	services	student	paper	emergency
results	content	strategies	educational	algorithm	disaster
networking	'social network'	customers	paper	problem	real
using	people	service	project	detection	youtube

Health	Sentiment Analysis	News	HCI	Influence	Methodology
health	content	news	systems	2015	purpose
information	springer	women	information	model	value
use	sentiment	study	privacy	influence	implications
patients	analysis	facebook	papers	al	findings
medical	user	posts	based	intention	limited
care	results	articles	music	et	paper
methods	negative	sexual	security	'et al'	methodology
results	generated	participants	personality	factors	approach
patient	online	page	cloud	perceived	publishing
participants	positive	young	alcohol	smoking	'publishing limited'
using	study	men	model	tobacco	emerald
related	opinion	stories	online	'2015 elsevier'	'emerald group'
internet	reviews	gender	include	satisfaction	'group publishing'
reported	comments	journalists	using	theory	practical
conclusions	switzerland	online	software	structural	originality
support	opinions	significantly	management	variables	design
used	'sentiment analysis'	female	proceedings	intentions	research
clinical	quality	group	discussed	equation	group
healthcare	users	exposure	contain	study	'originality value'
risk	media	pages	analysis	addiction	'methodology approach'

in social network analysis (rather than interface design, for example). While some of our topics match up well with the disciplines identified by Scopus, a few are more broad (e.g., 'Media Use') and most are more narrow (e.g., 'Sentiment Analysis'). This analysis provides a richer sense of the topics of interest to social media researchers. Finally, these topics emerged inductively without any need for explicit coding, such as classifying journals into disciplines. This final feature is a major benefit in social media research where text is rarely categorized for researchers ahead of time.

Topic modeling provides an intuitive, approachable way of doing large-scale text analysis. Its outputs can be understandable and theory-generating. The inductive creation of topics has advantages over traditional content analysis or 'supervised' computational methods that require researchers to define labels or categories of interest ahead of time. While models clearly lack the nuance and depth of understanding that human coders bring to texts, the method allows researchers to analyze datasets at a scale and granularity that would take a huge amount of resources to code manually.

There are, of course, limitations to topic modeling. Many of LDA's limitations have analogues in manual coding. One we have already mentioned is that researchers must choose the number of topics without any clear rules about how to do so. Although a similar problem exists in content analysis, the merging and splitting of topics can be done more intuitively and intentionally when using traditional methods. An additional limitation is that topic modeling tends to work best with many long documents. This can represent a stumbling block for researchers with datasets of short social media posts or comments; in these cases posts can be aggregated by user or by page to produce meaningful topics. The scope of documents can also affect the results of topic models. If, in addition to using abstracts about 'social media,' we had also included abstracts containing the term 'gene

splicing,' our twelve topics would be divided between the two fields and each topic would be less granular. To recover topics similar to those we report here, we would have to increase the number of topics created.

As with network analysis, a goal of LDA is to distill large, messy, and noisy data down to much simpler representations in order to find patterns. Such simplification will always entail ignoring some part of what is going on. Luckily, human coders and LDA have complementary advantages and disadvantages in this regard. Computational methods do not understand which text is more or less important. Humans are good at seeing the meaning and importance of topics, but may suffer from cognitive biases and miss out on topics that are less salient (DiMaggio et al., 2013). Topic models work best when they are interpreted by researchers with a rich understanding of the texts and contexts under investigation.

PREDICTING CITATION

A final computational technique is statistical prediction. Statistical prediction can come in handy in situations where researchers have a great deal of data, including measures of an important, well-defined outcome they care about, but little in the way of prior literature or theory to guide analysis. Prediction has become a mainstream computational approach that encompasses a number of specific statistical techniques, including classification, cross validation, and machine learning (also known as statistical learning) methods (Tibshirani, 1996). Arguably made most famous by Nate Silver (2015), who uses the technique to predict elections and sporting event outcomes, prediction increasingly colors public discourse about current events (Domingos, 2015).

There are many approaches to prediction. We focus on regression-based prediction because it offers a reasonably straightforward workflow. Begin by breaking a dataset into two random subsets: a large subset used as 'training' data and a small subset as 'hold-out' or 'test' data. Next, use the training data to construct a regression model of a given outcome (dependent variable) that incorporates a set of features (independent variables) that might explain variations in the outcome. Apply statistical model selection techniques to determine the best weights (coefficients) to apply to the variables. Evaluate the performance of the model by seeing how accurately it can predict the outcome on the test data. After selecting an appropriate model, assess and interpret the items that most strongly predict the outcome. One can even compare the performance of different or nested sets of features by repeating these steps with multiple groups of independent variables.

Interpreting the results of statistical prediction can be less clear-cut. The term 'prediction' suggests a deep knowledge of a complex social process and the factors that determine a particular outcome. However, statistical prediction often proves more suitable for exploratory analysis where causal mechanisms and processes are poorly understood. We demonstrate this in the following example that predicts whether or not papers in our dataset get cited during the period of data collection. In particular, we try to find out whether textual features of the abstracts can help explain citation outcomes. Our approach follows that used by Mitra and Gilbert (2014), who sought to understand what textual features of Kickstarter projects predicted whether or not projects were funded.

Our Application: Predicting Paper Citation

We use multiple attributes of the papers in our dataset, including text of their abstracts, to predict citations. About 42% of the papers (9,713 out of 23,131) received one or more citations ($\mu = 3$; $\sigma = 19$). Can textual features of the abstracts explain which papers receive

citations? What about other attributes, such as the publication venue or subject area? A prediction analysis can help evaluate these competing alternatives.

To begin, we generate a large set of features for each paper from the Scopus data. Our measures include the year, month, and language of publication as well as the number of citations each paper contains to prior work. We also include the modal country of origin of the authors as well as the affiliation of the first author. Finally, we include the publication venue and publication subject area as provided by Scopus. Then, we build the textual features by taking all of the abstracts and moving them through the following sequence of steps similar to those we took when performing LDA: we lowercase all the words; remove all stop words; and create uni-, bi-, and tri-grams.

We also apply some inclusion criteria to both papers and features. To avoid subject-specific jargon, we draw features only from those terms that appear across at least 30 different subject areas. To avoid spurious results, we also exclude papers that fall into unique categories. Specifically, we remove papers which are the only publications in a given language, journal, or subject area. These sorts of unique cases can cause problems in the context of prediction tasks because they may predict certain outcomes perfectly. As a result, it is often better to focus on datasets and measures that are less 'sparse' (i.e., characterized by rare, one-off observations). Once we drop the 8,494 papers that do not meet these criteria, we are left with 14,126 papers.

We predict the dichotomous outcome variable *cited*, which indicates whether a paper received any citations during the period covered by our dataset (2004–2016). We use a method of *penalized logistic regression* called the least absolute shrinkage and selection operator (also known as the *Lasso*) to do the prediction work. Although, the technical details of Lasso models lie beyond the scope of this chapter, it, and other penalized regression models work well on data where many of the variables have nearly identical values (sometimes called collinear variables because they would sit right around the same line if you plotted them) and/or many zero values (this is also called 'sparse' data) (Friedman, Hastie, & Tibshirani, 2010; James et al., 2013). In both of these situations, some measures are redundant; the Lasso uses clever math to pick which of those measures should go into your final model and which ones should be, in effect, left out.[4] The results of a Lasso model are thus more computationally tractable and easier to interpret.

We use a common statistical technique called cross-validation to validate our models. Cross-validation helps solve another statistical problem that can undermine the results of predictive analysis. Imagine fitting an ordinary least squares regression model on a dataset to generate a set of parameter estimates reflecting the relationships between a set of independent variables and some outcome. The model results provide a set of weights (the coefficients) that represent the strength of the relationships between each predictor and the outcome. Because of the way regression works (and because this is a hypothetical example and we can assume data that does not violate the assumptions of our model), the model weights are the best, linear, unbiased estimators of those relationships. In other words, the regression model fits the data as well as possible. However, nothing about fitting this one model ensures that the same regression weights will provide the best fit for some new data from the same population that the model has not seen. A model may be overfit if it excellently predicts the dataset it was fitted on but poorly predicts new data. Overfitting in this way is a common concern in statistical prediction. Cross-validation addresses this overfitting problem. First, the training data is split into equal-sized groups (typically 10). Different model specifications are tested by iteratively training them on all but one of the groups, and testing how well they predict the final group.

The specification that has the lowest average error is then used on the full training data to estimate coefficients.[5] This approach ensures that the resulting models not only fit the data that we have, but that they are likely to predict the outcomes for new, unobserved results. For each model, we report the mean error rate from the cross-validation run which produced the best fit.

Our analysis proceeds in multiple stages corresponding to the different types of measures we use to predict citation outcomes. We start by estimating a model that includes only the features that correspond to paper and author-level attributes (year, month, and language of publication, modal author country). We then add information about the first author's affiliation. Next, we include predictors that have more to do with research topic and field-level variations (publication venue and subject area). Finally, we include the textual features (terms) from the abstracts.

Results

Table 6.6 summarizes the results of our prediction models. We include goodness-of-fit statistics and prediction error rates for each model as we add more features. A 'better' model will fit the data more closely (i.e., it will explain a larger percentage of the deviance) and produce a lower error rate. We also include a supplementary error rate calculated against the 'holdout' data created from a random subset of 10% of the original dataset that was not used in any of our models. An intuitive way to think about the error rate is to imagine it as the percentage of unobserved papers for which the model will correctly predict whether or not it receives any citations. The two error rate statistics are just this same percentage calculated on different sets of unobserved papers. Unlike a normal regression analysis, we do not report or interpret the full battery of coefficients, standard errors, t-statistics, or p-values. In part, we do not report this information because the results

Table 6.6 Summary of fitted models predicting citation. The 'Model' column describes which features were included. The N features column shows the number of features included in the prediction. 'Deviance' summarizes the goodness of fit as a percentage of the total deviance accounted for by the model. 'CV error' (cross-validation error) reports the prediction error rates of each model in the cross-validation procedure conducted as part of the parameter estimation process. 'Holdout error' shows the prediction error on a random 10% subset of the original dataset not included in any of the model estimation procedures.

Model	N features	Deviance (%)	CV error (%)	Holdout error (%)
Controls	98	7	38	37
+ Affiliation	1909	23	39	37
+ Subject	2096	28	37	34
+ Venue	3902	55	34	30
+ Terms	4411	72	29	27

of these models are unwieldy – each model has over 2,000 predictors and most of those predictors have coefficients of zero! Additionally, unlike traditional regression results, coefficient interpretation and null hypothesis testing with predictive models remain challenging (for reasons that lie beyond the scope of this chapter). Instead, we focus on interpreting the relative performance of each set of features. After we have done this, we refer to the largest coefficients to help add nuance to our interpretation.

The results reveal that all of the features improve the goodness of fit, but not necessarily the predictive performance of the models. As a baseline, our controls-only model has a 37% classification error on the holdout sample. This level of precision barely improves with the addition of both the author affiliation and subject area features. We observe substantial improvements in the prediction performance when the models include the publication venue features and the abstract text terms. When it comes to research about social media, it appears that venue and textual content are the most informative features for predicting whether or not articles get cited.

To understand these results more deeply, we explore the non-zero coefficient estimates for the best-fitting iteration of the full model. Recall that the Lasso estimation procedure returns coefficients for a subset of

the parameters that produce the best fit and shrinks the other coefficients to zero. While it does not make sense to interpret the coefficients in the same way as traditional regression, the non-zero coefficients indicate what features the model identified as the most important predictors of the outcome. First, we note that among the 1,482 features with non-zero coefficients, only 2% are control measures (country, language, month, and year of publication). Similarly, 3% are subject features. In contrast, 15% are affiliation features, 34% are venue features, and a whopping 44% are textual terms. Once again, we find that publication venue and textual terms do the most to explain which works receive citations.

Closer scrutiny of the features with the largest coefficients adds further nuance to this interpretation. Table 6.7 shows the ten features with the largest coefficients in terms of absolute value. The Lasso model identified these coefficients as the most informative predictors of whether or not papers in our dataset get cited. Here we see that the majority of these most predictive features are publication venues. The pattern holds across the 100 features with the largest coefficients, of which 75 are publication venues and only two are textual terms from the abstracts. In other words, variations in publication venue predict which work gets cited more than any other type of feature.

Table 6.7 Feature, variable type, and beta value for top 10 non-zero coefficients estimated by the best fitting model with all features included. Note that the outcome is coded such that positive coefficients indicate features that positively predict the observed outcome of interest (getting cited) while negative coefficients indicate features that negatively predict the outcome.

Feature	Type	Coefficient
Multiple Sclerosis Journal	venue	−2.969
Nature Communications	venue	2.871
Journal of Information Technology	venue	2.762
CrossTalk	venue	2.543
21	term	−2.472
NICTA Victoria Research Laboratory	affiliation	−2.260
The Department of Education, Sookmyung Women's University	affiliation	−2.196
20th ITS World Congress Tokyo 2013	venue	−2.191
Electronics and Communications in Japan	venue	−2.085
British Journal of Nursing	venue	2.077

Discussion

The results of our prediction models suggest that two types of features – publication venue and textual terms – do the most to explain whether or not papers on social media get cited. Both types of features substantially improve model fit and reduce predictive error in ten-fold cross-validation as well as on a holdout sub-sample of the original dataset. However, venue features appear to have a much stronger relationship to our outcome (citation), with the vast majority of the most influential features in the model coming from the venue data (75 of the 100 largest coefficients).

As we said at the outset of this section, statistical prediction offers an exploratory, data-driven, and inductive approach. Based on these findings, we conclude that the venue where research on social media gets published better predicts whether that work gets cited than the other features in our dataset. Textual terms used in abstracts help to explain citation outcomes across the dataset, but the relationship between textual terms and citation only becomes salient in the aggregate. On their own, hardly any of the textual terms approach the predictive power of the venue features. Features such as author affiliation and paper-level features like language or authors' country provide less explanatory power overall.

The approach has several important limitations. Most important, statistical prediction only generates 'predictions' in a fairly narrow, statistical sense. Language of prediction often sounds like the language of causality and inferring process, but these methods do not guarantee that anything being studied is causal or explanatory in terms of mechanisms. We do not claim that a paper's publication venue or the phrases in its abstract *cause* people to cite it. Rather, we think these attributes of a paper likely index specific qualities of an article that are linked to citation outcomes. Just because something is predictive does not mean it is deterministic or causal. We also note that the sort of machine learning approach we demonstrate here does not support the types of inferences commonly made with frequentist null hypothesis tests (the sort that lead to p-values and stars next to 'significant' variables in a regression model). Instead, the interpretation of learning models rests on looking closely at model summary statistics, objective performance metrics (such as error rates), and qualitative exploration of model results.

CONCLUSION

In this chapter, we have described computational social scientific analysis of social media by walking through a series of example analyses. We began with the process of collecting a dataset of bibliographic information on social media scholarship using web APIs similar to those provided by most social media platforms. We then subjected this dataset to three of the mostly widely used computational techniques: network analysis, topic modeling, and statistical prediction. Most empirical studies would employ a single, theoretically-motivated analytic approach, but we compromised depth in order to illustrate the diversity of computational research methodologies available. As we have shown, each approach has distinct strengths and limitations.

We believe our examples paint a realistic picture of what is involved in typical computational social media research. However, these analyses remain limited in scope and idiosyncratic in nature. For example, there are popular computational methods we did not cover in this chapter. Obvious omissions include other forms of machine learning, such as decision trees and collaborative filtering (Resnick et al., 1994), as well as simulation-based techniques such as agent-based modeling (Macy & Willer, 2002; Wilensky & Rand, 2015).

Despite our diffuse approach, we report interesting substantive findings about the history and state of social media research. We discovered a number of diverse communities studying social media. We used different tools to identify these communities, including the categories provided by Scopus, the results of a community detection algorithm applied to the citation network, and the topics identified by topic modeling. Each analysis provided a slightly different picture of social media research. We learned that the study of social media related to media use and medical research is on the rise. We also learned that social network research was influential at the early stages of social media research but that it is not as influential in the citation network. All of these findings are complicated by our final finding that subject area is not as good a predictor of whether a paper will receive a citation as the publication venue and the terms used in the abstract.

In the process of describing our analyses, we tried to point to many of the limitations of computational research methods. Although computational methods and the promise of 'big data' elicit excitement, this hype can obscure the fact that large datasets and fast computers do nothing to obviate the fundamentals of high-quality social science: researchers must understand their empirical settings, design studies with care, operationalize concepts in ways that are valid and honest, take steps to ensure that their findings generalize, and ask tough questions about the substantive impacts of observed relationships. These tenets extend to computational research as well.

Other challenges go beyond methodological limitations. Researchers working with passively collected data generated by social media can face complex issues around the ethics of privacy and consent as well as the technical and legal restrictions on automated data collection. Computational analyses of social media often involve datasets gathered without the sort of active consent considered standard in other arenas of social scientific inquiry. In some cases, data is not public and researchers access it through private agreements or employment arrangements with companies that own platforms or proprietary databases. In others, researchers obtain social media data from public or semi-public sources, but the individuals creating the data may not consider their words or actions public and may not even be aware that their participation generates durable digital traces (boyd & Crawford, 2012). A number of studies have been criticized for releasing information that researchers considered public, but which users did not (Zimmer, 2016). In other cases, researchers pursuing legitimate social inquiry have become the target of companies or state prosecutors who selectively seek to enforce terms of service agreements or invoke broad laws such as the federal Computer Fraud and Abuse Act (CFAA).[6]

We advise computational researchers to take a cautious and adaptive approach to these issues. Existing mechanisms such as Institutional Review Boards and federal laws have been slow to adjust to the realities of online research. In many cases, the authority and resources to anticipate, monitor, or police irresponsible behaviors threaten to impose unduly cumbersome restrictions. In other cases, review boards' policies greenlight research that seems deeply problematic. We believe researchers must think carefully about the specific implications of releasing specific datasets. In particular, we encourage abundant caution and public consultation before disseminating anything resembling personal information about individual social media system users. Irresponsible scholarship harms both subjects and reviewers, and undermines the public trust scholars need to pursue their work.

At the same time, we remain excited and optimistic about the future of computational studies of social media. As we have shown, the potential benefits of computational methods are numerous. Trace data can capture behaviors that are often difficult to observe in labs and that went unrecorded in offline interactions. Large datasets allow researchers to measure real effects obscured by large amounts of variation, and to make excellent predictions using relatively simple models. These new tools and new datasets provide a real opportunity to advance our understanding of the world. Such opportunities should not be undermined by overly-broad laws or alarmist concerns.

Finally, much of computational social science, including this chapter, is data-focused rather than theory-focused. We would encourage others to do as we say, and not as we do. The great promise of computational social science is the opportunity to test and advance social science theory. We hope that readers of this chapter will think about whether there are theories they are interested in which might benefit from a computational approach. We urge readers with a stronger background in theory to consider learning the tools to conduct these types of analyses and to collaborate with technically minded colleagues.

Reproducible Research

Computational research methods also have the important benefit of being extraordinarily reproducible and replicable (Stodden, Guo, & Ma, 2013). Unlike many other forms of social research, a computational researcher can theoretically use web APIs to collect a dataset identical to one used in a previous study. Even when API limits or other factors prohibit creating an identical dataset, researchers can work to make data available alongside the code they use for their analysis, allowing others to re-run the study and assess the results directly. Making code and data available also means that others can analyze and critique it. This can create uncomfortable situations, but we feel that such situations serve the long-term interests of society and scholarly integrity. Although not every computational researcher shares their code (Stodden et al., 2013), there are movements to encourage or require this (LeVeque, Mitchell, & Stodden, 2012; Stodden et al., 2013; Bollen et al., 2015).

We have tried to follow emerging best practices with regards to reproducibility in this chapter. We have released an online copy of all of the code that we used to create this chapter. By making our code available, we hope to make our unstated assumptions and decisions visible. By looking at our code, you might find errors or omissions which can be corrected in subsequent work. By releasing our code and data, we also hope that others can learn from and build on our work. For example, a reader with access to a server and some knowledge of the Python and R programming languages should be able to build a more up-to-date version of our dataset years from now. Another reader might create a similar bibliographic analysis of another field. By using our code, this reader should able to produce results, tables, and figures like those in this paper. Data repositories, such as the Harvard Dataverse, make storing and sharing data simple and inexpensive. When thinking of the opportunities for openness, transparency, and collaboration, we are inspired by the potential of computational research methods for social media. We hope that our overview, data, and code can facilitate more of this type of work.

ONLINE SUPPLEMENTS

All of the code used to generate our dataset, to complete our analyses, and even to produce the text of this chapter, is available for download on the following public website: https://communitydata.cc/social-media-chapter/

Because the Scopus dataset is constantly being updated and changed, reproducing the precise numbers and graphs in this chapter requires access to a copy of the dataset we collected from Scopus in 2016. Unfortunately, like many social media websites, the terms of use for the Scopus APIs prohibit the public re-publication of data collected from their database. However, they did allow us to create a private, access-controlled, replication dataset in the Harvard Dataverse archive at the following URL: http://dx.doi.org/10.7910/DVN/W31PH5. Upon request, we will grant access to this dataset to any researchers interested in reproducing our analyses.

Notes

1   Technically, each paper is assigned to the modal (i.e., most frequent) country among its authors. For example, if a paper has three authors with two authors located in Canada and one in Japan, the modal country for the paper would be Canada. Any ties (i.e., if more than one country is tied for most frequent location among a paper's authors) were broken by randomly selecting among the tied countries.

2   This provides one example of how the details of missing data can be invisible or opaque. It is easy to see how missing data like this could impact research results. For example, if certain disciplines or topics are systematically less likely to include abstracts in Scopus, we will have a skewed representation of the field.

3   More complex approaches such as dynamic LDA (Blei & Lafferty, 2006) are often better suited to identify the temporal evolution of topics.

4   To put things a little more technically, a fitted Lasso model selects the optimal set of variables that should have coefficient values greater than zero and shrinks the rest of the coefficients to zero without sacrificing goodness of fit (Tibshirani, 1996).

5   For our Lasso models, cross-validation was used to select λ, a parameter that tells the model how quickly to shrink variable coefficients. We include this information for those of you who want to try this on your own or figure out the details of our statistical code.

6   See Sandvig's (2016) blogpost, 'Why I am Suing the Government,' for a thoughtful argument against the incredibly vague and broad scope of the CFAA as well as a cautionary tale for those who write software to conduct bulk downloads of public website data for research purposes.

REFERENCES

Arun, R., Suresh, V., Madhavan, C. E. V., & Murthy, M. N. N. (2010). On Finding the Natural Number of Topics with Latent Dirichlet Allocation: Some Observations. In *Advances in Knowledge Discovery and Data Mining* (pp. 391–402). Springer, Berlin, Heidelberg. https://doi.org/10.1007/978-3-642-13657-3_43

Asur, S. & Huberman, B. A. (2010, August). Predicting the future with social media. In *2010 IEEE/WIC/ACM International Conference on Web Intelligence and Intelligent Agent Technology (WI-IAT)* (Vol. 1, pp. 492–499). 2010 ieee/wic/acm international conference on web intelligence and intelligent agent technology (wi-iat). doi:10.1109/WI-IAT.2010.63

Barabási, A.-L. & Albert, R. (1999, October 15). Emergence of scaling in random networks. *Science, 286*(5439), 509–512. doi:10.1126/science.286.5439.509. pmid: 10521342

Bastian, M., Heymann, S., Jacomy, M., et al. (2009). Gephi: An open source software for exploring and manipulating networks. *ICWSM, 8*, 361–362. Retrieved July 20, 2016, from www.aaai.org/ocs/index.php/ICWSM/09/paper/viewFile/154/1009/

Binfield, P. (2012, February 29). *PLoS ONE and the Rise of the Open Access MegaJournal.* The 5th SPARC Japan Seminar 2011, National Institute for Informatics. Retrieved July 20, 2016, from www.nii.ac.jp/sparc/en/event/2011/pdf/20120229_doc3_ binfield.pdf

Blei, D. M. (2012, April). Probabilistic topic models. *Communications of the ACM, 55*(4), 77–84. doi:10.1145/2133806.2133826

Blei, D. M. & Lafferty, J. D. (2006). Dynamic topic models. In *Proceedings of the 23rd International Conference on Machine Learning* (pp. 113–120). ACM. Retrieved April 21, 2016, fromdl.acm.org/citation.cfm?id=1143859

Blei, D. M., Ng, A. Y., & Jordan, M. I. (2003). Latent Dirichlet allocation. *The Journal of Machine Learning Research, 3*, 993–1022. Retrieved December 3, 2015, fromdl.acm.org/citation.cfm?id=944937

Bollen, K., Cacioppo, J. T., Kaplan, R. M., Krosnick, J. A., Olds, J. L., & Dean, H. (2015, May). *Social, Behavioral, and Economic Sciences Perspectives on Robust and Reliable Science.* National Science Foundation. Retrieved from www.nsf.gov/sbe/ AC_Materials/SBE_Robust_and_Reliable_Research_Report.pdf

boyd, d. & Crawford, K. (2012). Critical questions for Big Data. *Information, Communication & Society, 15*(5), 662–679. doi:10.1080/1369118X.2012.678878

Chew, C. & Eysenbach, G. (2010, November 29). Pandemics in the age of Twitter: Content analysis of tweets during the 2009 H1N1 outbreak. *PLoS ONE, 5*(11), e14118. doi:10.1371/journal.pone.0014118

DiMaggio, P., Nag, M., & Blei, D. (2013, December). Exploiting affinities between topic modeling and the sociological perspective on culture: Application to newspaper coverage of U.S. government arts funding. *Poetics, 41*(6), 570–606. doi:10.1016/j.poetic.2013.08.004

Domingos, P. (2015). *The Master Algorithm: How the Quest for the Ultimate Learning Machine Will Remake Our World.* New York: Basic Books.

Friedman, J., Hastie, T., & Tibshirani, R. (2010). Regularization paths for generalized linear models via coordinate descent. *Journal of Statistical Software, 33*(1), 1–22. pmid: 20808728. Retrieved July 20, 2016, from www. ncbi. nlm. nih. gov/ pmc/articles/PMC2929880/

Fruchterman, T. M. J. & Reingold, E. M. (1991, November 1). Graph drawing by force-directed placement. *Software: Practice and Experience, 21*(11), 1129–1164. doi:10.1002/spe.4380211102

Ghosh, D. & Guha, R. (2013, March 1). What are we 'tweeting' about obesity? Mapping tweets with topic modeling and Geographic Information System. *Cartography and Geographic Information Science, 40*(2), 90–102. doi:10.1080/15230406.2013.776210

Hansen, D., Shneiderman, B., & Smith, M. A. (2010). *Analyzing Social Media Networks with NodeXL: Insights from a Connected World.* Burlington, MA: Morgan Kaufmann.

Hargittai, E. (2015, May 1). Is bigger always better? Potential biases of Big Data derived from social network sites. *The ANNALS of the American Academy of Political and Social Science, 659*(1), 63–76. doi:10.1177/0002716215570866

Hausmann, R., Hidalgo, C. A., Bustos, S., Coscia, M., Simoes, A., & Yildirim, M. A. (2014, January 17). *The Atlas of Economic Complexity: Mapping Paths to Prosperity.* Cambridge, MA: MIT Press.

Hood, W. W. & Wilson, C. S. (2001). The literature of bibliometrics, scientometrics, and informetrics. *Scientometrics, 52*(2), 291–314. doi:10.1023/A:1017919924342

James, G., Witten, D., Hastie, T., & Tibshirani, R. (2013). *An Introduction to Statistical Learning: With Applications in R.* New York: Springer.

Kessler, M. M. (1963, January 1). Bibliographic coupling between scientific papers. *American Documentation, 14*(1), 10–25. doi:10.1002/asi.5090140103

Kovács, A., Looy, B. V., & Cassiman, B. (2015, June 20). Exploring the scope of open innovation: A bibliometric review of a decade of research. *Scientometrics, 104*(3), 951–983. doi:10.1007/s11192-015-1628-0

Kozinets, R. V. (2002, February 1). The field behind the screen: Using netnography for marketing research in online communities. *Journal of Marketing Research*, *39*(1), 61–72. doi:10.1509/jmkr.39.1.61.18935

Lazer, D., Pentland, A., Adamic, L., Aral, S., Barabasi, A. L., Brewer, D., … Van Alstyne, M. (2009, February 6). Life in the network: The coming age of computational social science. *Science*, *323*(5915), 721–723. doi:10.1126/science.1167742. pmid: 19197046

Leskovec, J. & Krevl, A. (2014, June). *SNAP Datasets: Stanford Large Network Dataset Collection*. Retrieved from http://snap.stanford.edu/data

LeVeque, R. J., Mitchell, I. M., & Stodden, V. (2012). Reproducible research for scientific computing: Tools and strategies for changing the culture. *Computing in Science and Engineering*, *14*(4), 13–17.

Macy, M. W. & Willer, R. (2002). From factors to actors: Computational sociology and agent-based modeling. *Annual Review of Sociology*, *28*, 143–166. JSTOR: 3069238

Merton, R. K. (1968). The Matthew effect in science. *Science*, *159*(3810), 56–63. Retrieved September 27, 2014, from www. unc. edu/~fbaum/ teaching/ PLSC541_Fall06/ Merton_Science_1968.pdf

Mitra, T. & Gilbert, E. (2014). The language that gets people to give: Phrases that predict success on Kickstarter. In *Proceedings of the 17th ACM Conference on Computer Supported Cooperative Work & Social Computing* (pp. 49–61). CSCW '14. New York: ACM. doi:10.1145/2531602.2531656

Pedregosa, F., Varoquaux, G., Gramfort, A., Michel, V., Thirion, B., Grisel, O., … Duchesnay, É. (2011). Scikit-learn: Machine learning in python. *Journal of Machine Learning Research*, *12*, 2825–2830.

Pennacchiotti, M. & Gurumurthy, S. (2011). Investigating topic models for social media user recommendation. In *Proceedings of the 20th International Conference Companion on World Wide Web* (pp. 101–102). WWW '11. New York: ACM. doi:10.1145/1963192.1963244

Prier, K. W., Smith, M. S., Giraud-Carrier, C., & Hanson, C. L. (2011). Identifying health-related topics on Twitter: An exploration of tobacco-related tweets as a test topic. In *Proceedings of the 4th International Conference on Social Computing, Behavioral-cultural Modeling and Prediction* (pp. 18–25). SBP '11. Berlin, Heidelberg: Springer-Verlag. Retrieved July 19, 2016, fromdl.acm.org/citation.cfm?id=19646981964702

Resnick, P., Iacovou, N., Suchak, M., Bergstrom, P., & Riedl, J. (1994). GroupLens: An open architecture for collaborative filtering of netnews. In *Proceedings of the 1994 ACM Conference on Computer Supported Cooperative Work* (pp. 175–186). CSCW '94. New York: ACM. doi:10.1145/192844.192905

Rosvall, M. [M.], Axelsson, D., & Bergstrom, C. T. (2010, April 17). The map equation. *The European Physical Journal Special Topics*, *178*(1), 13–23. doi:10.1140/epjst/e2010-01179-1

Rosvall, M. [Martin] & Bergstrom, C. T. (2008, January 29). Maps of random walks on complex networks reveal community structure. *Proceedings of the National Academy of Sciences*, *105*(4), 1118–1123. doi:10.1073/pnas.0706851105. pmid: 18216267

Sandvig, C. (2016, July 1). Why I am suing the government. Retrieved October 23, 2016, fromsocialmediacollective.org/2016/07/01/why-i-am-suing-the-government/

Schwartz, H. A., Eichstaedt, J. C., Kern, M. L., Dziurzynski, L., Ramones, S. M., Agrawal, M., … Ungar, L. H. (2013, September 25). Personality, gender, and age in the language of social media: The open-vocabulary approach. *PLoS ONE*, *8*(9), e73791. doi:10.1371/journal.pone.0073791

Silver, N. (2015). *The Signal and the Noise: Why So Many Predictions Fail–but Some Don't*. New York: Penguin Books.

Small, H. (1973, July 1). Co-citation in the scientific literature: A new measure of the relationship between two documents. *Journal of the American Society for Information Science*, *24*(4), 265–269. doi:10.1002/asi.4630240406

Stodden, V., Guo, P., & Ma, Z. (2013, June 21). Toward reproducible computational research: An empirical analysis of data and code policy adoption by journals. *PLoS ONE*, *8*(6), e67111. doi:10.1371/journal.pone.0067111

Šubelj, L., van Eck, N. J., & Waltman, L. (2016, April 28). Clustering Scientific Publications Based on Citation Relations: A Systematic Comparison of Different Methods. *PLoS ONE*, *11*(4), e0154404. doi:10.1371/journal.pone.0154404

Tausczik, Y. R. & Pennebaker, J. W. (2010, January 3). The psychological meaning of words: LIWC and computerized text analysis methods. *Journal of Language and Social Psychology*, *29*(1), 24–54. doi:10.1177/0261927X09351676

Tibshirani, R. (1996). Regression shrinkage and selection via the lasso. *Journal of the Royal Statistical Society. Series B (Methodological)*, *58*(1), 267–288. JSTOR: 2346178

Wang, Y., Agichtein, E., & Benzi, M. (2012). TM-LDA: Efficient online modeling of latent topic transitions in social media (p. 123). New York: ACM. doi:10.1145/2339530.2339552

Wasserman, S. & Faust, K. (1994). *Social Network Analysis: Methods and Applications*. Cambridge: Cambridge University Press.

Wilensky, U. & Rand, W. (2015). *An Introduction to Agent-based Modeling: Modeling Natural, Social, and Engineered Complex Systems with NetLogo*. Cambridge, MA: MIT Press.

Yang, M.-C. & Rim, H.-C. (2014, July). Identifying interesting Twitter contents using topical analysis. *Expert Systems with Applications*, *41*(9), 4330–4336. doi:10.1016/j.eswa.2013.12.051

Zimmer, M. (2016, May 14). OkCupid study reveals the perils of Big-Data science. *Wired*. Retrieved August 31, 2016, from www.wired.com/2016/05/okcupid-study-reveals-perils-big-data-science/

7

Digital Discourse: Locating Language in New/Social Media

Crispin Thurlow

In this chapter, I introduce what is sometimes called computer-mediated discourse analysis or just digital discourse studies. This is a world of research that attends primarily to linguistic, sociolinguistic and discursive phenomena in new/social media. The chapter starts with a brief review of the field, referring to key moments, issues, and scholars. With this done, I move to identifying three broad organizing principles in digital discourse research: *discourse*, *multimodality*, *ideology*. A key objective with this overview is to show how digital discourse studies attends to both micro-level linguistic practices and more macro-level social processes; by the same token, scholars in the field are increasingly interested in understanding how language intersects with other modes of communication. New/social media have actually been pushing language scholars to rethink the foundations and boundaries of their work. In this regard, my chapter then turns to consider a selection of studies which exemplify a number of language-related issues, but which also demonstrate an analytic framework for understanding the way language takes place in new/social media as a *metadiscursive* resource, a *metrolingual* resource, a *transmodalizing* resource, and a *technologizing* resource. Recognizing the fuzziness of the labels 'new' and 'social', my chapter deliberately retains a dual new/social focus, not least because discourse scholars start from the premise that language is inherently and unavoidably social. Much of the research cited here is written in English and/or about English, even though the sites, topics and authors represent a far more diverse field. Unless specifically attending to different ways of speaking or writing, discourse studies is principally concerned with the uses of language in general rather than any particular language.

BACKGROUND

In the last decade there has been something of a boom in the broadly defined field of digital discourse studies – that is, scholars whose work centers on the language of new/social media within the even wider field of what is sometimes called Computer Mediated Communication. (No doubt the editors of this volume will have, from the outset, commented on the issues of labelling and terminology that plague academia generally and digital media studies in particular.) Some of the best examples of this digital discourse boom are listed below as ideas for further reading (see p. 143). To set the scene, however, I start here with little of the 'history' of the field, which is also a way for me to start introducing some of its major organizing principles.

Arguably the best known, internationally recognizable scholar of new media language is Susan Herring who, in 1996, edited a foundational English-language collection titled *Computer-Mediated Communication: Linguistic, Social and Cross-Cultural Perspectives* (Herring, 1996). Herring has always characterized her own work as *Computer Mediated Discourse Analysis* (or just CMDA; e.g., Herring, 2001) and is someone who retains one of the best overall perspectives on the field (see Herring, 2004, 2013, 2015; although see also Baron, 2008).[1] From the beginning, Herring helped establish the core linguistic variables needed for an analysis of new media language: structure (e.g., typography, spelling, word choice, sentence structure); meaning (i.e., of symbols, words, utterances, exchanges); interaction (e.g., turn-taking, topic development, backchannels, repairs); and social function (e.g., identity markers, humour and play, face management, conflict). In framing new media language, studies should also attend to key technological variables (e.g., synchronicity, persistence of transcript, channels of communication) and situational variables (e.g., number of participants, demographics, setting, purpose, topic). This basic framework continues to inform a great deal of digital discourse research. Scholars have, however, sought to push the field further; for now, I shall mention just two early examples.

Another foundational moment in the field was the publication in 2006 of a special issue of the *Journal of Sociolinguistics* on computer-mediated communication, edited by Jannis Androutsopoulos.[2] In his introductory paper, Androutsopoulos (2006) offered some important pointers for deepening digital discourse research; most notably, the need to move beyond an undue emphasis on the linguistic and orthographic features of digital media language, shifting towards more ethnographically-grounded user-related approaches. In more recent work, Androutsopoulos (e.g., 2010, 2011) has continued to promote the value of research shaped by this type of *discourse-ethnographic* rather than variationist-sociolinguistic approach; in other words, pushing us to pay less attention to the formal features of new media language (i.e., what it looks like) and more attention to the situated practices of new media language (i.e., what it does – or, rather, what people do with it). Along much the same vein, Alexandra Georgakopoulou (2006) offered her own recommendations for extending the field. These included: ensuring that the study of language is grounded in a concern for broader sociocultural practices and inequalities of communities; considering the connections between online and offline practices, and between different technologies; and emphasizing the contextual, particularistic nature of new media language. Once again, we see in Georgakopoulou's recommendations a growing preference for research that is more committed to the social meanings of technology and its particular (hence 'particularistic') significance for specific users, groups or communities. In many ways, this paradigm shift brings digital discourse analysis into line with similar shifts in new media studies more generally. In a nutshell, what we see is digital media language scholars turning away from the purely or distinctively 'linguistic' and towards a more properly discursive or communicative approach. And this brings me nicely to three organizing principles at the heart of digital discourse studies

CORE ORGANIZING PRINCIPLES

Most research on digital discourse nowadays responds either directly or indirectly to the kinds of paradigmatic issues and recommendations sketched above. Inspired by these priorities, I want now to offer three broader organizing principles which define the core work of new/social media language scholarship (Thurlow & Mroczek, 2011). For such an already interdisciplinary field – and in the context of an extremely interdisciplinary volume – these types of conceptual clarifications have the added benefit of making things a little more transparent and hopefully understandable.

Discourse

Putting 'language' in its place – and following the lead of those scholars already mentioned – it is essential to recognize that digital discourse is interested in language only in so far as it illuminates social and cultural processes (cf. Bucholtz & Hall, 2008, on 'sociocultural linguistics'). In other words, the primary concern is not with the abstract, grammatical language of linguistics, but rather the everyday functions and uses of language. It is for this reason that we tend to use the term *discourse*. (For excellent introductions to discourse studies, see Cameron & Panović, 2014; Jaworski & Coupland, 2014). In linguistically-oriented discourse analysis there is typically a shared commitment to the following: the social functions of language, the interactional accomplishment of meaning, the significance of communicator intent, and the relevance of context. This has two specific implications for digital discourse studies. First, we recognize the inherently *mediated* nature of all communication (Norris & Jones, 2005; Scollon 2001) and not just in the case of so-called computer-mediated communication; communication is always contextualized (i.e., mediated, embodied, emplaced) by, for example, relationship, setting, layout, gesture, accent and typography. The second implication of a social-cultural approach to language is a need to think also about its increasing *technologization* (cf. Fairclough, 1999). What is meant here is that we engage also with the historical-political context of contemporary language use: its commodification and its recontextualized use as a lifestyle resource to be sold back to us, or as a workplace tool used to manage us (see Cameron, 2000; Heller, 2003). This, as Pierre Bourdieu (1991) has famously discussed, recognizes language as a mode of symbolic power and why language is always a matter of political economy.

Multimodality

Multimodality is increasingly regarded as a core concept in and the study of discourse (e.g., Jewitt, 2014; Kress & van Leeuwen, 2001), which means attending to the way language interacts with – and is only made meaningful through its interaction with – other semiotic systems. This is especially germane given the growing complexity of the multi-media formats of contemporary communication, brought about by the inevitable *convergence* of "old" and "new" media and the *layering* of different digital media. In their efforts to redress the previous absence of linguistic issues in computer-mediated communication, digital discourse scholars have sometimes overlooked the fact that words are only ever part of the picture. All texts, all communicative events, are always achieved by means of multiple semiotic resources, even so-called text-based new media like instant- and text-messaging. Herein lies much of the potential in new media for *invention and creativity*; time and again, research shows how users overcome apparent semiotic limitations, reworking and combining – often playfully – the resources at their disposal. Well-known scholars of multimodality, Gunther Kress & Theo van

Leeuwen (2001: 11) use the bedroom for demonstrating the inherent multimodality of texts as well as the 'orchestration' of multiple semiotic modes. But another useful invocation of the bedroom is to be found in Rodney Jones' (2010) more literal reference to it as a common site for young people's digital media practices. In either case, digital discourse seeks to understand the situated, *spatialized* (which is also to say mobile) experiences of new/social media.

Ideology

Linguistically-oriented discourse studies, especially that falling under the rubric of Critical Discourse Studies, often also orients to the notion of Foucauldian discourses; as such, it combines both *d-discourse* and *D-discourse* (Gee, 2010). In practice, what this means is that scholars are interested in (a) the ways micro-level interactional and textual practices constitute our social worlds, and (b) the ways our everyday communicative/representational practices are structured by larger systems of belief and hierarchies of knowledge. In other words, we seek to understand how our uses of language feed ideological systems, just as we want to know how ideologies shape the way we use language. Of course, new/social media are themselves inherently ideological, both in terms of their political-economies of access and control (i.e., some have, some have none/less), but also in terms of their potential as mechanisms for both normative and counter-normative representation; they are used to control people, and they are used to resist control. This is quite apparent when one thinks of the symbolic power of the news and broadcast media, but no less is true of any number of seemingly mundane mechanical, medical or digital technologies. And, coming full circle, language too is fully ideological. Online or offline, spoken or typed, face-to-face or digitally 'mediated', what people do with language has

material consequence (cf. Foucault, 1981) and language is instrumental in establishing categories of difference, relations of inequality or, at the very least, the social norms by which we all feel obliged to live our lives. Whether it is done by academics, journalists, teachers or 'non-experts', talk about language (or *metalanguage*) always exposes the power/privilege: competing standards of 'correct', 'good' or 'normal' language; debates about literacy and occupational training; and the social categorization and disciplining of speakers. And, as work on *language ideology* (Woolard & Schieffelin, 1994) reminds us, talk about language is usually a matter of disciplining the bodies of speakers rather than the niceties of their speech.

These three organizing principles are clearly inter-related and they are presented here as a series of only loosely mapped statements. I should also add that different scholars orient differently to these principles, with some being more or less interested in questions of multimodality and/or ideology, for example. All, however, agree on the way we think about the language – that is, as discourse – even if we may decide to focus on different aspects of it. In this regard, I turn now to my proposal for a four-part framework for researching new/social media language.

ANALYTIC FRAMEWORK

In the real-world contexts of digital discourse, language emerges as a kind of figure-ground illusion, switching into and out of focus at different moments. Sometimes it feels as if language is everywhere, other times it is nowhere; it can be high-profile and dominant one minute, low-key and almost invisible the next. And this becomes increasingly true as our technologies keep evolving and converging, and, to some extent, approximating face-to-face communication with all its immediacy, complexity and variety (Which is certainly not to say that face-to-face communication is necessarily the best or highest order of human interaction). It is also true to say that the place of language in digital discourse is bound up with some deep-seated mythologies about the nature of language (see language ideologies above) and rooted in the global linguistic marketplace. In other words, we must remember that all ways of speaking/writing are not equal or treated as equal. With this in mind, I want to consider the place of the English language in digital discourse as a convenient way to think about a more comprehensive approach to understanding and/or studying language in new/social media.

Language as a Metadiscursive Resource

The language of digital media is often depicted in the news media and other public venues as a threat to the language; we hear that, for example, English is somehow being lost or that society is losing its control of 'good', 'proper' or standard English (Tagliamonte & Denis, 2008; Thurlow 2006). According to reputable news sources, new communication technologies 'ruin grammar' and 'beat up' or 'corrupt' languages. And this way of talking about digital discourse is fairly persistent even in spite of evidence to the contrary (Tagliamonte, 2016; Thurlow, 2014). The bottom line, of course, is that English cannot really be lost because it was technically never 'found' in the first place. There never was a neatly demarcated, unequivocally prescribed 'Golden Age of English' with a fully secured, unchanging standard. Take a look at this random sample of international newspaper headlines about texting:

- *Text-speak: language evolution or just laziness?*
- *Problems With Teens Texting Too Much*
- *Texting more popular than face-to-face conversation*
- *Are Teens Texting Away their Lives?*

- *Twtr? It's majorly bad! Leading headteacher condemns 'text speak'*
- *Is Texting Killing the English Language?*
- *Your Texting Addiction is Starting to Cost the Government*

These headline stories are all matters of social or moral judgement rather than linguistic ones. It is the *perception* of language threat – or language loss – that is real. In thinking about the place of English *vis-à-vis* new/social media, therefore, what we see here is language being taken up as a *metadiscursive* resource for telling a particular story about technology, but also about young people. In other words, this is "language about language" or rather discourse about discourse, written by adult journalists for (mostly) other adults. Language is, thus, not simply a way of communicating but a powerful resource for representing young people – so-called 'digital natives' – and a resource by which adults may perform their own identities as adults. As Deborah Cameron (1995) argues, none of this is especially new; every generation likes to complain about the next generation's communication practices. This is nonetheless an important context in which we see language taking place in and around new/social media.

Needless to say, telling an exaggerated story about digital discourse makes for good news. The story of a 'new language' or of 'language threat' sells much better than a story about the gradual, inevitable 'evolution' of English or about the ways young people's communication is actually being enhanced by new/social media. Which, of course, is precisely what a lot of empirical evidence reveals. Take a look at these messages – the first from the *Irish Times* (; see Thurlow, 2006), the second and third from my own empirical data (Thurlow, 2003; Thurlow & Poff, 2013):

In the news …

- *Mst f d tym dey usd ds knd f lng'ge 2 tlk 2 1 anthr nt 1ly n txt bt evn*
- *n wrtng ltrs 2*

In real life …

- *Have you had a shower today as I'm sure I can smell u from here!(Teehee)*
- *Where r u?We r by the bar at the back on the left.*

Unlike the kinds of completely fabricated, unrealistic 'examples' that often appear in news reports, the language of texting and other digital discourse is really surprisingly unremarkable. Regardless of their emoticons, abbreviations and non-conventional spellings, most messaging is far from hieroglyphic and unintelligible. Besides, as Tim Shortis (2007) has shown, most of the features thought to typify digital discourse have long-standing precedents in English anyway – even the supposedly iconic letter-number homophones (gr8). Digital discourse, while sometimes distinctive, is often far from unique. And this is precisely why studies of people's *actual* practices are always needed. English may well be changing but not in the ways – or to the extent – that news-makers would have us believe. Nor are old, conventionalized ways of doing English being straightforwardly or comprehensively replaced. Besides, it is not all about English anyway.

Language as a Metrolingual Resource

In digital discourse – but also in other contexts – English is increasingly dislodged and dislocated in all sorts of different ways. It is certainly less and less the *de facto* language of new/social media as it once was. If anything typifies digital English, it is the mixing of registers and styles, and the blending of vernacular and official ways of speaking/writing. (This is why teachers are sometimes driven to distraction by their students' emails.) In their large-scale study of text-messaging, for example, Christa Dürscheid and Elisabeth Stark (2011) amassed a compelling story of the multilingual nature of digital discourse.

Here is an example of one of their more striking text-messages:

> Olla fratello!!! Come stai? Wie geht's dir so? Immer noch so lange am arbeiten wie früher? Ich hab endlich mein eigenes Restaurant und mucho travajo aber macht mir extrem spass … ;-) allora amore, buona giornata und luegsch uf di, gäll …;-) peace (Dürscheid & Stark, 2011)

With four other languages being used, we see how English (underlined for clarity) figures as just one linguistic resource. Particularly given the *translocal* spaces of new media, where speakers/writers are often reaching beyond domestic spaces and national boundaries, digital discourse often resembles a linguistic 'mash-up' (see Leppänen et al., 2009). And these kinds of translocal, multilingual practices take place across a range of new/social media genres and contexts, as we see in examples from studies of microblogging by Carmen Lee (2011) in Hong Kong and by Saija Peuronen (2011) in Finland (again, English references underlined).

> WOW~~~WOW‾!!!!! 加油!!!! (Lee, 2011)

> Sanotaan näin et kyl voit chilli rullail kaupungil. Varmaan poljet nopeempaa kun mostly skedejät. Mut jos poljet rec(reational) rullaavien kavereiden kaa,jäät kyl harmittavan paljon jälkeen … ei nää oo niin opeet ku perus rullaimet. Mut voit kyl muutenki rullailla… Mut **rec** rullamil ET VOI grindata … et sinäänsä temppu rullat on only do it all skate! ☺ (Peuronen, 2011)

Here we have people dipping into and out of the global lingua franca, a language which may or may not be their own, at least not in straightforward ways. Nor is it straightforwardly 'languages' at play. As Peuronen demonstrates, the English that is used is not straightforwardly standard English, but rather particular varieties and subcultural styles of English. Indeed, digital discourse not only problematizes and challenges our tendency to overdraw the notion of languages (i.e., in practice, languages are not neatly separated or always easily distinguishable), but also our assumptions about the discrete nature of language itself (see next section). It is for this reason that digital discourse may be characterized by a term like *metrolingualism* (Otsuji & Pennycook, 2010), which tries to account for the creative, mix-and-match ways that people nowadays take up different ways of speaking as playful and transcultural resources.

It is also worth noting that the spaces – or cyberspaces – of English or any other language are certainly no longer neatly demarcated or ring-fenced. Anyone who travels will notice how ostensibly English-language texts are now constantly interpenetrated with the sounds and voices of other speakers, other languages. Opening up the *BBC News* homepage or my *World Time Buddy* page in Bern or Buenos Aires, I am immediately presented with a reconfigured linguistic landscape with, for example, local advertisements in local languages. New-media texts are often especially and explicitly *heteroglossic*, comprising multiple voices and multiple types of voices (Androutsopoulos, 2010, 2011). By the same token, they are also always multimodal.

Language as a Multimodal Resource

As a heavily keyboard-driven means of communicating, digital discourse is in some ways intensely verbal. Yet language is either secondary or marginal or altogether irrelevant to the kinds of everyday meaning making that happen with digital media. Any *Facebook* profile proves this point: they are often multilingual, and almost always multi-modal and multi-media. Indeed, one of the major problems with newspaper reporting about digital discourse is its noticeable and consistent disregard not only for the creativity of young people's language use, but also for the innovative, multimodal design-work that often characterize their new/social media

practices. By the same token, the problem with many language scholars is that they tend to single out language for isolated analysis.

> Two students chatting online [starts: 12:39am]
> …
> P1: is that who you went to the passion concert with?
> P2: YES
> P2: woooww
> P2: how did u know!?!?!?!?
> P1: lol you told me..?
> P1: how did you hear about passion anyway?
> P2: paul
> P2: paul invited me. and i listend to passions song on youtube
> P2: and i LOVED it
> P1: oh haha
> P1: haha is he flip
> P2: i love acoustic guitar
> P2: and piano
> P1: i knowwwwww
> P2: i have a picture with him hehe and his songs on my ipod

The extract above from two of my students chatting online clearly does not look like an email, a business letter, or an academic essay. (See Thurlow, 2012, for the complete extract and full discussion.) This is not formal, written English. Nor is it meant to be. More to the point, however, what is happening here is not simply a matter of language *per se*. The significance (in both senses of the word) of this exchange – its communicative force – lies as much in the visual as it does in the verbal. That the two have ever been separated for academic purposes says much about our own theoretical presuppositions and analytic conveniences. Words on the page or the screen have never, in practice, been simply verbal. No neat boundaries exist in digital discourse between standard written English and vernacular, spoken English or between global English and local English, or between English and other languages; by the same token, the symbolic and material properties of language can seldom be separated out. This is what Carmel Vaisman's (2011) research on the blogging 'language' of Israeli *Fakatsa* girls shows rather nicely (Figure 7.1).

Figure 7.1

Source: Vaisman (2011)

In this example, the line between the use of language and the *design* of language is very blurred. In recognizing and accounting for the creative, playful uses of language in new/social media contexts, we often witness unorthodox, experimental worlds – the kind of language practices that, following Evelyn Ch'ien (2004), we might think of as weird English or, in this case, weird Hebrew. (And to be clear: 'weird' here is meant as a good thing!) It is certainly the case that language is not neatly bounded in digital discourse and studies must always attend to – and account properly – for the ways it intersects with and relies on other modes of communication.

Language as a Technologizing Resource

I come now to the last of my four analytic frames for thinking about the place of language in digital discourse. In this regard, I want to draw attention to the ways language and communication are commodified, instrumentalized and *technologized* in new/social media contexts. In keeping with the work of Critical Discourse Analysts, therefore, we are obliged to consider how digital media are used in ways to shape and control our communicative practices (cf. Cameron, 2000; Fairclough, 1999). As a case in point, I offer *The British Monarchy* Facebook profile and the following excitable BBC News headline from October 2014: 'The Queen sends her first tweet through @BritishMonarchy'. And

the image accompanying this story? The British head of state, suitably behatted and wearing a matching Twitter-blue coat, stands in front of a podium with her forefinger tentatively outstretched towards a tablet screen – poised to tweet!

As I have argued before, this is not *social media* as many of us might understand or experience it (Thurlow, 2013). You certainly know something different is happening when one of the most detached, socially removed figureheads on the planet creates a Facebook profile or sends her first tweet. In fact, digital media – and especially social media – are increasingly used as tools for performing access, for staging participation and interaction. It is in this way that we see technology itself being taken up as a rhetorical resource. All of which is akin to what Norman Fairclough (1989) called *synthetic personalization*: the way businesses and organizations address mass markets/audiences as if they were all individuals. Technology is key to this process as we also see in automated customer-service systems designed to manage our interactions or in various apps offering to help us 'manage' our social lives (e.g., chatbots or 'conversational agents' like Apple's Siri or Amtrak's Julie; also *Swarm, Tinder* and other so-called 'social discovery apps'). All these are examples of how the social functions and meanings of language and communication are nowadays often disembedded and deployed as 'plug-ins' that skillfully blur the boundary between talk and technology. In effect, technology is presented to us as a stand-in for talk. It is for this reason also, and following what was said above about d-discourse and D-discourse, that a proper understanding of digital discourse requires that we be equally concerned with large-scale discourses (i.e., systems of power/knowledge) as we are with the linguistic specificities of discourse and everyday talk or writing.

Just as we find language and communication moving to center stage in our social and economic lives, many of our traditional, familiar ways of knowing and using language are being unsettled – not least due to the nature and impact of new/social media. And this is a challenge for scholars of language and for everyday language users alike. What I hope to have done in this chapter is to show some of the ways this is happening in the case of English and English-language research. Just as languages are less easily read as 'authentic' markers of identity and place, language itself is not so readily located in words and individual texts. Instead, we see language/s being recontextualized and resemioticized in different ways; that is, they are used outside their normal contexts, and used for a range of different purposes. Digital discourse, by no means a monolithic entity or practice itself, also demands a recognition of the relative place or importance of English and, indeed, the relative place or importance of language itself. Certainly, many of the people who use English on a daily basis have moved beyond monolingual, monolithic notions of English; they have also moved well beyond the notion of monomodal communication. And digital discourse is both evidence of these changes as well as a force that works to bring about these changes.

FURTHER READING

Like all new/social media research, the field moves quickly and changes constantly. In addition to the foundational literature sketched above and in addition to the studies cited here, I recommend the following handbook collections for a broader, more current survey of digital discourse research: Georgakopoulou and Spilioti (2015), Seargeant and Tagg (2014) and Herring et al. (2013). Two particularly useful texts are offered by Barton and Lee (2013) and by Page et al. (2014). In addition to papers published from time to time in *New Media & Society* and in the *Journal of Computer Mediated Communication*, two of the best journals for finding digital discourse research are the open-source *Language@Internet* (edited by foundational scholar Susan Herring) and *Discourse, Context & Media*.

ACKNOWLEDGEMENTS

As agreed with the volume editors, this chapter draws closely, but succinctly, on the introduction to my co-edited volume *Digital Discourse: Language and New Media* (Thurlow & Mroczek, 2011) and combines material from another recent piece published in Spanish (Thurlow, 2018).

Notes

1 In his *Language and the Internet*, David Crystal (2006) offers a very accessible summary of some core linguistic issues, drawing on a wide range of other people's research.

2 In the European context at least, scholars like Jannis Androutsopoulos are pivotal in connecting English-language research with research being done in other languages, and vice versa. Much the same role is played by someone like Ana Deumert (2014) who, while writing through English, is also a rare example of a prominent scholar engaging new/social media beyond the usual North-American/European contexts. In this regard, the work of people like Carmen Lee (e.g., 2011) and Yukiko Nishimura (e.g., 2011) has been key in extending our understanding of East Asian contexts. The fact remains, however, that digital discourse research continues to be driven by English-language publications with relatively little coverage of Latin America, Africa, Eastern Europe and South/South-East Asia.

REFERENCES

Androutsopoulos, J. (2006). Introduction: Sociolinguistics and computer-mediated communication. *Journal of Sociolinguistics*, 10(4), 419–438.

Androutsopoulos, J. (2010). Localising the global on the participatory web: Vernacular spectacles as local responses to global media flows. In N. Coupland (Ed.), *Handbook of Language and Globalization* (pp. 203–231). Oxford: Wiley-Blackwell.

Androutsopoulos, J. (2011). From variation to heteroglossia in the study of computer-mediated discourse. In C. Thurlow & K. Mroczek (Eds.), *Digital Discourse: Language in the New Media* (pp. 277–298). New York and London: Oxford University Press.

Baron, N. (2008). *Always On: Language in an Online and Mobile World*. Oxford: Oxford University Press.

Barton, D. & Lee, C. (2013). Language Online: Investigating Digital Texts and Practices. London: Routledge.

Bourdieu, P. (1991). *Language and Symbolic Power* (Trans. J. B. Thompson). Cambridge, MA: Harvard University Press.

Bucholtz, M. & Hall, K. (2008). All of the above: New coalitions in sociocultural linguistics. *Journal of Sociolinguistics*, 12(4), 401–431.

Cameron, D. (1995). *Verbal Hygiene*. London: Routledge.

Cameron, D. (2000). Good to Talk? Living and Working in a Communication Culture. London: Sage.

Cameron, D. & Panović, I. (2014). *Working with Written Discourse*. London: Sage.

Ch'ien, E. (2004). *Weird English*. Cambridge, MA: Harvard University Press.

Crystal, D. (2006). *Language and the Internet* (2nd ed.). Cambridge: Cambridge University Press.

Deumert, A. (2014). *Sociolingusitics and Mobile Communication*. Edinburgh: Edinburgh University Press.

Dürscheid, C. & Stark, E. (2011). *sms4science*: An international corpus-based texting project and the specific challenges for multilingual Switzerland. In C. Thurlow & K. Mroczek (Eds.), *Digital Discourse: Language in the New Media* (pp. 299–320). New York and London: Oxford University Press.

Fairclough, N. (1989). *Language and Power*. London: Longman.

Foucault, M. (1981). The order of discourse. In R. Young (Ed.), *Untying the Text: A Poststructuralist Reader* (pp. 48–77). London: Routledge & Kegan Paul.

Gee, P. (2010). An Introduction to Discourse Analysis: Theory and Method (3rd ed.). New York: Routledge.

Georgakopoulou, A. (2006). Postscript: Computer-mediated communication in sociolinguistics. *Journal of Sociolinguistics*, 10(4), 548–557.

Georgakopoulou, A. & Spilioti, T. (Eds.) (2015). *The Routledge Handbook of Language and Digital Communication*. London: Routledge.

Heller, M. (2003). Globalization, the new economy and the commodification of language and identity. *Journal of Sociolinguistics*, 7(4), 473–498.

Herring, S. C. (Ed.) (1996). *Computer-mediated Communication: Linguistic, Social and Cross-cultural Perspectives*. Pragmatics and Beyond series. Amsterdam: John Benjamins.

Herring, S. C. (2001). Computer-mediated discourse. In D. Schiffrin, D. Tannen & H. E. Hamilton (Eds.), *The Handbook of Discourse Analysis* (pp. 612–634). Malden, MA: Blackwell Publishers.

Herring, S. C. (2004). Slouching toward the ordinary: Current trends in computer-mediated communication. *New Media & Society*, 6(1), 26–36.

Herring, S. C. (2013). Discourse in Web 2.0: Familiar, reconfigured, and emergent. In D. Tannen & A. M. Tester (Eds.), *Discourse 2.0: Language and New Media* (pp. 1–25). Washington, DC: Georgetown University Press.

Herring, S. C. (2015). The co-evolution of computer-mediated discourse analysis and computer-mediated communication. Paper presented at the conference 'Approaches to Digital Discourse Analysis', University of Valencia, 18–20 November 2015.

Herring, S. C., Stein, D., & Virtanen, T. (Eds.) (2013). *Handbook of Pragmatics of Computer-mediated Communication*. Berlin: Mouton de Gruyter.

Jaworski, A. & Coupland, N. (2014). *The Discourse Reader* (3rd ed.). London: Routledge.

Jewitt, C. (2014). *The Routledge Handbook of Multimodal Analysis* (2nd ed.). London: Routledge.

Jones, R. H. (2010). Cyberspace and physical space: Attention structures in computer mediated communication. In A. Jaworski & C. Thurlow (Eds.), *Semiotic Landscapes: Language, Image, Space* (pp. 151–167). London: Continuum.

Kress, G. & van Leeuwen, T. J. (2001). Multimodal Discourse: The Modes and Media of Contemporary Communication. London: Arnold.

Lee, C. (2011). Micro-blogging and status updates on *Facebook*: Texts and practices. In C. Thurlow & K. Mroczek (Eds.), *Digital Discourse: Language in the New Media* (pp. 110–128). New York and London: Oxford University Press.

Leppänen, S., Pitkänen-Huhta, A., Piirainen-Marsh, A., Nikula, T., & Peuronen, S. (2009). Young people's translocal new media uses: A multiperspective analysis of language choice and heteroglossia. *Journal of Computer Mediated Communication*, 14(4), 1080–1107.

Nishimura, Y. (2011). Japanese *Keitai* novels and ideologies of literacy. In C. Thurlow & K. Mroczek (Eds.), *Digital Discourse: Language in the New Media* (pp. 86–109). New York and London: Oxford University Press.

Norris, S. & Jones, R. H. (Eds.) (2005). *Discourse in Action: Introducing Mediated Discourse Analysis*. London: Routledge.

Otsuji, E. & Pennycook, A. (2010). Metrolingualism: Fixity, fluidity and language in flux. *International Journal of Multilingualism*, 7, 240–254.

Page, R., Barton, D., Unger, J. W., & Zappovigna, M. (Eds.) (2014). *Researching Language and Social Media: A Student Guide*. London: Routledge.

Peuronen, S. (2011). Ride hard, live forever: Translocal identities in an online community of extreme sports Christians. In C. Thurlow & K. Mroczek (Eds.), *Digital Discourse: Language in the New Media* (pp. 154–176). New York and London: Oxford University Press.

Scollon, R. (2001). Mediated Discourse: The Nexus of Practice. London: Routledge.

Seargeant, P. & Tagg, C. (Eds.) (2014). *The Language of Social Media: Identity and Community on the Internet*. Basingstoke: Palgrave Macmillan.

Shortis, T. (2007). Gr8 txtpectations: The creativity of text spelling. *English Drama Media*, 8.

Tagliamonte, S. A. (2016). So sick or so cool? The language of youth on the internet. *Language in Society*, 45(1), 1–32.

Tagliamonte, S. A. & Denis, D. (2008). Linguistic ruin? LOL! Instant messaging and teen language. *American Speech*, 83(1), 3–34.

Thurlow, C. (2003). Generation Txt? The sociolinguistics of young people's text-messaging. *Discourse Analysis Online*, 1(1).

Thurlow, C. (2006). From statistical panic to moral panic: The metadiscursive construction and popular exaggeration of new media language in the print media. *Journal of Computer-Mediated Communication*, 11(3), 667–701.

Thurlow, C. (2012). Determined creativity: Language play, vernacular literacy and new media discourse. In R. Jones (Ed.), *Discourse and Creativity* (pp. 169–190). London: Pearson.

Thurlow, C. (2013). Fakebook: Synthetic media, pseudo-sociality and the rhetorics of Web 2.0. In D. Tannen & A. Trester (Eds.), *Discourse 2.0: Language and New Media* (pp. 225–248). Washington, DC: Georgetown University Press.

Thurlow, C. (2014). Disciplining youth: Language ideologies and new technologies. In A. Jaworski & N. Coupland (Eds.), *The Discourse Reader* (3rd ed.) (pp. 481–496). London: Routledge.

Thurlow, C. (2018). Enmarcando el lenguaje de los nuevos medios. In M. Giammatteo, P. Gubitosi & A. Parini (Eds.), *El Español en la Red: Usos y Géneros de la Comunicación Mediada por Computadora*. Madrid: Iberoamericana.

Thurlow, C. & Mroczek, K. (Eds.) (2011). *Digital Discourse: Language in the New Media*. New York and London: Oxford University Press.

Thurlow, C. & Poff, M. (2011). Text-messaging. In S. C. Herring, D. Stein & T. Virtanen (Eds.), *Handbook of the Pragmatics of CMC*. Berlin and New York: Mouton de Gruyter.

Vaisman, C. (2011). Performing girlhood through typographic play in Hebrew blogs. In C. Thurlow & K. Mroczek (Eds.), *Digital Discourse: Language in the New Media* (pp. 177–196). New York: Oxford University Press.

Woolard, K. A. & Schieffelin, B. B. (1994). Language ideology. *Annual Review of Anthropology*, 23, 55–82.

8

Ontology

Nick Couldry and Jannis Kallinikos

The methodology of any domain depends, first, on clarifying what types of object are being researched – indeed can exist – in that domain: that is, on clarifying the ontology of that domain. The ontology of social media might seem wholly unproblematic: social media *sites* are certainly infrastructures with considerable, even massive, presence in our lives, the focus of our everyday habits of checking and updating, circulating and sharing. When 1.5 billion people are active monthly users of one leading social media platform alone (Facebook), then the 'object' of study is hardly trivial. But what type of object are we studying exactly? Again from one point of view, the question seems straightforward: Facebook, Twitter, and other sites of social media activity are platforms (Gillespie, 2010), where social activity is supported generally by commercial operations.[1] The facts of such platforms – their design and other features – are important. But in this chapter we want to go beyond the platform 'surface' and ask a different

ontological question: what *are* social media from a sociological point of view? Or, more precisely, in what sense are 'social media' *actually* 'social', as opposed to merely being outputs *labelled as* 'social'? And, running behind that question, how should we interpret the related epistemological claims, made by various actors every day, that 'social media' provide evidence of '*the* social'? Those questions, it turns out, are far from straightforward, yet we cannot advance far in the study of social media without answering them. The answers will shape why we would want to spend our time studying social media at all rather than some other object.

Let us right away state the hypothesis of this chapter. Interaction in social media is organized along highly stylized activity corridors (e.g., sharing, tagging, liking) that essentially serve the purpose of *transforming* online forms of user participation into a computable and ultimately tradable data footprint. By these means, each user action is rendered a discrete data-token, a measurable click. Discrete data-tokens are then aggregated and several scores of user-choice affinities and relations are ceaselessly computed and fed back to users, thus establishing a dynamic context of interaction between user choice and sociality online. As a result, what happens on social media platforms cannot be regarded as unproblematic evidence of social activity *per se*.

Specifically, the spaces of social media are different from those of general social analysis. All social spaces, not just public spaces, have until now been analysed on the basis that they are 'spaces of appearances' (using Arendt's (1960) familiar term in a more general sense). We have assumed until now that 'appearance' in such spaces – presence-to-others, availability for interaction with and evaluation by others in that space – can be taken as a basic datum of social analysis. But this is no longer unproblematic, because 'appearance' is now the result of prior computer-based calculations and, worse, the result of calculations driven by a particular kind of economic motivation through which data from online forms of sociality are traded in a complex ecosystem of advertisers, data brokers and other interested stakeholders. *Put simply, there is on social media platforms no 'appearance-in-itself' but only ever appearance that is the derivative of prior processes of calculation.* The result is a challenge to the very basis of understanding the social: is Twitter, for example, best understood as a real space of social appearances, as we are tempted to see it, or rather a complex projection of intersecting calculative forces? If the latter, how *should* we treat Twitter and other platforms from a sociological point of view?

By asking these questions, we follow Jose van Dijck's scepticism about the term 'social media', insisting instead that the term 'social' is a site of contestation, aimed at the production of value. Rather than talk of an age of social media, Van Dijck (2013) insists we talk of a 'culture of connectivity', that is, of an industry-inflected *imperative to connect* on particular platforms, in order to generate specific types of value. This chapter builds on Van Dijck's approach, and is ordered as follows. First, we briefly review and distinguish between the main approaches to studying social media that have been taken in the scholarly literature. We argue that existing approaches need to be supplemented by a critical phenomenological approach that explores the contested status of social media platforms in social experience. Second, we ground this proposed critical approach in a discussion of the broad sociological nature of data operations as they occur in social media. Third, we discuss those data operations in greater detail, drawing out the problems they raise for any treatment of social media platforms as 'real' spaces of social interaction. Fourth, we consider the implications of our argument for the methodology of studying social media as an object within wider social experience. We follow this with a brief conclusion.

EXISTING APPROACHES TO SOCIAL MEDIA

There is no space here for a comprehensive review of the literature on social media. Instead, we aim, more modestly, to mark some distinctions between how various scholars have studied the 'object' of social media. The boundaries we draw are not exclusive, but they do, we suggest, indicate some important differences of emphasis in the existing literature.

The first important approach understands social media as sites where *social networks* are produced and sometimes generated (boyd and Ellison, 2008: 211). This made particular sense when, in the late 2000s and from diverse origins, the scale of social media platforms grew fast, and one of their most distinctive features was to provide the facilities whereby people built and/or sustained networks of friends and connections on an unprecedented scale. Some analyses focused in greater detail on the workings of this networking process, and its potential use as a source of social capital (Ellison et al., 2007; Ellison et al., 2011), suggesting a positive benefit for some types of users at least (Steinfeld et al., 20009). Other analyses sought to consider more broadly the consequence of such networking on wider social space, arguing that, under many conditions, the result was to foster the emergence of 'networked publics' (boyd, 2011): 'one way of interpreting the public articulation of connections on social networks is to see it as the articulation of a public' (boyd, 2011: 44). Note that boyd carefully does not rule out other uses; indeed a major strength of boyd's work is to be open to the multiple and multilevelled uses of social media (boyd, 2014). In another well-known essay, boyd (2008) analysed the meaning of the opportunities provided by social media platforms for US youth who are generally excluded from having voice in public space: 'they [go on social media] because they seek access to adult society. Their participation is deeply rooted in their desire to engage publicly' (2008: 137). boyd links explicitly to Arendt's (1960) concept of the 'sphere of appearances'. Such approaches do not disguise the constructed nature of social media platforms, and the difficulty of treating 'data' from one site as sociologically equivalent to 'data' from another (boyd, 2011; boyd and Crawford, 2012), and this scepticism is important to our argument. Nonetheless it is difficult to develop such a research agenda, while bracketing off entirely the term 'social': as some of these authors note in passing, 'social network sites provide rich sources of *naturalistic* behavioral data' (boyd and Ellison, 2008: 220, added emphasis), and 'networked technologies introduce new affordances for amplifying, recording, and spreading information and *social* acts' (boyd, 2011: 45, added emphasis). The question arises therefore how what we might call this 'social realist' approach to social media platforms can be combined with a more thoroughgoing scepticism *about* the 'social' produced there?

The second approach to social media platforms puts a primary emphasis on critique, but from a distinctive angle: this is the Marxist political economy approach championed by Christian Fuchs (2014). While this critique focuses on many points, its key argument is that social media are sites for unpaid labour (Fuchs, 2013) through which new forms of economic value are being generated as part of *capitalism's continuing struggle to reproduce itself*. On this account, the data aspects of social media platform operations are highlighted, and criticized as an aspect of a wider appropriation of social energies for economic ends. A strength of this analysis is to acknowledge in broad terms how social media both 'enable and constrain a social level of human societies' through a 'recursive organic relation between the technological and the social level of the media' (Fuchs, 2014: 37). This analysis is grounded in a broader social theory, and is highly critical of how some accounts of social media and their consequences (such as Castells' theory of 'network society': Castells, 2009) have become detached from social theory itself (Fuchs, 2014: Chapter 4). There is force to these arguments, and one of us has developed parallel arguments in other contexts (Couldry, 2012: Chapter 5; 2014). A limit, however, of Fuchs' approach is that, when it anticipates the possible future of social media, it is in terms of an unleashing of the social energies *seen within* social media: 'social media anticipate a full sociality of human existence, but in their corporate form this potential is limited by capitalist structures of ownership and capital accumulation' (Fuchs, 2014: 256). What is lost here is the possibility that the 'social' that is supposedly available *to be* unleashed has already been shaped by the operations of those platforms themselves.

A third approach developed particularly in sociological treatments foregrounds the possibility that the everyday use and embedding of social media platforms is ushering in *a transformation of both economy and society*: a transition from a 'linkage economy' to a 'like economy' where users now gain social currency from the public articulation of connections on social networking sites (Gerlitz and Helmond, 2014). Interestingly, one writer in this approach criticized the first approach for *too much* scepticism about the ontology of 'friends' on Facebook (Beer, 2008 520). Other work has discussed the implications of social media for our sense of social time (Kaun and Stierstedt, 2014; Weltevrede et al., 2014). Given the intensity of (and pressures towards) *self*-reproduction on social networking sites, there is clear scope to link such analysis to broader Foucauldian accounts of how subjects are produced in late modernity (Marwick, 2013). But what remains difficult in this approach is to clarify the reference-point from which this transformed 'social' is being analysed. If the social endlessly reproduces itself in ever-changing ways, how is critique possible, given that it must be developed from somewhere (where exactly?) inside the social?

This is where we find a fourth approach particularly helpful. This approach tries to get into view the whole process of social transformation through social media platforms, not as a 'done deal', but rather as a quite specific new inflection on, and *appropriation of*, the sorts of activities that broadly were once called 'social' in another very different, pre-platform context (Mejias, 2013; Van Dijck, 2013). Jose Van Dijck's critique of social media, for example, radically extends the work of cultural studies in an intertextual analysis of platform discourses and interfaces. From this analysis, Van Dijck develops an overall diagnosis that we have moved to a 'platformed sociality' (2013: 5) which is not equivalent to our 'social', but can, and must, be singled out for critical analysis. This fourth approach in our view goes furthest towards developing a critical ontology of social media. In its sceptical distance from current uses of the term 'social' in relation to social media platforms' activities, it comes close to philosopher Giorgio

Agamben's insight that the answer to our current involvement in what 'the apparatus' (by which he means our devices of technologically mediated connection) cannot be a simple acceptance or rejection, but must rather be 'the liberation of that which remains captured … by means of apparatuses, in order to bring it back to a possible common life' (Agamben, 2009: 17). That possible common life is not already 'there', visible and waiting to be released; it will have to be *reconstructed* from within the constrained context of today's platformed practices. However, a self-acknowledged limitation of Van Dijck's critique is that it does not encompass the views and accounts of users of social media.

Emerging from all these critical approaches to social media is the prospect of a critical phenomenology of social media, which takes distance from social media's appropriation of 'the social', while also tracing the *experience* of being connected through social media and its material conditions. This is what we try to develop in this rest of this chapter. First, however, we need to review some fundamental points about the sociology of data.

DATA

The interface which social media platforms present to a particular user is an array composed of various streams of content and activity-tokens; that array is not a display of everything and anything relevant to that user's use of that platform, but a particular composed *selection* produced on the basis of the platform's own criteria of importance (Van Dijck, 2013). Those criteria are shaped, above all, by the economic drivers of the platform. All activities shown on a social media platform must, to be shown at all, either originate in, or be translated into, 'formalized inscriptions' (Van Dijck, 2013: 6) in the format acceptable to that platform. Once in that format, they are treated by the platform in accordance with its own dynamics of selection, that is, in terms of the 'value' which that particular inscription has. As Van Dijck puts it: 'through social media, … casual speech acts [of everyday life] have turned into formalized inscriptions which, once embedded in the larger economy of wider publics, take on a different value' (2013: 6–7).

This *transvaluation* of everyday sociality may be blurred by platforms themselves who may be relaxed about blurring how long pre-existing friendships are equated with 'friendships' of previously unknown people formed only on the platform, as Van Dijck notes (2013: 13). This blurring is not the result of platforms' muddy thinking, let alone any mischief on their part, but follows simply from the more general principles about how their data are procured and ordered. Let us explore these briefly.

The database has a distinctive type of power which Bowker defines as 'jussive': an ordering power based on an 'exclusionary principle' that determines what can and cannot be stored in a particular form (Bowker, 2008 12). The consequences of database operations are in this sense final: 'what is not classified gets rendered invisible' (2008 153). Again, that is not (or at least not necessarily) the result of a prejudicial desire to exclude certain social entities, but simply the result of how databases *must* operate to function effectively. The point of the exclusions on which databases operate is to fix the *starting*-point from which data operations (counting, aggregating, sorting, evaluation) begin. In that sense, by being placed in a database, 'data' become 'unmoored' from the underlying detailed materials from which they were gathered (Kitchin, 2014: 72). The 'knowledge' that results cannot easily be separated out from the purposive selections that formed the database. Indeed, as Bowker notes, this is a feature of all archived social memory: 'our memory practices [are] the site where ideology and knowledge fuse' (2008 228). This, then, is the first key point about the ontology of social media: that what

appears as 'just having happened' to, and for, us on a social media platform (an apparently natural social 'datum') can only appear *as such* by virtue of its place in archives ordered according to principles quite different from those of everyday face-to-face social interaction (Alaimo and Kallinikos, 2016).

This might seem strange, but only if we forget that on social media platforms 'appearances' are always the result of prior processing. There must always be, therefore, as legal scholar Julie Cohen notes, a gap between the abstractions inherent to data functions – their 'processes of … representation and classification' – and the *experiential processes* in which those functions become, through platforms, embedded (Cohen, 2012: 24, 20). This gap is not accidental, or optional, but inherent to the type of appearance that 'platformed sociality' (Van Dijck, 2013: 5) provides.

As a result, the *basic* level of symmetry we take for granted in face-to-face social interaction cannot be assumed. This crucial point needs more explanation. When two native speakers of a language speak together, one speaks in the language in which s/he expects her/his interlocutor to respond, and so does the interlocutor, and from this follow many other more detailed symmetries of expectation and interpretation. The 'flow' of everyday conversation between those who share a language is based on two key assumptions that the great phenomenological sociologist Alfred Schutz called 'interchangeability of standpoints' and 'congruence of relevance systems' (Schutz and Luckmann, 1973: 60). In this way, the components in a stream of social interaction are treated by those involved as *continuous with* each other. But that symmetrical to-and-fro cannot be so easily assumed on social media platforms, where whatever can appear 'back' to us *must always already have complied with the external relevance-criteria of the platform, not those of the interlocutors*. In short-term exchanges, we might not notice any difference: our stream of interaction might seem to be frictionless and unimpeded, but on a larger scale the results may well be more misleading. We will discuss this in detail in the next section. As a result, there is a deeper asymmetry hidden within claims that data from social media platforms yield knowledge about the social. As Jose van Dijck puts it, 'it is easier to encode sociality into algorithms than to decode algorithms back into social action' (2013: 172), and yet this is exactly what we try to do, when we read social media datastreams as if they were simply an extension of our natural forms of sociality.

The pressures to treat what occurs on social media platforms as if they were the unmediated outcome of social interaction are indeed great. This too derives from the basic features of data processing understood as processes of categorization. Categories have been an important topic in social theory for more than a century. For Durkheim and Mauss (1969 [1902]), categories (as outputs of a system of classification in so-called 'primitive societies') were derivatives of the actual divisions of society itself, and of the very idea of society itself. In most subsequent accounts, the order of causality is reversed, with categories contributing to 'the built information environment of a society' (Bowker and Star, 1999: 5).

Categories do not just operate in isolation. They need to be held in place, as the anthropologist Mary Douglas pointed out, by processes of 'naturalization' (Douglas, 1986). However automated the operation of processes of categorizing, they also have wider effects as social actors react to them and to the implicit claims that the use of categories make about the way the underlying world is – that it exists in a form that *enables it to be* categorized in such a way. As Bowker and Star put it, every classificatory system 'represents the world "out there"' (1999: 61) in a particular and decisive way. Yet it may take time for objects, in everyday practice, to fit with the categories that are available for them in a particular community of interpretation, and so, Bowker and Star suggest, 'objects

exist [as members of categories] with respect to a community *along a trajectory of naturalization*' (1999: 299, added emphasis): that trajectory derives in part from the interactive nature of social categorization (Hacking, 1999). Over time, the processes of categorizing objects and using objects come together in a process of 'convergence': 'the mutual constitution of a person or object and their representation. People put things into categories and learn from those categories how to behave' (Bowker and Star, 1999: 311).

The relation between categories and the objects they categorize becomes more complex when categorization is automated, as with social media platforms, and must be inferred to operate 'behind the surface' of a platform, but there is no reason to expect anything other than naturalization. What one of us has called the 'computed sociality' of social media platforms (Alaimo and Kallinikos, 2016; Kallinikos and Tempini, 2014) therefore tends, over time, to appear natural. Research on social media has started to integrate the effects of this category-naturalization in its analysis, for example, of how we choose 'friends' in platforms such as Facebook (Bucher, 2012).

This can be understood finally also as a process of spatial organization. As Kitchin and Dodge (2011) analyse extensively in their book *Code/Space*, many spaces (physical, organizational, informational) are now 'coded', that is, their operations are structured through the software that processes data inputs of various sorts. The highly controlled space of the airport security queue is one clear example, entry into which is impossible without having met various data-related conditions in a prescribed sequence (2011: Chapter 7). But the same is true, even if less dramatically, with the 'spaces' of social media platforms. Social media platforms feel like 'spaces' where we can encounter others, but there would be no such spaces without the underlying operation of the platform software and its calculative infrastructure: those spaces are 'calculative publics' (Gillespie,

2014: 188–191) whose encounters depend entirely on the precondition of data-sorting, and whose 'space of appearances' derives from calculation. As a result, platforms organized around the category 'friends' are in no sense places for encountering friends naturalistically: rather, as Taina Bucher argues, 'friends have become a primary means through which *the production and occlusion of information* can be programmed' (Bucher, 2012: 49). How can we think further about the implications of this for social media platforms as 'social objects', and for our understanding of sociality itself?

ANATOMY OF SOCIAL MEDIA[2]

Two fundamental ideas emerge from what we have been claiming so far. First, user involvement and interaction on social media is heavily premised on the kind of institutional entities that social media platforms are. Access and use of social media functionalities on the part of users is embedded in a complex institutional matrix of relations, marked by the commercialization and trading of user activity and its data footprint. In other words, the patterns of interaction and the sociality that social media platforms afford are closely linked with the objectives of social media *qua* institutional (market) actors. Second, the premises of social interaction on social media platforms, and the consequent trading of its data footprint, are significantly shaped by the computational rendition of the operations of social media (Kallinikos, 2009) and the ways in which pervasive computational technologies, such as the database, function. As with most market-embedded exchanges, the pursuit of the commercial objectives of social media companies requires quantitative description and calculation. In an environment of large and shifting data volumes, these critical tasks can only be accomplished by the heavy involvement of computational technologies that provide

generic and specific solutions to the data-handling challenges that social media confront. Computational technologies, in turn, boost commercialization by affording, as we will see below, the multiple and contingent segmentation of the social *qua* data.

With few exceptions (e.g., Bucher, 2012; Gillespie, 2014; Van Dijck, 2013), these data-based operations supporting social media have tended to remain out of the limelight. For a variety of reasons, the social implications of the computational make-up of social media have been blackboxed. It seems to us important to submit to critical analysis the entanglement of institutional and technological forces at work here. This requires tracing the involvement of the backend data-handling techniques in the operations of framing, mapping and segmenting the social that characterize social media. The first step in this analysis is the recognition of the fundamental fact that the transposition of social relations on social media platforms presupposes, as already indicated, the drastic *simplification* of social activities and their *typification* or *categorization*. Social activity on social media has to be thus simplified and shaped so as the categorization and coding of social interaction delivers, reliably and systematically, standardized data-tokens that can be used as the basis for further operations of measurement and computation.

It is vital, always, to keep in mind the simple fact that on social media social interaction needs to be 'trans-substantiated' or 'trans-valued' into data. There is no other way that social media can operate. In some fundamental ways, therefore, social media are nothing but data entities. It is the data footprint of social interaction that provides the material for most calculative and marker operations performed by social media. The datafication of interaction is accomplished through the construction of narrow, heavily stylized, activity types (e.g., liking, sharing, tagging) that code user activity into data that can be recorded in distinct fields, and so indexed, counted, aggregated and computed.

Much data on social media is made of behavioural data of this sort, through which user activities are recorded as singular choices via clicking on specific activity types (Alaimo and Kallinikos, 2016, 2017). User-generated content that may matter more to some specific groups of users makes at present a less calculable body of data and is, for that reason, less often recycled in the calculative operations that define social media as institutional actors and organizations. Quantitative text analysis of unstructured, user-generated, content is of course possible and is used for certain purposes (e.g., sentiment analysis and marketing), but the bulk of operational data on social media is the outcome of recording single behavioural choices as orchestrated by the social media platforms themselves. The spine of social media operations is made of the collection and analysis of such behavioural data, not of user-generated content (Alaimo, 2014).

Left on its own, however, the data footprint of social interaction on social media procured by these means (simplification, categorization and coding) is not illuminating. As in most contexts where large data volumes are involved, data 'speak' only after they have been clustered, compared and analysed. It is the very detection of *relationships* between a user and other users, between one group of users and other groups, between past and present choices, whether of individual users or groups, that serves as the cognitive currency of social media. But the detection of such relationships requires that user choices *qua* clicks have been clustered and aggregated. Data aggregation is an essential operation of social media. The profile of the activities that users perform on social media and the connections they maintain with items and other users result from aggregating user choices *qua* clicks within and across activity types (liking, sharing, tagging, following, etc.). In this sense, on social media, users for practical purposes are not real persons but abstract operations enacted through the aggregation of singular data-points (Alaimo and

Kalinikos, 2016, 2017). On Facebook, for instance, a user is defined by, and is essential coterminous with, the aggregation of his or her likes on the basis of which he or she can be rendered as one entity comparable to others. On Last.fm or Spotify, a user is for most purposes defined by the aggregation of listening data (that is, clicks on tracks) and tagging data. The activity types of social media essentially split the unity of a person into well-defined acts and then reassemble it through the data aggregation that the performance of such acts delivers. Placed in this context, aggregation establishes *new* data entities through which the social fabric is *re-established* (Kallinikos, 2009) as an (apparent) relationship between individual users and groups of users, clustered and compared at various levels of abstraction or generality (Desrosières, 1998).

The result is a new and far-reaching *pliability* of social interaction on social media platforms, which constitutes a new ontology of the social, or at least of what passes for 'the social'. Novel ways of making sociality visible online are established as the data on platform social interaction can be sorted in a variety of ways that construct relationships and patterns between users and items. Abstractions of this sort and the numerical data they deliver have, of course, been inherent in many contexts and institutions of modernity (Cohen, 1982; Porter, 1996). States, markets and corporations have for a long time based their operations on large volumes of recombinant data, descriptive of carefully defined activities (e.g., expenditures, life styles) or people (e.g., consumers, tax payers) at individual and aggregate levels (Desrosières, 1998; Gandy, 1993; Hacking, 1990; Rose and Miller, 2013). Placed in this larger context, the ontology of aggregation and the status of aggregated entities (as real or nominal) have always been objects of dispute and controversy (Desrosières, 1998; Espeland and Sauder, 2007; Foucault, 1970). However, what is at stake today in the analysis of the ontology of social media goes further.

As earlier indicated, many of the naturalized categories that have served as the basis of institutional data collection in the past have been embedded in established social practices and, perhaps one can claim, in real-life contexts: the operations of class distinction (Bourdieu, 1984), medical professions and systems (Bowker and Star, 1999), other ritualized cultural orders (Douglas, 1986), practices and cultural conventions (Rosch, 1999; Rosch and Mervis, 1975). The relation of social media platforms' data collection to wider social reality is very different. Social media aggregate activity-tokens (user clicks) that encode narrowly defined activity-*types* (e.g., liking, tagging, following) whose basis in social interaction, as normally experienced and interpreted, is thin. None of these activity-types springs directly from experiences of social conventions. While aiming at mapping the trivial and everyday, social media go a considerable way towards *instituting* (Bourdieu, 1991) an artificial everyday that aims at *delivering* the data needed by social media platforms as market entities for counting, indexing and recombining what passes as 'the social'. This artificial everyday, constituted through the regular measurement and aggregation of its data footprint, is a defining attribute of social media, and indeed of the very ontology of the social that social media bring to being (Alaimo and Kallinikos, 2017).

This is only the beginning of a wider transformation. Aggregation further 'unmoors' data from the artificial platform-contexts in which it has originally been produced, and establishes the cognitive base upon which individuals and other data entities *are made commensurable* (through clicks being treated as equivalent) and thus comparable and measurable along various dimensions (Espeland and Stevens, 1998). Once aggregated, individual user-choices (e.g, liking, following, tagging) can be sorted and recomputed in a variety of ways. A user can be compared with other users at various levels of generality and patterning: like-minded

or similar users, similar or popular items or popular users generated. For instance, last.fm, a social media platform dedicated to music discovery, assembles categories of similar artists based on the number of tracks on which users click. The listening activity of users becomes the means through which artists can be grouped as more or less similar depending on the number of users they are counted to have in common; the more users they have in common, the more similar they are, and vice versa. These patterns of similarity can draw on aggregate data over longer or shorter periods and various permutations performed over artists and periods, tracks and users (geographical area, age or gender) that underlie the so-called personal recommendations so characteristic of social media.[3]

The pattern-extraction which such data permutations produce serves to establish a range of revenue-generating services all the way from marketing of specific items to credit-scoring. The business models through which this happens differ, but the underlying idea is to sell the data-patterns thus established to market actors. But it is also true that the extraction of these patterns serves as the basis for boosting platform activity by being carried over to users in the form of personal recommendations of various kinds that platforms assemble and which, on the top of any market purpose they may serve, incite further user action. It is important to underscore the critical nature of this last operation and the significance which a steady inflow of data plays in sustaining social media. Without a mass inflow of data (i.e., user activity and clicking) that is constantly produced *and reworked* in real time, the artificial reality that social media platforms have established risks losing touch with the institutional and market purposes that it is meant to serve (Kallinikos, 2007). The extraction of data-based patterns furthermore provides a *picture* of platform activity that can be the basis for improving platform functioning through the offer of novel functionalities to users.

USERS AND REACTIVITY AND POWER

How are users to be thought in the account of social media we have given above, the dimension that we noted even Van Dijck's critical perspective neglected? Even though the terms on the basis of which users join social media platforms are heavily shaped by the conditions outlined above, it is still reasonable to assume that personal, social and demographic factors play a significant role on how people react to these terms (e.g., boyd, 2008, 2014). The study of particular groups or communities of users might therefore be a much-needed complement to the picture we have painted in the preceding pages. Facets of the reality of social media platforms and the experiences they mediate are without doubt a local accomplishment that must be understood with reference to specific types of users and groups and their pursuits.

At the same time it is important to distinguish the different levels of reality to which one's arguments apply. The claims we have advanced in this chapter aim at unravelling the complex working machine that social media as institutional entities embody. Such a task, we admit, cannot be exhausted by the study of particular groups and the ways they receive, interpret or work around the structuring machine of social media. At any rate, the study of particular groups or communities of users cannot be meaningfully conducted without reference to the complex interplay between user groups and the structuring modalities of social media, and the ways in which social groups and social media as institutional entities accommodate one another. It is important to trace the distinct ways that groups of users or communities relate to, enact and are shaped by the structuring premises of social media platforms. Whether conceived as constraints or affordances, the technological and economic forces that define social media as institutional actors cannot be wished away.

In the account of social media offered in this chapter, user activity is an essential component of the apparatus of social media and so are the preferences and differences of users. Both user activity as a data-producing force and user-preferences (and absences of preferences) as a representation (in data form) of the social fabric are brought to a much higher level of abstraction or generality and shaped in ways that accommodate the objectives of social media platforms as institutional actors. In this context, the activity profiles of users and groups of users are captured by constantly placing them within a web of differences and similarities with other users or groups of users, in the same way perhaps that market forces regularly trade use for exchange value. It is *this play of similarity and difference worked out at aggregate levels*, and technically known as network analysis, that confers the social and market relevance of social media. As social media platforms expand and become active forces in contemporary societies, the highly selective and largely artificial ways (liking, tagging, following, sharing, posting) by which they orchestrate human activity become habitual and begin to congeal into a sort of self-evident or naturalized sociality. It is a critical research task to understand how these conditions interact with an alternative sociality that still has its roots in the traditional contexts of everyday life (Alaimo and Kallinikos, 2017).

Beyond the effects of habituation, it is critical to investigate the social implications of the personal recommendations and other comparisons that social media advance to users through the complex and largely invisible data machinery analysed above. The interactive and reactive status of this process has been repeatedly observed in other contexts of social life in conjunction with people's tendency to enact the distinctions and classifications that institutions impose on them (see, for example, Espeland and Sauder, 2007; Espeland and Stevens, 1998; Hacking, 1986, 1999).

Espeland and Sauder (2007: 6) define reactivity as 'individuals [that] alter their behavior in reaction to being evaluated, observed or measured', a conspicuously Foucauldian theme. The force of this reactive and self-reinforcing process is usually strongly correlated with the social embedment and solidification of the institutional matrix within which it takes place (Foucault, 1977, 1988; Hacking, 1999). In other words, the stronger the institutions and the relations they build with one another, the deeper and more persisting the effects which the distinctions and classifications they produce have on people, either directly through the provision of incentives for conforming to them or indirectly through mechanisms of enforcement and the construction of normative and legal orders. Even though social media may still be thought as thin institutions, and the measurements they produce lacking strong normative foundation, the growth and economic success they have acquired in barely more than a decade provide evidence of the importance of the institutional matrix (digital technologies, market entities, revenue generation) in which they are embedded. This matrix, without doubt, has social power of a sort, a power that fits well with Pierre Bourdieu's definition of symbolic power as a 'power of constructing reality' (1991: 166).

CONCLUSION

Several implications for the ontology of social media follow from our analysis. *First*, social media do not in fact map a social reality 'out there'. Rather, social media establish a kind of social reality by providing the means through which real persons *qua* users perform activities of very particular kinds that have largely been incited by social media platforms themselves. In other words, making media platforms 'social' in principle implies rendering sociality 'technical', as Van Dijck (2013: 12) has cogently claimed.

Second, what is recreated by these processes of social media is, overall, an ephemeral, real-time attuned, and perpetually changing 'everyday' that reorders the trivial pursuits and habits of individuals into groups, categories or profiles that can be used as the basis for generating revenues. These cognitive groupings or categories differ essentially from the categories established by conceptual means (taxonomies) and practical purposes in everyday life between social actors whose pursuits are not mediated by data processing. The cognitive clusters that social media deliver are contingent outcomes with little lasting value and significance. They are established, as it were, only to be shattered, and reassembled again into new configurations (Lévi-Strauss, 1962),[4] as the massive daily clicking of user crowds steadily reframes their value and market relevance (Kallinikos, 2007).

Third, what is thus accomplished takes, from the perspective of the collective understanding of the social, the form of a long analytical retreat, whereby the units of social action are disaggregated into discrete, singular and often artificial acts that are then computationally reassembled into larger social entities such as users, groups of users and short-term trends. This long trajectory of analytic reduction and – even we might say, pulverization – of the social is driven not by a collective attempt to understand our ways of living together, but by the computational capacities and constraints of current computing technologies, and the overall commercial context within which social media platforms operate. It also reflects the asymmetrical capabilities and powers on the basis of which the 'game' that social media platforms embody has been established and performed.

We need therefore to move beyond the study of particular groups of social media platform users, towards understanding social media as formations and institutional matrices that have larger effects on social life.

The 'big picture' in which social media are embedded cannot be exhausted by the study of particular groups or settings. It cannot be assembled unless one moves beyond the user interface and lays open the structuring and enduring effects which the entire apparatus of social media has on social life itself. Such a task is replete with empirical difficulties of varying complexity. On the one hand, access to empirical contexts in which economic success is built and revenues earned is not easily granted. On the other hand, there is the perennial challenge of how to demarcate meaningfully and study empirically digital infrastructures and ecosystems in which large numbers of actors, technologies (boundary technologies in particular, such as APIs, SDKs and social buttons) and processes are connected. Whatever the challenges, it is important to pursue research that is able to bring forward the logics by which social media platforms operate and the technologies and systems they deploy to shape the terms of user platform participation. Such a task requires prolonged immersion into particular research contexts (i.e., intensive case studies) that may provide the opportunity to unravel the design choices, technological systems and economic rationalities of social media platforms (Alaimo, 2014; Bucher, 2012). It is at this level that the evasive sociality of social media can begin to be pinned down, building on the various critical literatures on social media platforms discussed in the chapter's first main section (see, for example, Alaimo and Kallinikos, 2017). And it is against the background of analysis at this level that the projects of social actors who want to contest the power of this 'evasive sociality' and propose another one can, in turn, be explored (Couldry and Powell, 2014).

There is a deeper problem too: how can we design research to track the lineaments of an ongoing reshaping of the social as it is happening, and through the inevitably local and particular streams of social interaction to which as researchers we have access? The beginnings of the answer, at least, lie, we

suggest, in targeting in our research design the search for the elements of social interaction that precisely carry traces of the longer term: the *patterns* of action and categorization observable over time within a group of actors in a platform setting and acknowledged by those actors where we have access to them through interviews, observations or other means; reflections of actors of how across a range of platforms certain types of action are *incentivized* and others *disincentivized*, and how this evaluative patterning relates to their own broader sense of value and priorities; and, given how fast historically a social media 'habitus' has emerged, those actors' *memories* of actions they now do which seem to crowd out those that they once did. Each of these would be good starting-points, we suggest, for beginning to trace the logics of social media (Van Dijck and Poell, 2013) in action. But the task is a large one, and it is impossible to see beyond its beginnings at this point. Nonetheless, the fundamental ideas we have put forward in this chapter provide, we hope, some encouragement and guidance along the route towards opening up this new terrain for social inquiry.

Notes

1 The Chinese microblogging platform Weibo being an important example of a hybrid market/state platform.

2 Jannis Kallinikos wishes to acknowledge the contribution of Cristina Alaimo to developing the ideas that are presented from this section onwards. Much of what is presented here has come about as the result of our joint and protracted effort to understand the operational logics and technical conditions that sustain social media while retaining the focus on social processes and institutions.

3 This is accomplished by the technology of recommender systems by which affinities between users or items are produced and personal recommendations advanced. Amazon.com recommender system, which traces similarities and differences between transactions of users and advances recommendations of the type 'those that bought this item bought that item too', is a typical example. Such technologies, known as

Collaborative Filtering Recommender Systems, are widely used in social media.

4 This phrase is very similar to an epigraph of Franz Boas that Lévi-Stauss (1962) uses to open his great book on mythical classifications *La pensée sauvage* (*The savage mind*): 'It would seem that mythological worlds have been built up, only to be shattered again, and new worlds were built from the fragments'.

REFERENCES

Agamben, G. (2009) *What is an Apparatus? And Other Essays*. Stanford, CA: Stanford University Press.

Alaimo, C. (2014) *Computational Consumption: Social Media and the Construction of Digital Consumers*. PhD dissertation. The London School of Economics and Political Science (LSE).

Alaimo, C. and Kallinikos, J. (2016) Encoding the Everyday: The Infrastructural Apparatus of Social Data. In C. Sugimoto, H. Ekbia and M. Mattioli (Eds.), *Big Data is not a Monolith: Policies, Practices, and Problems* (pp. 77–90). Cambridge, MA: MIT Press.

Alaimo, C. and Kallinikos, J. (2017) Computing the Everyday: Social Media as Data Platforms. *The Information Society*, 33/4: 175–191.

Arendt, H. (1960) *The Human Condition*. Chicago, IL: University of Chicago Press.

Beer, D. (2008) Social Network(ing) Sites … Revisiting the Story so Far: A Response to danah boyd and Nicole Ellison. *Journal of Computer-Mediated Communication*, 13: 516–529.

Bourdieu, P. (1984) *Distinction: A Social Critique of the Judgement of Taste*. Cambridge, MA: Harvard University Press.

Bourdieu, P. (1991) *Language and Symbolic Power*. Cambridge: Polity Press.

Bowker, G. (2008) *Memory Practices in the Sciences*. Cambridge, MA: MIT Press.

Bowker, G. and Star, S. Leigh (1999) *Sorting Things Out*. Cambridge, MA: MIT Press.

boyd, d. (2008) Why Youth ♥ Social Network Sites: The Role of Networked Publics. In D. Buckingham (Ed.), *Youth, Identity and Digital Media* (pp. 119–142). Cambridge, MA: MIT Press.

boyd, d. (2011) Social Network Sites as Networked Publics: Affordances, Dynamics and Implications. In Z. Papacharissi (Ed.), *A Networked Self* (pp. 39–58). London: Routledge.

boyd, d. (2014) *It's Complicated: The Social Lives of Networked Teens*. New Haven, CT: Yale University Press.

boyd, d. and Crawford, K. (2012) Critical Questions for Big Data: Provocations for a Cultural, Technological and Scholarly Phenomenon. *Information, Communication and Society*, 15(5): 662–679.

boyd, d. and Ellison, N. (2008) Social Network Sites: Definition, History and Scholarship. *Journal of Computer-Mediated Communication*, 13(1): 210–230.

Bucher, T. (2012) The Friendship Assemblage: Investigating Programmed Sociality on Facebook. *Television & New Media*, 14(6): 479–493.

Castells, M. (2009) *Communication Power*. Oxford: Oxford University Press.

Cohen, J. (2012) *Configuring the Networked Self*. New Haven: Yale University Press.

Cohen, P. C. (1982) *A Calculating People: The Spread of Numeracy in Early America*. Chicago, IL: University of Chicago Press.

Couldry, N. (2012) *Media Society World: Social Theory and Digital Media Practice*. Cambridge: Polity Press.

Couldry, N. (2014) The Myth of Us: Digital Networks, Political Change and the Production of Collectivity. *Information Communication and Society*, 18(6): 608–626.

Couldry, N. and Powell, A. (2014) Big Data from the Bottom Up. *Big Data & Society*, 1(1). DOI: 10.1177/2053951714539277.

Desrosières, A. (1998) *The Politics of Large Numbers: A History of Statistical Reasoning*. Cambridge, MA: Harvard University Press.

Douglas, M. (1986) *How Institutions Think*. Syracuse, NY: Syracuse University Press.

Durkheim, E. and Mauss, M. (1969 [1902]) *Primitive Classification*. London: Routledge.

Ellison, N., Steinfeld, C. and Lampe, C. (2007) The Benefits of Facebook 'Friends': Social Capital and College Students' Use of Online Social Network Sites. *Journal of Computer-Mediated Communication*, 12(4): 1142–1168.

Ellison, N., Lampe, C., Steinfeld, C. and Vitake, J. (2011) Woth a Little Help from My Friends: How Social Network Sites Affect Social Capital Processes. In Z. Papacharissi (Ed.)

A Networked Self (pp. 124–145). London: Routledge.

Espeland, W. N. and Sauder, M. (2007) Rankings and Reactivity: How Public Measures Recreate Social Worlds. *American Journal of Sociology*, 113(1): 1–40.

Espeland, W. N. and Stevens, M. L. (1998) Commensuration as a Social Process. *Annual Review of Sociology*, 24(1): 313–343.

Foucault, M. (1970) *The Order of Things: An Archaeology of Human Sciences*. London: Tavistock.

Foucault, M. (1977) *Discipline and Punish: The Birth of the Prison*. London: Allen Lane.

Foucault, M. (1988) Technologies of the Self. In L. H. Martin, H. Gutman and P. H. Hutton (Eds.), *Technologies of the Self* (pp. 14–49). London: Tavistock.

Fuchs, C. (2013) Digital Presumption Labour on Social Media in the Context of the Capitalist Regime of Time. *Time & Society*, 23(1): 97-123.

Fuchs, C. (2014) *Social Media: A Critical Introduction*. London: Sage.

Gerlitz, C. and Helmond, A. (2013) The Like Economy: Social Buttons and the Data-Intensive Web. *New Media & Society* 15(8): 1348-1365.

Gillespie, T. (2010) The Politics of 'Platforms'. *New Media & Society*, 12(3): 347–364.

Gillespie, T. (2014) The Relevance of Algorithms. In P. Boczkowski, K. Foot and T. Gillespie (Eds.), *Media Technologies* (pp. 167–194). Cambridge, MA: MIT Press.

Hacking, I. (1986) Making up People. In T. C. Heller and C. Brooke-Rose (Eds.), *Reconstructing Individualism: Autonomy, Individuality, and the Self in Western Thought* (pp. 161–171). Stanford, CA: Stanford University Press.

Hacking, I. (1990) *The Taming of Chance*. Cambridge: Cambridge University Press.

Hacking, I. (1999) *The Social Construction of What?* Cambridge, MA: Harvard University Press.

Kallinikos, J. (2007) *The Consequences of Information: Institutional Implications of Technological Change*. Cheltenham: Edward Elgar.

Kallinikos, J. (2009) On the Computational Rendition of Reality: Artefacts and Human Agency. *Organization*, 16(2): 183–202.

Kallinikos, J. and Tempini, N. (2014) Social Data as Medical Facts: Web-based Practices of Expert Knowledge Creation. *Information Systems Research*, 25(4): 817–833.

Kaun, A. and Stiernstedt, F. (2014) Facebook Time: Technological and institutional affordances for media memories. *New Media & Society*, 16(7): 1154–1168.

Kitchin, R. (2014) *The Data Revolution*. London: Sage.

Kitchin, R. and Dodge, M. (2011) *Code/Space: Software and Everyday Life*. Cambridge, MA: MIT Press.

Lévi-Strauss, C. (1962) *La Pensée Sauvage*. Paris: Plon.

Marwick, A. (2013) *Status Update: Celebrity, Publicity and Branding in the Social Media Age*. New Haven, CT: Yale University Press.

Mejias, U. (2013) *Off the Network*. Minneapolis, MN: Minnesota University Press.

Porter, T. M. (1996) *Trust in Numbers: The Pursuit of Objectivity in Science and Public Life*. Princeton, NJ: Princeton University Press.

Rosch, E. (1999) Principles of Categorization. In E. Margolis and S. Laurence (Eds.), *Concepts: Core Readings* (pp. 189–206). Cambridge, MA: MIT Press.

Rosch, E. and Mervis, C. B. (1975) Family Resemblances: Studies in the Internal Structure of Categories. *Cognitive Psychology*, 7(4): 573–605.

Rose, N. and Miller, P. (2013) *Governing the Present: Administering Economic, Social and Personal Life*. London: Wiley.

Schutz, A. and Luckmann, T. (1973) *The Structures of the Life World. Volume II*. Evanston: Northwestern University Press.

Steinfeld, C., DiMocco, J., Ellison, N. and Lampe, C. (2009) Bowling Online: Social Networking and Social Capital within the Organization. In *Proceedings of the Fourth International Conference on Communities and Technologies* (pp. 245–254). New York: ACM.

Van Dijck, J. (2013) *The Culture of Connectivity*. Oxford: Oxford University Press.

Van Dijck, J. and Poell, T. (2013) Understanding Social Media Logic. *Media and Communication*, 1(1): 2–14.

Weltevrede, E., Helmond, A. and Gerlitz, C. (2014) The Politics of Real-time: A Device Perspective on Social Media Platforms and Search Engines. *Theory Culture & Society*, 31(6): 125–150.

9

Analysing Social Media Images

Simon Faulkner, Farida Vis
and Francesco D'Orazio

INTRODUCTION

According to Mary Meeker's 2016 *Internet Trends Report*, social media users shared more than three billion images every day during 2015 (Meeker, 2016).[1] As Meeker observes, image use on social media continues to grow rapidly, with a dramatic increase in image circulation occurring from 2013 onwards. Some have referred to this rapid increase as social media's 'visual turn' (Gibbs et al., 2015: 258). This visual turn involves the popularisation of image-centric platforms such as Instagram and Snapchat, as well as the circulation of images on other, less predominantly visual social media platforms and messaging apps, like Facebook and Twitter, WhatsApp and WeChat. Despite this growth in image sharing, academic research in this area has not yet developed to the same extent and depth as has research on text-based social media communication.[2] The research literature on social media images has been slowly developing over the last decade, particularly during the last few years. Significant early research has focused on Flickr (Van House, 2007; Burgess, 2009; Garduno Freeman, 2010; van Dijk, 2010), while more recent work has looked at the use of images on Twitter (Hjorth and Burgess, 2014; Vis et al., 2014; Thelwall et al., 2016) and Instagram (Alper, 2015; Borges-Rey, 2015; Gibbs et al., 2015; Kohn, 2015; Manovich, 2015, 2016; Highfield and Leaver, 2016; Tifentale and Manovich, 2016). Other recent work has examined particular types of image, such as selfies (Senft and Baym, 2015) and memes (Milner, 2013, 2016; Noony and Portwood-Stacer, 2014; Shifman, 2014).

The empirical aspects of this work have ranged from the analysis of large datasets to more qualitative interpretations of specific images. As in any field of research, different approaches have particular strengths and limitations. Computational methods have been used to analyse large sets of images, working with metadata, such as timestamps and geo-location. Such approaches have also been used to identify patterns within sets of images in terms of brightness, colour and hue (Hochman and Schwartz, 2012; Hochman and Manovich, 2013a, 2013b) as well as to identify objects or actions depicted within images (Delaitre, Laptev and Sivic, 2010). Such large-scale data analysis can identify patterns within sets of images, or map the networks through which images are distributed, but does not usually address the specific visual content and meaning of such images. Content analysis, which categorises images according to specific aspects of their content has been used by other researchers to examine more nuanced patterns within sets of images, but usually on a smaller scale (Seo, 2014; Vis et al., 2014; Kharroub and Bas, 2015; Thelwall et al., 2016). Yet it is generally through close interpretative work with small datasets that a sense of the richly intertextual meanings of images can be gained.

The analysis of social media images also presents challenges specific to the visual that are absent from research on written texts. Hence Highfield and Leaver's observation that such work 'requires more individual intervention and interpretation than samples of 140-characters' (Highfield and Leaver, 2016: 48). Although many social media images appear to be used conversationally (Gibbs et al., 2015: 264; Thelwall et al., 2016), the images themselves do not necessarily 'say' anything in the sense that words do. This does not mean that social media images cannot be analysed at a large scale without consideration of their socio-cultural contexts, but it means that images are difficult to address quantitatively in ways that are sensitive to the specificities and functions of their pictorial forms.

Given the variety of existing visual methods and theories, deriving from art history, photo theory, visual culture studies, visual sociology and anthropology, it is challenging to decide whether and how existing visual methods and theories can be adapted to the context of social media. Considerable theoretical and empirical work has been done on digital photography (Rubenstein and Sluis, 2008; Gómez Cruz and Meyer, 2012; Moschovi, McKay and Plouviez, 2013; Lister, 2013) and on cameraphone practices (Van House et al., 2005; Van House and Ames, 2006; Gye, 2007; van Dijck, 2008; Villi and Stocchetti, 2011; Villi, 2015). Further research examines the dynamic relationships between cameraphone use and locative media (Hjorth, 2014; Hjorth and Pink, 2014). Such scholarship can help us understand the specificities of online digital photography, and how people use cameraphones as an important aspect of their everyday lives. Yet it does not necessarily help researchers with the question of how to approach the interpretation of these shared images as examples of visual communication.

In the remainder of this chapter, we discuss three approaches to the analysis of social media images by reviewing recent research projects by the Software Studies Initiative that involved the collection and analysis of relatively large datasets, projects that involved working with images at different scales, and qualitative studies of memes relating to the Occupy Wall Street (OWS) movement in late 2011. We focus on specific work on Instagram and Twitter as well as on selfies and memes to further explore the strengths and limitations of these different approaches. The aim is not to prioritise one kind of approach over another, but rather to explore their advantages and limitations. The chapter will then discuss our own work on images circulated in response to the death of the Syrian refugee boy Alan Kurdi (initially misidentified as 'Aylan') in early September 2015, as an example of the kinds of approaches to visual social media that we advocate.

SURVEYING THE FIELD

Large-Scale Image Analysis

Several projects have focused on the large-scale collection and analysis of social media image-related data. The *Phototrails* and *Selfiecity* projects, developed by Lev Manovich and the Software Studies Initiative, are prominent examples. *Phototrails* began in 2011 and used 2,353,017 Instagram images uploaded in 13 cities[3] during specific periods of time. The primary period of data collection began in early 2011 and ended in April 2012, though further data was collected for particular cities during specific periods, for example during Hurricane Sandy in New York in November 2012. This extraction of city-specific data was based on the geospatial coordinates and time stamps of photographs taken on Instagram (Hochman and Manovich, 2013: 7). Images from the city-specific datasets were arrayed as visualisations on the project website (phototrails.net) to reveal what the project team described as the 'visual signatures' and 'rhythms' of these cities (Hochman and Manovich, 2013: 10, 16). This identification of 'signatures' and 'rhythms' involved the mapping of spatial and temporal patterns among the images as well as patterns relating to colour and hue. For example, the 23,581 images uploaded in Brooklyn, New York, during 24 hours of Hurricane Sandy between 29 and 30 November 2012, were visualised in the form of a semi-circular 'radial plot'. This involved positioning the images at different points in relation to the circumference of the semi-circle, depending on the time they were taken within the 24-hour period, and at different distances from the centre of the semi-circle, depending on the mean hue of the image. This revealed a 'demarcation line' marking the power outage in Brooklyn during the Hurricane, resulting in a decrease in the number of images and an increase in the darkness of their mean hue (Hochman and Manovich, 2013: 12).

The *Phototrails* team have made much of the fact that their visualisations are composites within which individual images remain visible (Hochman and Manovich, 2013: 4). However, it is clear that the orientation of the research has been towards the identification of macro-level patterns within the datasets, rather than towards the analysis of the pictorial content of individual images. Alise Tifentale and Lev Manovich have observed in retrospect that the project 'disregarded the content of the photos, the differences in compositions and other aspects of photographic aesthetics' (Tifentale and Manovich, 2015: 109). Although the *Phototrails* visualisations can tell us about the intensity with which images are uploaded to Instagram at certain times in specific places (Hochman and Schwartz, 2012: 2), they tell us little about what these images depict, and why people created and uploaded them.

In contrast to *Phototrails*, which involved working with different kinds of image, *Selfiecity* focused on the selfie as a specific image-type. The dataset for the project started out as 656,000 images extracted from Instagram between 4 and 12 December 2013, using their geo-tags to identify locations in the central areas of Bangkok, Berlin, Moscow, New York, and Sao Paolo. This initial dataset was reduced by random selection to 120,000 images (20–30,000 for each city). These images were then processed by Amazon Mechanical Turk (AMT) workers, who classified them according to whether or not they depicted a selfie of a single person.[4] The top 1,000 images from each city identified as a single selfie were resubmitted to AMT to be verified and classified according to the gender and age of the depicted person. These images were then examined by at least one member of the *Selfiecity* team to edit out mistakes, resulting in the selection of 640 selfies per city. The final corpus of 3,200 selfies was then processed using facial analysis software to classify them for face size, pose, emotional demeanour, the presence of glasses and smiles, whether the eyes or mouth are open or closed, as well as for gender and age (The Graduate Center, CUNY, 2014: 3–4; Tifentale and Manovich, 2015: 3). These classifications constituted the basis of a series of visualisations designed by Moritz Stefaner, and presented on the project website (selfiecity.net). As with *Phototrails*, the results were generally concerned with quantitative patterns within the corpus. For example, the researchers found that more selfies were taken by women and by younger people, and more people were identified as smiling in selfies from Bangkok and Sao Paulo than from Moscow. Although these findings involve a closer engagement with the visual content of the images than *Phototrails*, they remain limited by their focus on quantitative data at the expense of explanations that deal with the social uses of selfies. More recent work by Manovich and Tifentale has taken a more qualitative turn, attempting to identify different subjects and styles within previously collected datasets of Instagram images. This has involved linking these images to earlier developments within the history of photography (Manovich, 2015, 2016; Tifentale and Manovich, 2016). This work is interesting in that it attempts to ground a discussion of the format and content of Instagram image-types in the large-scale collection of images. Yet this discussion remains generic and consequently does not address the question of 'how to reconcile the "big data approach" with a close study of an object' (Tifentale, 2015: 6).

Working with Images at Different Scales

Other studies of social media images have grappled with both large image-based datasets and the specificities of particular images. The first of this kind is Larissa Hjorth and Jean Burgess' examination of images tweeted in response to the Queensland floods in Australia in December 2010 and January 2011. This study started with a dataset of 40,000 tweets containing the hashtag #qldfloods collected for a larger study of Twitter use in response to the disaster (Bruns et al., 2012). Tweets that contained links to visual images (hosted on photo sharing services such as twitpic and yfrog) were identified

and organised according to how many times they were retweeted. From here, Hjorth and Burgess analysed the top 100 most retweeted images, an approach also used in work presented later in this chapter, on the understanding that the frequency of their re-circulation was a measure of their cultural resonance (Hjorth and Burgess, 2014: 502). This focus on a final corpus of 100 images allowed the authors to address the specific content of the images in ways that would have been difficult with a larger set of images. The analysis explained photographic images in terms of Australian 'larrikin' humour, which functions as a culture-specific coping mechanism under conditions of stress (Hjorth and Burgess, 2014: 505).

The second study, which included two of the authors, was developed after the UK riots of August 2011 that occurred after police in London shot and killed a young black man called Mark Duggan (Vis et al., 2014). This work involved the analysis of a corpus of 10,001 tweets containing links to images, identified within a larger dataset of 2.6 million riot-related tweets.[5] The 10,001 tweets containing links to images were organised and categorised according to their basic denotative content using a content analysis approach. These images were also divided into two sets: one of images shared more than once, and the other of images shared only once. This overall image corpus was reduced to 3,466 multiply shared images and 235 single shares. These images were classified using 13 content analysis categories identified in relation to the original set of images, before focusing on 57 images coded under the category 'Bus', which referred to a bus set alight in Tottenham, London, where Duggan was shot and where the riots began. This focus on only 57 images allowed for the use of photographic theory to develop close readings of visual content. For example, screen grabs and cameraphone photos of TV news footage of the burning bus were discussed in relation to John Berger's understanding that the act of making a photographic image involves the basic statement 'I have decided that seeing this is worth recording' (Vis et al., 2014: 395). This movement from content analysis of a relatively large dataset to a close analysis of particular images involved a shift from a systematic analytical methodology to a relatively arbitrary choice of one category of images and of particular images within this category.

Both studies involved a mixture of methods that allowed for the derivation of insights from larger datasets, while also facilitating the close qualitative analysis of specific images. In both cases, researchers developed interpretative approaches that responded to the specific content and social context of the images under consideration. In the case of the Queensland flood, identifying appropriate cultural references specific to the Australian national context enabled the delineation of interdiscursive relationships between the images and wider cultural discourses. In the case of the London riots, this involved using ideas taken from photography theory. Both studies indicate that at the level of close qualitative work, researchers must make relatively intuitive case-specific choices about how to approach the analysis of images. This fits with Highfield and Leaver's (2016) point, quoted earlier, that the interpretation of images on social media requires more 'individual intervention and interpretation'. In both cases, the close analysis of specific images was dependent upon the collection and organisation of a larger dataset, but the qualitative analysis itself involved quite different interpretational decisions. This deployment of different forms of analysis is not a problem; rather, it constitutes the basis of the kind of complementary work with social media images at different scales we would encourage.

In-Depth Qualitative Analysis of Images

Studies that focus solely on the close reading of specific images are very different from both the large-scale data collection of Manovich and the Software Studies Initiative, and the quantitative aspects of the Hjorth and Burgess and Vis et al. studies. In contrast, studies of individual images generally do not involve the extraction and systematic processing of large quantities of image-related data from social media platforms. An example of this approach is Heidi Huntington's discussion of the Pepper Spray Cop meme, which circulated on social media in response to the Occupy Wall Street movement (Huntingdon, 2016). This meme was based on photographic images of police Lieutenant John Pike pepper spraying seated demonstrators during a student protest on the University of California Davis campus on 18 November 2011. Social media users responded to the original photographs by photoshopping the figure of Pike into other well-known images to create humorous and politically pointed conjunctions. Huntington focuses on the intertextual relationships between the meme and its cultural and political referents. For example, her discussion of one version of the meme, which involved the relocation of Pike into John Trumbell's famous painting of the signing of the US Declaration of Independence, involves both the physical location of the painting in the US Capitol Building and its relationship to the mythology of the American Dream. This allows her to suggest that the meme presents Pepper Spray Cop as 'an attack on the very essence of the American Dream and human liberty' (Huntington, 2016: 88). Huntington's analysis provides a strong example of how social media images are made meaningful through relationships to other cultural discourses that exist within and beyond social media. It also involves a detailed discussion of the specific ways the visual content of images produce meaning. This makes her work comparable to Art History analysis, which generally involves close readings of small numbers of images in terms of their formal qualities, symbolic content, and historical contexts. The qualitative analysis of social media images is also comparable to Art History when it comes to selecting images for analysis, which is often idiosyncratic and guided by individual research experience and intuition. Huntington does not discuss how she selected the images relating to the Pepper Spray Cop meme she addresses, but it is likely that she simply found the images by searching on social media platforms, via Google (image search) or websites like 'Know Your Meme'. This would make her method of corpus identification similar to that adopted by Ryan Milner in his study of OWS memes, which he gathered by 'visiting' social media platforms and other sites (Milner, 2013: 2370; see also Peck, 2014). Like Huntington, Milner focuses on the meanings of memes in terms of their intertextual relationships to socio-cultural contexts and their role within larger memetic conversations. Thus he states, 'OWS memes were interdiscursive, intertwining multiple texts and commentaries into complex collages' (Milner, 2013: 2367). Absent from both his and Huntington's analysis is the consideration of how, or on what scale, OWS memes circulated and were adapted through digital networks. Similar observations can be made about other articles that deal with this meme (Peck, 2014; Bayerl and Stoynov, 2016). These qualitative studies offer good examples of how the close interpretation of images can attend to the socio-cultural meanings of visual social media that are excluded by the methods employed by the Software Studies Initiative. Yet this work also excludes much in terms of the contexts through which images were communicated and the scale of their circulation. There are, however, other qualitative studies of memes that give more attention to their circulation via particular platforms (Pearce, 2015) and their adaptation across different national contexts (Shifman, 2014: 151–170).

CASE STUDY: THE DEATH OF ALAN KURDI ON TWITTER

The final part of this chapter explores the deployment of the three approaches discussed in the preceding sections and applies this to images relating to the death of Alan Kurdi. This case study allows for a focused consideration of the potential for bringing these different approaches together in a mutually supportive way. This understanding of the complementary potential of different approaches derives from the practices of the Visual Social Media Lab (VSML),[6] which we founded in 2014 in a conscious effort to create a meeting point for researchers from different sectors and disciplinary backgrounds, including Media and Communication Studies, Visual Culture, Art History, Software Studies, Sociology, Computer Science and Information Science. The aim of the VSML is to explore how different methods for the analysis of social media images can be combined or work in conjunction with each other. The findings presented here derive from the VSML's report *The Iconic Image on Social Media: A Rapid Research Response to the Death of Aylan Kurdi* (Vis and Goriunova, 2015).

Alan Kurdi was a three-year-old Syrian refugee who died with other members of his family in a failed attempt to cross the Mediterranean from Turkey to Greece. The Turkish photojournalist Nilüfer Demir photographed Alan's dead body after it washed up on Bodrum beach in Turkey, producing a series of photographs that depicted the body lying at the meeting point between the sea and the beach, or picked up, in the arms of a Turkish policeman. These photographs were widely published, first by Doğan Haber Ajansı (DHA) news agency in Turkey and circulated via mainstream and social media, triggering a significant on-the-ground response to the refugee crisis, including in the UK, which was the main focus of most chapters in the original report. This report involved 15 short articles by members of the VSML and other invited researchers with the aim of examining the online distribution and use of these images, their political impact and iconography, and the ethical implications of their publication and circulation.

DATA, RESEARCH QUESTIONS AND METHODS

Data was collected using Pulsar,[7] a commercial analytics platform that allows users to collect data from a range of different social media platforms (including Twitter, Facebook, Instagram, YouTube and Tumblr), news sources, forums, and blogs. Following collection, Pulsar offers a range of different ways to navigate and access the data, and to carry out different types of analysis, including network analysis. For Twitter, users can opt to pay for a full real-time or historic firehose sample. Pulsar was used to retrieve, analyse and visualise historic data for 1–14 September 2015. This query included data from Twitter, Tumblr, news, forums, and blogs, amounting to 2,843,274 posts in total, with the majority coming from Twitter. The report also included findings from Google search data, to get a sense of global search patterns during this period (Rogers, 2015). The Pulsar dataset was collected using a series of predominantly English language search terms and hashtags,[8] but included the Turkish hashtag #kiyiyavuraninsanli, which was translated as 'humanity washed ashore'. Including the child's first name (with various spellings) and last name as search terms meant that the dataset included many different languages, given the wide circulation of the boy's name by Twitter users. Below we outline the research questions and methods pertaining to the Twitter data.

Research Questions and Methods

In the broadest sense the report tried to explore three basic questions: Why this child? Why these images? Why this large-scale response now (given that so many refugees had already died)? Here we focus on three approaches, their associated research questions and methods. The first involved a large-scale analysis of the images shared on Twitter to map the spread of the images, key

networks, the rate of spread as well as the response images that were uploaded. We estimated that the images of Alan Kurdi spread to 20 million (Twitter) screens in the space of just 12 hours. To better understand the dynamics of this diffusion a set of network visualisations were created to show how and when the images were tweeted and retweeted over the first 12 hours after DHA put them online on the morning of 2 September. A subset of the data was created focusing on tweets containing at least one of the images of Alan Kurdi shared by DHA and posted on Twitter within the first 12 hours. Four diffusion phases were identified: the first hour (10.15am–11.15am); the first two hours (10.15am–12.15am); the first three hours (10.15am–13.15pm); and the first 12 hours (10.15am–22.15pm).

For each diffusion phase a network visualisation was created using the same methodology: Pulsar was used to create a network graph from the connections between tweets containing the Alan Kurdi images and their retweets. Pulsar also adds metadata to each tweet and retweet including: a code identifying a node as a tweet or a retweet; country; number of followers; Visibility score; number of retweets received by each tweet; and the betweenness centrality[9] of each tweet or retweet. The network graph was then processed with the network visualisation software Gephi, which uses the metadata added by Pulsar to each node as attributes to design the layout and visual appearance of the final visualisations. Before proceeding with the network design, additional metadata was added to each node using Gephi's statistical tools: Average Degree and Weighted Average Degree[10] of each node in the network. The metadata generated by Pulsar and Gephi and added to each node was used to design the network. In the network visualisations names of private users have been blurred. We have only identified Twitter users by name and handle where we felt it was clear that they were public figures tweeting in a public capacity.

In the visualisations, a node represents a tweet or a retweet while an edge represents a tweet/retweet relationship so that an edge only appears between two nodes when one of them is an original tweet and the other is a retweet of the original tweet. The size of the nodes indicates the impact of the tweet/retweet on the audience based on Pulsar's Visibility sco.[11] Visibility is a proprietary Pulsar algorithm designed to attribute an impact score to each tweet and retweet based on the number of retweets it receives and the level of reach it generates directly and indirectly (the size of the audience of the author plus the size of the audiences of anyone who has retweeted the original tweet). We also examined how the original photographic images of Alan were used to create response images and how this happened over time. Differentiating original images from adaptations involved a combination of manual identification and supported machine learning to more quickly identify identical images.

A second approach, working with images at different scales, sought to better understand the diversity of the 100 most shared Twitter images by lifting this smaller manageable sample from the larger dataset. To carry out this analysis, all 100 images were printed out so that smaller image collections could be built and easily organised for further inspection and analysis. We were particularly interested in the content, date and location of the images that were shared most frequently. Emphasis was also placed on the use of images showing Alan before and after death, adaptations and remediations of the original photographic images, and the circulation of images within the UK. This second approach relied on quantitative content analysis by manually coding the top 100 Twitter images. A limitation to this approach is that it effectively amplifies the 'loudest voices' by focusing on the most shared images and does not take into account less frequently shared images in other parts of the dataset (in the so-called 'long tail') (Eni et al., 2011; Vis, 2013). To more fully understand the diversity

of images shared additional sampling could have included a sample of images that were infrequently shared as well as images that were only shared once (Vis et al., 2014).

The final approach entailed an in-depth qualitative analysis of a smaller subset of images chosen from the top 1,000 Twitter images and selected for their individual visual qualities, in line with the researcher's individual interests. Key questions driving this approach included what people had done with the motif of Alan's body once they had removed it from its original photographic contexts, and how relocating Alan's body into new pictorial contexts through practices like Photoshop might be read. This approach involves something similar to classic art historical iconography, but is also similar to the qualitative work on memes discussed earlier.

FINDINGS

Large-Scale Image Analysis: The Spread and Diffusion of the Alan Kurdi Images

The Twitter journey of the Alan Kurdi images began on the morning of 2 September 2015, at 8.42am, when Turkish news agency DHA posted a report on their website concerning the death of 12 Syrian refugees, drowned while trying to travel from Turkey to the Greek island of Kos in a dinghy. This Turkish language article featured a gallery of 50 images taken that morning on or near Bodrum beach, by DHA photographer Nilüfer Demir, including four that showed the dead body of Alan Kurdi. Demir's photographs were examples of professional photojournalism intended for dissemination through news agencies and wires, and for publication in the press. When Turkish journalist and activist Michelle Demishevich took one of the images from a news agency website and uploaded it to Twitter at 10.23am[12] this changed. This

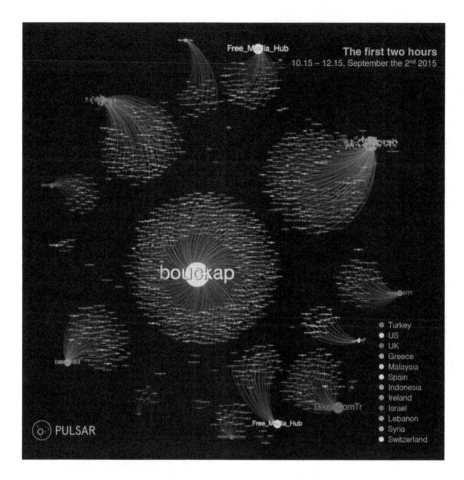

Figure 9.1   Diffusion graph B – two hours from the appearance of the first picture on Twitter. Size of the nodes indicates impact on the audience (Visibility Score). Colour of nodes and edges indicates country of the user

(*Source*: Pulsar)

post did not contain a link to a news source, featuring only a caption, the image, and five hashtags including #Refugeeswelcome and #Syrianrefugees. Over the next hour it was retweeted 33 times. Users in Greece and Spain started tweeting the same image. Between 11.00am and 11.30am the Turkish language press also began to report the story of the death of the refugees with more than 15 publications posting articles on their websites. But while the press was spreading the news to a mostly Turkish audience, the images of Alan's body began to embark on a very different international journey on Twitter in the following hour.

'The first two hours' network visualisation (Figure 9.1) is based on 1,382 nodes (tweets and retweets) and 1,320 edges (connections between a tweet and a retweet). The network has an Average Degree of 1.912 and an Average Weighted Degree of 0.956. The use of Twitter by journalists and media organisations was significant, with Turkish news agencies using Twitter to expand the local Turkish audience. When the images spread through the Middle East (Lebanon, Gaza and Syria), Lebanon became particularly important when Martin Jay, *Newsweek* Middle East correspondent in Beirut, suggested the images might be going viral (Figure 9.1: top left corner, third node

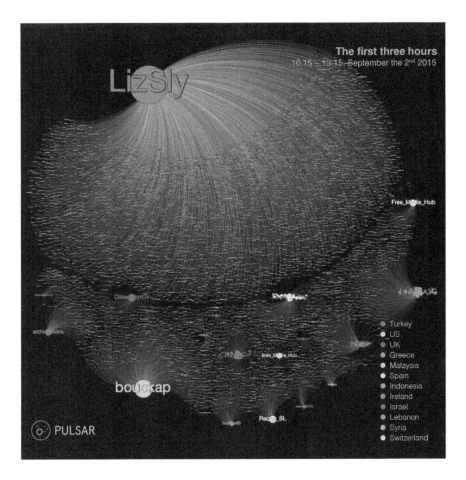

Figure 9.2 Diffusion graph C – three hours from the appearance of the first picture on Twitter. Size of the nodes indicates impact on the audience (Visibility Score). Colour of nodes and edges indicates country of the user

(*Source*: Pulsar)

from the left). Less than an hour later, Peter Bouckaert (@bouckap), the Geneva-based Emergency Director at Human Rights Watch, posted three images of Alan Kurdi, emphasising the need for an urgent plan to deal with the refugee crisis (Figure 9.1: central node). His tweet received 664 retweets from users located in a variety of countries (including the US, UK, Australia, Malaysia), signalling the spread of the images beyond the Middle East. By midday on 2 September the images had been shared fewer than 500 times (3 per cent of the total diffusion of the images by the end of the day). These tweets had reached a potential audience of 500,000 Twitter users

across 100 countries.[13] This situation changed at 12.49pm,[14] when Liz Sly, *Washington Post* Beirut Bureau Chief, posted a tweet that was retweeted 7,421 times; the most retweeted post in the dataset. Sly's tweet transformed the scale of the diffusion, generating in the first 30 minutes the same amount of retweets generated in the previous two hours (see Figure 9.2: @LizSly top left node). 'The first three hours' network visualisation is based on 7,028 nodes (tweets and retweets) and 6,689 edges (connections between a tweet and a retweet). The network has an Average Degree of 1.902 and an Average Weighted Degree of 0.952.

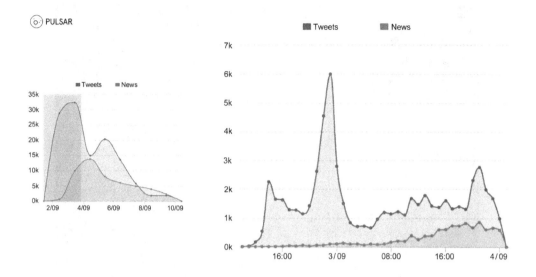

Figure 9.3   Tweet timeline vs News timeline by the hour, all tweets (2 September 2015, 08:00–3 September 2015, 23.59)

(*Source*: Pulsar)

The composition of the audience had also changed, with new tweets originating from Lebanon, Iraq, Palestine, Syria, the US, Switzerland, Spain, and retweeted by an audience that was now mainly outside of the Middle East (US (17 per cent), Spain (10 per cent), UK (9 per cent), India (4 per cent), Netherlands (3.4 per cent), and Greece (3.4 per cent)).

Almost five hours after the images were first published online, and three hours after they first appeared on Twitter, the Turkish press was the only national news media officially covering the story. In the absence of international news coverage, Twitter amplified the story to an international audience. Findings from the network analysis suggest that Twitter functioned as a decentralised catalyst that delivered this story to a highly relevant group of people (journalists, activists, politicians, and aid workers interested in the Middle East). It was this dynamic that underpinned the high engagement rate in the dataset (17 retweets for every single tweet posted).

This situation changed again at 1.10pm, when the UK newspaper the *Daily Mail* published an article on the death of Alan Kurdi. This story marked the beginning of a new phase of international diffusion, characterised by the heavy involvement of the international news media. Between the publication of the *Daily Mail* article and the end of 2 September, more than 500 articles were published online about Alan Kurdi and shared on Twitter. Compared to the preceding phase of the diffusion, the audience exposed to the story, sharing the images, and communicating about them was now 25 times larger. However, the mainstream news ecosystem 'owned' the story and used it to carry its own commentaries, along with the images of Alan. This trend continued on 3 September, when the volume of news media content continued to grow, fuelling an overall peak in tweets that reached 53,000 per hour at 8.00pm. At this point, both Twitter activity and the volume of news content decreased over the next 10 days, eventually reaching 50 per cent of the levels established on 2 September (see Figure 9.3).

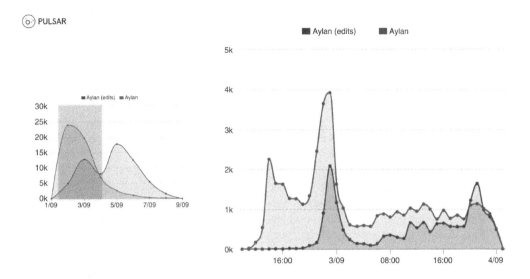

Figure 9.4   Alan Kurdi image tweets vs Variations image tweets by the hour (2 September 2015, 08:00–3 September 2015, 23.59)

(*Source*: Pulsar)

The findings from the network analysis show that during all these developments the diffusion of the story was consistently image-led. However, this did not mean that it was always the same images that were being distributed. Whereas the original press photographs of Alan dominated the first 48 hours of the diffusion cycle, from 4 September onwards they were replaced in terms of high volume of circulation by adapted versions the photographs (see Figure 9.4).

The mediation of Alan Kurdi's death was a process deeply entwined with the capacity of Twitter to act as a catalyst that allowed for the communication of emerging stories to relevant audiences. Twitter made it possible for global audiences to develop, connect, and propel the Alan Kurdi story into the mainstream, before the international press began to cover it. However, one should not forget that individual journalists initially broke and pushed the story on Twitter in the first place, thus facilitating a very effective diffusion dynamic.

Working with Images at Different Scales: The 100 Most Shared Alan Kurdi Images

Of the 100 most shared images, 11 were shared on the first day and most (68 of 100) were shared during the first three days (2 September–4 September). On 2 September this included the tweet from Liz Sly, the third most shared image, also highlighted in Figure 9.2. Of these 11 images shared on 2 September, six are one of the original images and five are not, indicating that on the first day a range of different types of image were already in circulation. These included images of Alan alive (alongside his older brother) as well as cartoons of Alan depicting him getting picked up from the beach by an angel. The remaining 32 images (of 100) were shared between 5 September and 14 September. Overall, just over one fifth (21 of 100) of the 100 most retweeted images were copies of one of the photojournalistic images of Alan's dead body. Of these top 21,

13 were images of Alan alone, lying face down in the surf. Less frequently shared were images showing his body with one or more Turkish policeman, or in the arms of one of the policemen (4 of 21). Following calls from Alan's aunt to share images of Alan before his death, journalists in particular started to encourage this type of sharing. Seventeen of the 100 most shared Twitter images depicted Alan alive. There were five variations on this theme: an image that shows Alan on his own (shared the most), standing at the top of a blue slide in a playground wearing a similar outfit to the one in which he died. Visually the viewer might be encouraged to imagine this scene as the child just before death: happy, smiling, full of life. The second image of Alan alone showed him about to kick a football. His outfit is again similar to the one he died in. Once more, one might assume this image was chosen and retweeted multiple times due to the similarity between the two outfits. Two images included Alan's older brother Ghalib: one where both boys are sitting on a sofa with a white toy bear between them, the other showing Ghalib with a protective arm around Alan. In both images the boys smile sweetly at the camera, most likely indicating it was taken by a family member. Only one image shows Alan with his brother and father, Abdullah Kurdi, and none show their mother. The images that show Alan before his death suggest a happy childhood and familial normality, in stark contrast to the images of his dead body on the beach.

Nearly a fifth of the most shared images (17 of 100) involved remediations of the original photograps of Alan's body on the beach. These included cartoons and photographs of sand sculptures or performances intended to be photographically documented, including one involving children in Morocco dressed in similar outfits to Alan emulating his pose in death by lying face down on the beach in Rabat.

Focusing on location, 24 images in the top 100 were shared from the UK and include

a wide range of different image-types. It is perhaps surprising that none of these images were the original press photographs. Instead, the original photographs were presented indirectly through the sharing of images of newspaper front pages, including compilation images that highlighted how individual newspapers had changed their stand on the refugee crisis. This was done, for example, by combining past and present front pages of *The Sun* newspaper to illustrate the paper's 'U-turn' from a staunchly anti-refugee position to a position temporarily sympathetic towards people fleeing from Syria. Another strategy was to present a compilation of front pages from papers across the political spectrum to emphasise a shared position on the refugee crisis. These images function as a kind of meta-commentary on the mainstream media. The compilation image of newspaper front pages from across the political spectrum was accompanied by a tweet that urged UK Prime Minister David Cameron to 'wake up' and for the UK to play a larger part in responding to the refugee crisis. Other users also urged the UK to do more, by posting infographics emphasising that the UK could and should take in more refugees, or highlighting how few refugees had been allowed to come to the UK so far. An image of Buckingham Palace was combined with text that indicated there was space in this building for at least 1,000 refugees, while another image suggested that all of the Syrian refugees allowed to enter the UK so far could fit into a single London Underground train.

Other UK-specific tweets involved sharing images of text containing comments mocking David Cameron's policy towards the refugee crisis. One in particular adopted a satirical approach to the change in UK policy after the widespread distribution of the photographs of Alan's body. This text adopted the voice of the UK Prime Minister, stating: 'Britain has a moral responsibility to help refugees, even though it didn't a couple of days ago'. There were also images depicting politicians, featuring images of their faces next to quotations of them pledging to play their full part in finding solutions to the crisis (Scotland's First Minister Nicola Sturgeon, tweeted from her own account), or showing politicians posing with 'Refugees Welcome' signs (Green Party MP, Caroline Lucas), as well as an image of Labour Party leader Jeremy Corbyn, tweeted from his account, showing him looking over a crowd gathered in Parliament Square in London. The text in this tweet highlighted that these people had gathered because they wanted a government that will respond properly to the crisis. Linked to this theme, two final images highlight moments in history when the UK did far more to help refugees from elsewhere in Europe. One of these was an appropriated black and white analogue photograph of a large steamship in Southampton dock. The text accompanying this image stated that it shows how the UK accepted 4,000 Basque children in 1937, asking: 'would we have let them drown?' The implication here is that in the past the UK accepted refugees from Southern Europe, but was now unwilling to accept refugees from the Middle East.

As was stated in the previous section, the original press photographs of Alan dominated the first 48 hours of the diffusion cycle, followed by the wide circulation of adapted versions of the originals. What this brief analysis of the 100 most shared images has shown is how content analysis can help gain further insight into the findings from larger-scale analysis, including during specific time periods. By further focusing on country-specific sharing, more nuance about the national socio-cultural situated-ness of this image sharing can be gleaned.

In-Depth Qualitative Analysis of Images: The Adaptation of the Original Alan Kurdi Images

This final section of the case study presents findings from a qualitative analysis of images that involved the creative adaptation of the original press photographs of Alan's body. This work involved manually identifying cartoons and photoshopped images among the top 1,000 most retweeted images within the dataset, without considering how much each individual image had been retweeted. This selection was then further reduced through the identification of two smaller sets of images that shared pictorial characteristics, the first involving the relocation of the motif of Alan's body lying on the beach to a different pictorial context and the second including the relocation of his body from the arms of the Turkish policeman to the arms of another figure. We selected examples from these two smaller sets of images for visual analysis. Like most iconic images, the original photographs of Alan's body on the beach and in the arms of the policeman are simple in terms of their visual content. The most significant element of the photos was Alan's body itself, with its easily identifiable clothing. Through practices of pictorial adaptation, Alan's body became a movable motif (much like Pepper Spray Cop) that was also metaphorically adaptable, as demonstrated by the examples from both sets of adapted images considered here.

The relocation of the motif of Alan's body lying on the beach to different contexts generated a range of unexpected associations that involved what appear to be attempts to establish relationships of moral culpability for the death of the child. In some examples this culpability involved the suggestion of responsibility for the conditions that caused the Kurdi family to become refugees and, by extension, for Alan's death. For example, in one image Alan's body was photoshopped into a scene of the family of Syrian ruler Bashar al-Assad sitting at a dinner table blowing out candles on a birthday cake, with the body replacing the cake. This photoshopped image produces a shocking visual conjunction between a family celebration and the death of a child. In other examples, different parties appear to have been identified as culpable for not acting to prevent Alan's death. One cartoon involved the relocation of his body to the centre of a large round table in a room decorated with the European Union emblem. Around this table sit a number of EU officials who are facing away from the body. The rhetorical implication of the cartoon is straightforward: the officials have failed to respond to the refugee crisis that caused Alan's death and are now refusing to see his corpse. This format was repeated in a photoshopped image that involved the relocation of the body to the United Nations Security Council Chamber. Although this time the council members face the body, they appear to not see its blatant presence on the floor. The theme of these images is not only culpability, but also the apparent contradiction between the high visibility of the image of Alan's body enabled by its mass circulation and the indifference of official bodies. But it was not only the EU and the UN which were identified as culpable through the visual relocation of the body to their meetings. Arab leaders and the Gulf States were also identified as failing in the face of the Syrian refugee crisis. Thus, Alan's body was relocated to composite images featuring the luxurious skylines of Qatar and Dubai. The body was also photoshopped into the middle of the Arab League meeting chamber and drawn in front of a set of Arab leaders, who appear to have dug a grave for the boy. These images function affectively through a form of guilt by visual association and attest to the transposable metaphorical power of the motif of Alan's body.

The images that involved the relocation of Alan's body from the arms of the policeman to the arms of another figure also entail different connotations. One cartoon depicted the body in the arms of a weeping crocodile that sits next to a wall topped with barbed wire, suggesting hypocrisy on the part of those who show concern for Alan's death while blocking the movement of other refugees. Another example, that appears to have been circulated specifically in the Middle East, involved the photoshopping of the body into the arms of Saddam Hussein, with a text in

Arabic at the bottom that read: 'If I was still alive this would not have happened'. The exact significance of this combination of text and image is unclear, though it appears to have arisen and gained its meaning from the contemporary political struggle in the region between Sunni and Shia communities, Saddam being identified here as a great Sunni leader. Given that Saddam was dead at the time of the creation of this image, the conjunction of him and Alan's body suggests their existence together in the afterlife. The meaning of this image was also contested in that it entered the dataset through its re-circulation by a Kurdish user who tweeted in English: 'Arabs are spreading this picture of Saddam Hussein holding #AlanKurdi, sure because Saddam loved Kurdish children …' In this tweet, the photoshopped image of Saddam holding Alan was combined with an image of children killed during the chemical weapon attack on the Kurdish city of Halabja enacted by Saddam's regime in 1988.

This qualitative analysis of pictorial re-contextualisations of Alan's body attests to how this motif was rapidly reframed in relation to very different cultural and political imaginaries and for different rhetorical purposes. As such, the use of the motif of Alan's body presented a particularly strong example of the 'migration' of images that has been a crucial aspect of their cultural function for millennia (Wittkower, 1977; Belting, 2011), but which has gained an accelerated intensity through social media. This discussion of adapted images also continues the general movement of the overall analysis from large to small scale, a movement that starts from the large-scale network analysis, continues with the analysis of the 100 most retweeted images, and ends with the close discussion of a much smaller selection of images. This analysis adds detail to the findings of the network analysis, namely the circulation of adapted images after the first 48 hours of the dispersion of the original photographs. Although this discussion does not examine when or how frequently particular images circulated, it provides some indication of what these images were and what they might have been intended to mean.

CONCLUSION

This chapter has discussed three methodological approaches to the analysis of social media images: large-scale image analysis; working with images at different scales; and in-depth qualitative analysis of images. The survey of the research literature provided examples of studies that analysed different datasets and subjects according to these three approaches. Our case study applied these three approaches to a single dataset and subject, demonstrating that they can be used to draw different insights from the same data and function in a mutually supportive way.

The network analysis segmented the larger dataset to create four distinct phases of diffusion concentrating on the first 12 hours after the images of Alan Kurdi were released by Turkish news agency DHA. This approach identified key actors in specific locations, tracing the spread of images from the Turkish Twittersphere to the eventual adoption of the story by the international mainstream media. This approach showed that Twitter was a key mechanism driving this story into the mainstream. Further analysis showed that these images were widely adapted and shared 48 hours after the originals had been circulated. This approach was thus able to give a top-level overview of how different images had spread and were shared on Twitter, but did not focus on their content or context.

By examining the content and some of the national context of the 100 most shared images, the network analysis was extended, both confirming and adding to the previous findings. It showed that while the image of Alan alone and dead on the beach was the most shared from 2 September onwards, additional images were also shared, including those of Alan still alive. As the 100 most shared images included images shared between 2 September and 14 September, the diversity of these images was discussed. A limitation of this approach remains that while it looked in more depth at the most shared images, this analysis was not able to shed light on images that were shared less frequently. On the other hand, while the final in-depth qualitative analysis did not systematically sample from the top 1,000 most shared images to identify the least shared images, the discussion still included images with very few shares. This analysis was also able to show far more context for individual images, highlighting the international nature of some images and how they might be interpreted.

This chapter has thus advocated that the study of visual social media may benefit from including a range of methods that, combined, can offer deep insight into a single dataset. While we have given examples of three specific approaches via the literature review and our case study, we do not wish to be prescriptive. Instead we have sought to show the possibility of productively combining approaches, which can help shape the next phase of this field of research.

Notes

1 Meeker's figure covers Snapchat, Facebook and Facebook Messenger, Instagram, and WhatsApp.
2 Highfield and Leaver recently observed something similar (Highfield and Leaver, 2016: 47).
3 San Francisco, Tokyo, London, Moscow, Tel Aviv, New York, Bangkok, Sydney, Istanbul, Singapore, Paris, Berlin, Rio de Janeiro.
4 The project's definition of a 'selfie' required a picture to be of a single individual's face (no group photos or photos of other body parts), and was contentious among qualitative selfie researchers, who noted this requirement excluded many photos the participants may have thought of as selfies.
5 This dataset was donated by Twitter to the 'Reading the Riots' project, a collaboration between *The Guardian* newspaper and a number of UK academics analysing Twitter use during the riots, which Vis et al. (2014) developed further, focusing on image use. See the original project here: www.theguardian.com/uk/reading-the-riots-blog/2011/oct/10/reading-the-riots

6 The Visual Social Media Lab (http://visualsocial-medialab.org) was set up as part of the Transformative Research project 'Picturing the Social: Transforming our Understanding of Images in Social Media and Big Data research'. ESRC grant reference: ES/M000648/1

7 www.pulsarplatform.com

8 #kiyiyavuraninsanlik · kiyiya vuran insanlik · #humanitywashedashore · humanity washed ashore · #refugeeswelcome · #refugeecrisis · #refugeescrisis · #aylankurdi · #alankurdi · #aylan · aylan · alan · kurdi · #nomoredrownings · no more drownings · #dyingtogethere · dying to get here · #syria boy · syria boy · #syrian boy · syrian boy · #syria child · syria child · #syrian child · syrian child · #syrianchild · #syrianboy · bodrum beach · drowned boy · drowned child · drowned toddler · refugees welcome · refugee crisis · refugees crisis

9 Betweenness centrality measures all the shortest paths between every pair of nodes and counts how many times a node is on a shortest path between two others.

10 Average Degree and Weighted Average Degree are options Gephi offers for the final rendering and centrality measures in your network visualisation.

11 According to Pulsar Visibility is a more accurate measure of the impact of a tweet than a simple retweet count. It also takes into account the estimated impressions generated by a tweet as a percentage of the potential audience that could have been reached if 100 per cent of the followers of an account who tweeted were reached by that tweet. In 2016 that percentage was estimated to be at 11.2 per cent of the total audience of the user posting a tweet.

12 Link to tweet: https://twitter.com/demishevich/status/639005592984649728

13 The Pulsar algorithm assesses the size of the audience of the author, plus the audiences of the people who have retweeted the original tweet. It applies a percentage of active users who are likely to see a tweet in their timeline based on the average activity benchmarks on Twitter re-assessed once a year.

14 Link to tweet: https://twitter.com/lizsly/status/639042438984699904

REFERENCES

Bayerl, P. S. and Stoynov, L. (2016) 'Revenge by photoshop: Memefying police acts in the public dialogue about injustice', *New Media & Society*, 18(6): 1006–1026.

Belting, H. (2011) *An Anthropology of Images: Picture, Medium, Body*. Princeton, NJ, and Oxford: Princeton University Press.

Bruns, A., Burgess, J., Crawford, K. and Shaw, F. (2012) *#qldfloods and @QPSMedia: Crisis Communication on Twitter in the 2011 South East Queensland Floods*. Brisbane: ARC Centre of Excellence for Creative Industries and Innovation.

Burgess, J. E. (2009) 'Remediating vernacular creativity: Photography and cultural citizenship in the Flickr Photo-sharing Network', in T. Edensor, D. Leslie, S. Millington and N. Rantisi (eds), *Spaces of Vernacular Creativity: Rethinking the Cultural Economy*. London and New York: Routledge, pp. 116–126.

Delaitre, V., Laptev, I. and Sivic, J. (2010) 'Recognizing human actions in still images: A study of bag-of-features and part-based representations', www.di.ens.fr/~josef/publications/delaitre10.pdf (accessed 10/11/2016).

Eni, M., Finn, S., Whitlock, C. and Metaxas, P. T. (2011) 'Vocal minority versus silent majority: Discovering the opinions of the long tail', paper presented at the IEEE SocialCom Conference, Boston, October 9–11.

Frosh, P. (2015) 'The gestural image: The selfie, photography theory, and kinesthetic sociability', *International Journal of Communication*, 9: 1697–1628.

Garduno Freeman, C. (2010) 'Photosharing on Flickr: Intangible heritage and emergent publics', *International Journal of Heritage Studies*, 16(4–5): 352–368.

Gibbs, M., Meese, J., Arnold, M., Bjorn, N. and Carter, M. (2015) '#Funeral and Instagram: Death, social media, and platform vernacular', *Information, Communication & Society*, 18(3): 255–268.

Gómez Cruz, E. and Meyer, E. T. (2012) 'Creation and control in the photographic process: iPhones and the emerging Fifth Moment of photography', *Photographies*, 5(2): 203–221.

Gye, L. (2007) 'Picture this: The impact of mobile camera phones on personal photographic practices', *Continuum: Journal of Media & Cultural Studies*, 21(2): 279–288.

Hariman, R. and Lucaites, J. L. (2007) *No Caption Needed: Iconic Photographs, Public Culture, and Liberal Democracy*. Chicago, IL, and London: University of Chicago Press.

Hess, S. (2015) 'The selfie assemblage', *International Journal of Communication*, 9: 1629–1646.

Highfield, T. and Leaver, T. (2016) 'Instagrammatics and digital methods: Studying visual social media, from selfies and GIFs to memes and emoji', *Communication Research and Practice*, 2(1): 47–62.

Hjorth, L. and Burgess, J. (2014) 'Intimate banalities: The emotional currency of shared camera phone images during the Queensland flood disaster', in G. Goggin and L. Hjorth (eds), *The Routledge Companion to Mobile Media*. New York and London: Routledge, pp. 499–513.

Hochman, N. and Manovich, L. (2013a) 'Visualizing spatio-temporal social patterns in Instagram photos', *GeoHCI Workshop at CHI 2013*: www-users.cs.umn.edu/~bhecht/geohci2013ps/paper_56.pdf (accessed 24/02/2016).

Hochman, N. and Manovich, L. (2013b) 'Zooming into the Instagram city: Reading the local through social media', *First Monday*, 18(7), 1 July: http://firstmonday.org/article/view/4711/3698 (accessed 24/02/2016).

Hochman, N. and Schwartz, R. (2012) 'Visualizing Instagram: Tracing cultural visual rhythms', The Workshop on Social Media Visualization (SocMedVis) in conjunction with the Sixth International AAAI Conference on Weblogs and Social Media (ICWSM-12). Dublin, Ireland: http://phototrails.net/research/ (accessed 28/10/16).

Huntington, H. E. (2016) 'Pepper spray cop and the American Dream: Using synecdoche and metaphor to unlock internet meme's visual political rhetoric', *Communication Studies*, 67(1): 77–93.

Kharroub, T. and Bas, O., (2015) 'Social media and protests: An examination of Twitter images of the 2011 Egyptian revolution', *New Media & Society*, 18(9): 1–20.

Kohn, A. (2015) 'Instagram as a naturalized propaganda tool: The Israel Defense Forces website and the phenomenon of shared values', *Convergence*, 23(2): 197–213.

Lister, M. (ed.) (2013) *The Photographic Image in Digital Culture*. London and New York: Routledge.

Manovich, L. (2015) 'Subjects and styles in Instagram photography (Part 1)', http://manovich.net/index.php/projects/subjects-and-styles-in-instagram-photography-part-1 (accessed 24/02/2016).

Manovich, L. (2016) 'Subjects and styles in Instagram photography (Part 2)', http://manovich.net/content/04-projects/090-subjects-and-styles-in-instagram-photography-part-2/lm_instagram_article_part_2_edited.pdf (accessed 24/02/2016).

Meeker, M. (2016) *2016 Internet Trends Report*, www.kpcb.com/blog/2016-internet-trends-report (accessed 5/11/2016).

Milner, R. M. (2013) 'Pop polyvocality: Internet memes, public participation, and the Occupy Wall Street Movement', *International Journal of Communication*, 7: 2357–2390.

Milner, R. M. (2016) *The World Made Meme: Public Conversations and Participatory Media*. Cambridge, MA, and London: MIT Press.

Moschovi, A., McKay, C. and Plouviez, A. (eds) (2013) *The Versatile Image: Photography, Digital Technologies and the Internet*. Leuven: Leuven University Press.

Nooney, L. and Portwood-Stacer, L. (2014) 'One does not simply: An introduction to the special issue on internet memes', *Journal of Visual Culture*, 13(3): 248–252.

Pearce, K. E. (2015) 'Democratizing kompromat: The affordances of social media for state-sponsored harassment', *Information, Communication & Society*, 18(10): 1158–1174. doi:10.1080/1369118X.2015.1021705

Peck, A. M. (2014) 'A laugh riot: Photoshopping as vernacular discursive practice', *International Journal of Communication*, 8: 1638–1662.

Rogers, S. (2015) 'What can search data tell us about how the story of Aylan Kurdi spread around the world?', in F. Vis and O. Goriunova (eds), *The Iconic Image on Social Media: A Rapid Research Response to the Death of Aylan Kurdi*. Visual Social Media Lab, http://visualsocialmedialab.org/projects/the-iconic-image-on-social-media (accessed 15/11/2016).

Rubinstein, D. and Sluis, K. (2008) 'A life more photographic: Mapping the networked image', *Photographies*, 1(1): 9–28.

Seo, H. (2014) 'Visual propaganda in the age of social media: An empirical analysis of Twitter images during the 2012 Israeli–Hamas conflict', *Visual Communication Quarterly*, 21(3): 150–161.

Senft, T. M. and Baym, N. K. (2015) 'What does the selfie say? Investigating a global phenomenon', *International Journal of Communication*, 9: 1588–1606.

Shifman, L. (2014) *Memes in Digital Culture*. Cambridge, MA, and London: MIT Press.

The Graduate Center, CUNY (2014) 'Selfiecity Project background', www.gc.cuny.edu/CUNY_GC/media/CUNY-Graduate-Center/PDF/Press%20Room/Selfiecity_Background_Factsheet.pdf (accessed 25/10/16).

Thelwall, M., Goriunova, O., Vis, F., Faulkner, S., Burns, A., Aulich, J., Mas-Bleda, A., Stuart, E. and D'Orazio, F. (2016) 'Chatting through pictures? A classification of images tweeted in one week in the UK and USA', *Journal of the Association for Information Science and Technology*, 67(11): 2575–2586.

Tifentale, A. (2015) 'Art for the masses: From Kodak Brownie to Instagram', *Networking Knowledge*, 8(6): 1–16.

Tifentale, A. and Manovich, L. (2015) 'Selfiecity: Exploring photography and self-fashioning in social media', in D. Berry and M. Dieter (eds), *Postdigital Aesthetics: Art, Computation, and Design*. Basingstoke: Palgrave MacMillan, pp. 109–122.

Tifentale, A. and Manovich, L. (2016) 'Competitive photography and the presentation of self", http://manovich.net/index.php/projects/competitive-photography-and-the-presentation-of-the-self (accessed 25/02/2016).

van Dijck, J. (2008) 'Digital photography: Communication, identity, memory', *Visual Communication*, 7(1): 57–76.

van Dijck, J. (2010) 'Flickr and the culture of connectivity: Sharing views, experiences, memories', *Memory Studies*, 4(4): 401–415.

Van House, N. A. (2007) 'Flickr and public image-sharing: Distant closeness and photo exhibition', http://people.ischool.berkeley.edu/~vanhouse/VanHouseFlickrDistantCHI07.pdf (accessed 5/11/2016).

Van House, N. A. and Ames, M. (2006) 'The social life of cameraphone images', http://citeseerx.ist.psu.edu/viewdoc/download?doi=10.1.1.137.4299&rep=rep1&type=pdf (10/11/2016).

Van House, N. A., Davis, M., Ames, M., Finn, M. and Viswanathan, V. (2005) 'The uses of personal networked digital imaging: An empirical study of cameraphone photos and sharing', https://pdfs.semanticscholar.org/2320/407a03c113401a3ac9436ba645c8774cd987.pdf (10/11/2016).

Villi, M. (2015) '"Hey, I'm here right now": Camera phone photographs and mediated presence', *Photographies*, 8(1): 3–21.

Villi, M. and Stocchetti, M. (2011) 'Visual mobile communication, mediated presence and the politics of space', *Visual Studies*, 26(2): 102–112.

Vis, F. (2013) 'Twitter as a reporting tool for breaking news', *Digital Journalism*, 1(1): 27–47.

Vis, F., Faulkner, S., Parry, K., Manyukhina, Y. and Evans, L. (2014) 'Twitpic-ing the riots: Analysis images shared on Twitter during the 2011 UK riots', in K. Weller, A. Bruns, J. Burgess, M. Mahrt and C. Puschmann (eds), *Twitter and Society*. New York: Peter Lang, pp. 385–398.

Vis, F. and Goriunova, O. (eds) (2015) *The Iconic Image on Social Media: A Rapid Research Response to the Death of Aylan Kurdi*. Visual Social Media Lab, http://visualsocialmedialab.org/projects/the-iconic-image-on-social-media (accessed 15/11/2016).

Wittkower, R. (1977) *Allegory and the Migration of Symbols*. New York and London: Thames and Hudson.

10

Ethnography

Jolynna Sinanan and Tom McDonald

Among a range of established social science research methods, ethnography claims distinctiveness by virtue of its commitment to achieving an especially deep engagement with participants through close observation of, and participation in, their social lives. Ethnography is the primary research method and methodology of anthropology, but ethnographically-informed approaches are used across a wide range of disciplines in contemporary scholarship, including those engaged with social media research. This chapter will examine the role that ethnography can play in understanding social media's impact upon social life, demonstrating ethnography's aptness for discovering new types of socialities and relationships that are made possible by social media. We will also discuss whether the migration of ethnographic methodologies to other disciplines (hastened as researchers across a broad range of fields grapple with understanding social media in the context of everyday action) poses a threat to the distinctiveness of anthropology itself.

Sanjek (2010) notes that ethnography has a distinctively dual nature, being both the main practice (undertaking fieldwork and participant observation) and product (in terms of ethnographic writing such as monographs and articles) of anthropological research. Therefore, rather than limiting our scope to ethnography as a tool for better understanding social media, this chapter will also examine how social media is changing ethnography. We demonstrate that the increasing ubiquity of social media in societies throughout the world not only constitutes a new focus of comparative ethnographic research, but is also profoundly reshaping how ethnographic research is conducted. This chapter does not provide readers with a 'how-to' guide for performing ethnography on social media, but argues that ethnography and social media should be considered as two sets of practices and artefacts that are themselves undergoing constant change and development, and are set on a course which will involve them becoming increasingly bound in interaction with each other, with important implications for how social research is conducted more broadly.

This chapter is divided into two parts. First, we examine ethnography as a practice, and second, as a product. In both instances, we give a concise summary of the literature that has informed the development of that aspect of ethnography, before considering relevant recent scholarship on researching social media through ethnography (largely from within the emerging subfield of digital anthropology, but also considering it's adoption by a range of cross-disciplinary scholars), placing this in context to other approaches to studying social m distinctiveness edia. We also draw on our own research from the *Why We Post* project,[1] conducted through University College London.[2] This study presented a unique opportunity to research social media ethnographically, involving nine anthropologists spread over eight countries.[3] Eight of the researchers lived for 15 months in towns with relatively small populations (18,000–25,000 people) in Brazil, Chile, North and South China, India, Italy, Trinidad and Turkey, and one lived close to his field site in England, across 2012–2014. The result was an in-depth, comparative study of the uses of social media (Miller et al., 2016) based on nine closely integrated ethnographies (Costa, 2016; Haynes, 2016; McDonald, 2016; Miller, 2016; Nicolescu, 2016; Sinanan, 2017; Spyer, 2017; Venkatraman, 2017; Wang, 2016). This chapter calls on some of our own practical experiences participating in the study, in addition to other recent scholarship that addresses this issue.

The chapter closes with a discussion of how social media brings the practice and product of ethnography together in a closer relationship. Although for the purposes of organising this chapter we have chosen to maintain this split between ethnography-as-practice and ethnography-as-product, in reality these two aspects have always influenced each other: decisions made on which ethnographic approach to adopt will inevitably dictate the nature of the final ethnographic product. Further, the presence of social media is progressively blurring the boundaries between these two aspects of ethnography. We argue that the future of anthropology as a discipline may be better safeguarded by embracing the opportunities offered by technologies such as social media in reshaping both ethnographic practice and product to better fit the contemporary world, rather than attempting to defensively confine ethnography within anthropology's disciplinary boundaries.

SOCIAL MEDIA AND ETHNOGRAPHIC PROCESS

It is the process, or method of ethnography where social media is arguably having the most noticeable and most discussed effects on how anthropologists go about their research. Postill and Pink (2012) helpfully identify three particular challenges created by the growth of social media, which will form the focus of this section:

> They [social media] create new sites for ethnographic fieldwork, foster new types of ethnographic practice, and invite critical perspectives on the theoretical frames that dominate internet studies, thus providing opportunities for re-thinking internet research methodologically. (Postill and Pink, 2012: 214)

In response to Postill and Pink's first challenge, we find that social media represents not only a new location for fieldwork, but is also increasingly becoming the explicit topic of anthropological research (see, for example, boyd, 2014; Miller, 2011; Miller et al., 2016; Postill, 2014). Such studies have precipitated a range of ethnographic insights on a wide variety of themes. They have made scholarly impacts by placing the global phenomena of social media within local contexts, and understanding how it is appropriated differently in different locales (Miller et al., 2016);

highlighting the reciprocity that underlies social media use (Miller, 2011); showing the divisions between parents and children with regard to social media use, and how parents often make the situation worse (boyd, 2014); documenting how people with disabilities develop their own social media practices to enable self-represesentation (Ginsburg, 2012); and detailing how user's selfhood can emerge through the configuration and reordering of online spaces (Horst, 2009).

With regard to Postill and Pink's (2012) assertion that social media create new types of ethnographic practice, we note that for the majority of anthropological researchers, social media are not their explicit focus of research; rather, these communication technologies increasingly impinge upon their own research topics by virtue of the fact that their participants make extensive use of many of these platforms. As a result, themes which are central anthropological concerns – including religion, politics, gender and kinship – are enacted on (or through the use of) these platforms. This carries important implications for all researchers carrying out ethnography, including those not explicitly focused on social media use. The ubiquity of these platforms in participants' lives necessitates that ethnographers should be proficient in conducting research on, about and around social media. The following review section will demonstrate that the literature regarding the practice of internet ethnography (rather than social media specifically) is relatively well developed and ever-expanding, albeit dominated by reflexive discussions of how to carry out research online.

Hine's *Virtual Ethnography* (2000) argues that attitudes towards the internet have important repercussions for the ways it is used or how individuals relate to it, once these beliefs are understood within broader cultural contexts (2000: 8). She sees the internet as a product of culture, and ethnography as a mode of engaging with practices within such contexts. This, she posits, is invaluable for deriving comparative understandings of how the internet connotes different cultural meanings to different people (2000: 29). However, Hine also asserts that internet ethnography does not necessarily involve physical immersion into a particular geographic location. Rather, internet ethnography is more concerned with experiential immersion into particular social spaces of the internet, where, similar to more traditional forms of ethnography, researchers negotiate access, observe different interactions and interact with participants themselves (2000: 45, 46). Hine later develops these ideas fully by challenging previous distinctions of immaterial 'virtual' space in opposition to material 'physical' space, claiming the internet is increasingly embedded, embodied, and everyday (Hine, 2015: 55). This leads Hine to call for an autoethnographic approach as the most apt way to engage with the mundane, unbounded and ubiquitous nature of the internet.

In *The Internet: An Ethnographic Approach*, Miller and Slater (2000) agree that uses of the internet are only meaningful when situated in particular places and wider generalisations about patterns of usage are better grounded within comparative ethnography. However, their ethnography differs in approach from Hine in the emphasis they afford to 'grounded' offline fieldwork. Based on research conducted in Trinidad and building on Miller's long-term engagement with the island, Miller and Slater conclude that the internet is a 'Trinidadian place' and refute the terms 'online', 'virtual' and 'cyber' when used to suggest the internet is a place separate from any physical one (2000: 4). Long-term involvement with individuals allowed the researchers to contextualise people's internet usage within other aspects of their social lives, which Miller and Slater argue is critical to understanding what the internet is and means in Trinidad (2000: 21).

Treating the internet as an immersive space in which to conduct fieldwork perhaps best culminates in Tom Boellstorff's (2008) study on Second Life, where he uses a traditional ethnographic approach, albeit while treating the online 'synthetic' world of Second Life as his field site. Creating an avatar called Tom Bukowski and a home called Ethnographia, Boellstorff observes, participates and interacts with others, using his own avatar as a means to research the social world of Second Life and the behaviours of those who inhabit it. One of the most significant contributions of the volume is Boellstorff's attempt to collapse the distinction between the 'virtual' and the 'real': he argues that the virtual should rather be thought of as an extension of the 'real' (through the flow of culture across on- and offline domains), and that our 'real' lives have, in fact, been 'virtual' all along (2008: 5).

In a similar vein, working from the assumption that digital spaces take their cue from their non-digital counterparts, Horst's study of teenagers and the social network site MySpace concludes that personal pages are far less about asserting individualism, but how 'individuals exist in alignment with highly socialised media of expression' (Horst, 2009: 99). Drawing on a material culture approach, Horst uses digital platforms to explore the relationship between places, persons and objects. By visiting teenage users in their homes and seeing their most private spaces – their bedrooms – Horst concludes that Facebook and MySpace are digital spaces that affirm physical and material relationships, tastes and values (2009: 108).

Responding to the proliferation of ethnographic studies in the mid-2000s, Coleman (2010) gives an excellent review on ethnographic approaches to digital media (non-analogue technologies, mobile phones, internet and software apps, but not social media in particular), in which she identifies interlinked and overlapping categories of scholarship. Studies of the cultural politics of digital media examine 'how cultural identities, representation and imaginaries, for example, youth, diaspora, nation or indigeneity are remade, subverted, communicated and circulated through individual and collective

engagement with technologies' (2010: 488). Coleman highlights how vernacular cultures of digital media typically focus on more incongruent phenomena, such as particular genres or groups, hackers, blogging, memes, migrant programmers and logics around properties of such media. She describes the 'prosaics' (or more mundane aspects) of digital media as how media are integrated into, reflect or shape other kinds of practices, such as economic exchange, finance or religious worship. Coleman historicises the studies she reviews within shifting theoretical trends, such as the anthropological concern with the impact of globalisation on localities and the emerging network society, and concludes that ethnography contributes to better understanding digital media in relation to history, context and lived experience (2010: 488–489).

The relationships between politics and social media (or previously, social networking sites) have also been given considerable attention to contextualise how digital activism and organisation has translated into physical activism and protest. Adopting a similar approach to Coleman, Postill (2014) highlights how contemporary trends in anthropology often conceptualise the 'global' in a way that is seen to encroach on the stationary, bounded spaces of the 'local' (2014: 414). He argues that social life understood ethnographically cannot simply be reduced to a community-versus-network binary, instead advocating for the use of ethnographic research to add depth and complexity to the theoretical debates surrounding concepts of community and network societies. Ethnographic studies of communities are not always best served by prolonged engagement in a single, clearly bounded field site: Tufekci and Wilson's (2012) ethnographic study of protest ecologies illustrates how following a protest movement within a physical context is far more challenging than analysing online political participation. They challenge the assumption that social media can contribute to resisting authoritarian regimes by emphasising that there are few accounts of how social media (or the internet more broadly) are used by protestors as events unfold in real time (2012: 363). Their study uses ethnographic methods in the aftermath of the 2011 Tahrir Square protests in Egypt to observe the protest's ecology and gain insider knowledge from participants; however, they note that encounters with participants, which occurred in semi-controlled public spaces such as cafés and parks around Tahrir Square, were characterised by anxiety, fear and panic. The main contribution of Tufekci and Wilson's study is to demonstrate how media ecologies during the protest movement reconfigured certain social relations from face-to-face conversations to social media chats, which rapidly accelerated the speed of the movement's social actions.

A number of scholars have speculated on different factors that may contribute to a social movement's success online. In his study of the Spanish 'indignados' political organisation, Postill (2014) coins the term 'media epidemiography' to explain how the movement suddenly gained momentum. He observed the protest directly in Barcelona, as well as following the techno-political context over Twitter, and concludes that throughout the movement activists showed 'selective uses of viral and non-viral contents both on and offline' (2013: 14). In a complimentary study, Lim (2013: 646) examines the relationship between users and social media for activism. Based on interviews and analyses of blog posts, Lim draws on her prior in-depth knowledge of the Indonesian social and historical context to identify the conditions where social media might lead to successful forms of activism. She argues that social media activism is more likely to mobilise individuals if the narratives of the cause are easy to understand, appeal to senses of nationalism and religiosity, and invite low risk action (2013: 638).

In reviewing this body of literature, one can be forgiven for thinking that the reflexive discussion of *how* to carry out research online

overtakes the desire to discover the actual use and transformation of digital platforms by research subjects, and the implications these have for how people understand their place in the world. Methodological reflections are clearly vital in strengthening critical engagement with regards to the validity and representativeness of research data. However, we are also keen to pair these discussions with our own experiences of conducting ethnography. In the *Why We Post* project, we did not seek out overt political engagement or activism as a focus of research, for example. Instead, our approach to politics was to uncover how and in what forms political engagement occurs through observations of social media use and daily interactions in our field sites (Miller et al., 2016: 142). In this sense, our topics of study were primarily driven by participants' actions, rather than presumed objects of inquiry.

The above examples demonstrate the emergence of a number of key anthropologists who have been influential in using ethnographic methods to understand social media, and in so doing establish the subfield of digital anthropology. A further key development has been the migration of ethnographic methods from the confines of the anthropological discipline and towards a broad range of scholars in fields such as human–computer interaction, media, communication and cultural studies. The result of this dispersion of ethnographic method into many subdisciplines has been a wide body of exemplary ethnographic publications that have greatly enriched our understanding of the impact of social media (and other ICT use) across a wide range of platforms and cultural settings. Examples include Baym's (1994) study of Usenet groups, Burrell's (2012) ethnography of Ghanaian internet cafés, Coleman's (2012) account of Debian hackers, and Kelty's (2008) study of open-source software, to name but a few. We, as authors of the current chapter, find this dispersion of the ethnographic approach particularly of interest given that our own personal trajectories have been very grounded within this central group of digital anthropologists (Sinanan originally completed her PhD in Development Studies, but conducted her Postdoctoral research in the Anthropology Department at University College London before joining RMIT University in Melbourne, while McDonald continuously trained as an anthropologist from undergraduate level). Our interest in the increasing adoption of ethnography in a wide range of disciplines lies not only in how data obtained through ethnographic methods are being used to address a range of questions beyond the traditional remit of convential anthropological topics, but also how this poses something of an existential challenge to anthropology's claim to disciplinary distinctiveness.

Postill and Pink (2012) also advocate a shift in the methodological emphasis of research away from specific 'objects' of study (e.g., communities and social network models), instead calling for increased attention to various forms of action (such as routines, mobilities and socialities). They posit that focusing on everyday, lived action can inform theoretical understandings of digital media, while keeping such explanations firmly 'grounded' in the realities of everyday life. Polymedia (Madianou and Miller, 2012, 2013) is an example of a theory having emerged from ethnographic inquiry, and in this section we will examine how polymedia applied to our own ethnographic findings.

Madianou (2015) argues that ethnography might be the only way to gain an in-depth understanding of how uses of social media are shaped by relational dynamics and context, and is thus essential for understanding the 'social' dimension of social media. Along with Miller, Madianou coined the term 'polymedia' (Madianou and Miller, 2012, 2013), which recognises that people use different forms of communication (e.g., phone calls as opposed to text messages) or different platforms according to the relationship to the person they are communicating with.[4] While Miller and Madianou concede that cost may

still be a factor in accessing digital media, they nevertheless argue that social media use has undergone rapid expansion in developing countries such as Trinidad and the Philippines (Madianou, 2015; Madianou & Miller 2013) that have also seen a growth of low-cost communication technologies. Polymedia is particularly ethnographic in nature as the concept recognises how different communications media are situated within their wider media ecologies. The concept recognises how each medium finds its place with respect to other media (Horst et al., 2010; Ito, 2010, Madianou and Miller, 2013; Slater and Tacchi, 2004), idioms of practice and media ideologies (Gershon, 2010).

One of the key differences between ethnographic approaches to studying social media and other methods, such as surveys, questionnaires and content analysis, is that the latter may become decontexualised from other forms of communication and lived relationships (Acquisti and Gross, 2006; Carpenter, 2012; Dwyer et al., 2007; Junco, 2012). In the *Why We Post* project, our ethnographic approach involved not only living in our respective field sites for an extended period of time, but becoming involved in the lives of the people we studied. In some cases, this meant volunteering in a local kindergarten or school, assisting with cooking for an event or helping with everyday work, in order to make genuine friendships. The underlying idea is a commitment to 'holistic contextualisation', where one aspect of a person, such as social media use, is examined in respect to other parts of a person's life that they might experience simultaneously (Miller et al., 2016: 28). We conducted formal interviews and questionnaires throughout the fieldwork, but most of the original insights came from spending extended periods of time with different people. Ideally, each researcher attempted to familiarise themselves with people from different social groups or geographical areas in their field site, so as to gain a more comprehensive knowledge of the place. Crucially, after identifying the most commonly used platforms in the site, each researcher aimed to befriend around 150 of their research participants on social media and follow their online activities, ideally for the entire course of the fieldwork. This chapter now turns to discuss a detailed example of how this process of forming relationships in the field became understood through an ethnography of – and on – social media.

RELATIONSHIPS OF TRUST TO INFORM GROUNDED THEORY

Sinanan discovered early in her fieldwork in Trinidad that asking to befriend someone on Facebook after having just met is more common than asking for a phone number. As each researcher had created a dedicated social media account for research, Sinanan found that participants were initially sceptical of her and were uncomfortable with being added as a friend to a research profile. Once she had populated the profile with some images from her 'normal' life in Melbourne, posted updates, chatted with new contacts and liked and commented on posts by others, she found that becoming friends on Facebook worked alongside getting to know people in her field site. By the end of her fieldwork, she had accumulated 267 Facebook friends, all of whom she had met face to face, and chatted with 38 people on WhatsApp. Having several research participants as contacts on different social media platforms, as well as spending time with them on a regular basis, enabled Sinanan to illustrate how a theory of polymedia unfolds in context.

In Sinanan's research, polymedia was useful not only to account for how Trinidadians relate to each other, but as a way for Sinanan to understand how she should relate to participants. As a social theory of media that has been developed from ethnography and anthropological theory, polymedia occupies a niche that addresses the uses of media in the context of relationships. One of the implications of the combination of media is that communications allow for the control of emotions and power asymmetries in relationships (Madianou and Miller, 2012; Miller and Sinanan, 2014). Polymedia suggests that media help to constitute social relationships. The example of the Trinidadian idiom 'liming' (below) demonstrates how forms of sociality that existed prior to social media translate to WhatsApp. In the case of liming, a spirit of egalitarianism and inclusion is important, so WhatsApp's group chat function affords each member of the group to be a potentially equal participant in the conversation. The second significant contribution of polymedia as a theory is that it emphasises content and *how* people also choose media to communicate particular messages, for example, why breaking up with a partner would be more appropriately done face to face than by text message. As a social theory of media grounded within ethnographic inquiry, Miller and Madianou's concept of polymedia compliments theories of relationships between media platforms proposed previously by a number of other scholars from a range of disciplines outside anthropology. Media multiplexity theory (Haythornthwaite and Wellman, 1998) and media ecologies (Fuller, 2005) are two notable examples. Polymedia may be distinctive in the way that it foregrounds the qualities of social relationships, which lends it to being used as a framework for making sense of ethnographic data.

There were clear implications and consequences for choosing which platform to communicate certain content to particular people. In Trinidad, the more dyadic nature of communication on WhatsApp made it more acceptable to conduct serious conversations over text on occasions where the other person was unable to speak owing to being in the company of others. Although a voice call, a video call, or face-to-face conversation was often described as being preferable to text, WhatsApp was viewed as a more acceptable text-based service for private and intimate conversations than

Facebook Messenger. WhatsApp was also understood in relation to its predecessor, BBM (BlackBerry Messenger). BlackBerry was arguably the first multimedia form of communication over a hand-held device for many Trinidadians, and when it declined in popularity Trinidadians were quick to adopt WhatsApp, which offered similar functions but could be used on many different brands of phones.

The configuration of media was also influenced by how participants viewed 'public' and 'private'. Over the duration of Sinanan's fieldwork, she observed an increase in closed, small-group chats between friends or family members on WhatsApp, which resonates with modes of socialising that were already widespread in Trinidadian society. The Trinidadian term 'liming' has a similar meaning to 'hanging out', but liming is considered integral to social life. Previously, liming was a predominantly male public activity, where men would lime in rum shops or on street corners, talking about politics and commenting on (or to) women passing by (Eriksen, 1990; Lieber, 1976). Today, men and women lime in both gendered and mixed groups, in homes, bars or more up-market clubs. On weekends, extended family or groups might lime at the beach or river. Several young men emphasised drinking as central to liming, but many enjoy liming for the sake of sharing company and relaxing without any impositions. Liming is also characterised by shows of bravado and performative banter for the entertainment of peers and was historically associated with street culture, which emphasises style and appearance to enhance a person's reputation (Burton, 1997; Miller, 1994a). The importance placed on appearance as defining a person takes on specific cultural importance in Trinidad, where individuals often emphasise character as residing on the surface of an individual rather than 'deep within' (Miller, 1994b). In this context, it is perhaps unsurprising that we found that people in the Trinidadian field site tend to post more images to Facebook, with

an average of 732 per person, than those in the English field site, for example, where the average is 450 per person.

Liming materialises through images of eating and drinking together or of empty alcohol bottles on Facebook, and it also appears through banter over WhatsApp. The importance of humour in Trinidad, and the ability to make others laugh, demonstrates a form of social inclusion achieved through sharing common references and experiences and reinforcing group norms as a form of everyday play (Eriksen, 1990; Lieber, 1976). Closed groups of extended family or friends on WhatsApp form a space where dynamics of liming are replicated through sharing banter, jokes, humorous memes and images from pop culture, and links to videos as a form of time spent together and bonding. One of the reasons for the greater popularity of group chats on WhatsApp compared to Facebook Messenger is because participants felt WhatsApp afforded them greater control over who saw specific content. In this example, we can thus see how ethnography of social media therefore does not set out to study how a particular platform is used, but, rather, starts with the field site and studies the platforms that are used within the context of social relationships in that place. Social relationships also influence the relationship to social media platforms and ethnographic research can then show how a platform can be localised rather than 'exported'. Such an approach takes a greater interest in content than the platform itself and emphasises that the norms and values they reveal are neither uniform nor universal.

Polymedia is a salient example of a theory of media that has been informed through the use of particular methods, illustrating how unique insight emerges from shifting the focus away from group or community formation, and instead towards specific practices or socialities. By considering the significance of liming and its inflections prior to the introduction of social media, Sinanan's case also confirms Coleman's (2010) assertion of the value of the process of ethnography for gaining detailed insights into the broader significance of digital media. Coleman argues that the ethnographic enterprise significantly contributes to digital media studies, as ethnography involves different frames of analyses, drawing attention to history and local contexts and the lived experiences that result from such contexts (2010: 488–489). The more abstract points of polymedia therefore become particularly concrete in Sinanan's comparison of how particular relationships correlated to particular forms of platform use within the Trinidadian social context, something that could only have been elucidated through ethnography. Relationships of trust and, ideally, long periods of immersion within people's everyday lives are beneficial for understanding uses of social media such as WhatsApp, which affords more dyadic communication between individuals and closed groups.

SOCIAL MEDIA AND THE ETHNOGRAPHIC PRODUCT

Throughout anthropology as a discipline, the relative weightings of three elements of ethnographic writing – ethnography, context and comparison – have shifted. Some of the earliest developments in ethnography came from Morgan (1851 [1962]), who aimed to depict the structure of society from his research participants' viewpoints in his writing. This was later bolstered by deeper ethnographic engagement which followed as researchers started learning their informants' languages (for example, Cushing 1883 [1988], 1920). Boas's (1888 [1964]) development of cultural anthropology in the US, guided by desires to 'salvage' cultures viewed under threat of disappearance, emphasised comparison over ethnographic description. Drastic reformulation accompanied Malinowski's (1922) work, which stressed active ethnographic engagement in participants' lives while also paying increased attention to the contextual element through charting linkages between supposedly separate domains, such as economics and magic. Evans-Pritchard's (1940) ethnography of the Nuer extended this by utilising vivid ethnographic accounts, to the extent that his work remains widely influential in anthropology today.

Traditionally, ethnography within anthropology is most commonly described as participant observation, although where this takes place has increasingly come under question. For Geertz (1973), ethnography defined anthropology in practice. He said that 'Anthropologists don't study villages (tribes, towns, neighbourhoods…); they study *in* villages' (1973: 22). Comaroff and Comaroff (2003: 151) bring into question the production of place, and the definition and boundaries of the field, as they argue that the local and global are now inseparable. The question of what constitutes place is an issue brought into sharp focus as a result of social media's presence, as people use these platforms to maintain both localised and transnational family relationships and friendships, as well as potentially expanding their own networks. Indeed, with the ubiquity of social media, where media stories, news and images from popular culture are circulated by users at a frequency comparable to that of direct messages between individuals, what constitutes 'global' and 'local' is increasingly problematised. In the 1990s, anthropological debates were concerned with the influence of economic globalisation and transnational media flows on the apparent reduction of the 'local' (Marcus, 1995). Ethnographic studies carried out towards the end of the twentieth century sought to understand whether global influences were making societies more homogenous (Foster, 1991, 1999; Wilk, 1995).

The ubiquity of social media has increased concerns with cultural homogenisation, but ethnographic research provides substantial comparative evidence that different societies appropriate social media into localised social norms, uses and meanings (Miller, 2011;

Miller et al., 2016). Viewing social media through ethnography complements research which associates social media with individualism, self-expression and ego-centred networking (Rainie and Wellman, 2012). Ethnography highlights issues of culture while remaining sceptical of both cultural and technological determinism.

The small selection of pivotal ethnographic texts discussed above are foundational reading in anthropology, and have thus spawned a multitude of further ethnographic research and writings, all of which have had to negotiate and merge these issues of ethnography, comparison and contextualisation.

Downloadable Digital Ethnography

Despite the various reconfigurations of the internal balance of ethnographic writings over the decades, the forms of research products have largely remained constant: published ethnographic monographs and academic journal articles. While digital publishing, e-books and online journals have changed how many people access this literature, the intended audience often remains much the same. Although steps have been taken to remove financial and technical barriers to accessing these publications, such as the welcome growth of open access publications within anthropology (Weiss, 2014), anthropologists have primarily emphasised maintaining (or even extending) the rigour and high academic standards of peer-reviewed ethnographic publications (Miller, 2012: 398), rather than enabling complimentary or alternative forms of scholarship.

The *Why We Post* project is attempting to challenge the 'traditional' ethnographic monograph as the main product of anthropological research. First, we committed to publish all of our monographs (Costa, 2016; Haynes, 2016; McDonald, 2016; Miller, 2016; Nicolescu, 2016; Sinanan, 2017; Spyer, 2017; Venkatraman, 2017; Wang, 2016) in

an open-access format through a leading academic publisher. This meant that they would be free to download by anyone in the world with an internet connection. Our own experience of conducting research in small towns in countries such as Brazil, India and China underlined the difficulties many have in accessing books and other educational resources.

However, our experiences showed us that simply providing access to the final ethnographic text was not enough. Merely being able to download a book free of charge does not necessarily equate to people *wanting* to download it or subsequently read it. To address this, we realised that we also had to change the form of the ethnographic product. For example, although the finished volumes are scholarly academic texts, we adopted an accessible and open style of writing, so that they could be understood by the genral public. We adopted a format that has more in common with historical writing than traditional anthropology, and decided to confine discussion of wider theory, academic issues and citations to endnotes. This means that reading the main body text provides the reader with a clear narrative of our findings, largely concentrating on the field site itself. For those who desire a more conventional academic book, the endnotes relate the evidence from each field site to the broader academic context and theoretical debates.

The methodological discussions around digital ethnography provide added insight into how digital ethnography, as a product, may be refined to reflect the actualities of people's everyday engagement with media forms. This methodological focus on what is taken for granted or perceived as normal in digital practices (Pink et al., 2016) necessitates an acknowledgement of the way that individuals perceive lived experience as entanglements, where aspects of life do not exist in separate categories (Ingold, 2008). Just as the *subjects* of ethnographies can no longer be caricatured as isolated social groups, those producing ethnography must also acknowledge that their *readers* (or audience) possess similarly complex and multivalent social lives. We argue, therefore, that any discussion of ethnography and social media must also rightfully consider the possibilities and challenges posed by new and alternative forms of ethnography, such as open-access publishing, filmmaking, and disseminating research findings and insights on social media platforms themselves.

Can A 'Tweet' be Ethnographic?

Above, we outlined a new format for ethnographic monographs that retains academic and theoretical rigour while focusing on specific results from a given field site. This is a small step towards making ethnographic research accessible to a larger audience. However, although this form emerged out of our ethnographic study of social media, it does not make use of social media itself.

Arguably, this a key area in which social media and ethnography are converging. Social media are an increasingly acceptable outlet for ethnographic writing, and in turn, a new ethnographic product. Researchers have shown willingness to use social media[5] to promote their own work and engage in theoretical and disciplinary discussion (Price, 2010). Anthropological organisations such as the *American Anthropological Association* and *Hau: The Journal of Anthropological Theory* are exemplary cases, with followers numbering in the tens of thousands. However, perhaps more interesting is how individual researchers are using social media, and how these platforms are used to share ongoing ethnographic reflections and embryonic theoretical ideas over the course of fieldwork.

This use of social media as an ethnographic product has transformed the process of reviewing field notes from a primarily internal and reflective stance to one that is potentially far more outwardly-directed and collaborative in nature. Social media

challenges the notion that there is such a thing as a 'final' ethnographic product. Instead, readers of a finished monograph may have followed the author's research project from afar for several years. Writing on the increasingly collaborative nature of the internet at the height of the 'Web 2.0' paradigm almost ten years ago, Bruns argued that 'the role of the "consumer" and even that of the "end user" have long disappeared, and the distinctions between producers and users of content have faded into comparative insignificance' (Bruns, 2008: 2). While Bruns' argument can be critiqued by arguing that such collaborative, open-ended production by users is in fact symptomatic of exploitative relationships between users and platform owners, we find the concept remains useful in understanding how the role of the 'producer-ethnographer' and 'consumer-reader' may become increasingly muddied once the researcher starts sharing their research project on social media.

Ethnographic social media postings are often less polished and theoretical than peer-reviewed books and articles, but it is often the untreated nature of these online ethnographic field notes-cum-realisations that makes them especially compelling. As such, these forms of ethnographic product challenge the implicit contradiction between the supposedly 'thick' nature of ethnographic description (Geertz, 1973) and a persistent public discourse which maintains that online forms of communication are, by nature, lacking in profundity and meaning.

A decade ago, Jenkins (2006: 18) argued that 'convergence requires media companies to rethink assumptions about what it means to consume media, assumptions that shape both programming and marketing decisions'. The same is true for ethnographers. The authors have directly experienced the benefits of using social media as an ethnographic product through a website, blog and social media profiles which were set up and maintained throughout their project. Social media postings related to the ongoing fieldwork added a reflexive, open aspect to the research process, and resulted in interest and feedback from fellow researchers and the wider public. Our blog resulted in invitations to present at conferences and workshops, to contribute articles regarding research to other outlets, among other benefits.

The ethnographic slant of our own research was complemented by a strong emphasis on social media's materiality – the physical nature of these platforms and their content, understood within the context of their social use. For instance, we paid careful attention to the increasingly visual nature of social media in each of our field sites. Our project dedicated an entire month solely to the study of our participants' social media profiles, systematically counting, analysing and categorising their postings (including status updates, shared images and video) across a range of platforms (including Facebook, Twitter, QQ and WeChat, depending on what was used by participants in each site). Although this approach may appear to represent something of a departure from the 'active engagement' in our participants' everyday lives, which ethnographic practice is supposed to typify, the majority of our researchers balanced this by remaining in the field site for the entire month in which they carried out this screen-based analysis. This meant that even during this period it was inevitable that we, as researchers, would encounter in social settings the very participants whose profiles we had been closely analysing with respect to the social media updates, affording a valuable opportunity to obtain narrative accounts of the context in which such postings had been made.

The result of this approach became clear in the case of baby photographs observed on social media in McDonald's field site. As McDonald systematically analysed the QQ (a popular social media platform in China) postings – a total of 1,214 postings from 55 participants – he gradually became aware of the prevalence of photos of participants' young children, especially babies, shared on

their QQ profiles. Before his systematic analysis was even complete, he began taking time in the evening to talk to the parents of these children about their rationale and motive for posting so many baby photos. McDonald was able to identify two distinct periods in the production of these baby photos: the first, self-produced photos that are taken by mothers and posted on social media to alleviate the boredom of the traditional 'sitting the month' period, where mothers are confined to the home with their newborn child; the second, a series of professionally produced baby photos that are taken when the child reaches a hundred days of age, and are then subsequently made into both a printed photo album and shared on social media.

Far from just considering these photos, their circulation online, and the subsequent implications of their sharing, being situated in the field site allowed him to examine how social media was changing the production of these images. McDonald spoke to the managers of several of the town's photo studios which specialised in offering this service, and started to understand that parents were so keen to upload the resultant hundred-day baby photos that photo studios were offering the uploading service within the studio itself, immediately after the initial photographs were taken. Furthermore, conversations with photo studio managers enabled him to understand how sharing these images on QQ represented the latest stage in the development of this photographic tradition, which had transformed over several decades following the introduction of photography in the town, and was also built upon a longer established tradition of banquets and gifting red envelopes filled with money to celebrate a child reaching his or her hundredth day.

In addition to charting the practice's historical roots, this focus on the social context of these images as material artefacts allowed for an understanding of how the practice related to conceptions of the future. Many 'successful' photo albums included photographs with a wide variety of different poses, facial expressions, outfits and props. Parents and photo studio managers explained that this variety was seen to reflect abundance and wealth and a desire to avoid monotony. This stood in contrast to baby photographs in the town taken in the 1970s, where most families were able to afford only a single black-and-white photograph. The increasing variety and complexity of photographic images reflected not only a desire to express their current wealth, but also an aspiration to bestow a certain material abundance upon their children. The images were also intended to serve as a record of parents' generosity towards their offspring at an early age, to be reviewed by these children when they reached adulthood, and contributing to informing traditional Chinese notions of parent–child reciprocity (see Stafford, 2000).

Despite being a single example, the case of baby photos shared on social media in China does demonstrate how a specific focus on the material content of postings, and systematic analysis thereof in light of their associated social context, can highlight seemingly mundane aspects of social media (that nevertheless tend to dominate participants' online activities), which, when subsequently combined with focused ethnographic research, illuminate the far-reaching effects of these practices: how they relate and contribute to the historical, economic, consumptive and material changes of people's lives. In this case, social media ethnography has to make sense of particular actions around social media within a much broader context of ongoing social transformation and how this interacts with people's own memories, concerns, morality, desires and aspirations.

However, this case gives us more than simply ethnographic insight. The postings studied in the course of the visual analysis are more than just objects to think with. They have also formed an integral part of the ethnographic findings of this project. The images that parents have shared online are reproduced (with their consent) in McDonald's (2016) monograph. With the help of a filmmaker,

McDonald produced a short documentary film about the photographic practice of taking photos to celebrate a baby reaching a hundred days, which included an interview with a photo studio owner and a parent, as well as examples of these postings shared online. The resultant film[6] is shared on the project's YouTube channel,[7] along with others from his field site. The implications of these baby photos were also discussed in the project's blog.[8] Although the traditions of using imagery to complement text in monographs, and the wider subdiscipline of visual anthropology are now well established, these kinds of social media postings and imagery provide a new feeling of presence in the field. They not only have an 'authenticating' quality, confirming to the audience that what is being spoken about actually exists, but they also invite viewers take part in a deeper, critical engagement with these reproduced artefacts, critically assessing the author's explanation of the item against their original account.

The case of baby photos on Chinese social media is perhaps most surprising because it demonstrates the new circularity that social media has brought to the ethnographic form. Photographs that were originally produced with the intention of being shared on social media are subsequently analysed in an attempt to understand *how* people use social media, and in addition to appearing in an ethnographic monograph, they subsequently become the subject of a documentary film which is shared and commented on upon social media. As the written ethnographic monograph becomes increasingly embedded in an environment of 'media convergence' (Jenkins, 2006), it is inevitable that the ethnographic 'product' will take on new and challenging forms.

CONCLUSION: WHAT DOES SOCIAL MEDIA MEAN FOR ETHNOGRAPHY?

Throughout this chapter we have seen how the ethnographic process and product are affected by the presence of social media. As social media become increasingly entangled in the daily lives of research participants, they become a mode through which many foundational themes in anthropology can be examined. This shift speaks to a broader change of methodological focus in relation to studies of social media, moving from studies of community formation to more 'action'-based analysis detailing how sociality, practice and mobility are being reshaped by social media. Polymedia, for example, emerged from modes of analysis which concentrated on the sociality associated with different platforms, and different practices of social media use.

In the second part of this chapter, we examined the changing nature of the ethnographic product, showing how social media has contributed to the latest phase in over a century's worth of shifting in the actual form of ethnographic product. We argued for acknowledgement of social media *itself* as a venue for a new type of ethnographic output, detailing how social media became an important venue for sharing our ethnographic experience and knowledge. To illustrate this, we turned to the example of Chinese baby photos, which highlighted the circularity of social media postings that were at once the focus of ethnographic inquiry, but which subsequently appeared as part of our ethnographic product in monographs and articles, but also on social media itself in the form of blog posts, YouTube videos and social media posts.

Ingold (2014) has recently highlighted the increasingly widespread use of the term 'ethnography', both within anthropology and its allied disciplines, claiming that the term has become so common that it has lost much of its meaning. He argues that our understanding of what constitutes ethnography ought to be confined to (largely written) attempts to 'chronicle the life and times of a people' (2014: 384). Ingold asserts that encounters with people, fieldwork, methods, and the knowledge emerging from these activities,

should *not* be regarded as ethnographic. Instead, he argues that many of these activities should simply be routinely referred to as participant observation. He stresses that participant observation involves the exploration of the human condition, rather than describing people's points of view or life world, and the *possibilities* of being human.

Ingold's positioning of anthropology – rather than ethnography – as a 'practice' or a type of exposure, and an exploration of humanness, is certainly an appealing one. We also sympathise with his concerns regarding the widespread appropriation of the use of the term 'ethnography' both within anthropology and elsewhere, ourselves noting that such use is extending to many settings outside academia, including by corporations in commercial settings (for example, Elliott and Jankel-Elliott, 2003; Thrift, 2006: 295).

We argue that anthropology's preservation is more likely to come from embracing, rather than resisting, the expansive nature of ethnography. This has been made especially clear through this chapter's examination of the relationship between ethnography and social media. The ubiquitous nature of social media means that they will be an essential tool for fieldworkers in nearly every environment regardless of their research site or theme. Social media and ethnography are already deeply embedded in one another, and will only become more so in the future. This process is not expected to be an easy one, as many of the changes that would be bought upon both the ethnographic process and product pose fundamental challenges to the way in which knowledge is constructed, the authority of the anthropologist, and the state of relations between the ethnographer, participants and readers. However, it is precisely for this reason, that rising to the challenge of a new social media-oriented ethnography has the potential to reinvigorate social science research more broadly, bringing it closer to the people they study both in the course of fieldwork and in the production and dissemination of knowledge.

Notes

1 www.ucl.ac.uk/why-we-post
2 This project was funded by the European Research Council (Grant number SOCNET Project 2011-AdG-295486).
3 China had two field sites, to account for the specificity of the country's distinctive social media platforms.
4 Madianou and Miller (2013) argue that polymedia can be said to apply in any given situation so long as access to different kinds of digital media are not majorly constrained by cost and usability.
5 Blogs have been included in this definition because of their 'social' commenting feature, but also because they frequently draw on online work.
6 http://youtu.be/_BQE1m1DQk8
7 www.youtube.com/whywepost
8 http://blogs.ucl.ac.uk/global-social-media/2013/11/19/qq-and-nationalism-is-qq-uniting-the-many-different-chinas/

REFERENCES

Acquisti, A. and Gross, R. (2006). Imagined communities: Awareness, information sharing, and privacy on the Facebook. In G. Danezis and P. Golle. (eds.) *Privacy enhancing technologies* (pp. 36-58). Berlin and Heidelberg: Springer.

Baym, N. K. (1994). From practice to culture on Usenet. *The Sociological Review, 42*(S1): 29–52.

Boas, F. (1888 [1964]). *The Central Eskimo.* Lincoln, NE: Bison Books/University of Nebraska Press.

Boellstorff, T. (2008). *Coming of age in Second Life.* Princeton, NJ: Princeton University Press.

boyd, d. (2014). *It's complicated: The social lives of networked teens.* New Haven, CT, and London: Yale University Press.

Bruns, A. (2008). *Blogs, Wikipedia, Second Life, and beyond: From production to produsage.* New York and Oxford: Peter Lang.

Burrell, J. (2012). *Invisible users: Youth in the Internet cafes of urban Ghana.* Cambridge, MA: MIT Press.

Burton, R. (1997). *Afro-Creole: Power, opposition and play in the Caribbean.* Ithaca, NY: Cornell University Press.

Carpenter, Christopher J. (2012). Narcissism on Facebook: Self-promotional and anti-social behavior. *Personality and Individual Differences, 52*(4): 482–486.

Coleman, E. G. (2010). Ethnographic Approaches to Digital Media. *Annual Review of Anthropology, 39*: 487–505.

Coleman, E. G. (2012). *Coding freedom: The ethics and aesthetics of hacking.* Princeton, NJ: Princeton University Press.

Comaroff, J. and Comaroff, J. (2003). Ethnography on an awkward scale: Postcolonial anthropology and the violence of abstraction. *Ethnography, 4*(2): 147–179.

Costa, E. (2016). *Social media in South East Turkey.* London: UCL Press.

Cushing, F. H. (1883 [1988]). *Zuni Fetishes.* Las Vegas, NV: KC Publications.

Cushing, F.H. (1920). *Zuni Breadstuff.* New York: Museum of the American Indian.

Dwyer, C., Starr, H. and Passerini, K. (2007). Trust and privacy concern within social networking sites: A comparison of Facebook and MySpace. *AMCIS 2007 Proceedings* (p. 339). http://aisel.aisnet.org/amcis2007/339.

Elliott, R. and Jankel-Elliott, N. (2003). Using ethnography in strategic consumer research. *Qualitative Market Research: An International Journal, 6*(4): 215–223.

Eriksen, T. H. (1990). Liming in Trinidad: The art of doing nothing. *Folk, 32*(1): 23–43.

Evans-Pritchard, E. E. (1940). *The Nuer.* Oxford: Oxford University Press.

Foster, R. J. (1991). Making national cultures in the global ecumene. *Annual Review of Anthropology, 20*: 235–260.

Foster, R. J. (1999). Melanesianist anthropology in the era of globalization. *The Contemporary Pacific 11*(1): 140–159.

Fuller, M. (2005). *Media ecologies: Materialist energies in art and technoculture.* Cambridge, MA: MIT Press.

Geertz, C. (1973). *The interpretation of cultures: Selected essays* (Vol. 5019). New York: Basic Books.

Gershon, I. (2010). *The Break-up 2.0: Disconnecting over new media.* Ithaca, NY: Cornell University Press.

Ginsburg, F. (2012). Disability in the digital age. In H. A. Horst and D. Miller (eds.), *Digital anthropology* (pp. 101–126). Oxford: Berg.

Haynes, N. (2016). *Social media in northern Chile.* London: UCL Press.

Haythornthwaite, C. and Wellman, B. (1998). Work, friendship, and media use for information exchange in a networked organization. *Journal of the Association for Information Science and Technology*, 49: 1101–1114.

Hine, C. M. (2000). *Virtual ethnography*. London: Sage.

Hine, C. M. (2015). *Ethnography for the internet: Embedded, embodied and everyday*. London: Bloomsbury.

Horst, H. A. (2009). Aesthetics of the self: Digital mediations. In D. Miller (ed.), *Anthropology and the individual: A material culture perspective* (pp. 99–113). Oxford: Berg.

Horst, H., Martinez, K. and Sima, C. (2010). Chapter 4: Families. In M. Ito (ed.), *Hanging out, messing around and geeking out: Kids living and learning with new media*. Cambridge, MA: MIT Press.

Ingold, T. (2008). Bindings against boundaries: Entanglements of life in an open world. *Environment and Planning*, 40(8): 1796–1810.

Ingold, T. (2014). That's enough about ethnography! *HAU: Journal of Ethnographic Theory*, 4(1): 383–395.

Ito, M. (ed.) (2010). *Hanging out, messing around, and geeking out: Kids living and learning with new media*. Cambridge, MA: MIT Press.

Jenkins, R. (2006). *Convergence culture: Where old and new media collide*. New York: New York University Press.

Junco, R. (2012). The relationship between frequency of Facebook use, participation in Facebook activities, and student engagement. *Computers & Education*, 58(1): 162–171.

Kelty, C. M. (2008). *Two bits: The cultural significance of free software*. Durham, NC: Duke University Press.

Lieber, M. (1976). 'Liming' and other concerns: The style of street embedments in Port-of-Spain, Trinidad. *Urban Anthropology*, 5(4): 319–334.

Lim, M. (2013). Many clicks but little sticks: Social media activism in Indonesia. *Journal of Contemporary Asia*, 43(4), 636-657.

Madianou, M. (2015). Polymedia and ethnography: Understanding the social in social media. *Social Media + Society*, 1(1). DOI 2056305115578675.

Madianou, M. and Miller, D. (2012). *Migration and new media: Transnational families and polymedia*. London: Routledge.

Madianou, M. and Miller, D. (2013). Polymedia: Towards a new theory of digital media in interpersonal communication. *International Journal of Cultural Studies*, 16(2): 169–187.

Malinowski, B. (1922). *Argonauts of the Western Pacific*. New York: Dutton.

Marcus, G. E. (1995). Ethnography in/of the world system: The emergence of multi-sited ethnography. *Annual Review of Anthropology*, 24: 95–117.

McDonald, T. (2016). *Social media in rural China*. London: UCL Press.

Miller, D. (1994a). *Modernity: An ethnographic approach*. Oxford: Berg.

Miller, D. (1994b). Style and ontology. In J. Friedman (ed.), *Consumption and identity* (pp. 53–70). Reading, UK: Harwood Academic Publishers.

Miller, D. (2011). *Tales from Facebook*. Cambridge: Polity Press.

Miller, D. (2012). Open Access, Scholarship and Digital Anthropology. *HAU: Journal of Ethnographic Theory*, 2(1): 385–393.

Miller, D. (2016). *Social media in an English village*. London: UCL Press.

Miller, D., Costa, E., Haynes, N., McDonald, T., Nicolescu, R., Sinanan, J., Spyer, J., Venkatramen, S. and Wang, X. (2016). *How the world changed social media*. London: UCL Press.

Miller, D. and Sinanan, J. (2014). *Webcam*. Cambridge: Polity Press.

Miller, D. and Slater, D. (2000). *The internet: An ethnographic approach*. Oxford: Berg.

Morgan, L. H. (1962 [1851]). *League of the Iroquois*. New York: Corinth.

Nicolescu, R. (2016). *Social media in southeast Italy*. London: UCL Press.

Pink, S., Horst, H., Postill, J., Hjorth, L., Lewis, T. and Tacchi, J. (2016). *Digital ethnography: Principles and practice*. London: Sage.

Postill, J. (2014). Democracy in an age of viral reality: A media epidemiography of Spain's indignados movement. *Ethnography*, 15(1): 1–19.

Postill, J. and Pink, S. (2012). Social media ethnography: The digital researcher in a messy web. *Media International Australia*, 145: 23–134.

Price, D. H. (2010). Blogging anthropology: Savage minds, zero anthropology, and AAA blogs. *American Anthropologist*, 112(1): 140–142.

Rainie, L. and Wellman, B. (2012). *Networked: The new social operating system*. Cambridge, MA: MIT Press.

Sanjek, R. (2010). Ethnography. In A. Barnard and J. Spencer (eds.), *The Routledge encyclopedia of social and cultural anthropology* (2nd edition) (pp. 243–249). Abingdon: Routledge.

Sinanan, J. (2017). *Social media in Trinidad*. London: UCL Press.

Slater, D. and Tacchi, J. (2004). *Research on ICT innovations for poverty reduction*. Paris: UNESCO.

Spyer, J. (2017). *Social media in emergent Brazil*. London: UCL Press.

Stafford, C. (2000). Chinese patriliny and the cycles of yang and laiwang. In J. Carsten (ed.), *Cultures of relatedness: New approaches to the study of kinship* (pp. 37–54). Cambridge: Cambridge University Press.

Thrift, N. (2006). Re-inventing invention: New tendencies in capitalist commodification. *Economy and Society*, *35*(2): 279–306.

Tufekci, Z. and Wilson, C. (2012). Social media and the decision to participate in political protest: Observation from Tahrir Square. *Journal of Communication*, *62*(2): 363–379.

Wang, X. (2016). *Social media in industrial China*. London: UCL Press.

Weiss, B. (2014). Opening access: Publics, publication, and a path to inclusion. *Cultural Anthropology*, *29*(1): 1–2.

Wilk, R. (1995). Learning to be local in Belize: Global systems of common difference. In D. Miller (ed.), *Worlds apart: Modernity through the prism of the local* (pp. 110–133). London: Routledge.

Venkatraman, S. (2017). *Social media in South India*. London: UCL Press.

11

Web History and Social Media

Niels Brügger

INTRODUCTION

Understanding social media as online computer networks that support social interaction, it becomes clear that histories of these media and the Web are closely entangled. On the one hand, online social media predate the Web. Online social activity took place in Newsgroups and Bulletin Board Systems as early as the 1980s, and not only did these pre-Web social media fuel an understanding in the general public of what it meant to 'be social' online with people on the other side of the globe, these early forms of online social media also continued to develop on the World Wide Web once it was established, and in this new medium they found their role in the emerging Web ecosystem, alongside all other use forms of the Web, including commercial, political, and civic use. On the other hand, the advent of Web 2.0 technologies in the early 2000s, and their extensive use in the development of social media platforms and companies such as Facebook, Twitter and YouTube,

have had a great impact on the development of the Web in general, for instance regarding the rapid spread of technologies used for content syndication such as RSS and practices like microblogging, which can be found not only on dedicated microblogging services, but have become widespread on the Web in general. Thus, if one wants to fully understand how Web and social media have become what they are, it is necessary to include their intertwined genealogies.

As any other digital media type the Web comes with two layers: on the one hand, the software code and the digital text treated by the software, and, on the other hand, the semantic elements we see on a computer screen, such as writing, images and video. The first layer is not understandable as such for the end user who reads a text or watches a video, but nevertheless it constitutes the condition for the manifest text since what is shown in a browser is created from the HTML code. Thus, when studying the Web focus can either be on HTML code, hyperlinks, and the entire digital ecosystem of the web, or on whatever is presented to the user on the screen – or on the relation between the two. It is also worth noting that although the Web code is not proprietary in itself, it allows for the creation of proprietary social media platforms that enables the creation of walled gardens on the Web.

However, studying the history of the Web more generally, before we even get to Web-based social media, can be a challenging task, in particular because Web content disappears rapidly, and therefore the archived Web becomes an important source. This chapter will discuss some of the particular methodological challenges related to the use of archived Web sources when studying social media on the Web of the past. First, the general characteristics of the archived Web and the consequences of these for its scholarly use are identified. Then attention is drawn to the specific challenges of the archived social media on the Web, followed by examples of how historical studies of social Web media are challenged when using archived Web sources. And, finally, future challenges are outlined.[1]

WEB HISTORY – WHAT IS THE DIFFERENCE?

The history of the internet has been studied for more than two decades (e.g., Abbate, 2000; Goggin, 2004; Goggin & McLelland, 2017; Hauben & Hauben, 1997; Naughton, 1999, 2012; Poole, 2005). However, much of the existing literature is about the internet in general, and not about the Web. If one wants to limit the scope to the Web, as is the case in this chapter, there exist only a few books about Web historiography (e.g., Brügger, 2010; Brügger & Burns, 2012; Gillies & Cailliau, 2000), but Web history constitutes a fast-growing field of study to which a number of forthcoming volumes attest (e.g., Brügger, 2017; Brügger & Milligan, 2018; Brügger & Schroeder, 2017).

This chapter is based on two meanings of the term 'Web history'. On the one hand, it can refer to the use of the Web of the past as a source in any kind of historical study and, on the other hand, it can refer to the study of the history of the Web itself (where the Web can also be a source). In other words, one can distinguish between writing history *with* the Web and writing histories *of* the Web.

In most respects Web historiography is no different from any other kind of historical study. The fundamental issues of historiography also apply for Web history (in both of the two senses outlined above), be they questions related to interpretation of the source material, to disciplines that can help the historical study, to theories of history, to periodization, to which forces drive history, as well as to general questions related to the source material: How, where and in what condition do we find it? Are the sources valid? Are they representative? Are they primary or secondary?

As with all types of historical studies, the nature and extent of available source material has a strong impact on which histories can be written. Histories of social media on the Web can be based on a variety of source types, from diaries, photos, and news stories to retrospective interviews, user statistics, log files, as well as studies of the Web and social media conducted in the past. However, the Web itself constitutes one of the most important sources, since it is the prime source for documenting what happened on the Web, what social media websites looked like, and which forms of interaction they allowed for. The problem with the Web is its ephemerality: content is frequently either updated or removed permanently, and layout, design and forms of interaction are changing rapidly. After just a short period, the Web of the past is likely to have disappeared, and it is only available if it has been archived. An illustrative example of a permanent disappearance of an important part of the Web is the decision by Yahoo in 2009 to close GeoCities and delete all user content; GeoCities partly survived in archived form only because of the effort made by the Archive Team, an archiving collective, and by the Internet Archive (Milligan, 2017).

However, as will be shown in the following section, the archived Web is a specific kind of historical source, and therefore it comes with a set of specific challenges.[2] Insofar as social media are part of the Web, they inherit the characteristics of the archived Web, including the array of challenges. But archived social media on the Web come with additional challenges of their own. First, the content on social media platforms is very often updated at an unprecedented pace, second, social media content is also often difficult to access because it is fenced-off, and, third, social media platforms often constitute very integrated digital media environments.

ARCHIVED WEB AS A SOURCE

For a scholar who wants to understand the history of social media in the future, the all-important challenge is that in most cases the Web of the past has disappeared.[3] Although other source types, such as the ones mentioned above (e.g., diaries, photos, or user statistics), may be useful, they cannot document the Web in the same manner as can the Web of the past itself. Therefore, scholars must hope that they are able to find versions of the Web that have been preserved, either by cultural heritage institutions, such as national or trans-national Web archives, by researchers, or on the online Web itself. But finding preserved Web material is only half a victory, because the form in which the Web was collected and preserved determines how it may be used as an object of study. Therefore, it is relevant to know more about some of the ways in which the Web can be preserved, and how each of these ways affects the possible studies to be conducted based on the material.[4]

From Online Web to Archived Web

Web archiving can be understood as 'any form of deliberate and purposive preserving of web material' (Brügger, 2011b, p. 25). On a general level, two approaches to Web archiving can be identified (Brügger, 2005, p. 10). On the one hand, there is macro Web archiving: Web archiving carried out by (trans-)national institutions with the remit of preserving the cultural heritage; and, on the other hand, micro archiving: Web archiving performed by a scholar or a group of scholars, for instance, with the aim of preserving the Web for scholarly purposes; or by anyone wanting to preserve the Web for whatever reason. In the main, macro Web archiving is carried out by professionals on a large scale, whereas micro Web archiving is carried out on a small scale by people with more limited technical knowledge. This distinction is important since knowledge about who preserved the Web, for what purpose, and how, may have an impact on how useful it is as a source as well as where to look for it.

The most important thing to have in mind when using the archived Web for historical studies is that for a number of reasons the archived Web is not necessarily identical to what was online at a certain point in time. On the contrary, it is better understood as an actively created and subjective reconstruction – that is, a version and not a copy. The reason for this is that it is not straightforward just to make a copy of the online Web, simply because this can be done in a number of very different ways, depending on which strategy for the archiving is adopted (e.g., where and when the archiving should start/stop), which choices are made on a more detailed level about how the archiving should be performed (e.g., in-/exclusion of specific file types, number of hyperlinks to follow, accessing other Web servers), and how the archiving of the Web actually unfolds (often involving technical problems, and challenged by the dynamics of updating).[5]

The Web of the past may have been preserved in one of the following three ways: (a) screen shots and individual webpages in a static form; (b) screen movies and downloaded video/audio; or (c) crawled web (cf. Brügger, 2005, p. 34). In the main, macro Web archiving is based on Web crawling, whereas micro archiving is often based on either one of the three types or on combinations.

Screen shots and individual webpages in a static form

Since the easiest way of capturing the Web is either to make a screen shot or to preserve an individual webpage in static form (Brügger, 2005, p. 47), the Web of the past may have been preserved in this form. A screen shot has preserved whatever was visible on the computer screen, whereas the webpage in static form was preserved by using specific software (a program or a browser add-on) where a Web address (a URL) was inserted, and the software has then retrieved the HTML content to be found at the URL and converted it to a static version of the webpage in question (typically a pdf file).

Although the result is the same in both cases, namely the output of a static image with no possibility of any kind of movement, the two are also different. In the first case, the parts of a webpage which were not visible on the screen were not preserved, and no scrolling on the webpage is possible, but as many open windows as it is possible to have on the screen can have been preserved, whereas in the latter case the webpage is preserved in its integrity and allows for scrolling. In addition, the screen shot is an adequate representation of what the screen actually looked like, whereas the pdf file may not be a perfect rendering of the webpage, especially if it is created with a print to pdf command. Finally, the two approaches also differ in that a screen shot does not have clickable hyperlinks and it is not searchable, whereas this is a possibility with a webpage preserved as a pdf file.

Screen movie and downloaded video/audio

The Web of the past can also be preserved in the form of a screen movie or a downloaded video/audio. A screen movie is a filmed record of what took place on the screen (in total or in part) (cf. Brügger, 2005, pp. 49–53), whereas a downloaded video/audio is moving images or sound in the form of video or audio files which have been part of a webpage (for instance, as an embedded video). Screen movies have been used with a view to preserving the interaction on a webpage or website, to preserving several parts of a website as they actually looked at the time they were visited, or to preserve streamed video, whereas the downloaded video/audio only preserves individual elements of a webpage, such as a video, and not the webpage as such. Neither of the two modes of preservation come with clickable hyperlinks.

Crawled Web

Finally, the Web of the past can be found in the form of crawled Web. Crawled Web was archived by the use of Web crawling software which contacted a Web server with a request for specific URLs from which the content was then downloaded as HTML or other file types. The software may have been configured to identify and follow hyperlinks from the URL in question and archive the link target, and this process can be repeated. The result of the Web crawling process is a compilation of HTML and other files from the Web server, and they can be displayed in a Web browser with clickable links and other forms of interaction, much like the online Web, either in a Web archive (if macro) or on the user's computer (if micro). Although Web crawlers should retrieve everything from the Web server, this is not always the case. Elements on a webpage are often not archived for technical reasons, including interaction based on java, rapidly updating content such as chat, video/audio (individual files, streamed), and flash, just to mention a few. In addition, the crawling process does not necessarily go as planned. In contrast to the two above mentioned forms of archiving, crawled Web is searchable and clickable.

Consequences

As outlined above the same Web entity of the past can have been preserved in a number of different ways, each of which has created their version of the same online Web entity, and each of which in their way impacts how the sources can be used in historical scholarly studies. In short, each of the ways the Web was preserved opens up their range of possible use scenarios where some types of study are made possible whereas others are precluded.[6]

Screen shots and individual webpages in a static form are very useful sources in research projects where it is important to have an exact image of what a webpage looked like, and how the different elements of expression actually appeared and were placed. For instance, this could be studies of the visual appearance of webpages, such as graphic design studies, or simply just studies where it is important to document or illustrate the exact content on a webpage at a given point in time. However, screen shots and webpages in a static form are not very useful in studies where access to the HTML code (including hyperlinks) is important, neither are they of any help if video, audio or any types of interaction on webpages are to be studied.

Screen-captured movies are useful sources in research projects where it is important to include the 'look and feel' of the Web as well as how the interaction could take place, or research projects where it is important that a rapidly changing content flow is documented, for instance, a chat. Downloaded audiovisual elements are very important for any study with a focus on these forms of expression. For instance, this could be studies of interaction, image, sound, or live streaming in

contexts such as anthropological studies, usability studies, or media studies. However, as was the case with screen shots and individual webpages, screen movies are not very useful when access to the HTML code is demanded, they are not searchable, and a screen movie can be difficult to navigate, because it follows the movements of the person who did the filming, which is not necessarily the way the person viewing the movie would like to move around in the website. In addition, downloaded audiovisual objects usually retain no trace of the webpage on which they were embedded or linked to or from, which is why it can be a challenge to establish the relationship between a given webpage and a given audiovisual element.

Crawled Web is an excellent source in research projects where a browsable version of the Web is needed, or where access to the HTML code is important. For instance, this could be studies where the exact look of the webpages plays a minor role, where missing elements are less important, and studies of the HTML code, including studies of hyperlinks. But crawled Web also comes with a number of shortcomings. As mentioned above, elements of expression and functionalities may be missing in crawled Web which can make a study of these features impossible.[7]

Where to Find the Web of the Past

The Web of the past can be found in several places, each of which influences the possible use of the material as a historical source.

Since the mid-1990s a number of professional Web archives have been established, in most cases with a view of preserving a cultural heritage, either on a national or a transnational scale.[8] In general, these archives are based on Web crawling, the material is of very high quality, and depending on the archiving strategies the material can be quite comprehensive. However, access restrictions may apply, ranging from online and open for all (as the Internet Archive or the Portuguese Web Archive) to only accessible for researchers, either at a physical location (as the UK Web Archive) or online (as the Danish Netarkivet). Other types of macro Web archiving initiatives are professional vendors who offer Web archiving services such as the Internet Archive's subscription service Archive-It, or the Internet Memory Research's Archivethe.Net. These companies are usually crawl based, and they are used by national Web archives as well as by researchers, universities, museums, institutions and companies, in the main by anyone with an interest in documenting the Web.

In addition to these professional Web archives, which are all based on a macro archiving approach, there exists an array of micro archiving-based collections of yesterday's Web. These Web collections include, on the one hand, collections archived by researchers in relation to research projects. This material may have been archived by the use of all the types of Web archiving mentioned in this chapter, and it is usually of high quality and well documented, but in many cases not publicly available, and since it was archived with a specific research project in mind it may be customized to such a degree that it is not usable in other studies. And, on the other hand, micro archived collections include a number of publicly available collections, archived by 'amateurs', with no explicit cultural heritage obligations, ranging from coherent collections such as The Archive Team Geocities Snapshot (www. archiveteam.org), or Common Crawl's open repository of Web crawl data (commoncrawl. org), both using Web crawling, to whatever can be found on the online Web, either old Web that someone has put there for whatever reason, such as screen shots of Facebook pages or screen movies, or old material that is simply still available on the Web (e.g., Tim Berners-Lee's first webpage). The coherent collections are usually of high quality and well documented, whereas it can be very challenging to determine the provenance of material found on the Web, but in many cases this material is the only source available (cf. the historical analysis of Facebook as a media/text in Brügger (2015), made on the basis of screen shots found on the Web).

Purposively Archived Web

To the scholar who wants to write Web history, including the Web history of social media, by including the Web of the past as a source, the main challenge is to find preserved versions of the Web. It is very likely that either no material is available or only partly relevant material can be found, and in either case the next step is to weigh to what extent the material makes it possible to perform the desired research and to answer the research questions, possibly by combining several source types which in itself is a challenge (cf. Brügger, 2005, pp. 40–41, 53–60). In general, what was archived, and how it was archived, is a function of the purpose identified by the institution, group or individual initiating the archiving. The purpose can be placed somewhere along a continuum with macro archiving at the one end and micro archiving at the other end. National and trans-national Web archives archive the Web with the purpose of preserving the cultural heritage, which implies that it is not preserved with any particular use in mind (one size fits all), whereas the preserved Web that can be found on the online Web is preserved for no specific reason, which is why it is unstructured and random. And in between these two ends of the continuum we have the micro archiving performed by researchers with a view to being used in a specific research project. In all three cases, the material may turn out to be of limited use. Although there is a lot of material to be found in the first case, it may not be preserved in exactly the form a scholar may later have wanted it to be, whereas in the latter two cases the material may prove to be too customized, either because it is simply archived and put online by anyone, or it was archived to fit only the specific research project to which it was archived.

SOCIAL MEDIA AND ARCHIVED WEB

The general characteristics of the archived Web as a source also apply to social media on the Web, but, as mentioned in the beginning of this chapter, social media raise at least three specific issues: social media content is very rapidly updated, it is often fenced off, and it is often integrated in larger digital media environments. These three characteristics also apply to the Web in general – webpages have always been dynamic, password protection as well as syndication and embeddedness were invented before modern social media – but they come in new extreme forms with today's social media, in part because of the scale of social media usage, and thereby because of the amount of content which is updated, fenced off, or syndicated and embedded. These three characteristics place special demands on how social media on the Web can be collected and preserved, and thus how they can be found and used later by a historian wanting to study the history of social media on the Web. The challenges related to these three characteristics are elaborated below, and in the following main section it is discussed how they affect the historiography of social media on the Web, with Facebook, Twitter and YouTube as illustration.

High-Speed Updating and APIs

If one wants to write a history of, for instance, a Facebook page where a close reading of status updates is needed, the three sources types identified in the previous section may not be of great help, simply because they have not been able to preserve the rapid update of huge amounts of data – for instance, Web crawling only preserves the immediately visible content on a webpage, whereas what will appear when scrolling down is not archived. Therefore, a fourth main source type will prove to be very valuable, namely the content archived via an Application Programming Interface (API), that is, a programing interface through which data can be requested directly from the provider's server. What is collected via an API is not a webpage as such, but rather some of the elements from which a webpage can be composed, such as posts, images, likes, and comments on Facebook, or tweets, re-tweets, and Favorites from Twitter, as well as information that was not necessarily visible to the users, for instance, information about geolocation when mobile media are used. Usually, the collected elements have to be organized in a database before they are ready for scholarly use.[9]

Material collected via an API also comes with a number of challenges (cf. Laursen et al., 2013). The first challenge is to find the material from the past. National Web archives usually do not use APIs when collecting the Web, so although this may change in the future it is not very likely that one can find API-based collections in existing Web archives. Archiving with APIs is widespread as micro archiving, performed by research projects or by individual researchers. However, it can be very difficult to find and be granted access to this type of material, and often it will be customized to fit the research project in question, which obviously is a challenge for a historical study with another research agenda. A final possibility for gathering material from the past via APIs is to fetch the material anew from the social media provider. This is possible as long as the material is still available, either by doing this oneself or by using a retail data outlet with extended access to, for instance, Twitter data. In either case, the social media company functions as a 'living Web archive'. But this solution also has its drawbacks. Using a data outlet can be costly, and no matter if one does the collecting one-self or a data outlet is used, it is not always clear to what extent a fully comprehensive dataset has been gathered because one has to rely on the provider (the social media company or the data vendor) actually providing what one thinks is provided. Social media companies often only provide random samples of the total data, they can have censored out or simply not included specific types of data, or they can have made changes to the API, which happens on a regular basis (Kumar et al., 2015, pp. 40–41; Lomborg & Bechmann, 2014, p. 260). In addition, since the material is not preserved elsewhere, there is no possibility of checking to what extent it is comprehensive (Bruns et al., 2013, p. 876; Lomborg & Bechmann, 2014, pp. 256–257). The impact of these two drawbacks grows as time goes by, because the social media platform in question may have made changes in their technical setup, content types may have disappeared and thereby no longer be available via the API, or content once online may have been removed (such as personal profiles) and may thus no longer be available either. The scholar who has found (or bought) Web material from the past, archived via API, may either find the material presented in a structured form in a database (for instance, done by a company), or it may be raw data. In the first case, the challenge is that one has to make do with the analytical possibilities enabled by the structured format of the material. In the latter case, it can be a challenge to manage the large quantities of data, just as a certain degree of computer skills is needed.

API archived Web material also enables some types of studies while disabling others. It is very usable for 'big data' studies of trends, structures, and the like, as well as studies of information otherwise hidden, such as geolocation, but it is less usable in cases where the focus is on how the elements retrieved by the API, such as images, status updates, tweets, etc., were displayed when they were originally online, for instance with a view to associating image and text elements present on a webpage at the same time (cf. Brügger, 2015; Weller, 2015).

Inaccessibility

It is a characteristic of social media that large portions of the material are not freely accessible, and such fenced-off Web material can be a challenge to historical studies based on the archived Web. Sources may not be accessible for two reasons.

First, the material was originally private and hence only accessible to the users contributing the content or their social networks, is in the case of Facebook profiles and networks of friends, or private profiles and direct messages on Twitter. This type of material can usually not be found in Web archives based on macro archiving, but it is more common to find such material as part of research projects, with the consequence that it is difficult to grant access to other people than the researchers who originally collected the material for their specific research purpose. However, some of the material from personal profiles may have ended up in national Web archives, because authors were not aware of the reach of their expressions, as seen with the syndication of content on personal profiles on Facebook which is automatically disseminated to other Facebook pages – or even beyond Facebook – through an opaque network of 'friends' and newsfeeds.

Second, the material was initially accessible, but later may not be freely accessible, either because the social media company denies access, or because the material is difficult to make accessible. This denial of access can come in different forms. For instance, between approximately 2009 and 2015 Facebook pages could not be found in the Internet Archive. The Internet Archive does respect website holders' wishes not to be included in the archive (a preference usually expressed in the robots.txt file), and this also applies retrospectively, which is why Facebook pages could no longer be found in the Internet Archive in the period mentioned above (cf. Brügger, 2015, p. 2). However, archived versions of public Facebook pages can often be found in national Web archives if the archive does not respect robots.txt (as is the case with the Danish Web archive Netarkivet). Another means of denying access is to block or prohibit the use of a social media company's API for archiving purposes. Social media companies may decide to close a researcher's access to the API for whatever reason. In addition, for instance, Twitter does not give access via their API to complete historical data, which is why this has to be purchased from a data outlet (cf. Kumar et al., 2015, p. 41). The Twitter collection at the Library of Congress is illustrative of the challenges of archiving social media data and making it accessible. Five years after Twitter and the Library of Congress announced that every public tweet would be made available to researchers, practical as well as policy challenges still prevent researcher access to this valuable archive (cf. Zimmer, 2015; see also Bruns and Weller, 2016).

Integrated Digital Media Environments

As mentioned above, social media often constitute very integrated digital media environments, where content is disseminated in a constant flow across websites via syndication, feeds, sharing, embeddedness and recommendations – Facebook feeds and tweets are syndicated or shared, and YouTube videos and images are embedded and recommended across the Web. This close networked integration adds an additional layer of complexity for anyone studying social media (Ellison & boyd, 2013, p. 165), but this is particularly challenging for the scholar who wants to study the history of social media, insofar as a study of one type of social media demands access to the social media to which it is related. But these may no longer be

accessible, either they are not preserved at all, or they may even be preserved, but are difficult to find and relate to the specific social media being examined. In short, with social media one has to study an integrated media environment of which the reach is opaque, and which it is probably impossible to find preserved anywhere in its integrity.

LOOKING BACK – EXAMPLES OF SOCIAL MEDIA WEB HISTORIES

Let us now turn to how all the above affect the historiography of the Web history of social media. As of today, the number of historical studies of social media on the Web is very limited, and with good reason since the phenomenon is quite new. However, a few social media studies with a historical approach have been made, but some of these were not using the Web of the past as a source, and only very few were based on archived Web. As for the studies not using the Web as a source, some were building on surveys and in-depth interviews (Archambault & Grudin, 2012; Steinfield et al., 2008), others were probably studying the material as it was still online, although this is not clearly stated (boyd & Ellison, 2008), and in a few cases it is not clear exactly what the empirical basis is (e.g., the historical overview in van Dijck (2013, pp. 3–23), or the study of Twitter's interface's mode of addressing and its changes in van Dijck (2011, pp. 336–338)). Regarding the studies actually based on archived Web, two are based on data collected by the scholars themselves, while the event they studied unfolded (Williams & Gulati, 2012), and this dataset was later used together with newly collected data (Gulati & Williams, 2013), hence, these studies were not using found archived Web. This is the case in only three studies, either based on previously collected datasets of Facebook (Page et al., 2013; Stutzman et al., 2012) or based on screen shots found on the Web (Brügger, 2015).

Thus, the existing literature only provides few answers to how the use of the archived Web affects the historiography of the Web history of social media. Therefore, another approach has to be adopted in the following, namely to put oneself in a future Web historian's place. How can scholars in 20 years' time write the history of social media on the Web if they have not preserved old Web material themselves? With a view not to imagining future studies out of nowhere, the point of departure will be already existing studies, and the question is how they could be re-made as historical studies in 20 years. The focus is on three main types of social media – Facebook, Twitter, and YouTube – which have been with us on the Web for quite some time, and which each place special demands on the use of archived Web as a source. A vast number of academic work about social media has been published over the last decade, and the following choice of illustrative examples does not claim any form of representativity *vis-à-vis* this body of literature.[10] In the following, the focus is primarily on the challenges related to the acquiring of the source material to be studied. Thus, relevant and important issues, such as research ethics and privacy, are not discussed.[11]

Facebook

A very large portion of the academic studies of Facebook focus on social interaction, use, social networking, behaviour, motives, and the like, and they are based on the inclusion of people being studied (respondents, people answering surveys, etc.), which is why they usually use methodological approaches that do not involve the Web, such as surveys, questionnaires, panels, interviews, focus groups, or experiments/labs. There also exist a considerable body of academic literature where the Web is actually analysed as a source in its own right, in the main in studies focusing on the semiotic content of webpages, using methods such as content analysis, rhetorical analysis, discourse analysis, or hyperlink studies.

Scholars who intend to write histories of Facebook on the Web in the future, with a focus on the semiotic, must take the following three points into consideration when looking for sources.

The first thing to consider is whether the object of study was a public or private Facebook page. If the study is about a publicly available Facebook page, such as the page 'Persian Gulf' (KhosraviNik & Zia, 2014), it may be possible to find sources to support a historical study in Web archives or even on the Web, such as screen dumps or pdfs. But if the study includes material on closed Facebook pages, such as profile photographs (Hum et al., 2011), or even a closed page belonging to a deceased person, a so-called memorialized page (Church, 2013), it can be almost impossible to make a historical study of exactly the same webpages because it is very unlikely that they have been preserved in any form. National Web archives usually do not preserve material which is not public, and finding screen shots or the like of closed profiles on the online Web is not very likely to happen.

Second, the number of webpages to include plays a role. If only one Facebook page is at the heart of the study (as in KhosraviNik & Zia, 2014), it is probably easier to find older versions of this webpage than if a much larger number is needed (as in Hum et al., 2011 (150 Facebook profiles)).

Third, the chance of finding relevant historical sources from Facebook is dependent on which parts of Facebook on the Web the historical study focuses on. For some studies it is important to have the entire layout (Hunt, 2015) or the entire page (Gulati & Williams, 2013) or the profile (Grasmuck et al., 2009), whereas others only need the wall posts (Church, 2013; Hunt, 2015) or a status update and the derived comments (Frobenius & Harper, 2015), and yet others study other elements on the Facebook pages, such as profile photographs (Hum et al., 2011) or hyperlinks

(Poell, 2014). In all these cases, the challenge is that the more specific the focus, the more difficult it is to find preserved material. Web archives based on Web crawling may not have preserved all elements, which is obviously a problem for someone wanting to study these elements, be that profile photographs or the continuous content flow on Facebook walls. An API-based dataset would be preferable for this kind of study, at the expense of losing the context in which the elements were displayed.

Twitter

Twitter has a very different communicative mode compared to Facebook. The form of expression has been limited to 140 characters for most of its history, tweets are in the main broadcast publicly, they can be re-tweeted (reposting another profile's tweet), and the relation between profile owners is based on followers, that is, social relations with asymmetric ties.

The biggest challenge for a scholar who intends to make a historical study of Twitter where the actual content is the main source is to find the material or, to be more precise, to find the correct material. For instance, if a scholar in 20 years' time wants to study the patterns of Twitter usage during political events (as in Bruns et al., 2013, or Johnson et al., 2013) the major problem is to find the right material to study. As mentioned above, Twitter's API makes it possible to retrieve data back in time, but at the expense that the researcher never knows exactly to what extent the collection is comprehensive (e.g., regarding the hashtags in question), and this problem increases the further back in time one goes (cf. Bruns et al., 2013, p. 876).

Another solution would be to go to a national Web archive. However, the challenge in this respect is that Twitter material has rarely been archived via API by these archives; rather, it is preserved through Web crawling. This implies that one cannot expect to find a comprehensive dataset of, for instance, all tweets, since Web archives usually only archive a selection of profiles (politicians, celebrities, or the like) or hashtags related to specific events, and not the entire communicative ecology with followers and re-tweets, which would enable 'big data' analyses of large amounts of data. However, having the profile pages may constitute an advantage if the study is about the historical development of profile pages (and not only the flow of tweets).

The last solution regarding finding old Twitter material would be to look for screen shots on the Web, but putting tweets on the Web is not as widespread as is the case with screen shots of Facebook, and screen shots will not allow for studies of larger trends and patterns.

If the scholar has succeeded in finding material, the three points mentioned above regarding Facebook also apply: finding old Twitter material from private profiles or direct messages is probably not easy; the more material is needed, the more difficult it is to provide this and the bigger the uncertainty as to the comprehensiveness; and the more specific the study (specific hashtags, only re-tweets, or the like), the more difficult it probably is to find relevant material.

YouTube

A scholar who intends to conduct a Web historical study of social media involving YouTube will in particular have to address three challenges.

First, if the historical study is about specific videos, for instance a study of the narratives used by extremist religious groups in YouTube videos (Vergani & Zuev, 2015), or in direct-to-consumer genetic testing (Harris et al., 2014), the major problem is to find archived versions of the videos, in the main because videos are usually not preserved by national Web archives, which base their collection on Web crawling. YouTube videos can be preserved, but it has to be done manually, which is why almost no Web archives do this, at least not in a systematic way. Videos may still be found on the online Web – either on YouTube or elsewhere – but as time goes by this will be more the exception than the rule.

Second, the historical study may want to include the context that originally surrounded the video when it was initially published on YouTube. This could, for instance, be a study of activist communication (Poell, 2014), which includes a hyperlink analysis of the outgoing links from YouTube's video webpages; or it could be a study with a focus on the commentaries on a webpage where a YouTube video was published, such as audience reactions to TED Talks, based on a content analysis of comments (Tsou et al., 2014), or the study of the comments to a singer's music video posted on YouTube (Davison, 2013). National Web archives may have archived these webpages, but in particular the commentaries are difficult to collect for a Web crawler (for technical reasons often only one page of comments is preserved). Thus, this type of study is only possible if someone has preserved the commentaries as screen shots or as a screen movie and made this accessible.

Third, if the historical study is not focused on the videos in their original context on YouTube, but rather on the videos as they were embedded in other types of Web environments (personal websites, news and media websites, other social media), for instance in a study of the use of YouTube in activist communication (as is the case in Poell, 2014), it can be very difficult to establish the link between the embedded hyperlink and the actual video, because the original YouTube video may no longer be at the same URL. And even if the original URL is known, it is difficult to find the video based on this information, be that in a Web archive or on the online Web.

More Social Media, More Complex Sources

Each of the examples above focus on one social media platform. However, future historians may very well want to study more social media at the same time, either in their closely integrated form, or just more social media in relation to a given topic.

The first is the case when closely integrated social media are studied, for instance a study of Facebook where focus is on the use of video, and these videos are embedded from YouTube. In such a project, one has to find not only the relevant Facebook and YouTube material, but the software-based connections between the two datasets also have to be established, which raises questions of space as well as of time: have we found the videos that were actually there on YouTube in the past? And is there temporal consistency between the video on YouTube and the embedded command on the Facebook page?

And the latter could be a study of an event where more social media are part of the analysis without having a focus on their technical integration, such as the study of how social media were used in activist protests at the 2010 Toronto G-20 summit, where the focus was on Twitter, YouTube, Flickr and Facebook (Poell, 2014).

In both cases, it is necessary to provide sources from different social media, and thereby probably different source types. Obviously, this increases the complexity, and the challenge is how these sources could be combined.

The Challenges When Looking Back

The available source material has a strong impact on which histories can be written, and, as demonstrated above, a number of histories of social media on the Web will be very hard to write, simply because no sources are available or the available sources are not usable.

A future Web historian who wants to write a Web history of social media based on the archived Web is facing the following mechanisms when looking for relevant and usable sources. The more fenced-off the material was originally, the more difficult it is to find archived versions of it. The more objects are to be included in the study, the more difficult it is to find all the necessary sources. And, finally, the more specific the study (specfic pages/profiles, videos, and/or periods in time), the more difficult it is to find relevant and usable sources. And the other way round: the more general the topic, the easier it is to find relevant sources. And when these three mechanisms are combined it becomes clear that, for instance, a historical study of 500 private Facebook profiles at three specific points in time in the past and their use of status updates may have a hard time finding something to study at all, whereas a historical study of general trends on 10 politicians' public Facebook pages may be an easier task. Therefore, the more difficult it is to find archived versions of social media, the bigger the need to base one's study on secondary source types, for instance studies of one's topic which were made in the past, at the time one wants to study (for an example, see van Dijck, 2011, pp. 338–341).

THE FUTURE

Although the history of social media on the Web is relatively short, a lot of decisive developments have already taken place, some of which point towards new challenges looming in the horizon of social media historiography. Concerning social media and the Web, three general waves of development can be identified.

The first wave of social media started on and developed with the Web, be that Facebook, LinkedIn, Twitter, YouTube, and others.

In the second wave, the existing Web-based social media began to expand to include mobile media, which takes place in three steps: first, with the mobile phone with a physical keyboard and no camera; second, with the camera-equipped mobile phone; and third, with the smart phone with touch screen, geolocation, still and video camera, and apps. In this second wave, social media not only supplement their already existing Web presence with a presence on mobile media in the form of apps, but this expansion also feeds back to the Web versions, because the mobile media enables new forms of expression and interaction that were not possible with laptops or desktop computers. For instance, the spread of amateur videos on YouTube is made possible by the smart phone (mobile video camera, high-speed internet access, apps) and the easy embedding in other social media.

The third wave is characterized by the emergence of a new generation of social media which has almost no attachment to the Web, but is exclusively based on the smartphone, and has a strong emphasis on images and video, in particular Instagram, Snapchat, and Tinder, whereas the Web still plays a role in Pinterest. Just as the 'old' social media were born with and on the Web, this third wave of social media is born with and on the mobile platforms. However, they are also entangled with the Web in the form of embedded content and functionality, be that on other social media or on any other website that has included a content feed such as a feed of status updates from Facebook.

It is important to stress that the three waves have not existed as separated waves. They overlap, and when the next wave hits land, the already existing social media types do not disappear; on the contrary, they co-exist with the new wave, but in a re-configured and reshaped form, prompted by the new wave. Although social media on mobile platforms have expanded, social media on the Web have not disappeared; rather, they have changed and have become embedded in a new social media ecology. However, the role of the Web will probably continue to change, with the usage patterns of the coming generations. For instance, in 2015, 91% of teens in the USA went online from a mobile device (Lenhart, 2015, p. 14), and the adoption of smartphones and tablet computers has grown in the period 2011–2015, whereas desktop and laptop computers has stayed flat (Anderson, 2015, p. 3).

Nevertheless, despite the rapid pace of change in social media (Ellison & boyd, 2013, pp. 165–166), the history of social media on the Web will probably be a relevant topic of study for many years. As a consequence, the need for archived Web materials will still be predominant. And so will all the challenges outlined above. But the last two waves of social media underline that it is imperative that the academic communities and the archiving institutions start to debate how these new mediated forms of social interaction should be collected and preserved, thus enabling future historians to study our age. Preserving the 'look-and-feel' of social media apps is still an unresolved problem, as is the preservation of social media, with a proclaimed aim of not being preserved, in particular Snapchat. Snapchat and apps can be collected by making either screen shots or screen videos, eventually combined with content retrieved via API, which may be useful for a research project, but which does not scale-up if the aim is to collect and preserve a national or trans-national cultural heritage. Thus, a study of today's Instagram (Seltzer et al., 2015) or Snapchat (Bayer et al., 2016) will be very difficult to transform into historical studies, if the problems of preserving these social media are not resolved.

In terms of finding historical sources of social media, future historians are facing a double challenge. Social media have developed and so has the preservation of the social media. But these two developments are almost always out of sync: the social media have a dynamic of their own, and so

has the archiving practices, be that macro as well as micro archiving. This means that the challenges above are very likely to have been supplemented by other challenges in 20 years' time. Not replaced, but supplemented, because the challenges of today do not disappear – today's archived material is still there – and the Web historian of the future will therefore experience an accumulation of old and new challenges which persist over time, and which constantly have to be negotiated.

As with any other type of historical study, the writing of social media histories is faced with the challenge of making do with what has been handed down from the past, either offline sources or archived Web material in cultural heritage institutions, in researcher-generated collections, within social media companies, or material that has survived on the online Web. There will, of course, be lacunae in the source material and some research questions may not be answered – or maybe not even asked – because of these gaps. Although this state of affairs has been a fundamental condition of historians' everyday lives for centuries, it will probably conflict with the expectations of future social media historians, who may find it difficult to understand that mediated social activities, which were somewhat archived while they took place, are no longer there. Thus, future historians have to come to terms with the fact that although Facebook, Twitter, and YouTube to a large extent come with their own archive while used today, this may by no means be the case 20 years later, and even finding relevant archived material may be difficult. But if expectations to the source material are kept at a realistic level, writing histories of social media on the Web is definitely a possibility – and a necessity for the understanding of social life from the 1990s onwards.

Notes

1   This chapter discusses methodological issues related to doing social media Web history based on preserved Web, but most of the points also

apply to studies of contemporary social media, since such studies must to some extent be based on preserved material which can be analysed and used to document the study. This is particularly important since contemporary social media change at a very rapid pace, as pointed out in Ellison and boyd (2013, pp. 165–167), although they do not identify the need to preserve previous versions, before changes were made.

2 For a detailed comparison of archived Web to digitized collections, see Brügger (2011a, 2017).

3 A couple of figures to illustrate this: the average life span of a web page is often said to be two months (Brügger, 2012, p. 318); almost 50% of .uk websites have disappeared again within a year (Jackson, 2015); out of 10 million mainly Japanese websites collected in 2001, 90% had disappeared in 2013 (Agata et al., 2014).

4 For a brief history of web archiving and an overview of web archiving strategies, see Brügger (2011b, pp. 29–32).

5 Each of these points is explained in greater detail in Brügger (2011b, pp. 32–38).

6 This section refers some of the insights in Laursen et al. (2013).

7 The crawled Web in Web archives has a number of other characteristics which are relevant to consider when using archived Web material, in particular big Web archives based on macro archiving. These are elaborated in detail in Brügger (2011a, 2011b, 2016).

8 For an overview of existing web archives, see Member Archives (n.d.), and List of Web archiving initiatives (n.d.). Cf. also Webster (2017) for a first attempt to write the history of web archiving initiatives.

9 Discussions about the use of APIs for academic purposes can be found in Lomborg and Bechmann (2014), and for Twitter in particular, see Kumar et al. (2015).

10 The examples have been chosen based on the criteria that they should represent a typical study of social media on the Web where the Web as such is to some extent included.

11 Some of the ethical issues related to using archived web for research purposes are discussed in Lomborg (2012) where a useful list of references can also be found.

REFERENCES

Abbate, J. (2000). *Inventing the Internet*. Cambridge, MA: MIT Press.

Agata, T., Miyata, Y., Ishita, E., Ikeuchi, A., & Ueda, S. (2014, September). Life span of web pages: A survey of 10 million pages collected in 2001. In *Proceedings of the 14th ACM/IEEE-CS Joint Conference on Digital Libraries* (pp. 463–464). Hoboken, NJ: Wiley/IEEE Press.

Anderson, M. (2015). *Technology Device Ownership: 2015*. Washington, DC: Pew Research Center.

Archambault, A. & Grudin, J. (2012). A longitudinal study of Facebook, LinkedIn, & Twitter use. Paper presented at CHI 2012, May 5–12, Austin, TX, USA.

Bayer, J.B., Ellison, N.B., Schoenebeck, S.Y., & Falk, E.B. (2016). Sharing the small moments: Ephemeral social interaction on Snapchat. *Information, Communication & Society*, 19(7), 956–977. DOI: 10.1080/1369118X.2015.1084349

boyd, d. & Ellison, N.B. (2008). Social network sites: Definition, history, and Scholarship. *Journal of Computer-Mediated Communication*, 13, 210–230. DOI: 10.1111/j.1083-6101.2007.00393.x

Brügger, N. (2005). *Archiving Websites: General Considerations and Strategies*. Aarhus: Center for Internet Studies.

Brügger, N. (ed.) (2010). *Web History*. New York: Peter Lang.

Brügger, N. (2011a). Digital history and a register of websites: An old practice with new implications. In D.W. Park, N.W. Jankowski & S. Jones (Eds.), *The Long History of New Media: Technology, Historiography, and Contextualizing Newness* (pp. 283–298). New York: Peter Lang.

Brügger, N. (2011b). Web archiving – between past, present, and future. In M. Consalvo & C. Ess (Eds.), *The Handbook of Internet Studies* (pp. 24–42). Oxford: Wiley-Blackwell.

Brügger, N. (2012). Web history and the web as a historical source. *Zeithistorische Forschungen*, 9(2), 316–325.

Brügger, N. (2015). A brief history of Facebook as a media text: The development of an empty structure. *First Monday*, 20(5), DOI http://dx.doi.org/10.5210/fm.v20i5.5423.

Brügger, N. (2016). Digital humanities in the 21st century: Digital material as a driving force. *Digital Humanities Quarterly*, 10(3).

Brügger, N. (Ed.) (2017). *Web 25: Histories from the first 25 Years of the World Wide Web*. New York: Peter Lang.

Brügger, N., & Milligan, I. (Eds.) (2018, forth-coming). *The SAGE Handbook of Web History*. London: Sage.

Brügger, N. & Burns, M. (2012). *Histories of Public Service Broadcasters on the Web*. New York: Peter Lang.

Brügger, N. & Schroeder, R. (Eds.) (2017). *The Web as History: Using Web Archives to Understand the Past and the Present*. London: UCL Press.

Bruns, A., Highfield, T., & Burgess, J. (2013). The Arab Spring and social media audiences: English and Arabic Twitter users and their networks. *American Behavioral Scientist*, 57(7), 871–898. DOI: 10.1177/0002764213479374.

Bruns, A. & Weller, K. (2016). Twitter as a first draft of the present – and the challenges of preserving it for the Future. WebSci '16, May 22–25, Hannover, Germany, DOI: http://dx.doi.org/10.1145/2908131.2908174.

Church, S.H. (2013). Digital gravescapes: Digital memorializing on Facebook. *The Information Society*, 29, 184–189. DOI: 10.1080/01972243.2013.777309.

Davison, P. (2013). On Avril Lavigne's missing YouTube comments. *Critical quarterly*, 55(4), 81–92.

Ellison, N.B. & boyd, d. (2013). Sociality through social network sites. In W.H. Dutton (Ed.), *The Oxford Handbook of Internet Studies* (pp. 151–172). Oxford: Oxford University Press.

Frobenius, M. & Harper, R. (2015). Tying in comment sections: The production of meaning and sense on Facebook. The self-explicative organization of communication acts on and through Facebook. *Semiotica*, 204, 121–143. DOI DOI 10.1515/sem-2014-0081.

Gillies, J. & Cailliau, R. (2000). *How the Web was Born: The Story of the World Wide Web*. Oxford: Oxford University Press.

Goggin, G. (Ed.) (2004). *Virtual Nation: The Internet in Australia*. Sydney: University of New South Wales Press.

Goggin, G. & McLelland, M. (Eds.) (2017). *The Routledge Companion to Global Internet Histories*. London: Routledge.

Grasmuck, S., Martin, J., & Zhao, S. (2009). Ethno-racial identity displays on Facebook. *Journal of Computer-Mediated Communication*, 15, 158–188. DOI: 10.1111/j.1083-6101.2009.01498.x.

Gulati, G.J. & Williams, C.B. (2013). Social media and campaign 2012: Developments and trends for Facebook adoption. *Social Science Computer Review*, 31(5), 577–588. DOI: 10.1177/0894439313489258.

Harris, A., Kelly, S.E., & Wyatt, S. (2014). Autobiologies on YouTube: Narratives of direct-to-consumer genetic testing. *New Genetics and Society*, 33(1), 60–78. http://dx.doi.org/10.1080/14636778.2014.884456.

Hauben, M. & Hauben, R. (1997). *Netizens: On the History and Impact of Usenet and the Internet*. Hoboken, NJ: Wiley/IEEE Computer Society.

Hum, N.J., Chamberlin, P.E., Hambright, B.L., Portwood, A.C., Schat, A.C., & Bevan, J.L. (2011). A picture is worth a thousand words: A content analysis of Facebook profile photographs. *Computers in Human Behavior*, 27, 1828–1833.

Hunt, D. (2015). The many faces of diabetes: A critical multimodal analysis of diabetes pages on Facebook. *Language & Communication*, 43, 72–86.

Jackson, A. (2015). Ten years of the UK web archive: What have we saved? http://netpreserve.org/sites/default/files/attachments/2015_IIPC-GA_Slides_03_Jackson.pptx

Johnson, G.A., Tudor, B., & Nuseibeh, H. (2013). 140 characters or less: How is the Twitter mediascape influencing the Egyptian revolution? *Middle East Journal of Culture and Communication*, 6, 126–148. DOI 10.1163/18739865-00503006.

KhosraviNik, M. & Zia, M. (2014). Persian nationalism, identity and anti-Arab sentiments in Iranian Facebook discourses: Critical discourse analysis and social media communication. *Journal of Language and Politics*, 13(4), 755–780. DOI: 10.1075/jlp.13.4.08kho.

Kumar, S., Morstatter, F., & Liu, H. (2015). Analysing Twitter data. In Y. Mejova, I. Weber & M.W. Macy (Eds.), *Twitter: A Digital Socioscope* (pp. 21–51). Cambridge: Cambridge University Press.

Laursen, D., Brügger, N., & Sandvik, K. (2013). Methods of collecting Facebook materials and their effects on later analyses. Paper presented at Nordmedia 2013: Defending Democracy, August, Oslo, Norway.

Lenhart, A. (2015). *Teen, Social Media and Technology Overview 2015*. Washington, DC: Pew Research Center.

List of Web Archiving Initiatives (n.d.), https://en.wikipedia.org/wiki/List_of_Web_archiving_initiatives.

Lomborg, S. (2012). Personal internet archives and ethics. *Research Ethics*, 9(1) 20–31. DOI: 10.1177/1747016112459450.

Lomborg, S. & Bechmann, A. (2014). Using APIs for data collection on social media. *The Information Society*, 30(4), 256–265. DOI: 10.1080/01972243.2014.915276.

Member Archives (n.d.), http://netpreserve.org/resources/member-archives.

Milligan, I. (2017). Welcome to the web: The online community of GeoCities during the early years of the World Wide Web. In N. Brügger & R. Schroeder (Eds.), *The Web as History: The First Two Decades*. London: UCL Press.

Naughton, J. (1999). *A Brief History of the Future: The Origins of the Internet*. London: Phoenix/Weidenfeld & Nicolson.

Naughton, J. (2012). *From Gutenberg to Zuckerberg: What You Really Need to Know about the Internet*. London: Quercus.

Page, R., Harper, R., & Frobenius, M. (2013). From small stories to networked narrative: The evolution of personal narratives in Facebook status updates. *Narrative Inquiry*, 23(1), 192–213. DOI 10.1075/ni.23.1.10pag.

Poell, T. (2014). Social media and the transformation of activist communication: Exploring the social media ecology of the 2010 Toronto G20 protests. *Information, Communication & Society*, 17(6), 716–731. DOI: 10.1080/1369118X.2013.812674.

Poole, H.W. (Ed.) (2005). *The Internet: A Historical Encyclopedia*. Santa Barbara, CA: ABC/Clio.

Seltzer, E.K., Jean, N.S., Kramer-Golinkoff, E., Asch, D.A., & Merchant, R.M. (2015). The content of social media's shared images about Ebola: A retrospective study. *Public Health*, 129, 1273–1277. DOI: http://dx.doi.org/10.1016/j.puhe.2015.07.025.

Steinfield, C., Ellison, N.B., & Lampe, C. (2008). Social capital, self-esteem, and use of online social network sites: A longitudinal analysis. *Journal of Applied Developmental Psychology*, 29, 434–445. DOI 10.1016/j.appdev.2008.07.002.

Stutzman, F., Gross, R., & Acquisti, A. (2012). Silent listeners: The evolution of privacy and disclosure on Facebook. *Journal of Privacy and Confidentiality*, 4(2), 7–41.

Tsou, A., Thelwall, M., Mongeon, P., & Sugimoto, C.R. (2014) A community of curious souls: An analysis of commenting behavior on TED Talks videos. *PLoS ONE*, 9(4): e93609. DOI:10.1371/journal.pone.0093609.

van Dijck, J. (2011). Tracing Twitter: The rise of a microblogging platform. *International Journal of Media and Cultural Politics*, 7(3), 333–348. DOI: 10.1386/macp.7.3.333_1.

van Dijck, J. (2013). *The Culture of Connectivity: A Critical History of Social Media*. Oxford: Oxford University Press.

Vergani, M. & Zuev, D. (2015). Neojihadist visual politics: Comparing YouTube videos of North Caucasus and Uyghur militants. *Asian Studies Review*, 39(1), 1–22. http://dx.doi.org/10.1080/10357823.2014.976171.

Webster, P. (2017). Users, technologies, organisations: Towards a cultural history of world web archiving. In N. Brügger (Ed.), *Web 25: Histories from the First 25 Years of the World Wide Web*. New York: Peter Lang.

Weller, K. (2015). Challenges in Archiving Social Media Data for Research: The Case of Twitter. Paper presented at the RESAW Conference 'Web Archives as Scholarly Sources: Issues, Practices and Perspectives'. Aarhus, 8–10 June.

Williams, C.B. & Gulati, G.J.J. (2012). Social networks in political campaigns: Facebook and the Congressional elections of 2006 and 2008. *New Media & Society*, 15(1), 52–71. DOI: 10.1177/1461444812457332.

Zimmer, M. (2015). The Twitter Archive at the Library of Congress: Challenges for information practice and information policy. *First Monday*, 20(7), http://firstmonday.org/ojs/index.php/fm/article/view/5619/4653.

12

The Incomplete Political Economy of Social Media

Siva Vaidhyanathan

In February 2016, the Telecommunication Regulatory Authority of India ruled that Facebook's plan to introduce a free service to underprivileged Indians via a partnership with one mobile company and a handful of commercial application services violated network neutrality, the principal that digital services should not favor one source of content over another. So 'Free Basics,' as Facebook had re-dubbed its ostensibly philanthropic effort 'Internet.org,' died quickly in a power struggle among a powerful American social media company, resentful Indian technology developers, overwhelmed regulators, sensitive nationalistic politicians, highly organized public interest activists, and rival mobile service providers. It was a remarkable tale of ideological hubris on the part of Facebook founder and CEO Mark Zuckerberg and the ambitions of Indian citizens and companies, who grew to resent the efforts and claims that Facebook made on behalf of poorer Indians (Bhatia, 2016). This story demonstrates the vast complexity of the political economy of social media. Issues such as neocolonialism, cultural imperialism, competition policy, political corruption, digital activism, class struggle, and the ideological foundations of Silicon Valley work to affect how social media function in our lives across the globe.

We think we understand social media. After all, we seem to increasingly live in and through them. The record of social media and their effects on global society and politics seems well documented. Since the rise of Facebook midway through the first decade of the 21st century, tyrants and tycoons alike have waxed anxiously about its influence over its more than 1.5 billion users. Twitter, although used by far fewer, has been credited with outsized influence on politics and culture. The fall of Myspace, with its youthful exuberance and inflated market capitalization, serves as a cautionary tale about poor investments and fleeting communities, and stands as the greatest financial blunder in Rupert Murdoch's long career.

But what are we to make of these technological tools and their influence on our lives?
How shall we assess the role of regulation
and the need for more? How empowered
are these 1.6 billion users? How powerful is
Facebook founder Mark Zuckerberg relative
to Rupert Murdoch, among others? And have
scholars fully grasped the trajectory of ideologically driven technological change that
almost instantly captured the attention of billions across the globe?

The study of the political economy of
social media in the first two decades of
the 21st century has been far less dynamic
than its subject of study. Scholarship is still
framed along the lines outlined by three
major schools of media analysis of the 20th
century: Frankfurt-School-inspired critical theory (Adorno, 2001; Habermas, 1984;
McCarthy, 1978); Marxian-inspired Critical
Political Economy (Golding and Murdock,
1997; Mosco, 2010); and Cultural Studies,
the strongest critical response to the two classic political economy schools (Grossberg,
2010; Hall, 1997). The most prolific scholar
of the political economy of social media,
Christian Fuchs (2009, 2012a, 2014a, 2015),
has staked out the claim that the Marxian-
inspired theories of the Frankfurt School and
Critical Political Economy suffice for full
understanding. And he has done great service
in outlining how we can revive and revise
concepts such as exploitation, surplus value,
and commodity fetishism while examining
how people and groups deploy and endure
social media platforms. But by merely revis-
ing and extending the arguments of the late
20th century, the study of the political economy of social media has failed to capture the
full range of consequences and rapid changes
in the field. More importantly, scholarship
has failed to influence how regulators and the
public view and influence social media platforms and the firms that promote it.

The study of political economy of social
media has largely been framed within and
among various interpretations of Marx-
influenced thought, whether echoing Gramsci

(Gramsci, Hoare and Nowell-Smith, 1971),
Adorno (2001), Habermas (1984), or Smythe
(1977). But has this been adequate and
appropriate? Have we used the best lenses
to examine a phenomenon as influential
and fast-growing as social media in the 21st
century? Social media platforms such as
Facebook, Twitter, Instagram, and even the
failed Myspace, demonstrate a more complex
and perhaps *sui generis* relationship among
firm, 'user' (as opposed to audience), labor
(which can include the 'user'), and states than
film and radio did in the time of the Frankfurt
School or television and early computers did
during the rise of Critical Political Economy.
The categories and assumptions of classic
political economy are largely based on static
categories. The major debates within the field
have too often turned inward on theory, making them more about the terms of debate than
the consequences of the subject and its exercise of power in the world.

I will offer one significant recent debate
that has occupied political economy scholars in recent years. In 1977 Smythe shook
up the study of both political economy and
media by publishing an article that challenged Marxist theorists to take communication seriously, as more than just the source
of ideology formation. Smythe posited that
the relationship of audience to advertising-
driven media industries could be captured
through a hybrid identity he called 'audience
commodity.' Smyth explained that the audience commodity is what television networks
(and radio stations and newspapers) sell to
advertising firms. But that's not all. The role
that audience members play in this transaction goes beyond that of a passive commodity
like cattle or wheat. The audience performs a
form of labor, Smythe argued, that enhances
the value of the media firms.

Smythe started an intense debate about this
concept among media scholars in the 1980s
and influenced the rise and tone of the Cultural
Studies response to political economy. As
Rigi and Prey (2015) explain, the debate
cooled until Fuchs (2010) revived it with a

strong case that social media users provide value and surplus value to firms because – beyond the ill-defined labor that Smythe asserted audiences performed – social media users clearly produce actual works of creative expression that social media firms frame and distribute. So in addition to serving as the sources of attention that social media firms sell to advertisers (so-called 'eyeballs'), users are also the chief labor force in the composition of the content that makes social media worthwhile, influential, and profitable. This is valuable insight that not only extends Smythe's argument but helps us grasp how the social media user is in fact different than the television or film audience member.

The immediate critical response to Fuchs was based not so much on whether Fuchs failed to describe the role of the user, but about whether Fuchs deployed Marx's (1992) labor theory of value appropriately. Arvidsson and Colleoni (2012) replied that the value of social media user activity is more centered in the social connections and affective expressions users produce than on labor *per se*. Fuchs (2012b) responded to their criticisms. Then Rigi and Prey (2015) recounted the debate and produced data that served to complicate and undermine Fuchs' argument. This entire debate was interesting, but more for the ways these scholars read Marx than for what they wrote about social media. In each of these accounts, social media services are static, stable, powerful, and valuable. They never rise, fall, fail, or corrupt. There is no action, only interpretation.

Perhaps by adding a perspective to these analytical lenses we can bring more clearly into view the role social media companies play in our lives and the ways that they affect – and are affected by – matrices of power and regulation across the globe. But to do this, we must examine the particulars of how social media companies and platforms have worked and failed in the world. And we should be open to going beyond defending or extrapolating one particular theory or another. As I have argued elsewhere (Vaidhyanathan, 2006), Political

Economy approaches can benefit greatly from adopting an appreciation of the meaning-making dynamics of users and audiences that Cultural Studies scholars have brought forth. And Cultural Studies scholars no longer have the luxury of suspending consideration of architecture, economic power, and regulation when considering how users and audiences perform their roles and organize themselves into discursive communities. Maintaining the boundaries between these schools of thought inhibits the fullest understanding of media and power. Schools and theories should supplement, not displace, each other. If media theorists don't look up to see what's coming next, we risk irrelevance and could fail to guide publics, markets, and states as we should.

WHAT DO SOCIAL MEDIA DO?

Social media may, as McLuhan (1964) predicted, contain streams of all previous media forms. They also foster new capabilities and concerns. They scramble the contexts in which we have grown comfortable, so mixing the personal, the political, the commercial, and the cultural that we have spent more than a decade trying to get our bearings and forge new norms and standards to deal with them (Nissenbaum, 2010).

Beyond those important observations, social media are not what we assumed they were just 10 years ago. Most scholarship, understandably and including this chapter, take Facebook and Twitter as the core subjects of study. The problem with this practice is that while both Facebook and Twitter are popular and important in 2016 (when this chapter was written) they might not be by 2020. Twitter, for instance, could be broke and gone by 2018. And they are very different services with different rules, norms, practices, and demands on users. Unsurprisingly, they function differently in users' lives. In addition, both Facebook and Twitter entered our lives first as Web-based platforms, experienced chiefly through desktop and laptop computers linked via relatively open networks. Use quickly and overwhelmingly shifted to proprietary mobile applications, which allow both companies to control much more of the user experience and successfully harvest more and more valuable user behavior records. The rise of 'mobile-first' platforms such as Instagram and Snapchat further complicates the story and study of social media. People use these differently than they do Facebook. Beyond the major services of North America and Western Europe, Weibo and WeChat, for instance, deserves significant and different study, simply because they are important social network services in the largest countries in the world. And examining social media as media also misses some important phenomena. For instance, as fitness applications connect with devices that sit on human bodies yet also connect users to each other, they qualify as 'social,' but maintain a distinct relationship between users and the firms that manage these exchanges.

So social media platforms are both singular and diverse in their nature, their architecture, their goals, the variety of uses to which they are put, and their ability to generate anxiety among parents, pundits, and politicians (boyd, 2014). Among other important phenomena, social media platforms also offer users (an unsatisfying term I deploy with full awareness of its inadequacy) new ways of defining and promoting themselves, thus imposing an ideology of 'self-branding' and capitulation to the demands of an 'attention economy' (Marwick, 2013).

For these reasons I must call for a fresh approach to studying the political economy of social media. Marx only takes us part of the way to clarity. As Fuchs (2014: 53) explains, such theory is grounded in the assumption that 'capitalism a) reduces humans to the status of being instruments for capital accumulation in the form of their role as wage workers and consumers and b) tries to make them believe in the feasibility of the overall system by using ideology as an

(attempted) silencing instrument.' This argument presumes that all institutions of capitalism operate the same ways everywhere and always, and that those of us who live, work, and dance under capitalism are blinded and silenced by the enforced parameters of debate that capital will allow.

But experience – whether in the form of Facebook, Google, and Twitter asserting that they espouse values distinct from the basest drives of capital accumulation, or global youth protesters harnessing social media platforms to rouse direct action against capitalism in 2011 and 2012 – tells us that there is much more going on. Some firms, if only temporarily and under ideal conditions, don't always follow the rules of capitalism.

We must have more to learn about this subject than Marxian theory allows us to consider. So in this chapter I invite readers to deploy different theoretical lenses, and offer as one example a theory largely ignored for much the past century: Institutional Economics, inspired by the work of an anti-Marxian yet culturally astute economist and social theorist, Thorstein Veblen. I don't offer Veblen as a replacement for Marx and the Marxian tradition. I merely hope to inspire political economists of media to look beyond the standard arguments and frameworks. And to inspire scholars to look beyond the Whiggish story of all-powerful and pervasive social media firms successfully exploiting users and corrupting states, I urge readers to examine the 2015 regulatory conflict between Facebook and the government of India. But first we must dissect our subject.

THE FACETS AND FUNCTIONS OF SOCIAL MEDIA: ARCHITECTURE AND INFRASTRUCTURE

At the core of every major social media system, whether Weibo or YouTube, are architecture and infrastructure. All major social media platforms operate by connecting devices to databases hosted in redundant proprietary server farms distributed across the globe. This centralization of search and hosting functions, as well as the indexing of content according to algorithmically-inscribed company values, results in a remarkable level of ideological control over user actions. While people experience only a light, inviting, shallow interface, the millions of lines of code, the miles of fiber-optic cable, the acres of air-conditioned server farms, the tons of aluminum, concrete, and glass all remain out of sight and thus out of mind. Users need not be burdened by knowledge of the environmental effects of the infrastructure. They should never communicate with a human being who has influence over the system. They should see no traces of human decision-making or labor. They also should never concern themselves with the location of the servers, despite the fact that states can heavily surveil and regulate social media services based on where servers sit. A server in Shanghai will generate different effects in the world than one sitting in Vancouver, largely because of the relative willingness of those governments to control and monitor activities over those servers.

We have been invited to describe this architectural choice – tapping into massive servers that sit perhaps half a continent away with instantaneous results on computers that fit into our palms – as accessing 'the cloud.' This metaphor has further alienated users from the architecture, infrastructure, and labor that enable social media activity. It has mystified the system. And it has undermined efforts to address negative externalities such as privacy violations and excessive control over content distribution (Pariser, 2011; Vaidhyanathan, 2011, 2015).

USER-GENERATED CONTENT

The second important facet of social media is 'user-generated content.' In 2005 Web and technology guru Tim O'Reilly declared the death of 'Web 1.0,' in which static and discreet pages were posted on small private servers distributed around the world, and the rise of 'Web 2.0.' This new vision for Web use and production harvested the labor of users who produced text, images, and links that sat on centralized corporate servers. Companies such as Google, O'Reilly predicted, would leverage the work of these billions of individuals into valuable 'user-generated content' that could be represented, indexed, and used as a template against which advertisements could be sold. The key concept to building value, O'Reilly argued, was that companies could exploit 'collective intelligence,' the belief that thousands, millions, or billions of discrete actions and interactions could generate patterns of preference and behavior, allowing firms to mine that data for optimal service to users (O'Reilly, 2005). On face, this manifesto granted some respect to users and their contributions to the fortunes of those who would build platforms on the World Wide Web (or, to use O'Reilly's term, use 'the Web as platform'). But ultimately, as Scholz (2013) and others argue persuasively, companies like Google, Facebook, and Twitter depend almost entirely on the creative labor of their unpaid volunteers. And as Fuchs (2014) asserts, this relationship constitutes exploitation in an almost classically Marxist fashion.

But through social media, the roles of 'producer' and 'consumer' are scrambled. Users are not so much consumers, or even labor, as they are commodities or raw material itself. What Google and Facebook sell is the monitored attention and habitual preferences of their users. Their users are thus the product as well as the producers. That complex relationship distinguishes the political economy of social media from that of broadcast media, for instance. A viewer is also the product that NBC or StarTV sells to advertisers. But that viewer does not also provide valuable content to a television network or service. Still, paying close attention to the rise of audience labor and other forms of informal and undercompensated labor such as the Amazon 'Mechanical Turk' system (Suri et al., 2016) allows us to move beyond the exclusion of 'audience' from traditional, 20th-century forms of political economy research while also curbing the idealization of the 'audience' that emerged from late 20th-century cultural studies work.

'User-generated content' models also allow firms to evade the risks and strictures of classic publishers. Traditional publishers such as *The New York Times* or Bertelsmann make editorial decisions, and thus face potential civil liability if their content violates privacy, copyright, or indecency laws. But in much of the world, Web and social media firms have convinced states to limit liability because they do not direct users to post particular content (17 USC Sec. 512, 47 USC Sec. 230). In fact, the transaction costs of policing thousands-to-millions of posts are so high that conforming to such laws would be impossible. The market would not provide services such as social media or search engines if these companies were held to the same legal standards as traditional publishers. However, in recent years, companies like Google have seen their officials held to standards closer to that of publishers for content their users have posted on social media sites. And both Google and Facebook have recently declared that their engineers will take a more active role in selecting content that users will see, with the goal of enhancing the news value of their services (Vaidhyanathan, 2011).

The dominant message proclaimed by Web enthusiasts, from the early days of Web 2.0 through the social and political uprisings around the Mediterranean Sea in spring 2011, was that 'user-generated' content performed democratizing, and even liberating, functions (Bruns, 2008; Jenkins, 2006; Shirky, 2008). No longer did promulgators of ideas need to convince traditional 'gate-keeping' media firms to publish their work (and assume the risk to reputation or fortune). Now the risks

to the host company (Facebook, Twitter, or Google) were lower, making it possible for more transgressive expression to flow. Communities could grow almost organically from collections of links, comments, retweets, follows, and 'likes.' But such user interaction also allows companies and states to monitor and track users, their preferences, and their associations on a much grander scale (Gerlitz and Helmond, 2013).

DATA HARVESTING

The ability of social media companies to harvest and analyze not only specific content created and posted by users, but the relationships between these pieces of expression, allows for the third essential facet of social media that political economy must consider: data harvesting. As early as 2002, leaders of Google realized that their impressive collection of user data allowed them to sharpen their search results and recommendations, keeping users satisfied that Google understood their desires and – perhaps – even read their minds (Vaidhyanathan, 2011). Once Google introduced its advertising programs soon after, the presence of such large and sophisticated records on each user and on groups of users proved lucrative. By 2008 Facebook was struggling to leverage its own special and massive collection of personal data and expressions of preferences to enable its own advertisement placement program. By 2012 Facebook had achieved the ability to use user data both for selecting and prioritizing content on users' news feeds and optimizing user-targeted advertising, making it possible for the company to generate significant revenue and turn a profit for the third year in a row (Greenfield, 2012; Thompson, 2009).

The practice of data harvesting and data retention did not come without costs. Facebook and Google faced regulatory challenges and investigations in Europe for their data retention practices (Levine, 2015). And after former US intelligence contractor Edward Snowden released select documents about US government data surveillance and mining programs in 2013, it became clear to citizens, states, companies, and terrorists around the world that the practices of social media companies to harvest, retain, and analyze data from their users tempted curious state actors to tap into those troves. As long as Facebook and Google retained valuable records of users' behavior and expressions, security services in both democratic and authoritarian governments would press both companies to reveal records, resorting to breaching the companies' security if they failed to gain cooperation (MacAskill et al., 2013). These revelations put the reputations of social media companies at great risk, as their utility as sites for collaboration and communication among dissident groups came into question.

The practice of data harvesting is largely hidden from users. There are no obvious clues from applications and platforms like Instagram or SnapChat that user data is being recorded, where and for how long it will be stored, and to what purposes it may be put. These and other services do offer vague, technical, and unhelpful 'privacy policies' that could answer some of these questions for users. But the policies are uninviting and not obvious. One must already be aware of the practice and its risks in order to engage with a privacy policy or adjust privacy settings. So for most users, the defaults work in the company's favor. Those most immersed in the cultures and practices of social media, teenagers and young adults, are often the most sophisticated and aware of data harvesting practices (boyd and Marwick, 2011).

In the current commercial, political, and regulatory environment, institutions have powerful incentives to collect, save, and analyze every trace of human activity. These incentives are not entirely new, of course. People have long been aware of the potential payoffs of tracing and tracking subjects (consumers, citizens, criminals, 'users'). To explain the relatively recent turn to data harvesting as a tool of choice, scholars and analysts have tended to emphasize the availability of appropriate technologies. Among these are huge server farms, algorithms designed to reveal patterns quickly within otherwise meaningless pools of data, and faster bandwidth and processing capacities. But this techno-centric analysis misses or downplays the role of significant changes in the global political economy and dominant ideologies since 1980. When securities markets and consultants praise 'efficiency' above all other values, when states place 'security' above all other public needs, and when mass-market advertising reaps, at best, murky returns for each dollar spent, the incentives to target, trace, and sift grow stronger.

When we examine the intentional opacity of such private surveillance systems and their vulnerability to capture by state security systems, we can forge a new sense of the privacy challenge in a socially mediated environment. No longer can we rely on the model of the 'panopticon,' the all-seeing central eye that forces us to acknowledge it, thus curbing our desires to act outside the norm (Foucault, 1995). Those who write about privacy and surveillance often invoke the Panopticon to argue that the great harm of mass surveillance is social control. Yet the Panopticon does not suffice to describe our current predicament. First, mass surveillance does not necessarily inhibit behavior: people often will act as they wish regardless of the number of cameras pointed at them. The thousands of surveillance cameras in London and New York City do not deter the eccentric and avant-garde, nor is there significant evidence that they deter crime (Greenberg and Roush, 2009; Welsh and Farrington, 2009). There is no empirical reason to believe that awareness of surveillance limits the imagination or stifles creativity in a market economy in an open, non-totalitarian state.

Instead we must confront a hidden and distributed system of surveillance that encourages us to find niche interests and express ourselves loudly and sincerely. The ideologies of Facebook, Google, and even Amazon guide us toward such niche expression. And 21st-century security services hope that we align ourselves with the fringe groups while assuming that no one is paying attention. Our current condition is therefore not at all like living under the gaze of a panopticon. Instead, we live within an invisible network or surveillance agents, both public and private. It's cryptic. So it's a cryptopticon (Vaidhyanathan, 2015).

ADVERTISEMENTS

Google and Facebook play very different roles in users' social media ecosystems. People use Facebook to keep up with family, friends, and colleagues. Facebook provides a news feed that displays items of demonstrated interest to users and allows people to discuss and debate the subjects that appear in those feeds. Google, on the other hand, serves as a source of knowledge. People seek answers, directions, recipes, and advice through Google. People seek products as well. Over time, Google has been much more successful than Facebook at leveraging its data riches to target advertisements effectively. But Facebook has recently improved its ability to target and tailor advertisements. Seeking advertisement revenue from companies is the chief way in which these two companies compete. While Facebook is the model of a successful social media company, Google provides services that could be described as successfully 'social' only through its YouTube platform, through which people subscribe to the feeds of their favorite video producers. Google, while largely failing as a social media enterprise, has set the standard and served as a model for selling advertisements through auction. Firms of all sizes can find consumers through Google. And since Facebook has adopted similar

practices it has also served that market well. These companies have significantly changed the advertising world and thus all the media economies that depend on advertisement (Auletta, 2009; Bell, 2016; Levy, 2011).

Targeted advertisements that reflect the various preferences expressed by users have the potential to shape not only consumer behavior but culture as well. If consumers are guided toward dependable products and brands that reflect the desires they have already expressed, they are unlikely to explore. If abused, the power to guide users toward particular products could generate anti-trust or competition issues. Even if not abused, users are subject to being profiled and funneled. And mass markets could be hard to define and exploit. A user's diet of news and information is filtered through an opaque system in which biases are undisclosed and unacknowledged. Even prices could differ between consumers for the same product based on different data points and histories (Turow, 2006, 2011).

The phenomenon of targeted advertisements has pulled other media companies closer to Facebook and its corporate sibling, Instagram. Newspaper and magazine companies see advantages to entering into partnerships that would allow Facebook to host the content in exchange for a portion of advertising revenue generated (Fitts, 2015).

CONTENT DISCRIMINATION

Advertisement-based partnerships between news organizations and social media platforms run the risk of determining which news sources reach certain people based on the desires of the companies involved rather than the desires or needs of the user. This undermines efforts to use digital media to construct a rich and dynamic public sphere through which civic engagement could thrive. By working through Facebook, media companies have relinquished any influence or control over who gets to see their content. This is a significant shift in power (Bell, 2016).

There are two methods of content discrimination within major social media platforms. We will limit our discussion to Facebook because it plays an outsized role in the news and information diet of users. Twitter, for example, does not deploy the methods that follow, as of the summer of 2016. The first method is filtering. Facebook positions items that its users have shared (from sites outside the Facebook ecosystem) or produced themselves (photos, text, video) within the news feeds of others. Those others could be 'friends' or merely 'followers' of the person who posted the content. Facebook algorithmically assesses the relevance or level of interest that the second person would have in the first person's posted content. Facebook's algorithms could consider factors such as shared interest (both parties have posted similar or the same item frequently in the past), shared friends (both parties are active on some mutual 'friend's' site and posts), or shared proximity (to a community of interest or a geographic location). Facebook is notoriously secretive about the values it embeds in its algorithm. But we know that over time, users form homophilous clusters and increasingly interact with each other. As each member of this cluster expresses herself or himself in richer and more elaborate ways, Facebook is able to make more granular judgments about what sort of material the person would like to see. If a person 'Likes' something, Facebook gives that person more of it. As Facebook structures usage, users see a narrower and narrower selection of materials. This creates the notorious 'filter bubble,' through which users increasingly retreat into ideological or other interest clusters and refrain from interacting with those significantly different than themselves. This, of course, has serious political, social, and cultural implications (Pariser, 2011).

The second method of content discrimination is a function of direct editing, which often demands human intervention. Female users of both Facebook and Instagram have found content removed and accounts closed after posting images or references to breast cancer, breastfeeding, or menstruation. In general, both Facebook and Instagram work to limit the exposure of women's bodies unless the users are celebrities or models. Women with more common body shapes often find their images suppressed. In addition, there have been accounts of images of refugees, warfare, and political groups being removed for violating vague guidelines (Chen, 2014; York, 2016). Because Facebook has an interest in limiting public criticism or inviting state censorship, it also has an interest in policing its own content in often clumsy ways. This practice generates problems because so many people now depend on Facebook to mediate their social and political lives.

SOCIAL ENGINEERING IN INDIA

In January 2012 Facebook released its first shares through an initial public offering of stock. Founder and chief operating office Mark Zuckerberg took that moment to issue a manifesto for his company. 'Facebook was not originally created to be a company,' Zuckerberg wrote. 'It was built to accomplish a social mission – to make the world more open and connected' (Zuckerberg, 2012). Zuckerberg's commitment to corporate social responsibility, to making the world a better place through connectivity, has found expression in his company's endeavors to expand its market into areas of the world in which significant numbers of people lack the access, skills, and money to sustain a digital presence.

Corporate social responsibility has risen in importance to global business culture since the 1970s. It has served as an organizational principal among corporate leaders who were not only concerned about their companies' influence on the Apartheid government of

South Africa, environmental disasters such as the deadly chemical accident at Bhopal, India, and struggles against ethnic and gender discrimination, but also about the image of their companies in the minds of a consuming public increasingly concerned about injustices around the world. Debates around corporate social responsibility have centered on the question of sincerity, of course. Are companies that engage in such promotions really concerned about human rights and a clean environment or are their efforts merely a marketing ploy? Within business culture and the scholarship on corporate social responsibility, the central question has been about the efficacy of such campaigns: Can a company leverage its efforts to be responsible to measurably improve its image and thus its standing in a market? Can companies have it all? (Vogel, 2006)

Facebook's corporate social responsibility stances reflect the common assumption among American technology companies, including Google and Microsoft, that there is no zero-sum choice between serving the interests of humanity and serving their shareholders. What is good for humanity is good for Facebook, and vice versa. Such firm belief in one's righteousness is both liberating and powerful. It can create a public message that generates admiration from users, consumers, regulators, workers, and competitors (Vaidhyanathan, 2011).

In India, Facebook found the limits of its self-regard. In 2014 Facebook launched a service it called 'Internet.org.' The choice of that brand name indicated that it should be considered distinct from Facebook itself. It would be about 'the Internet' itself, rather than one social media company. And it should be considered a not-for-profit venture (.org) rather than a commercial one (.com). The service was essentially an application interface – sort of a mobile operating system – that would work on any mobile device that allowed data connectivity. The operating system would allow access to a handful of Facebook-selected applications, including

the Bing search engine (Microsoft's competitor to Google and many other home-grown search engines), women's rights services, employment services, Wikipedia for reference, and weather information.

Importantly, these services would be offered at 'zero rating,' meaning that using data through them would not count against the paid data one would purchase for a mobile account. Using a competing service such as Google or an employment service not selected by Facebook would cost data and thus money for the user. If the user could not afford a data plan – and this service was ostensibly targeted at just those users – they would have to use the services that Facebook selected for Internet.org. Because zero-rating services necessarily favor some data streams over others they violate the principle of network neutrality that has been invoked as central to the development and success of Internet practices and industries around the world. Regulators have thus been busy trying to determine to what extent zero rating violates their laws and policies (Electronic Frontier Foundation, 2016; Nowak, 2016).

In each country in which Facebook launched Internet.org (42 countries by July 2016), Facebook enters into a partnership with one mobile service provider. Facebook promises that offering this service at no charge to consumers who do not currently have mobile data plans will inspire future paid use as users' financial status improves. This pledge rests upon the unquestioned assumption that access to information improves the prospects of users and the communities in which they live and work (Bhatia, 2016).

This challenge to network neutrality thus accompanies a more traditional threat to competition. India, unlike some of the other countries in which Facebook launched Internet.org, has deep traditions of democratic participation and a highly competitive private technology and telecommunications sector. Indian entrepreneurs would like to compete in areas such as mobile health information, search engines, and social media. And India has a vibrant collection of public interest activists who have been pushing to limit intellectual property protection for American and European firms while fighting for free speech and privacy protections through digital networks. So when Facebook brought Internet. org to India in 2014, complete with meetings between Zuckerberg and newly elected Prime Minister Narendra Modi and a massive public relations campaign, it did not expect that it would fail. Facebook officials not only underestimated the opposition within India, they failed to pay attention to the particulars of the Indian political economy.

Public interest activists were adept at using social media services – including Facebook but especially YouTube and Twitter – to rally support for network neutrality and opposition to what they saw as an arrogant move by a powerful American company in cahoots with Modi. Facebook officials, in contrast, were not nearly as effective as their opponents at deploying social media in their campaign to convince users and voters that their service would benefit India more than it would Facebook (Bhatia, 2016).

Everything Facebook officials did in their effort to thwart a strong network neutrality ruling by telecommunications regulators backfired. Billboards asking citizens to 'support a connected India' glowered at motorists stuck in traffic in cities across India. Facebook users in India were greeted by messages on the service asking them to send emails to regulators in support of Free Basics, what Facebook had renamed Internet. org in 2015. But regardless of whether a Facebook user actually agreed to send an email to regulators, Facebook would advertise to that user's 'friends' that he or she had done so. This angered many Facebook users. Ultimately, 16 million emails reached regulators, but their staff complained that these automatically generated emails failed to address the specific questions they had posed through the public comment process. News coverage focused on the clumsiness and high-handedness of the Facebook

campaign. Technology leaders noted the tone that Facebook was using with India and compared it to the promises that British East India Company leaders had deployed in the early days of the colonial project (Bhatia, 2016).

Complicating such matters, Facebook officials made tone-deaf statements. Chief Operating Office Sheryl Sandberg published an op-ed in the *Indian Express* newspaper in which she proclaimed that access to digital services can empower poor women to change their status (Sandberg, 2015). Unfortunately, the changing status of women is a controversial subject in India, so the op-ed served to alienate many traditional Hindus who voted for Modi to maintain traditional social relations intact. And economic competition is fierce for opportunities and resources as India's middle class has swelled over the past 30 years. So the prospect of inviting more poor people into the middle class did not appeal to many families that just recently purchased a scooter or an education. Sandberg and Facebook certainly meant well. But they were dealing with a society they did not understand, and one in which many of its citizens do not mean each other well. And the ruling BJP party represents just those citizens.

Immediately after Facebook lost its effort to stem strong network neutrality in India, Facebook board member Marc Andreesen, the founder of Netscape and a current venture capitalist, sent a Tweet complaining about the decision: 'Denying world's poorest free partial Internet connectivity when today they have none, for ideological reasons, strikes me as morally wrong.' In response to several Tweeted replies to this complaint, Andreesen proclaimed, 'Anti-colonialism has been economically catastrophic for the Indian people for decades. Why stop now?' This, understandably, set off a storm of resentment against Andreesen. Facebook officials quickly distanced the company from Andreesen's expression. And later that day Andreesen apologized for the Tweet and promised to refrain from discussing the history and politics of India on Twitter (Narayan, 2016). The Andreesen affair offered a glimpse into the ideology that too often guides decisions and campaigns dictated from Silicon Valley yet meant to benefit people far from its levels of wealth and power.

Examining the story of Facebook's failures to introduce Free Basics to India demonstrates the need for a sophisticated, multi-faceted, and open approach to the study of political economy. Facebook is not just a social media platform that operates on the Internet and mobile devices. It has designs to represent or stand in for the Internet and mask its intentions behind proclamations of public service. If it can't get Facebook.com in front of millions of underprivileged people, it will try to convince them that Internet.org is a good enough Internet for now.

This story is one of a wealthy and powerful company morphing and metastasizing. Traditional political economy theory fails to account for failure – specifically failure in part caused by activists using Facebook and competing social media platforms better than the master can use his own tools. Facebook's relationships with states, users, and other commercial services are dynamic and temporal. Traditional political economy theory fails to fully describe or challenge a company like Facebook as it enters its second decade of dominance.

BEYOND SOCIAL MEDIA: THE OPERATING SYSTEM OF OUR LIVES

Social media are no longer just social media. And all media firms and services are attempting to become 'social.' The permeable membranes among media services make accounts of social media done at a theoretical distance challenging. Observations and accounts of the political economy of Facebook in 2010 might not be relevant in 2020. What if 'social media' – and in fact 'media' – become something much more pervasive and powerful in

our lives over the next 20 years? Will political economy theory be able to keep up?

Consider the four most powerful digital companies in the United States (I am excluding Weibo, Ali Baba, Yandex, VK, and other powerful and important social media and Web search companies in places like China and Russia where Google and Facebook have struggled to establish markets): Facebook, Alphabet (the holding company for Google), Microsoft, and Apple. As of 2016 these four companies compete for highly trained and experienced labor. And they compete (and collaborate) for political influence in Washington, DC and Brussels. But they are not direct competitors. Facebook and Google do compete for Web and mobile advertising. But they harvest and sell our attention in different ways because we use these services in different ways. Apple still sells hardware for its core business. Microsoft still sells software to make most of its money. Areas of crossover competition, such as Bing with Google or Google + with Facebook, have not amounted to much beyond token efforts.

But each of these companies ha mounted efforts to achieve dominance in the next frontier of digital commerce: the data streams that would monitor, monetize, and govern our automobiles, homes, appliances, and bodies.

Often erroneously referred to as 'the Internet of Things' despite not resembling the Internet or being chiefly about things, these four companies are striving to become the operating system of our lives. Data, they predict, will soon flow from our clothing, our vehicles, and thus our bodies. The operating system of our lives is actually about people. As they steadily introduce personal assistants, new interfaces, thermostats, self-driving cars, glasses, watches, and virtual reality goggles, these companies hope to earn the trust of consumers and regulators such that they can set the standards for the transactions that can make this operating system work seamlessly and efficiently. If they realize this vision, there would be no clear distinction between media and non-media. There would be no distinction between content and objects. All objects and all bodies would be mediated content.

Such a prospect should alarm scholars of the political economy of media. How shall we confront such an effort? How shall we muster a vocabulary, a set of theories, and a set of rhetorical tools sufficient for such a challenge? Such a prospect makes the debate over whether Facebook's users add surplus value under Marxist theory rather quaint.

WHY VEBLEN MATTERS

Theory performs two major functions in intellectual life. As in the natural sciences and economics, theories attempt to so fully account for a phenomenon as to dependably predict the nature of change. If the theory fails to predict results, scientists revise or reject the theory. Over time a theory morphs into something more useful than the theory it replaced (Kuhn, 1970; Popper, 1959). In the realm of the study of societies and cultures, theories are useful as heuristics, shorthand methods of explanation. They help us focus our explorations and debates, providing questions and assumptions that save us time and energy. The risk of social and cultural theories lies in our dependence on them. Affection for a particular theoretical framework can limit the questions we ask and the subjects we explore a bit too well. We risk bracketing particular aspects of a subject of study to the exclusion of others, and thus we can fail to appreciate and account for the relationship between an aspect that 'counts' to a theoretical school and one that does not. So, for example, we might be obsessed with defining the extent to which social media users perform unpaid labor on behalf of exploitative firms (all true and important) yet ignore questions of whether that relationship flows from cultural or affective desires that are being widely or deeply satisfied through the platform. Investment in traditional political economy theory does not fully account for

complex and contradictory motivations, shifts in user norms and behavior over time, relative success and failure or particular firms and platforms, and differences in how certain groups (ethnicities, genders, sexualities, age cohorts, etc.) perform their roles in social media differently. What might serve us better is a fusion of Marxian political economy theory with what Mills (1959) called 'the sociological imagination,' a historical vision that appreciates the long curve of human expression, and an anthropological bend. Fortunately, we have a model for such a style. It lies in the diverse work of Thorstein Veblen.

Veblen lived from 1857 to 1929. An economist and sociologist, he witnessed a time of rapid technological change, globalization, imperialism, and concentrations of wealth. His chief contribution to economic theory was a critique of the Newtonian assumptions of neoclassical economics. Neoclassical analysis sees economic factors such as wages and prices seeking equilibrium, as if guided by laws of thermodynamics within closed systems. Instead, Veblen argued, economists should take inspiration from Darwin's accounts of change, stasis, successes, and failures among species (Veblen, 1904; Veblen and Horowitz, 2002). This attention to flow, change, and contingency should be embedded within an appreciation of the role of norms and values. People can make economic choices based on irrational or useless values – but they are relevant values nonetheless. From these arguments Veblen derived the familiar concept of 'conspicuous consumption' to describe economic decisions made to establish or proclaim status for the sake of status (Veblen, 1905; Veblen and Mills, 1953).

Veblen's work inspired a school of economic thought that strongly challenged both neoclassical theory and Marxist historical materialism. Institutional economics put its emphasis on transactions – commercial, political, and personal – and externalities – social, environmental, and cultural. It took seriously the persistence of communal values, and thus merged anthropology with political economy.

It also considered technological change, and thus merged historical analysis with political economy. For Veblen and those inspired by his approach and style, including John Kenneth Galbraith (1958), C. Wright Mills (1956), Deirdre McCloskey (2008) and Robert Frank (1985), political economy is never about abstracting data and research questions from the greater ecosystems of collective human behavior.

Veblen did not prescribe a method of analysis. Instead, his style serves as a model for interrogation and interpretation that goes beyond a facile call for 'interdisciplinarity.' It lives in a diverse, polyphonic world. So it struggles to make sense of a diverse, polyphonic world. It's pragmatic, in the sense that it eschews metaphysics and focuses on contingency. And it told stories, because it maintained a concern with both statics and dynamics. It was both empirical and theoretical, but never naively positivist or historicist. Consider what an analysis of the Free Basics campaign in India would look like with Veblen guiding it. A standard Marxian approach would limit the investigation to questions of ownership of the means of distribution and the modes of control that Facebook would have exercised over millions of Free Basics users. It would have generated a flat explanation of why Facebook failed: Indian telecommunication companies lined up on opposite sides of the regulatory question of whether Free Basics violated network neutrality and the more politically powerful companies prevailed. It also might invoke the anti-imperialist (or pro-protectionist or nationalist) backlash against Facebook's heavy-handed approach.

A fuller scholarly project, inspired by Veblen, would look for latent cultural values that might have influenced the protests against Facebook and for network neutrality. It would examine the content of the comments received by telecommunication regulators. It would include interviews with activists about their motivations and tactics. It would consider the long historical story of Indian technology firms and their efforts to establish markets under the shadow of larger American firms.

As we confront a global phenomenon like 'social media,' which always shifts and sifts through our analytical fingers, we should keep in mind that our theories must shift as well. We should embrace multiple approaches to the study of political economy. We should be open to abandoning the familiar and engaging with the unfamiliar. And we should move beyond doctrinal debates that freeze the subject we hope to confront.

REFERENCES

'17 U.S. Code § 512 – Limitations on Liability Relating to Material Online.' *LII / Legal Information Institute*. Accessed October 25, 2016. www.law.cornell.edu/uscode/text/17/512.

'47 U.S. Code § 230 – Protection for Private Blocking and Screening of Offensive Material.' *LII / Legal Information Institute*. Accessed October 25, 2016. www.law.cornell.edu/uscode/text/47/230.

Adorno, Theodor W. *The Culture Industry: Selected Essays on Mass Culture*. London; New York: Routledge, 2001. Print.

All India Bakchod. *AIB: Save The Internet*. N.p. Film.

Arvidsson, A., and E. Colleoni. 'Value in Informational Capitalism and on the Internet.' *Information Society* 28.3 (2012): 135–150. Print.

Auletta, Ken. *Googled: The End of the World as We Know It*. New York: Penguin Press, 2009. Print.

Baragar, Fletcher. 'The Influence of Thorstein Veblen on the Economics of Harold Innis.' *Journal of Economic Issues* 30.3 (1996): 667–683. Print.

Baym, Nancy K. *Personal Connections in the Digital Age*. Cambridge, UK; Malden, MA: Polity Press, 2010. Print.

BBC News. 'India Blocks Zuckerberg's Free Net App.' *BBC News*. N.p., n.d. Web. 3 July 2016.

BBC News. 'India Puts Brakes on Facebook's Free Basics Scheme.' *BBC News*. N.p., n.d. Web. 3 July 2016.

Bell, Emily. 'Facebook is Eating the World.' *Columbia Journalism Review*. N.p., n.d. Web. 1 July 2016.

Bennett, Lance. 'The Personalization of Politics: Political Identity, Social Media, and Changing Patterns of Participation.' *The Annals of the*

American Academy of Political and Social Science 644 (2012): 20–39. Print.

Bhatia, Rahul. 'The inside Story of Facebook's Biggest Setback.' The Guardian 12 May 2016. The Guardian. Web. 3 July 2016.

boyd, danah. It's Complicated: The Social Lives of Networked Teens. N.p., 2014. Print.

boyd, danah, and Alice E. Marwick. Social Privacy in Networked Publics: Teens' Attitudes, Practices, and Strategies. Rochester, NY: Social Science Research Network, 2011. papers.ssrn.com. Web. 1 July 2016.

Brabazon, Tara. 'Veblen Does the iPad: iPadification and the Technologies of Conspicuous Consumption.' Reconstruction: Studies in Contemporary Culture 13.3/4 (2013): 1–1. Print.

Brette, Olivier. 'Thorstein Veblen's Theory of Institutional Change: Beyond Technological Determinism.' European Journal of the History of Economic Thought 10.3 (2003): 455–477. EBSCOhost. Web. 29 May 2016.

Brousseau, Eric, and Jean-Michel Glachant, eds. New Institutional Economics: A Guidebook. Cambridge, UK; New York: Cambridge University Press, 2008. Library of Congress ISBN. Web.

Bruns, Axel (2008) Blogs, Wikipedia, Second Life, and beyond. New York: Peter Lang. Print.

Caraway, Brett. 'Audience Labor in the New Media Environment: A Marxian Revisiting of the Audience Commodity.' Media, Culture & Society 33.5 (2011): 693–708. mcs.sagepub.com. Web. 1 July 2016.

Chen, Adrian. 'The Laborers Who Keep Dick Pics and Beheadings Out of Your Facebook Feed.' WIRED. N.p., 23 October 2014. Web. 1 July 2016.

Commons, John R. Institutional Economics, Its Place in Political Economy. Madison, WI: University of Wisconsin Press, 1959. Web.

Dalrymple, William. 'The East India Company: The Original Corporate Raiders.' The Guardian 4 March 2015. The Guardian. Web. 10 April 2016.

Downing, John D. H. 'Towards a Political Economy of Social Movement Media.' Democratic Communiqué 26.1 (2013): 17–28. Print.

Dwyer, Paul. 'Theorizing Media Production: The Poverty of Political Economy.' Media, Culture & Society 37.7 (2015): 988–1004. mcs.sagepub.com.proxy.its.virginia.edu. Web. 29 May 2016.

Economist. 'From Weibo to WeChat.' The Economist 18 January 2014. The Economist. Web. 30 June 2016.

Electronic Frontier Foundation. 'Zero Rating: What It is and Why You Should Care.' Electronic Frontier Foundation. N.p., 18 February 2016. Web. 10 April 2016.

Encyclopedia of Social Media and Politics. 'The Political Economy of Social Media – Entry in Encyclopedia of Social Media and Politics.' N.p., n.d. Web. 10 Apr. 2016.

Fitts, Alexis. 'What Happens When Platforms Turn into Publishers?' Columbia Journalism Review. N.p., 24 March 2015. Web. 1 July 2016.

Foucault, Michel. Discipline and Punish: The Birth of the Prison. New York: Vintage Books, 1995. Print.

Frank, Robert H. Choosing the Right Pond: Human Behavior and the Quest for Status. New York; Oxford [Oxfordshire]: Oxford University Press, 1985. Print.

Fuchs, Christian. 'Information and Communication Technologies and Society: A Contribution to the Critique of the Political Economy of the Internet.' European Journal of Communication 24.1 (2009): 69–87. ejc.sagepub.com.proxy.its.virginia.edu. Web. 30 May 2016.

Fuchs, Christian. 'Labor in Informational Capitalism and on the Internet.' The Information Society 26.3 (2010): 179–196. Taylor and Francis+NEJM. Web. 1 July 2016.

Fuchs, Christian. 'The Political Economy of Privacy on Facebook.' Television & New Media 13.2 (2012a): 139–159. tvn.sagepub.com. Web. 10 April 2016.

Fuchs C. 'With or without Marx? With or without Capitalism? A Rejoinder to Adam Arvidsson and Eleanor Colleoni.' TripleC TripleC 10.2 (2012b): 633–645. Print.

Fuchs, Christian. Critique, Social Media and the Information Society. New York: Routledge, 2014a. Print.

Fuchs, Christian. Social Media: A Critical Introduction. N.p., 2014b. Print.

Fuchs, Christian. Culture and Economy in the Age of Social Media. N.p., 2015. Print.

Gagnon, Marc-André. 'Capital, Power and Knowledge According to Thorstein Veblen: Reinterpreting the Knowledge-Based Economy.' Journal of Economic Issues 41.2 (2007): 593–600. Print.

Galbraith, John Kenneth. The Affluent Society. Boston, MA: Houghton Mifflin, 1958. Print.

Gambs, John S. *Beyond Supply and Demand: A Reappraisal of Institutional Economics*. New York: Columbia University Press, 1946. Web.

Gehl, Robert W. *Reverse Engineering Social Media Software, Culture, and Political Economy in New Media Capitalism*. Philadelphia, PA: Temple University Press, 2014. *Open WorldCat*. Web. 29 May 2016.

Gerlitz, Carolin, and Anne Helmond. 'The Like Economy: Social Buttons and the Data-Intensive Web.' *New Media & Society* 15.8 (2013): 1348–1365. *nms.sagepub.com. proxy.its.virginia.edu*. Web. 1 July 2016.

Godwin, Mike. 'Facebook's Basic Instincts.' *Slate* 30 September 2015. *Slate*. Web. 10 April 2016.

Golding, Peter, and Graham Murdock. *The Political Economy of the Media*. Cheltenham, England; Brookfield, VT: Edward Elgar, 1997. Print.

Gramsci, Antonio, Quintin Hoare, and Geoffrey Nowell-Smith. *Selections from the Prison Notebooks of Antonio Gramsci*. New York: International Publishers, 1971. Print.

Greenberg, David F., and Jeffrey B. Roush. 'The Effectiveness of an Electronic Security Management System in a Privately Owned Apartment Complex.' *Evaluation Review* 33.1 (February 1, 2009): 3–26. doi:10.1177/0193841X08326468.

Greenfield, Rebecca. '2012: The Year Facebook Finally Tried to Make Some Money.' *The Wire*. N.p., Web. Dec. 14, 2012. Available at https://www.theatlantic.com/technology/archive/2012/12/2012-year-facebook-finally-tried-make-some-money/320493/ (accessed on 20 October, 2017).

Grossberg, Lawrence. *Cultural Studies in the Future Tense*. Durham, NC: Duke University Press, 2010. Print.

Grossberg, Lawrence, Cary Nelson, and Paula A. Treichler. *Cultural Studies*. New York: Routledge, 1992. Print.

Gruchy, Allan G. 'The Influence of Veblen on Mid-Century Institutionalism.' *American Economic Review* 48.2 (1958): 11. Print.

Habermas, Jürgen. *The Theory of Communicative Action*. Boston, MA: Beacon Press, 1984. Print.

Hall, Stuart. *Representation: Cultural Representations and Signifying Practices*. London; Thousand Oaks, CA: Sage, in association with the Open University, 1997. Print.

Hardy, Jonathan. *Critical Political Economy of the Media: An Introduction*. N.p. Web.

Harvey, Kerric. *Encyclopedia of Social Media and Politics*. N.p., 2014. Print.

Hemingway, Christine A. *Corporate Social Entrepreneurship: Integrity within*. N.p., 2013. Print.

Hemingway, Christine A. 'Personal Values as a Catalyst for Corporate Social Entrepreneurship.' *Journal of Business Ethics* 60.3 233–249. *link.springer.com.proxy.its.virginia.edu*. Web. 1 July 2016.

Hempel, Jessi. 'India Bans Facebook's Basics App to Support Net Neutrality.' *WIRED*. N.p., 8 February 2016. Web. 10 April 2016.

Highfield, Tim. *Social Media and Everyday Politics*. N.p., 2016. Print.

Jenkins, H. (2006) *Convergence culture: Where old and new media collide*. New York: New York University Press. Print.

Kangal, Kaan. 'The Karl Marx Problem in Contemporary New Media Economy: A Critique of Christian Fuchs' Account.' *Television & New Media* (2016): 1527476415622266. *tvn.sagepub.com*. Web. 10 April 2016.

Kirkpatrick, David. *The Facebook Effect: The Inside Story of the Company that is Connecting the World*. New York: Simon & Schuster, 2010. Print.

Kuhn, Thomas S. *The Structure of Scientific Revolutions*. Chicago, IL: University of Chicago Press, 1970.

Lee, Micky. 'Google Ads and the Blindspot Debate.' *Media, Culture and Society* 33.3 (2011): 433–447. Print.

Levine, Robert. 'Behind the European Privacy Ruling that's Confounding Silicon Valley.' *The New York Times* 9 October 2015. *NYTimes.com*. Web. 1 July 2016.

Levy, Steven. *In the Plex: How Google Thinks, Works, and Shapes Our Lives*. New York: Simon & Schuster, 2011. Print.

MacAskill, Ewen et al. 'NSA Files Decoded: Edward Snowden's Surveillance Revelations Explained.' *The Guardian*. N.p., 1 November 2013. Web. Available at https://www.theguardian.com/world/interactive/2013/nov/01/snowden-nsa-files-surveillance-revelations-decoded#section/1 (accessed on 20 October, 2017).

Manjoo, Farhad. 'Facebook, a News Giant that Would Rather Show Us Baby Pictures.' *The*

New York Times 29 June 2016. *NYTimes. com*. Web. 29 June 2016.

Marwick, Alice Emily. *Status Update: Celebrity, Publicity, and Branding in the Social Media Age*. N.p., 2013. Print.

Marx, Karl. *Capital: A Critique of Political Economy*. London, UK: Penguin, 1992. Print.

Marx, Karl, and Ben Fowkes. *Capital: A Critique of Political Economy*. New York: Vintage Books, 1977. Print.

McCarthy, Thomas. *The Critical Theory of Jürgen Habermas*. Cambridge, MA: MIT Press, 1978. Print.

McChesney, Robert Waterman. *The Political Economy of Media: Enduring Issues, Emerging Dilemmas*. New York: Monthly Review Press, c. 2008. Web.

McCloskey, Deirdre N. 'Not by P Alone: A Virtuous Economy.' *Review of Political Economy* 20.2 (2008): 181–197. *Taylor and Francis+NEJM*. Web. 30 May 2016.

McLuhan, Marshall. *Understanding Media: The Extensions of Man*. N.p., 1964. Print.

Mills, C. Wright. *The Power Elite*. New York: Oxford University Press, 1956. Print.

Mills, C. Wright. *The Sociological Imagination*. New York: Oxford University Press, 1959. Print.

Morozov, Evgeny. 'The Meme Hustler.' *The Baffler* 22 (2013): n. pag. Web. 30 June 2016.

Mosco, Vincent. *The Political Economy of Communication: Rethinking and Renewal*. London [UK]: Sage, 1996. Web.

Mosco, Vincent. *The Political Economy of Communication*. Los Angeles [u.a.]: Sage, 2010. Print.

Murdock, Graham, and Peter Golding. 'For a Political Economy of Mass Communications.' *Socialist Register* 10.10 (1973): n. pag. Web.

Napoli, Philip. 'Revisiting "Mass Communication" and the "Work" of the Audience in the New Media Environment.' *Media, Culture and Society* 32.3 (2010): 505–516. Print.

Narayan, Adi. 'Andreessen Regrets India Tweets; Zuckerberg Laments Comments.' *Bloomberg. com*. N.p., n.d. Web. 3 July 2016.

Nissenbaum, Helen Fay. *Privacy in Context: Technology, Policy, and the Integrity of Social Life*. Stanford, CA: Stanford Law Books, 2010. *Open WorldCat*. Web. 30 June 2016.

Nowak, Peter. 'Zero Rating: How ISPs Give Some Customers Preferential Treatment.' N.p., n.d. Web. 10 April 2016.

O'Reilly, Tim. 'What is Web 2.0.' *Oreilly.com*. N.p., 30 September 2005. Web. 30 June 2016.

Pariser, Eli. *The Filter Bubble: What the Internet is Hiding from You*. New York: Penguin Press, 2011. Print.

Parker, Ian. '"Commodity Fetishism" and "Vulgar Marxism": On 'Rethinking Canadian Political Economy."' *Studies in Political Economy* 10.1 (1983): 143–172. *Taylor and Francis+NEJM*. Web. 29 May 2016.

Peach, Jim, and William M. Dugger. 'An Intellectual History of Abundance.' *Journal of Economic Issues* 40.3 (2006): 693–706. Print.

Popper, Karl. *The Logic of Scientific Discovery*. London/New York: Hutchinson & Co., 1959. Print.

Rigi, Jakob, and Robert Prey. 'Value, Rent, and the Political Economy of Social Media.' *The Information Society* 31.5 (2015): 392–406. *Taylor and Francis+NEJM*. Web. 10 April 2016.

Sandberg, Sheryl. 'Sheryl Sandberg Writes: Empowering Women Economically is Good for Everyone.' *The Indian Express*. N.p., 8 December 2015. Web. 11 April 2016.

Scholz, Trebor. *Digital Labor: The Internet as Playground and Factory*. New York: Routledge, 2013. Print.

Scott, Mark. 'Europe is Expected to Approve E.U.–U.S. Data Transfer Pact.' *The New York Times* 29 June 2016. *NYTimes.com*. Web. 1 July 2016.

Seckler, David William. *Thorstein Veblen and the Institutionalists: A Study in the Social Philosophy of Economics*. Boulder, CO: Colorado Associated University Press, 1975. Web.

Shirky, Clay. (2008). *Here comes everybody: How change happens when people come together*. New York: Penguin Press. Print.

Smart, Barry. 'Good for Business, Good without Reservation? Veblen's Critique of Business Enterprise and Pecuniary Culture.' *Journal of Classical Sociology* 15.3 (2015): 253–269. *jcs.sagepub.com.proxy.its.virginia.edu*. Web. 29 May 2016.

Smythe, Dallas W. 'Communications: Blindspot of Western Marxism.' *Canadian Journal of Political and Social Theory/Revue canadienne de theorie politiqueetsociale* 1.3 (1977): 1–27. Print.

Suri, Siddharth et al. 'The Crowd is a Collaborative Network.' *Computer-Supported Cooperative Work and Social Computing* (2016): n. pag. *www.microsoft.com*. Web. 1 July 2016.

The Hindu. 'Facebook Campaigns to Defend 'Free Basics." *The Hindu*. N.p., 23 December 2015. Web. 10 April 2016.

Thompson, Derek. 'Facebook Turns a Profit, Users Hits 300 Million.' *The Atlantic* 17 September 2009. *The Atlantic*. Web. 1 July 2016.

Times of India. 'Net Neutrality: IAMAI Opposes Zero-Rating Plans – Times of India.' *The Times of India*. N.p., n.d. Web. 10 April 2016.

Tool, Marc R., ed. *Institutional Economics: Theory, Method, Policy*. Boston, MA: Kluwer Academic Publishers, 1993. *Library of Congress ISBN*. Web. Recent Economic Thought Series.

'TRAI Slams Facebook for Turning Consultation Paper on Differential Pricing into a 'Crudely Majoritarian and Orchestrated Opinion Poll' | Latest Tech News, Video & Photo Reviews at BGR India.' N.p., n.d. Web. 11 April 2016.

'TRAI Supports Net Neutrality, Effectively Bans Free Basics: All That Happened in This Debate | The Indian Express.' N.p., n.d. Web. 10 April 2016.

Trottier, Daniel. *Social Media, Politics and the State: Protests, Revolutions, Riots, Crime and Policing in the Age of Facebook, Twitter and YouTube / Fuchs, Christian; 1976-*. New York: Routledge, 2015. Print. Routledge Research in Information Technology and Society; 16; Variation: Routledge Research in Information Technology and Society; 16.

Turow, Joseph. *Niche Envy Marketing Discrimination in the Digital Age*. Cambridge, MA: MIT Press, 2006. *Open WorldCat*. Web. 10 April 2016.

Turow, Joseph. *The Daily You: How the New Advertising Industry is Defining Your Identity and Your Worth*. New Haven, CT: Yale University Press, 2011. Print.

Vaidhyanathan, Siva. 'Afterword: Critical Information Studies.' *Cultural Studies* 20.2–3 (2006): 292–315. *Taylor and Francis+NEJM*. Web. 10 April 2016.

Vaidhyanathan, S. (2011). *The Googlization of everything (and why we should worry)*. Berkeley, CA: University of California Press.

Vaidhyanathan, Siva. 'The Rise of the Cryptopticon: A Bibliographic and Filmographic Guide.' *HEDGEHOG REVIEW* 17.1 (2015): 72–85. Print.

Veblen, Thorstein. *The Engineers and the Price System*. New York: A.M. Kelley, bookseller, 1965. Print.

Veblen, Thorstein. *The Theory of Business Enterprise*. 1904. New York: A.M. Kelley, bookseller, 1965. Print.

Veblen, Thorstein. *The Theory of the Leisure Class, an Economic Study of Institutions*. New York: Macmillan, 1905. Web.

Veblen, Thorstein, and Irving Louis Horowitz. *The Vested Interests*. New Brunswick, NJ: Transaction Publishers, 2002. Print.

Veblen, Thorstein, and C. Wright Mills. *The Theory of the Leisure Class: An Economic Study of Institutions*. New York: New American Library, 1953. Print.

Veblen, Thorstein, and Richard F. Teichgraeber. *The Higher Learning in America: A Memorandum on the Conduct of Universities by Business Men*. N.p., 2015. Print.

Vogel, David. *The Market for Virtue: The Potential and Limits of Corporate Social Responsibility*. Washington, DC: Brookings Institution Press, 2006. Print.

Wasko, Janet Sousa. *The Handbook of Political Economy of Communications*. Chichester, West Sussex; Malden, MA: Wiley-Blackwell, 2011. Print. Global Handbooks in Media and Communication Research; Variation: Global Handbooks in Media and Communication Research.

Weingast, Barry R., and Donald A Wittman. *The Oxford Handbook of Political Economy*. Oxford; New York: Oxford University Press, 2006. Print.

Welsh, Brandon C., and David P. Farrington. 'Public Area CCTV and Crime Prevention: An Updated Systematic Review and Meta-Analysis.' *Justice Quarterly* 26.4 (December 1, 2009): 716–45. doi:10.1080/07418820802506206.

Winseck, Dwayne Roy, and Dal Yong Jin. *The Political Economies of Media: The Transformation of the Global Media Industries*. London; New York: Bloomsbury Academic, 2012. Print.

York, Jillian C. 'A Complete Guide to All the Things Facebook Censors Hate Most.' *Quartz*. N.p., 19 June 2016. Web. 1 July 2016.

Zuckerberg, Mark. 'Mark Zuckerberg's Letter to Investors: "The Hacker Way."' *WIRED*. N.p., 1 February 2012. Web. 11 April 2016.

Zuckerberg, Mark. 'Free Basics Protects Net Neutrality.' *Times of India Blogs*. N.p., 28 December 2015. Web. 10 April 2016.

PART III

Platforms, Technologies and Business Models

13

The Affordances of Social Media Platforms

Taina Bucher and Anne Helmond

In November 2015, social media platform Twitter changed the symbol of one of its core features – the 'favorite' button – to the great disbelief of many long-time users of the platform. The favorite button, symbolized by a star and once a main feature and part of Twitter's brand identity, was changed into a much more generic *like* button, indicated with a heart symbol. Described by the press as 'one of the biggest changes to its platform yet' (Clifton, 2015), the Twitter change caused a storm of reactions from its end-users:

'I hate the twitter heart so hard' – (@twocitylife, Nov 3, 2015)'[1]

'Twitter's acting like they invented the heart' – (@kumailn, Nov 3, 2015)'[2]

'Wait! What? When did they replace the favorite star with a heart? I'm now too scared to favorite in case somebody gets the wrong idea' – (@ForresterRobert, Nov 3, 2015)[3]

'I'm actually sad to see the "heart" feature on the mobile app. I'd hate to see Twitter start to lose its essence. I hope this is temporary' – (@deray, Nov 3, 2015)'[4]

'Twitter changing the "favorite" star to a "like" heart is everything that is wrong with capitalism, in icon form' – (@room34, Nov 3, 2015).[5]

Even Twitter engineers themselves seemed to be in disarray: 'I work at @twitter but even I can't believe how we replaced a completely value-neutral term like "favorite" with something so loaded' (@peterseibel, Nov 3, 2015).[6] A feature is clearly not just a feature. The symbols and the connotations they carry matter. Pressing a button means something; it mediates and communicates, or, as we will focus in this chapter, relates to different affordances. While this platform change may seem trivial – a controversy in the heat of the moment – it also shows how features are objects of intense feelings. Features are 'communicational actors' in the sense that they 'produce

نَوْر مِيزا
@Nawwarism

⚙ 👤 Follow

Dear star button,

Even if Twitter has replaced you with a heart button,

you're still my favourite.

RETWEETS	LIKES
1,902	1,026

6:02 AM - 3 Nov 2015

↩ ↻ ♥ •••

Figure 13.1   A Twitter user reacts to the change from stars to hearts.

meanings and meaningfulness' (Langlois, 2014: 52). That is, as software-produced visual elements on an interface, features such as the favorite and *like* button say and suggest things. What exactly these features suggest – or afford – is not set once and for all. Clearly these features suggest the action of clicking the button, but they also assign a variety of other possibilities and interpretations. As the user reactions exemplify, Twitter buttons are endowed with different meanings, feelings, imaginings and expectations. There is the official, corporate, attempt at stabilizing the meanings, 'the heart is more expressive, enabling you to convey a range of emotions and easily connect with people' (Kumar, 2015). According to this logic, the favorite does not allow for the same kind of expressiveness. However, many users seemed to disagree. As one user suggests, 'A fav means more than a like'.[7] For him the change only

'shows the homoginization [*sic*] of the Internet. Everything has to be LIKES' (Ibid.). Another user sees it in this way: 'Fav never meant favourite anyway. It means "I agree."', "That's funny, but not enough to RT.", or "Let's end the conversation here."'[8] Contrary to Twitter's official statements, many users saw the favorite as a more versatile feature than the somewhat generic concept of *like*. For others, it was precisely the fact that the favorite button wasn't a *like* that made the difference: 'Fav doesnt mean love/like. Fav means I want to look at the tweets after some time'.[9] So if users debunked the idea of a heart button allowing a greater range of expressiveness, why change the feature in the first place?

Ultimately the change was presented by the company to provide a clearer understanding of the function to new users: 'We want to make Twitter easier and more rewarding to use, and we know that at times the star could be confusing, especially to newcomers' (Kumar, 2015). By changing the name and icon of a feature linked to a core platform activity ('favoriting'), Twitter not only standardized a mode of engagement across its services ('liking'), but also affected the perceived range of possible actions linked to these features of the platform, or its *affordances*.

In this chapter we want to reflect on the concept of affordance as a key term for understanding and analysing social media interfaces and the relations between technology and its users. The concept of affordance is multivalent. Originally developed in the field of ecological psychology (Gibson, 2015) and later adopted in design studies (Norman, 1988), the concept of affordance is generally used to describe what material artifacts such as media technologies allow people to do. In outlining its specific intellectual trajectory from psychology, to technology and design studies, sociology, and communication and media studies, our intention is to focus on some of the many – and sometimes conflicting – ways in which affordance has been conceptualized and operationalized across various disciplinary boundaries. Even within the field of media and communication studies there is no single way that scholars have come to understand the concept of affordance. Following the renewed debates over affordances in recent scholarship on social media (see Ilten, 2015; McVeigh-Schultz and Baym, 2015; Nagy and Neff, 2015), this chapter addresses some of the new directions in which media and communication scholars have proposed to define and analytically deploy the concept. We first describe five different – but related – ways in which affordance has been conceptualized and subsequently address how it has been employed to analyse social media in particular. We then outline a platform-sensitive approach to affordance as an analytical tool for examining social media based on recent examples of changes to the Twitter platform.

CONCEPTUALIZING AFFORDANCES

Affordances as a Relational Property

The concept of affordance was originally conceived in ecological psychology by James Gibson to designate all kinds of action possibilities latent in the physical environment. Gibson first used affordance to refer to a specific kind of relationship between an animal and the environment. For Gibson, 'the *affordances* of the environment are what it *offers* the animal, what it *provides* or *furnishes*, either for good or will' (2015: 119, emphasis in original). Although this definition seems to privilege what specific environmental properties have to offer an animal, Gibson also emphasizes that affordances are to be understood as a *relational* property: 'I mean by it something that refers to both the environment and the animal in a way that no existing term does' (2015: 119). Gibson's aim was to propose a theory of visual perception based on the ways in which different species inhabit their surroundings. In his seminal book *The Ecological Approach to Visual Perception*, first published in 1979, Gibson takes up the question of 'how we see', Gibson was interested in exploring how 'we see the environment around us', particularly in terms of how 'we see its surfaces, their layout, and their colors and textures' (2015: xiii).

His key insight was that we do not perceive the environment as such, but rather perceive it through its affordances, the possibilities for action it may provide. Fire, for example, affords warmth, illumination, and cooking, but at the same time it may also afford injury to the skin. What delineates warmth from injury is not always clear and depends on the species' ability to detect the limit. What fire affords, then, is not merely a question of its physical properties, but its relation to a specific organism. As Gibson suggests, affordances 'have to be measured relative to the animal' (2015: 120). This does not mean, however, that affordances are indefinite. For Gibson, affordances are invariant, meaning that they do '*not change* as the need of the observer changes. The observer may or may not perceive or attend to the affordance, according to his needs, but the affordance, being invariant, is always there to be perceived' (2015: 130, emphasis in original). In its original meaning, an affordance is conceived as a relational property, one that 'points both ways, to the environment and to the observer' (Gibson, 2015: 121). The concept of affordance does not imply we can do anything with anything as 'different layouts afford different behaviors for different animals [...] Knee-high for a child is not the same as knee-high for an adult, so the affordance is relative to the size of the individual' (2015: 120). As Gibson put it, 'affordances do not cause behavior but constrain and control it' (1982: 411).

Perceived Affordances

While Gibson's ideas have been hugely influential in a variety of fields, the concept of affordance was most notably adapted in design studies and the field of Human–Computer Interaction (HCI) through the writings of Donald Norman. First introduced in his book *The Psychology of Everyday Things* (1988) – which was later published as *The Design of Everyday Things* (1990) – Norman defined affordances as 'the perceived and actual properties of the thing, primarily those fundamental properties that determine just how the thing could possibly be used' (1988: 9). Writing in the specific context of cognitive science and design, Norman's aim was to explore the relationship between human cognition and the design of devices and everyday things. As a cognitive scientist, Norman was interested in how the human mind works, especially in terms of human errors, wanting to teach people how to avoid making mistakes.

Norman proposes the concept of 'perceived affordance' (1990: 9, 1999: 38) to suggest that designers can and should 'indicate how the

user is to interact with the device' (1990: 8). As Norman contends, 'affordances provide strong clues to the operation of things [...] Knobs are for turning [...] Balls are for throwing or bouncing. When affordances are taken advantage of, the user knows what to do just by looking' (1990: 9). Poorly designed objects, so the message goes, would cause unnecessary problems for their users. With Norman, the concept of affordance was modified from Gibson's relational approach to accommodate design interests, suggesting that artifacts could be designed to suggest or determine certain forms of use through the notion of 'perceived affordances' (1990: 9). The question was no longer how organisms see, as was the case in Gibson's work, but rather how certain objects could be designed to encourage or constrain specific actions.

As others have noted (Maier et al., 2009; McGrenere and Ho, 2000; You and Chen, 2007), Norman's conceptualization of affordance became widely adopted within the design community, setting the standard for what would be considered good design and usability. For many designers and creative professionals, it was thus Norman's prescriptive formulation, not Gibson's work, which introduced them to the concept of affordance (You and Chen, 2007: 26). Unlike Gibson's relational understanding of affordance, Norman describes affordances as properties of things. Thus, power is placed in the hands of designers who have the power to enable and constrain certain action possibilities through their design choices. Whereas affordances may or may not be perceived in Gibson's view, according to Norman, the key is whether users actually *perceive* the intended possibilities for action inscribed into the design of an artifact. As Norman's concept of perceived affordances highlights, 'affordances are of little use if they are not visible to the users' (1999: 41). This notion of perceived affordances has been hugely influential in professional user experience design and interface design, within the digital media and tech industries where Norman's framework still serves as the working defini-tion of affordance. In their book *Universal Principles of Design*, authors Lidwell et al. provide design guidelines and considera-tions through a number of concepts, includ-ing affordance, and closely follow Norman in suggesting that 'good' affordances can enhance the usability of a design and influ-ence the way it is perceived (2010: 8–22).

Technology Affordances

Affordances are not just limited to the visible senses but can also be felt or heard. As William Gaver suggests, 'affordances are primarily facts about action and interaction, not perception' (1996: 114). For example, 'when door handles are turned the sound of the latch may reveal the affordance of moving the door' (Gaver, 1991: 82–83). For Gaver, affordances are not just waiting to be per-ceived; rather they are there to be actively explored. Building on Gibson's relational model of affordances, Gaver contributed one of the first thorough explorations of affordances within the field of HCI with his paper on 'Technology Affordances' (Gaver, 1991; McGrenere and Ho, 2000). According to Gaver, affordances 'are properties of the world defined with respect to people's inter-action with it' (1991: 80). It implies the 'complimentary of the acting organism and the acted-upon environment' (1991: 80). As Gaver exemplifies: 'whether a handle with particular dimensions will afford grasping depends on the grasper's height, hand size, etc. Similarly, a cat-door affords passage to a cat but not to me' (1991: 80).

Like Norman, Gaver thinks that technology and an artifact suggest different actions, but differs in his view that users know 'what to do just by looking' (Norman, 1988: 9). Gaver makes a separation between affordances and the perceptual information available about them, suggesting that affordances can be both perceptible and *hidden* (1991: 80). In the latter case, affordances must be inferred

from other evidence, possibly through experimentation and other actions that make affordances visible. In the case of a graphi-cal computer interface, for example, a hidden affordance could be revealed by the action of a mouse-over.

For Gaver, 'affordances exist not just for individual action, but for social interaction as well' (1996: 114). While the ecological approach to affordance stresses the relation-ship between the natural environment and the individual, 'how individual activities are shaped by the environment, and how individ-uals can orient to the relevant environmental attributes', Gaver is also concerned with 'the possibilities offered by the physical environ-ment for social interaction' (1996: 114). He points out, 'these are not social affordances […] but affordances for sociality' (1996: 114). In writing about the material features of technology, Gaver speculates about the differences between paper and electronic media, arguing that different affordances may have many effects on the social conven-tions that surround them. Contemplating the role of email, Gaver describes how moving from a high-bandwidth environment to a dial-up service dramatically changed the use and culture of email. 'The properties of email systems may not determine the communities that eventually form around them', Gaver suggests, 'but they do strongly constrain the cultures that might develop' (1996: 120). Although Gaver makes sure to distance him-self from accusations of technological deter-minism, the term 'technology affordances' establishes material qualities of technology as (partly) constitutive of sociality and commu-nicative actions in this view. Again, we need to recognize the particular context and aim of Gaver's conception of affordance. Whereas Gibson's aim was to propose a theory of visual perception and Norman's primary concern was to enhance good design, Gaver sought to 'challenge researchers to avoid the temptation of ascribing social behavior to arbitrary customs and practices, and to focus instead on discovering the possibly complex environmental factors shaping social interaction' (1996: 125). In doing so, Gaver considered the concept of affordances as a 'useful tool for user-centered analyses of technologies' (1991: 97).

Social Affordances

Gaver's aim of pointing researchers to the ways in which 'social activities are embedded in and shaped by the material environment' (1996: 125) might have paid off as many sociologists and communication scholars have subsequently used the notion of *social affordances* to refer to 'the possibilities that technological changes afford for social relations and social structure' (Wellman, 2001: 228) to talk about the ways in which 'technology affords social practice' (Hsieh, 2012). The term 'social affordance', however, might also seem confusing as it is primarily used to talk about the impact of technology, how technological properties enable and constrain sociality in certain ways. Social affordances are 'the social structures that take shape in association with a given technical structure' (Postigo, 2016: 5). Wellman et al. (2003) use the term to talk about the ways in which the internet may influence everyday life. Similar to how Gaver uses the notion of technology affordances to describe the changes in email culture effectuated by moving from high-bandwidth environment to a slower dial-up service, Wellman et al. (2003) use the notion of social affordance to describe how changes in broadband create new possibilities for communication. Using opposite prefixes, they both seem to be referring to the way in which technology affords sociality.

However, the notion of social affordance can also be understood in a much more general or relational sense without necessarily invoking technology explicitly. According to Gibson, 'the richest and most elaborate affordances of the environment are provided by other animals and, for us, other people'

(2015: 126). This is to say that how people behave, move, or simply exist in an environment afford important cues as to how others should behave, move or co-exist. Take the pedestrian sidewalk; people constantly adjust their own movements to other people in their pathway. While the environment may give structure to an organisms' existence, Gibson suggests that 'behavior affords behavior' (2015: 127). Importantly, 'what the other animal affords the observer is not only behavior but also social interaction' (2015: 36).

Communicative Affordance

Characteristic of many of the above conceptualizations of affordances is the question of how technology and society relate. For the sociologist Ian Hutchby (2001a, 2001b), the term 'affordance' provides a way to move beyond naïve technological determinism and strict social constructivism. Hutchby suggests that affordance provides a middle term that both takes into account the ways in which technologies are socially constructed and situated on the one hand, and materially constraining and enabling on the other hand. Specifically, Hutchby develops the concept of 'communicative affordances' referring to the 'possibilities for action that emerge from […] given technological forms' (2001a: 30). This definition emphasizes how affordances are both functional and relational; '*functional* in the sense that they are enabling, as well as constraining' and *relational* in terms of drawing 'attention to the way that the affordances of an object may be different for one species than for another' (Hutchby and Barnett, 2005: 151, emphasis in the original). Moreover, 'affordances can also shape the conditions of possibility associated with an action: it may be possible to do it one way, but not another' (Hutchby and Barnett, 2005: 151).

For Hutchby, the notion of communicative affordances is best understood as part of ordinary actions. While Gibson once observed that 'the walk-on-ability of a sur-face exists whether or not the animal walks on it', Hutchby and Barnett think 'it is never-theless the case that the surface's affordance of walk-on-ability becomes manifest when the animal walks on it' (2005: 152). In other words, affordances can best be observed in the course of agential actions. In the context of media and communications research, the actions that seem particularly apt to study are the ones that imply communication of some sort. Hence the relative usefulness of the term 'communicative affordances' as opposed to the very similar term 'social affordances'. While both of these terms describe the ways in which technology enable or con-strain social action, the term 'communica-tive affordances' focuses specifically on the 'impact of technology for communication' (Schrock, 2015: 1233).

The term 'communicative affordances' has most notably been used in research on mobile media (Boase, 2008; Helles, 2013; Hutchby and Barnett, 2005) as a way of describing how mobile devices 'alter communicative prac-tices or habits' (Schrock, 2015: 1232). While the mobile phone has often been described as a device for 'perpetual contact' (Katz and Aakhus, 2002), the affordance of availability on this account first and foremost alters the degrees and ways of being available. In terms of mobility or portability, Helles usefully sug-gests that 'the central affordance of mobile phones is not the mobility of the device per se, but rather the fact that the user becomes a mobile terminus for mediated communica-tive interaction across the various contexts of daily life' (2013: 14). As Humphreys (2005) showed in her work on mobile use in public, the range of social contexts in which mobile communication takes place afford new forms of social identity, as well as the modifica-tion of tacit codes of social interactions. The communicative affordance perspective thus moves away from Norman's applied perspec-tive of seeing affordances as features and instead focuses on more high-level abstrac-tions of what mobile devices afford.

SOCIAL MEDIA RESEARCH AND AFFORDANCES

As a concept that captures the relationship between the materiality of media and human agency, affordance continues to play an important role in media studies and social media research specifically (see Ellison and Vitak, 2015). Work in this area often uses an affordance approach to focus attention not on any particular technology, but on the new dynamics or types of communicative prac-tices and social interactions that various fea-tures afford. Whereas some scholars have used affordance almost synonymously with the features of technology (Graves, 2007), others have focused on the social structures that are formed in and through a given tech-nology (Baym, 2010; boyd, 2011; Postigo, 2016). Within the literature, social network sites and social media have often been ana-lysed in terms of having 'affordances and constraints' (e.g., Baym, 2010; boyd, 2011; Ellison and Vitak, 2015).

High-Level and Low-Level Affordances

Affordances tend to be conceptualized on either one of two distinct dimensions: an abstract high-level or a more concrete feature-oriented low-level. High-level affordances are the kinds of dynamics and conditions enabled by technical devices, plat-forms and media. As danah boyd argues in her work on social network sites as a form of networked publics (2011: 39), these sites are essentially shaped by four central affordances: persistence, replicability, scalability, and searchability (2011: 46). For boyd, these high-level affordances of SNSs structure the engagement of users in these environments (2011: 39–40). Comparably, Treem and Leonardi (2012) allocate four affordances of social media use shaping organizational com-munication processes: visibility, editability, persistence and association. Looking at what kinds of behaviours social media afford offers 'one way researchers can transcend the particularities of any technology or its features, and focus on communicative outcomes' (Treem and Leonardi, 2012: 147). Schrock also sees affordances as something much broader than 'buttons, screens and operating systems' (2015: 1233). For him, affordances exist on a higher-level, as exemplified through the kinds of dynamics or conditions enabled by the mobile phone. For Schrock, these affordances include: portability, availability, locatability and mulimediality (2015: 1229). In other words, what mobile media afford has nothing to do with a specific button, but rather with the kinds of communicative practices and habits they enable or constrain. In contrast, low-level affordances are typically located in the materiality of the medium, in specific features, buttons, screens and platforms. Interestingly, we find that many researchers use this low-level or design-oriented notion of affordance more in passing than in an analytical sense. As such, affordance becomes a way of talking about the technical features of a platform, for example, invoking the term to describe Twitter's 140-character limit or the ability to share a link using a *tweet* button. In a Gibsonian sense, technical features – understood as the furniture of the digital landscape – afford certain actions, such as clicking, sharing or liking.

More often than not, however, authors seem to combine a high-level understanding of affordance with a consideration of specific features or platforms. As boyd argues in her work, higher-level affordances are conditioned by the properties of bits, which essentially introduce new opportunities for interaction and communication (2011: 39). Comparably, Ellison and Vitak (2015) advocate for considering the high-level affordances of social media by conjoining this perspective with looking at specific features, such as the profile, to understand social capital processes. Conversely, Postigo uses

a low-level or feature-oriented conceptualization of affordance as a means of studying how YouTube's platform features create 'a set of probable uses/meanings/practices for users while serving YouTube's business interests' (2016: 332). Postigo thus starts his analysis by describing a set of architectural features and properties of the YouTube platform in order to describe its 'social affordances' (2016: 336).

While all conceptualizations of affordance take Gibson's original framing of the term as a starting point, they differ in terms of *where and when* they see affordances materializing (i.e., features, artifacts, social structures) and *what* affordances are supposed to activate or limit (i.e., particular communicative practices, sociality, publics, perception). By highlighting the difference between high-level affordances and low-level affordances, we want to emphasize what we see as one of the main ontological and epistemological differences in how the concept of affordance gets used. The Gibsonian understanding locates affordances *in* the relation between a body and its environment, whereas the low-level conception of affordance takes after Norman by locating affordances in the technical features of the user interface (Sun and Hart-Davidson, 2014: 3537).

Imagined Affordances

Despite the popularity and widespread usage of the term in social media research, recent contributions to the literature on affordance have called for more precise and nuanced definitions of the term, variously proposing additional concepts to better account for the complex relationships between technology and sociality (see Ilten, 2015; McVeigh-Schultz and Baym, 2015; Nagy and Neff, 2015). Nagy and Neff, for instance, have introduced the notion of 'imagined affordance' as 'a theory that better incorporates the material, the mediated, and the emotional aspects of human–technology interaction' (2015: 2). Imagined affordances, Nagy and Neff contend, 'emerge between users' perceptions, attitudes, and expectations; between the materiality and functionality of technologies; and between the intentions and perceptions of designers' (2015: 5). For Nagy and Neff, 'older' notions of affordance fail to address the complexity of cognitive as well as emotional processes. Simply locating the action possibilities of a social media platform in a set of features will not do, they claim, because users' perceptions, beliefs and expectations of what the technology does or what the platform suggests it is for 'shape how they approach them and what actions they think are suggested' (2015: 5). Imagined affordances may not just affect how users approach social media platforms, they may performatively help to shape the platforms themselves. As Bucher (2016) argues in her research on users' understanding and perceptions of algorithms in social media platforms, the ways in which users imagine and expect certain algorithmic affordances, affect how they approach these platforms. The feedback-loop characteristics of machine learning systems like Facebook make user beliefs an important component in shaping the overall system behaviour, as end-user activity is generative of the system itself.

Vernacular Affordances

In a similar vein, McVeigh-Schultz and Baym (2015) suggest linking the materiality of social media platforms to the sense-making processes of users when conceptualizing affordances. Developing the notion of 'vernacular affordance', McVeigh-Schultz and Baym emphasize 'how people themselves understand affordances in their encounters with technology' (2015: 1). Instead of researchers or designers assigning affordances to social media, they derive the affordances from users discussing how they engage with the technology. Such a perspective, they

state, infers affordances from a more 'vernacular' account of the users themselves, who may emphasize different aspects of the action possibilities of a platform. Interviewing key actors of NGOs involved in a campaign entitled 'Free Lunch for Children in China' (FL4C) on the Chinese microblogging platform Sina Weibo, researchers Zheng and Yu (2016) found that Weibo affords NGOs to scale their network, frame collective action, and establish the legitimacy of their campaign. Schools participating in the FL4C campaign had to post photographic evidence of the lunches provided to Weibo, thereby 'enforcing transparency', 'enhancing accountability' and 'enacting public scrutiny' (Zheng and Yu, 2016: 305), affordances which only revealed themselves through interviews and observing the practices of the actors involved in the campaign. In line with audience research more generally, the point with emphasizing the notion of vernacular affordances is to show how action possibilities cannot be determined once and for all, but need to be grounded in people's own perceptions and experiences. As McVeigh-Schultz and Baym argue in their study of how people use and make sense of the dating app *Couple*, 'affordances are not experienced in isolation, but rather in relation to a complex ecology of other tools with other affordances' (2015: 2). Thus, affordances simultaneously exist for people at multiple levels and across platform boundaries.

RE-ASSEMBLING AFFORDANCES

Our purpose with outlining the different conceptions of affordance was to point out its different intellectual history, ontological status and analytical value. It arguably makes a difference which conception of affordance is used – as it puts certain epistemological limits on what can be known about affordances and where to find them in the first place. When designers and designed artifacts are given priority, affordances are seen as part of the technological design. Following an understanding of affordance as communicative, however, locates affordances as part of communicative actions and can best be studied in and through the kinds of practices that technology allows for or constrains. Or, in the case of vernacular affordances, ways of knowing and analysing affordances requires an emphasis on users' own accounts of technology, where affordances become as much part of users' experiences and perceptions of technologies as of the technologies themselves.

A Relational and Multi-layered Approach to Affordances

The different concepts outlined above seem to focus on what technology does *to* users, and not, for instance, the other way around. Given the relational ontology of Gibson's original concept, it seems somewhat surprising that the relationality in question often seems to be applied rather unidirectional. The question is seldom what end-users afford or do *to* technology (not to be confused with the question of what users do *with* technology), or what platforms afford to other kinds of users besides end-users. In order to do the concept of affordance justice, we need to think much more relationally and in a multi-layered way about the concept, while retaining a sense of platform-sensitivity by taking the medium-specificity of platforms into account.[10] If Actor-Network Theory (ANT) and similar relational approaches to the relationship between technology and the social have taught us anything, isn't it to think in a more fully-fledged manner about agency and connectivity? ANT, while not a coherent approach, holds that agency is distributed and relational, and that nonhumans are actors with agency too. As Latour suggests, the agency of nonhumans refers to the ways in which 'things might authorize, allow, *afford*, encourage, permit, suggest, influence, block, render possible,

forbid, and so on' (2005: 72, emphasis added). As Latour acknowledged in a footnote to this much-cited reference on the idea of nonhuman agency, it is highly indebted to Gibson's notion of affordances and the question of what technology does to users. This may also be where some of the overemphasis on affordances as something seemingly tied to the agency of technological objects comes from. While the notion of nonhuman agency is important in studying social media platforms, we should also not lose sight of the multi-directionality of agency and connectivity at work in approaching questions of affordances. If one way of thinking more relationally about affordances on a par with Gibson's original conception means considering agency as pointing 'both ways, to the environment and to the observer' (2015: 121), then we want to suggest that thinking in a more multi-layered way about affordances means reconsidering the notion of the interface as well. Although providing a genealogy of the notion of the interface falls outside the scope of this chapter, let it suffice at this point to briefly explain what we mean by interface and why it is important to our current discussions.

While Gibson saw affordance as manifest in the surfaces and layout of the terrestrial environment, design studies and HCI in many ways have treated this as being analogous to graphical user interfaces, button and features in the context of digital environments. Following Branden Hookway (2014), however, we want to argue that surfaces and interfaces are not necessarily the same. A surface, Hookway suggests, 'exists primarily as an aspect of that which it surfaces'; it means 'a facing above' (2014: 12). The interface, by contrast, 'does not primarily refer back to a thing or condition but rather to a relation between things or conditions, or to a condition as it is produced by a relation' (Hookway, 2014: 13–14). While we do not want to go as far as Hookway in replacing all references to a web interface and the vernacular understanding of interface as the place of interaction between two systems with the term 'surface', we also want to stress that interfaces are not confined to this notion of a surface or a physical boundary of sorts. Following Hookway, interfaces should above all be understood as 'forms of relations'. If interfaces are not simply surfaces or computer screens, what does it mean to consider interfaces as sites of analysis for a study of affordances? Previously, Mel Stanfill (2015: 3) has proposed a method for analysing websites entitled 'discursive interface analysis', which takes a site's affordances as a starting point in order to analyse how they produce and make visible particular norms of use. However, following Hookway (2014), we wish to emphasize how interfaces produce and make visible particular *relations*. By moving beyond the surface and to platforms' distinct *inter*faces that mediate between different parties, we wish to draw attention not only to how affordances present and structure action possibilities for end-users in the graphical user interface, but also to how 'the interface privileges the question of how a relation may come into being and how it may produce behaviors or actions' (Hookway, 2014: 14). By approaching the question of affordance from a relational and multi-layered perspective, the question is not just *whose* action possibilities we are talking about, but also how those action possibilities come into existence by drawing together (sometimes incompatible) entities into new forms of meaningfulness. That is, there is nothing that necessarily warrants the analogous treatment of the Gibsonian animal or observer with the end-user. Correspondingly, we might wonder where in the course of the historical trajectory the properties of the natural environment that Gibson describes became synonymous with devices, technologies and the graphical user-interface?

Platforms as Environments

If the end-user is not necessarily equivalent to the Gibsonian animal, then who or what constitutes the animals of social media and how are we to think of the environment in this case? For Gibson, the terrestrial environment with its terrestrial features of paths, cliffs, barriers, water margins, etc. afford various ways of existing relative to the animal in question. In Gibson's terms, the 'earth has "furniture" […] it is cluttered' (2015: 123): 'Like the furnishings of a room', the environment is cluttered with objects and features, 'it is what makes it liveable' (2015: 71). For us, social media platforms constitute a form of environment too, composed of pathways and features in their own right. It is important to point out, however, that no two platforms are alike, although many tend to use similar features and functionalities such as likes, shares, comments or hashtags. While we focus specifically on Twitter as a platform in this chapter, and take its platform-specificity into account, the broader arguments about considering platforms as environments with its specific possibilities and constraints holds true for any social media platform of study.

Platforms, in their computational understanding, are seen as infrastructures that can be programmed and built on (Bogost and Montfort, 2009). In the context of Twitter, this programmability is facilitated by application programming interfaces (APIs), which enable interoperability and facilitate third-parties to employ platform data and functionality (Bodle, 2011; Bucher, 2013; Helmond, 2015). At the same time, APIs enable platforms to extend into the web by setting up data channels that make external web data flowing back to their databases 'platform ready' in order to fit the underlying economic business models of social media platforms (Helmond, 2015). Platforms are technologies or services that mediate interactions and relations between two or more parties (Rochet and Tirole, 2003), and social media platforms can be characterized as digital intermediaries that draw together and negotiate between different stakeholders, such as end-users, developers and advertisers, which each come with their own aims and agendas

(Gillespie, 2010). Social media platforms are characterized by the combination of their infrastructural model as programmable and extendable infrastructures, and their economic model of connecting end-users to advertisers (Helmond, 2015), where the 'politics of platforms' lies in the mediation of these stakeholder relations (Gillespie, 2010). For example, Facebook's Like button enables Facebook to extend into websites and apps, where the data produced on and collected through these external sources is sent back to the platform (Gerlitz and Helmond, 2013) and made available to advertisers through various advertising interfaces, such as the Facebook Marketing API.[11]

A PLATFORM-SENSITIVE APPROACH

If platforms are specific kinds of digital environments, and affordances reflect the complex co-evolution of users and environment, how are we to make sense of such contextual relationality in the concrete case of a social media platform? In the following we take the example of Twitter as a case in point to discuss what we term a platform-sensitive approach to the affordances of social media.

The Case of Twitter Platform Changes

Exactly ten years ago today, on 21 March 2006, Twitter's cofounder Jack Dorsey published the first tweet ever.[12] Since then, Twitter has grown into the most popular microblogging platform to date, with 320 million monthly users (Styles, 2016). Still, the alleged 'decay' of Twitter has been regularly pronounced, particularly in light of its loss of 'sociability' (Burgess, 2015), stalled user growth, and the many recent platform changes (see Topolsky, 2016; Tsukayama, 2016). Commentators have noted how declining user growth has prompted the platform to

change some of its most prevalent features and functionalities, including the favorite feature, as briefly discussed in the introduction of this chapter. When, in November 2015, the favorite was changed into a *like*, it was indeed presented as a way of making the service more comprehensible to new users (Kumar, 2015). The turn to hearts, or *likes*, was also motivated by a desire to standardize expressions across all Twitter products, as exemplified by Twitter's spokesperson, who put it in this way: 'You've embraced hearts in a big way on Periscope, and we're delighted to bring them to Twitter and Vine, making them the common language for our global community' (Kumar, 2015). A few months later, in February 2016, Twitter made another major change by enabling a new timeline ordering in which end-users would now receive 'the best Tweets first' by default in order to 'catch up on the best Tweets from people you follow' (About your Twitter timeline, n.d.). This change essentially transformed the curation and presentation of the feed, from that of a linear progression of tweets in a reverse-chronological order to a feed no longer exclusively organized around a linear flow of time. With the new feed introduced early in 2016, tweets would now be organized around various popularity and affinity metrics, including user interaction and their engagement with tweets through platform activities such as liking, retweeting and replying (About your Twitter timeline, n.d.). These two controversial changes were heavily discussed on technology blogs as well as on Twitter itself, where the rumoured introduction of what came to be widely discussed as 'the algorithmic timeline' of Twitter, prompted much outrage under the hashtag #RIPTwitter.[13] The question is what, if anything, these incidents have to do with affordances? As we will argue, much, indeed.

At first sight it might be tempting to interpret Twitter's claim that the favorite button is confusing to use, by evoking Norman's idea of good interface design. From a design-centred perspective the favorite button failed to communicate how the feature should to be used. The turn to hearts and *likes* could be read as an attempt to enhance the perceived affordances of the feature by indicating more clearly 'how the user is to interact with the device' (Norman, 1990: 8). However, if we tackle the question from the perspective of communicative or vernacular affordances it quickly becomes apparent that affordances cannot simply be understood in terms of good or bad design. What the many reactions to the change and previous studies attest to is that the favorite feature has been attributed various affordances beyond their original purpose of saving tweets you like (Stone, 2006). In their study of Twitter favoriting behaviour, Meier et al. (2014) identified 25 distinct motivations for using favorites, including showing agreement and relationship building. From the perspective of end-users, the favorite feature does not simply afford bookmarking a tweet, it also affords different types of sociality and communicative actions, e.g., favoriting as a form of communication to maintain relations, to show agreement, or to indicate the end of a conversation (cf. Meier et al., 2014). The change to hearts and *likes*, while technically not affording any new actions, certainly seems to suggest different communicative and social affordances. For some end-users, the change from a favorite into a *like* feature eradicated the wide range of 'communicative affordances' previously associated with the favorite (Newton, 2015). Others still, claimed the opposite, suggesting the importance of taking users' perspectives into account when analysing the affordances of social media. Simply approaching the favorite and like features on Twitter as examples of technical affordances will not do. While features clearly afford actions, only looking at what features allow users to do would quickly miss out on the multifarious meanings and communicative affordances these buttons entail. Although technically affording identical actions, taking into account what users say, believe and expect these features to be able to accomplish varies greatly.

Similar points could be made when considering the recent introduction of Twitter's 'algorithmic timeline' and the reactions that followed, particularly around the #RIPTwitter trending topic. Here, assessing affordances in terms of whether the Twitter feed is being used in the ways envisioned by designers in the vein of Norman would fail to acknowledge 'the role of the Twitter hashtag as a means of coordinating a distributed discussion among large numbers of users' and to explain the emergence of such 'hashtag publics' (Bruns and Burgess, 2015: 14). What a concept like imagined affordances usefully points to is that we also need to consider the ways in which the technology is imagined by its users (Nagy and Neff, 2015: 4). As Bucher (2016) has shown in her research on how Facebook's algorithms are imagined, people's expectations and perceptions of technology may affect behaviour as much as its material properties may do. Similarly, the #RIPTwitter reveals how multiple imaginings exist around what an algorithm is for, and what the prospects of an algorithmically curated timeline would do to the possibilities and constraints of Twitter.

Rather than introduce yet another concept of affordance, our aim in the remaining part of this chapter is to contribute one way of approaching the empirical analysis of affordances in social media by being sensitive to platform specificities. This specificity entails not merely looking at features that manifest on a graphical user interface, but considers how the affordances of platforms are relational and multi-layered.

Expanding the Notion of the User

Taking the specificity of platforms into account requires extending our notion of the 'user' as platforms cater to different users, actors or stakeholders. We argue for moving beyond the end-user-centred (e.g., Gaver, 1991: 97; Gibson, 2015) and designer-centred (e.g., Norman, 1990) approaches that have figured prominently within affordance theory. In the literature, the term 'user' is often used synonymously with the human end-user, the person for whom the website or app was originally designed. However, advertisers, developers and researchers are platform users in their own right too. Arguably, Twitter affords different things to an end-user than to a developer, advertiser or researcher. These different user types are predefined by Twitter, by addressing them via distinct interfaces, such as the end-user interfaces, including the website and Twitter apps, the Twitter APIs for developers and researchers, and the Advertising API for advertisers. In predefining these users, they could be considered the intended or designed-for user types. While end-users typically stress the communicative or social affordances associated with certain features available on the graphical user interface of Twitter, most developers would probably stress the importance of another interface altogether.

For developers, the action possibilities of Twitter are primarily related to its APIs, which affords them to build applications on top of the platform (Bucher, 2013). APIs afford developers, but also researchers,[14] advertisers and other users, access to and the possibility to re-use the data and functionality of platforms. Using the Twitter APIs,[15] a number of third-party services have been built on top of Twitter, including services like Favrd and Favstar, which have utilized Twitter's favorite feature. These services have made the act of favoriting public by aggregating favorite tweets, and by showing users who had favorited their tweets (MacManus, 2009). In doing so, Favrd turned the favorite from a personal bookmarking mechanism into a public popularity measure (MacManus, 2009). Favstar further enhanced the public nature of favorites by offering a social network around favorites through leader boards and other features (Paßmann et al., 2014). In this way, developers – in conjunction with end-users and their use

practices – have played an important role in shaping the action possibilities of the favorite button by envisioning new use case scenarios. The creation of third-party services built on top of the favorite feature, such as Favstar, shows how developers may conceive of new action possibilities which in their turn enable novel communicational dynamics outside the Twitter platform. It emphasizes the specificity of Twitter, as a platform which has a history of being fairly 'open' for third-party development, as an environment in which the generative potentials of end-users and developers should be taken into account when examining the platform's affordances.

In light of stalled user growth at Twitter, the change from favorites to *likes* should not just be seen as an attempt at catering to end-users' needs and practices (i.e., '*you've* embraced hearts', as Twitter's spokesperson has said), but also as an integrated approach to the standardization of expressions that enables or operates according to a dual logic of decentralization and recentralization that extends the 'environment' beyond the confines of the platform (Helmond, 2015). The Twitter APIs and their underlying logic of connectivity have enabled an ecosystem of third-party apps and services, weaving Twitter into the larger social media ecosystem (Van Dijck, 2013).[16] This includes creating connections between Twitter and other Twitter-owned services such as Periscope and Vine, as well as other social media platforms, e.g., through the practice of automatically cross-posting content to Facebook or LinkedIn, thereby extending Twitter's functionalities into the larger social media ecosystem. Furthermore, the change from favorite into *like* can be seen as a form of standardizing modes of engagement across various social media platforms, or as technology reporter Newton (2015) notes: 'likes and hearts have become a kind of universal currency of the social web, from Facebook to Tumblr to Instagram'.

The *like*, as a 'universal currency' in social media, is particularly important to advertisers, for whom the Twitter platform affords the promotion of content by targeting end-users and the measurement of engagement. While the *like* feature has certain communicative affordances, such as signalling support or sharing information with friends (Brandtzaeg and Haugstveit, 2014; Guy et al., 2016), for advertisers the feature and the actions it enables facilitates possibilities to tailor and personalize ads, and to measure engagement. Twitter's Ads API[17] connects Twitter, Twitter Official Partners[18] and advertisers to target end-users based on who they follow, information about the device they are using, such as IP address and installed apps, and interactions with tweets, including retweeting, replying and liking among other signals.[19] These activities are also used to predict the engagement rate for an ad in order to determine its relevancy for a user, and subsequently the ad's price.[20] Moreover, Twitter collects data from people engaging within the wider 'Twitter ecosystem' (Twitter Help Center, n.d.), by tracking end-users and non-Twitter users across the web via platform functionality such as Twitter buttons on external websites and apps (cf. Gerlitz and Helmond, 2013). This is what Heyman (2016: 143) calls the 'hidden affordances' (as defined by Gaver) of social media platforms since users do not perceive the action possibility of placing cookies to track users across the web.

Platform Users and their Interfaces

If the users of platforms are diverse and multiple, so are their points of contact. Users can form relations with the platform through multiple interfaces (or surfaces in Hookway's notion), such as the various APIs that have been discussed above. However, these are not isolated or separate points of contact between the Twitter platform and its different users. Rather, together they constitute the platform environment as a whole and enable relations between all users inside the platform, as well

as relations with users outside the platform's boundaries. Similar to the ways in which Gibson foregrounds the relationality between an animal and the environment in his conceptualization of affordance, Hookway's notion of interface privileges the formation of a relation, and how that relation in turn may become productive of certain actions. Social media platforms and their underlying logic of 'connectivity' (Van Dijck, 2013) also require a view on affordances that moves beyond the boundaries of the platform and takes the larger environment in which the platform operates into account. The notion of connectivity, José Van Dijck and Thomas Poell contend, refers to 'the socio-technical affordance of networked platforms to connect content to user activities and advertisers' (2013: 8). In the case of the Twitter platform and its users, the different APIs may provide some clues as to how different relationships come into being and the kinds of actions that are enabled. Importantly, these APIs also transform the domain and practices of advertising, research and marketing themselves insofar as they are now being channelled through Twitter. As our brief discussion of interfaces has shown, platforms address users differently and the possibilities for action are therefore relative to users (see Gibson, 2015; Hutchby, 2001a). The move from favorite to *likes*, we want to suggest, is symptomatic of this drive towards connecting various users together by standardizing the metric of endorsement across all Twitter products and places connected to those products (such as external websites or apps).

The Adaptability of Platform Surfaces

In addition to expanding the notion of the user and looking at different interfaces, a third important aspect of a platform-sensitive approach is to consider the specificity of the digital environment more explicitly. What distinguishes social media platforms from

Gibson's natural environment is the increasingly dynamic and malleable nature of these platforms. Following Gibson, platforms present themselves relative to their inhabitants, but contra Gibson, for whom the surfaces of the natural environment do not change as the needs of the observer changes, social media platforms adapt their surfaces to their users. These surfaces are optimized for web or mobile use and they can be adapted through platform settings and personalization features, which create personalized surfaces for end-users. In addition, the common practice of A/B testing, a technique to test the effectiveness of new features, functionalities or algorithmic recommendations with different groups of end-users of the platform, generates multiple platform surfaces. Platform surfaces are relative because they, in many cases, are personalized for each end-user and because platforms create and present multiple interfaces (as discussed in the previous section) that enable and constrain users' action possibilities.

A key question that we think social media researchers should be asking in terms of affordance theory is how the environment they are studying differs from the kind of environment studied by Gibson and other affordance theorists. When Gibson wrote about what the environment affords the animal, he was primarily thinking of its terrestrial features such as water margins, rocks and cliffs (2015: 31–36). A cliff offers certain things because of what it is, not because of the wishes bestowed upon it by an interlocutor (Gibson, 2015: 130). With the computational systems driving social media platforms, the environment takes on a different character that we think needs to be attended to. More specifically, it seems that an algorithmically organized environment challenges the invariant nature of affordances in important ways. As noted by Nagy and Neff, technologies are increasingly 'adaptive, learning, responsive, and changing along with the users they share an environment with' (2015: 5). While

Facebook has often been the exemplary case in terms of the adaptable and malleable nature of platforms, the move towards non-linear news feeds on platforms such as Twitter and Instagram[21] suggests a more general tendency towards a personalized furnishing (to use Gibson's words) of the social media environment. While the term 'algorithmic timeline' may be somewhat of a misnomer for a feed that technically speaking is already algorithmic in the sense that tweets are arranged in a reverse-chronological manner by an algorithm, the extent to which algorithms are used to organize feeds relative to users and their activities is new. This means that the digital environment does not merely offer something to its users, users' needs and individual likings and behaviours increasingly play a generative role in producing those very offerings in the first place.

(Non)human Agency Affording Things to Technology

The feedback-loops and generative role of users in shaping the algorithmically entangled social media environment brings us to our final point we want to make in terms of what we mean by a platform-sensitive approach to affordances. While affordance theory has mainly put emphasis on the question of what technology affords users, the socio-technical nature of social media platforms also begs the reverse question of what users afford to platforms? In the age of so-called big data fuelled by expansive data points and machine learning algorithms that respond to user input in an adaptive way, users serve quite literally as the 'action possibilities' of platforms. For example, Facebook uses machine learning for ranking search results, serving the most relevant ads, identifying faces, and predicting which memories people would like to view (Applied Machine Learning, n.d.). The platform feature 'On This Day' employs a machine learning model which learns in real time and continuously from people about which memories they would like to see in their News Feeds (Aziz and Paluri, 2016). In these cases, the question of who affords what and to whom seems increasingly more complex.

In order to do the relational view on affordances full justice, we need to consider the multi-directionality of agency and connectivity at play. More specifically, this means looking at what users afford to the environment, where users are understood in the expanded and typified ways explicated above. We have not been able to account for all the different forms of users above (nor do we believe such an exhaustive account is even possible), but want to stress that users are not confined to humans such as end-users and developers, but to nonhumans alike. As actors in their own right, algorithms can be considered 'hidden affordances' in Gaver's sense as their action possibilities shape our social relations and the content we see without being directly perceivable as such (Nagy and Neff, 2015: 3). Moreover, it's not only a question of what these algorithms afford to end-users, but also what they afford to the platform. In sorting and ranking content by displaying 'the best Tweets first' based on 'accounts you interact with most, Tweets you engage with, and much more' in order to 'catch up on the best Tweets from people you follow' (About your Twitter timeline, n.d.), algorithms are geared towards the creation and maintenance of participation and engagement. In light of Twitter's stalled user growth, the move towards an algorithmically sorted timeline can be interpreted as a corporate attempt at becoming more relevant, and therefore more engaging for its users.

As we see it, then, a platform-sensitive approach requires a socio-technical sensibility towards the distributed agency of humans and nonhumans at play. As Gibson himself pointed out, affordance 'cuts across the dichotomy of subjective–objective' (2015: 121). Rather than thinking of the affordances of social media platform as one-way

relationships whereby either the technology affords something to users or, as we might have suggested in this section, users afford things to technology, the presence of algorithms in particular suggests that such unidirectionality does not hold. By clicking and liking end-users fuel the algorithms, which in their turn generate the information flows fed back to end-users. Moreover, the clicks and *likes* fuel the interest and engagement of developers, researchers and advertisers, who help to keep the platforms in business.

Furthermore, the specific affordances of Twitter as an extendable platform, which includes Twitter's extension into the web and the app space through the Twitter button and Sign in with Twitter login feature, feeds data such as *likes* generated in external websites and third-party apps back into the platform. When Twitter end-users are browsing websites outside Twitter with Twitter Login or a Twitter button, they are still part of the 'Twitter ecosystem'.[22] Data about these website and app visits in the Twitter ecosystem flows back into the Twitter platform and is used to profile users based on the websites they have visited to suggest new people to follow who visit similar webpages. In other words, we might see how the activities of a diverse set of users, both inside as well as outside the platform's boundaries, afford back to the platform. Thus, a platform-sensitive approach to affordances should consider how a platform's infrastructure extends its affordances beyond its own environment and how they may be integrated in other platforms and services as well as how these activities afford back to the platform and its multiple users.

CONCLUSION

The notion of a platform-sensitive framework is meant to emphasize the specificity of platforms as socio-technological environments that draw different users together and which orchestrate the relations between different platform users. Such a perspective enables us to see how platforms may afford different things to various types of users, including end-users, developers and advertisers; and considers how they are connected through various possibilities for action. As demonstrated in our case study on two recent platform changes, the *like* provides distinct action possibilities for end-users (e.g., liking a tweet) and to advertisers (e.g., measuring engagement), enabling us to comprehend affordances *vis-à-vis* the economic underpinnings of platforms. In addition, we have emphasized how affordances extend across the boundaries of platforms and how both human and nonhuman users importantly afford something back to the platform. In the case of Twitter's new algorithmic timeline, it does not only afford end-users to receive relevant content first, but this relevance is in its turn established by those same end-users liking, replying and retweeting content, thereby affording things back to the algorithm and the platform. Thus, employing the concept of affordance to study social media requires explicating how the concept is used and considering the work it may do analytically. Furthermore, for the study of social media platforms, as we have argued throughout this chapter, we should take the specificity of platforms into account, which requires us to revisit earlier conceptualizations of affordance and to analyse critically how they may be employed or translated to platform environments.

Notes

1 https://twitter.com/twocitylife/status/661701885498294272
2 https://twitter.com/kumailn/status/661578296161800192
3 https://twitter.com/ForresterRobert/status/661568358651924480
4 https://twitter.com/deray/status/661597767052214272
5 https://twitter.com/room34/status/661627844422864896
6 https://twitter.com/peterseibel/status/661571212061990913
7 https://twitter.com/Longratter/status/661845126583590912
8 https://twitter.com/ultrabrilliant/status/661565224496009218
9 https://twitter.com/aisyahzaili/status/661637978360418304
10 We are not the first to propose a more complex understanding of the term. Gaver (1991) proposed notions of sequential and nested affordances, while McVeigh-Schultz and Baym (2015) suggest that affordances exist at various levels of abstraction, including: infrastructure, platforms and features.
11 https://developers.facebook.com/docs/marketing-apis
12 https://twitter.com/jack/status/20
13 http://knowyourmeme.com/memes/riptwitter
14 See Weltevrede (2016) on the notion of the 'research affordances' of social media platforms as enabled by APIs.
15 Twitter offers multiple APIs. Developers and researchers can employ the REST APIs for reading and writing Twitter data, and the Streaming APIs for accessing continuously updating or streaming Twitter data. Advertisers can employ the Ads APIs for integrating with Twitter advertising. See: https://dev.twitter.com/overview/documentation.
16 However, as of March 2011, Twitter started limiting the kind of third-party applications that could be built using its APIs, which has halted the growth of its rich developer ecosystem (Bucher, 2013). In October 2015, Twitter's CEO Jack Dorsey officially apologized to third-party developers and promised to improve its relationship with them (Lunden and Olanoff, 2015).
17 https://dev.twitter.com/ads/overview
18 https://partners.twitter.com/
19 https://business.twitter.com/help/how-twitter-ads-work
20 https://blog.twitter.com/2016/resilient-ad-serving-at-twitter-scale
21 http://blog.instagram.com/post/141107034797/160315-news
22 https://support.twitter.com/articles/20169421

REFERENCES

About your Twitter timeline (n.d.) *Twitter Help Center*. Available from: https://support.twitter.com/articles/164083 (accessed 10 February 2016).

Applied Machine Learning (n.d.) *Research at Facebook*. Available from: https://research.facebook.com/machinelearning (accessed 5 June 2016).

Aziz O and Paluri M (2016) Engineering for Nostalgia: Building a Personalized 'On This Day' Experience. *Facebook Code*. Available from: https://code.facebook.com/posts/1748968875380127/engineering-for-nostalgia-building-a-personalized-on-this-day-experience/ (accessed 5 June 2016).

Baym NK (2010) *Personal Connections in the Digital Age*. Cambridge, UK: Polity.

Boase J (2008) Personal Networks and the Personal Communication System. *Information, Communication & Society*, 11(4): 490–508.

Bodle R (2011) Regimes of Sharing. *Information, Communication & Society*, 14(3): 320–337.

Bogost I and Montfort N (2009) Platform Studies: Frequently Questioned Answers. In: *Proceedings of the Digital Arts and Culture Conference*. University of California, Irvine. Available from: http://escholarship.org/uc/item/01r0k9br.pdf (accessed 2 September 2012).

boyd danah (2011) Social Network Sites as Networked Publics: Affordances, Dynamics, and Implications. In: Z Papacharissi (ed.), *A Networked Self: Identity, Community, and Culture on Social Network Sites*. New York: Routledge, pp. 39–58.

Brandtzaeg PB and Haugstveit IM (2014) Facebook Likes: A Study of Liking Practices for Humanitarian Causes. *International Journal of Web Based Communities*, 10(3): 258–279.

Bruns A and Burgess J (2015) Twitter Hashtags from Ad Hoc to Calculated Publics. In: N Rambukkana (ed.), *Hashtag Publics: The Power and Politics of Discursive Networks*. New York: Peter Lang, pp. 13–28.

Bucher T (2013) Objects of Intense Feeling: The Case of the Twitter API. *Computational Culture* 3. Available from: http://computational-culture.net/article/objects-of-intense-feeling-the-case-of-the-twitter-api (accessed 6 May 2014).

Bucher T (2016) The Algorithmic Imaginary: Exploring the Ordinary Affects of Facebook Algorithms. *Information, Communication & Society*, 0(0): 1–15.

Burgess J (2015) Twitter (Probably) Isn't Dying, but is it Becoming Less Sociable? *Medium*. Available from: https://medium.com/dmrc-at-large/twitter-probably-isn-t-dying-but-is-it-becoming-less-sociable-d768a9968982#.jr4okd76o (accessed 20 May 2016).

Clifton D (2015) Why the Internet has no love for Twitter's 'like' button. *The Daily Dot*. Available from: https://www.dailydot.com/via/twitter-like-button-heart-star-favorite/ (accessed 22 June 2017).

Ellison NB and Vitak J (2015) Social Network Site Affordances and Their Relationship to Social Capital Processes. In: SS Sundar (ed.), *The Handbook of the Psychology of Communication Technology*. Boston, MA: Wiley-Blackwell, pp. 205–227.

Gaver WW (1991) Technology Affordances. In: *Proceedings of the SIGCHI Conference on Human Factors in Computing Systems*. New York: ACM, pp. 79–84. Available from: http://dl.acm.org/citation.cfm?id=108856 (accessed 20 January 2016).

Gaver WW (1996) Situating Action II: Affordances for Interaction: The Social is Material for Design. *Ecological Psychology*, 8(2): 111–129.

Gerlitz C and Helmond A (2013) The Like Economy: Social Buttons and the Data-intensive Web. *New Media & Society*, 15(8): 1348–1365.

Gibson JJ (1982) Notes on Affordances. In: *Reasons for Realism: Selected Essays of James J. Gibson*. London: Lawrence Erlbaum Associates, pp. 401–418.

Gibson JJ (2015) *The Ecological Approach to Visual Perception*. Classic Editions. New York: Psychology Press.

Gillespie T (2010) The Politics of 'Platforms'. *New Media & Society*, 12(3): 347–364.

Graves L (2007) The Affordances of Blogging: A Case Study in Culture and Technological Effects. *Journal of Communication Inquiry*, 31(4): 331–346.

Guy I, Ronen I, Zwerdling N, et al. (2016) What is Your Organization 'Like'? A Study of Liking Activity in the Enterprise. In: *CHI '16*, San Jose, CA: ACM. Available from: https://www.research.ibm.com/haifa/dept/imt/papers/Liking.pdf (accessed 24 March 2016).

Helles R (2013) Mobile Communication and Intermediality. *Mobile Media & Communication*, 1(1): 14–19.

Helmond A (2015) The Platformization of the Web: Making Web Data Platform Ready. *Social Media + Society*, 1(2). Available from: http://sms.sagepub.com/content/1/2/2056305115603080 (accessed 30 September 2015).

Heyman R (2016) Facebook & Users: Who is Using Who? A Material Semiotic Approach to the Irreversibilisation of Facebook as a Case of Lifeworld Colonisation by Social Media. PhD, Brussels, Belgium: Vrije Universiteit Brussel.

Hookway B (2014) *Interface*. Cambridge, MA: MIT Press.

Hsieh YP (2012) Online Social Networking Skills: The Social Affordances Approach to Digital Inequality. *First Monday*, 17(4). Available from: http://firstmonday.org/article/view/3893/3192 (accessed 20 January 2016).

Humphreys L (2005) Cellphones in Public: Social Interactions in a Wireless Era. *New Media & Society*, 7(6): 810–833.

Hutchby I (2001a) *Conversation and Technology: From the Telephone to the Internet*. Cambridge, UK: Polity Press.

Hutchby I (2001b) Technologies, Texts and Affordances. *Sociology*, 35(2): 441–456.

Hutchby I and Barnett S (2005) Aspects of the Sequential Organization of Mobile Phone Conversation. *Discourse Studies*, 7(2): 147–171.

Ilten C (2015) 'Use Your Skills to Solve This Challenge!': The Platform Affordances and Politics of Digital Microvolunteering. *Social Media + Society*, 1(2). Available from: http://sms.sagepub.com/content/1/2/2056305115604175 (accessed 11 February 2016).

Katz JE and Aakhus M (2002) *Perpetual Contact: Mobile Communication, Private Talk, Public Performance*. Cambridge, UK: Cambridge University Press.

Kumar A (2015) Hearts on Twitter. *Twitter Blogs*. Available from: https://blog.twitter.com/2015/hearts-on-twitter (accessed 27 November 2015).

Langlois G (2014) *Meaning in the Age of Social Media*. New York: Palgrave Macmillan US. Available from: http://link.springer.com/10.1057/9781137356611 (accessed 5 June 2016).

Latour B (2005) *Reassembling the Social: An Introduction to Actor-Network-Theory*. Oxford, UK: Oxford University Press.

Lidwell W, Holden K and Butler J (2010) *Universal Principles of Design, Revised and Updated: 125 Ways to Enhance Usability, Influence Perception, Increase Appeal, Make Better Design Decisions, and Teach through Design* (Second edition). Beverly: Rockport Publishers.

Lunden I and Olanoff D (2015) Twitter CEO Dorsey Apologizes to Developers, Says He Wants to 'Reset' Relations. *TechCrunch*. Available from: http://social.techcrunch.com/2015/10/21/twitter-ceo-dorsey-apologizes-to-developers-says-he-wants-to-reset-relations/ (accessed 5 April 2016).

MacManus R (2009) Favrd Shuts Down – Not Twitter's Last Laugh (Thank you, Textism). *ReadWrite*. Available from: http://readwrite.com/2009/12/06/favrd_shuts_down_show_goes_on_thank_you_textism (accessed 25 January 2016).

Maier JR, Fadel GM and Battisto DG (2009) An Affordance-based Approach to Architectural Theory, Design, and Practice. *Design Studies*, 30(4): 393–414.

McGrenere J and Ho W (2000) Affordances: Clarifying and Evolving a Concept. In: *Proceedings of Graphics Interface 2000*, Montréal, Québec, pp. 179–186. Available from: http://graphicsinterface.org/proceedings/gi2000/attachment/gi2000-24/ (accessed 20 January 2016).

McVeigh-Schultz J and Baym NK (2015) Thinking of You: Vernacular Affordance in the Context of the Microsocial Relationship App, Couple. *Social Media + Society*, 1(2). Available from: http://sms.sagepub.com/content/1/2/2056305115604649 (accessed 4 November 2015).

Meier F, Elsweiler D and Wilson ML (2014) More than Liking and Bookmarking? Towards Understanding Twitter Favouriting Behaviour. In: *ICWSM-14*, Ann Arbor, MI. Available from: www.cs.nott.ac.uk/~pszmw/pubs/icwsm2014-favouriting.pdf (accessed 27 November 2015).

Nagy P and Neff G (2015) Imagined Affordance: Reconstructing a Keyword for Communication Theory. *Social Media + Society*, 1(2). Available from: http://sms.sagepub.com/content/1/2/2056305115603385 (accessed 9 October 2015).

Newton C (2015) Twitter Officially Kills Off Favorites and Replaces Them with Likes. *The*

Verge. Available from: www.theverge. com/2015/11/3/9661180/twitter-vine-favorite-fav-likes-hearts (accessed 3 November 2015).

Norman D (1990) *The Design of Everyday Things*. New York: Doubleday Business.

Norman DA (1988) *The Psychology of Everyday Things*. New York: Basic Books.

Norman DA (1999) Affordance, Conventions, and Design. *Interactions*, 6(3): 38–43.

Paßmann J, Boeschoten T and Schäfer MT (2014) The Gift of the Gab. Retweets cartels and gift economies on Twitter. In: Weller K, Bruns A, Burgess J, et al. (eds), *Twitter and Society*, New York, NY: Peter Lang, pp. 331–344.

Postigo H (2016) The Socio-technical Architecture of Digital Labor: Converting Play into YouTube Money. *New Media & Society*, 18(2): 332–349.

Rochet J-C and Tirole J (2003) Platform Competition in Two-Sided Markets. *Journal of the European Economic Association*, 1(4): 990–1029.

Schrock AR (2015) Communicative Affordances of Mobile Media: Portability, Availability, Locatability, and Multimediality. *International Journal of Communication*, 9(0): 1229–1246.

Stanfill M (2015) The interface as discourse: The production of norms through web design. *New Media & Society* 17(7): 1059–1074.

Stone B (2006) Six More Twitter Updates! *Twitter Blogs*. Available from: https://blog.twitter. com/2006/six-more-twitter-updates (accessed 27 November 2015).

Styles K (2016) Twitter is 10 and It's Still Not a Social Network. *The Next Web*. Available from: http://thenextweb.com/opinion/2016/ 03/21/twitter-10-still-not-social-network/ (accessed 24 March 2016).

Sun H and Hart-Davidson WF (2014) Binding the Material and the Discursive with a Relational Approach of Affordances. In: *Proceedings of the 32nd Annual ACM Conference on Human Factors in Computing Systems*. New York: ACM, pp. 3533–3542. Available from: http:// dl.acm.org/citation.cfm?id=2557185 (accessed 20 January 2016).

Topolsky J (2016) The End of Twitter. *The New Yorker*. Available from: www.newyorker. com/tech/elements/the-end-of-twitter (accessed 24 March 2016).

Treem JW and Leonardi PM (2012) Social Media Use in Organizations: Exploring the Affordances of Visibility, Editability, Persistence, and Association. *Communication Yearbook*, 36: 143–189.

Tsukayama H (2016) The Death of Twitter as We Know It. *The Washington Post*, 11 February. Available from: www.washingtonpost. com/news/the-switch/wp/2016/02/11/the-death-of-twitter-as-we-know-it/ (accessed 24 March 2016).

Twitter Help Center (n.d.) FAQs about Tailored Suggestions. *Twitter Help Center*. Available from: https://support.twitter.com/articles/20169941 (accessed 15 March 2016).

Van Dijck J (2013) *The Culture of Connectivity: A Critical History of Social Media*. New York: Oxford University Press.

Van Dijck J and Poell T (2013) Understanding Social Media Logic. *Media and Communication*, 1(1): 2–14.

Wellman B (2001) Physical Place and Cyberplace: The Rise of Personalized Networking. *International Journal of Urban and Regional Research*, 25(2): 227–252.

Wellman B, Quan-Haase A, Boase J, et al. (2003) The Social Affordances of the Internet for Networked Individualism. *Journal of Computer-Mediated Communication*, 8(3). Available from: http://onlinelibrary.wiley. com/doi/10.1111/j.1083-6101.2003. tb00216.x/abstract (accessed 20 January 2016).

Weltevrede E (2016) Repurposing Digital Methods: The Research Affordances of Platforms and Engines. PhD, Amsterdam: University of Amsterdam. Available from: https://wiki.digitalmethods.net/Dmi/Repurposing-DigitalMethods (accessed 22 January 2016).

You H and Chen K (2007) Applications of Affordance and Semantics in Product Design. *Design Studies*, 28(1): 23–38.

Zheng Y and Yu A (2016) Affordances of Social Media in Collective Action: The Case of Free Lunch for Children in China. *Information Systems Journal*, 26(3): 289–313.

14

Regulation of and by Platforms

Tarleton Gillespie

Social media platforms rose up out of the exquisite chaos of the web. Their founders were inspired by or hoping to capitalize on the freedom it promised, while also hoping to provide spaces for the web's best and most social aspects. But as these platforms grew, that chaos and contention found its way back onto them – for obvious reasons: if I want to say something, whether inspiring or reprehensible, I want to say it where someone, maybe even everyone, might hear me. Today, we by and large speak on platforms when we're online. Social media platforms afford their users new opportunities to speak and interact with a wider range of people, organizing them into networked publics (boyd, 2011; Varnelis, 2008). Though the benefits of this may seem obvious, even seem utopian at times, the perils are also painfully apparent, more so every day: the pornographic, the obscene, the violent, the abusive, the illegal, and the hateful.

While scholars have long discussed the legal and political dynamics of speech online, much of that discussion preceded the dramatic move of so much of that speech onto social media platforms (Balkin, 2004; Godwin, 2003; Lessig, 1999; Litman, 1999). By *platforms*, I mean: sites and services that host, organize, and circulate users' shared content or social exchanges for them; without having produced or commissioned [the majority of] that content; beneath that circulation, an infrastructure for processing that data (content, traces, patterns of social relations) for customer service and for profit. This includes Facebook, YouTube, Twitter, Tumblr, Pinterest, Google+, Instagram, and Snapchat… but also Google Search and Bing, Apple App Store and Google Play, Medium and Blogger, Foursquare and Nextdoor, Tinder and Grindr, Etsy and Kickstarter, Whisper and Yik Yak. With this growing and increasingly powerful set of digital intermediaries, we have to revisit difficult questions about how they structure the speech and social activity they host, and what rights and responsibilities should accompany that

(DeNardis & Hackl, 2015; Gillespie, 2015; Grimmelman, 2015; MacKinnon et al., 2014; Obar & Wildman, 2015; van Dijck, 2013; Wagner, 2013).

Traditional private information providers – publishers, broadcasters, resellers, telecommunications – already have established legal obligations for the speech they facilitate, in the USA and elsewhere (Baker, 2001; Benkler, 1998; Braman, 2004; Entman & Wildman, 1992; Freedman, 2008; Hendershot, 1999; Horwitz, 1991a, 1991b; Streeter, 1996). But traditional communication policies have proven difficult to apply, honor, and enforce online (Bar & Sandvig, 2008; Braman, 2014; Castronova, 2015; Johnson & Post, 1996; Lessig, 1999; Tushnet, 2008). Even Internet-centric solutions formulated in an earlier moment, such as limited liability, safe harbor, and takedown measures for search engine and Internet Service Providers (ISPs), are arguably an ill fit for social media platforms (MacKinnon et al., 2014). Today, platforms face more vocal calls, from policymakers, from users, from foreign governments, from activists, and from the press, to both permit contentious speech and to curate it.

This essay begins with the governance *of* platforms: the laws and policies that have emerged in the past decade specifying their liabilities (or lack thereof) for the user content and activity they host. In the USA, these regulations are limited by a fundamental reluctance to constraint speech, whereas internationally, these same platforms face a wider array of restrictions. It will then consider the governance *by* platforms. This is related to the first, but is not the same. Social media platforms have increasingly taken on the responsibility of curating the content and policing the activity of their users: not simply to meet legal requirements, or to avoid having additional policies imposed, but also to avoid losing offended or harassed users, to placate advertisers eager to associate their brands with a healthy online community, to protect their corporate image, and to honor their own personal and institutional ethics.

Some of these interventions are welcomed by users, while others have been more contentious. The regulatory framework we impose on platforms, and the ways in which the major platforms enact those obligations and impose their own on their users, are settling in as the way public speech online is and will be privately governed.

REGULATION OF PLATFORMS

Platforms vary, in ways that matter both for the influence they can assert over users and for how they should be governed. It is deceptively easy in public debates, and in scholarship, to simply point accusingly at Facebook or Twitter and move on, without acknowledging the variety of purpose, scope, membership, economics, and design across the array of sites and services that call themselves platforms. In fact, 'platform' is a slippery term, in part because there may be little that unites different sites as a category, and in part because it gets deployed strategically, by stakeholders and critics alike (Gillespie, 2010). As shorthand, it too easily equates a site with the company that offers it, implies that social media companies act with one mind, and downplay the people involved. Platforms are socio-technical assemblages and complex institutions; they're not even all commercial, and the commercial ones are commercial in different ways. At the same time, 'platform' is a widely used term by the companies themselves. And many discourses of responsibility and liability (legal and otherwise) conceive of institutions as singular entities, and for good reason.

In the Middle

In the language of US information policy, 'platform' as a term has not enjoyed much traction. Most of the policies that currently apply to social media platforms were crafted before their emergence, to address a broader category of online services and access providers. The preferred term of art, 'online intermediaries,' which replaced an earlier and now archaic term, 'interactive computing services,' is broader. The Organization for Economic Co-operation and Development (OECD) definition helps highlight what's common to all these terms: 'Internet intermediaries bring together or facilitate transactions between third parties on the Internet. They give access to, host, transmit and index content, products and services originated by third parties on the Internet or provide Internet-based services to third parties' (OECD, 2010). The definition highlights two important aspects: (1) online intermediaries come between and facilitate the connection of others, and (2) the content they transmit is produced by others.

Contemporary social media platforms fit this category, but they also complicate it. They are not 'content producers' (though in practice they do produce lots of ancillary content along the way); rather, they host, store, organize, and circulate the content of others. While the hosting provided by platforms is more involved than that of ISPs, and the organizing of content provided by platforms is more involved than that of search engines, these differences are of degree more than of kind, given that all network services store and circulate content as part of their service, at least temporarily or incidentally.

By calling them intermediaries, let's recognize that social media platforms are fundamentally in the middle – that is, they mediate between users who produce content and users who might want it. This makes them similar to not only search engines and ISPs, but also traditional media. They too face a regulatory framework designed to oversee how they mediate between producers and audiences, between speakers and listeners.

Social media platforms are not only in the middle between user and user, and user and public, but between citizens and law enforcement, policymakers, and regulators charged with governing their behavior. Online, illicit activity can be difficult to pinpoint and difficult to police: users can enjoy the anonymity provided by some sites, and the obscurity provided by encryption and transient Internet connections; illicit content moves easily across regional jurisdictions and has oblique or cumulative effects. Since platforms gather people and collect traces of their activity, they present a compelling opportunity to policymakers to govern users through them. The regulation of platforms is marked by and struggles with this middle-ness, and the thorny questions of convenience and responsibility that come with it.[1]

Public and policy concerns around illicit content, at first largely focused on sexually explicit and graphically violent images, have expanded in recent years to include additional categories like hate speech, self-harm, and extremism; and to deal with the enormous problem of user behavior targeting other users, including misogynistic, racist, and homophobic attacks, trolling, harassment, and threats of violence. Questions about the responsibility of platforms are also expanding as the range of platforms expand: to social platforms that circulate goods (auction sites like eBay, exchange sites like Craigslist, and e-commerce platforms like Etsy), that circulate money or investment (Kiva, Venmo), that circulate labor (Amazon Mechanical Turk, Uber, Taskrabbit), or that trade access to physical services (AirBnB). Each of these intersects with other regulatory frameworks, but each also includes fundamental questions about whether and how platforms should be responsible for their (independent, amateur, non-salaried) users' speech and actions.

The Myth of the Impartial Platform

Social media platforms have long framed themselves as open, impartial, and noninterventionist – in part because their founders fundamentally believe it to be so, and in part to avoid liability and regulation. This fundamental mystification of the role of platforms began when platforms did: from the start they have often characterized themselves as open to all comers; in their promotional discourse they often suggest that they merely facilitate public expression, that they are impartial and hands-off hosts, with an 'information will be free' ethos, and that being so is central to their mission (Gillespie, 2010; Vaidhyanathan, 2011). Though users seem to be recognizing that platforms intervene in myriad ways and are growing increasingly concerned about it, platforms continue to perform their impartiality.

This is odd, considering that, from a different view, everything on a platform is designed and orchestrated. While social activity would exist without Facebook or Twitter, the kind of social activities that occur there depends powerfully on the space and structure they provide (Baym & boyd, 2012; Bruns and Burgess, 2015; Couldry & van Dijck, 2015; Gerlitz & Helmond, 2013; Langlois, 2013; Sandvig, 2015; Shepherd & Landry, 2013; van Dijck, 2013; Weltevrede et al., 2014). Platforms don't just mediate public discourse, they constitute it. They are designed to invite and shape participation, toward particular ends. This includes what kind of participation they invite and encourage; what gets displayed first or most prominently; how navigation tools direct the movement of users and content; how revenue models impose price mechanisms; and how they organize information through algorithmic sorting, privileging some content over others, in opaque ways. And it includes what is not permitted, and how and why that prohibition is enforced (Gillespie, 2015; Grimmelmann, 2015).

The Rise of Safe Harbor

In the mid-1990s, policymakers in the USA and elsewhere became aware of growing concerns about the proliferation of illicit content on the web, especially pornography and piracy.[2] In such cases, it proved difficult to directly pursue online 'publishers' for their illegal or illicit behavior, particularly when those publishers were individuals, usually amateurs, sometimes anonymous, and hard to locate and identify. Because of this, some lawsuits brought in the USA for defamation, publication of private documents, and the distribution of hate speech, began targeting not the individual user but the Internet service provider disseminating the content (Ardia, 2010; Kreimer, 2006; Mann & Belzley, 2005).

In the United States, Congress crafted its first legislative response to some of these issues, the Communication Decency Act (CDA), as part of a massive telecommunications bill. Passed in 1996, the CDA made it a criminal act to display or distribute 'obscene or indecent' material to minors. (It also imposed similar penalties for harassing or threatening someone online.) The law was ruled unconstitutional[3] by the Supreme Court only a year later. However, parts of the law survived, including the defenses it provided for 'interactive computer service providers' – safe harbors against any liability for harmful material their users might provide. Because these safe harbors were not at issue in the Supreme Court decision, they have remained a part of US telecommunication law, known as Section 230.

The Section 230 safe harbor has two parts (Mueller, 2015). The first assures that intermediaries cannot be held liable for the speech of their users, since they merely provide access to the Internet or other network services; they will not be considered 'publishers' of their users' content, in the legal sense. The implication was that, like the telephone company, intermediaries do not need to police what their users say and do. The second, less familiar part adds a twist: if an intermediary *does* decide to police what their users say or do, it does not lose its safe harbor protection by doing so. In other words, choosing to delete some content does not suddenly make them 'publishers,' nor does it require them to meet some standard of effective policing. This second half was crafted so that the safe harbor would not create legal jeopardy for intermediaries that chose to moderate in good faith, by making them no more liable for it than if they had simply turned a blind eye.

Section 230 extends a legislative distinction common to US telecommunication law, between publishers who *produce* information (and therefore can be held liable for it) and distributors that merely *circulate* the information of others (and should not) – commonly known as the 'content/conduit' distinction. Since ISPs offered 'access' to the Internet, and did not produce the content they help circulate, the law prioritizes the free movement of information, and limited their liability for the content users circulated through them.[4] As with telephone systems, holding a provider liable for what users say or do might encourage that provider to monitor users proactively and shut down anything that looked risky. This would be not only practically impossible and financially unbearable,[5] but also politically undesirable. Legislators and technologists feared that this might also discourage online innovation, as new ISPs or interactive computer services might not dare enter the market if the immediate legal risks were too costly (Center for Democracy and Technology (CDT), 2010).

Outside the USA, few nations offer the robust safe harbor provided in Section 230. MacKinnon et al. (2014: 42) dub the American approach 'broad immunity,' the most lenient of three types of intermediary liability regimes they identify. Most of the European Union nations, as well as Russia and most South American nations, offer intermediaries 'conditional liability,' which is more akin to the American rules for copyright. Platforms are not liable for what their users post or distribute, as long as they have no 'actual knowledge' of, and did not produce or initiate the illegal or illicit material, and they must respond to requests from the state or the courts to remove illicit third-party content.

China and many of the nations in the Middle East impose 'strict liability' (MacKinnon et al., 2014: 40), requiring Internet intermediaries to prevent the circulation of illicit or unlawful content. This generally means proactively removing or censoring, often in direct cooperation with the government. Without a regulatory bulwark against state intervention, these private actors are much more beholden to government demands, and in some cases even rules that prohibit political speech. Finally, some nations, for example in sub-Saharan Africa, have not instituted laws articulating the responsibilities of Internet intermediaries in any form, leaving intermediaries there uncertain about what they might or might not be liable for (MacKinnon et al., 2014: 52).

But while it is the most generous, even American safe harbor for intermediaries embodies conflicting views of online service providers (OSPs). As Mueller (2015: 805) writes, Section 230

> was intended both to immunize OSPs who did nothing to restrict or censor their users' communications, and to immunize OSPs who took some effort to discourage or restrict online pornography and other forms of undesirable content. Intermediaries who did nothing were immunized in order to promote freedom of expression and diversity online; intermediaries who were more active in managing user-generated content were immunized in order to enhance their ability to delete or otherwise monitor 'bad' content.

These competing impulses, between allowing intermediaries to stay out of the way and encouraging them to police their users, continue to shape the way we think about the role and responsibility of Internet intermediaries, and has extended to how we regulate social media platforms.

The Pressures on Safe Harbor

From a legal standpoint, broad and conditional safe harbors are profoundly advantageous for Internet intermediaries. Notice-and-takedown requirements generate real challenges for platforms, and are prone to abuse, but are far preferable for platforms than being held liable for what their users post (Urban et al., 2016). As Tushnet (2008: 1002) notes, 'Current law often allows Internet intermediaries to have their free speech and everyone else's too.' However, while safe harbor provisions have held up for two decades, three distinct challenges are revealing the limitations of the safe harbor provision, and in some cases are fueling calls for its reconsideration.

First and perhaps most obviously, most of these laws were not designed with social media platforms in mind. When Section 230 was being crafted, few such platforms existed. US lawmakers were addressing a web largely populated by ISPs and amateur web 'publishers' – amateurs posting home pages, companies designing websites, and online communities having discussions. Besides ISPs who simply provided access to the network, the only intermediaries at the time were ISPs that doubled as content 'portals,' like AOL and Prodigy; the earliest search engines like Altavista and Yahoo; and operators of bulletin board systems (BBS), chatrooms, and newsgroups. The law predates not just Facebook, but MySpace, Friendster, and Livejournal; not just YouTube, but Veoh and Metacafe; not just Soundcloud, but Last. fm and Lala, and Napster and its peer-to-peer brethren; even Google. Blogging was in its infancy, well before the invention of large-scale blog hosting services like Blogspot and Wordpress; eBay, Craigslist, and Match.com were less than a year old; and the ability to comment on a web page had not yet been modularized into a plugin.

Although they were not anticipated by the law, social media platforms have generally claimed that they enjoy its safe harbor. But many of the assumptions that animated intermediary liability (particularly the questions of whether the intermediary has knowledge of illicit content, could conceivably intervene in its circulation, and benefits financially from it) are tested by contemporary social media platforms. US regulatory traditions, such as protecting 'conduits' from liability so they are not encouraged to monitor or censor the content traveling through them, are an ill fit for YouTube's ContentID (which can automatically identify copyrighted music in user-submitted videos) or Facebook's NewsFeed algorithm (which constructs a curated feed from user posts designed to keep users interested and attentive to advertising) or the anonymous attacks possible with Yik Yak.

Second, while intermediary liability regimes are typically bound by nation or region, platforms largely are not. ISPs are almost exclusively located in the nation in which regulation is imposed and enforced, both in terms of the (physical and legal) location of the company, its material infrastructure, and its users. This is not the case for the likes of Twitter, Instagram, or Wikipedia. Most of the major social media platforms are, as corporate and legal entities, based in the United States, where they enjoy the broadest safe harbor, but they serve millions of users living in nations that impose much stricter liability or have specific requirements for responding to state or court requests to remove content.

Major social media platforms have had to develop their own policies on how to respond to requests from foreign governments to remove content. Google famously pulled out of China rather than filter its search results according to Chinese dictates (although there were certainly a variety of motivations for the move).[6] LinkedIn remained, by honoring the Chinese government's policies and seeking financial investment from Chinese firms.[7] Twitter removes tweets in response to government requests, but does so only for users in that nation rather than removing them from the entire service, and will indicate what has been removed and at whose behest.[8] Many of the major platforms publish data on the number of removal requests they receive, by country and by category of request. Some have even included 'warrant canaries' in their policy statements, a sentence stating that no government subpoenas had been served –

which they would remove when it was no longer true, alerting those in the know that a subpoena had been served without violating a gag order.

Because Western platforms have been cautious about how they respond to removal requests from foreign governments, some nations have threatened to block content they deem illegal or offensive. China and the Islamic nations of the Middle East and North Africa have been most aggressive in this tactic. This typically involves providing local ISPs with a 'blacklist' of pages deemed criminal or otherwise unacceptable. This is more complicated, of course, on massive platforms such as social networking sites and discussion platforms, where the offending post or video is just one element of a massive, complex, and constantly changing database. As Palfrey (2010) observes, this can result in 'overfiltering,' where a nation will threaten to block not a single YouTube video or Facebook user, but YouTube or Facebook in its entirety. What often follows is a high-stakes game of chicken: platforms do not relish being entirely blocked from an entire nation of users; at the same time, doing so is risky for the government as well, as it may have costs in terms of public sentiment. For countries with a stronger commitment to freedom of expression or independent telecommunications, this tendency to block legitimate content along with the offensive is an unpalatable one, but others may justify it as a bulwark against an unwelcome intrusion of Western culture and values.

Third, a slow reconsideration of platform responsibility has been spurred by categories of content particularly abhorrent to users and governments. These hesitations are happening in all corners of the world: even US policy, with the broadest safe harbor, has shifted in the face of specific concerns.

Most pressing has been, unsurprisingly, the issue of terrorism. Certainly, terrorist organizations have grown increasingly savvy in the use of social media platforms (Archetti, 2015).[9] At the same time, combatting

terrorism is a compelling justification for the imposition of policies that may have other political aims (MacKinnon, 2012). Even in the United States, where the ethos of the First Amendment typically provides information providers a powerful shield against government intrusion, terrorism can be an effective rhetorical counterargument. As ISIS and other extremist groups have taken to distributing gruesome beheading videos and glossy recruitment propaganda on YouTube and Twitter, and more quietly coordinated with supporters and looked to radicalize the disaffected, pressure from Western governments on social media to "crack down" on terrorist organizations has grown.

In Europe, this has meant an increasing expectation that platforms, once informed of terrorist content, must remove it quickly. Under the UK Terrorism Act of 2006, platforms have only two days to comply with a takedown request, otherwise they are deemed to have 'endorsed' the terrorist content.[10] Others have called for imposing fines on platforms for failing to remove terrorist materials, compelling them to cooperate more readily with police investigating terrorist incidents, and requiring them to share data with counterterrorist investigators. Several governments in the Middle East have instituted new anti-terrorism laws (or attempted to) that affect platforms. In Egypt, for example, a law drafted in 2014 gave authorities much wider latitude to intervene in and surveil online communication for suspected terrorist activity. Similar laws have been passed in Jordan, Qatar, and Saudi Arabia.[11] And in the United States, several lawsuits have been brought, though none have succeeded thus far, against Twitter or Facebook for providing "material support" to terrorist organizations, by the families of victims of terrorist attacks.

Hate speech and racial discrimination have also fueled debates about the obligations of social media platforms, particularly in Europe. Germany and France both have laws prohibiting the promotion of Nazism, anti-Semitism, and white supremacy. The French law produced one of the earliest online content cases, in which Yahoo was compelled to prevent French users from accessing online auctions of Nazi memorabilia.[12] More recently, when anti-Semitic comments began appearing on Twitter under the hashtag #unbonjuif, or 'a good Jew,' French courts pressed Twitter to turn over the user data behind the offending tweets (Mackinnon et al., 2014). Similar concerns have emerged in other parts of the world. In Argentina, in addition to their anti-discrimination law was considered that would require intermediaries to monitor and remove comments that were racist or discriminatory, and would even encourage them to remove the comment features of their sites entirely.[13]

Nations that do not share the American version of freedom of expression have been more willing to criminalize speech that criticizes the government or upsets public order. Some nations are limiting press freedoms for bloggers and amateur speech on social media platforms. Laws that curtail the press online have appeared in Egypt, Iran, Pakistan, Tunisia, and the United Arab Emirates.[14] In other nations, including Kuwait and Lebanon, laws that prohibit the disruption of public order have been applied to political activists.[15] Some countries prohibit speech directly criticizing their leaders, and in some cases these rules have been extended to social media platforms. In 2012, authorities in Brazil arrested the head of Google Brazil for refusing to remove YouTube videos that targeted Brazilian political candidates,[16] and Facebook now complies with Turkish law criminalizing defamation of the country's founder Mustafa Kemal Ataturk, or the burning of the Turkish flag, by removing any such content flagged by users.[17] Facebook works with Pakistan to remove online blasphemy, with Vietnam to remove anti-government content, and with Thailand to remove criticism of the royal family.

Other countries have used laws that exist purportedly to combat cybercrime, protect children, or prohibit terrorist content, to pressure platforms to remove politically contentious materials. Russia has been the innovator in this regard. In 2009, Russian law held that website owners are responsible for what users post in the comments on their site. In 2012, they developed a 'blacklist' of sites that include 'forbidden information' (illicit drugs, porn, suicide), requiring Russian ISPs to block these sites. ISPs were forced to respond to requests not only from the court or state regulatory authorities but also from regular citizens, including the 'Media Guard' youth group, which targeted gay teen forums and Ukrainian political organizations.[18] In 2014, the Russian government took a bolder step: a new dictate would require transnational platforms that have Russian users to store those users' data on servers located physically in Russia – otherwise, the whole platform would be blocked nationwide.[19] The revelations of National Security Agency (NSA) surveillance by Edward Snowden were the nominal justification, but many suspected that housing the data inside Russia's borders would make it easier for the government to access that data and squelch political speech. As of this writing, the (mostly US-based) platforms have refused, and Russia has extended the deadline for compliance. In addition, in 2015 Russia decreed that bloggers with more than 3,000 page views per day must register as media and follow Russian media laws. Though unclear, this seems to include users with over 3,000 daily visitors on Twitter and Facebook.[20]

The United States has by and large stayed true to the safe harbor protections first offered to online intermediaries. But growing concerns about terrorism and extremist content, harassment and cyber bullying, and the circulation of non-consensual pornography (commonly known as 'revenge porn') have tested this commitment. A number of platforms have developed specific policies prohibiting revenge porn,[21] modeled on the notice-and-takedown arrangements in copyright law: platforms are not obligated to proactively look for violations, but will respond to requests to remove them. This involves the kind of adjudicating platforms prefer to avoid: determining whether a complainant (who may not even be a user of that platform) is in fact the subject of the video or photo, whether the material was posted with or without the subject's consent, who owns the imagery and thus the right to circulate it, and so forth. In early 2016, the Obama administration urged US tech companies to develop new strategies for identifying extremist content, either to remove it or to report it to national security authorities.[22] Around harassment, pressure is coming from users, particularly women and racial minorities, who argue that the abuses have become so unbearable that platforms have an obligation to intervene (Kayyali and O'Brien, 2015; Matias et al., 2015).

Together, these calls to hold platforms liable for specific kinds of abhorrent content or behavior, and the increasing challenges posed by governments seeking to use platforms as a way to constrain political speech and activism, are undercutting the once sturdy principle of safe harbor articulated in Section 230 and elsewhere. As these platforms multiply in form and purpose, become more and more central to how and where users encounter each other online, and involve themselves in the circulation of not just words and images but goods, money, services, and labor, intermediary liability seems more and more insufficient. Platforms face both more vocal calls to permit contentious speech *and* more compelling reasons to curate it – not just under pressure from laws, but of their own accord.

REGULATION BY PLATFORMS

Social media platforms are eager to keep the safe harbor protections enshrined in Section 230. But at this point, all of them are taking advantage of the second half of its protection: nearly all platforms impose their own rules, and police their sites for offending content and behavior. In fact, their ceaseless and systematic interventions cut much deeper than the law requires. Both in terms of their impact on public discourse, and for the lived experience of its users, the rules these platforms impose themselves probably matter more than the legal restrictions under which they function. So, while part of the question must be how platforms are governed, an equally important question is how platforms govern (Citron, 2014; DeNardis & Hackl, 2015; Gillespie, 2015; Grimmelmann, 2015; Humphreys, 2013; Jeong, 2015; MacKinnon et al., 2014; Matias et al., 2015; Obar & Wildman, 2015; Reagle, 2015; Roth, 2015; Stein, 2013; van Dijck, 2013; Wagner, 2013).

There are clear reasons why social media platforms, though not legally required to do so, police the content of their sites and the behavior of their users – mostly economic reasons, though not exclusively so. Troubling content like pornography and graphic violence may scare off wary advertisers, who are not keen to see their products paired with an X-rated video or a xenophobic rant. Platforms worry about users leaving if they're overwhelmed by porn or trolls. No matter how successful or established or near-monopolistic, platforms all fear users flocking en masse to a competitor. While the major platforms have developed clever ways to keep users within their ecosystem, they remain haunted by the fact that alternatives are "just one click away." A graveyard of past social media services like MySpace and Digg linger in their discussions as cautionary tales, of how a successful platform can collapse when users decide that it is not serving their interests or that a better alternative exists. And, the content and behavior users may find perfectly acceptable does not always fit neatly with the platforms' effort to protect its public brand. Revisions of site policies often occur when a new company purchases a platform and struggles to incorporate its permissive ethos amid its other services.[23]

But even here, platforms face a double-edged sword: too little curation, and users may leave to avoid the toxic environment that has taken hold; too much moderation, and users may still go, either because what was promised to be an open platform feels too intrusive or too antiseptic. This is especially true as platforms seek to expand their user base: platforms typically begin with users who are more homogenous, share the goal of protecting and nurturing the platform, and who may be able to solve some tensions through informal means; as their user base broadens it also diversifies, and platforms find themselves hosting users and whole communities with very different value systems, and who look to the platform to police content and resolve disputes. And to be fair, these economic considerations are always intertwined with other kinds: the deeply felt commitment of the platform operators for nurturing a healthy community or encouraging the best creative output of their users; a sense of public obligation, especially as a platform grows and exerts greater influence on the public landscape; and in the face of criticism leveled by angry users, journalists, or activists.

These platforms must constantly police the pornographic, the harassing, and the obscene. There is no avoiding it entirely. But doing so can be a politically fraught exercise, particularly when the politics of visibility is involved (Bakardjieva, 2009; Couldry, 2015; Dahlberg, 2007; Gray, 2009; Gross, 2002; Thompson, 2005). I mean 'visibility' in the sense that groups seeking legitimacy sometimes struggle politically simply to be seen, against the wishes of those who would marginalize and silence them, such as around the issue of gay rights or public breastfeeding; visibility in the sense that some kinds of antagonism between groups go unnoticed or uncommented on, such as the culture of violence against women; visibility in the sense that one group's speech is silenced as potentially dangerous to others, as in fundamentalist Islamic propaganda; and visibility in the sense that some kinds of images are seen as potentially dangerous to those who choose to consume them, such as 'self-harm' images that may support anorexic, cutting, or suicidal behavior. I do not mean to equate these efforts. But they all, in some form or another and for very different ends, seek to be rendered visible, in places where visibility can be a step towards legibility and legitimacy. Sometimes visibility is not just a political accomplishment, but one that must also overcome the mechanics and governance of the medium through which they hope to appear (Bucher, 2012; Milan, 2015; Thompson, 2005).

With these unavoidable and perhaps unsolvable contentious politics increasingly inhabiting their sites, social media platforms have not only had to develop and refine their rules and develop more sophisticated means of policing their sites. They have also had to develop their own logics underpinning how and why they intervene. This is not to suggest that their policies are always conceptually coherent, in principle or in application; most have developed over time, often in an *ad hoc* fashion, often after having to face a contentious issue they were unprepared for. But out of each site composing this or that rule out of this or that thought process, there are certain kinds of approaches that seem to have coalesced.

Where the Lines are Drawn

When it comes to the specifics, the guidelines at the prominent, general-purpose platforms are strikingly similar. This makes sense: these platforms encounter many of the same kinds of problematic content and behavior, they look to each other for guidance on how to address them, and they are situated together in a longer history of speech regulation that offers well-worn signposts on how and why to intervene. Most have some rule prohibiting or limiting the following:

- sexual content and pornography
- representations of violence and obscenity

- harassment of other users
- hate speech
- representations of or promotion of self-harm
- representations of or promotion of illegal activity, particularly drug use.

Additionally, some platforms have rules about using a 'real' identity, or about what can and cannot be done under the cloak of anonymity. Some include advice or pointers for ensuring the smooth working of the site and the quality of its offerings. And some prohibit certain forms of commercial activity and self-promotion. Platforms differ on how they draw each of these lines, what kind of caveats they are willing to consider, and what kinds of consequences are leveled against offenders.

One might dismiss these guidelines as mere window dressing – performances of principles, ringing so clear and reasonable, that do not in fact have much to do with the actual enforcement of policy on the site, which can often be more slapdash, strategic, or hypocritical. I find it more convincing to say that these are statements of both policy and principle – struggled over by the platform operators at some moments and ignored at others, deployed when they are helpful and sidestepped when they are constraining. They do important discursive work, performing but also revealing how platforms see themselves as ambivalent arbiters of public propriety. These guidelines matter, not only when they are enforced, and not only to lend strength to the particular norms they represent. Platforms adjust their guidelines in relation to each other, and smaller sites look to the larger ones for guidance, sometimes borrowing language and policies wholesale. They perform, and therefore reveal in oblique ways, how platforms see themselves as public arbiters of cultural value. They are also by no means the end of the story, as no guidelines in the abstract could possibly line up neatly with how they are enforced in practice.

Looking at these guidelines together, it is clear that these platforms develop rules not just in anticipation of inappropriate content and activity, but in response to it. They undergo a routinized internal process: content policy teams must from time to time decide how to translate a new legal obligation into an actionable rule, react to the emergence of a category of content they would like to curtail, and respond to surges of complaints from users. Unanticipated kinds of content or behavior may be spotted first through the complaints of users, then formalized into new rules or written into existing ones. And changes can also come in response to outcries and public controversies. In these guidelines, we can see the scars of past challenges.

Enforcement and the Problem of Scale

While the law invited early platforms to enjoy a hands-off safe harbor like ISPs and other conduits, the operators of early platforms were also steeped in the tradition of online community management. In the early days of the web, while ISPs were fending off liability for pornography and copyright infringement, online communities quickly discovered that communities need care: they had to address the challenges of interpersonal conflict and obscene speech, and develop forms of governance that protected their community and embodied democratic procedures that matched their values and the values of their users. Community management was often the work of volunteers, either the webmaster or site manager, or participants in the communities who took on the role of moderation themselves (Postigo, 2009). Sometimes moderation emerged in response to a shock to the community: when, for example, a troll first dramatically disrupts a community that had, perhaps naively, assumed that everyone wanted the same things, and thus required no governance at all (Dibbell, 1993). Community management has taken many forms, perhaps as many forms as there were online communities:

from the benevolent tyranny of a webmaster, to public arbitration among an entire community, to *ad hoc* councils appointed to determine policies and dole out punishments. As communities grew and changed over time, new members and new conflicts challenged these forms of governance (Bergstrom, 2011; Kerr & Kelleher, 2015; Lampe et al., 2014; Shaw and Hill, 2014); sometimes they adjusted, sometimes the groups faltered and people moved on.

Such moderation persists in the contemporary equivalents of online communities. Many of the operators of early platforms were also steeped in the tradition of online community management, the set of practices and knowledges that emerged out of maintaining these online communities over time and in the face of growth, change, and challenge. But the key reason these approaches are ill-suited to social media platforms is scale. The moderation of online communities depended on community members who knew the webmaster, regulars who knew each other, and a history of interactions that provided the familiarity and trust necessary for a moderator to arbitrate when members disagreed.[24] Tough cases could be debated as a collective, policies could be weighed and changed together. This was the scale of the forum, rather than the *demos* (Forsyth, 2016). Some social media platforms that began at this scale continue to pursue forms of community moderation by retaining some structural form of groups within the platform. For instance, Reddit depends on volunteers to moderate particular subreddits, and Facebook expects the managers of a Facebook Group to moderate it (although the site will also respond to complaints about Groups just as it does any other kind of content). But as these platforms have grown in scale and ambition, the scale necessary for community moderation has become increasingly untenable.

In addition, on large-scale platforms there is simply too much content and activity being posted to support a proactive review process, where a moderator would examine each contribution before it appeared on the site. Apple is a notable exception, in that it reviews every iPhone app before making it available in their app store; but Apple fields hundreds of submissions a day, not hundreds of thousands. And it has certainly come under fire for failures in judgment, both for apps they rejected and ones they approved (Hestres, 2013). Nearly all platforms must embrace a 'publish-then-filter' (Shirky, 2008) approach: user posts are immediately public, without review, and platforms can remove questionable content only after the fact.[25] This means that even heinous content may get published, at least briefly, and criminal behavior may occur (and have its intended impact) before anything is done in response. Plenty of content that violates site guidelines remains online for days, or years, because of the sheer challenge of policing platforms as immense as these.

The approaches social media platforms take, not just to content moderation but to all the ways they manage information, are tied to this immense scale. Content is policed at scale, and most complaints are fielded at scale. More importantly, their understanding of the problems has been formed and shaped by working at this scale. What to do with a questionable photo or bad actor changes when you're facing not one violation but hundreds exactly like it and thousands much like it, but slightly different in a thousand ways. This is not just a difference of size; it is fundamentally a different problem. For large-scale platforms, moderation is industrial, not artisanal.

This raises a legal question, in that it is arguably impossible for a platform to assure that no illegal content or behavior will appear there. Section 230 answers this very well; any regime that replaced it would have to grapple with this challenge. And it raises an ethical challenge, in that users cannot avoid obscenity or be protected from harassers with complete certainty. I say it is arguably impossible because the resources that could be put toward this effort are limited only by convention. We can't imagine a platform employing enough people to review every piece of content before it is posted, but in principle they could; and given current expectations, users would probably be unwilling to accept the delay this would impose on their status updates and shared photos. These constraints are, in fact, movable. The Chinese government, for instance, employs hundreds of thousands of people to scour social media for political criticism and blocks many websites and keyword searches automatically.[26] I am not suggesting that China's approach is in any way ideal, nor that social media contributions should queue up to wait for publication. I am only noting that what counts as impossible only appears so to U.S. users. In the West, we accept that platforms cannot review content before it is posted, reject the delay that would impose, and yet also demand that platforms respond quickly and consistently to our complaints. In lieu of shifting these expectations themselves, social media platforms must accomplish the work of moderation within these limits.

The Human Labor of Content Moderation

Large-scale social media platforms have developed intricate and complex systems for conducting content moderation at scale. This requires immense human resources, if not at quite the Chinese scale.[27] These people generally labor in obscurity, some set at a distance from the platforms and its internal aims, and often with little oversight. And each layer of moderation introduces an element of ambiguity and potential bias into what remains a largely opaque process (Roberts, 2016).

At the top, most platforms have an internal policy team charged with overseeing moderation. They set the rules, oversee their enforcement, adjudicate the particularly hard cases, and craft new policies in response. These are, by and large, small teams, often just a

handful of full-time employees. At a few platforms they are an independent division, while at others they sit under the umbrella of 'trust and safety,' 'community outreach,' customer service, or technical support. At others, setting policy and addressing hard cases is handled in a more ad hoc way, by the leadership with advice from legal counsel; an engineer may find themselves asked to weigh in on what counts as harassment or stalking, in their spare time.[28] These groups are obscure to users, by design and policy. They are difficult for users to reach, and the statements and policy changes they generate are often released in the voice of the company itself. All together they are a surprisingly small community of people, based overwhelmingly in the San Francisco area, and individuals tend to move from platform to platform in their career.[29] At the scale at which most platforms operate, these internal teams would be insufficient by themselves. Still, they have an outsized influence on where the lines are drawn, what kinds of punishments are enforced, and the philosophical approach the team and the platforms take to governance itself.

At many companies, there is a substantially larger group of people who provide a frontline review of specific content and incidents beneath the internal moderation team. They might be employed by the platform, at the home office or in satellite offices around the world in places like Dublin and Hyderabad. But more and more commonly they are employed on a contract basis: as independent contractors through third-party 'temp' companies, or as on-demand labor employed through crowdwork services such as Amazon's Mechanical Turk, Upwork, or TaskUs – or both, in a two-tiered system.[30] These clickworkers are obscured, both intentionally and by circumstance. Many are in parts of the world where labor is cheap, especially the Philippines and India, far from both the platform and the users they are moderating; they are also distanced from the company through contract labor arrangements and the intervening interfaces of the crowdwork platforms that employ them and organize their labor.[31]

These clickworkers are used as a first response team, fielding complaints from users and making quick decisions as to how to respond. Quick can mean seconds per complaint, which means each user is getting very little attention, and clickworker moderators are facing a torrent of atrocities.[32] Most complaints are now fielded as a matter of course; only the most difficult to judge are directed up to the internal content team for further deliberation. Moderators are generally unaware of the identity of the user, and provided little of the surrounding context – the back and forth of a conversation, that user's previous posts, etc. Users may expect these judgments to weigh competing values, show cultural sensitivity, and appear to the user as fair and consistent. Instead, they are being distilled from their meaningful context and rushed under the pressure to be responsive to an enormous and endless queue of complaints. Some are beginning to worry about the psychological toll of this work: a lawsuit was recently brought against Microsoft by two content moderators suffering from post-traumatic stress since their work reviewing gruesome images and violent posts.[33]

Some sites continue to depend on community moderators in some form. Reddit, for instance, has smaller, persistent 'subreddits' that exist within the larger platform, each overseen by moderators, and Wikipedia has an 'administrator' class of superusers who do other kinds of back-end work on the platform. Facebook Groups give the founder of the group limited powers to include and exclude users, delete comments, etc. These community moderators are usually volunteers and thus independent of the platform itself, with their own commitment to the group for which they are responsible. They may be enforcing rules that were generated by and consented to by the community, with their help, making enforcement easier. On the other hand, they are typically volunteers, usually uncompensated and often underappreciated. In most cases, these moderators are given tools by the platform that make possible the enforcement of group policies, such as the ability to delete content or suspend users. Typically they do not have the authority to extend any punitive consequences beyond the group they're responsible for – they can ban a user from their specific group, but not from the entire platform – which significantly limits their scope, and allows troublemakers to move across groups and platforms with near impunity.In a tenuous position in relationship to the platform, such moderators are often overworked but undersupported, provided a weak mandate for the role they're expected to play, sometimes invited backstage and sometimes held at arms-length.[34]

Enormous platforms face an enormous moderation project, but they also have an enormous resource close at hand: users themselves. Most platforms now invite users to "flag" problematic content and behavior, generating a queue of complaints that can be fed to the platform moderators – typically, to its army of crowdworkers first – to adjudicate. And some give users tools to rate and block content, and designs mechanisms into the system to filter content towards those who want to see it, and away from those who don't. The implications of these two models are important, and I will address them in a moment. But in terms of a labor force, both depend on the crowd to police itself, though the populations on which they depend and the dilemmas each must grapple with are different.

Flagging is now widespread across social media platforms, and has settled in as a norm in the logic of the social media interface, alongside favoriting and reposting. A small icon or link beneath a post, image, or video offers the user a pull-down menu facilitating their complaint, often with submenus to classify the nature of the offense. In the earliest days of contemporary platforms, such mechanisms were nonexistent or buried in the help pages. Platforms have since made it easier and easier to find these flags, though in some cases criticism has dogged specific platforms for these mechanisms being inadequate.

On the one hand, flagging puts the work of complaining right at the point of offense, in front of those most motivated to complain. On the other hand, it is optional. This means that the population of users who deputize themselves to flag content are those most motivated to do so. Platforms also describe flagging as an expression of the community. But are the users who flag 'representative' of the larger user base, and what does it mean for the legitimacy of the system if they're not? Who flags, and why, is very hard to know. Platforms are tight-lipped about how many users flag, what percentage of those who do flag provide the most flags, how often the platform decided to remove or retain content that's been flagged, etc. (Crawford and Gillespie, 2016).

Recently, some platforms have experimented with granting some users the status of 'superflagger,' prioritizing their flags over others. These users might be law enforcement organizations, activist organizations concerned with a specific kind of violation or protecting a specific population of users, or long-time users who are recognized as reliable. Generally, who they are remains opaque to users. While platforms can gain insight over time into the reliability and evenhandedness of a particular group of flaggers, this can be extremely taxing on the people and groups who sign on to play this role (Matias et al., 2015).

The alternative is for platforms to ask users to rate their own content when it is first posted, and then provide filtering mechanisms so that users can avoid content they want to avoid. Unlike flagging, this enlists all users, which distributes the work more equitably and diminishes the concern that those doing the flagging do not represent the whole community. The challenge with this approach is achieving full participation and consistency. Platforms don't want to introduce too many steps at the moment a user posts, worried that an unwieldy and multi-click interface will discourage participation. So any user-rating process must either be lean and depend heavily on defaults, or it must happen less often. On Tumblr, for example, users are asked to rate their entire blog, rather than each post, and the default rating is 'safe.' While this makes the interface quite simple, the rating can only serve as a blunt instrument: a Tumblr user who rarely posts risqué content and a user who regularly posts pornography are rated the same, as 'NSFW' (Not Safe For Work). Users will inevitably have different interpretations of what is 'adult' or 'violent' or 'not for children,' especially regarding their own posts, leaving the platform with limited means for ensuring consistency across users. Many platforms penalize users for failing to rate adult material, or for doing so in ways that wildly differ from the platform moderator's opinion of it, or from users who come across it.

All of this labor, from the internal team setting the rules and adjudicating the hardest cases, to crowdworkers reviewing each bit of flagged content, to volunteer moderators overseeing groups within a platform, to flaggers lodging their complaints, to all users enlisted to rate content, represent a set of tiered solutions to the problem of scale. Many platforms use a combination of some or all, and the workflow that moves questionable content from one tier to the next may differ. Of course, there is the question of who does the judgment at each level and according to what criteria. But many of the problems with these systems of platform governance live in the uncertainties between this multi-tiered system: how are judgments at one level translated into consequences at another; how are criteria articulated at one level conveyed to another. And these uncertainties breed in the shadow of an apparatus that remains distinctly opaque to public scrutiny.

To Remove or to Filter

Platforms also have two choices for what to do with offending content: remove it, or mark it as such and help users avoid it. In practice, most platforms do some combination of both. Even permissive platforms remove the most heinous and illegal material, and even the most sensitive platforms often have a category of content that earns an age rating or warning. The difference tends to be where the balance is drawn between the two approaches, and how that balance is justified. But the two approaches have different implications as forms of governance.

It is commonplace for platforms to remove content deemed offensive and users deemed harassing. Content that offends one user is likely to offend others, so removing it addresses multiple points of offense; if it's gone, it cannot offend again. It demonstrates a decisive commitment to protecting the public, allows the platform to signal that it does not tolerate such content or behavior, and avoids associating the company brand with something offensive. And removal saves human resources later, having to adjudicate on the same content or user again and again.

On the other hand, removal comes with challenges. It is the harshest approach, in terms of its consequences. It renders the content or the user invisible on the platform. It is a blunt instrument, an all-or-nothing determination, removing that content for everyone, not just for those who were offended. And it runs counter to the principles of so many platforms: open participation, unencumbered interaction, and the protection of speech. Content policy managers are aware of this irony; several commented on how odd it is that, on a platform committed to open participation, their job is to kick some people off.

Disgruntled users who have had content removed or been banned from a social media platform sometimes cry "censorship." It is a powerful claim, but it is not entirely accurate. Users suspended by a platform, or even banned permanently, are not entirely shut out, as they can continue to participate on other platforms and on the broader web. This makes it hard to call this censorship in the strict sense. Moreover, "censorship"

presumes a right to speak, and usually the kind of legal speech rights enshrined in the US First Amendment and similar protections around the world. But the First Amendment and its corollaries elsewhere are protections against intrusions of the state, not private companies. There are currently no legal obligations requiring social media platforms to allow their users to speak, or preventing them from restricting their users' speech, even if those restrictions are capricious or unfair.

Still, removal from a social media platform matters. For a user, being suspended or banned from a social media platform can have real consequences – detaching them from their social circle and loved ones, interruptions in the professional life, and interrupting their access to other platforms. There may be other platforms available, but they cannot take with them their entire network of people, their accumulated history of interactions, or their personal archive of content. And being excluded from the highest-profile platforms, where the most valuable audiences can be built, matters especially. It's why the common admonition, "if you don't like it here, just leave" is insufficient when it comes to culturally and politically contentious speech. The longer we stay on platforms and the larger they grow, the more we are compelled to stick with them and the higher the cost to leave.

With this, the threat of removal, real or perceived, has real effects. And in that sense, removing content from a platform altogether represents a deeper cut in terms of the protection of speech. The US tradition of First Amendment jurisprudence has long established that preempting speech entirely is a more problematic intervention than imposing penalties for it after the fact – because it silences that speech in the process (Armijo, 2013; Balkin, 2014; Meyerson, 2001). Removing users does more than limit speech, it interrupts their ability to participate on that platform, and removes all of their future speech as well. At the same time, on most platforms suspended users can simply create a new profile and post again, turning platform governance into an endless game of whack-a-mole, where content reappears in slight variation, under new names, or from dummy accounts that can only be identified in hindsight.

Removals can also feel like – or be criticized as – a judgment of the user themselves. While the platform may have merely determined that the content in question was statistically similar to other deleted content, the person who posted it may feel that its deletion is a judgment of them. This is especially problematic when what was deleted was, from the user's perspective, a positive expression of themselves: for example, when users, especially women, post pictures that, while they do expose their bodies, represent a moment of physical triumph – giving birth, breastfeeding their newborn, surviving a mastectomy or other surgery – only to have those photos deleted as inappropriate or pornographic.[35]

Finally, because removal is so blunt an instrument, it opens platforms up to charges of subjectivity, hypocrisy, political conservatism, and self-interest. For the largest platforms, content moderation will never be complete or consistent, which means that any user who feels their deleted post or image was fine can easily find content still on the site that they think is worse. Explanations for why that more egregious content remains rarely give the platform the benefit of the doubt: in that inconsistency, aggrieved users see subjectivity, hypocrisy, and bias. And removals that seem to benefit the platform in some way can look self-interested – or, to put it less generously, platforms may remove content they want to do away with under the guise of content moderation, on behalf of their community. Editorial review can creep beyond its stated intentions. What may be justified as ensuring quality content (and may really be about establishing a way to extract fees) can drift into moral judgments. Having put themselves in a position of apparent or actual oversight, platforms can also find themselves saddled with some sense of responsibility, to users and to the public at large.

The second option is to allow obscene content or problematic users to stay, but rate them so that users who care not to encounter them will be automatically filtered away. This is arguably a less invasive approach. It allows platforms to proclaim their commitment to protecting the speech of their users, though it also opens them to criticism, ranging from being too permissive, even harboring pornographers and terrorists. If the right balance is struck, the platform can enjoy the traffic and revenue both generated by users seeking illicit content, and by users who want a 'clean' experience of the platform. For permissive platforms that have developed a sturdy community around adult interests, or pride themselves on allowing unfettered debate, or position themselves as hands-off when it comes to what users do, it offers a mode of governance aligned with these aims.

This is not unlike how adult content has sometimes been handled before: the adult movies in the back room of the video store, the magazines on the top shelf at the newsstand, the pornographic cable channels encrypted. But instead of a cashier looking at a driver's license at the point of sale, social media platforms must patrol users algorithmically. Some form of 'safesearch' mechanism must recognize which users are in a safe mode, and refuse to deliver to them the unsafe material. Instead of blocking content at the point of sale, they're blocked at the point of search, which means the very same mechanism we expect to help us find content is also being used by the platform to prevent us from finding it. This can have real cultural and political consequences, like when Tumblr blocked the term '#gay' because it is commonly associated with pornographic images, and thereby blocked all other non-pornographic content similarly tagged.[36]

This kind of technical choreography can be harder for users to see, and is not always where one might expect it. For instance, all of the major search engines offer users a "safesearch" mode – if I don't want to see pornographic results, I tick a box and the search engine filters them out. But the major search engines go one step further: even for users who have safesearch off, the search engines nevertheless filter out adult results – if they think your search query is an innocuous one, one that is not seeking adult content. In other words, even if I have safesearch off, if I search for 'movies' I will not see links to adult movie sites – it will deliver only non-explicit results, using the same algorithmic moderation as if I had safesearch turned on. If I search for 'porn movies,' then I get the adult content. Search engines assume all users do not want accidental porn: better to make the user actually looking for porn refine their query than to deliver porn to a user did not expect to receive. Reasonable, perhaps: but the intervention is a hidden one, and in fact runs counter to my stated preferences. Search engines not only guess the meaning and intent of my search, based on the little they know about me, they must in fact defy the one bit of agency I have asserted here, in turning safesearch off.

Finally, these filtering approaches can offer the platform compelling solutions to the legal demands of specific nations, but in ways that may differ from the intent of the law. For instance, when Germany, Singapore, and South Korea all complained to Flickr that, by allowing explicit content so long as the user rates it as such, it was violating their laws restricting access to pornography for minors, Flickr could have instituted a checkpoint requiring users to confirm their age. Instead, they simply designed the system so that users who are visiting Flickr from, say, a German IP address, simply cannot turn safesearch off. They will only ever see content rated "moderate" or "safe" photos, no matter their age. In other words, laws protecting minors become technical measures restricting adults. When the High Court of Pakistan ordered the entire Facebook site blocked for Pakistani users because of one particular Facebook group encouraging people to draw the image of Mohammed, Facebook removed the group – only from the search results of users located in Pakistan. For those users, the offending page was simply not there; even its removal was invisible. Technical measures that keep some users away from some content, while continuing to display it to others, are a convenient solution, but raise troubling questions about the power of social media platforms to offer different media to different publics, in ways that are hard to discern or criticize.

CONCLUSION: THE QUESTION OF RESPONSIBILITY

Questions about platforms and the harms they host are typically not framed in terms of responsibility – it is too often about liability and its avoidance. We tend to defend platforms as free conduits of speech until we are too troubled by something that freely moves through their system. When the government, or the aggrieved user, or the public at large, demands that the platform 'do something' about the problem, that request generally lies somewhere between a genuine belief in the platform's responsibility and a more practical hope that they are best positioned to intervene. It may be a convenience or a strategy: platforms do have the means to intervene in the circulation of abhorrent content and at the moment of abhorrent behavior. Pursuing individual bad actors is difficult, consumes time and resources, and has too little impact: getting a platform to intervene systematically promises to have a much broader impact. But platforms also make human behavior highly visible, leading to what Mueller calls a 'fallacy of displaced control': since the problem is most obvious there, we tend to assign too much blame to the platform itself. When this comes in the form of a legal imposition, it can look like a displacement of individual accountability: 'Instead of punishing bad behavior, we strive to control the tool that was used by the bad actor(s). Instead of eliminating illegal materials or activities, we propose to eliminate internet access to illegal materials or activities' (Mueller, 2015: 807). Platforms get the burden and the blame for what users say and do.

But, in principle, there might be good reason to think of platforms as bearing some responsibility. Copyright law points to at least two ways in which intermediaries could be held responsible for the activity of their users. First, if they gain financially from the illicit transaction, and second, if they have some material effect on the transaction, making it easier or expanding its scope.[37] In the case of offensive content and behavior, similar questions could be asked: does a platform pair advertising with offensive content? Do they materially enhance the ability of a bad actor to harass or threaten another user?

Then we might consider other versions of platform responsibility as well. Are they responsible because, by their very existence, they connect people who would not be connected otherwise? Do they have a responsibility (though this runs counter to Section 230) once they promise to moderate? Do they have a greater responsibility as they grow larger, as they displace other central venues of public life, or if they gain monopolistic power in a particular genre of services? Some of these questions depend on the role we think platforms play in shaping the activity and discourse they host, materially and institutionally. Some depend on what kinds of public obligations we are willing to impose on private institutions of any kind.

While Section 230 may have tried to provide both sides of a safe harbor from liability for user content and behavior – safe harbor from being held accountable for it, and the legal freedom to intervene on users' behalf without being then held accountable for how extensively they do so – platforms are in some ways hamstrung between these two positions. They are indeed intermediaries, stuck in the middle in both the legal and practical sense:

halfway between users with different values, halfway between policymakers and the people they seek to regulate, halfway between a conduit and a curator, and halfway between the pressure of internal aims and external demands. But they also get to play both sides, where they enjoy all the right to intervene, but with little responsibility about how they do so and under what forms of oversight.

The language of the impartial conduit is still powerful, though it seems to be diminishing in the glare of the most alarming content and egregious behavior being circulated through and perpetrated on these platforms, and in light of the different legal approaches around the world. Even in the West, with a robust safe harbor principle, we oblige platforms to remove illegal content like child pornography, and are considering other kinds of obligations, such as revenge porn and extremist content – governments and publics are not only willing to make exceptions, they are beginning to reconsider their starting assumptions about whether platforms should be responsible for what happens on them. And users, faced with direct harms coming at them on their chosen platform, quickly adjust their understanding of that platform, from an unfettered space in which to play to a responsible guardian failing to protect them. These are not just questions about the proper legal rules for intermediaries, they are broader societal questions about how bad something has to be to justify adjusting a general principle. This question falls heavily on platforms, sometimes asked not to intervene, sometimes required to, and shapes how we think about how to govern them, and how they govern.

In addition, the policies of the major social media platforms have themselves become a terrain for longstanding debates about the content and character of public discourse. It is not surprising that our dilemmas about terrorism and Islamic fundamentalism, about gay sexuality, about misogyny and violence against women, so front and center as public concerns, should erupt here too. The controversies these sites face can be read as a barometer of our society's pressing concerns about public discourse more broadly: which representations of sexuality are empowering and which are explicit, and according to whose judgment; what is newsworthy and what is gruesome, and who draws the line; do words do harm and exclude people from discussion, or must participants in public debate endure even caustic contributions; how do we balance freedom of speech with the values of the community, with the safety of individuals, with the aspirations of art, and with the wants of commerce.

For both reasons, it is high time to reconsider the responsibilities of platforms. This should include crafting a new principle of liability tailored for social media platforms, not borrowed whole cloth from a law designed for ISPs and search engines. It should include articulating normative expectations for what platforms are – legally, culturally, and ethically – not just passes for what they don't have to be. The aim would be to urge platforms to shift their fundamental approach: from being nominally impartial conduits that quietly intervene, to being the deliberate architects of public spaces of discourse, premised on specific rules of play, that they then obviously have the right to enforce. And it should include a new standard of transparency and accountability for how they do so: more information about the inner workings of the moderation process, more data provided about who flags and how those complaints are adjudicated, more transparency about the labor forces involved, and more public accountability about how and why the rules are made.

Notes

1   It is visible not only in the regulation of illicit content, but in legal efforts to protect user privacy, and in digital copyright law. Much of the way we think of intermediaries as protected legal entities was forged in the 'copyright wars' of the 2000s (Yu, 2003). This chapter will focus on the regulation of illicit content, though many of the tensions involved are relevant for ongoing concerns about copyright and privacy.

2   This was fueled by a vocal and urgent panic, in American culture, about the availability of pornography online, a concern not unwarranted but wildly overstated (Maddison, 2010; Marwick, 2008). Copyright infringement lawsuits began to appear (Ginsburg, 1995), but they were more concerned with images and private documents than music and movies, which would emerge as a problem later with the rise of peer-to-peer file sharing services like Napster (Litman, 2001; Yu, 2003).

3   *Reno v. American Civil Liberties Union*, 521 U.S. 844 (1997).

4   It is worth noting that Section 230 was for 'offensive material' and explicitly excluded 'cases involving federal criminal law, intellectual property law, and electronic-communications privacy law.' So the safe harbor it establishes for ISPs and platforms does not apply to these other concerns. This explains why the platform obligations for child pornography are very different than for other categories of harmful speech, because child pornography is a federal, criminal offense. It also explains why the arrangements are different for copyright infringement. The Digital Millennium Copyright Act, also passed in 1996, offered ISPs and search engines protection against a charge of contributing to copyright infringement as well, but this safe harbor comes with some obligations, the most notable being that intermediaries must comply with 'notice and takedown' requests from copyright owners who have identified their work as being circulated through their service (Fifer and Carter, 2004). In court cases that followed, peer-to-peer networks and other online services found they did not enjoy the DMCA safe harbor when they had 'materially' contributed to the circulation of pirated content, when they enjoyed some financial benefit from it, or even when they had 'induced' it by promoting their service as designed for piracy.

5   This is before innovations such as digital fingerprinting and other forms of automated content identification, techniques that now make it possible for platforms and ISPs to 'know' of illicit content on their service, even in real time.

6   Branigan, T. (2010). Google angers China by shifting service to Hong Kong. *The Guardian*, March 23. www.theguardian.com/technology/2010/mar/23/google-china-censorship-hong-kong

7   Mozur, P. and Goel, V. (2014). To reach China, LinkedIn plays by local rules. *New York Times*, October 5. www.nytimes.com/2014/10/06/technology/to-reach-china-linkedin-plays-by-local-rules.html

8   Chao, L. and Efrati, A. (2012). Twitter can censor by country. *Wall Street Journal*, January 28. www.wsj.com/articles/SB10001424052970204573704577185873204078142

9   Geller, E. (2016). Why ISIS is winning the online propaganda war. *The Daily Dot*, March 29. Retrieved from www.dailydot.com/politics/isis-terrorism-social-media-internet-countering-violent-extremism/. Waddell, K. (2016). The government is secretly huddling with companies to fight extremism online. *The Atlantic*, March 9. www.theatlantic.com/technology/archive/2016/03/the-government-is-secretly-huddling-with-companies-to-fight-extremism-online/472848/

10 JISC (Joint Information Systems Committee). (2007). *Hosting liability*. www.jisc.ac.uk/guides/hosting-liability

11 Radsch, C. (2015). Treating the Internet as the enemy in the Middle East, Committee to Protect Journalists. Apil 27. https://cpj.org/2015/04/attacks-on-the-press-treating-internet-as-enemy-in-middle-east.php

12 Lasar, M. (2011). Nazi hunting: How France first 'civilized' the Internet. *Ars Technical*, June 22. http://arstechnica.com/tech-policy/2011/06/how-france-proved-that-the-internet-is-not-global/

13 Bogado, D. (2015). No to Internet censorship in Argentina. *Deep Links* (Electronic Frontier Foundation), August 11. www.eff.org/deeplinks/2015/08/no-internet-censorship-argentina

14 Radsch, C. (2015). Treating the Internet as the enemy in the Middle East. Committee to Protect Journalists. Apil 27. https://cpj.org/2015/04/attacks-on-the-press-treating-internet-as-enemy-in-middle-east.php

15 Ibid.

16 Brooks, B. and Barbassa, J. (2012). Arrest of Google Brazil head stirs debate over web. Associated Press. http://finance.yahoo.com/news/arrest-google-brazil-head-stirs-debate-over-210814484–finance.html

17 www.hurriyetdailynews.com/zuckerberg-notes-turkeys-defamation-laws-over-ataturk-as-facebook-updates-rules.aspx?pageID=238&nID=79771&NewsCatID=359

18 Turovsky, D. (2015). This is how Russian Internet censorship works. *Meduza*, August 13. https://meduza.io/en/feature/2015/08/13/this-is-how-russian-internet-censorship-works

19 Sonne, P. and Razumovskaya, O. (2014). Russia steps up new law to control foreign Internet companies. *Wall Street Journal*, September 24. www.wsj.com/articles/russia-steps-up-new-law-to-control-foreign-internet-companies-1411574920

20 Luhn, A. (2015). Russia threatens to ban Google, Twitter and Facebook over extremist content.

The Guardian, May 20. www.theguardian.com/world/2015/may/20/russia-threaten-ban-google-twitter-facebook-bloggers-law

21 Daileda, C. (2015). Social media sites may be better than the law at blocking revenge porn. *Mashable*, March 18. http://mashable.com/2015/03/18/banning-revenge-porn/#E5HZfe5inkqd

22 Geller, E. (2016). White House and tech companies brainstorm how to slow ISIS propaganda. *The Daily Dot*, January 6. www.dailydot.com/politics/white-house-tech-companies-online-extremism-meeting/

23 Gillespie, T. (2013). Tumblr, NSFW porn blogging, and the challenge of checkpoints. *Culture Digitally*. January 14. http://culturedigitally.org/2013/07/tumblr-nsfw-porn-blogging-and-the-challenge-of-checkpoints/

24 Many thanks to Kevin Driscoll for this observation.

25 This excludes automated mechanisms for identifying problematic content. But such automatic filters, at this point, are generally only useful for identifying spam (based on its format and origins), child pornography (based on comparison to a collected database of examples), and profanity (based on simple language identification). Such tools have not yet been successfully extended to pornography, hate speech, or harassment such that they could be used to automatically remove content.

26 Hunt, K. and Xu, C. (2013). China 'employs 2 million to police internet'. *CNN*, October 7. www.cnn.com/2013/10/07/world/asia/china-internet-monitors/

27 Chen, A. (2014). The laborers who keep dick pics and beheadings out of your Facebook feed. *Wired*, October 23. www.wired.com/2014/10/content-moderation/

28 Dale Markowiz, How I Decide Who Gets Banned on OkCupid, *New York*, February 17, 2017. http://nymag.com/thecut/2017/02/banned-from-okcupid-sexting-moderation.html.

29 Rosen, J. (2013). The Delete Squad: Google, Twitter, Facebook and the new global battle over the future of free speech. *New Republic*, April 29. https://newrepublic.com/article/113045/free-speech-internet-silicon-valley-making-rules

30 Chen, A. (2014). The laborers who keep dick pics and beheadings out of your Facebook feed. *Wired*, October 23. www.wired.com/2014/10/content-moderation/. Buni, C. and Chemaly, S. (2016). The secret rules of the Internet: The murky history of moderation, and how it's shaping the future of free speech. *The Verge*, April 13. www.theverge.com/2016/4/13/11387934/internet-moderator-history-youtube-facebook-reddit-censorship-free-speech

31 Gray, M. (2016). Your job is about to get 'taskified'. *Los Angeles Times*, January 8. www.latimes.

com/opinion/op-ed/la-oe-0110-digital-turk-work-20160110-story.html

32 Ibid.

33 Stone, B. (2010). Policing the web's lurid precincts. *New York Times*, July 18. www.nytimes.com/2010/07/19/technology/19screen.html. Chen, A. (2014). The laborers who keep dick pics and beheadings out of your Facebook feed. *Wired*, October 23. www.wired.com/2014/10/content-moderation/. Day, M. (2017). Ex-workers at Microsoft claim jobs monitoring child porn, abuse caused PTSD. *Seattle* Times, January 11. www.seattletimes.com/business/microsoft/ex-workers-at-microsoft-claim-jobs-monitoring-child-porn-abuse-caused-ptsd/

34 Matias, J. N. (2015). What just happened on Reddit? Understanding the moderator blackout. *Social Media Collective*, July 9. https://socialmediacollective.org/2015/07/09/what-just-happened-on-reddit-understanding-the-moderator-blackout/

35 Collins, P. (2013). Why Instagram censored my body. *Huffington Post*, October 17. http://www.huffingtonpost.com/petra-collins/why-instagram-censored-my-body_b_4118416.html. Peters, L. (2014). What you need to know about Facebook and Instagram's war on motherhood. *The Daily Dot*, July 15. www.dailydot.com/opinion/why-we-need-stop-censoring-motherhood/

36 Baker-Whitelaw, G. (2013). New NSFW content restrictions enrage Tumblr users. *The Daily Dot*, July 18. www.dailydot.com/lifestyle/tumblr-nsfw-content-tags-search/

37 US copyright jurisprudence added a third, in the *MGM v. Grokster* decision, where the court held Grokster liable because it encouraged or 'induced' copyright infringement by advertising how easy it was to attain pirated music and movies through their software.

REFERENCES

Archetti, C. (2015). Terrorism, communication and new media: Explaining radicalization in the digital age. *Perspectives on Terrorism*, *9*(1).

Ardia, D. S. (2010). Free speech savior or shield for scoundrels: An empirical study of intermediary immunity under Section 230 of the Communications Decency Act. *Loyola of Los Angeles Law Review*, *43*(2), 373–506.

Armijo, E. (2013). Kill switches, forum doctrine, and the First Amendment's digital future. *Cardozo Arts & Entertainment Law Journal*, *32*, 411–469.

Bakardjieva, M. (2009). Subactivism: Lifeworld and politics in the age of the Internet. *The Information Society*, *25*(2), 91–104.

Baker, C. E. (2001). *Media, markets, and democracy*. Cambridge, UK: Cambridge University Press.

Balkin, J. (2004). Digital speech and democratic culture: A theory of freedom of expression for the information society. *New York University Law Review*, *79*, 1–55.

Balkin, J. M. (2014). Old school/new school speech regulation. *Harvard Law Review*, *127*(8), 2296–2342.

Bar, F., & Sandvig, C. (2008). U.S. communication policy after convergence. *Media, Culture & Society*, *30*(4), 531–550.

Baym, N. K., & boyd, danah. (2012). Socially mediated publicness: An introduction. *Journal of Broadcasting & Electronic Media*, *56*(3), 320–329.

Benkler, Y. (1998). Communications infrastructure regulation and the distribution of control over content. *Telecommunications Policy*, *22*(3), 183–196.

Bergstrom, K. (2011). 'Don't feed the troll': Shutting down debate about community expectations on Reddit.com. *First Monday*, *16*(8).

boyd, danah. (2011). Social network sites as networked publics: Affordances, dynamics, and implications. In Z. Papacharissi (Ed.), *A networked self: Identity, community, and culture on social network sites* (pp. 39–58). New York: Routledge.

Braman, S. (2004). Where has media policy gone? Defining the field in the twenty-first century. *Communication Law and Policy*, *9*(2), 153–182.

Braman, S. (2014). 'We are Bradley Manning': Information policy, the legal subject, and the WikiLeaks complex. *International Journal of Communication*, *8*, 2603–2618.

Bruns, A., & Burgess, J. (2015). Twitter hashtags from ad hoc to calculated publics. In N. Rambukkana (Ed.), *Hashtag publics: The power and politics of discursive networks* (pp. 13–28) New York: Peter Lang.

Bucher, T. (2012). Want to be on the top? Algorithmic power and the threat of invisibility on Facebook. *New Media & Society*, *14*(7), 1164–1180.

Castronova, E., Knowles, I., & Ross, T. L. (2015). Policy questions raised by virtual economies. *Telecommunications Policy*, *39*(9), 787–795.

Center for Democracy and Technology (CDT). (2010). *Intermediary liability protecting Internet platforms for expression and Innovation*. Washington, DC: Center for Democracy and Technology.

Citron, D. K. (2014). *Hate crimes in cyberspace*. Cambridge, MA: Harvard University Press.

Couldry, N. (2015). The myth of 'us': Digital networks, political change and the production of collectivity. *Information, Communication & Society*, *18*(6), 608–626.

Crawford, K., Gillespie, T. (2016). What is a flag for? Social media reporting tools and the vocabulary of complaint. *New Media & Society 18*(3), 410–428.

Couldry, N., & van Dijck, J. (2015). Researching social media as if the social mattered. *Social Media + Society*, *1*(2), 2056305115604174.

Dahlberg, L. (2007). Rethinking the fragmentation of the cyberpublic: From consensus to contestation. *New Media & Society*, *9*(5), 827–847.

DeNardis, L., & Hackl, A. M. (2015). Internet governance by social media platforms. *Telecommunications Policy*, *39*(9), 761–770.

Dibbell, J. (1993) A rape in cyberspace: How an evil clown, a Haitian trickster spirit, two wizards, and a cast of dozens turned a database into a society. *Village Voice*, December 23.

Entman, R. M., & Wildman, S. S. (1992). Reconciling economic and non-economic perspectives on media policy: Transcending the 'marketplace of ideas'. *Journal of Communication*, *42*(1), 5–19.

Fifer, S., & Carter, S. R. (2004). A tale of two safe harbors: The scope of ISP liability and the values of the Internet. *Journal of Internet Law*, *8*(2), 13–20.

Forsyth, H. (2016). Forum. In B. Peters (Ed.), *Digital keywords*. Princeton, NJ: Princeton University Press.

Freedman, D. (2008). *The politics of media policy*. Cambridge, UK: Polity Press.

Gerlitz, C., & Helmond, A. (2013). The like economy: Social buttons and the data-intensive web. *New Media & Society*, *15*(8), 1348–1365.

Gillespie, T. (2010). The politics of 'platforms'. *New Media & Society*, *12*(3), 347–364.

Gillespie, T. (2015). Platforms intervene. *Social Media + Society*, *1*(1), 2056305115580479.

Ginsburg, J. C. (1995). Putting cars on the 'information superhighway': Authors, exploiters, and copyright in cyberspace. *Columbia Law Review*, *95*(6), 1466–1499.

Godwin, M. (2003). *Cyber rights: Defending free speech in the digital age*. Cambridge, MA: MIT Press.

Gray, M. L. (2009). *Out in the country: Youth, media, and queer visibility in rural America*. New York: New York University Press.

Grimmelmann, J. (2015). The virtues of moderation: Online communities as semicommons. *Yale Journal of Law and Technology*, *17*(42).

Gross, L. (2002). *Up from invisibility: Lesbians, gay men, and the media in America*. New York: Columbia University Press.

Hendershot, H. (1999). *Saturday morning censors: Television regulation before the v-chip*. Durham, NC: Duke University Press.

Hestres, L. E. (2013). App neutrality: Apple's app store and freedom of expression online. *International Journal of Communication*, *7*, 1265–1280.

Horwitz, R. B. (1991a). The First Amendment meets some new technologies. *Theory and Society*, *20*(1), 21–72.

Horwitz, R. B. (1991b). *The irony of regulatory reform: The deregulation of American telecommunications*. New York: Oxford University Press.

Humphreys, S. (2013). Predicting, securing and shaping the future: Mechanisms of governance in online social environments. *International Journal of Media & Cultural Politics*, *9*(3), 247–258.

Jeong, S. (2015). *The Internet of garbage*. Forbes Media. Retrieved from www.forbes.com/ebooks/the-internet-of-garbage/

Johnson, D., & Post, D. G. (1996). Law and borders: The rise of law in cyberspace. *Stanford Law Review*, *48*, 1367–1402.

Kayyali, N., & O'Brien, D. (2015). *Facing the challenge of online harassment*. Retrieved from www.eff.org/deeplinks/2015/01/facing-challenge-online-harassment

Kerr, A., & Kelleher, J. D. (2015). The recruitment of passion and community in the service of capital: Community managers in the digital games industry. *Critical Studies in Media Communication*, *32*(3), 177–192.

Kreimer, S. F. (2006). Censorship by proxy: The First Amendment, Internet intermediaries, and the problem of the weakest link. *University of Pennsylvania Law Review*, *155*(1), 11.

Lampe, C., Zube, P., Lee, J., Park, C. H., & Johnston, E. (2014). Crowdsourcing civility: A natural experiment examining the effects of distributed moderation in online forums. *Government Information Quarterly*, *31*(2), 317–326.

Langlois, G. (2013). Participatory culture and the new governance of communication: The paradox of participatory media. *Television & New Media*, *14*(2), 91–105.

Lessig, L. (1999). *Code and other laws of cyberspace*. New York: Basic Books.

Litman, J. (1999). Electronic commerce and free speech. *Ethics and Information Technology*, *1*(3), 213–225.

Litman, J. (2001). *Digital copyright: Protecting intellectual property on the Internet*. Amherst, NY: Prometheus Books.

MacKinnon, R. (2012). *Consent of the networked: The worldwide struggle for Internet freedom*. New York: Basic Books.

MacKinnon, R., Hickok, E., Bar, A., & Lim, H. (2014). *Fostering freedom online: The roles, challenges and obstacles of Internet intermediaries*. New York: United Nations Educational.

Maddison, S. (2010). Online obscenity and myths of freedom: Dangerous images, child porn, and neoliberalism. In F. Attwood (Ed.), *Porn.com: Making sense of online pornography*. New York: Peter Lang.

Mann, R. J., & Belzley, S. R. (2005). The promise of Internet intermediary liability. *William & Mary Law Review*, *47*, 239–308.

Marwick, A. E. (2008). To catch a predator? The MySpace moral panic. *First Monday*, *13*(6).

Matias, J. N., Johnson, A., Boesel, W. E., Keegan, B., Friedman, J., & DeTar, C. (2015). *Reporting, reviewing, and responding to harassment on Twitter*. Women, Action & the Media. Retrieved from www.womenactionmedia.org/twitter-report/

Meyerson, M. (2001). The neglected history of the prior restraint doctrine: Rediscovering the link between the First Amendment and the separation of powers. *Indiana Law Review*, *34*(2), 295–342.

Milan, S. (2015). When algorithms shape collective action: Social media and the dynamics of cloud protesting. *Social Media + Society*, *1*(2), 2056305115622481.

Mueller, M. L. (2015). Hyper-transparency and social control: Social media as magnets for regulation. *Telecommunications Policy*, *39*(9), 804–810.

Obar, J. A., & Wildman, S. (2015). Social media definition and the governance challenge: An introduction to the special issue. *Telecommunications Policy*, *39*(9), 745–750.

Organization for Economic Co-operation and Development. (2010). *The economic and social role of Internet intermediaries*. Paris, France. April. Retrieved from www.oecd.org/dataoecd/49/4/44949023.pdf

Palfrey, J. (2010). Four phases of Internet regulation. *Social Research*, *77*(3), 981–996.

Postigo, H. (2009). America Online volunteers: Lessons from an early co-production community. *International Journal of Cultural Studies*, *12*(5), 451–469.

Reagle, J. (2015). *Reading the comments: Likers, haters, and manipulators at the bottom of the web*. Cambridge, MA: MIT Press.

Roberts, S. T. (2016). Commercial content moderation: Digital laborers' dirty work. In S. U. Noble & B. Tynes (Eds.), *Intersectional Internet: Race, sex, class and culture online*. New York: Peter Lang.

Roth, Y. (2015). 'No overly suggestive photos of any kind': Content management and the policing of self in gay digital communities. *Communication, Culture & Critique*, *8*(3), 414–432.

Sandvig, C. (2015). The social industry. *Social Media + Society*, *1*(1), 2056305115582047.

Shaw, A., & Hill, B. M. (2014). Laboratories of oligarchy? How the iron law extends to peer production. *Journal of Communication*, *64*(2), 215–238.

Shepherd, T., & Landry, N. (2013). Technology design and power: Freedom and control in communication networks. *International Journal of Media & Cultural Politics*, *9*(3), 259–275.

Shirky, C. (2008). *Here comes everybody: How change happens when people come together*. New York: Penguin Press.

Stein, L. (2013). Policy and participation on social media: The cases of YouTube,

Facebook, and Wikipedia. *Communication, Culture & Critique*, 6(3), 353–371.

Streeter, T. (1996). *Selling the air: A critique of the policy of commercial broadcasting in the United States*. Chicago, IL: University of Chicago Press.

Thompson, J. B. (2005). The new visibility. *Theory, Culture & Society*, 22(6), 31–51.

Tushnet, R. (2008). Power without responsibility: Intermediaries and the First Amendment. *George Washington Law Review*, 76, 101.

Urban, J. M., Karaganis, J., & Schofield, B. L. (2016). *Notice and takedown in everyday practice*. Retrieved from http://papers.ssrn.com/sol3/papers.cfm?abstract_id=2755628

Vaidhyanathan, S. (2011). *The Googlization of everything (and why we should worry)*. Berkeley, CA: University of California Press.

van Dijck, J. (2013). *The culture of connectivity: A critical history of social media*. Oxford: Oxford University Press.

Varnelis, K. (Ed.). (2008). *Networked publics*. Cambridge, MA: MIT Press.

Wagner, B. (2013). Governing Internet expression: How public and private regulation shape expression governance. *Journal of Information Technology & Politics*, 10(4), 389–403.

Weltevrede, E., Helmond, A., & Gerlitz, C. (2014). The politics of real-time: A device perspective on social media platforms and search engines. *Theory, Culture & Society*, 31(6), 125–150.

Yu, P. K. (2003). The escalating copyright wars. *Hofstra Law Review*, 32, 907–951.

Social Media App Economies

Rowan Wilken

INTRODUCTION

This chapter examines the global composition of social media app markets and economies. The conceptual frame that gives direction to this examination is that of the political economy of communication – an established and well-tested approach (Wasko, 2004; Mosco, 1996) that has been applied not only to the analysis of regulated broadcast media industries but also to the study of search (Van Couvering, 2011; Mosco, 2014), mobile (Goldsmith, 2014), locative (Wilken and Bayliss, 2015), and social media industries (Albarran, 2013), as well as to new forms of media consumption and distribution (Lobato and Thomas, 2015). This framework is productive for understanding higher-level transformations, financing arrangements, business models and other vested interests, and the political and social impacts of the media industries. When applied to social media app markets, a political economy approach directs our attention to the different

stakeholders involved with controlling and commercialising applications for mobile devices and, increasingly, the data that are generated in and through them. Who controls and benefits from commercial app development? How have Apple and Google managed to effectively create an app market? What are the financial arrangements, business models, and cross-platform and other data-sharing deals that make social media apps so lucrative and their end-user data so sought after?

Beginning with an overview of the mobile smartphone app economy and its two industry leaders, Apple and Google, the chapter shifts focus to social media applications and the revenue generation efforts of two large, US-domiciled firms: Facebook and Twitter. The second part of the chapter then argues for the importance of looking beyond the established US market to develop a fuller account of global social media app economies; specific attention is given to two of the larger BRICS nations, China and Russia. The chapter closes with consideration given to the importance of examining the interrelationships between firms (and their financing) if we are to develop a detailed account of the intricate structures of, and interconnections between, social media app markets and economies.

THE APP ECONOMY

Ben Goldsmith (2014: 171) explains that 'the first common use of "app" as shorthand for "software application" was in 1985, when Apple released the MacApp programming tool'. It was not until the launch of Apple's App Store in mid-2008, which Cheng (2012: 49) views as a revolutionary step in the 'development of a new type of market economy', that '"app" became commonly understood to refer principally to software designed to run on mobile platforms and devices' (Goldsmith, 2014: 171). As for the phrase 'app economy', Goldsmith (2014: 171) points out that its usage emerged as a way to describe 'the impressive revenues being earned, principally in the games sector, from sales of apps, in-app purchases, and in-app advertising either on Facebook, or via an app store'. A good example of such extraordinary app-based revenue generation in the games sector is *Angry Birds*, with the company behind it, Rovio, investing US$140,000 in initial development of the game for a profit of US$70 million (Cheng, 2012: 52). A crucial factor in understanding the app economy is recognising, as Michael Mandel points out, that it is in reality 'a collection of interlocking innovative ecosystems', and that at the heart of each ecosystem are three things: 'a core company, which creates and maintains a platform, and an app marketplace, plus small and large companies that produce apps and/ or mobile devices for that platform' (Mandel, quoted in Goldsmith, 2014: 171).

At present, there are two 'core' companies that control the platforms and app marketplaces at the heart of the larger mobile social

media app ecosystem: Apple, with its iOS platform and App Store; and Google, with its Android platform and Google Play app store. Traffic to each is driven, of course, by the astonishing growth of iOS and Android powered smartphones since the early 2000s. While accurate app store metrics are notoriously difficult to obtain, mobile industry analyst Benedict Evans argues that a close examination of the reporting offered by Apple and Google at their respective annual developer conferences does provide an overall picture of what is going on, although clear comparisons between the two app stores remain difficult to draw.[1] Looking at 2014 developer event data for both companies, Evans notes that, 'both Apple and Google gave numbers for the money they had paid to developers in their respective app stores: $5bn in the previous 12 months for Google Play and $10bn for the iOS App Store'. In interpreting these figures, Evans (2015) concludes that, 'given Android has double the user base of iOS, this meant that the average iOS user was worth around 4x the average Android user in app store revenue'. For Evans (2015), these payments also imply that, 'since Google Android has close to double the number of users', the 'average user is spending perhaps half as much as the average iOS user'. While this constitutes a change from the previous financial quarter, it is nonetheless still regarded as 'a big gap'. Subsequent interim figures released during 2015 by Google suggesting a slight increase in payments to developers, and Apple announcing an unchanged payment total in 2015 from the previous year, point to Google Play growing faster than and likely to overtake iOS (Evans, 2015). This statistic, alongside moves by Apple and competitors such as Google, Facebook and Snapchat 'to incorporate professional content [...] more deeply into their apps and services', may provide a clue as to why Apple was reported in mid-2015 to be contemplating 'new commercial terms with media companies' that would potentially 'alter the 70/30 "Apple tax"' – whereby a developer who sells an app or a digital good inside the app for $1 gets $0.70 of that sale and Apple takes $0.30 – that was pioneered by the late founder of Apple, Steve Jobs, to accompany the launch of the iTunes music store in 2003 (Bradshaw and Bond, 2015). Evans also records that Google Play had 50 billion downloads and the Apple App Store had 25 billion in the 2014–2015 financial year. When Play's greater number of users is accounted for, these figures imply 'roughly the same number of downloads per user on Android and iOS' (Evans, 2015). In overall terms, 'these numbers show annualized consumer spending on apps of around $25bn, and 75bn apps downloaded' in the 2014–2015 financial year (Evans, 2015).

There is also every indication that these figures will only continue to rise, especially beyond the US market. According to the International Telecommunication Union's 2015 report, 'there are more than 7 billion mobile cellular subscriptions, corresponding to a penetration rate of 97%, up from 738 million in 2000' (ITU, 2015). More tellingly in the context of the prospects of future social media app market growth is the fact that, despite significant pricing discrepancies that favour developed over developing countries, mobile broadband continues to be 'the most dynamic market segment', with 'mobile-broadband penetration' reaching 47% globally in 2015, 'a value that increased 12 times since 2007' (ITU, 2015). And, according to forecasts provided by app data analytics firm App Annie, 'the user base of smartphones and tablets will more than double to 6.2 billion by 2020', driven by cheaper smartphones and more accessible data plans, with much of the growth likely to come from India, Indonesia, China, Mexico, Brazil, and Turkey (Viita, 2016). This, in turn, is viewed as being likely to drive application store revenue up to US$101 billion within five years (Viita, 2016).

Setting aside the predicted growth of new smartphone app users, the immediate and longer term future of the global app economy also depends on the maintenance of good business relationships between the core platform and app market companies (Apple and Google) and mobile app developers and other interested parties. In short, there must be some tangible benefit in these arrangements to all parties who are involved – that is the fundamental premise of an ecosystem, after all. As Goldsmith argues, 'the restructuring of the mobile value chain' that Apple introduced with its App Store 'hinges on the ecosystem's attractiveness to developers'. In addition, there is the risk that, 'if third-party software applications and services cease to be developed and maintained for the [platform/ app market owner's] products, customers may choose not to buy the Company's products' (Apple 2012 Annual Report, quoted in Goldsmith, 2014: 174). Thus, as Goldsmith points out, 'the value of app stores for platform owners is not principally the income they generate, but rather the opportunity they provide to cultivate and manage an ecosystem' (2014: 175), even if the specific reasons for doing so differ from platform owner to platform owner (Pon, Seppälä, and Kenney, 2014). And yet,

> while it may be true that app stores 'are ecosystem control points, rather than revenue sources' for platform owners, as the number of paid-app downloads and in-app purchases increase, and despite the fact that most apps are downloaded for free, app stores *are* generating significant revenue for operators and for (some) developers. (Goldsmith, 2014: 175)

The 'some' that Goldsmith places in parentheses appears to be the operative word, as the app economy is by no means a level playing field. A 2014 VisionMobile study of developer economics collated responses from over 10,000 developers from 137 countries. Dividing app developers into the 'haves', the 'strugglers', the 'poverty-stricken', and the 'have-nothings', the study found that 50% of iOS developers and 64% of Android developers are operating below what they term the 'app poverty line' of US$500 per app per month (Perez, 2014b). In contrast, within the category of 'haves', 12% of developers make more than

US$10,000 per app per month, which is weighted in favour of iOS developers, 2% make between US$100,000 and US$500,000 per app per month, and 1.6% make more than US$500,000 per app per month.

A related study by Caribou Digital of the global distribution and concentration of the app economy discovered that '95% of the estimated industry value is being captured by just the top 10 producing countries', with the USA, Japan, and China dominant, and that 'the 19 lower-income countries [...] earned an estimated 1% of global app economy revenues' (Caribou Digital, 2016). Indeed, such is the level of concentration of app revenue generation that 'a small handful of firms earn so much that they outperform most of the countries' in the study, with the authors noting that Finnish game development company Supercell earned more than 28 of the countries in their sample, combined (Caribou Digital, 2016).

This uneven distribution of app revenue is associated with certain 'geographies of exclusion', to borrow David Sibley's (1995) term, that are not just a result of where a developer might live, but also of regional and national 'market-based factors' (e.g., that 'consumers in every market showed a preference for apps developed by local producers') and of 'platform-based factors' (Caribou Digital, 2016). Of the latter category, two such factors are worth noting here. The first concerns platform access restrictions. The report's authors point out that 'Google only allows developers in certain countries to monetize their products through the Google Play app store':

> Developers who want to earn revenue from Android apps on the Google Play app store are required to set up a merchant account, which is what links their bank account to Google so that they can receive funds from the app store. However, Google merchant accounts are not available in 74 countries, with half of sub-Saharan Africa and much of Latin America excluded. (Caribou Digital, 2016)

The second platform-based factor 'is the structuring of the app stores into discrete national stores' (Caribou Digital, 2016).

While this holds many compliance and other regulatory benefits for Apple and Google – it 'allows the platform to adhere to different tax laws, content regulations, and copyright licensing for music and other media' (Caribou Digital, 2016) – it carries other significant implications as well: it can lead to the exclusion of certain applications (as a result of local laws and cultural and political sensitivities); it can reinforce 'home field advantage'; contribute to a decrease in developer diversity and representation within app stores; and lead to a further concentration of revenues in the hands of only a few developers.

In the midst of this discussion of app developer revenues, one should not lose sight of who the major financial beneficiaries of the app economy actually are: the app marketplace owners themselves. In Apple's case, it recorded first quarter 2016 revenue of US$75.9 billion (up from $51.5 billion the previous quarter). In the same reporting period, Apple's install base (i.e., devices that have been used to interact with Apple's services within a 90-day period), which totals 1 billion, generated services revenue (which includes the App Store and iCloud, among others) of US$8.9 billion (Apple, 2016).[2] In Google's case, at the 2015 fiscal year end (first quarter 2016 figures were not released at time of writing) it earned US$74.5 billion in revenue for parent company Alphabet, with US$34.8 billion of this coming from the USA, US$7.1 billion from the UK, and US$33.1 billion from the rest of the world (USS&EC, 2015). Alphabet has since overtaken Apple as the world's most valuable company.

SOCIAL MEDIA REVENUE MODELS

Having provided this overview of the app economy, I want to sharpen the focus on social media apps by exploring briefly the revenue models and earnings of two globally dominant, publicly listed social media firms:

Facebook and Twitter. In an oft-quoted adage generally attributed to Silicon Valley entrepreneur Steve Blank (2010), a start-up is defined as 'an organization formed to search for a repeatable and scalable business model'. This is an apt characterisation of the social media-focused technology firms that were launched – post the 'dot.com' crash – in the 2000s, such as Facebook and Twitter. These firms were born into what writer Michael Lewis (2001) would term a post-Netscape era of fluid business models, where tech start-ups are backed by venture capital and other forms of investment, while developers and investors go about figuring out how best to monetise their assets (see also Lacy, 2009).

As these firms mature, however, the menu of available revenue generation options tends to be increasingly restricted. For social media firms, as José van Dijck notes, these options generally involve the fostering of data generation by users ('data generation has become the primary object rather than a by-product of online sociality'), and the subsequent utilisation of this data to 'influence traffic and monetize engineered streams of information' (van Dijck, 2013: 12). While the subtle differences in how each platform sets about extracting and monetising data are important considerations (Barreneche and Wilken, 2015), for Jiyoung Cha (2013) there are limited means by which revenue can be generated from end-user data, with each option tied to the core competencies of each firm. In the two cases explored here, these companies have matured to the extent that they are now both publicly listed, and, in terms of revenue generation, the strategies of both Facebook and Twitter have become somewhat more settled, but are far from stable, especially in the case of Twitter.

Facebook

In Facebook's case, Cha (2013: 71) argues, its three sources of revenue include advertising, commerce, and syndication. Given that Facebook's 'core competency [...] comes from its network size' (2013: 69), it is not surprising that advertising is the primary revenue source – the greater the market reach, the more desirable the platform becomes to advertisers, and the higher the advertising rates that can be imposed by the platform owners. Commerce in this context principally refers to within-platform transactions using Facebook Credits, while syndication concerns the linking of Facebook users' publicly available status updates with other search results (Cha, 2013: 72). Built around the company's 'three pillars' (newsfeed, timeline, and graph search) – and to which, I have argued elsewhere, we should add a fourth: geocoded data (Wilken, 2014) – Facebook has grown to become a highly lucrative social media business. Based on 2015 year-end figures, Facebook has 1.04 billion daily active users – 934 million of who are *mobile* daily active users (which is an increase of 13.2% from the previous quarter, and is attributed to take-up in emerging global markets) (Facebook, 2016). Facebook's reported revenue for 2015 was US$17.93 billion, which represents 'an increase of 44% year-over-year', for a profit of US$3.69 billion (Facebook, 2016). Mobile advertising accounts for 80%, or US$5.63 billion, of Facebook's overall advertising revenue. Also noteworthy here is that a sizeable portion of Facebook's ad revenue is derived from the Facebook Audience Network, which 'uses its data to target ads in other apps' (Constine, 2016a). Combined, this confirms Facebook as a major mobile advertising player and a significant challenger to the incumbent and long-established leader in online and mobile advertising, Google.

And, finally, to understand the scale of Facebook's corporate operations, and revenue potential this represents, it is also worth noting here the usage figures relating to its various services, including its subsidiaries. While Facebook reported 1.59 billion monthly active users, its other services are not far behind: WhatsApp has 900 million, Messenger 800 million, and Instagram 400 million. Of these, WhatsApp is interesting insofar as 'it doesn't make any money' (Statt, 2016). Facebook has dropped subscription fees, and made a commitment to keeping it ad free (the most obvious path towards monetisation). Instead, the longer-term plan is to turn it into 'a tool businesses can use to communicate with customers' (Zuckerberg, quoted in Statt, 2016).

Twitter

In Twitter's case, Cha (2013: 73) suggests there are two key sources of revenue: advertising and syndication. Twitter's ad revenue, Cha (2013: 73) writes, is based on three forms of ad delivery: promoted tweets, promoted accounts, and promoted trends. The cost of the first two is calculated on a cost-per-engagement basis, while the last is charged as a flat daily rate (Cha, 2013: 73). In the fourth quarter of 2015, Twitter earned US$641 million in revenue from these three forms of advertising combined (Twitter, 2015). The second source of revenue Cha mentions is syndication, whereby Twitter makes deals with search engine services (Google, Bing, Yahoo) to allow the integration of tweets with other search results. The deals struck with Google and Microsoft in 2009, for example, were said to be worth US$25 million for Twitter (Ante, 2009). Furthermore, in its 2011 renegotiations of its licensing arrangements with Microsoft, Twitter was reportedly seeking 'about [US]$30 million per year for its exhaustive real-time stream, a doubling of the previous fee,' as well as 'more user interface control, a larger cut of ads sold next to its tweets [on Bing] and more linking back to Twitter' (Gannes, 2011). While these figures are unconfirmed, and already somewhat dated, they are nevertheless indicative of the high commercial value that is placed on real-time

social media data for search and other more traditional media companies (Cha, 2013: 74).

Cha's account, however, neglects a third key source of Twitter revenue: monies earned through data licensing and analytics, including through social media API aggregation company Gnip, which Twitter acquired for US$134.1 million in April 2014. According to Twitter's fourth quarter 2015 figures, the company earned a healthy US$70 million from within its 'Data Licensing & Other' category (Twitter, 2015). As analysts have pointed out, it is important not to view these revenue streams and the technologies that facilitate each as unrelated; in the words of one commentator, 'analytics are essential to good advertising, and the data-licensing business is what's happening behind the scenes to create a strong advertising platform' (Neal, 2013). In overall revenue generation terms, however, the prospects for Twitter are looking somewhat less than rosy. While 'revenue was up 48% year-over-year' in early 2016 (Lynley and Constine, 2016), the company has not met industry earnings expectations, its stock has dropped nearly 70% in the past 12 months (fourth quarter (Q4) 2014 to Q4 2015), and, despite revenue of US$710 million, it has also recorded a net loss of US$90 million for fourth quarter 2015 earnings.

According to Goldman Sachs' Chief Operating Officer and President Gary Cohn, historically, in Silicon Valley, 'the mantra has been "grow at any cost – get bigger, get bigger, get bigger"' (quoted in Crowe, 2016). A key expectation for social media start-ups has been to grow user numbers year-on-year in the short-to-medium term, if not revenue and profit. The difficulty facing Twitter is that its new user growth has not only been 'flatlining', it has, in fact, also been shrinking (due to the loss of existing users, or 'churn'). This is especially evident if you exclude SMS-related user statistics – a point that requires some explanation. In Twitter's first quarter 2015 earnings documents, it was noted that the company had begun to include what they termed 'SMS Fast Followers' among their monthly average users (MAUs) statistics (Twitter does not provide daily average user statistics, as Facebook does). 'SMS Fast Followers' are users who 'access and use Twitter exclusively through text messages', an access technique that is primarily employed in emerging markets like India and Brazil. Twitter's embrace of this approach to user engagement was in part a result of their purchase in January 2015 of ZipDial, an Indian start-up whose focus was on marketing via text message (Purnell, 2015). Also known as 'missed call marketing', it works as follows:

> ZipDial allows consumers to dial a number for a company and hang up before connecting. The company then sends the caller a free text message containing advertisements and other information, without the users getting a charge. (Koh, 2015)

The idea for Twitter users in emerging markets such as India is that they can 'place a missed call to a Twitter account [and then] receive tweets on their mobile device'. This is viewed as having significant potential around large events, such as international cricket tournaments (Koh, 2015).

For analysts, the inclusion of these figures in Twitter's earnings reports has been viewed as an attempt by Twitter to 'goose its numbers' (Truong, 2015). By including these 'SMS Fast Followers' numbers in its MAUs within its first quarter 2015 earnings report, Twitter would 'suddenly have 6.4 million users' (Truong, 2015), a significant increase on what the figure would otherwise be. To return to fourth quarter earnings for 2015, 'Twitter's total user count is stuck at 320 million with zero growth this quarter', and, as *TechCrunch*'s Josh Constine (2016b) points

out, if you exclude 'SMS Fast Followers', Twitter's 'monthly user count went down from 307 million to 305 million in Q4' (see also, Smith and Popper, 2016). The difficulty for Twitter is that the path towards drawing revenue from these SMS users is long, slow, and difficult, even more so when set against Facebook's clear revenue growth in these same emerging markets. The silver lining for Twitter, it would seem, in what analysts otherwise view as a pretty gloomy Q4 2015 earnings report, is that Twitter's average revenue per monthly average user (ARPMAU) is considered to be quite strong, even when viewed against Facebook's ARPMAU (see Table 15.1).

Despite this financial silver lining, and despite its substantial existing user base, the harsh financial realities of the social media app economy mean that Twitter is faced with the prospect of having to either figure out how to foster significant new user growth, or convince investors that ongoing year-on-year growth is not a prerequisite for success and that it does not have to be the next Facebook in order to carve out a viable market niche (albeit perhaps at a reduced market valuation). Under present circumstances, there is significant pressure on Silicon Valley start-ups to achieve year-on-year new user growth if they are to attain, maintain, and further grow high market valuations. When new user growth shows signs of slowing, there is a strong temptation to tinker with platform design and core functionalities in an (often misguided) attempt to recapture user enthusiasm and attract new users, or, if this is not possible, to open up new revenue streams. This is precisely the path that Twitter has gone down, several times over. A viable, if somewhat less

Table 15.1   Comparison of Facebook and Twitter average revenue per monthly average user (ARPMAU) (amounts in US$)

	MAU	Revenue	ARPMAU	Market Cap ($B) as of February 10, 2016
Facebook	1,590,000,000	$5,841,000,000	$3.67	$286.90
Twitter	320,000,000	$710,000,000	$2.22	$9.90

attractive, alternative business strategy is to perhaps accept a reduced market valuation and concentrate efforts around retaining the core of the platform's present design success and a financially sustainable business model that seeks to keep running costs low, and user number and revenue streams steady.

BRICS AND BEYOND

In focusing on the aforementioned large-scale, US-domiciled social network services, despite their undisputed global reach, there is a still a risk that we become blinkered to other key global concentrations of social media activity[3] and other significant social media corporate players. Indeed, given the global reach of and fascination with social media, Gerard Goggin's and Mark McLelland's (2009) call that internet, social media, and mobile research move beyond 'Anglophone paradigms' remains as urgent as ever.

A useful starting point in broadening understanding of the global social media app economy is by accounting for the composition of the app economy within the BRICS (Brazil, Russia, India, China, and South Africa) group of nations. For a number of BRICS nations – specifically Brazil, India, and South Africa – the tale, on the surface at least, is an increasingly familiar one of Facebook entering and rapidly gaining sufficient traction to become the dominant social media service. This gloss, however, obscures a number of other potentially productive narrative trajectories that, if pursued, would likely draw out particularly striking features of, and issues pertaining to, each of these specific markets. In Brazil there is a potentially very interesting story to be told around the gradual demise of Google's Orkut and its supersession by Facebook, and failure in a Latourian sense, whereby a technology can be understood as failing not necessarily because any particular actor brought about

its demise, but because actors failed to sustain the technology through negotiation and adaptation to changing social (and, I would add, political economic) conditions (Latour, 1996). In India, there is the rich and fascinating tale concerning net neutrality and local entrepreneurial as well as regulatory resistance to Facebook's controversial 'Free Basics' programme (Ghoshal, 2016; see also Vaidhyanathan, Chapter 12 this volume), as well as the ensuing Twitter firestorm that erupted when prominent Silicon Valley venture capitalist and investor in Facebook, Marc Andreessen, expressed his displeasure at the failure of this programme, and the suggestion that Facebook represents a neo-colonial force in India, by tweeting that 'anti-colonialism has been economically catastrophic for India for decades' (Wadhwa, 2016). And, in South Africa, as elsewhere in the region, there is a quite different but equally fascinating tale to be told around infrastructural challenges, cultures of making do, and the complicated means by which platforms like Facebook and the locally-significant affordable instant messaging service MXit overlap and intersect (Walton, 2014). In the space available, however, I wish to touch on the cases of the two remaining BRICS nations: China and Russia.

China

The main Silicon Valley social media and search companies – Facebook, Twitter, Google – have by-and-large failed to gain a significant foothold in China. This should perhaps have come as no real surprise to those familiar with the mixed fortunes faced by other US-based companies attempting to enter the Chinese market. The trials and tribulations of advertising agencies in mainland China, for instance, have been well documented (see, for example, Sinclair, 2008). Rather, what has emerged in China since 2009 is a very concentrated social media market, dominated by three very big corporate players, Tencent Holdings, Weibo

Corporation, and Alibaba Group. In this analysis, I draw on a range of financial data: half-year 2015 figures in the case of Tencent, and second quarter (Q2) 2015 figures in the case of Weibo; at the time of writing, neither company had released full-year 2015 figures, which makes comparisons between them, and with Facebook and Twitter, difficult to draw.

Of the three big Chinese companies, Tencent is the largest. It has a 2015 market value exceeding US$200 billion and it is now the largest internet company in Asia (after Alibaba suffered a significant slump in its share value). Tencent Holdings, which is publicly listed on the Hong Kong stock exchange, controls the instant messenger services QQ and WeChat (known as Weixin in China), and the social media service QZone, plus a range of other QQ-badged services. According to its interim 2015 figures, Tencent generated RMB48.8 billion (US$7.4 billion) in revenue, with a gross profit of RMB27.8 billion (US$4.2 billion). As at 30 June 2015, QQ's monthly average users were 843.4 million (627 million of whom were accessing the service from a smart device), WeChat's were 600 million, and Qzone's were 659.2 million (573.5 million of whom accessed the service from a smart device). Unlike other social media companies, Tencent also reports the number of peak concurrent users of QQ (the highest number of people using the service within a predefined period of time), which for Q2 2015 was 233 million. And, in addition to chat and social services, a key component of Tencent's revenue generation operations is online gaming, the result of which is that Tencent also lists its fee-based value-added services (VAS) registered subscriptions, which were 84.3 million as at 30 June 2015 (Tencent, 2015).

In terms of revenue generation, to persist with Cha's (2013) categories, Tencent earns the lion's share of its revenue not from e-commerce, but from fee-based VAS-registered (gaming and social networks related) subscriptions, and, increasingly

rapidly, from advertising. With respect to the former, online games revenues grew by 17% and social networks revenues grew by 18%, while ad revenue grew from an initially low base, with online advertising revenues increasing by 97%, brand advertising revenues by 47% ('reflecting higher contributions from video advertising'), and performance-based advertising by 196% ('primarily due to performance-based social advertising on mobile devices') (Tencent, 2015). All of this, however, is not to underestimate the very real significance of commerce to Tencent: WeChat, for instance, is said to have recorded more mobile e-commerce transactions over the 2016 Chinese New Year than PayPal did during the whole of 2015 (McEleny, 2016).

Finally, a striking feature of Tencent's earnings is the concentration within China ('Revenues derived from external customers in Mainland China for the three and six months ended 30 June 2015 were RMB21, 590 million … and revenues derived from external customers in other regions were RMB1,839 million' (Tencent, 2015)). Given the take-up within China, this makes for very high active user and revenue figures, but also reveals that Tencent at present lacks the reach of other services, like Facebook. While there are clear growth opportunities for Tencent within a sizeable Chinese diaspora, it remains to be seen how successful the company will be at attracting a wider, international user base.

The second of the three firms is the long-running Chinese social media service, Sina Weibo, which is owned by parent company Weibo Corporation. Listed on the US NASDAQ stock exchange, Weibo recorded strengthened usage numbers and financial results by the halfway mark of 2015. Weibo's monthly active users (MAUs) were 212 million for June 2015, an increase of 36% year-over-year; 85% of these 212 million were mobile monthly active users (Weibo, 2015). Weibo also recorded daily average users of 93 million for June 2015, an averaged figure that, needless to say, is substantially less than its MAUs figure (Weibo, 2015). For the second quarter (Q2) of 2015, Weibo recorded net revenues of $US107.8 million, a reported increase of 39% year-over-year (Weibo, 2015). Like Tencent, Weibo earns the bulk of its revenue from advertising (US$87.9 million, which represents an increase of 37% year-over-year), and from Weibo Value Added Services (VAS) (US$20 million, a more modest increase of 13% year-over-year) (Weibo, 2015). These revenue increases are described in Weibo's financial reporting as the result of increased efforts to build their presence in 'lower tiered cities' in Mainland China, expanded partnerships 'with the television and movie industries' (Weibo, 2015), and elsewhere as the result of more aggressive longer-term efforts to push 'in-stream or news feed advertising', which was enabled, in part, through a strategic deal with Alibaba's Taobao e-commerce platform (Cutler, 2013). However, as *The Wall Street Journal* reports, these results are also the product of a 'critical transformative period to revamp [its] legacy business and diversify [its] business models' as a result of decline in 'portal revenue', and due to the threat posed by its rivals Tencent and Alibaba (Beckerman, 2015). While, for its investors, the financial results for the quarter ended June 2015 are encouraging, it is too early to tell what longer-term implications this 'revamp' will have for Weibo's social media business operations and corporate prospects.

Finally, in the case of Alibaba Group, despite dominating Chinese market share in the e-commerce sector, social media has been a particularly difficult nut for it to crack. Back in 2009, for instance, Alibaba attempted – albeit largely unsuccessfully – to graft social network functionality onto its e-commerce platform Taobao by creating a SNS subsidiary known as Taojianghu (Fletcher, 2009). In 2015, it tried to do so once again by launching DingTalk, a 'collaboration and messaging app for small-to-medium businesses' (Shu, 2015). However, its most significant moves towards building a social media presence are clearly its substantial US$586 million

investment in Sina Weibo (Custer, 2013), its US$215 million investment the following year in social messaging app Tango (Perez, 2014a), and its $US200 million investment in 2015 in Snapchat (Russell, 2015).

Russia

Turning from China to Russia, while Facebook dominates the social media landscape in many parts of the world, in Russia (and neighbouring countries), as in China, this does not hold true (Blinova, 2013). In Russia – as well as the Ukraine, Belarus, and Kazakhstan – Vkontakte (or VK.com) remains the most popular social media service ahead of Odnoklassniki, My World@ Mail.ru, and Facebook; it is also the second most visited website behind Yandex, the Russian search engine (Baran and Stock, 2015). Vkontakte (Russian for 'in touch', or 'keeping contact') was founded in 2006 by Pavel Durov, who was controversially ousted from the company in 2015 (Johnston, 2015). Vkontakte has a reported 67 million monthly active users.

Mail.ru Group, which is listed on the London stock exchange, dominates the Russian social media landscape. The holding company bought a 40% stake in VK.com in 2007, and then acquired the remaining shares in 2014 to become the sole owner of the leading Russian social media firm. Mail.ru also controls VK.com's two key rivals: Odnoklassniki and My World. For the six months ended June 2015, Mail.ru reported total revenues of RUB18 billion (US$248 million). In its reporting, Mail.ru divides revenues into five broad categories, with the RUB18 billion broken down as follows: 'Email, Portal, and IM [Instant Messaging]' (RUB1.9 billion); 'Social Networks (ex VK)' (RUB6.8 billion); 'Online Games' (RUB4.1 billion); 'VK' (RUB2.6 billion); and 'Ecommerce, Search & other' (RUB2.5 billion) (Mail.ru, 2015). What is striking about these figures is that, while VK.com remains the most popular social media service in Russia, it is by no means the most lucrative. One explanation for this is that VK.com earns revenues from app developer commissions and advertising, while Mail.ru's other social network businesses (Odnoklassniki and My World) from the quite lucrative e-commerce stream (in the form of user payments for virtual gifts), as well as from app developer commissions and advertising (Mail.ru, 2015).

Having provided the above accounts of the social media app economies of two key BRICS nations, China and Russia, I am reluctant to draw detailed comparisons between them. While examinations of media systems are sorely needed that compare 'the "East" with the "East"' (versus 'the "West" with the "Rest"'), to use Meng and Rantanen's (2015) terminology, any such analysis would be difficult to achieve in the space available here. As Meng and Rantanen (2015) argue, any nuanced comparative analysis of these two very complicated media markets requires 'historizing comparative media studies from non-Western perspectives' (p. 2), 're-conceptualizing the relationship between the state and media markets' (p. 2),[4] and critically 'rethinking the dynamics between the global, the national, and the local' (p. 8). Rather, in the space remaining I intend to add further detail to the emerging picture of global social media app markets and economies developed above by discussing the vitally important role that is played by cross-platform data-sharing and other arrangements in driving the commercialisation of social media applications. What these reflections aim to provide is some preliminary evidence of an emergent set of dynamics – shared by Facebook, Tencent and Mail.ru – that suggest a re-emergence of (and reinvigoration of the concept of) the *entrepôt*. This, I suggest, is facilitated by complicated (and difficult to track) cross-platform data-sharing agreements, increased global concentration of financial (cross-)investment, and the embrace of holding company-like

corporate structures (arrangements that are fuelled by corporate acquisitions driving greater horizontal integration of services and data-gathering capabilities).

'NETWORKED MEDIA': THE FACILITATION OF INTEROPERABILITY AND DATA-SHARING

In her book *Status Update*, Alice Marwick (2013: 6) remarks that, '"interoperability", the ability to port data from one site to another [… seems] quaint in the context of closed networks like Facebook, proprietary formats like the Apple App Store, and highly regulated environments like mobile carriers'. My suggestion here is that, contrary to this view, the facilitation of interoperability remains a vital concern for, and a key aspect of the economic ambitions of, the firms which control social media applications, regardless of whether these are 'closed networks', like Facebook, or other social media firms.

With respect to 'closed networks', Mark Andrejevic (2007: 299) points out that 'the model of enclosure highlights the ongoing importance of structures of ownership and control over productive resources'. Elsewhere I have attempted to draw out the strategic importance of this for Facebook, suggesting that a productive way of thinking about Facebook's location-driven acquisitions of Instagram and WhatsApp is via reference to an idea taken from international trade: that of the *entrepôt* (Wilken, 2014). This is a term that refers traditionally to 'a place or district which acts as an intermediary centre for trade between foreign countries' (Moore, c. 1963: 63). In a general – and, for my purposes, more apposite – sense, it also involves 'the receipt of goods from one part of the world and their distribution to another part; or a place where goods are temporarily stored' (c. 1963: 63). In the case of Facebook, we might think of its present relationship with Instagram and

WhatsApp, where these two (at least for now) enjoy relative independence from their parent company, as a form of application-based corporate – as opposed to transnational – *entrepôt* trade. A key difference from earlier conceptions of *entrepôt* trade, however, is that, in Facebook's case, the 'goods' are generated by end-users (in the forms of geotagged status updates, likes, and so forth), received and 'stored' by *entrepôt* intermediary centres (Instagram, WhatsApp), before flowing to the parent trader (Facebook) and into its places database and social graph. Of course, as with the historical development of *entrepôt* trade (Smith, 1910; Boon, 2013), control of the technological infrastructure facilitating this flow of 'goods' is crucial: for the British Empire this included railway, shipping, and other distribution technologies and channels; whereas, in Facebook's case, it involves propriety software and ranking and other algorithmic processes (Pasquale, 2015: 66) – especially those which facilitate the flow of data from Instagram and WhatsApp (among other sources) into Facebook's databases. The outcome for Facebook from this data flow, to adapt Mark Andrejevic's (2007: 296) words, is a portrait of 'user activity made possible by ubiquitous interactivity', especially social media-based interactivity, that is 'increasingly detailed and fine-grained, thanks to an unprecedented ability to capture and store patterns of interaction, movement, transaction, and communication'. Facebook and its subsidiaries, and Mail.ru and its subsidiaries, continue the tradition of *entrepôt* centres acting as key 'intermediaries' in the value chain. Traditionally, this would have linked manufacturers with consumers (see Feenstra and Hanson, 2004: 6–8); here, however, these arrangements are disrupted (Flew, 2008: 200–201), such that both ends of the value chain come to serve dual roles as both the suppliers and the consumers of rich, monetisable digital content. For Facebook, Tencent and Mail.ru, like for more traditional centres of trade, 'the income flow from these *entrepôt* activities is large' (Feenstra and Hanson, 2004: 4).

A key reason for the implementation and absorption by one platform of another's 'strategic interface modifications', José van Dijck explains (2013: 156), is that it is 'mutually beneficial' in 'driving traffic for all parties involved'. Clearly the main beneficiaries of these arrangements are the larger firms (Facebook, Tencent, Mail.ru). However, beyond large 'closed networks' like Facebook, the promotion and maintenance of interoperability – especially given a seemingly endless stream of app modifications and updates – remains a vital concern for social media firms, especially smaller firms (like Foursquare) and start-ups if they are to survive and thrive. Moreover, given the stakes involved, it is of little surprise that those who rely on interoperability 'have a vested interest in erasing the boundaries [between one service and another] and rendering its operational logic invisible' (van Dijck, 2013: 171). Van Dijck (2013: 163–164) describes these inter- and infra-firm arrangements as 'chains of microsystems'. This is a productive way of framing the various corporate arrangements that shape the flow and monetisation of data.

There are, I would suggest, two crucial further dimensions (at least) that might be added to future accounts of these social media 'chains of microsystems'. First, what is not included by van Dijck (2013) in her account, but is becoming increasingly important to understanding the internal logics of interoperability and data transfer, is focused consideration of the (often quite low profile) companies that form the links in these chains, the 'interstices between platforms' (2013: 156) – that is, those firms (like Button and IF) that provide infrastructural and service support so as to facilitate social media platform interoperability and data flow, and which form vital nodes in the larger networked app ecosystem and economy.[5] Second, I would like to further suggest that van Dijck's notion of 'networked media' might be extended productively by thinking through and exploring the place of venture capital investment within, and other forms of financial control of, these corporate 'chains of microsystems'.

One of the things that emerged most strongly from the research undertaken for this chapter was the clear and increasing sense of global concentration of investment in and ownership of social media businesses. For example, a key if little discussed firm is Naspers, a multinational internet and media group based in South Africa, with a market capitalisation of over US$66 billion. Naspers has a 34% stake in Tencent (as at 2014), and a 29% stake in Mail.ru (as at 2013), and a controlling stake in Russian classifieds site Avito (Khrennikov and Spillane, 2015). In addition, it is worth noting that Tencent and Alibaba, as well as DST Global (see below), all have significant stakes in Didi Kauidi, China's local rival to Uber.

My final example brings us back to Mail.ru Group. Back in June 2008, Estonian firm Forticom, owner of the Lithuanian social media service one.lt and quarter owner of Odnoklassniki, aquired a controlling stake in Polish social media service Nasza-Klasa for PLN200 million (US$92 million). Two years later, Russian firm Digital Sky Technologies, headed by the mercurial Russian entrepreneur Yuri Milner, took financial control of Forticom. Digital Sky Techologies was the operator of Mail.ru, and when the latter service was floated on the London stock exchange, Mail.ru Group became the new business name for both. As we have seen above, Mail.ru Group now owns VK.com, Odnoklassniki and My World, and thus controlling interests in Europe's largest (non-Facebook) social media services. It is also worth noting that Digital Sky Technologies made early investments in a number of now key tech firms, including Facebook (US$200 million in 2009), Groupon, and Zynga. Subsequent to the Mail.ru stock market float, Milner created a new firm, DST Global, to handle international investments, including US$800 million in Twitter, US$125 million in WhatsApp, stakes in Alibaba, Spotify, and AirBnB, further investments in Facebook

and Groupon, as well as financing many other ventures. These significant investments, and the sheer financial reach of firms such as Naspers and DST Global, are little understood and warrant careful future critical examination.

In addition to its investment reach, the Mail.ru Group is noteworthy for its holding company structure. It is one of a number of social media and search companies that have undergone corporate consolidation of this sort, most notably Alphabet Inc.; Facebook, too, while not formally operating as a holding company, increasingly has, I would suggest, holding company-like characteristics in the way that it manages its key subsidiary services.

A formal holding company structure carries a number of practical operational advantages for the firms involved (e.g., taxation benefits, a relaxation of certain forms of financial scrutiny, reduced risk, 'freedom of capital allotment', and so forth). Additional advantages to a holding company-like structure for social media and search firms can be grasped by briefly considering the situation facing the global advertising industry during the 1990s.

Prior to the arrival of the big holding groups (WPP, Omnicom, Interpublic, Publicis, Dentsu, Aegis, and Havas), the two basic functions of an ad agency – making and placing advertisements – were generally handled within one 'full-service' agency firm. The holding company structure, John Sinclair (2012: 39) has argued, led to an 'unbundling' of these core services, such that 'the business of strategically purchasing media space and time [were] hived off from the "creative" business of devising and executing advertising campaigns, in quite separate agencies'. These, alongside PR firms and specialised digital-strategy firms, became 'integrated under the one holding group'. One of the key drivers for these ad industry corporate reconfigurations was so that one holding group (such as Martin Sorell's WPP), could hold (or compete for) multiple accounts with different clients that are in direct competition with each other (such as Colgate-Palmolive and Proctor & Gamble) without there being any perceived or actual conflict of interest. What this enabled, in other words, was a kind of 'walled garden' that encouraged clients – multiple clients – to keep all their business (ad creation, media buying, PR work, etc.) within the one holding company family, and which, for that holding company, meant capturing a greater proportion of clients' overall ad- and media-spend budgets, as well as associated and invaluable client-related data.

This is not dissimilar to what Facebook has been doing through *entrepôt* trade that enables it to maintain ownership and control over [its] productive resources (Andrejevic, 2007: 299). Similarly, in the case of Mail.ru Group, the establishment of a holding company structure has enabled it to consolidate its dominance in a number of former Soviet countries – and, prior to this, in other 'semi-peripheral' markets (Toczyski, Krejtz, Ciemniewski, 2015) – where Facebook has struggled to gain a foothold, while maintaining service choice for end-users (VK.com, Odnoklassniki, MyWorld), and diversity of revenue generation.

CONCLUSION

This chapter has explored social media app markets and economies. Beginning with an overview of the app economy, in the first half of the chapter I examined the revenue options of two key US-domiciled firms, Facebook and Twitter. In the second part of the chapter, I argued for the importance of moving beyond these established business contexts to take into account other key markets. In making this argument, I focused on two of the BRICS nations: China and Russia. And, in the final part of the chapter I have suggested that, in developing an account of social media app economies, it is also important to account for the interrelationships between firms (and their financing).

While analysing the economics of mobile social apps, I have been conscious not to forget, as van Dijck (2013: 164) reminds us, that platforms are always fluid. Platforms change, as do their operations, end uses, business and revenue models, and their overall fortunes. Even so, a crucial stabilising factor is that there 'exists a ubiquitous technology [the mobile smartphone] that connects [...] to a central ecosystem' (Farbman, 2016), of which apps are a central part. Ecosystem 'stability' of this sort plays a crucial role in driving the current take-up of social media apps, as well as the present high levels of investment in social media services. One result of this, I have argued, is the emergence of forms of application-based corporate – as opposed to transnational – *entrepôt* trade.

Writing just after the turn of the twentieth century, J. Russell Smith (1910) makes the point that, while the days of a 'world *entrepôt*' have long since passed, new *entrepôts* are 'springing up all the time' (Smith, 1910: 712). What I have sought to argue in this chapter is that large social media firms, such as Facebook, Tencent, and Mail.ru, all effectively operate as *entrepôt* centres of trade. The emergence of new *entrepôts*, Smith suggests, is driven by economic imperatives, rather than by 'legislative statutes' or 'national whim' (1910: 712). While this may well still hold, in the case of the firms under examination here, it is becoming increasingly apparent that the growth of social media data *entrepôt* trade, and the consolidation of oligopolistic control of this trade, is, within many national contexts, of growing interest (and concern) across a range of areas (regulatory policy, economy, national security, etc.). Future work that systematically traces these corporate arrangements, the concomitant concentration in ownership and (cross-) financing of social media businesses, and the economic, policy, national security and other discourses that emerge in response to, and which circulate around, these developments is imperative, and will add additional, important layers to future critical understanding of 'networked media' and the complicated 'chains of microsystems' that structure their operations and interoperations.

Notes

1 A task that is made even more difficult by variable pricing of apps across app markets and mobile devices (Bensinger, 2013).
2 On the growing importance of iCloud to Apple's services, and to the app economy, see Mosco (2014).
3 For example, World Internet Project data reveals emerging areas where there is a notable concentration of internet users who visit social networking sites; one such concentration of high social media use is the MENA region, which includes countries such as Bahrain, Egypt, Jordan, Lebanon, Qatar, Saudi Arabia, the UAE, and Tunisia (WIP, 2016).
4 For an account of the many 'peculiarities' that inform this relationship in the Russian case, see Lehtisaari (2015).
5 On the former, see www.usebutton.com/; on the latter, see https://ifttt.com/

REFERENCES

Albarran, A. B. (ed.) (2013) *The Social Media Industries*. New York: Routledge.

Andrejevic, M. (2007) 'Surveillance in the digital enclosure', *The Communication Review*, 10: 295–317.

Ante, S. E. (2009, December 21) 'Twitter is said to be profitable after making search agreements', *Bloomberg.com*, www.bloomberg.com

Apple (2016, January 26) 'Apple reports record first quarter results', *Apple*, www.apple.com/au/pr/library/2016/01/26Apple-Reports-Record-First-Quarter-Results.html

Baran, K. and Stock, W. (2015) 'Facebook has been smacked down. The Russian special way of SNSs: Vkontakte as a case study', in *Proceedings of the 2nd European Conference on Social Media* (ECSM 2015), 9–10 July, Porto, Portugal. Reading, UK: Academic Conferences and Publishing Limited, pp. 574–582, www.phil-fak.uni-duesseldorf.de/fileadmin/Redaktion/Institute/Informationswissenschaft/heck/Baran_2015_ECSM_2015_Proceedings.pdf

Barreneche, C. and Wilken, R. (2015) 'Platform specificity and the politics of location data extraction', *European Journal of Cultural Studies*, 18(4–5): 497–513.

Beckerman, J. (2015, May 15) 'Sina revenue increases on Weibo growth: Weibo's monthly active users in March rose 38% from a year earlier', *The Wall Street Journal*, www.wsj.com/articles/sina-revenue-increases-on-weibo-growth-1431647742

Bensinger, G. (2013, March 3) 'The evolving economics of the app', *The Wall Street Journal*, www.wsj.com/articles/SB10001424127887323511804578300183961009070

Blank, S. (2010, January 25) 'What's a startup? First principles', *Steve Blank*, http://steveblank.com/2010/01/25/whats-a-startup-first-principles/

Blinova, M. (2013) 'Social media in Russia: Its features and business models', in M. Friedrichsen and W. Mühl-Benninghaus (eds), *Handbook of Social Media Management*. Berlin: Springer-Verlag, pp. 405–415.

Boon, G. C. (2013) *Technology and Entrepôt Colonialism in Singapore, 1819–1940*. Singapore: Institute for Southeast Asian Studies.

Bradshaw, T. and Bond, S. (2015, June 5) 'Apple rewrites app economies for media', *Financial Times*, www.ft.com/intl/cms/s/0/01a151fc-0b8b-11e5-8937-00144feabdc0.html#slide0

Caribou Digital (2016) *Winners and Losers in the Global App Economy*. Farnham, Surrey: Caribou Digital Publishing, http://caribou-digital.net/wp-content/uploads/2016/02/Caribou-Digital-Winners-and-Losers-in-the-Global-App-Economy-2016.pdf

Cha, J. (2013) 'Business models of most-visited US social networking sites', in Alan B. Albarran (ed.), *The Social Media Industries*. New York: Routledge, pp. 60–85.

Cheng, C.-W. (2012) 'The system and self-reference of the app economy: The case of *Angry Birds*', *Westminster Papers*, 9(1): 47–66.

Constine, J. (2016a, January 27) 'Facebook climbs to 1.59 billion users and crushes Q4 estimates with $5.8b revenue', *TechCrunch*, http://techcrunch.com/2016/01/27/facebook-earnings-q4-2015/

Constine, J. (2016b, February 10) 'Twitter's monthly user count actually shrunk if you exclude SMS', *TechCrunch*, http://techcrunch.com/2016/02/10/twitter-is-shrinking/

Crowe, P. (2016, February 11) 'Goldman Sachs: The "mantra" in Silicon Valley has changed', *Business Insider Australia*, www.businessinsider.com.au/cohn-says-the-mantra-has-changed-in-silicon-valley-2016-2?r=US&IR=T

Custer, C. (2013, April 30) 'Why did Alibaba invest $586 million in Sina Weibo?', *Tech in Asia*, www.techinasia.com/why-alibaba-invest-sina-weibo

Cutler, M. (2013, April 29) 'Sina Weibo, China's equivalent of Facebook and Twitter, gets $586m investment from Alibaba', *TechCrunch*, http://techcrunch.com/2013/04/29/sina-weibo/

Evans, B. (2015, June 14) 'The (lack of) app store metrics', *Benedict Evans*, http://ben-evans.com/benedictevans/2015/6/13/the-lack-of-app-store-metrics

Facebook (2016, January 27) 'Facebook reports fourth quarter and full year 2015 results', *Facebook*, http://investor.fb.com/releasedetail.cfm?ReleaseID=952040

Farbman, Z. (2016, January 28) 'The app ecosystem's new status quo', *TechCrunch*, http://techcrunch.com/2016/01/28/what-to-expect-from-the-app-ecosystem/

Feenstra, R. C. and Hanson, G. H. (2004) 'Intermediaries in entrepôt trade: Hong Kong re-exports of Chinese goods', *Journal of Economics and Management Strategy*, 13(1): 3–35.

Fletcher, O. (2009, August 6) 'China's Alibaba adds social networking to e-commerce', *Computerworld Hong Kong*, http://cw.com.hk/news/chinas-alibaba-adds-social-networking-e-commerce?page=0,0

Flew, T. (2008) *New Media: An Introduction* (3rd edition). South Melbourne, Vic.: Oxford University Press.

Gannes, L. (2011, July 15) 'With Google gone (for now), Twitter tries to come to terms with Microsoft's Bing', *All Things Digital*, http://allthingsd.com/20110715/with-google-gone-for-now-twitter-tries-to-come-to-terms-with-microsofts-bing/

Ghoshal, D. (2016, February 8) 'Why TRAI backed net neutrality – and killed Facebook's Free Basics in India', *Quartz*, http://qz.com/612159/why-trai-backed-net-neutrality-and-killed-facebooks-free-basics-in-india/

Goggin, G. and McLelland, M. (2009) 'Internationalizing internet studies: Beyond Anglophone paradigms', in G. Goggin and M. McLelland (eds), *Internationalizing Internet Studies*. New York: Routledge, pp. 3–17.

Goldsmith, B. (2014) 'The smartphone app economy and app ecosystems', in G. Goggin and L. Hjorth (eds), *The Routledge Companion to Mobile Media*. New York: Routledge, pp. 171–180.

ITU (2015) 'ICT facts & figures: The world in 2015', *International Telecommunications Union*, www.itu.int/en/ITU-D/Statistics/Documents/facts/ICTFactsFigures2015.pdf

Johnston, C. (2015, February 12) 'Crime, punishment, and Russia's original social network', *Motherboard*, http://motherboard.vice.com/read/v-for-vkontakte

Khrennikov, I. and Spillane, C. (2015, October 23) 'Naspers takes control of Russia's Avito in $1.2 billion purchase', *Bloomberg.com*, www.bloomberg.com/news/articles/2015-10-23/naspers-takes-control-of-russia-s-avito-in-1-2-billion-purchase.

Koh, Y. (2015, April 29) 'Twitter to enlarge user growth by counting SMS-only users', *The Wall Street Journal*, http://blogs.wsj.com/digits/2015/04/29/twitter-to-enlarge-user-growth-by-counting-sms-only-users/

Lacy, S. (2009) *Once You're Lucky, Twice You're Good: The Rebirth of Silicon Valley and the Rise of Web 2.0*. New York: Gotham Books.

Latour, B. (1996) *Aramis, or the Love of Technology*, trans. Catherine Porter. Cambridge, MA: Harvard University Press.

Lehtisaari, K. (2015, October) *Market and Political Factors and the Russian Media*. Working Paper. Oxford: Reuters Institute for the Study of Journalism.

Lewis, M. (2001) *The New New Thing*. New York: Penguin.

Lobato, R. and Thomas, J. (2015) *The Informal Media Economy*. Cambridge: Polity Press.

Lynley, M. and Constine, J. (2016, February 10) 'Twitter's user growth goes nowhere as it meets revenue expectations of $710m', *TechCrunch*, http://techcrunch.com/2016/02/10/twitters-user-growth-goes-nowhere-as-it-meets-revenue-expectations-of-710m/

Mail.ru (2015, June 30) 'Interim condensed consolidated financial statements', *Mail.ru Group Limited*, https://corp.imgsmail.ru/media/files/mail.rugroupifrsh12015.pdf

Marwick, A. E. (2013) *Status Update: Celebrity, Publicity, and Branding in the Social Media Age*. New Haven, CT: Yale University Press.

McEleny, C. (2016, February 9) 'WeChat had more mobile transactions over just Chinese New Year than PayPal had during 2015', *The Drum*, http://m.thedrum.com/news/2016/02/09/wechat-had-more-mobile-transactions-over-just-chinese-new-year-paypal-had-during

Meng, B. and Rantanen, T. (2015) 'A change of lens: A call to compare the media in China and Russia', *Critical Studies in Media Communication*, 32(1): 1–15.

Moore, W. G. (c. 1963) *A Dictionary of Geography*. Harmondsworth, Middlesex: Penguin.

Mosco, V. (1996) *The Political Economy of Communication*. London: Sage.

Mosco, V. (2014) *To the Cloud: Big Data in a Turbulent World*. Boulder, CO: Paradigm Publishers.

Neal, R. W. (2013, November 10) 'Twitter's hidden revenue stream: How the social media firm plans to turn every tweet we post and everything we reveal about ourselves into big profits', *International Business Times*, www.ibtimes.com/twitters-hidden-revenue-stream-how-social-media-firm-plans-turn-every-tweet-we-post-everything-we

Pasquale, F. (2015) *The Black Box Society: The Secret Algorithms that Control Money and Information*. Cambridge, MA: Harvard University Press.

Perez, Sarah (2014a, March 19) 'Mobile messaging app & gaming platform Tango raises massive $280 million Series D', *TechCrunch*, http://techcrunch.com/2014/03/19/mobile-messaging-app-gaming-platform-tango-raises-massive-280-million-series-d/

Perez, Sarah (2014b, July 21) 'The majority of today's app businesses are not sustainable', *TechCrunch*, http://techcrunch.com/2014/07/21/the-majority-of-todays-app-businesses-are-not-sustainable/

Pon, B., Seppälä, T., and Kenney, M. (2014) 'Android and the demise of operating system-based power: Firm strategy and platform control in the post-PC world', *Telecommunications Policy*, 38: 979–991.

Purnell, N. (2015, January 20) 'Twitter buys Indian mobile startup ZipDial', *The Wall Street Journal*, www.wsj.com/articles/twitter-to-buy-indian-mobile-marketing-startup-1421728561

Russell, J. (2015, March 12) 'Understanding Alibaba's Snapchat obsession', *TechCrunch*, http://techcrunch.com/2015/03/12/this-is-more-than-a-crush/

Shu, C. (2015, February 12) 'Alibaba launches enterprise messaging app DingTalk, its latest mobile software product', *TechCrunch*, http://techcrunch.com/2015/02/12/alibaba-dingtalk/

Sibley, D. (1995) *Geographies of Exclusion: Society and Difference in the West*. London: Routledge.

Sinclair, J. (2008) 'Globalization and the advertising industry in China', *Chinese Journal of Communication*, 1(1): 77–90.

Sinclair, J. (2012) *Advertising, the Media and Globalisation: A World in Motion*. London: Routledge.

Smith, J. R. (1910) 'The world entrepôt', *Journal of Political Economy*, 18(9): 697–713.

Smith, L. J. and Popper, B. (2016, February 10) 'Twitter's earnings report shows its user base is shrinking', *The Verge*, www.theverge.com/2016/2/10/10961776/twitter-q4-2015-earnings-user-base-stall-shrink

Statt, N. (2016, February 1) 'WhatsApp has grown to 1 billion users', *The Verge*, www.theverge.com/2016/2/1/10889534/whats-app-1-billion-users-facebook-mark-zuckerberg

Tencent (2015) '2015 interim report', *Tencent Holdings Limited*, www.tencent.com/en-us/content/ir/rp/2015/attachments/201501.pdf

Toczyski, P., Krejtz, K., and Ciemniewski, W. (2015) 'The challenges of semi-peripheral information society: The case of Poland', *Studies in Global Ethics and Global Education*, 3: 74–88.

Truong, A. (2015, April 28) 'Twitter is goosing its numbers by counting SMS-only users', *Quartz*, http://qz.com/393784/twitter-is-goosing-its-numbers-by-counting-sms-only-users/

Twitter (2015), 'Quarterly results 2015', *Twitter Inc.*, https://investor.twitterinc.com/results.cfm

USS&EC (2015, December 31) 'Alphabet annual report', *United States Security & Exchange Commission*, https://abc.xyz/investor/pdf/20151231_alphabet_10K.pdf

Van Couvering, E. (2011), 'Navigational media: The political economy of online traffic', in D. Winseck and D. Y. Jin (eds), *The Political Economics of Media: The Transformation of the Global Media Industries.* London: Bloomsbury Academic, pp. 183–200.

van Dijck, J. (2013) *The Culture of Connectivity: A Critical History of Social Media.* New York: Oxford University Press.

Viita, K. (2016, February 11) 'Cheap smartphones to propel app spending past $100 billion', *Bloomberg*, www.bloomberg.com/news/articles/2016-02-10/cheap-smartphones-to-propel-app-spending-past-100-billion

Wadhwa, V. (2016, February 16) 'Why Facebook and Marc Andreessen offended India with good intentions', *Financial Review*, www.afr.com/technology/why-facebook-and-marc-andreessen-offended-india-with-good-intentions-20160216-gmv4u4

Walton, M. (2014) 'Pavement internet: Mobile media economies and ecologies in South Africa', in G. Goggin and L. Hjorth (eds), *The Routledge Companion to Mobile Media.* New York: Routledge, pp. 450–461.

Wasko, J. (2004) 'The political economy of communications', in J. Downing, D. McQuail, P. Schlesinger, and E. A. Wartella (eds), *The SAGE Handbook of Media Studies.* Thousand Oaks, CA: Sage, pp. 309–329.

Weibo (2015, August 18) 'Investor relations – press releases', *Weibo Corp.*, http://ir.weibo.com/phoenix.zhtml?c=253076&p=irol-newsArticle&ID=2080444

Wilken, R. (2014) 'Friends nearby: Facebook as a location-based social media platform', *New Media & Society*, 16(7): 1087–1103.

Wilken, R. and Bayliss, P. (2015) 'Locating Foursquare: The political economics of mobile social software', in R. Wilken and G. Goggin (eds), *Locative Media*. New York: Routledge, pp. 177–192.

WIP (2016) *The World Internet Project – International Report* (6th edition). Los Angeles, CA: USC Annenberg School Center for the Digital Future.

16

Labor and Social Media: The Exploitation and Emancipation of (almost) Everyone Online

Jack Linchuan Qiu

INTRODUCTION

For most readers of this book and for average Internet users, the connections between social media and labor probably seem rather tenuous, if they appear to exist at all. Many would wonder, aren't social media purely about entertainment and leisure activities? Aren't we told that social media are all about fun and consumption and therefore act as a drain on productivity for employees, whose clicks and updates lead to endless procrastination? How on earth do they have anything to do with labor?

This lack of awareness should come as no surprise because modern media representations and discourse, as part and parcel of global capitalism, have for decades systematically suppressed, concealed, and twisted issues of labor (Mosco, 2011). As a result, members of the working class often orient themselves to individualism and consumerism, ignoring their collective interests and struggle. The sidelining of labor coverage and labor perspectives is common in media and communication research, where 'the relationship of labor and working people to mass media and information technologies is at best a peripheral item' (Mosco & Wasko, 1983, p. xx). This pattern characterizes not only western academia, but also the majority of media studies scholarship around the world, where conventional wisdom sees social media and smart devices (e.g., mobile phones and apps for teenagers) as socially constructed around discourses of leisure, fun, and consumption.

Yet, labor, employment, and questions of inclusion and equality in the digital economy have been classic topics in Internet studies from the beginning of the field (e.g., DiMaggio, Hargittai, Neuman & Robinson, 2001; Servon, 2002), following a much longer intellectual tradition that can be traced back to the seminal work by Daniel Bell in the 1970s and Manuel Castells since the 1980s (Qiu, 2013). As social media spread rapidly in the aftermath of the 2008–2009 global financial crisis, there has also been a revival of scholarly interests in 'digital labor', for instance, conceived in the new social and technological contexts of 'the Internet as factory and playground' (Scholz, 2013). Among others, Christian Fuchs (2014a, 2014b) has proposed that we need to re-imagine social media platforms as much more than places of entertainment and tools of consumption; that they are, instead, also instruments of capital accumulation as well as sites of struggles for 'the commons of society' (2014a, Loc 7772). Such arguments by Scholz, Fuchs, and colleagues shed light on new prospects for a socialist future and the emancipation of labor, broadly defined to include employees in social media industries and ordinary social media users as well. These ongoing debates about social media and labor, which this chapter will summarize, elaborate, and reflect upon, have ushered in a new phase of progressive academic intervention. Against a neoliberal backdrop, questions of collective and productive labor power have emerged paradoxically as issues of labor re-enter the world-historical limelight: social media workers of the world, unite!

The reality is, of course, much more complicated. This chapter shall guide readers through the key conceptual and empirical developments in (digital) labor studies and the research on social media, while making proposals for a new critical research agenda for social media and labor. The context of this discussion includes not only post-industrial societies but also the Global South at this very interesting time when 'the Internet is much less West-centric [than before], and rapidly diversifying as the world's populations engage with it in their own ways' (Wu & Taneja, 2016).

SHIFTING GROUNDS, SHIFTING PERSPECTIVES

Speaking of social media, José van Dijck writes:

> The very word 'social' associated with media implies that platforms are user-centered and that they facilitate communal activities, just as the term 'participatory' emphasizes human collaboration. Indeed, social media can be seen as online facilitators or enhancers of *human* networks – webs of people that promote connectedness as a social value. (2013, p. 11)

However, in the short span of a few years, the culture of human connectedness on social media platforms was transformed into what van Dijck calls 'the culture of connectivity' (2013) that is much more commercialized and privatized to the extent that critics such as Toby Miller now calls them 'anti-social' media (2015).

The shift of platform operations from mediated sociality and participatory culture to commerce and stock market performance is, of course, not the only dynamic that matters. There are also instances when the forces of marketization were stalled (e.g., Flickr) or remain ineffective (e.g., Wikipedia). But the sweeping influence of commercialization in social media industries has added to the imperative to highlight labor as an essential dimension of, and a persistently necessary approach to, social media. More than a binary opposition, the configuration of labor-capital relationship varies depending on the concrete market and/or power dynamics. This can be seen in systems of social media where van Dijck portrays 'the cat-and-mouse game between platform users and owners' as 'a struggle to define the conditions for online sociality' (2013, p. 109). More specifically, here she is analyzing Flickr, a prominent case when the force of commercialization toward 'connectivity' was unsuccessful due to resistance from 'platform users', i.e., the source of labor power.

Conceived as such, the particular meanings of social media vary greatly across time and space; so do their functions at the individual, communal (including in virtual communities), and societal levels. Extending an earlier argument (Qiu, 2013), I submit that that an oft-forgotten but always necessary demarcation line between different labor formations in social media is class. This idea builds on my earlier concept of 'working-class ICTs' (Qiu, 2009), by which I understand a large spectrum of low-end ICT tools such as cybercafés and inexpensive mobile devices, which serve disadvantaged populations from migrants and retiree to ethnic minorities and people with disabilities. Extending this idea, we can construe 'working-class social media' as a new category covering both the techno-logical tools serving working-class users and the social relations between such plat-forms and the working-class groups. These include, for example, platforms such as QQ in China, which shall be discussed in more detail below. In other words, the concept of 'working-class social media' is not just about Facebook, Twitter, Whatsapp and Instagram, although they have attracted working-class users as well. More importantly, it encom-passes cybercafés and their customers in Trinidad, Filipino domestic helpers Skyping home from Dubai, and Africans using Mxit to coordinate the transfer of remittances via M-Pesa.

Calling social media 'working-class' is not intended merely to highlight that the new digital platforms are used by people with lower socio-economic status; that they are cheap and sometimes unreliable. Moreover, it signifies that the media are in the hands of those who have 'less information overload or less commitment to the status quo' (Qiu, 2009, p. 13); that social media now serve more closely the existential needs of working people around the world, from job-seeking to access to reliable health services, rather than entertainment alone; and that the prospects remain for a working-class media landscape characterized by fairness, inclusiveness, non-rivalry, and mutual help.

FOUR MODES OF PRODUCTION

What then is labor? And where in relation to social media is labor to be located? Following Maxwell (2015), this chapter uses a broad definition of labor as productive human resources and social processes that generate wealth, wellbeing, and/or social relations in ways that may or may not benefit the laborers themselves. Labor, in this sense, is much more than 'work' as the latter usually oper-ates within the constraints of workplaces and work posts, whereas the former is much more generic and universal. More specifi-cally, social media and labor intersect each other in at least four 'modes of production', to use the classic Marxian term, which I term respectively (a) 'natural labor of sociality', (b) 'wage labor', (c) 'free labor', and (d) 'labor of struggle'. We will see that the con-crete meanings of labor are different, some-times even contradictory, in these four categories. In actuality, the four modes also overlap, clash, and combine into endless variations. This section describes the produc-tive forces in each mode and the relations of production therein.

Natural Labor of Sociality

In the theme song of their second CD album 'Ode to Labor' published in Beijing in 2007 (http://ow.ly/Z0MUo), the New Labor Art Troupe sings:

It is wrong to say that we have nothing
We have our wisdom and our hands
We build streets, bridges and high-rises with our
    wisdom and hands ... From now until forever
Glories to workers!

The lyrics reflect a concept of 'natural labor': labor before alienation and estrangement, when workers possess their labor power and means of production, be they intellectual or physical, and they control the benefits of production processes. Take this band as an example: it consists of migrant workers who happen to love music. They formed a coop-erative, adopted Creative Commons licenses, and published their CDs to support the ele-mentary school in their migrant-worker com-munity. By 2005 they had sold more than

100,000 copies of their first CD album. By 2016 they had published eight albums, all available on their own website 'Singing Aloud (*dashengchang*, www.dashengchang. org.cn/Music.htm)'. Their creative work would have been far less successful without social media, in this case, Weibo (the most popular Twitter-like service in China) and QQ (Qiu, 2009, pp. 121–123).

By using the descriptor 'natural', I frame sociality and acts of communication as innate to human nature. *Homo sapiens* are social animals; and communication is a concrete practice as well as systems of labor that generate use-value both for individuals and for collective social forces. To listen, to speak, to process information for oneself or one's family, to mobilize others to join a social cause – these all require labor as it is defined at the beginning of this section.

In terms of the history of the English language, Raymond Williams noted that '[t]he sense of labor as pain was applied to childbirth' from the sixteenth century (1983, p. 176). In a similarly natural mode of production, social media users communicate with each other without depending on capitalist platforms for the exchange of messages and the distribution of benefits. A case in point is Wikipedia and the Wikimedia networks in and across different societies, which to this day remain a non-commercial and collaborative commons. The Wikipedians may be toiling with their entries, but they are not doing it to enrich some private owners of the platform or to serve the interests of advertisers. Instead, they are creating value and meaning for themselves while providing a public good – like giving birth to children enriches society at large.

From ancient China to medieval Europe, the repetitive movements of manual labor have long been praised for their generation of use-value and as a source of genuine pleasure, of concerted efforts in workmanship, of musical rhythm and artistic value, for instance, in the mode of the 'mechanical arts' (Whitney, 1990). I hold that such a mode of labor, in its natural and pleasant forms, can still exist

in social media usage so long as the user sticks to her or his innate needs for sociality and exercise what Jean-Jacques Rousseau would call a 'natural sensibility' (Voirol, 2016). The nature that surrounded Rousseau (or the peasants for that matter) might differ considerably from the nature before human intervention, but still he was able to exercise his natural capacity, for example in appreciating the beauty of plants and thus improving his own wellbeing, despite the agricultural developments of his time. Similarly, in the man-made gardens of social media, it is still possible to perform natural labor despite structural constraints of corporate strategies and state regulation although mediated sociality and its unmediated forms are not the same. One may speculate that it is precisely the allure of such unalienated labor of sociality that attracts people to social media, who may or may not be aware of the other hidden dimensions of social media operations discussed below.

Wage Labor

In contrast to the idealized perception of labor as an innate, uplifting element of human nature, a much more familiar and widespread idea is to consider labor as unnatural, tedious, and agonizing. Being unpleasant, laboring thus requires monetary compensation or motivation; and hence, wage labor emerges.

Like any modern industry, the functioning of social media depends on the labor input of employees, who perform tasks that are essential to the business, such as programming, designing graphics, and office operations in the corporate headquarters of the social media companies. A notable trend in recent years is automation and its associated discourse, which promises to reduce the size of the human labor force through deploying advanced algorithms and cloud computing (Steiner, 2012; Lokot & Diakopoulos, 2015). Such processes of automation have resulted in

lay-offs, rising precarity, and increasing casualization of the workforce, which work both in
actuality and as a rhetoric to marginalize and
disempower those who are employed by the
social media companies. But as shown in the
infamous case of Facebook using journalism-
school graduates to conduct manual curation
of 'trending news' (Nunez, 2016), what looks
like automation on the surface may in fact be
low-paid precarious human employees working under degrading conditions.

This is of course not the first time we have
seen the persistence of wage labor in supposedly high-tech industries – wage labor in new
and old forms, at new and old locations, from
Indian programmers working in Australia
(Xiang, 2008) to Chinese engineers maintaining cloud-computing facilities (Mosco, 2014),
from commercial content moderators in the
Philippines (Roberts, 2014) to 'Google labor
aristocracy' (Fuchs, 2014a, Loc 5222) and
Facebook employees working on corporate
branding (Marwick, 2013) in Silicon Valley.

Despite the discourse of automation, none
of the social media platforms has succeeded in

getting rid of its employees entirely. Indeed,
none of them has really attempted to because
their founders and CEOs, like Facebook's
Mark Zuckerberg, know they cannot write all
the code themselves; nor can they exclusively
hire robots for sales, customer service, and
bookkeeping. For all these tasks, they have
to rely on wage labor that belongs to what
Maurizio Lazarrato refers to as the 'classic
forms' of 'immaterial labor' as in 'audio-
visual production, advertising, fashion, the
production of software, photography, cultural
activities' (1996, p. 133), which again in the
case of Facebook includes the journalism-
school graduates they hired to manually
curate 'trending news' (Nunez, 2016).

In addition to the full-time and part-time
employees directly on the payroll of social
media companies, there is a much broader
wage labor force that produces the tangible commodities and intangible services
that enable the social media industry. Fuchs
(2015) considers all of them as parts of the
International Division of Digital labor (IDDL)
and visualizes the framework in Figure 16.1.

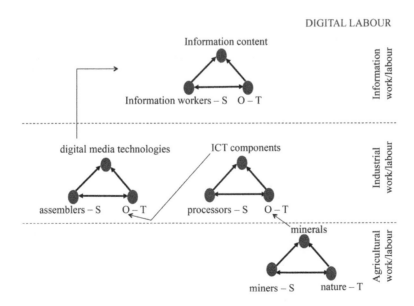

Figure 16.1 Cycles constituting the international division of digital labor

Source: Fuchs (2015, p. 88)

In this conceptualization, 'S' stands for subjects or workers providing labor power; 'O' stands for objects or means of production, including raw materials; 'T' stands for technology or the tools used by subjects to process objects and produce the desired commodities, which sit at the tip of the four triangular relationships represented in Figure 16.1.

In order for immaterial labor (e.g., Facebook workers) to produce content at the informational level of IDDL, there has to be an industrial system directly underpinning it and an agricultural/extractive system further below. Digital media technologies, such as laptops, smartphones, accessories, and servers, must be made, for example, by workers at Foxconn, the world's largest electronics contract manufacturer (Chan & Pun, 2010; Sandoval, 2013). But Foxconn doesn't produce all the ICT components, which instead have to be made elsewhere in mainland China, Taiwan, Korea, Japan, the UK, Germany, and the USA. The raw materials for ICT components come from the bottom of the IDDL, where key minerals for industrial ICT production are extracted: coltan from Congo, tin from Indonesia, gold from Peru. The most notorious case at the bottom level of IDDL is the usage of slave labor in the extraction of Congolese conflict-minerals (Steinweg & de Haan, 2007).

Industrial and agricultural workers in the middle and lower strata of the IDDL do not directly participate in the information labor system of social media. But their indirect involvement as wage labor provides the material basis for informational/immaterial work. Fuchs's diagram does not exhaust all forms of wage labor in the IDDL broadly defined, for instance, the infrastructure of fiber optics, electricity, and transportation systems delivering minerals to components makers, components to assembly factories, and computers to social media firms. All these infrastructures need to be built and maintained based on wage labor, whose scope can be greatly broadened beyond the shop floor of Foxconn or Facebook.

Within the informational labor system there is of course more than Facebook and similar social media firms that operate as for-profit companies or social enterprises, such as Fairphone, which strives to provide ethical alternatives to smartphone consumers (see www.fairphone.com/). Meanwhile, there are those employed in the public sector and state security bodies around the world, including those providing the essential labor power for surveillance operations. The most well-known among them is probably Edward Snowden, the former US National Security Agency (NSA) subcontractor who leaked information about NSA's spy program, Prism, and caused major scandal to the US intelligence services in 2013.

But state-based social media wage labor goes beyond surveillance. In China, authorities have hired people to put up pro-government posts to online forums or sending out anti-activism messages via popular social media platforms such as Weibo, WeChat, and Twitter. Initially they were nicknamed 'wumaodang' or '50-cents-party' for the piecework they performed at the wage of 50 cents per message. In a way not fundamentally different from Facebook's using manual workers to generate 'trending news' (Nunez, 2016), Chinese censors were found to be using intensive 'professional' human labor instead of automated programs in their efforts to suppress or skew Internet discussions (King, Pan, & Roberts, 2013). Over the years, the proactive online propaganda system has also expanded and upgraded into a full industry to monitor, analyze, and shape public opinion using new organizational as well as technological measures (Creemers, 2015), meaning that the authorities often need to hire more hands at higher wages.

Free Labor

Since Tiziana Terranova's foundational essay (2000), the oxymoronic concept of 'free labor' has been central to conceptions of

Internet and knowledge economy where 'productive activities that are pleasurably embraced and at the same time often shamelessly exploited' (p. 37). These oddly 'free' practices are arguably more pronounced in social media platforms than in other realms of Internet communication due to the pervasiveness and seemingly mundane nature of social media modalities.

We don't pay anything to use Twitter or QQ, or so we are told. Users, therefore, often see these services and the content they provide as completely free of charge. This is, however, incorrect as the platforms 'charge' users by accumulating valuable information about the users, their usage and other patterns, and profiting from it. Hence, in exchange for the seemingly 'free' stuff that we enjoy online, social media companies get our time, our attention, our UGC (user generated content), our social networks, and all kinds of meta data about us and our daily life, free of charge as well.

In addition to targeted advertising, much of the data gathered about us is used to improve our user experiences so that the social media platforms become more 'sticky', i.e., we would spend more time on these platforms, thereby generating even more data for the companies. On the one hand, we get more convenience and better online experiences; on the other hand, the social media platforms can have more effective corporate surveillance over us, thus making us more susceptible to targeted advertising. This is, however, an unequal barter because the companies almost always dictate the terms of exchange. As such, free labor in social media systems is ultimately about absorbing unpaid work contributed by Internet users and fans, which can be used to substitute traditional paid work in a wide variety of activities, such as programming and marketing (Terranova, 2000; Kücklich, 2005; Andrejevic, 2008; Fuchs, 2014a) in order to generate wealth for platform owners and stockholders. If a product goes viral through Facebook, even if it is part of a socially engineered campaign, the bulk of the promotional work is performed by unpaid social media users and their 'friends' through their clicking, forwarding, and commenting. This is an extreme mode for the casualization, valorization, and exploitation of media labor that 'allows companies to outsource paid labor time to consumers or fans who work for free' (Fuchs, 2014a, Loc 2957).

From a political economy perspective, Dallas Smythe offered a critique decades ago that the commercial model for advertising-funded mass media was to turn audiences into 'audience commodity' (1977, 1981). He wrote, 'As collectives these audiences are commodities. As commodities they are dealt with in markets by producers [media organizations] and buyers [advertisers]' (1981, p. 234). Unpaid audiences can in this sense be seen as 'workers': 'In "their" time which is sold to advertisers, workers (a) perform essential marketing functions for the producers of consumers' goods, and (b) work at the production and reproduction of labor power' (1977, p. 3).

With the spread of advertising-funded Internet and social media, Smythe's 'audience commodity' critique has received more scholarly attention in recent years. There are, on the one hand, strong objections, for instance from David Hesmondhalgh, who takes Smythe's view as 'crude, reductionist and functionalist' in seeing audience work (including via social media) as merely producing audience commodities for advertisers following a capitalist mode of production while 'totally underestimating contradiction and struggle in capitalism' (2010, p. 280).

On the other hand, Christian Fuchs (2015) extends Smythe's analysis to platforms relying on advertising, although not to other types of social media that do not rely on advertising. In so doing, Fuchs separates 'production workers' from 'circulation workers' in PR and advertising departments, who have a hidden division of labor in generating use-value, value, and symbolic value based directly on their unpaid work, and indirectly on paid employees and wage labor at Facebook and related companies (2015, pp. 89–90). The process generates a new social media audience commodity that adds to the effects of viral marketing campaigns and the consumption meanings of the products and services being promoted. In other words, from the perspective of the advertising industry, through social media they have gained new armies of volunteers who share their content (e.g., memes) and new expansive sets of social networks to further the goals of advertisers without considering themselves as being eligible for the payroll.

How large is the 'free labor' force working for Facebook? According to DMR (2016), Facebook has 1.59 billion monthly active users around the world, of whom 1.04 billion are active on daily basis. Meanwhile, Global Web Index found that, in January 2015, on average Internet users spend 1.72 hours on social network everyday (Mander, 2015). Considering active daily user population only, this means in 2015, Facebook has acquired 652.91 billion hours of labor power from its users globally. In comparison, this amount of labor power is more than 100 times larger than all the waged labor power accumulated by Foxconn, the world's largest electronics manufacturer with more than 1.3 million factory workers in China. Not only is Facebook 100 times 'bigger' than Foxconn in term of its total labor power acquisition, it is also 'free' because Facebook does not need to compensate Facebook users. 'One hundred per cent of their labor time is surplus labor time, which allows capitalists to generate extra surplus value and extra profits' (Fuchs, 2014a, p. 263). No wonder Facebook's business is more lucrative than Foxconn.

One way to connect 'free' social media usage and classic issues of labor is through the intellectual tradition of autonomist Marxism, for instance, Michael Hardt and Antonio Negri's influential idea of the 'multitude' (Hardt & Negri, 2005) about how immaterial labor working in an enlarged planetary 'social factory' can serve as the basis of world revolution. The root of this idea can be traced back

to Negri's *Red Notes*, published four decades ago, when he wrote presciently that, facing the crises of the 1970s, capitalism would need 'a project that is qualitatively different', one that separates production from circulation, aiming at creating a 'productive subject' incapable of collective action and solidarity (1979, p. 34). As revealed by Alice Marwick's ethnography in Silicon Valley, social media platforms such as Facebook serve exactly this function of the social factory in producing an individualist and consumerist subjectivity and 'ideal neoliberal selves' (2013, Loc 105). However, Negri and Hardt have gone further with a bold hypothesis that dialectically this social factory also sows the seeds of its own destruction by producing the multitude, subjects who serve as the social basis for a new worldwide communist revolution, who are now also connected via the Internet.

Meanwhile, an arguably more important, yet often forgotten, conception of 'free labor' is the feminist tradition *à la* Leopodina Fortunati (2007). Although conventional studies of labor often focus exclusively on wage labor, feminist scholarship has argued since the 1970s that women's unpaid work in domestic settings, such as cleaning, cooking and parenting, enabled the male breadwinners to be productive outside the home. As such, women's housework and carework are not a 'natural' attribute of womanhood, but they indeed produce economic value essential to modern society, not to mention their cultural values. Yet women's contribution is often rendered invisible because they are unpaid. Fortunati connects this critique more specifically to new technologies when she analyzes the 'mechanizing' of housework and immaterial labor more generally that includes various carework, communication work, affection, and labor of sociality. 'The mass possession of these intellective technologies represents an important ground for political experimentation and for a new theory and practice of communication, as well as a strategic moment of self-valorization' (Fortunati, 2007, p. 153).

Here, Fortunati is not only critiquing the bias against women's unwaged work. She also makes a key point that is often ignored in the analysis of social media globally: free labor is not limited to the core regions of western societies. Instead, '(g)lobalization separates the material elements from the immaterial ones of the same production process. The latter very often remains in the (post)industrialized countries while the former is located in developing countries, which brings the international division of labor to another level' (ibid., p. 154). Against this backdrop, free labor in the Global North and the Global South may seem to be identical in their outlook, but they are not. For the laboring subjects, female or male, the actual functions and meanings of their spending hours each day doing unwaged work online can be drastically different. The consequence of exchange-value overwhelming use-value may simply be more wealth for platform owners in Silicon Valley and less face-to-face interactions in western societies. But for those residing in the Global South, the same behavior may mean more serious malnutrition and livelihood problems in rural families, more work injuries and more deaths on the shop floor caused by sleep deprivation in the factory zones. The real-life cost of 'free labor' can be much, much higher for people in the developing world.

In her analysis of 'the Digital Housewife' (2016), Kylie Jarrett extends the feminist Marxist tradition into a full-fledged critique of digital labor and the economics of affect under conditions of Web 2.0 and social media. In so doing, she builds on, while transcending, the Automist Marxist argument about the 'social factory' (*à la* Hardt & Negri, 2005) as well as other classic conceptions of media and exploitation including Smythe's 'audience commodity'. According to Jarrett, 'Exploited in and vital to capitalist circuits, domestic work is often simultaneously socially meaningful and resistant to capture, particularly in its immaterial forms' (2016, p. 11). Like unpaid domestic work,

social media labor is a complex system of valorization that generates economic and cultural values that are vital to society. A typical social media user serves 'double duty' as s/he 'is unpaid and freely contributes content that provides these (social media) sites with their appeal to other users, while also generating readily repackaged data about consumer trends, tastes and desires. Moreover, s/he also produces shared meanings and builds social solidarity in those same interactions' (ibid., p. 10). More than merely reproducing labor itself along with the mode of production and consumption relations embedded in capitalism, this system of valorization examined through the lens of the Digital Housewife also serves as a basis for conceptual departure from patriarchic power relations and for activism against capitalism, whereby 'free labor' may be ultimately set free.

It is mportant to note that the trend toward 'free labor' is more than a feminist critique in the era of Web 2.0; and that it had been widespread in the media and cultural industries long before the emergence of social media. Mark Andrejevic's account of 'social network exploitation' (2008), for example, is not really about the latest technological innovations. Instead, it is about a consistent pattern stretching at least from reality TV to social media whereby amateur labor being paid either nothing or little more than token appreciation is asked to carry out tasks that used to be performed by professionals. Most importantly, 'social network exploitation' works when the amateurs 'willingly' accept the deal and perform 'happily' within the system.

Where does free labor lead us to? Is it Jacob Silverman's exclamation: 'I share, therefore I am – more interesting, more sociable, more desirable, more myself' (2015, p. ix)? Or is it Hardt and Negri's 'multitude' (2005), paving the way for world revolution? It is perhaps too early to make any conclusive remarks, although with Melissa Gregg, Kate Crawford and I have contended that the challenges are as great as the opportunities (Qiu, Gregg, &

Crawford, 2014); and that it is incorrect to see the two opposite directions of development as separate spheres.

Gregg, Crawford, and I developed a diagram called 'the circuits of labor' (ibid.) to visualize our argument while connecting many different conceptions of digital labor beyond the usual binaries of labor: material vs. immaterial, waged vs. free, progress vs. conservative (see Figure 16.2). On the left-hand side, economic capital dominates body and extracts surplus value generated in the lower hierarchies of the system, especially by blue- and grey-collar workers. ('Grey collar' is a term used in China for low-end informational workers). This is essentially the system

of wage labor and free labor under corporate control through physical discipline, monetary rewards, and/or socio-psychological domination that often leads to precarity and anxieties among workers. The top-down power inequality is expressed and guaranteed by formal agreements of labor contracts, market transaction records, and/or intellectual property right regimes.

On the right, the mode of production is more egalitarian from the perspectives of the laboring body, whereas capital is not only economic but also social and cultural, as conceived of by Bourdieu (1986). Workers – free social media labor included – engage in the 'natural labor of sociality' for their own

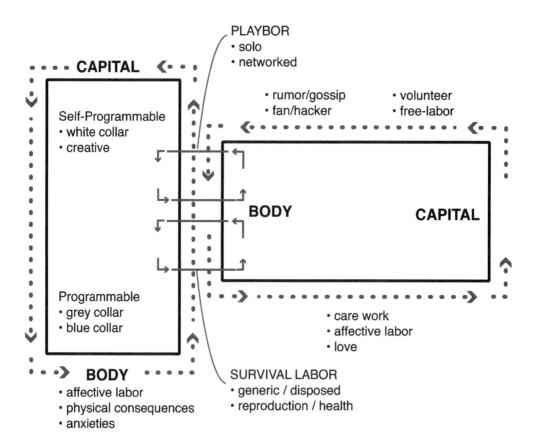

Figure 16.2   The circuits of labor (CoL): formal and informal exchanges

pleasure, survival, and collective formation. They may or may not require external compensation and the rewards can take many forms: social, cultural, political, rather than merely monetary. Due to the lack of top-down control, the labor involved can take many forms, such volunteer, hacker, care work, and love. Although affective labor and free labor appear in this circuit as well, the power relations differ considerably from the left-hand side because they are usually tacit knowledge and informal customs. Think, for example, an autonomous fan community or the network of a hackivist group.

The two circuits of labor (CoLs) – formal exploitation through vertical domination on the left, informal sociality through horizontal networking on the right – are short-circuited by 'playbor' (those who play online without being able to control the valorization processes and intellectual property rights, such as gamers; see Küklich, 2005) and 'survival labor' (those who are disposed of in capitalist modes of production, such as injured factory workers). Conceptualized as such, either the vertical system of formal CoL or the horizontal system of informal CoL can draw resources from the other. The flow of creativity and politico-economic energy is multi-directional and dialectical.

Due to space limitations, I cannot further explicate this model here, although interested readers can refer to Qiu, Gregg, and Crawford (2014). But the takeaway lesson is: the future of digital labor, including social media labor and free labor, is up to agentic human actors on both sides of the circuits – to resist top-down control that reduces us into subhumans and to expand our liberty and humanity through networking and innovative interventions.

Labor of Struggle

The term 'labor' has a fourth connotation in addition to the other three (something natural for human activities, something done in exchange for wages, and something 'free' to be exploited). That is, labor is an organized collective political force for workers to defend their rights and push for a better society.

In his article 'Social or anti-social media?', Toby Miller (2015) writes:

> When I interviewed people involved in Hong Kong's 2014 Umbrella Revolution, I found a very different story from the dominant Anglo narrative, which celebrated the social media's role in the uprising. Young and middle-aged activists alike told me that longstanding class-based organizations and democratic tendencies, and new interpersonal connections – experienced face to face – were more crucial organizational tools.

His observation reveals a pattern that is rather consistent with evidence from other parts of the world where long-lasting, on-the-ground labor struggle often not only predates social media uprisings but also serves as a crucial factor explaining if and how the social media uprising can be successful or not. Consider, for instance, Egypt and Tunisia, both with strong unionism tradition and face-to-face solidarity among workers on the one hand (Alexander & Bassiouny, 2014) *vis-à-vis* Libya and Syria, where such legacies were much weaker on the other hand, the fallout of the events can be much explained when we consider the strength of the existing labor movement above and beyond the oversimplified framework of social media diffusion (e.g., as reflected in the problematic phrase of 'Twitter revolution'; see Esfandiari, 2010).

How then do workers use social media to strengthen solidarity and extend it beyond the conventional scope of labor parties and unionism, especially during labor movements, old and new? To explore this question, I draw most of the following examples from China, where I conduct the bulk of my empirical work. By my understanding, China also has the world's longest-living working-class social media (i.e., QQ). In the third quarter of 2015, QQ has 850 million monthly active users (Wang, 2015). Most of these are members of the information have-less from the lower classes, including ordinary workers.

QQ started in 1999 as a copycat service of the then-popular instant messenger, ICQ. I first heard about it from a focus group that I conducted in Zhuhai, South China, among female migrant workers in 2002, when young office clerks were already using QQ for social networking and for instrumental goals such as learning how to use a new software. Chinese workers quickly discovered that QQ is well suited for organizing information and mobilizing peers at times of collective struggle. According to a work-injury victim who won the legal battle against his former boss and were helping fellow workers with their lawsuits:

> I like QQ because I can store phone numbers, legal documents, and all kinds of useful information in it. Here (in a factory zone of South China) it's so hot and humid, and it's cumbersome to have pen and paper with me all the time. But once I log onto QQ (through mobile phone), I see all the information I need.

QQ became a stronger tool for collective struggle when it started to offer the 'QQ Group (QQ qun)' service, which includes a full range of online community-building tools such as group chat, photo album, and file sharing.

In 2004, three major instances of labor uprising took place that marked the beginning of social media on the picket line (Qiu, 2016). Before then, nearly all strikes in China were kept under local information block-down by the authorities. But strikers in a textile factory of Xianyang, Shaanxi Province (Northwest China), and a military equipment factory in Chongqing (Southwest China) first used QQ and local forms to break the silence of censorship and call for national and international attention. Then workers at a Japanese-owned electronics factory in Shenzhen (South China) used QQ and Weblogs to publicize daily records of their struggle *vis-à-vis* the management. Their story made headlines, including in *The New York Times* (French, 2004). This was three years prior to China's middle class starting to use Internet tools

to organize collective action in landmark cases such as the 2007 Xiamen PX incident. Workers were leading the tidal wave of history probably not because they were technologically sophisticated but because they had the economic needs and political will.

During this early stage, workers were using basic texts and images to communicate. But soon they began to use poetry and videos. One good example is the Ole Wolff struggle during 2006–2009 in Yantai, Shandong Province, East China (China Labor News Translation, 2009). Ole Wolff is a Danish-owned factory. Their workers succeeded in organizing the first grassroots, independent workplace union in China, partly due to the national and international support mustered through their online videos. Their account at Sina Video, titled 'China Red Union (*zhongguo chise gonghui*)', had 29 videos. One of them that went viral is a 90-second video shot on a worker's mobile phone when a worker representative confronted a Danish manager and said, 'I despise this kind of behavior [by the employer]'. The video was unedited and not professional at all, but it was circulated widely via QQ Groups and blogs, and the management finally recognized the workers' union.

Another turning point was 2009–2010 with the diffusion of micro-blogging tools such as Sina Weibo, whose functioning is similar to Twitter. Initially Weibo was only popular among the more affluent users, but following a crackdown on labor movements, especially in South China during 2012–2013, more workers migrated to Weibo because there was less censorship on Weibo compared to online forums in South China, which were vulnerable to influence from local authorities. (Sina Weibo's headquarters is located in Beijing, North China). This was not to suggest that Weibo offers genuine freedom for workers to express themselves and to mobilize. Since 2013, the crackdown on Weibo-based activism has been greatly intensified nationwide. However, Weibo remains one of the most preferred tools for Chinese workers in struggle because it is openly accessible.

More recently, WeChat (WeiXin) has become the most widely used social media platform in China. It is also a product from Tencent, the company that operates QQ. WeChat is, however, mostly for interpersonal and small-group interactions among a small number of people, rather than publicly accessible communication like what Weibo allows. WeChat has a 'discussion group' mode that is similar to QQ Group chat, which workers often use to share logistical information, images, and call for action among their peers. Meanwhile, WeChat public account allows individual activists or labor NGOs to conduct one-to-many communication to their followers, almost like corporations using their company's Facebook accounts to talk to their followers. An influential WeChat public account is Pepper Tribe (jianjiao buluowww. jianjiaobuluo.com/) operated by and for female migrant workers, using innovative cartoons, videos, and games along with text-based stories and analytical articles to deliver a unique voice of labor, gender, and empowerment.

From QQ Instant Messenger and QQ Group to Weibo and WeChat, Chinese workers have actively adopted social media in their existing struggles for more than a decade. Although different platforms had different features and different periods had distinct working-class social media dynamics, overall the toolkit for picket line and other labor struggles has been enriched technologically because what we have seen is a cumulative process. Even to this day, QQ Group remains arguably the most important online mobilization and internal communication tool among workers, whereas Internet video, local and regional forums, Weibo and WeChat all add to social networking opportunities with more diverse audiences at critical moments when workers in struggle need to call for more public support and/or build a broader social basis.

Of course, worker struggles are highly diverse. The scope of social media applications is also remarkably broad under drastically different structural conditions, e.g., clampdown from the factory regime, local state censorship, pro-labor policy environment. As a result, the role of social media in labor struggles may look ambiguous and chaotic. I therefore developed a 2 × 4 typology (Figure 16.3) to provide a systematic overview of what I call worker-generated content (WGC). The typology is constructed from using three dichotomous variables: (a) 'collectivity', i.e., if the producer of the content is an individual worker or a group of workers; (b) 'activism orientation', i.e., if the content was created with the intention for social

		Collectivity			
		+		-	
		Empowerment		Empowerment	
		+	-	+	-
Activism orientation	+	1	2	5	6
	-	3	4	7	UGC

Figure 16.3 Seven types of worker-generated content (WGC)

change; and (c) 'empowerment', i.e., if at the end labor conditions of the workers involved were really improved.

Elsewhere (Qiu, 2015) I offer a more in-depth discussion on each type of WGC, as illustrated by workers' online video activities (each dot in the typology represents a specific instance of struggle). There are, however, two general arguments applicable to working-class social media in general. For one thing, if the content is generated by atomized individual workers without an activist orientation and does not improve labor conditions, then it still belongs to UGC (user-generated content) within the conventional system of platform capitalism operating according to the logic of 'the culture of connectivity' (van Dijck, 2013). Meanwhile, although the bulk of worker's social media practices still fall into the domain of individualistic, consumerist UGC, logically speaking there are seven possibilities outside UGC, of which five already have concrete instances of struggle materialized in the Chinese context. In other words, we need to look away from UGC to appreciate the diversity and liveliness of WGC, of social media being put to practical ends of labor in struggle.

CONCLUSION

This chapter contends that labor – broadly defined to include natural labor of sociality, wage labor, free labor, and labor of struggle – is arguably the most vital source of value and valorization in social media operations. Yet, it is often rendered invisible or marginalized through flashy and evanescent discourses of post-industrialism, consumer culture, and the stock market. It is therefore imperative to re-examine the relationship between social media and labor, which is, however, not a novel exercise. Classic conceptions of information society often include considerations of labor, e.g., Daniel Bell's 'meritocracy' (1976), and Manuel Castells's

'self-programmable labor' (2000). Since the turn to the twenty-first century, a new body of literature has materialized on 'free labor', immaterial labor, the IDDL, the Digital Housewife, and the WGC, all of which shed light on multiple connections between labor and social media. This literature was summarized and re-organized in order for readers to have a comprehensive view of the issues at state.

From a critical political economy perspective, the chapter highlights the need to transcend our constricted experiences *with* social media and *through* social media under circumstances of the Global North, and of the West. QQ, Orkut, Mxit, VK, Taringa, Weibo, WeChat – these platforms, albeit less known as Facebook or Twitter, have played prominent roles, and are likely to continue to do so, in shaping social media landscapes in the Global South and in societies beyond models of Eurocentrism. Each of these platforms has its unique features and lineage. There are major differences between them and their better-known Western counterparts, which deserve more systematic exploration in the future when it comes to issues of labor, from wage labor on the assembly line, free labor in the data mine, and in-between forms of labor power in the informal sectors and with increasing precarity.

For the populace of the expansive Global South, are social media a new chance of upward mobility or another curse of exploitation? The defeat of Facebook's 'Free Basics' initiative by civil society groups and start-ups in India is a case in point, demonstrating the complexity and importance of the issues at stake (Bose, 2016). While the challenge of the digital divide persists, technological diffusion has profoundly transformed the social class status of digital media the world over, changing it from elite platforms of highbrow discussion to grassroots spaces of mundane interaction and everyday networking as well as toolkits for workers and activists on the ground. Coming to terms with this vast, diverse, and rapidly changing realm of the world's social media platforms means we have to go beyond dichotomous thinking. Conventional binaries – material and immaterial labor, suppression and liberation, alienation and class-consciousness – still matter. But they have become insufficient. A 'circuits' model (Qiu et al., 2014) is, in this sense, a good example for what we need: holistic approaches to re-think issues of labor with highly diverse connections to social media.

REFERENCES

Alexander, A., & Bassiouny, M. (2014). *Bread, freedom and social justice: Workers and the Egyptian revolution*. London: Zed Books.

Andrejevic, M. (2008). Social network exploitation. In Z. Papacharissi (Ed.), *A networked self* (pp. 82–101). New York: Routledge.

Bell, D. (1976). *The coming of post-industrial society: A venture in social forecasting*. New York: Basic Books.

Bose, A. (2016, April 5). Why Facebook failed with Free Basics. *Techcrunch*. Available: http://ow.ly/k4AQ302Bs8A (accessed on July 26, 2016).

Bourdieu, P. (1986). The forms of capital. In J. Richardson (Ed.), *Handbook of theory and research for the sociology of education* (pp. 241–258). New York: Greenwood.

Castells, M. (2000). Materials for an exploratory theory of the network society. *The British Journal of Sociology*, *51*(1), 5–24.

Chan, J., & Pun, N. (2010, September 13). Suicide as protest for the new generation of Chinese migrant workers: Foxconn, global capital, and the state. *Japan Focus*, *8*(37). Available: http://ow.ly/OqWm302Bshc (accessed March 11, 2016).

China Labour News Translations (2009, March 10). Ole Wolff union struggle. Available: http://ow.ly/XIcl302Bso3 (accessed March 11, 2016).

Creemers, R. (2015). The pivot in Chinese cyberspace: Integrating internet control in Xi Jinping's China. *China Perspectives*, *4*, 5–13.

DiMaggio, P., Hargittai, E., Neuman, W., & Robinson, J. (2001). Social implications of the internet. *Annual Review of Sociology*, *27*, 307–336.

DMR – Digital Stats/Gadgets (2016, February 22). By the numbers: 200+ amazing Facebook statistics. Available: http://ow.ly/O0ELz (accessed March 12, 2016).

Esfandiari, G. (2010, June 8). The Twitter devolution. *Foreign Policy*. Available: http://ow.ly/CPQj302BqaN (accessed July 26, 2016).

Fortunati, L. (2007). Immaterial labor and its machinization. *Ephemera*, *7*(1), 139–157.

French, H. (2004, December 16). Workers demand union and Wal-Mart supplier in China. *New York Times*. Available: http://ow.ly/ZnbYa (accessed March 12, 2016).

Fuchs, C. (2014a). *Digital labor and Karl Marx*. London: Routledge.

Fuchs, C. (2014b). *Social media: A critical introduction*. Los Angeles, CA: Sage.

Fuchs, C. (2015). Digital labor: A comment on César Bolaño's *TripleC* reflection. *TripleC: Communication, Capitalism, Critique*, *13*(1), 84–92.

Hardt, M., & Negri, A. (2005). *Multitude*. New York: Penguin.

Hesmondhalgh, D. (2010). User-generated content, free labor and the cultural industries. *Ephemera*, *10*(3–4), 267–284.

Jarrett, K. (2015). *Feminism, Labour and Digital Media: The Digital Housewife*. London: Routledge.

King, G., Pan, J., & Roberts, M. (2013). How censorship in China allows government criticism but silences collective expression. *American Political Science Review*, *107*(2), 326–343.

Kücklich, J. (2005). Precarious playbour: Modders and the digital games industry. *The Fibreculture Journal*, 5. Available: http://ow.ly/jxCn302Bsr1 (accessed March 11, 2016).

Lazzarato, M. (1996). Immaterial Labor. In P. Virno & M. Hardt (Eds.), *Radical thought in Italy* (pp. 132–146). Minneapolis, MN: University of Minnesota Press.

Lokot, T., & Diakopoulos, N. (2015). News Bots: Automating news and information dissemination on Twitter. *Digital Journalism*, *13*: 1–18.

Mander, J. (2005, January 26). Daily time spent on social networks rises to 1.72 hours. *Global Web Index*. Available: http://ow.ly/NU8TZ (accessed March 11, 2016).

Marwick, A. (2013). *Status update: Celebrity, publicity and branding in the social media age*. New Haven, CT: Yale University Press.

Maxwell, R. (Ed.) (2015). *The Routledge companion for labor and media*. New York: Routledge.

Miller, T. (2015, December 17). Social or anti-social media? *APPS Policy Forum*. Available: http://ow.ly/YQ3v8 (accessed March 11, 2016).

Mosco, V. (2011). The political economy of labor. In J. Wasko, G. Murdock, & H. Sausa (Eds.), *The handbook of political economy of communications* (pp. 358–380). Malden, MA: Wiley-Blackwell.

Mosco, V. (2014). *To the cloud: Big data in a turbulent world*. New York: Routledge.

Mosco, V., & Wasko, J. (Eds.) (1983). *The critical communications review: Labor, the working class, and the media*. Norwood, NJ: Ablex.

Negri, A. (1979). *Red notes: Working-class autonomy and the crisis: Italian Marxist texts of the theory and practice of a class movement: 1964–79*. London: CSE.

Nunez, M. (2016, May 3). Want to know what Facebook really thinks of journalists? Here's what happened when it hired some. *Gizmodo*. Available at: http://ow.ly/u7J7302yXzy (accessed on July 25, 2016).

Qiu, J. L. (2009). *Working-class network society: Communication technology and the information have-less in urban China*. Cambridge, MA: MIT Press.

Qiu, J. L. (2013). Network societies and Internet studies: Rethinking space, time, and labor. In W. Dutton (Ed.), *The Oxford handbook of internet studies* (pp. 109–128). Oxford: Oxford University Press.

Qiu, J. L. (2015). Locating worker-generated content (WGC) in the world's factory. In R. Maxwell (Ed.), *The Routledge companion for labor and media* (pp. 303–314). New York: Routledge.

Qiu, J. L. (2016). Social media on the picket line. *Media, Culture & Society*, *38*(4), 619–633.

Qiu, J. L., Gregg, M., & Crawford, K. (2014). Circuits of labor: A labor theory of the iPhone era. *TripleC: Communication, Capitalism & Critique*, *12*(2), 564–581.

Roberts, S. T. (2014). *Behind the screen: The hidden digital labor of commercial content moderation*. Doctoral dissertation. University of Illinois, Urbana-Champaign.

Sandoval, M. (2013). Foxconned labor as the dark side of the Information Age: Working conditions at Apple's contract manufacturers in China. *TripleC: Communication, Capitalism & Critique*, *11*(2), 318–347.

Scholz, T. (Ed.) (2013). *Digital labor: The internet as playground and factory*. New York: Routledge.

Servon, L. (2002). *Bridging the digital divide*. Malden, MA: Blackwell.

Silverman, J. (2015). *Terms of service: Social media and the price of constant connection*. New York: HarperCollins.

Smythe, D. W. (1977). Communications: Blindspot of western Marxism. *Canadian Journal of Political and Society Theory*, *1*(3), 1–28.

Smythe, D. W. (1981/2006). On the audience commodity and its work. In M. G. Durham & D. M. Kellner (Eds.), *Media and cultural studies* (pp. 230–256). Malden, MA: Blackwell.

Steiner, C. (2012). *Automate this: How algorithms came to rule our world*. New York: Portfolio/Penguin.

Steinweg, T., & de Haan, E. (2007). *Capacitating electronics: The corrosive effects of platinum and palladium mining on labor rights and communities*. SOMO – Center for Research on Multinational Corporations. Available at http://ow.ly/LnBhM (accessed March 11, 2016).

Terranova, T. (2000). Free labor: Producing culture for the digital economy. *Social Text*, *18*(2), 33–58.

Van Dijck, J. (2013). *The culture of connectivity: A critical history of social media*. Oxford: Oxford University Press.

Voirol, O. (2016, February). Digital architectures of ostentation. Paper presented at the conference 'Digital Practices, Urban Space and Struggles for Visibility', Centre for Chinese Media and Comparative Communication Research, the Chinese University of Hong Kong.

Wang, A. (2015, November 16). Tencent in Q3 2015: QQ MAUs 850M, WeChat MAUs 650M. *China Internet Watch*. Available: http://ow.ly/lHZF302BsBK (accessed March 11, 2016).

Whitney, E. (1990). Paradise restored: The mechanical arts from antiquity through the thirteenth century. *Transactions of the American Philosophical Society*, *80*(1), 1–169.

Williams, R. (1983). *Keywords: A vocabulary of culture and society*. Oxford: Oxford University Press.

Wu, A. X., & Taneja, H. (2016, February 17). Reimagining the Internet as a mosaic of regional cultures. *The Conversation*. Available: http://ow.ly/Z0yyl (accessed March 11, 2016).

Xiang, B. (2008). *Global 'body shopping': An Indian labor system in the information technology industry*. Princeton, NJ: Princeton University Press.

17

Silicon Valley and the Social Media Industry

Alice Marwick

INTRODUCTION

The global center for venture-backed technology startups, both in terms of sheer numbers of companies, employees, and money, as well as mythological importance, is Silicon Valley in Northern California. When writing critically about the industry of social media, two things are difficult to avoid. First, it is tempting to adopt a dismissive or mocking stance. The peculiar combination of naive idealism and free market worship that characterizes tech startups is ripe for ridicule, especially when examined outside its Northern Californian context. The scramble to build the best laundry startup (Pressler, 2014), the recent $120 million venture capital (VC) investment in a $700 wi-fi enabled juicer (Ferdman and Ingraham, 2016), or venture capitalist Tim Draper's campaign to divide California into six states, of which Silicon Valley would be one (Wohlsen, 2014), seem goofball at best, clueless or juvenile at worst, making it easy to write off

modern tech culture as a clueless echo chamber. This misses the point. Despite its excesses, Silicon Valley functions as a global imaginary: it models what is considered a superior type of wealth-generating innovation for other places eager to replicate its success. Thus, we must take it seriously as attempts are made world-wide to replicate its practices.

Second, the conflation of 'Silicon Valley' with 'social media' is complicated. Most social media companies are venture-backed startups; some are public (Twitter, Facebook), some private (Pinterest, Snapchat), and some have been acquired by larger companies (Reddit, YouTube, Instagram, Tumblr). But most venture-backed technology startups do not produce social media. At the same time, many of today's most successful startups do build on the original concepts of 'social media' – user-generated content, peer production marketplaces, collaboratively generated information, datafication – to extend the logics and aesthetics of social media into new realms. As Tarleton Gillespie writes elsewhere in this volume, the model of 'platforms' that originated with social media now extends to labor (Uber, TaskRabbit, Postmates, Shyp), housing (AirBnB), finance (Venmo, Kiva), and direct-to-consumer goods (Casper, Everlane). The co-founder of mattress company Casper, for instance, told *Inc.* magazine that, 'In the beginning, it was "Let's disrupt the mattress industry. It's broken." That quickly morphed into "Let's invent an industry around sleep."' He says 'We consider ourselves a tech company first' (Welch, 2016). Affirming Silicon Valley's values of *disruption* and *innovation*, Casper positions themselves in conversation with other successful startups, rather than other mattress companies, who are implicitly written off as stodgy and out-of-touch with modern, technologically-savvy business practices. To understand the industry of social media, we must look at Silicon Valley's venture-based startups, their culture, and how this culture has been and is being exported – for better or for worse – around the world.

While the idea of digital networks spurs fantasies of 'virtual reality' and 'the cloud,' the production of software is very much grounded in place. Global sites of technological production such as Silicon Valley, as well as Tel Aviv, New York, Sydney, Bangalore, London, and Berlin, bring together bodies, technical infrastructure, and capital, creating particular sets of socio-economic circumstances under which software is created. The conditions of social media production are dominated by startups funded by venture capital, the most successful of which become mature, established companies, generating immense wealth for their founders and early employees.[1] Note that I use the term 'startup' in this chapter to mean 'venture-capital backed technology startup.' The term is sometimes used to denote a small business that is less than a year old (US Small Business Administration Office of Advocacy, 2016a), but startups and small businesses are distinct. The vast majority of entrepreneurs

in the United States, and around the world, start small businesses like barber shops, eBay storefronts, plumbers, and grocery stores. Most of these small business owners have no employees, and they are primarily self-financed (US Small Business Administration Office of Advocacy, 2016b). A startup, particularly a venture-capital-backed technology startup, is predicated on the ability to *scale* and the potential for very high growth (Henrekson and Sanandaji, 2014).

This chapter will provide context for the modern era of technology startups by examining the history of Northern Californian software development, specifically its libertarian-countercultural bent known as the 'Californian Ideology,' which combines a distrust of institutional structures with a deep belief in the potential of technology for social change (Barbrook and Cameron, 1996). This ideology has remained more-or-less constant through 60 years of boom-and-bust cycles, from transistors and micro-computers through to the dot-com boom and Web 2.0.

However, the cultures and values of contemporary technological practice, specifically how myths of meritocracy, openness, and entrepreneurialism function in the political economy of the tech industry, are crucial to understanding the discursive underpinnings of social media technologies, as are the way that space and place influence the conceptualization and building of startups. Silicon Valley, with a preponderance of young, wealthy men, creates many apps and services devoted to outsourcing homemaking and personal chores, while urban-exploration apps like Foursquare are designed for densely-populated, nightlife-heavy cities like New York. A global mythology of startups and entrepreneurship, spread through websites like Quora, Hacker News, Mashable, and TechCrunch, affects workers worldwide. Young men hold up Mark Zuckerberg and the late Steve Jobs as role models, mimic 'best practices' outlined on blogs and discussed on Twitter, and attend networking events modeled after those popular in major global cities. Several institutions in which such myths and cultural practices are replicated, namely hackathons, accelerators, and Startup Weekends, are re-enacted around the globe in an attempt to bring Silicon Valley values to local startup communities. In what follows, I outline the major mythologies of this discourse – entrepreneurialism, meritocracy, and openness – and how they contribute to specific conditions of technological production, such as funding rates and hiring practices. For example, 'pattern recognition' (venture capitalists assessing potential startups based on whether their founders resemble successful entrepreneurs in terms of gender, race, nationality, and education) and 'cultural fit' (one's ability to blend in with work cultures dominated by young white and Asian men) contribute to gender and race inequality in American startups, which in turn affects which technologies are developed and how target markets and user bases are conceptualized.

THE CALIFORNIAN IDEOLOGY AND THE HISTORY OF SILICON VALLEY

Social media is more popular than ever. Two-thirds of Americans use social media sites, up from only 7% ten years ago (Perrin, 2015). According to the Global Web Index, there are approximately 2.3 billion user accounts on social media services, representing 31% of the world's population (Chaffey, 2016). And much of this social media, with the significant exception of that popular in China,[2] is headquartered in Northern California. According to *Forbes*, 65 out of 174 of the 'unicorns' of the tech industry – privately-owned startups worth more than $1 billion US – are based in California. They include social media sites Snapchat, Pinterest, Nextdoor, and Slack, and social media-adjacent companies like AirBnB, Uber, and Buzzfeed (Nusca, 2016). (Of the rest, 42 are in China, 41 elsewhere in the United States,

19 in Europe, and eight in India; the rest are spread around the world (CrunchBase, 2016)). San Francisco and Silicon Valley represent more than 70% of US venture capital investment, most of it in software (Massaro, 2016). While San Francisco faces skyrocketing rents and a very visible homeless population, engineers at startups like Twitter, Facebook, Uber, and Slack are paid six-figure salaries, fed free healthy meals three times a day, and shuttled to and from work in private buses via Bay Area highways. As a result, the greater Silicon Valley area has lower unemployment, lower poverty rates, and higher wages than the rest of the United States (Massaro, 2016).

Santa Clara County, also known as Silicon Valley, encompasses the cities of Palo Alto, Mountain View, Cupertino, Sunnyvale, and San Jose. It is one of the United States' economic centers, with a long history of generating wealth from technological innovation, from transistors and micro-computers to video games, multimedia, and dot-com companies (Saxenian, 1996; English-Lueck, 2002). Silicon Valley proper boasts a diverse population with skilled immigrants, expensive real estate, well-funded public schools, and technological saturation (English-Lueck, 2002: 11). Its political sensibility is of a decidedly libertarian bent, emphasizing self-directed improvement, a belief in meritocracy and social mobility, and a lack of 'work-life balance' (Rogers and Larsen, 1984; Bronson, 2000; Borsook, 2001; English-Lueck, 2002). The mix of ethnic diversity and higher-than-average technology use has created an image of Silicon Valley as ultra-modern and representative of the future. English-Lueck writes, 'The things that make Silicon Valley distinctive – its technological saturation and complex range of identities – are not merely interesting cultural artifacts in themselves. They are significant because both the pervasiveness of technology and identity diversity are coming to define the emerging global culture' (2002: 8). Today, Silicon Valley is not only synonymous with the technology companies located there, such as Apple, Facebook, Google, and Yahoo, but has grown to include nearby San Francisco, which has historically been hipper, younger, and wilder than its more conservative southern suburbs (Marwick, 2013).

In *From Counterculture to Cyberculture*, cultural historian Fred Turner traced dense ties between 1960s counterculture movements like the New Communalists and the computer pioneers of Northern California (Turner, 2005, 2006; see also Markoff, 2005). This parallel history of both venture-backed capitalism and radical anti-establishmentarianism precipitated a discourse popularly known as 'The Californian Ideology' (Barbrook and Cameron, 1996). The Californian Ideology holds that an increase in computer technologies brings positive social consequences, that entrepreneurial technology culture rewards the smartest and the hardest workers, and that universal prosperity is best pursued through an unfettered free market. In previous work, I argued that the ethos of social media similarly combines countercultural ideology and neoliberal capitalism, positioning participatory technology as the solution to failing institutions (Marwick, 2013). Drawing from such disparate sources as the hacker ethic, Do-It-Yourself punk rock, zines, and 2000s anti-capitalist activism, the discourse of 'Web 2.0' identified Big Media as failing and faulty, and positioned social technologies as a more egalitarian alternative. When combined with Silicon Valley's strong foundation in libertarianism, free market capitalism, and venture-backed startups, social media begat a somewhat unholy alliance that emphasized the entrepreneur, the celebrity, or the brand as a model of subjectivity to combat economic woes – in other words, the incursion of economic principles into the most personal regions of selfhood and interpersonal relationships.

In its function as a global imaginary, Silicon Valley exports the Californian Ideology as a universal solution to localized problems. This project is articulated in various ways, some more overt than others. For instance, elsewhere in this volume, Siva Vaidhyanathan discusses Facebook's 'Free Basics' program, which provided mobile users in India with access to a limited number of Facebook-selected websites. Facebook ignored the local context and the Indian software and telecommunications industry in favor of a simplistic model of social change which presumed that access to information would intrinsically empower poor Indian people. Unsurprisingly, such an effort was criticized by Indian activists and media as tone-deaf and reminiscent of colonialism. However, in many places, social media technologies built in the United States have become deeply tied into local histories and cultures. As Miller et al. argue in their comparative analysis of social media use in eleven different countries, south Indian families, Chinese migrant workers, southeastern Turkish teenagers, and adults in rural Chile use social media quite differently based on local norms, geographies, and histories (Miller et al., 2016). Social media is articulated and experienced locally, but, as we shall see, the fantasy of technological solutionism is often taken up by countries and regions as a way to fiat economic success (Bresnahan, Gambardella, and Saxenian, 2001; Engel, 2014).

Beyond overt emulation of Silicon Valley by industries and governments, the media visibility and idealization of successful Northern California tech companies like Snapchat and Instagram have birthed a world-wide fan base that follows the business developments and social machinations of the scene through Hacker News, blogs, and Twitter feeds. San Francisco functions as a mythic center for entrepreneurs, academics, and venture capitalists across the world, who imagine themselves to be connected through technology, and thus beyond place, but still ground themselves in the Californian Ideology of the Bay Area. Social media workers from San Francisco, New York, Tokyo, Paris, Austin, and London stay in close touch via instant messenger, Slack, and social media, touching base at conferences and industry events, often forging strong personal and professional relationships between people who only meet in person once a year. SV therefore functions as a shared set of assumptions, beliefs, and norms that maintains common interests across geographical boundaries (Marwick, 2013).

MYTHS OF SILICON VALLEY

The tech industry is governed by a series of myths that function to justify the political economy of the technology industry: openness, meritocracy, and entrepreneurialism. As I outline below, they are rooted in a particularly American, and even more specifically Northern Californian, set of presumptions; they do not always function seamlessly when ported to another context.

Openness

'Openness' is an umbrella term for projects that emphasize collaboration, participation, and transparent governance, as in open-access journals or open-source software. Lilly Nguyen describes openness as 'a habituated moral view with particular aesthetics and sensibilities ... technologies are seen as open in their ability to generate the creation and production of new technical products, to enable the continuous circulation of these products, and to foster use and consumption independent of technical expertise' (2016: 640). In other words, openness is framed as desirable because it allows anyone to participate, fostering democratic involvement and boosting the tech industry's belief in itself as meritocratic. As Nathaniel Tkacz (2014) argues in his study of Wikipedia, while openness purports to be apolitical, this in itself is a political move, in that it sidesteps questions of inequality or power asymmetry. Indeed, most 'open' projects are, in reality, not particularly open, as

participation inevitably leads to hierarchy. Wikipedia, for instance, has a heavily striated structure of involvement, and those who are the most successful at navigating it are those able to convincingly manipulate its intricate body of rules (Tkacz, 2014). It is also overwhelmingly male-dominated.

The value of openness is also linked to a pleasurable, creative technical practice, which is acutely contextual to American internet culture. In her ethnographic work on technical practice in Vietnam, Lilly Nguyen discusses jailbreaking iPhones, which, in the Global North, is typically characterized as 'a moral commitment to generativity, openness, and transgressive self-expression' (2016: 640). However, during the time of Nguyen's fieldwork there was no service provider in Vietnam who could legally provide iPhone service. Thus, purchasing an iPhone from abroad and jailbreaking it for personal use represented a connection to a global technoculture, as well as a status symbol of modernity and luxury. While Northern hackers might see jailbreaking as a way to protest the 'tethered' system of Apple products (Zittrain, 2008), Vietnamese people saw it as a way to connect to the same system.

What this all presupposes, however, is that openness is still valued, which may be true in Western hacker or activist communities, but no longer seems true in the technology industry *per se*. 'Openness' is an ideal not necessarily of the tech industry as it exists today, but one left over from its previous iteration as 'Web 2.0' (Marwick, 2015). Most social media sites and apps (Facebook, Twitter, Instagram, Snapchat) are 'walled gardens' which deliberately make it difficult to port data from one platform to another – try exporting your Instagram photos to Snapchat, for instance – and use a number of techniques to keep users from clicking away from their site or switching to another application.[3] Proprietary technologies, from Apple laptops to wearables, are designed to facilitate 'lock in' to a particular system and make it difficult for people to move from one to another, so as not to lose audience and therefore ad sales. Platform content is often curated and organized by algorithms and, sometimes, human editors; determining the logic behind this creation is similarly black-boxed and difficult (Eslami et al., 2016). Openness is a vestigial remnant of Web 2.0, but is increasingly irrelevant in the eyeball-driven world of modern social media 'content.' Thus, it demonstrates how the political economy of the advertisement-driven web is extinguishing any ideals of libertarian tech culture that are incompatible. Despite this, several of the practices, like hackathons and Startup Weekends discussed later in this chapter, are open: since their basic structure is widely available online, anyone with the available resources can host one, and in theory anyone can attend. Within these contexts, freely sharing ideas and resources is not only normative, but explicitly taught to participants. Thus, openness is pedagogically reproduced, even if its value largely remains ideological.

Meritocracy

The term 'meritocracy' was coined by sociologist Michael Young in a 1958 satirical essay. Young described a dystopian Britain in which social class – status ascribed by birth – had withered away, to be replaced by social status achieved through education. Young was concerned that educational reforms would make it impossible for the working class to achieve high-up political positions, and instead stratify elitism so that the wealthy and powerful were also seen as the most 'deserving.' He was dismayed to see the word taken up enthusiastically – and non-ironically – by Tony Blair and his neoliberal New Labour party, bringing about the very dystopia he was attempting to guard against (Young, 2001). Meritocracy in its modern usage refers to the idea that people will be judged not on their gender, race, or background, but solely on their intelligence and talents. In other words, you get out of the system what

you put into it. Meritocracy is the underlying ideology of the American dream, which holds that each person can advance professionally and economically according to his or her merit. The ideal that the United States is a meritocracy is linked to its origin as a nation of immigrants, and stands in opposition to European birthright based on hereditary aristocracies (McNamee and Miller, 2009).

Despite considerable research showing that economic assets in the USA are not distributed according to merit, the term persists, particularly in Silicon Valley and the tech industry in general (Shih, 2006; English-Lueck, 2011; Bacon, 2013). Meritocracy functions to justify the immense inequity of wealth distribution in the technology industry, as its logical conclusion is that those who are worth millions, or even billions, of dollars are the smartest or the hardest-working (Marwick, 2013). It also provides a reason for the lack of African-American and Latino men, and women of all races (particularly women of color) in the industry: this discourse holds that they are simply not interested, or not skilled enough, to compete with white and Asian men.

In reality, Silicon Valley does not at all function as a meritocracy. Women are treated differently from men: they are subject to more harassment at work; they are left out of male-dominated mentoring networks; they are promoted less; their roles as mothers or care providers are seen as incompatible with the fast-paced world of technology; and their failures are seen as representative of their gender rather than individual (Cech and Blair-Loy, 2010; Hui, 2014). Moreover, practices like hiring based on 'culture fit' exclude people who don't enjoy or who have aged-out of the college dorm atmosphere of startups. Venture capitalists employ what they call 'pattern recognition' to determine who to fund, prioritizing entrepreneurs who look like people they've previously funded, excluding founders and products that don't fit into a particular (raced and gendered) archetype. In Johanna Shih's qualitative study of Silicon Valley workers, white women and Asian men and women experienced widespread gender and ethnic discrimination. They used job-hopping to circumvent bias: white women moved to companies recognized as good for women or to bigger companies with better work-life balance; Asian men and women joined minority-owned firms or started their own companies (Shih, 2006). In my own research in San Francisco, I found that women's accomplishments were systemically undervalued, whereas their appearance and relationships with men were emphasized (Marwick, 2013). Indeed, bias in the tech industry, whether based on race, gender, or geography, is significant, endemic, and structural.

As an explanation for social inequality, meritocracy justifies and reproduces inequality, and makes invisible its structural nature, precluding policy-making or other challenges to systemic inequity (Cech and Blair-Loy, 2010: 372). In other words, Silicon Valley's insistence that it is a home for the 'best and the brightest' and that those who don't succeed there simply aren't good enough masks very real barriers to entry and success.

Entrepreneurialism

The valorization of entrepreneurship may be the most cherished of Silicon Valley myths. The entrepreneur is a breed apart from normal men and women; he is fueled by passion and independence, with a deep desire to 'change the world.' Like Steve Jobs and Mark Zuckerberg, he is also usually a white guy in jeans and sneakers. The entrepreneur is also a key figure in the neoliberal paradigm. Sarah Banet-Weiser and Marita Sturken, in their study of street artist Shepard Fairey, write 'the entrepreneur … is understood as an ambitious individual, dependent on no one but him/herself, a person who "owns" his or her own labor and is thus accountable for not only profit but risks

accumulated by this labor' (2010: 273). The entrepreneur is presented as a subject position which anyone can and should step into.

Daniel Cockayne argues that this romanticized concept of entrepreneurship is simply an emotional attachment that justifies economic uncertainty. In other words, in order to rationalize the long hours, hard work, and negligible rewards of starting a company, one must have an emotional attachment to entrepreneurialism. Talking about being 'driven' or having a 'passion' for one's work excuses the obvious downsides (Cockayne, 2015). He writes:

> Affect functions through entrepreneurial forms of digital media work to produce and reproduce attachments to normative (and often precarious) working conditions. These affective attachments reinforce a privileged idea about what work 'should be', and how work ought to be practiced despite potentially deleterious effects on individuals' earning capacity, physical and mental health, and 'life' as a category broadly conceived. (Cockayne, 2015: 3)

In my earlier work, I found that even if employees at early stage startups were working under difficult, stressful, or uncertain working conditions, with only a vague possibility of success, they espoused platitudes of loving their job and changing the world. Being an entrepreneur was much higher-status than existing as a rank-and-file worker at Twitter or Facebook, even if the latter was much better paid. For the self-styled entrepreneur, working for others was anxiety-producing and unsatisfying.

This sense of entrepreneurial value extends beyond founding a company. Having personal projects demonstrates initiative and creativity. Participating in the larger community of technology enthusiasts, whether founding an event or developing an open-source tool, is highly respected in Silicon Valley, demonstrating 'community citizenship, generalized reciprocity, moral obligation, and pro-social behavior' (Tedjamulia et al., 2005), traits that are valued in many technology communities that prize information-sharing and collaboration. Similarly, contributing to free or open-source software projects demonstrates that the creator is technologically savvy, creative, and not motivated by money. But obviously not everyone can be an entrepreneur; all industries are comprised of levels of laborers, and those who do not run a company, or even know how to code, often live precariously without economic or social stability – such as the Uber driver. The emphasis on the entrepreneur obscures inequalities and exploitation within the neoliberal system of labor.

SILICON VALLEY AS GLOBAL IMAGINARY

Silicon Valley is a 'technopole,' or a model for technologically-aspiring regions (Castells and Hall, 1994). However, it is not enough to simply emulate software development or technology manufacturing; what must be emulated is the process of *entrepreneurship*. Jerome Engel writes that while SV functions as an exemplar for innovation-based economic development worldwide, often supported by local governments and businesses, this is not always successful:

> It is widely touted that the right combination of factors and policies can unleash the inherent entrepreneurial capacity of society, energize individual initiative, and create individual and collective benefit. However, the success of efforts to create innovation clusters has been uneven at best, and the regional economic scene is littered with Silicon Valley imitators. (Engel, 2014: 36)

These imitators, or *siliconia*, include Silicon Alley in New York, Silicon Gulf in the Philippines, Silicon Wadi in Israel, Silicon Saxony, Cwm Silicon in Wales, Silicon Beach, Silicon Corridor, and Silicon Prairie (Dawson, 2001; Wikipedia Contributors, 2009). Engel writes that to be successful, a 'Cluster of Innovation' must include universities, government support, VCs, entrepreneurs, investors, and a host of specialized service providers and professional resources, not to mention an emphasis on mobility and networking (Engel, 2014: 38). Indeed, Silicon Valley has a rich infrastructure of people, capital, and material developed over a 70-year history, and is thus extremely difficult to replicate (Lécuyer, 2006).

In their literature review of digital entrepreneurship in Latin America, Quinones, Nicholson, and Heeks (2015)explain that while policymakers and private investors throughout Latin America have supported a number of initiatives designed to increase the number of technology startups, such as Mexico Digital, Startup Chile, and Brazil Startup, these have mostly been unsuccessful. While they argue that the lack of research on the Latin American context makes it difficult to tell exactly what has prevented this success, it seems clear that much of it is contextual. The entrepreneurial infrastructure of Silicon Valley is characterized by 'incubators, spin-offs, informal networks, formal networks, physical infrastructure, and culture' (Quinones et al., 2015: 192). However, as Daniel Isenberg observes in a popular *Harvard Business Review* article (2010), outside the United States, successful entrepreneurial ecosystems have a different set of characteristics. Indeed, attempting to emulate Silicon Valley is impossible; not only is it a magnet for entrepreneurs who move there from all over the world, it has an 'overabundance of technology and technical expertise' that requires 'generations' to create. He writes:

> Even Silicon Valley could not become itself today if it tried. Its ecosystem evolved under a unique set of circumstances: a strong local aerospace industry, the open California culture, Stanford University's supportive relationships with industry, a mother lode of invention from Fairchild Semiconductor, a liberal immigration policy toward doctoral students, and pure luck, among other things. All those factors set off a chaotic evolution that defies definitive determination of cause and effect. (Isenberg, 2010: 3)

Instead of imitating Silicon Valley, Isenberg argues that entrepreneurial ecosystems should be shaped around local conditions. He says that Israel's successful startup culture, for instance, 'evolved haphazardly out of a combination of factors, including spillover from large military R&D efforts, strong diaspora connections to capital and customers, and a culture that prized frugality, education, and unconventional wisdom' (Isenberg, 2010: 4).[4]

Despite this, the desire to emulate Silicon Valley, its wealth, and its young, rock star entrepreneurs, remains strong. There is a folk belief in what Lilly Irani calls *entrepreneurial citizenship*: a model of selfhood 'celebrated in transnational cultures that orient toward Silicon Valley for models of social change' (2015: 3). She writes that 'work practices associated with software production have come to signify collaboration, voluntarism, optimism, and wealth, tested in software practice and ready to enter new domains of public life' (2015: 2). In other words, certain symbolic rituals and ideologies of modern software development are linked not only to financial success, but to an optimistic model of progressive production. In the next section, I look at how certain practices of the technology scene – Startup Weekends, hackathons, accelerators and incubators – are replicated world-wide in an attempt to spread the 'soft skills' that make up Silicon Valley.

Emulating Silicon Valley

In his study of Brazilian software developers, Yuri Takhteyev argues that to understand how globalization functions, we must examine 'worlds of practice' – 'systems of activities comprised of people, ideas, and material objects, linked simultaneously by shared meanings and joint projects' (2012: 2). Software development as a whole is certainly one of these worlds of practice, consisting of a shared set of values, technical knowledge, code, documentation, and the daily practice of creating software. Obviously, robust software industries exist world-wide. In countries like China, Taiwan and Israel, with

mature software industries, the 'brain circulation' (Saxenian, 2006) of engineers who move to Silicon Valley to work, gain expertise in work practice, and then return to their home companies complete with contemporary development practices, has been deeply influential. Beyond just software development, however, much of the 'soft infrastructure' (Haines, 2014a: 282) of Silicon Valley exists as a separate world of practice. More recent practices identified with venture-backed startups that blur the lines between work, play, and self, are deployed worldwide in a strategic attempt by institutions to attempt to create 'a culture of collaboration and innovation' (Cervantes and Nardi, 2012: 5). These practices are quite different from those of software development proper.

For instance, the SV nonprofit 'Startup Weekend,' owned and operated by the accelerator TechStars, conducts workshops around the globe teaching local would-be entrepreneurs about the culture of Silicon Valley startups. Startup Weekend brings engineers, entrepreneurs, venture capitalists, and educational institutions together in an attempt to create what SV refers to as an 'ecosystem' – a 'network of people, institutions, and resources needed to build startups' (Cervantes and Nardi, 2012: 7). In their ethnography of a Mexican Startup Weekend, Cervantes and Nardi argue that Mexico's software industry is characterized by service and manufacturing, and Startup Weekend is an attempt to create the type of 'startup companies that build innovative software products with global impact' (2012: 1). At Startup Weekend, Mexican entrepreneurs decry what they see as a risk-averse, distrustful, and non-collaborative local culture, and attempt to embrace the resourceful and collaborative spirit of Silicon Valley. It seems, however, that the spirit of SV leaks through in more ways than one; one team gets angry when their idea for a 'social network for cats' is pitched by another team. The Startup Weekend mentors calm them down, explaining that there are many social networks for pets, and that execution matters more than just ideas. One might question whether a social network for pets is the type of innovative product with global impact that will help transform Mexican industry; SV values and practices do not, in themselves, produce progressive solutions.

Another type of 'soft infrastructure' is the accelerator, a 'bootcamp for startups' where cohorts of small startups are mentored by successful entrepreneurs.[5] Small startups apply to join an accelerator, which accepts classes or cohorts of startups which go through a program for a fixed amount of time, and are provided with seed funding from the accelerator in exchange for equity, as part of a global network of venture capital funding. The goal of accelerators is for their alumni to get VC funding and eventually 'exit,' either through acquisition by a larger, wealthier company or with an Initial Public Offering (IPO). Because the accelerator takes a percentage of such exits, their success is judged by the monetary value of their alumni companies' exits. Some highly successful startups, including AirBnB, Reddit, Uber, and Taskrabbit, are accelerator alumni. Outside the USA, there are an estimated 200 accelerators in 33 countries worldwide; Haines observed accelerators in Singapore and Buenos Aires. She argues that these accelerators function as institutions that reproduce the social order of startups, providing young companies with funding, networking opportunities, and, perhaps most importantly, an acculturation into startup norms and communities of practice which, of course, are based on those of Silicon Valley (Haines, 2014b). In the accelerators she observed, she found that there were often cultural differences between the startup best practices taught by the accelerator and the norms of the local community. For instance, a Vietnamese startup quit their accelerator because they were uncomfortable with cold-calling potential investors (2014b: 292).

In her research on hackathons – intense, focused coding sessions held over multiple days, in which small teams of programmers create software prototypes – Lilly Irani argues that such events are significant not because they produce software (although they sometimes do), but because they produce *subjects*:

> They manufacture urgency and an optimism that bursts of doing and making can change the world. Participants in hackathons imagine themselves as agents of social progress through software, and these middle-class efforts to remake culture draw legitimacy from the global prestige of technology industry work practices. (Irani, 2015: 2)

To the middle-class Indian coders that Irani studied, hackathons primarily promoted entrepreneurialism. Just as the Mexican Startup Weekend reified Silicon Valley as an ideal model for economic development in Mexico, the 'open governance' hackathon extolled a model of social change based in Northern California as a way for India to develop nationally and progress globally. For participants, the hackathon, and its emphasis on 'design and social entrepreneurship' (Irani, 2015: 8), was a way to differentiate public sector development, which they characterized as slow and deliberative, from forward-thinking, market-driven solutions. The hackathon 'prescribed entrepreneurialism as a cure for ailments of global capitalism' (2015: 9). Given that at the time, however, only about 10 percent of Indians had internet access, a web-based solution to problems of governance would require the participation of NGOs and pre-existing activist networks. Despite their ideals, Irani's participants were unable to finish a demo in time, and the project went nowhere.

In other places, entrepreneurs were able to translate SV work practices into their local contexts with more success. Ali Mohajerani, Baptista, and Nandhakumar (2015) studied both innovative and traditional IT companies in Iran to examine the influence of Western social media on entrepreneurs. They found that the innovative firms, which 'used social media extensively to connect with others and learn new ways of doing business,' (Mohajerani et al., 2015: 23) used the internet to learn about the products, work practices, and values of companies like Google, Twitter, and Facebook. Rather, however, than adopting these practices intact, IT entrepreneurs 'localized practices and models, adding some features specific to their own contexts' (2015: 24). These innovations included American products like Dropbox and Google Apps, but also work practices like 'working from home' and prioritizing 'openness' as a company value. This was in sharp contrast to more traditional Iranian companies, which adhered to traditional values of family and religion, avoided the use of social media (much of which is prohibited by the Iranian government), and required employees to work in the office (2015: 24). The freely available resources online, from message boards to MOOCs, and the use of low-overhead, free or cheap collaboration technologies, helped the innovative companies grow faster and be more economically successful than their more traditional counterparts. In turn, this success spawned local Iranian communities, websites, and partnerships, especially in centers like Tehran. Thus, Iranian technology startups, in many ways, modeled themselves after successful Silicon Valley companies, 'portraying themselves as modern and innovative enterprises, emulating the best-practice management of global corporates' (2015: 25). However, these practices were translated and contextualized to the local context. It was the creativity and drive of Iranian entrepreneurs, not just the affordances of American social media, which led to these transformations.

CONCLUSION

While programmers and entrepreneurs worldwide still attempt to emulate Silicon Valley, the bloom is off the rose. Silicon Valley in the early twenty-first century exists both as something to mimic and something to parody. In New York, the 'Stupid Shit No One Needs

and Terrible Ideas Hackathon' mocked the propensity of the tech industry to tackle systemic problems like climate change through weekends spent building wearables and coding mobile apps. Categories like 'artisanal ad networks,' '3D printed drugs' and 'Using Slack to Raise Your Children' spawned projects such as 'Unfriend the Poors,' a plug-in that determines the wealth of your Facebook friends and then allows you to delete those who do not meet your socio-economic standards (inspired by a very real patent filed by Facebook that would use the social graph to determine Facebook user's credit risk); YOUrinate, a wearable that tells its user when they have to pee; and, infamously, Soylent Dick, a phallus made out of the meal replacement powder that shoots out Soylent when a phrase from the Soylent creator is typed in (Lavigne and Winger-Bearskin, 2016). Co-founder Sam Levigne told *Vice* magazine, 'Is a need being filled [by Silicon Valley] or is the need manufactured and then constantly reinforced?' (D'Anastasio, 2016). In entertainment media, the HBO show *Silicon Valley* takes broad shots at the nerdy, male-dominated culture where founders brag about being part of the 'three comma club' – worth a billion dollars – and hold meetings on bikes. Movies like *The Social Network* and *Steve Jobs* depict tech entrepreneurs as ruthless and socially challenged. The novel *The Circle*, by Dave Eggers (2013), depicts a dystopian world controlled by an unholy alliance of Facebook, Google, and Twitter. Despite the tech industry's massive financial success and uptake among regular Americans, its excesses and eccentricities are more visible than before.

Indeed, San Francisco has become the center of the country's debate about economic inequality, as the salary paid to technology workers, a lack of new affordable housing, and a constant increase in population displaced working people, activists, and artists from their neighborhoods and homes (Bort, 2015). The tech industry functions as a lightning rod for discontent over rising rents and gentrification, with protesters confronting private shuttle buses provided by Google, Facebook and Apple (LA Times Editorial Board, 2014). Wealthy tech workers fueled the fire by visibly confronting the city's homeless population. 'I know people are frustrated about gentrification happening in the city, but the reality is, we live in a free market society,' wrote Justin Keller, founder of a startup that makes it easier to manage data servers. 'The wealthy working people have earned their right to live in the city. ... I shouldn't have to see the pain, struggle, and despair of homeless people to and from my way to work every day' (Keller, 2016). Greg Gopman, founder of a company which organizes hackathons, posted on Facebook that 'In downtown SF the degenerates gather like hyenas, spit, urinate, taunt you, sell drugs, get rowdy, they act like they own the center of the city. Like it's their place of leisure. ... In actuality it's the business district for one of the wealthiest cities in the USA. It [sic] a disgrace' (Biddle, 2013). Publicly shamed for his post, a year later he proposed solving homelessness by building geodesic domes housing 'community transition centers' for shelter and 'personal development classes from computer programming to life coaching' (A Better San Francisco, 2015). To date, not a single transition center has been built.

Indeed, it's been a rough few years for the American tech industry. Not only have tech startups been subject to relentless criticism as the poster children for income inequality, misogyny, and bro-y cluelessness, but venture funding has dropped precipitously, and with it, the go-go conspicuousness of the Web 2.0 era (Samuel and Sanwal, 2016; Zaleski, 2016). 'It's no longer cool to throw a fifty-thousand-dollar party to celebrate your launch,' a recent SF transplant told me, complaining that the city's nightlife was sorely lacking compared to New York. Social media itself is cluttered with advertising and peppered throughout with tracking software, as apps and websites mine personal data and sell it to brokers (Angwin, 2014);

even the least savvy users are beginning to notice that visiting a website for slippers will cause said slippers to appear, as if by magic, on every site that you subsequently browse. On Facebook, Instagram, and, perhaps soon, Twitter, the News Feed displays only a sub-set of your Friends' posts, generated algorithmically based on what the company believes will make you the least likely to leave the site. Once lauded for its facilitation of increased cultural participation and democracy, social media now looks like nothing as much as the endless cycle of consumer want depicted in M. T. Anderson's 2002 dystopic YA novel *Feed*:

> But the braggest thing about the feed, the thing that makes it really big, is that it knows everything you want and hope for, sometimes before you even know what those things are. It can tell you how to get them, and help you make buying decisions that are hard. Everything we think and feel is taken in by the corporations ... and they can get to know what it is we need, so all you have to do is want something and there's a chance it will be yours. (Anderson, 2002: 40)

We must, then, consider the impact of Silicon Valley on the development of technology: where Silicon Valley is understood not just as a physical place but as a set of practices, ideologies, and beliefs. If these ideologies are uneasily compatible with social equality, yet are plugged as solutions to economic difficulties, what happens to them in other contexts? As we have seen, they often fail. But we may consider whether we want them to succeed at all.

Notes

1 While an alternative model exists in the form of the networked, non-profit collaborative culture of free/libre/open-source software, FLOSS projects rarely result in popular social media, with the notable exception of Wikipedia. See Gehl, Chapter 18 this volume, for more.

2 China has a very active social media population and an extremely robust startup sector. Generally US tech companies have a difficult time making inroads. The Chinese social media industry is

worthy of more attention than I can devote to it in this chapter. For more on Chinese social media, see Fuchs (2016), McDonald (2016) and Wang (2016).

3　This shift has been vigorously resisted in Europe, culminating in the passage of a 'right to data portability' as part of the European Union's General Data Protection Regulation (GDPR) passed in April 2016; it remains to be seen how social media platforms will respond to this imperative (Burton et al., 2016).

4　The Israeli government proactively supported a venture-capital backed startup market. For more on Israel's tech sector, see Avnimelech and Teubal (2006).

5　Both accelerators and incubators attempt to create or grow small startups. Accelerators are highly-selective programs with a fixed time-frame which require startups to apply; during the accelerator, the startup works with various mentors to improve their product and business, and is given a small amount of seed money in exchange for equity. Incubators, on the other hand, are co-working spaces in which people similarly focused on particular ideas or verticals are brought together in an attempt to nurture innovation. They rarely provide companies with money, and often work with startups much earlier in the process in an attempt to find a workable business model or product (Forrest, 2016).

REFERENCES

A Better San Francisco. 2015. 'Community Transition Centers.' www.transitioncenters.org/

Anderson, M. T. 2002. *Feed*. Cambridge, MA: Candlewick Press.

Angwin, Julia. 2014. *Dragnet Nation: A Quest for Privacy, Security, and Freedom in a World of Relentless Surveillance*. New York: Times Books.

Avnimelech, Gil, and Morris Teubal. 2006. 'Creating Venture Capital Industries that Co-Evolve with High Tech: Insights from an Extended Industry Life Cycle Perspective of the Israeli Experience.' *Research Policy*, 35(10): 1477–1498.

Bacon, Lauren. 2013. 'Once and for All: Tech is Not a Meritocracy.' *Quartz*, March 26. http://qz.com/66866/once-and-for-all-tech-is-not-a-meritocracy/

Banet-Weiser, S., and M. Sturken. 2010. 'The Politics of Commerce: Shepard Fairey and the New Cultural Entrepreneurship.' In Melissa Aronczyk and Devon Powers (Ed.), *Blowing up the Brand: Critical Perspectives on Promotional Culture* (pp. 265–85). New York: Peter Lang.

Barbrook, R., and A. Cameron. 1996. 'The Californian Ideology.' *Science as Culture*, 6(1): 44–72.

Biddle, Sam. 2013. 'Happy Holidays: Startup CEO Complains SF is Full of Human Trash.' *Valleywag*, December 11. http://valleywag.gawker.com/happy-holidays-startup-ceo-complains-sf-is-full-of-hum-1481067192.

Borsook, Paulina. 2001. *Cyberselfish*. New York: PublicAffairs.

Bort, Ryan. 2015. 'The Tech Industry is Stripping San Francisco of Its Culture, and Your City Could Be Next.' *Newsweek*, October 1. www.newsweek.com/san-francisco-tech-industry-gentrification-documentary-378628.

Bresnahan, Timothy, Alfonso Gambardella, and AnnaLee Saxenian. 2001. "Old Economy' Inputs for 'New Economy' Outcomes: Cluster Formation in the New Silicon Valleys.' *Industrial and Corporate Change*, 10(4): 835–860.

Bronson, Po. 2000. *The Nudist on the Late Shift*. New York: Broadway Books.

Burton, Cedric, Laura De Boel, Christopher Kuner, Anna Pateraki, Sarah Cadiot, and Sara G. Hoffman. 2016. 'The Final European Union General Data Protection Regulation.' *Bloomberg Law: Privacy & Data Security*, February 12. www.bna.com/final-european-union-n57982067329/

Castells, Manuel, and Peter Hall. 1994. *Technopoles of the World: The Making of Twenty-First-Century Industrial Complexes*. New York: Routledge.

Cech, Erin A., and Mary Blair-Loy. 2010. 'Perceiving Glass Ceilings? Meritocratic versus Structural Explanations of Gender Inequality among Women in Science and Technology.' *Social Problems*, 57(3): 371–397.

Cervantes, Ruy, and Bonnie Nardi. 2012. 'Building a Mexican Startup Culture over the Weekends.' In *Proceedings of the 4th International Conference on Intercultural Collaboration*, 11–20. New York: ACM. http://dl.acm.org/citation.cfm?id=2160884.

Chaffey, Dave. 2016. 'Global Social Media Statistics Summary 2016.' *Smart Insights*, February 16. www.smartinsights.com/social-media-marketing/social-media-strategy/new-global-social-media-research/

Cockayne, Daniel G. 2015. 'Entrepreneurial Affect: Attachment to Work Practice in San Francisco's Digital Media Sector.' *Environment and Planning D: Society and Space*, 263775815618399.

CrunchBase. 2016. 'The CrunchBase Unicorn Leaderboard.' *TechCrunch*, August 31. http://social.techcrunch.com/unicorn-leaderboard/

D'Anastasio, Cecilia. 2016. 'Inside the Stupid Shit No One Needs & Terrible Ideas Hackathon.' *Motherboard*, February 8. http://motherboard.vice.com/read/inside-the-stupid-shit-no-one-needs-terrible-ideas-hackathon.

Dawson, Keith. 2001. 'Siliconia.' *Tasty Bites from the Technology Frontier*, June 24. http://tbtf.com/siliconia.html

Eggers, Dave. 2013. *The Circle*. New York: Knopf Doubleday Publishing Group.

Engel, Jerome S. 2014. *Global Clusters of Innovation: Entrepreneurial Engines of Economic Growth around the World*. Northampton, MA: Edward Elgar Publishing.

English-Lueck, June Anne. 2002. *Cultures@Silicon Valley*. Palo Alto, CA: Stanford University Press.

English-Lueck, June Anne. 2011. 'Prototyping Self in Silicon Valley: Deep Diversity as a Framework for Anthropological Inquiry.' *Anthropological Theory*, 11(1): 89–106.

Eslami, Motahhare, Karrie Karahalios, Christian Sandvigt, Kristen Vaccaro, Aimee Rickman, Kevin Hamilton, and Alex Kirlik. 2016. 'First I 'Like' It, Then I Hide It: Folk Theories of Social Feeds.' In *Proceedings of the 2016 CHI Conference on Human Factors in Computing Systems* (pp. 2371–2382). New York: ACM. https://pdfs.semanticscholar.org/3411/f97b3ed4761f3d20fffaa0cbcdd62e76e650.pdf.

Ferdman, Roberto A., and Christopher Ingraham. 2016. 'This $700 WiFi 'Juicer' is Everything Wrong with Food Today.' *The Washington Post*, April 1. www.washingtonpost.com/news/wonk/wp/2016/04/01/this-juice-is-bananas/

Forrest, Conner. 2016. 'Accelerators vs. Incubators: What Startups Need to Know.' *TechRepublic*. Accessed April 13. www.techrepublic.com/article/accelerators-vs-incubators-what-startups-need-to-know/

Fuchs, Christian. 2016. 'Baidu, Weibo and Renren: The Global Political Economy of Social Media in China.' *Asian Journal of Communication*, 26(1): 14–41.

Haines, Julia Katherine. 2014a. 'Emerging Innovation: The Global Expansion of Seed Accelerators.' In *Proceedings of the Companion Publication of the 17th ACM Conference on Computer Supported Cooperative Work & Social Computing* (pp. 57–60). New York: ACM. http://dl.acm.org/citation.cfm?id=2556823.

Haines, Julia Katherine. 2014b. 'Iterating an Innovation Model: Challenges and Opportunities in Adapting Accelerator Practices in Evolving Ecosystems.' In *Ethnographic Praxis in Industry Conference Proceedings, 2014* (pp. 282–295). Wiley Online Library. http://onlinelibrary.wiley.com/doi/10.1111/1559-8918.01033/full

Henrekson, Magnus, and Tino Sanandaji. 2014. 'Small Business Activity Does Not Measure Entrepreneurship.' *Proceedings of the National Academy of Sciences*, 111(5): 1760–1765.

Hui, Kiana. 2014. 'The Obstacles of Female Entrepreneurship in Silicon Valley.' *Intersect: The Stanford Journal of Science, Technology and Society*, 7(2). http://ojs.stanford.edu/ojs/index.php/intersect/article/view/593

Irani, Lilly. 2015. 'Hackathons and the Making of Entrepreneurial Citizenship.' *Science, Technology & Human Values*, 40(5): 799–824.

Isenberg, Daniel J. 2010. 'How to Start an Entrepreneurial Revolution.' *Harvard Business Review*, 88(6): 40–50.

Keller, Justin. 2016. 'Open Letter to SF Mayor Ed Lee and Greg Suhr (Police Chief).' *Justin Keller on Svbtle*, February 15. http://justink.svbtle.com/open-letter-to-mayor-ed-lee-and-greg-suhr-police-chief.

LA Times Editorial Board. 2014. 'San Francisco's Bus Wars are a Proxy Fight against Gentrification.' *Los Angeles Times*, January 24. http://articles.latimes.com/

2014/jan/24/opinion/la-ed-google-bus-san-francisco-20140123.

Lavigne, Sam, and Amelia Winger-Bearskin. 2016. 'STUPID SHIT NO ONE NEEDS & TERRIBLE IDEAS HACKATHON.' *STUPID SHIT NO ONE NEEDS & TERRIBLE IDEAS HACKATHON*. www.stupidhackathon.com/

Lécuyer, Christophe. 2006. *Making Silicon Valley*. Cambridge, MA: MIT Press.

Markoff, John. 2005. *What the Dormouse Said*. New York: Penguin Books.

Marwick, A. 2013. *Status Update: Celebrity, Publicity, and Branding in the Social Media Age*. New Haven, CT: Yale University Press.

Marwick, A. 2015. 'Open Markets, Open Projects: Wikipedia and the Politics of Openness.' *Public Books*, July. www.publicbooks.org/nonfiction/open-markets-open-projects-wikipedia-and-the-politics-of-openness.

Massaro, Rachel. 2016. '2016 Silicon Valley Index.' San Jose, CA: Joint Venture Silicon Valley Institute for Regional Studies.

McDonald, Tom. 2016. *Social Media in Rural China*. London: UCL Press. www.ucl.ac.uk/ucl-press/browse-books/social-media-in-rural-china

McNamee, Stephen J., and Robert K. Miller. 2009. *The Meritocracy Myth*. New York: Rowman & Littlefield.

Miller, Daniel, Elisabetta Costa, Nell Haynes, Tom McDonald, Razvan Nicolescu, Jolynna Sinanan, Juliano Spyer, Shriram Venkatraman, and Xinyuan Wang. 2016. *How the World Changed Social Media*. London: UCL Press. www.ucl.ac.uk/ucl-press/browse-books/how-world-changed-social-media.

Mohajerani, Ali, João Baptista, and Joe Nandhakumar. 2015. 'Exploring the Role of Social Media in Importing Logics across Social Contexts: The Case of IT SMEs in Iran.' *Technological Forecasting and Social Change*, 95: 16–31.

Nguyen, Lilly U. 2016. 'Infrastructural Action in Vietnam: Inverting the Techno-Politics of Hacking in the Global South.' *New Media & Society*, 1461444816629475.

Nusca, Andrew. 2016. 'The Unicorn List.' *Forbes.com*, January 19.

Perrin, Andrew. 2015. 'Social Media Usage: 2005–2015.' *Pew Research Center: Internet, Science & Tech*, October 8. www.pewinternet. org/2015/10/08/social-networking-usage-2005-2015/

Pressler, Jessica. 2014. "Let's, Like, Demolish Laundry." *NYMag.com*, May 21. http://nymag.com/news/features/laundry-apps-2014-5/

Quinones, Gerardo, Brian Nicholson, and Richard Heeks. 2015. 'A Literature Review of E-Entrepreneurship in Emerging Economies: Positioning Research on Latin American Digital Startups.' In *Entrepreneurship in BRICS* (pp. 179–208). New York: Springer. http://link.springer.com/chapter/10.1007/978-3-319-11412-5_11

Rogers, Everett M., and Judith K. Larsen. 1984. *Silicon Valley Fever*. New York: Basic Books.

Samuel, Jennifer, and Anand Sanwal. 2016. 'Venture Capital Funding Activity Slows Drastically in Q4 '15: KPMG and CB Insights.' *KPMG Global*, January 22. https://home.kpmg.com/xx/en/home/media/press-releases/2016/01/vc-funding-slows-in-q4.html

Saxenian, AnnaLee. 1996. *Regional Advantage*. Cambridge, MA: Harvard University Press.

Saxenian, AnnaLee. 2006. *The New Argonauts: Regional Advantage in a Global Economy*. Cambridge, MA: Harvard University Press.

Shih, Johanna. 2006. 'Circumventing Discrimination Gender and Ethnic Strategies in Silicon Valley.' *Gender & Society*, 20(2): 177–206.

Takhteyev, Yuri. 2012. *Coding Places: Software Practice in a South American City*. Cambridge, MA: MIT Press.

Tedjamulia, S. J. J., D. L. Dean, D. R. Olsen, and C. C. Albrecht. 2005. 'Motivating Content Contributions to Online Communities: Toward a More Comprehensive Theory.' In *Proceedings of the 38th Annual Hawaii International Conference on System Sciences* (pp. 193b–193b). Hawaii.

Tkacz, Nathaniel. 2014. *Wikipedia and the Politics of Openness*. Chicago, IL: University of Chicago Press.

Turner, Fred. 2005. 'Where the Counterculture Met the New Economy.' *Technology and Culture*, 46(1167): 485–512.

Turner, Fred. 2006. *From Counterculture to Cyberculture*. Chicago, IL: University of Chicago Press.

US Small Business Administration Office of Advocacy. 2016a. 'What's New with Small Business.' Washington, DC: US Small Business Administration. www.sba.gov/sites/default/files/Whats_New_With_Small_Business.pdf

US Small Business Administration Office of Advocacy. 2016b. 'Small Business Finance Frequently Asked Questions.' Washington, DC: US Small Business Administration. www.sba.gov/sites/default/files/Finance-FAQ-2016_WEB.pdf

Wang, Xinyuan. 2016. *Social Media in Industrial China*. London: UCL Press. www.ucl.ac.uk/ucl-press/browse-books/social-media-in-industrial-china.

Welch, Liz. 2016. 'How Casper Became a $100 Million Company in Less than Two Years.' *Inc.*, February 25. www.inc.com/magazine/201603/liz-welch/casper-changing-mattress-industry.html

Wikipedia Contributors. 2009. 'List of Places with 'Silicon' names.' *Wikipedia, The Free Encyclopedia*. Wikimedia Foundation. http://en.wikipedia.org/w/index.php?title=List_of_places_with_%22Silicon%22_names&oldid=333653398

Wohlsen, Marcus. 2014. 'Silicon Valley's Plan to Split California into 6 States Just Might Succeed.' *WIRED*, July 16. www.wired.com/2014/07/silicon-valleys-plan-to-split-california-into-6-states-just-might-work/

Young, Michael. 2001. 'Comment: Down with Meritocracy.' *The Guardian*, June 29. www.theguardian.com/politics/2001/jun/29/comment

Zaleski, Olivia. 2016. 'Startup Funding Deals Fall to Lowest Level in Four Years.' *Bloomberg.com*, April 7. www.bloomberg.com/news/articles/2016-04-07/startup-funding-deals-fall-to-lowest-level-in-four-years

Zittrain, Jonathan. 2008. *The Future of the Internet – And How to Stop It*. New Haven, CT: Yale University Press.

18

Alternative Social Media: From Critique to Code

Robert W. Gehl

It's common to start any essay on social media with numbers, especially total numbers of users, as a means to establish their significance. So I will do the same here. These are the estimated registered members of several social networks:

- Ello: over 2,000,000
- *diaspora: 602,795
- Twister: 80,493
- GNU social: 25,823[1]

For anyone with a passing familiarity with the size of the user bases of Facebook, Twitter, Google+, or Pinterest, these numbers are not particularly impressive. However, for students of social media, these estimated numbers tell us that there is life outside the walls of the dominant social media platforms. Ello, *diaspora, Twister, and GNU social are part of a larger collection of sites meant to be alternatives to the mainstream. They are, as I call them, *alternative social media*.

What makes them 'alternative'? In this chapter, I suggest that these sites are not alternative in the sense of mere choice (as in, you have a choice between Coca-Cola and Pepsi). Rather, they are alternative in the same sense that 'alternative media' (Atton, 2002) are alternative: their internal operations, economics, and cultural practices are markedly different from what I call 'corporate social media.' In addition to providing users with a choice, they provide new ways of thinking about what 'social media' means. Alternative social media exist as a response to the criticisms of corporate social media: namely, their surveillance practices, their appropriation of user data, their emphasis on marketing messages over other forms of connection, and their algorithmic shaping of sociality, to name a few.

To highlight the differences between alternative social media (hereafter, ASM) and corporate social media (hereafter, CSM), in the first half of this chapter I will explore several academic critiques of corporate social media, tracing lines of argument through technical, economic, and cultural lenses. The lines of critique described below are not exhaustive, but they help illuminate differences between corporate social media and alternative social media. In the final half, I will explore how various alternative social media can be seen as responses to the criticisms leveled at CSM. Much of the second half is derived from my previous work on ASM, interviews with ASM makers and users, as well as my ongoing participant observation of multiple ASM systems.

CRITIQUES OF CORPORATE SOCIAL MEDIA

There are three lines of critique directed at corporate social media that have direct relevance for any exploration of alternative social media. These are: (1) *critiques of CSM technical infrastructures*, focusing on the network and software structures of CSM; (2) *critiques of the political economy of CSM*, focusing on how CSM monetize user activities and privilege marketing messages over other forms of communication; and (3) *critiques of the dominant cultural practices and uses of CSM*, focusing on social practices that are partly conditioned by CSM. As with anything to do with digital media, the lines between technical, economic, and cultural activities are blurred.

Technical Infrastructures

The goal of this line of critique is to map how CSM are 'primarily concerned with establishing the technocultural conditions within which users can produce content and within which content and users can be re-channeled through techno-commercial networks and channels' (Langlois et al., 2009). Thus, critical exploration of the technical infrastructures of CSM comports with traditional

media theory, which focuses on the medium over the message. Critics of CSM have largely focused on two main topics: the (en)closed structure of CSM network topologies, and their use of algorithms.

Much of the criticisms of the technical structures of CSM are directed at their centralized network topologies. Mark Andrejevic's (2007) criticism of Google's free wi-fi program as an example of 'enclosure' anticipates this line of critique. For Andrejevic, technology companies such as Google and Microsoft seek to enclose end users within a centralized network topology, drawing more and more user activity into corporate surveillance systems and policing the 'proper' uses of their respective technologies. Moreover, Andrejevic also notes that technology firms work to elide the internal details of their networks behind the (then proverbial, now ubiquitous) discourse of the 'cloud' (also see Mosco, 2014). 'The cloud' is in this case a fog that covers up the recentralized relationship between once relatively autonomous computer users and the manufacturers and service providers those computers now connect to. This relies on closed, proprietary code and protocols that end users cannot modify (Cabello et al., 2013: 340).

This critique of technology firms' double move of centralization and wiring shut (Gillespie, 2007) figures into later critical work exploring CSM. As Gerlitz and Helmond (2013) have shown, Facebook's centralized power is extending through the ubiquitous 'Like' button and Facebook's Connect login system. The Like button and Connect appear to be distributed across the Web in a decentralized manner; many sites allow for users to sign in with Facebook and Like items on their pages. This decentralizes the point of data gathering: one no longer needs to visit Facebook.com to have one's data tracked by Facebook. Yet, Gerlitz and Helmond argue that this distribution is always connected to the centralized data processing core of Facebook. This simultaneous, distributed centralization (Gehl, 2012), where end users' data is gathered across the Internet and drawn into centralized CSM, exemplifies the (en)closed line of critique: critics are finding that interaction is made more visible and transparent as users channel their social activities through social media. At the same time, the inner workings of social media – data analysis, storage, and sales – are increasingly closed and opaque. Everything flows to the logical center – large server farms and corporate headquarters – but the inner workings of that increasingly important and powerful center are obscured.

More recently, critical attention has turned to the use of algorithms to shape social and technical interactions within CSM platforms. The power of algorithms to shape online social interaction was quite visible during the 2014 controversy over the Facebook contagion study, where social scientists from Facebook, UC-San Francisco, and Cornell manipulated hundreds of thousands of Facebook users' social streams in order to elicit various emotional responses (Kramer et al., 2014). However, that controversy is only a more visible example of longstanding concerns over algorithmic shaping of culture. For example, Twitter's 'Trending Topics' algorithm has been criticized multiple times for perceived censorship of topics such as 'Occupy Wall Street' (Gillespie, 2011).

These controversies reveal anxieties over CSM's ability to algorithmically shape both the present and the future. Writing about the present, Weltevrede, Helmond, and Gerlitz (2014) have explored the technical construction of 'real time' within Facebook, Twitter, and Google, among other platforms. 'Real-time,' Internet critic Geert Lovink quips, 'is the new crack' (Lovink, 2012: 11). Weltevrede, Helmond, and Gerlitz show us how this 'crack' is algorithmically constructed, as well as how its addictive properties are tied to CSM imperatives. Denying any essential, a priori concept of time, they argue that Twitter, Facebook, and Google algorithmically engineer a sense of presence and immediacy within their specific sites:

'The organization of the pace of updates can be thought of as a pattern through which the continuous production of new content is being organized in ways that are aligned with the specific politics' (Weltevrede et al., 2014: 19) of systems such as corporate social media. CSM pushes out content, notifying us that there are five more Tweets, 10 more Likes, or 17 new Google+ messages. We turn to them to know what's going on now. However, Weltevrede, Helmond, and Gerlitz also note other temporalities that exist alongside these constant updates:

> In the case of Twitter, which simultaneously displays fresh, new content and relevant, featured results, relevance becomes a recommendation feature that alters the pace of the freshness stream, as these so-called Top Tweets are designed to produce future user engagement by making them sticky and able to stay on top of a fast-changing stream. (Weltevrede et al., 2014: 18)

These multiple temporalities – the constant appearance of fresh, user-generated content on the one hand, and curated trends on the other – are not accidental, but are tied to the desires of CSM to keep our attention both on streams of new content and the often sponsored 'sticky' messages that appear alongside.

These 'sticky' messages – trending topics, recommended reads, and the like – are the objects of multiple critics of CSM algorithms who focus on how CSM can shape the future. Ganaele Langlois (2014) has explored the 'recommendation engines' of corporate social media, seeing them as 'colonization of users' experiences of meaning' (Langlois, 2014: 85). Langlois finds that recommendation engines algorithmically shape what phenomenologists call 'protention' (i.e., our future expectations; see Langlois, 2014; Hansen, 2006: 304; and Turow, 2011). Similarly, Ted Striphas critiques 'algorithmic culture,' 'the enfolding of human thought, conduct, organization and expression into the logic of big data and large-scale computation, a move that alters how the category culture has long been practiced, experienced and understood' (Striphas, 2015: 396). Striphas sees CSM (and other large, centralized online systems such as Netflix and Amazon) as the new arbiters of culture, shaping our tastes through computer code. In other words, as more of our activities are channeled through CSM, CSM has more influence over our thoughts and actions as we move through space and time.

In sum, the criticism of the technical elements of CSM ties in their network topologies, use of closed-access code and databases, and their algorithmic shaping of both the present and future. The next line of critique, that of political economy, draws our attention to how these technical infrastructures relate to the profit motives of CSM.

Political Economy

When it comes to critiques of the political economy of corporate social media, perhaps the most fundamental concept is that of free labor. This concept, proposed by Tiziana Terranova (2000), describes how Web users contribute valuable labor to online applications. 'Simultaneously voluntarily given and unwaged, enjoyed and exploited, free labor on the Net includes the activity of building Web sites, modifying software packages, reading and participating in mailing lists, and building virtual spaces on MUDs and MOOs' (Terranova, 2000: 33). Terranova's argument holds that digital capitalism requires a large range of activities to keep it operating: moderating online communities, adding to open source code, or tagging objects, to name a few. These are done, for the most part, by unpaid volunteers, to the benefits of for-profit corporations who claim ownership over the results of users' labors.

This analytical concept had immediate applicability to specific instances of online social interactions. Hector Postigo (2003, 2009), for example, explores the America Online volunteers who did unpaid

work to maintain AOL forums. Mark Coté and Jennifer Pybus (2007) take up the concept to explore how MySpace managed its users, training them to profile themselves and contribute to the cultural, creative, and economic dimensions of the site. The promise of MySpace was that users who worked hard enough within its structures would become hypervalorized 'MySpace celebrities'; Coté and Pybus point to the example of Tila Tequila, a celebrity who used MySpace to promote herself and thus became a model laborer for other MySpace users to emulate. I myself take up the concept of free labor to contrast Facebook's management of its users as free laborers with MySpace, arguing that Facebook's more standardized structure helped make its free laborer/users more productive (Gehl, 2014b).

All of this begs questions: more productive for whom? Who benefits economically from the free labor of social media users? CSM relies on a basic exchange: you provide your personal information and your free labor, and in exchange CSM gives you access. While you have access, part of your attention must go to marketing messages. Therefore, marketers and advertisers are the primary beneficiaries of user free labor. Many critics suggest that users' constructions of their own profiles greatly benefit marketers and advertisers who previously had to do the work of profiling people (see Elmer, 2004). As Nick Couldry and Joseph Turow note, thanks to users doing the work of self-profiling themselves in Facebook and Twitter, 'It is ... now possible to buy the right to deliver an ad with a message tailored to a person with a specific profile at the precise moment that that person loads a Web page' (Couldry and Turow, 2014: 1714). As Maria Bakardjieva puts it, 'Thus we find our Facebook profile page populated with our friends' images, pronouncements, witty snippets and exclamations, all impishly mixed up with rider boots, cruise ships, designer clothes, eye-glass frames – you name it. In fact we have named it, directly or not – at some point in the recent past, and

Facebook is happy to oblige' (Bakardjieva, 2014: 376). Here we see a corollary to the 'realtimeness' that Weltevrede, Helmond, and Gerlitz (2014) found in their analysis of CSM technical structures: as users do the work of responding to real-time prompts (and therefore contribute to social streams), CSM sites mine their activities and sell their attention in real-time to marketers and advertisers who place targeted ads into end-users' social media screens.

But marketers and advertisers aren't the only ones benefiting from the free labor of users. The CSM platforms do, as well. Taina Bucher's (2012) analysis of Facebook's EdgeRank algorithm suggests that Facebook privileges constant user participation in the site, which in turn prompts other users to continue to provide content as they all work against becoming 'invisible' or drowned out by the constant stream of updates. Gerlitz and Helmond (2013) trace the 'Like economy' to find the ways in which such simple binary signals constitute a whole range of online practices. Participation in Facebook (liking, friending, commenting), Twitter (tweeting, retweeting, favoriting), or Google+ (+1ing, sorting contacts into circles) has a multiplicative effect: the resulting 'data and numbers have performative and productive capacities, they can generate user affects, enact more activities and thus multiply themselves' (Gerlitz and Helmond, 2013: 13). Bringing these works together, we see that CSM are structured to intensify user participation, with the benefit of more traffic on these respective sites, more user attention paid to them, and more data produced by users (which can then be sold to marketers).

CSM users who operate within these logics often internalize them and reflect them in their practices. Indeed, Alice Marwick and danah boyd's (2010) analysis of Twitter users find that many of them negotiate categories such as 'authenticity' and 'professionalism' in order to present themselves to their imagined audiences. 'These exemplify highly self-conscious identity presentations

that assume a primarily professional context. Revealing personal information is seen as a marker of authenticity, but is strategically managed and limited' (Marwick and boyd, 2010: 127). Building on these observations, both Marwick (2013) and I (Gehl, 2011) argue that the logic of branding and marketing has been folded back onto corporate social media users themselves, who are encouraged to think of themselves as 'personal brands.' Thus, CSM users not only do the work of building out the content of sites such as Facebook and Twitter, or the work of self-profiling so marketers no longer have to, they also construct themselves in idealized ways, mimicking the economic practices of corporate branding and attempting to control how their profiles influence other users' sentiments.

So far, I have traced the political economy line of critique with little regard for *polis*. However, several critics have addressed this topic, specifically the concern that the dominant CSM institutions (e.g., Facebook, Twitter, Pinterest, and Google) are peculiarly American, specifically Californian, companies. As Geert Lovink and Miriam Rasch (2013) note, 'Social media culture is belied in American corporate capitalism, dominated by the logic of startups and venture capital, management buyouts, IPOs, etc. Three to four companies literally own the Western social media landscape and capitalize on the content produced by millions of people around the world' (Lovink and Rasch, 2013: 367).

In an example of the critique of American dominance of CSM, Jack Bratich (2011) traces states of exception as the US State Department adjudicates between foreign media and home-grown media. In the case of Egypt, for example, 'we see an interesting divide here. In residual cold-war logic, the sovereign adversaries are said to have State-run mass media. The USA, meanwhile, has State-friended social media' (Bratich, 2011: 629). In other words, US political elites support Silicon Valley-native companies as they expand around the world, hailing their growth as media democratization, while condemning other nations' media systems as necessarily totalitarian and oppressive.

Thus, the technical structures explored by CSM critics link up with these political economic concerns: CSM are centralized, American, for-profit firms that deploy algorithms to intensify content production by users, appropriating and selling the resulting data to marketers and advertisers, supported by hegemonic governments. This has direct implications for how subjectivities are shaped in and through CSM. I take up the overdetermination between CSM technical structures, political economy, and cultural practices in the next section.

Cultural Practices

When we consider how culture – that is, day-to-day practices and subjectivities – is over-determined with technical and economic spheres, we see many articulations between network structures, algorithms, political economy, and the cultures of communication and sociality that are mediated in CSM. Cultural practices that have shaped, been shaped by, and emerged within the technical and economic imperatives of CSM have not gone unnoticed by critics.

The relationship between subjectivity, performance, and surveillance practices has perhaps been the single most explored topic for critical CSM scholars. Scholars have documented the various ways that CSM users perform, exhibit, and curate the self for others, whether those others be identifiable contacts or an imagined audience (Albrechtslund, 2008; Donath and boyd, 2004; Hogan, 2010; Marwick and boyd, 2010). In making performative declarations about hobbies, passions, friends, and desires, CSM users construct themselves in ways that previous media systems did not allow. However, users' knowledge that such performances are mediated, structured, and recorded has a particular

impact upon how they live their day-to-day lives. Dubrofsky (2011), for example, finds that Facebook normalizes surveillance as part of daily life:

> Facebook animates a seamless (unremarkable) integration of surveillance into the lives of users. ... Facebook effectively situates users as the master of their own surveillance and as the producers of their self under surveillance. On Facebook, surveillance is a practice of the self. (Dubrofsky, 2011: 120)

This normalization of surveillance is especially troubling when we consider the links between recorded and mediated performances of identity and the growing surveillance state. As Kirsty Best (2010) has shown, 'I have nothing to hide' is a prevalent attitude among everyday Internet users, even as a steady drumbeat about corporate and government surveillance sounds in the news (also see Solove, 2007). The normalized surveillance practices of CSM invite users to produce themselves through their data declarations, and, as Best notes, end users believe that they must be truthful and transparent in order to benefit from them.

Dubrofsky suggests that the self as constituted by surveillance produces a data-driven, profiled subject:

> The Facebook subject exists mostly through the data tracks it makes (there are few activities a subject can engage in that do not create data tracks traceable by either the makers of the site or by other users), which verify its existence as well as create its subjectivity: Facebook subjects are aggregates of traceable data. (Dubrofsky, 2011: 124)

Indeed, as attention to and funding for Big Data analysis increases, conceptions of who we are and what possibilities lie before us can be increasingly decided in relation to the data profiles we are building within CSM (Mackenzie, 2013). Given that centralized CSM systems have particular economic goals in mind (i.e., the abstraction and sale of our information and the direction of our attention to marketing messages), the sort of subjectivities that are being shaped within and through CSM are increasingly tied to those economic imperatives. Ultimately, I would suggest that the subjectivity preferred in CSM and produced through normalized surveillance is not that of the citizen, but of the consumer (Gehl, 2013).

Alongside the concerns about surveillance practices and the construction of the self, recent criticism of CSM, especially Facebook (but to a lesser extent Google+ and LinkedIn), has been directed at their requirement that users sign up with their real names. While early CSM saw the practice of 'Fakesters' (i.e., fake or pseudonymous profiles) (boyd, 2006), Facebook was able to create a culture of real-world identities, both through relying on third-party verification (college IDs at first, then later work-based emails) and through the use of the 'social graph' as a means to vet individuals (Gehl, 2014b: 85). Twitter of course does not have a real-name policy, but its increasing prominence as a place where media outlets, celebrities, and businesses promote themselves as 'brands,' as well as the badge of honor that is the 'verified account' status, are tied to a culture of authenticity within the site (Marwick and boyd, 2010). Google+ had a real-name policy, but dropped it under pressure from protesters (MacKinnon and Lim, 2014). As José van Dijck (2013: 200) argues, 'Platform owners have a vested interest in pushing the need for a uniform online identity to attain maximum transparency, not only because they want to know who their users are, but also because advertisers want users' "truthful" data.' A user signed up with a real-world identity is thus more valuable to marketers, and we might expect more demands for real names in CSM in the future, protests notwithstanding.

Indeed, this cultural practice has ossified into a policy: the 'real-world identity' policy of Facebook. Facebook's policy manifests in multiple ways, including the requirement of a government ID to sign up (if a user is unable or unwilling to provide a mobile phone number) as well as the recent controversy over the use of stage names by drag queens within

Facebook (Lux, 2014). Examining the latter, Jessa Lingel and Adam Golub (2015) explore how drag performers use social media. As they argue,

> Drag performers are tasked not only with fitting complex narratives of gender into rigid online interfaces, but with leveraging social media tools in service of personal, professional, and community objectives. While drag itself presents a dramatic form of complexity, there are more general layers of complexity around negotiating personal and professional life within a single platform. We argue that Facebook, like other dominant social media platforms, tends towards a design ethic of singularity and simplicity, fundamentally at odds with technological preferences (or needs) for complexity and mess. (Lingel and Golub, 2015: 537)

This 'design ethic of singularity and simplicity' runs counter to the identity-play that we presumably have in online interactions (e.g., Turkle, 1995). Instead, CSM's 'conflation of self-expression, self-communication and self-promotion into one tool, which is subsequently used for personality assessment and manipulating behavior, should raise the awareness of users in their different roles as citizens, friends, employees, employers and so on' (van Dijck, 2013: 213).

Similarly, the 'singularity and simplicity' of the term 'friend,' as it is used in CSM, has been critically explored. danah boyd (boyd, 2006; Donath and boyd, 2004), for example, has done pioneering work on the early CSM sites Friendster and MySpace, contrasting the vernacular meaning of friendship with the actual practices of users. Users of Friendster, for example, listed as 'Friends' 'fellow partygoers, people they knew (and people they thought they knew), old college mates that they hadn't talked to in years, people with entertaining Profiles, and anyone that they found interesting. Not everyone took the Friendship process seriously' (boyd, 2006). Despite this observation, rather than bemoaning the erosion of friendship and social interaction, boyd's valuable work has empirically examined new forms of sociality enabled by CSM, especially for teens and young adults.

However, even as critics have noted complex, emergent new forms of sociality in CSM, they also have evaluated the quality of those new social interactions. Some critics find them lacking. Bernard Stiegler, for example, draws on Aristotelian philosophy and decries the 'social engineering' of CSM:

> By (formally) declaring our 'friends' and our 'friendship,' and also operating a selection among our *friends, acquaintances, and contacts of all sorts*, here all lumped together under the appellation 'friends,' we trigger a profound alteration of *what used to be understood as social networks*: friends, family and relatives, acquaintances, chums, pals, old social structures, the very ones *creating* those networks and *depending* on them at the same time. (Stiegler, 2013: 20, original emphasis)

Stiegler goes on to suggest that the formal declaration of connection in sites like Facebook is the 'grammatization' (i.e., discretization, abstraction, and rationalization) of social relations, which can enable the modulation and control of populations and ultimately the 'destruction of the social' (Stiegler, 2013: 27).

Similarly, although she does not use Stiegler's term 'grammatization,' Maria Bakardjieva points to the discretization process:

> Twitter gives us the benefits of purging all words that do not represent the most direct means to an end. Facebook conveniently serves us with a button to register our 'likes', thus saving us the need to expend time and imagination on crafting an approving comment. (Bakardjieva, 2014: 374)

Ultimately, Bakardjieva concurs with Stiegler, criticizing the 'McDonaldization' of friendship: 'interpersonal sharing is mass-produced, standardized and automated. By claiming ownership over the notion of friendship, social media platforms seize the power to mold its cultural understanding in a formally rationalized manner' (Bakardjieva, 2014: 381).

There is certainly much more to be said about CSM, both from critical perspectives and from more celebratory frameworks. The lines of technical, economic, and cultural critique I offer here are germane to the next section: the exploration of alternative social media systems that have been built as a response to the growing body of criticism leveled at CSM.

FROM CRITICISM TO CODE

At its best, criticism – the active interrogation of cultural practices – opens up new possibilities of imagination and practice (Feenberg, 1986). But this opening up is also a key limitation of critique; very often the critic is satisfied with pointing out flaws, ruptures, and contradictions while leaving the construction of solutions to others.

To be fair to academic critics of CSM, most do not have the training or time to construct solutions to the problems in sites such as Facebook and Twitter. Nor are they likely to receive any institutional benefits from doing so. However, as I argue elsewhere (Gehl, 2014b), tackling sociotechnical problems requires more than critique; all of us need to learn from the knowledge gained by critical inquiry and apply it to specific, grounded, viable sociotechnical solutions, as well. This is a process I call 'critical reverse engineering.' Fortunately, there are a growing number of coders, software engineers, Web administrators, and users who are developing alternatives to CSM: what I call 'alternative social media' (Gehl, 2015c). ASM are technologies built as a critical response to CSM; they are new social media systems that replicate positive features of CSM while removing negative features.

The origin story of one such ASM site, diaspora*, illustrates this move from critique to code quite well. In February of 2010, lawyer, Internet scholar, and activist Eben Moglen spoke at a meeting of the Internet Society of New York at New York University (Moglen, 2010a, 2010b). In that talk, Moglen summed up many of the critiques of CSM detailed here: their centralization on server farms, their for-profit nature, and their '[degeneration of] the integrity of human personality' (Moglen, 2010a, 2010b). But after those critiques, Moglen made an impassioned plea:

> The problems are really bad. ... The solution is made of our parts. We've got to do it. That's my message. It's Friday night. Some people don't want to go right back to coding I'm sure. We could put it off until Tuesday but how long do you really want to wait? You know every day that goes by there's more data we'll never get back. Every day that goes by there's more data inferences we can't undo. Every day that goes by we pile up more stuff in the hands of the people who got too much. So it's not like we should say 'one of these days I'll get around to that.' It's not like we should say 'I think I'd rather sort of spend my time browsing news about [the] iPad.' (Moglen, 2010a, 2010b)

In the audience were four New York University students, Ilya Zhitomirskiy, Dan Grippi, Max Salzberg, and Raphael Sofaer, who took up Moglen's call and began diaspora*, one of the ASM projects I will detail below.

I point to this origin story as an example of the interface between critique and construction. This is an academic critic making the case for solutions to the problems of CSM and coders seeking a project they could pursue. Such meetings of critics and coders need to happen more often.

Here, I will trace a range of projects that have taken seriously the critiques leveled at CSM and have produced possible solutions in the form of alternative social media. Mirroring the above sections, I will examine ASM in terms of technical infrastructures, political economy, and cultural practices.

Technical Infrastructures

A great deal of innovative work has gone into addressing the criticism of CSM centralization. Because CSM are centralized – that is, they comport to a star network topology, where all data flows to a logical center – then ASM must decentralize.

Many ASM take one of two approaches to implement decentralization: *federation* and

distribution. The first approach, federation, is taken by systems such as diaspora*, rstat.us, and GNU social.[2] The federation approach modifies the server-client architecture so that multiple, independent Web servers can 'federate' into a larger network. In their paper on diaspora*, Bielenberg et al. (2012) explain:

> Rather than forcing users to store all their information on one central server or a collection of servers owned by one single entity, the Diaspora network users decide for themselves on which servers their information will be stored. Some users choose to maintain their own Diaspora servers in order to keep complete control of their data, while others might choose to join an existing server. (Bielenberg et al., 2012: 13)

Thus, a user might run diaspora*, rstat.us, or GNU social on her own server, or she might sign up on a server run by someone she trusts. Either way, users can communicate with one another across servers using protocols that are included with the software. diaspora* explains this process with the metaphor of seeds: diaspora*'s logo is a dandelion gone to seed. Metaphorically, a new server is a 'seed' planted by the overall project, blooming as new members join.

Distribution, on the other hand, is even more decentralized. Whereas federation employs the client-server architecture, distribution relies on peer-to-peer connections. In this architecture, there are no central servers; every device attached to the network (phone, tablet, laptop, or desktop computer) is both a server and a client. Given the prominence of peer-to-peer systems such as Napster in the early-to-mid-2000s, many computer scientists explored ways to build peer-to-peer social networks (e.g., Ackermann et al., 2008; Koll et al., 2014; Mahdian et al., 2011). However, there have been series of very difficult technical problems to solve, including authenticating users and the storage of data. Two viable solutions to these problems are bittorrent protocols and blockchain storage systems (such as the one used by Bitcoin). The project that has synthesized these technologies into a peer-to-peer ASM microblog is Twister (Freitas, 2015). Twister allows now-conventional microblogging practices (following, short messaging, repeating messages, and replying), but it does so as a fully independent node operating on the end users' devices.

I should note that not all ASMs use decentralized architectures, whether federated or distributed. Many operate as centralized client-server systems. Ello, for example, uses the standard centralized model. The dark web social network Galaxy2 operates as a Tor hidden service, which means that it runs on a centralized server, albeit one that has its geographic location hidden. As a 2012 critical survey of the economics and technical structures of decentralized architectures found, decentralization is a very difficult task (Narayanan et al., 2012). But even in the few years since that survey was released, decentralized networks are becoming the norm among ASMs.

A corollary to decentralization is the opening up of internal details. Whereas Facebook, Google, Twitter, and Pinterest store data and run code on server farms that are inaccessible to end users, making them, as Gillespie (2007) might put it, 'wired shut,' many ASM use Free, Open Source Software (hereafter FLOSS), or even Public Domain licensing schemes, enabling end users the ability to inspect, modify, and replicate their code. As a project sponsored by the Free Software Foundation, GNU social, for example, is free software. As GNU social founder Matt Lee explains:

> Free software is software that can be controlled by the users of the software, rather than the developers. Users of a free program can run, copy and modify the program to suit their own uses, and share copies with friends and colleagues. GNU social is a little different in that it is primarily used in a web browser, so we used a special free software license that extends these freedoms to users in a browser. (Quoted in Gehl, 2015c: 6)

Whereas Facebook, Google, Twitter, and Pinterest's software is obscured in a cloud, the lines of code comprising Free Software are open for inspection by all, including end users.

Finally, as for the algorithmic shaping of the present and future, the predominant response of ASM is simple: they don't use algorithms to shape social streams. For example, Ello proclaims, 'Ello doesn't use manipulative algorithms that control what you see' (Ello Dictionary, 2015). This might change as these systems grow, but in keeping with their status as alternatives, it is possible that ASM will approach the use of algorithms quite differently from CSM. In a personal interview, Twister creator Miguel Freitas noted that, in the future, users might demand algorithms to shape what they see in Twister. However,

> Because content is always delivered to your node unfiltered, that means that any content filter will have to be applied locally. Pretty much like those SPAM filters which for a while were built into POP3/IMAP clients. This hypothetical filter would be open for examination and configuration by the user. ... The user would always have the final word on what is filtered and how the algorithm works.

Thus, in contrast to the algorithms developed by data scientists and software engineers working for Facebook, Google, Pinterest, and Twitter, ASM algorithms would likely arise from end users (admittedly, end users with coding abilities). Moreover, because ASM tend to rely on FLOSS licensing, these algorithms would be open to end-user inspection and auditing.

The lack of ASM algorithms begs the question: why do CSM use them? The answer offered by executives at Facebook and Twitter is: we want users to see the most relevant items. Otherwise, users would drown in content. The fact that ASM can offer similar features to CSM without shaping streams with algorithms undermines the CSM executives' arguments. In my experience on a host of ASM sites, I have not encountered users complaining about the pace or volume of content, nor have I seen any users asking for algorithms to shape what they see. For now, ASM users enjoy 'raw' streams of updates and content from their fellow users.

Political Economy

In mid-2014, the social networking site Ello got a lot of attention, especially due to its manifesto, which read in its entirety:

> Your social network is owned by advertisers.
>
> Every post you share, every friend you make, and every link you follow is tracked, recorded, and converted into data. Advertisers buy your data so they can show you more ads. You are the product that's bought and sold.
>
> We believe there is a better way. We believe in audacity. We believe in beauty, simplicity, and transparency. We believe that the people who make things and the people who use them should be in partnership.
>
> We believe a social network can be a tool for empowerment. Not a tool to deceive, coerce, and manipulate – but a place to connect, create, and celebrate life.
>
> You are not a product. (Ello Manifesto, 2014)

Ello's manifesto was cited in a range of news outlets which proclaimed it to be a novelty: an 'ad-free social network' (e.g., Butcher, 2014). However, a marker of many ASMs, including those created prior to Ello, is their refusal to engage in the dominant political economy of the Internet: the sale of user attention to marketers. In other words, ASM refuse advertising.

As I suggest elsewhere (Gehl, 2015c), the refusal of advertising in ASM does two things: first, it denies moneyed speech – that is, statements that become more prominent because they are made by those who pay for the privilege. Even as CSM are lauded for allowing all of us to speak, they have built into their interfaces spaces for 'louder' voices – advertisers – whose messages get privileged positions on our screens. Second, and perhaps more importantly, refusing Internet advertising denies the entire socio-technical system that it stands in for: cross-site tracking, standardized exchanges, and organizational dynamics (such as having departments and engineers dedicated to improving advertising

response rates) (Turow, 2011). The anti-commercial ethos of ASM is in large part a reaction to the ways in which advertising has warped previous media systems, including CSM, radio, and print.

In addition, the lack of advertising on ASM alters ASM's relationship to free labor. Like CSM, ASM rely on the free labor of their users: users construct profiles, write posts, comment on each other's posts, declare connections, and signal affection (i.e., 'liking' or 'loving', depending on the system). Their affective work constitutes ASM, just as it does CSM. However, the ends to which this work is put are often different. For example, on a dark web social network I explored (Gehl, 2014a), a user and an administrator collaborated on a privacy policy, with other users commenting on drafts. Users who contributed did so out of a sense of duty to what they called their 'community.' Contrast this with the privacy policies of sites such as Facebook, which are not written in consultation with users and appear to be more about laying greater and greater claim to user data (Opsahl, 2010). Moreover, because ASM software is often licensed as FLOSS, users can contribute their free labor to the modification of the codebase.

Finally, in line with the decentralization of network topologies, there's a political decentralization happening in ASM, as well. While many ASM have been conceived of and developed in the United States (e.g., diaspora*, GNU social, rstat.us), they have been contributed to and greatly modified by people outside the USA. GNU social, for example, has been extensively modified by En Kompis Kompis, a Swedish team of software coders who have built Quitter.se, an ASM meant to challenge the power of the American firm Twitter. Likewise, according to https://podupti.me/, there are 93 diaspora* servers running worldwide as of this writing, and only 18% (17) of them are hosted in the United States. Many of them are located in Germany, Holland, and France.

But ASM are also being developed outside the United States. One key example was

Lorea, a federated ASM platform, developed to support the Occupy movement as it manifested in Spain and across Europe. Lorea, notably, was built specifically as a social networking system dedicated *for* such protest movements. This makes it unique; rather than being a pre-existing system appropriated for protest (as has happened with CSM such as Twitter), Lorea was built with the needs of protestors in mind (carolina, 2012).

Development of ASM outside the United States is important both as a challenge to the technological dominance of the USA and because of the recent revelations about US National Security Agency spying on non-Americans. Brazil, for example, has for years sought to protect its indigenous technology industries from the power of US firms such as Microsoft (Paiva, 2009). Moreover, it has reacted to leaked documents that reveal US surveillance of Brazilian leaders by intensifying the development of its own technology industry (Mari, 2013; Solon, 2013). Brazilian support for FLOSS is now presented as a national response to the centralized technological power of the United States.

This is more than simply keeping U.S. corporations at bay or blocking US spying. Many of the reforms made by the Brazilian government are radical changes to the dominant regimes of copyright and intellectual property. According to Simon Phipps, Brazil's new

License for Trademarks ... adds additional rights on top of those delivered by open source. It ensures that any trademarks used in the software can be freely used by the community and means that control of trademarks can't be used to chill the ability to exercise the four freedoms [of Free Software]. (Phipps, 2011)

This license is required of all government-sponsored software projects. Although Twister is not government-sponsored, it's not surprising that it has emerged from Brazil, complete with an Open Source software license and a distributed architecture meant to prevent American companies from being able to shut down communication in Brazil (or anywhere else, for that matter) (Gehl, 2015a: 8–9). Indeed, Twister appears to be growing in use among Chinese activists, possibly for these very reasons.

Cultural Practices

As I argue elsewhere (Gehl, 2015c), given the revelations about both corporate and government surveillance over the past few years, as well as the normalized surveillance practices of CSM themselves, we might conclude that ASM must be anti-surveillance. This, we might conclude, would lead to different day-to-day practices occurring in ASM, ones tied less to public performances of identity and more to other factors. However, this is not the case. Social media – corporate or alternative – is defined by its public, performative aspects. Both CSM and ASM share the three features proposed by Ellison and boyd (2013):

A social network site is a *networked communication platform* in which participants 1) have *uniquely identifiable profiles* that consist of user-supplied content, content provided by other users, and/or system-level data; 2) can *publicly articulate connections* that can be viewed and traversed by others; and 3) can consume, produce, or interact with *streams of user-generated content* provided by their connections on this site. (Ellison and boyd, 2013, original emphasis)

What distinguishes ASM from CSM is a more democratic form of surveillance: 'a wider negotiation of flows of vision and obfuscation than is allowed in CSM' (Gehl, 2015c: 7; also see Fuchs, 2012). This is clearest to see when we consider federated and distributed ASM (e.g., diaspora*, GNU social, Twister). Because these systems can be installed by end users, either on servers or local devices, the administrative control over them shifts from their creators to the end users. For example, I run Twister on several of my devices. This gives me, and me alone, administrative control; not even Twister founder Miguel Freitas could access my systems. Moreover, alongside this reduction in administrative surveillance capacity, users of ASM actively monitor the technical and policy decisions of administrators, critiquing their choices and demanding reforms if necessary.

The stated goal of many ASM is to allow censorship-free speech. Given that Facebook and Twitter users know that their statements are monitored both by other users, these respective CSMs, and state agents, and given that Facebook and Twitter have censored user posts many times (Gerstein, 2010; Pagliery, 2015), we might expect CSM users to carefully monitor what they say in order to avoid crossing a legal or normative line. In other words, we can expect a degree of self-censorship within CSM. This may not be a day-to-day concern of most CSM users (although Marwick and boyd (2010) have found evidence for this), but activists are quite aware of the pitfalls of CSM (Poell, 2014; Terranova and Donovan, 2013). Activists might be our proverbial 'canaries in the coal mine,' indicators of how deeply the internalization of the gaze of surveillance has penetrated into everyday users. In turn, following Foucault (1979), we can expect the internalization of the gaze to impact how we constitute ourselves as data subjects within CSM. In contrast, by building systems specifically to avoid censorship, ASM alter the parameters within which users can construct themselves through declarations and performances.

Where these altered parameters play out most prominently are in terms of real names and pseudonyms. In 2014, Facebook's real-name policy prompted public attention to Ello, revealing a major difference between ASM and CSM: there has never been a real-name policy in any ASM. Instead, ASM hearken back to an Internet before the real-name culture, a time of pseudonyms and the identity exploration that comes with them.

Finally, I turn to the critique of the quality of social interaction on CSM, which centers on the use of the term 'friend.' ASM have responded to criticisms of the reduction of all relationships to 'friendship' by working on new methods of connection. diaspora*, for example, pioneered the concept of 'aspects', where users can sort their contacts into various categories, such as friends, family, colleagues (All about aspects, n.d.). The activist-centric ASM Crabgrass used a completely different connective metaphor: the group (Sparrow, 2012). As ASM mature, we may see more such experimentation with both the granularity of social connection as well as new metaphors and approaches to connection.

However, such experimentation can only go so far; in other essays (Gehl, 2015b, 2015c), I suggest that ASM can experiment with existing social media conventions only up to the point when they begin to offer something distinctly different from social networking. Returning to Ellison and boyd's (2013) definition cited above, articulating connections is a *sine qua non* of social networking sites. Such practices are a source of the pleasures of social networking and online connection. Metaphors such as 'friends' and 'likes' are recognizable markers of these practices; thus ASM deploy them to signal to end users their purposes and goals.

CONCLUSION

As builders and activists Cabello et al. argue,

> Contributing to the design and development of technopolitical tools enhances 'technological sovereignty.' There are examples of such a rich contribution by citizens, for example the development of communal radio and television broadcasting, the launch of the first non-military satellite into orbit, the invention of free software and licenses, and even the first news portal on the Internet with an open and anonymous publication system, set up by the Indymedia network in 1999. (Cabello et al., 2013: 340)

Here, Cabello et al. articulate alternative social media (such as their project, Lorea) into a larger history of alternative media and technologies. Following them, I suggest that the best framework for understanding ASM is in terms of 'alternative media': media that challenge centralized media power (Couldry and Curran, 2003: 7). ASM do so by multiple means:

- Offering decentralized network topologies that do not enclose users or their devices into centralized star topologies;
- Opening up their code, including their algorithms, to inspection and modification;
- Allowing users, rather than central administrators, the ability to restructuring flows of transparency and opacity;
- Refusing to alter their technical or organizational structures to accommodate advertisers;
- Allowing for more play with online identity, especially in comparison with Facebook;
- Experimenting with new metaphors and means of connections.

However, ASM are not without their flaws. Most of the work put into them appears to be aimed at solving technical problems (i.e., the problem of both network and American centralization). The complexity of network decentralization often makes ASM systems technically challenging to use. Whereas CSM such as Facebook and Twitter are now so popular that there is a great deal of social knowledge on how use them, installing or running ASM can often be quite challenging to lay users. This can result in what I call cultures of 'techno-elitism' (Gehl, 2014a), where new users who ask for help are sometimes mocked by other, more experienced users. Moreover, if ASM become popular (as in the case of Ello in its early days), they can run into scaling problems as large numbers of new users sign up and overwhelm ASM servers or communications protocols.

In addition, the political economy problem of advertising is solved by many ASM merely through simple refusal: ASM often don't run advertisements, but do little else to consider financial viability. Less work has been done in ASM to make these systems financially stable, and in fact many ASM sites come and go

as funding depletes and coders lose interest (as has happened to many ASM sites, including Lorea, TalkOpen, Galaxy, and Crabgrass). Perhaps Ello's incorporation as a 'Public Benefits Corporation' is a viable economic model, or it could be that ASM can follow in Wikipedia's footsteps and become non-profit organizations funded through donations. Or, there may be a new model emerging in an as-yet largely unknown, experimental ASM. Twister, for example, allows users to volunteer spare computing cycles to verify its database, much in the same way that Bitcoin verification works. At the very least, this radically reduces the need for Twister to pay for storage and computational power by sharing these costs among users.

Perhaps most importantly, there are many problematic cultural practices that ASM have not directly addressed. For example, I have observed that the intense misogyny and racism found in Twitter (e.g., Mantilla, 2013) has in fact migrated to some ASM platforms. Under the banner of 'free speech,' some users have taken to ASM to rail against so-called 'Social Justice Warriors' who are seen as 'silencing' voices (predominantly of white men). Assuming they do not want such practices, ASM administrators and users must turn their attention away from technical problems and begin to focus more and more on the cultivation of particular cultures of interaction. Often, however, the overarching ideals of 'free speech' and 'open dialog' – many times coupled with technical barriers to controlling user activities – make ASM administrators hesitant to challenge sexist or racist speech.

Finally, the fact remains that ASM remain less popular than CSM. The numbers of registered members of various ASM I cited at the outset of this chapter are far, far lower than the reported monthly active users of Facebook and Twitter. The problems I'm pointing to here – techno-elitism, uncertain funding, and hateful speech of some ASM users – are not enough to explain this gap. The simplest explanation here is that of the network effect: the tendency for people to use communication technologies because people they know use them. In other words, people are on CSM because colleagues, friends, brands, and celebrities are, and people are not on ASM because colleagues, friends, brands, and celebrities aren't. But even network effects are no guarantee that CSM will always remain dominant. It is possible that present or future ASM system can become massively popular by combining new features with emerging media practices (such as augmented reality, virtual reality, or the Internet of Things), thus capturing a large userbase that continually attracts more and more users. Facebook, Twitter, Pinterest, and other CSM were once small projects, after all, and their dominance was never certain. One thing is certain, however: if critical reverse engineers *don't* make ASM, we will never see a decentralized, open, more democratic alternative to contemporary CSM. CSM are not going to become open and democratic on their own.

It is here that we academic critics can help. Comparative research between CSM and ASM, sustained ethnographic and social scientific study of ASM, the documentation and elaboration of new economic models, open participation by academics in ASM, and above all meetings of mind between critical coders and CSM critics can help to legitimate and mature these systems. This, I would suggest, is the best path forward for those of us who support contemporary alternative media and media justice.

Notes

1 Sources for these statistics: Ello (https://ello.co/dredmorbius/post/gxpvKs_tp-SL10nNJ1Rlbw); diaspora*: (http://pods.jasonrobinson.me/); Twister (http://yazgi.net/twister/users/charts); GNU social: (http://gstools.org/). Last visited 21 March 2016.

2 For more details on the alternative social media systems mentioned throughout this chapter, including URLs, see Appendix, as well as the S-MAP: The Social Media Alternatives Project (www.socialmediaalternatives.org).

REFERENCES

Ackermann M, Hymon K, Ludwig B, et al. (2008) Helloworld: An open source, distributed and secure social network. In *W3C Workshop on the Future of Social Networking-Position Papers*. www.w3.org/2008/09/msnws/papers/HelloWorld_paper.pdf. Checked: February, p. 2009.

Albrechtslund A (2008) Online social networking as participatory surveillance. *First Monday* 13(3). Available from: firstmonday.org/ojs/index.php/fm/article/view/2142/1949

All about aspects (n.d.) *The Diaspora* Project*, Blog. Available from: https://diasporafoundation.org/getting_started/aspects (accessed 14 October 2015).

Andrejevic M (2007) Surveillance in the digital enclosure. *The Communication Review* 10: 295–317.

Atton C (2002) *Alternative Media*. London: Sage.

Bakardjieva M (2014) Social media and the McDonaldization of friendship. *Communications: The European Journal of Communication Research* 39(4): 369–387.

Best K (2010) Living in the control society: Surveillance, users and digital screen technologies. *International Journal of Cultural Studies* 13(1): 5–24.

Bielenberg A, Helm L, Gentilucci A, et al. (2012) The growth of diaspora – a decentralized online social network in the wild. In *2012 IEEE Conference on Computer Communications Workshops (INFOCOM WKSHPS)*, pp. 13–18.

boyd danah (2006) Friends, Friendsters, and Top 8: Writing community into being on social network sites. *First Monday* 11(12). Available from: http://firstmonday.org/htbin/cgiwrap/bin/ojs/index.php/fm/article/view/1418/1336 (accessed 9 March 2009).

Bratich J (2011) User-generated discontent. *Cultural Studies* 25: 621–640.

Bucher T (2012) Want to be on the top? Algorithmic power and the threat of invisibility on Facebook. *New Media & Society* 14(7): 1164–1180.

Butcher M (2014) Ello, Ello? New 'no ads' social network Ello is blowing up right now. *TechCrunch*, Blog. Available from: http://

techcrunch.com/2014/09/25/ello-ello-new-no-ads-social-network-ello-is-blowing-up-right-now/ (accessed 25 September 2014).

Cabello F, Franco MG and Haché A (2013) Towards a free federated social web: Lorea takes the networks! In G Lovink and M Rausch (eds), *Unlike Us Reader: Social Media Monopolies and Their Alternatives*. Amsterdam: Institute of Network Cultures, pp. 338–346.

carolina (2012) Support free social network n-1. cc #lorea. *Take The Square*, Blog. Available from: http://takethesquare.net/2012/05/28/support-free-social-network-n-1-cc-lorea/ (accessed 21 March 2016).

Coté M and Pybus J (2007) Learning to immaterial labour 2.0: MySpace and social networks. *ephemera* 7(1): 88–106.

Couldry N and Curran J (2003) The paradox of media power. In *Contesting Media Power: Alternative Media in a Networked World*. Oxford, UK: Rowman & Littlefield, pp. 3–15.

Couldry N and Turow J (2014) Big Data, big questions| Advertising, Big Data and the clearance of the public realm: Marketers' new approaches to the content subsidy. *International Journal of Communication* 8(0): 17.

Dhekane R and Vibber B (2011) Talash: Friend finding in federated social networks. In *LDOW*. Available from: http://events.linked-data.org/ldow2011/papers/ldow2011-paper08-dhekane.pdf (accessed 14 October 2015).

Donath J and boyd danah (2004) Public displays of connection. *BT Technology Journal* 22(4): 71–82.

Dubrofsky RE (2011) Surveillance on reality television and Facebook: From authenticity to flowing data. *Communication Theory* 21(2): 111–129.

Ellison, Nicole B and boyd danah (2013) Sociality through social network sites. In W Dutton (ed.), *The Oxford Handbook of Internet Studies*. Oxford, UK: Oxford University Press, pp. 151–172.

Ello Dictionary (2015) *Ello*, Social network. Available from: https://ello.co/wtf/about/ello-dictionary/ (accessed 15 October 2015).

Ello Manifesto (2014) *Ello*, Social network. Available from: https://ello.co/wtf/about/ello-manifesto/ (accessed 13 October 2015).

Elmer G (2004) *Profiling Machines: Mapping the Personal Information Economy*. Cambridge, MA, and London: MIT Press.

Feenberg A (1986) *Lukács, Marx, and the Sources of Critical Theory*. New York: Oxford University Press.

Foucault M (1979) *Discipline and Punish*. New York: Vintage.

Freitas M (2015) Twister: The development of a peer-to-peer microblogging platform. *International Journal of Parallel, Emergent and Distributed Systems* 0(0): 1–14.

Fuchs C (2012) The political economy of privacy on Facebook. *Television & New Media* 13(2): 139–159.

Gehl RW (2011) Ladders, samurai, and blue collars: Personal branding in Web 2.0. *First Monday* 16(9). Available from: firstmonday.org/ojs/index.php/fm/article/view/3579/3041

Gehl RW (2012) Distributed centralization: Web 2.0 as a portal into users' lives. *Lateral* 1(1). Available from: http://lateral.cultural-studiesassociation.org/issue1/content/gehl.html (accessed 16 March 2012).

Gehl RW (2013) What's on your mind? Social media monopolies and noopower. *First Monday* 18(3–4). Available from: www.uic.edu/htbin/cgiwrap/bin/ojs/index.php/fm/article/view/4618/3421.

Gehl RW (2014a) Power/freedom on the dark web: A digital ethnography of the dark web social network. *New Media and Society* 18(7): 1219–1235.

Gehl RW (2014b) *Reverse Engineering Social Media: Software, Culture, and Political Economy in New Media Capitalism*. Philadelphia, PA: Temple University Press.

Gehl RW (2015a) Building a better Twitter: A study of the Twitter alternatives GNU social, Quitter, rstat.us, and Twister. *The Fibreculture Journal* (26): 60–86.

Gehl RW (2015b) Critical reverse engineering: The case of Twitter and TalkOpen. In G Langlois, J Redden, and G Elmer (eds), *Compromised Data: From Social Media to Big Data*. New York: Bloomsbury, pp. 147–169.

Gehl RW (2015c) The case for alternative social media. *Social Media + Society* 1(2): 2056305115604338.

Gerlitz C and Helmond A (2013) The Like economy: Social buttons and the data-intensive web. *New Media & Society* 15(8): 1348–1365.

Gerstein J (2010) Facebook censoring online activism? *Reader Supported News*, News. Available from: www.readersupportednews. org/off-site-news-section/69-69/3351-facebook-censoring-online-activism (accessed 18 September 2010).

Gillespie T (2007) *Wired shut*. Cambridge, MA: MIT Press.

Gillespie T (2011) Can an algorithm be wrong? Twitter Trends, the specter of censorship, and our faith in the algorithms around us. *Culture Digitally*, Blog. Available from: http://culture-digitally.org/2011/10/can-an-algorithm-be-wrong/ (accessed 2 November 2014).

Hansen MB (2006) Media theory. *Theory, Culture & Society* 23(2–3): 297–306.

Hogan B (2010) The presentation of self in the age of social media: Distinguishing performances and exhibitions online. *Bulletin of Science, Technology & Society*: 0270467610385893.

Koll D, Li J and Fu X (2014) SOUP: An online social network by the people, for the people. In *Proceedings of the 15th International Middleware Conference*. New York: ACM Press, pp. 193–204. Available from: http://dl.acm.org/citation.cfm?doid=2663165.2663324 (accessed 28 March 2015).

Kramer ADI, Guillory JE and Hancock JT (2014) Experimental evidence of massive-scale emotional contagion through social networks. *Proceedings of the National Academy of Sciences*: 201320040.

Langlois G (2014) *Meaning in the Age of Social Media*. New York: Palgrave Macmillan.

Langlois G, McKelvey F, Elmer G, et al. (2009) Mapping commercial Web 2.0 worlds: Towards a new critical ontogenesis. *Fibreculture* (14). Available from: http://journal.fibre-culture.org/issue14/issue14_langlois_et_al.html (accessed 18 October 2010).

Lingel J and Golub A (2015) In face on Facebook: Brooklyn's drag community and sociotechnical practices of online communication. *Journal of Computer-Mediated Communication* 20(5): 536–553.

Lovink G (2012) *Networks without a Cause: A Critique of Social Media*. Cambridge, UK: Polity Press.

Lovink G and Rasch M (eds) (2013) *Unlike Us Reader: Social Media Monopolies and Their Alternatives*. Amsterdam: Institute of Network Cultures.

Lux D (2014) Facebook real name policy: A front line battle report. *21st Century Burlesque Magazine*, Blog. Available from: http://21stcenturyburlesque.com/facebook-real-name-policy-meeting-drag-queens-performers-dottie-lux/ (accessed 25 September 2014).

Mackenzie A (2013) Programming subjects in the regime of anticipation: Software studies and subjectivity. *Subjectivity* 6(4): 391–405.

MacKinnon R and Lim H (2014) Google Plus finally gives up on its ineffective, dangerous real-name policy. *Slate*. Available from: www.slate.com/blogs/future_tense/2014/07/17/google_plus_finally_ditches_its_ineffective_dangerous_real_name_policy.html (accessed 29 June 2015).

Mahdian A, Black J, Han R, et al. (2011) MyZone: A next-generation online social network. *arXiv:1110.5371*. Available from: http://arxiv.org/abs/1110.5371 (accessed 9 May 2012).

Mantilla K (2013) Gendertrolling: Misogyny adapts to new media. *Feminist Studies* 39(2): 563–570.

Mari A (2013) Brazilian government to ditch Microsoft in favour of bespoke email system. *ZDNet*, Blog. Available from: www.zdnet.com/brazilian-government-to-ditch-microsoft-in-favour-of-bespoke-email-system-7000021929/ (accessed 18 June 2014).

Marwick AE (2013) *Status Update: Celebrity, Publicity, and Branding in the Social Media Age*. New Haven, CT: Yale University Press.

Marwick AE and boyd danah (2010) I Tweet honestly, I Tweet passionately: Twitter users, context collapse, and the imagined audience. *New Media & Society*. Available from: http://nms.sagepub.com/cgi/doi/10.1177/1461444810365313 (accessed 14 November 2010).

Miltenburg W and Leenaars M (2015) Functional breakdown of decentralised social networks. Available from: https://homepages.staff.os3.nl/~delaat/rp/2014-2015/p16/report.pdf (accessed 14 October 2015).

Moglen E (2010a) Freedom in the Cloud. *Software Freedom Law Center*, Blog. Available from: www.softwarefreedom.org/events/

2010/isoc-ny/FreedomInTheCloud-transcript. html (accessed 25 May 2012).

Moglen E (2010b) Freedom in the Cloud: Software freedom, privacy and security for Web 2.0 and Cloud computing. New York University. Available from: www.youtube.com/watch?v=QOEMv0S8AcA (accessed 7 October 2015).

Mosco V (2014) *To the Cloud: Big Data in a Turbulent World*. Boulder, CO: Paradigm.

Narayanan A, Toubiana V, Barocas S, et al. (2012) A critical look at decentralized personal data architectures. *arXiv:1202.4503*. Available from: http://arxiv.org/abs/1202.4503 (accessed 6 June 2012).

Opsahl K (2010) Facebook's eroding privacy policy: A timeline. *Electronic Frontier Foundation*, Blog. Available from: www.eff.org/deeplinks/2010/04/facebook-timeline (accessed 12 October 2015).

Pagliery J (2015) The 3 places where Facebook censors you the most. *CNNMoney*. Available from: http://money.cnn.com/2015/02/06/technology/facebook-censorship/index.html (accessed 14 October 2015).

Paiva E (2009) Use of Open Source software by the Brazilian government. *Open Source Business Resource* (May 2009).

Phipps S (2011) Brazil's new trademark license. *Computerworld UK*, Magazine. Available from: www.computerworlduk.com/blogs/simon-says/brazils-new-trademark-license-3569564/ (accessed 24 November 2014).

Poell T (2014) Social media and the transformation of activist communication: Exploring the social media ecology of the 2010 Toronto G20 protests. *Information, Communication & Society* 17(6): 716–731.

Postigo H (2003) Emerging sources of labor on the internet: The case of America Online volunteers. *International Review of Social History* 48(S11): 205–223.

Postigo H (2009) America Online volunteers: Lessons from an early co-production community. *International Journal of Cultural Studies* 12(5): 451–469.

Sevignani S (2013) Facebook vs. Diaspora: A critical study. In G Lovink and M Rausch (eds), *Unlike Us Reader: Social Media Monopolies and Their Alternatives*, Amsterdam: Institute of Network Cultures, pp. 325–337.

Solon O (2013) Brazilian government plans national 'anti-snooping' email system. *Wired UK*, Magazine. Available from: www.wired.co.uk/news/archive/2013-09/03/brazil-anti-snooping-email (accessed 18 June 2014).

Solove DJ (2007) *'I've Got Nothing to Hide' and Other Misunderstandings of Privacy*. SSRN Scholarly Paper. Rochester, NY: Social Science Research Network. Available from: http://papers.ssrn.com/abstract=998565 (accessed 14 October 2015).

Sparrow E (2012) Pitfalls of building social media alternatives (Debate). Amsterdam. Available from: http://vimeo.com/39257353 (accessed 7 June 2012).

Stiegler B (2013) The most precious good in the era of social technologies. In G Lovink and M Rasch (eds), *Unlike Us Reader: Social Media Monopolies and Their Alternatives*. Amsterdam: Institute of Network Cultures, pp. 16–30.

Striphas T (2015) Algorithmic culture. *European Journal of Cultural Studies* 18(4–5): 395–412.

Terranova T (2000) Free labor: Producing culture for the digital economy. *Social Text* 18(2): 33–58.

Terranova T and Donovan J (2013) Occupy social networks: The paradoxes of using corporate social media in networked movements. In G Lovink and M Rausch (eds), *Unlike Us Reader: Social Media Monopolies and Their Alternatives*. Amsterdam: Institute of Network Cultures, pp. 296–313.

Turkle S (1995) *Life on the Screen: Identity in the Age of the Internet*. New York: Simon & Schuster.

Turow J (2011) *The Daily You: How the New Advertising Industry is Defining Your Identity and Your Worth*. New Haven, CT: Yale University Press.

van der Velden L (2013) Meeting the alternatives: Notes about making profiles and joining hackers. In G Lovink and M Rausch (eds), *Unlike Us Reader: Social Media Monopolies and Their Alternatives*. Amsterdam: Institute of Network Cultures, pp. 312–322.

van Dijck J (2013) 'You have one identity': Performing the self on Facebook and LinkedIn. *Media, Culture & Society* 35(2): 199–215.

Weltevrede E, Helmond A and Gerlitz C (2014) The politics of real-time: A device perspective on social media platforms and search engines. *Theory, Culture & Society*: 0263276414537318.

APPENDIX: A SELECTION OF CURRENTLY ACTIVE ALTERNATIVE SOCIAL MEDIA

Here I offer URLs, short descriptions, and, where available, selected academic papers for many of the alternative social media systems discussed in this chapter.

For more information about these and other alternative social media, see the S-MAP: The Social Media Alternatives Project, at www.socialmediaalternatives.org

Diaspora*

URL: https://diasporafoundation.org/

Founded in 2010 by four students at New York University, diaspora* is a federated social networking system. Its code is open source and can be installed on any Web server. Early in its history, it was hailed in the news media as a 'Facebook Killer.' This was unfortunate, because it was too much to expect of a brand-new system. However, despite diaspora* not living up to that expectation, it has steadily grown. Moreover, it has incorporated as a non-profit in the United States.

Academic papers on diaspora*: Bielenberg et al. (2012), Sevignani (2013), van der Velden (2013).

GNU Social

URL: http://www.gnu.org/s/social/

Sponsored by the Free Software Foundation, GNU social is a Free Software package that can be installed on any Web server. GNU social began life in the late-2000s as Laconica, before being renamed

StatusNet and finally GNU social. GNU social is a microblogging service. A notable example of GNU social in action is the Swedish site Quitter.se, which is styled to mimic Twitter and thus be the 'methadone' to Twitter's 'heroin' (Gehl, 2015a: 7).

Academic papers on GNU social: Dhekene and Vibber (2011), Miltenberg and Leenaars (2015).

Twister

URL: http://twister.net.co/

Twister was created by Miguel Freitas in reaction to US National Security Agency spying, as well as the need for activists and protesters to have decentralized means of communication. Working as a peer-to-peer system, Twister runs on both the Bittorrent and Bitcoin protocols.

Academic paper on Twister: Freitas (2015).

Ello

URL: ello.co/

Ello was founded in 2014. It received a great deal of attention in news coverage due to its manifesto (quoted above) against advertising in social media. Unlike other ASMs, Ello is not open source, it is centralized, and in fact it is incorporated, albeit as a 'Public Benefit Corporation.' Ello's design is akin to Pinterest, with an emphasis on graphics over text.

Galaxy2

URL: http://w363zoq3ylux5rf5.onion/

Founded early in 2015, Galaxy2 is social network running as a Tor hidden service. It can only be accessed via Tor-based software such as the Tor Browser Bundle. Despite being hidden, Galaxy2 has grown to nearly 5,000 members. The site is built on Elgg, a popular open-source social networking package.

Academic paper on Galaxy2: Gehl (2015c).

Sone

URL: https://wiki.freenetproject.org/Sone

Sone is a social networking plugin for Freenet, an anonymous peer-to-peer network. Sone works much like Twitter: it uses a follower–followed relationship and relies on short posts. Much like Galaxy2, it cannot be accessed with a standard browser; the Freenet router is required.

PART IV

Cultures and Practices

19

Our Networked Selves: Personal Connection and Relational Maintenance in Social Media Use

Kelly Quinn and Zizi Papacharissi

Without question, social media platforms and applications like Facebook, Twitter, and Instagram have impacted the ways in which individuals relate to one another. Emerging media forms offer alternate avenues for connection and expression. In addition, they sustain digital traces and relational memory maps of evolving connections between individuals in everyday life. These practices and processes are not only important to understanding modalities of sociality, but are integral to understanding self-actualization through sociability.

This chapter explores personal connection and relational maintenance as they are accomplished through social media today. We examine these connections from a developmental perspective of interpersonal communication, which envisions interaction as becoming more personalized and complex over time (Parks, 2011b). This approach arises from the study of the behaviors of relational dyads and focuses on social aspects, the life course, and the self. In this chapter,

we focus on informal interpersonal relationships, or friendship, as our model, as this is perhaps the most common form of relational engagement. Friendship is distinct from other types of relationships due to its voluntary and non-exclusive nature; it contrasts with family relationships, which entail specific norms and obligations, and romantic relationships, which are exclusive and either have a finite duration or convert to a familial relationship. In this chapter, we address three major phases of relationship development as they occur through the lens of social media: relationship establishment or connection; relational management and boundary work; and relationship dissolution or disconnection. For each topic, we focus on how social media enable, challenge and figure in the negotiation of relationship and connection, and how performance of these processes connects with the concept of the networked self.

We use the concept of *the networked self* to describe modalities of sociality and identity performance that develop across online and offline platforms, interconnected and not (Papacharissi, 2011). Contemporary platforms of engagement, regardless of their materiality, support a sense of self that is networked: performed to networks and through networks. Such platforms of engagement frequently invite acts of expression and connection for the mere sake of doing so, no matter how mundane or ordinary those acts may be. As these acts of expression and connection are performed to audiences, actual and imagined, identity becomes increasingly performative. It must be understood that presentation as a performance is a typically subconscious act, rendered as we piece together learned behaviors to create a particular impression (Schechner, 2013). It is this increased theatricality afforded by social network sites – the drama of performance – that individuals frequently find most appealing (Parks, 2011a). Still, performances of the self enable sociability, and for the performer, these socially oriented performances must carry meaning for multiple publics and audiences without sacrificing one's true sense of self. These polysemic performances not only contain many layers of meaning, but are remixed and remixable, sampling digital traces of identity to piece together performative portraits of the self that are further remixed and reinterpreted by multiple audiences and publics.

The focus on friendship, combined with the emphasis on the networked self, allows us to blend distinct traditions in both the humanities and the social sciences toward understanding personal connections, relationships, and the self in contemporary societies. Our emphasis on connections, relationships and the self is essential in explicating how social relations are formed, grow, and are re-imagined through social media. Yet this emphasis permits us to explore how connections and relations with others play a part in self-expression, performance, and actualization. As mediated spaces – places across which these connections take form – evolve, expression, presentations, and representations

of the relational self attain a distinct texture, modality, and affect. It is these subtle adjustments to the fundamentals of social relationships that we are keen on exploring in this chapter.

FRIENDS, FOLLOWERS, AND CIRCLES: THE CHARACTERISTICS OF CONNECTION

Our line of thinking is informed by Wellman's (2001) work on *networked individualism*, which describes relational forms of engagement formed around looser networks and giving people a wider variety of ways to address social needs. As Rainie and Wellman (2012) explain, people are not 'hooked on gadgets but on each other,' in modalities of relational engagement that emanate from the individual as the autonomous center, and involve both multiple users and multithreaded multi-tasking. People use technologies to sustain a form of being that is primarily relational, even though, on occasion, their lives may be oversaturated with technology (Gergen, 2009). The networked self is a relational self (Hogan & Wellman, 2014), the center of a network of independent and overlapping social connections and expressive modalities.

Thus, in its simplest form, a relationship is the connectivity of a dyad, or two individuals linked through some context. In a traditional sense, how we characterize connection between individuals depends on the relationship's qualities. Such qualities include the level of intimacy between the two individuals, which typically falls on a continuum from passing acquaintance to close friend, or the degree to which a relationship is public and known to others. Relational contexts are important to understanding relationships as well, as they often reflect and suggest the forms of interaction that take place; some familiar forms are work colleagues, school mates, kin, and romantic partners.

For the networked individual, especially through the use of social media, relationships take on a tangible quality, as they are inscribed through publicly-articulated lists of connection that can be viewed and traversed by others (Ellison & boyd, 2013). Typically, these are designated as 'Friends,' 'Connections,' or 'Followers/Following,' depending on the platforms through which one engages. These graphical representations of individuals' social networks have spurred considerable research on sociability and social connection (e.g., Backstrom & Kleinberg, 2014). However, they distort representations of the totality of an individual's social connections in two important ways. First, these lists only reflect connections between individuals who participate in a particular social medium; hence, relationships that are important or significant to the individual may not be represented if one partner is not a platform user. For example, though a relationship with a grandparent may be important to a university student, this relationship may not be reflected in the student's Facebook Friends, as the grandparent may not participate in the medium. Second, some important relational qualities, including its context and strength, are not captured in the 'friends list' or list of followers. The invisibility of these qualities, coupled with the ability for relationships to be unidirectional, distinguish social media connection from other forms of interpersonal relationships, and reinforce that 'friends' on social media are not the same as 'friends' in the everyday sense (boyd, 2006).

Relational Context

Relational contexts provide information on how a given relationship is situated within an individual's network. These give relevance to connection and typically reflect an individual's social spheres (Simmel, 1955); typically, these contexts reflect how an individual 'knows' another, such as a through common worship or school community, or they may reflect a particular relational focus such as a place or activity (Feld & Carter, 1998). In the physical world, individuals use time and space to separate those contexts of their lives which may be incompatible with one another (Donath & boyd, 2004; Nippert-Eng, 1995), keeping separate, for example, professional colleagues from school friends. In social media, relational contexts are not visible to others, and, perhaps more importantly for the users of these media, relational contexts become jumbled and re-mixed in these digital spaces.

This melding of contexts has relevance as information about the self and one's relationships is created, commented on, and shared between individuals. Deemed as 'context collapse' for the individual (Marwick & boyd, 2014), this merging of audiences and relational contexts into a single digital space requires adjustments such as segregating relationships to specific platforms (Quinn, 2013; Wesch, 2009), curtailing the release of information about the self (Marwick & boyd, 2011), or even creating multiple profiles within a single social media platform to manage identity within groups of connections (Stutzman & Hartzog, 2012). To aid users in re-introducing context to their relationships, several social media platforms have introduced 'groups,' 'lists,' and 'circles' into their functionality. Grouping functionality benefits users by allowing for higher granularity in their consumption and dissemination of platform content. For example, the user can select specific groups of connection with which to share a photo or comment. But grouping functions provide little direction for outsiders for determining another's relational contexts, as these are often not visible to others.

One additional dimension of relational context can potentially be found in the use of a specific platform for connection. The meaning of a connection often varies between platforms, and is guided by the platform's focus, the social norms which predominate, and the platform's functionality. For example, a connection on LinkedIn may connote a professional context as the information highlighted on this platform is relevant to employment and commerce. Alternatively, following a Friend on Pinterest suggests a different relational context, as these often revolve around a common personal interest in a hobby or topic.

Relational Strength

The strength of a relationship is also a defining quality of the personal connections we sustain, and social media platforms typically lack information on this dimension. Both strong and weak relationships are important to an individual; strong ties (i.e., close friends and family) share resources and support, while weak ties (acquaintances and weaker contacts) expose an individual to different experiences and information (Granovetter, 1973). Strong relationships use multiple media forms to reinforce their relationships (Haythornthwaite, 2005), and social media technologies fit into this prototype by providing an additional means to communicate and maintain social connection. Social media also allow individuals to maintain weaker connections more easily, permitting a larger number of connections to be maintained (Donath, 2007). This ability to create and maintain weaker ties is considered a potential advantage of social media use; social media allow users to passively monitor weak connections without significant effort, and thus leaves open the possibility that weak relationships will become stronger, and thus more valuable, over time (Levin, Walter & Murnighan, 2010; Pearson, 2009).

Directionality

One additional characteristic of social media connection is directionality, that is, whether a relationship is acknowledged by only one or by both individuals. Among social media platforms, relationships can be mutual/ bi-directional, with both individuals consenting to the creation of the connection, or unidirectional, initiated by one individual and not reciprocated by the other. Mutual connections are typically referred to as 'friends,' 'connections,' or 'contacts,' and are acknowledged by both individuals in the relationship; they are commonly found in social network sites. Unidirectional connections characterize the initiating individuals as 'fans,' 'followers,' or 'subscribers,' and are initiated by one individual but do not need to be reciprocated by the other; these are often found in platforms that emphasize the sharing of user-generated content, such as microblogs or photo/video sharing applications.

It is assumed that mutual relationships are more durable (Li, Zhang & Bao, 2012), as they evidence an affirmation of the relationship from both partners. While some argue that unidirectional ties may be viewed as an initial step in establishing a mutual relationship (e.g., Westcott & Owen, 2013), they are probably closer in nature to latent ties (Haythornthwaite, 2002), or relationships that hold the potential for interaction in that they exist technically, but require a further reciprocating step of some form, such as a 'follow back' before they can be considered to have true substance.

MAKING FRIENDS: THE DYNAMICS OF CONNECTION

Traditional theories of interpersonal communication tend to examine relational trajectories as having a beginning, middle and end; they focus on relational development once a connection between two individuals has been made. Physical proximity, that is, the ability to 'bump into' one another, or social homophily, having similar tastes and interests, or both, are considered to be the key underlying factors for a connection opportunity. This approach to understanding relationships tends to diminish the role of third parties (such as a mutual friend) and social proximity (being a friend of a friend) for initial connection, although these factors are often critical for relationship establishment (Parks, 2007, 2011b). Social media have made the role of third parties and friends-of-friends in relational establishment more visible, if not more pronounced, and have highlighted the role that network structure plays in the formation of interpersonal relationships.

For the networked individual, social proximity and third parties are easily discerned as one navigates networks of visible connections in social media platforms. Individuals use a variety of strategies to find connections on social media, but three important mechanisms stand out: searching names of contacts using the platform's embedded search engine, relying on recommendations provided by the platform's algorithm, or examining the connection lists of existing contacts.

The use of embedded search engines to find connections in social media sites is often more successful than relying on independent search engines. Because social media profiles often contain personal details about an individual – employer, educational institutions, relationships with others – these tools enable a contextual form of search, associating more than just a name with an individual. This enables searches to be more precise and accurate, and provides more certainty for the searcher that the 'found' individual is definitively the correct and targeted person. For example, a user may search for people from their hometown or who graduated from the same high school to find friends from their teenage years.

Social matching algorithms, such as Facebook's People You May Know, provide an automated form of this contextual search by incorporating 'friends of friend' information into the recommendation (Zhang et al., 2015). The automated analysis of the larger network of an individual's connections, and the resulting systemic recommendations, facilitate and encourage relationship formation. Experiments suggest that the presence of high-quality algorithms result in larger connection networks for social media users, but also that this connection activity is enhanced when keywords from an individual's profile, such as musical interests, or their posting activity, such as the location of where photos are taken, are matched between potential connections (Chen et al., 2009). These friend-finding algorithms perform particularly well for locating known contacts who are not yet connected on a given social media platform, but are not as adept at sourcing novel or new connections for an individual (Chen et al., 2009).

Early research focused on the ways in which internet-based technologies helped overcome spatial and temporal limitations and thus facilitate connections between individuals that would otherwise not be possible or practical (Baym, 2015). These possibilities have come to fruition, as approximately 39% of social media users today are connected with at least one individual whom they have not met in person (Duggan et al., 2014). Nevertheless, social media, and social network sites in particular, largely replicate existing offline social connection patterns (Gershon, 2011; Mayer & Puller, 2008; Steinfield, Ellison, Lampe & Vitak, 2012), and offline friendships continue to be perceived as higher in quality than relationships initiated online or even those that are initiated online and move offline (Antheunis, Valkenburg & Peter, 2012). When compared to other possible uses of social media, such as seeking social information or maintaining existing relationships, its use to initiate new relationships is low (Ellison, Steinfield & Lampe, 2011), and correspondingly, the size of offline networks do not appear to be impacted through social media use (Pollett, Roberts & Dunbar, 2011).

Finally, the digital traces that remain from social media use, such as user activity logs or 'snapshots' of an individual's network taken at various points in time, have provided enhanced opportunity for examining connection refusals, or those requests for connection in a social media platform that are either denied or ignored by the recipient. Though sometimes grouped with practices of disconnection (e.g., Light, 2014), the avoidance (i.e., 'ignoring' a friend request) or an outright refusal of connection with others is frequently boundary work, or a mechanism to maintain and keep one's various social spheres separate (Malinen, 2015; Tokunaga, 2011; Wisniewski, Lipford & Wilson, 2012). Connection refusal on social media typically results in stress to the face-to-face relationship (McLaughlin & Vitak, 2011; Tokunaga, 2011) as there is a tangible quality to an incomplete connection; moreover, these relational consequences highlight how differences between traditional face-to-face and new online social norms associated with social media use are shaping relationships.

BIRTHDAY REMINDERS AND NEWSFEEDS: RELATIONAL MANAGEMENT AND BOUNDARY WORK

The convergence of technology and the sociality produced through social media use result in the ability to access and distribute social resources among local and remote spheres of family, friends, and acquaintances, no matter how loosely connected (Papacharissi, 2011). Relationships grow and are maintained through communication, and individuals spend more time maintaining relationships than in either their initiation or termination (Duck, 1988). Social media have provided an additional tool for individuals' communication media repertoires (Watson-Manheim & Bélanger, 2007). They empower the individual with more ways to communicate and thus maintain relationships, but also provide an ambient awareness of social information with which to nourish relational communication.

In the same vein, Stafford and Canary (1991) identified a typology of relational maintenance strategies between romantic partners, and later extended this to friend and kin relationships (Canary, Stafford, Hause & Wallace, 1993). They found that individuals use ten primary strategies to maintain relationships, such as being positive, open, and assuring; they share tasks and social networks, participate in joint activities, and make contact via cards/letters/calls. Sometimes they use avoidance and other anti-social behaviors, and they use humor. All of these strategies are performed through social media platforms: posting content and sending messages to connections (positivity); sharing news and disclosing important information about oneself (openness); sending congratulations and listing others as 'top friends' (assurances); coordinating events via chat and messaging (sharing tasks); adding friends of friends, especially those of a romantic partner (social networks); commenting on others' posts and tagging photos (joint activities); using chat and messaging functions to communicate as an additional medium (cards/letters/calls); blocking content or not responding to messages posted by others (avoidance); deliberately posting photos or comments intended to provoke (anti-social); and posting funny content or 'poking' others, a playful feature of Facebook intended to say hello or gain attention, (humor) (Bryant & Marmo, 2009). In addition, users of social media identify 'social surveillance,' or the use of social media platforms to monitor the events and activities of their connections, as an additional strategy to support relational interaction, by using the information found therein as a social lubricant to launch conversation or strengthen relationships (Bryant & Marmo, 2009; Lampe, Ellison & Steinfield, 2006). The significance of the plurality of relational strategies available to people is considerable, given the options available for creating and sustaining relationships. These options support an ambient form of sociability, which not only sustains 'always on' social environments, but also reconciles our need for individual autonomy with our inherent desire for social connection.

Architectural Qualities

Modalities of ambient, always-on sociability are further enhanced by the architectural features of the social environments sustained by these platforms. When used for social purposes, use of the net-based platforms results in larger numbers of social ties (Hampton, Sessions & Her, 2011; Zhao, 2006), and this is true of social media as well (Hampton, Sessions-Goulet, Rainie & Purcell, 2011). Dunbar's (2012) social brain hypothesis states that cognitive capacity and neocortex size limits complex social interaction, and therefore the size of social networks. He concludes that the 'natural' social group size for humans is approximately 150 individuals (Dunbar, 2012). But individuals maintain larger, and sometimes much larger, networks via social media platforms. For example, the average number of connections that a Facebook user maintains is 338 (Smith, 2014). This suggests that the mediation afforded by social network sites may aid in maintaining a greater number of relationships, although many of these do not involve regular interaction (Marlow, 2009). Social media possess key features that facilitate maintaining larger networks and extending an individual's ability to partake in complex sociability. These important qualities include *capacity for conversation, asynchronicity, persistence, and social reminding*.

First, social media enable individuals to broadcast information via news streams, tweets, and group shares. Importantly, however, this ability to broadcast is coupled with a capacity for reaction from others. Social media platforms literally invite interaction by providing the ability to comment on, like, favorite, and rebroadcast posted content. This coupling of these two qualities is extraordinarily powerful: it *enables conversation* to take place at once between individuals and groups (Kietzmann, Hermkens, McCarthy & Silvestre, 2011). Unlike unmediated conversation, which involves a maximum of about four individuals (Dunbar, Duncan & Nettle,

1995), social media conversation entails the flow of content across social media platforms and the mixing and remixing of local and remote social spheres (Papacharissi, 2011); this effectively expands the conversation into many-to-many interaction. The ability to monitor multiple conversation streams, which often incorporate the activities and life events of weaker relationships, without significant effort or cost keeps weaker ties in existence and fosters their maintenance (Vitak, 2014).

However, this ability to broadcast information, especially about the self, may come with some cost to some relationships too. Though self-disclosure has long been associated with increasing relational intimacy (Altman & Taylor, 1973), self-disclosure via social media can negatively impact relational quality. In a study of dyadic relationships, self-disclosure activity on Facebook was negatively associated with both relational satisfaction and liking (McEwan, 2013). Social media disclosures have the potential to make one's connections 'reluctant confidants' (Petronio, 2002), or involuntary recipients of personal and/or private information, and the broadcasting of these messages may be perceived as different from interpersonal interaction. This is an important area for future study, as it may highlight ways in which information flows through these platforms impact relational quality in both advantageous and deleterious ways.

A second important characteristic of social media as it relates to relational maintenance is *asynchronicity*, which is tied to the unidirectional nature of information transmission. Because information is sent in only one direction at a time, users recognize a time lag between the sending and receiving of messages and information. This lag allows individuals to carefully craft the information being sent for a desired effect (Tong, Kashian & Walther, 2011), permitting the ability to edit, revise or even delete before being seen by the recipient and thus preserves the ability to maintain a consistent presentation of self.

Unlike with synchronous media, such as a telephone, immediate responses and interaction are not expected when using social media platforms, giving users greater control over their disclosures and maximizing their ability to generate a desired image.

In addition, because social media permit users to compartmentalize conversations via threading and the use of hashtags, the asynchronous exchanges permit *multicommunicating* (Reinsch, Turner & Tinsley, 2008), or the simultaneous participation in multiple exchanges at once. Asynchronicity places the tempo of conversation under the control of participants; it enables the ability to catch up with conversations that transpired in one's absence, or while being engaged with others, and affords users some degree of time optimization in the maintenance of interpersonal relationships. It should be noted that the ability to handle multiple conversations at once is not unique to social media, as individuals can use technologies such as email, chat and phone at the same time. However, social media permit these multiple conversation possibilities to exist in a single social space, by offering multiple communication modalities such as messaging, wall posting and chat all within a single platform.

Persistence refers to the ways in which 'online expressions are automatically recorded and archived' (boyd, 2010: 46), in other words, the ways activity on social media is captured, preserved, and made available through time. Social media conversations are persistent, rendering them accessible at other places and at different times than when they transpired; this quality also makes such conversations searchable, browse-able, replayable, and visual (Erikson, 1999). Persistent conversation is difficult to remove once posted, but this accessibility also allows people to add or expand to conversations over time (Treem & Leonardi, 2012), enabling relational memories to be re-lived and remembered and sustaining relational closeness (Human & Lane, 2008). Moreover, persistence extends to the availability of

social media profiles, which maintain a single 'social address' through which connection might be maintained; profiles and connection persist in social media despite job changes, name changes prompted by marriage and divorce, and geographic relocation, factors which contribute to relational decay (Rose, 1984).

Finally, social media often perform *social reminding* functions, as algorithms and system-generated prompts nudge users to partake in the everyday relational practices necessary for maintaining relationships. Birthday and event reminders, updates from connections that appear in the newsfeed, and the highlighting of timeline anniversaries are digital artifacts that serve to encapsulate memory of the relationship and keep the 'promise' of the connection alive (Shklovski, Kraut & Cummings, 2008). Facebook goes as far as to systematically aggregate dyadic relational activity, such as photos in which two friends are tagged, their comment exchanges, and information about the beginning of their connection; while this feature provides a programmatic vision of the relationship and its importance (Bucher, 2013), it does serve as a tangible reminder of the relational connection. These mechanisms extend an individual's knowledge management and memory capabilities and enable the maintenance of shared interests and knowledge (Dunbar, 2012), elements critical to relational quality, and can assist in maintaining a minimal level of contact to sustain connection when one-to-one conversation is infrequent (Bryant, Marmo & Ramirez, 2011).

Boundary Work and the Rules of Social Media Connection

Social boundaries include the spatial, temporal and relational limits that define us as separate from one another (Ashforth, Kreiner & Fugate, 2000; Zerubavel, 1991). Boundaries are especially important to relational development (Altman & Taylor, 1983) and to the regulation of privacy (Petronio, 2002), and thus the ways in which they are created and sustained are critical to relationship management for two reasons: they maintain the integrity of individuals and relationships, and they also frame how information flows between individuals (Parks, 2011b). *Boundary work* refers to the strategies, principles, and practices by which we create and maintain these boundaries, and research in this area tends to center on cultural categories and role identity (Nippert-Eng, 1996).

The boundary work executed within social media entails not only the performance of one's identity, but also the ability to edit and redact it across multiple and converged audiences (Papacharissi, 2011). As connections consist of family, friends and acquaintances, strong and weak ties, in a singular social space, the networked individual must navigate these multiple audiences without sacrificing coherence or continuity in self presentation. But because the networked individual may be performing multiple roles in multiple relational contexts, recognition of the appropriate set of boundary expectations may be somewhat challenging (Parks, 2011b). Individuals often lack control of how information flows through social media platforms, and this can sometimes result in the communication of decontextualized content, in disclosures that travel beyond the imagined audience (Litt, 2012), or in context collapse (Marwick & boyd, 2014). In addition, the broadcast quality of social media platforms intersects with spatial boundary management processes, because it alters the level of control an individual has over the intended audience for disclosure (Tufekci, 2008). In turn, because information controls reflect such unpredictability, the ways in which individuals manage identity, interact with one another, and negotiate privacy are shaped in two important ways: boundary management extends beyond individual control to become a collective process; and the 'rules of friendship,' or the social norms and expectancies

regarding social relationships, become highly relevant to how weaker relational forms are negotiated and maintained.

Karr-Wisniewski, Wilson and Richter-Lipford (2011) identified five areas that challenge an individual's boundary regulation processes in social media environments: networks, territories, disclosures, relationships, and interactions. *Networks* refer to our social spheres, which often are distinct and sometimes require us to play roles that conflict with one another. Preventing these from overlapping, such as keeping work connections isolated from family connections, is an important boundary control mechanism. *Territories* refer to the ways in which individuals claim their own 'space,' by controlling the information that flows across and through social media spaces; individuals control these flows by limiting what is visible in one's own newsfeed or restricting the commenting that is permitted on one's profile. Unintended *disclosure*, or the revelation of information to unanticipated audiences, is a third area that challenges an individual's boundaries; individuals attempt to prevent or contain unintended disclosure through the use of privacy settings or by restricting the information that is shared to specific groups or individuals. *Relationships*, or the connection with others, are a source of boundary permeability and sometimes are seen as a reflection of the individual; a decision to connect/disconnect with an individual and the use of grouping functionality are both mechanisms for bounding interaction. Finally, limiting *interactions* with others provides the most direct mechanism for boundary control, and can be accomplished by disabling the ability of others to tag photos or blocking contact with specific individuals altogether. Taken together, these boundary control processes are used to preserve and maintain identity and regulate privacy. However, these mechanisms operate at the level of the individual and, while a significant way to control identity and privacy, are often underpowered in the convergent and fluid spaces of social media. To accomplish greater control over identity and privacy in social media spaces, a collaborative approach is frequently required.

Petronio's theory of communication privacy management identifies that privacy management, and therefore the regulation of social boundaries, is a social process that is based on rules and norms that operate at the individual, dyadic and group level (Petronio, 2002), and these requirements are amplified in social media spaces. Individuals often learn the norms of social media platforms by watching the behavior of others (Burke, Marlow & Lento, 2009), and thus learn and rely on explicit and implicit collaborative behaviors to enact boundaries in a networked environment (Lampinen, Lehtinen, Lehmuskallio & Tamminen, 2011). Explicit behaviors might include asking another's permission before posting certain information, such as a photo online, while implicit behaviors may include self-censoring information that might compromise another, such as not sharing photos of a weeknight party.

The concept of 'networked privacy' (Marwick & boyd, 2014) contextualizes this idea within the social media environment. Marwick and boyd effectively argue that the multiple contexts of audiences and the technical architecture of social media platforms alter mechanisms for disclosure. Because social media are networked, older models that envision privacy as a process of controlling access to information are incomplete; instead, new emphasis is placed on the importance of social coordination to accomplish privacy. According to Marwick and boyd, privacy is best maintained through shared social norms, yet social media platforms are poorly equipped to support such collaboration with others; instead this coordination activity, both as preventative and corrective measures, often takes place outside social media spaces, out of sight and to more private media (Wisniewski et al., 2012).

Despite this, the norms related to social boundary regulation in social media do appear to be coalescing into recognizable patterns (Lampinen et al., 2011; McLaughlin & Vitak, 2011; Peluchette, Karl & Fertig, 2013). Argyle and Henderson (1984) explored the 'rules' that are significant to relational development, and found agreement on four general rules that apply to all forms of friend relationships. Unsurprisingly, these rules center on social boundary control: don't criticize in public; keep confidences; don't criticize other relationships; and respect privacy. They found that these general rules were essential in order for non-friend relationships to develop into friendships, and that additional rules relating to reciprocal communication and support became important to sustaining friendship once it was established (Argyle & Henderson, 1984).

Bryant and Marmo (2012) explored how these rules applied in social media contexts and found, similarly, that 'rules of friendship' facilitate relationship stability and mitigate inter-relational conflict. Application of these rules varies with the level of the relationship, for example, close friends may be held to stricter adherence of the rules than casual friends or acquaintances. They found the influence of social media has led to both a focus on the appropriateness of various communication channels and the importance of impression management for the self and friend connections. The most significant rules center on requirements for reciprocal communication, respecting the social boundaries of the other person when posting content, and communicating outside social media platforms (Bryant & Marmo, 2012); they emphasize relationship maintenance through activities performed through social media, but at the same time acknowledge the importance of interaction outside the social media environment.

Interestingly, social media users are more apt to sever contact or delete a weaker connection that compromises one's self-image (Bryant & Marmo, 2012; McLaughlin & Vitak, 2011). This differs from strategies used with close friends, where confrontation or further conversation appears to be the accepted process for dealing with conflict and relational decline (Rose & Serafica, 1986). As individuals are more sensitive to the negative consequences of social exchange at earlier stages in the relational development process (Hays, 1989), Bryant and Marmo's (2012) findings suggest that the social media environment influences processes of relational development: the emphasis on communication outside the social media environment suggests that while relationships of lesser strength might be maintained via social media platforms in ways not possible without such mediation, realization of their potential for stronger connection may be constrained without supplemental forms of interactivity or, in other words, interaction outside the social media environment. This is further evidence of boyd's (2006) notion that 'friends' on social media are not the same as 'friends' in the everyday sense.

UNFRIENDING: THE ART OF RELATIONSHIP DISSOLUTION

Our relationships vary in temporality, both by their duration, or how long they last, as well as in the rhythms by which they strengthen and weaken over time. In the strictest sense, relationships end when the partners no longer have contact or influence each other in any way (Parks, 2007). In unmediated contexts, these endings occur for a variety of reasons: physical separation, as when partners relocate geographically away from one another; replacement by new relational partners; dislike, as when one partner's behaviors, criticisms or betrayals break the relational trust; and life events, such as gaining a romantic partner or having children (Rose, 1984; Rose & Serafica, 1986). The visibility of connection enabled by social media platforms makes processes of disconnection similarly visible, which in turn sculpts the practices surrounding relationship terminations and dissolutions.

Looking at social media activity from a rhetorical perspective emphasizes that communication is a goal-directed and strategic activity, and this is particularly true with regard to the end of a friendship. From this vantage point, three stages of this process are relevant: the personal decision-making that leads up to the decision to end a relationship; implementation of this decision (typically, we view this as a breakup); and the public presentation, to our broader social networks, that the relationship has ended (Baxter, 1987).

The personal decision-making stage of relationship dissolution involves an individual taking assessment of the relationship and why it is dissatisfactory (Baxter, 1987). Interviews with users find that disconnection on social media platforms is based on both online and offline reasons. The online reasons center on the posting of content and include reasons such as too many or frequent unimportant posts, polarizing posts, inappropriate posts, and everyday life posts about eating habits or children (Kwak, Chun & Moon, 2011; Malinen, 2015; Sibona & Walczak, 2011). Offline reasons for disconnection were typically due to specific disapproved behaviors or significant changes in the relationship; interestingly, disconnection for these behavioral reasons increases with greater offline contact and length of social media use (Sibona & Walczak, 2011).

The decision to disconnect on social media also considers the circumstances of a relationship's beginning too. There is some evidence that relationship initiators (i.e., those making the initial friend request) are more frequently disconnected than those receiving the connection request, and those receiving a connection request more frequently make the decision to disconnect the relationship (Sibona & Walczak, 2011). This tracks with research on patterns of connection behaviors: some users report that it is easier to accept a connection request from someone they have met, and then disconnect, rather than appear rude or unsociable (McLaughlin & Vitak, 2011). Alternatively, studies of social media use among older adults suggest that the decision to disconnect is viewed unfavorably as individuals age (Quinn, 2013, 2014), leading to reduced levels of disconnection activity (Madden, 2012). More work is required to understand the factors which influence disconnection decision-making in these media.

The second stage of relationship termination is decision implementation, or the stage in which the disconnection is actively negotiated (Baxter, 1987). Unlike unmediated contexts, whereby disconnection is negotiated between the partners, users confer relational disconnection directly with social media platforms, and not the other individual; direct negotiation with the other person may or may not take place, depending on the context of the unmediated relationship. Disconnection of social media relationships is not uncommon, particularly for weak connections, and typically results from connection being lost over time, relationships that are not perceived as close, or an interpersonal rift such as a break up or quarrel (Malinen, 2015). Women and younger persons are more likely to disconnect than other groups of social media users (Madden, 2012).

Prior to the advent of social media, researchers relied on self-disclosure to lend visibility to the processes of friendship termination; however, network logs and traces of digital connectivity have sparked new ways to view these activities, providing new insight into how relationships termination is accomplished. Factors such as embeddedness, or whether partners share common friends (Martin & Yeung, 2006), and homophily, or similarity among partners (McPherson, Smith-Lovin & Cook, 2001), factor importantly in whether a relationship ends. Logs of social network site activity reinforce the importance of these factors, and further highlight that some common personality traits, such as extraversion and neuroticism, also contribute reduced levels of disconnection (Quercia, Bodaghi & Crowcroft, 2012); this holds true for both social media platforms that feature mutual connections (i.e., Friends), as

well as directed platforms, or those that permit unidirectional connection (i.e., Followers). Tie reciprocity, or cases where unidirectional relationships are 'followed back,' is important to predicting tie persistence as well (Kivran-Swaine, Govindan & Naaman, 2011; Xu, Huang, Kwak & Contractor, 2013). While it is relevant that research on social media has confirmed the findings of prior work on friendship termination in unmediated contexts, it will be important for future work to uncover additional factors that might contribute to the end of relationships.

Whereas the decision implementation unbounds a relationship from the inside, the public presentation unbounds a relationship from the outside (Baxter, 1987). These involve actions or reactions that verify the dissolution of relationships, and on social media platforms these can take several forms, some visible to others and some not. Unsubscribing from updates, using lists to exclude the ex-friend, and using privacy settings are common mechanisms to employ.

Lopez and Ovaska (2013) divide these various strategies into 'soft' and 'hard' processes, according to their visibility to others; soft processes are relatively invisible to other parties, while hard processes target others directly. Soft processes include unsubscribing, using lists, and adjusting privacy settings, while hard processes include total disconnection and reporting an individual to the platform provider and/or blocking them from all communication. Networked individuals are more likely to take soft actions as a disengagement process than hard actions (Peña & Brody, 2014), as these soft processes remain silent to other users (Malinen, 2015). This silence holds distinct, relational preserving advantages, as users can claim plausible deniability of their action (Lopez & Ovaska, 2013). For example, because users interface with the social media technology, and not each other, 'the technology' can absorb some responsibility for any interactional failures, such as not seeing posted content. Likewise, use of the platform as an intermediary affords users ambiguity, which enables the saving of face, and reduces the social cost of disconnecting actions (Aoki & Woodruff, 2005).

Conversely, though formal notification does not take place, hard processes may still be detected by the disconnected partner, by examining one's connection lists or attempting to communicate directly. These hard processes embody a more visible and public character, as they can be witnessed by others (i.e., the lack of connection between individuals is visible, just as a connection is visible), so they result in greater social consequence than softer actions (Peña & Brody, 2014). Disconnections are viewed by the disconnected partner as an important, though often not unexpected, negative outcome of relationship de-escalation (Bevan, Ang & Fearns, 2014). Those who unfollow or unfriend others do not perceive a need to communicate such information to those who have been disconnected (Malinen, 2015), perhaps reflecting the mundane nature of disconnection activity. When disconnection is unanticipated, those who are on the receiving end of disconnection sometimes contact the initiator and report moderate to high satisfaction with the follow-up interaction (Bevan et al., 2014); this perhaps indicates appropriate relational closure. Perhaps most importantly, both hard and soft strategies leave open the possibility for relational reconnection at a future point.

CONCLUSION: CONNECTING THE NETWORKED SELF

Social media enable, challenge, and reconfigure relationship and connection in ways that mirror, and sometimes transform, more traditional understandings of friendship and the self. These technologies provide additional ways to relate to one another, while simultaneously offering tangibility and digital traces of our relational connections. To tease apart how these technologies have shaped interaction, we explored how three

major stages of relational development – the establishment of connection; relational management and boundary work; and relationship disconnection – transpire and occur through their use.

The sense of self sustained through these modes of connection and expression is reflexively adjusted across platforms, publics, and taste cultures to facilitate a narrative about the self. This narrative is sustained through social environment that sustain always-on, ambient modalities of sociability. The appeal of these environments lies in their ability to reassure our desire for individual autonomy with our need for relational support, but comes at a cost. As our ability to sustain connections is amplified, our social environment is further saturated with the potential for ever-growing social connection. For the self, this requires balancing a variety of relational narratives simultaneously without losing one's own sense of self. It requires developing a storytelling of the self that is both coherent and polysemic in nature; meaningful to the self and relevant to distinct and overlapping audiences. The management of this reflexivity, across spaces publicly private and privately public, generates both tension and opportunity for the individual. The ability to manage this reflexivity optimally, in a manner that balances tension with opportunity, rests upon redactional acumen. In crafting the relational self-portrait that establishes the basis of connection, people edit, adjust, revise, and reorganize behaviors and ensuing performances. As digital traces of identity assemble to form impressions of a relational self-portrait, redaction becomes an essential form of literacy.

Future research could focus on the following potential areas:

- Storytelling of the self, and the oralities that emerge as new modalities of storytelling develop.
- Literacies necessary in managing the relational contexts that online technologies frequently collapse.
- Emphasis on avenues for maintaining contextual integrity (Nissenbaum, 2010) as people develop

and manage personal connections, social relations, and self-actualization across spaces that do not draw a distinction between digital and non-digital, public and private, online and offline.

• Imagined audiences, aspirational selves, and the networks rendered as people perform aspirational selves to imagined communities of audiences.

• Augmented reality and relational maintenance across these contexts.

As research in this area moves forward, its emphasis centers on self-presentation, representation, and performance. The process of self-presentation, performance or self-portraiture (Donath, 2015) involves both production of performances and simultaneous or subsequent editing of these performances. Redaction enables the bringing together and editing of identity traces, to form and frame a coherent performance. It is essential in balancing and maintaining relationships within a social environment saturated with the potential for connection. Redactional acumen enables individuals to present a coherent and polysemic performance of the self that makes sense to multiple publics, without compromising one's authentic sense of self. This presents the modus operandi for the networked self and ambient, always-on sociability.

Early studies of communication across and within networks emphasized the interpersonal and relational context. While it remains meaningful to consider the relational dynamics of self-expression, it is worth considering digitally enabled performances of the self as ways of piecing together and maintaining a digital self-portrait, assembled out of relational references and interactions. We may understand this form of relational self-portraiture as part of the ongoing story or the reflexive project of the self (Giddens, 1991). The ongoing storytelling project of the self is not just a performative exercise; it is an existentially driven and ever evolving narrative, a live self-portrait of who we are and what our experiences and relations to others mean, online and offline.

REFERENCES

Altman, I., & Taylor, D. A. (1973). *Social Penetration: The Development of Interpersonal Relationships*. New York: Irvington.

Antheunis, M. L., Valkenburg, P. M., & Peter, J. (2012). The quality of online, offline, and mixed-mode friendships among users of a social networking site. *Cyberpsychology*, 6(3), 6. doi:10.5817/CP2012-3-6

Aoki, P. M., & Woodruff, A. (2005). Making space for stories: Ambiguity in the design of personal communication systems. In *Proceedings of the SIGCHI Conference on Human Factors in Computing Systems – CHI '05* (p. 10). New York: ACM Press. doi:10.1145/1054972.1054998

Argyle, M., & Henderson, M. (1984). The rules of friendship. *Journal of Social and Personal Relationships*, 1(2), 211–237. doi:10.1177/0265407584012005

Ashforth, B. E., Kreiner, G. E., & Fugate, M. (2000). All in a day's work: Boundaries and micro role transitions. *Academy of Management Review*, 25(3), 472–491. doi:10.5465/AMR.2000.3363315

Backstrom, L., & Kleinberg, J. (2014). Romantic partnerships and the dispersion of social ties: A network analysis of relationship status on Facebook. *Proceedings of the 17th ACM Conference on Computer Supported Cooperative Work & Social Computing* (pp. 831–841). New York: ACM Press. doi:10.1145/2531602.2531642

Baxter, L. A. (1987). Self-disclosure and relationship disengagement. In V. J. Derlaga & J. H. Berg (Eds.), *Self-Disclosure: Theory, Research, and Therapy* (pp. 155–174). Boston, MA: Springer US. doi:10.1007/978-1-4899-3523-6_8

Baym, N. K. (2015). *Personal Connections in the Digital Age* (2nd ed.). Cambridge, UK: Polity Press.

Bevan, J. L., Ang, P. C., & Fearns, J. B. (2014). Being unfriended on Facebook: An application of Expectancy Violation Theory. *Computers in Human Behavior*, 33, 171–178. doi:10.1016/j.chb.2014.01.029

boyd, d. (2006). Friends, Friendsters, and Top 8: Writing community into being on social network sites. *First Monday*, 11(12), 1–14. Retrieved from http://firstmonday.org/htbin/

cgiwrap/bin/ojs/index.php/fm/article/view/1418/1336

boyd, d. (2010). Social network sites as networked publics: Affordances, dyanmics and implications. In Z. Papacharissi (Ed.), *A Networked Self: Identity, Community, and Culture on Social Network Sites* (pp. 39–58). New York: Routledge.

Bryant, E. M., & Marmo, J. (2009). Relational maintenance strategies on Facebook. *Kentucky Journal of Communication*, *28*, 129–150.

Bryant, E. M., & Marmo, J. (2012). The rules of Facebook friendship: A two-stage examination of interaction rules in close, casual, and acquaintance friendships. *Journal of Social and Personal Relationships*, *29*(8), 1013–1035. doi:10.1177/0265407512443616

Bryant, E. M., Marmo, J., & Ramirez, A. (2011). A functional approach to social networking sites. In *Computer-Mediated Communication in Personal Relationships* (pp. 3–20). New York: Peter Lang.

Bucher, T. (2013). The friendship assemblage: Investigating programmed sociality on Facebook. *Television & New Media*, *14*(6), 479–493. doi:10.1177/1527476412452800

Burke, M., Marlow, C., & Lento, T. (2009). Feed Me: Motivating Newcomer Contribution in Social Network Sites. *Proceedings of the SIGCHI Conference on Human Factors in Computing Systems*, 945–954. Boston, MA: ACM Press. doi:10.1145/1518701.1518847

Canary, D. J., Stafford, L., Hause, K. S., & Wallace, L. A. (1993). An inductive analysis of relational maintenance strategies: Comparisons among lovers, relatives, friends, and others. *Communication Research Reports*, *10*(1), 3–14. doi:10.1080/08824099309359913

Chen, J., Geyer, W., Dugan, C., Muller, M., & Guy, I. (2009). Make new friends, but keep the old: Recommending people on social networking sites. *Proceedings of the 27th International Conference on Human Factors in Computing Systems – CHI '09* (pp. 201–210). New York: ACM Press. doi:10.1145/1518701.1518735

Donath, J. S. (2007). Signals in Social Supernets. *Journal of Computer-Mediated Communication*, *13*(1), 231–251. doi:10.1111/j.1083-6101.2007.00394.x

Donath, J. S. (2015). *The Social Machine*. Cambridge, MA: MIT Press.

Donath, J. S., & boyd, d. (2004). Public displays of connection. *BT Technology Journal*, *22*(4), 71–82. doi:10.1023/B:BTTJ.0000047585.06264.cc

Duck, S. (1988). *Relating to Others* (1st ed.). London: Open University Press.

Duggan, M., Ellison, N. B., Lampe, C., Lenhart, A., & Madden, M. (2014). *Social Media Update 2014*. Washington, DC: Pew Research Center. Retrieved from www.pewinternet.org/files/2015/01/PI_SocialMediaUpdate20144.pdf

Dunbar, R. I. M. (2012). Social cognition on the internet: Testing constraints on social network size. *Philosophical Transactions of the Royal Society B: Biological Sciences*, *367*(1599), 2192–2201. doi:10.1098/rstb.2012.0121

Dunbar, R. I. M., Duncan, N. D. C., & Nettle, D. (1995). Size and structure of freely forming conversational groups. *Human Nature*, *6*(1), 67–78. doi:10.1007/BF02734136

Ellison, N. B., & boyd, d. (2013). Sociality through social network sites. In W. H. Dutton (Ed.), *The Oxford Handbook of Internet Studies* (pp. 151–172). Oxford, UK: Oxford University Press.

Ellison, N. B., Steinfield, C., & Lampe, C. (2011). Connection strategies: Social capital implications of Facebook-enabled communication practices. *New Media & Society*, *13*(6), 873–892. doi:10.1177/1461444810385389

Erickson, T. (1999). Persistant conversation: An introduction. *Journal of Computer-Mediated Communication*, *4*(4). doi:10.1111/j.1083-6101.1999.tb00105.x

Feld, S. & Carter, W. C. (1998). Foci of activity as changing contexts for friendship. In R. G. Adams & G. Allan (Eds.), *Placing friendship in context*, (pp. 136-152). Cambridge: Cambridge University Press.

Gergen, K. J. (2009). *Relational Being: Beyond Self and Community*. New York: Oxford University Press.

Gershon, I. (2011). Un-Friend My Heart: Facebook, Promiscuity, and Heartbreak in a Neoliberal Age. *Anthropological Quarterly*, *84*(4), 865–894. doi:10.1353/anq.2011.0048

Giddens, A. (1991). *Modernity and Self-identity: Self and Society in the Late Modern Age*. Palo Alto, CA: Stanford University Press.

Granovetter, M. S. (1973). The Strength of Weak Ties. *The American Journal of*

Sociology, *78*(6), 1360–1380. doi:10.1086/225469

Hampton, K. N., Sessions, L. F., & Her, E. J. (2011). Core networks, social isolation, and new media. *Information, Communication & Society*, *14*(1), 130–155.

Hampton, K. N., Sessions-Goulet, L. S., Rainie, L., & Purcell, K. (2011). *Social Networking Sites and Our Lives*. Washington, DC: Pew Research Center. Retrieved from www.pewinternet.org/~/media//Files/Reports/2011/PIP - Social networking sites and our lives.pdf

Hays, R. B. (1989). The day-to-day functioning of close versus casual friendships. *Journal of Social and Personal Relationships*, *6*(1), 21–37. doi:10.1177/026540758900600102

Haythornthwaite, C. (2002). Strong, weak, and latent ties and the impact of new media. *The Information Society*, *18*(5), 385–401. doi:10.1080/01972240290108195

Haythornthwaite, C. (2005). Social networks and internet connectivity effects. *Information, Communication & Society*, *8*(2), 125–147. doi:10.1080/13691180500146185

Hogan, B., & Wellman, B. (2014). The conceptual foundations of social network sites and the emergence of the relational self-portrait. In M. Graham & W. H. Dutton (Eds.), *Society and the Internet: How Networks of Information and Communication are Changing Our Lives* (pp. 53–66). New York: Oxford University Press.

Human, R., & Lane, D. (2008). *Virtually Friends in Cyberspace: Explaining the Migration from FtF to CMC Relationships with Electronic Functional Propinquity Theory*. Conference Papers. San Diego, CA: National Communication Association.

Karr-Wisniewski, P., Wilson, D. C., & Richter-Lipford, H. (2011). A new social order: Mechanisms for social network site boundary regulation. In *Proceedings of the Seventeenth Americas Conference on Information Systems* (Paper 101). Detroit, MI. Retrieved from http://aisel.aisnet.org/amcis2011_submissions/101

Kietzmann, J. H., Hermkens, K., McCarthy, I. P., & Silvestre, B. S. (2011). Social media? Get serious! Understanding the functional building blocks of social media. *Business Horizons*, *54*(3), 241–251. doi:10.1016/j.bushor.2011.01.005

Kivran-Swaine, F., Govindan, P., & Naaman, M. (2011). The impact of network structure on breaking ties in online social networks. *Proceedings of the 2011 Annual Conference on Human Factors in Computing Systems – CHI '11* (p. 1101). New York: ACM Press. doi:10.1145/1978942.1979105

Kwak, H., Chun, H., & Moon, S. (2011). Fragile Online Relationship: A First Look at Unfollow Dynamics in Twitter. *Proceedings of the SIGCHI Conference on Human Factors in Computing Systems*, 1091–1100. Vancouver, BC, Canada: ACM Press. doi:10.1145/1978942.1979104

Lampe, C., Ellison, N. B., & Steinfield, C. (2006). A face(book) in the crowd. In *Proceedings of the 2006 20th Anniversary Conference on Computer Supported Cooperative Work – CSCW '06* (p. 167). New York: ACM Press. doi:10.1145/1180875.1180901

Lampinen, A., Lehtinen, V., Lehmuskallio, A., & Tamminen, S. (2011). We're in it together: Interpersonal management of disclosure in social network services. In *Proceedings of the SIGCHI Conference on Human Factors in Computing Systems – CHI '11* (pp. 3217–3226). Vancouver, BC, Canada. doi:10.1145/1978942.1979420

Levin, D. Z., Walter, J., & Murnighan, J. K. (2010). Dormant Ties: The Value Of Reconnecting. *Organization Science*, *22*(4), 923–939. doi:10.1287/orsc.1100.0576

Li, Y., Zhang, Z. L., & Bao, J. (2012). Mutual or unrequited love: Identifying stable clusters in social networks with uni- and bi-directional links. *Lecture Notes in Computer Science, 7323 LNCS*, 113–125. doi:10.1007/978-3-642-30541-2_9

Light, B. (2014). *Disconnecting with Social Network Sites*. London: Palgrave Macmillan.

Litt, E. (2012). Knock, knock. Who's there? The imagined audience. *Journal of Broadcasting & Electronic Media*, *56*(3), 330–345. doi:10.1080/08838151.2012.705195

Lopez, M. G., & Ovaska, S. (2013). A look at unsociability on Facebook. *Proceedings of the 27th International BCS Human Computer Interaction Conference*, 13. Dundee, UK: BCS Learning & Development Ltd. Retrieved from http://ewic.bcs.org/upload/pdf/ewic_hci13_full_paper12.pdf

Madden, M. (2012). *Privacy Management on Social Media Sites*. Pew Internet & American

Life Project. Washington, DC: Pew Research Center. Retrieved from www.pewinternet.org/2012/02/24/privacy-management-on-social-media-sites/

Malinen, S. (2015). 'Unsociability' as boundary regulation on social network sites. In *Proceedings of Twenty-Third European Conference on Information Systems (ECIS)* (Paper 128). Munster, Germany: AIS Electronic Library. Retrieved from http://aisel.aisnet.org/ecis2015_cr/128

Marlow, C. (2009, 9 March). Maintained relationships on Facebook [weblog post]. Retrieved from http://overstated.net/2009/03/09/maintained-relationships-on-facebook

Martin, J. L., & Yeung, K.-T. (2006). Persistence of close personal ties over a 12-year period. *Social Networks*, *28*(4), 331–362. doi:10.1016/j.socnet.2005.07.008

Marwick, A. E., & boyd, d. (2011). I tweet honestly, I tweet passionately: Twitter users, context collapse, and the imagined audience. *New Media & Society*, *13*(1), 114–133. doi:10.1177/1461444810365313

Marwick, A., & boyd, d. (2014). Networked privacy: How teenagers negotiate context in social media. *New Media & Society 16*(7), 1051–1067. doi:10.1177/1461444814543995

Mayer, A., & Puller, S. L. (2008). The old boy (and girl) network: Social network formation on university campuses. *Journal of Public Economics*, *92*(1–2), 329–347. doi:10.1016/j.jpubeco.2007.09.001

McEwan, B. (2013). Sharing, caring, and surveilling: an actor-partner interdependence model examination of Facebook relational maintenance strategies. *Cyberpsychology, Behavior and Social Networking*, *16*(12), 863–9. doi:10.1089/cyber.2012.0717

McLaughlin, C., & Vitak, J. (2011). Norm evolution and violation on Facebook. *New Media & Society*, *14*(2), 299–315. doi:10.1177/1461444811412712

McPherson, M., Smith-Lovin, L., & Cook, J. M. (2001). Birds of a feather: Homophily in social networks. *Annual Review of Sociology*, *27*(1), 415–444. doi:10.1146/annurev.soc.27.1.415

Nippert-Eng, C. E. (1995). *Home and Work: Negotiating Boundaries through Everyday Life*. Chicago, IL: University of Chicago Press.

Nippert-Eng, C. E. (1996). Calendars and keys: The classification of 'home' and 'work'. *Sociological Forum*, *11*(3), 563–582. doi:10.1007/BF02408393

Nissenbaum, H. (2010). *Privacy in Context: Technology, Policy, and the Integrity of Social Life*. Stanford, CA: Stanford University Press.

Papacharissi, Z. (2011). Conclusion: A networked self. In Z. Papacharissi (Ed.), *A Networked Self: Identity, Community, and Culture on Social Network Sites* (pp. 304–318). New York: Routledge.

Parks, M. R. (2007). *Personal Relationships and Personal Networks*. Mahwah, NJ: Lawrence Erlbaum.

Parks, M. R. (2011a). Social network sites as virtual communities. In Z. Papacharissi (Ed.), *A Networked Self: Identity, Community, and Culture on Social Network Sites* (pp. 105–123). New York: Routledge.

Parks, M. R. (2011b). Social networks and the life of relationships. In M. L. Knapp & J. A. Daly (Eds.), *The Sage Handbook of Interpersonal Communication* (4th ed., pp. 389–422). Thousand Oaks, CA: Sage.

Pearson, E. (2009). All the World Wide Web's a stage: The performance of identity in online social networks. *First Monday*, *14*(3). doi:10.5210/fm.v14i3.2162

Peluchette, J. V. E., Karl, K., & Fertig, J. (2013). A Facebook 'friend' request from the boss: Too close for comfort? *Business Horizons*, *56*(3), 291–300. doi:10.1016/j.bushor.2013.01.013

Peña, J., & Brody, N. (2014). Intentions to hide and unfriend Facebook connections based on perceptions of sender attractiveness and status updates. *Computers in Human Behavior*, *31*, 143–150. doi:10.1016/j.chb.2013.10.004

Petronio, S. (2002). *Boundaries of Privacy: Dialectics of Disclosure*. Albany, NY: State University of New York Press.

Pollet, T. V., Roberts, S. G. B., & Dunbar, R. I. M. (2011). Use of social network sites and instant messaging does not lead to increased offline social network size, or to emotionally closer relationships with offline network members. *Cyberpsychology, Behavior, and Social Networking*, *14*(4), 253–258. doi:10.1089/cyber.2010.0161

Quercia, D., Bodaghi, M., & Crowcroft, J. (2012). Loosing 'friends' on Facebook. *Proceedings of the 3rd Annual ACM Web*

Science Conference – WebSci '12 held in Evanston, IL (pp. 251–254). New York: ACM Press. doi:10.1145/2380718.2380751

Quinn, K. (2013). We haven't talked in 30 years!: Relationship reconnection and internet use at midlife. *Information, Communication & Society*, 16(3), 397–420. doi:10.1080/1369118X.2012.756047

Quinn, K. (2014). An ecological approach to privacy: 'Doing' online privacy at midlife. *Journal of Broadcasting & Electronic Media*, 58(4), 562–580. doi:10.1080/08838151.2014.966357

Rainie, H., & Wellman, B. (2012). *Networked: The New Social Operating System*. Cambridge, MA: MIT Press.

Reinsch, N. L., Turner, J. W., & Tinsley, C. H. (2008). Multicommunicating: A practice whose time has come? *Academy of Management Review*, 33(2), 391–403. doi:10.5465/AMR.2008.31193450

Rose, S. M. (1984). How friendships end: Patterns among young adults. *Journal of Social and Personal Relationships*, 1(3), 267–277. doi:10.1177/0265407584013001

Rose, S., & Serafica, F. C. (1986). Keeping and ending casual, close and best friendships. *Journal of Social and Personal Relationships*, 3(3), 275–288. doi:10.1177/0265407586033002

Schechner, R. (2013). *Performance Studies: An Introduction* (3rd ed.). London: Routledge.

Shklovski, I., Kraut, R., & Cummings, J. (2008). Keeping in touch by technology: Maintaining friendships after a residential move. In *Proceedings of the 26th Annual Conference on Human Factors in Computing Systems – CHI '08* (p. 807). New York: ACM Press. doi:10.1145/1357054.1357182

Sibona, C., & Walczak, S. (2011). Unfriending on Facebook: Friend request and online/offline behavior analysis. In *2011 44th Hawaii International Conference on System Sciences* (pp. 1–10). Piscataway, NJ: IEEE. doi:10.1109/HICSS.2011.467

Simmel, G. (1955) '*Conflict*' and '*The Web of Group-Affiliations*', trans. K. H. Wolff & R. Bendix, The Free Press, Glencoe, IL. (Original Works Published In 1908 and 1922, respectively)

Smith, A. (2014). *6 New Facts about Facebook*. Washington, DC: Pew Research Center. Retrieved from www.pewresearch.org/fact-tank/2014/02/03/6-new-facts-about-facebook/

Stafford, L., & Canary, D. J. (1991). Maintenance strategies and romantic relationship type, gender and relational characteristics. *Journal of Social and Personal Relationships*, 8(2), 217–242. doi:10.1177/0265407591082004

Steinfield, C., Ellison, N. B., Lampe, C., & Vitak, J. (2012). Online social network sites and the concept of social capital. In F. L. Lee, L. Leung, J. S. Qiu, & D. Chu (Eds.), *Frontiers in New Media Research* (pp. 115–131). New York: Routledge.

Stutzman, F., & Hartzog, W. (2012). Boundary regulation in social media. In *Proceedings of the ACM 2012 Conference on Computer Supported Cooperative Work – CSCW '12* (pp. 769–778). New York: ACM Press. doi:10.1145/2145204.2145320

Tokunaga, R. S. (2011). Friend me or you'll strain us: Understanding negative events that occur over social networking sites. *Cyberpsychology, Behavior, and Social Networking*, 14(7), 425–432. doi:10.1089/cyber.2010.0140

Tong, S. T., Kashian, N., & Walther, J. B. (2011). Relational maintenance and CMC. In *Computer-Mediated Communication in Personal Relationships* (pp. 98–118). New York: Peter Lang.

Treem, J. W., & Leonardi, P. M. (2012). Social media use in organizations: Exploring the affordances of visibility, editability, persistence, and association. In *Communication Yearbook 36* (pp. 143–189). Mahwah, NJ: Lawrence Erlbaum Associates.

Tufekci, Z. (2008). Can you see me now? Audience and disclosure regulation in online social network sites. *Bulletin of Science, Technology & Society*, 28(1), 20–36. doi:10.1177/0270467607311484

Vitak, J. (2014). Facebook makes the heart grow fonder. In *Proceedings of the 17th ACM conference on Computer supported cooperative work & social computing - CSCW '14* (pp. 842–853). Baltimore, MD: ACM Press. doi:10.1145/2531602.2531726

Watson-Manheim, M. B., & Bélanger, F. (2007). Communication media repertoires: Dealing with the multiplicity of media choices. *MIS Quarterly*, 31(2), 267–293.

Wellman, B. (2001). Physical place and cyber place: The rise of networked individualism. *International Journal of Urban and Regional Research*, 25(2), June, 227–252.

Wesch, M. (2009). YouTube and You: Experiences of Self-Awareness in the Context Collapse of the Recording WebCam. *Explorations in Media Ecology*, 8(2), 19–34.

Westcott, H., & Owen, S. (2013). Friendship and trust in the social surveillance network. *Surveillance and Society*, 11(3), 311–323. Retrieved from: https://ojs.library.queensu.ca/index.php/surveillance-and-society/article/view/friendship

Wisniewski, P., Lipford, H., & Wilson, D. (2012). Fighting for my space: Coping mechanisms for SNS boundary regulation. In *Proceedings of the 2012 ACM Annual Conference on Human Factors in Computing Systems – CHI '12* (p. 609). New York: ACM Press. doi:10.1145/2207676.2207761

Xu, B., Huang, Y., Kwak, H., & Contractor, N. (2013). Structures of broken ties. *Proceedings of the 2013 Conference on Computer Supported Cooperative Work – CSCW '13* (p. 871). doi:10.1145/2441776.2441875

Zerubavel, E. (1991). *The Fine Line: Making Distinctions in Everyday Life*. New York: The Free Press.

Zhang, Z., Liu, Y., Ding, W., Huang, W. (Wayne), Su, Q., & Chen, P. (2015). Proposing a new friend recommendation method, FRUTAI, to enhance social media providers' performance. *Decision Support Systems*, 79, 46–54. doi:10.1016/j.dss.2015.07.008

Zhao, S. (2006). Do internet users have more social ties? A call for differentiated analyses of internet use. *Journal of Computer-Mediated Communication*, 11(3), 844–862. doi:10.1111/j.1083-6101.2006.00038.

20

Television Viewing and Fan Practice in an Era of Multiple Screens

Rhiannon Bury

The year before Facebook co-founder Mark Zuckerberg was born, George Lucas co-founded THX, a system to ensure high-quality motion picture sound, first implemented in time for the 1983 release of *Star Wars: Return of the Jedi*. An early THX trailer included the slogan 'The audience is listening.' Today, thanks in part to Zuckerberg and other so-called Web 2.0 entrepreneurs, 'the people formally known as the audience' (Rosen, 2006) are sharing, liking, following, tweeting, blogging, reblogging, and otherwise engaging with popular media content produced by industry and fans alike. Of course, viewers and fans have always done more than passively consume media, but a convergence of digital technologies is playing a key role in bringing about 'a system of multiple producers/distributors/consumers, an entirely new configuration of communication relations in which the boundaries between those terms collapse' (Poster, 1995: 3). At its broadest, this chapter critically examines the ways in which media content

sharing sites such as YouTube, peer-to-peer file sharing networks, and social media platforms such as Facebook and Twitter are changing viewing and participatory fan practices.

In addition to drawing on the small but growing body of literature that addresses how social media is used in relation to viewing and fandom, I present relevant findings from my Television 2.0 project (henceforth referred to as TV 2.0). While the bulk of television studies scholarship has focused on digital convergence and its implications for the television industry in the *post network* era (Lotz, 2009), this study was designed to explore the ways in which patterns of reception and participation in fan culture are shifting as a result of engagement with timeshifting, streaming and downloading technologies as well as with social media. Through the collection of survey (n=671) and interview data (n=72), TV 2.0 fills a gap between the larger-scale quantitative studies, produced by audience measurement and marketing research companies such as Nielsen, government agencies such as OfCom (UK) and independent organizations such as the Pew Research Center (US), and the smaller-scale qualitative studies produced by fan studies scholars.

I begin the chapter by interrogating the very notion of the audience, and the distinctions made between audiences and fans as well as between participatory and non-participatory fans. I then deconstruct these binaries, instead placing viewing and online participatory practices on a continuum. Finally, I provide a detailed discussion of the ways in which platforms such as YouTube, Facebook and Twitter complicate and 'dirty' established fan practices associated with older internet technologies. Given the focus of my research, the reception and participation practices discussed below are in relation to television, although much of the analysis can be applied to engagement with other genres of popular media, such as film and music.

METHOD

The TV 2.0 project is a mixed methods study that is best classified as *quant-QUAL* (Morgan, referenced in Hesse-Biber and Leavy, 2011); it is primarily a qualitative study with a quantitative component. Data were collected over a two-year period beginning in September 2010. Individuals and online communities with scholarly, professional and/or personal interests in television were invited via email, listservs, and social media (Facebook and Twitter) to take the online survey questionnaire and were encouraged to share information about and the link to the survey. Purposive and snowball sampling were chosen not only to identify a reasonably diverse population of television viewers and fans, but also to seek out potential interview participants. SPSS software was used for statistical analysis. Of the 281 respondents who expressed interest in being interviewed by telephone or Skype,

110 confirmed their interest. The first 50 participants were selected in the order in which they responded; purposive sampling was then used after a review of the demographic variables to select the final set of participants to ensure a diverse sample. The interviews were semi-structured and ranged from 30 minutes to two and a half hours. All were transcribed and coded using QSR NVivo software. Participants were asked to choose a pseudonym; a few chose to use their own first names, initials, or social media 'handles.'

The demographic snapshot of the survey respondents is as follows: 66.3% were female, 22.3% were male and 1.3% self-identified as non-binary. The age of the respondents ranged from 18 (the minimum age to take part in the survey) to 75, with a mean of 34.6: 71% were under the age of 40. Respondents resided in a total of 33 countries, dominated by the USA (40%), Canada (18%), and the UK (13%). As for the interview participants, almost three-quarters were female (n=53) and two-thirds were under the age of 40. Just under half resided in the USA, 12 in Canada, 11 in the UK, six in Europe, five in Australia/New Zealand, two in South America (Brazil and Argentina) and one in India, Israel, and Malawi respectively.

THEORIZING AUDIENCES, FANS, AND PARTICIPATORY PRACTICE

What I call the *reception turn* of the early 1980s in mass communications (US) and cultural studies (UK) marked a major paradigm shift, from passive to active audience, from mindless consumer to engaged viewer and producer of meaning. With the emergence of fan studies and new media studies, the audience began to be displaced as an object of study in favour of participatory culture and the user/*produser* respectively (Bird, 2011). In his seminal work *Textual Poachers*, Henry Jenkins (1992) makes the distinction between the 'bystander' (a term first used by Ellis (1989) to describe the television viewer in relation to the cinema viewer) and the fan. He describes a set of collective practices, including the production of art, music, fiction and video, which form the basis of a participatory culture. At the heart of this culture is a desire for connection and community (Jenkins, 1992). Drawing on Toffler's notion of the prosumer, Axel Bruns coined the term *produsage* to describe 'the collaborative and continuous building and extending of existing content in pursuit of further improvement,' citing examples of open source software development, Wikipedia, and multi-user games (Bruns, 2006: 276. Later work by Jenkins (2006) on convergence culture and that of Bruns (2008) on video sharing and remix/mashup culture demonstrate that participatory fans are indeed some of the most active produsers. '*Fandom is the future*,' states Jenkins (2007: 361). 'Certainly there are still people who only watch the show, but more and more of them are sneaking a peak at what they are saying about the show on *Television without Pity*, and once you are there, why not post a few comments. It's a slippery slope from there.'

This so-called *fanification* (Nikunen, 2007) of the audience has been met with criticism for overestimating the numbers of fans involved in produsage (see Bird, 2011; Burgess, 2011). Yet counter-claims that fans make up a minority of television audiences are also unsubstantiated. Van Dijck, for exampled, makes reference to the 'emerging rule of thumb' that only one in a hundred viewers will actually produce online fan-based content (quoted in Bird, 2011: 504). Jenkins, Ford and Green (2013: 155) have tried to address these concerns, striving not to 'overstate the prevalence of many active audience behaviors'. At the same time, they maintain that even those who are 'just' viewing 'do so differently in a world where they recognize their potential to contribute to broader conversations about that content' (2013: 154–155). They cite findings from several

surveys conducted by the Pew Research Center that show that media production among teens is steadily increasing.

What seems to be taken for granted in this debate is that there is indeed an audience to be 'fanified.' While numerous reception scholars have followed the lead of Ien Ang (1991, 1996) to complicate or redefine the concept (see Abercombie and Longhurst, 1998; Fiske, 1992; Gorton, 2009; Livingstone, 2004), active audiences are as much a construct of the imaginings of others as are the passive audiences of the Nielsen Company or the Frankfurt School. They are what John Hartley calls *invisible fictions*:

> In no case is the audience 'real', or external to its discursive construction. There is no 'actual' audience that lies beyond its production as a category, which is merely to say that audiences are only ever encountered *per se* as representations. Furthermore, they are so rarely *self*-represented that they are almost always absent. (Hartley, 1992: 105, italics in the original)

It is this last point on self-representation that is key. Nation states are described by Anderson (1983) as imagined communities, their citizens invested in 'steady, anonymous, simultaneous activity' (Anderson, cited in Hartley, 1992: 104). Television audience members, on the other hand, are not invested in their collective existence. John Fiske takes a similar position to Hartley in declaring that the '"television audience" is not a social category. … Categories focus our thinking on similarities: people watching television are best modeled according to a multitude of differences' (Fiske, 1989: 56). Livingstone and Das (2013) echo Ang's position that the 'thingness' associated with the concept of audience is misleading. They argue that the audience is 'a noun that merely stands in as shorthand for the verbs that account for the textually/technologically mediated communicative processes that connect people' (Livingstone and Das, 2013: 111). I am arguing, however, that the audience cannot be decoupled from its history of thingness and that its use is overdetermined. Hence, the audience is always a *mass* audience, a fiction that is always in the process of being made 'real' through its measurement, monetization and commodification. While this process must be studied and critiqued in the era of Big Data (see Andrejevic, 2007), concept is best dispensed with altogether and attention paid to what Fiske (1987: 57) describes as 'the processes of viewing, that variety of cultural activities that take place in front of the screen,' and, today, in front of multiple screens as well as on the screen itself. The issue of 'fanification' raised at the beginning of this section therefore needs to be examined in terms of the relationship between viewing, participation and fandom.

Following Jenkins (1992), fan studies scholars, including myself (Bury, 2005), have focused on participation in relation to community making. This focus, in conjunction with the greater visibility of participatory culture afforded by the internet, has had the effect (even if not the intention) of not only rendering 'non-participatory' fans invisible, but measuring them against participatory fans and finding them lacking. In the TV 2.0 project, I set out to break down this binary by examining a selection of established online fan practices in the context of a continuum. On the one end are practices that involve lesser amounts of active involvement in fandom. These include information-seeking, or reading posts made on discussion forums but not posting. In the middle are practices such as engaging in some discussion on forums and possibly reading fan fiction or viewing fan 'vids' without being active members of fan communities. On the other end are interactive/interpretive practices as well as fan production and creativity in the context of community. To this end I asked the survey respondents to define themselves as fans based on their engagement with at least one of the following practices in the 12 months prior to taking the survey:

- Having watched the majority of episodes of at least one season of a particular series.

- Staying abreast of news about the series through traditional and new media.
- Accessing and/or using additional web content, such as webisodes, quizzes, or games.
- Discussing the series with other fans on discussion forums or social networking sites.
- Producing creative work (e.g., fiction, art, music, and/or videos) based on at least one favourite series.

Although I do not consider viewing on its own to be a participatory fan practice (which is not to say that viewing cannot be a social activity), I included it as part of the exclusion question to capture a minimal level of fannish commitment; those who answered in the negative were taken to the end of the survey, skipping the section on fan practices. Perhaps not surprisingly, 89% of the respondents identified as fans, 92% of women and 84% of men. The response to the first question in the section demonstrated that those who identified as fans were well above the minimal one-series threshold, having watched a mean of seven television series over the 12-month period. The next question in the section established how often they visited any type of online site, including social network sites, discussion forums, and social media platforms, in relation to the series of which they were fans: 12% answered never, 22% occasionally, 26% sometimes, and 41% frequently. When asked specifically about online discussion forums, 37% reported having visited at least one in the past year, but less than half (15%) had participated in a discussion. As for fan creative practices, 25% had read fan fiction and 13% had written it and shared with others online. The gap between 'consumption' and 'production' of fan vids is even more striking: whereas 31% had viewed at least one fan vid, only 3% had produced at least one and shared with others online (6% were unfamiliar with fan fiction and vids, respectively).

Taken together, these findings suggest that both the proponents and the critics of fanification are correct: the vast majority of viewers of popular television can be categorized as fans and as such their numbers have been underestimated. On the other hand, most fans are clustered on the 'less participatory' end of the continuum, doing more than just viewing a favourite program or series, but not directly engaging in the hallmark practices of participatory culture. The numbers of those clustered on the 'most participatory' end have therefore been overestimated. The next section will explore the ways in which content sharing platforms and social media further complicate the participatory continuum.

SOCIAL MEDIA AND THE POWER OF PARTICIPATORY DIRT

Hartley ascribes television's power as being 'located in dirt,' that is, a form of power that 'resides in the interfaces between individuals, in ambiguous boundaries' (Leach, cited in Hartley, 1992: 23). Television is dirty not only because it has traditionally challenged bourgeois aesthetics of taste (i.e., television as 'boob tube') but, in recent years, with the explosion of 'quality' television, it also refuses to stay on its side of the low culture boundary. I contend that its power of dirt these days also lies in the refusal of its content to remain on the television screen itself. Digital television is a boundary technology both 'window-on-the-world and portal, flow and database' (Bennett, 2008: 163). Streaming and downloading technologies enable multi-screen viewing, that is, the viewing of content on a computer, mobile device, or via a set-top box (e.g., Wii or Apple TV), connected to a television set. They also permit the widespread circulation of television and other media content by fans through a number of platforms, such as Vimeo, YouTube, iTunes and peer-to-peer file-sharing networks using BitTorrent clients (e.g., Pirate Bay). Social media platforms such as Facebook and Twitter are similarly 'dirty' because of the ways in which they alter established practices and enable new

ones. Furthermore, the boundary between the television viewer and new media user becomes blurred as it does between the 'real' spaces of viewing and cyberspaces. Below, I discuss four such dirty practices: *spreadability*, *second screen*, *liking and following*, and *creativity*.

Spreadability

When undertaken by fans, the sharing of television content can be understood as a practice of *spreadability* (Jenkins, Ford, and Green 2013), and its dirtiness is reinforced by an association with piracy. Despite YouTube's early identification with produsage, Burgess and Green (2009) found that the most 'favorited' and 'viewed' videos came from traditional media sources, most of which were almost certainly shared without copyright permission. (Interestingly, user-created content received the most comments.) According to the web publication *TorrentFreak*, *Game of Thrones (HBO)* was the most pirated TV show of 2016 for the fifth straight year in a row, followed by *The Walking Dead (AMC)* and Westworld *(HBO)*. (Van Der Sar, 2016). According to Newman, 'the existence of files of shows available for sharing is itself a token of the value of certain kinds of television' (2012: 466). PricewaterhouseCoopers surveyed just over 200 participants who admitted to pirating copyrighted media content. Over 80% said that they had streamed TV shows for free in the past six months and 61% said that they had downloaded shows for free (Bothun and Lieberman, 2011). My findings were similar. The TV 2.0 survey respondents streamed television programming more frequently than they downloaded it: 86% had streamed television programming from a network site (e.g., HBO.com) and 82% had used a 'third-party' site such as Netflix and YouTube, compared to 63% who had downloaded content (Bury and Li, 2015). The percentages of frequent streaming from both network and third-party sites and downloading were much closer: just over and just under 30% respectively. To comply with recommendations made by the Research Ethics Board at my university, however, I did not distinguish between unauthorized streaming or downloading activity in the questionnaire, and was careful not to ask direct questions in the interviews about the legality of such activity. Nonetheless, a quarter of the interview participants still made direct references to streaming entire TV programs via YouTube (as opposed to trailers or clips) or downloading them illegally with BitTorrent clients.

Bothun and Lieberman (2011) concluded that price was a driving factor for piracy, as was the popularity of the practice – the 'everybody does it' justification. Jenkins, Ford and Green, however, offer another perspective: 'piracy is as much a consequence of the market failures of media companies to make content available in a timely and desirable manner as it is a consequence of the moral failure of audience members' (2013: 16). This position is more in line with the TV 2.0 findings. Those participants who admitted or alluded to doing so gave examples of series that were not accessible in a timely fashion on broadcast television in their region of residence. William, for example, had already seen the numerous American series he was a fan of by the time they were broadcast in New Zealand. The following samples capture the frustration for those outside North America who are fans of American series:

> We've moved out of our traditional watching live to actually torrenting it so we are up-to-date with the US in *Top Chef Masters*. We couldn't stand it anymore. The wait for it was too long. .... [The same is true of] *The Killing* and *Game of Thrones*, neither of them are on New Zealand television. They are not even being pre-advertised as going to be on New Zealand television! (Khal)
>
> *Mad Men* here in Argentina got lots of news in the national newspaper and there is no way to see it other than the internet because no one bought it and there is not AMC here but there is a pretty big crowd of fandom. *Mad Men* is like an extreme case for me because it was like, I KNEW it aired on

Sundays or on Mondays. Then on Mondays I was like desperate and I woke up very early and said, 'PLEASE, download *Mad Men*!!' (Lauchita)

American viewers gave similar reasons for downloading British shows like *Doctor Who*, *Torchwood* and *Sherlock* before they were broadcast on BBC America (although now these series are broadcast almost simultaneously):

> I guess the one that I did seek out that they didn't show on BBC America was *Sherlock*. They didn't show it for a while. I did go get that one pretty quickly. Being a fan of Steven Moffat's writing I figured it would be pretty brilliant and of course, it was pretty brilliant. (Rene)

These responses offer an explanation for the *TorrentFreak* numbers. *Game of Thrones* most likely had the most downloads both because it airs on a speciality network, HBO, that requires a premium and therefore more costly cable/satellite package in Canada and the USA. Fans living in other countries do not even have the opportunity to view episodes at the time of original broadcast. Cost and timeliness are therefore interconnected factors that cannot be reduced to a desire to get something for nothing.

Heresluck is an interesting case of a 'cord cutter' who downloads everything she watches:

> As soon as I have the DVD's the downloads are obsolete. They are lower quality; I can't use them for vidding purposes very well. I mean, I can but they are a pain for various reasons. So yeah, they are obsolete as soon as I get the DVD's. I do typically keep them until the DVD's come out just in case I want to re-watch before I have the DVD's available. (Heresluck)

While cost is the primary reason for her not having a cable subscription, by purchasing the series of which she is a fan, she is, in her own words, an 'ethical pirate.'

Robert and Peter Parker were both anime fans and mentioned the extra step of 'subbing', a practice which involves the creation of English subtitles before an episode is uploaded to be shared with other fans.

M discussed the process by which Brazilian fans made *Lost* spreadable for other Portuguese-speaking fans:

> When *Lost* was still on, this is how it happened. You have that link to watch it on streaming, right? Then the episode would air around this time here now is 10:00 p.m. or 11:00 p.m. Then this group of fans, they would download the episode after it was aired and then they spent the whole night subtitling it. Translating and subtitling it. For me, for instance. I will wake up the next morning like 7:00 or 8:00 a.m. and the subtitle would already be done. It was ready to download. You could download it and watch it at home. (M)

Taken together, the quotations above demonstrate that while piracy may not be the future of TV, as De Kosnik (2010) claims, there can be no question that it is a global practice primarily driven by affective desire.

Second Screen

A laptop, tablet or smart phone that is used to access social media platforms while simultaneously watching television programming has come to be known as a *second screen*. According to the Nielsen Company (2012), 45% of American viewers watched television content while using a tablet at least once a day. Almost 70% reported doing so several times a week. These statistics, however, do not distinguish between attentive or fannish viewing (e.g., following a Twitter hashtag related to the program being viewed) and distracted or indifferent viewing (e.g., checking and posting status updates on Facebook with the program serving as background). A survey by the Pew Research Center found that 52% of Americans had used their smart phone as a second screen, with 20% reporting that they checked to see what others were saying about the program they were watching and 19% posting their own comments about the program (Smith, 2012). These findings are supported by Wilson (2016). The majority of her participants used social media 'as an adjunct to television viewing when not

fully immersed in a TV show' (Wilson, 2016: 184). For example, several families were watching the same program together but using social media unrelated to the program on their second screens. Others were connecting with absent family members who were watching different programs or not watching TV at all. Thus the large majority of second-screen users are connected but distracted viewers.

In 2010, faced with a marked decline in live viewing, American networks began to move beyond simply using Facebook and Twitter accounts to promote their popular series and entertainment events, to offering their audiences second-screen or two-screen experiences through three types of 'attractors': third-party apps, companion content on their websites, and the use of established social media platforms (Castillo, 2013). The first group includes apps such as Get Glue and Zeebox that let users 'check in' to shows, get stickers, and interact with other fans. These apps proved unsuccessful: Get Glue was sold, renamed as tvtag and finally shut down in January 2015; Zeebox was 'rebranded' to focus on celebrity news in April 2014 (Dreier, 2014). Companion content is a form of ancillary content provided by the networks that are designed to sync with viewing on the primary screen. AMC's Story Sync is one example, offering a series of quiz questions in relation to the scenes on the primary screen in combination with flashbacks to related scenes from previous episodes and promotional ties to other series. It debuted in 2012 with the second season of *The Walking Dead* and, according to the network's Senior VP Digital Media, use has grown steadily (Bishop, 2014), making it not only successful enough to use in the current sixth season of the series, but also to be developed for other popular series, such as *Breaking Bad* and *Better Call Saul*. These interactive apps and ancillary content, argue Lee and Andrejevic, 'play an important role in *reaggregating* audiences when programs air in real time and in generating "big data" alongside live and social entertainment' (2014: 43, emphasis mine). Wilson conducted the only qualitative study to date on fan engagement with these types of apps or companion content. She found that they have the potential to enhance viewing pleasure, particularly 'when they are already part of an existing social [viewing] situation' (Wilson, 2016: 187). Likely because the TV 2.0 data collection took place in the early days of companion content development, only Khal mentioned using the 'check in' app Miso, which shut down in September 2014. Kim mentioned entering an online contest during Season 2 of *The Walking Dead* to win a walk-on zombie role by entering a code shown on the screen during the original broadcast. Similar to Wilson's participants, both Khal and Kim were watching with their spouses and described the use of the app and entering the contest as a fun, social experience.

The juggernaut of the second screen is Twitter. As Highfield, Harrington and Bruns (2013) point out, Twitter is made up of two distinct but overlapping networks: those based on follower–followee networks and those based on hashtags. The practice of 'live tweeting' a broadcast of a program or event using hashtags can be traced at least as far back as the Obama–Clinton debate in February 2008 (Pure Visibility, 2008), which was within months of the first reported use of the hashtag in July 2007 (Kirkpatrick, 2011). A study of trending topics in November 2009 indicated that the largest percentage (27%) was related to entertainment (Hargittal and Litt, 2011). Deller (2011) observed that more than 50% of the trending topics in the UK in the evening were related to television programs being aired. Page (2012) also found that the hashtags that appeared most frequently in her corpus of tweets from June 2010 were related to sports, politics and television shows. According to Nielsen, 36 million unique US users tweeted about television in 2013 (Nielsen Company, 2014), enough to catch the Company's attention and form a partnership with Twitter. In October

2013, Nielsen Twitter TV Ratings launched, which measures 'not only "authors" – the number of people tweeting about TV programs – but also the much larger "audience" of people who actually view those Tweets' (Nielsen Company, 2013). It now claims to measure gender and age demographics (how its algorithm could accurately capture such information is another story) and publishes 'Daily Top Five' and 'Weekly Top Ten' lists of the most-tweeted telecasts on its Nielsen Social blog, and well as a report at the end of each television season. For their part, the broadcasting networks regularly promote the use of the 'official' hashtag for a particular series or event. It would seem that the reaggregation of the audience has come full circle.

Highfield, Harrington and Bruns (2013) describe the practice of live tweeting television series and events with hashtags, official or fan-created, as engendering 'distributed public conversations' that 'come to act as a kind of virtual loungeroom … where audience members can come together to discuss and debate in real-time, their responses to what they are watching' (2013: 317). Yet their findings, from a large data set of tweets collected during the airing of the 2012 edition of the Eurovision Song Contest, do not support this claim. Although their close analyses of some of the national clusters suggests ironic and political content, they did not attempt to distinguish between commentary and conversation.

Drawing on Bourdieu's notion of a linguistic marketplace, Page (2012) offers a more nuanced understanding of live tweeting as a participatory practice: 'Hashtags are a crucial currency which enables visibility and projects potential interaction with other members' (2012: 184). She suggests that what appears to be conversational may in fact be 'para-social simulations of conversationality found in broadcast talk' (2012: 184), in other words, people talking *at* each other rather than *to* each other. Her analysis of the Twitter data she collected showed that the 'one-to-many' update type of tweet was more popular than the 'addressed' tweet in which the @ symbol is used. For example, the subset of tweets that used #leadersdebate (2010 UK election) had 10 times more 'one to many' tweets than @ replies. That said, this does not preclude viewers who live tweet or read the tweets using the hashtag from feeling that they are part of a larger interpretive community or participatory culture. Zappavigna (cited in Page, 2012: 184) refers to this as *ambient affiliation*. Similarly, Wohn and Na (2011) analyzed over 1,000 tweets made during an October 2009 broadcast of *So You Think You Can Dance*. They mapped tweet patterns onto the content of the show, noting spikes in emotion, attention and opinion messages during commercial breaks, and when one of the dancers was injured. The rest of the program was dominated by informational tweets. Similar to Page (2012), they found very little interactivity, noting that less than 4% of the tweets directed at a specific user using the @ symbol were reciprocated. By using hashtags and retweeting, however, they suggest, as Page does, that these viewers are signaling their interest in being 'part of a larger group' (2012: 10).

Just over one-third of the TV 2.0 survey respondents, and nearly two-thirds of the participants interviewed, used Twitter to follow fan-related feeds or tweet as a fan. About one-third (n=14) of the latter engaged in the practice of live tweeting and/or followed television-related hashtags during a broadcast:

> I know there was quite a few weeks ago when *Supernatural* did their Super Uber Meta episode, as they billed it. So there was a ton of live tweeting of that one because everyone was just so excited and wanted to, I don't know – disseminate as much as possible and as quickly as possible and that seemed to be the way to do it. I don't remember the hashtag they used but it was trending pretty quickly and pretty high. (Rene)

> If you follow a hashtag on Twitter, like there is, I mean, I have been part of global 'oh, come on's'!! Where literally there are people and I have no idea who they are. They live in Montana, that's

awesome. And we are collectively going, 'Tony DiNozzo [NCIS] would never do that!!!' … I am not sure that I would have a satisfying TV experience if I couldn't immediately keyboard smash at people and go, 'Oh, God! How is this going to work?!' Or, 'That was brilliant!!' or 'That was terrible!' (Knitmeapony)

The above data samples capture the enthusiasm and excitement of ambient affiliation. Suzie made explicit the pleasures of this affiliation in relation to shows that she watched at home alone:

> I think there is this urge that we have in all of us to experience something together and so whether you call somebody on the phone or you go online with other people. Like my husband and son, they watch *Amazing Race* and *Survivor* but they don't watch the *Real Housewives* and when I watch *The Bachelor* they say, 'what is that?' … I think it's really nice that you can find a community of people who care about the show and talk about the show and they are just at your fingertips. (Suzie)

Not everyone, however, desires a shared viewing experience. Aimee told me that live tweeting held no appeal to her: 'I would rather focus on the storyline that's happening in front of me.' Farah was not interested in live tweeting because she was not interested in the opinions or reactions of others: 'I tend to just watch it and think what I want to think about it.' Heresluck was interested in the responses of others but not their live tweets:

> I mean I know that there are people who really enjoy things like say live tweeting a show while they are watching it and seeing all the tweets that other people are posting about *Supernatural* or whatever. I kind of don't care about that at all. I am much more interested in seeing someone's post about it a day or two later when they've had a chance to organize their thoughts and produce something sort of interesting and in-depth. That's my priority. (Heresluck)

Live tweeting is also problematic for those unwilling or unable to watch programming live:

> I frequently have to turn my Twitter off for 12 hours or 24 hours at a time during *Idol* season

or *Survivor* season because there is going to be discussion all over Twitter. I am going to be spoiled if I leave it on. And the same obviously, goes by extension to various other shows even non-competitive reality shows, you know. I had to be very careful while *Lost* was airing because inevitably people want to discuss it and it's going to be at least a couple of days before I am able to get the content and view it. (William)

This last set of quotes gestures to the unevenness of this practice and the varying conditions under which fans make meanings and pleasures from televisual texts as well as the differing levels of investment in a shared viewing experience. There can be no question that the second screen functions to blur the boundary between viewing and participation, whether through the use of a third-party app, ancillary web content, or social media platforms.

Liking and Following

Almost half the TV 2.0 respondents reported having liked a series on Facebook, making it the most popular practice included in the survey. Among those interview participants who used Facebook and/or Twitter as fans, there were variations in engaging in the practice. Some, like Sophie, liked or followed all the shows that they watched, while others were more selective. 'It depends on the hotness of the actor!' Bunny exclaimed. 'Usually just the ones that I really *really* super like. I have to really be into them to try to follow their feeds or anything like that.'

Liking or following also provides information about a favourite series and its showrunners, actors, and so on. Such information has always been important to fans. Fiske (1989) argues that secondary texts, including promotional material, professional and amateur criticism, insider information and 'biographical gossip' serve to extend the meanings and pleasures of the primary television texts. Facebook and Twitter's customized newsfeeds, however, are 'push oriented,' serving to

change 'pull-oriented,' browser-based information-seeking practices into information receiving and aggregation:

I get a lot of my fan news now from Facebook. So I follow all the shows that I like and a number of fan sites. So a fair chunk of my Facebook feed is either first order or second order fannish stuff. (Revan)

Twitter and Facebook are nice for immediate information about the stars themselves and I appreciate the TV stars. (Mary)

[Twitter] is more instantaneous. … I have got news sites on there but I have also got fandom people on there and you see a lot of useful links and news come by. (Vera)

There are a couple of news ones that I follow that have EVERY single thing that Adam Lambert or Kris Allen [*American Idol*] does. They will have a link to it or tweet about it. So I follow, like I get a lot of fandom information that way. (Anne, 164)

The appeal of Facebook and Twitter thus lies in the immediacy and extensiveness of the information afforded by the customized newsfeed.

The practice of liking and following is more than a way to receive and aggregate information; it provides the possibility of receiving news and information directly from showrunners, actors, and reality stars: 'Public figures can now seemingly speak directly to their fanbase without news or management filters' (Bennett, 2014b: 8). The research to date on this more direct relationship has been conducted primarily from the perspective of the artist/celebrity: Marwick and boyd (2011) did a close analysis of 20 Twitter-verified accounts, including those of well-known actors and musicians such as Mariah Carey. Baym (2012, 2015) interviewed more than 30 independent musicians to examine the complexities of their communications with their fans through Twitter. Bennett (2014a) examined Lady Gaga's tweets sent to her 'little monsters,' a term of endearment she uses for her fans.

Several TV 2.0 participants spoke enthusiastically about following the feeds of one's 'objects' of affection:

If Nathan Fillion is tweeting from the site of Castle then I am like, 'ahhh what's he's doing and this is so cool!' The guy who played Rodney McKay on Stargate is also a big Twitterer and he is hilarious. And Stephen Fry of course. I mean, I am a Jeeves and Wooster fan all the way up to him being on Bones. Just HUGE fan of that man. He is *massive* on Twitter. (Knitmeapony)

I follow Brent Spiner on Twitter and he tends to post a ton of things where fans ask questions about what he is doing, where he is, his experiences of playing Data [*Star Trek: The Next Generation*]. He is very sarcastic and very witty which is interesting. (Jayne)

I follow – oh what's his name? Sutter, Kurt Sutter. He's the guy that created and writes Sons of Anarchy. So he tweets a lot about the show and what's happening and where they are up to and so on with making the show. He also blogs about it. He follows some of the main players so I find that really interesting to get these kind of insights into what's going on as they produce the show. (Khal)

These quotes offer a glimpse into the ways in which Twitter in particular serves to alter established mediated producer–fan and actor/celebrity–fan relations and provides a new set of fannish pleasures.

Interactivity: It's Just a Tweet Away

With its reciprocal friending network and generous character limit, Facebook appears to be more suitable for discussion than Twitter with its non-reciprocal follower–followee network and its (in)famous 140-character limit. Yet few of the TV 2.0 participants, whether active in fandom or not, reported using either platform to engage in fannish discussion beyond a round or two of turn-taking. Just over 10% of the survey respondents had posted a comment on a Facebook page dedicated to a series of which they were fans. Few of the interview participants mentioned Facebook at all in this context.

Every once in a while on Facebook I will post an announcement saying I'm really looking forward to tonight's episode of *Dexter* and then somebody will write a comment to that. You know, say,

'Me too. It's one of my favourite shows.' So that's one minor way that I have the social connection but I have never had a really full-on elaborate conversation. (LWR)

Another reason for the lack of fannish interactivity on Facebook is related to spoilers (Bennett, 2014b). Buffy said that when she wanted to find out what her friends thought of an episode, she would post a comment, 'trying to make it as oblique as possible without revealing details … and then hoping your friends will respond in turn.' One exception, she recalled was the finale of *Lost*:

Everyone [was] taking to Facebook with their outrage at how bad that last episode was or how disappointed they were in where it went or happy. … I remember my feed turning into this string of responses to *Lost*. (Buffy)

On the other hand, Nem and Tarsus were members of Facebook groups (*X-Files* and *Star Trek* respectively) set up by fans (as opposed to official Facebook sites for series or actors).

Everybody kind of just gets to know everybody else. You are kind of, there will be times when people will just have little jokes with each other. You get to kind of know everybody's preferences and you will kind of go, 'Wow! Denise, look at this photo.' It's usually Zachary Quinto just being FABULOUS! 'Look at this. Isn't he wonderful?' And she will go, 'Yes, isn't he wonderful.' And then everybody will kind of join in. It's just really knowing what everybody kind of enjoys and everybody is going to find funny. (Tarsus)

Interactivity, as described above, clearly involves the kind of more extensive discussion that typically has taken place on listservs, Yahoo groups and discussion forums, and is the basis of community making (Bury, 2005). Indeed, Tarsus found out about this Facebook group from her Yahoo group.

Given Twitter's more restrictive design limitations, it is not surprising that a number of participants referenced its lack of suitability for interaction:

I am not anti-Twitter but I just don't see how it is, I don't see what it has to offer in terms of communicating between people. I find it a very useful information service. But I don't understand how people can use it to communicate with each other. (Diva)

The following participants reported interacting with others while live tweeting:

We make comments and so on when we are watching the show. It turns out there are other people around [New Zealand] that watch television the same way we do. So for instance, when Top Chef comes available or something like that we all tend to get it around the same time and you can have a conversation about it as you watch it. (Khal)

The BBC political debate program, Question Time…airs Thursday nights at half past ten and they have a hashtag … I find lots of my colleagues in those tweets. So it's a social thing as well. (Will)

Recalling the findings of Wohn and Na (2011) and Page (2012), which I cited in relation to the second-screen practices, it is unlikely that these exchanges were extensive. The few participants who did use Twitter to interact with other fans they knew and followed described the workarounds they used to have group conversations:

I actually do a lot of my fangirling and stuff on Twitter these days. … I have a lot of friends that I am into. Actually I talk a lot of podfic [fanfic recorded as a podcast by the author] on Twitter. I have mostly podfic people on my Twitter. We will get into like just discussions. How you have giant meta discussions all night in 140 characters. It drives me nuts but I've done it more than once. It gets really confusing because there are a lot of us. (Anne)

We @ at each other and links things to each other: did you see this? That kind of thing. Part of it is of being able to have live conversation about things that come out. New information comes out and you are able to talk about it. I GET my information from Twitter and then I am able to retweet and point other people to it and talk about it in that space rather than sort of like going to email or something like that. (Karen)

Honeycutt and Herring (2009) studied the use of the @ sign as a marker of addressivity. Their sample indicates that most of the exchanges that used the strategy of addressivity took place between two people and averaged 3–5 messages. The longest exchange in their sample was 32 messages between 10 participants, but it was the exception. As such, it serves to illustrate both the 'level of interactional complexity' that Twitter affords but also its 'limitations as a tool for conversation and collaboration' (Honeycutt and Herring, 2009: 8).

The possibility of communicating directly with showrunners, actors and celebrities was an exciting prospect for participants such as Anne, who saw it as 'the fourth wall … breaking down.' Yet, there is little evidence of such interactivity. Marwick and boyd (2011) note that Hollywood 'A-list' celebrities are either not on Twitter or, if they are, do not or rarely engage with fans directly. Mariah Carey never replies to fans publicly but some claim that she has sent them private direct messages (Marwick and boyd, 2011). Bennett's (2014a) analysis of Lady Gaga's tweets and the survey responses from her fans give no indication that the star interacts directly with them. Only one TV 2.0 participant reported interacting with a well-known celebrity:

Never in my life did I think that I would banter with George Michael on Twitter about politics which was what I was doing before you called! Because he is very involved in this scandal at the moment and he is just talking his head off and everybody is talking with him. (Vera)

Thus, it is fair to say that part of Twitter's appeal is the possibility of realizing the fantasy of interacting with the famous. The situation is somewhat different with less famous artists, entertainment workers and content producers. Bennett (2014b) mentions that American actor Orlando Jones regularly engages with fans. Baym interviewed Zoë Keating, an American new classical musician, who said that her fans expect her to reply to their tweets: 'It's not like "Oh my God, she actually wrote back." It's like "of course you wrote back"' (Baym, 2012: 293). Of the few TV 2.0 participants who mentioned tweeting an actor or showrunner, there was no sense that a reply was expected:

Joe Mantegna [*Criminal Minds*] said something about one of his movies being out and he simply tweeted, it will be out on such and such a day and I tweeted back, 'I have already pre-ordered mine.' Yeah that kind of thing. There was something about supporting veterans and I said, 'Thank you. My father's a veteran.' (Mary)

Mary had the following to say to fans who expected replies: 'Get it over it people … I don't expect somebody who is starring in a television show to send me a personal reply to anything. That's unrealistic. I appreciate what they do.' Libby did receive replies from showrunners Hart Hanson (*Bones*) and Shawn Ryan (*Chicago Code*) when she asked whether viewing on TV or online affected the amount that producers and actors were paid: 'I admit, it was pretty exciting when they actually wrote back to me. … I got all geeked about it and I was a little embarrassed.' Marwick and boyd (2011) suggest that fans tweet artists or actors that they follow not to receive a reply as much as to display an affective relationship.

To conclude, the dirty power of Facebook and Twitter is located in their potential to collapse the boundaries between information and interactivity: rather than visiting websites for information and/or forums to read or discuss, or even going to different sections on the same site, fans can move seamlessly from reading their newsfeed, liking or favoriting fan-related information to commenting or tweeting. They can also not only get information straight from the horse's mouth, so to speak, but engage the horse directly. Yet there are architectural limitations that constrain more extended interactions between and among fans as well as unequal relations of power that continue to constrain direct engagement between fans and the 'objects' of their affection.

Creativity

Fans have been collaborating on and sharing creative works online since the early days of

the internet via a combination of archives (e.g., fanfiction.net, Organization for Transformative Works' Archive of Our Own), listservs, Yahoo groups and Livejournal (Coppa, 2006). Such production reworks narratives, characterizations and relationships that are protected by intellectual property laws. As such, the unauthorized use of such content to create fan fiction and fan vids was already a dirty practice, as acknowledged by Jenkins (1992) through his deployment of De Certeau's concept of *poaching*. In the Web 2.0 era, Jenkins, Ford and Green (2013) argue that the spread of content is in itself integral to its remaking I contend, however, that fan fiction and vids are a part of a second-order of spreadability that alters the gift economy upon which fan production and sharing has been based. According to Booth (2010: 134), readers of fan fiction and viewers of fan vids are not expected to reciprocate in kind: 'what the gift in the digital age requires for "membership" into the fan community, is merely the obligation to reply.' This reply could take the form of a positive comment or piece of constructive criticism (Jenkins, Ford, and Green, 2013).

The operation of what Booth (2010) refers to as *digi-gratis*, however, is dependent on scale and restricted access to members of the creative communities. Second-order spreadability is enabled by sites like YouTube. As a result, 'fan producers are no more able to control the dissemination of their texts than corporate producers' (Russo, 2009: 127). According to Freda, an acafan who does research on vidding, there is 'a tension in the community [as to] whether vidding can exist outside of LiveJournal.' She admitted to being 'a bit of a snob': 'A lot of times if I see a vid and I don't know the vidder or, and this sounds really embarrassing, or if the vid is on YouTube I won't watch it.' In contrast, Anne was comfortable posting her vids to YouTube, although she also noted 'snobbery' around doing so:-

There are YouTube communities from what I have seen but there's also sometimes some snobbery involved where it's like if you post a YouTube you are not as good. Kind of like with fic and archives. A lot of people, especially on LiveJournal will be like, 'Well, I don't like going to archives. I would never post my fic to archives because archives have so much bad fic.' (Anne)

These comments highlight a longstanding concern about quality among those I have described elsewhere as 'elite' fans (Bury, 2005, 2008). From the expansion of the internet to include the AOL (America OnLine) bulletin boards in the early 1990s, elite fans have expressed concerned about a decline in standards of interpretation and creativity due to the participation of 'the masses,' who are seen as lacking the levels of cultural and linguistic capital needed to produce or engage with 'quality' works. Platforms like YouTube short-circuit the gift economy, the implicit value of which is founded on what Bourdieu (1993) calls *bourgeois aesthetics*. Outside the boundaries of fan communities, there is no guarantee of a 'quality' reply or feedback.

One positive effect of spreadability on this scale is that it affords the opportunity for 'view-only' fans as well as those fans on the 'less participatory' end of the continuumto become familiar with fan creativity.

Every now and then a friend of mine will post something on Facebook, for example, a fan vid but they don't know it's a fan vid. They don't know what it is; they don't know about fandom. It's like, 'I found this cool video. It's got House in it' or whatever is going on that day. At which point I usually have to educate them as to what it is they've found. Oh, look, you found a fan vid. This is what a fan vid does. (Rene)

Rene also engaged in second-order spreadability by posting the occasional fan vid to Facebook 'if I think it's a really good one.' Gene knew little about participatory fandom beyond a class he took in cultural studies. When he was asked to review a manuscript submitted to a scholarly journal analyzing fan-made reedits using scenes of a gay couple from *Verbotene Liebe* (*Forbidden Love*), a German soap with English subtitles, he went to view them on the YouTube channel where they were posted. When he found himself on extended bedrest, he went back to YouTube and watched all the original episodes of the soap and actively searched for other fan works not only featuring the couple, but other queer storylines from international and American series.

It was all foreign to what I do [as a communications scholar]. ... So it's been really exciting for me because it's the experience of being a fan, which I've never been or really understood. I mean, my earlier partner was a soap opera watcher and I would leave the room. I just couldn't stand the sound of it. (Gene)

Although Gene never became actively involved in fandom, and by extension the gift economy, the spread of creative fan works beyond the boundaries of fan communities made it possible for him and many other fans to value and take pleasure in these texts.

Beyond spreadability, there are a few creative practices worth noting that are specific to Twitter. The first is 'twitfic', mentioned by several TV 2.0 participants. As one might imagine, it is a very abbreviated work of fiction spread over a number of tweets. Anne's response pointed to the limitations of Twitter for such a practice: 'there is this one fic that I am constantly directed to that I like just can't work up the energy to read because it's in like 200 Twitter posts.' The other is the form of Twitter role-play that involves the creation of accounts for TV characters by fans (Bennett, 2014b). Jenkins, Ford and Green (2013) recount the reaction of AMC when Don Draper 'appeared' on Twitter, followed by the other main and supporting *Mad Men* characters, including the Xerox machine. After suspending the accounts as a violation of copyright, the network eventually heeded the advice of their marketing agency and relented. Wood and Baughman (2012) studied the tweets from 10 'character' accounts and their interactions with each other. They found that much of the tweeting was live and both supplemented the episode narratives as well as provided alternative narratives. Other fans who followed the character accounts would also get involved in the role-play at times, for example, taking on the role of a minor character but using their own account. While no TV 2.0 participants engaged in this creative practice, several mentioned following character accounts (Aimee), and reading character exchanges in relation to a series (Robert).

CONCLUSION

While communication relations between producers and consumers have yet to be entirely reconfigured as envisioned over 20 years ago by Poster (1995), Web 2.0 technologies have dirtied and disturbed the hierarchical binary relationship. As I have demonstrated, streaming and downloading protocols in combination with content sharing and social media platforms have blurred the boundaries between the television screen and mobile screens, viewing and participation, information and interactivity, and creativity and community. Much like the printing press in the fifteenth century, which increased the flow of communication and raised the likelihood that more people would have access to copies of printed materials (Graff, 1991), content sharing and social media platforms spread industry-produced content and fan creative works, increasing the opportunities for fans along the full range of the participatory continuum to find, view and engage with such content through legal and illegal means across national borders. While internet technologies made participatory culture more visible with the creation of fan-dedicated listservs, websites and discussion forums, Web 2.0 technologies make 'less participatory' fans more visible by enabling them to like, follow, post, and tweet without necessarily becoming active in fandom or, *pace* Jenkins (2007), even desiring to do so. When I asked the TV

2.0 participants on the 'less participatory' end of the continuum if they could see themselves becoming involved in online fan communities, writing a piece of fanfic, or creating a vid, few expressed interest in doing so. (Only those who were media scholars tried to rationalize why they were not actively involved in fandom.)

In placing the practices discussed above in the broader context of media reception and technology use, it is important to keep in mind that most people still predominately watch broadcast television. According to TV 2.0 survey results, only those respondents between the ages of 18 and 29 and those residing in continental Europe viewed as much programming online as they did on a television set (Bury and Li, 2015). As for social media use, according to the Pew Research Center, while 71% of US adult internet users are on Facebook, not even one quarter (23%) are on Twitter, less than on Pinterest (28 %) and Instagram (26%) (Duggan et al., 2015). The use of a second screen in relation to fannish engagement is therefore a marginal practice at best, the majority of the millions of tweets during live broadcast sent by a minority of the total viewing audience. Third-party apps and ancillary content were designed by the industry to encourage 'stickiness' (Jenkins, Ford and Green, 2013) and shore up the most traditional viewing practice of all – live viewing.

Moreover, as the TV 2.0 findings indicate, fans continue to use older platforms to find information, to interact with one another, and to share creative works. While social media platforms afford unique pleasures in terms of information aggregation and the possibility of direct communication with writers, showrunners, actors, and reality stars, the same is not true of interactivity. As I argue elsewhere, the in-depth, regular, sustained interaction enabled by older technologies ranging from listservs to LiveJournal, upon which community making in fandom was founded, casts the limitations of Facebook and Twitter into sharp relief (Bury, 2016).

Finally, this chapter does not capture the full range of participatory practices involving the use of social media. The reblogging platform Tumblr, for example, is popular among some fans. Bennett (2014b) notes its use for visual creativity, a claim supported by the TV 2.0 data. Participant opinions as to its usefulness for interaction were mixed as they were for Twitter. There are also several other established fan practices outside the scope of TV 2.0 project that now have a social media component: cosplay (dressing in character costume at conventions) (see Lamerichs, 2015) and fan activism (see Bennett, 2014a, 2014b). I also want to flag the emerging practice of crowdfunding or *fan-ancing* to quote Scott (2015). Fan-ancing relies on platforms such as Kickstarter to help finance not only independent creative projects, but those of creators of commercial film and television but which lack full industry backing (e.g., *Veronica Mars*) (see Bennett, Chin and Jones, 2015).

Taken together, content sharing and social media platforms have not replaced or displaced older platforms, or transformed participatory practices and participatory culture, as much as they have supplemented and extended them.

REFERENCES

Abercombie, N. and Longhurst, B. (1998) *Audiences: A sociological theory of performance and imagination*. London: Sage.

Anderson, B. (1983) *Imagined communities: Reflections on the origin and spread of nationalism*. New York: Verso.

Andrejevic, M. (2007) Surveillance in the digital enclosure. *The Communication Review*, 10(4): 295–317.

Ang, I. (1991) *Desperately seeking the audience*. London and New York: Routledge.

Ang, I. (1996) *Living room wars: Rethinking media audiences for a postmodern world*. London and New York: Routledge.

Baym, N.K. (2012) Fans or friends? Seeing social media audiences as musicians do. *Participations: Journal of Audience and Reception Studies*, 9(2): 286–316.

Baym, N.K. (2015) Connect with your audience! The relational labor of connection. *The Communication Review*, 18(1): 18–22.

Bennett, J. (2008) Television studies goes digital. *Cinema Journal*, 47(3): 158–165.

Bennett, L. (2014a) 'If we stick together we can do anything': Lady Gaga fandom, philanthropy and activism through social media. *Celebrity Studies*, 5(1-2): 138–152.

Bennett, L. (2014b) Tracing textual poachers: Reflections on the development of fan studies and digital fandom. *Journal of Fandom Studies*, 2(1): 5–20.

Bennett, L., Chin, B. and Jones, B., (Eds). (2015) *Crowdfunding the future: Media industries, ethics & digital society*. New York: Peter Lang.

Bird, S.E. (2011) Are we all produsers now? *Cultural Studies*, 25(4-5): 502–516.

Bishop, B. (2014) How a second-screen app made 'The Walking Dead' come alive. *The Verge*. Available at: www.theverge.com/entertainment/2014/2/13/5406498/how-a-second-screen-app-made-the-walking-dead-come-alive

Booth, P. (2010) *Digital fandom: New media studies*. New York: Peter Lang.

Bothun, D. and Lieberman, M. (2011) Discovering behaviors and attitudes related to pirating content. London: PricewaterhouseCoopers LLP. Available at: www.pwc.com/us/en/industry/entertainment-media/publications.html

Bourdieu, P. (1993) *The field of cultural production: Essays on art and literature*. New York: Columbia University Press.

Bruns, A. (2006) Towards produsage: Futures for user-led content production. In F. Sudweeks, H. Hrachovec and C. Ess (eds), *Cultural attitudes towards communication and technology*. Tartu, Estonia, pp. 275–284.

Bruns, A. (2008) *Blogs, Wikipedia, Second Life, and beyond*. New York: Peter Lang.

Burgess, J. (2011) User-created content and everyday cultural practice: Lessons from YouTube. In J. Bennett and N. Strange (eds), *Television as digital media*. Durham, NC: Duke University Press, pp. 311–331.

Burgess, J. and Green, J. (2009) *YouTube: Online video and participatory culture*. Cambridge, UK: Polity Press.

Bury, R. (2005) *Cyberspaces of their own: Female fandoms online*. New York: Peter Lang.

Bury, R. (2008) Textual poaching or game keeping? A comparative study of two *Six Feet Under* internet fan forums. In J. Machor and P. Goldstein (eds), *New directions in American reception study*. Oxford and New York: Oxford University Press, pp. 289–305.

Bury, R. (2016) Technology, fandom and community in the second media age. *Convergence: The International Journal of Research into New Media Technologies*. Epub ahead of print. DOI: 10.1177/1354856516648084

Bury, R. and Li, J. (2015) Is it live or is it timeshifted, streamed or downloaded? Watching television in the era of multiple screens. *New Media and Society*, 17 (4): 592–610.

Castillo, J. (2013) The rise of the second screen: Zeebox, GetGlue, Viggle, and more. *Streaming Media,* April/May. Available at: www.streamingmedia.com/Articles/Editorial/Featured-Articles/The-Rise-of-the-Second-Screen-Zeebox-GetGlue-Viggle-and-More-89008.aspx (accessed on 1 August, 2017)

Coppa, F. (2006) A brief history of media fandom. In K. Hellekson and K. Busse (eds), *Fan fiction and fan communities in the age of the Internet*. Jefferson, NC: McFarland & Co., pp. 41–59.

De Kosnik, A. (2010) Piracy is the future of television. White paper, Convergence Culture Consortium, 17 March. Available at: http://convergenceculture.org/research/c3-piracy_future_television-full.pdf

Deller, R. (2011) Twittering on: Audience research and participation using Twitter. *Participations: Journal of Audience and Reception Studies*, 8(1): 217–245.

Dreier, T. (2014) TVtag to shut down January 1st, marks decline in Social TV. *Streaming Media,*22 December. Available at: http://www.streamingmedia.com/Articles/News/Online-Video-News/TVtag-to-Shut-Down-January-1st-Marks-Decline-in-Social-TV–101242.aspx (accessed on 1 August, 2017)

Duggan, M., Ellison, N.B., Lampe, C., et al. (2015) *Social media update 2014*. Pew Research Center. Available at: www.pewinternet.org/2015/01/09/social-media-update-2014/

Ellis, J. (1989) *Visible fictions: Cinema, television, video*. London and New York: Routledge.

Fiske, J. (1987) *Television culture*. New York: Methuen.

Fiske, J. (1989) Moments of television: Neither the text nor the audience. In E. Seiter, H. Borchers, G. Kreutzner, et al. (eds), *Remote control: Television, audiences, and cultural power*. New York: Routledge, pp. 56–78.

Fiske, J. (1992) Audiencing: A cultural studies approach to watching television. *Poetics*, 21: 345–359.

Gorton, K. (2009) *Media audiences: Television, meaning and emotion*. Edinburgh: Edinburgh University Press.

Graff, H.J. (1991) *Legacies of literacy: Continuities and contradictions in Western culture and society*. Bloomington, IN: Indiana University Press.

Hargittai, E. and Litt, E. (2011) The tweet smell of celebrity success: Explaining variation in Twitter adoption among a diverse group of young adults. *New Media and Society*, 13(5): 824–842.

Hartley, J. (1992) *Tele-ology*. New York: Routledge.

Hesse-Biber, S.N. and Leavy, P. (2011) *The practice of qualitative research*. Thousand Oaks, CA: Sage.

Highfield, T., Harrington, S. and Bruns, A. (2013) Twitter as a technology for audiencing and fandom. *Information, Communication & Society*, 16(3): 315–339.

Honeycutt, C. and Herring, S.C. (2009) Beyond microblogging: Conversation and collaboration via Twitter. *International Conference on System Sciences*. Hawaii: IEEE.

Jenkins, H. (1992) *Textual poachers: Television fans & participatory culture*. New York: Routledge.

Jenkins, H. (2006) *Convergence culture: Where old and new media collide*. New York: New York University Press.

Jenkins, H. (2007) Afterword: The future of fandom. In J. Gray, C. Sandvoss and C.L. Harrington (eds), *Fandom: Identities and communities in a mediated world*. New York: New York University Press, pp. 357–364.

Jenkins, H., Ford, S. and Green J. (2013) *Spreadable media: Creating value and meaning in a networked culture*. New York: New York University Press.

Kirkpatrick, M. (2011) The first hashtag tweeted on Twitter: They sure have come a long way. Available at: http://readwrite.com/2011/02/04/the_first_hashtag_ever_tweeted_on_twitter_-_they_s

Lamerichs, N. (2015) The remediation of the fan convention: Understanding the emerging genre of cosplay music videos. *Transformative Works and Cultures*, 18: 1–16.

Lee, H. J. and Andrejevic M. (2014) Second-screen theory: From the democratic surround to the digital enclosure. In J. Holt and K. Sanson (eds), *Connected viewing: Selling, streaming & sharing media in the digital era*. New York: Routledge, pp. 40-61.

Livingstone, S. (2004) The challenge of changing audiences: Or what is the audience researcher to do in the age of the internet? *European Journal of Communication*, 19(1): 75–86.

Livingstone, S. and Das, R. (2013) The end of audiences? Theoretical echoes of reception amid the uncertainties of use. In J. Hartley, J. Burgess and A. Bruns (eds), *Companion to new media dynamics*. Hoboken, NJ: Blackwell, pp. 104–121.

Lotz, A. (2009) Beyond prime time: Television programming in the post-network era. New York: Routledge.

Marwick, A.E. and boyd, d. (2011) To see and be seen: Celebrity practice on Twitter. *Convergence: The International Journal of Research into New Media Technologies*, 17(2): 139–158.

Newman, M.Z. (2012) Free TV: File-sharing and the value of television. *Television and New Media*, 13(6): 463–479.

Nielsen Company. (2012) Advertising & Audiences Part 2: By demographic. *State of the Media*. Report, Spring 2012 Available at: www.nielsen.com/content/dam/corporate/us/en/reports-downloads/2012-Reports/nielsen-advertising-audiences-report-spring-2012.pdf

Nielsen Company. (2013) *Nielsen launches 'Nielsen Twitter TV Ratings'*. Available at: www.nielsen.com/ug/en/press-room/2013/nielsen-launches-nielsen-twitter-tv-ratings.html

Nielsen Company. (2014) Who's tweeting About TV. Nielsen Social. Available at: www.nielsensocial.com/whos-tweeting-about-tv/

Nikunen, K. (2007) The intermedial practises of fandom. *Nordicom Review*, 28(2): 111–128.

Page, R. (2012) The linguistics of self-branding and micro-celebrity in Twitter: The role of hashtags. *Discourse & Communication*, 6(2): 181–201.

Poster, M. (1995) *The second media age*. Cambridge, MA: Polity Press.

Pure Visibility. (2008) Yes we can twitter: Barack Obama supporters use social media to show their support. Blog. Available at: https://purevisibility.com/yes-can-twitter-barack-obama-supporters-use-social-media-show-support/

Rosen, J. (2006) The people formerly known as the audience. Available at: http://archive.pressthink.org/2006/06/27/ppl_frmr.html

Russo, J.L. (2009) User-penetrated content: Fan video in the age of convergence. *Cinema Journal*, 48(4): 125–130.

Scott S. (2015) The moral economy of crowd-funding and the transformative capacity of fan-ancing. *New Media and Society* 17(2): 167–182.

Smith, A. (2012) *The 'rise' of the connected viewer*. Pew Research Center 17 July. Available at: http://www.pewinternet.org/2012/07/17/the-rise-of-the-connected-viewer/

Van Der Sar, E. (2016) *'Game of Thrones' most pirated TV-show of 2016*. Available at: https://torrentfreak.com/game-of-thrones-most-torrented-tv-show-of-2016-161226/

Wilson S. (2016) In the living room: Second screens and TV audiences. *Television & New Media* 17(2): 174-191.

Wohn, Y. and Na, E.-K. (2011) Tweeting about TV: Sharing television viewing experiences via social media message streams. *First Monday*, 16(3). Available at: http://journals.uic.edu/ojs/index.php/fm/article/view/3368/2779

Wood, M.M. and Baughman, L. (2012) Glee fandom and twitter: Something new, or more of the same thing? *Communication Studies*, 63(3): 328–344.

21

Trolling, and Other Problematic Social Media Practices

Gabriele de Seta

I, TROLL

Ever since I started regularly accessing the Internet on my first personal computer in the late nineties, I've engaged in practices that today would be alternately called 'trolling', 'flaming', 'cyber-bullying', 'online harassment', 'social media abuse', and so on. I was fourteen years old, and I had finally convinced my parents to buy me a rather expensive Pentium III desktop computer so that I could play *StarCraft: Brood War* with some friends. The real-time strategy videogame had just come out, and sparring online with clanmates from all around Italy was my favorite activity, monopolizing a large chunk of my time out of school. Along with *StarCraft* came MSN Messenger, gaming forums, IRC channels, and a variety of other platforms mediating my online interactions.

Many of these interactions were quite quarrelsome: a regular multiplayer game with friends or strangers would customarily begin with a ritual exchange of greetings, then

escalate rapidly into racial offenses or sexual slurs, often dragged on through private messages until one of the participants blocked the other – losing a tournament game mattered quite a lot to us. Similarly, conversations with classmates, punctuated by rapid-fire MSN notification bleeps ringing across my house, often oscillated between the private plotting of pranks and more public gossip; the hazing and shaming of unfortunate victims moved seamlessly from schoolyards to group chats. Forums were even more confrontational. As my interests shifted from online gaming to death metal, I found myself comfortably at home in one small bulletin board mostly populated by people I had never met. Discussions about the latest album releases would quickly heat up into violent quarrels about personal taste, peppered by elaborate offenses singling out each other's mental health, political beliefs, sexual orientation, physical appearance, and so on.

Over several years of participation, discussions in this particular forum became less and less about music, and more a series of convoluted in-jokes drawing from a shared repertoire of ridiculous stories that occurred on public threads, private messages, and occasional meetups at metal festivals. When we discovered that it was possible to obtain embarrassing personal details about each other by impersonating this or that person on the community's IRC channel, some of us went beyond the line of what would be today dealt with in a civil court case. Yet, we found all of this to be worth the fun, and in self-reflexive discussions about our online community we sometimes marveled at how the absurdist abuse that we perfected as a form of sociality had in fact woven a tight texture of affects and memories between a group of people living across the country who would have never interacted, much less bonded, under different circumstances. '*Il forum è vita*', we often joked ironically when someone took an abusive session of online hazing too seriously: 'The forum is life'.

This bit of autoethnographic recollection from more than a decade ago, a time when I had no idea of what trolling – let alone autoethnography – meant, is neither a disclaimer nor an apology. Rather, it's an introduction to the central argument of this chapter. After familiarizing myself with the vast literature covering a variety of 'problematic', 'disruptive', 'abusive' and 'antisocial' practices on social media, as well as with the extraordinary visibility of trolling in contemporary popular media narratives, I felt the need to begin my discussion of the topic with some first-person memories. By taking stock of the socially mediated everyday that Georges Perec would call 'infra-ordinary' (1997, p. 177), I want to highlight how complicated arrangements of practices,

often reduced to shorthand terms, functional causes, and direct consequences, are always grounded in individual and self-reflexive experiences across time and space. For the same reason, I've decided to intersperse the text of this chapter with screenshots of posts by users participating in discussions about trolling that I purposely organized on two online image boards. By including a selection of posts collected from two structurally similar online platforms – 4chan and AC anonymous board, respectively enlivened by predominantly American and Chinese usebases[1] – I hope to undermine and destabilize my own academic writing, while welcoming social media users voicing personal interpretations of their own practices into the text (Figure 21.1).

QUESTIONS OF (BAD) FORM

Trolling, along with a shifting constellation of related or overlapping terms (flaming, spamming, cyber-bullying, online harassment, social media abuse, and so forth), belongs to the wider domain of social media practices that resulted from the popularization of Internet access and participatory digital media platforms. As Lee Rainie and Barry Wellman (2012) point out, the intense socially networked activities of digital media users, which include countless ways of creating, sharing, ranking and discussing content, inevitably imply a certain degree of personal disclosure, and easily lead to occasions for surveillance and sousveillance:

many internet users are leaving considerable digital footprints, advertently and inadvertently, for others to follow. And follow they do. [...] Not only

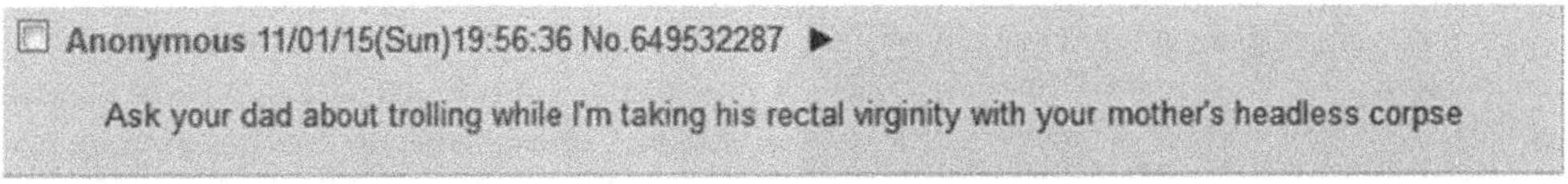

Anonymous 11/01/15(Sun)19:56:36 No.649532287 ▶

Ask your dad about trolling while I'm taking his rectal virginity with your mother's headless corpse

Figure 21.1 Anonymous reply to a discussion thread about trolling I opened on 4chan

are other users 'creeping' and 'stalking' each other, but also governments and large organizations have the capacity to surveil individuals. (Rainie & Wellman, 2012, p. 80)

Hurling insults across private messages in multiplayer games, embarrassing classmates in group chats, or impersonating users on IRC channels exemplify the tightening imbrication of social media and personal life. The rapid pace with which digital media platforms introduce new affordances for interpersonal interaction complicates this sociotechnical context, and along with evolving interactional norms and situational rules of etiquette emerge new ways of disturbing, harassing or abusing each other online.

In English-language media, trolling has become a placeholder for a stunning variety of practices (Hardaker, 2010, p. 224), ranging from mocking or taunting each other for fun (O'Neil, 2015) to disrupting large online communities (Pao, 2015), and from engaging in large-scale harassment campaigns (Allaway, 2014) to impersonating multiple identities engaging in extremist activities (Zavadski, 2015). Andrew Whelan (2013, p. 41) argues that the term 'troll', both as a noun and a verb, is widely appropriated by news media and recurrently used to sustain various moral panics about the abuse of networked communications. The incorporation of this term in the inventory of popular media narratives has resulted in overly simplified explanations of wildly different problematic social media practices. On the other side of the explanatory spectrum are the painstaking attempts of academic researchers to find a solid definition for these practices, often to counter the populist sensationalism of media panics (Jane, 2014, p. 532). Some examples testify to the variety of possible approaches to the topic:

Trolling is a game about identity deception, albeit one that is played without the consent of most of the players. The troll attempts to pass as a legitimate participant, sharing the group's common interests and concerns; the newsgroup members, if they are cognizant of trolls and other identity deceptions, attempt to both distinguish real from trolling postings and, upon judging a poster to be

a troll, make the offending poster leave the group. (Donath, 1999, p. 43)

To troll is to have negative intents, to wish harm or at least discomfort upon one's audience. To be trolled is to be made a victim, to be caught along in the undertow and be the butt of someone else's joke. (Bergstrom, 2011)

Internet trolls – a class of geeks whose *raison d'être* is to engage in acts of merciless mockery/flaming or morally dicey pranking. These acts are often delivered in the most spectacular and often in the most ethically offensive terms possible. (Coleman, 2012, p. 101, emphasis added)

Trolls are people who act like trolls, and talk like trolls, and troll like trolls because they've chosen to adopt that identity. (Phillips, 2013, p. 505)

Online trolling is a specific example of deviant and antisocial online behavior in which the deviant user acts provocatively and outside of normative expectations within a particular community; trolls seek to elicit responses from the community and act repeatedly and intentionally to cause disruption or trigger conflict among community members. (Fichman & Sanfilippo, 2015, p. 163)

This chapter is an attempt to pull together the three contexts sketched above: the multitude of practices experienced in one's infra-ordinary use of social media; the sensationalist narratives mustered under buzzwords throughout news media narratives; and the scholarly representation of a variety of practices often described as deceiving, confrontational, offensive, negative, disruptive, abusive, unethical, non-normative, deviant or antisocial. A reader might be expected to ask: What is trolling? Why do some social media users troll others? Is trolling good or bad? How can trolling be stopped? Unfortunately, my contribution is not meant to answer any of these questions. As I summarize in the first half of this chapter, more than twenty years of research into problematic social media practices have already tackled many of these interrogatives, providing a wide variety of comprehensive answers, and producing a rich and detailed cartography of the possibilities of academic approaches to trolling.

The broader theoretical question that this chapter addresses is, rather: Where next? How can we write about trolling, and about other problematic social media practices, while avoiding both the oversimplification of popular media narratives and the overdetermination that results from academic treatments? I attempt to answer these questions in the second half of the chapter, in which I present the results of a research project about trolling on Chinese social media platforms. I use this example to argue for the advantages that ethnographic accounts of infra-ordinary social media use, underpinned by a radical notion of underdetermination, might have for future discussions of problematic practices.

GOING META: REVIEWING LITERATURE REVIEWS

> Much of the attention that social uses of the computer has been given focused on outstanding incidents of sexual harassment, gender-switching, electronic cads who break women's hearts, flaming and other abuses, rather than the countless rewarding and routine non-problematic interactions (Baym, 1994, p. 29).

One of the quirkiest claims found in journal articles and book chapters dealing with trolling is that there hasn't been enough research on the topic (Leaver, 2013, p. 217). This lamented underrepresentation is usually explained with the scattering of existing literature across disciplinary domains (Buckels,

Trapnell, & Paulhus, 2014, p. 97), the conflation of radically different problematic practices under the same buzzword (Whelan, 2013, p. 48), the excessive technicality of research (McCosker, 2014, p. 204), or insufficient attention given to trolling in a particular discipline (Hardaker, 2015, p. 201). Dispersed across discursive communities or overlooked in specialist circles, trolling is described as an irremediably mysterious activity, an esoteric ritual practiced by folk devils in perpetual need of reconsideration and of innovative research approaches.

It isn't a coincidence that most treatments of trolling begin with a substantial literature review of the topic. Literature reviews of trolling research are fairly homogeneous, and largely agree in tracing the evolution of the problematic social media practices over two decades of sociotechnical change:

> In scholarly work, trolling has morphed from a description of newsgroup and discussion board commentators who appeared genuine but were actually just provocateurs, through to contemporary analyses which focus on the anonymity, memes and abusive comments most clearly represented by users of the iconic online image board 4chan, and, at times, the related Anonymous political movement. (Leaver, 2013, p. 216)

Even when slanted towards specific theoretical resources or disciplinary approaches, many reviews of existing scholarship propose a similar history of trolling research,

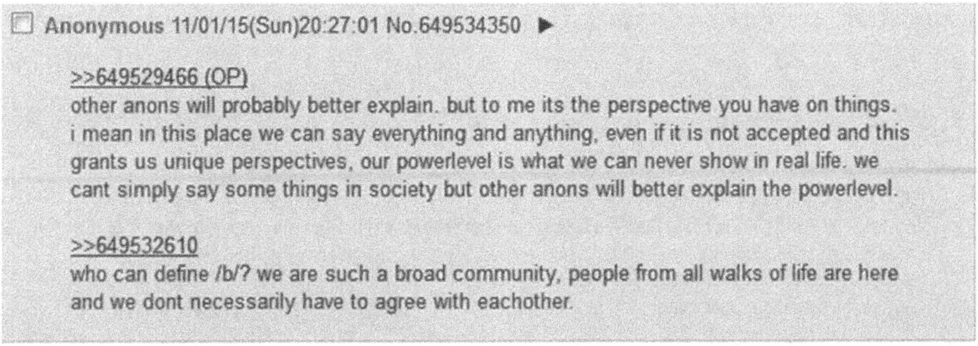

> Anonymous 11/01/15(Sun)20:27:01 No.649534350 ▶
>
> >>649529466 (OP)
> other anons will probably better explain. but to me its the perspective you have on things.
> i mean in this place we can say everything and anything, even if it is not accepted and this
> grants us unique perspectives, our powerlevel is what we can never show in real life. we
> cant simply say some things in society but other anons will better explain the powerlevel.
>
> >>649532610
> who can define /b/? we are such a broad community, people from all walks of life are here
> and we dont necessarily have to agree with eachother.

Figure 21.2 Anonymous reply to a discussion thread about trolling I opened on 4chan

dividing it into two major blocks: early explorations of conflict and impoliteness in computer-mediated communication and online communities, and more recent studies of problematic practices on contemporary social media platforms.

In this chapter I provide a more genealogical outlook on this body of research, arguing that trolling and similar social media practices have, in fact, been extensively studied across disciplines over a substantial period of time. The purpose of my genealogical approach, inspired by Foucault's lifelong work on the idea of genealogy, is to 'account for the constitution of knowledges, discourses, domains of objects, etc.' (Foucault, 1980, p. 117) rather than flattening them onto a transcendental history. A genealogy of trolling research seeks to identify the emergence of the definitions of certain practices (Rabinow, 2003, p. 55) and has the advantage of foregrounding how their problematization is structured and stabilized (Koopman, 2011, p. 539). In light of this, rather than pursuing strictly temporal or disciplinary categorizations, I map the existing research literature along three axes of controversies: the tension between descriptions of trolling as part and parcel of early Internet culture and its diagnoses as deviant online behavior (*Culture <-> Deviance*); the attempts at defining trolling versus the pursuit of contextual descriptions (*Definition <-> Contextualization*); and the debates between sympathetic appraisals of trolling versus critical condemnations of the practice (*Endorsement <-> Critique*). These axes define a three-dimensional domain of inquiry along functional, epistemological and ethical continuums, outline a comprehensive cartography of two decades of research into problematic practices on social media, and should provide a clear picture of the zones of opportunity for future inquiry.

Culture <-> Deviance

Actually, tell you what scares the shit out of me on the net. AFU (alt.folklore.urban). Now there's a newsgroup to dread. Posting as a newbie there should be one of those (often fatal) moves grouped under the same heading as accidentally shooting yourself through the private parts. (Anonymous Usenet user quoted in Tepper, 1997, p. 43)

The first axis of controversy outlines a functional tension between two possible repertoires of answers to the question 'what is trolling?' – one relying on insider accounts of the practice and defining it as an essential part of a culture of the Internet, and another observing its disruptive consequences and diagnosing it as a clear case of deviant behavior encouraged by computer-mediated interaction.

A certain impenetrable mystique has been an integral part of early descriptions of trolling, which chronicle a time when disruptive and uncivil practices in MOOs, newsgroups and chatrooms were often called flaming (Baym, 1995) or spamming (Marvin, 1995). Perhaps the earliest account of a case of trolling, Julian Dibbell's 'A Rape in Cyberspace'

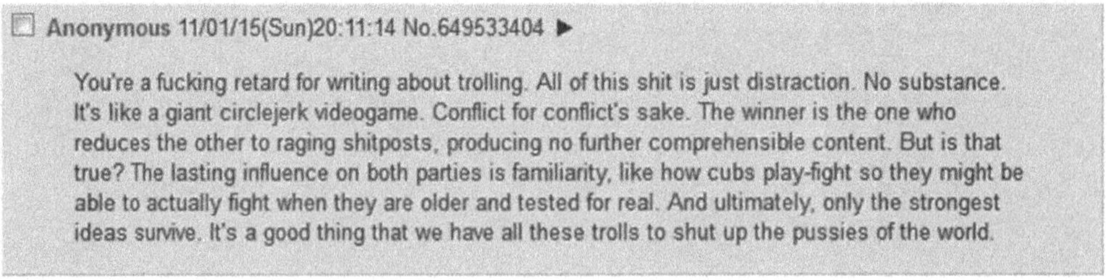

☐ Anonymous 11/01/15(Sun)20:11:14 No.649533404 ▶

You're a fucking retard for writing about trolling. All of this shit is just distraction. No substance. It's like a giant circlejerk videogame. Conflict for conflict's sake. The winner is the one who reduces the other to raging shitposts, producing no further comprehensible content. But is that true? The lasting influence on both parties is familiarity, like how cubs play-fight so they might be able to actually fight when they are older and tested for real. And ultimately, only the strongest ideas survive. It's a good thing that we have all these trolls to shut up the pussies of the world.

Figure 21.3   Anonymous reply to a discussion thread about trolling I opened on 4chan

(1993) presciently outlines all the major concerns that have echoed through two decades of academic research and public debate around problematic social media practices. 'They say he raped them that night', Dibbell begins, providing a poignant first-person account of harassment in cyberspace. The story is made even more uncanny and estranging by the distance separating the contemporary experience of ubiquitous and mobile social media from the textual environment of LambdaMOO, which the author describes as 'a very large and very busy rustic mansion built entirely of words' (1993, p. 1). The 'Bungle Affair', during which a MOO player called Mr. Bungle forced the in-game avatar of another player to engage in degrading sexual acts, is pitched by Dibbell as a case of online abuse that challenges techno-utopian visions of cyberspace. He begs readers to 'look without illusion upon the present possibilities for building, in the on-line spaces of this world, societies more decent and free than those mapped onto dirt and concrete and capital' (Dibbell, 1993, p. 1).

Dibbell's ethnographic attention to the political debates rippling across LambdaMOO in the wake of the Bungle Affair, which resulted in the deliberation of new community rules and in the emplacement of protective functions, is a clear example of how early descriptions of interaction in online communities contributed to the wider construction of an 'Internet culture'. In the classic definition by David Porter, the culture embodied by the Internet is theorized as a product of intense online interactions, 'a collective adaptation to the high frequency of anonymous, experimental, and even fleeting encounters familiar to anyone who has ventured into a newsgroup debate' (Porter, 1997, p. xi), which happens:

> not in the interface between the user and the computer, but rather in that between the user and the collective imagination of the vast virtual audience to whom one submits an endless succession of enticing, exasperating, evocative figments of one's being. (Porter, 1997, p. xiii)

A number of researchers identify flaming, spamming and trolling as integral parts of Internet culture, conflictual and imaginative interactions between users and their imagined networked publics (boyd, 2011) requiring constant adaptation and negotiation (Myers, 1987, p. 264). As Marvin (1995) notes, '[t]hese articulated aesthetics serve as rules for proper behavior, markers of experience and belonging, metaphors for poetic expression and resources for play and challenge within the community' but can at the same time be deployed for aggressive and even abusive purposes (Stivale, 1997, p. 134), resulting in a form of 'personal verbal violence' that is 'widely practiced and equally widely abominated' (Millard, 1997, p. 145). Progressively codified as a ludic in-group activity, trolling 'serves the double purpose of enforcing community standards and of increasing community cohesion by providing a game that all those who know the rules can play against those who do not' (Tepper, 1997, p. 40).

It's quite evident how early descriptions of flaming, spamming and trolling as integral components of an emerging Internet culture are predominantly based on certain locales (mostly the United States), platforms (mostly Usenet newsgroups and academic LISTSERVs) and userbases (mostly educated, middle-class males). This is not a coincidence, for '[i]n its early years, the only people using the internet were the ones developing it' (Baym, 2010, p. 17). Just as Dibbell's Mr. Bungle is revealed to be a communal account operated by residents of a NYU student hall floor (1993), confrontational interactions in online spaces appear to have been pioneered by the very same 'highly educated scholars and researchers' (H. Wang & Hong, 1996) who were writing extensively about the topic. In the earliest evaluations of the practice, flaming is in fact identified as an essential element of academic mailing lists: 'it educates the ignorant, polices cyberspace, brings order to the group, and scares away unwanted commercial advertising'

(H. Wang & Hong, 1996). University students and researchers were the first Internet trolls, and explained their practice by linking it to the 'high concentration of reflexive, reflective, anxious, and/or contentious personalities in academic communities' (Millard, 1997, p. 147).

On the opposite side of these self-reflexive observations about Internet culture made by early adopters of the medium are studies that correlate trolling and similar practices with psychological deviance or antisocial behavior (Fichman & Sanfilippo, 2015), a quite common response to emerging phenomena involving new technologies and youth (Yar, 2005, p. 387). Often grounded on technologically determinist arguments about the reduced social cues characterizing interactions mediated by the mostly textual interfaces of the early Web (Kiesler, Siegel, & McGuire, 1984), these treatments of trolling correlate disruptive, deceptive and abusive practices to psychological features such as sadism (Buckels et al., 2014), identify the behavior of victims of online harassment as coping strategies (Lee, 2005), and propose the introduction of protective systems and participatory incentives to discourage problematic behavior on social media platforms (Bishop, 2012).

Parallel inquiries in communication studies and sociology take a less prescriptive position, and approach trolling as a case study in interpersonal relationships, evaluating the emotional impact of 'messages that hurt' (Vangelisti & Crumley, 1998, p. 173). The resources most often underpinning this strand of scholarship are the *online disinhibition effect* and *deindividuation theory*. According to John Suler, a consequence of the anonymity, invisibility and asynchronicity characterizing online interactions is that 'some people self-disclose or act out more frequently or intensely than they would in person' (2004, p. 321), a form of online disinhibition which can in turn lead to disproportionately toxic behavior such as trolling. Following a similar technologically determinist argument, deindividuation theory correlates the anonymity and invisibility characterizing online interactions with anti-normative behavior, positing that '[b]eing unidentified and thereby unaccountable has the psychological consequence of reducing inner restraints and increasing behavior that is usually inhibited' (Postmes & Spears, 1998, p. 239). Anonymity, in the various degrees allowed by different social media platforms (Anonymous, 1998, p. 382), emerges as a key variable in discussions of problematic online practices (Tomita, 2005, p. 186), most recently and notably rehashed by the popularity of Anonymous, the collective movement supposedly emerging from the contentious and anti-normative environment of the 4chan image board (Bernstein et al., 2011, p. 53).

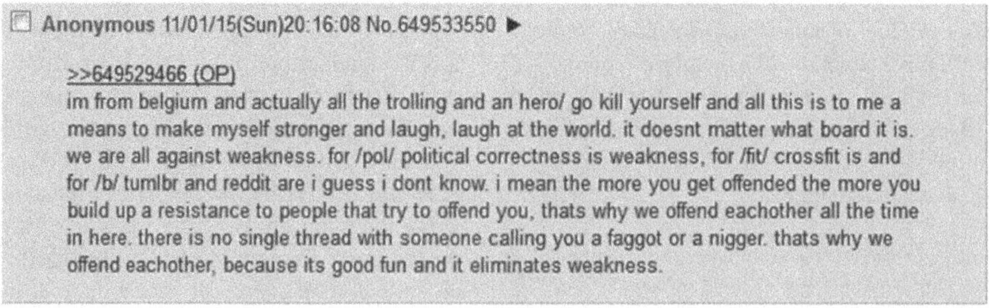

Anonymous 11/01/15(Sun)20:16:08 No.649533550 ▶

>>649529466 (OP)
im from belgium and actually all the trolling and an hero/ go kill yourself and all this is to me a means to make myself stronger and laugh. laugh at the world. it doesnt matter what board it is. we are all against weakness. for /pol/ political correctness is weakness, for /fit/ crossfit is and for /b/ tumlbr and reddit are i guess i dont know. i mean the more you get offended the more you build up a resistance to people that try to offend you, thats why we offend eachother all the time in here. there is no single thread with someone calling you a faggot or a nigger. thats why we offend eachother, because its good fun and it eliminates weakness.

Figure 21.4   Anonymous reply to a discussion thread about trolling I opened on 4chan

Definition <-> Contextualization

troll v.,n.
> To utter a posting on Usenet designed to attract predictable responses or flames. Derives from the phrase "trolling for newbies" which in turn comes from mainstream "trolling";, a style of fishing in which one trails bait through a likely spot hoping for a bite. The well-constructed troll is a post that induces lots of newbies and flamers to make themselves look even more clueless than they already do, while subtly conveying to the more savvy and experienced that it is in fact a deliberate troll. If you don't fall for the joke, you get to be in on it. (Andrew/, 1996)

The research literature mapped along the first axis of controversy in the previous section was chiefly concerned with the functional implications of trolling. Defining the practice itself – either as an essential component of early Internet culture or as a consequence of the technological constraints imposed by computer-mediated communication – appears to be a rather straightforward task. The definitions of terms like trolling, flaming, or spamming are directly lifted from the communities in which they are used (such as the explanation from *The Troller's FAQ* quoted above), interpreted by scholars who are at times part of these very same communities, and theorized either as activities contributing to online sociality, or as symptoms signaling the mediated occurrence of antisocial deviance. The second axis of controversy, introduced in this section, complicates the first, functional one by asking an epistemological question: should researchers strive to abstract trolling into a minimal, generalized definition, or should they rather pursue situated and contextual descriptions of problematic social media practices?

With the popularization of Internet access, the multiplication of online platforms, the advent of social media and the broadening spectrum of possible forms of networked participation, the definition of trolling becomes a problematic question in itself. As noted by Claire Hardaker, 'particularly within media and social networking circles,

it is possible to find widely divergent denotations and usages that make the creation of any clear definition [of trolling] almost impossible' (2015, p. 202). The dispersion of trolling across online communities, platform userbases and networked publics has resulted in two diametrically opposed epistemological approaches to this sort of social media practice: on the one hand, the effort to find a minimal definition of trolling that can be applied across disciplines and contexts; on the other hand, the choice to embrace differences and to focus instead on pragmatic explorations of what happens in particular socially mediated contexts.

The definitional effort is best represented by the work by O'Sullivan and Flanagin (2003) on what they call 'problematic messages'. In their paper, the authors lament the lack of 'precise conceptual and operational definitions of "flaming"' (O'Sullivan & Flanagin, 2003, p. 69), which leaves the discussion of problematic practices to popular opinion and news media, resulting in anxieties and moral panics about the Internet. O'Sullivan and Flanagin clearly write in reaction to existing academic literature, which they deem too technologically deterministic in its generalizing about different social media practices and defining them as antisocial, offensive, hostile or aggressive (2003, p. 72). Their solution comes from social semiotics: while recognizing that apparently hostile messages can be motivated by both antisocial attitudes and pro-social functions, the authors propose to ground their definition of a practice onto the context in which it occurs, supported by ethnographic attention to how users articulate local norms. O'Sullivan and Flanagin's definition of flaming – '*intentional (whether successful or unsuccessful) negative violations of (negotiated, evolving, and situated) interactional norms*' (2003, p. 84) – is by necessity minimal and open-ended, leaving room for changes of the practice in time and place, and for its adaptation to the analysis of other problematic social media practices such as online harassment, hate speech, and so on (2003, p. 88).

Claire Hardaker's extended research work on impoliteness in computer-mediated communication develops along similar vectors. By moving beyond deindividuation theory, she seeks to complicate the definition of impoliteness in online interactions through a careful mapping of its different nuances grounded on sociolinguistic evidence: 'a definition of trolling should be informed first and foremost by users discussions' (Hardaker, 2010, p. 215). Drawing on painstaking linguistic analyses of longitudinal activity in two Usenet newsgroups (*rec.equestrian* and *uk.sport.football*), Hardaker proposes her own definition of trolling: 'Trolling is the deliberate (perceived) use of impoliteness/ aggression, deception and/or manipulation in CMC to create a context conducive to triggering or antagonising conflict, typically for amusement's sake' (2013, p. 79). After honing in on this definition, Hardaker acknowledges that for many newsgroup members the identification of the practice is a similarly processual task: accusations of trolling are 'often co-constructed, sometimes through heated arguments spanning many days, involving dozens of users, and situated within a set of fluctuating, community-based norms' (2015, p. 205).

Approaches from the opposite end of the epistemological spectrum avoid the definitional problem altogether and begin from the situated contexts of different online communities and social media platforms. Over the past two decades, trolling has diversified beyond the well-documented acts of provocation and deception on mailing lists and newsgroups, and a wide variety of recent research has explored how problematic practices emerge and are dealt with on different online platforms (Fuller, McCrea, & Wilson, 2013, p. 4). In its most extreme formulation, this contextual approach argues that in the fluid ecologies of contemporary media, searching for a general definition of trolling might be a nearly futile exercise. In

his study of provocative humor shared on Facebook groups by Australian spectators of the 2012 London Olympic Games, Tama Leaver demands such a kind of epistemological contextualization as a prerequisite for any discussion of the topic: 'if trolling is situated as a practice to be addressed, then the term at least needs to be better explicated in each instance in order to ensure arguments and discussions of trolling are actually talking about the same thing' (2013, p. 221).

Grounding comparative descriptions of problematic social media practices onto the situated circumstances of use and their representation in popular media and academic discourses is necessary to understand what trolling is, and isn't, across different contexts. Moreover, trolling and similar terms are undeniably sites of prescription in themselves – similarly to the recurring anxieties around hacking or cybercrime, they can be 'actively *constructed* by governments, law enforcement, the computer security industry, businesses, and media' (Yar, 2005, p. 390). A classic example of the contextual approach to problematic social media practices is the work of Susan Herring and colleagues (2002) on a specific instance of trolling that caused trouble among the members of a feminist discussion board. Drawing on a detailed description of abusive interactions, the authors suggest a number of possible contextual interventions, such as the implementation of filtering functions and the improvement of community policies (Herring et al., 2002, p. 381, emphasis in original).

Similar studies demonstrate the variety of situational contexts and the importance of understanding local articulations of social media practices. For example, while Phillips (2011) demonstrates that trolling activity on Facebook memorial pages is underpinned by a critical attitude towards the platform's implementation of post-mortem profile pages and towards global media's obsession with tragedy, Shachaf and Hara (2010) find the trolling of entries on the Hebrew Wikipedia to be largely motivated by the boredom,

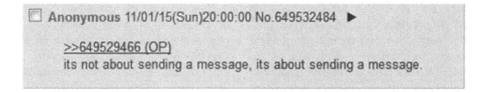

Figure 21.5   Anonymous reply to a discussion thread about trolling I opened on 4chan

attention seeking and vengeful resentment of a handful of users directly impacting on the community's well-being. Problematic practices not only differ across contexts, but might play out differently in structurally similar online environments: Binns (2012) describes the counter-strategies employed by online magazine editors to stymie trolling in comment sections and avoid disruption of the community atmosphere (2012, p. 554), but a study by Sindorf (2013) illustrates how similar moderation measures implemented by an online community newspaper to crack down on rude and insulting comments are widely perceived by the userbase as an overreaction and an attack on the democratic function of the comment section itself (2013, p. 195).

Endorsement <-> Critique

> [...] an entry in the prestigious Journal of Usenet Stupidasses written by an academic from the Department of Fine Malt Beverages at Bungmunch University. (Vrooman, 2002, p. 61)

The two axes of controversies outlined in the previous sections define a horizontal surface of inquiry concerned with the functional role of problematic practices and with the possible ways of knowing about these practices. Just like the epistemological axis complicates the functional one by questioning the researchers' definitions of trolling as an essential part of Internet culture or as an abject manifestation of antisocial behavior, the third axis proposed in this section complicates the previous two by introducing an ethical dimension: if problematic social

media practices are found to be socially productive for a certain community of users, should the sympathetic researcher take a stance and contribute to their defense from social stigma and mediated anxieties? If playful in-group activities become abusive and cause harm to individuals or communities, should the concerned scholar renounce impartiality and raise her voice to denounce these actions? In light of these ethical choices, how can researchers deal with communities that start talking back, reacting to their representation in academic discourse and media narratives?

An earnest sympathy for the emerging components of quickly changing social media cultures, combined with contextual attention to the local norms and functions of problematic practices, often results in scholars engaging in mildly defensive endorsements and ethical reappraisals of trolling. These sometimes hark back to histories of confrontational communication and disruptive performance in society, such as the long pedigree of rants and invective in American culture, which served 'an important social function in communicating social and political perspectives' (Vrooman, 2002, p. 56). Subcultural repertoires are another important point of reference for reassessments of problematic practices, and allow Coleman (2012) to position trolls within an extended history of technological mavericks, including phone phreakers and hackers. For Coleman, these figures of disruption can be interpreted as contemporary iterations on the mythical notion of the trickster, historical and fictional characters that recur across world cultures and are known for their 'acts of cunning, deceitfulness, lying, cheating, killing and destruction, hell raising, and as their name suggests, trickery' (Coleman, 2012, p. 115). This is a provocative genealogy, but as Boellstorff (2015) cautions, attempts at generalizing trolling by inscribing it in mythical archetypes can become functionalist tricks of perspective if they are not informed by anthropological evidence regarding the specific social implications and cultural contexts of tricksterism in world history and literature (2015, p. 394).

Also sympathetic towards trolling, but more mindful of the problematic politics of naming, are interventions that draw on first-hand involvement with different social media platforms and critical participation in networked publics. For Bergstrom (2011), the exaltation of disruptive figures should not obfuscate the fact that among many networked publics, the accusation of trolling is still deployed as an exclusionary category in itself, used 'as a justification for punishing those who transgress (or are accused of transgressing) an online community's norms'. Similarly, Sindorf (2013) warns that the very act of establishing the boundaries of trolling and incivility in increasingly commercialized online spaces requires prudent ethical positioning: 'who gets to decide what is and is not productive to debate? Are these distinctions that we feel comfortable making? Are these distinctions that we want someone else to make, especially when they may have financial motives at heart?' (Sindorf, 2013, p. 211). Ultimately, as McCosker (2014) argues through a study of media events and YouTube publics in New Zealand, defining problematic interactions on social media platforms as aberrant or antisocial can elide their participatory potential: 'provocation should be understood in context and examined in terms of the way it can not only problematise, but also productively intensify, vitalise and sustain publics within social media sites' (McCosker, 2014, p. 202).

Ethical choices not only determine researchers' positioning in relation to problematic practices, but the guiding metaphors they employ to describe social media. While authors leaning towards the reappraisal and endorsement of trolling tend to characterize online platforms as arenas for agonistic debate and democratic deliberation, scholars more concerned with the consequences of abusive interactions seek to ensure the existence of safe spaces (Herring et al., 2002) amidst the pervasively expanding hate space of the Internet (Shepherd, Harvey, Jordan, Srauy, & Miltner, 2015). The gendered nature of many online spaces and the predominance of sexist and misogynistic dimensions of abuse has been consistently traced from the early days of the medium, through hacking (Yar, 2005, p. 394) and gaming communities (Taylor, 2003, p. 37), to contemporary discussion boards and social media platforms (Phillips, 2013). In the case of 4chan's /b/ board, which Phillips identifies as a hotbed of trolling locked in a feedback loop of amplification with its own news media coverage, the difficulty in assessing user demographics behind the screen of anonymity should not hinder a recognition of 'the ways in which trolls' raced, classed and gendered bodies undergird and provide context for trolling behaviors' (Phillips, 2013, p. 495).

The work of Emma A. Jane presents a more radical critique of both trolling and of its appraisal in academic research. According to Jane, the numerous problematic practices described by scholarship about hostile communications on the Internet should be understood under the general header of 'e-bile', which she identifies as 'a type of vitriolic discourse notable for its hostile affect, explicit language, and stark misogyny' (Jane, 2015, p. 65). Besides agreeing with the claim that 'iterations of hate speech have become endemic to much online discourse' (Shepherd et al., 2015, p. 1), Jane argues that celebratory and dismissive scholarly accounts of abusive practices are complicit in overshadowing more ethically pressing questions about 'the real harms done to real victims in numerous real ways' (Jane, 2015, p. 70). Jane's evocative claim describing how 'toxic and often markedly misogynist e-bile no longer oozes only in the darkest digestive folds of the cybersphere but circulates freely through the entire body of the Internet' (2014, p. 532) stands in stark contrast to the functionalist folkloristics of flaming on academic mailing lists from two decades before.

Both the most apologetic chronicles of trolling and its most radical critiques are clearly speaking to a certain context – that of contemporary Anglophone cultural politics – and might seem puzzling to social media users from the increasingly diversified non-English language Internet. Yet, they suggest an important shift. As the editors of a recent journal issue about the topic argue, 'the way that we talk about trolls and trolling as a phenomenon of post-Internet culture places us in a broader, longer fight over the ethos, the history, and the politics of the digital' (Fuller et al., 2013, p. 2). Confronted with increasingly fluid media ecologies and expanding networked publics, academics are demanded to take ethical stances regarding problematic practices on social media, and to confront reactions from the communities that see their practices scrutinized and articulated by knowledge-producing outsiders (Figure 21.6).

THERE'S NO TROLLING IN CHINA

During my doctoral research I dedicated part of my ethnographic fieldwork on Chinese social media platforms to investigate the practice of trolling in a sociotechnical context noticeably distant from the Euro-American, Anglocentric media ecologies described by the majority of the existing scholarship on the topic (de Seta, 2013). The People's Republic of China hosts the world's largest Internet user population – 649 million users as of December 2014, 85.8% of which go online through a mobile device (CNNIC, 2015, pp. 25–28) – and the accelerated development of communication technologies in the country has been kept under close scrutiny as a key aspect to understand the growing prominence of the PRC in a global context (Zhou, 2006). The history of the Internet in China has been extensively chronicled over two decades of academic research both nationally and internationally (Qiu & Bu, 2013), with the majority of the literature focusing on the implications of the technology for online business, global Internet governance and local civil society (Herold & de Seta, 2015).

In terms of online platforms, the Chinese landscape is markedly shaped by the tight grip that the national authorities hold on Internet governance through incentives to the local industry, protectionist policies and outright censorship. Even though the impact of filtering systems and restrictive measures on user behavior is disputed (Taneja & Wu, 2014), it is undeniable that the situated predilections of hundreds of millions of local users result in a distinctly national Internet experience. Whereas contemporary narratives of the global Internet imagine the average user networking on Facebook, blogging on Twitter and Instagram, searching on Google or Yahoo!, chatting on Whatsapp or Snapchat, and watching videos on YouTube

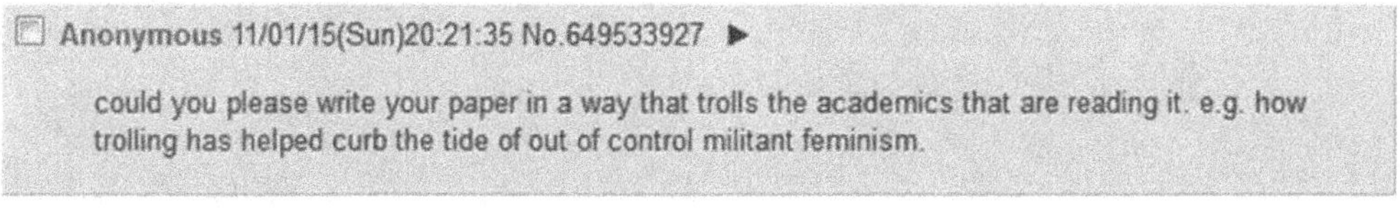

☐ Anonymous 11/01/15(Sun)20:21:35 No.649533927 ▶

could you please write your paper in a way that trolls the academics that are reading it. e.g. how trolling has helped curb the tide of out of control militant feminism.

Figure 21.6 **Anonymous reply to a discussion thread about trolling I opened on 4chan**

or Netflix, the majority of Chinese Internet users widely embrace homegrown services and platforms such as instant messaging software QQ, mobile social contact app WeChat, social networking websites QZone and Douban, microblogging platforms Sina Weibo and Tencent Weibo, search engine Baidu, video hosting service Youku Tudou, and so on. E-mail is rarely used, instant messaging plays an important role in everyday life, and online forums (locally called BBS, the acronym for bulletin board system) have remained popular since the early years of the medium (Wallis, 2011, p. 412), ranging from small communities to massive commercial or governmental platforms such as Baidu Tieba and Qiangguo Luntan (Damm, 2007, p. 413).

Besides the predominance of homegrown platforms and services, one of the most evident differences that I noticed at the beginning of my investigation was the absence of trolling in local media narratives. Whereas English-language popular media routinely describe trolling in terms of pranking, confrontation, harassment and abuse, in China mass-mediated anxieties related to the Internet tend to focus around a different set of practices and phenomena. During the time of my fieldwork (2013–2014), the most recurrent Internet-related anxieties were *renrou sousuo* [literally 'human-powered search'], a form of online vigilantism through doxing (F.-Y. Wang et al., 2010); the exploits of the *wumao dang* [fifty-cent party] of government-paid posters (Chen, Wu, Srinivasan, & Zhang, 2011); the activities of *shuijun* [literally 'water armies'] of

commercial astroturfers (Luo, 2010); and the propaganda department's push against loosely defined *yuyan baoli* [verbal violence] and *wangluo yaoyan* [Internet rumors] (Zhao, 2013). While these phenomena partially overlap with the problematic practices described in the first half of this chapter, the feelings and reactions articulated by local Internet users challenge simplistic equivalences with trolling. For example, recent surveys reveal the Chinese Internet users' widespread fear of becoming target of a *renrou sousuo* (Wallis, 2011, p. 421), while discussions with Chinese urban youth highlight anxieties about the potential dangers of emotional involvement with contentious online spaces, Internet rumors and personal attacks (Cockain, 2015, p. 59).

When I asked users of Sina Weibo, Douban, QQ and Baidu Tieba about trolling, I found myself in the awkward position of having to explain the meaning of the English language term through actual examples of problematic online interactions – often producing more confusion than clarity – which interviewees would interpret using a wide range of Chinese terms: 'this guy is just a *penzi*! [sprayer]', 'he is *zhao chou* [looking for trouble]', 'this post is *diaoyu* [fishing]', or 'this one is a *naocan* [braindamaged]' (de Seta, 2013, p. 308). While I regularly observed recurring instances of trolling across discussion boards and social media comment sections, these practices were never lumped under a single Chinese word that would directly translate to 'trolling', but were rather described through a range of specialized vernacular terms with well-documented popular etymologies (2013,

无标题 无名氏 2015-10-24(六)20:31:41 ID:hUvrWbC [举报] No.6922190

你这不就是在trolling吗

Figure 21.7 'Aren't you just trolling us with this thread?' Anonymous reply to a discussion thread about trolling I opened on the AC anonymous board

p. 310). As kindly explained to me by users of the AC anonymous board in a discussion organized during the writing of this chapter, among many possible contextual translations of trolling such as *hei* [to smear], *zhuonong* [playing with], *wunao pen* [mindless spraying], *diaoyu* [fishing] or *yinzhan* [to look for a fight], some originated from specific geographical areas and media environments – for example, in the case of *shua baimu* ['playing white eyes'], online gaming in Taiwan (Figure 21.8).

One of these many terms – *diaoyu*, which literally means 'fishing' – provides a clear example of how social media practices cannot be assumed to map smoothly across contexts. Suggested by many users as one possible translation of trolling, fishing is commonly practiced by posting *diaoyu tie* [fishing posts] or *diaoyu duanzi* [fishing bits], elaborated texts belonging to a vernacular repertoire of *diaoyu wen* [fishing literature]. *Diaoyu wen* includes fabricated news articles, carefully researched pseudo-scientific reports, and sensationalist social media posts written in specific stereotypical styles (de Seta, 2013, p. 311; Han, 2015, p. 1014). Here's a 'classic *diaoyu* bit' kindly

无标题 无名氏 2015-10-24(六)20:31:51 ID:MmQ8jTN [举报] No.6922192

黑

无标题 无名氏 2015-10-24(六)20:32:11 ID:GyppR8Q [举报] No.6922195

翻译就有～或者理解为捉弄(つдc)

无标题 无名氏 2015-10-24(六)20:32:49 ID:jCwO8jJ [举报] No.6922199

无脑喷。。。

无标题 无名氏 2015-10-24(六)20:33:56 ID:IAkcbQP [举报] No.6922205

釣魚、引|戰吧
台灣很流行lol, 裡面這個詞這意思就是要白目
故意亂玩讓對方贏之類的
其他就比較少看到這個字了

无标题 无名氏 2015-10-24(六)20:34:12 ID:m3c89qV [举报] No.6922207

就是钓鱼啊。。

Figure 21.8 'In Taiwan League of Legends is really popular, and the word used in that game is *shua baimu*, it means something like playing carelessly on purpose and letting the opponent win.' Anonymous replies to a discussion thread about trolling I opened on the AC anonymous board

shared with me by one user of the AC anonymous board:

> There're surely a lot of *wumao* here, is the sentence 'giving money to the people' enough to make you feel uncomfortable? Giving money to the people is always be better than giving it to the leaders, right? My classmate's father took part in the construction of the Three Gorges Dam, there was one time he drank too much and told me that the thing actually only cost less than five hundred million US dollars. So the question is, where did the remaining twenty billion dollars go? Just let your imagination fly. You shouldn't always indulge in comics and cartoons; if you have the chance, go learn how to cross the firewall, you will be able to see a different world. Since when we entered the month of July, it seems like a lot of people supporting the Party and the government have appeared around here, summer holidays did really arrive uh.

This *diaoyu duanzi*, known as *sanxia wuyi* [Three Gorges's Five Hundred Million], was originally posted in July 2012 as a comment to an article about the success of the Three Gorges Dam, and generated over one thousand responses for its outrageous claims based on hearsay (Moegirlpedia contributors, 2015). After being thoroughly debunked by members of the AC community, the comment has been incorporated in a repertoire of fishing literature, and its occasional reposting plays on multiple layers of humor. For uninformed audiences, the conceited prose reads as a smug mockery of discussion board users themselves, described as narrow-minded *wumao* ['fifty-cent' paid posters] who waste their summer holidays on comics and cartoons; when posted at the right time, this *diaoyu duanzi* might successfully elicit replies by outraged newcomers. For community members in the know, the reproduction of the post evokes the collective process of debunking the ungrounded allegations formulated by the original author, and stimulates further debate about the formal characteristics, discursive strategies and political leanings of fishing posts, consolidating the community's repertoire of *diaoyu wen*.

Compared with a similar practice on Usenet, where trolling posts are customarily explained as confrontational gatekeeping practices useful to protect specialized online communities from the unchecked influx of newcomers, *diaoyu* is interpreted by discussion board users as an occasion to engage in a collective fact-checking exercise in response to widespread anxieties about the dissemination of rumors and personal accusations by paid posters and propaganda workers, and about the radicalization of political conflict in online spaces (Wu, 2012, p. 2227). The communal creation of a repertoire of debunked rumors and failed provocations, maintained as a repository of community knowledge and disseminated for in-group amusement, evidences how tightly social

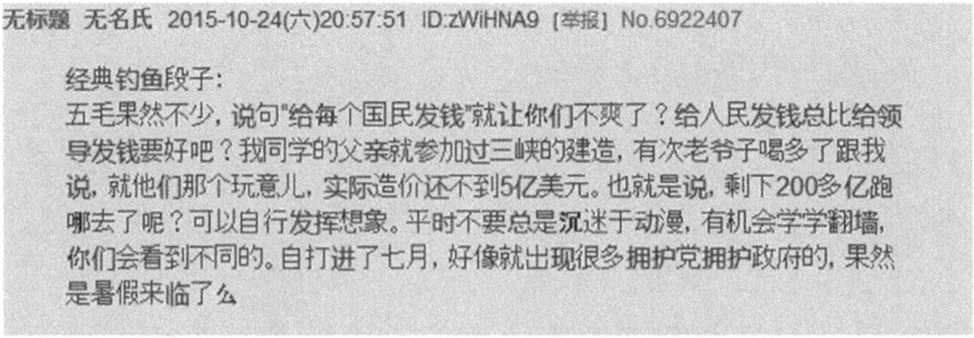

无标题 无名氏 2015-10-24(六)20:57:51 ID:zWiHNA9 [举报] No.6922407

经典钓鱼段子:
五毛果然不少,说句"给每个国民发钱"就让你们不爽了?给人民发钱总比给领导发钱要好吧?我同学的父亲就参加过三峡的建造,有次老爷子喝多了跟我说,就他们那个玩意儿,实际造价还不到5亿美元。也就是说,剩下200多亿跑哪去了呢?可以自行发挥想象。平时不要总是沉迷于动漫,有机会学学翻墙,你们会看到不同的。自打进了七月,好像就出现很多拥护党拥护政府的,果然是暑假来临了么

Figure 21.9 'A classic *diaoyu* bit.' Anonymous reply to a discussion thread about trolling I opened on the AC anonymous board

media practices are tied to local sociotechnical contexts and situated experiences of use across multiple scales. In the case of trolling in China, these include everything from the larger media ecologies of national platforms and services to the massive linguistic context of the Chinese-speaking Internet, down to the infra-ordinary experiences of discussion board users and their situated interpretations of specific media practices and texts.

SOCIAL, MEDIA, PRACTICES

Even though the Victorian Internet, a term coined by Tom Standage to refer to the telegraph system of the late nineteenth century, did not include such parasitical entities as worms and viruses, the discursive position of the anomalous was filled with other kinds of near-mythical instances of the uncanny. […] Often these were part of the folk culture of the new media rather than official concerns […]. Yet the short story "The Volcanograph" introduces how weird objects of network culture had already spread in the nineteenth century. The short story depicts "hobgoblins" who keep disturbing proper communicative events. The unwanted intruders that keep "breaking in" on the channels are given a lesson with the aid of a telegraphic bomb, a countermeasure of a kind. (Parikka, 2011, p. 268)

The mythologies of communicational disturbances uncovered by Jussi Parikka in the passages quoted above testify to the all-too-human propensity to make sense of problematic presences in technological networks by constructing folk cultures of new media populated by weird objects and uncanny figures. The difference between nineteenth-century hobgoblins disturbing telegraphic conversations and twenty-first-century trolls wreaking havoc on social media is that today, these near-mythical figures increasingly embody official concerns about a wide variety of media practices.

In this chapter I contended that social media practices commonly identified as problematic, confrontational, aggressive, abusive, or antisocial are an important topic of inquiry not simply due to their supposed resistive or recalcitrant qualities, but because they exemplify how much of contemporary media use is continuously constructed at the intersection of infra-ordinary experiences, popular media narratives, and academic discourses. If it's true that we (academics, journalists, social media users) talk about trolling only through *polemics* (Fuller et al., 2013, p. 1), then perhaps this chapter provides some directions to move towards more productive *problemizations* (Foucault, 1984, p. 384) of what the terms social, media and practices imply when they are used to articulate each other.

After recalling some first-hand experiences of problematic online interactions from my early years of Internet presence, I argued that social media practices are complex arrangements of technologies and usages, the articulation of which is unavoidably grounded in individual and self-reflexive experiences across time and space. Trolling, along with related problematic practices such as flaming, spamming, cyber-bullying and online abuse, belongs to a wider congeries of social media practices resulting from the popularization of Internet access and participatory digital media platforms. While portrayals of trolling in popular media have repeatedly oversimplified the phenomenon to foster anxieties and moral panics about networked communications, academic research has painstakingly attempted to account for the practice beyond such generalizations. In the first half of this chapter, I proposed a genealogy of two decades of research literature into problematic social media practices by distributing it along three axes of controversies: the tension between descriptions of trolling as functional component of Internet culture and its diagnoses as deviant online behavior (*Culture <-> Deviance*); the contrast between attempts to derive a general definition of the practice and efforts at emphasizing its situated circumstances (*Definition <-> Contextualization*); and the debates between sympathetic reappraisals of problematic interactions versus their critical condemnation (*Endorsement <-> Critique*).

Mapping a selection of the existing research literature along these three axes highlights the various theoretical and methodological contributions provided by scholarly treatments of the topic, and disproves the recurring claims that trolling is an inexorably understudied phenomenon. In actuality, a sustained cross-disciplinary engagement with problematic social media practices has resulted in important conclusions: trolling isn't a necessarily antisocial practice, but it can contribute to community cohesion as much as damage it; confrontational interactions don't directly result from the technological affordances of social media platforms, but can be mitigated with the implementation of ad-hoc measures; generalized definitions of problematic practices can be useful heuristics for further research, but risk flattening or misinterpreting their local articulations; and the positional and ethical choices made by the researcher ultimately determine which productive and abusive aspects are emphasized or obfuscated in academic accounts of problematic social media practices. The choice of distributing research literature along three axes describing functional, epistemological and ethical continuums is not presented as a definitive mapping of the field and can be expanded or reconfigured according to different dimensions, but has the advantage of opening up a wide variety of possible approaches to the topic while also hinting at zones of opportunity for future inquiry: when, and where, is trolling defined as such, and by whom? How is the problematization of a certain practice negotiated between communities of social media users and networked publics? What positionality does the researcher choose when confronted with problematic practices, and how are users portrayed in the research output?

In the second half of this chapter I presented a short overview of a research project about problematic interactions on Chinese social media platforms, highlighting how the loss in translation of the term trolling has lead my inquiry towards a rich repertoire of locally articulated practices tightly connected to different contextual scales. By focusing on the specific case of *diaoyu* [fishing] on a Chinese discussion board, I explained how the communal creation and dissemination of a repertoire of debunked rumors and failed provocations is linked to national media ecologies, informational anxieties and platform-specific interactional practices. Contrasting a predominantly Anglocentric research literature with a case study from China is not meant to be a call to de-westernize social media studies by presenting exotic social media contexts as sites of difference and otherness, but is rather intended as a way to question a practice by drawing on ethnographic attention to its situated articulations. Alireza Doostdar's account of *ebtezaar* [vulgarity] as a linguistic practice among Iranian bloggers (2004) and Sahana Udupa's work on the social and mediated construction of *gaali* [abuse] by Indian Twitter users (2015) are other examples of this research approach. According to Udupa's findings, for instance, accusations and dismissals of *gaali* are central concerns for Indian Twitter users who want to engage in highly confrontational debates around Hindu–Muslim politics. Unraveling the situated articulations of the practice reveals its grounding in India's history of political language play, its role in ritual social relationships during Hindu festivities, and its contemporary deployment as a gendered re-politicization of the domestic sphere (2015, pp. 7–14).

To conclude, it might be helpful to openly situate my own approach to problematic practices in terms of the same axes I used to distribute a substantial body of existing research, and to suggest some promising directions for future research endeavors. For my own inquiry, I adopt a neutral position on the functional axis (trolling is not a constitutive component of Internet culture nor necessarily deviant behavior), a radically contextual position on the epistemological axis (trolling has to be understood in situated social settings), and an agnostic position on the ethical axis (my representation of trolling doesn't side either with or against the practice). These choices lead to my preference for ethnographic and dialogic accounts of trolling and other problematic social media practices, a solution close to the one Whelan (2013, p. 57) derives from ethnomethodology: 'Naming behaviour as trolling is not deploying an objective and stable descriptor to convey a meaning about a social practice which is somehow itself before we get to it, it is a means of producing a social practice itself as meaningful.' Considering practices as being constantly produced by their own social and situated articulations is a promising starting point to engage with the mythical figures and folk cultures of new media beyond reductive dualisms and assumptions regarding the homogeneity of sociotechnical worlds (Crook, 1998).

Following these decisions, I take trolling as a starting point to understand 'the place of provocation in its multiple, highly contextualised and always changing forms' (McCosker, 2014, p. 202), and as an example of how problematic practices can be disentangled from the polemics developing around them. Another advantage of an ethnographic approach to social media practices is its sensitivity to the 'aspects of everyday internet use that often remain unnoticed' (Lovink, 2011, p. 10). The capacity of tuning into the trivial everyday that Georges Perec would call infra-ordinary as its extends into our sociotechnically mediated lives (Bassett, 2012, p. 111) allows ethnographically grounded inquiry to avoid both the over-simplification of popular media narratives and the overdetermination of disciplinary discourses. In times when media become increasingly fluid ensembles of technologies, platforms and forms of access, turning problematic practices into problemizations of the infra-ordinary experience of mediated sociality can be a fruitful strategy to gain a better understanding of the interrelation of media

and practice (Bräuchler & Postill, 2010). As Perec recognizes, turning towards the infra-ordinary results in research outcomes that appear fragmentary, apparently trivial, and 'barely indicative of a method, at most of a project' (1997, p. 178). This, I argue, is in fact what makes this turn essential: by moving towards the domain of the trivial and the infra-ordinary, I hope that my contribution provides a sense of 'how thoroughly social, how culturally and semantically articulated, how under-determined and contingent media production, reception and use are in practice' (Hobart, 2014, p. 517). Grounding ethnographic accounts of infra-ordinary mediated sociality on such radical notions of under-determination and contingency will become increasingly essential for future discussions of trolling and other problematic social media practices.

Note

1   4chan is an English-language bulletin board launched in 2003 and hosted in the USA. Modeled on the popular Japanese image board Futaba Channel, 4chan is divided into several thematic sections, does not require registration, and it has become known for its users' participation in various forms of disruptive activities. The AC anonymous board (AC *nimingban*) is a Chinese-language image board launched in 2011 by the video-sharing website AcFun and hosted in the People's Republic of China. Also modeled on Futaba Channel, the AC anonymous board is divided in numerous thematic sections, encourages anonymous participation, and at the time of writing moderates posting through timed cookies.

REFERENCES

Allaway, J. (2014, October 13). #Gamergate trolls aren't ethics crusaders; they're a hate group. Retrieved October 29, 2015, from http://jezebel.com/gamergate-trolls-arent-ethics-crusaders-theyre-a-hate-1644984010

Andrew/. (1996). The Troller's FAQ. Retrieved October 30, 2015, from https://web.archive.

org/web/20030105223101/http://www.
altairiv.demon.co.uk/afaq/posts/trollfaq.html

Anonymous. (1998). To reveal or not to reveal: A theoretical model of anonymous communication. *Communication Theory*, *8*(4), 381–407.

Bassett, C. (2012). The real estate of the trained-up self (Or is this England?). In R. Wilken & G. Goggin (Eds.), *Mobile technology and place* (pp. 104–120). New York: Routledge.

Baym, N. K. (1994). From practice to culture on Usenet. *The Sociological Review*, *42*(S1), 29–52.

Baym, N. K. (1995). The performance of humor in computer-mediated communication. *Journal of Computer-Mediated Communication*, *1*(2). http://doi.org/10.1111/j.1083-6101.1995.tb00327.x

Baym, N. K. (2010). *Personal connections in the digital age*. Cambridge, UK: Polity Press.

Bergstrom, K. (2011). 'Don't feed the troll': Shutting down debate about community expectations on Reddit.com. *First Monday*, *16*(8). Retrieved from http://firstmonday.org/ojs/index.php/fm/article/viewArticle/3498

Bernstein, M. S., Monroy-Hernández, A., Harry, D., André, P., Panovich, K., & Vargas, G. G. (2011). 4chan and /b/: An analysis of anonymity and ephemerality in a large online community. In *Proceedings of the Fifth International AAAI Conference on Weblogs and Social Media* (pp. 50–57). Barcelona, Spain: Association for the Advancement of Artificial Intelligence. Available at www.aaai.org/ocs/index.php/ICWSM/ICWSM11/paper/viewFile/2873/4398 (accessed on 1 August, 2017).

Binns, A. (2012). Don't feed the trolls!: Managing troublemakers in magazines' online communities. *Journalism Practice*, *6*(4), 547–562. http://doi.org/10.1080/17512786.2011.648988

Bishop, J. (2012). The psychology of trolling and lurking: The role of defriending and gamification for increasing participation in online communities using seductive narratives. In H. Li (Ed.), *Virtual community participation and motivation: Cross-disciplinary theories* (pp. 160–176). Hershey, PA: IGI Global.

Boellstorff, T. (2015). Audience, genre, method, theory. *HAU: Journal of Ethnographic Theory*, *5*(2), 391–397. http://doi.org/10.14318/hau5.2.023

boyd, danah. (2011). Social network sites as networked publics: Affordances, dynamics, and implications. In Z. Papacharissi (Ed.), *A networked self: Identity, community and culture on social network sites* (pp. 39–58). New York: Routledge.

Bräuchler, B., & Postill, J. (Eds.). (2010). *Theorising media and practice*. New York: Berghahn Books.

Buckels, E. E., Trapnell, P. D., & Paulhus, D. L. (2014). Trolls just want to have fun. *Personality and Individual Differences*, *67*, 97–102. http://doi.org/10.1016/j.paid.2014.01.016

Chen, C., Wu, K., Srinivasan, V., & Zhang, X. (2011). *Battling the internet water army: Detection of hidden paid posters*. Retrieved from http://arxiv.org/abs/1111.4297

CNNIC. (2015). *The 35th statistical survey on Internet development in China*. Beijing, China: China Internet Network Information Center. Retrieved from www1.cnnic.cn/IDR/ReportDownloads/201507/P020150720486421654597.pdf

Cockain, A. (2015). Regarding subjectivities and social life on the screen: The ambivalences of spectatorship in the People's Republic of China. In P. Marolt & D. K. Herold (Eds.), *China online: Locating society in online spaces* (pp. 49–66). Abingdon, UK: Routledge.

Coleman, E. G. (2012). Phreaks, hackers, and trolls: The politics of transgression and spectacle. In M. Mandiberg (Ed.), *The social media reader* (pp. 99–119). New York: New York University Press.

Crook, S. (1998). Minotaurs and other monsters: 'Everyday life' in recent social theory. *Sociology*, *32*(3), 523–540. http://doi.org/10.1177/0038038598032003007

Damm, J. (2007). The Internet and fragmentation of Chinese society. *Critical Asian Studies*, *39*(2), 273–294. http://doi.org/10.1080/14672710701339485

de Seta, G. (2013). Spraying, fishing, looking for trouble: The Chinese Internet and a critical perspective on the concept of trolling. *The Fibreculture Journal*, *22*, 301–317.

Dibbell, J. (1993, December 23). A rape in cyberspace. *The Village Voice*, pp. 36–42. New York.

Donath, J. S. (1999). Identity and deception in the virtual community. In M. A. Smith & P. Kollock (Eds.), *Communities in cyberspace* (pp. 27–59). London: Routledge.

Doostdar, A. (2004). 'The vulgar spirit of blogging': On language, culture, and power in Persian weblogestan. *American Anthropologist*, *106*(4), 651–662.

Fichman, P., & Sanfilippo, M. R. (2015). The bad boys and girls of cyberspace: How gender and context impact perception of and reaction to trolling. *Social Science Computer Review*, *33*(2), 163–180. http://doi.org/10.1177/0894439314533169

Foucault, M. (1980). *Power/knowledge: Selected interviews & other writings, 1972–1977*. (C. Gordon, Ed., C. Gordon, L. Marshall, J. Mepham, & K. Soper, Trans.). New York: Pantheon Books.

Foucault, M. (1984). Polemics, politics, and problemizations: An interview with Michel Foucault. In P. Rabinow (Ed.), *The Foucault reader* (pp. 381–390). New York: Pantheon Books.

Fuller, G., McCrea, C., & Wilson, J. (2013). Troll theory? *The Fibreculture Journal*, *22*, 1–14.

Han, R. (2015). Defending the authoritarian regime online: China's 'voluntary fifty-cent army'. *The China Quarterly*, *224*, 1006–1025. http://doi.org/10.1017/S0305741015001216

Hardaker, C. (2010). Trolling in asynchronous computer-mediated communication: From user discussions to academic definitions. *Journal of Politeness Research*, *6*, 215–242. http://doi.org/10.1515/JPLR.2010.011

Hardaker, C. (2013). 'Uh....not to be nitpicky,,,,,but...the past tense of drag is dragged, not drug': An overview of trolling strategies. *Journal of Language Aggression and Conflict*, *1*(1), 58–86. http://doi.org/10.1075/jlac.1.1.04har

Hardaker, C. (2015). 'I refuse to respond to this obvious troll': An overview of responses to (perceived) trolling. *Corpora*, *10*(2), 201–229. http://doi.org/10.3366/cor.2015.0074

Herold, D. K., & de Seta, G. (2015). Through the looking glass: Twenty years of Chinese Internet research. *The Information Society*, *31*(1), 68–82. http://doi.org/10.1080/01972243.2014.976688

Herring, S., Job-Sluder, K., Scheckler, R., & Barab, S. (2002). Searching for safety online: Managing 'trolling' in a feminist forum. *The Information Society*, *18*(5), 371–384. http://doi.org/10.1080/01972240290108186

Hobart, M. (2014). When is Indonesia? *Asian Journal of Social Science*, *41*(5), 510–529. http://doi.org/10.1163/15685314-12341315

Jane, E. A. (2014). 'Your a ugly, whorish, slut': Understanding e-bile. *Feminist Media Studies*, *14*(4), 531–546. http://doi.org/10.1080/14680777.2012.741073

Jane, E. A. (2015). Flaming? What flaming? The pitfalls and potentials of researching online hostility. *Ethics and Information Technology*, *17*(1), 65–87. http://doi.org/10.1007/s10676-015-9362-0

Kiesler, S., Siegel, J., & McGuire, T. W. (1984). Social psychological aspects of computer-mediated communication. *American Psychologist*, *39*(10), 1123–1134. http://doi.org/10.1037/0003-066X.39.10.1123

Koopman, C. (2011). Genealogical pragmatism: How history matters for Foucault and Dewey. *Journal of the Philosophy of History*, *5*(3), 533–561. http://doi.org/10.1163/187226311X599943

Leaver, T. (2013). Olympic trolls: Mainstream memes and digital discord? *The Fibreculture Journal*, *22*, 216–232.

Lee, H. (2005). Behavioral strategies for dealing with flaming in an online forum. *The Sociological Quarterly*, *46*(2), 385–403.

Lovink, G. (2011). *Networks without a cause: A critique of social media*. Cambridge, UK: Polity Press.

Luo, Q. (2010, November 26). Wodi shuijun riji [An undercover paid poster's diary]. Retrieved October 5, 2014, from www.infzm.com/content/52792

Marvin, L.-E. (1995). Spoof, spam, lurk, and lag: The aesthetics of text-based virtual realities. *Journal of Computer-Mediated Communication*, *1*(2). http://doi.org/10.1111/j.1083-6101.1995.tb00324.x

McCosker, A. (2014). Trolling as provocation: YouTube's agonistic publics. *Convergence: The International Journal of Research into New Media Technologies*, *20*(2), 201–217. http://doi.org/10.1177/1354856513501413

Millard, W. B. (1997). I flamed Freud: A case study in teletextual incendiarism. In D. Porter (Ed.), *Internet culture* (pp. 145–159). New York: Routledge.

Moegirlpedia contributors. (2015, March 13). Sanxia wuyi [Three Gorges' five hundred million]. In *Moegirlpedia*. Retrieved from http://zh.moegirl.org/%E4%B8%89%E5%B3%A1%E4%BA%94%E4%BA%BF

Myers, D. (1987). 'Anonymity is part of the magic': Individual manipulation of computer-mediated communication contexts. *Qualitative Sociology, 10*(3), 251–266. http://doi.org/10.1007/BF00988989

O'Neil, L. (2015, October 20). #BoycottStarWarsVII and why the Internet is trolling itself to death. Retrieved October 29, 2015, from www.esquire.com/entertainment/movies/news/a39017/boycottstarwarsvii-troll/

O'Sullivan, P. B., & Flanagin, A. J. (2003). Reconceptualizing 'flaming' and other problematic messages. *New Media & Society, 5*(1), 69–94. http://doi.org/10.1177/1461444803005001908

Pao, E. (2015, July 16). Former Reddit CEO Ellen Pao: The trolls are winning the battle for the Internet. *The Washington Post*. Retrieved from www.washingtonpost.com/opinions/we-cannot-let-the-internet-trolls-win/2015/07/16/91b1a2d2-2b17-11e5-bd33-395c05608059_story.html

Parikka, J. (2011). Mapping noise: Techniques and tactics of irregularities, interception, and disturbance. In E. Huhtamo & J. Parikka (Eds.), *Media archaeology: Approaches, applications, and implications* (pp. 256–277). Berkeley, CA: University of California Press.

Perec, G. (1997). *Species of spaces and other pieces*. (J. Sturrock, Trans.). London: Penguin.

Phillips, W. (2011). LOLing at tragedy: Facebook trolls, memorial pages and resistance to grief online. *First Monday, 16*(12). Retrieved from http://firstmonday.org/htbin/cgiwrap/bin/ojs/index.php/fm/article/viewArticle/3168/3115

Phillips, W. (2013). The house that Fox built: Anonymous, spectacle, and cycles of amplification. *Television & New Media, 14*(6), 494–509. http://doi.org/10.1177/1527476412452799

Porter, D. (1997). Introduction. In D. Porter (Ed.), *Internet culture* (pp. ix–xviii). New York: Routledge.

Postmes, T., & Spears, R. (1998). Deindividuation and antinormative behavior: A meta-analysis. *Psychological Bulletin, 123*(3), 238–259.

Qiu, J. L., & Bu, W. (2013). China ICT studies: A review of the field, 1989–2012. *China Review, 13*(2), 123–152.

Rabinow, P. (2003). *Anthropos today: Reflections on modern equipment*. Princeton, NJ: Princeton University Press.

Rainie, L., & Wellman, B. (2012). *Networked: The new social operating system*. Cambridge, MA: MIT Press.

Shachaf, P., & Hara, N. (2010). Beyond vandalism: Wikipedia trolls. *Journal of Information Science, 36*(3), 357–370. http://doi.org/10.1177/0165551510365390

Shepherd, T., Harvey, A., Jordan, T., Srauy, S., & Miltner, K. (2015). Histories of hating. *Social Media + Society, 1*(2), 1–10. http://doi.org/doi: 10.1177/2056305115603997

Sindorf, S. (2013). Symbolic violence in the online field: Calls for 'civility' in online discussion. *The Fibreculture Journal, 22*, 194–215.

Stivale, C. J. (1997). Spam: Heteroglossia and harassment in cyberspace. In D. Porter (Ed.), *Internet culture* (pp. 133–144). New York: Routledge.

Suler, J. (2004). The online disinhibition effect. *Cyberpsychology & Behavior, 7*(3), 321–326.

Taneja, H., & Wu, A. X. (2014). Does the Great Firewall really isolate the Chinese? Integrating access blockage with cultural factors to explain Web user behavior. *The Information Society, 30*(5), 297–309. http://doi.org/10.1080/01972243.2014.944728

Taylor, T. L. (2003). Multiple pleasures: Women and online gaming. *Convergence: The International Journal of Research into New Media Technologies, 9*(1), 21–46.

Tepper, M. (1997). Usenet communities and the cultural politics of information. In D. Porter (Ed.), *Internet culture* (pp. 39–54). New York: Routledge.

Tomita, H. (2005). Keitai and the intimate stranger. In M. Ito, D. Okabe, & M. Matsuda (Eds.), *Personal, portable, pedestrian: Mobile phones in Japanese life* (pp. 183–201). Cambridge, MA: MIT Press.

Udupa, S. (2015). Abusive exchange on social media: The politics of online Gaali cultures in India. *EASA Media Anthro E-seminar*. Retrieved from www.media-anthropology.net/file/udupa_abusive_exchange.pdf

Vangelisti, A. L., & Crumley, L. P. (1998). Reactions to messages that hurt: The influence of relational contexts. *Communication Monographs*, *65*(3), 173–196. http://doi.org/10.1080/03637759809376447

Vrooman, S. S. (2002). The art of invective: Performing identity in cyberspace. *New Media & Society*, *4*(1), 51–70.

Wallis, C. (2011). New media practices in China: Youth patterns, processes, and politics. *International Journal of Communication*, *5*, 406–436.

Wang, F.-Y., Zeng, D., Hendler, J. A., Zhang, Q., Feng, Z., Gao, Y., … Lai, G. (2010). A study of the human flesh search engine: Crowd-powered expansion of online knowledge. *Computer*, *43*(8), 45–53.

Wang, H., & Hong, Y. (1996). Flaming: More than a necessary evil for academic mailing lists? *Electronic Journal of Communication/La Revue Electronique de Communication*, *6*(1).

Whelan, A. M. (2013). Even with cruise control you still have to steer: Defining trolling to get things done. *The Fibreculture Journal*, *22*, 36–60.

Wu, A. X. (2012). Hail the independent thinker: The emergence of public debate culture on the Chinese Internet. *International Journal of Communication*, *6*, 2220–2244.

Yar, M. (2005). Computer hacking: Just another case of juvenile delinquency? *The Howard Journal of Criminal Justice*, *44*(4), 387–399.

Zavadski, K. (2015, November 9). 'Terrorist' troll pretended to be ISIS, white supremacist, and Jewish lawyer. Retrieved October 28, 2015, from www.thedailybeast.com/articles/2015/09/11/terrorist-troll-pretended-to-be-isis-white-supremacist-and-jewish-lawyer.html

Zhao, Q. (2013, August 24). Fazhi zilv xiang jiehe jiancheng wangluo yaoyan fanghuoqiang [The combination of rule of law and self-discipline to erect a firewall for online rumors]. Retrieved August 25, 2013, from http://news.xinhuanet.com/legal/2013-08/24/c_117078618.htm

Zhou, Y. (2006). *Historicizing online politics: Telegraphy, the Internet, and political participation in China*. Stanford, CA: Stanford University Press.

22

Internet Memes

Kate M. Miltner

INTRODUCTION

The fact that this chapter exists is somewhat remarkable. Not, of course, that approximately 8,000 words were written and published in a massive tome (although that does take quite a bit of effort), but the fact that a major academic publisher thinks that the topic of internet memes is canonical enough to include in a Handbook of Social Media. In 2010, you could count the number of scholars interested in internet memes on one, maybe two hands. Furthermore, most of those scholars had to consistently make their case as to why pictures of cats with misspelled captions or videos of New Jersey teenagers lip synching to Moldovan pop songs were worthy of academic inquiry.

In our current media landscape, such arguments are less necessary. In the space of a decade, internet memes have gone from quirky, subcultural oddities to a ubiquitous, arguably foundational, digital media practice. From Comedy Central's television program Tosh.0

to the endless listicles of Buzzfeed, an entire media infrastructure has developed to report on, disseminate, and dissect the newest piece of digital culture to emerge, whether that is weekly, daily, or hourly. As internet scholar Ryan Milner (2016, p. i) notes in the introduction to his new book on memes, 'it's hard to imagine a major pop cultural or political moment that doesn't inspire its own constellation of mediated remix, play, and commentary'. Similarly, digital culture scholar Limor Shifman (2013b, p. 3) has argued that our media landscape is governed by a 'hyper-memetic logic' where 'almost every major public event sprouts a stream of memes'.

However, while memes' omnipresence may make meme research more legible to both academic and lay audiences, it is not the key to their significance. Memes were important before they were ubiquitous because they represent a practice of vernacular creativity (Burgess, 2006), a blending of folk practices (such as storytelling) with contemporary media savvy and skill. In this way, they act like a funhouse mirror for culture and society, reflecting and refracting the anxieties and preoccupations of a variety of social groups across a series of national contexts. Memes have always been a method of circulating ideas and influencing discourse; they just do so now on a grander, more rapid scale than they did in the late 1990s and early 2000s. As Limor Shifman argues in her book *Memes in Digital Culture*, 'internet memes are like Forrest Gump. Ostensibly, they are trivial pieces of pop culture; yet, a deeper look reveals that they play an integral part in some of the defining events of the twenty-first century' (2013, p. 4).

This chapter is constructed as a primer on internet memes and internet meme research. It aims to provide a solid foundation in the theoretical and empirical work that has been done on internet memes up to this moment (2016), while simultaneously illustrating the significance of internet memes for students of communication, sociology, anthropology, cultural studies, or any other discipline invested in what has come to be known as participatory culture (Jenkins, 2006). It will discuss the theoretical origins and definition of memes, and trace the history of internet memes from the late 1990s to the current moment. It will examine memes as a political and activist practice in cultures across the world, and it will explore the process of commodification that memes have undergone as they moved from subcultural to mainstream media realms. Finally, it will discuss the current state of meme research and avenues for further scholarly investigation.

WHAT IS A MEME?

In 1976, evolutionary biologist Richard Dawkins published *The Selfish Gene*. In it, he made the case for a new unit, a 'cultural replicator' that spread ideas and behaviors in an infectious, gene-like fashion among individuals and populations alike. He called this unit the 'meme', short for 'mimema', an ancient Greek word meaning 'that which is imitated' or 'imitated thing.' The concept of the meme is based upon the principle of Universal Darwinism, which argues that any information that is varied and selected will produce design, whether that is biological or cultural. That is to say, Dawkins believed that information – whether in the form of a gene or a song – is interested in one thing, which is to be spread far and wide. Dawkins argued that these 'viruses of the mind' – which can be anything from the Happy Birthday song to religious beliefs – have a certain agency of their own, and propagate themselves to ensure their survival.

While Dawkins has since distanced himself from memetics, others took his ideas and developed them into a field of study. Scholars such as Richard Brodie (2009) and Susan Blackmore (2000) argued that humans are merely hosts and propagating machinery for memes. They maintain that humans developed to receive and spread memes, such as language – versus the other way around. From this point of view, information is selfish and strives to get copied, regardless of the consequences. While controversial, this position still has certain proponents; in 2014, *TechCrunch* journalist Josh Constine explained the results of a Facebook social influence study with the headline 'Facebook Data Scientists Prove Memes Mutate and Adapt Like DNA', stating that 'memes adapt to their surroundings in order to survive, just like organisms' (Constine, 2014).

In the internet studies/cultural studies world, memes are treated as media objects with particular characteristics and and associated practices instead of self-propelling ideas. Media scholar Limor Shifman (2013a) argues that Dawkinsian memes and internet memes are both social phenomena that are reproduced by various means of imitation and are diffused through competition and selection. However, Shifman (2013a, p. 367) contends that the issue of human agency is central to understanding internet memes, defining them as 'units of popular culture that are circulated, imitated, and transformed by individual Internet users, creating a shared cultural experience in the process.'

Similarly, Henry Jenkins, Sam Ford, and Joshua Green (2013) assert that internet memes, which they describe as 'spreadable media', are successful because they allow different audiences to make their own meanings from the same media artifact; the specific element within each internet meme that strikes a chord will differ from person to person. Internet memes are texts, and like any other text, different readers will interpret them and put them to use in varying ways. Other scholars (Miltner, 2014; Milner, 2016) have argued that internet memes succeed because of their 'emotional resonance' with audiences; people share memes not because they are mechanistically compelled to pass on a cultural replicator, but because they are emotionally compelled by some aspect of the media object with which they are engaging.

The media objects that come under the aegis of the term 'internet meme' are far from uniform, but they do tend to fall into specific categories. As Shifman (2013b, p. 99) quips, 'in theory, all Internet users are free spirits, individuals who take their unique path to the hall of digital fame. In practice, they tend to follow the same beaten tracks of meme creation.' These 'beaten tracks' are genres, 'socially recognized types of communicative action' (Yates and Orlikowski, 1992, p. 299) that are the 'keys to understanding how to participate in the actions of a community' (Miller, 1984, p. 165). There are dozens of genres of internet memes that have their own rules, structures, stylistic features, themes, topics, and intended audiences (Shifman, 2013b). Some of the most recognizable meme genres include flash mobs[1], recut trailers[2], rage comics[3], lip dubs[4], image macros[5], and exploitables[6].

However, no matter what the subgenre, Shifman (2013a) argues that internet memes have three main dimensions that can connect with audiences, or be used to create meaning: content, form, and stance. The content of internet memes refers to the 'ideas and the ideologies' that are expressed in the meme. The form involves the 'physical incarnation' of the meme; this includes the format (a video, a picture) and the 'genre-related patterns' of the format (such as font and text position, or whether the video is a lip dub or fake movie trailer). The stance of a meme has three sub-components: the participation structures, keying, and communicative functions. The participation structures of a meme involve who is entitled to participate and how; the keying of the meme involves the tone and style of communication; and the communicative functions involve the type of communication that is happening.

In order for a piece of content to become memetic, users need to modify at least one of these dimensions. This is the key difference between 'memetic' content and 'viral' content; if a piece of content is passed along intact and unaltered, it is considered to be viral. If a piece is altered or changed as it is passed along, it is considered to be a meme (Shifman, 2013b). For example, the 2009 performance of 'I Dreamed a Dream' by *Britain's Got Talent* contestant Susan Boyle is a viral video, since it was passed along without any alterations. However, 2012 K-Pop video *Gangnam Style* is considered a meme, as it inspired a series of spinoffs and imitations.

EARLY INTERNET MEMES

The exact origins of the very first internet meme are somewhat contested. As Lessig (2008) and Jenkins (1992) have argued, participatory culture did not start with the internet. In fact, some of the earliest and most popular memes were very similar to offline 'memes' from the 1970s and 1980s. One key example of this is the demotivational poster meme. Demotivational posters (or demotivators) were parodies of the motivational posters found in offices and classrooms across the United States. Despair, Inc. was a company that started selling demotivational posters in 1998, and later created their own online 'Parody Motivator Generator.'[7]

Many of the first internet memes took the form of 'single-serving sites' (Kottke, 2008), websites consisting of a single page with a domain name that matched the content of the site. One of the earliest and most popular single-serving sites was The Hampster Dance, a website featuring a series of animated hamsters rotating to a sped-up version of 'Whistle Stop' from Disney's animated version of *Robin Hood*. The Hampster Dance originally appeared on web community and hosting site GeoCities in 1998, gaining mainstream popularity in the early 2000s. Other famous single-serving sites included yourethemannowdog.com, a site that appeared in 2001 and featured a repeating clip of Sean Connery from *Finding Forrester* repeating his notorious line, 'You're the man now, dog' (Asuncion, 2010). You're The Man Now Dog (YTMND) developed into a repository of other single-serving sites, many of which turned into memes of their own.

A single-serving site featuring a gray cat is responsible for one of the internet's most longstanding memes: the LOLcat. In 2007, blogger Eric Nakagawa took a picture of Happy Cat, a grey cat originally featured in a Russian catfood ad, and superimposed the text 'I Can Has Cheezburger?' on top of it (Tozzi, 2007). He then posted the picture on icanhascheezburger.com, and an internet sensation was born. I Can Has Cheezburger was responsible for popularizing LOLcats, as well as the image macro genre. While image macros had been floating around subcultural web communities such as 4chan and Something Awful since the early 2000s, the popularity of I Can Has Cheezburger brought the image macro – and for many internet users, memes themselves – into the mainstream.

Many of the earliest internet memes in the US context seem to traffic in the random and bizarre: websites with repeating loops,

pictures of cats with misspelled captions, and silly bait-and-switch pranks, where the promise of an interesting news story turns out to be a video of Rick Astley's 1987 hit *Never Gonna Give You Up*. However, early memes were often cultural artifacts – sometimes playful, sometimes not – that served to erect and maintain in-and-outgroup boundaries within the communities from which they emerged. Many of these early memes were created by members of Something Awful[8] and 4chan[9], communities whose members were technologically skilled and valued absurdist and often off-color humor. Early memes that emerged from these collectives often reflected the tacit knowledge and technical skill required to appreciate their full meaning, making them inscrutable for outsiders. They also reflected a specific positionality; many memes emerging from what Whitney Phillips (2012) calls the 'meme/troll space' of 4chan and Reddit had decidedly misogynist and racist overtones (Milner, 2013). When memes like LOLcats moved from the subcultural to the mainstream, it was because their textual flexibility allowed them to be taken up and imbued with new meaning by different groups (Miltner, 2014).

Early memes in other areas of the world also reflected the cultural specificities of the contexts they came from. Animal-based memes in particular were genres that popularized the practice of meme generation and circulation. Early animal memes not only reflected regional humor, but cultural and political interpretations of certain animals that represented a specific national context. In Japan, for example, the popularity of early meme favorites OMGCat and Maru reflect the historical role that cats have played in Japanese culture and folklore. Some have argued that Maru closely resembles a *bake neko*, or spirit cat – a frequently humanized spirit guide with special powers who is also an emblem of good luck (Romano, 2013).

In Kenya, hyenas (*mafisi*) are animals that are seen as cowardly scavengers, and have lent their name to those who display an unseemly sexual desire: Team Mafisi (Kaigwa, 2015). In 2015, Kenyan lawyer Felix Kiprono Matagei was put on Team Mafisi when he offered 50 cows, 70 sheep, and 30 goats to marry sixteen-year-old First Daughter Malia Obama (Pleasance, 2015). In Latin America, the image macro Ola K Ase (an intentional distortion of 'hola que hace?' or 'what's up?') features a friendly llama, an animal that is indigenous to South America and has played a role in the economic life of the region since the pre-Columbian era (Berrin, 1997). While Ola K Ase is an example of the linguistic playfulness that accompanies many internet memes, it also has been used to comment on political and social issues, including corruption scandals and gender discrimination (Monroy-Hernandez, 2015) (Figure 22.1).

MEMES AS POLITICAL PRACTICE

As several meme scholars have noted (Milner, 2013; Shifman, 2013a, 2013b; Miltner, 2014), humor is a key component of many memes, and a large part of what helps them gain traction among online audiences. However, the humorous nature of memes also makes them an ideal venue for political critique and commentary. From the days of the court jester through to the political cartoon, humor has been a method for skewering both people and institutions in the highest echelons of power. Furthermore, as Pearce and Hajizada (2014, p. 68) have argued, humor can also 'make a difference in mobilization and dissent.' The use of Ola K Ase to make a political statement reflects a practice that has existed since the earliest internet memes, and continues to be one of the primary reasons that memes are created and circulated today.

Memes in Authoritarian Regimes

One key example of the political use of memes is one of China's earliest, most famous, and popular memes: the grass mud horse, or Cao Ni Ma. The grass mud horse is a rare breed of alpaca that lives in the Male Gobi Desert, which is constantly harangued by its nemesis, the river crab. It also interacts with the French-Croatian Squid and the Intelligent Fragrant Chicken. The story of the grass mud horse started off as a children's song, but now there are grass mud horse stuffed animals, animated videos, artwork, and even lines of clothing; it is truly beloved by many in China. While this little mythical creature may seem innocent on its face, it is

Figure 22.1 Ola K Ase

actually a deeply subversive symbol of resistance against the Chinese censored internet, the Great Firewall (Wines, 2009).

According to web scholar An Xiao Mina (2012b), the grass mud horse's name is pronounced 'cǎonímǎ' in Mandarin; this sounds very similar to 'càonǐ mā', which means 'fuck your mother.' The 'Male Gobi,' which is pronounced 'Mǎlè Gēbì', sounds like 'mālè ge bī', Mandarin for 'your mother's cunt.' The devious river crab, or 'héxiè', sounds like 'harmony' ('héxié') in Mandarin – a reference to the fact that the Communist Party refers to the censored internet as the 'harmonized internet.' The French-Croatian Squid is pronounced 'Fǎ Kè Yóu', and the Mandarin name for Intelligent Fragrant Chicken sounds remarkably close to the Mandarin for 'jacking off' (Mina, 2012b). As Shifman (2013b) points out, the humor of the grass mud horse is the incongruity between the way the lyrics are written (and meant to be read by the censors) and how they sound when spoken (or sung) aloud: the lyric 'on the vast and beautiful Male Gobi desert is a herd of grass mud horses' actually sounds like 'in your mother's vast and beautiful cunt is a group fucking your mother.' (Shifman, 2013b, p. 148)

The appearance of the grass mud horse appeared in concert with the Chinese government's 'Special Campaign to Rectify Vulgar Content' (Weiping, 2009). Its genius – and power – lies in the fact that although it is a rather dirty pun, its literal meaning is entirely benign; this means that it escapes the censors'

computers, as well as the government's ban on 'offensive' behavior (Wines, 2009). In a 2009 blog post, Beijing Film Academy professor Cui Weiping explained that the tone of the grass mud horse is one of sly obedience: 'I know you do not allow me to say certain things. See, I am completely cooperative, right? … I am singing a cute children's song – I am a grass-mud horse! Even though it is heard by the entire world, you can't say I've broken the law.'

The grass mud horse is just one example of an 'alternative political discourse' that is taking place in China with the help of internet memes. The *China Digital Times* has argued that internet memes have generated 'frames, metaphors, and narratives' that are an essential part of a 'resistance discourse' that undermine the authoritarian regime of the Chinese Communist Party, and as such, are an important venue for free expression and the development of civil society in China (Qiang, n.d., para. 2). However, China is not the only authoritarian regime where internet memes also play this role: dissenting groups in Iran, Egypt, and Russia (among others) have also used memes to speak out against those in power. In Azerbaijan, the use of internet memes takes on particular significance, as Azerbaijan was one of the first countries to arrest activists for creating and circulating digital humor (Pearce and Hajizada, 2014).

In September 2013, Azerbaijani youth activist Ilkin Rustemzade of the Free Youth Organization was arrested for 'hooliganism'

Figure 22.2   Grass mud horse

for posting a video of the Harlem Shake, a video dance meme. Pearce and Hajizada (2014) explain that while the video itself was non-political, the symbolism of Rustemzade's involvement with global internet culture (and its attendant political ideas) was perceived to be threatening to the government. This was not the first time such an arrest occurred. In 2009, 'donkey bloggers' Adnan Hajizada and Emin Milli were arrested for producing a YouTube video ridiculing the government for spending hundreds of thousands of dollars to import donkeys from Germany (Pearce and Hajizada, 2014), and in 2011, a group of Azerbaijani students were threatened with violence and military conscription for creating a fake talk show that critiqued Azerbaijani society and the government (ibid.).

The use of memes in Azerbaijan is an important case study, because it illustrates that while memes are often used as tools for speaking truth to power, they can also be used as tools of oppression. Katy Pearce (2015) has shown that memes are a powerful source of state-sponsored harassment in Azerbaijan. She argues that their effectiveness lies in the fact that memes are inexpensive and easy to make, and the lack of attribution usually associated with memes is an affordance

that the regime uses to put distance between themselves and the harassment they are conducting (Pearce, 2015 p. 1165). Several key opposition figures and activists have been the subject of memes that ridicule and disparage them in an attempt to undermine their credibility and authority, a weapon that is particularly effective in an 'honor society' like Azerbaijan.

Similar tactics have been used in Russia to humiliate and discredit Ukrainian leaders in the wake of the Russia–Ukraine conflict of 2015–2016. Ukrainian President Petro Poroshenko became the subject of a series of Russian memes after he photoshopped himself in the place of Russian President Vladimir Putin on a cover of *The Economist*. This prompted a flurry of photoshop memes where Poroshenko's head was put on a series of magazine covers, usually on the bodies of famous women: Kate Upton, Megan Fox, and even the Mona Lisa (Sharkov, 2016). However, the Russian government – and particularly President Vladimir Putin – has also been the subject of many memes. In 2011, a photo of Putin riding a horse while shirtless turned into a photoshop meme of Putin riding a variety of objects, including bears and spacecraft (Figure 22.3). Putin was

Figure 22.3   Putin riding bear

also the source of memetic ridicule when it was reported that voter turnout for the 2011 elections exceeded 140% in some regions (Abramovitch, 2011). For the Russian government, the use of humorous memes as a form of political critique is no laughing matter; in April 2015, the Russian government declared a ban on the use of high-profile figures in memes (Rothrock, 2015).

Memes in Democratic Regimes

The use of memes as parody and political statement is not relegated to authoritarian or otherwise repressive regimes. Memes have been a major part of the American electoral scene since artist Shepard Fairey created his famous Hope poster and Obama was subsequently coined 'the first meme President' (Beckwith, 2012). Memes were such a part of the political discourse during Obama's 2012 re-election campaign that it was dubbed 'The Meme Election' by a variety of media outlets, including *Salon* (Jurgenson, 2012) and *The Nation* (Melber, 2012). While memes had long been a part of online political discourse, this election brought the recognition that memes had a major role in shaping – if not outright dictating – the media narrative surrounding each candidate. From the 'live-GIFing'[10] of televised debates to the Obama campaign's meme-ridden Tumblr, memes started to be recognized as a powerful form of political expression, participation, and agenda-setting.

One of the most significant memes from the 2012 election cycle was Binders Full of Women, a meme created from a comment made by Republican candidate Mitt Romney during one of the presidential debates. When asked about the gender pay gap by a female voter, Romney responded that he was given 'binders full of women' to choose from when looking for qualified candidates to employ during his tenure as Governor of Massachusetts. The gaffe was instantaneously taken up by women across a variety of internet platforms and formats, from animated GIFs and image macros on Twitter and Tumblr to reviews for three-ring binders on Amazon.com. While Binders Full of Women was similar to other memes from the 2012 election in that it capitalized on a sound bite and was met with a satirical and parodic response, it had a longer shelf life. This was primarily because, as Carrie Rentschler and Samantha Thrift (2015, p. 332) have argued, the meme 'distilled a larger context of feminist critique of the Republican Party's war on women and increasingly vitriolic online misogyny' and provided the women who participated with an easy and humorous outlet to voice their frustration and displeasure.

While elections and electoral cycles are rich environments for the generation and circulation of poltical memes, they are only a small part of the political memescape. Like political memes in authoritarian regimes, most political memes in democratic regimes focus on critiquing, lampooning, and dissecting the quotidian goings-on of the people and institutions in positions of power. In his book *Social Media and Everyday Politics* (2016), media scholar Tim Highfield argues that memes outside the electoral cycle are simply how politics are discussed and dissected by social media-literate, politically engaged citizens. Just as in authoritarian regimes, memes in democratic nations are used to create new meanings and alternative framings of particular issues, events, and public figures. Highfield also argues that political content is often excellent fodder for the memetic logics (Milner, 2015) that increasingly pervade online cultural spaces. He also explains that because the endless media coverage of politicians provides boundless material for commentary and remix, even small moments can be turned into big memes if they are offbeat, unexpected, or ripe for mockery (Highfield, 2016).

One key example of this was the #davecalls incident on Twitter. In March 2014, British Prime Minister David Cameron posted a photograph of himself on the phone, ostensibly speaking to American President Barack Obama about the crisis in Crimea. The photo was ruthlessly mocked on Twitter, with users posting pictures of themselves in faux-serious poses with other objects held up to their ears in lieu of phones: stuffed animals, soda cans, beer glasses, and so on. Celebrities also joined in on the joke; in particular, when knighted actor (and prolific Twitter user) Sir Patrick Stewart joined in by holding a cylindrical container of wet wipes up to his ear, he gave the meme a serious boost. Eventually, Cameron himself got in on the joke, tweeting a picture of himself in a meeting with former President Bill Clinton to Stewart and quipping to Stewart, 'Talking to another US President, this time face to face, not on the phone.'

Cameron's photo represented a memeable moment for a variety of reasons. First, Cameron is not particularly popular with certain digitally savvy segments of the UK population, and there was a distinct sentiment among this group that Cameron was promoting himself and his leadership skills in a ridiculous and unnecessary manner with the photo. Furthermore, as Alexander (2010) has argued, Western citizens are deeply skeptical of political news coverage because they perceive it to be highly staged and choreographed. On top of being cartoonish, Cameron's picture played right into these perceptions.

ANOTHER KIND OF POLITICS: MEMES AS ACTIVIST PRACTICE

Humor is often an effective tool for commenting on the gaffes and hypocrisy of those in power, and many political memes are used to comment on politics in a humorous and parodic way. However, memes often reflect and invoke the rage of the subordinated;

Figure 22.4a   Cameron tweet

Figure 22.4b   Stewart tweet

Chinese film scholar Cui Weiping (2009) has referred to memes as one of the 'weapons of the weak' in our mediatized society. While that may be so, the impact of some activist memes illustrates just how powerful they can be.

While many early memes emerging from the 4chan subculture were prankish and puerile, they also had their roots in (and occasionally overlapped with) a hacker culture that resisted and rejected traditional power structures and norms. As Molly Sauter (2014) explained in *The Coming Swarm*, LOLcats featured prominently on the Low-Orbit Ion Cannon (LOIC), a tool used to engage in civil disobedience in the form of Distributed Denial of Service (DDoS) attacks on powerful individuals and institutions.

However, Chinese netizens were one of the first groups to clearly illustrate the activist power of memes. In July 2011, two high-speed rail trains collided in the suburbs of Wenzhou; 40 people died and over 192 others were injured. After the Chinese government claimed that there were no further survivors, rescue workers found two-year-old Xiang Weiyi alive in a train car that was being demolished; this led to a great deal of criticism of the government and the overwhelming sentiment that the government was more interested in covering its tracks than taking the rescue effort seriously (Ding, 2011). In response to the government's negligence, a series of memes began circulating about the train crash. Eventually, the outcry reached such a fever pitch that top Ministry of Railways officials resigned, and the government eventually issued a report on the cause of the crash. Artist and researcher An Xiao Mina described the involvement of memes in the government's response as 'a watershed moment', arguing that 'it forced the government to have more transparency' (quoted in Subbaraman, 2012).

Memes also played a major role in Chinese citizens' protest of activist lawyer Chen

Guangcheng being placed under house arrest in 2011. While Chen's name was officially censored from the 'harmonized' internet, Chinese citizens showed their support for Chen in other ways. One was by taking a Dark Glasses portrait, a project created by digital artist Crazy Crab, which exhorted Chinese internet users to post themselves wearing dark sunglasses or blindfolds to express their solidarity for the blind lawyer. Like the grass mud horse, this was designed to escape the censors, as it would be rather difficult to distinguish between a Dark Glasses portrait and a selfie on a sunny day. While Chinese censors eventually caught on, certain images escaped their grasp; there are still images of Chen circulating on photoshopped posters of *The Shawshank Redemption*. As An Xiao Mina (2012a) explains, the significance of the Chen Guangcheng meme is that it kept awareness of Chen's plight active and relevant in public discourse, a state of affairs that would have otherwise been difficult to achieve in such a censored environment.

Mina also notes that memes played a similar and equally important role in the case of Trayvon Martin. In February of 2012, seventeen-year-old Martin was fatally shot in Sanford, Florida. While Martin's murder is now a well-known event, there was originally very little media coverage surrounding his death. That changed after digital strategist Daniel Maree posted a video on YouTube encouraging people to wear hoodies in honor of Martin, who was wearing a hoodie when he was killed. Maree called his movement the Million Hoodie March, and it sparked a vibrant and intense discussion in American public discourse, a discourse that was further amplified when the Million Hoodie March moved offline into the streets. As Mina (2012a) explains, 'even in a democratic country with broad speech opportunities, it can be difficult to gather eyes and ears around an issue and even harder to sustain it in people's minds', and the hoodie meme helped amplify and sustain Martin's story – and the surrounding discussion of racial profiling

and violence – in the media, both social and broadcast.

Mina (2012a) also makes the important point that part of the success of the Trayvon Martin and Chen Guangcheng meme campaigns lay in the fact that they were organized: Crazy Crab and Daniel Maree provided clear instructions on how to participate, and they also provided a central repository in the form of dedicated websites to collect the images they were encouraging people to make. This sort of organization was also key for the success of Black Lives Matter (BLM),[11] the tour-de-force hashtag-turned-movement that changed the American discourse on racial justice and police brutality starting in 2015. In their seminal study of 40.8 million tweets, 100,000+ web links, and 40 interviews of BLM activists, Deen Freelon, Charlton D. McIlwain and Meredith D. Clark (2016) argued that one of the main contributing factors to BLM's success was that their core demand of 'stop killing us' was clearly articulated and agreed-upon from the start (Freelon et al., 2016, p. 83). The BLM movement has been incredibly successful in circulating narratives about police brutality and racial profiling that counter the 'neutral' narratives in the mainstream news media. Additionally, the content posted in connection with the #blacklivesmatter hashtag was remarkably successful in educating casual observers on Twitter, illustrating that 'under some political circumstances, political appeals on social media can do more than reinforce people's preexisting opinions' (ibid., p. 79).

THE MEME-INDUSTRIAL COMPLEX

As the many examples of political and activist memes illustrate, memes can be an efficient, high-impact method of spreading a message or idea, and they also have the potential to dominate popular culture during their time in the limelight. Both of these affordances make memes particularly appealing to people and groups interested in making money, whether that is advertisers, entrepreneurs, media companies, or other business interests.

Most successful memes are not created for the purpose of making money. Most memes are created for fun, to connect with a friend, or to express some kind of personally relevant statement, opinion, or joke (Miltner, 2014). As one meme creator put it, 'We're spending hours making these fun things for no compensation, and not even any recognition … just because of the inherent fun in it' (ibid.) Furthermore, the general lack of attribution that comes with the generation and dissemination of memes may be good for authoritarian governments looking to distance themselves from their harassment of dissidents, but it also makes it difficult to claim ownership – and consequently profit – from memes. Speaking to the collective nature of meme creation, one LOLcat enthusiast explained, 'You can never be like, "I'm the guy behind Ceiling Cat"' (ibid.). As Phillips (2015) relates, early memes – particularly those coming from subcultural community and 'meme factory' 4chan – required deep subcultural knowledge in order to both parse and participate in them. However, the fact that certain memes weren't designed to be mined for profit failed to deter those who saw them as an untapped commercial opportunity. As more accessible memes crossed into the mainstream and became more visible, their marketability also increased (Phillips, 2015, p. 139).

The first person to create a sustainable business model based on memes was Ben Huh, an entrepreneur who purchased LOLcat blog *I Can Has Cheezburger* (*ICHC*) in 2007. Huh recognized early on that *ICHC* was unique in the internet media ecosystem, and was able to pitch the uniqueness of *ICHC* to venture capitalists, eventually raising over US$2 million to purchase the site. In explaining his interest in *ICHC*, Huh said:

It was doing 500,000 page views a day for a cat picture site, that nobody understood, which I thought was fantastic. … And second, it was the incredible community. It had amazing buzz. We felt like that there was a pretty good possibility that we were buying into a cultural phenomenon, a shift in the way people perceived entertainment. (Cook, 2008)

Huh used the advertising profits from *ICHC* to acquire a collection of meme-related websites, including *FAIL*, *The Daily What*, *Memebase*, and meme encyclopedia *Know Your Meme*. Huh consolidated the websites under the aegis of Cheezburger, a corporation that received US$30 million in venture funding, made $4 million in yearly revenue, and employed 75 people at its peak (Erlich, 2011). Cheezburger has published five books – two of which are *New York Times* Bestsellers – and was the subject of *LOLwork*, a short-lived reality TV show on the Bravo network (Chard, 2010; Watercutter, 2012).

While some applaud Huh's savvy, the communities that were responsible for the generation of LOLcats and many of the other memes that populate the sites of Huh's meme empire were less enthusiastic. In 2010, Huh and 4chan founder Christopher 'moot' Poole were on a panel at internet culture conference ROFLCon, discussing the mainstreaming of meme culture. Towards the end of the panel, Poole accused Huh of being an 'oil tower', unfairly profiting off the unpaid labor of others,[12] and contributing to the destruction of the meme-creating subculture that he had helped establish. 'You can say "we're giving people tools to create LOLcats" and that's great and all', Poole said, 'but more or less you're giving people those tools so you can post them on your site because you monetize them with display ads. Do you feel like you put something back? Because I don't' (Phillips, 2015, p. 140).

Poole's sentiments were expressed in a less politic way by 4chan's /b/ board[13] in November 2010 with Operation Black Rage. Teen-oriented clothing retailer Hot Topic had started selling t-shirts with Rage Comics on them, a state of affairs that enraged /b/'s community and spurred them into vengeful action.

'The corporate slut that is Hot Topic has now decided that memes are to be the latest "cool" thing amoungst [sic] 13 year old emo consumer whores', the flier for Operation Black Rage groused. 'This is only the beginning, if this is allowed to continue then it'll only be a matter of time until /b/ starts getting raped of every meme to be turned into the next I Can Has Cheezburger? And before long? /b/ will die.' The plan for Operation Black Rage was to create a series of racist Rage Comics and subsequently encourage an outrage-fueled consumer boycott of Hot Topic until the shirts were removed from shelves. The plan originally worked, with Hot Topic agreeing to remove the shirts from their online store. The victory was short-lived, however; Hot Topic soon became wise to /b/'s campaign and reversed their decision.

In the end, /b/'s fears were warranted: Hot Topic's commodification of memes was only the tip of the iceberg. In the years that followed, British company Virgin Mobile used Success Kid[14] in a cable television campaign; American startup HipChat used Y U NO[15] on billboards around the San Francisco Bay Area, and Wonderful Pistachios used the Honeybadger[16] and Keyboard Cat[17] in television commercials. While some of these memes were created and popularized by a collective, such as Y U NO, many of them contain media that can be traced back to an original owner or creator; Keyboard Cat, The Honey Badger and Success Kid all had video or images that could be – and were – licensed. Other memes that were created by a single author have also successfully capitalized on their intellectual property. The creator of Nyan Cat[18], Christopher Torres, has monetized his creation through YouTube ads and Nyan Cat merchandise; the owner of Tardar Sauce, more commonly know as Grumpy Cat[19], has parlayed 'Tard's' popularity into toys, books, clothing, animated specials, pet food sponsorships, and even 'Grumppucino' iced coffee beverages. In Hong Kong, famous cat Brother Cream has also received sponsorships and book deals.

The road to meme monetization is not a one-way street; some advertising campaigns turned into memes of their own. Old Spice's 'The Man Your Man Could Smell Like' was a memetic success that inspired imitations on *Sesame Street*, Nickelodeon television show *iCarly*, and the ad campaign for *Shrek* spinoff *Puss In Boots*. The advertising spokesman for Dos Equis, The Most Interesting Man in the World, has long been the subject of his own image macro template. However, brands have generally not met with much success when it comes to creating truly successful memes. This is because memes created by marketers and advertisers are seen as inauthentic and 'forced'. Meme encyclopedia *Know Your Meme* defines a forced meme as a meme that is 'artificially created and spread … made with the intent of becoming a meme and aggressively promoted by its creator' ('Forced Meme', 2010).

MEMETIC FUTURES

By 2012, the commodification of memes combined with other shifts in the digital media ecosystem incited a series of dire proclamations and death knells for memes. At the 2012 Digital Life Design (DLD) conference, 4chan founder Christopher 'moot' Poole mourned the end of internet culture (Olsen, 2012). After the final ROFLCon later that year, technologist Andy Baio (2012) complained in *Wired* that the shift to mobile social (i.e., primarily accessing social media on a mobile phone) was quashing creativity. On his blog, *Know Your Meme* co-founder Chris Menning (2012) declared that 2012 was 'the year the meme died'. In his book, *World Made Meme*, internet scholar Ryan Milner (2016) tells a story of how in 2014, one of his second-year undergraduate students told him, 'I remember memes. They were really big in high school. Junior year.'

It's true that the body of texts that were readily identified as memes by a specific cohort of internet culture enthusiasts from the mid-2000s to approximately 2012 are no longer in vogue. LOLcats, Advice Animals, Rage Comics, Rickrolling and their ilk have fallen so out of favor that they have been given the meta-memetic label 'dank memes.' As Don Caldwell (2015) of *Know Your Meme* explains it, dank meme is 'an ironic expression used to mock online viral media and in-jokes that have exhausted their comedic value to the point of being trite or cliché'. As digital scholar Whitney Phillips pointed out in 2012, 'the meme/troll space of 2012 is very different from the meme/troll space of 2008. The question of whether or not that's a good thing is irrelevant – we are where we are, deal with it' (Phillips, 2012).

Much of the research on memes from 2014 onward has aimed to do just that – deal with the shifting memetic landscape and understand where we are now, although as Milner (2015) notes, 'it's easy to log in to Facebook, see yet another goddamn Minion, throw up our hands, and declare the death of the subculture.' For despite four years' worth of earnest declarations that memes are dead, the sheer volume of memes that permeate our media ecosystem illustrate that they are very much alive; or rather, as Milner (2016, p. 5) asserts, *memetic participation* is very much alive:

> Memetic media didn't start with 4chan, just as they didn't end with the final ROFLCon. Memetic practices persist, even if the specific resonant texts shift over time. If we're tired of stock character macros in 2015, it doesn't mean that 'memes are dead'; it indicates that those memes don't hold the specific cultural capital they did in 2010, or even that they hold cultural capital for people other than us.

As Milner, Highfield, Shifman, and others argued in an October 2015 series on *Culture Digitally*, much of our media engagement is governed by memetic logics, whether that is the platform vernacular of Twitter (Highfield, 2016); new modes of fundraising, like the Ice Bucket Challenge (Silvestri, 2015); and new forms of social mobilization in the form of #BlackLivesMatter. At the time of writing, as the American Presidential election of 2016 reaches fever pitch, so do the memetic texts generated about (and perhaps by the campaigns of) Hillary Clinton, Bernie Sanders, Donald Trump, and Ted Cruz. Whether we are watching Bad Lip Readings of the Republican debates or trying to #MakeDonaldDrumpfAgain at the exhortation of media critic and late-night host John Oliver, user-driven imitation, remixing, bricolage, and circulation are at the core of our media engagement. Furthermore, these behaviors and logics will continue to evolve and expand long after the election – or whatever media event is next – has ended. As Milner (2016, p. 15) reminds us, 'whether or not the subculture has lost its edge, memetic logics are as pervasive as ever.'

Notes

1 Flash mobs are coordinated events where a large number of people descend on a location for a short-lived purpose. Flash mobs are usually video recorded and posted online. For more, see http://knowyourmeme.com/memes/flash-mob

2 Recut trailers are parody videos that take movie trailers out of their original context and re-edit them to reflect different genres or narratives. For more, see http://knowyourmeme.com/memes/recut-movie-trailers-movie-trailer-remix

3 Rage comics are a series of stick figure comic strips used to humorously express anger about the frustrations and defeats of everyday life. For more, see http://knowyourmeme.com/memes/rage-comics

4 Lip dubs are videos that feature a person or group of people lip synching to a popular song, usually to comedic effect. For more, see http://knowyourmeme.com/memes/lip-dub

5 Image macros feature a picture or other image with text superimposed on it, usually in Impact font. For more, see http://knowyourmeme.com/memes/image-macros

6 Exploitables are image templates where a defining characteristic or key piece of content can be easily edited to make a joke or other humorous statement. For a full explanation of the various types of exploitables, see http://knowyourmeme.com/memes/exploitables

7 http://diy.despair.com/motivator.php

8 Something Awful is a shock image site and community that was an epicenter of early meme and trolling activity in the early 2000s. For more, see Phillips (2015).

9 4chan is an imageboard and community who's /b/ board, or 'random' board, is responsible for many of the memes that achieved mainstream popularity from 2008–2011. It is also known for being the origin site of the troll/hacktivist collective Anonymous. For a full explanation of 4chan and /b/'s role in meme culture, see Phillips (2015).

10 Live-GIFing is a practice, similar to live-blogging or live-tweeting, of creating content extemporaneously during a major media event. In 2012, Tumblr live-GIFed the Presidential debates, and in doing so helped frame the outcome of the debates in a way that was particularly friendly to Obama. For more, see Phillips and Miltner (2012).

11 For an in-depth explanation and discussion of Black Lives Matter and its accomplishments, see Freelon, McIlwain, and Clark (2016).

12 For a larger theoretical exploration of the unpaid labor of content creators online, see Terranova (2004).

13 /b/ is the 'random' board on 4chan. /b/ is responsible for many of the memes that achieved mainstream popularity from 2008 to 2011, and is also known for being the origin site of the troll/hacktivist collective Anonymous. For a full explanation of /b/'s role in meme culture, see Phillips (2015).

14 Success Kid is a reaction image macro used to express self-satisfaction or victory. For more, see http://knowyourmeme.com/memes/success-kid-i-hate-sandcastles

15 Y U NO is an image macro featuring a grotesquely-drawn stick character usually used to express frustration. For more, see http://knowyourmeme.com/memes/y-u-no-guy

16 The Honey Badger was originally a viral video featuring nature footage with irreverent commentary. For more, see http://knowyourmeme.com/memes/honey-badger

17 Keyboard Cat is a meme used to illustrate failure or incompetence, and featured home video footage of a cat 'playing' the piano. For more, see http://knowyourmeme.com/memes/keyboard-cat

18 Nyan Cat is an 8-bit animation of a grey cat with a Pop Tart for a body, flying through space with an accompanying song. For more, see http://knowyourmeme.com/memes/nyan-cat-poptart-cat

19 Grumpy Cat is a dwarf cat known for her perpetually unhappy expression. For more, see: http://knowyourmeme.com/memes/grumpy-cat

REFERENCES

Abramovitch, S. (2011, December 4). Putin clings to victory as Russia's voter turnout exceeds 146%. Gawker. http://gawker.com/5864945/putin-clings-to-victory-as-russias-voter-turnout-exceeds-146

Alexander, J. C. (2010). The performance of politics: Obama's victory and the democratic struggle for power. Oxford: Oxford University Press.

Asuncion, J. (2010). YTMND. Know Your Meme. http://knowyourmeme.com/memes/sites/ytmnd

Baio, A. (2012, September 5). Feels Bad Man: How mobile is stopping the lulz. Wired. www.wired.com/2012/05/opinion-baio-meme-decline/all/

Beckwith, R. T. (2012, October 24). Obama: The first meme President. Mercury News. www.mercurynews.com/politics-national/2012/10/obama-the-first-meme-president/

Berrin, K. (1997). The spirit of ancient Peru: Treasures from the Museo Arqueológico Rafael Larco Herrera. New York: Thames and Hudson.

Blackmore, S. (2000). The meme machine. Oxford: Oxford University Press.

Brodie, R. (2009). Virus of the mind: The new science of the meme. Carlsbad, CA: Hay House.

Burgess, J. (2006). Hearing Ordinary Voices: Cultural Studies, Vernacular Creativity and Digital Storytelling. Continuum: Journal of Media & Cultural Studies, 20 (2), 201–214.

Caldwell, D. (2015). Dank memes. Know Your Meme. http://knowyourmeme.com/memes/dank-memes

Chard, T. (2010, June 30). Cheezburger CEO Ben Huh on surrounding himself with more talent, and the future of the global humor blog network. Xconomy. www.xconomy.com/seattle/2010/06/30/cheezburger-ceo-ben-huh-on-surrounding-himself-with-more-talent-and-the-future-of-the-global-humor-blog-network/

Constine, J. (2014, January 8). Facebook data scientists prove memes mutate and adapt like DNA. Techcrunch. http://techcrunch.com/2014/01/08/facebook-memes/

Cook, J. (2008, November 6). Q&A: Ben Huh of I Can Has Cheezburger on tech, cats and more. Pugent Sound Business Journal. www.

bizjournals.com/seattle/blog/techflash/2008/11/QA_Ben_Huh_of_I_Can_Has_Cheezburger33692889.html

Dawkins, R. (1976). *The selfish gene*. New York and Oxford: Oxford University Press.

Ding, G. (2011, August 4). All your facts are belong to us. *ChinaGeeks*. http://chinageeks.org/2011/08/all-your-facts-are-belong-to-us/

Erlich, B. (2011). I Can Haz $$$: Cheezburger Network Scores $30 Million in Funding. Retrieved August 17, 2011, from Mashable: http://mashable.com/2011/01/18/cheezburgerfunding/

Forced Meme (2010). Know Your Meme. http://knowyourmeme.com/memes/forced-meme

Freelon, D. G., McIlwain, C. D., & Clark, M. D. (2016). *Beyond the Hashtags: #Ferguson, #Blacklivesmatter, and the online struggle for offline justice*. Washington, DC: Centre for Media and Social Impact. http://cmsimpact.org/resource/beyond-hashtags-ferguson-blacklivesmatter-online-struggle-offline-justice/

Highfield, T. (2016). *Social media and everyday politics*. Malden, MA: Polity Press.

Jenkins, H. (1992). *Textual poachers: Television fans and participatory culture*. Routledge.

Jenkins, H. (2006). *Fans, bloggers, and gamers: Exploring participatory culture*. NYU Press.

Jenkins, H., Ford, S., & Green, J. (2013). *Spreadable media: Creating value and meaning in a networked culture*. New York: New York University Press.

Jurgenson, N. (2012, October 28). What makes a meme. *Salon*. www.salon.com/2012/10/28/what_makes_a_meme/

Kaigwa, M. (2015) Kenya: Hyena. A Global Perspective (Animal Meme Map) [map], exhibited for How Cats Took Over The Internet (August 2015–February 2016). New York: Museum of the Moving Image.

Kottke, J. (2008, February 15). Single serving sites. *Kottke.org*. http://kottke.org/08/02/single-serving-sites

Lessig, L. (2008). *Remix: Making art and commerce thrive in the hybrid economy*. Penguin.

Melber, A. (2012, October 17). Why Romney is losing the meme election. *The Nation*. www.thenation.com/article/why-romney-losing-meme-election/

Menning, C. (2012). The year the 'meme' meme died. *Modern Primate*. www.modernprimate.com/2012-the-year-the-meme-meme-died/

Miller, C. R. (1984). Genre as social action. *Quarterly Journal of Speech*, 70(2), 151–167.

Milner, R. (2013). Hacking the social: Internet memes, identity antagonism, and the logic of lulz. *Fibreculture*, 22, 62–92.

Milner, R. (2015, October 27). Memes are dead. Long live memetics. *Culture Digitally*. http://culturedigitally.org/2015/10/01-memes-are-dead-long-live-memetics-by-ryan-m-milner/

Milner, R. (2016). *The world made meme*. Cambridge, MA: MIT Press.

Miltner, K. M. (2014). 'There's no place for lulz on LOLCats': The role of genre, gender, and group identity in the interpretation and enjoyment of an Internet meme. *First Monday*, 19(8).

Mina, A. X. (2012a, July 12). A tale of two memes: The powerful connection between Trayvon Martin and Chen Guangcheng. *The Atlantic*. www.theatlantic.com/technologyarchive/2012/07/a-tale-of-two-memes-the-powerful-connection-between-trayvon-martin-and-chen-guangcheng/259604/

Mina, A. X. (2012b, October 4). Five facts about the grass mud horse. *Impakt*. http://impakt.nl/archive/2012/essays/an-xiao-mina-five-facts-about-the-grass-mud-horse/

Monroy-Hernandez, A. (2015) Mexico: Llama. A Global Perspective (Animal Meme Map) [map], exhibited for How Cats Took Over The Internet (August 2015–February 2016), New York: Museum of the Moving Image.

Olsen, P. (2012, December 18). 4Chan's 'Moot' laments the death of Internet culture. *Forbes*. www.forbes.com/sites/parmyolson/2012/12/18/4chans-moot-laments-the-death-of-internet-culture/#4ab5cf3bd74d

Pearce, K. E. (2015). Democratizing kompromat: the affordances of social media for state-sponsored harassment. *Information, Communication & Society*, 18(10), 1158–1174.

Pearce, K., & Hajizada, A. (2014). No laughing matter: Humor as a means of dissent in the digital era: The case of authoritarian Azerbaijan. *Demokratizatsiya*, 22(1), 67–85.

Phillips, W. (2012, September 9). On shifting sands. *Billions and Billions*. https://billions-and-billions.com/2012/09/09/on-shifting-sands/

Phillips, W. (2015). *This Is Why We Can't Have Nice Things: Mapping the relationship between online trolling and mainstream culture*. Cambridge, MA: MIT Press.

Phillips, W., & Miltner, K. (2012, November 2). The meme election: Clicktivism, the Buzzfeed effect, and corporate meme-jacking. *The Awl*. www.theawl.com/2012/11/the-meme-election

Pleasance, C. (2015, May 27). Lawyer offers 50 cows, 70 sheep and 30 goats to marry Barack Obama's 16-year-old daughter Malia in Kenya… and says he has been 'interested' in her since she was 10. *The Daily Mail*.www.dailymail.co.uk/news/article-3098839/Lawyer-offers-50-cows-70-sheep-30-goats-marry-Barack-Obama-s-16-year-old-daughter-Malia-Kenya-says-interested-girl-10.html

Qiang, X. (n.d.). Grass-Mud Horse Lexicon old introduction: Translating the resistance discourse of Chinese netizens. *China Digital Times*. http://chinadigitaltimes.net/space/Grass-Mud_Horse_Lexicon_old_introduction

Rentschler, C. A., & Thrift, S. C. (2015). Doing feminism in the network: Networked laughter and the 'Binders Full of Women' meme. *Feminist Theory*, 16(3), 329–359.

Romano, A. (2013, August 13). The Internet's obsession with cats started in Japan. *The Daily Dot*. www.dailydot.com/lifestyle/japan-cat-maneki-neko-hello-kitty-lolcat/

Rothrock, J. (2015, April 10). The Kremlin declares war on memes. *Global Voices*. https://globalvoices.org/2015/04/10/russia-the-kremlin-declares-war-on-memes/

Sauter, M. (2014). *The coming swarm: DDOS actions, hacktivism, and civil disobedience on the Internet*. New York: Bloomsbury.

Sharkov, D. (2016, January 4). Ukraine's Poroshenko prompts meme craze in Russia after Twitter gaffe. *Newsweek*. www.newsweek.com/ukraine-president-russian-memes-411208

Shifman, L. (2013a). Memes in a digital world: Reconciling with a conceptual troublemaker. *Journal of Computer-Mediated Communication*, 18(3), 362–377.

Shifman, L. (2013b). *Memes in digital culture*. Cambridge, MA: MIT Press.

Silvestri, L. (2015, November 19). Beneficient memes. *Culture Digitally*. http://culturedigitally.org/2015/11/memeology-festival-08-beneficent-memes/

Subbaraman, N. (2012, May 7). Chinese political memes skirt censorship to make statements. *Fast Company*. www.fastcompany.com/1836506/chinese-political-memes-skirt-censorship-make-statements

Terranova, T. (2004). *Network culture: Politics for the information age*. Pluto Press.

Tozzi, J. (2007, July 17). Bloggers bring in the big bucks. *Bloomberg*. www.bloomberg.com/news/articles/2007-07-13/bloggers-bring-in-the-big-bucksbusinessweek-business-news-stock-market-and-financial-advice

Watercutter, A. (2012, November 7). I can has reality show? *LOLwork* brings cheezburger to TV. *Wired*. www.wired.com/2012/11/lolwork-ben-huh-reality-tv/

Weiping, C. (2009, March 1) Cui Weiping (崔卫平): I Am a Grass-Mud Horse. *China Digital Times*. http://chinadigitaltimes.net/2009/03/cui-weiping-%E5%B4%94%E5%8D%AB%E5%B9%B3-i-am-a-grass-mud-horse/

Wines, M. (2009, March 11). A dirty pun tweaks China's online censors. *New York Times*. www.nytimes.com/2009/03/12/world/asia/12beast.html

Yates, J., & Orlikowski, W.J. (1992). Genres of organizational communication: A structurational approach to studying communication and media. *Academy of Management Review*, 17(2), 299–326.

Self-Representation in Social Media

Jill Walker Rettberg

For millennia, humans have used media to represent ourselves. Children draw stick figures with a stick in the sand. Stone Age Australians blew ochre dust around their hands to leave marks in a cave. Vikings carved runes on sticks to tell the world their names. Our grandparents kept diaries hidden in drawers. Today we post selfies to Instagram or Snapchat and write updates on Facebook or Tumblr. With social media, ordinary people share their self-representations with a larger audience than ever before.

In this chapter, I will discuss three modes of self-representation in social media: visual, written and quantitative, building upon my book *Seeing Ourselves through Technology: How We Use Selfies, Blogs and Wearable Devices to See and Shape Ourselves* (Rettberg, 2014b). Visual self-representation includes selfies, of course, but also other images and icons that we use to express ourselves, such as the photos we choose to share on Facebook or the layout we choose for a Tumblr log. Written self-representations

can be blogs or online diaries, but also the many written status updates we share on sites like Facebook, Twitter or in comments on Instagram. The third mode I will discuss is quantified self-representation, which is becoming increasingly common as phones become step-counters and apps give us more and more opportunities to represent our lives through numbers and graphs. Quantified self-representation can mean extensive and deliberate self-tracking, as we see in the quantified self movement, or it can be something as simple as swiping right to add a filter to a Snapchat image showing the temperature where we are or the speed at which we are moving. Often the three modes overlap in social media, as with a Snapchat image that includes numerical information. A selfie with overlaid text uses both the visual and written modes of self-representation, and emoji can be understood both as part of an alphabet and as visual communication.

In social media, the social and communicative aspects of self-representations become very clear. But self-representations have always been social. When we see a self-portrait like Parmigianino's *Self-Portrait in a Convex Mirror* (1524) hanging in a gallery or shown on a website, we see it outside its original social context, and so it seems natural to understand it primarily as an object rather than as part of a conversation. In fact, Parmigianino used his self-portrait as an advertisement for his painting services, bringing it along when he spoke to potential patrons. Kings and queens used the paintings they commissioned of themselves to show their subjects their magnificent riches and power. The child of today who draws her mother a picture of the two of them together is creating a love letter, a charm to keep her mother close to her and to express her love. Even a private diary is written to an imagined reader: 'dear diary', we write, always imagining a recipient to whatever we write, even if that recipient is only a future version of our self (Lejeune, 2000).

Although self-representations are always about communication, they are frequently personal media, to use Marika Lüders' useful term (Lüders, 2008), and are often intended to be seen by only a few. Some forms of personal self-representation are intended to be shared with a limited audience, like the family photo album, which is a collective self-representation of a family that is kept in the home and shown to some but by no means all guests. Historically, personal letters and diaries were not necessarily kept completely private, but were often passed around or read aloud to family and friends (Humphreys et al., 2013). Sometimes personal self-representations become shared more widely than originally intended. Anne Frank kept her diary private during her lifetime, but it became very widely read once published after her death.

REPRESENTATIONS OR PRESENTATIONS?

Before discussing visual, written and quantitative kinds of self-representation in social media, we need to think about the term representation. Why are these forms of self-expression representations and not presentations? The short answer is that they can be seen as either, because the two terms provide two different ways of looking at this phenomenon. A representation is an object, a sign that is seen as constructed in some way, and that stands instead of an object to which it refers. Talking about representations lets us analyse the selfie, the tweet or the graph of a run. A presentation is an act, something that a person does, so talking about presentations allows us to analyse the way that the person acts to present themselves.

It's a little more complicated than this, unfortunately. The terms representation and presentation are used differently in different disciplines, making their use quite thorny in an interdisciplinary field such as internet studies.

Twentieth-century linguistics, with influential scholars like Ferdinand de Saussure and Charles Sanders Pierce, led to the semiotic understanding of representation as a system of signs, that is, sounds, words, images or objects that stand instead of a concept or a thing. For instance, the word 'tree' is a sign that refers to an actual tree. In his textbook *Representation* (1997), Stuart Hall describes three theories of representation: reflective, intentional and constructive. In the reflective approach, the sign or the representation is thought of as a reflection of reality: 'language functions like a mirror, to *reflect* the true meaning as it already exists in the world' (Hall, 1997: 24). In the intentional approach, one assumes that 'Words mean what the author intends they should mean' (ibid.: 25). However, both these theories are seen as flawed by most contemporary scholars. Most scholars today, including Hall, see representation as *constructed*. A representation cannot mirror reality because we all have different experiences and interpretations of 'reality'. Also, words and images and other representations can be interpreted very differently in different contexts or cultures. A suggestive message sent to a lover means something very different within that relationship than it means if it is displayed to work colleagues or tweeted to the world. When representations are shared out of context, their meaning is often constructed differently by the new audience. For instance, many media reports on police shootings of African-Americans use very informal photos of the victims. A teenager may think it is fun to show a silly or embarrassing party photo to friends, but this kind of image is interpreted quite differently when used by a newspaper to represent the victim in a police shooting. The #iftheygunnedmedown campaign on Twitter and Tumblr was a response to this. Participants posted two photos of themselves to Twitter, or to the *If They Gunned Me Down* Tumblr, where one photo was from a party or another informal setting, and the other photo was taken in a more formal or socially approved situation: a college graduation, or wearing a suit and smiling. The rhetorical question accompanying all the posts was which photo

the media would publish if 'they gunned me down', and the implied answer was of course that the media would use the less respectable-looking photo, making the African-American victim look less worthy of our respect than if a more formal photograph had been used (Korn, 2015; Jackson, 2016).

Semiotics, the study of signs, provides a large vocabulary for analysing images. The most liked image on Instagram in 2015 was a photo of Kendall Jenner lying on the floor in a white, lacy dress with her hair spread around her arranged into seven heart-shapes (Jenner, 2015) (Figure 23.1). The caption published with the image has no words, and consists of a single emoji, a rotated black heart: ▶, which is also treated as the title of the image in the web browser.

In semiotic terms my short description of the image and its caption is the *denotation* of the image and its caption. A denotation simply describes what is shown or states the literal meaning of the sign without interpretation. Jenner's photo is obviously not a selfie,

Figure 23.1 Kendall Jenner posted this photograph to Instagram on May 26, 2015

as her hands are visible in the frame, folded over her stomach as though she is laid out like a corpse. She couldn't have arranged her hair herself, either. The image can still be seen as a self-representation: deliberately staged, photographed, and posted to her Instagram account, where it gained over 3.5 million likes.

The most interesting semiotic analysis is not in the descriptive analysis of the denotation of the signs, but an analysis of their *connotations*. Connotations are common associations connected to a sign, not private associations that only one individual might have, but associations and references that are shared by larger cultures or groups. Jenner's image has some very obvious signs with well-established meanings or connotations in Western culture. The hearts that her hair has been shaped into connote love, and are echoed in the rotated black heart emoji in the caption. The choice of a black heart rotated sideways rather than the far more common upright red heart may suggest that though the image is about love, it is a darker, more complicated love than that signified by a red heart. The white lacy dress signifies a bride, which again signifies love, and, in a traditional sense, new, virginal but soon-to-be-consummated love in particular. The traditional wedding dress is white because white stands for innocence in Western culture. Jenner is laid out like a corpse, with her hands folded, as is traditional in Western funerals, and her eyes are closed. The floor is white with a black graphic pattern that could be interpreted as suggesting a river, although this is not an interpretation I would have arrived at had not the dead maiden with her outswept hair made me think of Ophelia, the girl who loved Hamlet and drowned herself. Paintings of the drowned Ophelia always show her hair floating out in the water she lies in, and her dress is often shown as white. Jenner's photo is an example of the way that death is frequently aestheticised in Western visual culture, and we could certainly take the analysis of the image much further by thinking about why a

photo showing Jenner as a dead virgin is the most liked photograph on Instagram. Gender and power relationships might be a place to start. A semiotic analysis always begins, though, by studying the image or the text itself and considering what signs it consists of and what those signs signify.

Seeing selfies and blog posts as representations is something that makes sense if you are considering them as texts to be interpreted or from the point of view of media studies. Another important theoretical tradition has its roots with the sociologist Erving Goffman, whose influential book *The Presentation of Self in Everyday Life* (1959) is heavily referenced in scholarship about social media. Writing well before social media, Goffman describes how we perform and present ourselves differently in face-to-face interactions with different groups of people. On Facebook, a typical user will be friends with quite different groups of people, such as close family, high school classmates, co-workers and distant relatives. Social media theorists have used Goffman to talk about how we try to manage these different audiences. It is often impossible to keep those contexts separate from each other, a phenomenon called 'context collision' by danah boyd (2011).

If we were to analyse Jenner's image as a presentation, rather than as a representation, we would focus less on its status as a set of signs, and more on the role Jenner was performing by posting this image, perhaps considering questions such as who the image was intended for, where and when it was posted, what responses it was met with and Jenner's motivations for creating and sharing the image. One approach would be to interview Jenner herself and perhaps also people who had seen, commented on or reposted the image, but it would also be possible to learn a lot from the image itself, from studying Jenner's other posts and from examining the comments and the contexts in which the image was republished or discussed. We might compare the image to other images posted by non-celebrities, or perhaps we might find a surge of homage images copying or playing upon the Jenner image. Often ethnographers and sociologists want to learn about practice across a group of people, and so a study of self-presentation rather than self-representation on Instagram might explore how users typically create and share images rather than focusing on individual examples like Jenner's image. Other scholars simply don't use the terms representation and presentation, like Katie Warfield, who prefers a phenomenological approach, arguing that focusing on the visual artefact of a selfie often means 'neglecting the fleshy producer of the image, who in the case of selfies, is also the heart of the image' (Warfield, 2015).

Presentation and representation are also used in different ways than those I have just described. Aristotle wrote about representation as *mimesis*, that is, an attempt to realistically mimic the world. This is similar to what Stuart Hall calls the 'reflective approach' to representation, as discussed earlier in this chapter. In theatre, some critics use the term representational acting to describe the 'naturalistic' form of theatre where actors do not acknowledge the presence of the audience. In this style of acting, there is an imagined 'fourth wall' between the actors on stage and the audience, and audience members are like flies on the wall observing the action. In presentational acting, on the other hand, actors acknowledge the audience and speak directly to them (Bakshy, 1923: 12). Often these modes of acting overlap, as in literature, where the narrator may invoke the 'dear reader' at times while at other times telling the story with no overt acknowledgement of any reader. Another use of the terms is found in the field of interpersonal communication, where John Fiske explains that representational codes produce a text that can stand alone, whereas presentational codes are 'indexical: they cannot stand for something apart from themselves and their encoder,' that is, the person who spoke or communicated (Fiske, 2010: 63).

Ultimately, there isn't necessarily any strict difference between the terms representation and presentation as they are used in scholarship on social media. In practice, most analyses will really view the material from both perspectives. In this chapter, I will primarily consider expressions of the self in social media as representations, but I use the term fairly broadly.

In the next sections of this chapter, I will discuss each of the three main modes of self-representation in social media, beginning with written self-representations, as seen in blogs, followed by visual and quantitative self-representations.

BLOGS AND WRITING ABOUT THE SELF

The first online diaries appeared around 1994, and were hand-coded by people who had taught themselves to create websites. One of the earliest online diaries was Justin Hall's *Justin's Links*, which is still active at links.net, though the style and content have changed considerably over the years. At first, the website took the form of a meandering hypertextual story about Hall's life, but in 1996 Hall began posting dated diary entries that still linked and intermingled with his hypertextual autobiography. Hall didn't call his site a weblog until much later, because 'web log' at that time was used to refer to the statistics available to website administrators showing the number of visitors to a website. In 1997, Jorn Barger proposed that the term weblog be used to refer to websites that post links to interesting material with commentary (Rettberg, 2014a: 8), and a number of hand-coded weblogs became popular. The style of these early weblogs was brief and although the comments usually had a clear individual voice and offered personal opinions, the content was not usually autobiographical. Weblogs were often seen as being different from online diaries, which were more confessional. In 1998, Open Diary became one of the first sites to provide easy web publication without users needing to know how to code or edit HTML (Rettberg, 2014a: 9). Instead, users picked a layout from a set of templates, and wrote their entries into text boxes. 1999 saw the launch of sites for easily publishing weblogs, or blogs as they became known, including Pitas and Blogger. Within a few years, the once quite separate genres of online diaries and blogs merged. Blog posts became longer and more essayistic, often using a more personal voice, and online diaries came to include more essayistic material and commentary in addition to the autobiographical content.

By 2004 blogs were so popular that 'blog' was named word of the year by the Merriam-Webster, much as 'selfie' was named word of the year by Oxford Dictionaries in 2013, and both declarations were much discussed in the mainstream media. Around this time, commercial blogging took off, and we saw corporate blogging as well as individuals who created their own profitable businesses by blogging about their lives or about products. Today microcelebrities (Marwick, 2013; Senft, 2013) and influencers (Abidin, 2015) tend to use multiple platforms rather than a single blog, as early bloggers did. A popular contemporary fashion blogger may have hundreds of thousands of readers a day, but often spread across platforms such as Instagram, Facebook, Snapchat and a blog.

Although much interesting work has been done researching people who have built their own careers online and become Instagram or blog celebrities or, to use Crystal Abidin's more general term, influencers, this chapter is primarily about the ways in which ordinary people represent themselves in social media. And yet the line can be difficult to draw. Abidin (2015) emphasises that influencers *are* ordinary people:

> Influencers are everyday, ordinary Internet users who accumulate a relatively large following on blogs and social media through the textual and visual narration of their personal lives and lifestyles, engage with their following in digital and physical spaces, and monetise their following by integrating 'advertorials' into their blog or social media posts.

The main thing that differentiates influencers from the majority of social media users is that influencers monetise their activity. They use advertising, sponsorship and advertorials to make money in social media, heavily using their online identities to make their message personal and intimate, and using emotions and designing empathetic communication (Lövheim, 2013) with their readers in order to establish strong, lasting relationships. Other celebrities may not directly monetise their self-representations in social media, but use them as platforms to increase their influence and money-making potential in other channels, for instance driving interest for their books, TV-shows, music, Etsy store or political cause.

Although it can be argued that social media forces, or at least encourages, users to promote themselves as brands (Marwick, 2013), most people do not monetise their social media use. Today people write about their lives on sites like Facebook, Twitter and Tumblr, as well as on traditional blogs, and use these platforms to express themselves and to build and foster connections with others.

Bloggers themselves have long recognised that blogging, over time, can be a way of becoming more sure of oneself and more aware of one's preferences and opinions. Rebecca Blood, a very early blogger, described her experience like this in an influential early essay:

> Shortly after I began producing *Rebecca's Pocket* I noticed two side effects I had not expected. First, I discovered my own interests. I thought I knew what I was interested in, but after linking stories for a few months I could see that I was much more interested in science, archaeology, and issues of injustice than I had realized. More importantly, I began to value more highly my own point of view. In composing my link text every day I carefully considered my own opinions and ideas, and I began to feel that my perspective was unique and important. (Blood, 2000)

A couple of years later, Steven Johnson, an author of popular science books, described blogging as being like a mental visit to the gym:

> I've actually been about twice as productive as normal since I started maintaining the blog. The more I keep at it, the more it seems to me like a kind of intellectual version of going to the gym: having to post responses and ideas on a semi-regular basis, and having those ideas sharpened or shot down by such smart people, flexes the thinking/writing muscles in a great way. (Johnson, 2002)

Viviane Serfaty's 2004 study of blogging connects blogs to the traditions of the English Puritans, who used diaries as 'a requirement of religious self- discipline', recounting 'a spiritual journey towards personal salvation' (Serfaty, 2004: 5). During the same period the Libertines developed the idea of 'an inner space devoted to internal deliberation' (ibid.: 5), which may be said to be one of the sources of the modern divide between the private and the public. Serfaty writes that both blogs and diaries are usually written more for the sake of the writer than for the sake of the reader. They are used as mirrors, she argues, to reflect upon the self, more than they are used to project a particular image to the public, as might, for instance, be the case in an autobiography intended for publication.

Serfaty's book was published in 2004, before the commercialisation of blogs (Rettberg, 2014a: Chapter 5) really began, and before social media went mainstream. While much of what she writes is still true of today's blogs, clearly many blogs are now much more about branding, monetisation or constructing a particular image of the self, while much other use of social media is more about keeping in touch with friends or sharing quick jokes or observations than about self-improvement or developing ideas. A lot of the discussion that previously happened in self-hosted blogs has shifted to corporate-owned spaces like Twitter and Facebook, where the space to write is far more limited

than in a traditional blog. Another shift is the increased emphasis on metrics: how many likes, shares or recommends did your post get? In the early days of blogging this was not visible to readers. You could see where discussions were taking place, but you couldn't calculate how important a blogger was based on numbers at the bottom of each post. Perhaps one of the reasons why Snapchat has gained influence is that people are relieved not to have to see how many likes and shares each snap they view has received. There are some metrics in Snapchat; for instance, you can see who viewed your own story, or who opened a private snap you sent, but you can't like or share somebody else's story, and you can't see how many views or likes somebody else's story has.

SELFIES AND VISUAL SELF-REPRESENTATIONS

As we approached 2010, smartphones with built-in cameras, good screens and cheap data plans became common, and images became increasingly important in social media. At the same time, platforms such as Facebook became mainstream forms of communication. It is easy to forget how recent these shifts are. The term 'social media' itself was not in popular usage until 2008. Before that, people talked about Web 2.0 and social networking sites, and before that, people simply talked about the web or the internet. Smartphones make taking, sharing and looking at images easier than typing or reading lengthy blog posts, and increasingly self-representation in social media has become visual.

Of course there were visual forms of self-representation online well before smart phones. ASCII graphics were used in discussion groups in the 1970s and 1980s, photos and animated gifs were used on early websites, bloggers and Myspace-users chose graphical templates and fonts that they felt represented them, icons and visual avatars were used in chatrooms (Thomas, 2004), 'camgirls' of the early 2000s used webcams to stream their lives online (Senft, 2008), and photo-sharing sites like Flickr (launched in 2004) were specifically created for image-sharing. In today's social media, users have less control of the overall look of the page, and visual control is generally limited to the choice of cover photos, profile pictures and other images shared. However, the images that are shared are given prominence and are the main point of many social media platforms.

Visual self-portraits are an age-old genre, and though there are many examples in art museums, the most interesting examples in the context of social media, namely those created by ordinary people and intended for the moment rather than posterity, are probably lost to us. It wasn't until the late fifteenth century, with Albrecht Dürer, that self-portraits became their own genre, rather than the slightly furtive insertion of the self into images that had other purposes (Borzello, 1998: 21). Self-portraits became promotional objects for artists, allowing a prospective client to assess the likeness between the painter and the self-portrait. They were also done for practice: even without access to a model, if an artist has a mirror available, they can always paint their own face.

Access to technology that would allow you to create a lasting self-portrait is a fairly recent development. A child can draw her face in the sand on a beach, but it will wash away with the next waves. To create a lasting image usually requires a material such as paper or marble or canvas and the tools to make marks on it, such as paints or pencils or tools for sculpture, and these things were not cheap until quite recently. Some artists have managed with much less, such as the Stone Age people who placed their hands on cave walls and blew ochre dust over them to make a hand print. But most of the self-portraits we have preserved, up until the last century or so, were created by professional artists.

Some of the first photographs ever taken were self-portraits. An early example is Hippolyte Bayard's *Self-Portrait as a Drowned Man* (1840), which is a carefully staged self-portrait showing the photographer slumped against a wall as though dead. Bayard claimed to have discovered photography before Daguerre, but was not recognised for this, and this photograph was presented as a criticism of the French Academy's failure to acknowledge Bayard's work. It was as though they had killed him, the image seems to say, thrown him, dead, into the gutters, and the words he scrawled on the back of the photograph confirm this: 'The Government which has been only too generous to Monsieur Daguerre, has said it can do nothing for Monsieur Bayard, and the poor wretch has drowned himself.'

This is not only one of the first photographic self-portraits; it is also a staged photograph, deliberately showing a scene that did not happen. As such the photograph is a useful reminder that self-representations are often staged and not always intended to be taken as truth, or at least not as literal truth. Bayard did not drown. But taking this photograph not only allowed others to see him as drowned, it allowed him to see himself as drowned. It allowed him to see himself as he could never see himself without technology that recorded and displayed a frozen image. We cannot see ourselves in a mirror with our eyes closed. Self-portraits can be a way to communicate with others, but they can also be a way for the photographer to imagine how he or she could be different.

When Kodak started marketing relatively cheap and easy-to-use cameras to amateurs in the late nineteenth century, family photographs and photo albums became personal media found in many homes. Photobooths also became popular as early as the 1910s or 1920s, first as amusement park attractions and later as fixtures in train stations and public spaces, where they were used to take the standardised portraits that had become necessary for identity papers, but also for fun (Pellicer, 2010). Photobooths allowed ordinary people to take photographs for themselves, and without a photographer being involved. If you search online, you will easily find many examples of old photos taken in photobooths, both of ordinary people and of celebrities, and it is fascinating to see how similar many of these images are to selfies taken today (Rettberg, 2014b: 42–44). People have a tendency to ham it up in photobooths, and, as with selfies, group portraits are common.

Twentieth-century photographers' self-portraits were often taken in mirrors, and often positioned the camera as a barrier between the viewer and the photographer (Borzello, 1998: 142). In their self-portraits, professional photographers like Kate Matthews (c. 1900) and Margaret Bourke-White (c. 1933) seem to hide behind their large cameras.

The great shift from these mirror self-portraits to today's selfies is that selfies are usually taken on a smartphone where the front-facing camera combined with the screen allows the photographer to simultaneously see and record herself (Warfield, 2014). The smartphone is a mirror that can capture our reflection, at any moment. Once you own a digital camera, you can take as many photos as you like without worrying about using up the film or having to pay to have the photographs developed. Perhaps it is almost as important that you can take photographs with the assumption that nobody else need ever see that photo. This assumption may not in fact be true, as we know from scandals where phones or private photo-sharing networks have been hacked and photographs posted publicly. But we can still take these photos in private, much as teenagers gaze into a mirror when nobody is looking to wonder who they are and who they might become.

A lot of interesting research on selfies has been published in the last few years. Anne Burns discusses the ways in which selfies are used to discipline young women in particular, using Foucault in her analyses (Burns, 2015). Katie Warfield interviewed women who take selfies and found that they use selfies as cameras, stages and mirrors:

> young women mediate between these various subjectivities at once trying to find a balance between an image that presents them as conventionally beautiful (the model), while also being an image that others would want to see (the self-conscious thespian) and finally an image that somehow represents a felt connection to the body and one's authentic sense of self. (Warfield, 2015)

Katrin Tiidenberg has analysed Tumblr communities that share erotic selfies (Tiidenberg, 2014; Tiidenberg and Gomez Cruz, 2015), while Crystal Abidin has written about the 'subversive frivolity' of influencers' selfies (Abidin, 2016).

Much of the research on selfies as visual artefacts or representations focuses on what Paul Frosh calls nonrepresentational changes: 'innovations in distribution, storage, and metadata that are not directly concerned with the production or aesthetic design of images' (Frosh, 2015: 1607). Frosh instead uses concepts from the theory of photography to argue that selfies are gestures, arguing that while photographs have previously been indexical primarily because they are traces of a material reality, selfies are indexical in that they point to a communicative action. The selfie 'says not only "see this, here, now," but also "see me showing you me." It points to the performance of a communicative action rather than to an object, and is a trace of that performance' (Frosh, 2015: 1610).

QUANTIFIED AND AUTOMATED SELF-REPRESENTATIONS

While written and visual self-representations have long, well-studied, pre-digital histories, quantitative self-representation was less common until personal computers became ubiquitous and powerful enough to make personal data collection easy. 'Self knowledge through numbers,' is the slogan of the quantified self (QS) movement. The idea of self-improvement through self-knowledge is a recurrent theme in self-tracking (Rettberg, 2014b: 62–68; Lupton, 2016: 64–69), as in social media in general. In *Status Update*, Alice Marwick writes that 'social media allows people to strategically construct an identity in ways that are deeply rooted in contemporary ideas that the self is autonomous and constantly improving' (Marwick, 2013: loc. 3091).

Benjamin Franklin's habit tracking, described in his autobiography, is an early, pre-digital example of the idea of self-improvement through self-tracking. To become a better person, he decided to track how well he adhered to thirteen virtues he had set out as especially important to him: temperance, silence, order, resolution, frugality, industry, sincerity, justice, moderation, cleanliness, chastity, tranquility and humility. He drew up a chart with a column for each day of the week and a row for each of the virtues, and gave himself a black mark for each day he felt he hadn't lived up to a virtue, and two black marks if he had done very badly. Looking at the chart in his autobiography, silence seems to have been a virtue he struggled with in particular, with two black marks on Sunday and one on Monday, Wednesday and Friday. Order was difficult for him too, but he did quite well at resolution (Franklin, 2007 [orig. 1791]).

Today's technology makes it easier both to track your personal data and to analyse that data. You might track how many cups of coffee you drink each day and compare that to how easily you fall asleep at night, or how many productive work hours you have, or how often you have a headache, and then use your findings to try to optimise your sleep, productivity or wellbeing by changing your coffee-drinking habits. This kind of analysis is made much easier by computers. Self-tracking has gone mainstream largely because it is built into many devices. Smartphones now have built-in step-tracking, and apps like Runkeeper, Strava and Endomondo let you track runs or other workouts, showing you how far and how fast you run as well as offering specific workout plans. Dedicated devices can measure how well you sleep, how good your posture is or how often you take deep breaths.

Several scholars have likened the increased quantification and measurement we see in social media to neo-liberalism, pointing out that using metrics to measure every aspect of our lives can make us cogs in a machine we do not control (Lupton, 2013: 28; Marwick, 2013: loc. 105; Grosser, 2014). Workplaces are increasingly requiring or expecting self-tracking of various kinds. Warehouses like Amazon's fulfilment centres track workers' every move. Other companies give health insurance discounts if workers log a million steps on their company-issued Fitbits. Sometimes tracking is required or encouraged by employers to document that a worker is getting enough exercise in order to be a healthy, productive worker (Till, 2014). Coerced quantified representations of ourselves may be required or expected by employers or schools. They are also generated and often displayed to others when we use social media: the number of likes a selfie posted to Facebook or the number of retweets we get on Twitter are displayed both to the person who posted the material and to anyone else who views it. In other cases, medical conditions such as diabetes require constant self-monitoring. Self-tracking is not always optional.

Quantified self-representations also include automated diaries, which are generated by apps you can install on your phone, or the algorithmic self-representations generated as summaries of your activities on various services (Rettberg, 2014b: 45–60). Often, these are generated without your having realised that your actions were being tracked as data that could represent you. For instance, at the end of each year, customised infographics are sent to users of Goodreads and Spotify showing an overview of the books the user read or the music they listened to. For the last few years, Facebook has generated 'Year in Review' videos and photo collages from posts from each user in the last year. Google Photos automatically stitches together videos and animations from users' photos and videos, using facial recognition, image search algorithms and metadata about time and location to automatically create, for instance, a video of a user's 'Christmas 2016' or of their 'Trip to Paris'. These sorts of representations are not necessarily seen as part of the quantified self-movement, but they are quantified self-representations because they represent an aspect of an individual using quantifiable data.

These algorithmically created diaries (Rettberg, 2018) are usually presented to the individual with a question: Would you like to share this? Services we use thus collect our data and present that data back to us as a possible self-representation. Sometimes, you might not even be aware that data about you are being added to your social media profiles. When Spotify posts a song you are listening to to your Facebook newsfeed, that becomes part of what others see as your self-representation on Facebook, but you might not have wanted the song to show up, and you might not even notice that it showed up (Kant, 2015). Sharing an infographic of the music you listen to can feel like quite a personal form of self-representation, but for the service that generated it (Spotify, GoodReads, Facebook or another company) it is also a mode of advertisement.

ABUNDANT SELF-REPRESENTATIONS

In the time of one-to-many communication, media were scarce. It was very expensive to write, edit, print and distribute books or newspapers, to make and distribute movies, or to create and broadcast television and radio, so gatekeepers like publishers and production companies made sure that only material that was either commercially viable or seen as aesthetically or ideologically important was published or broadcast. This meant

that we could assume a certain level of quality when we picked up a book or a newspaper, or turned on the television. Before the internet, individuals' production of personal media was also limited. While paper and pens for writing a personal diary were easily available in the twentieth century, it was expensive to buy film and to have it developed, so people were quite selective about what photographs they chose to take. That is why home photography generally centred around certain rituals, as Pierre Bourdieu described in his book on amateur photography, originally published in 1965 (Bourdieu, 1990). We took photos at birthdays and weddings, and of happy families in the sunshine at the beach, but not of our laundry or of walking the kids to school. We didn't often take photographs of ourselves.

With digital technology, media are no longer scarce. When everyone can create and distribute as much media content as they please, there will obviously be a lot of material available that is not particularly of high quality and that will never be of interest to most of the world. That's OK, many bloggers argued in the early 2000s (Mortensen and Walker, 2002). You don't have to read or look at blogs and photos you're not interested in. We all have a vast amount of media at our disposal. Of course, this also means that despite the potential for a huge audience, most social media content creators will never have very many people reading or looking at the material they publish. Andy Warhol famously said in the sixties that everyone has their fifteen minutes of fame. On the internet, Dave Weinberger and others have argued that it's more correct to say, 'Everyone is famous to fifteen people'.

And yet the accusation of shallow vapidity is one that recurs with every new form of self-representation online. Blogs and selfies have both been accused of being shallow, of being expressions of narcissism, of being boring. Back in 2002 when the first awards were established for blogs, bloggers Dave Linabury and Leia Scofield founded the

'Anti-Bloggies', an award created to ridicule bad blogs. They explained in an interview with *Wired* magazine:

> One of the things I don't like is the blog where someone says something like, 'Today I had a cheese sandwich.' That's the kind of thing you see in most of these blogs. You know, fascinating. I don't give a flying … whatever what you ate. Don't tell me you have a flat tire. And if this is how boring their writing is, I can't imagine how boring they must be to talk to in general. (Manjoo, 2002)

Similar criticisms have been levied at Twitter and Facebook as well. Much of our social interaction, whether online or offline, is banal. Perhaps more accurately, it is *phatic*: more about maintaining connections than about conveying information (Miller, 2008).

The quantified self-movement has not received the level of ridicule that blogs and selfies suffered when new. Perhaps its numerical basis gives it a sheen of objectivity, a sense of seriousness that blogs and selfies will never have. Perhaps selfies are dismissed because they are often seen as 'feminine' (Burns, 2015), whereas quantified self is seen as masculine and therefore more serious and worthy of attention.

Quantitative self data may appear objective, but we know that people negotiate with their data, retelling the stories of their days to make their own experience match up with the data. Researcher Minna Ruckenstein gave her informants heart-rate variation monitors, but didn't show them their data until after they had already told the researchers about their subjective experiences of the days they had worn the monitors. Heart-rate variation is an indicator of stress, and when the informants were shown the data, they changed their stories to fit (Ruckenstein, 2014). Data is always something that needs to be interpreted. It is not an objective window on truth, any more than visual or written self-representations are reflections of 'the true meaning as it exists in the world', to quote Stuart Hall again (1997: 24). Viviane Serfaty titled her 2004 book on personal blogs *The Mirror and the Veil*, arguing that bloggers use their blogs both as mirrors to reflect themselves and see themselves better, and as veils to hide behind. Self-representations are rarely about trying to tell the whole truth and nothing but the truth about ourselves. They are as much about constructing a truth or many truths about who we are and could be.

As objective as it may seem, even detailed counting does not necessarily tell you very much about a person's life. Sometimes the thing measured is not very interesting, as when Samuel Beckett mockingly let his character Molloy count farts in the novel *Molloy*:

> Three hundred and fifteen farts in nineteen hours, or an average of over sixteen farts an hour. After all it's not excessive. Four farts every fifteen minutes. It's nothing. Not even one fart every four minutes. It's unbelievable. Damn it, I hardly fart at all. (Beckett, 1994: 39)

Tracking farts is of course used as a mockery of obsessive self-tracking, or of excessive attention to oneself, and the idea of this useless obsession is echoed in the 2003 project *Statistics are Hot Air*, in which artist Ellie Harrison (2003) tracked her 'daily gaseous emission output' for a year. Harrison not only counted all her farts from January to June 2003, she visualised them both as a bar chart on a paper timeline hanging on her studio wall, and as a physical installation at Moor Street Station in Birmingham. The physical installation is a large, colourful bar chart on a glass window, and the vinyl stickers look like a purely decorative border at the bottom of the window. Visualisations of quantified self-representations do tend to have a decorative aesthetics that sometimes distracts from the data themselves, or that perhaps is ultimately more interesting to us than the data. We are driven by our desire for patterns and completed sequences: a gold star on every square on the star chart, or a graph showing we have gone for a run three times a week, every week.

The ultimately empty or purely decorative function of Harrison's chart of her farts can certainly be read as a critique of quantitative measurements in general. The title *Statistics are Hot Air* equates statistics to farts. Both are hot air, nothing at all, or worse, following the colloquial meaning of 'hot air', which the Oxford English Dictionary explains is 'Empty or boastful talk, pretentious or insubstantial statements or claims'.

The construction of meaning in quantified self-representations can also be seen in Molloy's fart-counting. He has counted exactly how many times he has farted that day, but is capable of interpreting that number as either high or low. The sentences immediately before the quote cited above read: 'I can't help it, gas escapes from my fundament on the least pretext, it's hard not to mention it now and then, however great my distaste. One day I counted them.'

Despite having arrived at the figure of three hundred and fifteen farts in nineteen hours, Molloy manages to conclude that this is 'nothing', adding 'Damn it, I hardly fart at all'. Like the informants in Minna Ruckenstein's study, Molloy is skilled at interpreting data in a way that suits him. Of course, knowing that the author of *Molloy* was Samuel Beckett, we can see that this is about a lot more than simply a critique of self-measurements. In her book *Narratives of Nothing in 20th Century Literature*, Meghan Vicks notes that 'Even when Molloy attempts to tabulate the most mundane facts about himself, he arrives at an ambiguity suggesting nothing' (Vicks, 2015: 123). The idea of nothingness and emptiness is important in Beckett's work.

Twelve years after Harrison's project, the CH4, an automated, wearable fart monitor that you slip into the back pocket of your jeans and that connects to an app on your smartphone, was pitched on Kickstarter, but failed to attract sufficient funding (Narciso, 2015). CH4 had a completely serious goal, and was apparently developed with no sense of irony or existential anxiety: the project aims to help people emit less gas by measuring how often they fart, comparing this to what they eat, and finding correlations between their diets and farts so as to help users to cut back on

the foods that increase wind. The interface of the app that shows the users' results contains more information than Harrison's colourful bar chart, but is still visually pleasing. The website and the device itself conform to contemporary tech startup aesthetics: the website has large, high-quality photographs, and responsive, scrolling design. The prototypes of the device itself are shown as square with rounded edges, and come in white as well as pink, blue and green. CH4 fits perfectly into the rhetoric of quantified self and tech startup cultures – except it is about something embarrassing: farts. Of course, farts are not simply embarrassing, as we have seen, they are also rich metaphors for nothingness, for meaninglessness, for pretentiousness.

Self-representations in social media are often mocked as vapid, self-obsessed, frivolous – or simply boring. This is perhaps where seeing them as *representations* can trip us up. Our everyday and scholarly tools for understanding representations carry with them a twentieth-century worldview where we expect media to be professionally created by the few for the many. We expect a representation to be carefully crafted and packed with meaning. Social media self-representations, on the other hand, are personal, social and often made for the moment, not for eternity. When I share a selfie or post a Snapchat story about my day, I am not usually trying to create immortal art or literature. Sometimes I may aim to impress or entertain an audience, or to put something deeply significant into words or images, but more often I am narrating or visualising my experiences so as to remember them better, or understand them better, or to strengthen a connection with my friends, or to ask for support, or simply to pass the time.

On the other hand, a self-representation is precisely a *representation*. It shows a certain aspect of ourselves, a certain way of seeing ourselves. A representation does not and never can share everything. We negotiate with our self-representations, whether like the informants in Minna Ruckenberg's study, retelling their days to suit the data, or by taking dozens of selfies before choosing the one we want to share. We choose what to share, which self-representations are appropriate, but we share far more than the rituals and the happy family situations that Bourdieu wrote about in the sixties. The social contract for what is photographable or sharable or representable is changing. New apps and devices and social media services are constantly being offered to us, and many fail. Others change our ideas of how to tell our stories. There will surely be more changes in years to come.

REFERENCES

Abidin, Crystal. 2015. 'Communicative ♥ Intimacies: Influencers and Perceived Interconnectedness.' *Ada: A Journal of Gender, New Media & Technology*, 8. http://adanewmedia.org/2015/11/issue8-abidin/.

Abidin, Crystal. 2016. '"Aren't These Just Young, Rich Women Doing Vain Things Online?": Influencer Selfies as Subversive Frivolity.' *Social Media + Society*, 2(2): 2056305116641342. doi:10.1177/2056305116641342.

Bakshy, Alexander. 1923. *The Theatre Unbound: A Plea on Behalf of the Ill-Used: The Actor, the Stage, and the Spectator*. London: C. Palmer.

Beckett, Samuel. 1994. *Molloy*. New York: Grove Press.

Blood, Rebecca. 2000. 'Weblogs: A History and Perspective.' *Rebecca's Pocket*, September. www.rebeccablood.net/essays/weblog_history.html.

Borzello, Frances. 1998. *Seeing Ourselves: Women's Self-Portraits*. London: Thames & Hudson.

Bourdieu, Pierre. 1990. *Photography: A Middle-Brow Art*. Stanford, CA: Stanford University Press.

boyd, danah. 2011. 'Social Network Sites as Networked Publics: Affordances, Dynamics and Implications.' In Zizi Papacharissi (Ed.), *Networked Self: Identity, Community, and Culture on Social Network Sites*. New York: Routledge.

Burns, Anne. 2015. 'Self(ie)-Discipline: Social Regulation as Enacted Through the Discussion of Photographic Practice.' *International Journal of Communication*, 9(May): 1716–1733.

Fiske, John. 2010. *Introduction to Communication Studies* (3rd ed.). London: Routledge.

Franklin, Benjamin. 2007 [1791]. *The Autobiography of Benjamin Franklin*. New York: Cosimo.

Frosh, Paul. 2015. 'The Gestural Image: The Selfie, Photography Theory, and Kinesthetic Sociability.' *International Journal of Communication*, 9: 1607-1628.

Goffman, Erving. 1959. *The Presentation of Self in Everyday Life*. New York: Anchor.

Grosser, Benjamin. 2014. 'What Do Metrics Want? How Quantification Prescribes Social Interaction on Facebook,' no. 4. http://computationalculture.net/article/what-do-metrics-want.

Hall, Stuart. 1997. 'The Work of Representation.' In Stuart Hall, *Representation: Cultural Representations and Signifying Practices*. Milton Keynes: The Open University Press.

Harrison, Ellie. 2003. 'Statistics Are Hot Air.' *EllieHarrison.com*.

Humphreys, Lee, Phillipa Gill, Balachander Krishnamurthy, and Elizabeth Newbury. 2013. 'Historicizing New Media: A Content Analysis of Twitter.' *Journal of Communication*, 63(3): 413–431. doi:10.1111/jcom.12030.

Jackson, Roni. 2016. 'If They Gunned Me Down and Criming While White: An Examination of Twitter Campaigns through the Lens of Citizens' Media.' *Cultural Studies ↔ Critical Methodologies*, March, 1532708616634836. doi:10.1177/1532708616634836.

Jenner, Kendall. 2015. '➤.' *Instagram*. May 25. www.instagram.com/p/3H0-Yqjo7u/.

Johnson, Steven. 2002. 'A Word from Our Sponsor.' Blog. *Stevenberlinjohnson.com*. December 26. www.stevenberlinjohnson.com/2002/12/a_word_from_our.html.

Kant, Tanya. 2015. '"Spotify Has Added an Event to Your Past": (Re)Writing the Self through Facebook's Autoposting Apps.' *The Fibreculture Journal*, no. 25. doi:10.15307/fcj.25.180.2015.

Korn, Jenny Ungbha. 2015. 'Towards Social Justice, against Media Bias: Creating Tumblr Content with Purpose through #IfTheyGunnedMeDown.' In *Proceedings of Internet Research 16 (IR16)*. Phoenix, AZ: Association of Internet Researchers.

Lejeune, Philippe. 2000. *'Cher écran...' Journal Personnel, Ordinateur, Internet*. Paris: Editions du Seuil.

Lövheim, Mia. 2013. 'Negotiating Empathic Communication.' *Feminist Media Studies*, 13(4): 613–628. doi:10.1080/14680777.2012.659672.

Lüders, Marika. 2008. 'Conceptualizing Personal Media.' *New Media & Society*, 10(5): 683–702. doi:10.1177/1461444808094352.

Lupton, Deborah. 2013. 'Understanding the Human Machine [Commentary].' *IEEE Technology and Society Magazine*, 32(4): 25–30. doi:10.1109/MTS.2013.2286431.

Lupton, Deborah. 2016. *The Quantified Self: A Sociology of Self-Tracking*. Cambridge: Polity Press.

Manjoo, Farhad. 2002. 'Blah, Blah, Blah and Blog.' *WIRED*. February 18. http://archive.wired.com/culture/lifestyle/news/2002/02/50443.

Marwick, Alice. 2013. *Status Update: Celebrity, Publicity, and Branding in the Social Media Age*. New Haven, CT: Yale Universsity Press.

Miller, Vincent. 2008. 'New Media, Networking and Phatic Culture.' *Convergence: The International Journal of Research into New Media Technologies*, 14(4): 387–400. doi:10.1177/1354856508094659.

Mortensen, Torill, and Jill Walker. 2002. 'Blogging Thoughts: Personal Publication as an Online Research Tool.' In Andrew Morrison (Ed.), *Researching ICTs in Context* (pp. 249–279). Oslo: InterMedia, University of Oslo. www.intermedia.uio.no/konferanser/skikt-02/docs/Researching_ICTs_in_context-Ch11-Mortensen-Walker.pdf.

Narciso, Rodrigo. 2015. 'Keep Track of Your Gases with CH4!' *Kickstarter*. www.kickstarter.com/projects/963861855/keep-track-of-your-gases-with-ch4.

Pellicer, Raynal. 2010. *Photobooth: The Art of the Automatic Portrait*. New York: Abrams.

Rettberg, Jill Walker. 2014a. *Blogging* (2nd ed.). Cambridge: Polity Press.

Rettberg, Jill Walker. 2014b. *Seeing Ourselves through Technology: How We Use Selfies, Blogs and Wearable Devices to See and Shape Ourselves*. Basingbroke: Palgrave.

Rettberg, Jill Walker. 2018. 'Apps as Companions: How Quantified Self Apps Become Our Audience and Our Companions.' In Btihaj Ajana (Ed.), *Self-Tracking: Empirical and Philosophical Investigations* (pp. 27–42). Basingbroke: Palgrave. doi:10.1007/978-3-319-65379-2_3

Ruckenstein, Minna. 2014. 'Visualized and Interacted Life: Personal Analytics and Engagements with Data Doubles.' *Societies*, 4(1): 68–84. doi:10.3390/soc4010068.

Senft, Theresa M. 2008. *Camgirls: Celebrity and Community in the Age of Social Networks*. New York: Peter Lang.

Senft, Theresa M. 2013. 'Microcelebrity and the Branded Self.' In John Hartley, Jean Burgess, and Axel Bruns (Eds.), *A Companion to New Media Dynamics* (pp. 347–355). Chichester, UK: Wiley.

Serfaty, Viviane. 2004. *The Mirror and the Veil: An Overview of American Online Diaries and Blogs*. Amsterdam: Amsterdam Monographs in American Studies.

Thomas, Angela. 2004. 'Digital Literacies of the Cybergirl.' *E-Learning*, 1: 358–382.

Tiidenberg, Katrin. 2014. 'Bringing Sexy Back: Reclaiming the Body Aesthetic via Self-Shooting.' *Cyberpsychology: Journal of Psychosocial Research on Cyberspace*, 8(1). doi:10.5817/CP2014-1-3.

Tiidenberg, K., and E. Gomez Cruz. 2015. 'Selfies, Image and the Re-Making of the Body.' *Body & Society*, 21(4): 77–102. doi:10.1177/1357034X15592465.

Till, Chris. 2014. 'Exercise as Labour: Quantified Self and the Transformation of Exercise into Labour.' *Societies*, 4(3): 446–462. doi:10.3390/soc4030446

Vicks, Meghan. 2015. *Narratives of Nothing in 20th-Century Literature*. New York: Bloomsbury.

Warfield, Katie. 2014. 'An Open Letter to Mass Media Explaining, Definitively, the Meaning of Selfies.' *Making Selfies/Making Self*. Accessed June 10. www.makingselfiesmakingself.com/an-open-letter-to-mass-media-explaining-definitively-the-meaning-of-selfies.html.

Warfield, Katie. 2015. 'Digital Subjectivities and Selfies: The Model, the Self-Conscious Thespian, and the #realme.' *The International Journal of the Image*, 6(2).

24

Sexual Expression in Social Media

Kath Albury

While there once was a time when it seemed easy to draw a boundary between 'cybersex' and offline sexuality, contemporary practices of courtship, dating, flirtation and sexual experimentation are explicitly and implicitly supported by social media platforms, particularly those offering affordances of picture sharing and geo-location. Contemporary practices, such as sharing sexy selfies, are not entirely new. Since the 1990s, new forms of sexual self-representation – such as text-based 'cybersex' (Atwood, 2013), or the 'peep-show' aspects of webcamming – have been supported by proto-social networking sites such as alt-sex bulletin boards and Pro/Am sites such as SuicideGirls (Senft, 2008; Paasonen, 2011). Within these spaces, mediated sexual practices that might previously have been associated with commercial sex work (or 'taboo' sexual subcultures) were adopted by 'ordinary' people (see Albury, 2002, 2004; McKee et al., 2002). Bulletin boards focusing on sex and sexuality emerged as spaces for aficionados of alternative (alt)

sexual practices and relationship style to chat, flirt and form new relationships. With the popularization of affordable home web-cams, sex-based sites expanded their capacity, evolving into spaces where users could not only discuss their favourite porn (or swap their favourite pictures and videos), but could actively participate in explicit live or pre-recorded interactions with other enthusiasts. Indeed, the rise of amateur or DIY porn enthusiasts in the 1990s sparked what was termed the 'pro-am' genre in commercial pornography, in which porn studios offered fans the opportunity to perform in 'candid' web-cam style videos with star performers (Albury, 2002).

Early internet scholars, particularly feminists and queer theorists, explored the possibilities of transcending or re-imagining embodiment, sexuality and gender in MUDs, MOOs and on alt-sex bulletin boards (for example, see Rheingold, 1991; Bornstein, 1994; Turkle, 1995). Despite this, as Gilbert Herdt and Cymene Howe note, 'as recently as the mid-1990s, experts reviewing sexuality research and policy completely ignored the Internet' (2007: 4). Much to the surprise of biomedically-focused sex researchers, online and mobile digital media spaces have become primary sites in which sexual cultures are made visible, with a multitude of websites, apps and social networking platforms proliferating commercial and non-commercial erotic images and written texts. These are intermingled with and scaffolded by sexual health information, activism, peer support, formal and informal pedagogy, and, in some cases, harassment and abuse (Herdt and Howe, 2007).

These practices have been condemned (and celebrated) as evidence of the rise of a 'pornified' culture – particularly within an Anglophone context (McNair, 2002). Some platforms, such as Grindr or Tinder, which primarily represent themselves as facilitating dating, but are seen to promote casual encounters or hook-ups, have been castigated in popular media as harbingers of a 'dating apocalypse' that will 'tear society apart' (Riley, 2015; Sales 2015). Others, such as Facebook and Instagram, are officially 'social networking sites', but are widely used for meeting new intimate and/or romantic partners, and buttressing existing relationships. In these 'unofficial' settings, reciprocal practices of liking and sharing non-explicit digital pictures (including profile pictures) can be an effective strategy for indicating, or confirming, a sexual and/or romantic interest (see Aziz, 2014; Lenhart et al., 2015).

Unsurprisingly, both media scholars and sexuality researchers are beginning to ask new questions regarding sexual expression in these spaces. How do the specific technological attributes or affordances of social networking services shape users' experience of sex, sexuality and gender? How do users shape (or resist) the codes and conventions of social media platforms? Are social media platforms facilitating new, or different sexual expression, particularly among vulnerable groups and stigmatized sexual subcultures?

Are they being used to control or coerce their users? Finally, what are the similarities and differences between sexual expression in contemporary social media cultures and other forms of online and offline sexual expression, such as early dating platforms and amateur webcam sites?

RECENT HISTORIES OF ONLINE SEXUAL EXPRESSION

A significant body of early research into sexual expression via mobile messaging and picture exchange focused on gay men. In his study of gay men's adoption of mobile messaging, Dowsett concludes that these practices suggest 'a remarkable shift in *inciting* desire rather than merely *representing* it' (2010: 269, original emphasis). Kreps (2009) and Mowlobocus (2007, 2010) explain eroticized picture exchange as a process of sexual identity formation, in which 'ordinary' men's bodies are re-contextualized with reference to pornographic genres of self-representation. Further, both Mowlobocus (2010) and Tudor (2012) observe that pictures are deployed as a form on non-verbal sexual negotiation, by which hook-up app or dating site users can easily indicate their 'preferred sexual roles, acts, practices, and fetishes' (Mowlobocus, 2010: 208). As Thomas Waugh's (1996) history of gay men's amateur cultures of erotic photograph shows, sexual representation, be it amateur or commercial, can take many forms. Each image, or collection of images, Waugh argues, may hold different meanings:

> from the nonsexual portrait of the loved one, to his unclothed body; explicit depictions of fucking, whether nonloving and mechanical or imbued with ... romantic patinas ...; both narrative representations (stories of desire) and nonnarrative (views of the object desired); not only depictions and narrations but also enunciations of desire ('I love you' – whether reciprocated, tolerated or unnoticed ...), performances ('here I am being desirable'), and even prescriptions ('here is how to

make love'); from the psychological or spiritual to the physiological, from the symbolic to the literal, from the exalted to the sleazy; from the embroidery of the fetish or symbol, to the look that strips bare. (Waugh, 1996: 7)

The history of heterosexual picture-sharing has been documented, too, and is found primarily in the field of 'porn studies', tracking DIY cultures of mediated sexual expression from the era of amateur photography described by Waugh, to the forums of Reddit or 4Chan (see van der Nagle, 2013; van der Nagel and Frith, 2015). From the mid-1990s, researchers have observed the increased visibility and accessibility of peer-to-peer, 'domesticated' online amateur porn sites and webcam communities, noting their similarities and differences to older analogue networks of classified advertising, mail-order catalogues and private newsletters (see Albury, 2004; McKee et al., 2008; Paasonen, 2011; Williams, 2004). Similarly, online 'sexseeker' sites, such as AdultFriendFinder, offer their subscribers the capacity to engage in online picture-swapping and webcam interactions, as well as facilitating offline hook-ups (Jacobs, 2010).

A range of researchers have documented accounts of heterosexual women's online participation in sexual cultures that pre-date contemporary NSFW (not safe for work) social media cultures. For example, Rival and colleagues' 1998 ethnographic study of an Internet Relay Chat (IRC) site for porn collectors found that female participants particularly enjoyed opportunities to not only discuss their favourite porn, but to participate in explicit chat and webcamming, in order to 'explore desires which are too taboo, embarrassing or dangerous for off-line life: mainly bisexuality, exhibitionism, group sex and promiscuity' (Rival et al., 1998: 301). Writing in 1997, US author Cleo Odzer described her participation in similar environments as 'the freedom to be anyone and do anything, I had sex with three men at once. I had sex with a woman… Posing as a man, I had sex with a man who was posing as a woman. I learned

all about S&M, as the sadist and as the masochist. I had all sorts of sex in every new way I could think of' (Odzer, in Waskul, 2003: 3–4). In their study of a heterosexual amateur webcam site, Kibby and Costello observed that it not only created a space for women to engage in sexual play and self-representation, but formed a community that both supported heterosexual women as voyeurs and promoted heterosexual men's exhibitionistic desires to perform for women (Kibby and Costello, 2001).

Early webcam communities served as a pleasurable space of play and fantasy, much as do contemporary social media sites that combine picture sharing with other forms of social communication (such as Reddit or FetLife). At the same time, these amateur porn and X-rated swap-sites seem to demonstrate that sex (even pornographic or taboo sex) is *interconnected* with everyday life. Not only did participants on the pic-trading site studied by Kibby and Costello discuss everyday domestic issues, the online space itself was 'domesticated' in participants' discussions. These included, for example, the collective formulation of guidelines for online sexual etiquette and tips for negotiating jealousy and competition between online and offline sex partners. As Rival and colleagues described it in 1998, 'the objectification of sexuality on-line appears to be fuelled at least as often by the urge to order sexuality (and IRC relationships and practices themselves) along ethical lines as it is to gratify it transgressively' (Rival et al., 1998: 316).

These early webcam and collector sites appear to have had much in common with contemporary social media feeds, in that researchers observed that 'many logged conversations move within minutes from tastes in porn to the problems of single-parenthood, money problems, dead-end jobs' (Rival et al., 1998: 304). Similarly, Kibby and Costello observed that webcam chat was 'often grounded in the ordinariness of everyday life as people discuss where they're from, their age, their marital status, their jobs, their computer problems and the weather, all the while displaying erotic images of their naked bodies' (2001: 364). This domestication, accompanied by a proliferation of explicit texts and images featuring 'ordinary' bodies and 'ordinary' lives, attracted both celebration and censure. On the one hand, DIY or cottage industry 'porn stars' were seen to promote representations of erotic diversity that were not common in more 'mainstream' areas of commercial media. On the other hand, they were critiqued for normalizing and homogenizing aspects of 'pornified' cultures, including the conflation of feminine 'sexiness' with a willingness to conform to hetero-centric norms of bodily display (see McKee et al., 2008). These tensions are still evident in discussions of sexual expression within contemporary social media cultures.

These 'cottage industry' modes of online sexual expression have been enhanced by the emergence of platforms such as YouTube, Wordpress, Instagram and Tumblr (Paasonen, 2011). Tumblr's affordance of anonymity has facilitated NSFW blogs, which serve a range of purposes. These include fan communities dedicated to sharing (or re-blogging) sexually explicit images and gifs appropriated from commercial pornography; and overtly queer and feminist blogging communities for whom creating and sharing 'sexy selfies' is a mode of political self-expression (see Fink and Miller, 2014; Tiidenberg and Gomez Cruz, 2015). As Tiidenberg and Gomez Cruz observe, while amateur NSFW selfie producers are not oblivious to broader cultural codes and conventions of sexual attractiveness, many experience their practices of sexual self -representation as a form of resistance to cultural double standards. As one blogger puts it:

> I have always stood by my Tumblr in terms of my rationale … because I'm not getting paid for this, I'm not representing a company, I'm not wearing Calvin Klein underwear, I'm not in any way marketing this. I am … this is a self exploration, this is a finding of myself, and I … feel … if I were ever to be … confronted with these images … my first

thing would definitely be: 'I don't see what's wrong with it because I was of age and I was exploring who I am as a person and I don't see what the difference is between Megan Fox doing it for Armani and me doing it for myself.' (Tiidenberg and Gomez Cruz, 2015: 93–93)

While some of Tiidenberg and Gomez Cruz's interviewees report feeling uncomfortable with the notion of 'performing' for their followers, other participants in DIY social media sex cultures actively seek out fans, and solicit ratings, likes and upvotes. For example, contributors to the Tumblr site *Critique My Dickpic* receive critical feedback, and are rated on their composition and aesthetics on a scale from A+ to D- (Holden, 2016; Sara, 2016).

As Paasonen (2011: 95) observes, a DIY or home-spun aesthetic is part of the branding of NSFW Tumblr or Blogger sites, and indeed the more 'domesticity, authenticity, amateurism and realness' the better. Australian porn performer Zahra Stardust describes how these representations of 'realness' and authenticity are highly stage-managed by professional producers:

> Alternative nude modeling site Suicide Girls gives calculated instructions on their website about the kinds of photos, make-up and aesthetic sets they accept: tasteful, picture perfect shoots with 'a little bit of face powder and mascara and freshly dyed hair, but specifically not cheap wig(s), top hats, stripper shoes, food or things that look cheesy, gross or creepy. Similarly, the girl next door look of the Australian all-female explicit adult site *Abby Winters* represents an alternative to glamour photography, featuring make-up-less, amateur adult models – but models are still required to cover up hair re-growth, remove piercings, and not have any scratches, marks or mosquito bites for the shoot in order to appear healthy. (Stardust, 2012)

At the same time, many contemporary amateur (or semi-amateur) sexual micro-celebrities (see Marwick, 2015) strive to reproduce the codes and conventions of commercial pornography, adhering, in the main, to conventional modes of youthful heterosexual femininity. As van der Nagle (2013) observes, while amateur nude/selfie forums such as reddit gonewild include tagging options for male, crossdresser and trans selfies, the site's algorithmic favoring of 'upvoted' images ensures that images of conventionally attractive, young, white women dominate the forum's 'frontpage'.

It is not the case, then, that amateur sexual self-representations are intrinsically 'authentic', while professional sexual representations should be dismissed as 'fake'. Instead, the various forms of sexual expression outlined above can be best understood in the broader context of what Burgess (2006) has termed the 'vernacular creativity' afforded by social media. As Burgess puts it, these forms of creativity are not rendered inauthentic by virtue of their references to commercial aesthetics or mass media culture. Rather, they represent 'a productive articulation of consumer practices and knowledges' (in this case, knowledge of mainstream pornographic aesthetics) 'with older popular traditions and communicative practices (storytelling, family photography, scrapbooking, collecting)' (Burgess, 2006: 207). Even where 'false' (or self-protective) practices such as the use of pseudonyms are deployed in amateur communities, these can be used to convey a sense of the user's personality. As van der Nagle and Frith (2011) note, such practices can promote intimacy in sexual communities.

SEXUALITY, INTIMACY AND SOCIAL MEDIA AFFORDANCES

Social media (a term I am using here to encompass both application and web-based platforms) offers particular technological opportunities and challenges to users' sexual expression. While sexual expression can be shaped or restricted by the affordances of a specific platform, including design features, Terms of Service, network reach, and so on, users may also need to find creative ways to negotiate, or work around, the platform's 'official' use.

As Gillespie (2010: 351) puts it '"platforms" are "platforms" not necessarily because they allow code to be written or run, but because they afford an opportunity to communicate, interact or sell'. However, while developers may design interfaces that *invite* certain kinds of usage, they cannot prescribe or enforce the ways that apps or other social media platforms are used. Platforms are always open to 'off-label' uses – hook-up apps can be used to find housemates, dating apps can be used by job-hunters searching for contacts, and gaming platforms deployed as secure messaging services (see Bercovici, 2014; Albury and Byron, 2016). As Joshua McVeigh-Schultz and Nancy Baym (2015: 1) observe, social media affordances are intrinsically relational, 'defined by the relationship between the materiality of technological artifacts and the lived practices of communication', and are therefore always open to everyday practices of improvisation and adaptation.

Drawing on Silverstone's domestication theory (1992), McVeigh-Schultz and Baym (2015: 2) focus on social media users' everyday sense-making practices in relation to the use of the 'microsocial' (two person only) dating/relationship app, Couple. In paying attention to Couple users' explanations of how they have learned to use and adapt the app within their relationship, the authors demonstrate the ways social media users express relational intimacy within a specific technological environment. Like other new users of social media, Couple users 'borrow not just from their conversational styles but also from how they already use other media' (McVeigh-Schultz and Baym, 2015: 3).

McVeigh-Schultz and Baym's study offers a useful framework for mapping the ways social media users might use platforms or apps to express sexual desire, curiosity and intimacy, and how these practices might be constrained or enabled by technical elements such as design features and Terms of Use. The authors draw on Sabine Trepte's

(2015) categorization of 'warm' and 'cold' affordances to unpack the contradictory experience of mediated sexual expression. On the one hand, as Trepte (2015: 1) argues, social media platforms offer 'warmth' by allowing users to connect with lovers, friends and strangers in familiar, but pleasurably enhanced ways. At the same time, users are constrained by 'cool' affordances. These are less intuitive, and include restrictive Terms of Use, in which, for example, developers claim the right to own (and commercialize) user content (Trepte, 2015: 1).

For Couple users, 'warm' interactions involved the development of intimate, and private 'patterns of communication, including photo taking as phatic communication, genres of sketching as gift exchange, and "selfie" videos shot and posted before bedtime' (McVeigh-Schultz and Baym, 2015: 5). Other affordances are more difficult to clearly categorize as either cool or warm, such as the 'forced reciprocity' imposed by time-stamping and 'Seen' notifications on messenger or chat apps. As McVeigh-Schultz and Baym observe, these affordances may cause one partner in a conversation to feel obliged to respond to a message at a time and place that may not suit them, because they know the other party (or parties) in a conversation has automatically received a time-stamped 'this message was seen...' notification (McVeigh-Schultz and Baym, 2015: 9).

OFF-LABEL USES AND WORKAROUNDS IN SEXUAL/ SOCIAL MEDIA

Yael Roth's research on gay hook-up apps raises further questions regarding the intended and unintended effects of not only social media affordances, but of Terms of Service and other regulatory frameworks that influence users' modes of sexual expression (Roth, 2012, 2015). Roth's work questions whether Terms of Use and Terms of Service

are simply reflections of broader market restrictions (for example, the legal guidelines for selling apps via the Apple Store or GooglePlay), or whether they are intended to reflect, or prescribe, normative expectations of sexual expression within particular communities. These 'cool' affordances are often not well understood by app or social network users, and only become visible where there is conflict or dissent regarding their interpretation (most notably in the case of Facebook's takedowns of pictures of women breastfeeding their children). Even when Community Standards, Real Name Policies and other such policies are explained by official spokespeople, the interpretation and policing of the rules or terms can be opaque (and unfair) from the users' perspective. As Roth puts it:

> Would even a well-informed reading of an ideally written policy correspond with the actual experience of using an application or service? The basic assumption is that there exists a necessary and direct correspondence between what a company says it does in its user agreements and what a company actually does – and, crucially, why it does it. Knowing the rules may not be enough. (Roth, 2015: 4)

There may be times, however, when the rules do not matter. Where social media users *do* know and understand the rules, they may still communicate via coded workarounds to signal specific sexual desires and interests, or to signal an interest in exchanging explicit messages and/or pictures with others, such as the use of eggplant emoji to flag 'dick pics'. This use of coded forms of communication, incorporating hashtags and emoji, can lead to a push/pull struggle between users and app developers, as content guidelines change to police new behavior, and users simply change their coding and practices. For example, as Roth outlines:

> [The gay hook-up app] Manhunt ... has specified the grammatical circumstances within which the term 'party' may be used, in an effort to combat drug references in user profiles: 'The term "party" isn't allowed when used as a verb or adjective, but

as a noun such as in "sex party", "dinner party" or "group party" it is allowed' (Manhunt, 2009b). These guidelines recognize the possibility that, in online spaces, users may attempt to subvert services' limitations on their conduct by encoding discussions of their practices in ways that are legible only to other members of the community – to circumvent the rules, albeit covertly. (Roth, 2015: 15)

These struggles are not limited to dating and hook-up apps. Users also circumvent Terms of Use and codes of conduct to adapt 'non-sexual' social media platforms for off-label sexual purposes. Journalist Beejoli Shah (2015) writes:

> though nudity is banned by Instagram's community guidelines, a cottage industry of illicit hashtags has sprung up to find and share these photos, everything from the more mundanely-phrased #seduced and #exposed for broad nudity, to the community-specific tags such as #femdomme and #daddydick, intended more for kink.

While Instagram has famously pushed back at 'wayward' users, banning or blocking sexualized hashtags, and other signifiers of nudity (such as the eggplant emoji), each ban has heralded the emergence of new workarounds (see Hess, 2015). Shah notes that while Tumblr and Reddit are also popular platforms for sharing nude selfies and other forms of amateur porn, Instagram's warm affordances – and popularity – make it easier to access via mobile devices. This is especially the case for users who combine Instagram accounts with the anonymous messaging (and sexting) app, Kik: 'Instagram's onboarding process is much easier – point, shoot, post – and cameras, Instagram and Kik are all on one device that goes anywhere its user goes' (Shah, 2015).

Social networking services such as Facebook are also deployed globally as dating or hook-up spaces. The 2015 anthology *Online Courtship: Interpersonal Interactions across Borders* (Degim et al., 2015), which includes accounts of digital flirtation and dating practices in the USA, Israel, France, India, China, Turkey, Cuba, and Portugal,

contains multiple accounts of creative uses of social media sites for romantic and sexual purposes. These practices are particularly common among those who can't afford to pay to access to commercial venues (such as bars and nightclubs), or apps with premium features. For example, Basile and Linne (2016) and Aziz (2014) have mapped the ways young urban heterosexuals in Bueno Aires and Paris, respectively, use Facebook to facilitate flirtation and courtship, particularly through practices of posting (and liking) selfies and group photos. Wen (2016) notes that single youth in Shanghai increasingly use social networking sites such as Renren to seek partners, rather than subscribing to commercial online dating sites. Wen suggests that many Chinese social networking sites have affordances that promote easy integration of meeting and flirting with strangers into quotidian social networking practices. For example, some sites allow users to filter 'friends of friends' by relationship status when searching for potential partners, while providing opportunities for everyday interactions with existing friends (including game-playing, picture-sharing and chat), without having to switch back and forth between apps (Wen, 2016: 107).

It should be noted, too, that sexual expression in social media is not limited to the pursuit of sexual and/or romantic relationships – it can also deliberate sharing of information for the purposes of peer support. Just as the overtly sexual webcam and IRC cultures studied by Rival and colleagues (1998) and Kibby and Costello (2001) included not just fantasy material, but also 'ordinary' discussions of domestic problems, narratives of same-sex attractions and first sexual encounters shared by Instagrammers and YouTube celebrities can be more than clickbait designed to elicit 'likes' (see Duguay, 2016a). In her ethnographic study of Singaporean 'Insta-famous' celebrity bloggers, Crystal Abidin observed practices of informal sexual pedagogy and peer-intimacy in an environment where formal sexuality is lacking, and open discussion of pre-marital sex and same-sex relationships are condemned by schools and other political institutions (Liew in Abidin, in press).

While these practices, which Abidin terms #sexbait, certainly can increase social media celebrities' fan-bases, and assist them in attracting sponsorship opportunities, these first-person accounts of sexual learning also can fill a knowledge gap for fans (Abidin, in press). For example, Abidin recounts celebrity blogger Naomi's disclosure of the conditions in which she lost her virginity (at age 15), and observes that following her blog post, she engaged with fans on Formspring and AskFM, giving sex advice, and answering questions about teen sex and contraception (Abidin, in press). This intimacy and reciprocity can be seen as a gendered expression of not only sexuality, but of care.

SOCIAL MEDIA AND THE MICROPOLITICS OF GENDERED SEXUAL EXPRESSION

More overtly eroticized social media cultures also involve reciprocity, although this can be more complicated in mixed-gender spaces. In their study of a pre-SNS webcamming subculture, Kibby and Costello (2001) observed that it is 'easier' for women to perform as part of a reciprocal culture of amateur exhibitionism, due to the centrality of women's bodies as erotic objects within mainstream pornographic aesthetics (as outlined above). As the authors observed, 'there is no sock equivalent to the fishnet stocking' (2001: 361). Further, cock-rings, uniforms, and other forms of masculine erotic costuming were commonly dismissed by male cammers as homoerotic. Interestingly, Kibby and Costello note that both male and female members of the 1990s webcam community were critical of male participants whose performances defaulted to what was termed 'crotch-cam', or the close-up framing of their

genitals to the exclusion of the rest of their bodies. This early ancestor of the dick-pic was not considered by community members to be a legitimate 'show', and female community members frequently refused to interact with crotch-cammers, who were regarded as 'selfish' (2001: 361).

It could be argued that aspects of hook-up app and selfie cultures have created tensions for heterosexual men, who are required to 'objectify' themselves in selfies that focus on abs or pecs, foregrounding their sexual desirability (Albury, 2015; Ringrose and Harvey, 2015). This transition to a (masculine) culture of visible desirability is not always easy. On platforms like Tinder, where the preliminary introduction is a profile picture (with or without significant accompanying text), heterosexual men must, like Kibby and Costello's webcammers, present themselves as objects of a female gaze.

The position of straight men in the social media 'marketplace' is somewhat different from the position of gay men, where, as a range of researchers have outlined, existing cultural practices such as cruising could be adapted into new digital repertoires (Gundelunas, 2012; Roth, 2014; Race, 2015). In their study of young Spanish heterosexuals' practices of exchanging selfies as within the context of 'digital seduction' via social media, Lasén and Garcia (2015: 719) noted the discomfort experienced by young men as they deliberately studied and cultivated practices of 'self-pornification'. The authors observed that visual traditions within Western art and pop culture (including pornographic examples of both genres) primarily depict women's bodies displayed for men's gaze. Faced with an absence of easy-to-mimic examples of hetero-masculine erotic self-representation, some young heterosexual men in their study (ambivalently) adopted poses from gay pornography in order to appear attractive to prospective partners (Lasén and Garcia, 2015: 720).

It could be argued that the upsurge of visual cultures of erotic flirtation and display (through social media picture exchange has provoked a micropolitical shift in normative heterosexual relational dynamics. William Connolly (1999) deploys the notion of micropolitics to argue that when even firmly held personal beliefs (such as gender norms) continue to be 'persuasive', a curiosity regarding the foundations of others' beliefs creates spaces and opportunities for 'uncertainties and paradoxes' to emerge (1999: 147). These uncertainties, in turn, may allow for a reconsideration of previously incontestable assumptions (that is, men do the looking/choosing, women are looked at/chosen) and a conflict within the self. As a result, 'what was heretofore nonnegotiable may now gradually become rethinkable' (1999: 147).

This does not mean, however, that heterosexual men's practices of 'self-pornification' are always undertaken for women's pleasure. While many incidents of picture-sharing are consenting and reciprocal, the proliferation of reports of women and girls receiving multiple, uninvited dick-pics suggests that such practices can be aggressive, and even threatening (for example, see Stevenson, 2016). This conflict between some social media users' drive for sexual expression versus others' non-consensual exercises of sexualized power and control is particularly vexed where participants are aged under 18.

YOUNG PEOPLE'S SEXUAL EXPRESSION: LEGAL AND ETHICAL AND SOCIAL CONTEXTS

Since the mid-2000s, concern has increased regarding young people's participation in the practice of sharing sexually suggestive (or sexually explicit) text and images (also known as sexting). This practice is not always facilitated via public social media spaces, but also in private groups, by direct messaging (or in-boxing), within chat and/or hook-up apps (such as SnapChat or Tinder), and by means of person-to-person text and picture messaging using portable devices.

At present, the most detailed quantitative information regarding the broadest context of young people's use of social media for sexual expression exists in the USA. According to the Pew Research Center's 2015 study of US teenagers' use of technology in relationships, between 30% and 50% of all US 13–17-year olds surveyed have used social media to flirt or otherwise interact with someone they are attracted to. As Baym (2015: 113) notes, there are wide-ranging (and longstanding) anxieties in the USA, and elsewhere, regarding the risks posed to both adults and young people interacting with – and possibly meeting – strangers online. Significantly, relatively few (about 8%) of US teens in the Pew study reported dating or hooking-up with someone they first encountered online. Of these, 'the majority met on social media sites, and the bulk of them met on Facebook' (Lenhart et al., 2015: 3). Participants without significant experience in romantic relationships tended to pursue a range of 'entry-level' practices when flirting on Facebook, such as 'liking' posts and photos, and sharing videos or songs (Lenhart et al., 2015: 4).

Around one-third of those who reported meeting a romantic and/or sexual partner or partners online described a purely 'virtual' relationship, that is 'a romantic relationship with someone online they never met face to face' (Lenhart et al., 2015: 12). Of those who did meet, many reported using multiple social chat platforms (including online gaming sites) before exchanging phone numbers and meeting in person (Lenhart et al., 2015: 18–21). This use of multiple platforms to establish trust and intimacy prior to meeting face to face, a process that might (to paraphrase van Dijck, 2013) be termed 'an intimate culture of connectivity' was also reported by Australian gay male participants in the *Young People and Sexting in Australia* study (Albury and Byron, 2016).

The Pew study notes that like the mobile phone messaging that preceded them, social media platforms can promote feelings of intimacy and closeness between romantic and/or sexual partners (see Gomez Cruz and Cristina, 2015). They can also provoke feelings of jealousy or lack of space between partners, or a sense that the relationship is overly exposed to the opinions of friends and peers (Lenhart et al., 2015: 5; see also Baym, 2015). A small percentage of those surveyed by Pew admitted using social media to monitor or control a partner, with 4% installing a tracking app in their partner's phone without their knowledge, and 11% admitting to accessing a 'mobile or online account of a current or former partner'. Ten per cent admitted to changing or deleting a partner's social media profile, and 10% 'impersonated a boyfriend, girlfriend or ex in a message' (Lenhart et al., 2015: 10). Almost a third of respondents reported experiences of being coerced or controlled by an intimate or romantic partner via social media.

As demonstrated throughout this chapter, practices of mediated sexual expression (including the consensual and non-consensual production and sharing of sexually suggestive or explicit pictures) are not limited to any particular age, gender or sexual orientation. Since the widespread global increase of smartphone ownership, however, concerns regarding 'sexting' (as opposed to picture sharing in general) have primarily focused on young people – particularly young heterosexual women in their teens. As a range of researchers have noted (see Albury, 2015) many young people do not use the term 'sexting' to describe this practice, referring instead to sexy selfies, pictures, or nudes. However, the term is widely used by educators, policy makers and commentators, so for the purposes of this brief discussion, both 'sexting' and 'picture-sharing' will be used, in conjunction with 'selfies'.

There is a range of legal, technical, and socio-cultural issues relating to young people's picture-sharing practices. In Australia, for example, the age of consent for all sexual activities is 16 or 17 (depending on State law). Since 2009, cases in Canada, the USA, Australia and the UK have highlighted the risk that such laws present for young people, who can be placed on 'sex offender' registers for producing or sharing a selfie, even when all aspects of production and distribution are undertaken with the consent of all participants. In Australia, Commonwealth law defines all under-18s as 'children', and consequently defines any sexual representation of under-18s as child pornography – even when the images are self-produced. These laws, however, are justified (by some, at least) as a lesser risk when compared to the risks posed by nonconsensual picture-sharing, known colloquially as 'revenge porn' (see Powell and Henry, 2014; Henry and Powell, 2015).

Where young people have been invited to comment on their perceptions of the role that consent plays in picture-sharing, their answers (like those of adults) range from clear-cut definitions of moral and ethical boundaries, to victim-blaming, to confusion – as demonstrated within the following extract from the *Young People and Sexting in Australia* study (Albury et al., 2013). The project invited school-aged young people, adult stakeholders and same-sex attracted young people aged 18–26 to comment on sexting laws, and offer feedback on educational resources and other media representations of sexting. In focus groups conducted with 16- and 17-year-olds, participants observed that sexy picture-exchange was undertaken on the basis of trust. However, that trust was too often breached, particularly where pictures were seen by young men as a trophy, by which they could display masculinity and/or sexual capital to others (see also Ringrose et al., 2013):

Male 1: This isn't my personal view, but it's – the moment a female sends – some guys see it as the moment she's – they send her – him a text – it's theirs. It's their photo. They can do what they want with it. She voided all rights to that photo, so – and they can – yes, they do whatever they want with it.

Male 2: It could be their photo, but it still counts as – they only gave them their photo as trust. That's why they did it.

Male 1: Yes, but that's not a lawful, binding agreement.

Male 2: Yes, not lawful, but...

Male 1: Yes, so it's based on morals.

Another group of young people debated the likelihood of young men sharing images that had been sent to them in the context of an intimate friendship, flirtation or romantic relationship:

Male 1: There's no guy who's been sent a naked photo of a girl who's, like, not shown their mates...

Male 2: They're not... no one's gonna ask... Unless it's like, just – no, but if you ask for it – if someone asks you for it, they're definitely going to show their friends.

Male 1: They might not send to anyone, but it's... they definitely would show...

Female 1: I think that's a bit of a generalisation though.
(G1)

The young men in this group began with a universal statement about their peers' behavior but, following a heated challenge from the young women in the group, sought to distinguish between young men who 'asked' for pictures (who were presumably more likely to share them without permission) and those who did not.

However, the 16- and 17-year-old participants generally agreed that picture-sharing was only 'offensive' in the absence of consent:

I think sending explicit text or photos to someone who doesn't want them sent to them is probably a problem, because usually, when I think about it, I think of both parties being consensual and both taking part in it.
(G1, F)

If it stays between the two consensual partners, yes, it's fine, because they both – they can trust each other. That's fine because it's their choice.
(G3, M)

All 16- and 17-year-old focus group participants opposed non-consensual production and sharing of sexual images, and indicated a general acceptance of legal penalties in these circumstances. Similarly, in a half-day consultation with adult stakeholders, the consensual production and exchange of pictures between young people of the same age was generally agreed to be unproblematic. There was, however, agreement among all participants that relationships between peers of the same age could be abusive, violent or exploitative; and that those under-18s who shared photographs without consent (or threatened to share them) in this context should face penalties. Interestingly, while all the school-aged participants agreed that both young men and women took naked or semi-naked selfies with a desire to 'look sexy', they distinguished between selfies that were intended to be shared with friends, either via direct messaging or social media (public selfies), and 'private selfies' that were intended solely for purposes of self-reflection or self-regard (see Albury, 2015).

GEO-LOCATION, SEXUAL EXPRESSION AND QUEER WORLD-MAKING

While teenagers (particularly teenage girls) are the focus of most academic and popular discourse around sexy selfies, picture-exchange (both explicit and non-explicit) is an essential aspect of intimate negotiation for many (if not most) adult dating/hook-up app users. At the same time, digital affordances such as geo-location are 'producing transformations in these practices and relations' (Race, 2015: 499). While geo-location is a significant aspect of 'mainstream' apps such as Tinder, it is particularly valued in apps targeting LGBTQ people who have traditionally relied on geographical and architectural markers such as bars, beats (or cottages) and 'gay villages' to establish safe(ish) spaces for dating and casual sex (see Gorman-Murray and Nash, 2016).

Both academic research and popular commentary on geo-locative dating/hook-up apps reports that users do not simply use apps to directly chat or hook-up with others, but to 'see' other same-sex-attracted people in specific geographical locations (see Albury and Byron, 2016). As Batiste (2013) describes it, by making the presence of registered users visible to others, apps present users with the ability to overlay 'queer cartographies' onto ostensibly heterosexual environments (see also Blackwell et al., 2014). However, as Brubaker and colleagues (2015) note (following Schwartz, 2011), while geo-locative apps can enhance a sense of community and connection for some, they can also amplify young same-sex-attracted users' feelings of disconnection in remote or rural areas. Moreover, in countries where homosexuality is illegal, same-sex-attracted men's hook-up apps have been used by police for the purposes of entrapment (Long, 2015). App users can be vulnerable to a range of violations of trust, ranging from racist abuse, shaming based on HIV status, sexual violence, blackmail and robbery (Cowburn, 2015; Power, 2016; Raj, 2016; Verass, 2016). Additionally, even anonymized information, such as weight, height and country of origin, can be seen to jeopardize user safety when it is de-contextualized beyond an app. For example, *Daily Beast* editor Nico Hines, who identifies as a married heterosexual man, caused considerable alarm among LGBT commentators when he shared Olympic athletes' personal details gleaned from his use of Grindr within the Rio Olympic Village in an 'Olympic hookups' story (Rodriguez, 2016).

Apps, therefore, could be seen to facilitate not only dating or sexual encounters, but other forms of positive and negative sociality and sociability, via a process of off-label use (see Castañeda, 2015; Albury and Byron, 2016). As Roth notes, these queer cartographies can change users' relationship to space and place: 'coding spaces as "gay" or "straight" becomes less important when

an application's grids of nearby profiles can be overlaid atop any space where a user has a cellular data connection' (Roth, 2014: 2127). One 23-year-old same-sex-attracted participant in the *Young People and Sexting in Australia* project described the multiple forms of 'queer world-making' she and her friends practiced as follows:

> The app, for same-sex-attracted people, was a way of making friends
>
> when they were just coming out ... I know my friend who just moved to
>
> [a new city], he got straight on there. He has a partner of like, years, but
>
> he got straight on Grindr when he went down there to meet gay guys
>
> who could be his friends down there. So I guess yeah, I think we use it
>
> more for friendship than straight people a little bit, if that's possible.

This same participant reported using hook-up apps with her friends while on road trips, to 'see' the presence of other same-sex-attracted people in ostensibly 'straight' regional cities. She also searched for local same-sex-attracted women whenever she visited her mother. Her aim was not to make contact, but simply to affirm their presence and reduce her feeling of isolation in the suburb where she grew up (Albury and Byron, in press). This use of hook-up apps is not exclusive to younger people, as 51-year-old *Advocate* columnist Jeff Daniel reports. Daniel recounts his surprise (and pleasure) at activating Grindr in his 'working-class, blue-collar' neighborhood for the first time, only to discover he had radically underestimated the number of same-sex-attracted men living nearby. As Daniel put it:

> I doubt I'll ever meet most of the people behind the smiling faces staring up at me from my smartphone, but it's comforting to know that I have so many gay and bisexual brothers surrounding me, and I'm sure that the younger generation of LGBT people in my neighborhood feel comforted as well. (Daniel, 2015)

While these off-label uses of geo-locative apps can be seen to promote feelings of sexual belonging or sociability, it is the exchange of chat and images that most characterizes contemporary sexual expression within social networking spaces. These practices can operate quite differently within different sexual cultures, however. As Murray and Sapnar Ankerson (2016) observe in their study of Dattch (an app for same-sex-attracted women), the design features of hook-up and dating apps may invite users to participate in picture-sharing in order to promote particular kinds of sexed and gendered interaction. What works well for gay and same-sex-attracted men may not meet the needs of lesbian and same-sex-attracted women.

According to Murray and Sapnar Ankerson, while Dattch's developers initially offered an interface that was similar to Grindr, they found that same-sex-attracted women did not necessarily want to hook-up quickly, rather they wanted to 'get to know' each other quickly (Murray and Sapnar Ankerson, 2016: 59). With this in mind, the developers deliberately 'pinterestified' the app's interfaces and enriched the capacity for users to build visually rich profiles, in order to speed up the 'process of sociality by applying the success of the highly feminized space of fashion and shopping' (2016: 59). The authors argue that the aesthetics produced by these design choices created an implicitly white, a-political, hyper-feminine 'ideal' user (2016: 66), an identity that was amplified when the app was re-badged with a gendered pronoun in 2016: Her (2016: 66). This case study illustrates the pressures and contradictions that emerge when commercial platforms seek to standardize – and monetize – the subtleties of non-heteronormative courtship and sexual expression.

SEXUAL COMMUNITY, SAFETY AND STIGMA

Platforms such as Gaydar, Grindr, OKCupid and FetLife not only support interaction between prospective sexual and romantic partners, but also provide spaces for engaging in 'identity work' through advertising and business networking, social chat, peer support, health promotion, commercial and scholarly research recruitment, and links to 'offline' social events and networking opportunities (for example, see Castañeda, 2015; Wargo, 2015). These spaces have been recognized as being especially supportive for users whose sexual desires and/or modes of gender expression are highly stigmatized or subject to repressive legal restrictions (see Bezrah et al., 2012).

As outlined previously, exchange of both sexual and non-sexual pictures on platforms like Tinder and Grindr can form part of sexual negotiations with new partners, serving as a means of establishing 'authenticity', familiarity and trust before a face-to-face meeting (see Albury and Byron, 2016; Duguay, 2016b). In these circumstances, the exchange of 'face pics' may be perceived as more intimate than an exchange of anonymous torso or genital pictures. However, while exchange of face pics and personal details can promote intimacy and trust, such exchanges also increase users' vulnerability to predators and persecution.

While more mainstream platforms such as Facebook facilitate the organization of affinity-based groups and social and political events, the Facebook Terms of Service can restrict users' capacity for sexual self-representation. Facebook's Real Names policy increases the risk of what Marwick and boyd (2011) have termed 'context collapse' for same-sex-attracted and gender-diverse users who are not 'out' to family, schoolmates or workmates (see Lingel and Golub, 2015). Similarly, members of BDSM, kink or fetish subcultures and communities can be outed when group memberships, pictures or 'likes' are inadvertently made public. While kink-focused hook-up apps (such as Whiplr) are available, many kink practitioners have sought out the broader social media experience of Fetlife, which could be described as 'kinky Facebook'.

SEXUALITY, STIGMA AND SECURITY IN SOCIAL MEDIA: THE CASE OF FETLIFE

While platforms such as Tumblr and Instagram allow members of sexual subcultures to deploy pseudonyms, their Terms of Service are not always supportive of explicit sexual expression. In contrast, the kink-focused social network FetLife not only permits the use of pseudonyms, but actively allows (and encourages) posting of explicit sexual pictures and chat. In a 2014 interview, CEO John Baku described the site as 'Facebook meets *50 Shades of Grey*' (in McCabe, 2015: 1), while the site's Terms of Use explains that 'FetLife is a social network for kinksters and people curious about exploring their sexuality' (FetLife ToU). The site operates under a freemium model, with most discussion groups and events freely available, while a number of 'Kinky and Popular' posts (including photos, videos and text) sit behind a paywall (McCabe, 2015: 10). As Fay and colleagues observe, FetLife is explicitly *not* a dating site, lacking the usual affordances of such platforms, but merges the characteristics of both dating/hook-up platforms and social networking sites (Fay et al., 2015: 3). It does this by promoting 'sexual interaction (present in dating websites, absent in typical social networks such as Facebook) but in the presence of a social context (absent in dating websites)' (Fay et al., 2015: 3). Fay and colleagues note that most FetLife members' social connections are local, rather than global, which reflects a use of the site to chat and keep up-to-date with 'offline' events and workshops, allowing them to 'bootstrap their fetish sex life' (Fay et al., 2015: 9).

Given that BDSM practices (and imagery) are illegal in many international jurisdictions, it is not surprising that FetLife not only permits users to use pseudonyms, but promotes its encryption policies and 'fetish for security' on its welcome page. The security policy has been criticized, however, with kink community bloggers reporting significant flaws in FetLife's code over a period of several years (see McCabe, 2015). The site's security has been severely compromised several times, including a 2014 incident in which an external party named Mircea Popescu published what he termed a 'Meat List' of 'female-identified FetLife users under the age of 30' which included 'usernames, ages, preferred BDSM roles, and number of FetLife friends, as well as their sexual orientations and locations' (Massey, 2015).

In 2015, Baku and BitLove (the Canadian company behind FetLife), were subjected to mainstream scrutiny by publications *The Daily Dot* and *The Atlantic* – perhaps sparked by the increased visibility of BDSM via the *50 Shades* franchise. While *The Daily Dot* drew attention to the deficiencies in the social networking site's code, *The Atlantic* reported on ongoing concerns within the BDSM/kink community regarding FetLife's refusal to allow members to 'name and shame' users who had sexually assaulted and/or violated the sexual boundaries of others (see McCabe, 2015; Morris, 2015). Those who supported FetLife's policy of forbidding 'criminal accusations against another member in a public forum' argued that if the site's owners allowed members to be publicly named (perhaps falsely), both Baku and BitLove would be subject to unreasonable legal risks (see MacAulay Millar, 2012).

In contrast, users who supported naming abusers argued that FetLife's Terms of Use allowed abusers to offend repeatedly within the online and offline BDSM community without consequence. As many researchers and community members have noted, the illegality of many kink practices and the stigmatized nature of BDSM sexuality has built a culture in which external legal frameworks are distrusted (see Stryker, 2011). Consequently, word-of-mouth recommendations and warnings, mentoring relationships, and community self-policing have been preferred practices for safe-guarding consent and excluding dangerous or predatory community members (Weiss, 2011). These practices previously tended to be covert or discreet. Thanks to FetLife's archiving functions, these discussions are archived for future members, provoking significant debate regarding the ways that the platform's affordances (including the cool affordances of the Terms of Use) both reflected and departed from traditional 'offline' modes of self-governance within kink subcultures.

CONCLUSION

While online dating sites, like newspaper classified advertising before them, have allowed for an element of geographic filtering of prospective partners, the geo-locative capacity of contemporary dating and hook-up apps facilitate a level of precision in sorting that adds a cartographic dimension to digital sexual expression. Importantly, digital sexual expression does not always involve self-representation in the form of selfies or public/private sex chat, but can also take place within fan spaces, via the exchange of fan fiction, or photo-shopped manips (manipulations) of popular television or cinematic characters mashed up with explicit porn images, and posted on social media sites, personal blogs and Tumblr pages (Fink and Miller, 2013).

As outlined above, the variety of modes of sexual expression afforded by social media are not 'new' – online sex chat, networking, peer support and erotic and/or explicit picture exchange have been part of digital spaces since the early days of the internet. While these evolving practices of sexual expression have promoted freedom of expression for sexual minorities, they have also raised legitimate concerns regarding the costs of increased visibility for a range of groups, including young people, LGBTQ people, and members of BDSM and kink subcultures. As these practices have evolved, particularly as they become more accessible

to young people aged under 18, they have provoked increasing anxiety regarding the privacy and security (or lack thereof) afforded to users.

As platform developers have sought to promote or constrain particular kinds of sexual expression, however, they have been challenged by both consumer advocates calling for alternative modes of regulation (as in the case of FetLife), and by 'creative' users who have developed workarounds and off-label media practices to support their sexual cultures. This chapter has therefore offered a snapshot of a particular historical moment in the history of digital sexual expression. While this account of the present (and recent past) cannot claim to predict the future, it can suggest some possible trajectories for future research and inquiry. As suggested in the introduction, sexual expression is not necessarily limited to sexual exhibitionism, or the pursuit of erotic or romantic encounters; it also includes practices of identity formation and the building of communities of care. The ethical concerns raised both in teen sexting debates and among users of FetLife intersect with broader socio-cultural and legal conversations regarding the intersection between online and offline expressions of sexuality, gender and power – particularly as they relate to questions of safety and consent among stigmatized populations. Social media makes these ethical (and sometimes uncomfortable) conversations visible in new ways, and this, I suggest, is what makes it such a productive and intriguing space of inquiry.

REFERENCES

Abidin, C. (in press) #sexbait: Sex talk on commercial blogs as informal sexuality education. In L. Allen and M. Rasmussen (Eds.), *The Palgrave handbook of sexuality education*. London: Palgrave.

Albury, K. (2002) *Yes means yes: Getting explicit about heterosex*. St Leonards, NSW: Allen & Unwin.

Albury, K. (2015) Selfies, sexts and sneaky hats: Young people's understandings of gendered practices of self-representation. *International Journal of Communication*, 9: 1734–1745.

Albury, K. and Byron, P. (2014) Queering sexting and sexualisation. *Media International Australia*, 153: 138–147.

Albury, K. and Byron, P. (2016) Safe on my phone? Same-sex-attracted young people's negotiations of intimacy, visibility and risk on digital hook-up apps. *Social Media + Society*, 2(4), October–December. Available at: http://sms.sagepub.com/content/2/4/2056305116672887.full (accessed 22 October 2016).

Albury, K., Crawford, K., Byron, P. and Mathews, B. (2013, April) *Young people and sexting in Australia: Ethics, representation and the law*. ARC Centre for Creative Industries and Innovation, Journalism and Media Research Centre, The University of New South Wales, Australia.

Attwood, F. (2013) Cybersexuality and online culture. In J. Hartley, J. Burgess and A. Bruns (Eds.), *A companion to new media dynamics*. Chichester, UK, and Malden, MA: Wiley-Blackwell (pp. 341–345).

Aziz, F. (2014) Visual transactions: Facebook, an online resource for dating. *Études Photographiques*, 31. Available at: http://etudesphotographiques.revues.org/3490 (accessed 30 September 2014).

Basile, D. and Linne, J. (2016) The virtual nightclub: Adolescents from low-income sectors search for their couples through Facebook. In I. A. Degim, J. Johnson and T. Fu (Eds.), *Online courtship: Interpersonal interactions across borders*. Amsterdam: Institute of Network Cultures (pp. 47–56).

Batiste, D. P. (2013) '0 feet away': The Queer cartography of French gay men's geo-social media use. *Anthropological Journal of European Cultures*, 22(2): 111–132.

Baym, N. (2015) *Personal connections in the digital age*. Cambridge, UK: Polity Press.

Bercovici, J. (2014) LinkedIn for love, Tinder for business and other off-label technology uses. *Forbes*. Available at: www.forbes.com/sites/jeffbercovici/2014/05/06/linkedin-for-love-tinder-for-business-and-other-off-label-technology-uses/#414033b3372a (accessed 30 November 2015).

Bezreh, T., Weinberg, T. S. and Edgar, T. (2012) BDSM disclosure and stigma management: Identifying opportunities for sex education. *American Journal of Sexuality Education*, 7(1): 37–61.

Blackwell, C., Birnholtz, J. and Abbott, C. (2014) Seeing and being seen: Co-situation and impression formation using Grindr, a location-aware gay dating app. *New Media & Society*, DOI 1461444814521595.

Bornstein, K. (1994) *Gender outlaw: On women, men, and the rest of us*. New York: Routledge.

boyd, d. and Ellison, N. (2007) Social network sites: Definition, history and scholarship. *Journal of Computer-Mediated Communication*, 13(1): 210–230.

Burgess, J. (2006) Hearing ordinary voices: Cultural studies, vernacular creativity and digital storytelling. *Continuum: Journal of Media & Cultural Studies*, 20(2): 201–214.

Castañeda, J. (2015) Grindring the self: Young Filipino men's exploration of sexual identity through a geo-social networking application. *Phillipine Journal of Psychology*, 48(1): 29–58.

Clark-Flory, T. (2012) When safe-words are ignored. *Salon*. Available at: www.salon.com/2012/01/29/real_abuse_in_bdsm/ (accessed 12 January 2016).

Connolly, William (1999) *Why I am not a secularist*. Minneapolis, MN: University of Minnesota Press.

Cowburn, A. (2015) Armed gang using gay dating app Grindr to target and rob men in London. *The Independent*. Available at: www.independent.co.uk/news/uk/crime/armed-gang-using-gay-dating-app-grindr-to-target-and-rob-gay-men-in-london-a6779526.html (accessed 12 January 2016).

Daniel, J. (2015) Giving Grindr a go at age 51. *The Advocate*. Available at: www.advocate.com/commentary/2015/12/10/giving-grindr-go-age-51 (accessed 10 December 2015).

David, G. and Cambre, C. (2016) Screened intimacies: Tinder and swipe logic. *Social Media + Society*, April–June: 1–11.

Degim, I. A., Johnson, J. and Fu, T. (2015). *Online Courtship: Interpersonal Interactions across Borders*. Amsterdam: Institute of Network Cultures. Available at: http://networkcultures.org/blog/publication/no-16-online-courtship-interpersonal-interactions-across-borders/ (accessed xx Month 2016).

de Seta, G. and Zhang, G. (2016) Stranger stranger or lonely lonely? Young Chinese and dating apps between the locational, the mobile and the social, In I. A. Degim, J. Johnson and T. Fu (Eds.), *Online courtship: Interpersonal interactions across borders*. Amsterdam: Institute of Network Cultures (pp. 167–185).

Dowsett, G. W. (2010) Dancing with daemons: Desire and the improvisation of pleasure. In P. Aggleton and R. Parker (Eds.), *A handbook on sexuality, health and human rights*. London: Routledge (pp. 264–270).

Duguay, S. (2016a) Dressing up Tinderella: Interrogating authenticity claims on the mobile dating app Tinder. *Information, Communication & Society*, http://dx.doi.org/10.1080/1369118X.2016.1168471.

Duguay, S. (2016b) Lesbian, gay, bisexual, trans and queer visibility through selfies: Comparing platform mediators across Ruby Rose's Instagram and Vine Presences. *Social Media + Society*, April–June. DOI: 10.1177/2056305116641975.

Fay, D., Haddadi, H., Seto, M. C., Wang, H. and Kling, C. (2016) An exploration of fetish social networks and communities. In *Advances in Network Science*. New York: Springer (pp. 195–204).

Felizi, N. and Varon, J. (2015) *Safer nudes: A sexy guide to digital security*. Available at: www.codingrights.org/wp-content/uploads/2015/11/zine_ingles_lado2.pdf (accessed 9 December 2015).

Fink, M. and Miller, Q. (2014) Trans media moments Tumblr, 2011–2013. *Television & New Media*, 15(7): 611–626.

Gillespie, T. (2010) The politics of 'platforms'. *New Media & Society*, 12(3): 347–364.

Gomez Cruz, E. and Cristina, M. (2014) I'm doing this right now and it's for you: The role of images in sexual ambient intimacy. In M. Berry and M. Schleser (Eds.), *Mobile media making in an age of smartphones*. London: Palgrave Connect (pp. 139–148).

Gorman-Murray, A. and Nash, C. (2016) LGBT communities, identities and the politics of mobility: Moving from visibility to recognition in contemporary urban landscapes. In K. Browne and G. Brown (Eds.), *The Routledge research companion to geographies of sex and sexualities*. Abingdon, UK: Routledge (pp. 247–256).

Gudelunas, D. (2012) Generational differences among gay men and lesbians: Social and media change. Paper presented at the International Communication Association Virtual Preconference, May, Phoenix, AZ.

Henry, N. and Powell, A. (2015) Beyond the sext: Technology-facilitated sexual violence and harassment against adult women. *Australian and New Zealand Journal of Criminology*, 48(1): 1104–1118.

Herdt, G. and Howe, C. (2007) Introduction. In G. Herdt and C. Howe (Eds.), *21st century sexualities: Contemporary issues in health, education and human rights*. London: Routledge.

Hess, A. (2015) Move over, banana: How the eggplant became the most phallic food. *Slate*. Available at: www.slate.com/articles/technology/users/2015/04/eggplant_rising_how_the_purple_fruit_surpassed_the_banana_as_the_most_phallic.html (accessed 12 September 2015).

Holden, M. (2016) Critique my dick pic. Available at: http://critiquemydickpic.tumblr.com/ (accessed xx Month 201x).

Jacobs, K. (2010) Lizzy Kinsey and the Adult-Friendfinders: An ethnographic case study about internet sex and pornographic self-representation in Hong Kong. *Culture, Health and Society*, 12(6): 691–703.

Kibby, M. and Costello, B. (2001) Between the image and the act: Interactive sex entertainment on the Internet. *Sexualities*, 4(3): 353–369.

Kreps, D. G. (2009) Performing the discourse of sexuality online: Foucault, Butler, and videosharing on sexual social networking sites. Paper presented to Fifteenth Americas Conference on Information Systems, 6–9 August, San Francisco, CA.

Lasén, A. (2015) Digital self-portraits, exposure and the modulation of intimacy. In J. R. Carvalheiro and A. Serrano Tellerí (Eds.), *Mobile and digital communication: approaches to public and private*. Covilhã: LabCom Books (pp. 61–68).

Lasén, A. and García, A. (2015) '…but I haven't got a body to show': Self-pornification and male mixed-feelings in digitally mediated seduction practices. *Sexualities*, 18(5/6): 714–730.

Lasén, A. and Gómez Cruz, E. (2009) Digital photography and picture sharing: Redefining the public/private divide. *Knowledge, Technology & Policy*, 22(3): 205–215.

Lenhart, A., Smith, A. and Anderson, M. (2015, October) *Teens, technology and romantic relationships*. Washington, DC: Pew Research Center.

Liew, W. M. (2014) Sex (education) in the city: Singapore's sexuality education curriculum. *Discourse: Studies in the Cultural Politics of Education*, 35(5): 705–717.

Lingel, J. and Golub, A. (2015) In face on Facebook: Brooklyn's drag community and sociotechnical practices of online communication. *Journal of Computer-Mediated Communication*, 20(5): 536–553.

Long, S. (2015) Entrapped! How to use a phone app to destroy a life. *A paper bird: Sex, rights and the world*. Available at: https://paper-bird.net/2015/09/19/entrapped-how-to-use-a-phone-app-to-destroy-a-life/ (accessed 12 January 2016).

MacAulay Millar, T. (2012) There's a war on Part 6: Anti-Sunshine League. *Yes Means Yes*. Available at: https://yesmeansyesblog.wordpress.com/2012/05/07/theres-a-war-on-part-6-anti-sunshine-league/ (accessed 12 December 2015).

Marwick, A. E. (2015) Instafame: Luxury selfies in the attention economy. *Public Culture*, 27: 137–160.

Marwick, A. E. and boyd, d. (2011) I tweet honestly, I tweet passionately: Twitter users, context collapse, and the imagined audience. *New Media & Society*, 13: 96–113.

McKee, A., Albury, K. and Lumby, C. (2002) *The porn report*. Carlton, Vic.: Melbourne University Publishing.

McNair, B. (2002) *Striptease culture: Sex, media and the democratization of desire*. London: Psychology Press.

McVeigh-Schultz, J. and Baym, N. K. (2015) Thinking of you: Vernacular affordance in the context of the microsocial relationship app, Couple. *Social Media + Society*, 1(2). Available at: http://sms.sagepub.com/content/1/2/2056305115604649.full (accessed 10 December 2015).

Mowlabocus, S. (2007) 'Gay men and the pornification of everyday life. In S. Paasonen, K. Nikunen and L. Saarenmaa (Eds.), *Pornification: Sex and sexuality in media culture*. New York: Berg.

Mowlabocus, S. (2010) 'Look at me! Images, validation, and cultural currency on Gaydar. In C. Pullen and M. Cooper (Eds.), *LGBT identity and online new media*. New York: Routledge.

Murray, S. and Sapnar Ankerson, M. (2016) Lez takes time: Designing lesbian contact in geosocial networking apps. *Critical Studies in Media Communication*, 33(1): 53–69.

Paasonen, S. (2011) *Carnal resonance: Affect and online pornography*. Cambridge, MA: MIT Press.

Powell, A. and Henry, N. (2014) Blurred lines? Responding to 'sexting' and gender-based violence among young people. *Children Australia*, 39: 119–124.

Quiroz, P. A. (2013) From finding the perfect love online to satellite dating and 'Loving-the-one-you're near': A look at Grindr, Skout, Plenty of Fish, Meet Moi, Zoosk and assisted serendipity. *Humanity & Society*, 37(2): 181–185.

Race, K. (2015) Speculative pragmatism and intimate arrangements: Online hook-up devices in gay life. *Culture, Sexuality and Health*, 17(4): 496–511.

Raj, S. (2015) Grindring for justice, right now: Homan rights in Australia. Available at: http://rightnow.org.au/topics/asylum-seekers/grindring-for-justice/ (accessed 18 March 2016).

Rheingold, H. (1991) *Virtual reality: Exploring the brave new technologies*. New York: Simon & Schuster.

Riley, N. (2015) Tinder is tearing society apart. *New York Post*, 16 August. Available at: http://nypost.com/2015/08/16/tinder-is-tearing-apart-society/ (accessed 2 September 2015).

Ringrose, J. and Harvey, L. (2015) Boobs, back-off, six packs and bits: Mediated body parts, gendered reward, and sexual shame in teens' sexting images. *Continuum*, 29(2): 205–217.

Rival, L., Slater, D. and Miller, D. (1998) Sex and sociality comparative ethnographies of sexual objectification. *Theory, Culture & Society*, 15(3): 295–321.

Rodriguez, M. (2016) 'Daily Beast' editor Nico Hines used Grindr at 2016 Rio Olympics: It's a homophobic mess. *Mic*, 16 August. Available at: https://mic.com/articles/151282/daily-beast-editor-nico-hines-used-grindr-at-2016-rio-olympics-it-s-a-homophobic-mess#.pnmlF9se8 (accessed 20 October 2016).

Roth, Y. (2014) Locating the scruff guy. *International Journal of Communication*, 8: 2113–2133.

Roth, Y. (2015) 'No overly suggestive photos of any kind': Content management and the policing of self in gay digital communities. *Communication, Culture & Critique*, 8(3): 414–432.

Sales, N. (2015) Tinder and the dawn of the dating apocalypse. *Vanity Fair*. Available at: www.vanityfair.com/culture/2015/08/tinder-hook-up-culture-end-of-dating (accessed 1 September 2015).

Sara, M. (2016) 'Critique My Dick Pic' is a body positive approach to sexting: BUST interview (NSFW). *BUST*. Available at: http://bust.com/sex/16085-critique-my-dick-pic-interview.html (accessed xx Month 201x).

Schwartz, R. (2011) Out of the grind? Grindr and teen queer identity work in rural US. Paper presented at the American Anthropological Association Invited Session, Montréal, QC, Canada, 17 November.

Senft, T. M. (2008) *Camgirls: Celebrity and community in the age of social networks*. New York: Peter Lang.

Shah, B. (2015) Inside Instagram's long guerrilla war on porn – and the users who keep coming back. *Medium*. Available at: https://medium.com/the-slice/inside-instagram-s-long-guerrilla-war-on-porn-and-the-users-who-keep-coming-back-32cbc67137d5#.59unm3kvg (accessed 12 December 2015).

Shaw, A. and Sender, A. (2016) Queer technologies: Affordances, affect, ambivalence. *Critical Studies in Media Communication*, 33(1): 1–5.

Stardust, Z. (2012) Authenticity issues in the sex trade. *Arts & Opinion*, 11(6). www.artsandopinion.com/2012_v11_n6/stardust.htm (accessed 1 October 2016).

Stryker, K. (2011) Safe/Ward: I never called it rape. *Kitty Stryker*. Available at: http://kittystryker.com/2011/07/07/safeward-i-never-called-it-rape/ (accessed 12 December 2015).

Tiidenberg, K. and Gomez Cruz, E. (2015) Selfies, image and the re-making of the body. *Body & Society*, 21(4): 77–102.

Trepte, S. (2015) Social media, privacy, and self-disclosure: The turbulence caused by social media's affordances. *Social Media + Society*, 1(1). DOI: 10.1177/2056305115578681.

Tudor, M. (2012) Cyberqueer techno-practices: Digital space-making and networking among Swedish gay men. MA thesis, Stockholm University.

Turkle, S. (1995) *Life on the screen: Identity in the age of the internet*. New York: Simon & Schuster.

van der Nagel, E. (2013) Faceless bodies: Negotiating technological and cultural codes on reddit gonewild. *Scan | Journal of Media Arts Culture*. Available at: http://scan.net.au/scn/journal/vol10number2/Emily-van-der-Nagel.html (accessed xx Month 201x).

van der Nagel, E. and Frith, J. (2015) Anonymity, pseudonymity, and the agency of online identity: Examining the social practices of r/Gonewild. *First Monday*, 20(3). Available at: http://firstmonday.org/ojs/index.php/fm/article/view/5615/4346 (accessed xx Month 201x).

van Dijck, J. (2013) *The culture of connectivity: A critical history of social media*. New York: Oxford University Press.

Verass, S. (2016) Racism on Grinder: Indigenous man screenshots racial abuse online. *NITV/SBS.com.au*. Available at: www.sbs.com.au/nitv/sexuality/article/2016/04/14/man-shares-experiences-of-racism-on-grinder (accessed 14 April 2016).

Waskul, D. D. (2003) *Self-games and body-play*. New York: Peter Lang.

Waugh, T. (1996) *Hard to imagine: Gay male eroticism in photography and film from their beginnings to Stonewall*. New York: Columbia University Press.

Weiss, M. (2011) *Techniques of pleasure: BDSM and the circuits of sexuality*. Durham, NC: Duke University Press.

Wen, C. (2016) The advertising and profit model of leading dating sites in China: A comparison of Jianyuan, Baihe and Zhenai's targeting and advertising. In I. A. Degim, J. Johnson and T. Fu (Eds.), *Online courtship: Interpersonal interactions across borders*. Amsterdam: Institute of Network Cultures (pp. 106–116).

25

Privacy and Surveillance

Daniel Trottier

We like to think that we have control over our social media presence. Yet the fact that users are typically always connected to these profiles means that a single oversight can lead to drastic consequences. A college student I interviewed on this topic was shocked to discover that her mother was, as it turned out, her Facebook friend. While acknowledging that she must have consciously 'friended' her at some point in time, coming to terms with this connection was a lesson in social media visibility:

> I had no idea she had Facebook first of all ... And I was like, 'That is so creepy!' Like, I had no idea I had my mom as a friend and I have no idea how long she has been creeping my Facebook! ... And it turned out she'd been like looking at my Facebook almost every day for like five months.

While the fallout of this connection was relatively benign, this young user vowed to be more vigilant about her friendship ties, especially with people she did not know. Social media platforms like Facebook, Twitter, and Instagram allow users to circulate personal information, such as photographs and geolocative details, as well as articulate interpersonal and professional relationships. Individual users and other social actors are perpetually coming to terms with the consequences of accumulating and circulating this information. This chapter presents an overview of contemporary surveillance practices that occur on social media, focusing on how these practices force a reconsideration of privacy as a legal and cultural value.

I introduce surveillance as a social scientific concept to underline how collecting, processing and acting upon information about individuals and groups of individuals is an organizational logic of virtually every social sphere, including policing, marketing, interpersonal relations and the workplace, all of which are also present on social media. Framing social media in terms of surveillance evinces a number of concerns to be addressed. First, the asynchronous and distributed nature of information exchange on platforms like Facebook results in forms of visibility that are both unverifiable and unanticipated. Indeed, visibility can be knowingly harnessed as a means to harm others. Second, the cross-contextual nature of many platforms results in surveillance creep, whereby personal information provided in one context is repurposed for new practices. Users rely on terms like 'creeping' and 'creepy' to make sense of such unwanted forms of exposure. Recent scholarship in the area of social media and surveillance underscores that contemporary surveillance practices may be participatory (Albrechtslund, 2008), lateral (Andrejevic, 2005), and social (Marwick, 2012). These concepts complicate panoptic understandings of surveillance, since individuals who were traditionally framed as the *object* of surveillance are active agents on social media, who may nevertheless contribute to their own visibility as well as that of other social actors. Institutions also exploit these platforms; individual use may mutually augment institutional surveillance and vice versa (Trottier, 2012).

Both users and researchers believe that social media surveillance endangers privacy. The emergence and domestication of social media has augmented these concerns by pushing personal information into the public eye. However, focusing exclusively on privacy overlooks the social complexities of social media. This chapter considers ways of understanding and resisting contemporary surveillance that fully consider privacy, but go beyond it. It will provide an overview of relevant accounts of and approaches to privacy, including legal and rights-based interpretations, performative and enacted approaches, as well as approaches that consider context and culture as key elements. These perspectives highlight controversies linked to the use of social media platforms, for example when users' expectations of privacy diverge from a platform's technical configuration. In this chapter, I also consider scholarly critiques of privacy. Public discourse typically frames privacy as an individual concern, with a narrow sense of responsibility that precludes caring for others (Lyon, 2001). Attempts to assert privacy on social platforms may also justify surveillance practices against others. Finally, privileging privacy may come at the expense of awareness of other social harms linked to surveillance, including categorical discrimination and a chilling effect on public speech.

INTRODUCING SURVEILLANCE AND VISIBILITY

Surveillance, which implies watching over others, is performed by individuals and organizations. David Lyon defines surveillance as 'processes in which special note is taken of certain human behaviors that go well beyond idle curiosity' (2007: 13). Surveillance processes can be broken into various steps: collecting personal data about individuals, processing that data, profiling those individuals or groups of individuals, and the social consequences stemming from that assessment. This distinction is worth noting due to temporal and contextual gaps between these steps. For example, an individual may write a series of tweets expressing her political views in the context of a controversial election. Years later, they may be used by a potential employer to assess that she is not a good 'fit' (Walker, 2012).

Surveillance is often understood through dystopian literature and movies, such as George Orwell's *1984* and Steven Spielberg's *Minority Report*. A well-known model in surveillance studies is the panopticon, a prison model by the 19th-century English utilitarian philosopher Jeremy Bentham, and made famous by Michel Foucault, a 20th-century French philosopher. In the panopticon, all prisoners can be viewed from a central tower, whose guards cannot be seen. Surveillance becomes both all-encompassing and uncertain, as inmates never know when they are being watched by prison guards. This uncertainty pushes inmates to watch over themselves (Foucault, 1977: 221). This self-scrutiny is evident in contemporary society, as individuals are broadly expected to watch over their own behavior. While people are aware that their lives are visible to others, notably through socializing on social media, a lack of self-awareness may still lead users to commit a social gaffe by uploading discrediting content into the public realm (Ronson, 2015). Yet high-profile coverage of these gaffes compels everyone else to be vigilant in their self-scrutiny. For example, when a former vice-president at a public relations firm was invited to FedEx's headquarters in Memphis to give a talk about digital media, he issued a disparaging tweet about the city, offending his host (and client) in the process (Andrews, 2009). Unknowingly, this social media expert delivered an important lesson about the consequences of self-expression online.

In addition to Orwell and Foucault, surveillance studies stems from the study of police practices (Marx, 1988), emerging technologies (Norris and Armstrong, 1999; Lyon, 2009), and micro-level interactions to manage one's identity (Goffman, 1959). These studies support the view that surveillance is more than just a strategy for espionage and undercover policing, but rather a broader organizational strategy for knowing and directing a given population. In fact, gathering personal information is a dominant logic for modern governments and organizations (Dandeker, 1990), as evidenced in developments such as the census as well as modern boulevards that rendered citizens and their movements more visible. Surveillance is ubiquitous, not just because of ubiquitous technologies, but because watching and assessing pervades 'virtually every enduring social relationship' (Rule, 2011: 64). Thus, some of the dimensions that render social media 'social', including the digitization of pervasive social relations, are precisely what facilitate surveillance practices on platforms like Facebook. Many scholars contend

that the rise in contemporary surveillance is partly explained by large-scale migration to urban centers. As individuals were no longer rooted in a fixed setting, people turned to modes of verification that sought to make up for the fleeting and unverifiable nature of social relations (Lyon, 2001). When reputations become less tangible, social actors may seek additional measures to ensure trust. This is most apparent in login, reputation and verification measures on social media platforms. Some users suggest that Facebook marks a return to a small town dynamic, in the sense that everyone knows everyone else's business (Trottier, 2012). Yet social media are a more enhanced form of surveillance when compared to the rural dwelling, as digital information is retained indefinitely, rendered searchable, and hosted on platforms like Facebook that are unstable and ever-changing. In other words, these social platforms are part of an emerging global techno-commercial infrastructure that greatly augments the capacity and persistence of surveillance practices through these platforms.

Surveillance processes typically target personal information, which is understood as a source of revenue to corporations (CBC, 2015), a strategic asset for security agencies (Brelsford, 2015), and a burden for individuals to manage. Personal information refers to biographical data (date of birth, nationality), but also transactional data (recent online purchases, GPS coordinates). This covers a broad range of behavioral and attitudinal measures that can be aggregated and utilized far beyond the context in which they first emerge. For example, insurance companies use social media to find evidence of fraud (Millan, 2011) or determine nebulous measures such as 'quality of life.' An insurance company asserted that a Canadian woman's presence on Facebook, including photos 'showing her having a good time at a Chippendales bar show, at her birthday party and on a sun holiday' demonstrated that she was not depressed enough to receive compensation (CBC, 2009). Quality of life is difficult to quantify, and this ruling took place at a time when legal systems were uncertain about how much importance to attribute to Facebook evidence. Although these investigations were controversial, they demonstrate that social media content is increasingly scrutinized, and that courts make rulings based on this content. Sites like Facebook are also a prime source of information for divorce lawyers (Popken, 2011). Here, it is not the individual's profile that is scrutinized, but a combination of that presence and the spouse's access to their network of friends. A broad section of the divorced couple's social life is made visible through their use of social media. Visibility once reserved for trusted peers has crept into public sphere, and into investigative work.

Scholars recognized the pervasive and determinant nature of the profile long before social media users were updating and maintaining theirs (Gandy, 1993). The profile is the principal online interface between users and their social contacts, but also between individuals and corporations, governments and other organizations. Profiles refer to any accumulation of information of an individual by an organization, and are therefore key to online sociality as they enable users to build and maintain a consistent identity. Individual profiles range from online identities on social media, to customer profiles in loyalty card systems, to medical records within a healthcare scheme. Yet they may bear troubling consequences for users who lack control over their data or even the ability to view what an organization has collected about them. Such profiles are not operated by the user, but operate on behalf of the user, who may in turn struggle to fix disparities and cope with assessments made against them on the basis of such profiles. Likewise, vital aspects of social media profiles are beyond the individual's direct control, including tagged photos and posts on Facebook, negative reviews on Airbnb, and peer recommendations on LinkedIn.

Profiles are a quasi-involuntary construction and representation of the self. Yet the term 'profile' refers to a wide range of other 'data doubles' (Haggerty and Ericson, 2000: 606), including racial profiles for policing and geodemographic profiles based on postal codes (Burrows and Gane, 2006). Upon moving to a specific postal code, an individual may be categorized by a market research group as a 'newlywed or nearly dead' or as embracing a 'shotguns and pickup trucks' lifestyle. Again, these profiles serve as stand-ins for – or simulations of (Bogard, 1996) – the actual person, and these simulations have tangible consequences for individuals. Cumulative disadvantage (Gandy, 2009) occurs when an individual is negatively profiled, and the consequences of this profiling impact life chances, further reinforcing the negative profile. The expansion of surveillance schemes is fueled by a 'phenetic fix' (Lyon, 2002): a desire by organizations to classify and govern aspects of social life. Surveillance is a concern not only because people's social lives are visible in ways that are unanticipated, but also because models, profiles, and simulations stand in for individuals, who in turn endure the consequences. What remains unclear for both users and scholars is the extent to which their social media activity, as well as that of their peers, feeds into invisible but determinant categories in any number of social contexts. As a result, seemingly inconsequential forms of self-expression, like semi-serious conversations with friends online, feed in to a kind of permanent – and pervasive – record.

Another theme that cuts across surveillance studies is the balance between care and control. Surveillance practices are assumed to be a branch of social control, but many of these practices are implemented for the sake of ensuring a safe environment. This serves as a reminder that not all surveillance practices are received as repressive. For instance, a cyclist may value aerial cameras that monitor speeding motorists, who in turn may be thankful for the CCTV cameras in their parking garage. Likewise, social media visibility affords innumerable social benefits to those who engage with these platforms. Yet the semblance of care is also used to justify increasingly invasive procedures, and a greater concern with personal lives. The boundary between care and control is also difficult to pinpoint, for example, when a parent who once used a baby monitor, later monitors their child's mobile phone activity, and eventually installs a tracking device in their first car (Steeves and Jones, 2010).

AN EMERGING TYPOLOGY OF USER-LED SURVEILLANCE PRACTICES

Surveillance on social media primarily concerns users' personal data. Yet these individuals themselves play a crucial role in the production and circulation of this information. Recent scholarship on this topic reveals insights about how user information is being repurposed through new practices and expectations, and how users themselves manage and even initiate these developments. In referring to social surveillance, Marwick suggests that platforms like Facebook and Instagram 'are characterized by both watching and a high awareness of being watched' (2012: 379). Social surveillance thus speaks to relationships where those who watch over others on social media are also rendered visible through these very same platforms. In practice these users balance out seemingly conflicting desires for exposure and privacy. Unlike the relationship between an employer and employee, social surveillance is a product of everyday power differentials, rather than more rigid power asymmetries. These dynamics speak to contemporary visibility on social platforms, and how in particular they inform interpersonal relationships.

Through social media, watching and being watched are bundled together, as are curating a visible and a private self. Scholars may wonder how these practices co-exist – and perhaps are co-constructed – with surveillance practices led by states and other institutional actors. Trottier (2012) refers to *mutual augmentation* to consider how formerly distinct surveillance practices by different actors in separate social contexts manifest online. Noting that many institutional actors drew from interpersonal experiences and skillsets when using social media, Trottier argues that various surveillance practices may now share the same interface, information and even the same tactics. By converging on platforms like Facebook, these different types of surveillance amplify and enhance each other. For example, recognizing that prospective employers may access their profile, job candidates may scan their friends' content with an 'employability' lens, thus internalizing and extending the gaze of the job interview. Likewise, a campus security officer may turn to a university gossip page on Facebook, taking advantage of the interpersonal scrutiny between students. As social media are governed by a logic of connectivity that relies on social media affordances to algorithmically link users to other users, content, advertisers and platforms (Van Dijck and Poell, 2013), information authored with one audience in mind has the tendency to take on an unanticipated afterlife, often to a completely different audience.

Participatory surveillance refers to a process whereby social media users knowingly share information about themselves, and derive some form of empowerment from this sharing (Albrechtslund, 2008). This perspective serves as an important intervention to scholarly and journalistic accounts that assume that users unknowingly violate their own privacy when uploading content to social platforms. Indeed, users often yield specific pleasures and values from online sharing, such as sharing exercise logs or calorie intake with an online fitness community (O'Hara, Tuffield and Shadbolt, 2008). However, it is conceptually and practically important to consider whether a user can fully consent to share personal data, given the ever-changing visibility of platforms, along with other users' unanticipated intentions. As such risks become embedded in public awareness, we can imagine that these are factored in as a kind of transaction cost associated with participatory surveillance.

Another departure from the typical watcher/watched framework is through Mann's theory of sousveillance (Mann, Nolan and Wellman, 2003). This refers to a reversal of the surveillant gaze, whereupon the relatively powerless social actor watches (and typically records and transmits footage of) the more powerful actor. Such practices are linked to recent political movements, including Edward Snowden and Chelsea Manning's revelations about government surveillance schemes, as well as cop-watching initiatives, the latter of which takes advantage of social media to render police misconduct visible. While mobile devices and social platforms are used in key political interventions, scholars may question whether these uses contest or confirm traditional power differentials over the long term. In the case of cop-watching initiatives, consider police adoption of body-worn cameras that aim to provide a more authoritative account of the same incidents (Brucato, 2015; Sandhu and Haggerty, 2015), as well as the fact that visibility of police abuse does not readily translate into accountability.

Finally, lateral surveillance refers to a broader cultural condition of individuals watching other individuals (Andrejevic, 2005). As this concept is not limited to social media platforms, it underlines a broader media culture characterized by a lack of trust in the other, coupled with a savvy subject position that compels individuals to bypass their peers' self-presentation through a series of techniques and technologies, including nanny cams and home drug test kits. Faced with the ever-present possibility that a peer may misrepresent themselves online or in-person, this media culture privileges interpersonal surveillance (and the knowledge this might yield) over what the peer under scrutiny might claim, for instance, on a blind date. A social dynamic that crosscuts

these concepts is that individuals are watching over other individuals, using the same technologies and practices to simultaneously watch over themselves. This implies a heightened preoccupation with information flows in almost any interpersonal setting. It also speaks to a blurring of the boundary that would otherwise distinguish socializing and surveillance, as both now involve the asynchronous overview of aggregated personal data on social platforms.

WHAT DOES SURVEILLANCE BRING TO OUR ATTENTION?

Approaching social media practices from a surveillance studies perspective reveals a number of features. First, the prevalence of information sharing speaks to a *datafication* of sociality on social media platforms. Surveillance studies is ultimately concerned with the use and appropriation of personal information in a range of social contexts. These concerns are heightened when discussing social media, where every click and 'like', alongside thousands of images, messages and other user inputs, contributes to an ever-growing and semi-public record. Even the absence of an active profile, along with attempts to delete data and remove one's presence, generates digital traces and thus contributes to this record. As these data are largely contained on a limited number of privately owned platforms, we may consider the latter to be a series of digital enclosures where online activity is contained, managed and brokered (Andrejevic, 2009).

Users may accept surveillance practices in some contexts, but not others. Yet the boundary between acceptable and unacceptable use is actively eroded. Consider the notion of 'function creep' and the spread of surveillance practices from one context to another (Winner, 1977; Lyon, 2007). Seemingly intrusive technologies typically emerge in airports, casinos, and other locations that can justify a heightened scrutiny of individuals. This scrutiny is then normalized, and spreads to other contexts. Likewise, exceptional events can justify the unveiling of surveillance technologies. If a multinational company hires a social media expert, it would seem reasonable for them to scrutinize the social media presence of their short list of candidates. However, they may decide to extend this practice to all future hires. What users accept in one context may provoke unease in slightly different circumstances. Indeed, it comes as no surprise that early Facebook users drew upon this term to describe the ever-shifting landscape of information sharing (Trottier, 2012). The term 'creep' stands as a cogent way of sensing and expressing surveillance concerns.

Surveillance studies is also deeply concerned with the convergence of formerly distinct surveillance regimes. This includes merging databases and individual profiles, whether through technological innovation (Jenkins, 2006) or through post 9-11 legislation (for example, the 2001 USA PATRIOT Act; Bill C-51 in Canada). This suggests a kind of surveillant assemblage (Haggerty and Ericson, 2000) that leads to all-encompassing and seemingly irrefutable profiles, by leaking information from one context to another. The notion of the assemblage draws from postmodern contributions to theories of social control that consider the prevalence of temporary connections between discrete entities, allowing for the strategic information 'flows' and 'leaks'. Although censorship still occurs online, a generalized desire to get individuals to speak and implicate themselves is a more effective strategy for asserting a particular social order. This can be traced back to the role of the 'confession' in the Catholic church (Foucault, 1980), but it extends into contemporary culture through reality television tropes, notions of interactivity as 'empowering', and social media interfaces that solicit personal information. In some contexts, posting inflammatory content could negatively impact someone's life chances, if,

for instance, they are denied employment or are unable to cross a border. Despite recent public conversations about information leaks on social media, we may be compelled to have a presence on these sites by our peers, the telecommunication industry and even our employers, and the absence of one could also lead to social harms. For example, in cities such as New York and San Francisco, landlords have refused to provide housing for tenants who don't have a visible social media presence (Morozov, 2013).

Surveillance in the context of social media underscores how all interactions on platforms like Twitter and Instagram are about the strategic and often unanticipated exchange of personal details. Perhaps more importantly, the collection and use of this information maintains a particular social order, including power asymmetries. In fact, asymmetrical visibility feeds into asymmetrical power relations. For example, the company behind a social media platform may have access to data about users that the users themselves cannot access – even if this breaches data protection laws. On the other hand, those same users may possess only minimal knowledge about the platform and its owners' intentions. They might not know how their information is being used, who views their profile, or how future platform redesigns will impact how they engage with the site. If we view the relationship between user and technology companies as adversarial, the latter has a strategic advantage that stems directly from this asymmetrical visibility.

Yet users can also harness social media visibility as a kind of weapon. During the 2011 Vancouver riot, users uploaded images and videos of suspected rioters in real time. They invited others to provide not only names, but any other available personal information, including address, employment, and scholarships. This was done to bring suspects to the attention of the police, but also to shame them and prevent others from committing similar acts (Schneider and Trottier, 2013).

This campaign took advantage of networked and distributed sociality to crowd-source a pervasive form of surveillance. Unlike earlier forms of vigilantism, these actions take advantage of the diffuse, sped-up and far-reaching circuits of visibility on social media platforms. This kind of response is becoming more common when it comes to identifying and shaming suspected child exploiters, terrorists, and those deemed guilty of minor social gaffes such as bad parking and poor public transit etiquette (Trottier, 2014). Along with 'doxxing' practices (Massanari, 2015) and the 'human flesh search engine' in China (Cheung, 2009), these cases suggest that users are harnessing networked sociality and online visibility to gather and broadcast information about targeted individuals as a type of online vigilante justice.

The above developments force a reconsideration of the prevalence and relevance of a so-called big brother in the age of social media. Those who watch over others online are dispersed in their social and political intentions, as well as their access to various forms of capital. We may instead speak of little brothers and sisters (Andrejevic, 2004). Yet little sisters do not displace big brothers. Rather, the relation between them is mutually augmenting. Little sisters may take advantage of the social visibility effected by big brother, such as using tax records to publically shame corporations. Likewise, police following a violent crime may use dozens of mobile video recordings posted by witnesses on YouTube. The uneasy co-existence of big and little siblings will remain a troubling dynamic in the study of social media surveillance.

While the following section addresses privacy, it is already evident that surveillance and data collection are concerning for reasons that extend beyond privacy. Surveillance regimes are indeed ubiquitous, multi-contextual, and increasingly converging. Public exposure is a concern, yet surveillance also contributes to profiling, a foreclosure of life chances, and patterns of discrimination.

PRIVACY AND SOCIAL MEDIA: A PRIMER

Privacy is central to both the study and personal experience of surveillance. It is a legal concern linked to individual and collective rights, but is also performed through everyday social interactions. In practice, individuals have various conceptual models of privacy which are balanced against other priorities. Privacy's relevance in modern law was identified by Warren and Brandeis, who defined it as 'the right to be let alone' (1890), that is, freedom from surveillance and scrutiny. Alan Westin also shaped the contemporary understanding of privacy in his 1967 book *Privacy and Freedom*. Westin describes privacy as 'the claim of individuals, groups, or institutions to determine for themselves when, how, and to what extent information about them is communicated to others' (1967: 337). This definition implies a degree of control over personal information flows that has been greatly complicated by social media.

While privacy is an abstract concept, it is also a cause that is championed by activists and policy makers (Bennett, 2008), as well as managed in everyday contexts by individuals (Nippert-Eng, 2010). Macro-level advocacy shapes laws, policies, and best practices through an international network of governmental and non-governmental actors. A micro-level understanding of privacy is informed by Erving Goffman's work on self-presentation (1959). His dramaturgical approach underscores the performative nature of social interactions by framing social life in terms of roles, stages and audiences. Goffman argues that individuals are deliberate and strategic in their social interactions. This is partly for the sake of cooperating with others to maintain a cohesive understanding of the world, but also to remain in good standing with others. He distinguishes between front stages, locations and contexts where social performances occur, and back stages where performances are managed. These regions map very well with a cursory understanding of 'the public' and 'the private,' and are embedded in architectural designs (for example, most service sector workplaces have a clear barrier separating front and back stages), as well as social media interfaces, where the distinction may be more fluid.

The construction and performance of identity gains salience when considering another one of Goffman's sociological contributions: stigma (Goffman, 1963). Stigma refers to personal attributes that an individual wishes to hide from others, ranging from biographical details (a criminal record), a physical trait (a skin condition), or a social quality (an inability to understand the rules of football). Goffman contends that individuals go to great measures to hide stigmatizing information from public scrutiny, and that the privacy of the back stage is paramount for concealing these stigmas. Moreover, stigmas are as ubiquitous as the technologies and processes that risk uncovering them:

> ...There is only one complete unblushing male in America: a young, married, white, urban, northern, heterosexual Protestant father of college education, fully employed, of good complexion, weight and height, and a recent record in sports. (Goffman, 1963: 128)

An oft-repeated critique of privacy concerns is that if you have nothing to hide, you have nothing to fear. Based on the pervasive nature of categorical discrimination, Goffman stresses that social interactions are typically a high-stakes affair.

Privacy is a relevant social concern. It is a legal right, and it is also a requisite for maintaining one's dignity. Yet there is more to information technologies and accountability than simply ensuring privacy rights. As a starting point, consider the many ways that individuals understand privacy. Though some of these perspectives are more nuanced than others, they all hold some degree of conceptual and empirical purchase. An initial approach to privacy is based on a private/public distinction. Such binaries are tangible, conceptually elegant ways of making sense of the social world. We can return to Goffman's front and back stages in order to understand how individuals divide the social world into 'private' and 'public'. For instance, Facebook users readily make distinctions between private regions like their inbox and public regions like an event wall. Likewise, users experience privacy violations when information in a private space leaks to a public one. While this distinction is helpful for comparative purposes, not all private spaces are identical. An initial corrective would move away from absolutes like private and public, and instead situate privacy on a continuum. Users do make these distinctions in a comparative sense: an inbox message on Facebook is private compared to a wall post, but it is still public in the sense that it has been shared with an audience of one or more. Likewise, a photo on an event page may be considered public, but could be subject to further public exposure if it were published in a newspaper.

Some scholars believe that a private/public continuum fails to fully address social complexity, and instead advocate for a contextual understanding of privacy (Nissenbaum, 2009). Users may be comfortable sharing some information with a marriage counselor, and other information with close friends. Yet having either type of information cross over to the other context might cause embarrassment and harm. Users on contextually broad platforms like Facebook or Twitter encounter this challenge as they struggle to find information they are comfortable sharing with friends, co-workers, family, and others simultaneously. Multi-contextual services need to develop privacy settings that are robust enough to maintain contextual boundaries. Perhaps the most important contextual violation is the transition from online to offline. Individuals may still expect a boundary that separates the two, yet this boundary is more permeable and requires greater effort to maintain. The now-iconic 'on the internet, nobody knows you're a dog' cartoon published in 1993 by *The New Yorker* is indicative of an antiquated understanding of privacy.

Another perspective considers how people may value privacy, yet compromise their own due to competing or conflicting values. In other words, people may choose to expose private information for the sake of achieving publicity. In a set of interviews on how users come to terms with online visibility, a college freshman likened social media to reality television and describes Facebook as: 'our own little form of entertainment where we can get a glimpse of everyone's life. ... It's like our own little video camera following us around and taking snapshots of our life, for everyone to see.' Not only is the public exposure of otherwise private information seen as desirable, but it is also a reciprocal activity among peers. Users describe watching others in the same breath as being watched by others, to the extent that one practice informs and justifies the other. They acknowledge that they may regret this visibility later on – if not immediately – but that this regret is offset against other values and priorities. They do not necessarily want their personal information to be public, but they want social ties and validation, and exposure via social media is the most tangible way to obtain these things. Other users may go public for the sake of feeling secure. As one student user reports:

> By having a Facebook profile – I mean, you're agreeing to have this information posted. Like, all this information available to people. Obviously if you're posting it, you want people to see it. Because why else would you put it up there? ... It's almost like an insecurity thing. And it's kind of like a way of saying, 'Oh, look at me. Look at my life. Look at all the friends that I have and look at all of the people that want to talk to me' and I don't know. I guess in that way it made me really self-conscious about Facebook.

Interpersonal security is a positive value that pushes users to compromise their online privacy. In other instances, they feel social pressure from their peers to have a public presence on social media. Among the 30 young users interviewed, there was consensus that they joined Facebook at the behest of their friends, and now maintain an active presence because of this social pressure (Trottier, 2016).

Privacy is an elusive concept, for scholars as well as social media users. Users invoke different kinds of imagery to make sense of their experiences and values on social media. These often represent some blend of compliance and discomfort with social media visibility. One set of users we interviewed initially likened their Facebook photo albums to real-life photo albums, and described privacy concerns as though strangers were breaking into their homes to browse through their photos. Others objected to this imagery, treating Facebook instead as a whiteboard on a residence door. The profile is public, fundamentally social, and meant to be shared. This imagery still links the profile to the individual's integrity, as it is still subject to abuse. Still other participants drew links between being on Facebook and being outdoors. This suggests that users should have limited expectations of secrecy, but still not be subject to invasive or humiliating encounters. Social media research often rests on the assumption that users' motivations to harness social media are tempered by privacy concerns (Ellison et al., 2011). It assumes people deliberately seek a safe space to be sociable. Yet the range of contexts and practices that we observed on social media instead suggest that other social values conflict with or compromise users' desires for privacy. Many users are not concerned with privacy when building a presence on social media; some will develop an awareness of these concerns only if they experience privacy violations. Yet many will be oblivious to privacy, regardless of how private or public they regard their information. Users often recognize that this may be contextual: while university students feel privacy invasions are not an immediate concern, they acknowledge that privacy will likely be more important when they move on to the next stage in their lives. Conversely, users who value privacy may not be concerned with it on a per-use basis. These findings speak to the risk of ubiquitous, everyday technology. On social media, even vigilant users may compromise their privacy simply through continuous engagement.

SOCIAL MEDIA PRIVACY IN PRACTICE

Popular discourse often suggests that social media and privacy are incompatible, or at least that continued use of these platforms is linked to a general disavowal of such concerns. We may also consider a paradoxical distinction between a concern for privacy in principle and a willingness in practice to routinely disclose personal information online (Barnes, 2006). Yet recent scholarship not only considers how users articulate and perform privacy in the wake of significant legal, technical and market-based pressures (boyd and Marwick, 2011), but also how privacy – or lack thereof – on social media is further shaped by seemingly contradictory enactments on these platforms.

Users may first consider their privacy on social media when configuring their so-called privacy settings. These settings enable the user to choose with whom they consent to share specific types of personal information. On platforms like Facebook, these settings have expanded in response to user outrage, as well as government criticisms following an unanticipated and prolonged contextual expansion of the site (FBNewsroom, 2006, 2009). To be sure, Facebook's privacy settings in 2017 are more granular than they were in 2007, and users may feel overwhelmed by these changes. Yet by navigating through these settings, many users are compelled to think about their privacy in practice (boyd and Marwick, 2011). In addition, some platforms, like Snapchat, are expressly designed for ephemeral communications (Poltash, 2013), while others, like Twitter and Instagram, are primarily framed as tools for public expression. Yet even Snapchat's claims of ephemerality have been

compromised by users intentionally leaking private data to the public, alongside the discovery that the platform itself retained photos that were meant to be deleted (FTC, 2014). Note that individuals are not typically bound a single platform, and may choose one over the other at a particular moment on the basis of perceived privacy affordances.

User understandings of privacy are partially shaped through platform engagement, particularly the default privacy settings (boyd and Hargittai, 2010). However, users adopt a variety of privacy-protective behaviors that are independent of privacy settings. For example, boyd and Marwick (2011) document how youngsters may conceal their thoughts and feelings in plain sight by posting song lyrics. If such lyrics are familiar to their peers, these peers will understand what the user is expressing, while parents and other unintended audiences will not access the meaning of that coded message. Other tactics include relying on pseudonyms, as well as maintaining multiple accounts that may distinguish professional roles from personal ones (Trottier, 2012). Several platforms and service providers, such as Facebook and Google, have explicitly targeted these practices through adopting 'real name' policies. These efforts have in turn been met by protest from communities such as transgender people and drag performers (Lingel and Golub, 2015). User tactics also include norms and expectations in embodied contexts; for example, the expectation that house-party attendees will not be photographed and tagged online.

When mapping the myriad ways social media privacy is understood and enacted, it bears noting that these platforms are almost entirely privately owned, which in turn confers a distinct set of rights and entitlements to the platform owners. 'Private' in this context pits platform owners' accumulation of personal data against users' expectations of self-determination in the outcomes of that data. While platforms may retain users' personal information as per their terms of service, this entitlement may conflict with users' cultural and even legal articulations of privacy rights. To further complicate privacy concerns, social media platforms are frequently conceived of as a public sphere, even if this ideal is not actualized in practice (Fuchs, 2014). This evokes dilemmas for users as well as other concerned actors: social recognition and self-expression are desirable values, and are key motivations for social media users to upload personal information (Shao, 2009). Indeed, even those who have significant privacy concerns may still seek out a public presence on social media. Surveillance and privacy studies must therefore avoid reductionist accounts of private–public 'tradeoffs', instead focusing on the complex arrangement of motivations (which typically map on to fundamental rights) that govern use and exposure online.

CRITICAL ENGAGEMENTS WITH PRIVACY

Privacy holds purchase as a scholarly concept as well as in public discourse. Users' experiences and concerns on social media are relatively novel, and blend familiarity and unease in a manner that is typical of domesticated technologies (Silverstone and Haddon, 1996). Privacy has become a salient term to describe these experiences. Yet approaching social media visibility exclusively in terms of privacy limits the scope of a social scientific analysis and raises a number of concerns. To begin, privacy is typically conceived as an individual matter, typically overlooking precisely how the social dimensions of social media may put other social actors in harm's way. User privacy often framed as an individual responsibility, and privacy settings for social media as well as public recommendations by advocacy groups support the assumption that it is the user's responsiblity to govern their own data. Yet control over what personal information is knowable to what social actors is a form of autonomy that is largely beyond individual control. Scholars should consider interpersonal dynamics that are crucial to its functioning. In particular, the idea of collaborative identity construction (Trottier and Lyon, 2011) underscores how social media interfaces encourage users to speak on behalf of other users. Through wall posts, tags, and comments, users routinely disclose information about their peers, exposing others to public scrutiny. Concern for the self should extend to a concern for how others are subject to exposure through our own actions.

Related to this individualistic bias in privacy discourse, managing one's own privacy often results in the increased scrutiny of others. Individuals will understandably take measures to safeguard their privacy, notably in the maintenance of private spaces which necessitate securing boundaries, carefully monitoring those who enter and exit that space. Consider the gated community equipped with security cameras and facial recognition software, or the private social media platform that requires visitors to identify themselves and make their actions visible while interacting with others. Likewise, upon finding out that their privacy could be compromised on social media, young users I interviewed reported that they began watching over content their friends would post, taking active steps to manage or sanction them (Trottier, 2012). These measures exemplify the internalization of the surveillant gaze (Foucault, 1977) applied outwards to peers, in the name of self-preservation.

A further limitation of privacy is that it is too easily conceived of as a resource or commodity, which means that those with greater capital or purchasing power will be able to make use of privacy, while others will simply have to cope with unwanted and unanticipated exposure. Privacy thus becomes a luxury good instead of a fundamental right. In defining privacy as the absence of embarrassing and harmful forms of exposure, it is evident that detached houses afford residents more privacy than apartments, and first-class airport lounges are a comparatively safer space than a crowded concourse in which to commit a jetlag-fueled gaffe. On social media, navigating interfaces and combing through content requires particular sets of media literacy, and also costs time, to say nothing of hardware and services. Many users simply do not have enough of either, and will be disproportionately subject to invasive scrutiny. Public relations efforts on social media are informed by high-profile cases involving politicians, celebrities and other public figures. This arguably constitutes a normalization of strategic identity management, along with a proliferation of online reputation management services and consultancies. While legal debates and political advocacy focus on establishing fundamental privacy and data protection rights and legislation, commoditizing privacy can circumvent a collective and rights-based preservation of privacy.

Finally, focusing on privacy in public discourse often comes at the expense of other pressing social concerns linked to surveillance and exposure on social media, including discrimination and social sorting. Privacy concerns may reduce our focus to visible and tangible artifacts, such as a user's most recent tweets. Such a focus overlooks the aggregate effect that this body of information has over 10 or 20 years, as well as the myriad of ways in which such aggregated data can be repurposed. If a user's social media presence – including their social graph of connections with others – can be used to determine their employability (Walker, 2012), or their eligibility for a bank loan (Kestler D'Amours, 2015), then it bears focusing on how these personal data feed into pervasive and opaque social categories that govern individuals. Another concern is self-censorship and the broader chilling effect that social media exposure may have on self-expression. As users come to terms with the fact that public and private speech on social media is under watch, they will adjust their behavior accordingly (Trottier, 2012). One aspect of

internalizing this gaze is that they may withhold content they would otherwise wish to share with their colleagues, out of fear of unverifiable and undesirable outcomes. At an aggregate level, the increased unwillingness of users to express themselves online means that their potential for service in the public sphere is further compromised. Finally, the above concerns point to fundamental inequities when it comes to our understanding of social media platforms, and in particular user understanding of how their information is repurposed. The actions users may take to mitigate visibility and privacy, such as deleting content or closing an account, may fail to prevent these harms, especially when information remains on the platform's servers, and therefore remains vulnerable to hacks and leaks (Thomsen, 2015). As stated above, asymmetry of control and of knowledge is a primary condition that informs user experiences of privacy, of visibility and of everyday and exceptional moments of surveillance.

CONCLUSION

This chapter considers surveillance and privacy as they relate to social media and a broader digital media landscape. A surveillance studies approach locates privacy as a primary societal concern, one that is both nuanced and paradoxical. Addressing this complexity necessitates cross-disciplinary and multi-perspective research that interrogates how individuals are exposed through social media, and the risks and harms associated with this exposure. Privacy matters, as does publicity, autonomy, and the broader mix of priorities and values that motivate users to build a presence (or not) on social media platforms. It is equally important to consider the design and redesign of these platforms. The continued expansion, transformation and acquisition of sites like Twitter and Instagram shape engagements by scholars, users and policy makers. These changes challenge any definitional or functional understanding of social media, and in particular suggest that user consent at one moment in time should not extend automatically if, for instance, the platform's user base expands tenfold, or if it is repurposed as a marketing resource.

Along with scholarly engagement, public education and outreach efforts may be effective to promote relevant forms of media literacy. Technologies and their surrounding practices are dynamic, and users are not always aware of the consequences of these changes. A lot of data schemes work by opt-out rather than opt-in, and many users only have a partial understanding of these agreements. This speaks to the weakness of individual consent (Rule, 2011), and awareness campaigns are a potential remedy for dense and largely overlooked privacy statements. Students who share these concerns may wish to examine how social media users of varying backgrounds envision and utilize privacy settings in practice, as well as how they discover and respond to violations of their privacy and informational autonomy. Likewise, the fact that many users remain active on these platforms for extended periods means that the conditions of visibility that they embraced at an earlier stage of their lives may provoke discomfort or social harms at a latter stage. Students of social media and surveillance may also wish to develop an empirically based understanding of how these users respond to such discomfort. Finally, scholarly research should not only focus on how users are coping with these developments, but also re-direct the outputs of these efforts back to users, for example by addressing the consequences of technologically-mediated transparency to a broader public (see Bennett et al., 2014).

REFERENCES

Albrechtslund, Anders. 2008. Online social networking as participatory surveillance. *First Monday*, 13(3): http://firstmonday.org/article/view/2142/1949.

Andrejevic, Mark. 2004. Little Brother is watching: The webcam subculture and the digital enclosure. In A. McCarthy and N. Couldry (Eds.), *Mediaspace: Place, scale, and culture in a media age* (pp. 109–124). New York: Routledge.

Andrejevic, Mark. 2005. The work of watching one another: lateral surveillance, risk, and governance. *Surveillance & Society*, 2(4): 479–497.

Andrejevic, Mark. 2009. Privacy, exploitation and the digital enclosure. *Amsterdam Law Forum*, 1(4): http://amsterdamlawforum.org/article/view/94/168.

Andrews, James. 2009. True confession but I'm in one of those towns where I scratch my head and say 'I would die if I had to live here!' 14 January. https://twitter.com/keyinfluencer/statuses/1119553072.

Barnes, Susan B. 2006. A privacy paradox: Social networking in the United States. *First Monday*, 11(9): http://firstmonday.org/article/view/1394/1312.

Bennett, Colin J. 2008. *The privacy advocates: Resisting the spread of surveillance*. Cambridge, MA: MIT Press.

Bennett, Colin J., Kevin D. Haggerty, David Lyon and Valerie Steeves. 2014. *Transparent lives: Surveillance in Canada*. Edmonton: Athabasca University Press.

Bogard, William. 1996. *The simulation of surveillance: Hypercontrol in telematic societies*. Cambridge, UK: Cambridge University Press.

boyd, danah and Eszter Hargittai. 2010. Facebook privacy settings: Who cares? *First Monday*, 15(8): http://journals.uic.edu/ojs/index.php/fm/article/view/3086/2589.

boyd, danah and Alice Marwick. 2011. Social privacy in networked publics: Teens' attitudes, practices, and strategies. *A decade in internet time: Symposium on the dynamics of the internet and society*. September. http://papers.ssrn.com/sol3/Papers.cfm?abstract_id=1925128.

Brelsford, Paul. 2015. *White Paper: Employing a social media monitoring tool as an OSINT platform for Intelligence, Defence & Security*. www.eurosint.eu/system/files/employing_social_media_monitoring_tools_as_an_osint_platform_for_intelligence_defence_security.pdf.

Brucato, Ben. 2015. Policing made visible: Mobile technologies and the importance of point of view. *Surveillance & Society*, 13(3/4): 455–473.

Burrows, Roger and Nicholas Gane. 2006. Geodemographics, software and class. *Sociology*, 40: 793–812.

CBC. 2009. Depressed woman loses benefits over Facebook photos. *CBC.ca*, November 21. www.cbc.ca/news/canada/montreal/story/2009/11/19/quebec-facebook-sick-leave-benefits.html.

CBC. 2015. Windows 10 raises privacy concerns. *CBC.ca*, September 10. www.cbc.ca/news/technology/windows-10-1.3223168.

Cheung, Anne S. Y. 2009. China Internet going wild: Cyber-hunting versus privacy protection. *Computer Law & Security Review*, 25(3): 275–279.

Dandeker, Christopher. 1990. *Surveillance, power and modernity: Bureaucracy and discipline from 1700 to the present day*. New York: St Martin's Press.

Ellison, Nicole B., Jesica Vitak, Charles Steinfeld, Rebecca, Gray and Cliff Lampe. 2011. Negotiating privacy concerns and social capital needs in a social media environment. In S. Trepte and L. Reinecke (Eds.), *Negotiating privacy concerns and social capital needs in a social media environment* (pp. 19–32). Berlin: Springer.

FBNewsroom. 2006. Facebook launches additional privacy controls for news feed and mini-feed. *Facebook Newsroom*. September 8. http://newsroom.fb.com/news/2006/09/facebook-launches-additional-privacy-controls-for-news-feed-and-mini-feed/.

FBNewsroom. 2009. Facebook announces privacy improvements in response to recommendations by Canadian Privacy Commissioner. *Facebook Newsoom*. August 27. http://newsroom.fb.com/news/2009/08/facebook-announces-privacy-improvements-in-response-to-recommendations-by-canadian-privacy-commissioner/.

Foucault, Michel. 1977. *Discipline and punish: The birth of the prison*. London: Allen Lane.

Foucault, Michel. 1980. *The history of sexuality*. New York: Vintage Books.

FTC. 2014. Snapchat settles FTC charges that promises of disappearing messages were false. *Federal Trade Commission Press Releases*. May 8. www.ftc.gov/news-events/press-releases/2014/05/snapchat-settles-ftc-charges-promises-disappearing-messages-were.

Fuchs, Christian. 2014. Social media and the Public Sphere. *triple*, 12(1): 57–101.

Gandy, Oscar H. 1993. *The panoptic sort: A political economy of personal information*. Boulder, CO: Westview Press.

Gandy, Oscar H. 2009. *Coming to terms with chance: Engaging rational discrimination and cumulative disadvantage*. Farnham, UK: Ashgate.

Goffman, Erving. 1959. *The presentation of self in everyday life*. New York: Anchor Books.

Goffman, Erving. 1963. *Stigma: Notes on the management of spoiled identity*. New York: Simon & Schuster.

Haggerty, Kevin D. and Richard V. Ericson. 2000. The surveillant assemblage. *British Journal of Sociology*, 51: 605–622.

Jenkins, Henry. 2006. *Convergence culture: Where old and new media collide*. New York: New York University Press.

Kestler D'Amours, Jillian. 2015. How Facebook could affect your chances of getting a loan. *The Toronto Star*, August 10.

Lingel, Jessa and Adam Golub. 2015. In face on Facebook: Brooklyn's drag community and sociotechnical practices of online communication. *Journal of Computer-Mediated Communication*, 20(5): 536–553.

Lyon, David. 2001. *Surveillance society: Monitoring everyday life*. Milton Keynes, UK: Open University Press.

Lyon, David. 2002. Editorial. Surveillance studies: Understanding visibility, mobility and the phenetic fix. *Surveillance & Society*, 1(1): 1–7.

Lyon, David. 2007. *Surveillance studies: An overview*. Cambridge, UK: Polity Press.

Lyon, David. 2009. *Identifying citizens: ID cards as surveillance*. Cambridge, UK: Polity Press.

Mann, Steve, Jason Nolan and Barry Wellman. 2003. Sousveillance: Inventing and using wearable computing devices for data collection in surveillance environments. *Surveillance & Society*, 1(3): 331–355.

Marwick, Alice. 2012. The public domain: Surveillance in everyday life. *Surveillance & Society*, 9(4): 378–393.

Marx, Gary T. 1988. *Undercover: Police surveillance in America*. Berkeley, CA: University of California Press.

Massanari, Adrienne. 2015. #Gamergate and the Fappening: How Reddit's algorithm, governance, and culture support toxic technocultures. *New Media & Society*. Published online before print (October 9). doi:10.1177/1461444815608807.

Millan, L. 2011. Insurers and social media: Insurers' use of social networks impinges on privacy rights. *The Lawyers Weekly*, March 25. www.lawyersweekly.ca/index.php?section=article&volume=30&number=43&article=2.

Morozov, Evgeny. 2013. The folly of technological solutionism. LSE Public Lecture, March 21. London.

Nippert-Eng, Christena. 2010. *Islands of privacy*. Chicago, IL: University of Chicago Press.

Nissenbaum, Helen. 2009. *Privacy in context: Technology, policy, and the integrity of social life*. Palo Alto, CA: Stanford University Press.

Norris, Clive and Gary Armstrong. 1999. *The maximum surveillance society: The rise of CCTV*. Oxford: Berg.

O'Hara, Kieron, Mischa M. Tuffield and Nigel Shadbolt. 2008. Lifelogging: Privacy and empowerment with memories for life. *Identity in the Information Society*, 1(1): 155–172.

Poltash, Nicole A. 2013. Snapchat and sexting: A snapshot of baring your bare essentials. *Richmond Journal of Law & Technology*, 29(4): 1–24.

Popken, B. 2011. Facebook is number one tool for divorce lawyers. *The Consumerist*, May 18. http://consumerist.com/2011/05/facebook-is-number-one-tool-for-divorce-lawyers.html.

Ronson, Jon. 2015. How one stupid tweet blew up Justine Sacco's life. *New York Times Magazine*, February 12. www.nytimes.com/2015/02/15/magazine/how-one-stupid-tweet-ruined-justine-saccos-life.html?_r=0

Rule, James. 2011. 'Needs' for surveillance and the movement to protect privacy. In Lyon David, Kirstie Ball and Kevin D. Haggerty (Eds.), *Routledge handbook of surveillance studies* (pp. 64–71). New York: Routledge.

Sandhu, Ajay and Kevin D. Haggerty. 2015. Policing on camera. *Theoretical Criminology, Theoretical Criminology* 21(1): 78–95.

Schneider, Christopher and Daniel Trottier. 2013. Social media and the 2011 Vancouver riot. *Studies in Symbolic Interaction*, 40: 335–362.

Shao, Guosong. 2009. Understanding the appeal of user-generated media: A uses and gratification perspective. *Internet Research*, 19(1): 7–25.

Silverstone, Roger and Leslie Haddon. 1996. Design and the domestication of information and communication technologies: Technical change and everyday life. In R. Mansell and R. Silverstone (Eds.), *Communication by design: The politics of information and communication technologies* (pp. 44–74). Oxford: Oxford University Press.

Steeves, Valerie and Owain Jones. 2010. Surveillance, children and childhood. *Surveillance & Society*, 7(3/4): 187–191.

Thomsen, Simon. 2015. Extramarital affair website Ashley Madison has been hacked and attackers are threatening to leak data online. *Business Insider UK*, July 20. http://uk.businessinsider.com/cheating-affair-website-ashley-madison-hacked-user-data-leaked-2015-7?r=US&IR=T.

Trottier, Daniel. 2012. *Social media as surveillance: Rethinking visibility in a converging world*. Farnham, UK: Ashgate.

Trottier, Daniel. 2014. Vigilantism and power-users: Police and user-led investigations on social media. In D. Trottier and C. Fuchs (Eds.), *Social media, politics and the state: Protests, revolutions, riots, crime and policing in the age of Facebook, Twitter and YouTube* (pp. 209–236). New York: Routledge.

Trottier, Daniel. 2016. Caring for the virtual self on social media: Managing visibility on Facebook. In I. van der Ploeg and J. Pridmore (Eds.), *Digitizing identities*. London: Routledge.

Trottier, Daniel and David Lyon. 2011. Key features of a social media surveillance. In C. Fuchs, K. Boersma, A. Albrechtslund and M. Sandoval (Eds.), *The internet and surveillance: The challenge of Web 2.0 and social media* (pp. 89–109). New York: Routledge.

Van Dijck, José and Thomas Poell. 2013. Understanding social media logic. *Media and Communication*, 1(1): 2–14.

Walker, Joseph. 2012. Meet the new boss: Big data. *The Wall Street Journal*. Retrieved September 20. http://online.wsj.com/article/SB10000872396390443890304578006252019616768.html.

Warren, Samuel and Louis D. Brandeis. 1890. The right to privacy. *Harvard Law Review*, 15(5).

Westin, Alan. 1967. *Privacy and freedom*. London: Atheneum.

Winner, Langdon. 1977. *Autonomous technology: Technics out of control as a theme in human thought*. Cambridge, MA: MIT Press.

PART V

Social and Economic Domains

26

Social Media Marketing

Michael Serazio
and Brooke Erin Duffy

INTRODUCTION

The story of advertising in the 21st century might be summarized in two words: *lost control*. This is, at least, the conventional, received wisdom among industry professionals who view the technological, economic, and cultural upheaval wrought by digitization through such a narrative prism. In their reckoning, the mass media of the analogue era offered a comparatively predictable model of audience habits, platform monitoring, and content output; accordingly, advertisers functioned as 'top-down communicators, in control of what information is released, to whom and when, as well as the channels of communication themselves' (Spurgeon, 2008: 1).

Marketers' confidence and sense of authority within this traditional model might well be nostalgically overstated: audiences were never really that docile; large-scale persuasion never that assured. Nonetheless, this rather crude framing – top-down versus bottom-up – maps emblematically onto the structural transition from mass media to social media as the ideal means for commercial coaxing. Audiences, long regarded by the industry as passive recipients for mediated advertising messages, are now articulated as *co-creators* in a fluid, digital brand conversation; what had been a one-way flow of content through 30-second TV spots, full-page glossies, and roadside billboards is being complemented (and, in some cases, supplanted) by online initiatives configured for two-way interactivity. If mass media advertising had to interrupt content in order to reach audiences, social media advertising offers a different approach, both philosophically and operationally: It tries not to seem overly commercial and instead operates, guerrilla-style, to blend seamlessly with social patterns, streams, and platforms (Serazio, 2013).

Against this backdrop, it is perhaps not surprising that marketers – more than 97 percent, according to a 2014 industry survey of professionals throughout North America, the UK, and Australia – utilize social media as part of their overall communications strategy (Stelzner, 2014). The seismic growth in social media expenditures is both staggering and telling. Forrester Research pegged US spending at $12 billion in 2015 – an increase from just $2 billion in 2010 and en route to an estimated $27 billion by 2020 (Miglani, 2015). Globally, eMarketer projected 2015 spending would inflate to $24 billion – more than doubling from just two years earlier (eMarketer, 2015). These figures, while clearly a testament to the sprawling digital media landscape, also reflect widespread disillusionment with more traditional techniques of and channels for persuasion. Thus, before examining how social media communication is reconfiguring marketing discourses and practices, it is useful to take a look back at the recent history of the advertising-media system.

CONTEXTUAL CRISES

An appraisal of the contemporary state of advertising provides the necessary backstory to understanding the allure of social media. Though admittedly painting the industrial history in broad strokes, a series of escalating threats to the traditional advertising model have compelled marketers to explore alternative opportunities to deliver their messages. Chief among these fears and laments is the proliferation of ad-skipping technologies. From 1980s-era worries over the VCR and remote control to more recent anxiety directed at spam filters, DVR recordings, and 'Do Not Call' registries, these tactics of avoidance represent – to marketers, at least – a 'backlash' against unwanted commercial exposure (Evans, 2012: 12). One recent estimate holds that more than 200 million people worldwide regularly employ some kind of ad-blocking software and, given the presumed impatience of younger Web users, those rates are only projected to increase (Block shock, 2015). Together, these forces

have hastened various eulogies about 'the death of advertising' as we know it (Rust and Oliver, 1994).

The pervasive sentiment that there is more advertising than ever to evade – as consumers wade through the thickets of a 'mature sign economy' within advanced capitalist nations – has also prompted advertisers to rethink traditional communicative approaches (Goldman and Papson, 1996: 8). Tallying a precise figure for advertising exposure has long been an inexact science, with widely varying definitions, methodologies, and contexts for assessing 'clutter.' One of the more extreme – though often cited – estimates from market research firm Yankelovich suggests that people now face as many as 5,000 ads competing for their attention on a daily basis (Story, 2007). Critiquing the promotional overload that seems to define contemporary environments, cultural critic James Twitchell (1996: 56) contends, 'Almost every physical object now carries advertising, almost every human environment is suffused with advertising, almost every moment of time is calibrated by advertising.' Naturally, then, the rise of social media has lent itself to the latest frontier in this persistent 'colonization' of communication formats (McAllister, 1996).

These patterns of ad-skipping and commercial clutter have, moreover, taken shape amidst a fragmentation of media and society that has meant smaller segments of the audience pie for advertisers to divvy up (Turow, 1997). For nearly a quarter-century, advertisers could count on the vast majority of American homes tuning into one of just three television networks during prime time scheduling. By the start of the new millennium, cable channels had collectively garnered bigger audiences than the network share and, a decade later, studies showed the time that Americans spent with digital media had surpassed the amount watching television (Delo, 2013b; Jenkins, 2006). Such findings mirror the patterns of audience fragmentation in other geo-national contexts, such as the UK (Oliver & Ohlbaum, 2011). If advertising once bought and sold audiences in 'tonnage' bulk – and if 'it seemed logical to use media vehicles to mass-produce customers in the same way that the factories mass-produced the merchandise' – then the new conditions ushered in by Facebook and Twitter demand a more nimble, targeted commercial alternative (Turow, 2005: 108–109). With widespread audience immersion in these networked, co-creative media contexts, advertising professionals have adopted the rhetoric that 'the age of mass advertising is over' and that social media might offer a necessary solution (Deuze, 2007b: 126).

When articulating their motivations for exploring social media strategies, practitioners routinely cite all three of these conditions – avoidance, clutter, and fragmentation – as part of a churning industrial maelstrom. It is, however, a fourth challenge – trustworthiness – that makes traditional advertising so comparatively lacking and social media opportunities so enticing. One recent survey reveals that only four percent of Americans believe that marketers conduct themselves with integrity (defined as 'always keeping promises') (Morrison, 2015). Scholarly research has further found that consumers do not particularly trust advertising in any of the dominant forms of mass media (e.g., TV, newspapers, radio, magazines, and the internet); rather, consumers deploy an automatic cynicism to deal with advertising within those confines (Friestad and Wright, 1994; Soh et al., 2007). At the same time, a global study of trust in advertising by Nielsen, an audience measurement company, confirmed the long-standing truism that personal recommendations from friends and family rate the highest as compared to professionally created messages (Nielsen, 2013). Naturally, then, advertisers would begin to turn toward settings wherein this personal communication flourishes. As a writer for *Inc.* magazine emblematically enthused:

> Often we think of social media as a way to drive traffic to websites, or build brand awareness or as another channel for marketing communications … but one of the best outcomes with social media is how it can *build trust in customers and the general public that ultimately adds to your bottom line.* (Campbell, 2014, para. 3, italics added for emphasis)

PROTO-HISTORY

Despite the upbeat euphoria over this seemingly innovative approach to promotion, social media marketing – both theoretically and as an industrial practice – needs to be placed within a timeline that well predates the rise of Facebook, YouTube, and Instagram. Before these digital platforms emerged, the strategy of deploying peer influence was known simply as 'word-of-mouth' or 'buzz' marketing (see Serazio, 2013, for expanded detail of this summary). An early incarnation of these techniques can be traced as far back as the First World War, when the Committee on Public Information enlisted opinion leaders ('Four Minute Men') in communities across the United States to propagandize their neighbors to build military support (Ewen, 1996). Such tactics inspired Edward Bernays (1928), frequently hailed as the 'father of public relations,' to leverage the authority of third-party intermediaries in the hope of swaying public opinion; today, social media strategists attempt to achieve much the same. Though perhaps best known for spearheading the 'Torches of Freedom' campaign, which exploited the women's suffrage movement to position cigarette smoking as a conduit to gender equality, Bernays also famously increased bacon sales by convincing physicians to recommend it to their patients under the guise of a 'hearty' breakfast (Cutlip, 1994). Similarly, beauty and kitchenware companies like Avon and Tupperware found success by targeting female consumers through their social networks – recruiting respectable women of the community and organizing party dates to embed sales strategies (Clarke, 1999; Manko, 1997). Over the years, such schemes also found their way into both political 'astroturfing' (i.e., implanting grassroots momentum) and pop music promotion – the assumption being that fans and supporters can do the best and most authentic shilling on behalf of campaigning candidates and record labels (Serazio, 2013, 2014, 2015, 2017). Youth, in particular, have been pursued through these proto-social media machinations – as seen in 'teen peer-to-peer marketing' (Quart, 2003). By the early 2000s, this industry had grown fast enough that a Word-of-Mouth Marketing Association could be formally chartered.

Yet even as marketers were 'discovering' the utility of everyday social practices among consumers – concomitant with the waning of faith in mass media efficacy – scholars had long since established these patterns as fundamental to understanding how interpersonal influence flows throughout society. Word-of-mouth marketing – and, later, its social media stepchild – exists largely because of diffusion: the theory that ideas and trends spread over time from innovative individuals through to mass adoption (Rogers, 1962). Moreover, a related 'two-step flow' concept holds that there are 'opinion leaders' found in every social network that facilitate the outreach of those mass media messages (Katz and Lazarsfeld, 2006 [1955]). Such individuals are imbued with significant 'social' or 'subcultural' capital, depending on the theoretical formulation (Bourdieu, 2001; Thornton, 1996).

Marketers, unsurprisingly, lust after these opinion leaders and hope to draw them in as brand evangelists; one of the largest word-of-mouth firms, BzzAgent, boasts upwards of a million participants across the US, Canada, and the UK (www.bzzagent.com, 2015). As brand ambassadors, individuals receive free products to try out, talk about with friends, and then provide feedback to clients about those interactions (Balter and Butman, 2005). One practitioner who has hired barflies, doormen, Little League moms, and mass transit commuters to show off such samples likens the strategy to 'real life product placement' (Eisenberg, 2002).

With the rise of the internet – and the explosion of user-generated content enabled by digital tools – word-of-mouth sparked interest in a 'word-of-mouse' equivalent (Word of mouse, 2007). The voracious market for 'interactive' or 'two-way' communication emerges at a moment when the *network* – rather than *broadcasting* – is upheld as the 'core organizing principle of this [new] communication environment' (Bruns, 2008: 14). Between Amazon reviews, Facebook updates, and YouTube commentary, conversations that had been private and ephemeral are now rendered more public and quantifiable than ever before. Advertisers, particularly those clinging tightly to the rhetoric of 'lost control,' endeavor to secure part of this market 'share' by deftly managing social media communication. But how do these professionals strategize and coordinate their efforts amidst the heady brew of digital options? To what extent have they been able to regain control of the social media conversation? How might these practices challenge and/or reaffirm existing power relations, including those between producers and consumers of advertising content? And what are the socio-cultural implications of these changes for consumer-citizens who increasingly live their lives *in and through* (digital) media (Deuze, 2012)?

The following sections find answers to these questions by illustrating the new holy trinity of social marketing: earned media (i.e., promotion-driven publicity); owned media (i.e., content channels directly controlled by marketers); and paid media (i.e., the traditional purchase of ad time and space). And quite symptomatic of the emergent logics animating 21st-century marketers, 'neither earned media nor owned media *explicitly involves advertising*' (Turow, 2012: 133).

SOCIAL MEDIA MARKETING'S HOLY TRINITY

Earned Media

Within this much-hyped marketing triad, earned media represents word-of-mouth promotion that is amplified by the networked capability of digital platforms. Simply put, earned media signals online buzz: It is the one-off YouTube clip that goes viral; the glowing product review posted on a blog or Amazon; the auspicious brand-centric moment that suddenly rouses the Twitterverse. 'Authentic' and 'organic' are frequent euphemisms for earned media; as one popular social media marketing guidebook exhorts:

> The best social media marketing is always going to be done by your fans, not by you, so get out of their way. ... Motivate your fans to create content on social networking sites for you. Organic content is much more convincing. (Zarrella, 2010: 67, 76)

Such 'motivat[ion]' may take many forms. A felicitous earned media exemplar comes from the British supermarket chain Sainsbury's: In 2011, '3 ½' year-old Lily Robinson wrote a letter inquiring why the company's 'tiger bread' was named as such, rather than what she considered the much more apt 'giraffe bread' (Stevens, 2012). Chris King, a Sainsbury's customer service representative, responded to the toddler's query with a letter concurring, 'I think renaming tiger bread giraffe bread is a brilliant idea – it looks much more like the blotches on a giraffe than the stripes on a tiger, doesn't it?' King included a £3 Sainsbury's gift card with his charming response, which was signed 'Chris King (age 27 and 1/3).' When Robinson's mother posted the letter exchange on her blog, the 'giraffe bread' story went viral, garnering significant mainstream press coverage along with more than 150,000 Facebook 'likes' and nearly 50,000 'shares.' Indeed, the response was so profound that a representative for the company later announced it was officially changing the appellation of the bread. From a strategic planning perspective, it is difficult to imagine that Sainsbury's could have predicted the extent to which a happenstance exchange could burnish their public image.

However, earned media isn't necessarily *unanticipated*, and many companies go to great lengths to try to steer the online conversation about their brand or product. Emulating the offline seeding practices described above, marketers distribute their wares to social media *influencers* – the voguish term for those with substantial clout in the digital arena (e.g., followers, friends, subscribers). Traditionally, bloggers represented one of the first amateur groups targeted by marketers, likely owing to the platform's ascendance prior to other social networking sites; increasingly, though, 'blogger' activities take place across a raft of social platforms. Given advertisers' deep-rooted assumptions about women as chiefly 'social' shoppers, companies have been especially eager to curry favor with bloggers who have cultivated a following in the fashion, beauty, and parenting realms (Duffy, 2013b). In 2008, relatively early on in marketers' attempts to leverage digital influence, consumer goods behemoth Procter & Gamble invited more than a dozen 'mommy bloggers' to their corporate headquarters for an event orchestrated by their Pampers brand. Dispelling the claim that the company was trying to 'buy their loyalty' with this all-expenses paid trip, an external relations representative explained – in terms indicative of social media marketing's commercial self-effacement – 'We've made it clear that this is not really about pitching products per se ... but exploring areas of common interest, such as baby development and how to help moms in this topsy-turvy time in their lives' (Neff, 2008).

More recently, as these sorts of influencer programs have become a central part of marketers' strategies, they have expanded in both size and scope. The fashion industry, in particular, has become notorious for comping products to high-ranking bloggers and Instagrammers in hopes of scoring favorable publicity among the sartorially inclined. In her exposé of the gifting suites at Sundance, an independent film festival held annually in Park Springs, Utah, *New York Times* reporter Sheila Marikar (2015) explained how fashion bloggers, Viners, and Instagrammers are eclipsing traditional celebrities as public taste-makers.

To woo these social media personalities, some of whom boast readership in the millions, advertisers and publicists furnished them with brand-named clothes, shoes, tech accessories, and even an all-expenses-paid trip to Aruba. In exchange for the gratis, the digital influencers were expected to share photos and reviews of the Sundance swag with their social media friends and followers in an 'organic' way. Highlighting the financial boon of this system to marketers, a public relations representative explained, 'We see higher conversions off those girls than we do with celebrity placement that we might have paid money for' (ibid.). Here, the rep nods to an assumption that underpins the earned media imperative: persuasive communication is deemed 'authentic' precisely because it is not paid.

To be sure, discourses of authenticity have long been at the heart of commercial strategy, particularly in the US context. By the time Coke was famously touted as the 'real thing' to American consumers in the early 1970s, marketers understood the value of using authenticity-draped pitches as a response to the consumerist desire for expressive individualism (Duffy, 2013a; Frank, 1997). Yet 'authenticity' as a cultural construct seems to have taken on a particular salience in the social media era; as Alice Marwick (2013: 248) argues of the Web 2.0 ethos, 'Authenticity has become an axiom that primarily differentiates user-generated brands from each other'. Thus, the authority of fashion bloggers and other 'influencers' comes not from traditional markers of expertise or prestige but, rather, from their ability to position themselves as 'relatable' throughout their arsenal of social media content (Duffy, 2013b, 2013c). Yet as we discuss below, this rhetoric of 'relatability' effectively veils some of the covert marketing strategies deployed to peddle products – *for pay*.

Owned Media

If earned media is meant to connote 'authenticity,' then an apt euphemism for owned media might be the equally buzzy term 'engagement.' Recall that owned media are channels that are under marketers' direct control: webpages, mobile sites, and brands' 'official' or 'verified' social media destinations. British luxury retailer Burberry, oft-regarded as a pioneer among prestige brands on the digital frontier, has been delivering content through the company's Facebook page since 2009; posts include 'behind-the-scenes' photo shoots, footage from catwalks, product images, and store opening announcements. Above all, this kaleidoscope of imagery, videos, and text is designed to be 'sharable,' which is all the more vital considering their Facebook page has close to 17 million followers across the globe (Swire, 2014). The retailer's more recent forays into social media marketing include a Twitter account dedicated exclusively to customer service inquiries, a YouTube channel that has amassed more than 180,000 subscribers, and an Instagram account that includes live video footage from its runway shows. To further engage fans in their owned media content, Burberry maintains a micro-site, 'The Art of the Trench,' populated by images of 'real people' donning their iconic line of coats. Created in 2009 and re-launched in 2014, this user-generated initiative includes features that allow users to filter the style of the garment by style, color, and gender; recordings of 'up-and-coming artists' provide a soundtrack for the site.

To date, legions of companies have – like Burberry – launched micro-sites that leverage the content, publicity, and networked capacity of social media users. In the ever-popular 'contest' model for social media participation, corporations invite photo and video submissions featuring fans with branded goods. Doritos' 'Crash the Super Bowl Contest' might be the most prominent example, in which competitors create ads in the hopes of landing them in a television break during the US's most widely watched sports event. Initiatives such as this fit quite cozily into the wider context of convergence culture, where the boundaries between production and consumption are blurring and power is ostensibly being redeployed to the 'newly empowered consumers' (Jenkins, 2006: 19). Though such initiatives are upheld in the popular imagination as potential springboards to fame and creative success, they have also been critiqued for the extent to which they rely upon the unpaid labor of brand ambassadors (Carah, 2011; Duffy, 2010). After all, traditional media and advertising companies don't need to bankroll researchers, producers, and promoters if self-enterprising 'co-creators' are willing to do the work for free (or the oft-deterred promise of 'exposure') (Burgess and Green, 2009).

In another example of using owned media to solicit co-creative content, *Cosmopolitan* targeted a young, socially connected female audience with their 2010 'Fun, Fearless, Female' user-generated campaign (see Duffy, 2013b, for an overview). A multi-platform promotion, the contest invited women around the world to 'be the star' of a *Cosmopolitan* ad campaign that was timed to coincide with the magazine's international expansion. The initiative was announced on the brand's YouTube channel with a video featuring then-editor-in-chief Kate White, publisher Donna Kalajian Lagani, and singer Jordin Sparks, among others. Signaling the increasingly global nature of the brand, 'readers and users around the planet' could upload their photos on the website, cosmofff.com, and 'see themselves as part of the campaign,' Lagani announced. After submitting a personal photo on the website – using either a Facebook photo or another digital image – visitors were immersed in a digital simulation of a '*Cosmo* Photo Studio' and given virtual 'makeovers.' Young women were then encouraged to share their mock photo shoots with their friends via Facebook, a nod toward the growing utility of social networks as promotional and data-generating tools. Furthermore, the contest section of the campaign required participants to provide their names, home and email addresses – personal information that could then be harvested by corporate partners. As this example suggests, the ambition in launching such initiatives is twofold: both capturing detailed personal information about consumer preferences and also seeding 'authentic' buzz into social network communities.

Paid Media

'Paid media' in the digital world harkens back to its analogue antecedents: marketers *pay for* time and space while taking full advantage of the customizable, trackable potential of the internet. Positioning the unique benefits of 'paid media' as a mechanism for industrial control, a social business strategy executive summarized, '[Such] initiatives usually target prospects in an effort to create brand awareness or new customer acquisition. ... While it can certainly be expensive, you have complete control over the creative, content and marketing' (Brito, 2013). To date, most, if not all, of the top social media platforms are ad-supported, although their technological and targeting capacities continue to evolve in rapid succession.

Although it has become the biggest beneficiary of social media marketing, Facebook appeared initially cautious, preferring to build up its user base (and the enormous sums of time spent on the site) before monetizing those eyeballs and hours of interaction through advertising intrusion (van Dijck, 2013). As with almost any form of advertising, what began confined to the margins (e.g., banners on the side) has increasingly crept into and colonized more central spaces (e.g., sponsored updates in the 'News Feed' timeline) (Delo, 2013a). No doubt attentive to eye-tracking research that reveals habitual blind spots in places that advertising regularly appears – and building upon a central thesis here, that advertisers seek to co-opt people for their pitches – Facebook began exploiting the names of users' friends in the ad content, if they had 'liked' a particular product or brand. Once again, the exploitation of the credibility and social capital of ordinary individuals – as though 'micro-celebrities' in their own right – is a central ambition and tension in this space (Marwick, 2013).

Twitter played it similarly coy in its early days, before expanding the opportunities for sponsored tweets and promoted trends to interested partners; the 'real-time' immediacy of the network (and, therefore, potential for on-the-fly messaging responsiveness) has been one of its most sought-after assets (Learmonth, 2013). The progressive evolution of these platforms from non-commercial to ad-subsidized has set the stage for marketing on newer, and more spectacularly visual, social networks. Pinterest, for instance, has rolled out 'promoted pins,' and more recently 'cinematic pins,' both of which are positioned as ways to engage captive users who may potentially 'click through' and purchase the displayed product. The YouTube model, by contrast, is heavily dependent on pre-roll advertisements, which have a historically low viewership because of their skippable feature. Consequently, advertisers have responded by trying to craft slicker ads that reach people in the crucial, initial five-second viewing window. Geico, in particular, has been lauded for creative spots that 'specifically tailor ads to pre-roll,' an indicator that marketers are trying to work *with*, rather than against, digitally enabled ad-avoidance technologies (Nudd, 2015). Here, too, 'lost control' – and the adaptation to a more complicated social media set of commercial circumstances – resonates with advertisers.

EVALUATING THE SOCIAL MEDIA MARKETING MIX

Of course, as the previous discussion makes clear, the boundaries between earned, owned, and paid media are often quite fluid as marketers attempt to optimize impact on social

media denizens. In the 'contest' model described above, for instance, both paid (i.e., ads promoting the contest) and owned (i.e., the contest micro-site) media strategies are implemented in an effort to mobilize consumers to become (un/under-paid) promotional channels (earned media). As Pepsi's vice president for marketing explained of a social media contest they organized soliciting fan photos, 'A Pepsi brand communication going from friend to friend is much more powerful than brand to consumer' (Zmuda, 2013). In other cases, these pillars of the social media marketing mix are integrated into more comprehensive marketing plans that also involve traditional media. Such is the case with 'alternate reality marketing' schemes, which, like *The Dark Knight*'s 'Why So Serious?' promotion, tend to be elaborate, cross-platform, interactive, puzzle-like experiences that are frequently employed on behalf of films and video games (Serazio, 2013: 143).

Among the more insidious forms of this blurring, and owing much to the stealth marketing programs of yesteryear, are paid media initiatives that are deployed under the pretense of earned or 'organic' media. So-called 'native advertising' tries to pass advertising content off as editorial news or entertainment, much like traditional magazines have done through oft-disparaged (and presumably ignored) *advertorials*. The immensely popular Buzzfeed, a so-called 'laboratory for viral content' that draws 150 million viewers each month, is a prime exemplar of this tactical blurring: The start-up boasts a 75-person division that is 'dedicated to creating for brands custom video and list-style advertising content that looks similar to its own editorial content' (Isaac, 2014). This breach of church–state ideals threatens to leech journalistic credibility much as Facebook and Twitter have leeched off our interpersonal credibility with their efforts to blur social and commercial content.

It is this very same logic, or perhaps, more accurately, surreptitiousness, that has powered the tremendous growth of paid influencer programs, wherein digital media personalities receive payment to puff various goods among their social media audiences. Although regulatory bodies in several Western countries now require bloggers to disclose these payment deals (as we discuss in a later section), the extent to which this actually happens is unclear. So-called 'influencer marketing programs' have become so pervasive that a whole industry has sprung up to broker deals between brand marketers and social media producers. Often, the latter are selected, evaluated, and compensated on the basis of their digital metrics: followers, shares, views, and more – a testament to the new currency that increasingly drives commercial activity the social media age.

And, indeed, the advertising industry as a whole has begun to reconsider its system of evaluation: Rather than simply judge return-on-investment based upon how many audiences are *'reached by'* a given campaign, firms now privilege how many people *'reached out'* with convergence contributions including likes, shares, retweets, submissions, and comments (Serazio, 2013: 126, italics in original). Messages circulated from peer-to-peer (in what quickly came to be known as 'viral' advertising) are held in greater esteem than those simply forced by a mass media outlet onto a 'passive' receiver.

The incredible abundance of personal information that is available through social media channels naturally captivates advertisers who have implemented profiling and targeting practices. Two case studies, in particular, stand out as exemplary of these ambitions. In 2011, the Polish vodka brand, Ultimat, released 'The Social Life Audit,' the first-ever Facebook app that scans and rates a user's profile and content across a dozen dimensions, including 'social status' (photos posted per week), 'crew size' (number of people counted in those photos, through facial recognition software), 'trendiness' (check-ins at popular locations), 'nocturnality' (check-ins tracked late at night), and even

'good times' (percentage of smiling faces in photos) and 'hookup' potential (percentage of photos tagged with single people). The app won plaudits from *Mashable* and *Creativity* magazine, with the latter acknowledging that, 'In the social media age, you are what you put on Facebook' (Creativity Online, 2011; Wasserman, 2011). In effect, the campaign represented a branded variation on the 'Klout Score,' a social media analytic standard which measures the interactivity and influence of users across a variety of online platforms; with the 'Audit' app, Ultimat aimed for opt-in viral circulation, social comparison, increased partying (tips were given to improve low scores), and affiliated mindshare along the way.

On the other hand, Amnesty International New Zealand's 'Trial By Timeline' app exemplified much the same means of social media-derived profiling and targeting, but toward very different ends. The 2013 campaign, which was meant to drum up a sense of empathy for and solidarity with political prisoners and human rights victims worldwide, developed an algorithm to similarly scan a Facebook user's timeline 'to an unprecedented level' and '[take] note of anything that could be used against you,' including likes, postings, friendships, demographic information, and political and religious views. It subsequently delivered a summary of hundreds of punishments that would have been administered in countries around the world where such behavior is outlawed (e.g., 'stoned for drinking alcohol, imprisoned and beaten just for talking to the opposite sex, or hung for premarital sex') (Trial by timeline, 2014). The campaign claimed a total reach of 15 million people, being particularly effective in reaching 'key online influencers' on Twitter (e.g., those sharing results had an average of more than 1,500 followers), and it garnered the top prize that year in Facebook's non-profit awards category. The potential demonstrated by these two campaigns – one to incentivize bacchanalia, the other to caution about the international consequences of it – show how much advertisers have to gain in systematically plumbing social media data for personalized insights and attention-grabbing content. Whether any governmental authorities will step in to oversee access to and manipulation of that data is another matter.

REGULATING SOCIAL MEDIA CONTENT

As commercial logics make further inroads into various aspects of online life, there is growing concern about the extent to which advertisers are monitoring and harnessing consumer information – a fear pithily summarized as the 'creep factor' (Turow, 2012). Such apprehension about marketers' access to and control over personal data has triggered backlash from grassroots advocacy groups and consumer protection agencies alike. In 2013, for instance, thousands of Facebook members rallied against the social network through the 'Say NO to suggested posts' community page. Group members denounced Facebook's move to better tailor ads through the site's 'suggested posts' feature; however, participation in the group waned after a few months. More recently, in a *New York Times* op-ed critiquing Facebook's data monitoring practices, internet scholar Zeynep Tufecki (2015) proposed a novel economic model where users could pay a fee to *opt out* of the network's surveillance activities. Based on a calculation that Facebook makes about 20 cents per user each month in advertising revenue, Tufecki envisioned a micropayment system wherein social media users could contribute a small fee for an ad-free experience.

Government organizations have a more formal charge to uphold the rights of citizen-consumers in the digital age. Yet the velocity of change and complexity of activities involved in social media marketing means that regulators have struggled to keep pace

with the industry's rapid innovations. Questions and concerns have revolved primarily around the appropriate means of disclosing the commercial origin of social media speech and the recommended protections for consumers' digital data (Hayes, 2013). Overall, Europe's system of regulating digital advertising is considered much more robust than that of the US (Delo, 2012). European policies tend to limit the kind of information companies can collect and use to deliver hyper-targeted social media messages. Moreover, Europeans are more likely than Americans to opt out of online behavioral tracking and block advertising in those spaces (Sloane, 2015). In the United States, by contrast, marketers are afforded more leeway to self-regulate; as such, privacy watchdogs believe that the nation 'has lagged behind other countries when it comes to protecting consumer privacy rights' (Arbel, 2016). In 2016, the Federal Communications Commission proposed a series of rules that would constrain the ability of internet service providers to share customer data with advertisers; perhaps not surprisingly, the projected plan generated significant backlash from broadband networks (ibid.).

Guidelines governing the appropriate means of disclosing the commercial nature of social media messages, such as the earlier mentioned 'native advertising,' also vary by country. In the United Kingdom, the Advertising Standards Authority (ASA), the industry's self-regulatory organization, has aggressively pursued cases of surreptitious marketing. In 2014, the ASA ruled that vloggers must clearly disclose the paid nature of their relationships with brand sponsors; the decision came in the wake of a social media promotion for Oreo cookies that involved several British YouTube stars. Though some of the social media celebs nodded toward the company's involvement with elusive statements thanking Oreo 'for making this video possible,' the ASA ruled that such acknowledgments were 'insufficient to make clear the marketing nature of the videos' (Sweney,

2014). Two years later, the ASA banned the *Buzzfeed* listicle, '14 Laundry Fails We've All Experienced,' which was actually a paid advertorial by British fabric care company Dylon (Sweney, 2016). Also in 2016, the Advertising Standards Authority of Ireland announced its own set of directives for sponsored blog content; the guidelines hold bloggers to the same ethical standards as other forms of 'media,' in part by ensuring that 'consumers know when they're receiving marketing material' (Cullen, 2016).

The Federal Trade Commission (FTC) is the key regulatory body responsible for overseeing social media marketing in the US. In 2013, the FTC issued a report stressing that advertising embedded in online spaces needed to disclose itself as such 'clearly and conspicuously' to prevent consumer deception; moreover, claims had to be truthful and substantiated, as has been mandated – albeit, if not always upheld – for offline content (Federal Trade Commission, 2013: 6). The updated FTC rules also required bloggers to disclose any products, services, or samples they received for free. Of course, by requiring that a posting be identified as advertising via an #ad or #sponsored hash-tag preface, the FTC cuts against that which marketers and clients value most about social media in the first place: the fact that its messages can *avoid* seeming like advertising (Serazio, 2013). Although the FTC has only punished a handful of violators (see, for example, Learmonth, 2012; Morrison, 2014), one of the most high-profile cases involved luxury department store Lord & Taylor. As part of a promotion for their new spring clothing line, the retailer paid 50 fashion influencers to showcase a new dress on their Instagram feed; however, none of the bloggers (who reportedly received between $1,000 and $4,000 for the post) disclosed their compensation. The FTC ruled that this slickly produced promotion was misleading to consumers, and Lord & Taylor subsequently got a 'slap on the wrist' before a settlement was reached (Coffee, 2016; Moran, 2016). Other

examples include a music instruction software company that was punished $250,000 for paying for fake online reviews, and Sony settled with the FTC following charges that its advertising agency enlisted employees to boost Twitter buzz about a new PlayStation device without disclosing their affiliation (Learmonth, 2012; Morrison, 2014).

To be sure, any review of the legal oversight of these efforts that can be offered here will have to be temporary and certainly subject to revision as new codes are written (and new platforms inevitably take shape confounding the clarity of those codes). At the same time, there are certain spaces where marketers routinely err on the side of caution, particularly concerning children. Indeed, despite the massive growth of the youth market for social networking and gaming sites – including Moshi Monsters with its tens of millions of members worldwide – many remained surprisingly ad-free, given the perceived risk of minors' privacy (Slutsky, 2011).

CONCLUSION

As this chapter has shown, the meteoric ascent of social media has altered the promotional landscape of the advertising world in profound and complex ways. Industry professionals, once bound by the temporal and spatial constraints of analogue formats – newspaper column inches, radio spots, and TV commercial lengths – now have a dizzying array of channels through which to communicate with potential consumers – seemingly anytime, anywhere. On the surface, at least, the staid era of mass persuasion has been eclipsed by a networked era of individualized, interactive communication. And contemporary advertisers have swiftly become deft (and insidious) experimenters as they jockey for consumers' eyeballs in the aptly named 'attention economy.'

These changes dovetail with a new, or perhaps renewed, industry vernacular that centers on the much-hyped ideals of authenticity and engagement. What underpins these ideals is the realization that brand communication is increasingly dialogical, a shift which cannot be understood apart from the ostensible 'democratization' of brands. Beginning in the aughts, as more media content could be conceptualized along a scale from 'open' to 'closed' in terms of the degree of participation elicited from audiences (versus control maintained by corporations), advertising professionals began to scoff at the 'myth' that they 'owned and orchestrated' their own brands (Deuze, 2007a; Hanna et al., 2011: 266). And, to be sure, the social media marketing ideal seems much more populist: It stresses 'grassroots' dialogue over mass media monologues; hails a consumer who is 'in charge' of the brand; and venerates ambitions like genuineness, spontaneity, decentralization, and egalitarianism. Further, by taking a more polysemic approach to the brand (in that it is dependent on diverse interpretations fostered in social media), marketers ostensibly relinquish tight control of the message in favor of hoping to see a variety of messages spread further and, presumably, more credibly. For these reasons, scholars have variously theorized the brand as an 'open-ended object,' a 'platform for action,' a 'building block,' and a 'cultural resource,' because 'brands work by enabling consumers, by empowering them in particular directions' (Arvidsson, 2006: 8, 68; Holt, 2002: 83; Lury, 2004: 1, 151).

For example, some of the activities profiled in this chapter testify to such rhetorical and operational openness and serendipity: the letter from a (very) young consumer that prompts a product rebranding or the spontaneous product review from an uber-hip social media influencer. In other cases, though, marketers have been able to effectively harness consumer 'control' and interactivity in more deliberate ways. Among the best examples is the deployment of 'real people' as un- or under-paid brand ambassadors in user-generated content schemes: marketers leverage the *earned* buzz of these programs while

capitalizing on the laboring activities of co-creators. To critical scholars, these practices exploit participants in the digital labor system (Andrejevic, 2008; Scholz 2012) and tend to exacerbate existing industrial hierarchies, including those related to gender (Duffy, 2010, 2013c). Accordingly, we close by raising the possibility that the infectious rhetoric of 'lost control' is in many ways a convenient myth that helps to conceal the extent to which traditional players still exert their influence. While the breakneck clip of social media technologies continues to reshape the relationship between marketing producers and consumers, the power ascribed to the latter might perhaps be more illusory than currently hyped.

REFERENCES

Andrejevic, M. (2008) Watching television without pity the productivity of online fans. *Television & New Media*, 9(1), 24–46.

Arbel, T. (2016) New privacy rules expected for Internet providers. 10 March. *Associated Press*. Available from: www.bigstory.ap.org/article/c10739f7f8cc4848b0bb823b5d53baac/new-privacy-rules-expected-internet-providers.

Arvidsson, A. (2006) *Brands: Meaning and value in media culture*. London: Routledge.

Balter, D. and Butman, J. (2005) *Grapevine: The new art of word-of-mouth marketing*. New York: Portfolio Hardcover.

Bernays, E. L. (1928) *Propaganda*. New York: Horace Liveright.

Block shock (2015) *The Economist*, 6 June. Available from: www.economist.com/news/business/21653644-internet-users-are-increasingly-blocking-ads-including-their-mobiles-block-shock

Bourdieu, P. (2001) The forms of capital. In M. Granovetter and R. Swedberg (Eds.), *The sociology of economic life* (pp. 96–111). Boulder, CO: Westview Press.

Brito, M. (2013). Your content strategy: Defining paid, owned and earned media. *Hootsuite*. Available from: http://blog.hootsuite.com/converged-media-brito-part-1/.

Bruns, A. (2008) *Blogs, Wikipedia, Second Life, and beyond: From production to produsage*. New York: Peter Lang.

Burgess, J. and Green, J. (2009). *YouTube: Online video and participatory culture*. Chichester, UK: John Wiley & Sons.

Campbell, A. (2014) Trust: The often over-looked benefit of social media. *Inc*, 4 September. Available from: www.inc.com/comcast/trust-the-often-overlooked-benefit-of-social-media.html.

Carah, N. (2011). Breaking into The Bubble: Brand-building labour and 'getting in' to the culture industry. *Continuum: Journal of Media & Cultural Studies*, 25(3), 427–438.

Clarke, A. J. (1999) *Tupperware: The promise of plastic in 1950s America*. Washington, DC: Smithsonian Institution Press.

Coffee, P. (2016) FTC slams Lord & Taylor for not disclosing paid social posts and native ads. *Adweek*. Available from: www.adweek.com/news/advertising-branding/ftc-slams-lord-taylor-deceiving-customers-not-disclosing-its-native-ads-170229.

Creativity Online (2011) Ultimat Vodka: Social life audit. Available from: http://creativity-online.com/work/ultimat-vodka-social-life-audit/25279.

Cullen, C. (2016) Irish bloggers must now tell their fans when they have been paid to pro-mote a product. *Independent (Ireland)*, 25 January. Available from: www.independent.ie/entertainment/banter/trending/irish-bloggers-must-now-tell-their-fans-when-they-have-been-paid-to-promote-a-product-34394353.html.

Cutlip, S. M. (1994) *The unseen power: Public relations, a history*. Hillsdale, NJ: Lawrence Erlbaum Associates.

Delo, C. (2012) You are big brother (but that isn't so bad). *Advertising Age*, 23 April. Available from: http://adage.com/article/news/marketers-big-brother-bad/234290/

Delo, C. (2013a) Has Facebook lost faith in social ads? *Advertising Age*, 1 April. Available from: http://adage.com/article/digital/facebook-lost-faith-social-ads/240633/.

Delo, C. (2013b) U.S. adults now spending more time on digital devices than watching TV. *Advertising Age*, 1 August.

Deuze, M. (2007a) Convergence culture in the creative industries. *International Journal of Cultural Studies*, 10(2), 243–263.

Deuze, M. (2007b) *Media work*. Cambridge, UK: Polity Press.

Deuze, M. (2012) *Media life*. Cambridge, UK: Polity Press.

Duffy, B. E. (2010) Empowerment through endorsement? Polysemic meaning in Dove's user-generated advertising. *Communication, Culture & Critique*, 3(1), 26–43.

Duffy, B. E. (2013a) Manufacturing authenticity: The rhetoric of 'real' in women's magazines. *The Communication Review*, 16(3), 132–154.

Duffy, B. E. (2013b) *Remake, remodel: Women's magazines in the digital age*. Champaign, IL: University of Illinois Press.

Duffy, B. E. (2013c) The new 'real women' of advertising: Subjects, experts and producers in the interactive era. In M. McAllister and E. West (Eds.), *The Routledge companion to advertising and promotional culture* (pp. 223–236). New York: Routledge.

Eisenberg, D. (2002) It's an ad, ad, ad, ad world. *Time*, 160(10), 38. Available from: http://content.time.com/time/magazine/article/0,9171,344045,00.html.

eMarketer (2015) *Social network ad spending to hit $23.68 billion worldwide in 2015*. Available from: www.emarketer.com/Article/Social-Network-Ad-Spending-Hit-2368-Billion-Worldwide-2015/1012357.

Evans, D. (2012) *Social media marketing: An hour a day* (2nd ed.). Indianapolis, IN: John Wiley & Sons.

Ewen, S. (1996) *PR!: A social history of spin*. New York: Basic Books.

Federal Trade Commission (2013) *.com disclosures: How to make effective disclosures in digital advertising*. Available from: www.ftc.gov/sites/default/files/attachments/press-releases/ftc-staff-revises-online-advertising-disclosure-guidelines/130312dotcomdisclosures.pdf.

Frank, T. (1997) *The conquest of cool: Business culture, counterculture, and the rise of hip consumerism*. Chicago, IL: University of Chicago Press.

Friestad, M. and Wright, P. (1994) The persuasion knowledge model: How people cope with persuasion attempts. *Journal of Consumer Research*, 21(1), 1–31.

Goldman, R. and Papson, S. (1996) *Sign wars: The cluttered landscape of advertising*. New York: Guilford Press.

Hanna, R., Rohm, A. and Crittenden, V. L. (2011) We're all connected: The power of the social media ecosystem. *Business Horizons*, 54(3), 265–273.

Hayes, N. (2013) *The social media legal and regulatory landscape*. Available from: www.forrester.com/The+Social+Media+Legal+And+Regulatory+Landscape/fulltext/-/E-RES99883?docid=99883.

Holt, D. B. (2002) Why do brands cause trouble? A dialectical theory of consumer culture and branding. *Journal of Consumer Research*, 29(1), 70–90.

Isaac, M. (2014) 50 million new reasons buzzfeed wants to take its content far beyond lists. *New York Times*, 10 August. Available from: www.nytimes.com/2014/08/11/technology/a-move-to-go-beyond-lists-for-content-at-buzzfeed.html?_r=1.

Jenkins, H. (2006) *Convergence culture: Where old and new media collide*. New York: New York University Press.

Katz, E. and Lazarsfeld, P. F. (2006 [1955]) *Personal influence: The part played by people in the flow of mass communications* (2nd ed.). New Brunswick, NJ: Transaction Publishers.

Learmonth, M. (2012) As fake reviews rise, Yelp, others crack down on fraudsters. *Advertising Age*, 1 October. Available from: http://adage.com/article/digital/fake-reviews-rise-yelp-crack-fraudsters/237486/.

Learmonth, M. (2013) When did Twitter grow up? *Advertising Age*, 25 February. Available from: http://adage.com/article/digital/twitter-grow/239992/.

Lury, C. (2004) *Brands: The logos of the global economy*. International library of sociology. London: Routledge.

Manko, K. (1997) 'Now you are in business for yourself': The independent contractors of the California Perfume Company, 1886–1938. *Business and Economic History*, 26(1), 5–26.

Marikar, S. (2015) Sundance courts a new celebrity crowd. *New York Times*, 30 January. Available from: www.nytimes.com/2015/02/01/style/sundance-courts-a-new-celebrity-crowd.html?_r=0.

Marwick, A. (2013) *Status update: Celebrity, publicity, and branding in the social media age*. New Haven, CT: Yale University Press.

McAllister, M. P. (1996) *The commercialization of American culture: New advertising, control and democracy*. Thousand Oaks, CA: Sage.

Miglani, J. (2015) *Forrester research social media forecast, 2015 to 2020 (US)*. Available from: www.forrester.com/Forrester+Research+Social+Media+Forecast+2015+To+2020+US/fulltext/-/E-RES122290.

Moran, C. (2016) Lord & Taylor gets slap on wrist for paying Instagram 'influencers' to run secret ads. *Consumerism*. Available from: https://consumerist.com/2016/03/15/lord-taylor-gets-slap-on-wrist-for-paying-instagram-influencers-to-run-secret-ads/.

Morrison, M. (2014) In a first, FTC charges social campaign as deceptive. *Advertising Age*, 8 December. Available from: http://adage.com/article/news/ftc-sony-deutsch-la-deceived-consumers/296004/.

Morrison, M. (2015) No one trusts advertising or media (except Fox News). *Advertising Age*, 24 April. Available from: http://adage.com/article/media/marketers-media-trusts/298221/.

Neff, J. (2008) P&G relies on power of mommy bloggers. *Advertising Age*, 14 July. Available from: http://adage.com/article/digital/p-g-relies-power-mommy-bloggers/129580/.

Nielsen (2013) *Nielsen global trust in advertising*. Available from: www.nielsen.com/us/en/insights/reports/2013/global-trust-in-advertising-and-brand-messages.html.

Nudd, T. (2015) Ad of the day: Geico makes clever preroll ads that are basically unskippable those first five seconds are key. *Adweek*, 2 March. Available from: www.adweek.com/news/advertising-branding/ad-day-geico-makes-clever-pre-roll-ads-are-basically-unskippable-163233.

Oliver & Ohlbaum Associates (2011) The fast pace of change in UK media. Report available from: http://stakeholders.ofcom.org.uk/binaries/consultations/tv-advertising-investigation/responses/attach1.pdf

Quart, A. (2003) *Branded: The buying and selling of teenagers*. Cambridge, MA: Perseus Publishing.

Rogers, E. M. (1962) *Diffusion of innovations*. New York: Free Press.

Rust, R. T. and Oliver R. W. (1994) The death of advertising. *Journal of Advertising*, 23(4), 71–77. Available from: www.jstor.org/stable/4188952.

Scholz, T. (Ed.) (2012) *Digital labour: The internet as playground and factory*. New York: Routledge.

Serazio, M. (2013) *Your ad here: The cool sell of guerrilla marketing*. New York: New York University Press.

Serazio, M. (2014) The new media designs of political consultants: Campaign production in a fragmented era. *Journal of Communication*, 64(4), 743–763.

Serazio, M. (2015) Managing the digital news cyclone: Power, participation, and political production strategies. *International Journal of Communication*, 9, 1907–1925.

Serazio, M. (2017) Branding politics: Emotion, authenticity, and the marketing culture of American political communication. *Journal of Consumer Culture*, 17(2), 225-241.

Sloane, G. (2015) Here's how Europe is stifling the ad business for Google, Facebook and others. *Adweek*, 16 April. Available from: www.adweek.com/news/technology/heres-how-europe-stifling-ad-business-google-facebook-and-others-164103.

Slutsky, I. (2011) Kids flock to social nets, but few advertisers dare to follow. *Advertising Age*, 20 June. Available from: http://adage.com/article/digital/togetherville-moshi-monsters-hot-advertisers-follow/228289/.

Soh, H., Reid, L. N. and King, K. W. (2007) Trust in different advertising media. *Journalism & Mass Communication Quarterly*, 84(3), 455–476.

Spurgeon, C. (2008) *Advertising and new media*. London: Routledge.

Stelzner, M. A. (2014) 2014 social media marketing annual report. *Social Media Examiner*. Available from: www.socialmediaexaminer.com/SocialMediaMarketingIndustryReport2014.pdf.

Stevens, J. (2012) Giraffe bread hits the shelves! Sainsbury's officially changes name of tiger variety after three-year-old's letter goes viral. *The Daily Mail*, 1 February. Available from: www.dailymail.co.uk/news/article-2094564/Giraffe-bread-Lily-Robinson-3-gets-Sainsburys-change-tiger-variety-viral-letter.html.

Story, L. (2007) Anywhere the eye can see, it's likely to see an ad. *The New York Times*, 15 January. Available from: www.nytimes.com/2007/01/15/business/media/15everywhere.html?_r=0.

Sweney, M. (2014) Vloggers must clearly tell fans when they're getting paid by advertisers, ASA rules. *The Guardian*, 26 November. Available from: www.theguardian.com/media/2014/nov/26/vloggers-must-tell-fans-paid-adverts-asa-rules.

Sweney, M. (2016) BuzzFeed breaks UK ad rules over misleading advertorial. *The Guardian*, 12 January. Available from: www.theguardian.com/media/2016/jan/13/buzzfeed-breaks-uk-ad-rules-over-misleading-advertorial.

Swire, R. (2014) Why is Burberry's digital strategy so good? *Parralax*, 28 April. Available from: https://parall.ax/blog/view/3047/why-is-burberry-s-digital-strategy-so-good.

Thornton, S. (1996) *Club cultures: Music, media, and subcultural capital*. Hanover, NH: Wesleyan University Press.

Trial by timeline (2014) *Facebook Awards*. Available from: www.facebook-studio.com/gallery/submission/trial-by-timeline.

Tufecki, Z. (2015) Mark Zuckerberg, let me pay for Facebook. *The New York Times*, 4 June. Available from: www.nytimes.com/2015/06/04/opinion/zeynep-tufekci-mark-zuckerberg-let-me-pay-for-facebook.html.

Turow, J. (1997) *Breaking up America: Advertisers and the new media world*. Chicago, IL: University of Chicago Press.

Turow, J. (2005) Audience construction and culture production: Marketing surveillance in the digital age. *The ANNALS of the American Academy of Political and Social Science*, 597(1), 103–121.

Turow, J. (2012) *The daily you: How the new advertising industry is defining your identity and your worth*. New Haven, CT: Yale University Press.

Twitchell, J. B. (1996) *Adcult USA: The triumph of advertising in American culture*. New York: Columbia University Press.

van Dijck, J. (2013) *The culture of connectivity: A critical history of social media*. Oxford, UK: Oxford University Press.

Wasserman, T. (2011) Facebook app gives you Klout-like score for your social life. *Mashable*, 18 November. Available from: http://mashable.com/2011/11/18/klout-score-social-life-app/#PxQ62ZwTumq3.

Word of mouse (2007) *The Economist*, 8 November. Available from: www.economist.com/node/10102992.

Zarrella, D. (2010) *The social media marketing book*. Sebastopol, CA: O'Reilly Media.

Zmuda, N. (2013) Pepsi puts public in Super Bowl spot. *Advertising Age*, 7 January. Available from: http://adage.com/article/special-report-super-bowl/pepsi-puts-public-super-bowl-spot/239023/.

27

Social Media and Journalism

Alfred Hermida

INTRODUCTION

When Apollo 11 landed on the Moon on the night of July 20, 1968, 125 million Americans were glued to their TV sets to watch astronaut Neil Armstrong set foot on the grey landscape. By the time of the live broadcast of the Moon landings, television had become the dominant form of media for news, information and entertainment in the US. The TV set was a fixture in nine out of 10 American homes. Television was the defining medium for the Baby Boomer generation in the US. Now in their fifties and sixties, this generation continues to turn to television for political news (Mitchell, Gottfried and Matsa, 2015).

Television has proved to be remarkably resilient as a source for news. In their analysis of four years of cross-national data on news habits, Newman, Levy and Nielsen (2015) found that significant audiences continue to tune in to the news on TV. The overall figures mask generational differences that point to the emergence of social media as spaces

for news and information. People born in the 1980s and early 1990s have grown up with the internet. For this millennial generation, research suggests that social media are what TV was for the Baby Boomers. Six out of 10 online millennials in the US cite Facebook as their source for political news (Mitchell et al., 2015).

The social practices that have developed alongside social media have led to shifts in how publics discover and consume the news. First is the rise of social media platforms as spaces for the circulation of news and information. While TV and online remain as key sources for news, audiences for print newspapers dropped off as the importance of social media as gateways to the news has risen (Newman et al., 2015). In particular, Facebook, with 1.71 billion monthly active users by June 2016, has emerged as the significant force in news discovery. In 2010, a third of internet users in the US were distributing or discussing news on networks like Facebook (Purcell et al., 2010). By 2015, two-thirds of Facebook users across 12 countries cited the social network as a place where they find, read, discuss or share news, indicating 'a quickening of the pace towards social media and mobile news' (Newman et al., 2015: 7).

If the Moon landing were taking place today, millions would, no doubt, be tuned into the live broadcast on television. Alongside, though, people would be checking live updates and feeds on the web, on mobile devices and on social platforms. They would be recommending and commenting on links, photos and video on Facebook and Twitter. They would be distributing, discussing and dissecting news tidbits about the landings on social platforms, from Facebook to Twitter and from WhatsApp to WeChat.

These platforms, created as networks for people to connect, communicate and create, have taken on some of the functions of the traditional news media, from newsgathering to publication. This chapter examines the interplay between social platforms, journalistic norms and routines and media institutions. It examines how the development and growth of social media platforms have impacted news flows, before going on to consider how journalists and media institutions have responded to the changing dynamics around the discovery, selection, publication and distribution of news and information.

SOCIAL MEDIA AND THE NEWS

Social media tools, platforms and services may be a relatively new phenomenon but it is important to note that media have always had a social element. People were discussing, commenting on and sharing news long before Facebook, using the communication systems available at the time, from talking on the doorstep with neighbours to sending newspaper cuttings in the mail. In 1961, playwright Arthur C. Miller was quoted in *The Observer* newspaper as saying that 'a good newspaper,

I suppose, is a nation talking to itself'. Donath (2004) notes that the roots of sociable media can be tracked back to the advent of letter writing on clay tablets 4,000 years ago. Her definition of sociable media as media that kindle communication and the formation of social ties can be overlaid to digital platforms such as Facebook or Twitter.

The growth of social media and concurrently social practices of sharing have led to increased interest in the concept of 'sharing' in communication and media studies (Brake, 2014; Hermida, 2014; John and Sützl, 2015; Stalder and Sützl, 2011; Sützl et al., 2012). In the context of social media, sharing is inextricably related to communication. The sharing of news serves as a form of social currency, with publics taking advantage of the communication tools and spaces available at the time to filter, manage and exchange information, and in the process form and foster relationships. On social platforms, the act of posting information about a matter of public interest or sharing a link to a news story is an exchange of cultural and symbolic capital that strengthens social relationships (*New York Times*, n.d.; Robinson, 2011). The context for these exchanges is shaped by what Rainie and Wellman call the triple revolution: the prevalence of 'social networks, the personalized internet and always-available mobile connectivity' (2012: ix).

As a result, news has become a pervasive, persistent and perpetual commodity, never more than a click away through a social media app on a smartphone. The impact on journalism goes beyond the enhanced and expanded social discovery of the news. These spaces enable citizens to reinterpret and contextualize messages from institutional media organizations by adding their own comments on a Facebook post or a specific hashtag to frame an issue (Hinsley and Lee, 2015; Meraz and Papacharissi, 2013). Moreover, citizens are able to craft, circulate and consume their own media messages (Callison and Hermida, 2015: Papacharissi and de Fatima Oliveira, 2012), taking on some of the institutional practices of journalists. The most dramatic and visible example is the capacity of people to share their experiences of a breaking news event. Twitter, alone, has emerged as a major channel for the dissemination of first-hand reports on major events from the 2008 Chinese earthquake to the Arab Spring in 2011 (Bruno, 2011; Hermida, 2014). As Marwick and boyd note, on social media, 'the networked audience has a clear way to communicate with the speaker through the network' (2011: 129).

Social media, then, are a fundamental element of the digital media environment that has been conceptualized as a hybrid space, where 'the personnel, practices, genres, technologies, and temporalities of supposedly "new" online media are hybridized with those of supposedly "old" broadcast and press media' (Chadwick, 2011: 7). On social media, and particularly on Twitter, news and views from journalists, institutions and publics are intermingled in incessantly updated and refreshed social awareness streams, in what Hermida (2010) describes as ambient journalism. Journalism has become literally ambient as a backing track to daily life, with news intermingled in streams of content generated by professionals and the public. For Papacharissi, these are affective news streams, with the news 'collaboratively constructed out of subjective experience, opinion, and emotion, all sustained by and sustaining ambient news environments' (2015: 34). Journalists and media organizations contend with operating in what Callison and Hermida (2015) describe as a contested middle ground, when the weight in institutional elites such as reporters and news outlets is challenged and counteracted by the networked actions of a diverse public.

The proliferation of social media and the development of social practices around the use of these technologies have combined to affect the context for journalism. Not only are they having multifaceted consequences for journalistic norms and practices, they have also unsettled established relationships and hierarchies in the newsroom and in the traditional producer–consumer relationship between the journalist and the audience. The result has been both opportunities and challenges as traditional and novel norms, practices and contexts blend in a hybrid media environment. As with earlier media technologies, such as the telegraph and television, the digital technologies of social media have had a significant impact on what journalists do, how they do it and why they do it, as well as on the institutional frameworks in which they have traditionally operated.

THE PROFESSIONAL ADOPTION OF SOCIAL MEDIA

Since the rapid growth of Facebook and Twitter, social media have increasingly become part of the toolkit of journalists. Industry reports have tracked the growth in the number of journalists on social media (Cision, 2010, 2015). A survey from the UK suggested it has become an everyday professional tool for virtually all journalists (Cision, 2013). A study of journalists in four European countries, including the UK, shows similar results (Gulyas, 2013). News organizations have created new positions for social media editors as well as setting up training programmes and developing guidelines for journalists operating in this area (Newman, Dutton and Blank, 2012).

Moreover, media organizations have sought to capitalize on the network effort by encouraging readers to share news stories with their social circles. Social discovery and recommendation has increasingly become a significant way to reach audiences, especially those with only a passing interest in the news (Newman et al., 2015). Tools encouraging users to like, share or recommend a story have become commonplace (Ju, Jeong and Chyi, 2014; Singer, 2014).

While top-level figures suggest that social media have become everyday in the newsroom, it is important to acknowledge that these figures can mask differences over the degree of use. For example, Hedman and Djerf-Pierre (2013) found that 85 per cent of Swedish journalists say they use social media, but went on to highlight that only one in 10 journalists posted to Twitter on a daily basis.

Digging into the numbers reveals how Twitter developed as the social media platform of choice for journalists, despite its relatively small user base compared to Facebook. A 2009 headline on the *American Journalism Review* decreed 'The Twitter Explosion' in the profession (Farhi, 2009), while a report published at the same time noted that 'the last few years have seen Twitter sweep through newsrooms on the back of its convenience, utility and immediacy' (Newman, 2009: 47). Media organizations have encouraged their journalists to be active on Twitter, with the guide to social media produced by Swedish Radio noting that the platform was 'a strategic choice for spreading our material', adding that 'with the help of Twitter you can quickly reach the "right" people' (quoted in Hedman, 2016).

The appeal of Twitter to journalists lies in its stream of news, comments and analysis, mixed in with professional and personal updates, snippets of little consequence and self-promotional activities. For Bruns and Burgess, it is 'both a social networking site and an ambient information stream' (2012: 803). This conceptualization builds on Hermida's suggestion of Twitter as 'an awareness system that offers diverse means to collect, communicate, share and display news and information, serving diverse purposes' (2010: 301).

Since its launch in 2006, Twitter has moved away from its initial prompt of 'What are you doing?' to privilege event-based and event-driven content, becoming increasingly influential as a platform for news. In 2011, it launched an official Twitter for Newsrooms guide, followed by best practice guidelines for journalists. By 2015, its 'About' page featured a stream of events happening at the moment, with the service describing itself as 'your window to the world,' that provides 'real-time updates about what matters to you' (Twitter, n.d.). In tracking the development of Twitter, van Dijck found how the 'subtle but meaningful change in Twitter's interface indicates a strategy that emphasizes (global, public) news and information over (personal, private) conversation in restricted circles' (2012: 340–341).

Much as journalists have tended to gravitate towards Twitter, so have scholars. By 2011, there were at least 14 academic texts dedicated to the platform (Pérez-Latre, Portilla and Sánchez Blanco, 2011). Most of the studies into how journalists and media organizations are responding to social media have focused on Twitter (see Hermida, 2013, for an overview). Yet, such studies may not be representative of the practices of the majority of journalists. Research has tended to look at strategic samples based on the most active, prominent or influential media professionals on Twitter (Artwick, 2013; Lasorsa, Lewis and Holton, 2012; Noguera-Vivo, 2013; Vis, 2013) or have relied on self-selected, non-representative samples (Gulyas, 2013; Jordaan, 2013). While most journalists talk about using social media in their work, only a minority share, like or tweet constantly throughout their workday (Hedman and Djerf-Pierre, 2013). As a result, there is a lack of broad, representative studies that reflect the nuances of professional practices in diverse contexts across the full range of social media platforms.

SOCIAL MEDIA AND JOURNALISM PRACTICES

The picture that emerges from the existing body of literature on social media and journalism reveals simultaneous and contradictory processes of resistance and renewal taking place. In line with previous changes in journalism, much of the response from the profession has been to resist change and instead adapt new ways of working on social media to fit within long-held, established practices. Such processes of normalization have been evident in the development of online news (for an overview, see Mitchelstein and Boczkowski, 2009). Similarly, journalists held on to their traditional gatekeeping role during the emergence of participatory media technologies such as blogs or comments on stories (Hermida and Thurman, 2008; Singer, 2005; Singer et al., 2011).

With the arrival of social media, a similar pattern has emerged. Newsgathering and sourcing routines have been adapted to take advantage of the visibility and reach of social media to find story tips, eyewitness material or sources, above all at times of breaking news. By and large, news organizations have adopted what Bruno describes as an 'opportunistic' model (2011: 66). It has become commonplace for journalists and news organizations to scour social media and then publish what they evaluate as newsworthy material based on long-standing news values. First-hand accounts, photos and videos shared on social media by people caught up in major events such as a natural disaster or terror attack are the most valued by news organizations (Williams, Wardle and Wahl-Jorgensen, 2011). Such material fills the news vacuum that can follow a major event until professional journalists are on the ground.

In what Bruno dubbed as the 'Twitter effect', newsrooms are able 'to provide live coverage without any reporters on the ground, by simply newsgathering user-generated content available online' (2011: 8). For example, *The Guardian*, the BBC and CNN used extensive social media from the audience in the immediate aftermath of the 2010 Haiti earthquake but stopped once their own journalists had arrived at the scene (Bruno, 2011). In their study of the BBC, Williams, Wardle and Wahl-Jorgensen concluded that the public service broadcaster had

been 'harnessing audience material in order to fit within existing long-established processes of journalistic production' (2011: 94). The notion of using social media to engage with audiences in the co-construction and co-creation of the news is a minority activity (Cozma and Chen, 2013; Noguera-Vivo, 2013). One study on two South African newspapers epitomized that general trend in journalism with editors largely ignoring discourse on social media in their daily news decisions (Jordaan, 2013). By and large, it is journalism as usual, with journalists firmly in charge of deciding the news.

Sourcing practices have followed the same trajectory. Traditionally, journalists have turned to people in power as sources for information, privileging elites with institutional authority and credibility, such as government officials, police officers or business leaders (Gans, 1979; McNair, 1998; Tuchman, 1972). Moreover, journalists face operational impediments, such as proximity of sources, the acceleration of news cycles and reduced newsroom resources (Boczkowski, 2010), that tend to reinforce traditional sourcing practices. A growing body of research on social media and activism shows how these platforms can serve as channels for non-traditional sources to rise to prominence (Callison and Hermida, 2015; Lotan et al., 2011; Papacharissi and de Fatima Oliveira, 2012). Such studies point to the potential of social media to expand the range of actors involved in the construction of the news.

However, research into journalistic sourcing practices on social media indicates little change in established approaches. In their study, Lariscy, Avery, Sweetser and Howes (2009) found that business journalists did not use social media as a way to find sources for stories. As for reaching out to members of the public, journalists have tended to replicate existing practices, except instead of interviewing people on the street, they are taking comments off Twitter. Tweets by members of the public are used to capture and represent the *vox populi* (Broersma and Graham, 2012;

Knight, 2012). The notion of engaging with audiences via social media is the exception, rather than the rule. For example, in her study of Swedish journalists on Twitter, Hedman (2016) found that only 1 per cent made explicit appeals to audiences.

Once the business of gathering and producing the news is complete, news organizations have gravitated towards social platforms as distribution mechanisms. They approached social platforms as tools to promote published content, reach a greater audience and potentially build brand loyalty. Research in this area found that the overwhelming approach of news organizations was to post a headline with a link back to the online story (Herrera-Damas and Hermida, 2014; Messner, Linke and Eford, 2012). As Revers notes in his study of Twitter adoption at a US newspaper, 'news corporations viewed Twitter as a way to promote consumer loyalty, which can be monetized' (2014: 822).

As with the early days of online, when much of the content was print 'shovelware', news organizations have shifted away from automated tweets to crafting posts for the range of social platforms available. At times, the process was automated so that a headline was posted on Twitter when a story was published online, even if some words were cut off due to the 140-character limit on tweets (Blasingame, 2011). Overall, though, the approach remains a one-way flow of information from the journalist to the audience. While the use of social media is framed as engaging and connecting with audiences, there is little in the way of an exchange of information, responding to comments or discussing issues. As Bullard concluded, 'to take full advantage of social media's potential, news outlets must interact with audiences beyond simply posting links to stories' (2015: 180).

At an individual level, journalists have by and large adopted similar approaches, taking advantage of social media as channels to promote their work or the work of their organization (see, for example, Lasorsa et al., 2012). However, there are studies that point to differences in approaches based on news beats. Cozma and Chen (2013) found that foreign correspondents shared mostly news stories, approaching platforms such as Twitter as an ersatz wire service. Sports reporters, on the other hand, seemed far more at ease with going beyond headlines, placing greater emphasis on sharing bits of opinion and commentary rather than breaking news (Sheffer and Schultz, 2010).

Such studies suggest that the norms and practices within specific domains of journalism are a factor in shaping how social media is integrated into daily routines. Against the backdrop of normalization of new communication technologies, with journalists shaping social media to fit within established ways of working, there are indications of how the platforms are shaping journalistic practices. As the environment in which journalism takes place changes, so do approaches to journalism. The rise of social media as a source for breaking news, and the speed at which information is disseminated has contributed to a compression of the news cycle (Bruno, 2011; Newman, 2009). It has become common for journalists to share snippets of information on an event as it unfolds, at times providing the first reports via social media.

Such minute-by-minute reporting online pre-dates social media – for example, the *Guardian* newspaper offered live reports on soccer matches on its website as early as 1999 (Thurman and Walters, 2013). Since then, platforms such as Facebook and Twitter have emerged as ready-made spaces for the transmission of brief chunks of text, photos or video to the audience. By 2009, trade publications were noting that 'reporters now routinely tweet from all kinds of events – speeches, meetings and conferences, sports events' (Farhi, 2009: n.p.). In the same year, Newman suggested 'a new grammar is emerging of real-time news coverage' (2009: 34).

Twitter, in particular, emerged as the key channel for journalists to distribute blow-by-blow accounts of the news. Sharing morsels of information in 140 characters, photos or video as events such as political rallies, courtroom cases or sporting occasions has become part of news routines (Hedman and Djerf-Pierre, 2013; Lasorsa et al., 2012). For example, journalist Brian Stelter described how he was 'trying to tweet everything I saw' when despatched in May 2011 by *The New York Times* to the town of Joplin, Missouri, in order to portray the aftermath of a devastating tornado (Stelter, 2011: n.p.). Stelter is an example of how journalists have taken to Twitter as a means to provide immersive, immediate and impressionistic reporting direct to the public. In her exploratory study of the use of Twitter by two journalists during the London riots of 2011, Vis found that the platform functioned as an effective reporting tool, as well as a 'rich source for story leads and material' (2013: 43). Other studies suggest that journalists see the ability to offer real-time updates via social media and other platforms in a positive light, saying it allows them to be more responsive to audience interests (Thurman and Walters, 2013; Zeller and Hermida, 2015).

The disaggregation of the news has given rise to new digital formats that curate the fragments of information into a more coherent whole, designed to tame the deluge of content on social media. Constantly updated live blogs or live pages have been adopted by leading news organizations such as the BBC and *The New York Times* in response to breaking news events. Live pages present information in text and audio-visual formats in reverse chronological order, with latest updates first. The format 'combines conventional reporting with curation, where journalists sift and prioritize information from secondary sources and present it to the audience in close to real time, often incorporating their feedback' (Thurman and Walters, 2013: 83).

Live pages mark a shift away from journalism as a finished product towards journalism as process, capturing the confusion and uncertainty that often surrounds breaking news. They echo the type of breaking news coverage of 24-hour TV news channels where a story is reported as it unfolds. In contrast to TV news, readers are able to go back and track the twists and turns of a story. As *Guardian* journalist Matthew Weaver suggests, 'on a live blog you are letting the reader in on what's up there, and say: look, we're letting you in on the process of newsgathering. There's a more fluid sense of what's happening' (quoted in Bruno, 2011: 44). Journalism as a practice becomes less about manufacturing a definitive rendering of events and instead a tentative and iterative process where audiences can follow how information is considered, challenged and corrected in near real-time (Hermida, 2012).

The live pages format points to a greater co-construction of the news by journalists and audiences than in legacy media formats, as public material is routinely integrated into the stream of updates. Live pages take news that is happening on social media, outside the structures of institutional news structures, and reintegrate it into spaces governed by professional norms and practices. The traditional gatekeeping function becomes one of gatewatching (Bruns, 2005), with journalists monitoring social media to select and amplify content considered newsworthy and relevant.

How far journalists open up the editorial process and involve the public in decisions on what is newsworthy is an emerging area of research. To date, the most high-profile example of a journalist actively involving the public in the co-construction of the news is Andy Carvin, a former social media strategist at NPR (Hermida, Lewis and Zamith, 2014). While at the public service broadcaster, he covered the 2011 uprising in the Middle East through social media platforms. For him, Twitter served as both newswire and newsroom. On it, he shared updates, photos and video, facilitated discussions, appealed for information, and collaborated with others to verify reports floating on social media. Hermida, Lewis and Zamith argue that Carvin functioned as a central hub in a networked media environment, working in a 'distributed and networked newsroom where knowledge and expertise are fluid, dynamic, and hybrid' (2014: 495).

Research to date suggests that processes of continuity and change are taking place alongside each other, with differences emerging depending on the group of journalists under scrutiny. There is little doubt that journalists are normalizing social media platforms to fit within traditional practices, similar to the adoption of blogs in journalism (Hermida, 2009; Singer, 2005). But, as with blogging there is evidence of shifting practices shaped by the logics of the new platforms. What is still open to question is how far media professionals who are changing the way they work are a sign of things to come, or whether they represent outliers. As Hedman posits, perhaps the most engaged journalists active on Twitter 'act as *journalism's avant-garde*, pointing in the direction of what journalism may become' (2016: 294, emphasis in original). To address this question, the next section of this chapter will consider how far fundamental norms of the profession are being impacted by social media.

SOCIAL MEDIA AND JOURNALISM NORMS

Social media platforms exist as spaces beyond the institutional constraints of journalistic enterprises. Journalists are representing their host news organization yet publishing their material on third-party platforms, leading to tensions over what have been comparatively constant norms in journalism in Western liberal democracies (Singer et al., 2011; Tuchman, 1972; Weaver, 1996). For Lasorsa, Lewis and Holton, this means that they 'do not face the same level of oversight nor the same necessity to stay on-topic journalistically' (2012: 24). Professional norms of objectivity, impartiality and accuracy are being bent, and to some extent subverted, in

social media spaces. Singer's observations that blogging challenges the notion of the journalist 'as a nonpartisan gatekeeper of information important to the public' (2005: 74) could have easily been said about social media platforms such as Facebook and Twitter. Moreover, as she adds, a new format 'also offers journalists the potential for expanded transparency and accountability' (Singer, 2005: 74).

One area where these tensions have arisen is objectivity. Admittedly, objectivity is a contested idea in journalism research. And professional objectivity need not necessarily exclude public displays of subjectivity by journalists, such as emotional reactions to traumatic news events. Yet the notion of objectivity has long been held as one of the central tenets in journalism (Kovach and Rosenstiel, 2007; Schudson, 2001). Trust in journalists draws on the assumption that they have kept their own point of view out of their reporting and are instead offering an impartial and neutral assessment of events. Professional publications go to great lengths to distinguish the spaces for commentary and opinion from those for the news. Social media platforms break down such boundaries, with facts and fiction, and observations and opinions, in the mix.

News organizations have sought to reinforce norms around objectivity and impartiality through training and social media guidelines. For example, *The Washington Post* urged its journalists that 'nothing we do must call into question the impartiality of our news judgment' (quoted in Hohmann, 2011: 4). Another leading US newspaper, *The Los Angeles Times*, warned against expressions of partisanship, 'just as political bumper stickers and lawn signs are to be avoided in the offline world, so too are partisan expressions online' (quoted in Currie, Bruser and van Wageningen, 2011: 2). Despite the boundaries delineated by organizational guidelines, individual journalists are going beyond just the facts on social media. A growing body of research into what journalists do on Twitter suggests the line between the professional and the personal is being blurred (Hedman, 2016; Molyneux, 2014; Vis, 2013). One analysis of US journalists' tweets from March 2010 showed that nearly 43 per cent of the tweets contained some degree of opinion, while nearly 16 per cent were primarily opinions (Lasorsa et al., 2012). The study also found that 20 per cent of tweets were unrelated to work and instead discussed personal life. The factors related to more personal disclosure on social media are a growing area of research. For example, female journalists appear to be more willing to share personal details (Hedman, 2016; Lasorsa, 2012).

Such research highlights the dilemma for journalists operating in a space where the norms of behaviour are different from the institutional spaces for the news. On social media, there is an expectation to move away from the traditional voice of authority that has marked much of journalism for the last century. As a space, it privileges personal expression so much so that crafting a personality on social media is predicated on being 'human' (Marwick and boyd, 2011). Herrera and Requejo (2012) go as far as recommending that journalists and news outlets use a personal and human tone. The reward for journalists is that audiences prefer individual to institutional accounts (Hermida et al., 2012). Those who keep their accounts strictly professional tend to have fewer followers (Hedman, 2016).

Being more open has significant implications for journalism. Traditionally, journalists would have expected the public to trust them, drawing on the contested idea of objectivity. Just saying, 'trust me, I'm a journalist', is ill-suited to a media space where audiences can check, criticize and condemn the media, particularly, if as Robinson (2011) posits, journalism is increasingly about relationships with audiences. Transparency, rather than objectivity, then emerges as an important way of connecting with audiences and gaining their trust (Hayes, Singer and Ceppos, 2007; Plaisance, 2007). Mapping how transparency

unfolds on social media is an underdeveloped area of research. One study found a quarter of journalists practised some form of transparency on Twitter, mostly engaging in disclosure transparency by talking about their work and in personal transparency by sharing morsels about their lives (Hedman, 2016). Key questions going forward concern how journalists navigate the personal and professional as transparency, rather than objectivity, emerges as a way to engender trust and accountability.

Related to the notion of objectivity is verification. Both norms have traditionally been associated with a journalist's claim to a special kind of authority and status, forming part of the professional ideology of journalism in Western liberal democracies. For Kovach and Rosenstiel, verification is 'the essence of journalism' (2007: 71). For its part, the Society of Professional Journalists' code of conduct urges journalists to 'test the accuracy of information from all sources and exercise care to avoid inadvertent error' (1996). While speed has been an issue in journalism since the invention of the telegram, the visibility, volume and velocity of information facilitated by social media platforms have magnified the tensions over verification. Moreover, social media weaken the gatekeeping role of the media, as information can rapidly circulate beyond the realms of professional publications, especially during breaking news events. When details are changeable, confused and contradictory, reliable information is at a premium. It is at these times that prominent news organizations have been caught out publishing incorrect information.

Some studies suggest that news organizations are relaxing the rules on verification (Bruno, 2011; Thurman and Walters, 2013). Arguably, though, verification was never an absolute, even before social media. Rather, the discipline of verification has been uneven and inconsistent, adapted to suit the story and circumstances (Shapiro et al., 2013). Getting the story right remains an ideological imperative in journalism and the cost of getting it wrong has a reputational impact on news organizations. Verification is being reconfigured, rather than abandoned, through 'processes of reinforcement, rearticulation, and reinvention' (Hermida, 2015: 41). Approaches to reinforce verification range from the institutional frameworks to elicit and vet material from social media, to outsourcing the process, to the development of automated tools.

At the same time, the concept is being rearticulated through guidelines that urge journalists not to share information that hasn't been verified or confirmed. In practice, holding off publication may not be a viable strategy, as audiences may already be aware of details being circulated on social media. The reputational cost of appearing ignorant about tweets, photos or videos surfacing on Twitter or Facebook is weighed against the cost of publish then verify. An emerging approach to resolve these tensions is the use of attribution to separate unconfirmed details from material that has been professionally verified (Hermida, 2015). Labels such as 'unverified' or 'unconfirmed' signal to audiences that the material has not undergone a rigorous vetting process, yet are a signifier that a news organization attaches to it some degree of significance. Such disclaimers allow news organizations to expand the range of material they publish while maintaining a professional line of defence.

There are indications that verification is being reinvented into what Lewis describes as a willingness 'to find normative purpose in transparency and participation' (2012: 851). Journalism has traditionally been based on providing an accurate, authenticated and authoritative rendering of events, with facts checked before publication. On social media and emerging formats such as live pages, the process of filtering and checking information is more open, collaborative and iterative (Hermida et al., 2014; Thurman and Walters, 2013). News accounts are based on the synthesis of reports, commentary and perspectives from journalists and the public in near

real-time, where verification takes place in public through a constantly updated stream of news. Trust and authority are derived from being transparent about the veracity or otherwise of information, and from involving the public in sourcing, filtering and confirming facts (Hermida et al., 2014).

LOOKING AHEAD

Journalism norms and practices are continuously impacted by the societal shifts that accompany the emergence of new communication technologies. Social media platforms have not only affected time-honoured news routines, but also elicited ambiguities over professional values and the nature of journalistic identity. Most of the research into these tensions has focused on Twitter, as it has developed as the leading platform for news organizations and journalists (Hermida, 2013). Yet the news activities of journalists and audiences are not limited to Twitter, which is relatively easy to study. Looking ahead, there is scope for more research into other social media platforms, such as Snapchat and WhatsApp, even though the characteristics of some platforms present considerable questions for scholars. In these proprietary, closed networks, shared content may be designed to be ephemeral or be visible only to a distinct set of connections. Journalist Alexis Madrigal (2012) used the term 'dark social' to describe such social media sharing that is difficult to track. In a sense, these spaces recreate the fleeting exchanges of news and information that have long taken place in physical social spaces such as cafés, bars and parks, without a permanent record for analysis.

For now, much of the research on journalism and social media points to processes of normalization at play, in line with previous technologies such as blogs. But they also highlight that the introduction and use of social media have been a contested and uneven process, with examples of novel and hybrid forms of news making that depart from traditional narrative structures and diverge from established norms. The interplay between emerging forms of storytelling that deviate from print-based narrative forms and established norms and practices offers a rich area for study.

Such research would look beyond individual works of journalism and instead take into account storytelling as a distributed service consumed across social media platforms at different times in different contexts. First is investigating how journalists and news organizations intervene across distributed social media services, raising questions over how such activity is recorded, studied and analyzed. Second is examining how audiences appreciate and react to novel forms of journalism distributed across diverse social media spaces which may have their own media logic. For example, there are opportunities to define, measure and analyze what is considered in-depth, impactful journalism in social media contexts where the work may be spread across different platforms and consumed over a period of time. Such research would shed light on whether audiences can acquire depth over time through coming across a wide range of content on a topic over the course of a day or week on distributed platforms, rather than more established notions of in-depth journalism related to the length of a single story.

Social media operate as a space outside the institutional and hierarchical structures of publication of journalism. Given the widespread popularity of these platforms, they are the land of opportunity for both news organizations and journalists. They present new avenues to expand their reach, engage with new audiences, build profile and foster brand loyalty at both an individual and institutional level. But the research also highlights the tensions for both journalists and news organizations in operating outside the framework of institutional journalism.

Social media generate 'a contested middle ground for relevance, meaning and interpretation' (Callison and Hermida, 2015: 713) where journalism as an institution is one element in a shared and hybrid media environment. Not only are journalistic norms and practices strained, but the framing and representation of the news are challenged in processes 'characterized by conflict, competition, partisanship, and mutual dependency, in the pursuit of new information that will propel a news story forward and increase its newsworthiness' (Chadwick, 2011: 19).

In these contested environments, the interactions on social media can propel a crowdsourced elite to prominence, together with the articulation of a counter-narrative at odds with mainstream media reporting (Callison and Hermida, 2015; Papacharissi and Meraz, 2012). As Papacharissi (2015) suggests, 'claims to agency are discursive, crowdsourced to prominence, networked, and sometimes ephemeral, enabling a variety of actors to tell stories'. There are significant questions over long-standing journalistic sourcing practices in such circumstances where authority and influence are open to negotiation. How sourcing practices evolve is an area for further study, as journalists go beyond the standard approach of quote tweets as ersatz for the *vox populi*.

At an institutional level, news organizations face a loss of control over the news. The rise of social discovery and recommendation weakens the agenda-setting function of the media, as audiences take on the role of secondary gatekeeping (Singer, 2014). Social media platforms have themselves emerged as gatekeepers, fast becoming the intermediaries between a news organization and its potential audience. Their value to news organizations as novel distribution channels is balanced by uncertainties over loss of revenue and of brand awareness.

Above all, there are questions over the power of platforms in the filtering, selection and promotion of news and information, with some disquiet over how far the public service ideals of journalism mesh with the values of commercial companies such as Facebook or

Google (Ananny and Crawford, 2015). Of particular concern are automated processes of news selection through proprietary algorithms, with calls for further research into the impact of algorithmic manipulation on the news diet of audiences (Anderson, 2011; Gillespie, 2014; Tufekci, 2014). Research into the response of an industry built on control of the means of production and distribution of news is underdeveloped. The disaggregation and fragmentation of the news product from its original publication opens avenues for study over the traditional relationship between readers and a news outlet, with significant implications for the institutional power of the media in the future.

Despite these tensions, news organizations and journalists have incorporated social media into what they do. Platforms such as Facebook and Twitter are complementary to legacy media platforms. But they are also in competition with legacy media. And they both need each other. News organizations need the audiences and social platforms need content. But it is debatable how far this is a partnership of equals, particularly given the growth of technology giants such as Facebook at a time of cutbacks in the mainstream media. There is a similar trade-off for individual professionals. The opportunities for greater audiences and a higher profile are offset by the simple fact that they are essentially providing free content for social media platforms.

While news is everywhere on social media, that is not the primary function of these networks. News is incidental to the daily use of these platforms to communicate and connect. It is important to note that legacy media still outweigh social media as sources for news (Nielsen and Schrøder, 2014). As social platforms become embedded in everyday communicative practices, so too may everyday news consumption. With it come implications not only for the practice of journalism, but for the financial models that have sustained it in the past and for its assumed function in society in the future.

REFERENCES

Ananny, M. and Crawford, K. (2015) 'A liminal press: Situating news app designers within a field of networked news production', *Digital Journalism*, 3(2): 192–208.

Anderson, C.W. (2011) 'Deliberative, agonistic, and algorithmic audiences: Journalism's vision of its public in an age of audience', *Journal of Communication*, 5: 529–547.

Artwick, Claudette G. (2013) 'Reporters on Twitter', *Digital Journalism*, 1(2): 212–228.

Blasingame, D. (2011) 'Gatejumping: Twitter, TV news and the delivery of breaking news', *#ISOJ Journal: The Official Journal of the International Symposium on Online Journalism*, 1(1).

Boczkowski, P.J. (2010) *News at work: Imitation in an age of information abundance.* Chicago, IL: The University of Chicago Press.

Brake, D. (2014) *Sharing our lives online: Risks and exposure in social media.* Basingtoke: Palgrave Macmillan.

Broersma, M. and Graham, T. (2012) 'Social media as beat: Tweets as a news source during the 2010 British and Dutch elections', *Journalism Practice*, 6(3): 403–419.

Bruno, N. (2011) *Tweet first, verify later: How real-time information is changing the coverage of worldwide crisis events.* Oxford: Reuters Institute for the Study of Journalism, http://reutersinstitute.politics.ox.ac.uk/publication/tweet-first-verify-later.

Bruns, A. (2005) *Gatewatching: Collaborative Online News Production.* New York: Peter Lang.

Bruns, A. and Burgess, J. (2012) 'Researching news discussion on Twitter', *Journalism Studies*, 13(5–6): 801–814.

Bullard, S.B. (2015) 'Editors use social media mostly to post story links', *Newspaper Research Journal*, 36(2): 170–183.

Callison, C. and Hermida, A. (2015) 'Dissent and resonance: #Idlenomore as an emergent middle ground', *Canadian Journal of Communication*, 40(4): 695–716.

Chadwick, A. (2011) 'The political information cycle in a hybrid news system: The British prime minister and the "Bullygate" affair', *The International Journal of Press and Politics*, 16(1): 3–29.

Cision (2010) '2010 Social journalism study', http://feed.ne.cision.com/wpyfs/00/00/00/00/00/12/53/B7/wkr0005.pdf.

Cision (2013) 'Social journalism study 2013', www.cision.com/de/wp-content/uploads/2014/04/Social-Journalism-Study-2013-14-Grossbritannien.pdf.

Cision (2015) '2015 Global social journalism study finds journalists increasingly rely on social media to complete daily activities and improve productivity', 22 July, www.cision.com/us/about/news/2015-press-releases/2015-global-social-journalism-study-finds-journalists-increasingly-rely-on-social-media-to-complete-daily-activities-and-improve-productivity/.

Cozma, R. and Chen, K. (2013) 'What's in a Tweet?', *Journalism Practice*, 7(1): 33–46.

Currie, T., Bruser, B. and van Wageningen, E. (2011) 'Guidelines for personal activity online', Canadian Association of Journalists, 4 February, www.caj.ca/?p=1347.

Donath, J. (2004) 'Sociable Media', in W.S. Bainbridge (ed.), *The Berkshire Encyclopedia of Human-Computer Interaction.* Great Barrington, MA: Berkshire Publishing Group.

Farhi, P. (2009) 'The Twitter explosion', *American Journalism Review*, 31(3): 26–31, http://ajrarchive.org/Article.asp?id=4756.

Gans, H.J. (1979) *Deciding what's news: A study of CBS Evening News, NBC Nightly News, Newsweek, and TIME.* New York: Pantheon Books.

Gillespie, T. (2014) 'The relevance of algorithms', in T. Gillespie, P. Boczkowski and K. Foot (Eds.), *Media technologies: Essays on communication, materiality, and society.* Cambridge, MA: MIT Press.

Gulyas, A. (2013) 'The influence of professional variables on journalists' uses and views of social media: A comparative study of Finland, Germany, Sweden and the United Kingdom', *Digital Journalism*, 1(2): 270–285.

Hayes, A.S., Singer, J.B. and Ceppos, J. (2007) 'Shifting roles, enduring values', *Journal of Mass Media Ethics*, 22: 262–279.

Hedman, U. (2016) 'When journalists tweet: Disclosure, participatory, and personal transparency', *Social Media + Society*, 2(1): 1–13.

Hedman, U. and Djerf-Pierre, M. (2013) 'The social journalist: Embracing the social media life or creating a new digital divide?', *Digital Journalism*, 1(3): 368–385.

Hermida, A. (2009) 'The blogging BBC: Journalism blogs at "the world's most trusted news organisation"', *Journalism Practice*, 3(3): 268–284.

Hermida, A. (2010) 'Twittering the news', *Journalism Practice*, 4(3): 297–308.

Hermida, A. (2012) 'Tweets and truth: Journalism as a discipline of collaborative verification', *Journalism Practice*, 6(5–6): 659–668.

Hermida, A. (2013) '#Journalism: Reconfiguring journalism research about Twitter, one tweet at a time', *Digital Journalism*, 1(3): 295–313.

Hermida, A. (2014) *Tell Everyone: Why we share and why it matters.* Toronto: Double-Day Canada.

Hermida, A. (2015) 'Nothing but the truth: Redrafting the journalistic boundary of verification', in Matt Carlson and Seth C. Lewis (Eds.), *Boundaries of journalism: Professional, practices and participation* (pp. 37–50). New York: Routledge.

Hermida, A., Fletcher, F., Korell, D. and Logan, D. (2012) 'Share, like, recommend', *Journalism Studies*, 13(5–6): 815–824.

Hermida, A., Lewis, S.C. and Zamith, R. (2014) 'Sourcing the Arab Spring: A case study of Andy Carvin's sources on Twitter during the Tunisian and Egyptian revolutions', *Journal of Computer-Mediated Communication*, 19(3): 479–499.

Hermida, A. and Thurman, N. (2008) 'A clash of cultures: The integration of user-generated content within professional journalistic frameworks at British newspaper websites', *Journalism Practice*, 2(3): 343–356.

Herrera-Damas, S. and Hermida, A. (2014) 'Tweeting but not talking: The missing element in talk radio's institutional use of Twitter', *Journal of Broadcasting & Electronic Media*, 58(4): 481–500.

Herrera-Damas, S. and Requejo, J.L. (2012) '10 good practices for news organizations using Twitter', *Journal of Applied Journalism and Media Studies*, 1(1): 79–95.

Hinsley, A. and Lee, H. (2015) '#Ferguson strategic messaging: How local journalists and activists used Twitter as a communication tool', *#ISOJ Journal: The Official Journal of the International Symposium on Online Journalism*, 5(1).

Hohmann, J. (2011) '10 best practices for social media', *American Society of News Editors*, http://asne.org/portals/0/publications/public/10_Best_Practices_for_Social_Media.pdf (accessed 24 March).

John, N.A. and Sützl, W. (2015) 'The rise of "sharing" in communication and media studies', *Information, Communication & Society*, 19(4): 1–5.

Jordaan, M. (2013) 'Poke me, I'm a journalist: The impact of Facebook and Twitter on newsroom routines and cultures at two South African weeklies', *Ecquid Novi: African Journalism Studies*, 34(1): 21–35.

Ju, A., Jeong, S.H. and Chyi, H.I. (2014) 'Will social media save newspapers: Examining the effectiveness of Facebook and Twitter as news platforms', *Journalism Practice*, 8(1): 1–17.

Knight, M. (2012) 'Journalism as usual: The use of social media as a newsgathering tool in the coverage of the Iranian elections in 2009', *Journal of Media Practice*, 12(1): 61–74.

Kovach, B. and Rosenstiel, T. (2007) *The elements of journalism: What newspeople should know and the public should expect* (rev. ed.). New York: Three Rivers Press.

Lariscy, R.W., Avery, E.J., Sweetser, K.D. and Howes, P. (2009) 'An examination of the role of online social media in journalists' source mix', *Public Relations Review*, 35(3): 314–316.

Lasorsa, D. (2012) 'Transparency and other journalistic norms on Twitter', *Journalism Studies*, 13(3): 402–417.

Lasorsa, D., Lewis, S.C. and Holton, A.E. (2012) 'Normalizing Twitter: Journalism practice in an emerging communication space', *Journalism Studies*, 13(1): 19–36.

Lewis, S. (2012) 'The tension between professional control and open participation: Journalism and its boundaries', *Information, Communication & Society*, 15(6): 836–866.

Lotan, G., Graeff, E., Ananny, M., Gaffney, D., Pearce, I. and Boyd, D. (2011) 'The revolutions were tweeted: Information flows during the 2011 Tunisian and Egyptian revolutions', *International Journal of Communication*, 5: 1375–1405.

Madrigal, A. (2012) 'Dark social: We have the whole history of the web wrong', *The Atlantic*, 12 October, www.theatlantic.com/technology/archive/2012/10/dark-social-we-have-the-whole-history-of-the-web-wrong/263523/ (accessed 10 April 2016).

Marwick, A. and boyd, d. (2011) 'I tweet honestly, I tweet passionately: Twitter users, context collapse, and the imagined audience', *New Media & Society*, 13: 114–133.

McNair, B. (1998) *The sociology of journalism*. London: Arnold.

Meraz, S. and Papacharissi, Z. (2013) 'Networked gatekeeping and networked framing on #egypt', *International Journal of the Press and Politics*, 18(2): 1–29.

Messner, M., Linke, M., and Eford, A. (2012) 'Shoveling tweets: An analysis of the microblogging engagement of traditional news organizations', *#ISOJ: The Official Research Journal of the International Symposium on Online Journalism*, 2(1): 76–90.

Mitchell, A., Gottfried, J. and Matsa, K.E. (2015) 'Millennials and political news: Social media – the local TV for the next generation?' Washington, DC: Pew Research Center, www.journalism.org/2015/06/01/millennials-political-news/.

Mitchelstein, E. and Boczkowski, P.J. (2009) 'Between tradition and change: A review of recent research on online news production', *Journalism*, 10 (5): 562–586.

Molyneux, L. (2014) 'What journalists retweet: Opinion, humor, and brand development on Twitter', *Journalism*, 16: 920–935.

Nielsen, R. K. and Schrøder, K. C. (2014) 'The relative importance of social media for accessing, finding, and engaging with news', *Digital Journalism*, 2(4): 472–489.

Newman, N. (2009) *The rise of social media and its impact on mainstream journalism*. Oxford: Reuters Institute for the Study of Journalism.

Newman, N., Dutton, W.H. and Blank, G. (2012) 'Social media in the changing ecology of news: The fourth and fifth estates in Britain', *International Journal of Internet Science*, 7(1): 6–22.

Newman, N., Levy, D.A.L. and Nielsen, R.K. (2015) *Digital news report 2015: Tracking the future of news*. Oxford: Reuters Institute for the Study of Journalism.

New York Times (n.d.) 'The psychology of sharing, New York Times insights', *The New York Times*, http://nytmarketing.whsites.net/mediakit/pos/.

Noguera-Vivo, J.M. (2013) 'How open are journalists on Twitter? Trends towards the end-user journalism', *Communication & Society/Comunicacion y Sociedad*, 26(1): 93–114.

Papacharissi, Z. (2015). *Affective publics: Sentiment, technology, and politics*. Oxford: Oxford University Press.

Papacharissi, Z. and de Fatima Oliveira, M. (2012) 'Affective news and networked publics: The rhythms of news storytelling on #Egypt', *Journal of Communication*, 62(2): 266–282.

Papacharissi, Z. and Meraz, S. (2012) *The rhythms of Occupy: Broadcasting and listening practices on #ows*. Salford, UK: Association of Internet Researchers.

Pérez-Latre, F.J., Portilla, I. and Sánchez-Blanco, C. (2012) `Social networks, media and audiences: A literature review', *Communication & Society*, 24 (11), 63–74.

Plaisance, P.L. (2007) 'Transparency: An assessment of the Kantian roots of a key element in media ethics practice', *Journal of Mass Media Ethics*, 22: 187–207.

Purcell, K., Rainie, L., Mitchell, L., Rosenstiel, T. and Olmstead, K. (2010) 'Understanding the participatory news consumer', Pew Internet and American Life Project. Washington, DC: Pew Research Center, www.pewinternet.org/Reports/2010/Online-News.aspx.

Rainie, L. and Wellman, B. (2012). *Networked: The new social operating system*. Cambridge, MA: MIT Press.

Revers, M. (2014) 'The Twitterization of news making', *Journal of Communication*, 64: 806–826.

Robinson S. (2011) 'Journalism as process: The labor implications of participatory content in news organizations', *Journalism & Communication Monographs*, 13(3): 138–210.

Schudson, M. (2001) 'The objectivity norm in American journalism', *Journalism Studies*, 2(2): 149–170.

Shapiro, I., Brin, C., Bédard-Brûlé, I. and Mychajlowycz, K. (2013) 'Verification as a strategic ritual: How journalists retrospectively describe processes for ensuring accuracy', *Journalism Practice*, 7(6): 657–673.

Sheffer, M.L. and Schultz, B. (2010) 'Paradigm shift or passing fad? Twitter and sports journalism', *International Journal of Sport Communication*, 3: 472–484.

Singer, J.B. (2005) 'The political j-blogger: "Normalizing" a new media form to fit old norms and practices', *Journalism*, 6(2): 173–198.

Singer, J.B. (2014) 'User-generated visibility: Secondary gatekeeping in a shared media space', *New Media & Society*, 16(1): 55–73.

Singer, J.B., Domingo, D., Heinonen, A., Hermida, A., Paulussen, S., Quandt, T., Reich, Z. and Vujnovic, M. (2011) *Participatory journalism: Guarding open gates at online newspapers*. New York: Wiley Blackwell.

Society of Professional Journalists (1996) *Code of ethics* [online]. Indianapolis, IN: Society of Professional Journalists, www.spj.org/ethicscode.asp/.

Stalder, F. and Sützl, W. (2011) 'Ethics of sharing', *International Review of Information Ethics*, 15(2).

Stelter, B. (2011) 'What I learned in Joplin', *The Deadline*, 27 May, http://thedeadline.tumblr.com/post/5904630983/what-i-learned-in-joplin (accessed 28 May 2011).

Sützl, W., Stalder, F., Maier, R. and Hug, T. (Eds.) (2012) *Media, knowledge and education: Cultures and ethics of sharing*. Innsbruck: Innsbruck University Press.

Thurman, N., and Walters, A. (2013) `Live blogging: Digital journalism's pivotal platform?', *Digital Journalism*, 1(1): 82–101.

Tuchman, G. (1972) 'Objectivity as strategic ritual: An examination of newsmen's notion of objectivity', *The American Journal of Sociology*, 77(4): 660–679.

Tufekci, Z. (2014) 'Engineering the public: Big data, surveillance, and computational politics', *First Monday*, 19(7), http://firstmonday.org/ojs/index.php/fm/article/view/4901/4097.

Twitter (n.d.) 'About Twitter', https://about.twitter.com/.

van Dijck, J. (2012) 'Tracing Twitter: The rise of a microblogging platform', *International Journal of Media and Cultural Politics*, 7(3): 333–348.

Vis, F. (2013) 'Twitter as a reporting tool for breaking news', *Digital Journalism*, 1(1): 27–47.

Weaver, D.H. (1996) 'Journalists in comparative perspective', *The Public*, 3(4): 83–91.

Williams, A., Wardle, C. and Wahl-Jorgensen, K. (2011) 'Have they got news for us?', *Journalism Practice*, 5(1): 85–99.

Zeller, F. and Hermida, A. (2015) 'When tradition meets immediacy and interaction: The integration of social media in journalists' everyday practices', *About Journalism/Sur le Journalisme*, 4(1): 106–119.

28

Social Media and the Cultural and Creative Industries

Terry Flew

CREATIVE INDUSTRIES AND SOCIAL MEDIA: CLOSE FRIENDS OR DISTANT RELATIVES?

At one level, it makes a lot of sense to discuss social media and the cultural and creative industries (CCIs) together. The creative industries policy discourse emerged in the late 1990s, just as the new breed of Internet companies were emerging whose platform innovations were no longer tied to information and communication technology (ICT) hardware production. The first Creative Industries Mapping Document (Department of Culture, Media and Sport, 1998) was published in the UK in 1998, the same year in which Larry Page and Sergey Brin established Google as an incorporated private company. The processes of digital disruption that have been central to the evolution of the Internet, and of digital and social media, have also been those that have forced innovation in the media, arts and entertainment industries, related to

products (making content readily accessible in digital formats), processes (unbundling traditional production chains and reorganizing the workforce) and services (generating convergent media content that can be accessed across multiple devices in ways more driven by user preferences rather than distributional conventions). For incumbent businesses in the media and related industries, the challenge of 'born digital' competitors such as Google, Apple, Facebook, Amazon, Netflix and others has been substantial, and has undermined traditional models of revenue generation through users paying for content, traditional advertising channels, and copyright revenue streams associated with the durability of quality content over time and restrictions over how it can be accessed.[1]

At the same time, there has often been a surprising lack of overlap between creative industries debates and those surrounding digital and social media. Despite some attempts to think about creative industries and the digital revolution in tandem – Hartley

(2005) being a notable example – the two fields as often as not went in separate directions, with creative industries being associated (both positively and negatively) with economic rationales for supporting the arts and cultural activities, and digital media being largely associated with technological innovation. In their overview for the National Endowment for Education, Science and the Arts (NESTA) of UK creative industries policy from the 1990s to the present, Bakhshi et al. (2013) made the point that while these policy documents were certainly aware of the transformative impact of digital technologies, few substantive recommendations flowed through into actual sectoral policies. In another overview of the period, Hewison (2014) argued that one reason for this was that the new generation of user-driven content platforms such as YouTube – what would subsequently be termed Web 2.0 (O'Reilly, 2005) – had not yet come into existence at the time in which key ideas about creative industries were emerging.

But the divide between creative industries and digital and social media also spoke to deeper intellectual, conceptual and policy divides. A common criticism of the early DCMS reports concerned their inclusion of the software industries among the creative industries, which critics saw as artificially inflating the size and significance of the creative industries in the UK economy. In a critique of creative industries policies that was illustrative of these divides, Nicholas Garnham saw attempts to associate CCIs with digital technologies creative industries as a contrivance, to associate cultural policies with theories of the information society (Bell, 1980) in order to 'capture the current prestige of this theory of innovation … for a sector and a group of workers to whom it does not really apply' (Garnham, 2005: 22). Bakhshi et al. noted that policy makers concerned with the creative industries had little input into important changes in broadcasting and telecommunications laws in the UK, despite obvious links between digital content innovation and the quality and speed of broadband infrastructure. Indeed, in those sectors which came to be labeled as part of the creative industries, the response to digital disruption was often litigious and defensive, seeking stronger copyright laws, and more vigorous enforcement, as a way of protecting long-established business models in the copyright-based industries (Knopper, 2009; Flew, 2015).

In considering the international development of cultural and creative industries debates, there are some notable features, including: the question of whether to refer to 'cultural industries' or 'creative industries'; whether it is better to refer to a system-wide 'creative economy' than to the application of creativity in defined industries; and the substantial differences in related policy discourses in different parts of the world (e.g., the UK and Europe as compared to the US or to China). It is also apparent that one element of the apparent disconnect between creative industries and digital and social media is that the field of CCI research is often ambivalent about questions of digital disruption, and associated policy issues. Of these, the most significant are the future of copyright and intellectual property laws in a digital economy context, and the battles between incumbent media interests and emergent digital/social media platform and service providers.

In this chapter, I will consider the extent to which the cultural and creative industries benefit from, as well as feel threatened by, digital media. The chapter will begin with an overview of the various academic and policy debates that have surrounded the cultural and creative industries. This is focused upon partly because it is a contested intellectual space – particularly with regards to 'arts as industry' questions and how 'culture' is being defined – but also because concepts like intellectual property have been key points of friction in debates around digital media and the creative industries. It will then discuss how, in different contexts, social media have been variously seen as an amplifier, a disruptor and a transformer of different CCIs. The chapter will conclude with a consideration of how best to retool thinking about the cultural and creative industries for the context of a digital economy.

CULTURAL AND CREATIVE INDUSTRIES: ACADEMIC AND POLICY DEBATES

As was noted in the introduction, creative industries policies were first developed in the United Kingdom, and it is around that experience that the most detailed academic analyses have been developed (e.g., O'Connor, 2010; Flew, 2012; Hewison, 2014; Hesmondhalgh et al., 2015). With the election of the Labour Government led by Tony Blair in 1997, the newly-created Department of Culture, Media and Sport (DCMS) undertook a mapping exercise of the size and significance of the creative industries to the UK economy, finding that it had considerably greater economic size and significance than had previously been assumed. Rather than seeing the arts as publicly subsidised activities bracketed off from the wider economy and culture, the DCMS reports proposed that the creative industries were now at the forefront of an increasingly post-industrial UK economy. The creative industries were also at the forefront of a wider attempt by Tony Blair and 'New Labour' to promote cultural modernization as part of a wider narrative associated with the politics of the 'Third Way', between free market capitalism and traditional European social democracy.

Creative industries is an interesting case study in policy discourse that ran well ahead of academic debates in the cognate fields of arts, media and cultural policy. The DCMS defined the creative industries as 'those activities which have their origin in individual creativity, skill and talent and which have the potential for wealth and job creation through the generation and exploitation of intellectual property' (quoted in Flew, 2013: 3–4). In linking cultural achievement to economic performance, the DCMS followed cultural policy statements in other parts of the world, such as Australia's *Creative Nation* statement, published in 1994, which proposed that 'culture creates wealth ... [and] adds value [and] makes an essential contribution to innovation, marketing and design', and is therefore 'essential to our economic success' (Department of Communication and the Arts, 1994: 7).

In the early 2000s, there was substantial uptake of the creative industries concept internationally (Flew, 2012), and it also generated significant academic debate in fields such as media and cultural studies, as well as in cultural economics and cultural policy studies (Throsby, 2010; Towse, 2010). MIT scholar Jing Wang (2008) observed that the term 'creative industries' had itself become an effective piece of British global brand promotion, while the cultural studies scholar Andrew Ross noted that 'few could have predicted that the creative industries model would itself become a successful export' (Ross, 2007: 18). In the extensive debate that has followed, a number of issues have continued to arise that have impacted upon the uptake of the concept internationally as well as its general policy trajectory:

- The question of why *creativity* should be seen as being primarily located in those industries defined as 'creative', particularly as it is also seen as increasingly important to value-adding through all sectors of the economy (the importance of design to automobiles or mobile phones, to take two examples). Andy Pratt (2005: 33) made the point that 'it would be difficult to identify a non-creative industry or activity', while Bilton and Leary (2002: 50) pointed out that 'every industry would surely lay claim to some measure of individual creativity, skill and talent'.
- The question of the *breadth* of the categories. Is it too broad, for instance, to include computer software and advertising along with music and crafts? By contrast, could it be too narrow:

should tourism be included, or sport, or the libraries, galleries and museum sectors?

- The *depth* with which the industry sectors are being understood. A UNESCO (2013) study observed that the activities of these industries are underpinned by significant cultural infrastructure, that includes buildings and facilities, physical equipment, the archiving and preserving of materials, and the vital role played by educational and training institutions in preparing people for these industries and in their ongoing sustainability.
- The question of whether there has been an *overemphasis upon tangible and primarily economic measures of value*, as distinct from forms of cultural value, including aesthetic, spiritual, historical, symbolic and other forms of value that are more intangible and difficult to quantify (Banks & O'Connor, 2009; Throsby, 2010: 17–22).
- The focus on *individual creativity*, when many of the industries listed clearly rely upon team-based processes to develop complex cultural goods and services (Caves, 2000: 85–170), and a misleading association of the creative industries with romantic notions of artistic genius (Bilton, 2007).
- Whether the focus upon *intellectual property* as a cornerstone of the creative industries was misleading at a time when digital networks were enabling new modes of peer-based, collaborative and often non-market forms of production and distribution of information, knowledge and culture. Authors such as Lessig (2004) and Benkler (2006) made the argument that copyright and intellectual property laws had decisively moved from being enablers to being constraints on creative production in a digitally networked age, and a time when 'the removal of the physical constraints on effective information production has made human creativity and the economics of information … core structuring facts in the new networked information economy' (Benkler, 2006: 4).

Many of these debates point back to critiques of instrumentalism in the arts, and the relationship between cultural and economic value, that return to the roots of cultural policy, and even to the Romantic critique of the Industrial Revolution (Williams, 1963). But the relationship of CCIs to intellectual property is a decidedly contemporary one, arising in the context of dramatic transformations in how information is produced, distributed and reproduced in the context of ICTs and digital networks. In terms of the international uptake of cultural and creative industries policies in the early 2000s, the emergence of the concept was timely in that it arose at a time when earlier debates about ICT policies for the 'new economy' were flagging. In the wake of the Clinton Administration's commitment to a National Information Infrastructure (NII) for the US in 1993, and the subsequent Buenos Aires agreement for a Global Information Infrastructure (GII) in 1994, a plethora of reports, policies and strategies for information policy and an information society emerged around the world (Henten & Skouby, 2006).

The crash of the NASDAQ stock price index in 2001 saw a resulting deflation of digitally based 'new economy' discourses, but this was matched by a growing awareness that investment in broadband infrastructure and digital capacity was a necessary but not sufficient condition for engagement with new ICT-based industries. In an influential statement of the need to think in terms of a *creative economy*, the British writer John Howkins distinguished between an *information society* 'characterized by people spending most of their time and making most of their money by handling information, usually by means of technology', and a *creative society* where expanded access to information and data is complemented by 'the need to be active, clever, and persistent in challenging this information … to be original, skeptical, argumentative, often bloody-minded and occasionally downright negative – in one word, creative' (Howkins, 2005: 117–118).

In such a context, creative industries as a policy discourse proved to have considerable capacity for policy transfer (Pratt, 2009; Alasuutari, 2013). The earliest uptake was in countries that shared English language and/or post-colonial links to the UK, most notably Australia, New Zealand, Singapore and

Hong Kong (Flew, 2012: 42–44, 50–52). In the Asian context, creative industries was a particularly strong urban policy discourse, as cities such as Singapore, Hong Kong, Seoul, Singapore, Taipei, Shanghai and Beijing sought to become the leading global cities in the fast-growing East Asian region, developing place competitiveness in order to attract global capital and creative talent. In this respect, the 'normative creative economy script' proved attractive to urban policy makers, in cities 'which had already established national broadcasting, arts and cultural industries, but [had] aspirations for "world city" status' (Gibson & Kong, 2005: 550). In some instances, most notably Singapore, earmarked creative industries policies that were developed as part of the 2002 *Renaissance City* strategy had devolved by the late 2000s into more sector-specific policies for the arts, media and design (Lee, 2010; Kong, 2012).

In the case of South Korea, there was a massive investment in the promotion of Korean cultural products worldwide under the banner of *Hallyu*, the 'Korean Wave', through agencies such as the Korean Creative Content Agency (KOCCA) (J. Walsh, 2014; Jin, 2016). In Japan, the concept of 'Gross National Cool' was embraced (Iwabuchi, 2015), as promotion of local CCIs was combined with strategies to 'rebrand' Japan and exercise 'soft power' globally, and particularly in the Asia-Pacific region.

Perhaps the most surprising uptake of CCI policy discourse was in China. With the policy objectives of reducing China's cultural trade imbalance with the West, developing new industries in local and regional economies, and making media and cultural institutions less dependent upon the state, the hybrid concept of *cultural creative industries* was taken up strongly in China. Creative clusters such as Beijing's 798 Art Zone and Shanghai's Tianzifang developed as concentrated sites of cultural production and arts consumption. As Keane (2013) has argued, the concept of CCIs walks an interesting line in China, between those who identify the marketization

of culture as being associated with creative innovation and the integration of culture and technology, and those who see the cultural industries as inherently tied to state power and the preservation of a distinctive Chinese national culture, and who perceive 'creativity' as a 'Trojan Horse' for Western cultural hegemony and neo-liberal ideas. In that respect, there are parallels between debates about creative industries in China and those about social media: both potentially point in the direction of reduced state control and greater individual freedom, but for precisely that reason, both are closely monitored by the Chinese party-state.

Europe has adopted the CCI concept, both at a regional level (European Commission, 2010), and in its nomination of 'Capitals of Culture', in order to revivify post-industrial economies around the arts, media, cultural tourism and cultural entrepreneurship. At the same time, the terminological distinction between 'cultural industries' and 'creative industries' has been quite sharp within Europe; in some nations, such as Germany, the term 'industry' is associated with the industrialization of culture, and the associated negation of aesthetics. In its policy documents, the European Union (European Commission, 2010) has used the 'concentric circles' approach derived from Throsby (2010: 26–27), where 'cultural industries' are seen as those where artistic inputs are paramount (e.g., performing and creative arts, music), whereas 'creative industries' are seen as those with primarily commercial motivations in terms of how creativity is applied (e.g., advertising, architecture, commercial broadcasting).

The term 'creative industries' did not gain policy traction in the United States, but the 'creative cities' movement, spearheaded by academic/policy entrepreneurs such as Richard Florida, had great influence among urban policy makers, and was a significant catalyst for investment in the arts and culture (Florida, 2002; Grodach, 2013). It has been notably associated with the revitalization of urban centers through investment in new cultural institutions, development of creative clusters (particularly in decommissioned industrial spaces), and the development of a bohemian ambiance, with a thriving community of bars, music venues, live events and urban nightlife. The group that Florida termed the 'creative class', who are those whose work he saw as being most associated with the application of creativity in business as well as in the arts, have been seen as having a catalytic role in the development of creative cities: they are also the group most likely to be extensively networked through social media.

SOCIAL MEDIA AND THE CCIS: THREE SCENARIOS

While creative industries discourses and the development of social media have developed along parallel yet distinct paths, social media have profoundly shaped the cultural and creative industries themselves. We can identify three ways in which the uptake of social media has transformed the CCIs: (1) as *amplifier*, or as a means of expanding reach and/or engagement; (2) as *disruptor*, being connected to processes that undermined traditional media and creative business models; and (3) as *transformer*, leading to the emergence of new types of media and creative businesses within established industries. In developing this three-fold typology, I am drawing upon the Weberian notion of ideal-types, that combines the subjective understanding of agents themselves with an interpretation of underlying causal logics or systemic forces, to generate models that can be compared against empirical evidence (Weber, 1978: 18–22; Aronovitch, 2012). It is also apparent that there is not one type of force necessarily dominant in one industry and a different one in another. Rather, the three ideal-types need to be seen as common force-fields operating across the spectrum of cultural and creative industries.

Social media as Amplifier: Broadcasting and Twitter

The case of *social media as amplifier* refers to those instances where the use of social media in a manner complementary to existing business models has added value to those cultural goods and services produced by and through the cultural and creative industries. One example would be the ways in which social media platforms such as Facebook and Twitter enable *second screen engagement* with television content. In particular, Twitter has enabled real-time interaction on a large scale with television programs, in ways that have the scope to add value to TV content by developing user communities and social networks around particular programs and personalities.

Katie Walsh (2014) observed that such real-time interaction can be of value to audiences, producers, TV networks and social media companies simultaneously. For audiences, 'live-tweeting television (and recapping and commenting after an episode) is a way for fans to participate in the show itself: to insert themselves into the game of television via technology and social networks' (K. Walsh, 2014: 13). For producers, they are better 'able to cater (or not) to the fan response that they receive on their shows, ensuring fan appreciation and loyalty, but almost more importantly, online audience visibility has seemed to solve the other issue of counting audiences' (K. Walsh, 2014: 13). For the television networks, 'Tweets become tangible evidence of audience attention, which serves as a commodity to be bought and sold, and as a new metric for counting audience metrics' (K. Walsh, 2014: 11). Social media interaction could thus provide verifiable third-party data on audience engagement that can be presented to advertisers as evidence of those to whom they can potentially appeal with their messages. Finally, evidence of large-scale interaction is valuable to the platforms themselves. In Twitter's 2014 IPO, this live-tweeting 'was ... the number one way that a billion-dollar company was going to prove its value', meaning that while 'social networking sites and new media services may be groundbreaking, but they are still turning to legacy media such as television as a way to monetize their services. While TV might be grasping onto Twitter in order to engage audiences, Twitter is just as dependent on TV for a business model' (K. Walsh, 2014: 15).

For the television industry, the great boon of social media is the emphasis upon the value of live-ness in broadcasting, and hence on the value of advertising during programs. A vast array of technological devices has enabled audiences to move away from the 'tyranny of scheduling' and time-dependent access to television content, including Digital Video Recorders (DVRs), streaming services such as Netflix and Hulu, and online catch-up services. All of these typically provide users with the capacity to filter out advertisements. This has been one reason why advertising revenues have held up most strongly for programming such as sports, where viewing the event as it happens is most critical. Platforms such as Twitter have been valuable in sports broadcasting, although Billings (2014) has questioned claims that they provide better insight into the interests of the 'average' sports fan. One area where the impact of social media has been critical is that of political television, where opinionated hosts and guests frequently trigger 'Twitter talk', and where social media platforms enable congregations of like minds and the dissemination of views to a wider public (Himelboim, 2014). The impact of social media has been significant for both traditional political television formats and for satirical television that engages with political issues (Gray et al., 2009; Harrington, 2013).

The focus thus far has been on the positive aspects of the relationship between social media and broadcast television. Katie Walsh (2014) has made the point that, in the US context, there is little correlation between the most watched US television programs and those which attract the most Twitter

comments. This should not surprise, as the most active users of social media tend, on average, to be younger, better educated, and more likely to have a wider range of entertainment options available to them than the most frequent television viewers. There is also the issue of control over the platform itself. Whereas broadcast television has typically been characterized by a high degree of control over when and how content is distributed, the social media environment tends to one where content is more *spreadable* across platforms and among users (Jenkins et al., 2013). Moreover, distributors cannot control what is said on social media platforms. For example, the Australian interactive political panel program *Q&A*, which encourages its viewers to tweet during the program and screens a selection of the tweets during the show, has often found itself open to allegations of political bias when a message has gone across the screen that a panel guest found offensive or inappropriate (Flew & Swift, 2015). In response to this, broadcasters have sometimes created their own apps, enabling participation within a 'walled garden' environment, where comments are closely monitored by the provider themselves, rather than relying upon the moderation practices of third parties such as Twitter.

Social Media as Disruptor: The Continuing Crisis of News

While social media have clearly created new possibilities in some CCIs, they have also profoundly disrupted others. The concept of *disruptive innovation* comes from the work of Harvard Business School Professor Clayton Christensen (2003), and refers to the ways in which changing market and technological dynamics can lead to once successful companies losing their dominance in industries, as the underlying foundations of economic relationships and associated business models are radically transformed. The concept of disruptive innovation has resonances in the evolutionary economics of Joseph Schumpeter (1950), who described capitalism as an economic system based upon 'gales of creative destruction', where the core dynamic of competition was less about marginal price changes in markets than it was about entrepreneurs continually transforming economies, firms, industries, institutions and jobs in the relentless search for new sources of profit. Capitalism is an economic system where 'creative destruction fosters economic growth but also ... undercuts cherished human values' (McCraw, 2007: 349).

Digital technology industries are particularly prone to disruptive innovation, as there is a highly fluid and variable relationship between rates of uptake of new technologies and digital services, due to the interaction between user adoption of new technologies and the manner in which the associated products and services improve over time (Flew, 2014: 150–153). In some instances, there is significant *first-mover advantage*. The rise of Amazon as one of the world's largest internet companies came from the realization of founder Jeff Bezos in the 1990s that the Internet enabled a new way of selling books, as it greatly expanded global market reach while simultaneously allowing for greatly reduced inventory costs. There was thus the scope to benefit from *long tail economics* (Anderson, 2009) by offering for sale a much wider range of titles that had more niche readerships than conventional bookstores could offer: Amazon also pioneered user recommendation systems as a means by which consumers could get valuable third-party information about particular titles. In other cases, the primary benefits have gone to second movers. In the music industry, the rise of Napster threatened conventional music businesses by allowing for free downloads of songs. The major music labels responded by driving Napster out of business for copyright infringement, but Apple successfully adopted the core elements of the Napster business models – namely, that people wanted individual songs in digital

formats rather than bundled CDs – and came to dominate the music industry in the 2000s. Its primary competitors, such as Spotify, today offer individual songs as part of subscription packages, meaning that the music business in the 2010s has little in common with the form it took in the 1990s (Knopper, 2009; Wikström, 2013).

One sector where social media have had a particularly disruptive impact has been news. News organizations were early adopters of digital media, recognizing the value of the Internet as providing a new channel for news distribution, as well as providing superior means for checking information and allowing for greater content sharing within the organization. But while there was adaptation to the new digital environment within newsrooms, underlying elements of journalistic practice and culture remained unchallenged, namely that: (1) journalists produced content for a single outlet, and in a single format (print, radio, television, etc.); (2) they worked for established news mastheads; (3) they were the only trusted sources of news, on the basis of their skills and professional accreditation; and (4) their work-related communication was primarily with their news sources rather than with their readers, viewers or listeners.

Jane Singer (2010: 103) has pointed out that, by the late 2000s 'none of those things were true', as the traditional boundaries were breached to the point where:

> Deadlines are continuous, and stories are updated whenever new information becomes available. Content of all sorts flows in from everywhere and everyone, and even the bits produced by journalists are no longer necessarily routed through a newsroom (or an editor) before appearing online. The unmanaged and perhaps unmanageable nature of the network itself, with its myriad intertwined links and updates every nanosecond, creates an essentially infinite, unbounded product. (Singer, 2010: 107)

The crisis in traditional journalism has had the hardest impact on newspapers. There has been a significant decline in the readership of newspapers as readers increasingly turn to online sources for news. It has been estimated that time spent reading newspapers fell by about one-third worldwide between 2010 and 2017, with particularly sharp declines in established news media markets such as the United States (globally, such trends are offset in part by growth in countries such as India and China, where rising literacy levels have led to increased newspaper readership) (Zenith OptiMedia, 2015). Many newspaper titles have closed, while others have gone to online only. In the online environment, traditional news titles face strong competition from a range of new online sites, including *Huffington Post*, *VICE*, *BuzzFeed* and others, that are often more attuned to the habits and interests of younger users. There has also been significant internationalization of online news, with globally recognized brands such as *The Guardian*, *Daily Mail*, *Wall Street Journal* and *The New York Times* generating sites for new markets in Asia and in countries such as Australia.

International broadcasters have also expanded their worldwide operations, often under the *aegis* of the national governments seeking to expand the 'soft power' influence in world affairs: the BBC, China's CCTV, Russia Today, Japan's NHK and several other broadcasters have been expanding both their online operations and their international reach (Sparks, 2016). In areas such as sport, clubs and code administrators have themselves developed significant news websites, that make it less relevant to go to generalist news sources to get information such as the results of matches. Journalists themselves have lost their privileged status as the sole providers of news, as a range of bloggers, citizen journalists and others circulate information online to their specialist readerships, in a process greatly enhanced by distribution and sharing across social media content platforms.

By far the most disruptive impact of social media upon news organizations, and indeed upon all media industries, has been upon their traditional business models. The traditional newspaper relied upon a mix of three sources of revenue: (1) direct sales; (2) advertising; and (3) classifieds. All three of these were significantly eroded over the first decade of the 2000s. Classified revenues dried up as specialist online sites proved to be far more effective means of promoting and selling those products and services that had traditionally used classified advertising: real estate, car sales, job advertisements, trade services, etc. With regards to content, social media platforms are built around sharing: the ability to circulate and share content invites users to continue to engage with the platforms, and is also central to building the profile and 'brand identity' of those who create the original content, as well as those who re-circulate it (Markham, 2016). This means that the content that is most popular on social media sites is that which is most easily shared, and a core condition for that is that it is freely available. This has presented media businesses with a core contradiction. To boost their own profile, and hence their audiences, sales and revenues, they need to make their content widely available and easily accessible, which generally correlates with making it available for free. When online news sites have responded by establishing paywalls and subscriber-only content, they have generally experienced a sharp loss in their readerships, unless their content is truly unique and hence able to command a premium price. However, making content freely available undercuts the ability to employ staff and resources to generate new content, as there are not revenue streams associated with the new content. News organizations have responded by cutting staff, downsizing newsrooms, sharing content, and outsourcing activities such as sub-editing, but this has risked generating a downward spiral, as they have less internal capacity to generate the original and compelling content that would draw readers to their sites, in an environment with a greatly expanded degree of user choice (Doyle, 2013: 76–98).

This has meant that traditional media businesses have had to put a greater reliance upon advertising as a source of revenue, hoping that distribution of content through social media platforms will drive new user traffic to their sites, thus being successful for the 'competition for eyeballs' in the *attention economy* (Lanham, 2006; Webster, 2014). Phenomena such as 'clickbait' (content with sensational headlines or pictures that encourage readers to click through out of curiosity) and 'churnalism' (re-use of pre-packaged content such as media releases) arose in this environment, as cheap ways of attracting readers online to sites: celebrity stories and scandals have been reliable means of attracting the relatively disengaged online user through such techniques (Davies, 2008; Jackson & Moloney, 2015). But advertising has proven to be an ever less reliable means of funding content as proliferation of content, combined with access on the part of clients to ever more detailed demographic data about those who view content online, has led to the price that can be charged for online advertising falling dramatically. It has become increasingly apparent that, the big winners from online advertising spend are increasingly the online platforms themselves, rather than the content providers (Knapp, 2014). This is because they operate in multi-sided markets, where they can be positioned as the mediating platform providers for multiple producers and consumers, none of whom has equivalent market power in relevant transaction spaces (Bauer, 2014). The growing use of adblocker software by users also hits the content-based sites harder than platform-based ones, as the latter typically have their advertising already embedded within the site (so-called 'native advertising'), rather than as unrelated material that hangs off the main site.

Social Media as Transformer: Algorithmic Screen Media

The final context to be considered is that where social media act as a transformer of media and creative industries. The digital transformation of CCIs has elements of both amplification and disruption about it, as can be seen with the case of new forms of distribution of screen media content that combine digital delivery and traditional long-form formats for media such as film and television. For other broadcasters, as well as the cable industry, new streaming media services such as Netflix, Hulu and Amazon TV, as well as China's iQiyi and LeTV and a variety of other streaming services around the world, challenge and potentially undermine traditional media industry business models. While the major revenue sources for broadcast media have been advertising revenue, subscription to a bundle of channels, and taxpayer funding, the new models offer a different type of subscription service, more akin to being a member of a 'club', where membership offers access to a wider range of content than is the case with traditional broadcasting, but less than the large bundle of often unrelated channels provided by cable services. At the same time, these new services are highly supportive of new content developers, being prepared to invest large amounts of money in the commissioning of original content. This is different from the relationship of services such as Facebook to news producers, where they amplify distribution but do not invest in the creation of new content (Cunningham & Silver, 2013). High-budget, and highly acclaimed, productions such as *House of Cards*, *Transparent* and *Orange is the New Black* were developed by Netflix and Amazon as part of their strategies to build a new subscriber base.

At the core of the 'Netflix model' is the new relationship established between algorithmic sorting and 'Big Data' on the one hand, and cultural production and distribution on the other. Broadcast media have traditionally relied upon rating data as the basis for programming decisions, basing judgements on data derived from relatively small sample sizes and a high propensity for various forms of bias and unreliability (Balnaves &

O'Regan, 2002). By contrast, Netflix has drawn upon the kinds of recommendations technologies developed by social media companies such as Facebook, e-commerce sites such as Amazon, and a wide range of online dating sites. The 'recommendation algorithm' (Hallinan & Striphas, 2016) draws upon the invitations Netflix offers its customers to rate content online, through both a one-to-five star ratings system and the opportunity to comment on the material viewed. As Hallinan and Striphas have noted, this entails a shift in cultural authority from those who have traditionally judged the nature of 'good works' (critics, academics, award judges, etc.) to 'the realm of technique and engineering, where individuals with no obvious connection to a particular facet of the cultural field (i.e., media) are developing frameworks with which to reconcile those difficult questions' (Hallinan & Striphas, 2016: 122).

The 'Netflix model' is also associated with a shift in marketing practices, and programming practices which aim to attract advertisers, from broad demographics and socio-graphics (age, gender, ethnicity, income, etc.) towards an understanding of individuals as nodes within social networks, where the art of programming involves the identification of overlaps between different types of preference. In developing a program such as *House of Cards*, where Netflix apparently offered $US100 million and outbid cable channels such as HBO, Netflix 'took a factor-based approach … using its algorithms to decompose the property to determine whether an audience might exist for some combination of "David Fincher," his "style," the collection of genres across which he has worked, "Kevin Spacey," the specific genre of political thriller, and so forth' (Hallinan & Striphas, 2016: 128).

The wider implications of algorithmic culture are open to debate. If its ability to generate content such as *House of Cards* and *Orange is the New Black* is an indication, it may provide a formula for more effectively meeting the tastes of niche audiences than either broadcast television, which sought to maximize overall audience share, or cable channels, which have sought to aggregate audiences around particular program genres. This process of 'leveraging crowd wisdom' (Striphas, 2015: 407) in order to generate content tailored to revealed subscriber preferences may be, as the platform providers sometimes imply, a democratization of public culture. But the reality is that it is almost impossible to know what the algorithms are, guarded as they are by patent law, trade secrets, non-disclosure agreements, and so forth (Gillespie, 2010). In such a context, the claims to '"crowd wisdom" is largely just a stand-in … for algorithmic data processing, which is increasingly becoming a private, exclusive and indeed profitable affair … and why companies like Amazon, Google and Facebook are fast becoming, despite their populist rhetoric, the new apostles of culture' (Striphas, 2015: 408).

CONCLUSION

In this chapter, we have considered the relationship of social media to three trends in the cultural and creative industries, using applied case studies. The first trend is that of *amplification*, where social media can both expand the reach and enhance the appeal of creative product by allowing for second-screen communicaion about the content. This has been most successfully applied in the area of television, although the appeal of social media engagement differs significantly across program types and genres. The second has been that of *disruption*, as social media, and digital media platforms more generally, fundamentally change how we consume media content, to the disadvantage of incumbent media and creative industries. The impact of social media on journalism is a strong case in point. Finally, there are cases of fundamental *transformation* of how cultural and creative industries operate. The impact of algorithmic sorting and other developments enabled by

'Big Data' and automation is at a relatively early stage, but the relationship between such consumer information and new forms of screen content, as seen with cases such as Netflix, points towards the possibility that we are at the early stages of much wider transformations.

The case of new recommendation-based and data-driven models of media such as Netflix, and their equivalents in fields such as music, news and other cultural and creative industries, reveals the growing significance of algorithmic culture. In this respect, the relationship between the cultural and creative industries and digital and social media is becoming an ever closer one. It has been argued in this chapter that the relationship has indeed been close in practice, even if CCI debates and those surrounding digital technologies have frequently occurred along parallel paths. It is now essential to conceive of the CCIs as being enmeshed in a wider digital economy, but one where the value of creativity remains significant, and where those fields through which developments in the CCIs are critically evaluated, such as the academic disciplines associated with the arts, media and design, retain a key role in how we think about phenomena associated with social media, such as algorithmic culture and the 'sharing economy'. While many of the most intense debates around the intersection between creative industries and digital culture have been around the changing status of intellectual property, and associated legal, ethical and policy issues, they are increasingly likely to be turning to questions around the political economy of the networked digital and social media platforms themselves.

Note

1 In this chapter, I will focus primarily upon digital media companies, particularly those which provide platforms for digitally-mediated communication. It will not focus exclusively upon those companies that are considered to be primarily in the 'social media' space, such as Facebook and Twitter. This recognizes that many of the companies that have had the most disruptive impact upon the creative industries are not necessarily engaged in providing platforms to facilitate person-to-person online communication.

REFERENCES

Alasuutari, P. (2013) 'Spreading global models and enhancing banal localism: The case of local government cultural policy development', *International Journal of Cultural Policy*, 19(1), 103–119.

Anderson, C. (2009) *The Long Tail: How Endless Choice is Creating Unlimited Demand*. London: Random House.

Aronovitch, H. (2012) 'Interpreting Weber's ideal-types', *Philosophy of the Social Sciences*, 42(3), 356–369.

Bakhshi, H., Hargreaves, I. & Mateos-Garcia, J. (2013) *A Manifesto for the Creative Economy*. London: NESTA.

Balnaves, M. & O'Regan, T. (2002) 'Governing audiences', in M. Balnaves, T. O'Regan & J. Sternberg (Eds.), *Mobilising the Audience* (pp. 10–28). Brisbane: University of Queensland Press.

Banks, M. & O'Connor, J. (2009) 'After the creative industries', *International Journal of Cultural Policy*, 15(4), 365–373.

Bauer, J.M. (2014) 'Platforms, systems competition, and innovation: Reassessing the foundations of communications policy', *Telecommunciations Policy*, 38, 662–673.

Bell, D. (1980) 'The social framework of the information society', in T. Forester (Ed.), *Microelectronics Revolution* (pp. 500–549). Cambridge, MA: MIT Press.

Benkler, Y. (2006) *The Wealth of Networks: How Social Production Transforms Markets and Freedom*. New Haven, CT: Yale University Press.

Billings, A. (2014) 'Power in the reverberation: Why Twitter matters, but not the way most believe', *Communication & Sport*, 2(2), 107–112.

Bilton, C. (2007) *Management and Creativity: From Creative Industries to Creative Management*. Malden, MA: Blackwell.

Bilton, C. & Leary, R. (2002) 'What can managers do for creativity? Brokering creativity in the creative industries', *International Journal of Cultural Policy*, 8(1), 49–64.

Caves, R.E. (2000) *Creative Industries: Contracts between Art and Commerce.* Cambridge, MA: Harvard University Press.

Christensen, C.M. (2003) *The Innovator's Dilemma: When New Technologies Cause Great Firms to Fail* (2nd ed.). Boston, MA: Harvard Business School Press.

Cunningham, S. & Silver, J. (2013) *Screen Distribution and the New King Kongs of the Online World.* Basingstoke, UK: Palgrave.

Davies, N. (2008) *Flat Earth News: An Award-winning Reporter Exposes Falsehood, Distortion and Propaganda in the Global Media.* London: Vintage.

Department of Communication and the Arts (1994) *Creative Nation: Commonwealth Cultural Policy.* Available at: http://pandora.nla. gov.au/pan/21336/20031011-0000/www.nla. gov.au/creative.nation/contents.html (accessed 28 March 2016).

Department of Culture, Media and Sport (1998) *Creative Industries Mapping Document.* Available at: www.gov.uk/government/ publications/creative-industries-mapping-documents-1998 (accessed 25 March 2016).

Doyle, G. (2013) *Understanding Media Economics* (2nd ed.). London: Sage.

European Commission (2010) *Unlocking the Potential of Europe's Cultural and Creative Industries.* Available at: http://eur-lex.europa. eu/legal-content/EN/TXT/?uri=CELEX: 52010DC0183 (accessed 28 March 2016).

Flew, T. (2012) *The Creative Industries, Culture and Policy.* London: Sage.

Flew, T. (2013) *Global Creative Industries.* Basingstoke: Palgrave Macmillan.

Flew, T. (2014) *New Media: An Introduction* (4th ed.). Melbourne, Vic.: Oxford University Press.

Flew, T. (2015) 'Copyright and creativity: An ongoing debate in the creative industries', *International Journal of Cultural and Creative Industries*, 2(3), 4–17.

Flew, T. & Swift, A. (2015) 'Engaging, persuading, and entertaining citizens: Mediatization and the Australian political public sphere', *The International Journal of Press/Politics*, 20(1), 108–128.

Florida, R.L. (2002) *The Rise of the Creative Class and How It's Transforming Work, Life, Community and Everyday Life.* New York: Basic Books.

Garnham, N. (2005) 'From cultural to creative industries', *International Journal of Cultural Policy*, 11(1), 15–29.

Gibson, C. & Kong, L. (2005) Cultural Economy: A Critical Review. *Progress in Human Geography*, 29(5), 541-561.

Gillespie, T. (2010) 'The politics of "platforms"', *New Media & Society*, 12(3), 347–364. doi: 10.1177/1461444809342738.

Gray, J., Jones, J. & Thompson, E. (2009) *Satire TV: Politics and Comedy in the Post-network Era.* New York: New York University Press.

Grodach, C. (2013) 'Cultural economy planning in creative cities: Discourse and practice', *International Journal of Urban and Regional Research*, 37(5), 1747–1765.

Hallinan, B. & Striphas, T. (2016) 'Recommended for you: The Netflix prize and the production of algorithmic culture', *New Media & Society*, 18(1), 117–137.

Harrington, S. (2013) *Australian TV News: New Forms, Functions, and Futures.* Bristol: Intellect.

Hartley, J. (2005) 'Creative industries', in J. Hartley (ed.), *Creative Industries* (pp. 1–43). Malden, MA: Blackwell.

Henten, A. & Skouby, K.E. (2006) 'New media and trade policy', in L. Lievrouw & S. Livingstone (Eds.), *Handbook of New Media: Social Shaping and Social Consequences of ICTs* (pp. 386–404). Los Angeles, CA: Sage.

Hesmondhalgh, D., Oakley, K. & Lee, D. (2015) *Culture, Economy and Politics: The Case of New Labour.* Basingstoke: Palgrave Macmillan.

Hewison, R. (2014) *Cultural Capital: The Rise and Fall of Creative Britain.* London: Verso.

Himelboim, I. (2014) 'Political television hosts on Twitter: Examining patterns of interconnectivity and self-exposure in Twitter political talk networks', *Journal of Broadcasting & Electronic Media*, 58(1), 76–96.

Howkins, J. (2005) 'The Mayor's Commission on the creative industries', in J. Hartley (Ed.), *Creative Industries* (pp. 117–125). Malden, MA: Blackwell.

Iwabuchi, K. (2015) 'Pop-culture diplomacy in Japan: Soft power, nation branding and the question of "international cultural exchange"',

International Journal of Cultural Policy, 21(4), 419–432.

Jackson, D. & Moloney, K. (2015) 'Inside Churnalism: PR, journalism and power relationships in flux', *Journalism Studies* (online first), DOI: 10.1080/1461670X.2015.1017597.

Jenkins, H., Ford, S. & Green, J. (2013) *Spreadable Media: Creating Value and Meaning in a Networked Culture*. New York: New York University Press.

Jin, D.Y. (2016) *New Korean Wave: Transnational Cultural Power in the Age of Social Media*. Urbana-Champaign, IL: University of Illinois Press.

Keane, M. (2013) *Creative Industries in China: Art, Design, Media*. Cambridge: Polity.

Knapp, W. (2014) *Why are CPM Rates for Ads Falling?* Available at: www.clickz.com/clickz/column/2354801/why-are-cpm-rates-for-ads-falling (accessed 28 March 2016).

Knopper, S. (2009) *Appetite for Self-destruction: The Spectacular Crash of the Record Industry in the Digital Age*. London: Simon & Schuster.

Kong, L. (2012) 'Ambitions of a global city: Arts, culture and creative economy in "post-crisis" Singapore', *International Journal of Cultural Policy*, 18(3), 279–294.

Lanham, R.A. (2006) *The Economics of Attention: Style and Substance in the Age of Information*. Chicago, IL: University of Chicago Press.

Lee, T. (2010) *The Media, Cultural Control and Government in Singapore*. London: Routledge.

Lessig, L. (2004) *Free Culture: How Big Media Uses Technology and the Law to Lock Down Culture and Control Creativity*. New York: Penguin.

Markham, T. (2016) *Media and Everyday Life*. Basingstoke: Palgrave Macmillan.

McCraw, T.K. (2007) *Prophet of Innovation: Joseph Schumpeter and Creative Destruction*. Cambridge, MA: Harvard University Press.

O'Connor, J. (2010) *The Cultural and Creative Industries: A Literature Review*. Available at: www.creativitycultureeducation.org/the-cultural-and-creative-industries-a-literature-review (accessed 28 March 2016).

O'Reilly, T. (2005) *What is Web 2.0?* Available at: www.oreilly.com/pub/a/web2/archive/what-is-web-20.html (accessed 28 March 2016).

Pratt, A.C. (2005) 'Cultural industries and public policy', *International Journal of Cultural Policy*, 11(1), 31–44.

Pratt, A.C. (2009) 'Policy transfer and the field of the cultural and creative industries: What can be learned from Europe?', in L. Kong & J. O'Connor (Eds.), *Creative Economies, Creative Cities: Asian–European Perspectives* (pp. 9–23). Dordrecht: Springer.

Ross, A. (2007) 'Nice work if you can get it: The mercurial career of creative industries policy', in G. Lovink & N. Rossiter (Eds.), *MyCreativity Reader* (pp. 17–39). Amsterdam: Institute of Network Cultures.

Schumpeter, J.A. (1950) *Capitalism, Socialism, and Democracy* (5th ed.). London: Allen and Unwin.

Singer, J. (2010) 'Journalism in a network', in M. Deuze (Ed.), *Managing Media Work* (pp. 103–110). Thousand Oaks, CA: Sage.

Sparks, C. (2016) 'Global integration, state policy and the media', in T. Flew, P. Iosifidis & J. Steemers (Eds.), *Global Media and National Policies: The Return of the State* (pp. 49–73). Basingstoke: Palgrave Macmillan.

Striphas, T. (2015) 'Algorithmic culture', *European Journal of Cultural Studies*, 18(4–5), 395–412.

Throsby, D. (2010) *The Economics of Cultural Policy*. Cambridge: Cambridge University Press.

Towse, R. (2010) *A Textbook of Cultural Economics*. Cambridge: Cambridge University Press.

UNESCO (2013) *United Nations Creative Economy Report 2013: Widening Local Development Pathways*. Available at: www.unesco.org/new/en/culture/themes/creativity/creative-economy-report-2013-special-edition/ (accessed 28 March 2016).

Walsh, J. (2014) 'Hallyu as a governmental construct: The Korean Wave in the context of economic and social development', in Y. Kuwahara (Ed.), *The Korean Wave: Korean Popular Culture in Global Context* (pp. 13–31). New York: Palgrave Macmillan.

Walsh, K. (2014) 'What does Twitter really offer TV audiences, and at what cost?', *Spectator – The University of Southern California Journal of Film and Television*, 34(2), 11–15.

Wang, J. (2008) *Brand New China: Advertising, Media, and Commercial Culture*. Cambridge, MA: Harvard University Press.

Weber, M. (1978) *Economy and Society* (2 vols). Eds. G. Roth and C. Wittich. Berkeley, CA: University of California Press.

Webster, J.G. (2014) *The Marketplace of Attention: How Audiences Take Shape in a Digital Age*. Cambridge, MA: MIT Press.

Wikström, P. (2013) *The Music Industry: Music in the Cloud* (2nd ed.). Cambridge: Polity Press.

Williams, R. (1963) *The Long Revolution*. Harmondsworth: Penguin.

Wright, S., Newbign, J., Holden, J. & Kieffer, J. (2009) *After the Crunch*. London: Counterpoint.

Zenith Optimedia (2015) *Media Consumption Forecasts*. Available at: www.zenithoptimedia.com/shop/forecasts/media-consumption-forecasts-2015/ (accessed 28 March 2016).

29

Politics 2.0: Social Media Campaigning

Jessica Baldwin-Philippi

Although 2008 marks a watershed moment for digital electoral campaigning, the practices that were widely extolled as revolutionary have a much longer history. Campaign websites have played a role in US communications efforts since the mid-1990s, when the Clinton/Gore and Dole/Kemp campaigns developed the first presidential campaign websites. The voter data programs that campaigns now use daily have their roots in tools developed in the late 1980s, and have benefitted from evolution and infrastructure building within parties. The very data such programs rely upon still involve opinion polls, which have been a meaningful part of campaigns since the 1960s.[1] Although campaigns were slow to adopt the participatory, reciprocal affordances that were tenets of web 2.0 (O'Reilly, 2005), the 2004 Dean campaign and 2008 Obama campaigns' use of social platforms such as Facebook, Meetup, and Myspace marked a more fundamental shift: the rise of social media campaigning.

Social media campaigning marks both an evolution of traditional campaign practices and a space of opportunity for new strategies and norms to emerge. In the years since 2008, campaigns of all sizes have had to grapple with the adoption of digital tools to supplement their existing methods of persuasion and mobilization, which has led to strategic and technical innovation, as well as the solidification of some existing practices. This chapter highlights what social media strategies look like now that the dust of the revolutionary 2008 elections has settled, what effects these emerging strategies have had on a variety of campaign goals in both the American and European context, and how the on-the-fly adoption of new tactics and tools has resulted in unintended consequences for campaigns. Specifically, this chapter drills down further into three particular social media campaign strategies and their unintended consequences – opening up campaign content to public feedback while encouraging citizens to 'talk back,' the adoption of widely available, popular social media platforms, and the increase in campaigns' attention to analytics.

To investigate these practices, this research combines a review of quantitative campaign research that draws primarily on US and European cases with original qualitative research investigating campaign tactics, professional trainings for political consultants and staffers, and campaign messages in the US. It draws on data spanning the years 2010–2014, including ethnographic observations of a federal-level campaign in 2010, in-depth interviews of over 40 campaign consultants following the 2010 and 2012 campaigns, brief interviews with an additional 15 staffers and consultants following the 2014 election, and textual analysis of training sessions at professional consulting conferences over the course of those four years (Baldwin-Philippi, 2015). The original research in this chapter is devoted to the US, although it attempts to draw attention to similarities and differences in uses across national contexts to highlight the ways country-context matters and can influence strategic choices.

As campaign practices evolve over time and adoption differs across national contexts, this chapter draws on actor-network theory (Latour, 2005) to situate the emergence of new practices as a product of individual staffers and consultants as well as the technologies they deploy, and emphasizes both the material aspects of social media as well as their patterns of use. In line with calls for communication studies as a discipline to more deeply investigate the material aspects of communication technologies (Boczkowski & Lievrouw, 2008), this chapter also focuses on the affordances and interfaces of social media and analytics platforms in order to illuminate the ways platform changes result in shifts in strategy or priorities for campaigns. Though deductive and quantitative approaches still drive most political communication research, the adopted inductive approach allows for investigation into the socio-technical interactions between campaigns and technologies. Such an inquiry can illuminate the causes and consequences of emerging campaign strategies, and, in turn,

develop digitally-situated theories of political participation and institutional politics, as has been called for in recent years (Bennett & Iyengar, 2008; Karpf, Kreiss, Nielsen, & Powers, 2015).

Combining a review of quantitative, international literature with qualitative work in the US context, this chapter seeks to explain how social media campaigning builds on and influences prior campaign strategies. First, it will illuminate the current state of cutting-edge social media strategy in the US and explain how social media platforms are currently used in other countries, while also focusing on the impact of this use on citizens. Second, it highlights the problem of unintended consequences in the adoption of new social media platforms: changes to both the user interface and backend of Facebook and Twitter from 2010 to 2014 have played a vital role in the development of social media content and impacted strategic decisions. Third, this chapter will discuss the normative, democratic implications of these practices.

WHAT ARE CAMPAIGNS DOING?

Obama's 2008 campaign has been dubbed the Facebook election by academics and journalists alike (Harfoush, 2009; Lutz, 2009; Sabato, 2009; Trippi, 2008), as it was the first to make use of social platforms that are now commonplace in political campaigns, and harness user-created content in these spaces. Although other examples of pioneering digital campaigns exist, such as Australian Labor Party (ALP) Leader Kevin Rudd's 2007 use of Myspace to garner support en route to the ALP's victory and become Prime Minister, the Obama campaign was perceived as the first to combine use of social media platforms with on-the-ground mobilization in a wide-scale and effective manner. The Obama 2008 team used YouTube to provide volunteers with backstage videos from campaign staffers and the candidate himself, and the user-created video, 'I got a Crush On Obama' was so popular that it was later named a top ten meme of the decade by *Newsweek* (Allison, 2009). The Obama campaign had over 2 million Facebook followers and more than 112,000 Twitter supporters, to John McCain's 600,000 and 4,600 respectively (Dutta & Fraser, 2008), and they also made use of blogging networks and other more niche platforms like Flickr, Digg, LinkedIn, BlackPlanet, and MiGente. While these platforms themselves were less robust than they are now, the Obama campaign created groups to which supporters could subscribe in order to show their support, receive campaign updates, and find sharable images with Obama's campaign logo, website and picture on them..[2] Despite these new tools that the campaign deployed, the successes of the Obama campaign and the national Democratic party more broadly were, as Daniel Kreiss (2012b) has detailed, rooted in the party's adoption of technology in the following election cycle. Moreover, as Rasmus Kleis Nielsen's work has shown (2012), while social media were exciting and highly visible in campaigns in 2008, campaigns relied much more heavily on using voter data to make in-person contact with potential voters through traditional mobilization efforts like canvassing.

Following the Obama campaign's wide margin of victory, and the perception that social media was a driving force of the campaign's success, political campaigns at all levels proceeded to get on board, campaigning through social media. Despite the fact that political campaigns' goals remain the same in an age of social media campaigning – electing a candidate through a combination of persuasive messaging, mobilizing fundraising and volunteer efforts, and getting out the vote (GOTV) – social media platforms have allowed campaigns to make slight changes to the ways they go about these goals, and have even catalyzed the adoption of a handful of new ones as well.

All of these changes are due not only to the availability of social media tools and their increasingly widespread adoption by campaigns, but are also a product of the changing technological affordances of these platforms. Insofar as social media are provided by privately-run companies, decisions about what to allow campaigns (or any account manager) to do, how and when paid-programming can purchased, and even the visual layout of the user interface are out of the campaigns' control. As campaigns adopt these social media platforms and their changing technological affordances, their own strategies and emphases concerning how and when to use such tools change as well.

Social Media Adoption

In the years since the Obama campaign's 2008 victory and the subsequent coronation of social media campaigning in American politics, campaigns' use of social media tools – social networking systems like Facebook and Twitter, as well as less socially-oriented platforms like YouTube – has increased rapidly. In 2010, as statewide and local campaigns began to grapple with the adoption of digital media, the presence of campaign-controlled social media accounts was clear, but not ubiquitous, with 78% of Senate and House campaigns using official YouTube channels, 71% using campaign Twitter accounts, and 82% using campaign Facebook accounts (Williams & Gulati, 2011). Just two years later, the use of such platforms had become nearly universal, with 97% of Senate campaigns and 90.2% of Congressional campaigns using an official Facebook account (Gulati & Williams, 2015), and has stayed stable.

In contrast, European political campaigns have been slower to take up social media platforms at both the candidate and party level. In 2010, social media campaigning was said to have 'failed to fire' in Germany (Marcinkowski & Metag, 2014) and the UK

(Aldrich, Gibson, Cantijoch, & Konitzer, 2016), with only 30% of campaigns using social networks. By 2013, these numbers had risen only to 76.6 % of campaigns having profiles on either Twitter or Facebook, with a slightly lower number (72.3%) actively maintaining those accounts (Hinz, 2014). Similarly low use numbers for elections occurring in 2010 and 2011 occurred in the Netherlands (32%) and Finland (19% of candidates) (Vergeer & Hermans, 2013). Not only did many European candidates and parties refrain from the immediate post-Obama-'08 uptake in social media; in many cases this trend continued in the years to come. In 2013, only 26.2% of Australian candidates were on Twitter, and that percentage was largely composed of candidates who were party spokespeople or 'frontbenchers' (Bruns & Highfield, 2015). Similarly, Norway's 2013 election saw only 24% of candidates with social media accounts, and Sweden's election that same year saw a meager 19% (Larsson, 2015). Across most countries, candidates belonging to opposition parties, or those not in power, are more likely to adopt Twitter as a channel to get out their message (Jungherr, 2016).

Although European candidates' use of social media looks considerably different from candidates in the US, these countries' party-centric parliamentary systems and subsequently reduced need for candidates to craft personal political identities are the likely reason for such vast differences. Indeed, we see that parties' use of social and digital media is widespread, and perceptions of its importance are similar across European nations. Signaling the adoption of what Andrew Chadwick (2013) has called the hypermedia style, the use of social tools do spread from the US, outward, even if specific tactics and strategies are influenced by the local political contexts (Lilleker, Tenscher, & Štětka, 2015). Candidates in the European context, in contrast to the US, do not seem to provide voters with personal information, in social media content or elsewhere (Hermans & Vergeer,

2013; Kriesi, 2012). The phenomenon of candidate or party adoption of professionalized, consultant-based campaign strategies is not limited to the adoption of social media tools. Campaigns also use analytics software to assess the impact of digital campaign communications. As McKelvey and Piebiak (2014) have shown, off-the-shelf analytics tools like NationBuilder, which were developed and first used in US campaigns, are now widely used in Canada.

Persuasion in Social Media

As campaigns increasingly adopt social media and discover best practices for crafting content that is popular and persuasive, social media messages have emerged as a genre that in some ways mirrors traditional broadcast messaging, while making small changes that allow campaigns to take advantage of networked relationships. Campaigns' early use of social media saw a repetition of traditional communications strategies, as campaigns in 2010 often used Facebook and Twitter as places to amplify the same persuasive messages they were used to creating, rather than developing new norms of content. As a result, their social media accounts were often overrun with press releases and campaign ads. In 2010, out of fourteen Senate and Congressional level campaigns in Illinois that had an active social media presence, nine of their Facebook accounts had a plurality of traditional content such as event coverage, press releases, and links to stories on their own campaign websites. Not only was the content often identical across these platforms, with campaigns taking advantage of programs that automatically pushed content from one platform to the other, but campaigns also used it as a way to link back to their own campaign websites. As one communications director from a Congressional race explains it, 'Capturing people and getting them stuck in something like flypaper – they go to your website …

then they're looking at your education plan, and go to the Facebook page, and the Facebook takes them to the Twitter feed, Twitter feed takes them to the YouTube page ... they're continuing to browse and they're staying on your message' (personal communication, January 18, 2011).

Similar findings showed that both US (Gerodimos & Justinussen, 2015; Hemphill, Otterbacher, & Shapiro, 2013) and European campaigns used social media for unidirectional, broadcast communication, including the UK (Graham, Broersma, Hazelhoff, & van 't Haar, 2013) and Germany (Jungherr, 2016). Additionally, in a small study of how elected officials' from the US Congress, European Parliament, and Korean National Assembly used Twitter as of 2012, Otterbacher, Shapiro, and Hemphill (2013), found that interactive features such as tagging, @replying, retweeting, use of pictures and videos, and so on, are not widely used. Despite studying only a handful of representatives, their findings indicated that the European MEPs and Korean assembly members used more of these interactive features than their counterparts in the US Congress. A much larger-scale study of US campaigns' use of Twitter by Jason Gainous and Kevin Wagner found that challengers and Republicans were more likely to use those features (2013).

Interestingly, while social media messages take the form of unidirectional, broadcast messages, their content is not an exact duplication of campaigns' mass media strategies. Major differences lie in the fact that social media content is less issue-based, and more often used to draw attention to campaign events and opportunities to get involved with campaigns, and that it is more positive than television advertisements (Bode et al., 2011). Moreover, these same findings show that external political factors that have historically made it likely a campaign will use negative ads, such as incumbency or closeness of the race, do not make it any more or less likely that these same candidates will publicize negative content in social media

spaces. While social media content has been increasingly image-driven since 2010 and those images have become more professional in their aesthetics and composition (Baldwin-Philippi, 2015), political campaigns have also begun to harness the popularity of memes in social media, crafting content that is humorous and that encourages citizens to create similar content of their own (Graef, n.d.).

As campaigns and advocacy groups alike adopted networked communication platforms, they innovated the channels through which they dispersed their broadcast-style messages. Not only were they publishing content on social media platforms, but the flow of campaign communications became networked as well. As Daniel Kreiss (2012a) has shown, the Obama campaign used bloggers on the activist left to break news stories that would likely damage the opposition. A related practice also spread in the subsequent election cycles, with campaigns commonly feeding stories to partisan political bloggers when they could not get the subject picked up by more mainstream reporters with wider circulation. Beginning in 2010, most campaigns also directly enlisted supporters to spread, pass along, and share social content – even before the practice was so widespread that Facebook introduced a 'share' button to make the practice even easier (Baldwin-Philippi, 2015).

Social media platforms became especially productive means through which campaigns could identify and directly contact opinion leaders and/or surrogates, crafting a new, networked version of the two-step-flow of information (Katz & Lazarsfeld, 1955). Campaigns saw digital opinion leaders as especially valuable precisely because they expanded the population of valued opinion leaders beyond that of mainstream media, to include more diverse outlooks and critics of traditional media institutions. Similarly, while Twitter is most obviously a platform for publicly broadcasting a message to a campaign's supporters and followers, it has also been used as a way to directly reach out to individuals who may be engaging in political discussions online and persuade in more direct, interpersonal ways. This was a tactic that was sporadically deployed among the most tech-savvy digital consultants in 2010, but it was refined and routinized by the 2012 Obama campaign, when the campaign directly emailed Twitter users they had deemed opinion leaders on the platform to ask them to 'Join the Obama 2012 Twitter Team [...] help turn out the vote for President Obama [...] Retweet! Retweet! Retweet!'" Communications and digital consultants who began this practice in a haphazard way as early as 2010 described seeking out undecided voters on Twitter in the weeks and days leading up to an election and reaching out to them directly in efforts to persuade (personal communication, March 4, 2011). To do so, however, required specialized targeting of more supportive members, which meant more precise data and advanced technical skill, and was thus a tactic used only by more advanced staffers and consultants. By 2012, the social network analyses and social media analytics that were both integral to locating these individuals were becoming a routine part of major presidential campaigns in the US. This level of data strategy was largely absent in European countries.

Micro-targeting and Mobilization

One of the most fundamental changes to digital strategy since 2008 has been the increasingly specific ability to target messages to individuals through email, social networks, and even individual online ads. This practice of micro-targeting has its roots in highly-segmented public opinion polls of the 1996 Clinton campaign, and has only increased with the advent of digital advertising. As social media platforms have become places where people disclose a large amount of personal information, campaigns are able to gain access to much of it when purchasing social

media ads, and use it to categorize people based on geography, interests, issue-salience, or demographic information. Social media platforms allow campaigns to better know their audience, locate specific audiences, define and create their own audiences, and then target them with specifically tailored ads. This was a widely used tactic at the Congressional level as early as 2010. In terms of persuasive messaging, social media can be used to broadcast messages in the traditional, public sense, and to simultaneously micro-target those same messages to increasingly small slices of relevant potential audiences.

While the 2008 Obama campaign used Facebook to both broadcast and target their messages via public posts and advertisements respectively, the platforms and strategies for doing so have changed dramatically over the past eight years. In 2010, the line between public and targeted content was clearly drawn – posts were public (unless sent directly and privately to individuals), and advertisements were available to be targeted based on users' location, age, gender, and interests. Though many campaigns engaged in both tactics, they were sometimes surprised and often frustrated at the difference in affordances, and their inability to use the targeting tools they used for advertising to target regular public posts or messages (Fieldnotes, August 31, 2010; September 1, 2010). By the 2012 campaigns, however, the line between the two had blurred. While there were still both advertisements and public posts, campaigns' pages were given the ability to 'promote' (now 'boost') individual posts to audiences that could be targeted based on user location, age, gender, and interests. Social platforms like Facebook and Twitter have continued to blur the line between advertising and content by allowing campaigns to pay to promote their posts to larger audiences and target the populations who make up that audience. At the same time, micro-targeting has become even more common.

Mobilization efforts of all kinds, whether they be geared toward fundraising, soliciting volunteers for campaign needs or getting out the vote, now involve activities that take place both on- and offline. While many of campaign's most fundamental needs, such as getting out the vote, still necessarily rely on boots-on-the-ground volunteers, campaign field operations have also radically expanded the amount and types of data and analytics they rely on to know which doors to knock on and which hands to shake. Similarly, both persuasive and mobilizing messages have benefitted from the increasingly precise data used to identify and separate audiences and target them with different, pertinent messages.

Campaigns see social media not as an automatic conduit to increasing turnout or support, but as a way to increase the amount and depth of engagement they get from citizens. Since 2010, campaigns have been concerned with getting people engaged in easily enacted forms of political participation, which they hoped would lead to greater and more involved forms of activism later on. This constant, escalating ask is known to campaign and advocacy leaders as the 'ladder of engagement', and is central to campaigns' digital strategy. 'Once we know you'll sign a petition, we can try to get you to forward them to friends, or donate money. ... So you want to turn people who are on your email list into donors and/or volunteers; you want to turn donors and/or volunteers into super-volunteers. It's a constant ask' (personal communication, May 20, 2011). Recent research has supported the logic of this strategy, showing that the more citizens access political information online and use social media to express themselves politically, the more likely they are to take subsequent, more difficult mediated political actions (Vaccari et al., 2015).

Another major effort to directly combine online and offline mobilization has been the development of organizing platforms or action 'hubs' that citizens can log into, keeping track of their own acts of participation and sometimes taking action directly.

These, like 2008's MyBarackObama.com (known as MyBO) or Cruz's Crew, the activism app from the 2016 Republican presidential primary candidate Ted Cruz, not only gave campaigns data, but made participation easy. While most campaigns below the presidential level lack the resources necessary to develop fully-fledged original social activism platforms, in 2012, top-tier campaigns began to enlist the services of consulting firms to provide the same tools. More often, firms would design campaigns' official websites so they had the look and feel of a platform – they could link to phone banking directions or volunteer signups – without needing to devote time to the complex development task of credentialing users with their own accounts. During her first run for US Senate in 2012, the campaign website of Elizabeth Warren, rising star of the Democratic Party, contained an Action Center with nearly all of the same options for action provided by BarackObama.com, from receiving information or calling others, to joining groups within the campaign or attending events hosted by other citizens. This workaround enabled smaller-scale campaigns to draw on the rhetorical and aesthetic qualities of an original social activism platform and mobilize citizens, while working within their resource constraints. By April of the 2016 primary campaign, with help from tech-savvy volunteers, Senator Bernie Sanders' campaign had not only developed a website that acted similarly to an action hub – FeelTheBern.org – but refined home phone banking technology, enabling volunteers to make over 47 million calls from their homes – on pace to surpass the Obama 2012 camapign's numbers from the entire election (Issenberg, 2016; Scola, 2016). On the Republican side in 2015, the Cruz campaign added elements of gamification – points, leaderboards, and badges – to its action hub (and mobile app) to further motivate users to take more actions, such as calling potential voters or tweeting about the candidate.

As studies have tried to measure the impact of social media campaigning on persuasion, mobilization, and general voter behavior, the findings have been inconclusive at best. At the most basic level, despite the immense amount of energy put into digital campaign communications, these messages go largely ignored by the public (Nielsen & Vaccari, 2013). When they are attended to, no relationship between campaign success and either overall number of followers or growth in followers has been found (Dimitrova & Bystrom, 2013; Vaccari & Nielsen, 2013). Despite little research in the area, early analysis of what kind of social media content drives citizen participation shows people are likely to engage with substantive issue-oriented posts (as measured by shares, likes, and comments), and that tone and timing also affect this (Gerodimos & Justinussen, 2015; Xenos, Macafee, & Pole, 2015). Such findings highlight the fact that digital campaigning's benefit is unlikely to lie in its ability to reach and persuade new voters, but in its ability to mobilize, as was the case with prior digital tools as well (Bimber & Davis, 2003). At the same time, many other types of participation are increasing as well. Not only are people taking action online, but they are also engaging in what Chadwick (2009) has called high-threshold activities – canvassing, presence at rallies, phone banking, etc. – and low-threshold activities, such as signing petitions, donating, etc. (Vaccari et al., 2015). The use of digital tools to upgrade or personalize traditional strategies, such as using SMS text messages to get out the vote, rather than emails, mail or robo-calls, have been shown to increase turnout by a handful of percentage points (Malhotra, Michelson, Rogers, & Valenzuela, 2011). Early data from the 2016 primaries indicate that new digital engagement tools have facilitated more political participation in the form of small dollar donations, phone banking calls and voter contacts than in prior election cycles (Scola, 2016).

Overall, as adoption of social media has become nearly ubiquitous, both the subsequent use of additional technologies and the development of new communications strategies have followed. On the one hand, social media content remains largely broadcast-oriented and relies on much of the same information as press releases. On the other hand, this content is also different from that of traditional mass media, as it is more positive, relies on photographs and infographics, and, at the local level, also tends to be more oriented toward announcing and recapping events than focusing on issues. Broadly, much of this content is concerned with mobilizing supporters rather than persuading the undecided. Micro-targeting ads and emails have enabled campaigns to focus on persuasion in these spaces, and simultaneously allow for more efficient mobilization efforts. These efforts, in turn, have been even more supported by the rise in proprietary tools like action hubs and mobile apps that use social elements to encourage people to take action over time and away from campaign headquarters.

The democratic implications for these new forms of campaigning are much debated. On the one hand, many have pointed to the use of analytics and micro-targeting as a form of controlling or managing citizens (Howard, 2006; Kreiss, 2012b). Despite these very real tendencies, others have argued that these changes imply new views of how citizens are organized in relation to one another and to political institutions (Wells, 2015), and that even actions that are managed by campaigns can act as openings for participatory citizenship (Baldwin-Philippi, 2015). In cases where citizens are actively discussing politics on social media platforms, there is increasing concern that these discussions are emblematic of polarization rather than deliberation and debate (Conover, Gonçalves, Flammini, & Menczer, 2012), although recent work, drawing on data from Germany, Spain, and the US, shows that social media can also reduce polarization (Barberá, 2015). Additionally, digital media outreach that focuses on the less politically-interested and less mobilized may be a potential answer to polarization by mobilizing those with tempered perspectives (Prior & Stroud, 2015). While this chapter does not focus on advocacy campaigns, they offer additional reasons to be optimistic about the effects of digital and social strategies. Because they are removed from electoral time constraints and the zero-sum stakes of winning/losing an election, advocacy campaigns are better equipped to engage citizens in digital organizing, wherein they learn activist skills and facilitate the development and deepening of political social networks. This form of networked activism not only leads to productive structural changes to organizations that make them more focused on participation (Karpf, 2012), but facilitates actualized citizenship (Bennett, 2008; Wells, 2015). In all cases, the optimistic views on the possibility for digital and social tools to improve political life largely rely upon participatory and interactive methods of engagement.

THE UNFORESEEN CONSEQUENCES OF ADOPTING DIGITAL STRATEGY

As campaigns adopt social media, they also necessarily encounter new forms of content and opportunities for political communication that cause them to question old ways of doing things. This section examines three of these instances of emerging campaign strategies that have resulted in unintended consequences. They are a product of human agency and constraints of material technologies; they are driven by individual and organizational decisions and platform interfaces that are difficult (and in some cases impossible) to change; and, taking a wider view, they are also a product of the daily decisions campaign staffers make, and the larger economic environment of US campaigning that is constantly short staffed and short on funds. This section first discusses the changing norms surrounding campaign message control and citizen participation and discussion in campaign-supplied public forums (social media, commenting sections, etc.). It then turns toward analysis of the constraints imposed on all campaigns by their use of publicly available, proprietary platforms. Finally, it discusses the emerging use of analytics in campaigns, and the limits to their use in everyday campaigning.

Inviting Participation, Losing Control

While the 2008 campaign was dubbed 'the Facebook election,' the Facebook that the Obama and McCain campaigns dealt with was a different version of Facebook than we know today. The social norms and affordances surrounding commenting had yet to be as popular and user-friendly as they became in the following six years. Sharing content among friends, for instance, was neither common nor made particularly easy by the platform. The 2008 Obama campaign did deal with comments in its MySpace page, but the population of users there was much fewer in number than contemporary social media or commenting sections, and therefore the risk of allowing vitriolic comments (or those that were supportive, but inappropriate) was not as great as it is now. Within Facebook, the number of user-generated comments grew exponentially with each election cycle since 2008, as commenting became a dominant social practice on the platform. In 2010, a candidate running for a close Senate race was likely to receive one to two dozen comments per social media posts. For example, Alexi Giannoulias, Democractic candidate for the Senate in Illinois had an average of 13.50 comments per post, with the highest numbers coming from posts specifically requesting comments. Four years later, a comparably competitive Senatorial race in New Hampshire resulted in hundreds of comments per post for both Scott Brown (Republican) and eventual winner, Jean Shaheen (Democrat). Even in 2010, campaigns began to see the strategic, community-building value of encouraging the public to comment and hold discussions within their platforms. To facilitate this, campaigns even encouraged feedback, asking supporters how they felt about issues, for feedback on advertising spots, and polling on policy questions (personal communication, May 19, 2011). While campaigns had no intention of allowing feedback to influence their strategic decisions or issue stances (or even that they would have time to comb through the answers), they saw benefit in asking citizens to talk back.

Encouraging citizens to speak up and talk back to campaigns might be good for ideals of deliberative democracy, but it posed a problem for campaign staffers who wanted to control the message. While campaigns saw that deleting citizens' comments on their Facebook posts or blog comments was dangerous and not strategically beneficial, staffers disagreed on how else they should shape user contributions. In 2010, Facebook allowed administrators of campaign pages to control whether people could make direct posts to a candidate's wall, who was able to comment on the campaign's post, and which posts visitors would see first – posts by the campaign, the campaign and the public, or just the public. As social media platforms offer an array of controls, conversations about what choices to make have divided campaign staffers within as well as across campaigns. Exactly how much control was the campaign willing to let go of, and what leeway should the public be given in their commentary, input, and criticism of campaigns? As campaigns developed on-the-fly answers to these questions, the new strategic opportunities also exposed an unforeseen rift between staffers.

Consultants saw opening forums like commenting sections on Facebook and campaign blogs as beneficial not because of the intrinsic value of open, democratic spaces, but because of the potential downsides of closed spaces, and the consequences of being perceived as untrustworthy and inauthentic.

One digital director stressed these downsides, saying, 'people would begin to hate that if you [censored lots of content]. You don't want to do that. People will talk about that' (personal communication, May 19, 2011). Yet another communication director described the backlash from citizens that deletions caused. 'They came back stronger, we learned not to do that quickly' (personal communication, May 20, 2011). Although fear of downsides of exerting control were dominant, some staffers – largely those hired into newer positions on Digital teams – also argued for the moral value of leaving platforms' commenting sections open and uncontrolled. As one digital staffer explained, 'I come from the sort of generational culture, the tech culture, whatever that believes in openness and more transparency' (personal communication, June 9, 2011).

Such disagreements became catalysts for organizational rifts between two of the major players within campaigns: Communications and Digital teams. The digital director quoted above contrasted his view specifically with that of his Communications counterparts, adding: 'whereas the comms shop comes from the opposite culture: "Don't say anything unless you have to"' (personal communication, June 9, 2011). These disagreements were not only the purview of local campaigns, nor did they resolve themselves after a chaotic 2010 election; the 2012 Obama campaign was also plagued by them, despite its widely lauded digital strategy. As detailed in post-campaign journalistic debriefs, Obama's digital team clashed with their communications counterparts over this very issue (Madrigal, 2013). Even as European campaigns tend more toward the broadcast model of communication within social media platforms, the fact that comments are becoming a part of the social fabric of the platform itself make this issue unavoidable. While stronger norms of civility and deliberation may provide Europeans with less of a threat to control, there is little reason to think they will not deal with the same issues and navigate the internal divisions those choices are likely to reveal.

Inviting participation from volunteers eager to help campaigns also held the potential for problems, even as they took action that aided the campaign. As campaigns dealt with the problems associated with relinquishing control of their social media spaces, one productive strategy was seeking out volunteers to take on opposition in public forums and commenting spaces, sometimes going as far as to call them 'ambassadors' and give them a more meaningful, though symbolic, place in the campaign (personal communication, March 4, 2011; personal communication, June 22, 2011a). Another communications director described this as especially helpful if people from the opposition got heavily involved, saying 'We'll immediately go into full recruit mode for getting more of our like-minded people to join the page to balance it out' (personal communication, June 22, 2011b). While these tactics were productive and saved campaigns time responding, they also raised concerns of volunteers going off message, and staffers' anxiety about volunteers staying on message were constant. Such concern over well-meaning volunteers' ability to stay on message or allow campaigns to control engagement tools they have created is not unfounded. In 2008, technically-savvy and politically-active Obama supporters supplemented the campaign with grassroots-created websites, social media posts, YouTube videos and more. Although these efforts generated publicity, showcased the dedication and enthusiasm, and held the potential to persuade and motivate voters, they also were outside campaign control and thus causes of concern for the campaign and its goals of ensuring a cohesive message. In May 2007, the Obama campaign took over the MySpace page for their candidate, much to the dismay of the grassroots supporter, Joe Anthony, who had run the page for two years. Following a legal dispute over the page's ownership, the campaign was ultimately left with control of the official page, but none of the followers

Anthony had amassed (Sifry, 2007). In 2016, grassroots supporters of Senator Sanders had similarly created organizing websites, such as FeelTheBern.org, which links back to the official Sanders campaign site to facilitate donations, volunteer efforts, and information about upcoming Sanders events, but is not affiliated with the campaign, or any supporting PACs.

Public Platforms and Changes to Interfaces

The landscape of digital tools that campaigns can enlist is overwhelming. From tools to procure and analyze data to social media platforms that connect directly with potential voters, campaigns can choose from a wealth of options that include campaign-developed proprietary tools (e.g., My.BarackObama.com), purchasable, off-the-shelf software packages that sometimes also include consulting help (e.g., NationBuilder, CiviCRM, Salsa Labs, etc.), or publicly available, privately-owned platforms like Twitter, Facebook and Wordpress. Increasingly, campaigns are paying for software to record and organize data that will improve their persuasion and mobilization efforts, but popular social media platforms are still vital to all campaigns because potential voters already spend time within these spaces. Moreover, the economic realities of races below the presidential level means that most campaigns are reliant on social media tools. As these platforms are privately owned and controlled, campaigns are unable to control what data, controls, and affordances such platforms provide them.

By now, the public is generally aware that social media platforms use algorithms to filter content and provide more relevant results to users (Gillespie, 2014, as well as in this volume). As a result, campaign consultants often apply strategies to 'game' the algorithm and make their posts visible to a higher number of their followers. While the specifics of these algorithms are proprietary, some variables are known to be important, enabling consultants and staffers to learn what content the algorithm is known to reward. With every major change in the algorithm comes a flurry of concerns and discussions on consulting listervs and trade publications, writing on how best to post content in this new configuration. A prominent recent example of this are the changes to Twitter's once-purely-chronological algorithm. First, the platform added content 'favorited' by others to a users' feed, then it introduced 'Recaps' or 'While you were away' – an algorithmically-curated collection of tweets the user is likely to enjoy, based on popularity of a tweet, the account tweeting, and the engagement between the user and other accounts. As this algorithmically curated part of Twitter became more widely distributed by Twitter, consultants were forced to consider the value of creating content that will draw engagement versus constant tweeting (relevancy over recency). While we have yet to see how campaigns will respond to this change, the very fact that campaigns are reliant upon a privately owned platform and not in control of its affordances highlights the problem of unforeseen consequences of social media adoption. More visible changes to social media platforms can also 'disrupt' campaigns' strategies and abilities, and force them to change their practices.

In 2011, Facebook, for example, changed its user interface from what had been a more text-heavy layout that highlighted many of users' (and friends') posts at the same time to what the company called 'Timeline,' an image-heavy design. This change did more than just move all users into an interface that afforded visual content; it changed campaigns' ability to control where and if users could post comments and information on official campaign pages. Before the 2011 change, campaigns could choose to allow users to post on their page, could specify whether all users or just fans could do so. Moreover, if campaigns allowed fans or users

to post, they could also choose from three options of how visible those posts would be, in effect, allowing campaigns to discreetly control how visible citizen-created content would be. Campaigns could set a default view to show only their own posts, those of only users, or all posts. Thus, a campaign could allow anyone to post content to their own page, but also make it so audiences would have to flip through a filter in order to see everyone's posts. It could also prevent users who were not fans from commenting on other posts or creating their own post.

When Facebook made its change to the Timeline layout in 2011, these options were reduced. In this new layout, campaigns still had the ability to limit whether users could post directly to the page, including limiting whether users who had become 'fans' or 'friends' of the page could do so, or if anyone could. However, campaigns lost the ability to limit users' comments on posts the campaign published themselves. While the campaign can delete or hide individual comments, there is no backend control of limiting comments in the first place; any post a campaign makes is open to the public for commenting. Additionally, the design of the Timeline layout meant that campaign-produced content was front and center, while visitors' or fans' posts were relegated to a side column. Thus the change allowed campaigns to highlight their own content, but simultaneously prohibited campaigns from exerting a type of discreet control over the comments on that content.

Limits to Data and Analytics

Data and analytics have long been useful and necessary aspects of campaigning, from the use of local and national polls to gauge public opinion to dial tests used to measure reception of particular messages or arguments, to the micro-targeting practices discussed previously. While these uses of data to craft persuasive messages are commonplace, in the years following the 2008 presidential election, discussions of the importance of 'data-driven campaigning' and the importance of a 'culture of analytics' have gained traction among political professionals working in both advocacy and campaign environments. In many ways, communications offices have made leaps and bounds in the time between 2010 and 2014. In 2010, campaigns were only on the cusp of making sense of the new digital tools at their disposal. Campaigns rarely used analytics to test messages or develop strategy, and they were struggling with the basics, such as how to increase circulation in new social media spaces or reach desired populations. In one example, a communications director of a major Congressional campaign found himself confused and frustrated upon seeing that he could not target direct messages to citizens because he incorrectly assumed that the affordances of Facebook advertisements could be used for public posts and messages as well (Fieldnotes, September 1, 2010). As a result of this inability to target messages, he questioned the usefulness of the entire platform. Another Chicago-area campaign that was in an extremely tight race described being so concerned with gaining Facebook friends that a member of the communications/digital team purchased additional friends. This strategy held many problems, not least of all that it failed to reach actual voters, and staffers had to subsequently spend additional hours manually deleting the campaign's Facebook page of fake friends (personal communication, March 27, 2011). Here, social media benchmarks that seemed important to campaigns directly impeded other strategic goals.

Even in 2010, those in federal races were using targeted email lists, and occasionally deployed an A/B test for special occasions or initial website development. In one case, a campaign tested three options to determine the content of a splash page that preceded the campaign website during the final two weeks of the campaign, but that was their only A/B test of the final month of the campaign (Fieldnotes, October 18, 2010). Generally, communications directors for Senate and Congressional campaigns were well versed in targeting email lists, but only those at the Senate level were testing those messages in order to determine what type of subject header, content, and images were best at gaining attention or mobilizing constituencies (Baldwin-Philippi, 2016).

Much has happened since 2010 – analytics are increasingly automated, or 'baked in,' and displayed to the messages' creators with clarity, simplicity, and aesthetic appeal. Without much effort, staffers can use email management systems to catalog what audiences do with the messages, collecting data on whether an email was opened, if it was shared in other social media spaces, and/or what links were clicked. Likewise, domain hosts and free analytics provide basic web traffic data for campaign websites that also tells campaigns where visitors are located, and what linked them to the site. Campaigns gravitate toward these tools, even if they are not always deployed in statistically rigorous ways, largely because they are easy to access and interpret. Because time is always of the essence in a campaign, data that update immediately and can be quickly interpreted are of great benefit. One communication consultant explained how baked-in analytics are the most practical in the time crunch of a campaign, saying, 'I don't have to take time to set something up before posting a message […] I can look at the numbers when I have the time, and still use that [finding] the next time we need to post a message' (personal communication, December 3, 2014). Others echoed the benefit of their immediate presence and the obvious usefulness, with one noting 'They're right there! You can just take a quick look and see what type of messages perform well' (personal communication, December 18, 2014).

Notably, these analytics focus on popularity, highlighting the amount of impressions content makes, how many times it is liked or favorited, and how often it is shared about other metrics. Visually, the native analytics of Facebook overwhelmingly emphasize these very measures. In each of these, the number of likes, the reach (total impressions), and 'engagement' (a combination of likes, comments, shares, and how many times links are clicked) are provided. These engagement analytics begin to provide insight that is deeper than popularity of topics or issues, but also require more advanced strategies in combination with other forms of analytics to understand if other actions, such as donating or signing up for a newsletter, are taken. Facebook highlights notifications specifically for likes and shares and bar graphs that visually represent the amount of people reached. While it also measures additional actions such as engagement, or if audiences click on links provided, the system itself cannot track analytics of more action-oriented behavior, such as which users donate once a link is clicked, or how long they stay on that page. Twitter, on the other hand, provides people with an overview that is more concerned with how the campaign as a whole is doing, highlighting how well tweets are doing over multiple weeks, rather than only focusing on particular messages. Although retweets and favoriting mirror the drive for popularity seen in Facebook's analytics, Twitter's engagement metric is a sum of all replies, retweets, and mentions, and speaks more to how much a campaign is being discussed by the public of users than merely what type of content is popular. While Twitter provides data on a user's audience through a 'followers' section of their analytics, that information is a click deeper than analytics displaying an account and individual tweet's impressions, retweets, favorites, or an account's mentions.

Just as the material constraints of privately-owned platforms impacted campaigns' ability to control and sensor public commentary, they also constrain campaigns' ability to work with analytics. The data that platforms like Facebook and Twitter automatically provide to users – especially the data that they choose to visually represent and make the most easily interpretable – will be the data that campaigns turn to, and that therefore drives content creation. Popular social media analytics packages such as SproutSocial, CrowdTangle, Attentive.ly, and so on, provide more complex metrics of 'engagement' than those baked into social media platforms themselves, like Facebook Insights. In these third-party tools, algorithms rank combinations of measures such as likes, shares, attention, users' networks, and so on, and sometimes compare them with other similar pages. These uses of analytics are certainly an important beginning step into testing messages and engaging analytics more rigorously, but their limited use results in attention to the type of content that encourage campaigns to focus on messages that are popular, rather than mobilizing.

IMPLICATIONS AND CONCLUSION

Campaigns' use of social media was solidified in the wake of the 2008 Obama campaign, and this use has continued to increase in the international context. Currently, the parliamentary context breeds widespread use of social media by party accounts, approaching that of candidates in the US case, and individual politicians' are increasingly turning toward social media campaigning. Although most campaigns' and parties' use of social media involves the unidirectional broadcasting of messages, there is also a substantial minority of campaign strategy designed specifically around using social media to mobilize individuals to take both online and offline action. Beyond the traditional mobilization-oriented campaign goals of increasing voter turnout, fundraising, attendance at campaign events, a new goal of getting supporters to participate in online discussions and deliberations has also emerged. Overall, early research gives reason to be hopeful that engagement with campaigns on social media leads to further, deeper political action as well. However, social media do not provide unmitigated aid to campaigns; as this this chapter points out, there are often unintended consequences to adoption. This chapter points to three such instances of unintended consequences of social media adoption: (1) the rise of citizens who talk back and loss of campaign message control; (2) the decision to use privately-created platforms such as Twitter and Facebook, even when necessary, limits campaigns' ability to control messages and understand data; (3) the difficulties posed by the drive toward data and analytics and the default options that campaigns gravitate toward.

This assessment of unforeseen consequences serves as neither an optimistic nor pessimistic assessment of the future of campaign communication and digital democracy. Rather, it points to the possibility of both. Sometimes, as was the case with campaigns' unraveling ability to control public feedback, actions taken by staffers and changes in campaign technology lead to a rupture in the tight control campaigns have long wielded over citizens. What campaigns see as a loss of control is, to citizens, a space that is open and encourages them to voice their opinions, provide support (and dissent) for policies and candidates, and give feedback on political information. It is true that the content of this feedback may not reach the high standards of reasoned, rational, and consensus-oriented debate that are indicative of deliberative democracy. That said, deliberation is not the only democratic ideal that can be gained from speaking on political issues. The act of giving voice to political beliefs and stances via social media necessarily involves engaging others in your social network in political speech and information, and is itself participatory, and part of the ladder of engagement. Even as some campaign staffers have found such spaces dangerous and desired to reduce their availability, campaigns' decisions to engage with citizens via the popular social media platforms of Facebook and Twitter

have left them hamstrung. We can surely consider ways to improve the potential for voice-giving in these spaces, but the particular platforms of Facebook and Twitter have forced campaigns to deal with – and even encourage – citizens' voices in ways that are unparalleled.

Other campaign strategies offer less room for optimism. As campaigns routinely turn to social media platforms, they also embrace the analytics that the platforms provide in order to assess how successful the content they create has been, and anticipate what content will be successful in the future. Many of the ways campaigns use this data – especially at the level of local and state-wide campaigns – incentivize simplistic views of campaign goals that also motivate a turn toward superficial forms of democratic engagement. As these analytics highlight popularity – how many individuals a message reaches, how many likes, favorites, or shares it gets, the number of comments rather than their content, and so on – social media platforms motivate the production of content that will bring popularity, rather than alternative, more participatory options, such as mobilizing citizens or identifying new opinion leaders. While creating popular content could motivate supporters to deepen their commitment, the fact that these metrics do not highlight or provide clear, legible data on such effects limits campaigns' ability to see mobilization as a tangible outcome of social media messaging. Further, because popular content is not always that which is the most successful at persuading or mobilizing particular acts of political participation like donating, volunteering, or turning out at events, what counts as visible 'success' within the world of social media content may not be the most important to campaigns' immediate needs.

These unforeseen consequences are occurring as social media platforms play an increasingly widespread role in campaigns – popular standards like Facebook, Twitter, and YouTube are now near-ubiquitous. Campaigns experiment with emergent platforms such as

Snapchat and Periscope and even their own mobile applications; more time, money and staffers are devoted to the messages produced for and circulated within and across social media platforms. As these tools continue to be important sites of engagement for campaigns, inspection of their ability to affect the types of participation allowed and encouraged is necessary. This chapter is not meant to slow the adoption of social media campaigning – not only will campaigns continue to rush toward and even develop new tools that might give them the slightest edge, but I am generally hopeful for the democratic opportunities offered by the vast majority of such tools. Instead, this is a call for consideration of the strategic choices campaigns might be making in the moment and for deeper attention to the long-term consequences of technology adoption and strategy development. This is especially important as international campaigning may be driven to catch up with the US cases that currently drive most innovation, and as US campaigns continue to develop new tools that will be improved, adopted, and deployed in campaign cycles to come.

Notes

1 Many have written accounts of the history and evolution of these aspects of campaigning, which are due far more consideration than this chapter is able to give. For accounts of the emergence and changing practices around campaign websites, see Stromer-Galley (2014), Foot and Schneider (2006) and Vaccari (2013). For discussions of the emergence of campaign database technologies in the US, Philip Howard (2006) provides an overview of tools used across electoral and advocacy campaigns to better target members of the public and Daniel Kreiss (2012b) provides an account that charts the practice of infrastructure building within the Democratic Party. Colin Bennett (2015) has detailed emerging trends in voter surveillance and data collection in the European context.

2 Many more books have been written about the 2008 Obama campaign's social media strategy. For information on the various types of message created for various social platforms, see Harf-

oush (2009). For a discussion of data and analytics, see Issenberg (2012). For a study of the race that contextualizes the campaign's use of media within more traditional concerns of political communication such as candidate narratives and voter behavior, see Kenski, Hardy and Jamieson (2010).

REFERENCES

Aldrich, J. H., Gibson, R. K., Cantijoch, M., & Konitzer, T. (2016). Getting out the vote in the social media era: Are digital tools changing the extent, nature and impact of party contacting in elections? *Party Politics*, 22(2), 165–178.

Allison, J. (2009). 20/10: The decade in rewind. Internet memes: #3 Obama Girl. *Newsweek*, December 3, 2009. *Internet Archive https:// web.archive.org/web/20100110003943/ http://2010.newsweek.com/top-10/internet-memes/obama-girl.html.*

Baldwin-Philippi, J. (2015). *Using Technology, Building Democracy: Digital Campaigning and the Construction of Citizenship*. New York: Oxford University Press.

Baldwin-Philippi, J. (2016). The cult(ure) of analytics in 2014. In J. A. Hendricks & D. Schill (Eds.), *Communication and Midterm Elections: Media, Message, and Mobilization*. New York: Palgrave Macmillan.

Barberá, P. (2015). How social media reduces mass political polarization: Evidence from Germany, Spain, and the US. Paper presented at the American Political Science Association 2015 Annual Meeting, San Francisco, CA.

Bennett, C. J. (2015). Trends in voter surveillance in western societies: Privacy intrusions and democratic implications. *Surveillance & Society*, 13(3/4), 370–384.

Bennett, W. L. (2008). Changing citizenship in the digital age. In W. L. Bennett (Ed.), *Civic life online: Learning how digital media can engage youth*. Cambridge, MA: MIT Press.

Bennett, W. L., & Iyengar, S. (2008). A new era of minimal effects? The changing foundations of political communication. *Journal of Communication*, 58, 707–731.

Bimber, B., & Davis, R. (2003). *Campaigning online: The Internet in US elections*. New York: Oxford University Press.

Boczkowski, P., & Lievrouw, L. (2008). Bridging communication studies and science and technology studies: Scholarship on media and information technologies. In E. H. O. Amsterdamska (Ed.), *The Handbook of Science and Technology Studies* (Vol. 3, pp. 949–977). Cambridge, MA: MIT Press.

Bode, L., Lassen, D., Kim, Y. M., Shah, D., Fowler, E. F., Ridout, T. N., & Franz, M. (2011). Social and broadcast media in 2010 Midterms: The expanding repertoire of Senate candidates' campaign strategies. Paper presented at the American Political Science Association 2011 Annual Meeting, Seattle, WA.

Bruns, A., & Highfield, T. (2015). Social media in selected Australian federal and state election campaigns, 2010–15. Paper presented at the Internet Research 16: 16th Annual Meeting of the Association of Internet Researchers Conference (AOIR16), Phoenix, AZ.

Chadwick, A. (2009). Web 2.0: New challenges for the study of e-democracy in an era of informational exuberance. *I/S: Journal of Law and Policy for the Information Society*, 5, 9–41.

Chadwick, A. (2013). *The hybrid media system: Politics and power*. New York: Oxford University Press.

Conover, M. D., Gonçalves, B., Flammini, A., & Menczer, F. (2012). Partisan asymmetries in online political activity. *EPJ Data Science*, 1(1), 1.

Dimitrova, D. V., & Bystrom, D. (2013). The effects of social media on political participation and candidate image evaluations in the 2012 Iowa Caucuses. *American Behavioral Scientist*, 57(11), 1568–1583.

Dutta, S., & Fraser, M. (2008). Barack Obama and the Facebook election. *US News & World Report*, November 19. Retrieved from: www.usnews.com/opinion/articles/2008/11/19/barack-obama-and-the-facebook-election

Foot, K., & Schneider, S. (2006). *Web campaigning*. Cambridge, MA: MIT Press.

Gainous, J., & Wagner, K. (2013). *Tweeting to power: The social media revolution in American politics*. New York: Oxford University Press.

Gerodimos, R., & Justinussen, J. (2015). Obama's 2012 Facebook campaign: Political communication in the age of the like button. *Journal of Information Technology & Politics*, 12(2), 113–132.

Gillespie, T. (2014). The relevance of algorithms. In *Media Technologies: Essays on Communication, Materiality, and Society*. Cambridge, MA: MIT Press.

Graef, E. (n.d.). Binders full of election memes: Participatory culture invades the 2012 US election. Retrieved from: http://civicmediaproject.org/works/civic-media-project/binders-full-of-election-memes-participatory-culture-invades-the-2012-us-election

Graham, T., Broersma, M., Hazelhoff, K., & van 't Haar, G. (2013). Between broadcasting political messages and interacting with voters. *Information, Communication and Society*, 16(5), 692–716.

Gulati, G., & Williams, C. B. (2015). Congressional campaigns' motivations for social media adoption. In V. A. Farrar-Myers & J. S. Vaughn (Eds.), *Controlling the Message: New Media in American Political Campaigns*. New York: New York University Press.

Harfoush, R. (2009). *Yes We Did! An Inside Look at How Social Media Built the Obama Brand*. New York: New Riders Press.

Hemphill, L., Otterbacher, J., & Shapiro, M. (2013). What's congress doing on Twitter? In *Proceedings of the 2013 Conference on Computer-supported Cooperative Work*. New York: ACM Press.

Hermans, L., & Vergeer, M. (2013). Personalization in e-campaigning: A cross-national comparison of personalization strategies used on candidate websites of 17 countries in EP elections 2009. *New Media & Society*, 15(1), 72–92.

Hinz, K. (2014). Campaigning on Facebook and Twitter: Information provision of candidates in the social web during Germany's federal election campaign 2013. Paper presented at the ECPR Graduate Student Conference, Innsbruck, Austria.

Howard, P. (2006). *New Media and the Managed Citizen*. New York: Cambridge University Press.

Issenberg, S. (2012). *The Victory Lab: The Secret Science of Winning Campaigns*. New York: Crown Books.

Issenberg, S. (2016). The meticulously engineered grassroots network behind the Bernie

Sanders revolution. *Bloomberg Politics*, February 24. Retrieved from: www.bloomberg. com/politics/features/2016-02-24/behind-bernie-sanders-revolution-lies-a-meticulously-engineered-grassroots-network

Jungherr, A. (2016). Twitter use in election campaigns: A systematic literature review. *Journal of Information Technology & Politics*, *13*(1), 72–91.

Karpf, D. (2012). *The Moveon Effect*. Princeton, NJ: Princeton University Press.

Karpf, D., Kreiss, D., Nielsen, R. K., & Powers, M. (2015). Qualitative political communication| introduction ~ The role of qualitative methods in political communication research: Past, present, and future. *International Journal of Communication*, *9*(0), 19.

Katz, E., & Lazarsfeld, P. (1955). *Personal Influence*. Glencoe, IL: Free Press.

Kenski, K., Hardy, B., & Jamieson, K. H. (2010). *The Obama Victory: How Media, Money, and Message Shaped the 2008 Election*. New York: Oxford University Press.

Kreiss, D. (2012a). Acting in the public sphere: The 2008 Obama campaign's strategic use of new media to shape narratives of hte presidential race. *Media, Movements, and Political Change: Research in Social Movements, Conflicts and Change*, *33*, 195–223.

Kreiss, D. (2012b). *Taking Our Country Back: The Crafting of Networked Politics from Howard Dean to Barack Obama*. New York: Oxford University Press.

Kriesi, H. (2012). Personalization of national election campaigns. *Party Politics*, *18*(6), 825–844.

Larsson, A. O. (2015). Pandering, protesting, engaging: Norwegian party leaders on Facebook during the 2013 'Short campaign'. *Information, Communication & Society*, *18*(4), 459–473.

Latour, B. (2005). *Reassembling the Social: An Introduction to Actor-Network-Theory*. New York: Oxford University Press.

Lilleker, D. G., Tenscher, J., & Štětka, V. (2015). Towards hypermedia campaigning? Perceptions of new media's importance for campaigning by party strategists in comparative perspective. *Information, Communication & Society*, *18*(7), 747–765.

Lutz, M. (2009). *The Social Pulpit: Barack Obama's Social Media Toolkid*. Chicago, IL: Edelman.

Madrigal, A. (2013). When the nerds go marching in. *The Atlantic*, November 16.

Malhotra, N., Michelson, M. R., Rogers, T., & Valenzuela, A. A. (2011). Text messages as mobilization tools: The conditional effect of habitual voting and election salience. *American Politics Research*, *39*(4), 664–681.

Marcinkowski, F., & Metag, J. (2014). Why do candidates use online media in constituency campaigning? An application of the theory of planned behavior. *Journal of Information Technology & Politics*, *11*(2), 151–168.

McKelvey, F., & Piebiak, J. (2014). Porting the good campaign. Paper presented at the 2014 International Communication Association Annual Conference, Seattle, WA.

Nielsen, R. K. (2012). *Ground Wars: Personalized Communication in Political Campaigns*. Princeton, NJ: Princeton University Press.

Nielsen, R. K., & Vaccari, C. (2013). Do people 'like' politicians on Facebook? Not really. Large-scale direct candidate-to-voter online communication as an outlier phenomenon. *International Journal of Communication*, *7*(0), 24.

O'Reilly, T. (2005). What is Web 2.0. *O'Reilly Media*. Retrieved from: www.oreilly.com/pub/a/web2/archive/what-is-web-20.html

Otterbacher, J., Shapiro, M., & Hemphill, L. (2013). Interacting or just acting? A case study of European, Korean, and American politicians' interactions with the public on Twitter. *Journal of Contemporary Eastern Asia*, *12*(1), 5–20.

Prior, M., & Stroud, N. J. (2015). Using mobilization, media, and motivation to curb political polarization. In N. Persily (Ed.), *Solutions to Political Polarization in America*. New York: Cambridge University Press.

Sabato, L. (2009). *The Year of Obama: How Barack Obama Won the White House*. New York: Longman.

Scola, N. (2016). Inside Bernie Sanders' vast virtual ground game. *Politico*. Retrieved from: www.politico.com/story/2016/04/bernie-sanders-virtual-ground-game-221748

Sifry, M. (2007). The battle to control Obama's MySpace. Retrieved from: http://techpresident.com/blog-entry/battle-control-obamas-myspace

Stromer-Galley, J. (2014). *Presidential Campaigning in the Internet Age*. New York: Oxford University Press.

Trippi, J. (2008). *The Revolution will not be Televised: Democracy, the Internet, and the Overthrow of Everything.* New York: Harper.

Vaccari, C. (2013). *Digital Politics in Western Democracies: A Comparative Study.* Baltimore, MA: Johns Hopkins University Press.

Vaccari, C., & Nielsen, R. K. (2013). What drives politicians' online popularity? An analysis of the 2010 US Midterm elections. *Journal of Information Technology & Politics*, *10*(2), 208–222.

Vaccari, C., Valeriani, A., Barberá, P., Bonneau, R., Jost, J. T., Nagler, J., & Tucker, J. A. (2015). Political expression and action on social media: Exploring the relationship between lower- and higher-threshold political activities among Twitter users in Italy. *Journal of Computer-Mediated Communication*, *20*(2), 221–239.

Vergeer, M., & Hermans, L. (2013). Campaigning on Twitter: Microblogging and online social networking as campaign tools in the 2010 general elections in the Netherlands. *Journal of Computer-Mediated Communication*, *18*(4), 399–419.

Wells, C. (2015). *The Civic Organization and the Digital Citizen.* New York: Oxford University Press.

Williams, C., & Gulati, G. (2011). Social media in the 2010 Congressional elections. Paper presented at the Annual Meeting of the European Consortium for Political Research, Reykjavik, Iceland.

Xenos, M. A., Macafee, T., & Pole, A. (2017). Understanding variations in user response to social media campaigns: A study of Facebook posts in the 2010 US elections. *New Media & Society*, *19*(6), 826–842.

30

Social Media and New Protest Movements

Thomas Poell and José van Dijck

From the Arab Spring to the Occupy movement and the Gezi Park protests, major contemporary protest movements have been accompanied by intense social media activity. Millions of social media users have become involved in the rapid and widespread production and circulation of activist materials, including everything from protest hashtags, second-hand rumours and photoshopped images, to first-hand eyewitness reports and video evidence. In January and February 2011, the opposition against the dictatorial regimes in Tunisia and Egypt especially used Facebook and text messaging to share reports on the events in the streets, while Twitter played a vital role in the transnational communication on these revolutions (Bruns et al., 2013; Lim, 2012; Lotan et al., 2011; Tufekci & Wilson, 2012). Inspired by the Arab Spring, large protests subsequently erupted in Spain, the US, and Italy during the summer and fall of 2011. Again major social media platforms were used for mobilization and communication purposes (Castells, 2012;

Gerbaudo, 2012). And in following years, similar spikes in social media activity could be observed during protests in Turkey, Hong Kong, Brazil, and other countries (Göle, 2013; Kuymulu, 2013; Lee & Chan, 2016; Saad-Filho, 2013).

This chapter discusses how the intensive use of social media transforms the organization and communication of protest. The starting point of this discussion is the idea that traditional modes of organization in social movements (with structural features like identifiable leaders and persistent collective identities) have been largely replaced by more distributed and emergent mass user activity enabled by social media platforms (Bennett & Segerberg, 2013; Castells, 2012; Margetts et al., 2016). We will show how this argument has been questioned and complicated from two angles. First, through detailed studies on social media protest practices, researchers have demonstrated that leadership and collective identities continue to play a vital role in online contention. Second, based on the exploration of the techno-commercial architecture of social media, it has been argued that these platforms not only enable activist social media activity, but also fundamentally shape it.

Reviewing these arguments, we will combine insights from different fields of research. We not only build on social movement studies, but also on work in political communication, platform and software studies, and political economy. Furthermore, we profit from a wide range of available case studies on protest and social media, which have been published over the past years. These studies trace in detail how social media protest practices have taken shape in different parts of the world. In turn, this allowed us to develop a nuanced understanding of how social media platforms become involved in protest. Finally, we build on our own research, especially using material from case studies on social media communication during the 2011 Egyptian and Tunisian uprisings, which many scholars consider as the start of the current wave of popular protests (Poell et al., 2016; Poell & Darmoni, 2012). We also draw from an earlier inquiry into the techno-commercial shaping of social media protest activity (Poell & van Dijck, 2015).

A NEW MODE OF PROTEST

Reflecting on recent protests and uprisings, various scholars, most prominently Castells (2012), Bennett and Segerberg (2012, 2013), and Margetts et al. (2016), have proposed that social media user activity is at the heart of a fundamental transformation of activism. These theorists see social media platforms enabling more bottom-up, distributed forms of protest mobilization, organization, and communication. It is important to emphasize that none of these authors considers social media activity in isolation or gives this activity primacy over 'offline' protest practices. In fact, as much current research shows, the

distinction between the 'online' and 'offline' can no longer be made. Since many protestors carry smartphones and have continuous access to online platforms to share their content and observations, protest simultaneously unfolds on the ground *and* online. Thus, the key question is not whether the activity on social media is more important than street protests, or whether the rise of these media is somehow the 'cause' of popular uprisings, as was suggested by some of the press reports on the 2011 Arab Spring protests. Instead, the question is how the widespread use of social media platforms affects the organization and communication of contemporary protest (Shea et al., 2015).

Responding to this question, Castells argues in *Networks of Outrage and Hope* (2012: 232) that today's protest movements should be seen in the context of a 'culture of sharing', enabled by social networking sites and the internet more generally. In this culture, people construct horizontal networks that simultaneously take shape locally on streets and squares and globally on social media platforms. For Castells, these networks transform the dynamic of activism, as they support 'cooperation and solidarity while undermining the need for formal leadership' (2012: 225). Crucially, they 'create togetherness', which allows people to 'overcome fear and discover hope'. This togetherness does not, however, constitute community, because 'community implies a set of common values', whereas 'most people come to the movement with their own motivations and goals' (ibid.). Thus, following Castells, new social movements revolve around both solidarity and individuality.

Lance Bennett and Alexandra Segerberg (2012, 2013) have articulated the most developed theory of how social media sharing practices transform the dynamic of activism. They maintain that new protest movements are driven by 'the self-motivated (though not necessarily self-centered) sharing of already internalized or personalized ideas, plans, images, and resources with networks of others' (2012: 753). Sharing activist content becomes self-motivated because it is a form of 'personal expression' and 'self-validation' (2012: 752–753). The mass sharing of 'personal action frames' facilitates, according to Bennett and Segerberg, a new type of action, which they label 'connective action' (2012: 744). From this point of view, the communication process itself provides key organizational resources, allowing large crowds to act together with little need for prominent leaders, formal social movement organizations, and collective action frames, which require individuals to share common identities and political claims (2012: 747).

The latest major contribution to the argument that social media enable bottom-up, distributed forms of mass protest has been made by Margetts et al. (2016). On the basis of large-scale data analysis of contemporary protest events, they come to the conclusion that 'social media extend the range of political activities that citizen can undertake, lowering the cost to an extent whereby people are offered the opportunity to make micro-donations of time and effort to political causes' (2016: 196–197). As such, social media platforms provide what the authors call 'zero-touch coordination' for micro-donations, altering the costs and benefits of political actions (2016: 199). While micro-donations might seem insignificant, Margetts and colleagues emphasize that they are politically of great importance, as they can and occasionally do scale up to mass mobilizations. The authors label this new mode of popular contention 'chaotic pluralism', which constitutes an individualization of collective action, and 'injects turbulence into every area of politics, acting as an unruly, unpredictable influence on political life' (2016: 200).

These theories on how social media enable distributed forms of protest mobilization, organization, and communication have had a lot of impact on current scholarship. Many case studies on particular protests build on them, citing similar observations (see, for example, Anduiza et al., 2014; Caraway, 2016;

Dessewffy & Nagy, 2016; Lim, 2013; Wright, 2015). At the same time, as discussed in the following sections, a growing number of studies question some of the key assumptions underpinning these theories. By staging a debate between the different interpretations of the role of social media platforms in contemporary protest, we gain a more precise understanding of both the intricacies of social media protest practices and the techno-commercial infrastructures through which such practices are articulated. We will start by looking at the question of leadership and collective identity.

LEADERSHIP AND COLLECTIVITY

Whereas the theorists discussed above examine how social media platforms enable mass self-organization and self-communication by individuals, various other scholars observe the emergence of new forms of hierarchy and leadership. Research on transnational social media communication during the Tunisian and Egyptian uprisings, for example, shows that prominent users, mostly activists, bloggers, and journalists, deployed carefully planned tactics. These tactics included promoting particular hashtags and accounts, and collecting protest information from Facebook and on-the-ground social networks; it also involved translating, distributing, and curating this information on Twitter, YouTube, and various independent blogs. In these translation and distribution efforts, core users strategically employed different languages, most prominently Arabic, English, and French, to address publics ranging from Arab youth to international news media (Della Ratta & Valeriani, 2014; Lotan et al., 2011; Papacharissi, 2015; Poell & Darmoni, 2012).

Such protest tactics were not just used on social media platforms, but also on the streets. Research on the build-up to the Egyptian uprising demonstrates how leading activists from different protest networks, loosely organized through social media platforms, distributed tens of thousands of flyers, circulated calls for mobilization in public transport, and organized feeder marches in the working-class neighborhoods of Cairo (Gerbaudo, 2012; Lim, 2012). Crucially, most of these mobilization tactics were not invented on the spot, but developed in the years before the uprising in transnational activist networks, facilitated by international NGOs (Aneja, 2011; Kirkpatrick et al., 2011; Tufekci & Wilson, 2012).

These examples suggest that, even though formal social movement organizations were mostly absent in the mobilization of the Arab Spring uprisings, strategizing and leadership were still essential to protest organization and communication. Small groups of activists, centrally positioned in social media-facilitated networks, fulfilled many of the functions traditionally associated with social movement leaders, that is: strategically framing protest activity and connecting previously separate individuals and groups in common action. Furthermore, these actors were essential in so-called information politics: translating, diffusing, and curating protest information (Della Ratta & Valeriani, 2014; Poell et al., 2016; Tremayne, 2014; Tufekci, 2013). Reflecting on these practices, Della Ratta and Valeriani (2014) have labeled these top social media users as 'connective leaders': leaders who are focused on connecting people and information.

Although such connective leaders fulfill many functions traditionally associated with social movement leaders, theirs is a fundamentally different type of leadership. Some of the key characteristics of connective leadership in a social media environment can be identified by examining the interactions between administrators and users of the Egyptian 'Kullena Khaled Said' (We are all Khaled Said) Facebook page. This page was created in June 2010 by Wael Ghonim, the Dubai-based head of marketing for Google Middle East and North Africa. He developed

the page, in close collaboration with journalist and activist AbdelRahman Mansour, to protest the murder of Khaled Said, a young middle-class Egyptian man from Alexandria who was beaten to death by Egyptian security forces (Ghonim, 2012). The page received 250,000 likes during its first three months and rapidly developed into a stage where users shared grievances about the Mubarak regime (Lesch, 2011; Lim, 2012). Having initiated and guided this process of online contention, Ghonim and Mansour can be considered prominent examples of connective leaders (for the full discussion, see Poell et al., 2016).

Examining the activities of the two administrators in detail, it is striking how hard they tried to remain anonymous and not be labeled as activist leaders. This corresponds with a more general trend in contemporary activism. In contrast to social movement leaders of previous decades, some of which figured prominently in the mass media, most leading actors in social media protest communication do not want to be publicly recognized as leaders (Coleman, 2014). With varying measures of success, such actors have tried to remain out of the limelight. They do so partly for security reasons – certainly a major concern of Ghonim and Mansour – but also to maintain the image of a spontaneous people's movement. By presenting their movements as bottom-up, contemporary protestors seek to transcend traditional political alignments. Making protest leaders publicly visible would undermine this narrative. This even applies to leading social media users in transnational protest communication, some of whom have developed into so-called microcelebrities. As Tufekci (2013: 868) points out, 'the networked microcelebrity activist' remains an integral part of protest movements. As she writes, 'Without necessarily an institutional role or a claim to legitimacy through established, institutionalized means, the activist's position within the movement remains that of a peer whose political acts are visible and can be challenged from within the movement' (ibid.). This is in clear contrast to social movement leaders of the past who became mass media celebrities, such as the leaders of the Civil Rights Movement or the anti-war movement in the US (Gitlin, 1980).

Furthermore, the analysis of Kullena Khaled Said suggests that connective leadership revolves around inviting, connecting, steering, and stimulating, rather than directing, commanding, and proclaiming. Instead of recruiting members willing to 'follow', as social movements have historically sought to do, Ghonim and Mansour explicitly cultivated the page to be 'participatory'. The admins actively invited user contributions, which informed further initiatives and activities developed through the page. A prime example of this was a call to users to photograph themselves holding up the 'Kullena Khaled Said' sign, a tactic which was, a year later, replicated on a much larger scale during the Occupy protests with the 'We are the 99%' slogan (Gerbaudo, 2015; Milan, 2015a). Moreover, Ghonim and Mansour regularly held polls to determine what further activities the users were interested in developing through the page. More generally, the admins systematically read user comments to be able to adequately respond to user feedback. Thus, active user engagement, as enabled by social media, does not contradict the exercise of leadership, or make leadership obsolete. Instead, triggering, shaping, and incorporating user contributions are part and parcel of how this type of leadership is exercised.

Although connective leaders facilitate and steer the participation of social media users in protest communication and mobilization, this type of leadership is certainly not without its problems. First, connective leaders command little, if any, loyalty because they do not and cannot publicly identify themselves as leaders. And given the completely open character of social media communication, their activities can also be easily monitored and undermined by authorities. This became very clear on the Khaled

Said page when supporters of the Mubarak regime effectively hijacked the communication on the page from the moment the mass protests started on January 25, 2011. With newly created Facebook accounts, these supporters began spreading false rumors and accusing the administrators of being foreign agents, secretly working for Israel. Second, as Gerbaudo (2017) has demonstrated, the contradiction between leadership in social media protest communication and the ideology of horizontality and leaderlessness that characterizes new protest movements often leads to conflicts among connective leaders. Examining the small teams that managed the Twitter, Facebook, Tumblr, and Livestream accounts of Occupy Wall Street in the US, the Spanish Indignados, and the UK Uncut movements, he observes that 'disputes about the management of activist power accounts have seen competing factions fighting to secure control over these assets, with activists engaging in the banning of rivals, and in mutual accusations of "hi-jacking" collective resources' (Gerbaudo, 2017: 11). He maintains that such conflicts, which occur in virtually every major contemporary protest movement, significantly undermine these movements and hasten their decline.

These tensions point towards a fundamental dilemma facing the leadership of today's social movements. As Melluci (1996) already pointed out 20 years ago, to ensure the survival of social movements particular tasks, which require some form of leadership, have to be fulfilled. At the same time, in the current cultural setting of individualization and rejection of hierarchy, it is impossible to make leadership explicit, as this would lead to the breakdown of the 'interpersonal relations' and 'solidarity' on which movements are built (1996: 345). According to Melucci, movements try to resolve this dilemma by minimizing and concealing decision-making and representative functions (ibid.). This strategy can clearly be observed in the attempts by connective leaders in social media protest communication to remain anonymous, or at least refrain from identifying themselves as leaders. Accordingly, today's movements present themselves as the 'people', as 'we' the '99%'. Evidently, these strategies don't permanently revolve the dilemma, as leadership functions continue to be exercised, even in highly distributed forms of social media protest communication. Any time these functions become explicit, conflicts are likely to occur.

While this analysis of the articulation of leadership doesn't invalidate arguments about connective action, micro-donations, and a culture of sharing, it does complicate these ideas. The challenge for researchers studying contemporary protest communication, mobilization, and coordination is not just to explore how these processes take shape through distributed user practices, but also to trace how these practices are steered through new forms of leadership. Examining these relationships, it is important to see that activist leadership and social media protest activity are not necessarily contradictory, but can be mutually reinforcing.

Collectivity

The second major question is whether collectivity still plays a key role in today's protest movements. Castells (2012) suggests that most people join social movements with their own motivations and goals. And Bennett and Segerberg (2012) argue that connective action does not revolve around 'collective action frames', which require negotiating common interpretations of collective identities. Instead, connective action is driven by the rapid sharing of personal action frames through social media platforms. Various other researchers have, however, begun to question this interpretation, arguing that a 'collective sense of self' does emerge in the mass sharing of protest slogans and materials on social media platforms. This collective sense of self can be understood as a manifestation of collective identity (Bakardjieva, 2015; Coretti & Pica,

2015; Gerbaudo, 2015; Kavada, 2015, 2016; Monterde et al., 2015).

Recognizing that social media protest communication has a vital 'affective' or 'emotional' dimension is an important step towards identifying collectivity. Mass protest, as Juris (2008: 63) emphasizes, produces through its 'highly unpredictable and confrontational nature … powerful affective ties'. Such ties are especially crucial 'within fluid, network-based movements that rely on non-traditional modes of identification and commitment' (ibid.). In the absence of social movement organizations to provide stability, it becomes difficult, as Juris (2008) makes clear, to sustain a mobilization process without strong affective ties. This suggests that the 'personal action frames' highlighted by Bennett and Segerberg (2012) are not sufficient to bring together large protesting masses.

Studying protest mobilization on social media platforms, various scholars have indeed observed instances in which powerful affective appeals were made to larger collectives. For example, in their exploration of Twitter communication during the 2011 Egyptian uprising, Papacharissi and de Fatima Oliveira (2012: 275) detected 'overwhelming expressions of solidarity' in the stream of news reports. In fact, it 'became difficult to separate factual reports from expressions of camaraderie' (ibid.). Gerbaudo (2016: 256), in turn, makes similar observations in his analysis of the interaction on large Facebook pages central to the 2011 Egyptian and Spanish protest movements. In the mass interaction on these pages, he noticed 'moments of digital enthusiasm', 'in which the emotions of thousands of Web users fuse into a collective sense of possibility'. Acting as connective leaders, the administrators of these pages played a key role in boosting enthusiasm by producing 'hopeful narratives', which set in motion processes of 'emotional contagion' as users reinforced these narratives (Gerbaudo, 2016: 254).

Having established the presence and importance of emotions and affective relations in contemporary protest communication, the question, subsequently, becomes whether moments of emotional connectivity can be understood in terms of 'collective identity'. In their introduction to a special issue on social media and protest identities, Gerbaudo and Treré (2015: 867) strongly argue in favor of such an assessment. They maintain that the mass adoption of hashtag #wearethe99percent in the Occupy protest, the transformation of the 'lady in red dress' picture into a protest symbol during the Gezi Park protests, and other similar protest sharing practices are effectively 'manifestations of collective identity'. Correspondingly, Milan (2015a: 894) argues that as such practices take shape on social media, they produce 'collective narratives' that score high in terms of 'bridging' personal viewpoints and experiences and 'building' and 'reproducing' 'communication-based social capital'.

However, scholars observing such instances of collectivity emphasize that these relations are by no means stable. A collective 'we' can suddenly emerge, but just as quickly disappear. Juris (2012: 266) calls this the 'logic of aggregation', in which a mass of individuals quickly comes together, but can fall apart at any moment. When today's protestors interact with each other through social media platforms, they often forge 'a collective subjectivity'. Yet, as Juris points out, this 'is a subjectivity that is under the constant pressure of disaggregation into its individual components' (ibid.). Consequently, he emphasizes the importance of offline interaction and community building on the ground for those interested in building more sustainable collectives.

This brings us to the second angle from which we need to complicate the idea that contemporary protest movements are propelled and shaped by self-motivated social media sharing practices. We will show that the techno-commercial architecture of platforms fundamentally steers how users connect and interact with each other, and, consequently, how social media protest organization and

communication unfolds. While many scholars working on contemporary protest movements devote some attention to the particular technological features of platforms, such as hashtags, like buttons, and algorithms, this area of research remains underexplored. There is little research that systematically examines how social media user practices, technologies, and business models mutually articulate each other, or that explores the consequences for the character and dynamic of today's protest movements.

TECHNO-COMMERCIAL STRATEGIES

Reflecting on how social media steer popular contention, it is vital to observe that these platforms are not primarily developed and managed to facilitate protest. Reading the celebratory accounts in the press and some of the academic literature on the vital role of social media platforms in protest mobilization and communication, it is easy to forget that platforms are, above all, developed to facilitate the systemic collection and analysis of user data to enable various forms of targeted advertising and services (Couldry, 2015; Fuchs, 2011; van Dijck, 2013). There is a constant tension between these techno-commercial platform strategies and activist tactics and values.

To explore this tension, we need to turn to what Gillespie calls 'governance by platforms' (see Chapter 14, this volume), which refers to the ways platforms curate the content and police the activity of their users. One crucial method through which social media corporations 'govern' is through their Terms of Service (ToS). Youmans and York (2012) provide one of the few studies that examines how such a form of governance can obstruct activist communication. Drawing from several case studies, the authors demonstrate that the policies and user agreements of social media platforms, including those of Facebook, YouTube, and Twitter, have resulted in the banning of activist users, the removal of activist content and accounts, and the handing over of sensitive activist user information to governments.

One crucial example of this are the attempts by leading social media corporations to prohibit the use of pseudonyms, also known as real-names policies, requiring users to identify themselves through their legal name. In the case of the above-discussed 'Kullena Khaled Said' Facebook page, this policy caused substantial problems. When Wael Ghonim created the page, he used the pseudonym 'ElShaheed' ('the martyr'). As we have discussed, Ghonim and his collaborators tried hard to remain anonymous. They did so both for security and to maintain the image of a spontaneous people's movement. However, as Facebook does not allow the use of pseudonyms, Ghonim's account and, more importantly, the page, which had become a highly popular oppositional platform, were suddenly deactivated in November 2010 (Youmans & York, 2012: 318–319). Although the page was relatively quickly restored, this incident reveals a fundamental tension. For many activists it is important to remain anonymous, whereas social media platform owners – generally American corporations – have a strong interest in knowing users' real identities, which can be monetized more easily.

Friction is also generated by attempts to police the content and activity on social media platforms in accordance with particular 'community standards'. Virtually all platforms impose rules to regulate offending content and behavior, most prominently pornography, graphic violence, hate speech, and trolling. Again there is an obvious economic interest to do so, as such content and behavior might discourage some groups of users and, more problematically, deter advertisers, who do not want their products associated with potentially offensive content. Platforms rely on a combination of automated detection of problematic content and on users flagging and blocking such content (Crawford &

Gillespie, 2016). These policing efforts, while necessary to protect users and the economic viability of a platform, can undermine activist communication. Youmans and York (2012: 320–321) give the example of various popular activist YouTube videos from Syria and Egypt, which showed graphic violence by authorities and were removed from the platform for this reason. As in the case of the Khaled Said page, these videos were eventually restored after complaints by journalists and activists. These examples illustrate, on the one hand, how social media corporations put up serious efforts to accommodate activist interests. On the other hand, they also show that these corporations have a structural economic interest to systematically police the activity and content on their platforms in ways that do not always correspond with activists' politics of visibility (ibid.; Milan, 2015b).

Whereas various studies illustrate the tension between activism and content policing by platforms, more systematic research is needed to understand how frequent such cases are and how they affect protest mobilization and communication. Even more complex is the question how the particular technological architectures of platforms – their user and programming interfaces, as well as their algorithmic selection mechanisms – shape the character and dynamics of protest. In other words, how to 'weigh' the power of algorithms versus the power of users to steer online attention and relations? This is a complex question as it is impossible to precisely determine how algorithms enhance or decrease the visibility of specific protest issues and actors, nor is it possible to exactly pin down how different technologically enabled practices, such as hashtagging, retweeting, liking, following, and friending, promote particular types of connection and exchange between activists. At the same time, as work in platform and software studies shows, it is clear that the technological architectures of social media do fundamentally shape how users connect and interact with each other

(Berry, 2011; Gillespie, 2014; Langlois et al., 2009). Consequently, there is a strong need to critically explore social media protest activity as a particular set of socio-technical practices, even though such an exploration will to some extend remain speculative.

Acceleration

The first development we would like to highlight concerns the acceleration of activist communication propelled by social media. In combination with the ubiquitous availability of advanced mobile communication devices, social media platforms allow users on the move to exchange information in real time. As various researchers have observed, the Web is transforming from a relatively static environment primarily focused on information retrieval to a highly dynamic ecology of data streams, which constantly feed users with new information (Berry, 2011; Hermida, 2010; Weltevrede et al., 2014).

This transformation greatly speeds up the exchange of information between activists. On the one hand, acceleration can be interpreted as a form of empowerment. Social media platforms allow activists to document (almost in real time) unfolding protest events, and massively share their feelings about these events (Papacharissi & de Fatima Oliveira, 2012; Poell & Borra, 2012). Papacharissi and de Fatima Oliveira use the term 'instantaneity' to describe the instant online recording and communication of unfolding events, as well as the tone and urgency of the language individuals employ on social media platforms. Such real-time and ubiquitous forms of protest communication are of great strategic importance to activists. Social media protest communication not only shows the larger world the violence committed by authorities, but they also allow protestors to coordinate their activities. As Earl et al. (2013: 472) have pointed out in their research on the protests against the 2009 G20 summit in Pittsburgh, such use of social media has the potential 'to reduce information asymmetries between protesters and police'.

On the other hand, though, protesters' social media practices tend to focus attention on the violence and spectacle that accompanies many protests. Historically, alternative activist media have been considered especially important because these allowed activists to highlight the larger issues at stake in political contestation. In the early 2000s, NGO sites and alternative online news outlets, such as Indymedia, were celebrated precisely because they facilitated the long-term articulation and polarization of protest issues. By discussing such issues and linking alternative sites to each other as well as to corporate and governmental sites, activists constituted 'issue networks' (Bennett, 2004; Dean, 2002; Marres and Rogers, 2005). As Jodi Dean wrote in 2002, such networks make it possible to move away from the 'drive for spectacle and immediacy that plagues an audience oriented news cycle' as they 'work to maintain links among those specifically engaged with a matter of concern' (2002: 172–173). Evidently, the event-oriented focus and 'real-time' nature of social media protest communication runs the risk of shifting the perspective of online activist communication from the actual protest issues to the protest spectacle.

It is crucial to note that the event-oriented focus of social media communication is not merely the result of specific user practices, but is also prompted by the technological architectures underpinning social media platforms. Various social media sharing mechanisms, such as 'liking' and 'retweeting', are promoted by the platforms themselves, as well as by many mainstream and alternative news sites in the form of social buttons (Gerlitz & Helmond, 2013). Omnipresent sharing features encourage users to spread and repeat breaking news. Further adding to the newsy character of social media platforms are the 'hashtag' and 'trending topic' features, which are particularly prominent in the Twitter architecture, but have more recently also been taken up by Facebook. Hashtags instigate users to share and search for news on specific subjects, whereas trending topics further highlight breaking news. Most notably, Twitter has developed their trending feature into a sophisticated popular news barometer by identifying the 'most breaking news', and by allowing users to break down trending topics by region, country, and city.

Given how this event-oriented focus is fundamentally built into social media platforms' architectures, it will be very difficult to reverse or adjust the perspective of social media communication. This becomes especially difficult as activists increasingly build their communication and organization strategies around social platforms' sharing mechanisms and orient these strategies towards the platforms' specific mechanisms of algorithmic selection. Activists' practice of promoting particular hashtags, such as #g20report in the case of the G20 protests, #sidibouzid during the Tunisian revolution, and #25jan in the early stages of the Egyptian revolution, exemplifies this tendency. More generally, such strategies can be understood as symptomatic of a more general tendency among 'producers of information to make their content, and themselves', in the words of Gillespie (2014: 184), 'recognizable to an algorithm'.

Personalization and Virality

The second development we would like to reflect on is the 'personalization' of public communication, which many scholars have associated with the rise of social media (Bennett & Segerberg, 2011; Couldry & Turow, 2014; Kennedy & Moss, 2015; Lovink & Rasch, 2013; Pariser, 2011). As discussed, the question of how this development affects protest has triggered a lot of debate, with some researchers seeing contemporary protest as revolving around personal action frames, whereas others observe powerful moments of collectivity in social

media protest communication. Yet, these observations are primarily based on research that focuses on social media user practices. To advance this debate, it is important to also examine how personalization is shaped by the *techno-commercial architecture* of platforms.

From such a perspective, personalization involves social media platforms prompting users to explicitly make 'personal' connections and stimulating them to create their persona by constantly posting and sharing new content. Moreover, personalization uniquely depends on these platforms' propensity to algorithmically connect users to content, advertisers, and each other (van Dijck & Poell, 2013: 9). The development of the Facebook News Feed, YouTube's recommended videos, and Twitter's Top search results show how social media corporations are constantly trying to more precisely tailor content to users' specific interests. Algorithmic curation is, however, not only about serving each user with a personal diet of content, ads, and friend suggestions, but also about connecting users with content that is generating engagement in the larger networks in which they are situated. Research on the algorithmic selection mechanisms used by the main US-based social media platforms suggests that these mechanisms take both individual and collective user signals into account. As such, social media platforms *steer* users towards personalized connections, while at the same time introducing viral dynamics in public communication that *produce* moments of collectivity. Let's briefly look at each side of the equation in a bit more detail.

Major social media platforms such as Facebook, Twitter, and YouTube personalize the user experience on a number of levels. First, they push users to create and extend their personal networks by 'following' or 'friending' other users or accounts. They also enable users to create their own communication spaces, for example, through hashtags such as #egypt, #sidibouzid, or

#OccupyWallStreet, or in the form of Facebook groups and pages, like 'Kullena Khaled Said'. Finally, social media platforms algorithmically select for each user the content that is most likely to meet their interests, hence serving customized media diets. Thus, the techno-commercial flipside of personalization is customized services that steer users towards particular types of connections, content, and ads.

At the same time, social platforms are found to promote virality (Goel et al., 2015; Papacharissi, 2015; Sampson, 2012). They do so by providing users with omnipresent like, share, and retweet buttons to quickly and easily share content with other users. These user signals are subsequently processed through platform algorithms, which tend to privilege items that rapidly generate a lot of user engagement, in the form of trending topics and most relevant content. While processes of algorithmic selection do frequently highlight protest-related communication during large demonstrations, occupations, and uprisings (because of their newsworthiness), there is certainly no guarantee that they will do so. As the Occupy protestors found out, social media algorithms can conflict with what users themselves consider relevant. In the fall of 2011, at the height of the occupations, protestors noticed that despite their intense use of #OccupyWallStreet and #OccupyBoston, these hashtags trended almost anywhere in the US except for New York and Boston, whereas less popular Occupy-related terms and hashtags made it into the trending topic lists of the two cities. Suspicious Occupiers subsequently accused Twitter of manipulating its trending topics. However, as Gilad Lotan (2011) has demonstrated, no censoring appears to have taken place; it was the 'outcome of a purely algorithmic mechanism', pointing out that the consistent attention given to #OccupyWallStreet and #OccupyBoston in NYC and Boston did not result in attention spikes. As Lotan explains, trending topics are not simply determined on the basis of the volume of tweets containing a particular hashtag

or term. Instead, 'the algorithm adapts over time, based on the changing velocity of the usage of the given term in tweets. If we see a systematic rise in volume, but no clear spike, it is possible that the topic will never trend' (ibid.) Similar observations can be made concerning Facebook's News Feed algorithms (McGee, 2013).

In other words, social media promote viral communication over sustained long-term public attention for specific topics. Not coincidentally, this predilection towards virality corresponds with the business strategies of the major social platforms, which try to derive income from (third party) data services that detect, in real time, emerging topics of popular interest as well as shifts in public sentiment. Building on such real-time analytics, Twitter and especially Facebook are developing personalized systems of targeted advertising, which pick up on the specific interests of particular user aggregates (Cheney-Lippold, 2011; Turrow, 2012; Wilken, 2014).

In light of these techno-commercial mechanisms, which underpin the socio-cultural forms of personalization, it should come as no surprise that activist communication and mobilization processes based on social media have generated loosely connected protest networks, which just as quickly fall apart as they are stitched together. Personalization, real-timeness, and virality are part of social media's DNA. The technological architectures and business models of these media are geared towards the viral dissemination of affective messages through personal networks. For activists this is both a blessing and a curse. As social media penetrate deeply into everyday personal communication in ways alternative media have never been able to do, activists can reach people who would otherwise not be reached by activist communication. At the same time, the interactions and interests that tie dispersed social media users together to form protest movements, generating instant moments of togetherness, tend to dissolve when social platforms algorithmically connect users to the next wave of trending topics.

Alternative media are technologically and intellectually designed to sustain interest in particular social and political issues and to build communities and publics around such issues. By contast, on social media there is a constant tension between community building and commercial interests and strategies. Many of the major social media platforms, on the one hand, invest in the development of community features, Facebook groups and pages are a prime example of this. On the other hand, to sustain their structural commercial appetite for online engagement, these platforms also continuously introduce the next set of topics that satisfy user interests, whatever these interests might be. From this perspective, we suggest that while social media enable powerful moments of collectivity, communities and publics are destined to remain ephemeral in social media environment, always already on the point of giving way to the next set of trending topics and related sentiments.

CHALLENGES FOR FUTURE RESEARCH

The key challenge for future research on the evolving relationship between social media and the organization and communication of protest is to develop a comprehensive approach that is sensitive to the innovative ways in which users self-organize, create, and share new protest-related material, and how collectivity and leadership are articulated in such practices. At the same time, it is crucial to critically interrogate how these practices are steered by the techno-commercial strategies of corporations. So far, researchers have tended to either focus on specific sets of socio-cultural or techno-commercial practices and strategies. This has produced a lot of valuable insights, but has also limited our ability to understand the overall dynamic of contemporary protest. Without a thorough examination of creative activist social media

practices it is hard to understand the vitality and impact of platform-mediated protest. And vice versa: without a critical examination of the techno-commercial strategies of platforms we cannot fully understand why protest messages and activity can spread very quickly, but also suddenly disappear from the public limelight (for examples of research that tries to do both, see Galis & Neumayer, 2016; Milan, 2015b; Poell, 2014; Shea et al., 2015).

In a further complication for studying these interrelated practices, both platform and protest strategies are continuously evolving. As has been extensively documented, social media corporations constantly tinker with the algorithms they use to determine 'relevant' content. Substantial changes in, for example, Facebook's News Feed algorithm or Twitter's trending topics algorithm are usually publicly announced, but social platforms also make small changes on a daily basis. Furthermore, from time to time these platforms introduce new features, which transform how users can express themselves and connect with each other. Prominent examples of this were the launch of Facebook's News Feed, and the integration of retweeting and @mentioning in Twitter's architecture. And finally, new popular platforms regularly emerge, such as Snapchat and WeChat a few years ago, while other platforms, like Flickr or Friendster, become less popular or disappear altogether. All of these changes bring about shifts in how protests are mobilized and communicated. Exploring such evolving socio-technical relations, it is important to realize that platform affordances do not determine how users employ social technologies, but that they rather guide this use. How particular social media protest activities unfold is also very much shaped by the creativity and reflexivity of users. Connective activist leaders, as discussed in this chapter, have over the years developed a range of communication and mobilization strategies in using social platforms. These strategies – ranging from promoting particular hashtags to selecting particular platforms to pursue core objectives – are changing over time as well.

Thus, for researchers, the challenge is to trace how changing activist practices and evolving techno-commercial platform strategies mutually articulate each other. Such inquiry should allow for a more precise understanding of the current dynamic of protest organization and communication, but also how this dynamic has changed over time. Doing this type of inquiry is by no means easy, as researchers need to take the specific political-cultural settings of the protests they are studying into account as well. Evidently, it matters for activist social media use whether a protest is directed at an authoritarian state, as in the case of the Egyptian protests discussed in this chapter, or at a liberal democratic state. From the mid-2000s onwards, as the Berkman Center has documented in detail, states have made extensive efforts to control online communication (Deibert et al., 2010, 2012). These efforts deeply affect how activists connect with each other on social platforms. While the relations between states and new protest movements are beyond the scope of this chapter, case studies on particular protests will need to take these relations into account.

This brings us back to the call for interdisciplinarity with which we started this chapter. To understand how the character and dynamic of social media activity enables and shapes new protest movements, we need to combine insights from different fields of research. While social movement studies remains an important starting point for investigating protest, it is also crucial to draw from work in political communication, software and platform studies, as well as from political economy, surveillance, and censorship research. It is only through interdisciplinary research that we can comprehensively explore the complex political-cultural and socio-technical relations in which new protest movements take shape.

REFERENCES

Anduiza, E., Cristancho, C., & Sabucedo, J. M. (2014). Mobilization through online social networks: The political protest of the indignados in Spain. *Information, Communication & Society*, 17(6), 750–764.

Aneja, A. (2011). Protest movements in West Asia: Some impressions. *Strategic Analysis*, 35(4), 547–551.

Bakardjieva, M. (2015). Do clouds have politics? Collective actors in social media land. *Information, Communication & Society*, 18(8), 983–990.

Bennett, L. (2004). Communicating global activism: Strengths and vulnerabilities of networked politics. In W. van de Donk, B. Loader, P. Nixon, & D. Rucht (Eds.), *Cyberprotest: New media, citizens and social movements* (pp. 123–146). London: Routledge.

Bennett, W. L., & Segerberg, A. (2011). Digital media and the personalization of collective action: Social technology and the organization of protests against the global economic crisis. *Information, Communication & Society*, 14(6), 770–799.

Bennett, W. L., & Segerberg, A. (2012). The logic of connective action: Digital media and the personalization of contentious politics. *Information, Communication & Society*, 15(5), 739–768.

Bennett, W. L., & Segerberg, A. (2013). *The logic of connective action: Digital media and the personalization of contentious politics*. Cambridge: Cambridge University Press.

Berry, D. (2011). *The philosophy of software: Code and mediation in the digital age*. New York: Springer.

Bruns, A., Highfield, T., & Burgess, J. (2013). The Arab Spring and social media audiences: English and Arabic Twitter users and their networks. *American Behavioral Scientist*, 57(7), 871–898.

Caraway, B. (2016). OUR Walmart: A case study of connective action. *Information, Communication & Society*, 19(7), 907–920.

Castells, M. (2012). *Networks of outrage and hope: Social movements in the Internet age*. Hoboken, NJ: John Wiley & Sons.

Cheney-Lippold, J. (2011). A new algorithmic identity soft biopolitics and the modulation of control. *Theory, Culture & Society*, 28(6), 164–181.

Coleman, G. (2014). *Hacker, hoaxer, whistleblower, spy: The many faces of anonymous*. London: Verso.

Coretti, L., & Pica, D. (2015). The rise and fall of collective identity in networked movements: Communication protocols, Facebook, and the anti-Berlusconi protest. *Information, Communication & Society*, 18(8), 951–967.

Couldry, N. (2015). The myth of 'us': Digital networks, political change and the production of collectivity. *Information, Communication & Society*, 18(6), 608–626.

Couldry, N., & Turow, J. (2014). Advertising, Big Data and the clearance of the public realm: Marketers' new approaches to the content subsidy. *International Journal of Communication*, 8, 1710–1726.

Crawford, K., & Gillespie, T. (2016). What is a flag for? Social media reporting tools and the vocabulary of complaint. *New Media & Society*, 18(3), 410–428.

Dean, J. (2002). *Publicity's secret*. Ithaca, NY: Cornell University Press.

Deibert, R. J., Palfrey, J. G., Rohozinski, V., & Zittrain, J. (Eds.) (2010). *Access controlled: The shaping of power, rights, and rule in cyberspace*. Cambridge, MA: MIT Press.

Deibert, R. J., Palfrey, J. G., Rohozinski, V., & Zittrain, J. (Eds.) (2012). *Access contested: Security, identity and resistance in Asian cyberspace*. Cambridge, MA: MIT Press.

Della Ratta, D., & Valeriani, A. (2014). Remixing the Spring! Connective leadership and read-write practices in the 2011 Arab uprisings. In C. Padovani & A. Calabrese (Eds.), *Communication rights and social justice* (pp. 288–304). Basingstoke, UK: Palgrave Macmillan.

Dessewffy, T., & Nagy, Z. (2016). Born in Facebook: The refugee crisis and grassroots connective action in Hungary. *International Journal of Communication*, 10, 23.

Earl, J., McKee Hurwitz, H., Mejia Mesinas, A., Tolan, M., & Arlotti, A. (2013). This protest will be tweeted: Twitter and protest policing during the Pittsburgh G20. *Information, Communication & Society*, 16(4), 459–478.

Fuchs, C. (2011). *Foundations of critical media and information studies*. New York: Routledge.

Galis, V., & Neumayer, C. (2016). Laying claim to social media by activists: A cyber-material détournement. *Social Media + Society*, 2(3), e2056305116664360-e2056305116664360.

Gerbaudo, P. (2012). *Tweets and the streets: Social media and contemporary activism*. London: Pluto Press.

Gerbaudo, P. (2015). Protest avatars as memetic signifiers: Political profile pictures and the construction of collective identity on social media in the 2011 protest wave. *Information, Communication & Society*, 18(8), 916–929.

Gerbaudo, P. (2017). Social media teams as digital vanguards: the question of leadership in the management of key Facebook and Twitter accounts of Occupy Wall Street, Indignados and UK Uncut. *Information, Communication & Society*, 20(2), 185-202.

Gerbaudo, P., & Treré, E. (2015). In search of the 'we' of social media activism: Introduction to the special issue on social media and protest identities. *Information, Communication & Society*, 18(8), 865–871.

Gerlitz, C., & Helmond, A. (2013). The like economy: Social buttons and the data-intensive web. *New Media & Society*, 15(8), 1348–1365.

Ghonim, W. (2012). *Revolution 2.0: The power of the people is greater than the people in power: A memoir*. Boston, MA: Houghton Mifflin Harcourt.

Gillespie, T. (2014). The relevance of algorithms. In T. Gillespie, P. J. Boczkowski & K. A. Foot. *Media technologies: Essays on communication, materiality, and society* (pp. 167-194). Cambridge, MA: MIT Press, 2014.

Gitlin, T. (1980). *The whole world is watching: Mass media in the making & unmaking of the new left*. Los Angeles, CA: University of California Press.

Goel, S., Anderson, A., Hofman, J., & Watts, D. J. (2015). The structural virality of online diffusion. *Management Science*, 62(1), 180–196.

Göle, N. (2013). Gezi-anatomy of a public square movement. *Insight Turkey*, 15(3), 7.

Hermida, A. (2010). Twittering the news: The emergence of ambient journalism. *Journalism Practice*, 4(3), 297–308.

Juris, J. S. (2008). Performing politics: Image, embodiment, and affective solidarity during anti-corporate globalization protests. *Ethnography*, 9(1), 61–97.

Juris, J. S. (2012). Reflections on# Occupy Everywhere: Social media, public space, and emerging logics of aggregation. *American Ethnologist*, 39(2), 259–279.

Kavada, A. (2015). Creating the collective: Social media, the Occupy Movement and its constitution as a collective actor. *Information, Communication & Society*, 18(8), 872–886.

Kavada, A. (2016). Social movements and political agency in the digital age: A communication approach. *Media and Communication*, 4(4), 8–12.

Kennedy, H., & Moss, G. (2015). Known or knowing publics? Social media data mining and the question of public agency. *Big Data & Society*, 2(2).

Kirkpatrick, D. D., Sanger, D. E., Fahim, K., El-Naggar, M., & Mazzetti, M. (2011). A Tunisian–Egyptian link that shook Arab history. *The New York Times*, February 14, p. A1.

Kuymulu, M. B. (2013). Reclaiming the right to the city: Reflections on the urban uprisings in Turkey. *City*, 17(3), 274–278.

Langlois, G., Elmer, G., McKelvey, F., & Devereaux, Z. (2009). Networked publics: The double articulation of code and politics on Facebook. *Canadian Journal of Communication*, 34(3), 415.

Lee, F. L., & Chan, J. M. (2016). Digital media activities and mode of participation in a protest campaign: A study of the Umbrella Movement. *Information, Communication & Society*, 19(1), 4–22.

Lesch, A. M. (2011). Egypt's Spring: Causes of the revolution. *Middle East Policy*, 18(3), 35–48.

Lim, M. (2012). Clicks, cabs, and coffee houses: Social media and oppositional movements in Egypt, 2004–2011. *Journal of Communication*, 62(2), 231–248.

Lim, M. (2013). Framing Bouazizi: 'White lies', hybrid network, and collective/connective action in the 2010–11 Tunisian uprising. *Journalism*, 14(7), 921–941.

Lotan, G. (2011) "Data Reveals That "Occupying" Twitter Trending Topics is Harder Than it Looks!" *SocialFlow*, 12 October 2011. Accessed on September 10, 2013. http://blog.socialflow.com/post/7120244374/data-reveals-that-occupying-twitter-trending-topics-is-harder-than-it-looks

Lotan, G., Graeff, E., Ananny, M., Gaffney, D., & Pearce, I. (2011). The Arab Spring| the revolutions were tweeted: Information flows during the 2011 Tunisian and Egyptian revolutions. *International Journal of Communication*, 5, 31.

Lovink, G., & Rasch, M. (2013). *Unlike us reader: Social media monopolies and their alternatives* (No. 8). Amsterdam: Institute of Network Cultures.

Margetts, H., John, P., Hale, S., & Yasseri, T. (2016). *Political turbulence: How social media shape collective action*. Princeton, NJ: Princeton University Press.

Marres, N., & Rogers, R. (2005). Recipe for tracing the fate of issues and their publics on the web. In B. Latour & P. Weibel (Eds.), *Making things public: Atmospheres of democracy* (pp. 922–935). Cambridge, MA: MIT Press.

McGee, M. (2013). EdgeRank is dead: Facebook's news feed algorithm now has close to 100K weight factors. *Marketing Land*, August 16. http://marketingland.com/edgerank-is-dead-facebooks-news-feed-algorithm-now-has-close-to-100k-weight-factors-55908 (accessed on October 14, 2013).

Melucci, A. (1996). *Challenging codes: Collective action in the information age*. Cambridge: Cambridge University Press.

Milan, S. (2015a). From social movements to cloud protesting: The evolution of collective identity. *Information, Communication & Society*, 18(8), 887–900.

Milan, S. (2015b). When algorithms shape collective action: Social media and the dynamics of cloud protesting. *Social Media + Society*, 1(2), 2056305115622481.

Monterde, A., Calleja-López, A., Aguilera, M., Barandiaran, X. E., & Postill, J. (2015). Multitudinous identities: A qualitative and network analysis of the 15M collective identity. *Information, Communication & Society*, 18(8), 930–950.

Papacharissi, Z. (2015). *Affective publics: Sentiment, technology, and politics*. Oxford: Oxford University Press.

Papacharissi, Z., & de Fatima Oliveira, M. (2012). Affective news and networked publics: The rhythms of news storytelling on# Egypt. *Journal of Communication*, 62(2), 266–282.

Pariser, E. (2011). *The filter bubble: What the Internet is hiding from you*. Harmondsworth, UK: Penguin.

Poell, T. (2014). Social media and the transformation of activist communication: Exploring the social media ecology of the 2010 Toronto G20 protests. *Information, Communication & Society*, 17(6), 716–731.

Poell, T., Abdulla, R., Rieder, B., Woltering, R., & Zack, L. (2016). Protest leadership in the age of social media. *Information, Communication & Society*, 19(7), 994–1014.

Poell, T., & Borra, E. (2012). Twitter, YouTube, and Flickr as platforms of alternative journalism: The social media account of the 2010 Toronto G20 protests. *Journalism*, 13(6), 695–713.

Poell, T., & Darmoni, K. (2012). Twitter as a multilingual space: The articulation of the Tunisian revolution through# sidibouzid. *NECSUS. European Journal of Media Studies*, 1(1), 14–34.

Poell, T., & van Dijck, J. (2015). Social media and activist communication. In C. Atton (Ed.), *The Routledge companion to alternative and community media* (pp. 527–537). London: Routledge.

Saad-Filho, A. (2013). Mass protests under 'left neoliberalism': Brazil, June–July 2013. *Critical Sociology*, 39(5), 657–669.

Sampson, T. D. (2012). *Virality: Contagion theory in the age of networks*. Minneapolis, MN: University of Minnesota Press.

Shea, P., Notley, T., & Burgess, J. (2015). Entanglements–activism and technology: Editors' introduction. *Fibreculture Journal*, 26, 1–6.

Tremayne, M. (2014). Anatomy of protest in the digital era: A network analysis of Twitter and Occupy Wall Street. *Social Movement Studies*, 13(1), 110–126.

Tufekci, Z. (2013). 'Not this one': Social movements, the attention economy, and microcelebrity networked activism. *American Behavioral Scientist*, 57(7), 848–870.

Tufekci, Z., & Wilson, C. (2012). Social media and the decision to participate in political protest: Observations from Tahrir Square. *Journal of Communication*, 62(2), 363–379.

Turow, J. (2012). *The daily you: How the new advertising industry is defining your identity and your worth*. New Haven, CT: Yale University Press.

van Dijck, J. (2013). *The culture of connectivity: A critical history of social media*. New York and Oxford: Oxford University Press.

van Dijck, J., & Poell, T. (2013). Understanding social media logic. *Media and Communication*, 1(1), 2–14.

Weltevrede, E., Helmond, A., & Gerlitz, C. (2014). The politics of real-time: A device perspective on social media platforms and search engines. *Theory, Culture & Society*, 31(6), 125–150.

Wilken, R. (2014). Places nearby: Facebook as a location-based social media platform. *New Media & Society*, 16(7), 1087–1103.

Wright, S. (2015). Populism and Downing Street E-petitions: Connective action, hybridity, and the changing nature of organizing. *Political Communication*, 32(3), 414–433.

Youmans, W. L., & York, J. C. (2012). Social media and the activist toolkit: User agreements, corporate interests, and the information infrastructure of modern social movements. *Journal of Communication*, 62(2), 315–329.

31

Lively Data, Social Fitness and Biovalue: The Intersections of Health and Fitness Self-tracking and Social Media

Deborah Lupton

INTRODUCTION

The fitness-tracking platform Strava calls itself 'The social network for athletes' on its Twitter account. Its Twitter feed is filled with screenshots of the routes that members of the platform have taken on their bicycle rides, swims or runs, and accounts of how many kilometres they have travelled and how fast they have done so. These images and comments contribute to the social media functions of the site. The Strava website lists the opportunity for members to 'socialize' by following friends and their activities, joining or creating clubs and 'pushing' each other by commenting on people's data and giving them kudos for their achievements. A new Strava feature encourages members to upload photos of their trips to the platform to share with other members. These are entitled 'Strava Stories', and the most recent photos are displayed at the top of members' profiles, framing their other data.

In my current research on people who use platforms and apps like Strava for tracking their physical activity, many participants commented on the pleasures they derived from the social networking functions of such software. The possibilities of recording information about their activities, sharing these with members of the site or with friends on social media sites, comparing their data with other athletes, engaging in challenges and competitions and providing encouragement to others were viewed as motivating, encouraging and adding a social dimension to their pursuits. These findings are echoed in researchers' work on self-tracking physical fitness pursuits (Rooksby, Rost, Morrison and Chalmers, 2014; Epstein, Jacobson, Bales, McDonald and Munson, 2015; Stragier, Evens and Mechant, 2015).

As the example of Strava demonstrates, there are growing entanglements between the practices of self-tracking human bodies and engaging in social media networks and relationships. The expanded array of digitised devices that are available for self-tracking, and the capacity of many of these technologies to interact with social media platforms, has encouraged self-trackers to share the details that they collect about themselves with others. In addition to physical activity, this personal information may include biometrics such as heart rate, body temperature, body weight, sleep patterns, mood, blood glucose levels, blood pressure, menstrual and ovulation cycles, sexual activity and pregnancy. As part of their general ethos of promoting the sharing of personal information, mainstream social media platforms such as Instagram, Twitter, YouTube and Facebook offer opportunities for people to share the data that they generate from these self-tracking practices, whether these are photos, videos, maps of their movements in space or quantitative data. In turn, some self-tracking platforms have incorporated tailored social media elements as part of their customised offerings. The pleasures and affordances of the networking capabilities of these media promote a culture of sharing what are often very intimate details about people's bodies and their movements in space. These data have use value that extends well beyond the individuals who generate these details about themselves and their social networks. As contributors to large datasets of information about people's activities and movements in space, these self-trackers are imbricated within the digital data economy.

In this chapter, I focus on these intersections, drawing out their sociocultural and political implications. The chapter begins with a brief review of the theoretical perspectives that underpin my analysis. After describing the range of technologies that are available for physical activity, health and medical self-tracking, I then discuss the concept of 'social fitness' and its broader implications. This is followed by an analysis of the new forms of value that personal health and medical data have attracted and the political implications of encouraging people to participate as socially fit citizens.

THEORETICAL FOUNDATIONS

My approach here is underpinned by a perspective that recognises the sociomaterial status of digital devices, software and the data that they generate (Rogers, 2013; Kitchin and Lauriault, 2014). Digital devices that generate personal data participate in the formation of digital data assemblages, in which technologies and humans work together to create new configurations of information. The digital data generated by self-tracking may be conceptualised as 'lively' in various ways (Lupton, 2016c). First, these data are generated from life itself by documenting humans' bodies and selves. Second, as participants in the digital data economy, they are labile and fluid, open to constant repurposing by a range of actors and agencies, often in ways in which the original generators of these data have little or no knowledge. Third, these data are lively due to the advent of algorithmic authority and predictive analytics that use digital self-tracked data to make inferences and decisions about individuals and social groups. These data, therefore, have potential effects on the conduct of life and life opportunities. Fourth, by virtue of their growing value as commodities or research sources, the personal data that are derived from self-tracking practices have significant implications for livelihoods (those using these data in the data-mining, insurance and data science industries, for instance).

The recognition of the sociocultural and political implications of the use of people's personal data by other actors and agencies is also a key theoretical tenet of my discussion here. The term 'prosumption' is often used to describe users' engagement in the digital data economy as both consumers and producers of digital data content (Beer and Burrows, 2010; Ritzer, 2014). The taken-for-granted definition of social media relates to platforms or apps that facilitate and promote prosumption: the sharing of personal information with other users and opportunities to comment on or respond to others' content. However, any form of personal data that is generated using digital technologies now becomes 'social' by these data's transmission to and storage in databases on the computing cloud. These data inevitably enter into the circulations, flows and fluxes of the digital data economy. As part of big data, they contribute to social relations and social selves and the management of social institutions and have potential social effects.

Theories of surveillance are also highly pertinent to understanding personal digital data assemblages. The role played by digital technologies in surveillance, or watching, of people is a central feature of contemporary data practices. As scholars in surveillance studies have emphasised, there are many different modes of dataveillance, or conducting modes of watching people using data-generating technologies (van Dijck, 2014). Some are covert and non-consensual: the subjects of these modes do not realise that they are being watched and have not given their permission. These covert modes include the dataveillance conducted by security and policing agencies, some forms of commercial collection of personal digital data and the dataveillance that is conducted by hackers or cybercriminals. Other modes of dataveillance are open and voluntary. These include the self-surveillance that people may undertake of their own bodies and lives using mobile and wearable devices, apps and other software (Lupton, 2016c); the intimate surveillance that they may conduct on friends and family members as part of their social relationships or caregiving practices (Levy, 2015); and the social surveillance that is part of people's interactions of social media platforms, in which they watch each other (Marwick, 2012).

Early versions of social media platforms focused on the ideals of sharing and participatory democracy; the free exchange of information for the mutual benefit of all users (Beer and Burrows, 2010; John, 2013). Several critical scholars have drawn attention to the ways in which this participatory and communal ethos is now harnessed to commercial, managerial and surveillance imperatives that seek to exploit people's prosumption activities (van Dijck, 2013; Fuchs, 2014; van Dijck, 2014; Zuboff, 2015; Banning, 2016). Zuboff (2015) uses the term 'surveillance capitalism' to refer to what she characterises as a new era in capitalist economic systems, in which personal digital data as part of big data have taken on immense value as commodities. As I will go on to outline in this chapter, the value of personal biometric data has significant implications for how self-trackers use and share their data with others on social media and also for how they may lose control of their data as they enter the digital data economy.

SELF-TRACKING AND THE QUANTIFIED SELF

Self-tracking is an enterprise that involves individuals observing and, in many cases, recording details of their bodies and lives, often for achieving self-knowledge, self-reflection and self-improvement. Monitoring and measuring details of their bodies' physical activities and functions is a common focus for many self-trackers. In recent years, the practices of self-tracking using digital devices have received growing attention from the popular media and in academic research. While self-tracking has taken place for millennia, new digital technologies facilitate the collection of ever-more detailed personal information. Self-trackers are drawing on the capacities of new technologies to generate increasing quantities and diverse forms of information about their bodies and selves (Rooksby et al., 2014; Ruckenstein, 2014, 2015: 6; Barta and Neff, 2015; Epstein et al., 2015; Lomborg and Frandsen, 2015; Stragier et al., 2015).

Terms other than self-tracking are used to refer to self-monitoring practices: lifelogging, personal analytics, personal informatics and the quantified self. The 'quantified self' is a relatively new term, but has become popularly used. *Wired* journalists Gary Wolf and Kevin Kelly invented it in 2007 to describe the practices that they had observed among friends and colleagues involving the use of digital technologies to monitor and measure themselves. Wolf and Kelly went on to establish the Quantified Self website (*Quantified Self*, 2016) and to establish the associated Quantified Self Labs to facilitate the development of technologies directed at self-trackers. Since then, the 'quantified self' or 'quantifying the self' terms have been taken up in the popular media and some of the academic literature to refer to various methods of self-tracking and especially those that involve using digital devices to generate numerical data (Lupton, 2013c). I prefer to use 'self-tracking' in my work, as it is a broader term that encompasses all the different types and practices of self-monitoring, including collecting both metrics and qualitative data.

All forms of self-tracking involve data practices, or ways of generating, engaging with, interpreting and applying the insights developed from personal data, and data materialisations, or ways of representing data (Lupton, 2016c). When self-trackers use methods such as journal keeping or writing down numbers, it is difficult to analyse these data for their patterns. Digital data devices and apps and other software provide the opportunity to access and analyse personal details efficiently and quickly. These technologies also let users combine different data sets to identify patterns in ways that were not achievable in the past. Indeed, the difficulty now faced by self-trackers is the overwhelming mass of data that they may have to deal with, given the infinite number of ways in which data sets can be combined with the aim of generating insights.

TECHNOLOGIES FOR SELF-TRACKING FITNESS, HEALTH AND MEDICINE

New digital technologies are increasingly incorporated into healthcare delivery and health promotion initiatives. Telemedicine and telehealth initiatives offered to patients have emphasised self-monitoring as part of patient self-care for chronic conditions such as diabetes and high blood pressure for over two decades. Well before the advent of digital technologies, patients were encouraged to keep track of their blood glucose level or blood pressure using technologies that they could operate themselves, and to take note of the readings as part of managing their condition and treatment regimen. The latest versions of telemedicine offer continuous real-time self-monitoring, wireless data transfer and cloud computing storage facilities that reduce the expense and expertise required for the proprietary systems that were characteristic of earlier technologies. Self-care strategies using digital devices have become incorporated in the ideal of the digitally engaged patient, who is willing and able to take up these devices for self-monitoring (Lupton, 2013a). Patient self-monitoring technologies that are now available include digital pills embedded with sensors that monitor the body from within by sending signals to a patch worn on the user's arm. Continuous wearable monitoring devices measure such bodily features as physical movement, blood glucose levels, body temperature, sleep patterns, heart rate and function, lung function, blood pressure and oxygen saturation and brain activity. Sensor pads are available to place under mattresses or in chairs to monitor heart rate, breathing and body movement and mobility. These data can then be transmitted wirelessly to healthcare providers or caregivers as part of remote monitoring programs (for overviews of these technologies, see Swan, 2012a, 2012b; Lupton, 2013a, 2014b; Topol, 2015).

Health and physical activity self-monitoring also takes place among healthy populations using new apps and wearable technologies. Thousands of apps for the self-tracking of human bodies are available for downloading. By late 2015, 160,000 health and medical apps had been placed on the market, most of which (65 per cent) focus on promoting wellness, diet and exercise, with nearly a quarter directed at the self-management of chronic diseases such as diabetes, high blood pressure and mental health conditions. One in ten have the capability to connect to a monitoring device or sensor, while a third can connect to social media networks. There are a small number of very popular, highly-downloaded apps, such as some of the fitness tracking or calorie counting apps, period trackers or medical information apps such as WebMD (IMS Institute for Healthcare Informatics, 2015).

Digital devices that are available for self-tracking include wireless body weight scales and blood pressure monitors and wearable trackers. The range of wearables offered by the Fitbit, Misfit, Nike and Jawbone companies include wristbands, headbands, pendants or devices clipped to clothing. Many of these wearables either interact with customised apps or sync with platforms such as Runkeeper, Strava and MapMyFitness. Smartwatches also now offer biometric tracking. For example, the new Apple Watch includes a range of sensors, such as geolocation, accelerometer, gyroscope and heart rate monitors that facilitate self-tracking. It offers two pre-loaded apps, Workout and Fitness, which record the wearer's levels of physical activity. There is also a range of smart clothing and sporting equipment on the market, including shirts, helmets, bats and balls equipped with sensor-based technologies for monitoring and measuring exercise and sporting activities. Several self-tracking device developers are finding ways of incorporating their technologies into the Internet of Things so that these devices can interact with other monitoring digital technologies. For example, the Misfit company is working on integrating its wristband self-tracking device that currently facilitates sleep and physical fitness monitoring with Nest, 'smart home' monitoring software that regulates the home thermostat. The users' sleep data can then be incorporated into the home thermostat system to regulate air temperature based on the occupant's sleeping patterns and time of awakening in the morning.

Self-tracking initiatives focusing on health and fitness are spreading from the clinic into insurance and the workplace. Some health insurance companies are taking up self-tracking initiatives as part of user-based insurance policy calculations, encouraging their clients to upload their health and fitness data to receive incentives or reduced premiums. In the USA, these programs are often linked to the provision of health insurance by the employers, who therefore have a financial incentive to motivate their employees to take part. The manufacturers of self-tracking devices are approaching American workplaces to use their technologies in their corporate 'wellness programs' (Olson, 2014; Zamosky, 2014). Children and young people are also encouraged to engage in health and fitness self-monitoring endeavours. Several wearable device manufacturers offer child-sized devices that parents can purchase as part of nudging their children to be more physically active. Some schools are introducing self-tracking as part of physical education and health classes. Initiatives such as the UNICEF Kid Power program involve recruiting children and young people to monitor their physical activity using a digital wristband and use the points they earn to play games that unlock therapeutic food packets for malnourished children.

PERSONAL HEALTH DATA AND SOCIAL MEDIA

The use of social media for medical and health-related purposes has become widespread. Patient online discussion groups and blogs written by healthcare providers or institutions and patients are long-established modes of digital health communication and interaction. The role played by websites in providing health and medical information to lay people ('Dr Google') has been well recognised for some years (Fox and Duggan, 2013; Kivits, 2013). Online searching remains a dominant source of information about medical conditions, with the top websites, such as WebMD, receiving tens of millions of users each month (eBizMBA, 2016). The newer social media platforms are often represented in the medical and public health literature as an extension of Dr Google: a means by which lay people can continue to seek information about health, illness and medicine online and, importantly, easily share their experiences with others. Sometimes these initiatives are promoted by patients and related lay person organisations (Lupton, 2014a). As part of championing the ideal of digital patient engagement (Lupton, 2013a), healthcare and public health professionals have also frequently called for lay people to collect information on themselves and share these on social media (Swan, 2012a; Lefebvre and Bornkessel, 2013; Househ, Borycki and Kushniruk, 2014).

Twitter has been used to facilitate information sharing among people interested in specific health and medical topics or conditions, including lay people as well as healthcare professionals and officials and pharmaceutical and medical device companies. Condition-specific Facebook pages promote the interaction of patients with each other. Patients can upload videos to YouTube about their illness experiences. Many examples of surgical techniques are available on that platform, including demonstrations by medical professionals, tand also videos made by lay people seeking to display 'do-it-yourself' surgery. Several patient-oriented platforms, such as PatientsLikeMe, Treato and CureTogether, offer opportunities for patients to join condition-specific communities and to record their symptoms and treatments. These data are then aggregated to provide information for users about trends among other members of the site. Some initiatives have been developed to encourage people to use sensor technologies to track their local environment as part of citizen science projects. There are also opportunities for people to use social media to rank and rate their medical care providers. The Patient Opinion platforms in the UK and Australia, for example, encourage patients to provide feedback on the care that they receive in their national healthcare systems. In the USA, platforms like ZocDoc (with associated apps for mobile devices) help patients find doctors and dentists in their local area and make appointments online, as well as read reviews of doctors by other users.

People who track their biometric data for health-promoting purposes often use social media. Facebook is one major social media platform in which self-trackers share their latest information with others. They can post regular updates on exercise routines and achievements with Facebook friends or contribute to specialised pages that have been set up to establish communities around specific exercise or sporting interests. Twitter, Instagram and Tumblr offer further opportunities for people to share their information and images with other. They can employ a relevant hashtag to draw attention to their data and contribute to a community of people with shared interests. More specialised platforms, such as Fitocracy, Daily Mile and Strava, encourage users to share their fitness achievements with other members, emphasising the competitive dimension of comparing numbers. The weight-loss platform Extra Pounds combines 'body logs' with access to support groups, while PumpUp focuses on users uploading selfies to document their fitness achievements and sharing healthy recipes with each other. Several health and fitness self-tracking app developers have worked on making the social media elements of their apps more prominent and easy to use. A survey of health and medical apps published in 2015 found that recent apps were more likely, when compared with apps available two years ago, to offer the functions of connecting to another device or wearable or social media (Comstock, 2015). The MapMyFitness app, for example, is now integrated with Facebook, and users can create or join groups of other users to share routes and training plans, organise events and compare progress.

Patient self-care, voluntary self-tracking and social media use are coming together in some initiatives. In medicine and health informatics (a field devoted to understanding the best ways of generating, storing and using health and medical information) the term 'patient generated data' has begun to be employed (Huba and Zhang, 2012). This term describes the various ways in which patients or their lay caregivers produce information about the patients outside the clinic setting, through self-tracking efforts, using remote monitoring self-care devices or uploading material to social media platforms or as part of routine transactions online. For their part, healthcare providers and public health workers use social media as part of their working lives. Healthcare professionals employ LinkedIn, Twitter and closed Facebook pages to join specialised groups, discuss cases with each other and provide advice. Hundreds of YouTube channels, Facebook pages and Twitter accounts have been set up by hospitals and healthcare organisations as part of public relations strategies.

The phrase 'social fitness' is used to refer to these practices of sharing personal data to facilitate motivation and achieving personal goals. This is particularly clearly outlined on the Strava website. As is contended on the website, 'Strava lets you experience what we call social fitness – connecting and competing with each other via mobile and online apps' and thereby providing 'motivation and camaraderie'. The overt and broader meaning of social fitness has its roots in physical exercise training or weight loss regimes and encouraging people to join groups as a means of mobilising the support of others to achieve their goals. The importance of social networks as part of motivation in health promotion has frequently been employed in psychological models of behaviour change (see, for example, Bandura, 2004). In recent times, the field of persuasive computing has employed these types of models in designing interventions for behavioural change relate to health (Purpura, Schwanda, Williams, Stubler and Sengers, 2011). When it is employed more specifically to online health and fitness self-tracking, the newest version of social fitness refers to sharing personal data and engaging in online communities for the same ends. Social fitness has become integral to corporate 'wellness programs'. Some workplaces have instituted competitions requiring participating employees to upload and display to all other workmates data they have collected on their bodily movements and weight loss using self-tracking devices as part of efforts to motivate them to achieve higher fitness levels (Zamosky, 2014). The Jawbone company (Jawbone, 2016) offers the 'Up Group' package to employers seeking to institute wellness programs. On its website, Jawbone argues that promoting competition between different teams in an organisation will motivate individuals to exercise more, sleep better and eat healthier food. Team members are encouraged to view the data on their apps showing how their team is performing against other teams and to upload supportive comments and emoticons to motivate other team members.

The Quantified Self website (Quantified Self, 2016) provides an online social medium by which people interested in self-tracking can share experiences. A Facebook page and Twitter account also link to the website. The co-founders of the Quantified Self movement have asserted from its inception that one of its integral elements is to develop community among its members and encourage them to share with other members details of their self-tracked data and the lessons that they have learnt from self-tracking. In his first article on the Quantified Self for *Wired* magazine, Gary Wolf (2009) stated that self-tracking involves the sharing of data and collaboration on ways of using them. An important dimension of the Quantified Self movement, meetups and conferences is the 'show-and-tell' mode of communication. Many 'show-and-tell' videos appear on the Quantified Self website. They typically feature an individual standing in front of a group talking about their self-tracking experiences. The Quantified Self also includes numerous examples of data visualisations that members have generated, allowing them to share these visualisations with other members. In several blog posts on the Quantified Self website, Gary Wolf (for example, Wolf, 2014) has argued for the importance of 'our data', or the pool of aggregated data collected from self-trackers. Other commentators who champion the notion of 'the quantified us' privilege the ways in which aggregated personal data sets can contribute to self-tracking communities. Writing in *Wired* magazine, Jordan and Pfarr (2014) claim that: 'Ultimately the Quantified Us can help people take better care of themselves, more often – and feel more connected to each other in the process.'

I have developed a typology of the five distinctive modes of self-tracking that have emerged in recent times. This identifies the different uses of self-tracking data and the diverse range of actors and agencies involved (Lupton, 2016b, 2016c). When self-monitoring is self-initiated and purely voluntary, responding to self-directed objectives and goals, it conforms to the mode that I entitle 'private self-tracking'. This mode is perhaps the most public and well-known face of self-tracking, particularly in portrayals of the Quantified Self phenomenon. 'Pushed self-tracking' departs from the private self-tracking mode in that the initial incentive for engaging in self-tracking comes from another actor or agency. People may take up self-tracking voluntarily, but initially in response to external encouragement or advocating. 'Imposed self-tracking' involves the imposition of self-tracking practices upon individuals by other actors and agencies primarily for these others' benefit. 'Communal self-tracking' describes the voluntary sharing of a tracker's personal data with other people as a central feature of self-tracking practice.

'Exploited self-tracking' refers to the ways in which other actors and agencies repurpose people's personal data from self-tracking practices. As this section has outlined, the private, pushed, imposed and communal modes are apparent in self-tracking practices for fitness, health and medical purposes. The data generated from all of these modes can be exploited by other actors and agencies, as I detail in the next section.

THE EXPLOITATION OF PERSONAL HEALTH DATA

Many commercial, research and managerial uses of the types of personal health and medical data that are uploaded to social media sites have been identified. Health insurance companies, government bodies, pharmaceutical and medical technology companies, healthcare organisations, self-tracking device developers and entrepreneurs, researchers and employers are finding ways of exploiting people's personal data from self-tracking.

Healthcare, pharmaceutical and biotechnology companies frequently use social and other digital media for marketing and public relations purposes, or 'building their brands' (Belby, 2015). This takes place in a variety of ways, from the traditional explicit type of marketing, such as sponsoring banner ads and conferences, to the covert, like attempting to influence social media discussions on platforms such as Facebook or Twitter. Some pharmaceutical companies employ researchers to harvest data from blogs written by people about an illness or medical condition they have or Twitter exchanges by patients about their conditions and therapies. Using this material, the companies' employees then attempt to influence conversation threads (Robinson, 2014). Healthcare professionals and organisations employ patient-generated data for purposes such as health profiling for targeting treatment and illness prevention strategies. In the USA, the Affordable Care Act promotes payment systems that reward keeping patients out of the hospital system. Hospitals have begun to invest in big data technologies to construct new risk models of patients. Information about patients is entered into hospital data systems, including biometric and treatment details from their medical records and patient self-monitoring activities at home and demographic characteristics such as race or ethnicity, age and gender. These data are used to predict which patients are more likely to require readmission for medical care (Humphries, 2013).

Health promoters have experimented with using social media sites to disseminate information about preventive health, collect data about people's health-related behaviours and attempt to 'nudge' members of target groups to change their behaviour. Public health professionals employ various social media tools to disseminate information about health risks and disease outbreaks and to collect data on the incidence of illness and disease. One example is the digital tool HealthMap. The software can search the web for disease reports from online news reports, blogs, social media platforms and official reports and can represent disease outbreaks visually on a digital map. It includes an app that users can download to their mobile digital devices so that they can identify what region is experiencing an outbreak of infectious disease or report cases that are then followed up.

Crowdsourcing health and medical data is often championed in discussions of how such big data can benefit not only the patients themselves who contribute their information to such sites, but also other patients with the same condition, healthcare providers, caregivers and commercial bodies such as pharmaceutical and medical device companies. Patient support and opinion platforms have become increasingly commercialised. The data generated by people contributing their experiences of illness and treatments on many of these platforms are now routinely harvested by the developers and on-sold to

third parties (Lupton, 2014a). For example, the Treato website landing page boasts that membership of the site is over two million patients (Treato, 2016). The site focuses on harvesting patients' accounts of drug therapies across the spectrum of social media and other digital platforms, including seeking out accounts of how well drugs work, their side-effects and why patients may switch one brand for another. Treato provides free access to the general data that are collected, but also offers a more targeted service to pharmaceutical companies that incurs fees. The PatientsLikeMe site also offers members the opportunity to enrol directly into clinical trials of new pharmaceuticals.

Data privacy and security problems have emerged in relation to the generation and sharing of personal biometric details. People's very intimate bodily details that they upload to apps and social media sites may be disclosed to others without their knowledge or consent. It has been demonstrated that many developers of health and fitness tracking apps fail to secure the personal data uploaded to the apps and that these apps often leak personal data in covert ways (Adhikari, Richards and Scott, 2014; Huckvale, Prieto, Tilney, Benghozi and Car, 2015). There are also many privacy threats involved with uploading personal health and medical information to social media platforms, including the misuse of the data, accidental data releases, disclosures to third parties and user profiling across sites (Li, 2015). Data-mining and data brokering companies and advertisers have a vested interest in health and medical data. Some of these agencies use the data to construct detailed profiles or predictive analytics that may be used to make decisions about people's eligibility for employment, insurance and credit. Profiles of people with conditions such as sexually transmissible diseases, HIV/AIDS, cancer and mental illnesses and who have been victims of sexual assault are regularly developed by data miners and brokers for sale to advertising agencies, potential employers and financial institutions (Pasquale, 2014). If used in these ways, the kinds of personal data that are generated by self-tracking and shared on social media may, therefore, have significant implications for people's life chances (Crawford and Schultz, 2014; Rosenblat, Wikelius, boyd, Gangadharan and Yu, 2014).

The exploitation of personal health and medical data is taking place in legal ways, but also on the part of hackers and cyber-criminals, who seek to access illegally these data for financial gain. Criminal breaches of medical digital data sets are becoming common. Such data can be used in identity theft, fraudulent health insurance claims and to gain access to pharmaceuticals and medical equipment (McCarthy, 2013; Humer and Finkle, 2014). In early 2015, for example, confidential information about 80 million patients was accessed illegally on the database of the American healthcare provider Anthem Inc., which had failed to encrypt this information (Symons, 2015).

DISCUSSION: DIGITISED BODIES, SURVEILLANCE AND BIOCAPITAL

Self-tracking for health and medical purposes is just one way, among a plethora of others, to render fleshly bodies into digital data. The digitised data assemblages that are configured via self-tracking technologies are the newest forms of 'informatic bodies' (Waldby, 2000). Accounts of self-tracking for health and medical purposes are beginning to describe a data entity generated from an individual's different personal data sets. Thus, writing recently for *Nature*, Kish and Topol (2015) describe the 'external wisdom of the body' that these data sets comprise, while Swan (2013) makes reference to the 'extended exoself' configured by self-tracking data. These metaphors draw on age-old representations of human bodies as machines and, more lately, as computerised information systems (Lupton, 2012b, 2013c). In responding to the

new affordances of the digitised human as part of the Internet of Things, these metaphors represent the human body as an entity that constantly generates digital data and pushes these data out into the increasingly interconnected digital world of smart things and simultaneously incorporates these data back as the individual responds to their data and makes changes to their lives.

The data that self-tracking practices generate have different forms of value for different actors and agencies. For the individual self-tracker, these data are opportunities to acquire self-knowledge, engage in self-reflection and optimise their lives. Self-trackers often seek to make meaning from their data. The practice is not simply about collecting data, as this suggests, but also attempting to engage with such issues as what should be done with these data, how they should be presented and interpreted, and what the implications are for self-trackers' identity and future life prospects and success (Nafus and Sherman, 2014; Ruckenstein, 2014; Lupton, 2016c). In so doing, self-trackers are engaging in voluntary self-surveillance. The process of meaning making may be facilitated by engaging in data sharing practices. For those who participate in the communal mode of self-tracking, these data offer a means of entering into exchanges of personal information for the mutual benefit of other users or the opportunity to contribute to aggregated big data sets that promise to reveal insights that may be of use to themselves and others (Barta and Neff, 2015; Lupton, 2016c). When self-trackers engage in these practices, they are inviting the surveillance of others and are thus engaging in social surveillance.

When self-tracking practices enter into social media platforms they draw on deeply felt desires for becoming part of communities, connecting and sharing with others, exchanging common experiences and opening private details about oneself to others in the interests of altruism, creating social bonds and solidarity, contributing to stocks of new knowledge as well as learning more about oneself

(Barta and Neff, 2015; Banning, 2016). As I argued in my introductory remarks, self-trackers can gain much pleasure from their participation in social surveillance, enjoying feeling part of a community of like-minded people and the often playful dimensions of demonstrating their achievements to others, motivating and supporting others or engaging in competitive endeavours with other members (Whitson, 2013; Lomborg and Frandsen, 2016).

The skilful manipulation and portrayal of personal data is a key factor of this type of social surveillance. The 'show and tell' presentations on the Quantified Self and other self-tracking forums are often very complex and aesthetically appealing, conforming to the appeal of the 'data spectacle' (Gregg, 2015). The pleasures of 'showing and telling' in these formats, therefore, include engaging in the opportunity to let other interested people know about the insights about oneself that the tracker has garnered, as well as displaying prowess in making these data beautiful or easy to understand. Such communications of personal data seek to attract the interest and attention of other people and in the communal and sharing ethos that is an integral dimension of the Quantified Self movement. They have strong performative dimensions in revealing both how a presenter's self-tracking efforts have improved their lives and also how adept they are at manipulating self-tracking technologies and data materialisations and thereby facilitating the sharing of their data with others (Nafus and Sherman, 2014; Barta and Neff, 2015; Lupton, 2016c).

Indeed, it could be argued that yet another type of surveillance is demonstrated in self-trackers' engagements on social media: that of ludic surveillance, involving these pleasurable elements of competition and play. As part of the general 'ludification' of many aspects of social life and selfhood (Frissen, Lammes, de Lange, de Mul and Raessens, 2015), self-tracking of human bodies has become progressively oriented towards these elements as a way of engaging users and maintaining their participation. This is even evident in apps that allow people to monitor, measure and then share details of their pregnancies (Lupton and Thomas, 2015; Thomas and Lupton, 2015) or sexual activities (Lupton, 2015).

As outlined in the Introduction, the uploading and sharing of personal information that occurs on online platforms, however, is no longer confined to a community of like-minded individuals seeking to help each other. As knowledge in the form of digital data has become increasingly valuable for commercial, research and managerial purposes, the participatory, sharing and playful ethos of social media has become commodified and exploited by a multitude of actors and agencies. The progressive commercialisation of the sharing economy has implications for digitised self-tracking practices. Actors and agencies other than those collecting their personal information have compelling reasons for wanting to access and harvest these data. The data generated by practices of voluntary self-surveillance, social surveillance and ludic surveillance are now often available to the surveillance and exploitation of these actors and agencies. Unlike previous forms of self-tracking, in which personal data could be kept private, digitised data assemblages cannot easily be protected from the gaze or use by others.

As the digital data economy has expanded, and entrepreneurs, researchers, managers, businesses and cybercriminals have recognised the possibilities of digital data, personal information such as that uploaded to health and medical social media sites has taken on a new form of commercial value – that of 'biovalue' (Lupton, 2014c, 2016c). Biovalue is produced from the surplus commercial value that is attributed to biological objects such as human body tissues, cells and organs (Waldby, 2000; Mitchell and Waldby, 2006; Rose, 2007a). Just as this human fleshly matter is now a commodity traded for financial profit, the data about human bodies, their functions and behaviours that are generated by self-tracking devices have become valuable entities. The fact that these data are about 'life itself' has become exploitable in new ways. The biovalue that is generated by personal digital data is yet another form of surveillance capitalism.

The incorporation of biometric self-tracked data into the digital data economy and the subsequent exploitation of these data is an instance of biopolitics and biopower. As originally outlined by Foucault (for example, 1988, 1991, 2008), biopolitics and biopower are exercised in and through human bodies. They are modes of power relations that rely on concepts of human subjectivity and embodiment in which practices of self-care, self-knowledge and self-optimisation are privileged (Lupton, 1995; Rose and Novas, 2005; Rose, 2008). The social media platforms that have been developed to promote the uploading of these data, the sharing of these data and their subsequent entry into the digital data knowledge economy provide routes for the translation of biodata into a new form of biovalue that generates digital biocapital.

When thinking about the entanglements of biometrics, biovalue and biopolitics, the concept of social fitness takes on an expanded form of meaning. Programs directed at preventive medicine, patient self-care and health promotion have traditionally relied on a discourse of ideal citizenship that melds private objectives with the public good, the self with the community. Notions of idealised 'biocitizenship' (Rose and Novas, 2005) in the contemporary neoliberal state emphasise self-responsibility and the entrepreneurial management and optimisation of one's life, including promoting and maintaining good health and physical fitness (Lupton, 1995; Petersen and Lupton, 1996; Rose, 2007b, 2008). When digital technologies designed for self-tracking biometric data enter into this field, these ideals are elaborated in response, configuring the ideal of the 'socially fit citizen', a new, digitised form of biocitizenship. More recent forms of self-administered

health promotion and patient self-care have focused attention on the ways in which digital technologies can be employed to achieve good health, supporting the notion of the digitally engaged patient. The discourses of 'patient empowerment' and 'engagement' and the importance of people taking responsibility for their health recur in such accounts (see, for example, Swan, 2009; Househ et al., 2014). In these programs, morality, responsibility, accountability and concepts of health and illness are inextricably intertwined (Lupton, 2012a; 2013a, 2013b, 2016a). These practices are emphasised to the exclusion of other ways of caring for human subjects, such as collective or state-supported initiatives (McGregor, 2001).

When the meaning of social fitness is expanded to incorporate the use of new digital media for facilitating social interactions and networks, these moral meanings also enter into digitised sharing and participation systems. Idealised biocitizens are socially fit because they are appropriately socially-engaged using technologies such as social media, as well as performing the attributes of healthy and responsible citizens who are willing to share their data for the interests of others or to provide encouraging feedback about other people to help motivate them. Socially fit biocitizens take steps to employ self-tracking devices and technologies as well as social media to contribute to personalised digital data assemblages that enable them to manage and optimise their bodily health and wellbeing. They may encourage others on social media by engaging in communal self-tracking, or contribute their personal data to large data sets that are then used to develop new knowledges about health and medicine. In this discourse, the 'self-knowledge' championed by the Quantified Self movement and other advocates for self-tracking should not only benefit the individual: it should also contribute to collective knowledge stores.

The affordances of new digital media and their intersections with the digital data economy, however, complicate and extend the potentialities and consequences of social fitness. There is a fine line between voluntary, pushed and imposed self-tracking. When financial incentives are offered, or social pressures are brought to bear on individuals to engage in self-tracking, there is often little room to make a choice. In the case of employees who are encouraged to engage in fitness self-tracking as part of corporate wellness programs, or children who are handed heart rate monitors in physical education lessons, encouragement can quickly become imposition. People who do not participate or who fail to meet pre-set targets for fitness or other health- or productivity-related data may be discriminated against with social disapproval or financial penalties. Given that the impetus in these instances does not come from the individual but from those in positions of power, this also raises the question of how effective such practices are in helping people achieve self-knowledge or change their lives for the better. Forcing change on people is likely to be far less effective than allowing them to make a choice (Frakt and Carroll, 2014).

All three of these modes can be taken up in communal or exploited self-tracking modes. The possibilities of the types of use of personal health and medical information that I have outlined are rarely raised by actors and agencies who are seeking to encourage (nudge or even coerce) people to engage in self-tracking. The ways in which personal value that self-trackers gain from developing their self-knowledge in the quest for self-optimisation is expropriated for the profit of others or used to discriminate against people tend not to be highlighted in the discourses of sharing and caring that recur in social fitness discussions. Self-trackers may not be aware of who is viewing or using the types of personal information that they share on social media.

FUTURE DIRECTIONS

Important questions emerge from the analysis I have presented here. If moral precepts are brought to bear on people to encourage them to engage in self-tracking and personal data sharing as socially fit biocitizens by government, research and commercial agencies, what are the attendant precepts that should be highlighted by these agencies to alert or warn people of the potential uses (both legal and illicit, both overt and covert) of the highly intimate personal data that are produced by these practices? What are the ethics and values that need to be confronted and assessed in this situation? What responsibilities should be borne by those who advocate for the socially fit citizen? To what extent will it become increasingly difficult for people to opt out of participating in social fitness programs, and what are the possible harms that may eventuate from this form of pushed or coerced self-tracking? What are the ways in which self-tracking can be used for radical activist purposes that challenge existing norms and assumptions concerning personal responsibility for health status? How will the expansion of the Internet of Things contribute to the generation of increasingly detailed information on people's bodies and everyday practices and the exchange of these data between humans and between inanimate 'smart' objects? All of these questions provide the basis for future critical analysis of the entanglements of social media with self-tracking technologies.

REFERENCES

Adhikari, R., Richards, D. and Scott, K. (2014) Security and privacy issues related to the use of mobile health apps. *25th Australasian Conference on Information Systems*, Auckland, New Zealand.

Bandura, A. (2004) Health promotion by social cognitive means. *Health Education & Behavior*, 31: 143–164.

Banning, M.E. (2016) Shared entanglements: Web 2.0, info-liberalism & digital sharing. *Information, Communication & Society*, 19: 489–503.

Barta, K. and Neff, G. (2015) Technologies for sharing: Lessons from Quantified Self about the political economy of platforms. *Information, Communication & Society*, 19(4), 518–531.

Beer, D. and Burrows, R. (2010) Consumption, prosumption and participatory web cultures: An introduction. *Journal of Consumer Culture*, 10: 3–12.

Belby, J. (2015) How healthcare can use social media effectively and compliantly. *Forbes*. www.forbes.com/sites/joannabelbey/2015/01/21/how-healthcare-can-use-social-media-effectively-and-compliantly/ (accessed 23 September 2015).

Comstock, J. (2015) IMS: 1 in 10 health apps connects to a device, 1 in 50 connects to healthcare providers. *Mobi Health News*. http://mobihealthnews.com/46863/ims-1-in-10-health-apps-connects-to-a-device-1-in-50-connects-to-healthcare-providers/ (accessed 18 September 2015).

Crawford, K. and Schultz, J. (2014) Big data and due process: Toward a framework to redress predictive privacy harms. *Boston College Law Review*, 55: 93–128.

eBizMBA. (2016) Top 15 most popular health websites May 2016. *eBIZMBA*. www.ebizmba.com/articles/health-websites (accessed 25 May 2016).

Epstein, D.A., Jacobson, B.H., Bales, E., McDonald, D.W. and Munson, S.A. (2015) From 'nobody cares' to 'way to go!': A design framework for social sharing in personal informatics. *Computer Supported Cooperative Work and Social Computing (CSCW 15)*. Vancouver: ACM Press, pp. 1622–1636.

Foucault, M. (1988) Technologies of the self. In L. Martin, H. Gutman and P. Hutton (Eds.), *Technologies of the Self: A Seminar with Michel Foucault*. London: Tavistock, pp. 16–49.

Foucault, M. (1991) Governmentality. In G. Burchell, C. Gordon and P. Miller (Eds.), *The Foucault Effect: Studies in Governmentality*. Hemel Hempstead: Harvester Wheatsheaf, pp. 87–104.

Foucault, M. (2008) *The Birth of Biopolitics: Lectures at the Collège de France, 1978–79*. Basingstoke, UK: Palgrave Macmillan.

Fox, S. and Duggan, M. (2013) Health online. *Pew Research Internet Project*. www.pewinternet.org/2013/01/15/health-online-2013/ (accessed 12 December 2013).

Frakt, A. and Carroll, A.E. (2014) Do workplace wellness programs work? Usually not. *The New York Times*. www.nytimes.com/2014/09/12/upshot/do-workplace-wellness-programs-work-usually-not.html?_r=0 (accessed 29 June 2016).

Frissen, V., Lammes, S., de Lange, M., de Mul, J. and Raessens, J. (2015) Homo ludens 2.0: Play, media and identity. In V. Frissen, S. Lammes, M. de Lange, et al. (Eds.), *Playful Identities: The Ludification of Digital Media Cultures*. Amsterdam: University of Amsterdam Press, pp. 9–50.

Fuchs, C. (2014) *Social Media: A Critical Introduction*. London: Sage.

Gregg, M. (2015) Inside the data spectacle. *Television & New Media*, 16: 37–51.

Househ, M., Borycki, E. and Kushniruk, A. (2014) Empowering patients through social media: The benefits and challenges. *Health Informatics Journal*, 20: 50–58.

Huba, N. and Zhang, Y. (2012) Designing patient-centered personal health records (PHRs): Health care professionals' perspective on patient-generated data. *Journal of Medical Systems*, 36: 3893–3905.

Huckvale, K., Prieto, J., Tilney, M., Benghozi, P.-J. and Car, J. (2015) Unaddressed privacy risks in accredited health and wellness apps: A cross-sectional systematic assessment. *BMC Medicine*, 13. www.biomedcentral.com/1741-7015/13/214 (accessed 26 September 2015).

Humer, C. and Finkle, J. (2014) Your medical record is worth more to hackers than your credit card. *Reuters US*. www.reuters.com/article/2014/09/24/us-cybersecurity-hospitals-idUSKCN0HJ21I20140924 (accessed 26 July 2015).

Humphries, C. (2013) A hospital takes its own big-data medicine. *MIT Technology Review*. www.technologyreview.com/news/518916/a-hospital-takes-its-own-big-data-medicine/?goback=%2Egde_2181454_member_276737924#%21 (accessed 28 September 2013).

IMS Institute for Healthcare Informatics. (2015) *Patient Adoption of mHealth: Use, Evidence and Remaining Barriers to Mainstream Acceptance*. Parsipanny, NJ: IMS Institute for Healthcare Informatics,.

Jawbone. (2016) *UP by Jawbone*. Available at: https://jawbone.com/up.

John, N. (2013) Sharing and Web 2.0: The emergence of a keyword. *New Media & Society*, 15: 167–182.

Jordan, M. and Pfarr, N. (2014) Forget the quantified self: We need to build the quantified us. *Wired*. www.wired.com/2014/04/forget-the-quantified-self-we-need-to-build-the-quantified-us/ (accessed 12 June 2014).

Kish, L. and Topol, E. (2015) Unpatients – why patients should own their medical data. *Nature biotechnology*. www.nature.com/nbt/journal/v33/n9/full/nbt.3340.html (accessed 12 September 2015).

Kitchin, R. and Lauriault, T. (2014) Towards critical data studies: Charting and unpacking data assemblages and their work. *Social Science Research Network*. http://papers.ssrn.com/sol3/papers.cfm?abstract_id=2474112 (accessed 27 August 2014).

Kivits, J. (2013) E-health and renewed sociological approaches to health and illness. In K. Orton-Johnson and N. Prior (Eds.), *Digital Sociology: Critical Perspectives*. Basingstoke, UK: Palgrave Macmillan, pp. 213–226.

Lefebvre, R.C. and Bornkessel, A.S. (2013) Digital social networks and health. *Circulation*, 127: 1829–1836.

Levy, K. (2015) Intimate surveillance. *Idaho Law Review*, 679. www.uidaho.edu/law/law-review/articles (accessed 31 October 2015).

Li, J. (2015) A privacy preservation model for health-related social networking sites. *Journal of Medical Internet Research*, 17. www.jmir.org/2015/7/e168/ (accessed 11 July 2015).

Lomborg, S. and Frandsen, K. (2016) Self-tracking as communication. *Information, Communication & Society*, 19(7): 1015–1027.

Lupton, D. (1995) *The Imperative of Health: Public Health and the Regulated Body*. London: Sage.

Lupton, D. (2012a) M-health and health promotion: The digital cyborg and surveillance society. *Social Theory & Health*, 10: 229–244.

Lupton, D. (2012b) *Medicine as Culture: Illness, Disease and the Body*. London: Sage.

Lupton, D. (2013a) The digitally engaged patient: Self-monitoring and self-care in the digital health era. *Social Theory & Health*, 11: 256–270.

Lupton, D. (2013b) Quantifying the body: Monitoring and measuring health in the age of mHealth technologies. *Critical Public Health*, 23: 393–403.

Lupton, D. (2013c) Understanding the human machine. *IEEE Technology & Society Magazine*, 32: 25–30.

Lupton, D. (2014a) The commodification of patient opinion: The digital patient experience economy in the age of big data. *Sociology of Health & Illness*, 36: 856–869.

Lupton, D. (2014b) Critical perspectives on digital health technologies. *Sociology Compass*, 8: 1344–1359.

Lupton, D. (2014c) Self-tracking modes: reflexive self-monitoring and data practices. Social Science Research Network. Available at https://papers.ssrn.com/sol3/papers.cfm?abstract_id=2483549 (accessed 23 June 2017).

Lupton, D. (2015) Quantified sex: A critical analysis of sexual and reproductive self-tracking using apps. *Culture, Health & Sexuality*, 17: 440–453.

Lupton, D. (2016a) Digitized health promotion: Risk and personal responsibility for health in the Web 2.0 era. In J. Davis and A.M. Gonzalez (Eds.), *To Fix or To Heal*. New York: New York University Press, pp. 152–176.

Lupton, D. (2016b) The diverse domains of quantified selves: Self-tracking modes and dataveillance. *Economy and Society*, 43(1): 101–122.

Lupton, D. (2016c) *The Quantified Self: A Sociology of Self-Tracking*. Cambridge: Polity Press.

Lupton, D. and Thomas, G.M. (2015) Playing pregnancy: The ludification and gamification of expectant motherhood in smartphone apps. *M/C Journal*, 18. http://journal.media-culture.org.au/index.php/mcjournal/article/viewArticle/1012 (accessed 22 October 2015).

Marwick, A. (2012) The public domain: Social surveillance in everyday life. *Surveillance & Society*, 9: 378–393.

McCarthy, M. (2013) Experts warn on data security in health and fitness apps. *British Medical Journal*, 347. www.bmj.com/content/347/bmj.f5600 (accessed 27 February 2014).

McGregor, S. (2001) Neoliberalism and health care. *International Journal of Consumer Studies*, 25: 82–89.

Mitchell, R. and Waldby, C. (2006) *Tissue Economies: Blood, Organs, and Cell Lines in Late Capitalism*. Durham, NC: Duke University Press.

Nafus, D. and Sherman, J. (2014) This one does not go up to 11: The Quantified Self movement as an alternative big data practice. *International Journal of Communication*, 8: 1785–1794.

Olson, P. (2014) Get ready for wearable tech to plug into health insurance. *Forbes*. www.forbes.com/sites/parmyolson/2014/06/19/wearable-tech-health-insurance/ (accessed 21 June 2014).

Pasquale, F. (2014) The dark market for personal data. *The New York Times*. www.nytimes.com/2014/10/17/opinion/the-dark-market-for-personal-data.html (accessed 8 April 2015).

Petersen, A. and Lupton, D. (1996) *The New Public Health: Health and Self in the Age of Risk*. London: Sage.

Purpura, S., Schwanda, V., Williams, K., Stubler, W. and Sengers, P. (2011) Fit4life: The design of a persuasive technology promoting healthy behavior and ideal weight. *Proceedings of the SIGCHI Conference on Human Factors in Computing Systems*. Vancouver: ACM Press, pp. 423–432.

Quantified Self. (2016) *Quantified Self*. Available at: http://quantifiedself.com/.

Ritzer, G. (2014) Prosumption: Evolution, revolution, or eternal return of the same? *Journal of Consumer Culture*, 14: 3–24.

Robinson, R. (2014) The power of the hashtag. *PharmaVoice*. www.pharmavoice.com/content/digitaledition.html?pg=24 (accessed 4 May 2014).

Rogers, R. (2013) *Digital Methods*. Cambridge, MA: MIT Press.

Rooksby, J., Rost, M., Morrison, A. and Chalmers, M.C. (2014) Personal tracking as lived informatics. *Proceedings of the SIGCHI Conference on Human Factors in Computing Systems*. Toronto: ACM Press, pp. 1163–1172.

Rose, N. (2007a) Molecular biopolitics, somatic ethics and the spirit of biocapital. *Social Theory & Health*, 5: 3–29.

Rose, N. (2007b) *The Politics of Life Itself: Biomedicine, Power, and Subjectivity in the Twenty-First Century*. Princeton, NJ: Princeton University Press.

Rose, N. (2008) The value of life: Somatic ethics and the spirit of biocapital. *Daedalus*, 137: 36–48.

Rose, N. and Novas, C. (2005) Biological citizenship. In A. Ong and S. Collier (Eds.), *Global Assemblages: Technology, Politics and Ethics as Anthropological Problems*. Malden, MA: Blackwell Publishing, pp. 439–463.

Rosenblat, A., Wikelius, K., boyd, d., Gangadharan, S.P. and Yu, C. (2014) Data & civil rights: Health primer. *Data & Society Research Institute*. www.datacivilrights.org/pubs/2014-1030/Health.pdf (accessed 16 December 2014).

Ruckenstein, M. (2014) Visualized and interacted life: Personal analytics and engagements with data doubles. *Societies*, 4: 68–84.

Ruckenstein, M. (2015) Uncovering everyday rhythms and patterns: Food tracking and new forms of visibility and temporality in health care. In L. Botin, C. Nohr and P. Bertelsen (Eds.), *Techno-Anthropology in Health Informatics*. Amsterdam: IOS Press, pp. 28–40.

Stragier, J., Evens, T. and Mechant, P. (2015) Broadcast yourself: An exploratory study of sharing physical activity on social networking sites. *Media International Australia*, 155: 120–129.

Swan, M. (2009) Emerging patient-driven health care models: an examination of health social networks, consumer personalized medicine and quantified self-tracking. *International Journal of Environmental Research and Public Health* 6: 492–525.

Swan, M. (2012a) Health 2050: The realization of personalized medicine through crowdsourcing, the quantified self, and the participatory biocitizen. *Journal of Personalized Medicine*, 2: 93–118.

Swan, M. (2012b) Sensor mania! The Internet of Things, wearable computing, objective metrics, and the Quantified Self 2.0. *Journal of Sensor and Actuator Networks*, 1: 217–253.

Swan, M. (2013) The quantified self: Fundamental disruption in big data science and biological discovery. *Big Data*, 1. http://online.liebertpub.com/doi/abs/10.1089/big.2012.0002 (accessed 2 March 2014).

Symons, X. (2015) Privacy 1: Security flaws. *BioEdge*. www.bioedge.org/index.php/bioethics/bioethics_article/11318 (accessed 8 February 2015).

Thomas, G.M. and Lupton, D. (2015) Threats and thrills: Pregnancy apps, risk and consumption. *Health, Risk & Society*, 17: 495–509.

Topol, E. (2015) *The Patient Will See You Now: The Future of Medicine is in Your Hands*. New York: Basic Books.

Treato. (2016) *Treato*. Available at: http://treato.com/.

van Dijck, J. (2013) *The Culture of Connectivity: A Critical History of Social Media*. Oxford: Oxford University Press.

van Dijck, J. (2014) Datafication, dataism and dataveillance: Big Data between scientific paradigm and ideology. *Surveillance & Society*, 12: 197–208.

Waldby, C. (2000) *The Visible Human Project: Informatic Bodies and Posthuman Medicine*. London: Routledge.

Whitson, J. (2013) Gaming the quantified self. *Surveillance & Society*, 11: 163–176.

Wolf, G. (2009) Know thyself: Tracking every facet of life, from sleep to mood to pain, 24/7/365. *Wired*. http://archive.wired.com/medtech/health/magazine/17-07/lbnp_knowthyself (accessed 12 October 2013).

Wolf, G. (2014) Access matters. *Quantified Self*. http://quantifiedself.com/page/5/ (accessed 4 September 2014).

Zamosky, L. (2014) Digital health tools are a growing part of workplace wellness programs. *iHealthBeat*. www.ihealthbeat.org/insight/2014/digital-health-tools-are-a-growing-part-of-workplace-wellness-programs (accessed 2 August 2014).

Zuboff, S. (2015) Big other: Surveillance capitalism and the prospects of an information civilization. *Journal of Information Technology*, 30: 75–89.

32

Social Media Platforms and Education

José van Dijck and Thomas Poell

INTRODUCTION

What is the impact of social media on education and learning in schools? This very broad question has been addressed by academics from a variety of disciplines. In this chapter, we will first give an overview of the different ways in which this question has been tackled. Most scholars have studied the impact of social media as *tools*, assessing their immediate impact on learning. While some predict they may potentially revolutionize education, others see them as potential minefields. We want to introduce an approach to social media that does not just regard them as tools, but as *platforms*, driven by a complex interplay between technical architectures, business models, and mass user activity. These automated architectures, models, and activities introduce new mechanisms in social life (van Dijck & Poell, 2013). Beyond affecting student behaviour and teaching practices, they also impact the organization of schools and universities and, one might argue,

(public) education as such. We will highlight two mechanisms that are increasingly relevant in online teaching environments: *datafication* and *commodification*. To illustrate our approach, we will first focus on primary education, then on higher education.

To illustrate how datafication affects education, we discuss a Californian initiative called AltSchool, a platform that is currently gaining traction in the US. AltSchool, which has been touted the 'Uber for primary education', is an interesting case because it is an initiative that is potentially scalable to other countries and is backed by major Silicon Valley investors. The platform thrives on datafication: learning processes are translated into data processes and turned into tracking systems that continuously relate individual progress to standardized performance. The technological architecture of the platform directly informs its pedagogical philosophy of personalized data tracking – a mechanism that dominates the entire ecosystem of connective media. We will identify and discuss the pros and cons of data-driven personalized educational platforms such as AltSchool in primary education.

Next, we will focus on how commodification operates as a mechanism in Massive Open Online Courses (or MOOCs) in higher education; MOOCs such as Coursera deploy the same principles of datafication and personalization as AltSchool, but their impact can be observed outside American universities, in Europe and other continents. MOOCs are promoted as an efficient and effective form of higher education – allegedly cheaper than courses and curriculums offered by brick-and-mortar universities. Zooming in on the principle of commodification, we argue that MOOCs operate business and governance models that are very similar to social media platforms. The ways in which MOOCs incorporate social media mechanisms may affect the pedagogical and economic value of (institutional) college education.

Beyond pedagogy and economics lies the question of *education as a public good*. How do online educational platforms relate to key public values sustaining school systems? These values are subject to fierce contestation, raising fundamental questions such as privacy protection and academic independence. Online education has become an intricate battleground for waging private, corporate, and public interests in an online economy where technological interoperability is expedited by larger social trends such as privatization and globalization. These disputes are likely to have a substantial impact on the definition of online education as a public good.

SOCIAL MEDIA'S IMPACT ON EDUCATION: TOOLS OR PLATFORMS?

Since their emergence, the role of social platforms in all types of education has been extensively debated by academics and professionals (for an overview, see Davis et al., 2012). Disputes on the 'promises and perils' of social media and their impact on classroom learning have intensified in accordance with the growth of these media since 2004. On the 'promises' side, researchers have investigated whether social networking platforms can be turned into efficient and effective tools for knowledge enhancement and classroom discussion (Tess, 2013). The ubiquity of social media in virtually every aspect of children's and teenager's lives has led teachers to reflect on how to purposefully integrate these tools into curricular activities (Gikas & Grant, 2013; Mao, 2014). Some argue that social media use plays a key role in helping students with particular educational tasks, such as information retrieval (Hrastinski & Aghaee, 2012). On the 'perils side' of the debate, social media platforms have been identified as a constant cause of dismay to teachers, triggering disruptions in the classroom (Junco, 2012). Others conclude that the potential of social media as a means of sharing academic knowledge has not been actualized yet (Forkosh-Baruch & Hershkovitz, 2012). Both sides in this debate adopt a social media-as-tools approach: social media are considered as technical tools that may either enhance or disrupt learning experiences. So far, however, empirical evidence on the efficacy and efficiency of social media use in the classroom has been rather scarce in the academic literature.

A second approach to social media in relation to education and learning has been the 'civic engagement' approach. Large social media networks such as Facebook and Twitter have been hailed as drivers of a new, socially engaged educational experience, fostering the capacity for discussion and connection among youngsters (Friesen & Low, 2012; Vanwynsberghe & Verdegem, 2013). Twitter, particularly, has been found helpful in fostering in-class discussions and engaging students with their learning tasks (Kassens-Noor, 2012). Most discussions on how social media nurture student engagement fit the larger argument on online media and civic engagement, a discussion meticulously described by Bennett (2008) and Jenkins (2009). Bennett argues that social media are not simply 'tools' for engagement, but they are themselves part of a changing institutional and political landscape where they may embody both supportive and critical attitudes towards education. According to Bennett, researchers should examine social media networks not apart from institutional changes, but as an integral part of socio-economic and political transformations.

The approach taken in this chapter extends Bennett's ideas on civic engagement, regarding social media not as (technical) tools but as *platforms*. Online social media platforms are more than mere technical facilitators: they are simultaneously technological, economic, and socio-cultural frameworks for managing online social traffic (Gillespie, 2010). Thousands of platforms have proliferated on the Web since the turn of the millennium, forming an ecosystem of connective media through which people perform a large part of their everyday lives, including communication and educational activities (van Dijck, 2013a). All platforms are equally defined by a set of mechanisms, which we have described in more detail elsewhere (van Dijck and Poell, 2013). In the remainder of this chapter, we want to analyze how these mechanisms shape education, affecting not online learning and teaching in school environments, but the organization of primary and higher education more generally. In doing so, we will concentrate on two mechanisms in particular: datafication and commodification.

Datafication – the tendency to quantify all aspects of social interaction and turn them into code – is one of the basic mechanisms undergirding social platforms (Mayer-Schoenberger & Cukier, 2013; van Dijck, 2014). This principle is becoming more popular in school curriculums at every stage of education, from kindergarten to university. Indeed, as Selwyn (2015: 66) argues, 'schools, colleges, universities and other educational contexts now function increasingly

along "data driven" lines'. Large quantities of data are generated and collected on a daily basis, not only by and through schools, but also by (or in collaboration with) companies that are keen on gathering information from youngsters. Data sets range 'from the often ad hoc "in-house" monitoring of students and teachers to the systematic "public" collection of data at local, state and federal levels' (Selwyn, 2015: 66).

As educational assessment is increasingly quantified, student performance gets governed by numbers (Robert-Holmes, 2015). Quantitative learning analytics, grounded in large numbers of students' online behavioral data, involve data *tracking* (real-time analytics) as well as *predictive* analytics (Tempelaar, Rienties & Giesbers, 2015). For instance, data tracking can be used to register fine-grained information about the amount of time a student needs to solve a problem, to record the cognitive stages in problem solving, to measure the amount of instruction needed, and to trace student interaction (Koedinger, McLaughlin & Stamper, 2014a). Predictive analytics may result in algorithmic calculations defining an individual's chances for academic success based on average scores and a number of variables. These emerging digital policy instruments transfer the assessment of didactic and pedagogical values from teachers and classrooms to (commercial) online platforms deploying real-time and predictive analytics techniques. The general idea of data-driven platform services is to allow for modification and corrective action of learning activities; they provide the as of yet unrealized potential to radically transform learning processes and pedagogies (Maull, Godsiff & Mulligan, 2014).

The ability to monitor individuals and groups at a microlevel obviously includes competence scores and performance levels, but may also pertain to stress levels, speed variations, and heart rates. The sheer unlimited combination of data sets may cause a paradigm shift in education. Some researchers have hailed the datafication of educational processes, emphasizing how personalized data analytics informs learning design and may facilitate specific pedagogical action (Lockyer, Heathcote & Dawson, 2013). Others have pointed out how a growing emphasis on datafication through online platforms and platform services can have serious impact on the organization of education and increase managerialism and dataveillance (Selwyn, 2015). Finally, a number of researchers have pointed towards the ethical and legal challenges involved in data collection and interpretation in educational contexts, including privacy and data ownership (Siemens, 2013; Slade & Prinsloo, 2013).

Datafication as a mechanism that drives social media platforms is closely intertwined with the mechanism of *commodification*: the monetization of online social traffic through business models and governance structures. Social media platforms are propelled by a limited number of business models that are mainly based on data as connective leverage to generate economic value. Commodification in the context of educational platforms often involves the processing of learning data by large data hubs that render big data streams monetizable and potentially profitable. The center of educational governance, as Williamson (2016: 123) argues, 'is being distributed and displaced to new digitized "centres of calculation"'. Massive information transfer to 'calculation centres' and data hubs tallies with the concentration power in a few large data companies which may serve commercial rather than pedagogical interests (Lawson, Sanders & Smith, 2015).

Educational platforms cannot and should not be seen apart from the larger ecosystem of connective media through which they thrive – an ecosystem that is gradually transforming all sectors of society and that is steered by the same set of mechanisms. However, this system is not a level playing field as some platforms are more powerful than others. Facebook, Google, Apple, Amazon and Microsoft are pivotal gatekeepers in the data flows that fuel the 'platform society'. Their

economic interests in educational platforms are huge and it should come as no surprise that they heavily invest in the development and distribution of online education.

In the next two sections, we will analyse *how* these two dominant mechanisms of social media platforms – datafication and commodification – increasingly penetrate the processes and institutional contexts of education. In the US in particular, datafication has been hailed as a new paradigm in primary education, and AltSchool is a case in point. Commodification is surfacing as a structuring principle in online platforms targeting higher education across the globe, a development illustrated by Coursera. Although AltSchool and Coursera are mere examples, we think that these platforms may elucidate the larger trend of how social media mechanisms affect the transformation of the educational sector in a platform-driven society.

DATAFICATION: ALTSCHOOL AS A PLATFORM FOR PRIMARY EDUCATION

Primary schools in the US increasingly incorporate educational software into their curricula, from math and language apps to customized online lessons. Along with educational software came data trackers and 'dashboards'; instruments that record and analyze thousands of pieces of data about each student, catering to their abilities and tastes, have become increasingly popular. Proponents of quantitative learning analytics claim they are a significant quality booster for students' learning (Ebner & Schön, 2013; Reamer et al., 2015). Real-time data about individual learning processes help instructors monitor students' progress and allow for corrective feedback. Personalized data allegedly provide unprecedented insights into how individual students learn and what kind of tutoring they need. If the data show that one student is better at solving verbal math problems than abstract equations, software developers can adapt the assignments and implement personalized variations. Aggregated data about learning behavior provide the input for individual 'adaptive learning' schemes. As some advocates argue, continuous measuring of performance levels may enhance the quality of instruction (Maull, Godsiff & Mulligan, 2014). Taking a cue from the social media world, some schools are fully embracing datafication and personalization as the core principles of their pedagogy, and are eager to team up with tech entrepreneurs to explore the datafied learning concept.

AltSchool is a Californian initiative founded in 2013 by Google's former head of personalization Max Ventilla; it has drawn much attention, if not for its educational philosophy, then certainly for the names of its financial backers, including Mark Zuckerberg's education-focused non-profit foundation and the Founder's Fund of entrepreneur and venture capitalist Peter Thiel. AltSchool envisions and enacts a one-classroom setting populated by teachers but without administrators; AltSchool offers no facilities except for an iPad or Chromebook for each child. Instructed through a weekly 'playlist', each pupil engages in individual or group activities that are tailored toward their unique capabilities. Independent projects have replaced direct group instruction. Teachers supervise the learning process; student performance is monitored through tracking systems that minutely analyze each child's tasks and results. Informed by these data, teachers keep cards of each child's progress and setbacks, and use them to make weekly personalized learning plans for each child. This means for some pupils that math gets prioritized over reading skills, and for others, the other way around (Lapowsky, 2015). Proponents hail the process of datafication as a means to make education more efficient by cutting out ineffective tasks for each child individually.

More than just a classroom, AltSchool is an experimental lab where teachers and students are minutely observed: every activity is videotaped and analyzed. A large technical staff develops customized educational software and tweaks learning analytics to optimize each part of the learning process. The tools developed by this team are remarkably similar to those deployed by social media companies: a recommendation algorithm, not unlike Netflix or Amazon, that takes into account everything a child has already learned; data analytics that eliminate the need for constant testing; and reputation mechanisms that rate the personal input of children while measuring their relative scores.

Although AltSchool is currently still in its experimental stages and has only been tested in small sections of privileged Bay Area districts, there is every intention of scaling and spreading this model once it gets beyond the testing phase. In terms of educational philosophy, AltSchool favors technology over teachers; online personalized learning takes over classroom instruction; and the primacy of predictive analytics downgrades teachers' professional judgment. In addition, individualized learning schemes are taking priority over the notion of a curriculum as the cornerstone of education. All these principles arguably undermine the conventional pedagogical model still dominant in most brick-and-mortar schools across the US. The comparison with a disruptive platform uprooting the taxi sector inevitably pops up when educators speak of 'Uber-education.'

Detractors of AltSchool have pointed out how the principle of datafication advances a pedagogical perspective also known as 'learnification.' Many data-driven, personalized education initiatives focus on *learning* rather than education, and on *processes* rather than on teachers and students. The (social) activity of learning is broken into quantifiable cognitive and pedagogical units, such as instruction, short quizzes, assignments, deliberation with other students, and tests. The learnification model is predicated on the real-time, short-term process of learning rather than its long-term outcome, which is, in most schools, to provide an education. Education, as critics argue, involves simultaneous nourishing of intellectual, social, technical, and cognitive skills. The 'learnification' of education, according to some social scientists and philosophers, sprouts from the idea that learning can be managed, monitored, controlled, and ultimately modified in each student's personal mind (Attick, 2013; Biesta, 2012; Mead, 2014).

Datafication appears to be a double-edged sword. Indeed, personalized assignments based on quantitative measurements help improve each individual's learning process and outcomes. However, personalization algorithms are based on *inference* of users' needs or interests – supporting the prediction of needs rather than solving the demand for remedial teaching. A by-product of personalized learning algorithms may be that they 'filter out what is not designated as being of interest to users and rather presents to them only what fits the system's belief of what their interests are' (Ashman et al., 2014: 824). In addition, the biggest challenge that software developers face is the rather paradoxical demand of *mass individualization*: the question is how the AltSchool approach will scale up to schools populated by thousands of students. Will it benefit not just privileged Bay Area students whose parents are able to afford the experimental school's hefty fees, but also children from underprivileged and underfunded schools?

Besides the ideological criticism concerning this learnification paradigm, researchers have raised various other concerns, such as privacy violations and selective ranking (Siemens, 2013). Students enrolled in AltSchool and similar initiatives are prone to constant monitoring, to the extent that they become (unwitting) participants in continuous lab experiments. Over the past years, online education has shown a conclusive shift toward continuous behavioral experiments (Ebben & Murphy, 2014). Using students for research experiments is nothing new. However, the continuous tracking of young

children raises important ethical questions; issues of privacy and repurposing of data have raised concerns from parents and regulators alike (Ashman et al., 2014; Selwyn, 2015). Student and teacher performance are increasingly monitored through dashboards and assessments are based on behavioral tracking mechanisms and automated classroom surveys – techniques already introduced in many elementary schools throughout the United States and that have triggered serious controversy (Rich, 2015; Singer, 2015).

Datafication and personalization mechanisms such as reputational ranking or recommendation systems are informed by the techno-commercial logic of social media platforms. On most social networking sites, such as Facebook or Google+, assessments happen *instantly* and *continuously*, mostly on the basis of *perception* or *likability*. Other popular platforms, such as Uber and Airbnb, deploy user recommendations to anchor reputation and trustworthiness: customers review their drivers or hosts, who, in turn, can check their customers' online reputations (Coetzee et al., 2014). But what happens when we transfer this principle to an online learning environment? And how does it affect the traditional (hierarchical) dynamics between teacher, students, and institution? Educating is a process very different from liking or recommending. Students do not always like what they learn; learning often requires endless practice or involves unexpected encounters with content that only much later turns out to be very valuable. In short, the instantaneity of recommendations and likability of perceptions – the need for instant gratification – may be squarely at odds with long-term pedagogical values of curriculum-based education.

Also unresolved are the ethical issues involved in the ownership of (meta)data and their accessibility, which can be quite thorny. One of the advantages claimed by online courses is that students' performance is not just assessed in terms of grades or learning outcomes, but can be evaluated in terms of learning curves and social adaptability. Datafication of the learning process – minutely monitoring the interactive and cognitive behavior of pupils – yield an abundance of data beyond mere test results. How fast do students answer a quiz question? How autonomous or collegial are they when it comes to problem solving? Behavioral data are a sort of by-product of continuous monitoring, and students are barely aware of these data being accumulated, interpreted, and repurposed (Ashman et al., 2014). In fact, dashboards may produce behavioral information that is far more interesting than a straightforward grade point average. It is already completely normal for employers to scrutinize a potential employee's postings on Facebook and LinkedIn and reject candidates on the basis of social media appearances (Swallow, 2011 van Dijck, 2013b). Therefore, it is not at all difficult to imagine that future employers might request a full performance record from kindergarten up to college to assess an employee's intellectual and social adaptability.

COMMODIFICATION: COURSERA AND THE IMPACT OF MOOCS ON HIGHER EDUCATION

Many of the same mechanisms involving datafication and personalization can be identified in the platforms for higher education that we have come to call Massive Open Online Courses (MOOCs). Platforms like Coursera, Udacity, and edX started to penetrate the higher education sector in 2012. In this section, we want to focus on the mechanism of *commodification*: the transformation of objects, activities, and ideas into data streams with the intent to turn them into tradable commodities. Over the past four years, MOOCs have become popular vehicles for online learning, and they frequently promote themselves as future alternatives to or even replacements of college education. A large

number of universities, both in the US and in Europe, have started to collaborate with mostly American-based MOOCS. For the purpose of this chapter, we want to zoom in on Coursera as an example of a successful platform whose business model is strikingly similar to the dominant socio-economic principles connecting all platforms on the social Web.

Coursera is a for-profit platform that started in 2012 out of Stanford, and has offered online courses to students worldwide. Initially backed by four American universities, it engages in partnerships with universities in Europe, South America and Asia. Over the past four years, Coursera has experimented with various business models and is still finetuning some of its monetizing schemes. Similar to Facebook, Google, and other major platforms, Coursera offers content that is free to end-users; students can enroll and follow videotaped lectures, engage in online exercises, and take tests. Typically, a university organizes the educational content featured in courses, while Coursera provides the online means for attracting a mass audience. User acquisition is critical to achieve network effects, as we have learned from social media platforms (Clow, 2013). Similarly, MOOCs have a vested interest in massive numbers of users in order to obtain large sets of (learning) data and student profiles. Students and young professionals are arguably the most coveted target population of data industries, and their attention is very valuable. To optimize their metrics, it is crucial for Coursera to attract large quantities of students with free content. The more (meta) data they collect, the more they learn about users (Koedinger, McLaughlin & Stamper, 2014b).

Still in the early stages of its development, Coursera deploys a variety of value-capture strategies, one of which is the freemium model. A premium variant expands the free option by offering extra paid-for services such as so-called 'signature tracks', where students pay for certificates of completion, proctored exams, and identity verification. Proctored exams and verified certificates are gradually developed into – potentially profitable – units that can be marketed globally. Another business model is to collect and trade user data. Coursera's user policy states that it may collect 'student-generated content, such as assignments you submit to instructors, peer-graded assignments and peer grading student feedback … course data, such as student responses to in-video quizzes, standalone quizzes, exams and surveys' (Coursera Privacy, 2015). It is unclear whether Coursera is currently monetizing its wealth of student data, sharing it with third parties. Advertising in online content is another option which Coursera has not utilized yet, but which, as some point out, may be a lucrative value proposition (Kalman, 2014). Like most MOOCs, Coursera is fully absorbed in the ecosystem of connective media where Facebook and Google dominate online advertising.

Part of Coursera's revenues comes not from end-users but from universities. First, universities pay for the content offered on the site, and with an average of US$50,000 per online course, MOOCs do not come cheap. According to Bogen (2015), Coursera's contracts with universities 'promise 6–15% in revenue-sharing per course with the university and 20% of gross profits on aggregate sets of courses, paid out every quarter.' Coursera thus draws over 80% from its online course profits. Universities consorting with Coursera pay for the development of their course content as well as for instructors who process student feedback and questions – a massive effort that is not always recognized properly. In 2015, Coursera started to offer a degree MA-program in collaboration with Georgia Tech University in exchange for an unknown percentage of tuition fees. Universities, in other words, invest heavily in Coursera's business model.

How does a MOOC's value proposition differ from (and profit from) the pricing system that sustains traditional universities? Regular universities offer a 'bundled' educational experience – an experience that comes complete with lecture halls, facilities, and libraries and labor-intensive courses where instructors give feedback and for which they proctor and grade exams to result in a diploma degree (in some instances, course certificates and transfer credits). For this all-inclusive package, students pay tuition and fees; in the case of public education, taxpayers fund the institutions to make higher education more affordable to citizens. The conventional business model reflects the ideology of higher education as a curriculum-based, comprehensive experience that offers an education at a price that includes not only lectures or course content but certification, advising, tutoring, and testing (Boullier, 2012; Decker, 2014).

Coursera's value proposition runs parallel to social media platforms' revenue models. Content is free to end-users; money is made from offering premium services and from leveraging data value to interested third parties. By the same token, Coursera's model parallels the way Facebook and Google promote the 'unbundling' of content, for instance news and publishing industries: news articles and advertisements no longer come in a bundled package, but are resdistributed via Facebook's News Feed and Google's PageRank algorithms. The intricate intertwining between datafication and commodification as underpinning mechanisms illustrates how the ecosystem of connective platforms is fueled by techno-economic forces. As we saw in the example of AltSchool, the accumulation of behavioral learning data culled from participants all over the world can be sold to businesses competing for global talent. The appetite for educational data as valuable resources on the data market is enormous. Combined with other data, such as social media profiles or health and fitness data, the availability of learning data may render CVs to future employers virtually obsolete. The repurposing of student data in the US context is a large grey legal area.

As Young (2015) points out, privacy law is simply outdated when it comes to platforms like AltSchool and Coursera or other MOOCs.

The widespread distribution and adoption of educational platforms promoting a dynamics based on these mechanisms will likely affect not only students' and teachers' relationship towards learning, but also towards the institutions of education. As Kalman (2014: 11–12) convincingly argues, the logic of MOOCs tends to strip down higher education to its most traditional and visible components – video lectures and examinations – some of which are offered for free to users. Partnering institutions pay for the costly infrastructure that comes with higher education. Coursera as a platform charges a percentage of course revenue – if there is any – in exchange for using its format and global distribution function, but they do not contribute anything towards the 'collective' costs of producing education. So whereas the educational content is entirely generated and paid for by universities, Coursera's added value comes from unbundling and then rebundling content, and offering this to students worldwide. The real costs of massive open online courses remain obscure, because they are largely paid for by academic partner institutions and by students in the form of private data. Not unlike Uber and Airbnb, Coursera can trade off valuable information to third parties using student data as currency. It is precisely this connective platform model that has caused the disruption of entire sectors, such as newspaper publishing and the music industry (Dellarocas & van Alstyne, 2013).

THE PLATFORMIZATION OF EDUCATION

The mechanisms of datafication and commodification, adapted from the ecosystem of social media platforms, may foreshadow a profound shift in the organization of education. Of course, single platforms like AltSchool or Coursera can never account for an entire institutional transformation, but they do signal a larger trend. While few people believe Altschool and Coursera pose a serious threat to brick-and-mortar educational institutions the way Uber and Airbnb have disrupted the transportation and hospitality sectors, they are likely to have a strong impact on the educational sector. Although it is impossible to predict how deeply the dynamics of 'platformization' will penetrate the traditional structures of higher education, three potential implications follow from the analysis above. First, educational platforms tend to subjugate their pedagogical principles to social media mechanisms; second, the efficacy of educational software and data tracking systems in schools and universities have so far been poorly tested but are nevertheless presented as much-needed fixes to outdated educational institutions; and third, the incorporation of online education in a global world of commercial high-tech platforms may transform the notion of education as a public good.

To start with the first potential implication: schools and didactic online systems tend to blend in with the techno-economic and socio-cultural mechanisms of social platforms, particularly the mechanisms of datafication and commodification. Social networks like Facebook and Google+ have already deeply penetrated the everyday lives of pupils and students (Tess, 2013). Inside and outside schools, youngsters are growing up immersed in the compelling social interaction these platforms offer in terms of connecting, liking, rating and following each other. Platforms like Facebook are predicated on mass individualization, allowing personalized content and many-to-many communication at the same time. Besides, various platforms developed by Google have a significant presence in students' lives, offering free services such as Gmail, Scholar, Books, and LibraryLink to students, teachers, and universities. For funding-deprived institutions, these propositions are increasingly hard to resist, and the result is that corporate platforms such as Google, Facebook, LinkedIn, and Microsoft are able to position themselves strategically, at the gateways of educational infrastructures such as libraries, administrative and communication systems. Free cloud services offer students the expediency and convenience of online tools that they can access for 'free' (Center on Law and Information Policy, 2013). Advantages notwithstanding, it is increasingly difficult for students to 'opt out' of an educational environment that is inundated with connective tools if they feel uncomfortable about trading privacy for access and dataveillance for convenience.

Second, many online educational tools are currently celebrated as much-needed fixes of a crumbling institution that has been, to a large extent, underfunded. However, few of the (expensive) online solutions have been properly tested; their short-term gains in learning progress may be valued intuitively over long-term pedagogies. Indeed, online learning tools undoubtedly add value to the arsenals of teachers and researchers (Gikas & Grant, 2013; Rennie & Morrison, 2013). Online tools, if carefully mixed with proven pedagogical methods in blended learning environments, may enhance the learning process not only for already advantaged students, but also for those who are less gifted and need more training. Pedagogical instruments and funding contexts are interdependent variables. Education has always been and will always be a labor-intensive, local, and costly affair, but costs and benefits are not a zero-sum game. The compelling rhetoric used by Coursera's and AltSchool's promoters often makes them appear as 'technological solutionism' to the problem of disadvantaged students all over the world (Morozov, 2013). However, online educational platforms are more than a story of technology; they are part of the socio-economic conditions in which education is embedded in a town, state, or nation (Stohl, 2014).

Finally, we need to reflect on how the incorporation of learning tools in a global world of commercial high-tech platforms may transform the notion of (public) education. The educational sector is equally prone to disruptive innovation as the hospitality and transportation industries, but education is fundamentally different from hotels or cars in that it is also a *public good*. For instance, when it comes to accreditation, standardized credits, and valorized diplomas, education is still largely governed through national systems, which are regulated and validated by government institutions and subject to democratic control. Particularly in Europe, education is still largely a public sector, while in the US, private schools and universities are taking up a proportionally larger share. The pressure to open up educational standards and regulation to global commercial high-tech companies is an important strategy pursued by education platforms such as AltSchool and Coursera and their owners. Using these platforms as examples may help us understand how education is increasingly defined as a technological challenge developed by tech companies and decreasingly as a service carried out by dedicated teachers and funded by taxes (Kolowich, 2013; Meister, 2013).

At a time when schools, universities, and students are facing serious challenges in terms of funding, a proposition that seemingly reduces the cost of teaching, attracts large enrollments, and offers free courses to students seems irresistible. So it should come as no surprise that the 'scalable' and 'free' logic of online learning modules is finding inroads into many (private as well as public) school systems. As we have learned above, AltSchool is a private school financially backed by Google, attracting a high-end class of pupils in Silicon Valley. In September 2015, Facebook's Mark Zuckerberg announced he would start to fund the Summit Public Schools in San Francisco – an initiative that develops software to help individual children learn at their own pace. Just like AltSchool,

Facebook's new platform-based initiative promises to help create tailored lessons and projects, and administer individualized quizzes that special software can grade and track. Developing educational software is a crucial strategy to integrate the underpinning mechanisms of social platforms into the everyday lives of young children and their institutional environments.

Facebook and Google are also both heavily investing in developing and financially supporting MOOCs, such as Coursera, Udacity, and edX. Although they often invest in educational platforms indirectly, through nonprofit initiatives, it is clear that the intricate interwovenness between educational platforms and major connective platforms lies in their interlocking dynamics. In sum, the battle for domination in the world of online education is as much about technological and economic mechanisms as it is about pedagogy, effective learning strategies, and quality teaching (Beetham & Sharpe, 2013). Even if online platforms will never replace schools or universities, they will likely have a substantial impact on how education becomes redefined as a public good. By regarding social media as *platforms* rather than just tools, we wanted to draw attention to the power of its underpinning dynamics. Online platforms do not only affect basic processes of learning and teaching, but also impact the ways in which education is organized in a society that is increasingly data-driven and platform-based.

REFERENCES

Ashman, H., Brailsford, H., Cristea, A. J., Sheng, Q. Z., Stewart, C., Toms, E. G., & Wade, V. (2014). The ethical and social implications of personalization technologies for e-learning. *Information and Management*, 51, 819–832.

Attick, D. (2013). Education is dead: A requiem. I. *Critical Questions in Education*, 5(1), 1–9.

Beetham, H., & Sharpe, R. (Eds.). (2013). *Rethinking pedagogy for a digital age: Designing for 21st century learning*. New York: Routledge.

Bennett, W. Lance. (2008). Changing citizenship in the digital age. In W. L. Bennett (Ed.), *Civic life online: Learning how digital media can engage youth* (pp. 1–24). Cambridge, MA: MIT Press. doi: 10.1162/dmal. 9780262524827.001.

Biesta, G. (2012). Giving teaching back to education: Responding to the disappearance of the teacher. *Phenomenology and Practice*, 6(2), 35–49.

Bogen, M. (2015). Coursera flipped the classroom, but can it turn a profit? *Open Forum*, April 22. Retrieved from: https://openforum. hbs.org/challenge/understand-digital-transformation-of-business/business-model/coursera-flipped-the-classroom-but-can-it-turn-a-profit.

Boullier, D. (2012). The MOOCs fad and bubble: Please tell us another story. *Inside Higher Ed*, December 18. Retrieved from: www.inside-highered.com/blogs/globalhighered/moocs-fad-and-bubble-please-tell-us-another-story.

Center on Law and Information Policy. (2013). *Privacy and cloud computing in public schools*. New York: Fordham University. Retrieved from: www.fordham.edu/info/23830/research/5917/privacy_and_cloud_computing_in_public_schools.

Clow, D. (2013). MOOCs and the funnel of participation. In *Proceedings of the Third International Conference on Learning Analytics and Knowledge* (pp. 185–189). New York: ACM Press.

Coetzee, D., Fox Marti, A., Hearst, A., & Hartmann, B. (2014). Should your MOOC forum use a reputation system? In *Proceedings of the 17th ACM Conference on Computer Supported Cooperative Work and Social Computing* (pp. 1176–1187). New York: ACM Press.

Coursera Privacy. (2015). Home page. Retrieved from: www.coursera.org/.

Davis, C., Deil-Amen, R., Rios-Aguilar, C., & Gonzalez-Cranche, M. (2012). *Social media in higher education: A literature review and research directions*. University of Pennsylvania: Selected Works Charles Davis. Retrieved from: https://works.bepress.com/hfdavis/2/.

Decker, G. (2014). MOOCology 1.0. In S. D. Krause & C. L. Lowe (Eds.), *Invasion of the MOOCs: Promises and perils of the new massive open online courses* (pp. 3–13). Anderson, SC: Parlor Press.

Dellarocas, C., & van Alstyne, M. (2013). Money models for MOOCs. *Communications of the ACM, 56*, 25–28.

Ebben, M., & Murphy, J. S. (2014). Unpacking MOOC scholarly discourse: A review of nascent MOOC scholarship. *Learning, Media and Technology, 39*(3), 328–345.

Ebner, M., & Schön, M. (2013). Why learning analytics for primary education matters! *Bulletin of the IEEE Technical Committee on Learning Technology, 15*(2). http://lttf.ieee.org/issues/april2013/Ebner.pdf.

Forkosh-Baruch, A., & Hershkovitz, A. (2012). A case study of Israeli higher-education institutes sharing scholarly information with the community via social networks. *The Internet and Higher Education, 15*(1), 58–68.

Friesen, N., & Lowe, S. (2012). The questionable promise of social media for education: Connective learning and the commercial imperative. *Journal of Computer Assisted Learning, 28*(3), 183–194.

Gikas, J., & Grant, M. (2013). Mobile computing devices in higher education: Student perspectives on learning with cellphones, smartphones and social media. *The Internet and Higher Education, 19*, 18–26.

Gillespie, T. (2010). The politics of platforms. *New Media and Society, 12*(3), 347–364.

Hrastinski, S., & Aghaee, N. (2012). How are campus students using social media to support their studies? An explorative interview study. *Education and Information Technologies, 17*(4), 451–464.

Jenkins, H. (2009). *Confronting the challenges of participatory culture: Media education for the 21st century*. Cambridge, MA: MIT Press.

Junco, R. (2012). The relationship between frequency of Facebook use, participation in Facebook activities, and student engagement. *Computers & Education, 58*(1), 162–171.

Kalman, Y. (2014). A race to the bottom: MOOCs and higher education business models. *Open Learning, 29*(1), 5–14.

Kassens-Noor, E. (2012). Twitter as a teaching practice to enhance active and informal learning in higher education: The case of sustainable tweets. *Active Learning in Higher Education, 13*(1), 9–21.

Koedinger, K. R., McLaughlin, E. A., & Stamper, J. C. (2014a). MOOCs and technology to advance learning and learning research: Data-driven learner modeling to understand and improve online learning. *Ubiquity, 3*, 1–13.

Koedinger, K. R., McLaughlin, E. A., & Stamper, J. C. (2014b). MOOCs and technology to advance learning and learning research: Data-driven learner modeling to understand and improve online learning (Ubiquity symposium). *Ubiquity.* DOI=http://dx.doi.org/10.1145/2591682

Kolowich, S. (2013). As MOOC debate simmers at San Jose State, American U. calls a halt. *Chronicle of Higher Education*. Retrieved from: http://chronicle.com/article/As-MOOC-Debate-Simmers-at-San/139147/.

Lapowsky, I. (2015). Inside the school Silicon Valley thinks will save education. *Wired*, May 15. Retrieved from: www.wired.com/2015/05/altschool/.

Lawson, S., Sanders, K., & Smith, L. (2015). Commodification of the information profession: A critique of higher education under neoliberalism. *Journal of Librarianship and Scholarly Communication, 3*(1): eP1182. http://dx.doi.org/10.7710/2162-3309.1182.

Lockyer, L., Heathcote, E., & Dawson, S. (2013). Informing pedagogical action: Aligning learning analytics with learning design. *American Behavioral Scientist, 57*(10): 1439–1459.

Mao, J. (2014). Social media for learning: A mixed methods study on high school students' technology affordances and perspectives. *Computers and Human Behavior, 33*, 213–223.

Maull, R., Godsiff, P., & Mulligan, C. E. (2014). The impact of datafication on service systems. *Proceedings of the 47th Hawaii International Conference on System Science* (pp. 1139–1201). Waikoloba, Hawaii, January 6–9. New York: IEEE Computer Society. Retrieved from: www.computer.org/csdl/proceedings/hicss/2014/2504/00/2504b193-abs.html.

Mayer-Schoenberger, V., & Cukier, K. (2013). *Big data: A revolution that will transform how we live, work, and think*. London: John Murray.

Mead, K. (2014). The hidden costs of MOOCs. In D. Krause & C. D. Lowe (Eds.), *Invasion of the MOOCs: The promises and perils of massive open online courses* (pp. 45–55). Anderson, SC: Parlor Press.

Meister, B. (2013). *Can venture capital deliver on the promise of a public university?* Davis, CA: Council of UC Faculty Associations. Retrieved from: http://cucfa.org/news/2013_may10.php.

Morozov, E. (2013). *To save everything click here: The folly of technological solutionism.* New York: Public Affairs.

Reamer, A. C., Ivy, J. S., Vila-Parrish, A., & Young, R. (2015). Understanding the evolution of mathematics performance in primary education and the implications for STEM learning: A Markovian approach. *Computers in Human Behavior*, *47*, 4–17.

Rennie, F., & Morrison, T. (2013). *E-learning and social networking handbook: Resources for higher education.* New York: Routledge.

Rich, M. (2015). Some schools embrace demands for education data. *The New York Times*, May 11. Retrieved from: www.nytimes.com/2015/05/12/us/school-districts-embrace-business-model-of-data-collection.html?_r=0.

Robert-Holmes, G. (2015). The 'datafication' of early years pedagogy: If the teaching is good, the data should be good and if there's bad teaching, there is bad data. *Journal of Education Policy*, *30*(3), 302–315.

Selwyn N. (2015). Data entry: Towards the critical study of digital data and education. *Learning, Media and Technology*, 40(1): 64–82, DOI: 10.1080/17439884.2014.921628.

Siemens, G. (2013). Learning analytics: The emergence of a discipline. *American Behavioral Scientist*, *57*(10), 1380–1400.

Singer, N. (2015). Tools for tailored learning may expose students' personal details. *The New York Times*, August 30. Retrieved from: www.nytimes.com/2015/08/31/technology/tools-for-tailored-learning-may-expose-students-personal-details.html?ref=technology&_r=1.

Slade, S., & Prinsloo, P. (2013). Learning analytics: Ethical issues and dilemmas. *American Behavioral Scientist*, 57(10), 1510-1529.

Stohl, C. (2014). Crowds, clouds, and community. *Journal of Communication*, *64*(1), 1–19.

Swallow, E. (2011). How recruiters use social networks to screen candidates. *Mashable*, October 23. Retrieved from: http://mashable.com/2011/10/23/how-recruiters-use-social-networks-to-screen-candidates-infographic/.

Tempelaar, D., Rienties, B., & Giesbers, B. (2015). In search for the most informative data for feedback generation: Learning analytics in a data-rich context. *Computers in Human Behavior*, *47*, 157–167.

Tess, P. A. (2013). The role of social media in higher education classes (real and virtual): A literature review. *Computers in Human Behavior*, *29*(5), A60–A68.

van Dijck, J. (2013a). *The culture of connectivity: A critical history of social media.* New York: Oxford University Press.

van Dijck, J. (2013b). 'You have one identity': Performing the self on Facebook and LinkedIn. *Media, Culture and Society*, *35*(2), 199–215.

van Dijck, J. (2014). Datafiction, dataism and dataveillance: Big data between scientific paradigm and secular belief. *Surveillance and Society*, *12*(2), 197–208.

van Dijck, J., & Poell, T. (2013). Understanding social media logic. *Media and Communication*, *1*(1), 2–14. Retrieved from: www.librelloph.com/mediaandcommunication/article/view/MaC-1.1.2.

Vanwynsberghe, H., & Verdegem, P. (2013). Integrating social media in education. *Comparative Literature and Culture*, *15*(3), Article 10.

Williamson, B. (2016). Digital education governance: Data visualization, predictive analytics, and 'real-time' policy instruments. *Journal of Education Policy*, *31*(2), 123–141.

Young, E. (2015). Educational privacy in the online classroom: FERPA, MOOCs, and the big data conundrum. *Harvard Journal of Law & Technology*, *28*, 549–593.

33

Scholarly Communication in Social Media

Katrin Weller and Isabella Peters

INTRODUCTION

Lately, blogs have been increasingly used by researchers as tools to reflect upon their latest readings or other everyday workflows, and Maitzen (2012) concludes that academic blogging is a 'forum for developing and testing ideas'. Similarly, Twitter is used by many researchers for live reporting of academic conferences and networking (e.g., Weller, Dröge & Puschmann, 2011) or sharing links to scholarly publications (Eysenbach, 2011). In some disciplines, researchers' activities on social media platforms have covered up to 97% of the relevant scholarly literature, which means that in those cases more articles can be found in the social reference manager Mendeley than in the traditional bibliographic databases, for example Web of Science or Scopus (Li, Thelwall & Guistini, 2012). In fact, more than 60,000 scholarly articles are shared or discussed every week (Adie, 2015).

Therefore, alongside the traditional world of formal papers and official journals, there is a lively parallel universe bustling with new forms of and outlets for scholarly communication – one that needs to be explored for both its potential and its perils. Thus, this chapter provides an overview of how social media platforms are used by academics in different contexts and on the reasons and purposes of researchers in attending to social media. Particularly, we look at platforms that are being used by scholars – this can be common platforms such as Facebook, Twitter, and blogs or specific platforms explicitly aiming at academic audiences, such as Mendeley, Academia.edu and ResearchGate. We will ask about the role these platforms play in academia and outline the positive and negative effects of social media activity on scholarly communication. The chapter demonstrates similarities between traditional forms of scholarly communication – expressed mainly in form of publications and citations – and new ways of communicating through social media. In both cases researchers leave different forms of traces which have the potential to measure activity and impact and which shape the (digital) identity of a researcher. At the end of this chapter we will take a closer look at the footprints and shadows as traces academics leave while using social media – and explain how this relates to new approaches of measuring academic impact and how the study of these 'altmetrics' contributes to the understanding of scholarly communication in social media.

Basics of Scholarly Communication

Scholarly communication is traditionally based on academic writing that is published and thereby shared with the academic community. Researchers communicate by reading, reflecting on and finally referencing other researchers' publications. The flow of information within the scholarly community can be retraced by studying the citations, which connect different publications: an author who includes a reference to another publication in their work is assumed to have received the information from that original publication. Hence, scholarly communication can be characterized as perpetual loop of publishing and citing of scholarly literature.

By participating in scholarly communication and generating its products researchers create their academic identities. The primary outcomes of academic writing (publications) can be considered as *footprints* (Bar Ilan et al., 2012; Goodier & Czerniewicz, 2015) that the author leaves in the landscape of scholarly knowledge. As a whole they mirror what the researcher does professionally – their scientific contribution – and draw a picture of their expertise. Publications are always linked to the author, who is bringing them into reality. As such the author initiates the publication and influences the appearance of this part of their academic identity. Those self-initiated footprints form the essential foundation for scholarly exchange.

On the other side, it is the citations that show the impact a publication has on other authors (Cronin, 1984). This results in a citation identity of every author (Cronin & Shaw, 2002) reflecting how other researchers perceive their work and, again, ends up in a certain impression of the author. Goodier and Czerniewicz (2015) speak of *shadows* that are initiated by people other than the researcher. Accordingly, this part of the academic identity cannot be controlled by the researcher herself/himself. Interestingly, in scholarly communication, leaving footprints and creating shadows are two sides of the same coin. Since authors publish original material by referencing known literature, they automatically develop shadows of other researchers.

Moreover, citations indicate some sort of topical relation between publications and can thus be used to 'navigate' through masses of publications, for example with special search engines that enable searching for all publications which cite a specific paper, or searching for works that are cited in (or citing) the same set of publications, or by ranking publications based on citations. The ability to retrieve relevant publications is a key for successful scholarly communication. Academics usually have to search for publications on a topic of interest, and to find ways to constantly monitor new publications in a given field to select those that are relevant. While solutions such as subscriptions to journals' table of contents or search alerts can help to monitor the field, the challenge of selecting which publications to read remains. And as publication output grows exponentially (De Solla Price, 1963; Larivière, Haustein & Mongeon, 2015), new strategies for keeping up with new publications and selecting the most relevant in one's field of research are needed to face the challenge of information overload. Peer-based recommendations, for example through social media, may become a welcome support in this effort.

It should also be noted that citations have become a sort of currency in academic life. They are no longer a mere trace of information flows between different researchers and their publications, but have become one of the most frequently used units for creating indicators of scholarly impact (De Bellis, 2009). The effects this may have and the drawbacks and limitations of different citation-based metrics are discussed and studied in the fields of scientometrics and bibliometrics (Cronin & Sugimoto, 2015; Leydesdorff, 1995).

Traditionally, monographs and journal articles have been the most common publication formats (Harmon & Gross, 2007; Meadows, 1974), though preferences may vary across disciplines and additional formats (e.g., conference papers) have emerged over time. Traditional publication processes rely on professional publishers as outlets. In addition, peer review has widely been adapted as a standard way for quality control of what should be published and what not. Both, the commercial role of publishers and the peer review process, have been subject to public critiques recently. Peer review processes have been criticized for being slow, biased or insufficient to identify flaws in scientific studies. Publishers are being criticized for overcharging access to academic publications and for thus dividing the research community into those who can afford access fees and those who cannot, which has in turn led to the formation of the 'open access' movement, postulating novel modes for financing publishing processes to enable access to the resulting publications free of charge for the reader (apparently already with some effect on scholarly communication as a whole as open access articles appear to attract more citations [Davis & Walters, 2011; Eysenbach, 2006]).

While academics publish at a growing rate and speed, and while dissatisfaction with publishing formats and access, citation counts and peer review is constantly expressed, new developments can be observed which already have a significant influence on scholarly communication.

Effects of Social Media in Scholarly Communication

The activities that make the researcher part of the scholarly communication ecosystem and that form the academic identity of an author consist of countable units, for example the number of publications and citations. These output units are inevitably linked to the elements of the research life-cycle of writing, consuming, understanding, and referencing publications. The publication and referencing structures that have been well established over centuries are increasingly being challenged by new tools and practices in online communication environments. As we will see below, different social media platforms – such as blogs, wikis, and the various types of social networking sites – are having different effects on scholarly communication – in general, we can speak of a positive feedback loop of more output units (e.g., publications acting as footprints as introduced above) generating more units of visibility (i.e., shadows like citations) leading to a better findability (of footprints), as well as increased reputation (of footprints via shadows). As such, social platforms are influencing at least the following seven dimensions of scholarly communication (modified from Peters & Heise, 2014):

1 *The production of published material.* Social media and other collaborative platforms allow for new ways of working together in groups. Although tools for collaborative writing existed before the term social media was made popular (Digital Research Tools, n.d.), new possibilities to work together on a manuscript have come up as the landscape of social media tools grew richer. Researchers may share their drafts and ideas with co-authors through various channels (e.g., via Academia.edu's comments), or may have (near to) real-time conversations while writing collaboratively (e.g., via chat in Google Docs).

2 *The process of searching for information or of monitoring a research field.* Researchers may use their peers (through social media) as indicators for relevant literature and recommendations

of what to read. Researchers may comment on useful literature via Facebook, Twitter or blogs. Academic social networking platforms like Academia.edu or ResearchGate are used to recommend publications. Increasingly, the personal network on the social media platforms is also used to – illegally – obtain articles published behind a paywall (e.g., via Twitter hashtag '#icanhazpdf').

3   *The ways to increase visibility of research results and self-promotion.* As social media platforms are growing into systems that are used to spot relevant publications, they can also be used, in reverse, to broadcast one's own publications. By communicating about academic work through social media it may even become possible to reach other than the core academic audiences (e.g., via hashtags on Twitter, by addressing blogs at a broader public audience, by including references in Wikipedia articles, or by answering FAQs on ResearchGate).

4   *The ways to connect with or to keep in touch with other academics.* Social networking sites such as Facebook are used to establish or maintain relationships with peers and other acquaintances and serve the need for comfortable, informal and fast communication. Given that there are several social network platforms on the market with different purposes and target groups, scholars often choose the platform, their persona and tasks carried out carefully, for example, differentiating between private and professional use on Facebook and LinkedIn (Siegfried, Mazarakis & Peters, 2015). Since most social networking sites allow people to build groups or categorize users via tags or lists, efficient information exchange and dissemination is possible by channeling information to relevant users or filtering out what is of no interest.

5   *The available publication formats and their accessibility.* Blogs, status updates in social networks, wiki articles all serve different purposes of scholarly communication and can be used to publish pieces of information of different sizes, formats and styles. This may also include multimedia formats, for example, videos of a talk on YouTube that supports a written paper. Access to social media contents is typically not restricted through paywalls. But other restrictions may be imposed by the different access settings in social media that may make content only visible to certain groups of users.

6   *The ways to respond to academic publications across a variety of social media channels.* With different publication formats also come different ways to respond to publications. It is possible to respond to a journal article through commenting in tweets, blog posts or other status updates. Sometimes comments are also encouraged ahead of a formal publication as new forms of open peer review.[1] And of course it is also possible to use a tweet to comment on a blog post, to blog about a scholarly talk published on YouTube or to apply other cross-platform types of response (Hall et al., 2016). In this way, citations in social media environments are getting much more complex than in traditional publication formats (Mahrt, Weller & Peters, 2014).

7   *The ways to measure publication output and impact of scholarly work.* As new publication formats and new ways to cite them emerge, it should also be reassessed how scholarly output is being measured and evaluated. The term 'altmetrics' has been coined to refer to new indicators based (among others) on social media data (Priem et al., 2010).

ACADEMIC USES OF SOCIAL MEDIA PLATFORMS

As the *Time* magazine prominently put it in 2006, social media is about 'YOU'.[2] The fundamental property of social media is the ego and the content or activity the person generates on the web (Schmidt, 2009). Usually, a user profile is the entry ticket to the social media platform, allowing only registered users to approach other users and access the available content. Around these profiles the online identity of the person emerges, since the social media platforms track, record and display all user activities performed by the user himself or her contacts. These contacts can either be established via a mutual relationship (e.g., friends on Facebook) or a one-sided relation (e.g., followers on Twitter). Besides setting up a profile and generating original content, social media platforms always also allow for sharing, that is re-distributing or forwarding

(Puschmann & Peters, 2015) content produced by other users of the platform. Both generating and sharing content are characteristic for social media. And both also fit well into the context of scholarly communication, which is about sharing and consuming content as well as about establishing 'profiles' for individual researchers.

The following selection of prototypical social media platforms reflect these characteristics particularly well and therefore will be discussed against the background of their use in academia. The most popular social media platforms are not focusing on a specific target audience. Facebook, YouTube, blogs or Twitter are popular across many different demographic populations (although Facebook was initially created for university students). And of course some of their users are also academics. Many of them may have started using social networks like Facebook for private purposes – before more and more colleagues would connect with them and private and professional communication became increasingly inseparable. While some scholars may simply improvise how they use social media in their daily routines, others turn to specific guidelines for academic usage of social media, such as, for example, the one by Bik and Goldstein (2013). There even exist guidelines for specific platforms targeted at scholars from specific disciplines, like König's (2012) guidelines for historians. Some may try to keep professional communication and private communication separate – either by establishing different accounts within the same platform or by turning to different social media platforms for different purposes – and some may have given up on these efforts after a while.

The use of social media platforms is strongly task-driven. Hence, researchers can have profiles on different platforms and use them in a varying intensity (Pscheida et al., 2014; Siegfried, Mazarakis & Peters, 2015). Some initiatives aim at systematically allocating social media tools to the elements and activities of the research life-cycle, reflecting what platform is used for which task (e.g., 101Innovations.wordpress.com). However, truly distinct assignments are difficult to make, mainly due to the broad spectrum of functionalities the social media platforms offer. Literally, most of them successfully serve more than one purpose (Peters & Heise, 2014).

However, as social media platforms evolve over time and their user communities also constantly develop new practices, studies on the adoption of social media platforms in academia (such as the ones by Procter et al., 2010a and 2010b, or Pscheida et al., 2014) can always only capture a certain snapshot at one point of time – and are often also confined to specific subgroups of academics, for example in specific countries or specific disciplines. Among the existing studies, some contain evidence that uptake on social media usage in academia has been rather slow in many cases, while some disciplines appear as early adopters. For example, Procter et al. (2010b: 4044) observed that 'computer science researchers are more likely to be frequent users and those in medicine and veterinary sciences less likely'. Given the case study nature of many findings, generalizability of such research has to be discussed and backed up with more evidence.

Furthermore, determining the value of social media in scholarly communication by using data about active users, or by counting how many academics have user accounts on specific platforms, is problematic in itself. Besides the lack of reliable data in many cases (e.g., when there is no open application programming interface [API] available), it is also of interest who consumes content from social media sites, which in the case of reading blogs or Wikipedia can be done without registering and can be considered much more common than active contributions (Weller et al., 2010). As Allen et al. (2013) point out, social media in academic contexts are more about pushing information (tailored to users' interests) to the public, which distinguishes them from traditional literature databases where users would usually pull information by active searching. Allen et al. (2013) also conclude that this is how social media increased dissemination of scholarly publications in the health and medical domains. Thus, given the assumingly large share of passive users or lurkers (Nielsen, 2006) on social media platforms, within this chapter we will look at practices rather than at usage statistics.

In particular, we are distinguishing the more text-based platforms that can be considered as pioneers in the earlier years of social media (mainly blogs and Wikipedia) from the later platforms that are more centered around network structures and can combine content-sharing of different media formats (e.g., multi-media formats in Facebook posts). Furthermore, we distinguish platforms that specialize on academic users from those addressing a general audience.

TEXT-BASED SOCIAL MEDIA PLATFORMS AS ADDITIONS TO SCHOLARLY PUBLICATIONS

Blogs have been among the earliest phenomena to be labelled as elements of 'Web 2.0' or the Social Web, and therefore are among the first social media that were believed to challenge traditional (scholarly) communication structures (Nardi et al., 2004). The idea was that blogs could open up new possibilities for sharing scholars' work independently from traditional publishers. Blog posts may look very similar to research articles, as both are text-based and may include figures, tables and references. Blogs offer a platform to write about research, and to reach out to academic and non-academic audiences alike, to cross-reference through the use of hyperlinks, and to receive immediate feedback from the community (Shema, Bar-Ilan & Thelwall, 2015).

Blogs rather seem to complement traditional publications than to aim at replacing them. Being free from constraints in traditional formats, blogs have been used and interpreted in different ways by the academic community. Mewburn and Thomson (2013) suggest that academic bloggers rather write about academic work conditions than about their own research findings, and that they like to give advice or share useful information with their audience. They also report on their workflows in everyday lab-life or latest readings, and use their blogs to informally develop and test ideas (Maitzen, 2012). Halavais (2006) uses several images to illustrate academic uses of blogs: the 'notebook' (a place for work in progress), the 'coffee house' (a place for discussing with [often like-minded] academics), and the 'opinions page' or 'editorial page' (for more general forms of public communication). Walker (2006) distinguishes blog types into 'public intellectuals', 'research logs' and 'pseudonymous blogs about academic life' (and blogs that combine these different genres). Quite interesting is the phenomenon of anonymous/pseudonymous blogging to talk about everyday academic life and the frustrations it may bring.

Overall, it remains hard to define what precisely constitutes an academic blog, or research blogging. In addition, the term 'science blogging' is often used to describe blogs covering scientific topics in general, independent of whether their authors are tenured professors, grad students, high school teachers, interested laymen, or journalists (Mahrt & Puschmann, 2014). Colson (2011) points out that there is a strong interrelation between blogging researchers and science journalists who interact through blogs. Her study also shows that academics may turn to blogging in order to bypass traditional journalism in broadcasting research findings to a broader public, while journalists consider blogs by researchers as useful and trustworthy sources (Colson, 2011). Of course, blogging, as with many other online activities, is not only hard to categorize, it is also evolving over time (Karpf, 2012). Walker (2006) reports how her personal blogging practice changed – from her first experience as a blogging grad student to being a tenured faculty member – and how blogging in general became more popular.

In some cases, blogs may be used to publish novel research results. Compared to journal articles (where the publication process may take years), blogs have the advantage of a much faster publication process – in fact, they are often instantly available. There are still more indications that blogging is not used for the same purposes as traditional publications. Buschman and Michalek (2013) explain that researchers use blogs to share background information about their work, which may also include approaches that led to negative results. Negative research results are important for the advancement of science, but have recently been less frequently published in traditional publications (Fanelli, 2012). Although new journals have been founded which particularly focus on negative results (e.g., *Journal of Negative Results in Biomedicine*, http://jnrbm.com), they are not universally available for all disciplines. It is therefore positive when blogs help to fill the gap and provide information of this kind. Blogging is also used in addition to traditional papers, for example, to attract more attention to them. Several researchers reported on positive effects of having blogged about their research. Terras (2012) experienced an increased download rate of papers discussed in her blog in comparison with papers that were only published traditionally. Hoang et al. (2015) found that blog articles receive up to 14 times more page views than journal articles on the same topic. Therefore, they conclude that 'dissemination of scientific material on a radiology blog promoted on social media can substantially augment the reach of more traditional publication venues [and] … researchers in radiology should not ignore opportunities for increasing the impact of research findings via social media' (Hoang et al., 2015: 760).

It remains an ongoing question to what extent references in Wikipedia might also help to increase the impact and visibility of research publications. Similar to blogs, wikis in general and Wikipedia in particular can be considered as early examples of social media. Wikipedia as a collaboratively created online encyclopedia reflects a form of public understanding of science. It has thus found its very own place within the ecosystem of scholarly communication: Wikipedia articles quote scholarly work and therefore become part of the scholarly communication life-cycle. On the other hand, many academics would not consider Wikipedia as a reliable source that can be quoted. Nielsen (2007) uses the number of Wikipedia references to peer-reviewed articles as a proof for the quality of Wikipedia content. Luyt and Tan (2010) have analyzed the credibility of Wikipedia articles and found numerous statements of Wikipedia articles on history topics lacking any form of valid reference. They still conclude that Wikipedia is valuable, as it offers a gateway to academic knowledge that is otherwise often hidden behind paywalls that prevent access to scholarly publications for a general public and even for many researchers. It is, however, unclear whether Wikipedia articles really help to transfer knowledge from behind academic publishers' paywalls to a broader community. For example, Teplitskyi, Lu and Duede (2015) arrive at the conclusion that there is an effect of open access literature being overrepresented on Wikipedia.

NETWORKING AND CONTENT-SHARING PLATFORMS FOR GENERAL AUDIENCES THAT ARE USED BY ACADEMICS

Blogs and Wikipedia focus primarily on longer texts as their dominant form of content. User profile pages and connections between users are of minor relevance. During the evolution of the social media landscape, networking elements have gained importance and by now there is a vibrant landscape of various social networking platforms that are utilized by researchers in specific ways. Facebook can be considered the biggest social networking platform worldwide (Statista, 2016), although in some countries different social networks have grown popular instead, such as Vkontakte in Russia or renren, Weibo or WeChat in China. Other social networking platforms, such as Google+ (Henderson, 2012), may include similar features as Facebook, but are less popular in general. LinkedIn is popular among academics in different countries, but has a slightly different set of features as it is mainly targeted as professional usage. Given that in June 2016 Microsoft announced that it had acquired LinkedIn, it remains to be seen how usage numbers and functionalities will develop or merge with existing services.

The high number of users is Facebook's biggest advantage – as with typical network goods, the number of users determines its value for the individual user (Katz & Shapiro, 1985). Thus, Facebook establishes a common ground for connecting with others with little effort. Facebook is highly popular with researchers of different disciplines (Van Noorden, 2014), but little is known about whether researchers are more likely to have a Facebook account than other groups, whether they connect with more people via Facebook, or have more international connections. The facts that researchers tend to travel a lot, often work in international environments, or even move on to different places of residence over the years, suggest that they could particularly benefit from platforms that support connections internationally. It has, however, been shown that use of Facebook often takes place in private settings (Pscheida et al., 2014; Van Noorden, 2014), reflecting that researchers perceive the *audiences* and *affordances* (Norman, 1988) they find on the platform in a specific, yet too narrow, way, preventing them from using it professionally.

In fact, Facebook offers several useful features for academics (Nentwich & König,

2014): it allows group communication and one-to-one communication and supports synchronous as well as asynchronous communication channels. Facebook enables different profile pages for academic institutions (universities, scholarly associations, etc.) and for individuals, offering different functionalities for interaction with followers (of pages) and friends (of users). Posts on Facebook are of flexible length and can contain multimedia features. Another asset is the diversity of user groups with whom researchers can get in touch and with whom they can communicate their work. On the other hand, all this comes at a cost: Facebook is frequently criticized for intransparent privacy settings (e.g., Liu et al., 2011). Furthermore, Facebook's features and options for individual settings are constantly changing, which may require that users constantly spend time and effort on keeping up to date. Another potential drawback can be the fact that students also largely use Facebook, which may challenge traditional authoritative structures. Goodband et al. (2012) report a case of a student group that got in conflict with the broader mathematics community.

Another platform that combines social networking features with personal status updates is Twitter. Several guidelines for scholarly uses of social media have portrayed microblogging with Twitter as useful for diverse academic purposes and contexts (Herwig et al., 2009; Mollett, Moran & Dunleavy, 2011). There are also several studies that investigate the use of Twitter in scholarly communication (an overview can be found in Mahrt, Weller & Peters, 2014), though often focusing on specific case studies. However, surveys with researchers have indicated a rather low uptake of Twitter among academics (e.g., Gu & Widén-Wulff, 2011; Harley et al., 2010; Ponte & Simon; 2011), while there appear to be some disciplinary differences.

Twitter's strength is in specific usage scenarios, such as in being used during academic conferences as a tool for live reporting and interconnecting (e.g., Letierce et al., 2010; Ross et al., 2011; Weller, Dröge & Puschman, 2011). In this specific context and connected to a conference-specific hashtag, Twitter facilitates exchange not only among existing networks of scholars, but also around shared interests. It enables new contacts in an informal and low-threshold manner. This is supported by the fact that Twitter does not require relationships between users to be reciprocal. Another typical use of Twitter is the sharing of URLs that point to interesting Web content or scholarly publications (Eysenbach, 2011; Priem & Costello, 2010). It thus plays a major role in the study of alternative metrics for measuring scholarly impact, as we will see below.

Other platforms that target a general audience but are also used by academics for professional purposes include, among others, SlideShare, YouTube or GitHub. These three platforms are mainly selected to illustrate the broader spectrum of academic content that is being shared online, including videos, slideshows and programming code. They are, however, not the only examples of tools used for these purposes. On SlideShare researchers may share presentation slides used during conference talks. In principle, it can also be an outlet for teaching material, although a survey by Herath and Hewagamage (2015) indicates that SlideShare is only rarely used for teaching purposes. In general, rather little is known about the academic use of SlideShare or other platforms that enable the sharing of presentation slides. Some more insights are available on the scholarly use of YouTube, which also features videos taken at academic conferences and online lectures. Furthermore, YouTube videos are being cited both in traditional scholarly publications (Kousha, Thelwall & Abdoli, 2012) and in academic tweets (Thelwall et al., 2012). GitHub can be described as an open software repository, where users may share their scripts and code with an interested audience. As such, it is being studied as an example of social coding (Dabbish et al., 2012; Marlow,

Dabbish & Herbsleb, 2013), where one may get insights not only into sharing behavior, but also into collaboration in creating new code.

Researchers can also be found communicating in various online forums. Another case of particular interest is reddit. This platform includes several sections (subreddits) that are dedicated to current scientific findings and recent scholarly publications as well as academic life and career choices (e.g., www.reddit.com/r/academia or www.reddit.com/r/Professors/). There are even subreddits that call out cases of misinterpretations of scientific findings (e.g., www.reddit.com/r/badscience). With all this, reddit combines features of blogs and bookmarking systems with a broader networked community and thus has a significant potential for advancing scholarly communication. However, not much insight is available on the actual role reddit is currently playing in academia.

SPECIFIC SOCIAL MEDIA PLATFORMS FOR ACADEMIC AUDIENCES

In addition to the popular general platforms, some social media platforms are specifically addressing academics as their target audience. Few of them even focus on specific disciplines, for example, http://hypotheses.org, a blog aggregator for the humanities and the social sciences. But more popular are those that address the academic community as a whole, like Academia.edu, Mendeley and ResearchGate.

All of the latter include some principles of social bookmarking. The idea of social bookmarking platforms (Henning & Reichelt, 2008) is relatively simple yet powerful: they enable their users to create bookmarks for web contents which they want to retrieve later. Often they include functionalities of social tagging so that users assign content-descriptive keywords ('tags') to their bookmarks for adding structure and enhancing retrieval options (Peters, 2009). Social book-marking platforms started as tools for gener-ally saving all sorts of links on the Web, for example, through platforms like CiteULike or Delicious. They were soon also taken up by users who wanted to share and keep track of scholarly literature on the Web, which lead to specialized bookmarking systems for this type of resources and turned platforms into social reference managers. Platforms like Bibsonomy (Zoller et al., 2016) or Zotero include functionalities such as, for example, directly importing bibliographic metadata via identifiers (e.g., DOI or ISBN numbers).

Moreover, Academia.edu, ResearchGate and Mendeley have used functionalities of social networking platforms and com-bined them with bookmarking principles in order to attract an academic user com-munity. Users can set up profile pages with information on their affiliations and other biographical details as well as research interests and expertise. They may then also connect with other researchers (e.g., also by browsing for topics or affiliations), and fol-low their updates. In this way, one may, for example, be informed about new publica-tions from specific researchers. Publication lists are becoming part of the user profiles too. And usually, researchers are enabled to also upload manuscripts directly. This leads to another core feature of these platforms: they may count in-platform citations of pub-lications as well as numbers of article views, downloads and of course bookmarks. They also use these counts to promote platform services through addressing the academics' vanity fair, that is the tendency of academics to constantly compare themselves and their works against those of their peers - which is increasingly criticized (Murray, 2014).

There are more critical voices, especially concerning the increasingly commercial nature of these platforms. Academia.edu is criticized for using the .edu domain without being an educational institution. And since Mendeley was bought by Elsevier in 2013, this has also raised many concerns for future

developments and led to calls for boycotting the reference management system (although almost no effect can be seen in the user num-bers[3]). Others criticize these platforms for their lack of transparency and for locking in user data. For example, ResearchGate's underlying metrics are intransparent and influenced by spam (Kraker & Lex, 2015). Single approaches exist for making the underlying user data transparent and open. Mendeley, for example, offers an open appli-cation programming interface (API) that allows users to download their contribution, whereas ResearchGate and Academia.edu do not offer this option. To overcome this problematic situation, William Gunn from Mendeley, in a comment to Matthews (2016), advises us to 'embrace the idea of a [sic.] eco-system of applications, each interoperating with the other to provide a flexible range of functions that fit the diverse needs of various scholarly fields rather than one monolithic site which aims to be all for everyone'. It should be noted, however, that similar prac-tices and methods to ensure exclusivity have been known in scholarly communication for years – most prominently those fought about in the 'Elsevier boycott'[4] – and they are not immanent challenges of social media use.

Despite some limitations in accessibil-ity, the overall existence of different usage statistics also makes these platforms inter-esting in the exploration of novel metrics to measure scholarly impact – as we will also discuss below. Indeed, from research in this field we learn that these academic bookmark-ing/networking platforms have achieved notable coverage of scholarly literature. In selected samples from different scholarly domains, Mendeley includes more than 80% (and up to 97%) of published research papers (Haustein et al., 2013: Haustein, Larivière et al., 2014; Li, Thelwall & Giustini, 2012; Priem et al., 2012). Although coverage of publications appears broad on social media platforms, there may be specific omissions and biases (especially regarding the disci-plines and types of articles covered). Given that articles shared on social networking platforms like ResearchGate are subject to the platforms' terms and services, those publishing approaches can also not be compared to institutional repositories and true open access initiatives for several reasons, such as that they do not support long-term availability of the data or allow for text mining.

Also, some researchers explicitly avoid using these platforms for these reasons or consider profiles only as a 'me too-presence' (Nentwich & König, 2014: 113) to signal readiness to network. This leads to the next question on the validity of usage data. Do registered researchers actively use the platforms at all? Little is still known about who is active. In terms of number of profiles, 'ResearchGate is more than twice as popular as Academia.edu. Usage of ResearchGate particularly outweighs that of Academia.edu in China and Japan, in the sciences and among the most senior researchers. Overall, 61 per cent of respondents who have published at least one paper use ResearchGate, while 28 per cent use Academia.edu, and just 0.2 per cent apparently use Mendeley' (Matthews, 2016). Studies like these are just the first step towards understanding how social media influence the perceived impact and relevance of a researcher or their individual digital identity. Much more work is needed to fully assess the impact of social media on scholarly communication and researchers' careers.

CHALLENGES AND DRAWBACKS OF USING SOCIAL MEDIA IN ACADEMIA

We have now seen that social media platforms offer a variety of opportunities for researchers to connect and engage and that, overall, their functionalities well meet the goals of scholarly communication. However, to complete the picture of scholarly communication with social media we must also consider the drawbacks and challenges that every tool entails. First, the appearance of social media platforms in academic environments may lead to new tasks and efforts that may challenge researchers personally. The increased availability and amount of products of scholarly communication can lead to an information overload that leaves the consumers of research results with all the effort of searching and compiling information. Moreover, since in social media environments traditional indicators and institutions commonly guaranteeing a certain quality standard of the research product may not work any more, the entire process of quality assurance (e.g., peer review) and relevance assessment is loaded on to the consumer side. Here, education and tools need to be developed to assist researchers and other stakeholders in wading through the flood of information. On the other side, it might be problematic and time-consuming for researchers to engage in social media-based scholarly communication in order to maintain their profiles on social networking sites and keep every representation of their digital image up to date. Some researchers may decide just to focus on single platforms and will not register on other platforms. On the other hand, this means that one single platform will rarely be able to provide a complete picture of researchers in one field.

Second, there are other reasons why researchers may decide to not use specific platforms. It should not be underestimated that most of the social media platforms used for scholarly communication are, although free for use, private companies still searching for business models and revenue. This means that content put on their platforms is subject to the company's terms and services – sometimes allowing the company forms of manipulation, re-use, and ownership. Moreover, since the platform providers usually control appearance, functionalities and algorithms of their services, they also massively influence how (as well as if and what) scholarly content is presented and consumed. Matthews (2016) reports that researchers fear 'tunnel vision' if only popular and mainstream articles are displayed and only a narrow view of the landscape of scholarly publications is provided. Although social media-based platforms are able to increase accessibility to scientific content, openness is interpreted differently by the providers.

Finally, social media use may be approached differently by different researchers. Some may be more successful in drawing attention to their own activities. This can lead to a 'rich gets richer' phenomenon, where those who already have succeeded in gaining attention for their social media profiles will continue to do so, while others will struggle to ever reach a similar level. Also, researchers with a higher academic age and/or longer lists of publications may have an advantage over beginners, since it is easier to find them or their contributions on the social media platforms. This has been confirmed by earlier research: senior scholars appear to attract more page views on Academia.edu (Thelwall & Kousha, 2014), and have a higher perceived impact (Li & Gillet, 2013). As mentioned before, this effect is amplified by the algorithms underlying the social media platforms that often provide more visibility for researchers and contributions that have already gained a lot of attention in the past.

Considering this, it is most crucial that we improve our understanding of attention economics in scholarly social media use. A first step towards this can be achieved by critically investigating social media usage related to academia. Currently, such efforts can mainly be found as parts of a broader community that aims at developing novel indicators for measuring scholarly communication through novel data (not only) from social media.

ASSESSING SCHOLARLY COMMUNICATION WITH SOCIAL MEDIA METRICS

We have seen how different social media platforms can be used in academia and that social media complement platforms of scholarly communication since they offer authors even more possibilities to present themselves, publish content, exchange arguments and to set up an online academic identity. As such, they enable researchers to leave new types of footprints that can be exploited in scholarly communication, for example, user profiles, posts, tweets. The next question is whether there are ways to measure how the platforms are actually affecting scholarly communication. Defining what counts as acts of scholarly communication in platforms such as Twitter, Facebook or Wikipedia is not always trivial. In social media environments scholarly conversation and exchange of arguments evolve around profiles, footprints, and shadows of all contributors to the research life-cycle. In the following, we will consider scholarly communication in social media as reflected through three dimensions: (1) the dimension of actively leaving footprints in social media; (2) the dimension of passively casting shadows which are reflected through the activities of others; and (3) the dimension of creating a digital identity that is composed of the previous two dimensions.

Footprints, Shadows and Digital identities

Every researcher leaves their footprints through numerous activities. In traditional scholarly communication, the act of leaving footprints is relatively clear to define – and typically happens very consciously: a researcher actively publishes a paper or a book, gives a talk at a conference, provides a list of references with a publication, edits a collection, etc. All these acts can be traced back to the researcher and thus shape his or her identity as an actor in the respective scholarly community. A more complicated case is participation in blind review processes, where actions of one researcher – writing a review – leave footprints, but cannot normally be traced back to the person directly. However, reviewing also shapes the presented identity of a researcher if membership on reviewer boards or program committees is included in the CV. All of these footprints can be counted – and most of them are increasingly being counted in order to measure scholarly activity (e.g., to justify spending of tax money for research, etc.).

Researchers also cast their shadows, an act that is more passive because it cannot be influenced – shadows emerge where others react to one's own activities. In traditional scholarly publication, this usually happens through citations. If my own work is being cited in another scholar's paper, a shadow of my work has been created. There are thus two sides on how to view a single researcher within the system of scholarly communication: based on the profile he/she has created himself/herself or based on how others see her/him reflected through citations and other types of shadows (which can, for example, be book reviews or mass media articles referring to scholarly work). Again, most of this can be and is being counted. In terms of citations, counting is to some degree automated on platforms like Google Scholar, Scopus or Web of Science; in other cases, researchers may have an interest to count themselves how often they are mentioned in reviews or mass media. This is because the respective numbers are also increasingly being viewed as a part of an academic identity; they are believed to illustrate how influential a researcher is. Of course, focusing on aggregated counts as indicators of activity and influence, and therefore as true reflections of an academic identity, can be criticized, especially if numbers are viewed out of context (e.g., disciplinary context) (see the Leiden Manifesto: Hicks et al., 2015).

In the digital world, new types of footprints and shadows emerge, not all of them happening equally consciously and not all of them in a countable format (yet). A researcher who actively publishes a blog post, posts a comment on Facebook, or publishes a tweet is leaving a footprint. A researcher who downloads the pdf file of an article, likes a Facebook post, retweets a tweet, or links to a blog post is also leaving footprints in social media. Shadows of researchers' activities can consequently appear in the form of received likes, retweets, pingbacks, or mentions on Wikipedia, as well as in download statistics, Mendeley readership and other forms of reactions to traditional publications that are represented in social media platforms. Again, footprints and shadows contribute to the perceived identity of a scholar. The digital identity of a researcher with all the facets is based on footprints and shadows that are visible online – and only on those that are visible online, that is presentations or publications and activities that are not tracked and publicly published online do not shape the *digital* identity of a researcher.

All this leads to new important questions: As researchers' identities do no longer build on footprints and shadows of purely traditional forms of scholarly communication, do we need new ways to measure and quantify digital forms of footprints and shadows? And to which degree are both dimensions, digital and traditional, similar or different in what they represent?

Metrics to quantify scholarly communication have long been subject to critiques. Researchers concerned with scholarly metrics have acknowledged several drawbacks and limitations, among others, that citations need time to accumulate, that they do not reflect the motivation of the citation, that they only reflect impact on other *authors* instead of all *readers* of the publication, and that citation behavior varies between disciplines (MacRoberts & MacRoberts, 1989; see also Haustein & Larivière, 2014). Consequently, with scholarly communication reaching the Internet, approaches for also measuring these activities were explored. Early approaches have been labeled 'webometrics' (Thelwall, 2008) in reference to the earlier terms 'bibliometrics' and 'scientometrics'. Webometric approaches for calculating metrics are mainly based on Web links or download numbers.

In 2010, the term 'altmetrics' was introduced when Jason Priem, Dario Taraborelli,

Paul Groth and Cameron Neylon (2010) published their Altmetrics Manifesto (Priem et al., 2010), after Priem first suggested the name altmetrics in a tweet. The authors of the manifesto report different motivations for their call for new metrics: they describe altmetrics as a possible tool to guide researchers through the huge amount of potentially relevant information on the Web (acknowledging that 'no one can read everything', Priem et al. [2010], highlight the role of social media as pointers to interesting literature), and envision that evaluation of researchers may in the future also consider output and influence in social media environments. Altmetrics are still not or only very rarely used officially in evaluation processes such as funding or hiring decisions, but some in the altmetrics community have been advocating for this idea (Galligan & Dyas-Correia 2013; Lapinski, Piwowar & Priem, 2013; Piwowar, 2013b).[5] Not all researchers, believe that social media activities will be considered in evaluative contexts in the future (Procter et al., 2010a), and there is no knowledge about how many would want social media to be included in evaluation processes. Even more crucial may be the fact that it is hardly known what types of activities and influence of scholarly communication would actually be measured through data from social media and altmetrics based upon them – a problem that is also inspiring different broader initiatives to better understand altmetrics. One of the most notable developments in this field is the NISO Alternative Assessment Metrics (Altmetrics) Initiative[6] by the National Information Standards Organization (NISO).

WHAT DO SOCIAL MEDIA METRICS MEASURE – AND HOW?

Since the publication of the Altmetrics Manifesto (Priem et al., 2010), and even before this, quite a significant number of studies have focused on measuring different

scholarly footprints and shadows through social media data with the aim to better understand why and how researchers make use of different social media platforms. Overall, it is assumed that altmetrics will measure different phenomena than traditional metrics for scholarly communication. Social media are expected to respond to scholarly publications much quicker than traditional citations, which means that 'many online tools and environments surface evidence of impact relatively early in the research cycle, exposing essential but traditionally invisible precursors like reading, bookmarking, saving, annotating, discussing, and recommending articles' (Haustein et al., 2013: 2). Consequently, social media metrics can be obtained quicker than traditional citations; they are 'available immediately after publication – and even before publication in the case of preprints – and offer a more rapid assessment of impact' (Thelwall et al., 2013). Piwowar (2013a: 9) sees four advantages of altmetrics/social media metrics in that they: (1) provide 'a more nuanced understanding of impact', (2) provide 'more timely data', (3) include the consideration of alternative and 'web-native scholarly products like datasets, software, blog posts, videos and more', and (4) serve as 'indications of impacts on diverse audiences'. While Piwowar (2013a) speaks of nuances for measuring impact, this also poses additional challenges, as long as little is known about the different nuances and their meanings. Similarly, Lapinski Piwowar and Priem (2013: 292–293) discuss different 'impact flavors' as 'a product featured in mainstream media stories, blogged about, and downloaded by the public, for instance, has a very different flavor of impact than one heavily saved and discussed by scholars' (Lapinski et al., 2013: 292–293). But what is the 'flavor' of a retweet, a blog post, or a Wikipedia reference? What are the motivations behind these different social media activities? To what degree do they represent a commitment comparable to a citation in a published article? A lot of the current research in altmetrics attempts to assess the quality and scope of altmetrics indicators, with case studies comparing metrics across platforms (either alternative or traditional) or across specific disciplines.

Answering questions on how social media metrics relate to traditional forms of scholarly communication, altmetrics research faces the same challenges as all social media studies: with these media evolving quickly and users changing their practices at the same time, one is studying a moving target (Karpf, 2012). Altmetrics studies also face similar technical challenges as social media research in general: data have to be obtained from social media platforms, for example, via the application programming interface (API), which is often restricted by the companies behind the platforms (Gaffney & Puschmann, 2014). Also, many third-party tools that allow for data collection from social media act as black boxes: it is hard to understand how data have been collected and prepared and to assess whether a tool is reliable and the data are complete or representative (Haustein, Peters et al., 2014). Stakeholders involved in altmetrics (Weller, 2015) have assembled some specialized tools, sometimes based on the involvement of big publishers such as Elsevier (who bought Mendeley in 2013). Liu and Adie (2013b: 153) have summed up the current state of the art as follows: 'All of the tools are in their early stages of growth. Altmetrics measures are not standardized and have not been systematically validated; there has been no clear consensus on which data sources are most important to measure; and technical limitations currently prevent the tracking of certain sources, such as multimedia files'.

So, currently, different approaches to measure scholarly communication are being explored, different indicators are being combined and different tools are being developed. At the same time, research in altmetrics is conducted to better understand the relations between user behavior, tools and new indicators. Before we take a look at some examples of this kind of research, it may be useful to take a step back and – on a meta-perspective – distinguish different levels of assessing user activities in social media through altmetrics. In particular, we can distinguish the following approaches (modified from Weller, 2015):

- *Article-level metrics.* This summarizes approaches to measure the impact of traditional scholarly articles through the shadows they cast in social media platforms, especially by aggregating all types of citation for a specific publication (such as, for example, traditional citations plus mentions on Twitter).
- *Metrics based on alternative forms of interactions.* Some shadows resemble traditional citations less, but reflect other forms of engaging with a publication (e.g., readership statistics, likes or bookmarks). Again, these can be aggregated with other metrics on the article-level.
- *Metrics for new output formats.* A next step is not only to measure the impact of traditional publications, but to consider all kinds of footprints, including a researcher's output in social media platforms, such as blog posts or academic YouTube videos, or software commits (e.g., Github and Depsy [see http://depsy.org]).
- *Aggregated metrics for researchers.* If all kinds of footprints and shadows are combined for one researcher, the aggregated metrics can also be used to inform us about their digital identity.

For the key question of whether social media mentions predict subsequent traditional citation rates (or whether they at least correlate to some degree with traditional citation metrics), the most comprehensive study has been conducted by Thelwall et al. (2013), who looked at eleven different social media resources. They concluded that the metrics collected from different sources were not able to predict subsequent citations. We thus have to assume that social media metrics represent different phenomena of scholarly communication than traditional metrics, although in this mostly case-based area of research, slightly varying values may be found for some platforms or for specific disciplines. For example, for Mendeley, several studies found a moderate to significant correlation of readership and counts of traditional citation (Haustein et al., 2013; Li et al., 2012; Priem et al., 2012; Zahedi et al., 2014).

In another example, Zahedi et al. (2014) compared article-level altmetrics aggregated for journals across disciplines and showed how journals from different disciplines are represented to a very different extent on Mendeley, Wikipedia, Twitter, and Delicious. Holmberg and Thelwall (2014) compare Twitter usage across 10 different scholarly disciplines. And, as mentioned above, social media have to be considered as a moving target – the field of social media metrics is still developing, as Haustein, Peters et al. (2014) demonstrated: in 2012 around 20% of biomedical papers were mentioned in at least one tweet on Twitter, twice as many as in 2011.

On the other hand, research indicates that social media activities do have a potential to really influence scholarly communication. For example, tweeting about a scholarly paper increases its download statistics (Shuai, Pepe & Bollen, 2012) – which could mean that social media are rather linked to readership than to citations and that researchers do indeed use their peers' social media activities as recommendations for useful literature. One needs to be careful with very popular content on social media, though. Haustein, Peters et al. (2014) show that papers with unusually funny titles are much more popular on Twitter (e.g., 'Penile fracture seems more likely during sex under stressful situations').

This case is a reminder that altmetics research has not yet fully revealed what social media metrics are measuring exactly – scholarly impact or other forms of interestingness, popularity, or buzz. Another crucial step in order to shed light on this situation will be to get a more complete picture of who is using different social media platforms: Who is using Twitter, Facebook, YouTube, Mendeley and co.? Are users of different academic disciplines represented equally across platforms? What are the user demographics and how do they develop? How well are we able to capture data from different platforms with the tools we have? How can we compare conceptually different units of user interaction, for example, retweets versus likes?

CONCLUSION

In the last decade, new formats and means of publishing, communication and exchange have evolved. These tools and publications, driven by developments in the social media market in particular, have brought a plethora of options that have fundamentally changed the way researchers engage in scholarly discourse and that have proposed, among others, the following benefits for scholarly communication:

- They offer new venues for all elements of scholarly communication.
- They provide more timely and direct conversations and feedback.
- They enable faster and more efficient access and exchange of scholarly information.
- They increase availability of scholarly information.
- They increase visibility of researchers and their scientific contribution.
- This results in a positive feedback loop of visibility and reputation of research products and researchers.
- They enable quick feedback on the relevance of scholarly products via altmetrics.

Social media-based scholarly communication has resulted in diverse products concerned with research outcomes (e.g., blogs or tweets) which in specific cases are much better publication formats for research findings (e.g., videos of scientific experiments). It has also enabled showcasing as well as the acknowledgement of all types of research output (e.g., data papers on GitHub). Moreover, this development has offered a multitude of alternatives for reacting to those publications (e.g., via likes or retweets, which then also become elements of the scholarly discourse). Social media now offer researchers endless possibilities to express themselves and to develop scholarly identities that are truly digital. Research showed that scholars make conscious decisions when choosing social media for scholarly communication, that they differentiate between tools that address a general public (e.g., Facebook) or peers (e.g., Academia.edu), and that they are well aware of what platforms serve which purposes and what footprints they leave.

Tracing shadows that other scholars create in traditional, web and social media environments may not have moved into the center of most researchers' attention so far. But it will gain importance given that forms of reaction to scholarly content and engagement with publics on the Social Web have been proposed as complementary ways of measuring impact of research (Priem et al., 2010). Besides traditional forms of publication and scholarly communication, which surely will keep their space in the ecosystem of publishing and referencing because of their long-earned reputation, social media-based products have gained in popularity and are seen as one of the driving forces behind Science 2.0 and Open Science (European Commission, 2016). It is believed that access to research results and other outcomes of the research life-cycle, as provided by social media platforms and other tools (preferably in an as open as possible way), is of immense benefit for science as a whole and will accelerate innovation and progress (European Commission, 2016).

Social media have put new players in the field of scholarly communication, consequently making it more difficult for traditional providers of scholarly content to get their shares of the market, but also making the publication landscape more complicated and opaque for researchers and consumers of scholarly content. Given the success of social media-based communication practices and their still-increasing uptake among researchers, the scholarly community as well as society have to fundamentally rethink how science is performed, presented and assessed. In the end, the community has to decide on which publishing modes are valued the most and should persist, and which processes should be revised.

Notes

1 For example during this workshop: http://ascw. know-center.tugraz.at
2 Time Magazine Person of the Year 2006: https:// en.wikipedia.org/wiki/You_(Time_Person_of_ the_Year)
3 http://tech.eu/features/762/mendeley-elsevier
4 http://thecostofknowledge.com/
5 One example for the use of altmetrics in evaluation can be found here: http://guides.mclibrary. duke.edu/c.php?g=217135&p=1434259
6 NISO Alternative Assessment Metrics (Altmetrics) Initiative: www.niso.org/topics/tl/altmetrics_initiative/

REFERENCES

Adie, E. (2015). Bad science: detecting research errors. Retrieved August 14, 2016 from www.internationalinnovation.com/bad-science-detecting-research-errors.

Allen, H.G., Stanton, T.R., Di Pietro, F., Moseley, G.L., & Sampson, M. (2013). Social media release increases dissemination of original articles in the clinical pain sciences. *PLoS One*, 8(7), e68914.

Bar-Ilan, J., Haustein, S., Peters, I., Priem, J., Shema, H., & Terliesner, J. (2012). Beyond citations: Scholars' visibility on the Social Web. In *Proceedings of the 17th International Conference on Science and Technology Indicators*, Montréal, Canada (pp. 98–109). Retrieved August 14, 2016 from http://arxiv.org/abs/1205.5611.

Bik, H.M., & Goldstein, M.C. (2013). An introduction to social media for scientists. *PLoS Biology*, 11(4), e1001535. DOI: http://dx.doi.org/10.1371/journal.pbio.1001535.

Buschman, M., & Michalek, A. (2013). Are alternative metrics still alternative? *Bulletin of the American Society for Information Science and Technology*, 39(4), 35–39.

Colson, V. (2011). Science blogs as competing channels for the dissemination of science news. *Journalism*, 12(7), 889–902.

Cronin, B. (1984). *The Citation Process: The Role and Significance of Citations in Scientific Communication*. London: Taylor Graham.

Cronin, B., & Shaw, D. (2002). Identity-creators and image-makers: Using citation analysis and thick descriptions to put authors in their place. *Scientometrics*, 54(1), 31–49.

Cronin, B., & Sugimoto, C.R. (eds) (2015). *Scholarly Metrics under the Microscope: From Citation Analysis to Academic Auditing*. Medford, NJ: Information Today Inc.

Dabbish, L., Stuart, C., Tsay, J., & Herbsleb, J. (2012). Social coding in GitHub: Transparency and collaboration in an open software repository. In *Proceedings of the ACM 2012 Conference on Computer Supported Cooperative Work* (pp. 1277–1286). New York: ACM Press.

Davis, P.M., & Walters, W.H. (2011). The impact of free access to the scientific literature: A review of recent research. *Journal of the Medical Library Association*, 99(3), 208–217.

De Bellis, N. (2009). *Bibliometrics and Citation Analysis: From the Science Citation Index to Cybermetrics*. Lanham, MD: Scarecrow Press.

De Solla Price, D.J. (1963). *Little Science, Big Science*. New York: Columbia University Press.

Digital Research Tools (n.d.). *Writing*. Retrieved June 17, 2016 from http://dirtdirectory.org/tadirah/writing.

European Commission Directorate-General for Research and Innovation (2016). *Open Innovation, Open Science, Open to the World*. Brussels: EC. DOI: 10.2777/061652.

Eysenbach, G. (2006). Citation advantage of open access articles. *PLoS Biology*, 4, e157. DOI: http://dx.doi.org/10.1371/journal.pbio.0040157.

Eysenbach, G. (2011). Can tweets predict citations? Metrics of social impact based on Twitter and correlation with traditional metrics of scientific impact. *Journal of Medical Internet Research*, 13(4), e123.

Fanelli, D. (2012). Negative results are disappearing from most disciplines and countries. *Scientometrics*, 90, 891–904. DOI: 10.1007/s11192-011-0494-7.

Gaffney, D., & Puschmann, C. (2014). Data collection on Twitter. In K. Weller, A. Bruns, J. Burgess, M. Mahrt & C. Puschmann (eds), *Twitter and Society* (pp. 55–68). New York: Peter Lang.

Galligan, F., & Dyas-Correia, S. (2013). Altmetrics: Rethinking the way we measure. *Serials Review*, 39(1), 56–61.

Goodband, J.H., Solomon, Y., Samuels, P.C., Lawson, D., & Bhakta, R. (2012). Limits and potentials of social networking in academia: Case study of the evolution of a mathematics Facebook community. *Learning, Media and Technology*, 37(3), 236–252.

Goodier, S., & Czerniewicz, L. (2015). Academics online presence: A four-step guide to taking control of your visibility. Retrieved June 17, 2016 from http://openuct.uct.ac.za/sites/default/files/Online%20Visibility%20Guidelines.pdf.

Gu, F., & Widén-Wulff, G. (2011). Scholarly communication and possible changes in the context of social media: A Finnish case study. *Electronic Library*, 29(6), 762–776.

Halavais, A. (2006). Scholarly blogging: Moving toward the visible college. In A. Bruns & J. Jacobs (eds), *Uses of Blogs* (pp. 117–126). New York: Peter Lang.

Hall, M., Mazarakis, A., Peters, I., Chorley, M., Simon, S., Mai, J-E. & Strohmaier, M. (2016). Following user pathways: Cross platform and mixed methods analysis in social media studies. In *Proceedings of the 2016 CHI Conference Extended Abstracts on Human Factors in Computing Systems*, Santa Clara, USA (CHI EA '16) (pp. 3400–3407). New York, NY: ACM. DOI: 10.1145/2851581.2856500.

Harley, D., Acord, S.K., Earl-Novell, S., Lawrence, S., & King, C. J. (2010). *Assessing the Future Landscape of Scholarly Communication: An Exploration of Faculty Values and Needs in Seven Disciplines*. Berkeley, CA: Center for Studies in Higher Education. Retrieved June 17, 2016 from http://escholarship.org/uc/item/15x7385g.

Harmon, J.E., & Gross, A.G. (2007). *The Scientific Literature: A Guided Tour*. Chicago, IL: Chicago University Press.

Haustein, S., & Larivière, V. (2014). The use of bibliometrics for assessing research: Possibilities, limitations and adverse effects. In I.M. Welpe, J. Wollersheim, S. Ringelhan & M. Osterloh (eds), *Incentives and Performance: Governance of Research Organizations* (pp. 121–139). Cham: Springer.

Haustein, S., Larivière, V., Thelwall, M., Amyot, D., & Peters, I. (2014). Tweets vs. Mendeley readers: How do these two social media metrics differ? *It – Information Technology*, 56(5). DOI: http://doi.org/10.1515/itit-2014-1048.

Haustein, S., Peters, I., Bar-Ilan, J., Priem, J., Shema, H., & Terliesner, J. (2013). Coverage and adoption of altmetrics sources in the bibliometric community. *Scientometrics*, 101(2), 1145–1163.

Haustein, S., Peters, I., Sugimoto, C.R., Thelwall, M., & Larivière, V. (2014). Tweeting biomedicine: An analysis of tweets and citations in the biomedical literature. *Journal of the American Society for Information Science and Technology*, 65(4), 656–669.

Henderson, J. (2012). Google Plus: A tool for academic collaboration. In T. Amiel & B. Wilson (eds), *Proceedings of World Conference on Educational Multimedia, Hypermedia and Telecommunications 2012* (pp. 905–911). Chesapeake, VA: AACE.

Henning, V., & Reichelt, J. (2008). Mendeley. A Last.fm for research? In *Proceedings of the 4th IEEE International Conference on eScience*, Indianapolis, IN (pp. 327–328).

Herath, H.M.C.T., & Hewagamage, C. (2015). Analysis of ICT usage for the teaching and learning process by the academics. *International Journal of Computer and Information Technology*, 4(5), 803–808.

Herwig, J., Kittenberger, A., Nentwich, M., & Schmirmund, J. (2009). Microblogging und die Wissenschaft: Das Beispiel Twitter [Microblogging and Academia: The Example of Twitter]. Retrieved June 17, 2016 from http://epub.oeaw.ac.at/ita/ita-projektberichte/d2-2a52-4.pdf.

Hicks, D., Wouters, P., Waltman, L., de Rijke, S., & Rafols, I. (2015). The Leiden Manifesto for research metrics: Use these 10 principles to guide research evaluation. *Nature*, 520, 429–431. DOI: 10.1038/520429a.

Hoang, J.K., McCall, J., Dixon, A.F., Fitzgerald, R.T., & Gaillard, F. (2015). Using social media to share your radiology research: How effective is a blog post? *Journal of the American College of Radiology*, 12(7), 760–765.

Holmberg, K., & Thelwall, M. (2014). Disciplinary differences in Twitter scholarly communication. Scientometrics, 101(2), 1027–1042.

Karpf, D. (2012). Social science research methods in internet time. *Information, Communication, and Society*, 15(5), 639–661.

Katz, M.L., & Shapiro, C. (1985). Network externalities, competition, and compatibility. *American Economic Review*, 75(3), 424–440.

König, M. (2012). Twitter in der Wissenschaft: Ein Leitfaden für Historiker/innen. Retrieved June 17, 2016 from: http://dhdhi.hypotheses.org/1072.

Kousha, K., Thelwall, M., & Abdoli, M. (2012). The role of online videos in research communication: A content analysis of YouTube videos cited in academic publications. *Journal of the American Society for Information Science and Technology*, 63(9), 1710–1727.

Kraker, P., & Lex, E. (2015). A critical look at the ResearchGate score as a measure of scientific reputation. In Quantifying and Analysing Scholarly Communication on the Web (ASCW '15), Web Science Conference, Oxford, GB. DOI:10.5281/zenodo.35401

Lapinski, S., Piwowar, H., & Priem, J. (2013). Riding the crest of the altmetrics wave: How librarians can help prepare faculty for the next generation of research impact metrics. *College and Research Libraries News*. Retrieved June 17, 2016 from http://crln.acrl.org/index.php/crlnews/article/view/8960/9708

Larivière, V., Haustein, S., & Mongeon, P. (2015). The oligopoly of academic publishers in the digital era. *PLoS One*, 10(6), e0127502. DOI:10.1371/journal.pone.0127502.

Letierce, J., Passant, A., Breslin, J., & Decker, S. (2010). Understanding how Twitter is used to spread scientific messages. In *Proceedings of the WebSci10: Extending the Frontiers of Society On-Line*, Raleigh, NC. Retrieved June 17, 2016 from http://journal.webscience.org/314/2/websci10_submission_79.pdf

Leydesdorff, L. (1995). *The Challenge of Scientometrics: The Development, Measurement and Self-organization of Scientific Communication*. Leidon: DSWO.

Li, N., & Gillet, D. (2013). Identifying influential scholars in academic social media platforms. In *Proceedings of the 2013 IEEEACM International Conference on Advances in Social Networks Analysis and Mining* (pp. 608–614). New York: ACM Press.

Li, X., Thelwall, M., & Giustini, D. (2012). Validating online reference managers for scholarly impact measurement. *Scientometrics*, 91(2), 461–471.

Liu, J., & Adie, E. (2013a). Five challenges in altmetrics: A toolmaker's perspective. *Bulletin of the American Society for Information Science and Technology*, 39(4), 31–34.

Liu, J., & Adie, E. (2013b). New perspectives on article-level metrics: Developing ways to assess research uptake and impact online. *Insights: The UKSG Journal*, 26(2), 153–158.

Liu, Y., Gummadi, K.P., Krishnamurthy, B., & Mislove, A. (2011). Analyzing Facebook privacy settings: User expectations vs. reality. In *Proceedings of the 2011 ACM SIGCOMM Conference on Internet Measurement* (pp. 61–70). New York: ACM Press. DOI: http://dx.doi.org/10.1145/2068816.2068823.

Luyt, B., & Tan, D. (2010). Improving Wikipedia's credibility: References and citations in a sample of history articles. *Journal of the American Society for Information Science and Technology*, 61(4), 715–722.

MacRoberts, M., & MacRoberts, B.R. (1989). Problems of citation analysis: A critical review. *Journal of the American Society for Information Science*, 40(5), 342–349.

Mahrt, M., & Puschmann, C. (2014). Science blogging: An exploratory study of motives, styles, and audience reactions. *Journal of Science Communication*, 13(3), A05.

Mahrt, M., Weller, K., & Peters, I. (2014). Twitter in scholarly communication. In K. Weller, A. Bruns, J. Burgess, M. Mahrt & C. Puschmann (eds), *Twitter and Society* (pp. 399–410). New York: Peter Lang.

Maitzen, R. (2012). Scholarship 2.0: Blogging and/as academic practice. *Journal of Victorian Culture*, 17(3), 348–354.

Marlow, J., Dabbish, L., & Herbsleb, J. (2013). Impression formation in online peer production: Activity traces and personal profiles in github. In *Proceedings of the 2013 Conference on Computer Supported Cooperative Work* (pp. 117–128). New York: ACM Press.

Matthews, D. (2016, April 7). Do academic social networks share academics' interests? Retrieved June 17, 2016 from www.timeshighereducation.com/features/do-academic-social-networks-share-academics-interests.

Meadows, A.J. (1974). *Communication in Science*. London: Butterworths.

Mewburn, I., & Thomson, P. (2013). Why do academics blog? An analysis of audiences, purposes and challenges. *Studies in Higher Education*, 38(8), 1105–1119.

Mollett, A., Moran, D., & Dunleavy, P. (2011). Using Twitter in university research, teaching and impact activities: A guide for academics and researchers. [Blog]. London: London School of Economics. Retrieved June 17, 2016 from http://blogs.lse.ac.uk/impactofsocialsciences/files/2011/11/Published-Twitter_Guide_Sept_2011.pdf.

Murray, M. (2014). Analysis of a scholarly social networking site: The case of the dormant user. In *Proceedings of the 17th Annual Conference of the Southern Association for Information Systems* (SAIS). Retrieved June 17, 2016 from http://aisel.aisnet.org/sais2014/24.

Nardi, B.A., Schiano, D.J., Gumbrecht, M., & Swartz, L. (2004). Why we blog. *Communications of the ACM*, 47(12), 41–46.

Nentwich, M., & König, R. (2014). Academia goes Facebook? The potential of social network sites in the scholarly realm. In S. Bartling & S. Friesike (eds), *Opening Science* (pp. 107–124). Berlin: Springer.

Nielsen, F.A. (2007). Scientific citations in Wikipedia. *First Monday*, 12(8). DOI: http://doi.org/10.5210/fm.v12i8.1997.

Nielsen, J. (2006). The 90-9-1 Rule for participation inequality in social media and online communities. Retrieved August 14, 2016 from www.nngroup.com/articles/participation-inequality.

Norman, D. (1988). *The Design of Everyday Things*. New York: Basic Books.

Peters, I. (2009). *Folksonomies: Indexing and Retrieval in Web 2.0*. Berlin: De Gruyter/Saur.

Peters, I., & Heise, C., (2014). Soziale Netzwerke für Forschende. In *Handbuch Co-Science*. Retrieved June 17, 2016 from https://osl.tib.eu/w/Handbuch_CoScience/Soziale_Netzwerke_f%C3%BCr_Forschende.

Piwowar, H. (2013a). Altmetrics. What, why and where? *Bulletin of the American Society for Information Science and Technology*, 39(4), 8–9.

Piwowar, H. (2013b). Altmetrics: Value all research products. *Nature*, 493(7431), 159.

Ponte, D., & Simon, J. (2011). Scholarly communication 2.0: Exploring researchers' opinions on Web 2.0 for scientific knowledge creation, evaluation and dissemination. *Serials Review*, 37(3), 149–156.

Priem, J., & Costello, K.L. (2010). How and why scholars cite on Twitter. In C. Marshall, E. Toms & A. Grove (eds), *Proceedings of the*

73rd ASIS&T Annual Meeting on Navigating Streams in an Information Ecosystem, Pittsburgh, PA (Article No. 75). New York: ACM Press. DOI: http://doi.org/10.1002/meet.14504701201.

Priem, J., Piwowar, H., & Hemminger, B. (2012). Altmetrics in the wild: Using social media to explore scholarly impact. Retrieved June 17, 2016 from http://arxiv.org/abs/1203.4745.

Priem, J., Taraborelli, D., Groth, P., & Neylon, C. (2010). *Altmetrics: A Manifesto*. Retrieved June 17, 2016 from http://altmetrics.org/manifesto/.

Procter, R.N., Williams, R., Stewart, J., Poschen, M., Snee, H., Voss, A., & Asgari-Targhi, M. (2010a). *If You Build It, Will They Come? How Researchers Perceive and Use Web 2.0*. London: Research Network Information. Retrieved June 17, 2016 from http://wrap.warwick.ac.uk/56246.

Procter, R., Williams, R., Stewart, J., Poschen, M., Snee, H., Voss, A., & Asgari-Targhi, M. (2010b). Adoption and use of Web 2.0 in scholarly communications. *Philosophical Transactions of the Royal Society A: Mathematical, Physical and Engineering Sciences*, 368(1926), 4039–4056. DOI: http://doi.org/10.1098/rsta.2010.0155.

Pscheida, D., Albrecht S., Herbst, S., Minet, C., & Köhler, T. (2014). Nutzung von Social Media und onlinebasierten Anwendungen in der Wissenschaft. Erste Ergebnisse des Science 2.0-Survey 2013 des Leibniz-Forschungsverbundes 'Science 2.0', Dresden. Retrieved June 17, 2016 from http://nbn-resolving.de/urn:nbn:de:bsz:14-qucosa-132962.

Puschmann, C., & Peters, I. (2015). Informationsverbreitung in sozialen Medien. In J.-H. Schmidt & M. Taddicken (eds), *Handbuch Soziale Medien* (pp. 1–23). Wiesbaden, Germany: Springer Fachmedien.

Ross, C., Terras, M., Warwick, C., & Welsh, A. (2011). Enabled backchannel: Conference Twitter use by digital humanists. *Journal of Documentation*, 67(2), 214–237.

Schmidt, J. (2009). *Das neue Netz: Merkmale, Praktiken und Folgen des Web 2.0*. Konstanz: UVK Verlagsgesellschaft.

Shema, H., Bar-Ilan, J., & Thelwall, M. (2015). How is research blogged? A content analysis approach. *Journal of the Association for Information Science and Technology*, 66(6), 1136–1149.

Shuai, X., Pepe, A., & Bollen, J. (2012). How the scientific community reacts to newly submitted preprints: Article downloads, Twitter mentions, and citations. *PLoS One*, 7(11), e47523. DOI:10.1371/journal.pone.0047523.

Siegfried, D., Mazarakis, A., & Peters, I. (2015). *Usage of Social Media Services in Economics*. Kiel: ZBW – Deutsche Zentralbibliothek für Wirtschaftswissenschaften – Leibniz-Informationszentrum Wirtschaft. Retrieved June 17, 2016 from www.zbw.eu/fileadmin/pdf/presse/2014-zbw-study-usage-social-media.pdf.

Statista (2016). Leading social networks worldwide as of January 2016, ranked by number of active users (in millions). Retrieved June 17, 2016 from www.statista.com/statistics/272014/global-social-networks-ranked-by-number-of-users/.

Teplitskiy, M., Lu, G., & Duede, E. (2015). *Amplifying the Impact of Open Access: Wikipedia and the Diffusion of Science*. Retrieved June 17, 2016 from http://arxiv.org/abs/1506.07608.

Terras, M. (2012). The impact of social media on the dissemination of research: Results of an experiment. *Journal of Digital Humanities*, 1(3). Retrieved June 17, 2016 from http://journalofdigitalhumanities.org/1-3/the-impact-of-social-media-on-the-dissemination-of-research-by-melissa-terras.

Thelwall, M. (2008). Bibliometrics to webometrics. *Journal of Information Science*, 34(4), 605–621.

Thelwall, M., Haustein, S., Larivière, V., & Sugimoto, C. (2013). Do altmetrics work? Twitter and ten other social Web services. *PLoS One*, 8(5).

Thelwall, M., & Kousha, K. (2014). Academia.edu: Social network or academic network? *Journal of the Association for Information Science and Technology*, 65(4), 721–731.

Thelwall, M., Kousha, K., Weller, K., & Puschmann, C. (2012). Assessing the impact of online academic videos. In G. Widén & K. Holmberg (eds), *Social Information Research* (Vol. 5, pp. 195–213). Bingley, UK: Emerald Group.

Van Noorden, R. (2014). Scientists and the Social network. *Nature*, 512, 126–129.

Walker, J. (2006). Blogging from inside the ivory tower. In A. Bruns & J. Jacobs (eds), *Uses of Blogs* (pp. 127–138). New York: Peter Lang.

Weller, K. (2015). Social media and altmetrics: An overview of current alternative approaches to measuring scholarly impact. In I.M. Welpe, J. Wollersheim, S. Ringelhan & M. Osterloh (eds), *Incentives and Performance: Governance of Research Organizations* (pp. 261–276). Cham: Springer.

Weller, K., Dornstädter, R., Freimanis, R., Klein, R.N., & Perez, M. (2010). Social software in academia: Three studies on users' acceptance of Web 2.0 services. In *Proceedings of the 2nd Web Science Conference* (WebSci10), Raleigh, NC, USA.

Weller, K., Dröge, E., & Puschmann, C. (2011). Citation analysis in Twitter: Approaches for defining and measuring information flows within tweets during scientific conferences. In *Proceedings of Making Sense of Microposts Workshop 2011* (pp. 1–12). Retrieved June 17, 2016 from http://ceur-ws.org/Vol-718/paper_04.pdf.

Zahedi, Z., Costas, R., & Wouters, P. (2014). How well developed are altmetrics? A crossdisciplinary analysis of the presence of 'alternative metrics' in scientific publications. Retrieved June 17, 2016 from http://arxiv.org/abs/1404.1301.

Zoller, D., Doerfel, S., Jäschke, R., Stumme, G., & Hotho, A. (2016). Posted, visited, exported: Altmetrics in the social tagging system BibSonomy. *Journal of Informetrics*, 10(3), 732–749.

Index